The Papers of
HENRY CLAY

The Papers of
HENRY CLAY

Robert Seager II
Editor

Melba Porter Hay
Associate Editor

Volume 8
CANDIDATE, COMPROMISER, WHIG
March 5, 1829-
December 31, 1836

THE UNIVERSITY PRESS OF KENTUCKY

*"My ambition is that we may enter a new
and larger era of service to humanity."*

Dedicated to the memory of
JOSIAH KIRBY LILLY
1861-1948
President of Eli Lilly and Company
Founder of Lilly Endowment, Inc.

Whose wisdom and foresight were
devoted to the service of
education, religion, and
public welfare

ISBN: 0-8131-0058-5
Library of Congress Catalog Card Number: 59-13605

Copyright © 1984 by the University Press of Kentucky

Scholarly publisher for the Commonwealth,
serving Bellarmine College, Berea College, Centre
College of Kentucky, Eastern Kentucky University,
The Filson Club, Georgetown College, Kentucky
Historical Society, Kentucky State University,
Morehead State University, Murray State University,
Northern Kentucky University, Transylvania University,
University of Kentucky, University of Louisville,
and Western Kentucky University.

Editorial and Sales Offices: Lexington, Kentucky 40506-0024

CONTENTS

PREFACE

In addition to the people mentioned on the dust jacket and the title page, the names and labors of others who have contributed their time, energy, and skills to Volume 8 of *The Papers of Henry Clay* must gratefully be acknowledged.

Mackelene G. Smith has continued her important work as senior research and editorial assistant. Assisting her from February to August, 1983 was Mary A. Moloney. Margaret Spratt-Wyatt has contined her effective labors as research associate and indexer extraordinary. Contributing to the project in many useful ways, mainly with proof-reading, typing, and photocopying, have been Ingrid Hansen, Julie A. Kruse, and Mary N. Baird. The professional dedication and tirelessness of the entire staff has contributed importantly to the dispatch and efficiency with which this volume has been produced.

The editors have continued to implement the editorial philosophy and methodology that guided them in Volume 7 (see 7:vii-viii). In addition, they have decided to summarize a few of Clay's less important letters in this volume. Also summarized here is almost all of his incoming mail as well as his remarks on the Senate floor. These items, as well as his outgoing letters, have been extensively cross-referenced and subject indexed. It should be especially noted in this regard that the editors have continued to bracket into the text of summarized documents cross-references to helpful and relevant Clay materials found in other volumes in the series. In non-summarized documents the cross-references are found in the footnotes. So there will be no confusion between summarized items and those documents presented in full, as apparently there was in Volume 7, the former have been set in smaller type. Also, a calendar of marginal and peripheral Clay materials has again been employed.

Every Clay document for 1829-1836 about which the editors know has been printed in full, summarized, or calendared herein. No Clay item has been consciously omitted.

The chief editorial decision that had to be made in Volume 8 was how best to handle Clay's almost daily participation in Senate debate during those thirty-two and a half months between December 5, 1831, and December 31, 1836, when Congress was actually in session. This participation was recorded in Joseph Gales & William W. Seaton's, *The Register of Debates in Congress*, and, somewhat less extensively, in Francis P. Blair & John C. Rives's, *The Congressional Globe*, which began publication in December, 1833. To edit and reprint Clay's voluminous Senate remarks in their entirety was clearly not feasible from a labor, space, and cost-efficiency standpoint, especially since the *Register* and/or *Globe* can be found in almost all good public and academic libraries. On the other hand, to eliminate any, some, or all of this interesting material would be to deny the reader the historical context in which the impact and meaning of Clay's personal correspondence can best be judged.

In the best tradition of a Henry Clay compromise, the decision was to summarize *all* of Clay's remarks on the floor of the Senate, using the account in the *Register* as the preferred source. These summaries attempt to identify the main subject under discussion, provide the general thrust of Clay's contribution to the debate, and capture, in short quotes, something of the flavor of his language.

To help the reader distinguish at once between the casual and the formal in Clay's Senate participation, between the ephemeral and the extensive, the editors have separated his observations into three categories — Remark, Comment, and Speech. His *Remark in Senate* is a brief, off-hand, unprepared statement; the *Comment in Senate* represents a more sustained, thoughtful (though extemporaneous) involvement in the main business of the day's session; the *Speech in Senate* is generally an extensive, carefully prepared declaration of Clay's position on an important national political issue — a major policy statement or partisan attack of the sort often picked up by the newspapers or later printed in pamphlet form for political purposes.

The summarization process, no matter how carefully and conscientiously executed, whether applied to Clay's own letters, to those of his correspondents, or to the records of his participation in Senate debate, is a decidedly subjective undertaking. Different editors will summarize identical texts differently and in different language. It should be remarked also that the present editors have exercised varying degrees of verbal latitude in fashioning these summaries since their goal in Volume 8 is to render the background, content, meaning, and historical context of all summarized documents as clear to the reader as possible. But since such latitude has been exercised, scholars will want to proceed with caution. Should the need for semantic precision in their research arise, they will want to go directly to the original document for a full rendition of all that Clay wrote, received in the mail, or had to say on a given subject on a given day. Copies of these documents are on file in Special Collections, King Library, University of Kentucky. The originals may be found in the manuscript repositories noted on each document. The full texts of Clay's speeches are in the *Register of Debates* or the *Congressional Globe*.

Once again the editors wish to thank the National Historical Publications and Records Commission staff, particularly Dr. Frank G. Burke and Dr. Roger A. Bruns, for their assistance, encouragement, and support during difficult economic times. For similar support we are extremely grateful to Dean Wimberly C. Royster and the University of Kentucky Research Foundation and to Dr. Otis A. Singletary, President of the University of Kentucky.

Robert Seager II
Melba Porter Hay
December, 1983

SYMBOLS & ABBREVIATIONS

The following symbols are used to describe the nature of the originals of documents copied from manuscript sources.

AD	Autograph Document
AD draft	Autograph Document, draft
ADI	Autograph Document Initialed
ADS	Autograph Document Signed
AE	Autograph Endorsement
AEI	Autograph Endorsement Initialed
AES	Autograph Endorsement Signed
AL	Autograph Letter
AL draft	Autograph Letter, draft
ALI	Autograph Letter Initialed
ALI copy	Autograph Letter Initialed, copy
ALI draft	Autograph Letter Initialed, draft
ALS	Autograph Letter Signed
ALS draft	Autograph Letter Signed, draft
AN	Autograph Note
AN draft	Autograph Note, draft
ANI draft	Autograph Note Initialed, draft
ANS	Autograph Note Signed
Copy	Copy not by writer (indicated "true" is so certified)
D	Document
DS	Document Signed
L	Letter
L draft	Letter, draft
LI draft	Letter Initialed, draft
LS	Letter Signed
N	Note
N draft	Note, draft
NS	Note Signed

The following, from the *Symbols Used in the National Union Catalog of the Library of Congress* (9th ed., rev.; Washington, 1965), indicate the location of the original documents in institutional libraries of the United States.

CSmH	Henry E. Huntington Library and Museum, San Marino, California
Cty	Yale University, New Haven, Connecticut
DeGE	Eleutherian Mills Historical Library, Greenville, Delaware
DLC	Library of Congress, Washington, D.C.
DLC-HC	Library of Congress, Henry Clay Collection
DLC-TJC	Library of Congress, Thomas J. Clay Collection
DNA	United States National Archives Library, Washington, D.C. Following the symbol for this depository the letters A. and R. mean Applications and Recommendations; M, Microcopy; P. and D. of L., Publication and Distribution of the Laws; R, Reel; and RG, Record Group.

ICHi	Chicago Historical Society, Chicago, Illinois
ICN	Newberry Library, Chicago, Illinois
ICU	University of Chicago, Chicago, Illinois
In	Indiana State Library, Indianapolis, Indiana
InHi	Indiana Historical Society, Indianapolis, Indiana
InU	Indiana University, Bloomington, Indiana
Ky	Kentucky State Library and Archives, Frankfort, Kentucky
KyDC	Centre College of Kentucky, Danville, Kentucky
KyHi	Kentucky Historical Society, Frankfort, Kentucky
KyLoF	The Filson Club, Louisville, Kentucky
KyLxT	Transylvania University, Lexington, Kentucky
KyU	University of Kentucky, Lexington, Kentucky
MB	Boston Public Library, Boston, Massachusetts
MBAt	Boston Athenaeum, Boston, Massachusetts
MCM	Massachusetts Institute of Technology, Cambridge, Massachusetts
MdBP	Peabody Institute, Baltimore, Maryland
MdHi	Maryland Historical Society, Baltimore, Maryland
MeHi	Maine Historical Society, Portland, Maine
MH	Harvard University, Cambridge, Massachusetts
MHi	Massachusetts Historical Society, Boston, Massachusetts
MiD-B	Detroit Public Library, Detroit, Michigan, Burton Historical Collection
MiDW	Wayne State University, Detroit, Michigan
MiU	University of Michigan, Ann Arbor, Michigan
Mi-U-C	University of Michgian, Ann Arbor, Michigan, William L. Clements Library
MoHi	Missouri State Historical Society, Columbia, Missouri
MoSHi	Missouri Historical Society, St. Louis, Missouri
MS	City Library, Springfield, Massachusetts
Ms-Ar	State Department of Archives and History, Jackson, Mississippi
NbHi	Nebraska State Historical Society, Lincoln, Nebraska
NBuHi	Buffalo Historical Society, Buffalo, New York
NcD	Duke University, Durham, North Carolina
NcU	University of North Carolina, Chapel Hill, North Carolina
NhD	Dartmouth College, Hanover, New Hampshire
NhHi	New Hampshire Historical Society, Concord, New Hampshire
NHi	New York Historical Society, New York City
NIC	Cornell University, Ithaca, New York
NjHi	New Jersey Historical Society, Newark, New Jersey
NjP	Princeton University, Princeton, New Jersey
NN	New York Public Library, New York City
NNC	Columbia University, New York City
NNPM	Pierpont Morgan Library, New York City
OC	Public Library of Cincinnati and Hamilton County, Cincinnati, Ohio
OCHP	Historical and Philosophical Society of Ohio, Cincinnati, Ohio
OClW	Western Reserve University, Cleveland, Ohio
OClWHi	Western Reserve Historical Society, Cleveland, Ohio

OFH	Rutherford B. Hayes Library, Fremont, Ohio
OHi	Ohio State Historical Society, Columbus, Ohio
PCarlD	Dickinson College, Carlisle, Pennsylvania
PHC	Haverford College, Haverford, Pennsylvania
PHi	Historical Society of Pennsylvania, Philadelphia, Pennsylvania
PP	Free Library of Philadelphia, Pennsylvania
PPAmP	American Philosophical Society, Philadelphia, Pennsylvania
PPiU	University of Pittsburgh, Pittsburgh, Pennsylvania
PPL-R	Library Company of Philadelphia, Ridgeway Branch, Philadelphia, Pennsylvania
PPPrHi	Presbyterian Historical Society, Philadelphia, Pennsylvania
RPAB	Annmary Brown Memorial Library, Providence, Rhode Island
RPB	Brown University, Providence, Rhode Island
THi	Tennessee Historical Society, Nashville, Tennessee
ViHi	Virginia Historical Society, Richmond, Virginia
ViU	University of Virginia, Charlottesville, Virginia
WM	Milwaukee Public Library, Milwaukee, Wisconsin
Wv-Ar	West Virginia Department of Archives and History Library, Charleston, West Virginia

The following abbreviations are used in the footnotes of this volume:

AQR	*American Quarterly Review*
BDAC	*Biographical Directory of the American Congress 1774-1961. Washington: United States Government Printing Office, 1961.*
BDGUS	*Biographical Directory of the Governors of the United States 1789-1978. Robert Sobel and John Raimo, eds. Westport, Ct.: Meckler Books, 1978.*
CAB	*Cyclopedia of American Biography.* James G. Wilson and John Fiske, eds. New York: D. Appleton & Company, 1888.
DAB	*Dictionary of American Biography.* Allen Johnson, ed. New York: Charles Scribner's Sons, 1927, 1964.
DH	*Delaware History*
DNB	*Dictionary of National Biography.* Sir Leslie Stephen and Sir Sidney Lee, eds. London: Oxford University Press, 1917.
EB	*Encyclopaedia Britannica.* 15th ed. Chicago: Helen Hemingway Benton, 1974.
EHR	*English Historical Review*
FCHQ	*Filson Club History Quarterly*
FHQ	*Florida Historical Quarterly*
HRDUSA	*Historical Register and Dictionary of the United States Army 1789-1903.* Francis B. Heitman, ed. 2 vols., 1903. Reprint. Urbana: University of Illinois Press, 1965.
IMH	*Indiana Magazine of History*
JMH	*Journal of Mississippi History*
JNH	*Journal of Negro History*
JSAH	*Journal of the Society of Architectural Historians*
JSH	*Journal of Southern History*
LH	*Labor History*

LHQ	*Louisiana Historical Quarterly*
MHM	*Maryland Historical Magazine*
MHR	*Missouri Historical Review*
MPP	*A Compilation of the Messages and Papers of the Presidents 1789-1902.* James D. Richardson, comp. 10 vols. Washington: Bureau National Literature and Art, 1904.
MVHR	*Mississippi Valley Historical Review*
NAR	*North American Review*
NCAB	*National Cyclopaedia of American Biography.* New York: James T. White & Company, 1898.
NEHGR	*New England Historical and Genealogical Register*
NEQ	*New England Quarterly*
NHSQB	*New-York Historical Society Quarterly Bulletin*
OHQ	*Ohio Historical Quarterly*
PMHB	*Pennsylvania Magazine of History and Biography*
PSQ	*Political Science Quarterly*
RIH	*Rhode Island History*
RKHS	*Register of the Kentucky Historical Society*
SCHM	*South Carolina Historical Magazine*
SHQ	*Southwestern Historical Quarterly*
USMA, Register	*Register of Graduates and Former Cadets, United States Military Academy* West Point: The West Point Alumni Foundation, Inc., 1960.
VMHB	*Virginia Magazine of History and Biography*
WMQ	*William & Mary Quarterly*
WPHM	*Western Pennsylvania Historical Magazine*
WVH	*West Virginia History*

Note: Volume and page numbers of dictionaries, encyclopedias, and registers arranged alphabetically are not included in citations.

The Papers of
HENRY CLAY

To MARGARET BAYARD   Washington, March, 1829
[Mrs. Samuel Harrison] SMITH

You desire, my dear Madam, some line of friendly remembrance. What shall I say? You have asked me to record something of the celebrated Madame [Anne Louise] de Stael. She was the most extraordinary woman of this or any other age, blending the philosophy of our sex with the imagination of yours. She was a person of whom both may be justly proud. She seems to have been bestow[e]d on our race to vindicate the equal claim of the female mind to intellectual excellence. I knew this remarkable woman in Paris. I first met her at a ball given on the occasion of the Peace of Ghent at the banker Hottinguer's

"Ah, Mr Clay," she said, "the English have been much incensed against you. I have been lately pleading your cause at London. Do you know they contemplated at one time sending the Duke of Wellington to command their armies against you?"[1] I told her that I was aware of the exertion of her eloquence in our behalf, and I thanked her heartily for it. I added that I wished the British Government had sent the Duke. "Why," she inquired with much surprise. "Because Madame, had we beaten the Duke, we should have gained immortal honor, whilst we should have lost none, had we been defeated by the Conqueror of Napoleon."

I next saw Mme de Stael at her own house where she introduced me to the Duke of Wellington, and related to him the above conversation. He remarked, with much apparent feeling and grace, that he should have placed a most noble feather in his cap had he beaten so gallant a people as the Americans.

Copy. DLC-Carl Schurz Papers (DNA, M212, R22). For Margaret Bayard Smith, see Gaillard Hunt, ed., *The First Forty Years of Washington Society* (New York, 1906), *passim*, a collection of her letters; and *Notable American Women*.   1. See Philip Guedalla, *The Duke* (Montreal, 1931), 254-55; George Hooper, *Wellington* (London, 1908), 201-2.

From Robert Lee *et al.*, Rahway, N.J., March 4, 1829. Write, as a committee for the citizens of Essex and Middlesex, to tender their high regards and to assure Clay that even though he is leaving office, they will retain "a recollection of your services in the cause of general liberty, in both the Northern and Southern hemispheres, and your zealous and unwearied labors to promote every great interest of your country, and especially the interest of the manufacturers, so essential to our national prosperity and independence." State: "Much as we regret that the Republic should be deprived of your experience . . . much more do we regret the manner in which the recent change has been effected. Henceforth no purity of Character, no extent of services, no abilities . . . can shield the public officer from attack." Add that they are not "condemning the administration of General Jackson in advance" and "hope for the sake of the Republic, that he will govern well." Maintain, however, that "ages spent in administering our Government with angel-like perfection, never could erase from honorable minds, the

1

repulsive feeling that the executive office was obtained by the charge of bribery and corruption." Copy. Printed in Lexington *Kentucky Reporter*, May 6, 1829.

Clay replied to Lee *et al.* on March 6, thanking them for their flattering expression. Continues: "All human life is exposed to vicissitudes — they are common to Republics, and to public men. The change which has recently occurred, whatever may have been the impropriety of the means sometimes employed to produce it, has been the consequence of the regular action of our institutions. The will of the majority has been constitutionally expressed. . . . We should merge the passions and the prejudices by which most of us were probably affected whilst the contest raged, in an anxious desire now that it has terminated, that its issue may tend to the prosperity of the nation. . . . Whilst we should neither condemn nor approve the new administration in advance, we ought to give it a fair trial, and estimate it according to the nature of its measures."

Assures them of his continuing support of the protective tariff and promises "Wherever I may be, during the residue of my life . . . be assured that my heart will beat not less strong than it has heretofore in the cause of civil liberty." *Ibid. Niles' Register* (April 18, 1829), 36:125 dates this letter March 9, 1829.

From James L. Hawkins, Baltimore, March 5, 1829. Suggests that on his trip home to Lexington he travel by way of Baltimore to Frederick, Md., since the roads directly to Frederick from Washington are now "in a Very Bad State." Remarks that his friends in Baltimore will want to entertain him while there. ALS. DLC-HC (DNA, M212, R3).

In declining an invitation from William Dorne *et al.* to attend a "Collation" at Rockville, Md., Clay responded, *ca.* March 9, that he was proceeding home by way of Baltimore because of poor roads. Added: "My anxious hope [is] that an early provision may be made by Congress for the improvement of the road from Rockville to Frederick." Copy. Printed in *The Gazette* (Martinsburg, Va.), Supplement, April 2, 1829.

From Joseph Gales, Jr., & William W. Seaton, Washington, March 6, 1829. Request a copy of his instructions to the U.S. ministers — Richard C. Anderson, Jr., and John Sergeant — to the Panama Congress [5:313-44] that it might be published in the Washington *Daily National Intelligencer*. ALS. DLC-HC (DNA, M212, R3).

Clay responded to Gales and Seaton, adding Peter Force as a recipient, *ca.* March 10. He pointed out that since Adams had sent a copy of the instructions to the Senate prior to its adjournment, it had become a public document and could therefore be published. He enclosed copies and asked "that you will publish it in your respective papers." ALS. KyU. Force published the document in his Washington *Daily National Journal* on March 20, 1829. It was published in the Washington *Daily National Intelligencer* on March 21, 1829. See Fendall to Clay, March 24, 1829.

Clay earlier, in an undated letter, *ca.* March 1, had written to John Q. Adams "suggesting for your consideration the propriety of a communication of the [Panama] instructions to Congress," pointing out that the "nation has a right to know what their Executive intended at that Congress." ALS. MHi-Adams Papers, Letters Received (MR490).

In another undated letter, *ca.* late February or early March, Clay wrote either to Adams or to Congress that "I transmit to Congress a copy of the [Panama] instructions. . . . They are submitted with more satisfaction, because they will afford additional evidence to the world of the liberality which always distinguishes the Govern't. of the U.S. in their intercourse with foreign powers." *Ibid.*

From THOMAS I. WHARTON   Philadelphia, March 6, 1829
I rec'd your Letter of the 3d with the check enclosed of $150 to the Adv of T[homas]. H Clay. Your former enclosure of $100 to my Adv. also came safe to hand and has been appropriated as follows

For 6 weeks boarding to the 8th of February	$30.00
For Medicines	3.50
Paid his order for small debts &c	15.00
Paid do do	6.00
Paid for a set of Kent's Commentaries[1] pr him	12.00
Leaving in my hands a balance of $33.50	66.50

I bought the Commentaries for him at his particular request & in the hope that he would Apply himself to his studies again of which there seemed a reasonable prospect. I fear that his discharge cannot be obtained before the expiration of the 3 months from his imprisonment in about the 26th or 27th of April, & it being necessary to give 15 days notice after the expiration of the 3 months his Actual enlargement in Course of law Cannot take place before the 10th or 15th of April. I have caused a suggestion to be made to Hieskell[2] that he will get nothing by keeping him in prison, but I Am assured this will not produce any effect. If he remains until the 15th of April there will be due for boarding about $50 towards which I will apply the balance in my hands. I wish the $150 now sent could be secured so that the balance may be paid out of it, as it is to be feared that on his enlargement & perhaps under temptation to dispose of it otherwise this debt may be forgotten. I will at all counts do my best to effect this and to induce him to repair immediately to Kentucky. Dr. C's[3] efforts to the same result will not be wanting.[4]

I congratulate you on your emancipation from the fatigues of an onerous office and on the dissolution of a co-partnership which boded evil from the first which I took the liberty earnestly to remonstrate against and which tied you to the fortunes of a person [John Q. Adams] whom I believe all the efforts of man could not keep afloat. For me I trust we shall hear no more of him, & on your reappearance on the stage a year or two hence, which I hope will take place with restored health, we shall be ready to give you a clear board and stand by you with clear consciences — which I confess I have not been well able to do these last 4 years considering all I had thought & said respecting the late incumbent.

ALS. DLC-HC (DNA, M212, R3).   1. James Kent, *Commentaries on American Law*. Philadelphia, 1826.   2. Apparently Hieskell had Thomas jailed for failure to pay for lodging at Hieskell's City Hotel, located at 43 N. 3rd Street, Philadelphia. For Hieskell see *PMHB*, 46:363-64 and 1829 *Philadelphia City Directory*, 37.   3. Probably Dr. Nathaniel Chapman. 4. Wharton reported to Clay on March 24 that young Thomas had been released from jail on common bail when Hieskell accepted "his note for the Amount," and had left for Kentucky on March 22 "under repeated promises to proceed without stopping to Lexington." Of the $250 Clay had sent him, he had $137.55 in his pocket when he left Philadelphia. This sum, Wharton instructed him, was "to be applied to the purchase of a great coat and to the payment of his expenses home." ALS. DLC-TJC (DNA, M212, R13).

From Gustavus H. Scott, Washington, March 7, 1829. Takes fond leave of Clay and Samuel L. Southard, whom, he says, he will never "renounce" even though "My name may be presented to the Genl [Jackson] some day or other for an appointment — not by myself or by any one who is not fully apprized of my attachment to those whom he execrates" and "so ardently wishes to destroy." Remarks that he too leaves Washington hardly able to "say whether I go home most grieved at my own, or the situation of my country." ALS. DLC-HC (DNA, M212, R3).

Scott had attended the farewell party for Clay at the Mansion Hotel earlier that day. Jones to Clay, March 6, 1829. *Ibid*.

SPEECH AT FAREWELL DINNER   Washington, March 7, 1829

In rising,[1] Mr. President [Walter Jones], to offer my respectful acknowledgement for the honors of which I am here the object, I must ask the indulgence of yourself and the other gentlemen now assembled, for an unaffected embarrassment which is more sensibly felt than it can be distinctly expressed. This City has been the theatre of the greater portion of my public life. You and others whom I now see have been spectators of my public course and conduct. You and they are, if I may borrow a technical expression from an honorable profession, of which you and I are both members, jurors of the vinciage. To a judgment rendered by those who have thus long known me, and by others, though not of the pannel, who have possessed equal opportunities of forming correct opinions, I most cheerfully submit. If the weight of human testimony should be estimated by the intelligence and respectability of the witness, and the extent of his knowledge of the matter on which he testifies, the highest consideration is due to that which has been this day spontaneously given. I shall ever cherish it with the most grateful recollection, and look back upon it with proud satisfaction.

I should be glad to feel that I could with propriety abstain from any allusion, at this time, and at this place, to public affairs. But considering the occasion which has brought us together, the events which have preceded it, and the influence which they may exert upon the destinies of our Country, my silence might be misinterpreted, and I think it therefore proper that I should embrace this first public opportunity which I have had of saying a few words, since the termination of the late memorable and embittered contest. It is far from my wish to continue or revive the agitations with which that contest was attended. It is ended for good or for evil. The Nation wants repose. A majority of the people has decided, and from their decision there can and ought to be no appeal. Bowing as I do with profound respect to them, and to this exercise of their sovereign authority, I may nevertheless be allowed to retain and to express my own unchanged sentiments, even if they should not be in perfect coincidence with theirs. It is a source of high gratification to me to believe that I share these sentiments in common with more than half a million of freemen, possessing a degree of virtue, of intelligence, of religion, and of genuine patriotism, which, without disparagement of others, is unsurpassed in the same number of men, in this or any other Country, in this or any other age.

I deprecated the election of the present President [Jackson] of the U States, because I believed he had neither the temper, the experience, nor the attainments requisite to discharge the complicated and arduous duties of Chief Magistrate. I deprecated it, still more, because his elevation, I believed, would be the result exclusively of admiration and gratitude for military service, without regard to indispensible civil qualifications. I can neither retract, nor alter, nor modify any opinion which, on these subjects, I have, at any time heretofore, expressed. I thought I beheld in his election an awful foreboding of the fate which at some future (I pray to God that, if it ever arrives, it may be some far distant) day was to befall this infant Republic. All past history had impressed on my mind this solemn apprehension. Nor is it effaced or weakened by contemporaneous events passing upon our own favored Continent. It is remarkable that, at this epoch, at the head of eight of the nine Independent Governments established in both Americas, military officers have been placed or have placed themselves. General [Juan] Lavalle has, by military force, subverted the republic of La Plata. Genl. [Andres] Santa Cruz is the Chief Magistrate of Bolivia; col. [Francisco] Pinto of Chile; Genl. [Jose de] La Mar [*sic*, Lamar] of Peru; and Genl. [Simon] Bolivar of Colombia. Central America, rent in pieces, and bleeding at every pore from wounds inflicted by contending military factions, is under the alternate sway of their Chiefs. In the Government of our nearest neighbour [Mexico], an election, conducted according to all the requirements of their Constitution, had terminated with a majority of the States in favor of [Manual Gomez] Pedraza, the Civil candidate. An insurrection was raised in behalf of his military rival the cry, not exactly of a bargain, but of corruption was sounded, the election was annulled and a reform effected by proclaiming Genl [Vicente] Guerrero, having only a minority of the States, duly elected President. The thunders from the surrounding forts, and the acclamations of the assembled multitude, on the fourth [March], told us what Genl. was at the head of our affairs. It is true, and in this respect we are happier than some of the American States, that his election has not been brought about by military violence. The forms of the Constitution have yet remained inviolate.

In respecting the opinions which I hold, nothing is further from my purpose than to treat with the slightest disrespect those of my fellow Citizens here or elsewhere who may entertain opposite sentiments. The fact of claiming and exercising the free and independent expression of the dictates of my own deliberate judgment, affords the strongest guaranty of my full recognition of their corresponding priviledge.

A majority of my fellow citizens it would seem does not perceive the dangers which I apprehended from the example. Believing that they are not real or that we have some security against their effect which antient and modern Republics have not found, that majority, in the exercise of their incontestible right of Suffrage, have chosen for Chief Magistrate a Citizen who brings into that high trust no qualification other than military triumphs.

That citizen has done me much injustice — wanton, unprovoked and unatoned injustice. It was inflicted, as I must ever[2] believe, for the double purpose of gratifying private resentment, and promoting personal ambition. When, during the late canvass, he came forward, in the public prints, under his proper name, with his charge against me, and summoned before the public tribunal his friend and his only witness [James Buchanan] to establish it, the anxious attention of the whole American people was directed to the testimony which that witness might render. He promptly obeyed the call, and testified to what he knew. He could say nothing, and he said nothing, which cast the slightest shade upon my honor and integrity. What he did say was the reverse of any implication of me. Then all just and impartial men, and all who had faith in the magnanimity of my accuser, believed that he would voluntarily make a public acknowledgement of his error. How far the reasonable expectation has been fulfilled let his persevering and stubborn silence attest.

But my relations to that Citizen, by a recent event, are now changed. He is the Chief Magistrate of my Country, invested with large and extensive powers, the administration of which may conduce to its prosperity, or occasion its adversity. Patriotism enjoins as a duty, that whilst he is in that exalted Station he should be treated with decorum and his official acts be judged of in a spirit of candor. Suppressing as far as I can a sense of my personal wrong; willing even to forgive him, if his own conscience and our common God can

5

acquit him; and entertaining for the majority which has elected him, and for the office which he fills all the deference which is due from a private Citizen, I most anxiously hope that, under his guidance, the great interests of our country, foreign and domestic, may be upheld, our free institutions be unimpaired and the happiness of the nation be continued and increased.

Whilst I am prompted by an ardent devotion to the welfare of my country sincerely to express this hope, I make no pledges, no promises, no threats, and, I must add, I have no confidence. My public life, I trust, furnishes the best guarranty for my faithful adherence to those great principles of external and internal policy, to which it has been hitherto zealously dedicated. Whether I shall ever hereafter take any part in the public councils or not depends upon circumstances beyond my control. Holding the principle that a Citizen, as long as a single pulsation remains, is under an obligation to exert his utmost energies in the service of his Country, if necessary, whether in private or public station, my friends here and every where may rest assured that, in either condition, I shall stand erect, with a spirit unconquered, whilst life endures, ready to second their exertions in the cause of liberty, the Union, and the National prosperity.

Before I set down I avail myself, with pleasure, of this opportunity, to make my grateful acknowledgements for the courtesies and friendly attentions which I have uniformly experienced from the inhabitants of this City. A free and social intercourse with them, during a period of more than twenty years, is about to terminate without any recollection on my part of a single painful collision, and without leaving behind me, as far as I know, a solitary personal enemy. If, in the sentiment with which I am about to conclude, I do not give a particular expression to the feelings inspired by the interchange of civilities and friendly offices, I hope the Citizens of Washington will be assured that their individual happiness and the growth and prosperity of this City will ever be objects of my fervent wishes. In the sentiment which I shall presently offer they are indeed comprehended. For the welfare of this city is independently associated with that of our Union, and the preservation of our Liberty.

I request permission to propose, Let us never despair of the American Republic.[3]

AD, in Clay's hand. DLC-HC (DNA, M212, R3). Endorsed by Clay on verso: "For Mr. [Peter] Force." Printed in Force's Washington *Daily National Journal*, March 10, 1829; also in *Niles' Register* (March 14, 1829), 36:39-40. 1. On March 6 Walter Jones invited Clay to the dinner in his honor at the Mansion Hotel at 5:30 p.m. on March 7. ALS. DLC-HC (DNA, M212, R3). The Washington *Daily National Journal* on March 10, reported that "upwards of a hundred persons" attended. The toast to Clay, before he rose to speak, is in DLC-HC (DNA, M212, R3). The Rev. John L. Barger wrote Clay, *ca.* March 8, that while he "could not conscienciously drink to you a toast," he had offered up a silent prayer in Clay's behalf. *Ibid.* (R4). 2. Phrase "am compelled to" struck through and "must ever" substituted. 3. Following his remarks, "Mr. C. who appeared to be suffering from a severe col[d] almost immediately retired." However, the social enjoyments of the evening were "prolonged for some-time by the company with great vivacity." Washington *Daily National Journal*, March 10, 1829.

From LAFAYETTE   Paris, March 8, 1829

A precious Book, Beautifully Bound, and Containing Several of Your Admirable Speeches,[1] Has Been Lately presented to me, By Your Excellent Brother [in-law] Mr [James] Brown, as a New token of Your friendship. that it Has Been Received with Every Sentiment of Affection and gratitude. I need not, I know, to assert, But I want to Express, and So I want to Add that While I am

Happy to Acknowledge Your personal kindness along with Your public Eloquence, there is one Speech, strongly tinctured with Both, which altho' not Recorded in the Book, as it Relates to a more private object, shall ever be Engraved in My Heart.

Four days are now elapsed, my dear friend, Since You Have Been Restored to a Life of Repose; it will probably not last long, and I anticipate the Approaching time when You will be Returned to Congress and probably to the Chair of the House. I Hope the intervals will Be Consecrated to the Restoration of Your Health, above Which, and also above Every thing that concerns Yourself and family   I Beg You to Give me frequent and minute informations. They Become the more necessary to me as We are going to loose Mr and Mrs Brown, a loss that is deeply felt By Every American on this side of the Atlantic, By None More than By me, and my family who are Attached to them By Every tie of Gratitude, affection, and Respect. Mrs [Anne Hart] Brown's Health is now Better than when they took the Resolution to Return Home. We Have Been much alarmed on Her Account; it is now over, as to danger, and a few days ago she Looked quite well. But all the particulars Relative to Her Health she, no doubt, gives to Her Sister [Lucretia Hart Clay], and these lines will go By the Same Opportunity. Packets now run three times in the month. Miss [Susan] Brown who lives with them is a Most Amiable young lady.

Of the affairs of Europe You Have, in Your Official Capacity, Heard a Great deal, and much of them is to Be found in the public papers. it Appears the two great despots of the East [Russia and Turkey] will try the fortune of War. The Conduct of the french government Has Been Liberal and disinterested. Not so with the Rulers of England; they strive to Contract the limits and independence of Greece. Their Connexions with Don Miguel and late behaviour at terceira[2] Have Roused a General Cry against them. The American Stars Have Lately lighted on a dexterous and Honorable private attempt of which I feel very proud. Austria is as Bad as Ever. italy deserves the Leaden inquisitorial yoke. it is impossible for Spain and portugal to go on as they are now governed. the downfall of the [Jean] Villele Administration, and a Better Chamber of deputies Which did occasion it, Has Set the interior Affairs of france on a Somewhat improved line of March. But very slow, timid steps indeed. far even from what Could Be done Within the So Very limited Circle of an *octroid charter*. Yet, I think it a duty to Assist in the little progressive Good that Can Be obtained.

On Reading Again Your observations on our Colonization Society,[3] of which to Have Been chosen a vice president is to me a Great Honor, and a more Highly valued Gratification, I Have thought You Will employ Some of Your time of leisure in promoting the More important object that it remains, in my opinion, for our part of America finally to obtain. The Settlement of Liberia may in future times Civilise Affrica [*sic*, Africa] and facilitate a Gradual abolition of slavery. I Have Seen With much pleasure that measures of the kind were talked of for the District of Colombia [*sic*, Columbia]. You know that while I feel, as much as any man, the Cursed evil Entailed upon America By Great Britain I am not insensible of the immense difficulties, But think that if an incessant attention, in the Southern States, to that momentous object of Self interest as well as of Humanity, is directed that way, Means may Be found out Consistent with prudence and possession, to limit, lessen, and

7

perhaps, in time to Eradicate that only obstacle to Southern improvements, that only objection to the example proposed to the world in the Superior State of American Civilization. I am told our friend Mr [John Q.] Adams intends to Remain With His Family in the District of Colombia; if You See them, and Your former Colleagues in the Cabinet Remember me very affectionately to them all. [P.S.] My Son [George Washington Lafayette] requests me to present His Best Respects. Le Vasseur[4] is now a partner in a Bookselling firm under the name of Malker and Co faubourg St. Germain Where he has Settled His family and Himself. You know that M. david,[5] one of the first Statuaryes in the World, and the first in paris, member of the institute etc. Has presented Congress, With a marble Bust, made on purpose to be offered as a tribute to them. it Has been much admired By the Artists of paris.

ALS. DLC-HC (DNA, M212, R3). Printed in Calvin Colton, *The Life, Correspondence, and Speeches of Henry Clay*, 6 vols. (New York, 1864), 4:223-25. Hereafter cited as Colton, *Clay Correspondence*.
1. *The Speeches of Henry Clay, Delivered in the Congress of the United States*. . . . Philadelphia, 1827.
2. See 7:388, 431. 3. See 6:83-97 for Clay's speech to the American Colonization Society which was included in *The Speeches of Henry Clay*, 331-39. Lafayette, who attended the annual meeting of the society in 1825, was made an honorary vice president of it on that occasion. P. J. Staudenraus, *The African Colonization Movement, 1816-1865* (N.Y., 1961), 118. 4. Auguste Levasseur was secretary to Lafayette during the latter's American tour in 1824-25. He was author of *Lafayette in America, in 1824 and 1825; or Journals of Travels in the United States*, N.Y., 1829. 5. For Pierre Jean David, see *NBG*, 7:234-35. His bust of Lafayette and Washington is in the Great Hall of Congress.

From Luke Tiernan *et al.,* Baltimore, Md., March 11, 1829. Asks that his friends be permitted "a public demonstration of our personal affection and political confidence" when he stops in Baltimore on his way home. Notes that "We have just passed through a most arduous and Extraordinary political contest, a peculiar characteristick of which was a personal impeachment of your motives and proceedings," but assures Clay "that our reliance on your integrity never faltered for a moment." ALS. DLC-HC (DNA, M212, R3).

On March 10, William K. Mitchell *et al.* of Baltimore, describing themselves as "managers of the *Fancy Rag ball*," invited Clay to a public dinner with them when he came to town. Copy. Printed in *Niles' Register* (April 4, 1829), 36:90.

On March 14, while in Baltimore, Clay wrote Mitchell. He declined the invitation with thanks and with regret, since his stay in Baltimore would be so short. *Ibid.*

To FRANCIS T. BROOKE
Washington, March 12, 1829

I have not written you very lately, because, having nothing to communicate which the papers did not contain, I did not wish to make you pay postage for the thousand rumors with which this city has been filled. Among the official corps here there is the greatest solicitude and apprehension. The members of it feel something like the inhabitants of Cairo when the plague breaks out; no one knows who is next to encounter the stroke of death; or which, with many of them is the same thing, to be dismissed from office. You have no conception of the moral tyranny which prevails here over those in employment. It is, however, believed that the work of expulsion will not begin till after the adjournment of the Senate.

It is said that Amos Kendall, of Kentucky, is to be appointed an auditor, and Tom Moore minister to Colombia![1]

I take my departure to-morrow. My inclination at present is not to return to the next Congress, but I shall reserve a final decision of the question, for a consideration of all circumstances, after my return home. The major part of my friends, whom I have consulted, think a seat in the next Congress inexpedient. Among them all the best spirit prevails, and high and confident hopes are cherished by them. Every movement of the President, though dictated by personal resentment toward me, conduces to my benefit, especially his Kentucky appointments.

Let me hear often from you. . . .

Copy. Printed in Colton, *Clay Correspondence*, 4:225-26.   1. Kendall's initial job in the Jackson administration was that of fourth auditor in the Treasury Department. For his subsequent career, see *DAB*. Thomas P. Moore of Ky. (see *BDAC*) replaced William Henry Harrison as U.S. minister to Colombia. See 7:621.

From Thomas McGiffin, Washington, Pa., March 12, 1829. Urges him to stop in Washington on his way home so that his many friends there might have an "opportunity of Testifying their respect to you." Points out that the "state of the roads" will have made the "journey fatiguing to yourself," that a "day or two nights rest" will refresh him, and that the low water in the river at this season will render "your passing down the river" to Kentucky a difficult task. ALS. DLC-HC (DNA, M212, R3).

While in Hancock, Md., on March 23, Clay wrote Alexander Wilson *et al.*, accepting with pleasure a dinner invitation in Washington, Pa., on March 28, and pointing out that he would likely be spending the previous evening in Brownsville, Pa. ALS. ICHi.

From John Currey *et al.*, Hagerstown, Md., March 14, 1829. Writing as the "Mechanics of Hagerstown and vicinity," a "class of citizens who have been the peculiar objects of the aid and encouragement afforded by your public and patriotic labours," invite Clay to a public supper at the Town Hall on March 20 at 8:00 p.m.   ALS, by S. Herbert. DLC-HC (DNA, M212, R3). Addressed to Clay at Frederick, Md.

It was at this affair in Hagerstown that Clay was later [May 5, 1841] quoted by Amos Kendall as having said: "If authority shall be accompanied with a spirit of relentless proscription, expelling from public employment men of tried capacity & integrity, & filling their places with others—and if all these evils shall flow from the councils of secret, unseen and unworthy and irresponsible advisers, then those who co operated to bring about the late event will have just cause to lament their success." *Kendall's Expositor*, May 5, 1841, pp. 107-8.

From Ferdinand R. Hassler, New York, March 14, 1829. Refers to the "two papers relative to the northern boundary line which I had the honor to communicate to You, the one at Your office the last day of [18]28.   the other sent from here are for me documents of importance upon my agency in that business, which, as You know, I must be ready at any time to justify. I regretted in time." Asks that they be returned to him "after perusal" by the hand of Secretary Samuel L. Southard. Does not want them left in the papers of the State Department. ALS. DLC-HC (DNA, M212, R3). For Hassler, first superintendent of the United States Coast Survey, and his relationship to the Northeast Boundary "business," see *DAB*.

From ROBERT WICKLIFFE   Lexington, March 15, 1829

I am truly distressed at an event which took place the other day   Charles [Wickliffe] imprudently got in to an encounter with the editor [Thomas R. Benning] of the [Lexington *Kentucky*] Gazette & the poor fellow attempting to use his cane Shot him mortally.[1] He was arrested & I became his bail but owing to the State of political excitement & the bias of the sheriffs I have consented to the advice of my friends that he shall not appear on tomorrow. My recognizance of Course will then be forfeited but I still wish to have it over at farthest next Court yet I am much embarrassed for the want of Counsel & never did I feel the want of you more. I am beset by the villains in a new mode & assailed through the misfortunes of a child

This unfits me to act, were I the subject of prosecution or punishment I should feel happy & defy their malice but I have a fathers fears a fathers weakness   I write this that you may receive it a weelling & hasten to Kentucky.

The whole has been the work & villany of the prince of villains *Jno* [John M.] *McCalla*   The Cowardly Scoundrel Skulked from responsibility while the Printer lived & Charles was in a situation to chastise him but after he has Caused the death of the Printer & as he hopes the r[u]in of my child he comes out [the] Hero & avows himself the auth[or] of the piece for which the Printer died   You know that I cannot be a judge of the affair. But It does seem to me that — if provacation & assault can Justify a boy that Charles — ought to be excused & I hope that when you learn even from their own witness[es] & creatures (for none others were present) the whole facts that you will think that Charles has not acted dishonrably much less feloneously. . . . P S. I fear nothing but Party

ALS. KyU. Addressed to Clay at Wheeling, Va. (W. Va.), with the envelope notation: "Should Mr Clay have passed Wheeling the Post Master will send it on to him."   1. Young Wickliffe shot Benning when he refused to identify the anonymous author (John M. McCalla) of a printed attack on his father, Robert. Clay, John J. Crittenden, and Richard H. Chinn represented Charles Wickliffe at the trial which began on June 30. On July 4, Wickliffe was acquitted by a jury that deliberated only a few minutes. The origin, development, and politics of the case are discussed in Dwight L. Mikkelson, "Kentucky Gazette, 1787-1848," Ph.D. dissertation, University of Kentucky, 1963, pp. 211-19. It can also be traced in the Lexington *Kentucky Gazette*, March 6, 13; June 19, 26; July 31, 1829. When George J. Trotter became editor of the *Gazette* in September, and made unflattering remarks about Charles Wickliffe's murder of Benning, Wickliffe called him out. On Oct. 9, Trotter killed him in their duel. J.W. Coleman, *Famous Kentucky Duels* (Frankfort, 1953), 69-83. McCalla complained that when addressing the jury Clay had "condescended to take particular notice of me," and that "all his powers of declamation, of wit, and of satire, were exerted to demolish my humble standing in society." He also called Clay "this windy orator of the West." Lexington *Kentucky Gazette*, July 31, 1829.

From Charles D. Knox, Wheeling, Va. (W. Va.), March 16, 1829. Writes again, as the spokesman of the "Manufacturers and Mackenicks of this place," asking Clay "to give to our Citizens an opportunity of manifesting the attachment and respect they feel for you personally and their approval of your political course." Mentions that an earlier (March 6) letter addressed to him in Washington must have arrived after he had left the city. Directs this letter to Hagerstown, Md.   ALS. DLC-HC (DNA, M212, R3).

Similar letters, all lauding Clay personally, castigating the Jacksonians, variously praising Clay's American System, his patriotism, and his statesmanlike posture during the recent bitterly-fought election, invited him to stop, take dinner with, or otherwise greet his friends as he made his way home to Kentucky. Such invitations were received from John Dawson, Uniontown, Pa., March 17, 1829; Martin Rizer *et al.*, Cumberland, Md., March 19, 1829; John Armstrong *et al.*, Maysville, Ky., March 22, 1829; D. L. Collier *et al.*, Steubenville, Ohio, March 26, 1829 (two letters of this date); and Kedick McKee, Wheeling, Va., March 26, 1829, with postscript dated March 27. All in *ibid.*

Clay wrote D. L. Collier *et al.* from Washington, Pa., on March 30, declining the Steubenville invitation with regret because the town was off the route he was taking on his way home. "You are right," he told Collier and his Committee of Arrangement, "in supposing that one of the objects of the slanders to which I have been exposed, has been accomplished; but another remains to be achieved, and until that also is decided, or until I shall have paid the common debt of nature, I shall be the object of ceaseless vituperation and malignant calumny. — With an approving conscience, sustained by a large and respectable portion of the virtuous and good among my fellow citizens, and witnessing the prosperity of my country under the practical operation of that policy which I have zealously supported, I shall disregard the abuse yet reserved for me, and rest in full confidence of final justice." Condemns the Jackson administration for launching a "system of intolerance and propscription" which can only lead to the "most pernicious consequences." Copy. Printed in Washington *Daily National Journal*, April 18, 1829.

His letter to Adam Beatty, Maysville, April 3, 1829, declined a dinner invitation there because of "the desire of my family and myself to reach home." ALS. NIC. He reached Lexington on April 6, 1829.

From Jesse B. Harrison, Lynchburg, Va., March 18, 1829. Explains his view of the meaning of the election of Andrew Jackson: "The *rationale* of this grand revolution is merely this: we have had the first grand triumph of the *rowdy* principle in the U. States — a triumph which, about once every twenty years, will, I venture to predict, constantly occur. The term and the idea are wholly Irish, but marvellously well adapted to the American soil. Behold a triumph of which foul ambition is the impulse among the leaders, and absolute bêtise, among those who follow! and that too in our century, and in America!" Assures Clay, however, that "most of our friends in Virginia will be very well content to abide by their avowed principles, and feel that the sentiments which befit a virtuous minority" will appeal more to honest men than the "swollen arrogance of the majority." As for Clay's own political future, guesses "that you cannot yourself decide what part you are to take in the coming events. I hope you do not consider our emancipation from the Jackson party as hopeless. Such is not the sentiment of our friends in Lynchburg. And I cannot but reflect that altho' J's majority of Electoral votes was overwhelming; yet every vote that went to make up the 95 [margin] was narrowly gained: so in fact the struggle was very critical. Let our friends but stand firm, & we will see a brighter day soon. And be assured, we trust much to that intensity of purpose, that vehemence of soul which have always characterized you. In the December of 1824 I was at Monticello — Mr. [Daniel] Webster was there also. Speaking of your enthusiasm in high designs, Mr. Jefferson with great emphasis said, 'Quisquid [*sic*] vult, valde vult'; the words were so apt, the tone so deep, and falling from him on a mute audience, that I scarcely wondered when Mr Webster involuntarily moved his lips after the sage! and repeated the glowing words. It is a rare effect of successful oratory to force your auditor to utter your *words*, as they fall from your mouth!" ALS. DLC-HC (DNA, M212, R3). The Latin phrase translates, "whatever he wants he wants badly." Harrison, who aspired to a teaching position in modern languages at the University of Virginia, eventually practiced law. *VMHB*, 80:320-21. See Clay to Henry Clay, Jr., April 19, 1829.

SPEECH AT FREDERICK, MD.   March 18, 1829
[Thanks the assembled diners for their invitation and the warmness of their reception. Continues:]

The prominent measures of the general government, in which I have participated, are, the late war with great Britain; the peace of Ghent by which it was concluded; the recognition of Spanish American independence, the cause of internal improvements; the settlement of the Missouri question; the protection of American industry; and most of the important public transactions of the last four years. I look back upon my agency, on those various occasions, with entire satisfaction, and without the slightest feeling of self-reproach. And I now quit the public councils of our country without any personal regret growing out of the part which I have, at any time, acted in public affairs. I have often, indeed, sincerely regretted the necessity which I have felt myself under of differing from friends and fellow citizens, for whom I entertained the greatest respect and esteem. I quit the public councils not only without any personal regret, but with the highest of all human consolations—that which is not only superior to any other, but the want of which cannot be compensated by the united possession of all others—which lies deeply embosomed in the heart, beyond the reach of human injustice—the consciousness of having faithfully, zealously and constantly discharged my public duties. [Mr. C. was here interrupted by the most enthusiastic applause.]

The honest, experienced and enlightened statesman, who was lately charged with the chief magistracy, and those who were associated with him in his administration, carry with them into retirement other cheering consolations. They carry with them the blessings and the approbation of a large and respectable part of the wise and the good of the American public. They carry with them the proud satisfaction of having transferred the executive government from their hands to those of their appointed successors, with the republic in the highest state of prosperity.

During the administration of that illustrious but persecuted citizen, the honor and the rights of the nation have been maintained abroad, whilst at home all our great domestic interests have been fostered and improved.

They leave the government, without a speck of war in the political horizon, at peace and in friendly intercourse with all nations. During their administration, many treaties, founded upon the most liberal and enlightened principles of friendship, commerce and navigation, have been formed.—The conclusion of several of these has been sought at the seat of the federal government, where, during the last four years, more have been actually signed than had been during the thirty-six previous years of the existence of our present constitution. Whilst a ceaseless opposition has discovered real or imaginary objection to almost every important measure of the late administration, these treaties have not only escaped all animadversion, but have commanded unanimous approbation. Our relations with Great Britain especially—that great power with which we come into contact and collision in so many points, on sea and on land—are perfectly friendly; and I bear, with pleasure my testimony to the conviction that the British government, equally with all the foreign governments, desires to cultivate peace and friendship with us. She will adhere, as sometimes perhaps she has, in a spirit of jealousy and rivalry, to her own interests; but I believe her to be animated, at present, by a sincere wish for the preservation of peace. And I hope that her example, in maintaining national rights, will not be lost upon us.

If we withdraw our attention from foreign states, and direct it to the internal condition of our country, we behold abundant cause of patriotic felicitation. Under the late administration, the constitution has been inviolably respected, and the laws faithfully executed. Our extensive fortifications have been nearly completed, and important additions and improvements have been made to our gallant navy, that safe and justly cherished arm of the national defence. The public debt has rapidly melted away, by the aid of an undiminished revenue, steadily and economically applied—so rapidly as to place the day of its entire extinction near at hand, and to give rise to wild propositions for distributing the surplus, which will soon not be wanted to fulfill our engagements. Our American system, which was at once both to destroy foreign commerce, and to dry up the sources of the public income, has disappointed all the predictions of its foes, and assures us of the speedy arrival of the day when our national independence will be consummated. The manufactures of our country have now struck such deep and strong root, that the hand of violence itself can scarcely tear up and destroy them. [Great applause.] Their twin-sister, internal improvements, has not been neglected. Large and liberal appropriations, in every part of the union, have been made to that beneficent object.

Such are some of the fruits of the late abused administration. Whilst, throughout its whole progress, it was assailed by a bitter, vigilant, intelligent and powerful opposition, members of which were not wanting to avow a readiness to condemn either of the alternatives, in public measures, which were presented to the executive choice.

A majority of the people of the United States, in the exercise of the highest of human privileges, has decreed a transfer of power from the hands which lately held it to those of one of our fellow citizens, who enjoys a greater share of their affection and confidence. This change was personal and not intended to be one of policy. — Brought about by the regular action of our free institutions, those even who regret, ought to acquiesce, in it. Whether we comprise a part of the crew, or are in authority in the national ship, we should most anxiously wish it a prosperous voyage, under its new commander. [Cheering.] The love of the country ought to predominate over all selfish and party views and interests. [Applause.] We shall hasten to forget all the personal collisions and angry contentions which arose out of the recent contest. That contest often divided father from son, and brother from brother, and embittered the most intimate private relations. Not one of principle so much as of personal preference, we should all strive to obliterate a recollection of painful incidents, to gather together the scattered fragments of society, and to again blend and unite them in one harmonious structure. [Applauses.] Let us henceforward substitute to mere personal contests, the higher and nobler struggle for principle, for liberty, for sound measures of national policy. [Applauses.] By the standard of these we may safely try the new administration. By its neglect or devotion to these ought it to be approved or condemned. I seize with pleasure, the opportunity of expressing my sense of the liberality of those now here, who, actuated by those patriotic sentiments, honor me by their presence, although we differed in the late contest. [Applause.]

I avail myself of this opportunity to express my deep sense of the many obligations under which I have been placed by the people of Maryland. I can never forget that to their love of truth and justice, to their generous sympathies, and to their hatred of calumny and persecution, I stand as much if not more indebted than to the people of any other state. [Loud cheering.] It was here that the people, in resolutions and addresses, adopted at public meetings, first expressed their affection and confidence towards me, and their indignant feelings towards my persecutors and calumniators. This high minded conduct has made a grateful impression on my heart which can never be effaced. And I beg leave to propose a sentiment which I most sincerely entertain.

Health, happiness and prosperity to the people of Maryland.

[Mr. Clay resumed his seat amidst loud and reiterated plaudits.][1]

Copy. Printed "in substance" in *Niles' Register* (April 18, 1829), 36:124-25. The dinner company numbered 213 gentlemen.   1. On March 20, Clay, writing from Hagerstown, Md., sent to Samuel Barnes and Dr. William Bradley Tyler of Frederick, what he described as "a rough sketch of my remarks at the dinner in Frederick, hastily prepared, amidst Circumstances the most unfavorable for composition. It is characterized by as much fidelity as is compatible with their extemporaneous nature." ALS. Courtesy of St. George L. Sioussat, Washington, D.C.   Barnes and Tyler were members of the local arrangements committee. Tyler was incorrectly identified [7:33] as M. Bradley Tyler.

SPEECH AT HAGERSTOWN, MD.   March 20, 1829

[Thanks the audience for their toasts to the American System, John Quincy Adams, William Henry Harrison, and himself, and for the gracious invitation to address them on this occasion. Continues:]

A nation may possess the advantages of a genial climate and a fertile soil, its granaries may be full to overflowing, its fields may teem with the finest flocks, it may abound in all the varied productions of the earth; but if the arts are not introduced and successfully cultivated, or if they are suffered to languish for the want of due encouragement, that nation cannot be comfortable, great and powerful, nor, I will add, independent.

It was this reflection that prompted me long ago to enlist under the flag, bearing the inscription of Domestic Manufactures and Internal Improvements, which adorns the wall behind me. The nation wisely adopted the policy, and the nation is now reaping the rich harvest of the forecast of Congress. Is there, in this wide spread country, a patriotic heart that does not swell with pride at the contemplation of the rapid progress of the arts, and the high degree of perfection which they have already attained under the fostering care of government? And yet he must be an inexperienced or sleeping mariner, who does not see a gathering storm that threatens, at no distant day, to destroy that system under which the mechanic and manufacturing arts have so greatly prospered. It would be folly and madness to shut our eyes and conceal from ourselves the fact, that a great, and I fear, a doubtful struggle is just at hand. The Hall of the House of Representatives will be its theatre; and at the next session of Congress the tug of war will be there exhibited.

I hope the American System may survive the impending contest. Sustained, as in my humble judgment it is, both by the Constitution and by the soundest policy, it ought to prevail. But, if in its origin it had been doubtful; if it had been even wiser to have disregarded the experience of all great nations, and to have suffered the infant arts to make their unassisted way, against the overwhelming competition from the practised skill and long accumulated capitals of rival nations, the question, which is now presented, is totally different. The policy of protection has been solemnly adopted and proclaimed by the Government, not only once, but again and again. Under faith of it, capital has been invested, large establishments formed, and the industry of thousands of our fellow citizens applied. To abandon, at this time, the policy thus sanctioned, would manifest no unsteadiness and caprice discreditable to Government. It would inflict the greatest injustice and cruelty on individuals, and be productive of calamity to the nation. In the affairs of Government, there is a vast difference between the institution and the abolition of measures of national policy. When a scheme to advance the general prosperity is first proposed, it may be conscientiously opposed by a statesman who, after it has been carried into practical operation, would not feel himself justified in voting its repeal.

We have, fellow citizens, just terminated a long, arduous, and embittered contest for the office of Chief Magistrate of our country. It raged with a violence which we ought to hope will not be often exhibited. During its continuance society was shook to its centre, and the most intimate ties of connexion were rent asunder. The will of the majority has been expressed, and the will of

14

the majority should be respected. In our free institutions, popular elections are, happily, frequent. — But unless we mean to perpetuate feuds, and render immortal animosities excited in the heat of the struggle, it should be the wish and the aim of all to tranquilize society, and to restore its harmony, after the decision of the majority has been fairly pronounced. This effort to heal wounds and reunite brethren who have been separated by passion or misconception, is perfectly consistent with the duty of watching, in future, over our rulers, and of bringing their measures to the standard of reason.

Happily, the past Administration of our country are sure guides to the present, if it choose to follow them, and furnish to the people unerring tests by which to judge the conduct of the new Cabinet. If the peace of the nation is preserved with foreign powers, whilst its honor and its rights are firmly maintained; and if the domestic policy which has been hitherto pursued shall be still continued, the country may have no cause to regret the recent change. But if we should be involved in unnecessary war, or any of our rights should be abandoned, or our honor tarnished; if the interests of our navigation or commerce shall be sacrificed; or if the protection of our manufactures shall be abandoned; the improvement of our country be neglected, and the public treasure misapplied, those, who did not concur in that change, will find some of their worst fears realized. If misrule shall be accompanied by a spirit of relentless proscription, expelling from public employments men of tried capacity and integrity, and filling their places with others devoid of the requisite attainments, and if all these evils shall flow from the counsels of secret, unseen, unworthy, and irresponsible advisers, then those who cooperated in bringing about the late event will have just cause to lament their success. Above all, the people of this country are not prepared, and I trust in God will never be prepared, to set up any human idol to be worshipped, nor to consider all the duties of patriotism as comprehended in blind devotion to such an idol. If an edict shall be sent forth, requiring that, instead of great and enduring principles of liberty and policy, attachment to the name of an individual shall constitute the sole passport to public confidence, and that all who do not profess it shall be excluded from public situations, my life upon it such an edict will never be registered in the hearts of American freemen.

[Concludes with a toast to the Constitution of the United States, "as it has been, and as it ought to be always expounded, affording protection to our arts as it gives vigor to our arms, in all collisions with Foreign Powers." Following another series of toasts by diners present, Clay added: "The Irish Catholic — success to his struggles for liberty."]

Copy. Printed in Washington *Daily National Journal*, March 31, 1829. Dinner speech given to "about two hundred persons . . . consisting of gentlemen of the various branches of business and the arts, and of the various learned professions."

From Stephen Duncan, Natchez, Miss., March 22, 1829. In response to an inquiry from Clay dated March 9, says he "would not like to fix on the price of your rope." He would be willing, however, to buy "at a fair price," Clay's total production if it can be delivered in May and paid for on January 1, 1830. Remarks that he needs 6,000 lbs. Adds: "The rope I got of you last year. was not as good as you supposed it to be: it was in fact, a cent per lb inferior to the supply of the year previous. I am well awares that you were ignorant of this. and I did not consider it necessary to complain." Concludes that he is "verry apprehensive we shall have a War with G. Britain — and that before the 1st. of July. I think much will depend on the character & disposition of the special

Messenger. War would be ruinous to this section of country. —" ALS. InU. For Duncan, one of the South's wealthiest plantation owners, see D. Clayton James, *Antebellum Natchez* (Baton Rouge, 1968), 150-53. The "special Messenger" was Louis McLane of Delaware. See F. Lee Benns, *The American Struggle for the British West India Carrying Trade, 1815-1830* (1923; reprint ed., Clifton, N. J., 1972), 163.

From PHILIP R. FENDALL   Washington, March 24, 1829

The unexpected manner in which the Senate retreated from Mr. [Littleton W.] Tazewell's maneuvre,[1] having placed the Panama instructions within the reach of the Public,[2] and consequently prevented the contingency on which I was to deliver to the Editors of the [Washington *Daily National*] Journal and [Washington *Daily National*] Intelligencer your joint note with its accompaniments. I determined to withhold from them those papers. After Mr. [Peter] Force, however, had caused about one half of the Instructions to be transcribed from the Senate copy, I lent him the residue in order to expedite the printing. As we carefully collated the proof with the Ms., I trust you will find no material errors in the impression in the Journal of the 20th. inst., nor in that of the Intelligencer of the following day., But one opinion exists so far as I can learn, in regard to those Instructions; always excepting from the unanimity, the patriotic objections of Gen. Jackson and Gen. [Duff] Green.

The Journal of this morning copies from a Frederick town [Md.] paper an account of the proceedings connected with your visit to that place.[3] We are all here expecting anxiously some Reports of your speech, and also of the proceedings at Hagerstown,[4] where, we learn from letters received here both a dinner and an evening entertainment were given.

In a late number of [Mordecai M.] Noah's paper [New York *Enquirer*], is a passage which means either that you are now sixty years old, or that Jackson is to remain in office till you are superannuated. The [Providence, R.I.] Literary Subaltern of the 17th inst. introduces your speech [March 7, 1829] at. the dinner here with an article written in the spirit which distinguished the better days of its Editor [Sylvester S. Southworth], and which there is no reason to doubt, animates the People of New England. I herewith send the paper. All your intelligent friends whom I see are constant, devoted and confident.

The newspapers will have informed you that the work of Reform, commenced by the substitution of Mr [Thomas] Moore for Gen. [William Henry] Harrison, has been continued by that of Messrs: [William B.] Lewis, [Isaac] Hill and [Amos] Kendall, for Messrs [William] Lee, [Richard] Cutts and [Tobias] Watkins.[5] Lewis tried, I believe, to certify the Hero out of some discreditable speculations;[6] Hill slandered Mr and Mrs Adams;[7] and Kendall, besides his base ingratitude to his benefactor, had the farther merit of having committed a perjury.[8] It seems to be the determination of the Imperial mind, to honour vice, to reward friends and to punish enemies. Various reports connected with this determination are afloat, but they rest on such insufficient authority, and the course of the Executive is so vacillating, that it is not worth while to [illeg. word] with them. The government is supposed [illeg. words] in the hands of Duff Green and Mr [John H.] Eaton [illeg. word] Green is often, and it would seem confidentially, with the President. The only sumptom [*sic*, symptom?] of Anti Reform yet vissible, is the appointment of a Mr. [Benjamin] Williams to be warden of the [District of Columbia] Penitentiary, and of one or two friends of Mr. [John Q.] Adams to the board of Director[s]. Williams, it is understood, was the candidate preferred by the late President.

Jackson has been very sick for several days, but is now recovering. Dr. [Tobias] Watkins, who does not bear his ejection very well, is making an effort to get possession of the [Washington *Daily National*] Journal. Mr. [Samuel L.] Southard, who has had the misfortune to lose one of his children [Ann], is now at his friend Mr. R J Coxes,[9] in a state of health which I am sorry to believe is extremely alarming. Mr. [John Q.] Adams and Mr. [Richard] Rush, whom I see occasionally, are in good health.

You would oblige me, Sir, by offering my respectful compliments to Mrs. Clay. I will not attempt to express the gratification which I shall receive by being honored with any commands from you which I may be capable of executing, nor my anxiety to testify the attachment to you which on every personal and public ground. I must always and profoundly feel.

ALS. DLC-HC (DNA, M212, R3). Addressed to Clay at Wheeling, Va. (W. Va.).   1. Tazewell's attempt to have Clay's Panama instructions [5:313-44] printed was defeated by the Senate on March 16, 1829, by a vote of 18 to 13. Thomas H. Benton, *Abridgement of the Debates of Congress From 1789 to 1856* (New York, 1859), 10:256-57. For Tazewell's earlier attempts to get the instructions published, see *Register of Debates*, 20 Cong., 2 Sess., 75-76, 80.   2. Gales and Seaton to Clay, March 6, 1829.   3. Speech at Frederick, Md., March 18, 1829.   4. Speech at Hagerstown, Md., March 20, 1829.   5. Thomas Moore replaced Harrison as minister to Colombia; William B. Lewis of Tenn. replaced William Lee as second auditor in the Treasury Dept.; Isaac Hill of N.H. replaced Richard Cutts as second comptroller; Amos Kendall of Ky. replaced Tobias Watkins as fourth auditor. Washington *Daily National Journal*, April 9, 1829.   6. Having to do with leasing the salt lick on the Chickasaw cession in 1818. See 7:488-89; and John S. Bassett (ed.), *Correspondence of Andrew Jackson*, 7 vols. (Washington, 1926-35), 2:443-44.   7. The allegation that while serving as U.S. minister in Russia in 1809-14, Adams had procured a woman for the pleasure of Tsar Alexander I.   Isaac Hill had included the story in his campaign biography of Jackson, *Brief Sketch of the Life, Character and Services of Major General Andrew Jackson. By a Citizen of New England*. Concord, N.H., 1828.   8. See 7:306-7, 327-31, 379-80.   9. Richard J. Coxe had worked with Southard as a solicitor in the Navy Department.

From Otho H. N. Stull, Hagerstown, Md., March 28, 1829. Reports that he has just seen a letter from former Postmaster General John McLean to "a particular friend of mine, but a *quondam* bitter enemy of yours," dated March 15, 1829, in which McLean wrote: "Under other *circumstances*, I should have remained in the department, as I prefer political life to the *Bench*. It is my *determination* not to abandon *the field of politicks*, but to return to it when a *suitable* opportunity offers." The "underscores," Stull continues, "are my own." Interprets McLean's statement to mean that "the *circumstances* alluded to" were related to the fact that McLean "peremptorily refused to subscribe to the terms of uniform proscription [of Adams's appointees], as the only condition upon which he could retain his place"; and that on this point, what Clay had "gathered orally, was here written down in plain characters." Concludes: "The attempt to deceve the publick mind in relation to the true character of Mr McLean's *elevation to the Bench* [U.S. Supreme Court], displays in a still more perspicu[ous] light the extreme depravity of 'the powers that be,' thro[ugh] their organ the 'attrocious Duff [Green].'" ALS. DLC-HC (DNA, M212, R3). Stull was postmaster at Hagerstown.

From HENRY CLAY, JR.   West Point, March 29, 1829

Your favour of the 3d Inst enclosing a ckeck on the Branch Bank of the U.S. at New York for $150 has long since come to hand—I should have acknowledged the receipt of it before had it not been for my uncertainty as to the place to which it should be directed—The sum which you have sent me I have no doubt will be quite sufficient to defray all the necessary expences of the journey to K'y and to supply me with Citizen's clothes. I am delighted at your kind desire to have me with you next encampment; I shall most certainly avail myself of the opportunity to visit you at Ashland. I wrote to Anne [Brown Clay Erwin] some time since persuading her to meet me in Ky and in her answer she tells me that she will spend all the sickly season at home and expresses *almost* a readiness to go to Ky by way of New York and West Point. How pleasant it will be to assemble once more around our own fireside, to conve[r]se about times that have passed by, stations that have been filled with honour and to relate the amusing adventures which each of us has engaged in and which, in relation, will be interesting to all of us

I am more glad now than ever that your vote was given against Gen. Jackson. His conduct since his election to the Presidency has shown clearly that all the disqualifications of a hasty temper, want of discrimination in the selection of officers and an untiring obstinacy which have been imputed to him do really exist. The last parpagraphs of his inaugural address,[1] if written by him, evince feelings of sore resentment, which however well they might become the man should be banished by the President—

I am rejoiced to see by the papers that Maryland has extended to you her hospitality—It must be cheering to you to have the generous flow of kindly feeling which seems to pervade all classes and which is characteristic of the state directed towards you.

I devote a great deal of my time to literary composition. Since you have given your consent to my studying law—I have had but one desire, that of appearing a practitioner at the Bar. I do not know that I shall suceed but if I do not, I shall be eminent in no other profession; for I do sincerely believe that my mind is better adapted for the Law than for any thing else.

I have lately recd a letter from Theodore [Wythe Clay], it shall be answered immediately. I would be glad if you would ask him to enquire if I shall have the honour of receiving a degree of A.M. at the approaching commencement.[2] If [William C.C.] Claiborne [Jr.] be with you, Remember me to him but do not ask him to write to me this he seems too little inclined to do. Tender my sincere regards to my mother and to all of our friends & relations. . . . P.S. I thought of sending some of my own drawings to the family by Mr Davies[3] who will go to the West in a short time, but I believe that it will be better to bring them myself—These will exhibit greater improvement in the graphic art, as our erudite Teacher of drawing [Thomas Gimbrede] says, than I can perhaps boast of in many other departments, And I hold it a maxim always to carry evidence of improvement about one whether it be in the mind or hand—

ALS. Henry Clay Memorial Foundation, Lexington, Ky.   1. *MPP*, 2:436-38.   2. Henry Clay, Jr., received the M.A. degree from Transylvania University at commencement exercises on July 29, 1829. Lexington *Kentucky Reporter*, August 5, 1829.   3. Cadet Thomas Alfred Davies of N.Y., U.S.M.A., class of 1829.

From Eliza Sibley [Mrs. Josiah S.] Johnston, Louisville, March 29, 1829. Describes her trip from Washington en route to New Orleans. Notes that the boat they took at Wheeling was forced to stop in Louisville where they have remained for five days. States that if only "could I have had the hope of seeing you I should have reconciled myself" to stay "a week longer." Mentions that she has received "many civilities from the ladies here," and describes the women as "quite pretty & well informed, but awkward, & dress badly." Complains of being unable to sleep ("a distressing disease"), and adds that she is "tired of everything—the good people of Kentucky must certainly have some subject of interest among themselves, but I should die of Ennui, very soon—I have not heard anything that I did not know before or seen anything to interest since my arrival."

Describing her friendly personal feelings, comments: "I did think of you the first Sunday Eveg, till my head & heart ached & I went sick to bed." Adds that "I have had many political contests on the Boat & elsewhere, during the journey my blood glows, when you are unkindly spoken of & I defend you with all my mite of eloquence." Concludes by asking him to "pray tell me all your plans for the future—confide in me, as formerly, I shall be faithful to my trust & betray nothing imprudent." ALS. DLC-HC (DNA, M212, R3).

To PHILIP R. FENDALL　　　　Wheeling, Va. (W. Va.), March 31, 1829

I received here and thank you for your favor of the 24 instant. Upon the whole, I am glad that the Panama instructions have been published in the manner they have been,[1] which prevents an objection which would have been raised, if my authority for their publication had been used. I am amused with the squeamishness of the majority of the Senate, lest they should be considered, by ordering the publication of them, as giving any sanction to their objects etc. When before was the order of the Senate or of the House, a mere matter of course, constr[ai]ned as an approval of the message or document directed to be printed? The majority would have been safe against any such imputation, from the elevated views of the instructions; but it deserves nevertheless severe animadversion for its factitiousness.

I have been greatly distressed, on their account, by the removal of Mess. Cutts, Watkins and Lee.[2] Why is not that a subject of severe censure? Those officers hitherto have been considered as a sort of judicial officer. Millions annually depend upon their honest liquidation of accounts. If the President, without any official misconduct, removes that description of officer, can there be a greater abuse? Where is the safety in their passing or rejecting a/cs. according to the Presidential will?

My journey, throughout its whole progress, has been a kind of triumphant march.[3] Every species of demonstration has been made of warm attachment. Stages, taverns, tollgates have been generally thrown open to me, without charge; and I have literally had a free passage. I must refer to the paper for further details. I attend a dinner here today, and a ball tonight. Tomorrow or the next day I shall descend the Ohio river. Yesterday, saturday and today are the first Spring days we have had.

Let me hear from you frequently, and communicate all the details of passing events. Do not forget to tell Mr. [Peter] Force to send me the tri weekly [Washington *Daily National*] Journal.

ALS. KyU.　　1. Fendall to Clay, March 24, 1829; also 7:628.　　2. Fendall to Clay, March 24, 1829. Also for Watkins, see Clay to Hammond, May, 27, 1829.　　3. See 7:633.

Speech at Wheeling, Va. (W. Va.), March 31, 1829. Thanks his audience for its kindness to him and then, according to the reporter on whose notes the speech is based, "proceeded at considerable length to expatiate on the policy of the protection of American Industry." Reviews the constitutional arguments for tariff protection and the importance of the latter to the growth of American industry. Predicts that "Congress would shortly be the theatre of a serious attempt to subvert the established policy of the Government, in regard to Domestic Manufactures," as is "evident from all the signs of the times." Regrets that President Jackson "in his recent exposition of the principles by which he intends to be guided, during his administration, has not been less ambiguous, on this subject." Points out that a paragraph in the president's inaugural address "lays down the rule against the policy of protection." Charges that during "the late Presidential canvass," Jackson represented himself "in all the Tariff states" as a "friend of the American System . . . a warmer and more unreserved friend than his competitor."

He should now, therefore, reassure Pennsylvania, Ohio, and Kentucky, states he carried handily, on this point. Argues that the "Western Section" of the nation is most concerned with Jackson's true stance on this issue.

Demands that the "Cumberland Road . . . constructed by National means, for great National purposes" should be "protected, repaired and preserved by National authority." The road is a "Bond of Union" designed to "connect, by an indissoluble chain, the two great sections of our country. It was made more particularily for the comfort and benefit of the Western States." It is also "our only comfortable pass of the Mountains which divide our country. It is the Thermopylae of the people of the West, not in a military, but in a civil and social sense." Discusses its importance to Wheeling. Argues, further, that its maintenance is a national obligation not to be "turned over to local, subordinate and inferior jurisdictions." Hopes that a branch of it will be built through Kentucky and Tennessee to the Gulf of Mexico. As a system of such extensions develops, the "preservation and protection" of the whole must be "enforced . . . by *one* controlling will!" Copy. Published in Lexington *Kentucky Reporter*, April 22, 1829. No manuscript copy of the speech has been found.

To ELIZA & JOSIAH S. JOHNSTON
Wheeling, Va. (W. Va.),
April 1, 1829

W. C. C. Claiborne [Jr.] having decided rather suddenly to throw himself on board a Steam boat about departing for Louisville, I have only time to say that we reached this place the day before yesterday, nine days after you, in good health. I found here Mr. Johnston's letter, informing me of your journey &c. The same snow that you left in the Mountains remained and smoothed our passage over them, altho' it rendered us somewhat uncomfortably Cold.

My journey has been marked by every token of warm attachment, and cordial demonstration. I never experienced more testimonies of respect and confidence, nor more enthusiasm. Dinners, Suppers, Balls &c. I have had litterally a free passage. Taverns, Stages, Toll gates have been generally thrown open to me, free from all charge. Monarchs might be proud of the reception with which I have been every where honored.

The work of proscription has commenced at Washington and elsewhere. Our poor friend Mr. [Richard] Cutts, [Tobias] Watkins and [William] [L]ee are among the sufferers. Editor [Isaac] Hill has succeeded the first, Editor [Amos] Kendall the second, and Majr. [William B.] Lewis the last.[1] So we. . . .

ALS. PHi. Letter multilated and incomplete. Printed in Colton, *Clay Correspondence*, 4:226.
1. Fendall to Clay, March 24, 1829.

From Otho W. Callis, Prince George's County, Md., April 4, 1829. Identifies himself as a veteran officer of the War of 1812 who is attempting to raise a company of "fifty of my countrymen" to accompany him to Mexico to serve in the Mexican Army as soldiers of fortune. Asks Clay to recommend him for a captaincy in that army. Believes Clay is the nation's best friend as well as "the friend of all Mankind," as he proved in 1824 when he "held the destinies of the world" in his hands. Adds: "Please tell me what I must do to procure the desired imployment in Mexico?" ALS. DLC-HC (DNA, M212, R3). Written from "Palmers Tavern."

From JOHN F. HENRY
Hopkinsville, Ky., April 8, 1829

I presume from the accounts I have received of your movements, that by the time this reaches Lexington, you will be quietly seated at Ashland, enjoying the respect of all honorable men, and the consciousness of having struggled with firmness, against the tide, which has overwhelmed almost all the virtue and talents of the Country. — If any thing had been wanting to convience [*sic*] the thinking part of the community of his utter unfitness for the Station, which he occupies, the Hero has furnished evidence, in the selection of his Cabinet, & Foreign Ministers, and in the indiscriminate removal of every man who opposed his Election, which none but the most blind and devoted can question. This course is however strangely captivating to his supporters, who, no doubt *expected to be rewarded* for their loyalty and zeal. — I cannot but fear, that the worst effects will result from the introduction of so many new and inexperienced men, who bankrupt in character and fortune, will go into office, with the intention of fattening upon the public spoil, and, thus averting the destiny, which awaits them admidst this general regret nothing affords me any pleasure, except the circumstance of his having removed from Kentucky three or four of the most pestiferous vermin who ever infested our counsels. —

I have heard but one opinion among your friends, of this section of the State which is, that you should resume your Station in Congress, where you can still be the rallying point of the friends of the American System. No doubt can, I think, be entertained as to the policy of the new administration on the various points involved in relation to that system; and unless you are in Congress to sustain the measures, which even you would admit you have been chiefly instrumental, in promoting. We very much fear the most disastrous changes —

[Suggests, at length, that if Clay resumes his law practice in Lexington, he will consider hiring Henry's brother, Gustavus A. Henry, to assist him. Points out that his brother is a graduate of Transylvania University who read law under Judge John Boyle.]

ALS. DLC-HC (DNA, M212, R3).

From Francis Johnson, Bowling Green, Ky., April 8, 1829. Asks him to visit among his friends in the Bowling Green area, noting that the "Current has begun to set strong for you — the Hero [Andrew Jackson] has greatly disappointed his friends and many have become disaffected with him: but they do not yet like to own it openly —" Has learned that Presley Edwards, brother-in-law of John Pope, is a candidate for the state senate. Notes that Edwards "was known to be your enemy and to have, espoused the cause of Jackson, because Adams had appointed you Secretary." But since he "is desirous of being Elected — and the strength of Public Opinion [is] in your favor," he has "come out, sort of half way for you —" Further, both Edwards and Pope have suggested that "I would become a candidate for Congress," a position that indicates his (Johnson's) belief that "Pope is desirous of a reconcilliation between you & himself —"

Discusses his thinking on running for Congress, as he has been "exceedingly pressed" to do, against "the late incumbent [Joel Yancey]." Reports that he definitely does not want the job, but that, since Ephraim M. Ewing and Judge Christopher Tompkins seem reluctant to run, he may have to offer himself. Says his only political ambition is to return to the state legislature a year hence, in order to make a speech "giving an *account* or *sketch* of the *Heros* cabinet and appointments."

Assures Clay "this section of the State is permanently & unchangably for you, against the *world* — [Chittenden] Lyon I heard has declared for you — Judge [Alney] McLean I learned would probably oppose [Thomas] Chilton, and if so he beats him." Has discovered that in Louisville "Many prominent Jackson men" are urging him to run. Remarks that the "prevailing disposition in: our freinds seem to be, that I should beat the 'returned Member' [Yancey] in preference to any one else —"

Concludes with this advice to Clay: "Now as it regards yourself, suffer me to say a word, and give to it what weight it shall seem to deserve — I am decidedly opposed to your entering into public life, in any office or station whatever for the present. everybody knows you can be Elected by the people of this state or any part of the State to what office you please—That public affairs are to go awry I have no doubt; and if you remain a year or two out of public employment, the more intensely will the public eye be cast toward [you]—In Legislature matters your fame is fule—to meddle in Legislative state matters, would afford a ground for the enemies to build up some thing against you—for the truth is not regarded by them—To go to Congress, will not do: at the head of the Government [Jackson], I consider we have a Robrtspeire [sic, Robespierre], a Danton & a Marat: Van Buren is the Danton & [Samuel] Ingham the Marat: they are surrounded, by some of the most unprincipled & base men in the Nation; [Amos] Kendal [sic, Kendall], [Isaac] Hill &c. and others no doubt, will be brought into the public employment—We have seen how ready they are at invention and how strong to swear & prove whatever they project—You are the Mordecai, to the whole phalanx—And if your person could be safe amid such a phalanx of devouring & cunning monsters, could you expect to escape altogether, again you could not expect to controul the Measures of the Government and they would ascribe, with unblushing impudence, every evil to your Opposition, for they would have you opposed, openly or secretly—every wise & prudent consideration in my opinion, dictates that you should not return to Washington, as a Member of Congress—You might spend a winter there, attending the Supreme Court if you chose." [P.S.] "10th. April: I have recd a letter from Judge Tompkins to day he declines becoming a a [sic] candidate—And of necessity, I shall have to oppose the late incumbent—" ALS. InU. Edwards won the Logan County senate seat in the August 3 election. He was the brother of Ninian Edwards and husband of Hester Pope. Johnson had lost a congressional election to Yancey in 1827. The latter, in Johnson's eyes, was thus "the late incumbent," or the "returned Member." He challenged Yancey for his seat in the August, 1829, congressional elections and lost again. Chittenden Lyon was returned to his seat in the U.S. House without opposition. Chilton, in the eleventh district, won reelection to the U.S. House over his opponent, James Crutcher, by 1,903 votes. Lexington *Kentucky Gazette*, May 8; September 11, 1829; Frankfort *Argus of Western America*, July 8; September 2, 1829; Louisville *Public Advertiser*, August 29, 1829. The reference to Mordecai is from the *Book of Esther*.

From THOMAS H. BLAKE   Louisville, April 9, 1829

I left Washington on the 31st. of March and Baltimore on Friday last, and reached this place last night. The last removal from office which I heard of was that of [Edward] Jones, the chief clerk of the Treasury Department, and learnt at the same time that Asbury Dickens [sic, Dickins], was put in his place. Who is to succeed Dickens I did not learn, nor did I consider it important to enquire.[1]

On the day I left Baltimore, I was overtaken at Fredericktown [Frederick, Md.] by Mr. [John] McLean the late Postmaster General, who came through Montgomery, and was on his way with his family to establish their residence at Cincinnati. In a conversation I had with him in the publick sitting room, as he appeared disposed to be communicative, I endeavored to ascertain from him his state of feeling towards the present administration, and his views of their late conduct in making so many removals from office, and which I said, I had heard would be persisted in. Mr. McLean in the course of his remarks said, that "his principles and General Jacksons were the same, as the General had avowed them to him, but that it was yet to be seen whether the General would practice upon these principles. Sir, (said he) misrepresentations, have been made to General Jackson—he is deceived. No man should be proscribed for an honest opinion, under our government, and if the course begun by this administration should be persisted in, there must be a reaction. This government should look to its moral force to sustain it, and not to the gratification of party." I named Mr. [Martin] Van Buren to him, stating that he had now arrived at Washington, and that it was expected *he* would put a stop to removals from office. & to this Mr. McLean answered with an emphasis, which I thought indicated bitterness of feeling towards the individual, that "those who had such an expectation of Mr. Van Buren would be disappointed, for that so far from Mr. Van Burens putting a stop to removals from Office, he was one of those very men who would be for supporting and encouraging such a course." I have thought it proper to communicate this conversation to you, which took place by accident, as it may possibly assist you to discern the course which Mr. McLean may hereafter pursue, and as I thought it due to you to be more acquainted with what seemed to me, a change in Mr. McLean, and not only a willingness, to abandon the present administration, but also a willingness to oppose it.

I shall leave this in a day or two for Terre Haute, and believe that I shall accept the invitation which the citizens of the county [Vigo] in which I live have given me, to represent them next winter in the Legislature of the State,[2] and where I can do much more in promoting what may be required for the publick good, than it would be possible for me to do in the next Congress.[3] [P.S.] The report in this town to day is, that [Shadrach] *Penn* has been offered the appointment of postmaster in the place of [John T.] Gray, but that he will not accept.[4] What is the country coming to? I am inclined to think it is mere rumour or I should have heard it at Washington.

ALS. DLC-HC (DNA, M212, R3).   1. Dickins had been a clerk in the Treasury Dept. before replacing Jones as chief clerk; Samuel M. McKean took Dickins' previous position. *Biennial Register*, 1829, p. 18.   2. Blake ran for the state legislature and was elected.   3. Blake, unsuccessful candidate for reelection in 1828 to the twenty-first Congress, declined to run for a seat in the twenty-second. *BDAC.*   4. Gray was replaced as Louisville postmaster in 1829 by John P. Oldham.

To JAMES ERWIN   Lexington, April 9, 1829

[Reports that "we reached home, all in pretty good health," on April 6. Discusses business affairs in New Orleans. Continues:][1]

We are just beginning to keep house at Ashland again. Although we have very little furniture there, Mrs. Clay prefers being on the spot; and I have this moment learnt that two waggon loads of furniture and effects expedited from Washington *are now* between Frankfort and this place. In less than two weeks we shall be comfortably re-established at Ashland. We hear, with great pleasure, that you and Anne and your children will join us in May. We shall be delighted to have you with us. And I hope you will prevail upon [Martin] Duralde to accompany you.

[William C.C., Jr.] Claiborne will be with you long before this letter reaches you. He will tell you all about us that I have not time now to write. And I hope that he also will visit us this spring or summer with you.

I must refer to the News papers for all public affairs.

ALS. NHi.   1. See 7:614-15.

From GEORGE F. WARFIELD   Baltimore, April 9, 1829

We have much pleasure in hearing of the favorable attentions to you at every public place & Town on your Journey, homeward, & we watch with increased delight the gratefull expressions of feeling towards you, by an honest & Intelligent people. — The deceptive glair by which the late Change has been effected in the Counsils of the Nation will soon pass away, & retributive justice is close at hand to measure back to the Enemy a full Merit of the peoples resentment; & the lights that will now be spread, will I trust convince the honest part of the late opposition; of the Purity, Integrity & Wisdom of the late administration, and will bring home to their understandings the duplicity which has been practiced upon them by the worst spirits in our Country, & they will be stricken with Consternation & astonishmt. at their having been made the dupes of such political magicians as are now in power — The People have already begun to repent of the great error they have commited, & time which unfolds all things will do justice to the demands of the late talandt. dignified & Virtuous administration, & history will record the means Employed to bring about the present state of Public affairs; when the hiden Monster will be made to appear in all its deformity. It is likely we shall suffer, & perhaps it is good for us we should suffer for a time, & with patience; until the Eyes of the Nation is fully opened to the abuses which may be brought on us, it will then be, the people will look back upon what has just passed, with regret & astonishment for the grate Sins they have Commited, by Elevating such men to power —

The letter of Mr. Adams in reply to the N. Jersey Committee[1] is sought for, & read with much interest by all classes; & by your friends (in particular) with delight, & many of the Jackson party openly admit that you have been unjustly persecuted & that is the Connection is now disolved between you & Mr. Adams they will support you at the next Presidential Election for President — I think but a short time must convince the people of their unjust distrust & they will be brought back to sound principales — The late changes made in the subordinate offices by the Jackson Cabinet, has already produced, disorder in their Camp & many among them disapprove of the Proscription system & consider the Example a dangerous Policy — depend on it Maryland will stand Erect & do her duty at the next Election for Members to the assembly,[2] as allso for Congress. — We are just informed that Jackson Committee will bring out [John van Laer] McMahon & [Elias] Brown (Brown is the late Jackson Elector for this district) to oppose [Peter] Little & [John] Barney — as both of the present incumbents stand high with his Constituents & have a large number of personal friends in the Jackson ranks, I trust they will not be deserted by them on party grounds alone & I think the opposition will not succeed — [3] By the time the Electors convene the name of Jackson will loose much of its Charm all over our state — your friends in Maryland look up to you, as If you were the last hope for their safety, & a Confidence is expressed that you will be Elected to [Congre]ss in August next, in the place of Judge [James] Clark who it is said will resign on account of bad health — we do sincerely hope such Expectations may be realised — They must be closely watched in all their first movements & Exposed when rong & no man in the Nation can do it with better effort than yourself — you will Excuse this liberty, taken I felt a desire to write you at this moment, & hope you will Excuse it, & shall not again trouble you, as I presume you will be heavily burthened by your numerous friends. . . .

ALS. DLC-HC (DNA, M212, R3).   1. In a letter of March 11, Adams thanked the citizens of Essex and Middlesex counties in New Jersey for their past support. Praising each member of his Cabinet, he argued that the internal harmony of his administration was greater than that of any of its predecessors. Also in this letter, Adams, for the first time, publicly defended Clay from the charge of bargain and corruption. Said he: "Before you, my fellow citizens, in the presence of our country and of Heaven, I pronounce the charge totally unfounded. This tribute of justice is due from me to him, and I seize with pleasure the opportunity afforded me by your letter of discharging the obligation." Challenges anyone who questions his motives in appointing Clay secretary of state to name one more qualified. See Washington *Daily National Journal*, April 6, 1829; Clay to Adams, April 16, 1829; Lee to Clay, April 22, 1829.   2. In the Maryland election of Oct. 5, the Jackson forces won 11 seats in the state senate, to 4 for their opponents and 39 seats in the house of delegates to 41 for their opponents. See *Niles' Register* (Oct. 10, 1829), 37:122.   3. Barney and Little were defeated for Congress by Benjamin C. Howard and Elias Brown. McMahon was not a candidate. *Ibid.*, 100.

From William Browne, Washington, April 10, 1829. Reports that "On settling my Salary account for the last quarter, I discover that in computing the amount due you for the last three days of your service as, Secretary of State, I adopted an incorrect principle, by which means you received $16.67 too much." Explains the arithmetic of his calculations and asks that Clay remit the overpayment. Notes that this error was "happily one of the few official errors I have to confess the commission of, during your Secretaryship." Blames it on the "gloomy anticipations" in his office following Jackson's election. Says he should not discuss politics, "yet cannot refrain from expressing a hope, common to all your freinds, that after a night of four years, we may (however 'against the use of nature,') look to the *west* for *day*." ALS. DLC-HC (DNA, M212, R3).

From GEORGE SWEENY, Washington, April 10, 1829. Thanks Clay, "in the name of the religious fraternity to which I belong [The Association of the Friends of Ireland]" for the "kindly" reference in his Hagerstown, Md., speech [March 20, 1829] to the "efforts of the Catholics of Ireland." Confesses that "I was not originally amongst the number of your political friends," but feels now that because of Clay's "great worth" and on "account of the unparalleled persecution with which you have been pursued, that I can truly say, (I hope without impiety) as was once said on a more solemn and important occasion — 'If all leave you, I will not leave you —'" ALS. DLC-HC (DNA, M212, R3).

From DAVID LEE CHILD   Boston, April 11, 1829
[Notes the "enthusiastic demonstrations of affection & respect with which your approach & presence have been hailed in the various towns & cities thro which you have passed" on your way home from Washington. Because of such spirit on the part of the people, "I never will 'despair of the American Republic.'" Continues:]

We are all quiet in this quarter. Our friends, the late administration party, stand firm & erect. You will see that there has been a very slight & scarcely percepictible increase of the Jackson party. I hope the designation of "National Republican"[1] will be acceptable to friendly & patriotic persons every where. It satisfies & does not offend the most fastidious. It forms a good *antithesis* to Jackson Republican. If we ever do obtain relief from the ruffian[s] who have possessed themselves of the Government, I for one am satisfied that we must act on principles & under a name broad enough to comprehend *all* honest & patriotic citizens. [John] Binns of the [Philadelphia] Demo[cratic] Press, with all his industry & ability appears to me to have had a mischievous influence & will hereafter have it, if he does not alter his style. The present dissentions as well as the past struggle in Pennsylvania demonstrate that the old parties exist only in name: & that the names, tho they may be beneficial to *individuals* (& there lies one danger) can but be perni[cious] to the nation or to any party. I do not know that other[s] entertain these views, or that with an intimate knowledge of others states, they would entertain them. In this state the name of "National Republican" has taken well. It seems to have a latent allusion to the

National or "American" policy. I should feel gratified & honored by a letter from you, but wish above all that you should have repose & recreation.

ALS. DLC-HC (DNA, M212, R3). This letter enclosed in Clay to J.Q. Adams, April 12, 1829, below.   1. Party names were still in a state of flux in 1829, although the name "National Republicans" had been adopted by the conservative, pro-administration group in Massachusetts as early as 1827. See Florence Weston, *The Presidential Election of 1828* (Philadelphia, 1974), 95; and Arthur B. Darling, *Political Changes in Massachusetts 1824-1848* (New Haven, 1925), 52-54.

To JOHN Q. ADAMS   Lexington, April 12, 1829

I reached home on the 6h. inst.   I found here a letter from Mr. [David Lee] Child which is enclosed together with my answer which, after perusing it, I will thank you to seal and cause it to be dropt in the post office.

What think you of the idea of applying the epithet Federalist to the opponent of the Tariff and I[nternal]. Improvements, and claiming for their supporter that of Republican? Will it not counteract the aim now making to revive old names for other purposes?

I believe I shall remain, in retirement, for the present. My friends are much divided as to the propriety of my returning to Congress. One portion of them is very anxious that I should, whilst another thinks I had better not. Both are however entirely disposed to acquiesce in my own determination. Although I could be elected, I believe without an opposing Candidate, I shall not offer. The care of my health (which is already improved) the necessary attention to my private affairs, and the want of rest, both for body and mind, entitle me, I think, after a public service so protracted, to pursue the direction of my own inclination.

The appointments and the proscription of the new Administration are operating here very much against it. That of little Tom Moore is most condemned because he is here best known. . . . [P.S.] Where and how is poor [Samuel L.] Southard? [Be] pleased, if with you, to tell him that [I] feel greatly interested in the recovery of his health.

ALS. MHi-Adams Papers, Letters Received (MR 491).

To JOHN Q. ADAMS   Lexington, April 16, 1829

When I wrote you a few days ago [April 12] I had not seen your letter of the 11h. Ulto., addressed to the Citizens of Essex and Middlesex in New Jersey,[1] or I should not have so soon again written to you. I have since perused it, with a satisfaction which my feelings will not allow me to forbear expressing to you. Forming as I do so prominent a subject of the letter, it does not become me to speak of its merits, but I may, at least, say to you that the highest praises of it are in the mouths of every body I meet. And I may express my own gratitude for the testimony which it bears in my behalf. I am sensible that you could not, with propriety, in reference to the exalted office which you lately filled, have earlier testified in regard to the slander alluded to in your letter. At no time could you have spoken with more decisive effect. Your testimony was, perhaps, wanted to complete the circle of proof, and to eradicate forever the calumny. The public now has it, and I have no doubt it will make a general and lasting impression.

So far was I, in voting for you as President, from being influenced by any personal or selfish consideration, that I felt and I stated, at the time, that, if I knew and *disapproved* every member of your Cabinet, I should still greatly prefer you to Genl. Jackson. All that I have since seen and known in respect to both of you has tended to strengthen and confirm that preference. I wish that my worst apprehensions in regard to the present Chief Magistrate may not be realized.

From all the parts of this State, from which I have yet received intelligence, I obtain the most encouraging information. Not a doubt is entertained by any of those whose opinions have been communicated to me that the State, by an overwhelming vote, would support me, if it shall be deemed proper to present my name as the successor of Genl. Jackson. Leading Jackson men in various parts have proclaimed such to be their preference. And several of the present members of Congress, favorable to Jackson, yielding to public sentiment in their districts, have declared in my favor. My opportunities of mixing with the people, since my return, have been as yet too limited to enable me to speak with certainty as to public predilections throughou[t] the State.

I have been agreeably occupied, since my return, in superintending repairs of my house, directing improvements in the surrounding grounds and preparing for a Crop on the farm. The season has been very unfavorable to rural avocations. It is at least a fortnight behind. . . . P.S. I understand that my Successor [Martin Van Buren] has waited upon you. Pray has your's [Jackson]? Or does the nonintercourse continue?

ALS. MHi-Adams Papers. 1. Warfield to Clay, April 9, 1829.

To JOHN F. HENRY   Lexington, April 16, 1829

I hasten to acknowledge the receipt of your favor of the 8h. instant, which I have just received.

The sentiments expressed by you in relation to the new Cabinet, and late appointments of the new Administration are every where entertained. They are not confined to those who were opposed to the election of Genl. Jackson, but are entertained and expressed by thousands who supported him. No administration ever lost so much of the public confidence, in so short a time.

My present determination, which I do not think I shall change, is to remain in private life, at least for a season. On the question, whether I ought to offer for Congress, my friends are much divided in opinion, every where, in and out of the State. There is here a general disposition to acquiesce in whatever decision I may make. If I were to offer there would be probably no opposition. The utility of my public service, in the H. of R, is very doubtful at this time. It is true that on each side of the question much may be said. That being the state of it, I think I am at liberty to attend to my private affairs and to the care of my health. I want tranquillity. It is necessary to the entire restoration of my health. I want also to see my fellow Citizens of Kentucky. I have been too much separated from them. I wish them to know me, as I desire to know them personally. With this view, and as travelling is conducive to my health, I mean to move about as much as I can this summer. Having some business also in several quarters of the State, I shall be carried thither by that. You must not be surprized to see me at Hopkinsville.

I have not yet resolved to resume the practice of the Law; and if I can avoid it, I shall not enter it again. But if I do, it would not be with an intention to engage in business generally. The kind of practice which I should prefer would be simply to argue causes previously prepared. The state of professional

business in this Country would not, I apprehend, afford me profitable employment of that description. The Court of Appeals has most of it; but there the
docket is so full, with trifling as well as important causes, that I am almost
deterred, by the too great consumption of my time, from practising in the
Appellate Court.

Under these circumstances, you will perceive that, if I return to the Bar, I
shall have no occasion for an associate in the practice. I have had very favorable accounts of your brother [Gustavus A. Henry], independent of yours.
And I should have been very happy if we could have been mutually beneficial
to each other; but with views such as I have I feel sure that I can offer him no
adequate inducement.

ALS. Courtesy of William P. Foster, Portland, Oregon. Letter marked "Confidential."

From ABDUHL RAHAHMAN

Cape Montserada, Africa,
April 16, 1829

We sailed in the ship Harriett from Norfo[lk]. with 160 souls[1] on b[oar]d. for
this place on the 9h. Feb: from Hampton Roads & after a moderate passage of
37 days arrived on 19h. ult. all in good health &c. since our landing have lost
many valuable souls from among us, and many others are dangerously indisposed with the Coast fever so fatal to Northern constitutions.

Thanks to the Omnipotent that his benign munificence is extended
towards me & my wife as no more than a slight indisposition has affected us,
but are at present in the perfect enjoyment of good health.

I would ever be rendered one of the most obnoxious & diabolical Creatures My Dr: Sir were I not to render you a suitable return of grateful homage
and respectful attention for the friendship manifested by you in the mo[st]
sanguine exertions in procuring my release & restoring me to my long lost
Country You are well aware my Inestimable Friend the affections of a
parent are only to be app[re]ciated but by those who are parents themselves —
and therefore [I] entreat you to befriend me, in the possibility of retaining the
whole of my family, Viz) children & Grandchildren in a Train of Emancipation & thereby Obtain their general release; that they may be restor[ed] to
their parent's Arms in the land which gave him birth — As my younger brother
has been King 3 Years, I have recd. advices of his favorable disposition
towards me & expect e'er long to have more official communications with him.
We are 15 days journey apart, Viz) On foot & 10 days by a water conveyance,
which precludes the more frequent communications & hope it will shortly be
within the compass of my reach to establish a line of communications directly
from hence to my Brother's dominions

Be pleased to accept the mo: grateful homamage of a very high consideration and and [sic] am unalterably until Death. . . .

ALS. DNA, RG59, Misc. Letters (M179, R67). Signed "Prince Rhahamman." Clay spelled the
name "Rahahman," as did Thomas Foster, Rahahman's former owner. Another spelling is
Rahhaman. His slave name was "Prince."   1. See 7:30-31; Mechlin to Clay, April 22, 1829.

From MARK HARDIN

Near Shelbyville, Ky., April 17, 1829

[Notes that God will look after the nation in the coming difficult years, and that it
is "a precept of his divine law that Christians forgive their enemies." Continues:]

I may now proceed to the object of this communication — your own advancement in our Sister States will grow with the same rapidity that it does at

home — There is an awful bitterness of disappointment amongst Mr [John Q.] Adams late opponents, the moment of the first impulses of this disappointment, is the propitious time to profit by it — It is easier to go over to Mr Clays standard than turn right round and go for Mr Adams, there is not that inconsistincy in it which men dislike — I hold that the first step to be gained is a real (not a nominal) mutual forgiveness between you [and John] Pope — It is needless to state that a press — funds and indefatigable industry are removed from annoying you — How is this to be done? It is the Lions part to advance towards the object   As an earnest of your sincerity in wishing this event, make an effort to get the Governor [Thomas Metcalfe] to enquire of him if after the first of June (to which time his last nominations for Chief Justice was laid on the table) he is appointed Chief Justice he will accept — [1] I believe he will   The Court will not be better filled — He will not probably remain there long — There will be no difficulty in his ascertaining how & why he was appointed — He feels that [Thomas R.] Moore & [William T.] Barry & [John] McLean & [George M.] Bibb have been lifted over his head & he also appreciates his own claims as prior to either of these men   I say this not because that I know he has ever said so — But beca[use] it is a fact — I as [sic] know that upon a reconciliation he has many warm friends about Lexington who will become openly avowedly and devotedly your *firm* friends not holliday friends, they see your predictions fulfilling — They appreciate your sagac[ity] and would be glad to see you commence rising even upon the ruins of the Hero [Andrew Jackson] they so lately confided in bu[t] who they confess has disappointed them — I hold that the sooner you have a decided, an overwhelming majority for you in the State the better — I hold that my advice is not the caprice of the moment — Do as you love your Country adopt it. . . . [P.S.] The Revd Mr [Nathan H.] Hall of your town was with me yesterday — I ventured to suggest my wishes to him on this subject — It so turned out that he had also thought on the subject, and we are mutually determined to effect this object, or to throw the blame at your own doors — If I succeed in this first effort I will thereby be encouraged to commence other efforts in a different quarter Should I fail I must be content that my best Judgment my warmest wishes have been disappointed — I should like to hear from you — I should like to see you and converse with you.

Copy, written and signed by author. Courtesy of R. S. Sanders, Lexington, Ky. Letter marked "(Confidential)." The original, less legible ALS version is in DLC-HC (DNA, M212, R3). 1. In the fall of 1828 Pope had been responsible for securing the approval by the state senate of Metcalfe's nominations of George Robertson and Joseph R. Underwood for the Ky. Court of Appeals. This action so aroused the Jackson forces in the legislature that Pope chose not to be a candidate for the U.S. Senate. In Dec. 1828, George M. Bibb, the chief justice of the Ky. Court of Appeals, was elected to the Senate. Underwood and Robertson comprised the court until near the end of 1829 when Richard A. Buckner's nomination was approved. Metcalfe did not appoint Pope to the court, because Jackson appointed him governor of the Arkansas Territory in late March, 1829. He accepted the position in April. See Orval W. Baylor, *John Pope, Kentuckian* (Cynthiana, Ky., 1943), 317-33; Lewis and Richard H. Collins, *History of Kentucky*, 2 vols. (Cynthiana, Ky., 1874), 2:497; and 7:583-84.

To HENRY CLAY, JR.   Lexington, April 19, 1829

Your [*sic*, you] perceive that my letter is dated at home. We reached here tomorrow will be a fortnight. We found the house and grounds out of repair but not more so than was to be expected. We shall have them in nice order by the time you will join us.

I received your letter of the 29h. Ulto. the perusal of which afforded me much satisfaction. I am delighted to find that you are so firmly resolved upon attaining eminence at the Bar. I am well persuaded that you have it in your power to make yourself any thing you please. "Quicquid vult, valde vult." You know that I am not versed in latin, and I cannot therefore answer for the correctness of my quotation.[1]

But to attain the highest place, or even a respectable rank, in the profession of Law, you must make up your mind to labor incessantly. I never studied half enough. I always relied too much upon the resources of my genius. If I had life to pass over again, and, with my present information, could control my movements, I would not appear at the Bar before 24 or 25, nor until after two or three years, at the least, of close study. You must not however let your eagerness to enter upon the study of law occasion you to remit your efforts in your present pursuits. Of these, I am well convinced, you will profit in all the vicissitudes of your future life.

I hope you will not neglect to bring with you some of your own drawings, according to your intention. We shall be happy to see them, and any specimens of your composition that you may choose to shew.

The Spring has been uncommonly backward; but a few days of sun and rain have brought out the grass, and the trees also begin to bloom. In a short time Ashland will look very well.

Thomas [H. Clay] joined us on the journey out. He and Theodore [W. Clay] are both now here. The want of employment, or rather the want of some business which promises comfort and support to them, affects them both. Other causes have operated to give Thomas an unpleasing appearance.

W[illiam C. C.]. Claiborne [Jr.] accompanied us as far as Maysville, where we parted. He went to New Orleans, but I think it probable he will accompany Anne [Brown Clay Erwin] and Mr. [James] Erwin on their intended visit to us.

James [Brown Clay] enters the preparatory department of Transylvania tomorrow, and John [Morrison Clay] and [Martin] Duralde are under the care of Mrs. [Charlotte] Mentelle.

All the family unite in love to you—

ALS. Henry Clay Memorial Foundation, Lexington, Ky.   1. According to Latin scholar William J. Hogan of Keysville, Va., the phrase "Quicquid vult, valde vult" translates as "whatever he wants he wants badly." Clay acquired the phrase from Jesse B. Harrison who had incorrectly spelled it "quisquid." Harrison to Clay, March 18, 1829.

To THOMAS I. WHARTON   Lexington, April 19, 1829

I recd. your favor of the 24h. Ulto.   Thomas [H. Clay] unexpectedly joined us at Cumberland and accompanied us the residue of our journey home. He is now here with better 'though not perfectly restored health. I transmit enclosed a ten dollar note to correct the excess you paid him. How I shall acquit myself of the obligation under which you have placed me I know not. I can at least express my gratitude, which is also extended to Mr. Badger[1] for the kindness which he displayed without neglecting his duties to his client.

You perceive I am at home. We reached here about a fortnight ago. We are beginning to keep house again. When I left here four years ago we disposed of most of our furniture; and altho' we brought some articles from Washington we want many more to complete our establishment. Among those we want are some Sofas. And I have to request that you will purchase for me one Ottoman, and two Greecian (so I believe those are called which are open at one end) hair Sofas; and have them carefully boxed by the Cabinet maker and sent to Allen and Grant Commission merchants Pittsburg[h] to be forwarded to this place. We want plain neat ones, without any extra finishing. I think I gave for such an Ottoman as I want about 40 or $45 — And that the price of the Greecians is about 25$ or $30. Be pleased to charge the Cabinet maker to be very careful in boxing them, as they will have a Land carriage of three hundred and seventy miles. And the sooner they are sent (the next day if you please after this is received) the better, because we want and [need] them, and because the navigation of the Ohio is very uncertain. You will be pleased to negotiate a draft on me at sight for the amount, which you can do at the B. of the U.S., or I will remit it to you the moment I am informed of it, as may be best.

My whole journey was marked by the strongest testimonies of respect and attachment, not limited at all by the old divisions of party. All the information which I have received, since I came to the West, tends to confirm my opinion of its unshaken adherence to me. Leading Jackson men have come out, in various quarters, with declarations of their future friendly purposes. &c   Have you seen Mr. [John Q.] Adams's New Jersey letter?[2] It has produced a strong sensation in Kentucky.

ALS. KyLoF.   1. Possibly William Badger, a Philadelphia lawyer. *PMHB*, 62:517. 2. Warfield to Clay, April 9, 1829; Clay to Adams, April 16, 1829.

From CHARLES S. TODD

Stockdale, Shelby Co., Ky., April 19, 1829

Your esteemed favor of the 20h. Dec with its enclosure, was only received and as I had concluded to decline for the present any further publication as to the Conduct of General Jackson at the Chickasaw Treaty   I have not as yet acted on your suggestion as to the allusion made to you by General Jackson in the interview with Col. [Leslie] Combs.[1] I felt that any agitation of the subject, after it seems to have passed from the eye of the public, would only have the effect to bring upon you a renewal of the shameless and unmerited abuse with which you have been visited —

I have concluded to send an Extract of your letter to General James Shelby for his information in order that he may pursue such Course in relation to it as he may deem proper and I have deemed it, with due submission to your better judgment, the most satisfactory plan to address a letter to you on the Subject which you Can use at any time you shall think necessary. The statement is accordingly enclosed and I presume you will hear from Genl. Shelby on the Subject.

The "Journal"[2] is just such a paper as we expected to See; containing no reference whatever to the principal matters charged on the General, although the obliquity of his perceptions or his contempt of the public discernment has permitted him to say "it proves the declarations made by T. H. Shelby and myself of Gov. [Isaac] Shelby's opinions to be *positively untrue*." In this case as in the reference to Mr. [James] Buchanan the General has relied entirely on the weight which he supposed the people attached to his name and Services.[3] In no other way can we account for his readiness to rely on a position so utterly groundless and inconclusive —

Allow us to congratulate Mrs. Clay and yourself on your safe return to your old friends in improved health. — May you enjoy in the amplest sense "Otium cum dignatate" until the returning good sense of the Nation, shall call you to its first office. I understand you will open a Law office in Lexington and it is conjectured by all parties that you will go into the Legislature or into Congress —

Be pleased to accept my acknowledgements for the spirited and elevated views contained in your Speech at Washington [March 7, 1829] and on your route to the West; they cannot fail to add a Niche in the Temple of your Fame whatever may be your future destinies — The sentiments lately expressed by Mr. [John Q.] Adams in reply to the address from Ohio & New Jersey do him great honor. — [4] I see that those who control the [United States] "Telegraph" at Washington are very jealous of his residence there, lest he may be contribute to the promotion of your interests — The opinion which he has pronounced on your merits in terms so beautiful and splendid is worth much more than the vote which General Jackson received.

ALS. DLC-HC (DNA, M212, R3). Letter postmarked at Shelbyville, Ky. No. 1 of this date.
1. Combs had interviewed Jackson at the Hermitage on October 14, 1828, on behalf of James Shelby concerning the controversy over the Chickasaw Treaty. Gov. Isaac Shelby's sons and his son-in-law, Charles S. Todd, claimed that one James Jackson possessed some highly important facts in relation to the treaty which he would not disclose unless permitted to do so by Gen. Jackson. Combs's object at the interview was to secure this permission. Jackson reportedly told him that everyone concerned with the treaty "might say what they pleased." See Lexington *Kentucky Gazette*, Oct. 24, Nov. 14, 1828; and Todd to Clay, April 19, 1829, no. 2 of this date.
2. "The Secret Journal" kept at the Chickasaw Treaty. See 7:488-89. 3. See 6:839-41, 884-89, 948-49. 4. Warfield to Clay, April 9, 1829. 5. Duff Green was owner and editor of the Washington *United States Telegraph*.

From CHARLES S. TODD   Shelby County, Ky., April 19, 1829

In a communication addressed by General Jackson to the Editor of the "Nashville Republican" on the 31st. of October last, he undertakes to give his recollections of an interview[1] with Colonel [Leslie] Combs in the latter part of which he states that "with the close of this sentiment we walked into the passage when I observed I was well advised how all this matter was managed; that had not such a man as Henry Clay existed, Thomas Shelby and [Charles S.] Todd would never have put forth such falsehoods — In making this remark, I had reference to particular information contained in a confidential letter received from Kentucky."

I deem it an act of justice to you to state explicitly and unequivocally that so far as I was concerned I know, and so far as other Members of the family participated I believe, you neither promoted nor advised any of the measures which we felt ourselves bound to adopt in relation to the opinions of Governor [Isaac] Shelby as to the Conduct of General Jackson at the Chicksaw Treaty.[2] My letter to you[3] in which the Subject was first noticed, was dictated by the Consideration already avowed before the public and the determination to forward it was solely and exclusively the Suggestion of my own judgment and feelings. — In so far, then as the assertion made by General Jackson and his confidential authority in this State would convey the insinuation that You prompted or advised the course which we adopted. I pronounce that assertion to be utterly destitute of any foundation in truth. — In one sense only can it have any pretense to be considered probable — "Had not such a Man as Henry Clay existed." General Jackson could not have uttered and published against him the slanders which he did; nor would your friends have considered it a duty to communicate to the public conversations held with you which repudiated the idea of any necessity on your part to bargain for your vote in relation to the Presidency and in this sense the General may have been indeed, *"well advised how this matter was managed"* as the "origin of it was at his own fireside"

ALS. DLC-HC (DNA, M212, R3). No. 2 of this date; enclosed in Todd to Clay, April 19, 1829, no. 1 of this date.   1. Todd to Clay, April 19, 1829, no. 1.   2. See 7:488-89.   3. *Ibid.*

From JOHN Q. ADAMS   Washington, April 21, 1829

Your favour of the 12th inst. enclosing a Letter to you from Mr [David Lee] Child, with your answer has come to hand. The Letter to Mr Child has been forwarded to him as you desired

I have no design or wish that old party distinctions should be revived, and do not believe that they will or can be. A struggle by certain individuals of the old federal party to recover the ascendency they had lost — may render a re action of the republicans necessary for their own defences; it can be necessary for no other purpose of which I am aware; and I have no wish to fortify myself by the support of any party whatever

The objection here appears to me to be against applying the denomination of federalists to the opposers of protection to manufactures and internal improvement is that I believe the fact to be otherwise — The old federalists were generally friendly to those Interests — Washington was pre-eminently so. The remains of the federal party now are divided upon those questions, as they are upon all others of present political interest. They have now no public principle peculiar to themselves. The federalists have generally supported the measures of the two last Administrations — Those Administrations have adopted, and practised upon many of their favourite opinions — most of the New. England manufacturers are federalists, and would hardly be gratified by the application of their name to their opponents.

The composition of the new Administration indicates the intention to conciliate the South — Perhaps means will be found also of propitiating the West — New England will not be a favourite nor it would seem will Virginia, but there is now no propensity to opposition in either.

You will have time between this and next August, to fix your opinion whether it will be advisable for you to come to the House or not   I have no doubt your presence here will be salutary — But whether at the present Congress a Seat in the house would conduce to your health or comfort, may admit of doubt. . . .

ALS. DLC-HC (DNA, M212, R3). Printed in Colton, *Clay Correspondence*, 4:226-27.

From Richard Henry Lee, Washington, D.C., April 22, 1829. Congratulates Clay on the personal and political enthusiasm he encountered from the people on his trip home from Washington, noting that "the gloom in which you left us here, was dispelled by the events of your journey." Reports that John Quincy Adams is in "fine health and spirits" and has "very much gratified his friends, by his letter to the Citizens of New Jersey." Continues: "The irony of the last paragraph was keen, and just towards him, who, on *such an occasion,* had the indecorum to charge him, with corruption and abuse of Office, and to libel half a million of his fellow Citizens. . . . That letter has blistered the tribes of error, in all their gradiations —"

Hopes that Clay will soon return to the House of Representatives. Assures him that in less than two years, there will be a movement in his behalf in Virginia "to accept your pledge to serve your country, which will be signified by public Meetings. . . . I expect to return to my native state in two years, and to mingle my efforts in giving impetus to these movements."

Says he has abandoned his plan to write a history of the Adams administration because "my relation, Mr. [Philip R.] Fendall had anticipated me. He will *execute* this just & grateful task, while *we* will compare our views and unite our researches." ALS. DLC-HC DNA, M212, R3). Printed in Colton, *Clay Correspondence*, 4:227-29. In the last paragraph of his March 11 letter to the citizens of New Jersey (Washington *Daily National Journal*, April 6, 1829), Adams promised his congratulations to Jackson if he succeeds in reforming the "abuses which have escaped the vigilance of my observation." He pledged also "to extend to the administration every reasonable indulgence which they may need, and to give them credit for every good deed they may perform." See Warfield to Clay, April 9, 1829. There is no evidence that either Lee or Fendall wrote a history of the Adams administration.

From Joseph Mechlin, Jr., Colony of Liberia, April 22, 1829. Reports the death of "Principal Agent Dr. Rich. Randall" on April 19. Has assumed the duties of his office pending further instructions from the American Colonization Society. Relates that Abduhl Rahhaman (Rahahman) and his wife arrived in the ship *Harriet* on March 17 in good health; but that Rahahman soon contracted "coast fever" from which he has recovered [Rahahman to Clay, April 16, 1829]. Because of the onset of the rainy season, Rahahman cannot proceed to his own country, Morocco, via Sierra Leone, until November. Mentions that he has "drawn on your [State] Depart a Bill at Sight for Two hund and fifty dollars" to support Rahahman until his departure. ALS. DNA, R659, Misc. Letters (M179, R67). Received June 29, 1829, after Clay had left the State Department, but see Rahaman to Clay, April 16, 1829. For Joseph Mechlin and Richard Randall, see P. J. Staudenraus, *The African Colonization Movement*, 162, 164.

It may have been this letter that Clay forwarded to Secretary of State Van Buren from Lexington on July 8, 1829, noting in his letter of transmission that though it was "private in form," it "relates to a subject of public nature (Prince Rhahamman)" and probably ought "to be put on file in the Dept. of State." ALS. DNA, RG59, Misc. Letters (M179, R67).

From John Rodgers, Steamboat *Huron*, Cincinnati, April 24, 1829. Announces that he is enroute to visit the recently established navy yard at Pensacola and takes this "opportunity of enclosing to you the certificate I promised to send you previous to your departure from Washington, in relation to the Jacks, and which I hope may be a means of rendering them somewhat more valuable to you." ALS. Josephine Simpson Collection, Lexington, Ky.

On March 13, 1829, Clay had traded his Washington, D.C., lot, "fronting a public Square," to Commodore Rodgers for "a Jack and Jenny and their produce."

Rodgers to Clay, March 13, 1829, is an endorsed receipt. DS. Courtesy of M. W. Anderson, Lexington, Ky.

From MARK HARDIN   Near Shelbyville, Ky., April 27, 1829

In mine to you of the 17th Inst I perhaps predicated my wishes more upon my own knowledge of facts than I should have done, leaving you more of a field of conjecture to range in than was proper.

It is therefore necessary to state that a decided majority of Jackson men occupied the lower house of our Legislature, a controuling voice of that party were also in the Senate — [1]So long as there is a contest between them and the

Governor [Thomas Metcalfe] the parties must necessarily exist. This party composed chiefly of New Court men will continue to be turbulent so long as there is any hope for them to keep or gain the ascendency — Give to them a member of the Appellate Court[2] and the ostensible matters of contention is done away — Look no further than simply to the quiet of Ky and it is an object which all peace loving men should desire — Look amongst the Jackson men (forgetting private feuds) and who stands more prominent than Mr [John] Pope, I confess I had taken it for granted under all the circumstances as a matter of State policy, that it would present itself very nearly allied to a duty we owed to the peace of the Country — I do not view it I could not view it as a price, for the friendship of any man or any party, but would simply consider it as an evidence that for the moment every thing else was forgotten except the object of getting a Court composed of two parties and of the best materials on of the parties afforded — I had hoped this would have been effected last Session so that the seeds of discord would not have brought forth fruit at the next August election and that no marked line of distinction might cross the Legislative Hall next Session — If it could even now be done I should hope to see the benefit of it —

I can see no mean compliances in such a course, but the spirit of calumny purchance might ferret out bargain sale and corruption in it

Copy, written and signed by author. Courtesy of R. S. Sanders, Lexington, Ky. 1. After the August, 1828, election for members of the Ky. General Assembly, the Jackson forces controlled the senate 20-18 and the house 57 to 42 with 1 member neutral. Frankfort *Argus of Western America*, August 27, 1828. 2. Hardin to Clay, April 17, 1829.

From FRANCIS T. BROOKE

Near Frederickburg, Va.,
April 29, 1829

I may now congratulate you on your safe arrival with your family at Lexington and on your triumphal journey from Washington to your peaceful home The unsolicited and unbought respect and affection of numerous bodies of your fellow citizens must much inhance the feelings which hath (a conciousness of having discharged faithfully, your duties to your country, inspires you and gives an example to others which will stimulate them to do the like, in despite of the Slanders that may annoy them you will see by the papers the efforts that are making to sustain the administration in Virginia, after what has so recently passed I cannot trust myself to pronounce what will be the issue, I venture to say however, that it cannot name, I think the meeting of the convention in the fall[1] in which it is now probable there will be a majority of anti Jacksonians[2] will give a new tone to the public mind and do much to bring the people back to their confidence in those whom they had deserted, when you write me let me know your opinion of the State of things in your States, should they be as favorable as is calculated on by your friend Beal [*sic*, Beall][3] from Louisville and Some others we may expect to See you in the next Congress. . . .

ALS. DLC-HC (DNA, M212, R3). Extract printed in Colton, *Clay Correspondence*, 4:229. 1. See 7:575-76. 2. Contemporary commentary suggests that party differences were not of primary importance in choosing delegates to the Virginia Constitutional Convention. Noting the results of the convention election, the Richmond *Constitutional Whig* stated: "It ought to be known, to the eternal honor of the people of Virginia, that they have not permitted party or federal politics to have the smallest influence over their suffrages for members of convention. . . . Jackson and anti-Jackson districts, have indifferently chosen, in many instances, gentlemen opposed to them on the question." *Niles' Register* (July 4, 1829), 36:300. See also Charles H. Ambler, *Sectionalism in Virginia From 1776 to 1861* (New York, 1964), 145. 3. Probably Norborne B. Beall.

From **Clifton R. Thomson** *et al.*, Lexington, April 30, 1829. Invite Clay to deliver the anniversary oration of the Union Philosophical Society of Transylvania University in July. ALS. DLC-HC (DNA, M212, R3). There is no evidence that Clay accepted this invitation.

From THOMAS I. WHARTON
Philadelphia, May 1, 1829

I have recd. your letter of the 19th of April with its enclosure. I am glad to hear of you & your sons [Thomas H. Clay] safe arrival and of what might have been anticipated—Your cordial reception to the west. As yet there are no indications here by which the course of the political Currents can be prophicized Although there is a good deal of dissatisfaction expressed with the appointments especially Among those who have been called Federalists. Are we to see you in Congress next session or do you mean to reserve yourself for the following one when I presume the present "coalition" will have fallen to pieces?

I endeavoured to execute your Commission for the furniture immediately as you requested but without success. I could not meet with any of the articles ready made of a quality that was pro [?] to send you—such things being generally like Peter Pendais razors made to sell. I have therefore ordered of one of our best Cabinet makers An Ottoman & two Grecian sofas to be Completed with all dispatch & I hope they will be found of the kind you requested. There was some difficulty however in understanding precisely from you description the particular article required as the appellations are sometimes different in Philada. & Washington. About the Ottoman I believe there can be no mistake but both for that & the Lounges or Grecian Sofas I shall have to give rather more than the sums you have mentioned. I cannot persuade one Workman to Send you any other than an article of the best construction and finish. The prices you have mentioned are such as they get for the inferior workmanship sometimes sent to the Southern Cities for sale. They will be plain and sent without any extra ornament. The Ottoman will cost about $50 and the Grecian Sofas about $35 each and they are to be ready in 2 or 3 weeks at the furthest when I will have them dispatched without delay. Bye the bye if you were still in the department of State I should consider this order of an Ottoman as 'Confirmation strong' of the reports concerning the projected treaty with the Sublime Porte—[1] if it were not for the Grecian Sofas which if you will excuse a bad pun might be considered as a sort of *set-off* against the other.

[Asks Clay to ask John J. Crittenden if he has received a letter from Wharton dealing with a legal matter in Philadelphia.]

ALS. DLC-HC (DNA, M212, R3). 1. The Treaty of Adrianople, signed Sept. 14, 1829, ended the Russo-Turkish War.

From JOHN Q. ADAMS
Washington, May 2, 1829

I have received your obliging Letters of the 16th. and 19th. ulto. the latter covering a copy of my correspondence with the New Jersey Committee printed upon Satin.[1] I am happy that my Letter was Satisfactory to you; and I have learnt that it has been generally gratifying to our friends—There was a testimony due from me to all the members of the late Administration, and in a Special manner to you—No better opportunity could have been afforded me to give it than that presented me by the New Jersey Address and I availed myself of it with pleasure.

The Catholic Question has assumed in England an aspect entirely new;[2] and is presenting appearances quite unexpected. Brought forward in Parliament by the Duke of Wellington and Mr [Robert] Peel, carried in the House of Commons by a Majority of more than two to one, it is almost doubtful whether it will yet overpower the cry of "No Popery" in the House of Peers, among the People and with the King [George IV]—Mr [Albert] Gallatin who is here, and called upon me a few days Since, thinks it will pass the *House* of Lords by a small majority

11. May 1829

I was interrupted in the writing of this Letter, by information of a domestic calamity of which you will have Seen Some account in the Newspapers and which has disqualified me for the time even for the performance of Some of the duties of Social life—[3] The loss of my eldest Son has been followed by an aggravation of the infirm health of his mother [Louisa Johnson Adams], and by an effect upon my own Spirits, calling for more than the consolation of philosophy.

Mr [Samuel L.] Southard before he left this City had met with an affliction Similar in its nature, though not equally Severe, in the loss of his youngest daughter [Ann]—He has returned home, and I have learnt is recovering his health—Mr [Richard] Rush has Sailed for England.

I expect to leave this place towards the close of this month—I have no intercourse with any member of the Administration; and am a Silent observer of passing Events.

ALS. DLC-HC (DNA, M212, R3). Printed in Colton, *Clay Correspondence*, 4:229-30.   1. Warfield to Clay, April 9, 1829.   2. The shift of position on the issue by George IV. See Philip Hughes, *The Catholic Question 1688-1829* (London, 1929), 300-13; and Philip Guedalla, *Wellington* (New York, 1931), 382-86.   3. George Washington Adams died on April 30, 1829, apparently committing suicide by jumping from the ship *Benjamin Franklin*. He had a history of emotional problems. Aida and David Donald (eds.), *Diary of Charles Francis Adams* (Cambridge, Mass., 1964), 372; Martin B. Duberman, *Charles Francis Adams* (Cambridge, Mass., 1961), 5.

From John L. Lawrence, New York, May 2, 1829. Reminds him of their association at Gottenburg (Göteborg, Sweden) in 1814. Asks if a rumor reaching New York on April 30 that he and John Pope had fought a duel, "which terminated fatally to you," was true. Hopes not, since the election of Jackson has caused "the eyes of the largest portion of the intelligent and reflecting, [to] turn to you, as the instrument of our deliverance." Comments on the mixed national sentiment regarding dueling, noting that "Your own affair at Washington [5:208, 211-12], was perhaps unavoidable, situated as you then were: But your position has materially changed with the times. . . . I apprehend that it is a necessary recourse only when one's character for personal courage might Suffer by declining. This motive cannot operate in your case." Reminds Clay that "The new administration is essentially *belligerous*; and without a corps of Sharp Shooters its arrangements would seem incomplete. It might, peradventure, be imagined by some self-constituted legion of *honour*, that your removal from 'this world of woe' were a meritorious service!" Warns him, therefore, not to get involved in duels. ALS. DLC-HC (DNA, M212, R3). Printed in Colton, *Clay Correspondence*, 4:229-32.

To JOHN H. EWING
Lexington, May 4, 1829

I received your favor of the 28h. Ulto. informing me of your having purchased for me, at the Sale of the late Mr. [Richard W.] Meade, fifty head of Merinos, and requesting any directions that I may have to give concerning them. I am very glad that you have made the purchase, and thank you for your kind attention to the matter. I am perfectly satisfied with the terms.

My wish is to have the sheep sent by water to the care of Mess January & Co. commission merchants at Maysville as soon after they are sheared as you think they ought to be removed.[1] As the warm weather of the summer will soon be here it is I think expedient that they should commence their voyage whenever they can safely. I spoke to Mess Forsythe Dobbins & Co. at Wheeling about superintending their shipment, and they promised to attend particularly to it. But perhaps there may be some other point of the Ohio above Wheeling more convenient to embark them from than Wheeling. If you are of that opinion and can see to their shipment, it is left to your direction whether to send them to Wheeling or not. Whenever they leave you be pleased to inform me by a letter transmitted by the mail. I will take due care that the amount of the purchase shall be remitted to you before payment is to be made. I have to request, my dear Sir, that you will not omit to charge me with the full amount of whatever expences you may have incurred or shall incur under this agency, including the keeping of the sheep after the purchase. Whenever I am informed of the sum, it shall be immediately forwarded.

Is it practicable to get a Shepherds dog, or, which would be better, a pair of them in your neighbourhood? If you can, I should esteem it a great favor if you would procure me one or a pair (as you may be able) and send them with the Sheep. I would willingly pay a reasonably price for them. The dogs are some times very destructive with Sheep in this quarter, and have already destroyed the greater part of my lambs that dropt this Spring.

I am thankful for the political part of your letter. I have heard enough, since my return home, to satisfy me that if my name should be held up as the successor of Genl. Jackson there is not a doubt about my receiving the vote of this State. Many Jackson men have already given in their adhesion. And whenever the contest should be between any other man and myself, not excepting the Hero, I believe a large majority (less in case he were the candidate) would be for me. Whether it will be expedient or proper to use my name at the seasonably time must depend upon the decision of my friends throughout the Union. Whatever that may be, there will be perfect acquiescence in it on my part.

As I intimated to Mr. [Thomas] McGiffin and yourself, I have determined not to offer for Congress. I could have been elected almost by acclamation. There would have been no opposition. Many of the Jackson party expressed a wish that I would offer. But the reasons for retirement appeared to me too strong to be resisted.

I will thank you to make my best regards to Mr. McGiffin, and tell him that I received his letter by Mr. Frazier, communicating the purchase of the Sheep.

I hope to hear from you again shortly. . . .

ALS. KyU. Addressed to Ewing at "Meadow Lands near Washington Pennsylvania." 1. Clay wrote Ewing again on July 11, 1829, reporting that the sheep had not arrived and wondering what the cause of the delay might be. ALS. KyU. On Sept. 5 he informed Adam Beatty that Ewing had reported that the sheep had left Washington, Pa., on August 26. ALS. Courtesy of Earl M. Ratzer, Highland Park, Ill. Printed in Colton, *Clay Correspondence*, 4:240-41.

To James Taylor, Frankfort, May 5, 1829. Thanks him for a recent letter in which Taylor asked Clay to represent him in a suit against the United States. Declines the offer, explaining: "I do not mean to engage immediately in the practice of the Law, if I do at all. Should I return to it, I will not forget your wish." ALS. KyHi. Addressed to Taylor at "Belle Vue," Newport, Ky.

From Francis Johnson, Bowling Green, Ky., May 6, 1829. Invites Clay to make a political swing through the "district," perhaps in June. Thinks "that your presence would be of service to yourself, we are not afraid of an available excitement being produced in the Election in consequence of your visit to this Country — It is true, they are trying all in their power to raise the question *& fan up party flames* again — I mean such candidates, as have no hope but party excitement." Notes that some "Jackson men" are drifting back into the fold, "and a concilliatory course on our part, will probably unite the most of them, with us—" These people are "Conscious no doubt of the errors &c. he [Jackson] has already committed, they are glad we have not already *pounced* upon him. . . . let them have time to breathe and fall out a little among themselves." Thinks Clay will be invited also to visit Bardstown, Elizabethtown, and Russellville on his way to or from Lexington or Louisville to Bowling Green. ALS. InU. See Johnson to Clay, April 8, 1829, for the August 3 congressional election in Johnson's district. Clay did not make his swing through western Kentucky before the congressional election; however, he visited Bowling Green, Russellville, Hopkinsville, and Glasgow in September and October. See Lexington *Kentucky Reporter*, September 16, 30; October 10, 14, 21, 1829.

To FRANCIS T. BROOKE   Lexington, May 12, 1829

Your favor of the 29h. Ulto. is duly received. I must refer you to the public prints for the incidents of a journey which though performed at an unpleasant season and over bad roads was full of gratification, on account of the testimonies of esteem, public and private, by which it was attended. On Saturday next [May 16] I am to attend a public dinner,[1] which promises to be the largest ever given in this State.

I have been much occupied, since my return, with repairs to my house, grounds and farm. As far as I have yet been able to learn the state of public feeling and sentiment towards me it is far from being unfavorable, except with a few of the most violent of the Jackson party. Many of them have come out openly for me, and several of the prominent of them in this district have communicated their wishes that I would offer for Congress. I could not only be elected with the most perfect ease, but I have reason to believe that there would be no opposition from any quarter whatever. The public, nevertheless, confiding perhaps too much in my judgment as to what is best to be done, is entirely disposed to acquiesce in any resolution I may take. That which I have adopted is to offer for no office, at present, and until I can see more distinctly than I do now how I can be useful, but to remain in private life, attending to the care of my private affairs and the re-establishment of my health. I was consulted repeatedly to know if I would serve in the Legislature, but I thought it best to decline.

There is enough, in passing events, God knows, to alarm, to arouse, and to urge to the most strenuous exertions; but if I were to put myself forward my motives and my aims would be questioned, and perhaps the re-action so desirable would be retarded instead of being accelerated. Others I think had better take the lead, who stand in attitudes less likely to excite passion and prejudice. Above all, we must rely upon the reflections, and convictions among the Jackson party themselves. Already they begin to repent, that is many of the better portion of them. Pride restrains them from denouncing openly with their mouths an administration which they detest from their hearts. As time elapses, and new events are developed, they will take courage, and finally concur in restoring the Civil rule.

I have not determined to return to the practice of my old profession; and nothing but necessity will compel me to put on the harness again. That I hope to be able to avoid.

I must request that you will keep me informed of all that relates to your Convention,[2] it's composition, &c &c. Will you have the goodness to desire [John H.] Pleasants to put me down as a Subscriber to the [Richmond *Constitutional*] Whig, and send it to me?

ALS. KyU. Printed in Colton, *Clay Correspondence*, 4:232-33, which omits the last sentence. 1. May 16 at Fowler's Garden, in Lexington. 2. See 7:575-76.

From Eliza Sibley [Mrs. Josiah S.] Johnston, New Orleans, May 12, 1829. Reports at length on social functions she has attended since returning to New Orleans, especially "several Evegs." at the home of James and Anne Brown Clay Erwin. Remarks that "Col. [Thomas Hart] & Mrs. Benton were here   they took their departure two days since for St Louis. I think they must have remarked the difference between *their* reception & that of the friends of Mr. [John Quincy] Adams   I met them at dinner, *but once*, altho we have been out almost every day, & in fact believe, that very few of the genteel or fashionable people called upon them." Discusses at length a tiff she has had with Mrs. Horace Holley, "whose jealousy I presume, had been excited from my having received many more visits than herself during the day—" Announces that she and her husband will attend a wedding in Cincinnati in June, and that Mr. Johnston hopes Clay will meet him there, since "he has much to say." Envies the pending visit of the Erwins to "Ashland," and mentions that she has had a letter from Henry Clay, Jr., at West Point. Considers him "a dear, affectionate boy, & we must all love him, & express our interest for his future welldoing—" ALI. DLC-HC (DNA, M212, R3).

To JOHN H. EWING   Lexington, May 14, 1829

I ought to have mentioned to you in my last [May 4], but I hope it will occur to you, that I may find a demand or use for the rams among the lambs of the Ewes which you purchased for me; and that therefore I do not wish them castrated. Several have already applied to me for rams, and I shall have no difficulty in disposing of them upon some terms or other. If they shall not have been changed, before you receive this, letter, I request that they may be sent unaltered.

I daily receive further information in regard to public feeling and sentiments towards me, in this State; and I can speak, with great confidence, in stating that there is a decided & large majority favorable to me. On Saturday next there is to be a great dinner, when I am assured there will be many Jacksonians present.[1]

ALS. Courtesy of Lexington Galleries, Lexington, Ky.   1. Fowler's Garden Speech, May 16, 1829.

From H. Blanton & P. Dudley, Frankfort, May 15, 1829. In their capacities as treasurer and president, respectively, of the Frankfort Bridge Company, they certify that Clay is "entitled" to purchase 40 shares "in the Capital and joint stock" of the company. ADS. DLC-TJC (DNA, M212, R16). See Mount Vernon Phillips, "History of the Independent Toll Bridge in Kentucky 1792-1850," M.A. thesis, University of Kentucky, 1930.

On July 18, 1829, Dudley sent Clay five shares, "which is all I have, as yet, obtained for you," quoting a price of $50 per share, but noting that a dividend of $3.00 per share had been declared on July 1. "Your dividend is subject to your order," he said. Adds in a postscript: "I do not believe there is the slightest cause even to doubt the success of [John J.] Crittenden's election—I put his majority at 100." ALS. DLC-TJC (DNA, M212, R10). In the August, 1829, elections in Franklin County to the Ky. General Assembly, Crittenden defeated Ezra Richmond by 85 votes. Lexington *Kentucky Reporter*, August 12, 1829.

On July 19, 1829, Dudley certified Clay's entitlement to the five shares. ADS. DLC-TJC (DNA, M212, R16). On July 28, he certified Clay for an additional 27 shares, accepting $1,350 in payment. *Ibid.*

Also on July 28, he congratulated Clay for having made such a good investment. "I do not believe there is another share to be had on any terms," he wrote. In a postscript to this same letter, he also reaffirmed his confidence in Crittenden's election "by a majority of from one to two hundred—Crittenden told me this morning he thought his majority would be at least 150." ALS. DLC-HC (DNA, M212, R3).

FOWLER'S GARDEN SPEECH   Lexington, May 16, 1829

I fear, friends and fellow-citizens, that if I could find language to express the feelings which now animate me, I could not be heard throughout this vast assembly. My voice, once strong and powerful, has had its vigor impaired by delicate health and advancing age. You must have been separated, as I have been, for four years past, from some of your best and dearest friends, with whom, during the greater part of your lives, you had associated in the most intimate friendly intercourse; you must have been traduced, as I have been, after exerting, with zeal and fidelity, the utmost of your powers to promote the welfare of our country; and you must have returned among those warm-hearted friends, and been greeted and welcomed and honored by them, as I have recently been, before you could estimate the degree of sensibility which I now feel, or conceive how utterly inadequate all human language is to pourtray the the grateful emotions of my heart. I behold gathered here, as I have seen in other instances, since my return among you, sires far advanced in years, endeared to me by an interchange of friendly office and sympathetic feeling, beginning more than thirty years ago. Their sons, grown up during my absence in the public councils, accompanying them; and all, prompted by ardent attachment, affectionately surrounding and saluting me as if I belonged to their own household. Considering the multitude here assembled, their standing and respectability, and the distance which many have come personally to see me, and to testify their respect and confidence, I consider this day and this occasion as the proudest of my life. The tribute, thus rendered by my friends, neighbors and fellow-citizens, flows spontaneously from their hearts, as it penetrates the inmost recess of mine. Tendered in no servile spirit, it does not aim to propitiate one in authority. Power could not buy or coerce it. The offspring of enlightened and independent freemen, it is addressed to a beloved fellow citizen, in private life, without office, and who can present nothing in return, but his hearty thanks. I pray all of you, gentlemen, to accept these. They are due to every one of you for the sentiment just pronounced, and for the proceedings of this day. And I owe a particular expression of them to that portion of my friends who, although I had the misfortune to differ from them in the late contest, have honored me by their attendance here. I have no reproaches to make them. Regrets I have. But I give, as I have received from them, the hand of friendship as cordially as it is extended to any of my friends. It is highly gratifying to me to know that they, and thousands of others who cooperated with them in producing the late political change, were unaffected towards me by the prejudices attempted to be excited against me. I entertain too high respect for the inestimable privilege of freely exercising one's independent judgment, on public affairs, to draw in question the right of any of my fellow citizens to form and to act upon their opinions, in opposition to mine. The best and wisest amongst us are, at last, but weak and fallible human beings. And no man ought to set up his own judgment as an unerring standard by which the correctness of all others is to be tested and tried.

It cannot be doubted that, with individual exceptions, the great body of every political party that has hitherto appeared in this country, has been honest in its intentions and patriotic in its aims. Whole parties may have been sometimes deceived and deluded, but, without being conscious of it; they no doubt sought to advance the welfare of the country. Where such a contest has existed as that which we have recently witnessed, there will be prejudices on the one side and predilections on the other. If, during its progress, we cannot calm the passions, and permit truth and reason to have their undisturbed sway, we ought, at least, after it has terminated, to own their empire. Judging of public men and public measures in a spirit of candor, we should strive to eradicate every bias, and to banish from our minds every consideration not connected with the good of our country.

I do not pretend to be more than other men exempt from the influence of prejudice and predilection. But I declare most sincerely that I have sought, in reference to the present administration, and shall continue to strive, to discard all prejudices, and to judge its acts and measures as they appear to me to affect the interests of our country.

A large portion of my friends and fellow citizens from whom I differed on the late occasion, did not disagree with me as to the foreign or domestic policy of Government. We only differed in the selection of agents to carry that policy into effect. Experience can alone determine who was right. If that policy continues to be pursued under the new administration, it shall have as cordial support from me, as if its care had been confided to agents of my choice. If, on the contrary, it shall be neglected or abandoned, the friends to whom I now refer will be bound by all the obligations of patriotism and consistency to adhere to the policy.

We take a new commencement from the fourth of March last. After that day those who supported the election of the present Chief Magistrate were left as free to judge on the conduct of his administration as those who opposed it. It will be no more inconsistent in them, if he disappoints their expectations, to disapprove his administration, than it will be in us to support it, if, disappoint·ing ours, he should preserve the established policy of the Nation, and introduce no new principles of alarming tendency.

They bestowed their suffrages, upon the supposition that the Government would be well administered; that public pledges would be redeemed, solemn professions be fulfilled, and the rights and liberties of the people be protected and maintained. If they shall find themselves deceived, in any of these respects; should principles avowed during the canvass be violated during the Presidency, and new principles of dangerous import, neither avowed to, nor anticipated by them, be put forth, they will have been betrayed; the distinguished individual for whom they voted will have failed to preserve his identity, and they will be urged by the most sacred of duties to apply the proper corrective.

Government is a trust, and the officers of Government are trustees. And both the trust and the trustees are created for the benefit of the people. Official incumbents are bound, therefore, to administer the trust, not for their own private or individual benefit, but so as to promote the prosperity of the people. This is the vital principle of a Republic. If a different principle prevail, and a government be so administered as to gratify the passions or to promote the interests of a particular individual, the forms of free institutions may remain, but that government is essentially a monarchy. — The great difference between the two forms of Government is, that in a Republic all power and authority and all public offices and honors emanate from the people, and are exercised and held for their benefit. In a monarchy, all power and authority, all offices and honors, proceed from the monarch. His interests, his caprices and his passions influence and control the destinies of the kingdom. In a Republic the people are every thing, and a particular individual nothing. In a monarchy, the monarch is every thing, and the people nothing. And the true character of the Government is stampt not by the forms of the appointment to office alone, but by its practical operation. If, in one, nominally free, the Chief Magistrate, as soon as he is clothed with power, proceeds to exercise it so as to minister to his passions, and to gratify his favorites, and systematically distributes his rewards and punishments, in the application of the power of patronage, with which he is invested for the good of the whole, upon the principle of devotion and attachment to him, and not according to the ability and fidelity with which the people are or may be served, that Chief Magistrate, for the time being, and within the scope of his discretionary power, is in fact, if not in form, a monarch.

It was objected to the late administration, that it adopted and enforced a system of proscription. During the whole period of it, not a solitary officer of the Government, from Maine to Louisiana, within my knowledge, was dismissed on account of his political opinions. It was well known to the late President that many officers, who held their places subject to the power of dismission, were opposed to his re-election, and were actively employed in behalf of his competitor. Yet not one was discharged from that cause. In the commencement and early part of his administration, appointments were promiscuously made from all the parties in the previous canvass. And this course was pursued until an opposition was organized, which denounced all appointments from its ranks as being made for impure purposes.

I am aware that it may be urged, that a change was made in some of the publishers of the laws. There are about eighty annually designated. Of these, during the four years of the late administration, about 12 or 15 were changed. Some of the changes were made from geographical or other local considerations. In several instances one friend was substituted for another. In others, one opponent for another. —

Several papers among the most influential in the opposition, but otherwise conduced with decorum, were retained. Of the entire number of changes, not more than four or five were made on account of the scurrilous character of their papers, and not because of the political sentiments of the Editors. It was deemed injurious to the respect and moral influence, which the laws should always command, that they should be promulgated in columns of a public paper, parallel with which were other columns, in the same paper, of the grossest abuse of the Government and its functionaries.

On this subject I can speak with certainty, and I embrace with pleasure this opportunity for explanation. The duty of designating the printers of the laws appertains to the office which I lately filled. The selection is usually made at the commencement of every session of Congress. It was made by me without any particular consultation with the President or any member of his Cabinet. In making it, I felt under no greater obligation to select the publisher of the laws of the previous year, than an individual feels himself bound to insert a succeeding advertisement in the same paper which published his last. The law does not require it, but leaves the Secretary of State at liberty to make the selection according to his sense of propriety. A publisher of the laws is not an officer of Government. It had been judicially so decided. He holds no commission. The accuracy of the statement, therefore, that no officer of Government was dismissed, by the late administration, in consequence of his political opinions, is not impaired by the few changes of publishers of the laws which were made.

But, if they had been officers of Government, who could have imagined that those, who objected to the removals, would so soon have themselves put in practice a general and sweeping system of exclusion?

The President is invested with the tremendous power of dismission, to be exercised for the public good, and not to gratify any private passions or purposes. It was conferred to prevent the *public* from suffering through faithless or incompetent officers. It was made summary because, if the slow process of trial before a judicial tribunal were resorted to, the public might be greately injured during the progress and prior to the decision of the case. But it never was in the contemplation of Congress, that the power would or could be applied to the removal of competent, diligent and faithful officers. Such an application of it is an act of arbitrary power, and a great abuse.

I regret extremely that I feel constrained to notice the innovation upon the principles and practice of our institutions now in progress. I had most anxiously hoped, that I could heartily approve the acts and measures of the new administration. And I yet hope that it will pause, and hereafter pursue a course more in unison with the spirit of a free government. I entreat my friends and fellow citizens, here and elsewhere, to be persuaded that I now perform a most painful duty; and that it is far from my wish to say one word that can inflict any wound upon the feelings of any of them. I think, indeed, that it is the duty of all of them to exercise their judgments freely and independently on what is passing; and that none ought to feel themselves restrained, by false pride, or by any part which they took in the late election, from condemning what their hearts cannot approve.

Knowing the imputations to which I expose myself, I would remain silent if I did not solemnly believe that there was serious cause of alarm in the principle of removal which had been recently acted on. Hitherto, the uniform practice of the government has been, where charges are preferred against public officers, foreign or domestic, to transmit to them a copy of the charges, for the purpose of refutation or explanation. This has been considered an equitable substitute to the more tedious and formal trials before judicial tribunals. But now persons are dismissed, not only without trial of any sort, but without charge. And, as if the intention were to defy public opinion, and to give to the acts of power a higher degree of enormity, in some instances the persons dismissed have carried with them, in their pockets, the strongest testimonials to their ability and integrity, furnished by the very instruments employed to execute the purposes of oppression. If the new administration had found these discharged officers wanting in a zealous co operation to execute the laws, in consequence of their preference at the preceding election, there would have been ground for their removal. But this has not been pretended; and to show that it formed no consideration; they have been dismissed, among its first acts, without affording them an opportunity of manifesting that their sense of public duty was unaffected by the choice which they had at the preceding election.

I will not dwell on the injustice and individual distress which are the necessary consequences of these acts of authority. Men who accepted public employments entered on them with the implied understanding that they would be retained as long as they continued to discharge their duties to the public honestly, ably, and assiduously. All their private arrangements are made accordingly. To be dismissed, without fault, and without trial; to be expelled, with their families, without the means of support, and, in some instances, disqualified by age or by official habits from the pursuit of any other business; and all this to be done upon the will of one man, in a free government, was surely intolerable oppression.

Our institutions proclaim, reason enjoins, and conscience requires, that every freeman shall exercise the elective franchise freely and independently: and that, among the candidates for his suffrage, he shall fearlessly bestow it upon him who will best advance the interests of his country. The presumption is that this is always done, unless the contrary appear But, if the consequence of such a performance of patriotic duty is to be punishment; if an honest and sincere preference of A to J is to be treated as a crime, then our dearest privilege is a mockery, and our institutions are snares.

During the reign of Bonaparte, upon one of those occasions in which he affected to take the sense of the French people as to his being made Consul for life, or Emperor, an order was sent to the French armies to collect their suffrages. They were told, in a public proclamation, that they were authorized and requested to vote freely, according to the dictates of their best judgments and their honest convictions. But a mandate was privately circulated among them importing that if any soldier voted against Bonaparte he should be instantly shot.

Is there any other difference, except in the mode of punishment, between that case and the arbitrary removal of men from their public stations for no other reason than that of an honest and conscientious preference of one Presidential candidate to another? And can it be doubted, that the spirit which prompts these removals is restrained from being extended to all, in private life, who manifested a similar preference, only by barriers which it dare not yet break down? But should public opinion sanction them, how long will these barriers remain?

One of the worst consequences of the introduction of this tenure of public office will be, should it be permanently adopted, to substitute for a system of responsibility, founded upon the ability and integrity with which public officers discharge their duties to the community, a system of universal rapacity. Incumbents, feeling the instability of their situations, and knowing their liability to periodical removals, at short terms, without any regard to the manner in which they have executed their trusts, will be disposed to make the most of their uncertain offices, whilst they hold them. And hence we may expect innumerable cases of fraud, peculation, and corruption.

President Jackson commenced his official career on the 4th of March last, with every motive which should operate on the human heart to urge him to forget the prejudices and passions which had been exhibited in the previous contest, and to practice dignified moderation and forbearance. He had been the choice of a considerable majority of the people, and was elected by a large majority of the Electoral votes. He had been elected mainly from the all powerful influence of gratitude for his brilliant military services, in spite of doubts and fears entertained by many who contributed to his elevation. He was far advanced in years; and, if fame speak true, was suffering under the joint infirmities of age and disease. He had recently been visited by one of the severest afflictions of Providence, in the privation of the partner of his bosom, whom he is represented to have tenderly loved, and who warmly returned all his affection. He had no child on whom to cast his honors. Under such circumstances, was ever man more imperiously called upon to stifle all the vindictive passions of his nature, to quell every rebellious feeling of his heart, and to dedicate the short residue of his life to the God who had so long blessed and spared him, and to the country which had so greatly honored him?

I sincerely hope that he will yet do this. I hope so for the sake of human nature, and for the sake of his own reputation. Whether he has, during the two months of his administration, so conducted himself, let facts tell and history pronounce. Truth is mighty and will prevail.

It was objected to Mr Adams that, by appointing several members of Congress to public places, he endangered the purity of the body, and established a precedent fraught with the most mischievous consequences And President Jackson (no, he begged his pardon, it was candidate Jackson) was so much alarmed by these appointments for the integrity and permanency of our institutions, that in a solemn communication which he deliberately made to the Legislature of Tennessee, he declared his firm conviction to be, that no member of Congress ought to be appointed to any office except a seat upon the bench. And he added that he himself would conform to that rule.

During the four years of Mr. Adams's administration, the whole number of appointments made by him, from Congress, did not exceed four or five. In the first four weeks of that of his successor, more than double that number have been appointed by him. In the first two months of President Jackson's administration, he has appointed more Members of Congress to public office than I believe were appointed by any one of his predecessors during their whole period of four or eight years. And it appears that no office is too high or too low to be bestowed by him on this favored class, from that of a Head of a Department down to an inconsiderable Collectorship, or even a subordinate office under a Collector. If I have not been misinformed, a Representative from the greatest commercial Metropolis in the United States has recently been appointed to some inferior station, by the Collector of the port of New York.

Without meaning to assert, as a general principle, that in no case would it be proper that a resort should be had to the Halls of Congress to draw from them tried talents and experienced public servants, to aid in the Executive or Judicial departments, all must agree that such a resort should not be too often made, and that there should be some limit both as to the number and the nature of the appointments. And I do sincerely think that this limit has, in both particulars, been transcended beyond all safe bounds, and so as to excite serious apprehensions.

It is not, however, my opinion, but that of President Jackson, which the public has now to consider. Having declared to the American People, through the Tennessee Legislature, the danger of the practice; having deliberately committed himself to act in consonance with that declared opinion, how can he now be justified in violating this solemn pledge, and in entailing upon his country a perilous precedent, fraught with the corrupting tendency which he described?

It is in vain to say that the Constitution, as it now stands, does not forbid these appointments. It does not enjoin them. If there be an inherent defect in the theoretical character of the instrument, President Jackson was bound to have redeemed his pledge, and employed the whole influence and weight of his name to remedy the defect in its practical operation. The Constitution admitted of the service of one man in the Presidential office during his life, if he could secure successive elections. That great Reformer, as President Jackson describes him, whom he professes to imitate, did not wait for an amendment of the Constitution to correct that defect; but, after the example of the Father of his Country, by declining to serve longer than two terms, established a practical principle which is not likely to be violated.

There was another class of citizens upon whom public offices had been showered in the greatest profusion. I do not know the number of Editors of newspapers that have been recently appointed, but I have noticed, in the public prints, some fifteen or twenty. And they were generally of those whose papers had manifested the greatest activity in the late canvass, the most vulgar abuse of opponents, and the most fulsome praise of their favorite candidate. Editors are as much entitled to be appointed as any other class of the community: but if the number and the quality of those promoted be such as to render palpable the motive of their appointment; if they are preferred not on account of their fair pretensions, and their ability and capacity to serve the public, but because of their devotion to a particular individual, I ask if the necessary consequence must not be to render the Press venal, and in time to destroy this hitherto justly cherished Palladium of our Liberty.

If the *principle* of all these appointments—this monopoly of public trusts by Members of Congress and partisan Editors—be exceptionable, (and I would not have alluded to them but from my deliberate conviction that they are essentially vicious,) their effects are truly alarming. I will not impute to President Jackson any design to subvert our liberties. I hope and believe that he does not now entertain any such design. But I must say that if an ambitious President sought the overthrow of our Government, and ultimately to establish a different form, he would, at the commencement of his administration, proclaim, by his official acts, that the greatest public virtue was ardent devotion to him. That no matter what had been the character, the services, or the sacrifices of incumbents or applicants for office, what their experience or ability to serve the Republic, if they did not bow down and worship him they possessed no claim to his patronage. Such an ambitious President would say, as monarchs have said, "I am the state." He would dismiss all from public employment who did not belong to the true faith. He would stamp upon the whole official corps of Government one homogeneous character, and infuse into it one uniform principle of action. He would scatter, with an open and liberal hand, offices among Members of Congress, giving the best to those who had spoken and written and *franked* most in his behalf. He would subsidise the press. It would be his earnest and constant aim to secure the two greatest engines of operation upon public opinion, Congress and the press. He would promulgate a new penal code, the rewards and punishments of which would be distributed and regulated exclusively by devotion or opposition to him. And when all this powerful machinery was put in motion, if he did not succeed in subverting the liberties of his country, and in establishing himself upon a throne, it would be because some new means or principle of resistance had been discovered which was unknown in other times or to other Republics.

But if an administration, conducted in the manner just supposed, did not aim at the destruction of public liberty, it would engender evils of a magnitude so great as gradually to alienate the affections of the people from their government, and finally to lead to its overthrow. According to the principle now avowed and practised, all offices vacant and filled within the compass of the Executive power, are to be allotted among the partisans of the successful candidate. The people and the service of the State are to be put aside, and every thing is to be decided by the zeal, activity, and attachment, in the cause of a particular candidate, which were manifested during the preceding canvass. The consequence of these principles would be to convert the nation into one perpetual theatre for political gladiators. There would be one universal scramble for the public offices   The termination of one Presidential contest would be only the signal for the commencement of another. And on the conclusion of each we should behold the victor distributing the prizes and applying his punishments, like a military commander, immediately after he had won a great victory. Congress corrupted, and the press corrupted, general corruption would ensue, until the substance of free government having disappeared, some Pretorian band would arise, and, with the general concurrence of a distracted people, put an end to useless forms.

I am aware that the late acts of administration on which it has been my disagreeable duty to animadvert (I hope without giving pain to any of my fellow-citizens, as I most sincerely wish to give none) were sustained upon some vague notion or purpose of reform. And it was remarkable that among the loudest trumpeters of reform, were some who had lately received appointment to lucrative offices. Now it must be admitted that, as to them, a most substantial and valuable *reform* had taken place; but trust that something more extensively beneficial to the people at large was intended by that sweet sounding word. I know that, at the commencement, and throughout nearly the whole progress of the late administration, a reform in the constitution was talked of, so as to exclude from public office members of Congress, during the periods for which they were elected, and a limited term beyond them. This proposition appeared to be received with much favor, was discussed in the House of Representatives, session after session, at great length and with unusual eloquence and ability. A majority of that body seemed disposed to accede to it, and I thought for some time, that there was high probability of its passage, at least through that house. Its great champion (General [Alexander] Smyth of Virginia) pressed it with resolute perseverance. But, unfortunately, at the last session, after the decision of the Presidential question, it was manifest that the kindness with which it had been originally received, had greatly abated. Its determined patron found it extremely difficult to engage the House to consider it. When, at length, he prevailed by his frequent and earnest appeals to get it taken up, new views appeared to have suddenly struck the reformists. It was no longer an amendment in their eyes, so indispensable to the purity of our constitution; and the majority which had appeared to be so resolved to carry it now by a direct or indirect vote, gave it the go by. That majority, I believe, was composed in part of members, who, after the fourth of March last, gave the best practical recantation of their opinions, by accepting from the new President lucrative appointments, in direct opposition to the principle of their own amendment. And now General Smyth would find it even more impracticable to make amongst them proselytes, to his conservative alteration in the constitution, than he did to gain any to his Exposition of the Apocalypse.

Reform, such as alone could interest a whole people, can only take place in the constitution, or laws, or policy of the government. Now and then, under every administration, and at all times, a faithless or incompetent officer may be discovered, who ought to be displaced. And that in all the departments of Government. But I presume that the correction of such occasional abuses could hardly be expected to fulfil the promise of reform which had been so solemnly made. I would then ask, what was *the reform* intended? — What part of the Constitution was to be altered? What law repealed; what branch of the settled policy of the country was to be changed? The people have a right to know what great blessing was intended by their rulers for them, and to demand some tangible practical good, in lieu of a general, vague, and undefined assurance of reform.

I know that the recent removals from office are attempted to be justified by a precedent drawn from Mr. Jefferson's administration. But there was not the most distant analogy between the two cases Several years prior to his election, the public offices of the country had been almost exclusively bestowed upon the party to which that at the head of which he stood was opposed. When he commenced his administration he found a complete monopoly of them in the hands of the adverse party He dismissed a few incumbents for the purpose of introducing in their places others of his own party, and thus doing equal justice to both sects. — But the number of removals was far short of those which are now in progress. When President Jackson entered on his administration, he found a far different state of things There had been no previous monopoly. Public offices were alike filled by his friends and opponents in the late election. If the fact could be ascertained, I believe it would be found that there was a larger number of officers under the government attached than opposed to his late election.

Further — in the case of Mr. Jefferson's election, it was the consequence of the people having determined on a radical change of system. There was a general belief among the majority, who brought about that event, that their opponents had violated the constitution in the enactment of the alien and sedition laws; that they had committed other great abuses, and that some of them contemplated an entire change in the character of of [*sic*] our government, so as to give it a monarchical cast. I state the historical fact without intending to revive the discussion, or deeming it necessary to examine whether such a design existed or not. But those who at that day did believe it, could hardly be expected to acquiesce in the possession by their opponents, the minority of the nation, of all the offices of a government to which some of them were believed to be hostile in principle. The object of Mr. Jefferson was to break down a pre-existing monopoly in the hands of one party, and to establish an equilibrium between the two great parties. The object of President Jackson appears to be to destroy an existing equilibrium between the two parties to the late contest, and to establish a monopoly. The object of President Jefferson was the Republic, and not himself. That of President Jackson is himself and not the State.

It never was advanced under Mr. Jefferson's Administration, that devotion and attachment to him were an indispensable qualification, without which no one could hold or be appointed to office. The contrast between the inaugural speech of that great man, and that of his present successor, was remarkable in every respect. Mr Jefferson's breathed a spirit of peace. It breathed a spirit of calm philosophy and dignified moderation. It treated the nation as one family. "We are all republicans, all federalists." It contained no denunciations; no mysterious or ambiguous language; no reflections upon the conduct of his great rival and immediate predecessor. What is the character of the inaugural speech of the present Chief Magistrate, I shall not attempt to sketch. Mr Jefferson, upon the solemn occasion of his installation into office, laid down his rule for appointment to office — "Is he honest; is he capable; is he faithful to the constitution?" But capacity and integrity and fidelity, according to the modern rule, appear to count for nothing, without the all absorbing virtue of fidelity to President Jackson

I will not consume the time of my friends and fellow-citizens with observations upon many of the late changes. My object has been to point your attention to the principle which appears to have governed all of them, and to classes. I repeat, that I would not have touched this unpleasant topic but that it seems to me to furnish much and just occasion for serious alarm   I hope that I have treated it in a manner becoming to me, without incurring the displeasure of any one now present. I believe the times require all the calm heads and sound hearts of the country. And I would not intentionally say one word to excite the passions.

But there are a few cases of recent removal, of such flagrant impropriety, as I sincerely think, that I cannot forbear alluding to them   Under no administration prior to the present, from the commencement of the Government, have our Diplomatic Representatives been recalled from abroad, on account of the political opinions which they entertained in regard to a previous Presidential election. Within my recollection, at this time, there has been but one instance of recall of a foreign Minister, under the present Constitution, on account of any dissatisfaction with him   But President Washington did not recall Colonel Monroe (the case referred to) from France, on his individual account, but because he was not satisifed with the manner to which he performed the duties of the mission. President Jackson has ordered home two of our foreign Ministers, one filling the most important European mission, and the other the most important of our missions on this Continent. In both cases the sole ground of recall is, that they were opposed to his election as President. And as if there should be no possible controversy on this head, one of them was recalled before it was known at Washington that he had reached Bogota, the place of his destination; and consequently before he could have possibly disobeyed any instruction or violated any duty.

The pecuniary effect of these changes is the certain expenditure, in outfits, of $18,000, and perhaps more than triple that sum in contingencies. Now it does seem to me that (and I put it to *your* candid judgments whether) this is too large a sum for the public to pay because two gentlemen had made a mistake of the name which they should have written on a little bit of paper thrown into the ballot boxes. Mistake! They had in fact made no practical mistake.

They had not voted at all, one being out of the United States, and the other out of his own State, at the time of the election. The money is therefore to be paid because they made a mistake in the abstract opinions which they held, and might possibly, if they had been at home, have erroneously inscribed one name instead of another on their ballots.

There would be some consolation for this waste of public treasure, if it were compensated by the superiority of qualification on the part of the late appointments in comparison with the previous. But I know all four of the gentlemen perfectly well, and my firm conviction is, that in neither change has the public gained any intellectual advantage. In one of them indeed, the victor of Tippacanoe and of Thames, of whose gallantry many who are now here were witnesses, is replaced by a gentleman who, if he possess one single attainment to qualify him for the office, I solemnly declare it has escaped my discernment.

There was another class of persons whose expulsion from office was marked by peculiar hardship and injustice. Citizens of the District of Columbia were deprived of all actual participation in the elections of the United States. They are debarred from voting for a President or any member of Congress. Their sentiments, therefore, in relation to any election of those officers are perfectly abstract. To punish them, as in numerous instances has been done, by dismissing them from their employments, not for what they *did*, but for what they *thought*, is a cruel aggravation of their anomalous condition. I know well those who have been discharged from the Department of State, and I take pleasure in bearing testimony to their merits. Some of them would have done honor to any bureau in any country.

We may worship God according to the dictates of our own consciences. No man's right in that respect can be called in question. The Constitution secures it. Public offices are happily, according to the theory of our Constitution, alike accessible to all, Protestants and Catholics, and to every denomination of each. But if our homage is not paid to a mortal, we are liable to a punishment which an erroneous worship of God does not bring upon us. Those public officers, it seems, who have failed to exhibit their devotion to that mortal, are to be visited by all the punishment which he can inflict, in virtue of laws, the execution of which was committed to his hands for the public good, and not to subserve his private purposes.

At the most important port of the United States the office of Collector was filled by Mr. [Jonathan] Thompson, whose removal was often urged upon the late Administration by some of its friends, upon the ground of his alleged attachment to Gen Jackson. But the late President was immovable in his resolution to deprive no man of his office in consequence of his political opinions or preferences. Mr. Thompson's removal was so often and so strongly pressed, for the reason just stated, that an inquiry was made of the Secretary of the Treasury into the manner in which the duties of the office were discharged. The Secretary stated that there was no better Collector in the public service; and that his returns and accounts were regularly and neatly rendered, and all the duties of his office ably and honestly performed, as far as he knew or believed. This meritorious officer has been removed to provide a place for Mr. [Samuel] Swartwout, whose association with Colonel [Aaron] Burr is notorious throughout the United States. I put it to the candor of all who are here, to say if *such* a change can be justified in the port of New York, the revenue collected at which amounts to about ten millions of dollars, more than one third of the whole revenue of the United States.

I will detain the present assembly no longer upon subjects connected with the General Government. I hope that I shall find, in the future course of the new Administration, less cause for public disapprobation. I most anxiously hope that, when its measures come to be developed, at the next and succeeding sessions of Congress, they shall be perceived to be such as are best adapted to promote the prosperity of the country. I will say, with entire sincerity, that I shall be most happy to see it sustaining the American System, including Internal Improvements, and upholding the established policy of the Government at home and abroad. And I shall ever be as ready to render praise where praise is due, as it is now painful to me, under existing circumstances, to participate in the disapprobation which recent occurrences have produced.

No occasion can be more appropriate than the present, when surrounded by my former constituents, to say a few words upon the unimportant subject of myself Prior to my return home I had stated, in answer to all inquiries whether I should be again presented as a candidate to represent my old district in the House of Representatives, that I should come to no absolute decision until I had taken time for reflection, and to ascertain what might be the feelings and wishes of those who had so often honored me with their suffrages. The present representative of the district [James Clark] has conducted himself towards me with the greatest liberality; and I take pleasure now in making my public acknowledgements, so justly due to him. He had promptly declined being a candidate, if I would offer, and he warmly urged me to offer.

Since my return home, I have mixed freely as I could with my friends and fellow citizens of the district — They have met me with the greatest cordiality. Many of them have expressed a wish that I would again represent them. Some of the most prominent and respectable of those who voted for the present Chief Magistrate, have also expressed a similar wish. I have every reason to believe that there would be no opposition to me from any quarter or any party, if I were to offer But if I am not greatly deceived in the prevailing feeling throughout the district, it is one more delicate and respectful towards me, and I appreciate it much higher than if it had been manifested in loud calls upon me to return to my old post. It referred the question to my own sober judgment. My former constituents were generally ready to acquiesce in any decision I might think proper to make. If I were to offer for Congress they were prepared to support me with their accustomed zeal and true-heartedness. I thank them all, from the bottom of my heart, whether they agreed or differed with me in th late contest, for this generous confidence.

I have deliberated much on the question. My friends in other parts of the Union are divided in opinion about the utility of any services which I could render, at the present period, in the National Legislature. This state of things, at home and abroad, left me free to follow the impulse of my own feelings and the dictate of my own judgment These prompted me to remain in private life. In coming to this resolution, I did not mean to impair the force of the obligation under which every citizen, in my opinion, stood, to the last flickering of human life, to dedicate his best exertions to the service of the Republic. I am ready to act in conformity with that obligation whenever it shall be the pleasure of the people, and such a probability of usefulness shall exist as will justify my acceptance of any service which they may choose to designate.

I have served my country now near thirty years. My constitution, never very vigorous, requires repose. My health, always of late years very delicate, demands care. My private affairs want my attention. Upon my return home, I found my house out of repair; my farm not in order, the fences down, the stock poor, the crop not set, and late in April the corn stalks of last year's growth yet standing in the field, a sure sign of slovenly cultivation.

Under all circumstances, I think that, without being liable to the reproach of dereliction of any public duty to my country or to my friends, I may continue at home for a season, if not during the remainder of my life, among my friends and old constituents, cheering and cheered by them, and interchanging all the kind and friendly offices incident to private life. I wished to see them all; to shake hands cordially with them; to inquire into the deaths, births, marriages, and other interesting events among them; to identify myself in fact as I am in feeling with them, and with the generation which has sprung up whilst I have been from home serving them. I wish to put my private affairs to rights, and if I can, with the blessing of Providence, to re-establish a shattered constitution and enfeebled health.

It has been proposed to me to offer for a seat in the Legislature of the State. I should be proud of the selection if I believed that I could be useful at Frankfort. I see, I think, very clearly the wants of Kentucky. Its finances are out of order, but they could be easily put straight by a little moral courage on the part of the General Assembly, and a small portion of candor and good will among the people. Above all, we want an efficient system of Internal Improvements adopted by the State. No Kentuckian who travelled in or out of it could behold the wretched condition of our roads, without the deepest mortification We are greatly to the rear of almost all the adjacent States, some of which sprung into existence long after we were an established commonwealth. Whilst they are obeying the spirit of the age, and nobly marching forward in the improvement of their respective territories, we are absolutely standing still, or rather going backwards. It is scarcely credible, but nevertheless true, that it took my family, in the month of April, near four days to travel, through mud and mire, a distance of only sixty-four miles, over one of the most frequented roads in the State.

And yet our wants, on this subject, are perfectly within the compass of our means, judiciously applied. An artificial road from Maysville to the Tennessee line, one branch in the direction to Nashville, and a second to strike the mouth of Cumberland or Tennessee river: an artificial road extending from Louisville to intersect the other somewhere about the Bowling Green; one passing by Shelbyville and Frankfort to the Cumberland Gap; and an artificial road extending from Frankfort to the mouth of Big Sandy, compose all the leading roads which at present need the resources of the State. These might be constructed, partly on the M'Adams' method, and partly by simply graduating and bridging them, which latter mode can be performed at an expense less than $1,000 per mile. Other lateral, connecting these main roads might be left to the public spirit of the local authorities and of private companies.

Congress, without doubt, would aid the State, if we did not call upon Hercules without putting our shoulders to the wheel. But without that aid we could ourselves accomplish all the works which I have described. It would not be practicable to complete them in a period of less than seven or eight years, and of course not necessary to raise the whole sum requisite to the object in one year. Funds drawn from executed parts of the system might be applied to the completion of those that remained. This auxiliary source, combined with the ample means of the State, properly developed, and faithfully appropriated, would enable us to construct all the roads which I have sketched, without burthening the people.

But, solicitous as I feel on this interesting subject, I regret that I have not yet seen sufficient demonstrations of the public will to assure me that the judgment of the people had carried them to the same or similar conclusions to which my mind has conducted me. We have been, for years past, unhappily greatly distracted and divided. These dissensions have drawn us off from a view of greater to less important concerns. They have excited bitter feelings and animosities, and created strong prejudices and jealousies I fear that from these causes the public is not yet prepared dispassionately to consider and to adopt a comprehensive, I think the only practicable system of Internal Improvements, in this State. A premature effort might retard instead of accelerating the object. And I must add that I fear extraneous causes would bias and influence the judgment of the Legislature.

Upon the whole, I must decline acceding to the wishes of those who desired to see me in the Legislature. Retirement, unqualified retirement, from all public employment, is what I unaffectedly desire. I would hereafter, if my life and health are preserved, be ready at all times to act on the principles which I have avowed; and whenever, at a more auspicious period, there shall appear to be a probability of my usefulness to the Union or to the State, I will promptly obey any call which the people may be pleased to make.

And now, my friends and fellow-citizens, I cannot part from you, on possibly this last occasion of my ever publicly addressing you, without reiterating the expression of my thanks from a heart overflowing with gratitude. I came among you, now more than thirty years ago, an orphan boy, pennyless, a stranger to you all, without friends, without the favor of the great. You took me up, cherished me, caressed me, protected me, honored me You have constantly poured upon me a bold and unabated stream of innumerable favors. Time, which wears out everything, has increased and strengthened your affection for me. When I seemed deserted by almost the whole world, and assailed by almost every tongue and pen and press, you have fearlessly and manfully stood by me, with unsurpassed zeal and undiminished friendship. When I felt as if I should sink beneath the storm of abuse and detraction, which was violently raging around me, I have found myself upheld and sustained by your encouraging voices and your approving smiles. I have doubtless committed many faults and indiscretions, over which you have thrown the broad mantle of your charity. But I can say, and in the presence of my God and of this assembled multitude I will say, that I have honestly and faithfully served my country; that I have never wronged it; and that, however unprepared I lament that I am to appear in the Divine presence on other accounts, I invoke the stern justice of His judgment on my public conduct, without the smallest apprehension of His displeasure

Mr. Clay concluded by proposing the following toast:

The State of Kentucky. — A cordial union of all parties in favor of an efficient system of Internal Improvements adapted to the wants of the State.

Copy. Printed in Washington *Daily National Journal*, June 13, 1829, which version is used here; and in Lexington *Kentucky Reporter*, June 3, 1829. Excerpts reprinted in *Kendall's Expositor* (Washington, D.C.), May 5, 1841.

From HENRY CLAY, JR.   West Point, N.Y., May 19, 1829

I am glad to see by your letter that you have reached home. In the papers[1] I had seen this before and also, which gave me great satisfaction, that your old constituents had acted like themselves.

You caution me against remitting my efforts in my present pursuits, in my eagerness to enter upon the study of Law. I hope and at present feel confident that I shall preserve my rank in my class. The course of studies of this year is by no means so difficult as that of the last or of the coming year. I now find time to attend to some studies which I believe will be useful to me when I commence the study of Law, I am reading Montesquieu's spirit of Laws.[2] I take much interest in it. The subjects treated of are such as would present themselves continually to a man's mind in our country of laws an[d] of free enquiry. the style of the work is very different from the general style of the French, for it is both concise and comprehensive

I shall be with you by the 1st of July. Remember me to our friends. . . . P.S. I would be glad if you would send me an application by you for a furlough for me. I believe that I have not mentioned this to you before although it ought to have been done, for by a regulation of the Academy it is required that the application of the parent or guardian should be handed in together with that of the cadets on the 1st of June

ALS. Henry Clay Memorial Foundation, Lexington, Ky. Printed in Colton, *Clay Correspondence*, 4:233-34, without first paragraph.   1. In 1825 Clay had taken out for his son a four-year subscription to the Washington *Daily National Intelligencer*. It was mailed to him at West Point. Clay to Gales and Seaton, May 5, 1829. D, partially printed. DLC-TJC (DNA, M212, R16).   2. Charles Louis de Secondat Montesquieu, *De l'Esprit des Lois*.

From George Howard *et al.*, Mount Sterling, Ky., May 20, 1829. Invite Clay to a public dinner in his honor at Mt. Sterling so that they may express their "unqualified approbation of your public labors." Believe that posterity in its "unbiased decision, will place you among the most conspicuous and able supporters of human liberty throughout the world." Copy. Printed in Lexington *Kentucky Reporter*, June 24, 1829.

Clay replied on May 28, postponing acceptance of the invitation to speak in Montgomery County until sometime during the summer. Thanks them for "the approbation that you have expressed of my public labor." Recalls that Montgomery County was "one of the first in which I commenced the career of the profession of law" and "is endeared to me by many early associations and agreeable recollections." *Ibid.*

To UNKNOWN RECIPIENT   Lexington, May 23, 1829

I have [word missing] [d]uly [r]eceived your favor of the 15h. Ulto. [How] the ridiculous story of my fall, in a duel with Mr. [John] Pope, came [to] be put in circulation I know not;[1] but I assure you most seriously that I am not dead, and that I am happy to have survived to witness the generous sympathies and regrets of my New England friends, on account of my death. After all, there was quite as much foundation for the story as for many others about me that have been put forward of late.

The ferocious spirit of universal proscription seems to be in full operation. If the principle and the practice are sanctioned by the people, and become the prevailing usage hereafter, our institutions will not be worth preserving. I perceive that it has been extended to you, as well as many other of our friends. I cannot concur with those friends who are pleased with it, because of the beneficial results which may flow from it. They are not certain, whilst the amount of individual suffering is positive and great.

In a late Speech[2] which I addressed to a small dining party of between three and four thousand gentlemen I animadverted pretty freely on passing events, perhaps too freely for policy, though not enough so for the atrocity of the proceedings or the warmth of my feelings. The Speech will be published.

From all that I have heard and seen, since my return, I entertain no doubt of the issue of any future contest, to which I should be a party, in this State. Many have avowed that, in supporting Genl. Jackson, they did not intend to affect me. That unfortunate discrimination was made much more extensively than I was aware of. Some of the leaders have [declared] [word missing] and many more [words missing] contest between Jackson [words missing] prevail. [All my] friends are aware here [words missing] something more certain than [words missing] facts on my side ought to be opposed to facts apparently against me. These they say shall be furnished in due season. As the termination of the late election is yet so near, and the next so distant, it may be impracticable, during this summer, to make the people perceive the utility of agitating the question, and of inducing them to turn the elections on that pivot. Still many will be placed on that ground, and I have no doubt that in the course of the next if not in that of the present year the requisite demonstrations will be given.

I could have been returned to the H. of R. without any opposition; but, for reasons some of which are stated in the above Speech, and others are known to my friends in N. England, I declined being a Candidate.

On the point of a nomination of me by the Legislature of Massachusetts at their Spring Session (respecting which you are pleased to ask my views), I can only say that it is not *now* necessary for any effect in this quarter; that I am inclined to think it premature; and that I believe it would be better to postpone it until next winter, after the developement in Congress of the policy of the new Administration. Still my friends will act upon their better views. They are much more competent to judge than I am in a matter so nearly concerning me.

As to the general course of Opposition to the administration it appears to me that attack should not precede cause of attack; that as errors are committed they should be exposed in as strong colors [as] [missing words] [t]ruth will justify; tha[t] [words missing] against the counseller [words missing]; that his imbecility [words missing] be [words missing] [de]licacy; that it should be [word missing] to appear as I believe the fact to be, that he is abso[lutely] destitute of all energy, except when acting under a gust of vindictive passion, or rewarding some devoted and unprincipled favorite; and that Duff Green &c should be rendered as odious as he is rapacious and monstrous.

I have not received the Circular of the Bunker hill association[3] to which you refer. I am not rich, but I would with pleasure contribute any thing in my power to that patriotic object.

My New England friends may be assured that they do not entertain a stronger abhorrence of the practice of duelling than I do. It would not be proper to make a pledge that, under no possible circumstances, would one engage in such an affair. But the difficulty would be much greater to draw me, now that I am fifty two, into one, than I could have been at a less advanced age; and nothing would provoke me to meet any Subaltern. . . . . P. S. Things are working well in respect to the gentleman suggested by you for V. P.[4] He is more and more alienated. But it would be better to wait a little longer before he should be nominated.

ALS. KyU. Portions at top of pages missing. Letter marked "Confidential."   1. Lawrence to Clay, May 2, 1829.   2. At Fowler's Garden, Lexington, May 16, 1829.   3. *Bunker Hill Monument Association Circular* (Boston, 1824) which explained the design of the association & solicited support for the erection of the monument.   4. Reference obscure.

From **ROBERT WICKLIFFE**   Frankfort, May 23, 1829

I have reflected with much concern on the situation of my son [Charles][1] since you were here & my mind has come to the conclusion that It would greatly promote my security if you will consent to appear for him & If you do not differ in opinion & feel willing to appear it will in a great measure relieve my fears as to the result — If However you think it not comparable with your views of propriety I cannot urge you to do so   Of the effect I know that it will excite both my friends & your own for you to step forward as his defender and of my enemies I ask nothing & It is a rule of my life never to fear them or to count them & I do believe that a firm and resolute course in Charles, Case will do more than Policy or Concession, Of yourself I can scarcely think that it will lessen you in the estimation of your friends or enemies on the Contrary it will command the one & endear that of the other for them to believe; that your course is not decided by an apprehension of political effect   If my friends are his triers I expect justice for him   If he fall into the hands of my own and your enemies I consider my condemnation Certain & nothing but that boldness of Temper & firmness in effect that you are so capable of will excuse him from the trap which is set for him please to signify by an answer to this if you can appear.
. . .

ALS. DLC-HC (DNA, M212, R3).   1. Wickliffe to Clay, March 15, 1829.

From **THOMAS SPEED** *et al.*   Bardstown, Ky., May 26, 1829

[Invite Clay to a public dinner at Bardstown. Continues:][1]

In executing the duty thus assigned us, we take occasion to say, that to the recent change, by which the people have confided to other hands the management of the executive department of their government, and by which our beloved country has for a season been deprived of your useful labors, it becomes us to submit — yet, we cannot withhold the expression of our opinion, that the late administration has been excelled by none that preceded it, for the wisdom of its policy, or the disinterested application of the national resources to their legitimate objects.

In casting a retrospective view to the circumstances which have led to this change, we see nothing derogatory to the enlightened and patriotic head and members of the late administration. Though many causes may have contributed to this change, we attribute it, mainly to two — 1st. To that watchful jealousy of the people over their rulers, so common in republics, and so essential to their existence — and secondly, to a misconceived opinion in the southern section, that there is a confliction of interest between that section, and the balance of the union, upon the subject of protection to the manufacturing labor of our citizens.

Peculiarly situated as to their laboring force, and hence not prepared to participate extensively in the immediate profits of manufacturing industry, secure (to a great extent) in a foreign market, for the few articles of agricultural product by which they are enabled abundantly to supply themselves with all the manufactured articles they need — that highly respectable and patriotic portion of our country have little felt, and, therefore, have not been able duly to appreciate the value, and the necessity of the mechanic arts, to supply to the great majority of their countrymen (less favored in soil and climate) numerous indispensable articles of manufacture. They have not perceived the correctness of the principle of extending (by duties on foreign fabrics) that same protection and preference to the manufacturing industry of American citizens which foreign governments extend to theirs.

Deluded by the fallacious idea of an adverse interest, it was determined by the leaders of the southern section to make a stand against this long established and well-settled policy, of a decided majority of the people of these states. Upon what other hypothesis can we account for the unanimity of the opposition displayed in the south against the late administration, avowedly favorable to the protecting policy?

It was as one of the most ardent and efficient advocates of that policy, that you, individually, became peculiarly obnoxious to its opposers. To destroy, therefore, your political influence in the national councils, became as necessary to the opposers of that policy, as it was to certain political aspirants to arrest the progress of your growing popularity; and hence the avidity with which those "combined" opponents seized upon the circumstance of your vote in the election of the late president, to impeach your political integrity.

This insidious attempt has so far succeeded, as in some degree, and for a time, to render you a victim of suspicion, the concomitant of republican vigilance—but reflection and experience will not fail to evince that an enlightened and patriotic discharge of public duty, in the selection of talents, virtue and experience, for the highest of all political trusts, was not an act to merit censure or to deserve reproach. The firm and steady efforts of the late administration for the protection of the industry of the people, the advancement of the internal improvement of the country, and the great reduction of the public debt, when viewed without the prejudice of party excitement, must be approved. And, then, let those who, from sinister motives, in the absence of proof, have unjustly excited the suspicions of the people, expect to receive the sentence of their stern retributive justice.

Thus impressed, we look with an assured hope to your speedy restoration to the favor and confidence of the people in every section of this union. It is as citizens of the union we address you as an American statesman—as one who has shown an equal wish to afford protection to the planter and sugar manufacturer of the south; the farmer of the western and middle section, as to the navigator and manufacturer of the north and east; as a friend to the union; as a supporter of the independence of your country, and of the industry of her citizens in every quarter, that we tender to you this testimony of our high approbation and sincere regard.

Awaiting your answer as to the desired visit, we remain. . . .

Copy. Printed in *Niles' Register* (July 18, 1829), 36:335.   1. In a letter to Speed and his committee dated June 9, 1829, Clay accepted this invitation. In his reply, Clay agreed with Speed's assessment of the causes of Jackson's victory in the 1828 election, adding: "I believe that, if the friends of the policy of protecting the products of our own industry against similar rival productions of foreign countries, had been as united and zealous as their opponents, the change of administration would not have been made." Notes, further, that "our southern brethern attribute" to protection "evils which belong to other causes. If the policy were abandoned, and our manufacturing establishments were put down, their great staple [cotton], the price of which has been reduced by an excess of supply beyond the joint demand both in Europe and America, would further decline in value." Because of his belief in the principle of protection, "I have, in some degree, shared the fate of the unpopularity of the tariff, where it is unpopular. Other motives have cooperated in exciting prejudices against me." *Ibid.*, 336.

To CHARLES HAMMOND   Lexington, May 27, 1829

Your obliging letter of the 13h instant was either not delivered to me by Mr. Moses, its bearer, or it was handed by him in a crowd, under such circumstances as to prevent my cultivating his acquaintance. That crowd was collected on the occasion of a public dinner given to me; and, as I embraced the opportunity of a public address [May 16] to it, to say all that I ought to have said about myself, and perhaps much more, I will decline repeating here what, in a few days, you will see in the public prints. The substance of it was that I shall offer neither for Congress nor the Legislature, but remain at home to take care of my health and my private affairs.

I said a great deal also on the subject of late removals from office; and perhaps here also oversteped the bounds of prudence. But I was a great way on this side of the limit of my feelings of abhorrence, on account of the compound of embicility, tyranny and hypocrisy, which the Cabinet at Washington now exhibits, and that was enough for me.

You appear discouraged by passing events. And I must own that their tendency is to produce despondency. Still we ought to resist that effect. You seem to think that they will be deceived who calculate on the virtue and intelligence of the people. Then I shall be deceived. Are those happier and better off (even supposing them right) who have no confendence in the virtue and intelligence of the people? They must admit that we who hold to that faith are at least under a most pleasing delusion. And, if it be finally dissipated, we are then no worse off than the unbelievers. That is to say, after having for a long time enjoyed some most agreeable dreams we wake and find ourselves where the unbelievers have all along known themselves to be, in the midst of an ignorant vicious and incompetent race.

But, my dear Sir, I not only have confidence in the virtue and intelligence of the people, notwithstanding the event of the late election, but I think those qualities are beginning to operate. You must recollect that the smoak is almost yet in view which rose from the Cannon fired in exultation of President Jacksons election. You must estimate the restraining power of pride and mortification. And then I think you will be prepared to allow that the number of changes, and of penitents, and the number who are on the anxious seat, which you have seen, or of which you have heard, is quite considerable. Reform, real and substantial, very different from the mock reform at Washington, I believe to be now going on throughout the whole Country. Its progress may be slow, for some time, but its ultimate accomplishment I believe to be certain.

You infidels in the virtue and intelligence of the people require too much. You require that the people should never err, but be always right. I require them only to be *generally* right. The late election I look upon as an exception. You make it the rule.

I must acknowledge that the late error was very great, but I hope it is not incurable. It was symptomatic of a disease which has too often proved mortal in Republics; but then there is great improvement in the moral constitution of the patient, and in the science of the physician.

You have grouped a number of alarming causes of public discontent, if not of disunion. There will be no war with Mexico. We shall not get Texas. The Tariff won't be repealed. The system or rather the power of Internal Improvements I hope will not be abandoned. The worst of all the enumerated subjects is that of the public lands. An influential Southerner lately asked a

Western friend of mine   Will you of the West give up the Tariff if we give up to you the public lands? What an abominable project!

With you I am grieved at the affair of Dr. W.[1] I know nothing about it but what I gather from the papers. Only one friend has alluded in his letter to the subject (I mean from Washn.) and his account is not better than that in the papers. We shall soon hear. Whatever it may be, it must be *his* personal matter without affecting others.

I wish you would send me your paper [Cincinnati *Gazette*], if you will trust me for it—I mean your paper published two or three times a week, not your daily paper, the advertisements in which I do not want to read.

I should be glad to see you over here. Can't you come this way?

ALS. InU.   1. Dr. Tobias Watkins, fourth auditor under the Adams administration, was indicted and convicted on three counts of defrauding the government of some $3,050. He was sentenced to nine months in jail and fined $3,050. See *Niles' Register* (August 22, 1829) 36:421.

To THOMAS LAW   Lexington, May 28, 1829
[Discusses a land title case in Kentucky in which Law is interested and refers him to George M. Bibb for information about it. Continues:]

The picture of public affairs at Washington, which you have drawn, is truly distressing. From what I saw prior to my departure from that City, and from what I have since heard and seen, I have no doubt that it is not too high colored. A similar, though not an equally aggravated state of things exists in every part of the Country. It is discouraging, but I do not think that we ought to despond. Two reforms are going on. One at Washington, which is nominal and for purposes of deception; and another, throughout the Country which is real and I hope will prove effective. The progress of this latter reform can not be expected as yet to be rapid. The smoak of the cannon, fired in exultation of the Election of President Jackson, has hardly yet vanished. Mortification and pride prevent many from expressing their regrets and disappointments, on account of their having supported him. But people will soon take courage. They are now reflecting; and many have taken the first step towards weaning themselves from their infuriated attachment, and returning to common Sense. I endeavored to aid this process, in a speech [May 16] which I lately addressed to a mixed party of about three or four thousand gentlemen with whom I dined. It will appear in the papers next week, and I will send you a Copy.

I regret, my dear Sir, that you should have ever witnessed the afflicting scene now exhibiting at Washington. I know how it must shock your benevolence. You have done well to retire to Tusculum,[1] where you will be able to enjoy the tranquil scenes of rural life, in spite of all the wickedness, violence, and hypocricy which at present disgrace the Metropolis.

ALS. ViU.   1. Law's "county seat." See Delas H. Smith, "A Forgotten Mansion—Tusculum," *Columbia Historical Society Records*, 50:159-65.

To JOHN L. LAWRENCE   Lexington, May 28, 1829
It is true that, since our separation at Gottenburg [Göteborg, Sweden], the opportunities for personal intercourse, as stated in your very obliging letter of the 2d. inst. have been rare. I have nevertheless not been inattentive to your progress or indifferent to your welfare. That letter affords gratifying proof of your interest in mine. The principal subject of it (the rumored duel between Mr. [John] Pope and me) had quite as much foundation as many other reports

concerning me circulated of late years, that is not the slightest. The only regret I feel about it is that it should have occasioned the least uneasiness to any of my friends.

On the subject generally of personal combats I think as you think, and as all rational men think. And, although I can not persuade myself that the Nation at large has any very deep interest in the preservation of a life, now chiefly spent; and although I cannot pledge myself that under no possible state of things, would I engage in such an affair, this much I will say that I detest the practice; that I will not, now that I am turned the corner of fifty two, be easily drawn into it; and that if unfortunately I ever should be, on any political account, it shall not be with any subaltern.

I should be glad to see the compound of imbecility, tyranny, and hypocricy, now in operation at Washington, put down. I should be happy to be instrumental, in any honorable way, in opening the eyes of the public to its shocking enormity. But whether I shall live or not to witness the restoration of reason, order, law and good government is far from certain. But if I die before the accomplishment of that desirable *reform*, I shall die in the confident hope that posterity may achieve it

ALS. NHi.

From James Brown, Paris, May 29, 1829. Reports that his intended departure for the United States on June 1 has been delayed because of his wife's illness. Plans now to leave before the end of May. Has heard nothing from the State Department, but has been told by his successor, Edward Livingston, that "as it is not very convenient to come immediately he regrets that I cannot prolong my stay." Remarks that Livingston, who has been successful in business, will discover that he will "require something more than his Salary to enable him to live in a suitable style at this Court unless he possesses means of economy to which [Albert] Gallatin & I have been strangers."

Notes that the Russians "with all their immense preparations" move but slowly against the Turks. But should Constantinople be menaced, "I think it not improbable that England and Austria and perhaps France may interfere to terminate the strife."

Has heard that Clay will run again for the House and that "I have no doubt of your maintaining your coveted rank in that body." Comments that in removing James Barbour and William Henry Harrison from their diplomatic posts, the new administration has treated them "very unceremoniously." Predicts that "These cases will revolt Virginia pride." Thinks, too, that "The Printers seem to be a priviledged or rather a favored corps and your friend Amos [Kendall] has made his debut by a brilliant display of economy which will never be forgotten by his Country men — But enough of this. You hear too much of it —"

Concludes with the observation that he is becoming "very anxious to return as my private affairs may require more attention. My last crop was excellent and lands fit for sugar are reported as having greatly increased in value." ALS. DLC-HC (DNA, M212, R3). Printed in *LHQ,* 24:1142-44. Addressed to Clay at Lexington. Amos Kendall, the new fourth auditor, issued a circular on March 24 announcing that henceforth all letters to others enclosed in letters to him to be sent out under his franking privilege would be returned to the post office. He also stated that subscriptions had been cancelled to 20 newspapers which were being paid for with public money for use in the office of the fourth auditor. See *Niles' Register* (April 18, 1829), 36:125-26.

To JOHN SLOANE   Lexington, May 30, 1829

I received your obliging letter of the 27h. Ulto. and perused with much interest its contents. The course of the new administration is so far worse than its worst enemies could have anticipated. I think it is producing considerable effect among the Jackson party. It is however too early yet to expect that many of them will over come the pride of consistency, the mortification which they experience, and their *disappointments* (I use the word in both its senses) to admit to their adversaries their error. As time elapses they will take courage and speak out. In the mean time we should rather appeal to their reason and patriotism than excite their passions by reproach and sarcasm. I do not know that you will think I have myself conformed to that rule in a Speech which I delivered two weeks ago [May 16] to an assembly of three or four thousand, on the occasion of a public dinner with which they honored me. The Speech will be published in the [Lexington *Kentucky*] Reporter of next week,[1] and I must refer it to you for some of the reasons which have induced me, for the present, to decline all public employment. One of the most influential of them, which is not stated, was the opinion of yourself and other friends mentioned by you and communicated to me by Mr. [Josiah S.] Johnston, I am not sure that I have decided right, but I thought it was best. I could have been elected to the H. of R. with great ease, and probably without any opposition.

My reception in K. has fully equalled my most sanguine hopes. The unfortunate discrimination between Mr. Adams and me is now openly avowed by many of the Jackson party. Many of them declare that they would support me against Jackson. And the belief of my friends and my own belief is that I could now beat him without difficulty in this state—Some of them take the further ground that they supported him for one term only and that they will oppose his re-election.

In respect to the elections to Congress from this State I am not yet in possession of full information. In [Thomas] Moore's district there is at this time great probability of the election of a Jackson man [John Kincaid] friendly to me, in opposition to the Candidate of the Jackson party. In this district, [James] Clarke [*sic*, Clark] has as yet no opposition; and probably will have none.   In [Robert P.] Letcher's there is no opposition.   F[rancis]. Johnson it is believed will beat [Joel] Yancey. It is doubtful whether Col. R[ichard] M. Johnson will be elected. [Richard] Buckner declines, and several candidates are out. Among others Col. [Tunstall] Quarles, late Speaker and Jackson elector, who declares himself, I understand, for me. [Chittendon] Lyon will have to do the same, if as reported he has not already done it, or be beaten. In [John] Chambers's district we are in danger from two Candidates on our side, neither of whom will give way. I have nothing certain from the other districts.[2]

It is believed that there will be a Legislature friendly to me. But I am not sanguine on that point owing to the difficulty of getting the elections to turn on the question, at this early day.

All the appointments in K. are serviceable to me. The selections made by the President &c with a different motive cannot fail to operate in my favor. I hope often to hear from you. And particularly in respect to public opinion in your State [Ohio].

I should be greatly distressed if I did not trust that I should live to see the imbecility, tyranny &c hyprocricy at Washington put down.

ALS. MH.   1. Published in Lexington *Kentucky Reporter*, June 3, 1829.   2. Bridges to Clay, July 12, 1829; Clay to Whittlesey, August 6, 1829; Clay to Southard, August 9, 1829; Johnson to Clay, April 8, 1829; Buckner to Clay, June 13, 1829; Clay to Beatty, June 2, 7; July 9, 1829.

To SAMUEL STUART GRIFFIN   Lexington, June 1, 1829

[Discusses Griffin's interest in purchasing land near Lexington and calls his attention to a 900-acre tract which can currently be bought for $20 per acre. Continues:]

Land of the first quality within say eight or ten miles of Lexington sells from $20 to 26$ per acre. It is slowly but certainly rising. There is a very fine tract of 500 acres within three miles of Lexington, belonging to James D'Wolf of Rhode Island in market at $26. 25$ have been refused.

My opinion is that I have never seen so fine a Country as this. I believe judicious Cultivation of hemp (where it can be water rotted, and the above mentioned tract of 900 acres possesses great facilities for that process) would be as profitable as the culture of Sugar Cane, without requiring one fifth part of the Capital

Corn and grass grown luxuriantly, and raising or grazing Stock is found very profitable.

Lexington is pretty well supplied with physicians. Some of the most eminent of them are professors in the [Transylvania University] Medical School, and they do not all practice. One of the most popular of the faculty[1] is very old and cannot pursue the profession much longer. Another might squeeze in, but the degree of his success would depend upon circumstances.

There is no better society than Lexington affords, at least in a place no larger. Virginia manners and habits prevail, with a slight modification produced by our intercourse with the Northern Capitals. As to the expence of living, I should think that it is about one half of what it may be at Richmond [Va.], in the same conditions of life. Rents are very low, and markets quite cheap. Beef sells from ½ to 3 Cents per lb.

But my dear Sir, without extending this letter, as I could do to great length, my advice to you is to come here and view the Country. No one can judge for another as well as he can for himself. And a step so important as a permanent removal for life ought not to be taken, without an examination, made by the emigrant himself, of the Country to which he goes.[2] If you will go to Wheeling you can be at Lexington in three days after, taking passage in a Steam boat which can be procured in one of some size or other almost the whole. You ought however if practicable to get there in all this month.

If I had recd. your letter a few days sooner I could have obtained full information from Maj [William] Taylor respecting his agency, as I saw him last Monday; but he is gone home, some seventy or eighty miles distant from me. . . . P.S. You may do well here with your slaves. Good male hands sell [for] about $400. Young females at [Ms. torn] 00. Boys from 12 to 18 at from 300 to $400. Men hire at 60 or 70$. Women at from 30 to $40.

ALS. KyU. Addressed to Dr. Griffin at Williamsburg, Va.   1. Not identified, but see Robert Peter, *The History of the Medical Department of Transylvania University* (Louisville, 1905), 166 and *passim* for a list of the faculty in the medical school and their years of service.   2. Griffin evidently chose not to move to Lexington. He died in Williamsburg, Va., on Dec. 19, 1864. See *WMQ*, (Series 1, 1930), 10:48.

To ADAM BEATTY   Lexington, June 2, 1829

I have lately purchased in Washn. Co Pennsa. fifty full blooded Merino Ewes, the choice out of three hundred, part of one of the finest flocks in the Country which belonged to the late Mr. R[ichard]. W. Meade, whose persecution and sufferings were so well known in Spain.[1] The choice was made by a friend of mine [John W. Ewing], himself one of the largest Sheep owners in Pennsa., and one of the best Judges that I know of. There are about sixteen or eighteen lambs with them, and I suppose an equal portion of rams. I expect them all at Maysville in the course of eight or ten days, on their way to my residence.

It is my intention to let a few of my particular friends have about a dozen of them, at reasonable prices. If you wish any of them, you may have your choice of an ewe with the ram lamb belonging to her at 25 dollars for both. Should you decide to take them, you may shew this letter to Messrs. January &c. as their authority for delivering them to you.

Is there not danger, my dear Sir, of an adverse result to the Congressional Election in your district?[2] I fear it. And I hear perhaps some things that you do not. There is much dissatisfaction among our friends in Bourbon [County], as I regret to learn. They think that they are entitled to the Member. Can you not device some plan to collect and concentrate public opinion, in behalf of *one* Candidate of the party of our friends? There is no one in the district that I should be more happy to see elected than yourself; and I hope, if you continue to offer, that you may be. But if it be impracticable, from any cause, perseverance might display resolution, without leading to any good issue. Perseverance indeed, without success, might lead to the worst consequences to yourself and to the district. It might give a permanently unfriendly character to the district. Such I have several times observed to be the effect of divisions elsewhere among our friends.

There is always danger, which I trust I need not guard you against, of the opposite party practising deception in regard to the prospects of Candidates among their opponents.

I pray you my dear Sir to appreciate the friendly motives which have dictated these observations, to which you will give just so much weight as they deserve. . . .

ALS. Courtesy of Earl M. Ratzer, Highland Park, Ill. Printed in Colton, *Clay Correspondence*, 4:234-35.   1. For Meade's difficulties in Spain, including two years of imprisonment, see *DAB*.   2. Beatty's second congressional district comprised Bourbon, Bracken, Mason, and Nicholas counties. Beatty and Nicholas Coleman were the two major candidates in the August 3 election. Coleman defeated Beatty by a vote of 2,541 to 2,519 with the other contenders— George M. Bedinger and Dr. James G. Leach—receiving a combined vote of about 550. Coleman carried Nicholas and Bracken counties while Beatty carried Mason and Bourbon. Lexington *Kentucky Reporter*, June 17; August 12, 1829; Frankfort *Commentator*, June 30, 1829.

To JESSE B. HARRISON   Lexington, June 2, 1829

I duly received your obliging letter of the 18th. March and perused its contents with much satisfaction. I should have earlier acknowledged it but for the want of something interesting to say or to communicate, which I regret even the delay has not supplied me with. I was sorry that you could not execute the plan of your German residence,[1] because I was persuaded that benefit would have accrued from it both to yourself and ultimately to our Country. As it is, you remain with us to behold the afflicting scenes of public affairs which a grateful but deluded people have contributed to produce by placing, at their head, a most incompetent but vindictive C[hief]. Magistrate. You rightly conceive my feelings in supposing that on *my own* account I care not for late events. But how is it possible to be indifferent to what concerns the character and the prosperity, possibly the free institutions of our Country? This feeling prompted me on a late occasion [May 16] of addressing a public meeting to say much (the prudent portion of my friends will perhaps think quite too much) on passing events. I have directed a Copy of the Speech to be forwarded to you and the Mail which carries this letter ought to take. I have said so much, in that Speech, both in respect to public affairs and to myself that but little remains to add in this letter on either of those topics.

You think that our delivery from Jackson thraldom is not hopeless. I hope so too. If I believed it were; if I believed that the compound of imbecility, tyranny and hypocrisy which now disgraces our Metropolis would be approved by the people of the U. States, when they come to understand it, I should have to renounce one of the most pleasing and deeply rooted sentiments of my life, that of the competency of Man to self government.

But although I have still great confidence in the public condemnation of the men whom the public have lately directly or indirectly elevated, I cannot yet perceive clearly where or when this salutary work of reform will begin. With us indeed it has commenced. Many changes have been made and are openly avowed. Many have been made, which are not yet avowed. And many are on the anxious seats. I do not believe that the vote of this State would now be given to Jackson, even in a contest with Mr. Adams.

Kentucky cannot alone, however, accomplish the work of reform. Without Virginia, or Pennsa. or N. York it cannot be effected. And I have not seen any indications in either of those States of repentance in consequence of the part which it took in the late Election. I know that it is too early now, when the smoak of the Cannon fired in exultation of that event, has scarcely vanished, to expect much change. But the enormity of the principles and practices of the Cabinet at Washington I had supposed would have aroused more indignation, at least in Virginia, than I have seen displayed.

Let us not despair. Reason and truth must prevail, if liberty be not a dream and free Government a mockery. I receive from all quarters the most encouraging and flattering accounts, in regard to myself. I have thought, indeed, in some instances, where I regretted that I should be consulted, that it was expedient to restrain what appeared to me would be premature.

We shall all now look with the deepest attention to the composition of your contemplated Convention,[2] and then to the time of its assembling and its proceedings. I perceive, with great pleasure, that it is likely to contain most of your ablest men. In bringing into it, such men as Mr. [James] Madison, Mr [John] Marshall and Mr [James] Monroe, you appear to have drawn, in some sort, upon our Ancestors as well as our Contemporaries. You have my most fervent prayers that it may realize all the hopes of our Native State.

I hope you will not be discouraged from occasionally writing to me by the delay which I have suffered in answering your letter. It will afford me great pleasure to hear from you. . . .

ALS. DLC-HC (DNA, M212, R21). A typewritten copy, with minor variations in capitalization and spelling, is in *ibid*. (R3). Addressed to Harrison in Lynchburg, Va.   1. Harrison had planned to go abroad to continue his study of modern languages. See Harrison to Clay, Oct. 20, 1829.   2. See 7:575-76.

From William C. C. Clairborne, Jr., New Orleans, June 5, 1829. Reports that Mr. [James] and Mrs. [Anne Brown Clay] Erwin will leave New Orleans in a "few days" for Ashland. Thanks Clay for his "kind invitation," but regrets he cannot accompany them to Kentucky. Hopes, however, that "nothing will prevent your intended visit to New Orleans next winter," since "very many" people, "activated only by admiration of your public character and gratitude for your services," want to greet you. Concludes: "The Creole population here are very indignant at the system of proscription; in all the changes that have taken place here, not one of them has been appointed to office. From the tone of the Jackson Bull dogs in the camp, it seems to have been determined among them, that the old Brute himself is to be run against you, as a derniere resort: so much the better, I would rather you would beat him than any other of them, and If you do *not* beat him, why, I think we will *have* to give up your Motto, we *must* 'despair of the American Republic'; And to adopt that of your rival, we *must* 'judge of the Tree by its fruit.'—Institutions that will allow the rabble, and the corrupt, to create, to foster, and to hold in power such an infernal party as that, to domineer over honest & patriotic men, must be defective. The tree that can produce such fruit, must be rotten some where. But we must look forward to a glorious regeneration, and await the issue once more, 'ere we condemn.'" ALS. DLC-HC (DNA, M212, R3).

To ADAM BEATTY   Lexington, June 7, 1829
I have been mortified by the late movements in Bourbon [County] in bringing out Mr. [Thomas A.] Marshall for the H. of R. lest you might suppose that when I wrote you a few days ago [June 2] I had some knowledge that they were in contemplation. Such a supposition would be very far from the fact. I had no more knowledge or information, about them, when I wrote that letter than the man in the moon. I had indeed understood from Mr. Marshall himself that he would not be a Candidate, and I was well pleased with that decision, because I believed it to be in conformity with the best interests of his family. And now I have no doubt, indeed I have heard, that he has been brought out, most reluctantly on his part, in consequence of the state of things to which I alluded in my last as existing in Bourbon.

I derived information of that state of things principally from Mr. Rain [*sic*, John B. Rains], the Sheriff of Bourbon, and Mr. Spiers [*sic*, Abraham Spears], who were at my house the day after the dinner at Fowler's garden [May 16]. They both represented the dissatisfaction in Bourbon, among our friends, to be very great, because a Candidate was not selected from that County; and they both concurred in expressing the belief that they could not be prevailed upon to rally at the polls on any Candidate out of Bourbon, Mr. R. expressing that opinion with more and Mr. S. with less confidence. I urged them to support you. They said that they hoped some measure would be yet adopted to collect the sense and unite the exertions of our friends throughout the district. I of course supposed that that measure would be some such as was adopted last year. I went to Madison on Tuesday last, and it was not until my return on Thursday that I learnt what had transpired in Bourbon.

I have thought these statements due to our long and warm friendship, and I hope they will be received in the spirit in which they are made.

I have not yet heard of my Sheep having been started.[1]

ALS. Courtesy of Earl M. Ratzer, Highland Park, Ill. Letter marked "(Confidential)." Printed in Colton, *Clay Correspondence*, 4:235-36.   1. Clay to Beatty, June 2, 1829.

From Charles King, West Point, N.Y., June 8, 1829. Reports that he "happened to be present at" West Point when Henry Clay, Jr., took his final examination. Explains that he is at West Point to enter his eldest son, Rufus, in the academy. Remarks that he heard young Clay's examination and wants his father to know "how well and intelligently he acquitted himself, and how deservedly high he stands in our institution." Notes that the examiner was Major William M. Davis of Kentucky—"a member I believe of your Legislature and at any rate a very *good* friend of yours, tho a Jackson man—" Recounts a political conversation with Davis in which the Major "appears to me to stand by you." Concludes from this that "there are many 'red-hot Jackson men'" who will do the same when the time comes. Hopes, therefore, that Clay "may yet successfully run the race where less worthy Coursers will contest with him—In this part of the Country and that East & North the feeling is as good as Can be desired—" thanks to the "course . . . the present Administration is pursuing." Has asked Davis to write him from Kentucky about political matters since "It may be of consequence to me to have such a correspondent in the West—" ALS. DLC-HC (DNA, M212, R3). For Rufus King's subsequent military career, see USMA, *Register*, 185.

From THOMAS PATTERSON · Hagerstown, Md., June 8, 1829

I[1] spent last week in Washington City. I can assure you I never did expect that such a state of things was to take place in my day I often feared that our children might live long enough to see and feel tyrany. but it now rages with most frightfull sway in the City of Washington—men who have been long employed by the government with large and helpless families are almost daily dismissed from employ and some days by half dozens—Those who are yet continued are in a state of terror and alarm—each man counting at equal chances to meet his dismissal on his desk every morning when he goes to the office—no qualification of capacity or faithfulness gives the least security—If by the strictest inquiry he is found to have been even in opinion friendly to the late administration. that is his condemnation. Some have had thoughts of resigning at once who are in better circumstances. but I believe all now intend to continue till they can carry with them their certificate. we may as we have reproached the British government for her test law and religious tyrany but she can throw in our teeth the charge of political test laws. — They charged you and Mr Adams with corrupting the press. — that being a process which might be practised they have addopted it. They charged you with cohorting upon the patronage of the government as being all powerful in sustaining the dominant party — they are determined to exert its utmost force — pity and mercy seem to have been banished from their code of virtue & morality — I am well satisfied that where freedom of opinion is tolerated some liberty must exist but if a man is to be put under the ban of the empire for enjoying and exercising it — it must exist in a very unhealthy condition — It still seems to me that you are a great eye sore to the party — they cry out Clay is done — he is down — I think they are very anxious to have your head still deeper under the water — a reaction will take place It will not yet do to say the world was made for Cazer [*sic*, Caesar] — & Genl. Jackson I do hope will before two years find he cannot do as he pleases — I think a large number of his friends feel allarmed at his course though few of them speak out yet — I am glad you have determined not to come into the next Congress it would have only have stimulated their rage & prevented reflection — & no doubt they would have insulted you as far as they dare in the House — but I trust the succeeding Congress will have your presence — When the people have come to see better what Jacksonism means — I think you lose no friends in Maryland but I hope they are on the increase — we shall make no effort in this District this fall for congress — Whether I shall be dismissed or not I cannot tell — It is now no disgrace to receive a certificate of discharge — City proprty is deeply affected by the present state of things those who are turned out of office sell off—those who come in do not purchase as all Such cases of appointment expect to be turned out—& those who have been terned out by Jackson restored again if—the present party do not succeed in the next Presidential election—The opinion appears to be that—wherever Jackson has put out & put in—the successor if opposed to the Jackson party—will go so far as to reinstate in every possible case & no further—some reports which I have heard though probably not true restrain me from suscribing my name. . . . [P.S.] [Otho] Stull is still P[ost]. M[aster]. here [Hagerstown]—Young Mr Barnes Mason has taken a most active stand in his behalf—some lett[e]rs have passed betwixt him Mason & Mr Barry old Tom Kennedy[2] wants the office for his son not yet of age by 2 months probably Stull will be permitted to occupy the place till then—Old Tom is down here but he courts the Cabinet

AL. DLC-HC (DNA, M212, R3).　　1. Patterson was a clerk for the House of Representatives. See Patterson to Clay, Dec. 13, 1829.　　2. Thomas Kennedy had served as postmaster at Hagerstown from 1822-27 when Stull succeeded him. Stull served until Nov. 17, 1829, and was succeeded by Tom Kennedy's son, Howard. John Scharf, *History of Western Maryland* (Philadelphia, 1882), 2:1004. William T. Barry was Jackson's postmaster general.

From ROBERT R. RICHARDSON　　　　　　　　Baltimore, June 12, 1829

I shall make no appology for writing this letter I merely wish to inform you what is passing in this quarter. The whole Jackson corps is thrown into confusion by the declaration of J V L Mc Mahon being a candidate for congress they cannot fix upon their man, [if] Mc Mahon is to go into the post office at this place it will be the unkindest cut of all to the Jackson men, that they could *not* retain [John S.] Skinner.[1] Your dinner Speech [May 16] has just arrived it will be read with great interest, The Eyes of this community are turned upon you as their next President, if it is agreeable to you I will from time to time write you what is passing, and you may rely on profound silence. . . . [P.S.] I recd the [Lexington *Kentucky*] Reporter and shall use it to effect

ALS. DLC-HC (DNA, M212, R3).　　1. John Van Laer McMahon did not run for Congress nor did he get the post office appointment; Skinner retained the latter. See Warfield to Clay, April 9, 1829.

From RICHARD A. BUCKNER　　　　　　　Greensburg, Ky., June 13, 1829

We have been informed that you intend to visit Russelville [*sic*, Russellville]—If so, an earnest desire is expressed by some of your friends, that you should give us a call going or coming—It would be productive of beneficial consequences　It is very important, to get such a legislature, as will by a respectable majority, present your name to the nation, for the Presidency. I have good hopes of every county in this district—[1] Had I been a candidate, my success would have been certain and easy.

　　Should you consent to come, there will be an immense congregation Prospects are encouraging, I hope, for your triumph, over all the malignity, with which you have been persecuted. . . .

ALS. DLC-HC (DNA, M212, R3).　　1. District eight was comprised of Adair, Casey, and Cumberland counties. Nathan Gaither defeated his chief opponent, Martin Beatty, by 2,267 to 2,168 in the August election. G. Glenn Clift, "Kentucky Votes 1792-1894," typescript in KyHi.

From Isaac Hendershott, Piqua, Ohio, June 13, 1829. While not personally known to Clay, feels that he must comment on the dangers to the nation posed by the new

Jackson administration. "I do think enough has transpired to produce at least, *a fearful looking for*, among the American people. — A *crisis* seems to have arrived, that places in jeopardy the freedom of our institutions, and threatens to reduce the sacred principles of honour, of reason, and of justice, to the mere *pantomine* of Executive favour and partiality. — " Develops this theme at length noting that the Jackson party's use of patronage is "a monstrous and shocking perversion of every right notion of Government and of law. and all this is affected to be done under the specious and imposing, but solemnly deceptive, title of *Reform!*"

As for the important issues of "*Domestic Manufactures*, and *Internal Improvements*," wonders whether the president "Will recommend and approve of those measures or not, at least in their present liberal and qualified form. from the indecisive, and equivocal tone of his mind, prior to his Election, and the fact of its being under the influence of a strong Southern bias, avowedly hostile to the American System, there is just grounds of apprehension, that the present Administration" will undo the work of its predecessor.

Asks that Clay visit Dayton during the coming summer or fall so that his many friends there and in Piqua may "see you, and take you by the hand," and give thanks for your services to "their beloved country." ALS. DLC-HC (DNA, M212, R3).

From Manning Goodwin & Henry Kilbourn, Hartford, Conn., June 15, 1829. Admit that they are strangers to Clay, but wish to thank him for his role in "one of the most virtuous Administrations our country could ever bost." Regret that he has been the victim of so much personal abuse. Criticize Jackson's appointment to his cabinet of men, "most of whom were little known, whose patriotism consists in a desire for office, and whose love of country extends only to those minions of party who have assisted in raising them to power." Note, further, that already the Jacksonians "have thrown off the mask and talk of the re election of the 'chieftain,' although they so lately contended the the [*sic*] presidential Office should hereafter be held by one person but for a single time." Do not believe that the people of the United States will long submit to "the system of proscription and persecution which characterizes the present Administration," but instead will soon "drive the demagogues from the places they have so unworthily obtained." Attribute to Clay and to the American System the "present prosperity and happiness" of the nation. Conclude: "We wish, Sir, to see you at the head of our national government." ALS. DLC-HC (DNA, M212, R3).

To CHARLES R. VAUGHAN   Lexington, June 18, 1829
I have, according to my promise, procured for you a genuine Kentucky rifle, every part of which, except the lock, was manufactured near me. It is neat and not expensive, carrying about 90 or 100 balls to the pound. I will forward it to you as soon as practicable.[1]

I congratulate you on the final success of the measure for the emancipation of the Irish Catholics.[2] By its adoption, Lord Wellington has secured for himself more imperishable fame than all his splendid military victories could entitle him to.

I request you to communicate my warmest to my late diplomatic associates at Washington. . . .

ALS. Codrington Library, All Souls College, Oxford University.   1. Vaughan to Clay, July 1, 1829.
2. Adams to Clay, May 2, 1829.

To Nathaniel Hardy & Worden P. Churchill, Louisville, June 22, 1829. Declines, on the basis of "prior engagements," an invitation to march in a "public procession" of Masons on June 24 in Louisville. "I pray, you, Brothers to be assured of my grateful sensibility to your kind and fraternal attention." ALS. KyLoF. For Hardy, see Collins,

History of Kentucky 1:525; for Churchill see Lexington *Kentucky Gazette*, June 5, 1829; Louisville *Public Advertiser*, May 27, 1829; and *RKHS*, 36:314.

From JOHN ARMSTRONG   Maysville, Ky., June 26, 1829

Dear Sir at the desire of the Stock Holders of the Maysville & Wash[i]ngton Turn Pike road Company[1] I am requested to Invite yr. Honour to the Participation of A Publick Dinner on the 4th of July on which day the above road is to be commenced, and as this road is considered an Entering wedge to A General System of Improvents thr. this Section of the State, and as this Place in all Probability will be a Point at which a Branch of the Great National road Passing through Ohio may terminate, in order to give a zest to Such Improvemts the Presene of our chief Magistrates, and off those, who like *your Honour* have contributed So largely is of Much Importance. I have therefore addressed this day A note to Gov. [Allen] Trimble [Ohio] & Gov. Metcalf [*sic*, Thomas Metcalfe] to meet us on the day Spoken off. I hope Sir If you can make it conveint you will do us the Honour of your company On that day.[2]

ALS. DLC-TJC (DNA, M212, R10).   1. For the Maysville Road issue see 2:569; and Carlton Jackson, "The Internal Improvement Vetoes of Andrew Jackson," *THQ* (Fall, 1966), 25:261-79.   2. Clay did not attend the ceremonies on July 4. On July 6, he wrote Armstrong apologizing for not having been able to attend. In this letter, he wished success to the venture, hoping it would be funded "under the joint aid of Congress and individual enterprize." He viewed the Maysville Road, he told Armstrong, "as a section of what I have thought deserved to be considered as an essential National chain." Copy. Printed in Maysville *Eagle*, July 14, 1829.

To JOSIAH S. JOHNSTON   Louisville, June 26, 1829

I quit this City with much regret on account of my not seeing you. The trial of young [Charles] Wickliffe,[1] fixed for tuesday next, and the preparations incident to it, oblige me to go. I have during five days been in constant expectation of your arrival. I am informed by rumor only of your being on board the Hibernia.

I have not time to enter into details on public affairs. Unless my friends are greatly deceived, there is not a particle of doubt about the disposition of Kentucky to support me. And although it is too early to draw the line between those who are for and those who are against me, we have reason to hope the friendship of a majority of the next Legislature.

I should be extremely delighted to see you at Ashland. Can you not visit us? If not do let me hear from you.

ALS. PHi. Addressed to Johnston, "expected at Louisville." Printed in Colton, *Clay Correspondence*, 4:236.   1. Wickliffe to Clay, March 15, 1829.

From "New England," July 1, 1829. Assumes the right as "a native American Citizen" to remind Clay "of your obligations to your country and to tell you what she expects of you in return for her favors." Instructs Clay: "Look back, Sir, on the last thirty years of your life, and you will perceive that you have not merely labored ambitiously in the public service but you have also partaken liberally of public honors. A Senator . . . a Representative . . . an Ambassador . . . the first cabinet minister . . . all this you have been, and all this, — you may say with a pride of heart and intellect . . . 'all this is MY work.' I have ventured to call your attention to these facts in order to remind you, that, from one, who has proved that he can do so much for himself, something is expected for your country. That country will not permit you to retire from her service. She looks to you for the accomplishment of that great and important plan of protection to domestic industry, by which alone her perfect independence can be established and the prosperity and happiness of her people made permanent."

Says that the question "now agitating the thoughts and the passions of the people" is whether or not they will be permitted to develop their own resources and "to feed and clothe ourselves by the exercise of our own faculties and the employment of our own possessions—or must we continue to contract debts in Europe which we cannot pay, that the population of that region may be sustained at our expense?" Continues: "You have been called, Sir, the *Father of the American System*. . . . But, Sir, the American System did not originate with you.—Its leading principle teaches men to refrain from purchasing of others what they can make for themselves, and impelled our fathers, before you and I were born, to seek independence in the exercise of their own strength and ingenuity. . . . But think not, Sir, that I would deprive you of a particle of that honor you have derived from your efforts to finish and perpetuate [the American System]. . . . Though not the parent, you are the no less honored advocate of that only System of political economy which can give prosperous independence to this people and memorable permanency to its government."

Admonishes Clay, as "the *champion* of the American System," of his duty to help overcome the crisis which threatens domestic manufactures. Notes that "From the well known characters of the men composing the national cabinet, it is manifest, also, that no measures of relief will be devised by them." Indeed, they "have not yet . . . had opportunities to display their skill or expose their weakness in any affairs of greater magnitude than the removal of collectors, postmasters, clerks, and auditors; but who can doubt their entire subserviency to the views of despots . . . and their promptness to execute whenever the decree shall go forth to destroy one of the most popular branches of domestic trade and to change the whole policy, which the government has successfully pursued from its organization." Urges Clay to use his influence, either in or out of office, to support the American System. Copy. Printed in Lexington *Kentucky Reporter*, July 1, 1829. Date of composition not known.

From Charles R. Vaughan, Washington, July 1, 1829. Thanks Clay for procuring for him "a genuine Kentucky Rifle" and looks forward to its arrival in Washington "about the time of the meeting of Congress, if not before." Has had a letter from Christopher Hughes, dated May 10, "when he was waiting with anxiety to know his fate . . . . by this time he must be aware that he is to be superceded by Mr. [William P.] Preble, and I do not yet hear what other appointment he is likely to get." Reports that he is "perfectly satisfied with the conduct & feelings of the present President [Jackson] in all communications which I have had with his Govmt. as British Minister." Notes that in carrying through the "Catholic Relief Bill [Adams to Clay, May 2, 1829]" the Duke of Wellington has overcome difficulties "insurmountable for any other man." ALS. DLC-HC (DNA, M212, R3). Printed in Colton, *Clay Correspondence*, 4:236-37. For Christopher Hughes's fate, see 7:565-67.

Vaughan wrote Clay on December 18, 1829, reporting that he had received the rifle "& it seems to me to be in workmanship, most perfect, & I am as well pleased with it as any child you ever saw with a new Toy." Scolds Clay for refusing to accept reimbursement for the rifle, adding "The only way in which you can sooth me, is, by telling me what article you want or would covet from England. . . . I shall ever be proud of the Rifle as a memorial of your friendship." ALS. DLC-HC (DNA, M212, R4).

Clay replied on December 29 saying he was happy that Vaughan was pleased with his rifle. "I instructed the artist to make a good one, which could be perfectly relied on for its accuracy, and not to aim at mere show. Unless he has deceived me, it will prove a good shot. It cost a mere trifle, not worthy of being mentioned, and I am sorry you should think of it. But if it will be more agreeable to you to send me some article, in return, I should be glad to have a plain English fowling piece, with a single band, not to exceed in cost 30 or 40 dollars. I could not receive it without the latter condition is observed." Thanks Vaughan for the Christmas day toast in his honor. ALS. Codrington Library, All Souls College, Oxford University.

To SAMUEL L. SOUTHARD   Lexington, July 7, 1829

It has been a long time since I heard from you. Through Mr. Adams I learnt that your health had improved. I sincerely hope that it may be entirely re-established, and should be glad to have directly from yourself such an assurance. Mine has been improved, since my return home.

Do tell me all about the case of Dr. [Tobias] Watkins.[1] I have obtained no satisfactory information; that which has reached me through the papers being imperfect. Is it possible that we were all deceived in him, and that he has wanted probity?

The course of the new administration has produced great effect in the West. Many who voted for Jackson openly express their regrets, and thousands of others feel what their pride restrains them from expressing. Without some fortunate turn in public affairs, for him, I consider that he never can again obtain the support which he received last fall in the Western States. My friends believe, and I believe, that in a contest between us I should certainly prevail in this quarter. I find that a discrimination existed, much more extensively than I had supposed, between Mr. Adams and myself. However much it is to be regretted, the fact is nevertheless incontestible.

How does the land lie in New Jersey? What are you doing? What are your prospects, in the line of your profession? I need not assure you of the deep interest I feel in all that concerns you. . . .

ALS. NjP. Letter marked "(Confidential)."   1. Clay to Hammond, May 27, 1829.

To GEORGE W. DAWSON   Lexington, July 8, 1829

I have waited with some anxiety for information as to the disposition made of the petition of Lotty for freedom [7:622-24, 631-33]; and I should be glad if you would have the goodness to furnish it. If it were not tried, be pleased to inform me when it will be? Should it be necessary to take any depositions on the Eastern Shore [of Md.], Mr. Henry Page of Cambridge [Md.],[1] Atto. at Law, will attend to the business for me. Is it thought to be necessary to take the deposition of Mr. [James] Condon, from whom I purchased the woman? If so be pleased to inform me, and transmit directions as to the manner of having it done.

I write to you instead of Genl. Jones,[2] in the hope that your engagements will admit of your more promptly communicating the desired information than he could do.

To enable me to read Condons' deposition it might be necessary for me to release him, which I would have no objection to doing. His responsibility I regard as nominal.

ALS. KyLoF. Dawson was an attorney in Washington.   1. For Page, see Elias Jones, *History of Dorchester County Maryland* (Baltimore, 1902), 391.   2. Probably Roger Jones, adjutant-general of the army, 1825-52. *CAB.*

From JOSIAH S. JOHNSTON   Maysville, Ky., July 8, 1829

The low state of the Water, has prevented My ascending the River, & I shall be compelled to take a long & fatiguing journey by Land   I have left Mrs J. at Cincinnati, while I shall make a Short visit to My friends & I am now on the Bank of the River, looking anxiously for a Boat to return—I remained in Cincinnati Long enough to witness the procession & escape the oration on the 4h. And arrived here too late for the Celebration of the day—

It is the opinion of the people every where from Maine to Louisiana, that you will be a Candidate for the Presidency, & there is a general impression, a Sort of Presentiment, that you will be the President—I found this idea prevailing among the Moderate Men of both parties, while the violent ones of the Jackson party, evince that it is [the] only thing they dread—

On My Way from the Capitol I found a general disapprobation of the Cabinet—There Were some violent partizans perhaps Silent, but all Who spoke were very frank & honest in their Declarations of disappointments. As far as I recollect, I have not met one man who ventured to oppose or defend—I [*sic*, It] augured favorably of this fact, it evinced still some independence of Opinions, some freedom of action, some respect for principle & it goes far to redeem the people from the fears entertained of them—I confess I have better hopes of the people, although I never dispaired of them—

The subsequent measures of the admn—have produced a more strong & general feeling—of disapprobation—all the promises of reform, have dwindled down to removals from Office—all the abuses resolve themselves in to a vindictive persecution of [Tobias] Watkins—[1] & the professions of economy, and in paltry savings in News papers—The whole power of the Executive has been wielded to reward friends & punish enemies—in removing the most faithful & experienced officers, to provide rewards & places for the most violent & the most dispicable of the party—There is a general Sense of disappointment in the Whole Course—arising more from the character of the men, whom he has selected—than from the principle it involves, or Sympathy with the distress it produces—although both have their effect—The delusion about the General has banished—The Idea prevails more generally among his friends, (although they are Silent) than we are aware of, that he has undertaken a task, above his ability—that he is above the advice & Controul of the leading Men of his party—That he is in the hands of a desperate adventurer—They see, what they must be unwilling to acknowledge, that he is a Weak old Man—with a designing favorite, fostering his prejudices—& influencing his resentments—& directing his Course—That he is surrounded by a full & distracted Cabinet—That his Whole Admn. so far is Completely a failure—Nay Worse, it must be disapproved on principle & will be disavowed by the people—

This state of things, has already made a deep impression on the public mind & has changed the opinions of many of the intelligent, reflecting & honest men of the Country & has turned the minds of men very much towards you—& the changes are going on daily

But we must not suppose the party has changed—It exists in its full vigour & every thing will be done to hold it together, in order to Concentrate it at some future time on some other point & wield its force—. It is held together by views to the future & by hostility to you   If you were out of the way, the party would instantly divide & dissolve—But disaffection is Weakening their force, while the seeds of disunion are deeply sown in their ranks—It will require all the art & address of the Managers, to Keep together—all the pliancy & Suavity of the Secretary to hold his place—& all their talent to maintain themselves before the people—

The spirit of the party, which consists in wielding the power & patronage of the Govt. & in hostility to you, yet remains, though some what impaired—the spirit of Jacksonianism is much subdued—And the poison is working its death. The party will survive, & we must prepare to meet it, under Whatever name or guise it may present itself—The *Leaders*, the office holders, the Editors the *politicians* will never come over to you & they will always rally a strong party—But they can be beaten & will—Jackson Calhoun Van Buren & probably McLane will be against you as they will be against each other—or any body else   Genl. Jackson does not mean to retire   He is not to be put aside—Until he pleases voluntarily to withdraw—If he lives, this is certain. 1st. Because he wills it—2ndly. because they can not agree on any other person—3d. if they Could he Could not succeed   4th. Because you must be Kept out—But it is My opinion he Can be beaten—The Next Winter will shew the Course of events—

There is much difficulty & Collision among them at Washington, Which they partially conceal but private anecdotes leak out occasionally—Duff [Green] is odious to all the Cabinet—but they are afraid of him—Van Buren is ill at ease—& [John] Eaton has his troubles—But of Which I will give you a better account, when I visit there—

There is not a man that I have seen or heard of from Tennessee who does not openly object to Eaton & I understand the fact has been made known that the Ladies of Nashville will not receive Madam [Eaton] if they visit that place—[2]

He [Eaton] has written to Mr. [George] Graham, that "if he does not make his Wife, hold her tongue, he hold him responsible"—

A Major in the Army with his Lady, being great friends of the General; in order to be with him, boarded at Oneils [*sic*, O'neale] some time ago—Where the Lady said Some thing she did not approve & of Which she spoke to some of her friends—The Officer & Lady were Lately in Washington & did not pay their [word illeg.]—After they had left the City—The Lady recivd a very insulting, anonymous Letter, Which Concluded by Saying that if her husband had not left the City, He would have received a severe Chastisement—On the receipt of this strange Letter, being well satisfied from whence it came, the Officer felt bound in honor to return & meet his unknown enemy—he returned, Walked the streets several days, but not finding his man he proceeded on his journey—But I understand his friends are very Candid with him & the Ladies very divided—

To turn from Gay to Grave—I congratulate you on the Acquittal of [Charles] Wickliffe—[3]It has given great pleasure every Where, but to no one more than myself—We have a very gratifying account of the defense, Which is said to be very able   I know your Objection to Long Letters, but the Boat will not Come—The trouble this will give you is nothing to the suspense & [word illeg.] I shall suffer When I quit Writing to Look up the River in vain for a Conveyance to Cincinnati—

The difference about [Thomas A.] Marshal[l] & [Adam] Beatty is difficult to adjust,[4] the friends of both are obstinate & induce it is a delicate question—But I can say to you very Confidentially, that in my opinion if Beatty Can not be elected his friends will persuade him to withdraw & make a merit of the sacrifize to the party—Beatty is now in Bourbon & reports that he is strong there—But if it is ascertained, that Bourbon will not support him he ought to withdraw—If Beatty can get a strong support there Marshal[l] ought not to defeat both—I think it will yet be arranged—otherwise [Nicholas] Coleman will defeat both

I have seen [Joseph] Vance—He gives the most favorable account of Ohio—Proscription has done the Work there—The changes are very great—He told me he would write you—so I will say no more

ALS. DLC-TJC (DNA, M212, R13). 1. Clay to Hammond, May 27, 1829. 2. Johnston to Clay, Sept. 9, 1829. 3. Wickliffe to Clay, March 15, 1829. 4. Clay to Beatty, June 2, 7; July 9, 1829; Clay to Johnston, July 18, 1829.

To ADAM BEATTY   Lexington, July 9, 1829

I duly received and have attentively read your favor of the 26h. Ulto. with its enclosure, the address to the voters of the Second Congressional district.[1] I entertain no doubt that you have correctly represented the purport of your interviews with Majr. Allen, and that you have been unjustly dealt by on account of them.

I view, with inexpressible regret, the state of things in your district,[2] and I should be most happy to learn that any mode had been adopted to concentrate on yourself, or any other friend, the votes of those who concur in their political principles. Can no such mode be fallen upon? Is it not yet practicable to convene persons together from all parts of the district? Of what avail to the present Candidates on the same side can it be to persevere, with the *certainty* of defeat, before them all? How will the honor of any one of them be *vindicated* by such a course? Defeat can neither gratify friends, nor the Candidate himself. It may display his resolution, but it can prove nothing else. Most certainly neither of the Candidates can feel gratified by being the instrument (should such be the result) of the failure of his competitor on the same side.

The existing state of things can afford pleasure to none but our opponents. They alone will profit by it. And I fear that it may lead in your district to pernicious consequences permanently.

I have not seen nor heard directly from Mr. [Thomas A.] Marshall since he was announced. I believe him utterly incapable of deception; and I therefore feel confident that he has been brought out contrary to his wishes; for he told me in April that he has no desire whatever to be a Candidate. I do not know him, if he would not concur in any honorable expedient by which a member can be returned favorable to those views of National policy which both he and you entertain.

But I must leave this painful subject, fearing, I confess, that owing to the unhappy divisions among friends we are destined to add another to the long catalogue of defeats, from the same cause, which we have sustained within a few years.

I have been disappointed in not receiving the Merino Sheep which I presume have been kept to be sent when the weather is somewhat cooler. You shall be advised of their arrival.

ALS. Courtesy of Earl M. Ratzer, Highland Park, Ill. Letter marked "(Confidential)." Printed in Colton, *Clay Correspondence*, 4:236-37. 1. The June 2 Address to the Voters of the Second Congressional District from John G. Martin *et al.* explained why Bourbon County had nominated Thomas A. Marshall for Congress. Lexington *Kentucky Reporter*, June 17, 1829. 2. Clay to Beatty, June 2, 7, 1829; Clay to Johnston, August 26, 1829.

From Eliza Sibley [Mrs. Josiah S.] Johnston, Cincinnati, July 10, 1829. Comments at length on her health and her disappointment in not having seen Clay. Lauds his "successful effort, in defence of Mr. [Charles] Wickliff[e], (altho you fancied yourself unprepared [Wickliffe to Clay, March 15, 1829], — " Discusses the vacation plans of herself and husband. Notes that Judge John McLean and his family are in Cincinnati and that "he expresses, openly, his disappointment at Genl. Jacksons conduct — I have conversed much with him, but cannot find out who he likes, & do think (entre nous) that he has high views for himself . . . he must surely fail." Reports that it is "the opinion of many, of a great many persons, with whom I have met, of good sense, & judgement — that it would be better, if possible, for you, to avoid public dinners, or at all events, avoid making those exciting addresses . . . they all think it best to see the people in a more quiet way travel as much in your own state as you can — & let us all try, to conciliate as much as possible, which you know can be done, without losing the smallest portion of dignity — " ALS. DLC-HC (DNA, M212, R3).

From FRANCIS T. BROOKE
Near Fredericksburg, Va.,
July 11, 1829

I have delayed writing you since the receipt of your letter of the 12th of May Seeing by the papers that you were not at home nothing could be more gratifying to your friends in this quarter, than the impression you are you [sic] making in Kentucky and Ohio, of which we have daily accounts   that there has been a great reaction in Virginia also there can be no doubt   the affair of Watkins[1] may have shaken it in some degree under the plastic hand of [Thomas] Ritchie, and other means will no doubt [be] used by the governm[en]t to turn the current, but nothing I believe now will do unless it comes out boldly the next Session against the tariff and internal improvemts.   indeed I understood before I left Richmond from a Jackson man that that would be redeeming measure of the governm[en]t as regards Virginia, the Election of the committee[2] has had a happy effect, the people came back to those again by whom they had been faithfully   Such you will have seen who constitute it, a large proportion if not a majority will be found to be anti Jackson, as an example of the change in Virginia, you will be surprised to hear that [Thomas Walker] Gilmer of Albemarle and [J.A.H.] Davis the late Editors of that infamous, paper[3] have come out boldly against the Adminisn   I wished I had known you were going down to Livingston & I would have troubled you with my matters in that quarter, and if I do not hear favorably from [Robert] Triplet as to the condition of my land near Madisonville I shall yet be obliged to do so. . . . N B   I have just had a letter from [Samuel L.] Southard who is at Washington, he has been terribly *persecuted* by the case of Watkins, who at one time in givings out, had implicated our *friend* but the rascal retracted every thing on Southard appearances   is it true as I was told by a Jacksonian, that McClane [sic, John McLean] is now one of your warm friends, I hope he is, because I shall then return to my first opinion of him

ALS. DLC-HC (DNA, M212, R3).   1. Clay to Hammond, May 27, 1829.   2. Delegates had recently been chosen to the 1829 Virginia Constitutional Convention. *Niles' Register* (July 4, 1829), 36:300.   3. *The Virginia Advocate.*

From John L. Bridges, Harrodsburg, Ky., July 12, 1829. Reports that from a political standpoint "Things are going on as well in this quarter as could be expected. . . . I have no doubt of the Election of Capt [John] Kincaid, *our Old* friends [Robert] McAfee and [Samuel] Daviss [sic, Daveiss] have been *compeled* to go into port, and I think it will be years before they will venture upon another political cruise." Assures Clay that he has "many more friends in this Section than you expect and they are not without their influance and will to exert it when it Shall become necessary." Has heard rumors that

Clay will visit Harrodsburg at the end of July, but thinks mid-August might be a better time. ALS. DLC-HC (DNA, M212, R3). Kincaid, McAfee, and Daveiss were among the candidates running for Congress from the 7th district. McAfee and Daveiss withdrew before the election and Kincaid defeated his opponent, William O. Booker, by a margin of 822. Lexington *Kentucky Gazette*, April 24; May 22, 1829; *Niles' Register* (September 26, 1829), 37:68; Lexington *Kentucky Reporter*, August 12, 1829.

To JOSIAH S. JOHNSTON   Lexington, July 18, 1829

I received your obliging letter of the 8h. instant under date at Maysville, and I perused with great satisfaction the information and reflections which it contains. Although I have an aversion to some *long* letters, it does not extend to such as that; and you would greatly oblige me by frequently writing me similar ones. I agree with you in most of the reflections which you have communicated. The elements undoubtedly exist for a serious if not doubtful struggle at the next Presidential election. I believe with you that, in certain contingencies, Genl. Jackson will be again brought forward. But whether he should be or not, if the party that elected him can be kept together, in any considerable extent, it will be formidable, whoever else it may happen to betake up. The next Session of Congress will, I think, greatly add to the dissolvents of that party which are now operating. Whatever the President may say or recommend, or forbear to recommend, in his message to Congress, his friends in the body must divide on certain leading measures of policy. Each section of it will claim him as belonging to it, if he should be silent; and a quarrel between them is inevitable. On the contrary, if he speak out his sentiments (probably the safest course for him, whatever they may be) he must throw from him all of his party who are opposed to his sentiments, and those, thus cast off, must sooner or later attach themselves to the party who has all along been adverse to the General. If, for example, he comes out for the Tariff, the South leaves him, and will try another change if it can effect it, of the office of Chief Magistrate. If he comes out in opposition to the Tariff, there will be such an opposition to him in the Tariff States as must prevent his re-election.

The worst course, for those who were opposed to his election and are now unwilling to see him re-elected, is that he should declare himself unequivocally for the Tariff. The best course for them is that he should come out clearly against the Tariff. In the former case, it would be difficult to detach in sufficient number the friends of the System from him, and make them comprehend the expediency of supplanting the head of an Administration favorable to their views. This was done in the case of Mr. [John Q.] Adams, but that was an exception, from various causes. In the latter supposition, it would not I think be at all difficult or impracticable to unite the friends of the Tariff and place at the head of the Administration one who would promote their policy. In short, I think matters have come, or are rapidly tending to such a state of things, that those, who are in favor, or those, who are against, certain measures of policy must govern. Masks must be cast, and the real color and complexion of men and their opinions must be seen.

In respect to my future personal movements, I hope to so conduct myself as to satisfy my friends. I appeared for young [Charles] Wickliffe, with some reluctance. I would have avoided doing so, if I could have avoided it honorably. But the case had such a triumphant issue that I have been greatly benefited by it, in this State, instead of being injuriously affected.

I will write you after the result of the August elections is certainly known. Prospects continue very good, but they are better for the State Legislature than for Congress. In [John] Chambers's late district, you saw what they were. Mr. [Thomas A.] Marshall has declined, but [Adam] Beatty's Election is still regarded uncertain.[1]

I shall be glad often to hear from you; and I repeat the hope that you will not forbear to write me any and every thing that occurs, without entertaining the smallest apprehension of your letters every being unwelcome.

Be pleased to deliver the enclosed to Mrs. Johnston. . . .

ALS. PHi. Addressed to Johnston at Northampton, Mass. Printed in Colton, *Clay Correspondence*, 4:238-40.   1. Clay to Beatty, June 2, 7; July 9, 1829.

From JOHN SERGEANT   Philadelphia, July 20, 1829

I have often thought of writing to you since we parted at Washington, but never had any thing to say, unless it were to repeat the assurance, of continued respect and good wishes. Tho' still in the same predicament, yet I really wish to hear from you—we hear of you every day, and in a manner highly gratifying to your friends. It is some satisfaction to know that this is not all.   You give great uneasiness to your enemies. They seem to be haunted by continual fear, and I hope not without good cause. It would be premature yet to indulge in speculation, and I am the less inclined to it from having been lately so painfully mistaken. I think it very clear, however, that we are not to consider all as your enemies who supported Genl. Jackson. Many, I have no doubt, preserved their good feelings towards you throughout the contest, and many more have found them revive[d] since the contest ended. To these, we may add, I hope, very many who will return to a right sense of what is due to the honour and welfare of the Country, and, (*least* as well as *last*) not a few who have their own particular disgusts and griefs to indulge—Much is to depend upon future movements, of which nothing will be discernible 'till after the meeting of Congress. In the mean time, however, you are losing nothing, certainly, and I think you are decidedly gaining. Among our old friends, there is not the least symptom of distraction or division. They all look to you, and when the proper period arrives, you will find them all as zealous as your warmest and most affectionate neighbours would wish.

At Washington, if we are to judge from concurring reports, there is deplorable imbecility in the head, and some disorder among the members. Society is in a wretched state, and the prosperity of the City most effectually checked. The new administration has so far been nothing but a scourge.

In Pennsylvania, chaos seems to be come[ing] again. There is an open and furious rupture in the Jackson party in the City and County of Philada. AntiMasonry is disturbing other parts of the State. In a short time, it will be difficult to tell who is who, or what the divisions really are. [George] Wolf is as yet without a competitor, except the Anti-Masonic candidate [Joseph] Ritner. If the latter should gain any considerable strength, it is not impossible that some other candidate may be taken up and run in between them—perhaps Governor [John A.] Shulze.[1]

Pray let me hear from you. . . .

ALS. DLC-HC (DNA, M212, R3).   1. On Oct. 14, 1829, Wolf was elected governor of Pennsylvania by a large majority over Ritner. *Niles' Register* (Oct. 24, 1829), 37:132. For Ritner see *DAB*; for Wolf and Ritner see *BDGUS*, 3:1302-303.

To GEORGE WATTERSON   Lexington, July 21, 1829

Prior to the receipt of your obliging letter of the 10h. instant I had seen, with mingled sentiments of indignation and regret, your removal from the office of Librarian [of Congress]. It was a step in keeping with the despotism which now rules at Washington, and it has a precedent in that act by which the famous Alexandrian librarian[1] was reduced to ashes. In your particular case, as in some others, I have been inexpressibly grieved by the reflection that friendship for me may have been one of the causes which led to this exercise of vengeance upon you and upon them. I rejoice however, my dear Sir, to perceive that you possess a soul which is not to be subdued by the exertion of tyranny. There is happily a returning sense of patriotism, and judgement, already manifest throughout the Union; and I hope both you and I shall live to see the Nation rid of its present misrule, and the Jacksons and the [Duff] Greens and the [John] Eatons and the host of kindred spirits driven back to their original stations and insignificance. If such men and such measures are to be sanctioned and continued, our hopes of free institutions, with their concomitant blessings, would be forever destroyed. I am glad to find that you are resolved to contribute all in your power to produce the desirable change. The Journal[2] has been edited, I think, with much spirit and great ability. It combines the two best qualities of an efficient paper, that of presenting excellent Editorial articles, and a most judicious selection from other prints. I think that paper has strong claims to public patronage.

No more successful means could be pursued to open the eyes of the people than to make more and more evident at Washington, the fact, which I believe to exist, that Duff Green is the practical President.

I should be sorry that the Chronicle[3] should be applied to the political purpose you mention, unless it should prove to be for the interest of its publishers. On that subject, it will be well to confer with my Congressional friends next winter.

I have only had an opportunity of consulting with one Editor as to his disposition to engage and compensate you for the correspondence which you suggest. He would be glad to do so, during the sitting of Congress. In its vacation, he thinks he could not afford to offer any thing worthy of your acceptance. I will make further enquiries and let you know the result.

I have been long acquainted with and grateful for your friendly attachment to me. And I repeat how much I have been afflicted by your removal, from a comfortable situation, in consequence of my fears that it has been occasioned by that attachment. I wish it were in my power to do something. . . .

ALS. DLC-George Watterson Papers (DNA, M212, R22).   1. Letters "ian" superimposed on "y."   2. Two weeks after his dismissal from the Library of Congress, Watterson joined the staff of the Washington *Daily National Journal* and the following year became its editor. *DAB.* 3. Possibly the Washington (D.C.) *Chronicle*, published from 1828-32 by A. Rothwell and T.W. Ustick.

From Elisha Whittlesey, Canfield, Ohio, July 21, 1829. Expresses his alarm at the "acts of the present administration," noting that "So sensible are capitalists of this. That the manufacturers of the country, even those that are amply protected by the tariff, are at a stand." Does not believe that a move to "repeal the duties immediately" will be made. Such repeal "will be delayed until Gen Jackson is *'immortalized'* by paying off the public debt, or nearly so . . . and that when the public debt is extinguished, an attempt will then be made to repeal all duties, except enough to carry on the ordinary expences of the government; and if successful, the manufactures of the country will be broken down, and the system of internal improvement will be suffered to languish." At this point, "Southern or foreign policy will then triumphantly prevail." Reports that some of Ohio's "moderate Jacksonians . . . begin to fear they have abandoned principles for men, while the most violent sympathize with the South, and begin to declare their doubts, whether it is beneficial for us to manufacture for ourselves." Calls Clay's attention to the address sent to candidates for the Pennsylvania state legislature by "the mechanics at Pittsburgh" and states that Henry Baldwin, "who has considerable influence in Pennsylvania, and particularly in the western parts of it," was behind it. Its purpose was "to defeat the plans of the [John C.] Calhoun party" in Pittsburgh. Advises Clay that Baldwin has high personal regard for him and can be weaned from "his late political connections." Urges personal approaches to that end. Reports a decline in Jackson sentiment in Mercer, Pa. ("they began to distrust the story of 'bargain and sale'") and the fact that Calhoun is "generally unpopular" there. Assures Clay that his friends in Trumbull County, Ohio, remain firm, but feels that the Jacksonians may carry "some of their candidates in the [Western] Reserves at the approaching election for State Representatives." Laments that it is "extremely difficult to bring out the moral, sober and industrious part of our citizens to the polls," or make them see "the importance the election may have, on the measures of the General government either immediately or remotely — or on the state of parties hereafter." Remarks that Clay's "address at Lexington [May 16], has been well received by our citizens." Reports that Jesse B. Thomas, who is "more personally, than politically opposed to you," will come to have "considerable influence in this State." Since Thomas does not like either Martin Van Buren or Calhoun, "I most ardently could wish, that some measures could be taken to reconcile his feelings." ALS. DLC-HC (DNA, M212, R3). See Clay to Whittlesey, August 6, 1829. For the "Address of the Mechanics and Manufacturers of Pittsburgh" in support of the protective tariff see *Niles' Register* (July 25, 1829), 36:346, 352-54. The Anti-Jackson forces won most of the legislative seats, including Trumbull County's in Ohio's Western Reserve. Cincinnati *Daily Gazette*, November 11, 1829.

From Samuel L. Southard, Trenton, N.J., July 23, 1829. Comments on his own poor health, that of his wife, and the death of his daughter, Ann, prior to leaving Washington. Discusses at length the Tobias Watkins embezzlement scandal pointing out that "pressed by his wants created by extravagant living, & I fear by gambling also, he sought temporary relief by drafts on several of the Navy Agents." These amounted to seven in number and $7,300 in sum and were executed "while I was absent" from the office. Thinks it "doubtful," however, "whether the criminal prosecution will be successful. It has been very badly conducted."

Reports that his prospects at law are excellent and that he will soon have "the best practice in the State" if his health permits.

Notes that in politics in New Jersey "our friends are dispirited & do not desire an early struggle. The friends of the General [Jackson] are silent, & do not zealously defend him. If we could pass our next election, without much conflict, all matters would go right." Anticipates conflict between Calhoun and Van Buren within the Jackson administration. Reports that Van Buren is organizing in New Jersey, but that his progress is slow. "At this time he could not carry the State — nor do I believe he will, at any time."

Concludes: "I have heard a good deal from various parts of the Union & I think it manifest, that you are the great object with the present opposition. The only question with yourself is, when you ought to be formally announced, for the first office. The toasts on the 4 July indicate, that you are, at this time of more interest to both parties than any man in the Union. It is a matter of some moment to you who shall be associated with you as V.P. — I have been consulted from several quarters & solicited to permit my name to be mentioned — but have given one uniform answer — that it would not suit me — I am too poor & do not desire the Office — I think it unwise to take me from so small a State. My wishes run in the different direction. The Society at Washn.

is greatly changed & gloom hangs over the whole City. The course of the Govt. has carried distress into almost every house—depreciated real estate—& affected seriously the business of the Place." ALS. DLC-HC (DNA, M212, R3). Letter marked "(Confidential)." For the Watkins scandal, see Clay to Hammond, May 27, 1829.

Bardstown Speech, July 30, 1829. Disclaiming an intent to interfere with or affect the approaching state elections, declares "that, however divided we unhappily had been, or might now be, on particular questions," there are "some cardinal points" on which all are united. Among these are "our Union; our constitution; our republican institutions, and uncompromising hatred of tyranny and of tyrants; and an ardent, unextinguishable love of liberty." Argues that despotism depends not so much on the quantity of power as upon the manner in which it is used, and that the great superiority of a constitutional, limited government consists in the fact that it offers a more solid security for public happiness and prosperity. If, however, a magistrate in a constitutional government uses his power for himself and not for the community, "surrendering himself to the influence of wicked and unprincipled men,—such a magistrate whatever may be, the extent of his authority, is an oppressor."

Discusses the need for internal improvements, advocating that both the state and federal governments do all they can for this purpose. Turns to his chief topic—the protective tariff—describing its origins, purpose, and accomplishments. Argues it is intended "to develope the resources, to cherish the arts, and to protect the industry of our own country; to increase our domestic markets, and to ensure a certain and cheap supply of articles required by our wants, and essential to our independence of foreign powers." Contends "that *competition at home*" will "at no distant day supply us with articles in greater abundance, cheapness and perfection, than we had been in the habit of purchasing from Europe; and, that in the mean time . . . a home market would be created." Refers to the current depression in the textile industry, saying "this embarrassment, resulting from the excess of production, is relied on to destroy our manufactures by the very men who denied its competency to produce a bare supply." Warns that when the public debt is paid, tariff opponents will attempt to repeal the duties under the guise of lowering taxes. "If our rulers will repeal duties on any objects not produced by our own industry, they will be entitled to our thanks. . . . But if our burthens are to be lightened by the overthrow of our system of protection, if taxes are to be dispensed with, on articles of European fabrication coming in competition with rival articles of American origin—our rulers will inflict curses instead of bestowing blessings upon us." Concludes with a warning against the formation of a treaty, now rumored with Great Britain, in which the productions of the two countries would "be admitted in the ports of each at a rate of duty, not exceeding a limited maximum." Such a treaty would make the United States a province and dependency of Britain. Summary printed in Lexington *Kentucky Reporter*, September 2, 1829. No manuscript text of Clay's speech in Bardstown has been found.

From Sidney Breese, Kaskaskia, Ill., July 30, 1829. Informs Clay that "a large and . . . most respectable portion" of the American people, as well as "thousands who were angered against you but lately are now turning their eyes toward you, as the most probable successor of the present 'Demigod [Jackson]'." Notes that he should inform his friends of his intentions with respect to "the Coming election" at an early date. Believes that Clay can carry the West and argues that if the "Dominant party" attacks the tariff in the next session of Congress he can also count on the support of Pennsylvania and New York. Reports that "the original Jackson men" in Illinois are quite unhappy with the president's "course thus far," particularly with his "Proscriptive system." Has been told that his own removal from his job as U.S. district attorney for Illinois was "owing to a suspicion that I was friendly to you." Assures Clay that the charge is correct and that "under any state of circumstances you can count on me as an auxiliary in any course you may adopt directed to the one great Object." ALS. DLC-HC (DNA, M212, R3).

From Samuel J. Browne, Cincinnati, August 1, 1829. In closing the books on the Cincinnati *Emporium,* "now changed to the Centinel," bills Clay for $14.00 owed. Remarks that the "perservering aid" he has rendered "the American system has been Expensive with the disappointment by the elevation of A Jackson" which "has dampened my ardour for the present." Assures Clay, however, that the publisher of the Cincinnati *Sentinel,* "Mr. [John] McCalla is your warm advocate and will continue to give you every aid to the upsetting of those whose patriotism is for gain; and their love o[f] country, the hope of office. I trust the 4th. M[arch] of 1833 will place *one* in the chair of state, whose private and public character will be an honor to the nation." ALS. DLC-HC (DNA, M212, R3). The weekly Cincinnati *Emporium* had commenced publication early in 1824. McCalla's Cincinnati *Sentinel* was apparently short-lived, because the only known copy in existence is the issue of August 20, 1829, located at OClWHi. For Browne, see *CAB.*

From DAVID LEE CHILD   Boston, August 4, 1829

I received your favor from Ashland in due season, and should have long ago acknowledged it, if I had not been afraid that even to ask you to peruse a letter, from a distant and comparatively unknown friend, while you was so much occupied with your family, your farming, & the receiving & reciprocation of visits, might seem like intrusion.

Permit me to thank you as thousands in Massachusetts do for your [May 16] speech at Fowler's Gardens. It seemed to me that if you had made it before the Senate & Chief Justice on the trial of *an impeachment,* it could scarcely have failed of success. It was in great demand here & was issued *in an extra* on the Evening of its arrival. On looking back upon the events of the last spring & viewing the present happy *prospect,* I feel deeply impressed with wisdom & propriety of the disposition which you made of my suggestions on an important subject. The true, natural & effectual cure is now taking place. At any rate, if the present cure be not effectual, it will prove that the *subject* is not worth curing. The state of things in this place is singular. The new PM,[1] who is a most worthless creature and obtained his office by mere faction (aided it is said by deception practised upon the president) refuses to admit others to offices in his department upon the same claim by which he obtained it. This produces clamor & mutual recrimination. I have been made the depository of some of the secrets of the Jackson party in consequence of the schism from the above and from other causes I am in possession of the whole history of the publication of the "Cunningham correspondence"[2]   A [word illeg.] Ghent Commissioner is implicated[3] both in purse & character, tho an acknowledged bankruptcy on the latter score can leave to friends or enemies little to hope or fear whatever may betide   However the deep infamy of that transaction which extends rather beyond the immediate actors & visible agents, may possibly be so developed & commented on as to bear on existing questions. & the active politicians of these days. You will occasionally see something & possibly a *good* deal upon this subject in the Mass Journal. One of the agents who paid a large sum of money on the faith of persons at Washington & in Massachusetts has written to demand of each his proportion, (they having hitherto fulfilled old promises by *new* ones.) and if it does not come you will see some curious memories *pour servir a l'histoire.* In the [Washington *Daily*] National Journal you will see some letters from Boston giving anecdotes of Jacksonism here. — The meeting of Boston Merchants, was started & conducted by *Jackson men*.[4] The crowd who attended showed a profound conviction of the inexpediency & injustice of the present policy. Wishing you entire health and *present* tranquility, as much for the sake of my country as for your own and that of your family & social circle.

ALS. DLC-HC (DNA, M212, R3).   1. Postmaster for Boston, Nathaniel Green.   2. See 3:500-502.   3. John Q. Adams. See Hecht, *John Quincy Adams*, 376.   4. For "anecdotes of Jacksonism," which discuss the decline of the Jackson party in Massachusetts, see Washington *Daily National Journal*, July 24, 25, 30, 1829; for the "meeting of Boston merchants" which condemned the Jackson administration removals from the custom house in Boston, see *ibid.*, August 14, 1829.

To ELISHA WHITTLESEY   Lexington, August 6, 1829

Your favor of the 21st. Ulto. is thankfully received. I have perused it with much attention. The state of relations between Mr. [Henry] Baldwin and me has always been friendly, and is so now, as far as I know. Our separation prevents me from cultivating it, except I were to write to him, which I should not like to do, without first hearing from him. You know the state of my relation to the other gentleman [Jesse B. Thomas] alluded to by you. It is not unfriendly, and there is no obstacle on my part to its being more so. But he once wronged me by his vote, and, therefore, from my knowledge of human nature, I am induced to fear that he can never be very cordial in his attachment to me.

My return home and mixing with the People has had good effect. Hundreds and thousands of those who voted for Jackson have openly avowed their attachment to and confidence in me. Our elections terminated yesterday, and, as far as we have yet heard, their result demonstrates the existence of a powerful reaction. The [Thomas P.] Moore party is defeated in the adjoining Congressional district, and a friend of the American System and to me (Mr. [John] Kincaid) is elected.[1] Wickliffe is defeated or run so close that his triumph is a defeat.[2] Clarke [*sic*, Clark] is re-elected by a much larger majority than he ever received before.[3] J. J. Crittenden is probably elected to our State Legislature.[4]

There is every reason to believe that both branches of our Legislature will be composed of majorities friendly to the late administration, and still larger majorities friendly to me. There will probably be adopted a resolution nominating me *or*. . . .

AL. OClWHi. Letter incomplete. Marked "(Confidential)."   1. Bridges to Clay, July 12, 1829.   2. Charles A. Wickliffe defeated Richard Rudd for Congress in the 9th district by the margin of 675. Louisville *Public Advertiser*, August 15, 1829.   3. James Clark defeated Matthew Flournoy for Congress in the 3rd district, 2,605 to 1,045. Lexington *Kentucky Reporter*, August 12, 1829.   4. Crittenden defeated Ezra Richmond 586 to 501. *Ibid.*

From Stephen W. Marston, Newburyport, Mass., August 7, 1829. Informs Clay that he has just finished reading the correspondence between John S. C. Knowlton, editor of the Lowell (Mass.) *Journal* and Amos Kendall, fourth auditor, which was published in the Boston *Courier* on July 30. Remarks that while he is an "utter stranger" to Clay, he is forwarding the correspondence. Points out that he and Kendall had been classmates at Dartmouth College; and that after they left school in 1811, "I often heard of Mr Kendall," and considered him "exceedingly fortunate in having obtained the good opinion, patronage and friendship of the Hon Mr Clay." Says it was to him a "surprise" later to learn that Kendall had come to the support of "Genl. Jackson's pretensions to the highest office in the gift of this people." Continues: "The story of his ingratitude towards you & your family has long been familiar to his friends & your friends in N. England. By your friends it never has been doubted, nor by him, or his friends publickly denied until the appearance of the above correspondence. The letter was intended to suit the meridian of his native state N.H. & is calculated to do mischief there as well as else where. . . . he has not, in any respect satisfied me, by his own showing, that the charge of *ingratitude* towards you is without foundation. . . . I make no attempts to criticize Mr Kendall'[s] letter here. It is now public property, & the public journals are the proper place to discuss the nice & novel distinctions which he has drawn between the hospitality & friendship which he received at Mrs Clay'[s] table & fireside, in the absence of her husband in a foreign Country, & those which Mr Clay did not personally bestow himself. But in vindicating himself Mr K has no right unjustly to represent others." Concludes with the observation "that with our N. England people, no man, as I trust and believe, in this section, stands on more elevated ground than yourself. & nothing would give me more pleasure than conscious ability to serve you in attaining, under this government, that public station—which is alone equal to your merit." ALS. DLC-HC (DNA, M212, R3). In his reply to Knowlton, Kendall denied that Clay had ever been his benefactor as Knowlton had claimed, saying: "I never needed, asked, or received Mr. Clay's charities. . . . He never gave me money; never loaned me money, except at usury." Furthermore, he never benefitted from Clay's counsel in any way and regrets only that his consideration for Mrs. Clay's earlier kindnesses kept him from speaking out against the Adams-Clay coalition in 1825. Both Knowlton's and Kendall's letters are published in Lexington *Kentucky Reporter*, August 26, 1829.

To SAMUEL L. SOUTHARD   Lexington, August 9, 1829

I recd. your very acceptable favor of the 23d. Ulto. I am highly pleased to hear of your professional prospects and sincerely hope they may be all realized; and I am particularly happy to learn the improvement of your health. Mine is decidedly better and perhaps is as good as one fast getting old ought to expect. Your domestic loss, prior to your departure from Washington had reached and afflicted us.

I congratulate you on the honorable manner in which, friends and foes agree, you acquitted yourself of the painful duty of giving evidence in the unfortunate case of Dr. [Tobias] Watkins. How much have we all been deceived in him!

Our elections are just over. We have not heard the result generally. In those for Congress, owing to bad arrangements, with the detail of which I will not trouble you, it is not as favorable as it might have been. But as far as we have yet heard that of our members of the State Legislature has far exceeded our most sanguine expectations. We shall have, I think, a large and a practical majority in both of its branches. J. J. Crittenden has been elected from a County [Franklin] hitherto decidedly Jacksonian, and many similar elections have taken place. There has been operating in all parts of the State a powerful reaction, which, in the instance of some of the congressional elections, was counteracted by local causes, but which has been demonstrated in most of the State elections. Where we had majorities, our majorities are now greater. Where we had them not, we have now got them, or greatly diminished the majorities against us. Clarke's [*sic*, James Clark] majority in this district is upwards of 1500,[1] and if, in consequence of its certainty, it had not produced some apathy; and if the election had been as well attended this year as the last, his majority would have been 2500. [Robert P.] Letcher has been elected without opposition.[2] From most of the other Congressional elections we have not yet heard the certain results, except in Tom Moore's district, where his faction has been completely routed by the election of Mr. [John] Kincaid, a friend of mine.[3]

In relation to the affair of V-P. I have no fixed opinions as to the person whom it will be most expedient to run. The selection ought to be made upon full consultation and comparison of sentiments and information. I think you ought to let matters take their course, without a positive decision against it.

My son Henry [Clay, Jr.] passed the season of encampment with us. He leaves us in a few days for West point, and if he goes by Trenton will call on you. We are much obliged by your friendly invitation to him.

During our next Legislature there will a question among the members whether they shall nominate me or pass a resolution simply declaring their confidence, their discredit of Calumnies, and the readiness of K. to co operate, at a *suitable time*, with other States in securing my election. Some such resolution as the last[4] would probably command the largest vote. Either, unless I am deceived, could be passed. Which is best? Or is it best to adopt neither? Are they not, in effect equivalent?

ALS. NjP. Letter marked "(Confidential)." 1. Clay to Whittlesey, August 6, 1829. 2. From fourth congressional district. 3. Clay to Whittlesey, August 6, 1829. 4. On Nov. 18, 1822. See 3:301.

From John G. Simpson, Lexington, Ky., August 10, 1829. Receipt for $422, "being the price of a negro woman named Alice and her two children this day sold by me as Commissioner under a decree of Fayette Circuit Court." DS, in Clay's hand. DLC-TJC (DNA, M212, R16).

On August 18 Clay was able to hire from John E. Cooke a slave named Anthony for $5 per month from mid-April to mid-August, 1829. *Ibid.*

Sometime in late 1831, Henry Clay, Jr., in his diary, spoke of his father's views on slavery in the following terms: "A conversation between my father and several gentlemen from the Eastern States on the subject of slavery. My father said that Mr [William] Lowndes told him some years ago that in S. Carolina the profit upon the increase of slaves was about 8 per cent; and He (H.C.) said he presumed it must be 6 or 7 at present in Ky. He was one of the minority who at the last remodelling of the Ky. Constitution [1799] made strenuous efforts to rid Ky of slavery. They did not effect their great object. But their exertions and the discussions of the day in the popular contest conducted in conversation, newspapers &c. caused several clauses to be introduced which would not perhaps have otherwise been inserted—slavery shall not be abolished without compensation to the owners of slaves: They shall be treated with humanity &c: They shall not be made subjects of merchandise: This last clause however has not been entirely observed: For slaves are brought into the state to this day by negro-traders. One of the gentlemen present regretted that the public goods were used by the traders to secure their property: But H.C. thought that it was better so, for otherwise private depots would be established without the advantage of the responsibility of officers acting under the supervising public eye. The traders, H.C. thought, act as scavengers for the public: carrying off the vicious and incorrigible to another country where new characters may be formed with better habits and propensities. This view was taken from the consideration that the evil exists and the public should suffer as little detriment from it as possible." Manuscript diary of Henry Clay, Jr. KyU.

From 1829 through 1836 Clay's financial transactions involving the buying, selling, and leasing of slaves were as follows:

Purchases from Leroy L. Hill, no price given, a female slave named Mary, aged 19 or 20. Hill to Clay, October 20, 1829. DS. DLC-TJC (DNA, M212, R16).

Buys from John G. Simpson, out of the estate of George Taylor, the female Alcey, age about 26, and her two children, Mary and John, for $422. Simpson to Clay, November 9, 1829. *Ibid.* Clay paid Simpson the money on November 11, 1829. ADS. *Ibid.* (R19).

Leases out seven of his slaves (Shadrack, Meredith, Henry, Aaron, Nathan [Nace], Logan, and James) to George W. Anderson & Co. for $500 from January 1, 1830, to December 25, 1830. George W. Anderson & Co. to Clay, December 30, 1829. *Ibid.*

Buys from William McLane a slave child named John or Johnny, age about seven, for $150. McLane of Clay, May 31, 1830. *Ibid.* (R17).

Buys from James Hatter for $450 a slave, age about 22, named John. Hatter to Clay, August 13, 1830. *Ibid.*

Purchases from Leroy Hill and Elizabeth Haley a slave woman named Sibby, age about 35, for $275. Hill and Haley to Clay, September 24, 1830. *Ibid.*

Sells to Maslin Smith four men and boy slaves (Meredith, Henry, Nace, and Logan) presently hired out until December 25, 1831. Date of delivery to be December 25, 1831. Price: $1,780; also leases to Smith the slave, Shadrack, from January 1 to December 25, 1831, for $70. Clay to Smith, December 3, 1830. ADS. KyLxT.

Purchases at auction from John M. McCalla two slaves, a boy named Winston and a girl named Betsey, children of Adam and his wife Melly (or Pamella) for $280. McCalla to Clay, December 20, 1830. DS. DLC-TJC (DNA, M212, R17). On this same day, December 20, Clay bought a mule for $22.50. *Ibid.*

For Clay's desire to purchase three or four young Maryland slaves, in particular ages 17 to 21, see Clay to Washington, July 24, 1831. ALS. MeHi.

Buys slave, Abraham, from estate of Robert Carey for $400; and on same date joins with Hezekial Ellis and Joseph Carey to lease Abraham to Joseph Carey for one month for $10. September 14, 1831. DS. DLC-HC (DNA, M212, R17).

Asks Francis T. Brooke on July 19, 1832, if he could purchase in the Fredericksburg, Va., "neighbourhood a negro boy ten or twelve years old at a reasonable price? I want such an one to ride out [to Kentucky from Washington] a Maltese Jack." ALS. NcD.

Leases slave Abraham to Gabriel Morton on June 12, 1832, for 50 cents per day; David hired to General Taylor on July 4, 1832, for $6.00 per mo.; Jane leased to Samuel Long, Jr., on September 1, 1832, for $20 per year. Memorandum by William Martin, *ca.* September 1, 1832. AD. DLC-TJC (DNA, M212, R17).

Proposes to Mr. Helm, clerk of Lincoln County, "to have the three slaves purchased by Osborne Henley . . . sold at public sale, in conformity with the decree of Lincoln" County Court. Authorizes Helm to have someone purchase the slaves for him if the price does not exceed $385. Clay to Helm, September 20, 1832. ADS. NN. The preceding enclosed in a note to Helm of September 24, 1832, instructing Helm to inform Clay concerning the date of the sale, "as I may possibly attend." ALS. *Ibid.*

As executor of the estate of Thomas Hart, sells to Susannah Price at public auction in Lexington for $200 "one Negro woman named Jane or Jenny about forty years of age and her daughter named Peggy—about seven years of age." Clay Announcement, September 29, 1832. AD. Courtesy of Eleanor Marshall Turner, Louisville, Ky.; see also Susannah Price to Clay, September 22, 1832. DS, in Clay's hand. DLC-TJC (DNA, M212, R17).

Leases out six of his slaves for the coming year at the annual rate of $80 to $100 plus their food and lodging. Clay to Martin, September 20, 1833. Copy. Printed in *JSH* (February, 1949), 15:91-95.

Instructs son-in-law James Erwin to handle a possible transaction between Sen. George A. Waggamann (La.) and former Gov. James Barbour (Va.) in which the former wants to buy slaves from the latter "and would go higher than $300, but not to $500 each." Clay to Erwin, December 21, 1833. ALS. NcD.

In March, 1835, A.B. and Gabriel J. Morton conclude an agreement with Clay to pay on January 1, 1836, the sum of $140 to Clay "for the hire of his negro man

Abraham" and to "bind ourselves to pay the taxes and clothe the said man in the customary manner." A.B. and Gabriel Morton to Clay, March, 1835. DS. Ky.

Purchases from George Lansdowne "one negro girl named Hannah" for $400. Lansdowne to Clay, August 10, 1835. DS, in Clay's hand. DLC-TJC (DNA, M212, R17).

Purchases from Harriet Rogers for $1,200 "two negro slaves," Washington, aged 22 or 23 years, son of Major, and "a negro girl named Barbara, the wife of Washington, aged about sixteen or seventeen." Also pays Rogers the "hire of Washington" up to the time of his outright purchase on September 15, 1835. Two bills of sale, September 15, 1835. *Ibid.*

Sues to collect from A.B. and Gabriel Morton $140 plus damages for failure to pay for the hire of Clay's slave Abraham. Complaint, dated February 6, 1836. DS. Ky. On the same day, February 6, the sheriff of Fayette County was commanded to summon the Mortons to appear before the judge of the Fayette Circuit Court on March 3, 1836, to answer the complaint. *Ibid.*

By Henry Clay *et al.*, Lexington, August 11, 1829. Memorandum of meeting of board of trustees of Transylvania University, signed by Clay and nine others, authorizing the payment of $120 to Prof. Thomas J. Matthews to defray "his expences in procuring money, Books & Aparatus for Trans. University from the citizens of Boston, New York Phila and such other places as he may think proper to visit." DS. KyLxT.

On August 12, 1829, Clay wrote to Josiah Quincy, introducing Matthews, and mentioning the fire that motivated his journey to the East. ALS. MHi. See John D. Wright, Jr., *Transylvania: Tutor to the West* (Lexington, 1975), 124-26 for an account of the fire at Transylvania on May 9, 1829, and Matthews's subsequent fund-raising expedition to pay for the replacement of lost equipment.

To CHARLES HAMMOND   Lexington, August 12, 1829

I receive your very acceptable favor of the 9h. instant just at the moment of preparations for an excursion to the Olympian Springs, for which I start tomorrow, and where I shall remain until the 21st. or 22d. Why can't you come there? You would find good water, good venison, and possibly good company.

I have read your account of the political state of things in Ohio with much attention, but with some regret. I regret to hear, on every account, that a prospect should exist of the Jackson party getting possession of the Govt. of Ohio. It will be bad for you; and it will be bad for the rest of the Union, if we are right in our belief of what is best for the whole. If it can be prevented it would in my opinion be bad policy not to prevent it, at all honorable hazards.

In all political movements, within the respective States, but with reference to the Union at large, two questions ought for ever to be considered 1st. what is best for the particular State and 2dly. what is best for the exterior. If the contemplated movement can reconcile both interests so much the better. If one only that which is most important should always be prefered. But the loss of the State Government is, in my humble judgment, good for neither of those two interests. If it can't be prevented, then submission is the only alternative. But if it can be, depend upon it that an ounce of prevention is worth a pound of cure.

In human affairs generally, as in War, there are two great principles or guides in action. According to one we attack; to the other, we parry or defend. The first most generally succeeds, the last never, unless it be favored by very peculiar circumstances. But if we depend upon the divisions of our Opponents and seek by stratagem to foment and aggravate them, we pursue the latter policy.

We must never forget that we cannot make them lose sight of me, or cease to apprehend me, unless I die, run away, or in some other manner become a non combatant. I cannot veil myself. I cannot withdraw from the gaze of the public eye. I cannot, except in the above contingencies, prevent my being looked to as a Candidate for the Presidency. Nor is it possible for my friends secretly to cherish hopes about me which shall elude the searching vigilance of our opponents.

Besides; if benefit would accrue from our opponents' supposing me withdrawn or unthought of, by their divisions, that benefit would be more than counterbalanced by the injury resulting from the despair and consequent abandonment of friends. If unfurling a standard unites enemies, so it does friends. If the striking of colors disarms the enemy, it no less discourages the ally.

Sometimes I have indeed thought that, as it seems, I cannot die (unless I commit an act of suicide) I would publicly renounce for ever public life. That I am ready to do, if my friends advise it. That I would do, whether they advised it or not, if I believed that it would be for the good of our common Country. My heart may deceive, but it does not, such is its feeling.

To apply some of these general observations. I know it is the wish of our friends in the Eastern States (New England especially) that some favorable demonstrations shall be made in the West, Kentucky most particularly. I think our friends were right in doing nothing towards that object at Columbus last Court. You tell me that you are in danger of losing the Legislature. In that event, we must not only not expect any friendly manifestations, but the very reverse. To give the Jackson party a majority in your Legislature is to place in their hands moral power and the means of retaining the majority.

In this State we have done badly in the Congressional elections, but extremely well in those for the General Assembly. In our H. of R our majority is about two thirds, and in the Senate not much less. I think a resolution of nomination, or one expressive of confidence will be proposed, either in a formal or informal meeting. They appear to me to be nearly equivalent. You think the first inexpedient; what think you of the second? Kentucky, during all the late contest (I mean the Genl. Assembly) was silent. It not only did or said nothing in my behalf, but a most extraordinary species of exparte trial, in my absence, was instituted in her Senate.[1] I am now a private man. Does she not owe something to an injured fellow Citizen; something to her own justice?

If K. remain silent, with a majority of her representation in Congress in favor of the present administration; and if moreover Ohio shall present a Jackson majority in her Legislature will not our distant friends be absolutely discouraged? Will they retain or acquire courage from our *opinions* of what those States will finally do, when those opinions are opposed by stubborn facts? Will they not tell us that our *opinions* which were formerly erroneous may again be founded in mistake?

It appears to me that we should preserve all the strength we can in the Legislatures of the several Western States, and act or not, during the next winter according to circumstances. Jackson may come out against the Tariff, or may attempt its destruction by negotiation. He may decline a re-election &c &c. In any or all of these or other contingencies it may be expedient to act.

You do not surprize me by the course of the late P.M.G. [John McLean] But he deceives himself. The hour when he was deprived of that office stript him of all prospects of the higher situation. He has lost the confidence of the

Jackson party without having acquired that of the other. He may be restless in his present situation [U.S. Supreme Court], but there he is, and there he will remain unless he dies or resigns.

I should be glad to hear from you again shortly. I have now hardly time to read what I write. . . .

ALS. InU. Letter marked "(Confidential)." 1. See 7:54.

From Michael Allen & George Grant, Pittsburgh, August 14, 1829. Send Clay a statement of his account with them. Comment that "politics are hot again here, as for the writer he has been Solicited to enter the ranks again but has assured them that he will change his mind for if he on any occasion votes until he votes for you as President of the United States." ALS. DLC-TJC (DNA, M212, R10).

From Samuel C. Browne, Philadelphia, August 16, 1829. Says that he has just visited Washington which he found "Filled with Scoundrelly beggars — and pitiful sycophants — the former prostrating themselves to obtain and the latter cringing to retain a place and sustain a loathsome existance —" Reports on the gossip about and activities of various people in the city known to Clay. Thinks that Dr. Tobias Watkins will be sentenced to six months on each of the three indictments against him [Clay to Hammond, May 27, 1829]; but notes that Samuel L. Southard's testimony in the Watkins case "is approved highly by all. He saved the reputation of the last administration." Reports that there have been "mixed desertions from our camp," citing Dr. Thomas P. Jones, late superintendent of the Patent Office, as a case in point. By declaring his loyalty to the new administration, Jones managed to salvage "an under clerk's office" that Martin Van Buren gave to him thinking he would be "of use to him in his work." What really saved Jones was President Jackson's view "that he was an unfaithful servant to Mr. A[dams]." Notes that half the personnel of the Patent Office has been replaced, including Clay's friend William Elliott who refused to renounce Adams and left with his head high. Notes that among the various people he met at his hotel while in Washington, Clay's "greatest enemy or rather most noisy and . . . mischievous enemy is a young Wilson. . . . a messenger in the Land Office. . . . He is a favorite with [Duff] Green — it is said." Concludes that it is "hoped by all" that Clay's health has improved and that "you will live to do justice [to] Jackson . . . before March, 1830 —" ALS. DLC-HC (DNA, M212, R3).

From Caspar W. Wever, Ellicotts Mills, Md., August 22, 1829. Assures Clay "that public sentiment here is undergoing a change very favorable to your future prospects. Your old friends are becoming more ardent and sanguine, whilst many of the heroites [Jacksonians] are drooping their heads at the conduct of their chief & gradually sliding into opposition." Has heard it rumored that the Kentucky General Assembly is likely to nominate Clay for the presidency. "This my friend I fear would be bad policy. You are as much nominated now as if all the Legislatures in the Union had proclaimed your name to the people. I would suggest that the adoption of a resolution approbatory of your public conduct without a word about the presidency would probably do some good if it can be passed by a handsome majority. —" Concludes with the "candid" advice that "some of your friends here do not think it good policy in you to make so many speeches. To the north of this region the people are entirely hostile to the system and it is the only matter for the Jackson prints to pass upon. It is also conceived bad policy to deal so harshly with the administration." ALS. DLC-HC (DNA, M212, R3).

To JOSIAH S. JOHNSTON Lexington, August 26, 1829
The result of our Congressional Elections was not as favorable as might have been, owing to bad arrangements. [Adam] Beatty was beaten by a majority of

only 12, owing to [George M.] Bedinger's perseverance as a Candidate and his own want of tact.[1] In Tom Moores old district our triumph is complete.[2]

In both branches of our General Assembly we have large majorities, bordering upon two thirds in each, of friends of the late admon. The majorities friendly to me are still larger.

Ought our Legislature to do any thing and what at the ensuing Session? Let me know your opinion, and that of our friends in your quarter.

It may adopt either of two courses. Make a direct nomination, or, avoiding that, limit itself to an expression of undiminished confidence and attachment, and a discrediting of calumnies &c &c. Which is best? Or is it best to embrace neither course?

My health continues good. Mrs. [Anne Brown Clay] Erwin remains at Ashland, but I shall accompany her to Russellville about the 10h. of next month. . . .

ALS. PHi. Letter marked "(Confidential)." Addressed to Johnston in Washington. Printed in Colton, *Clay Correspondence*, 4:240.   1. Clay to Beatty, June 2, 7; July 9, 1829.   2. Clay to Whittlesey, August 6, 1829.

From William B. Lawrence, New York, August 31, 1829. Thanks Clay for his support and good opinion while he was U.S. chargé in London.

Calls his attention to an anonymous letter to the editor that had appeared in the Washington *United States Telegraph* on August 21 in which "I am made to express in the most extravagant terms, my gratification at discovering the extensive knowledge and attainments of the present President, as evinced in a recent interview" with the author of the letter. Reports that in the New York papers "the words imputed to me" have been used "by the Administration papers not only to announce my conversion," but are "relied on as evidence" of General Jackson's great qualities as a statesman. In reflecting where this fabrication might have originated, recalls that shortly after his return to the U.S. in mid-July he had gone to Washington to settle the accounts of his London office. There he had "my only interview with the President," as well as a "casual conversation with a Mr. [Jonathan] Elliot, formerly Editor of a newspaper through whom I had obtained some Congressional documents." Elliot had represented himself as "an ardent friend of the late [Adams] Administration and after speaking in the strongest terms of Genl. Jackson's ignorance, asked me a few questions which led me to observe that the President was not altogether so badly informed as I had supposed, & that he had conversed with me a good deal on European matters, especially in relation to the war in Turkey." Assures Clay that he "never uttered the silly language" attributed to him in the newspapers, and hopes that Clay's opinion of him has not suffered because of this event. "Nor need I comment on the admission of Genl. Jackson's insufficiency for his station, as evinced by the desire of his partisans to catch at any phrase however equivocal coming from an officer of the late Admin., that may be turned to his advantage."

Comments on the destructiveness of Jackson's policy of proscription and thinks it will surely damage him before the next presidential election. Believes that in the New York state elections in the autumn "it will be the policy of the opponents of the present Administration to avail themselves of some local questions, instead of meeting the whole force of the Jackson party." Speculates that such a local question might be "a law proposed by Mr. Van Buren, when Governor, making all the Banks in the State in a measure responsible for each other." Notes the unpopularity of that proposal in New York City and thinks it will "afford an opportunity" politically there. Mentions that he may run for the senate of New York. ALS. DLC-HC (DNA, M212, R3). Jonathan Elliot had been editor of the Washington *City Gazette* until 1827 [6:572-74]. For Van Buren's banking bill which proposed establishment by contributions from each bank of a "safety-fund" to insure the notes of all banks, see Edward M. Shepard, *Martin Van Buren* (Boston, 1890), 144-45. See also Porter to Clay, March 30, 1834.

From HENRY CLAY, JR.　　　　　　　West Point, N.Y., September 1, 1829

I arrived here on the 28th Ultimo, the day specified in my furlough; and have already commenced study. My course of this year will be by far more difficult, and will therefore require much stricter application, than those of the preceding years: It embraces Mechanics, Natural Philosophy, Chemistry, Pencil Drawing & Topography or Pen Drawing.

I am now glad that I came back. I feel that I shall be pleased with the studies to be pursued this year and the next. Good fortune had again favoured me. Last night an officer in my class was reduced to the ranks and at parade by an order of Col [Sylvanus] Thayer I was appointed in his place—The office that I have obtained is an excellent one, and although it is not so elevated in point of rank, still on account of the privileges attached to it I think it is preferable to the one that I should have had, had I not gone on furlough. That, that I now enjoy is Colour bearer to the Battalion of Cadets.

When in Lexington I forgot to suscribe any thing for the benefit of the Union Society.[1] If you would present 5 or 10 Dol's in my name you would much oblige me.

ALS. Henry Clay Memorial Foundation, Lexington, Ky.　　　1. Union Philosophical Society of Transylvania University.

To HENRY CLAY, JR.　　　　　　　Lexington, September 3, 1829

I received your letter dated on board the Steam boat near Pittsburg[h], on the 21st. Ulto. narrating the numerous mishaps that occurred to you, in ascending the river. If you had disembarked at the mouth of Guyandotte you would have avoided them all, although you might have encountered others on that route.

I rejoice to learn that you are becoming satisfied about West Point. I hope that this letter will find you entirely reconciled to it. Desiring nothing more ardently than your success in life, and believing that it will greatly conduce to it, if you continue at the Point, I naturally feel much solicitude concerning it. Still, as I have repeatedly said to you, I do not wish to force you to remain there. You are now old enough to think correctly and act for yourself. My opinions I wish you to receive not as commands but as advice flowing from one who loves you much, and who possesses no other advantage over you than that of having lived some what longer.

Anne [Brown Clay Erwin] leaves here this day week. I shall go with her to Russellville [Ky.]. She and your mother are now in Woodford [Ky.]. All are well, except that my health is not quite as good as when you left us.

ALS. Henry Clay Memorial Foundation, Lexington, Ky.

To WILLIS FIELD　　　　　　　Lexington, September 3, 1829

I received your favor of the 29h. Ulto.　I had hoped to see you at Versailles this week, but I have been disappoint[ed] in going down.

My Pensa. sheep have not yet arrived, but I expect them shortly. I have agreed with three friends to let each of them have a ewe with a ram lamb at twenty five dolla[rs] for both; and I should be glad to supply you with a pair on the same terms. I lately bought of a Mr. Atkinson[1] twelve ewes and four rams. I would let you have one of the rams and four or five of the Ewes at six dollars a piece, which is the price they cost me. I would think it might be for your interest to take one of these rams for immediate use, and the ewe and lamb from

Penasa. for future service. I have greater confidence in the Pennsa. sheep, altho' I believe those which I procured from Mr. Atkinson are full blooded and of good quality. I can furnish you with an uncommonly fine bull calf about five months old or with one about four years old. you see I can equip you in the Stock way

I think it will be best for you to come and stay a night with me, after the arrival of my Sheep, and judge for yourself. I will send you word when they come.

Copy. KyU.   1. Possibly Thomas Atkinson.

From William H. Russell, Carlisle, Ky., September 4, 1829. Explains that during "the late electioneering canvass" the Jacksonians had put out a story that he (Russell) had turned against Clay, that this story had helped defeat him in his bid for state office, and that the charge was vicious and contemptible. Says Clay is "gaining ground" in Nicholas County and throughout the state. Concludes: "I doubt not that the present course of proscriptive punishment pursued by the general administration will be sufficient in one or two years more to produce a total change." Believes Clay's "cause will by no means abate," and gives assurance that he will firmly support Clay. ALS. DLC-HC (DNA, M212, R3). For Russell and his later connection with Clay, see *DAB*. Russell was defeated in his bid for the Nicholas County seat in the Kentucky house of representatives by incumbent James Parks. Ky. H. of Reps., *Journal* . . . 1829-1830, p. 4. He won the seat in the 1830 canvass. In 1831, he migrated to Missouri.

From Elisha Whittlesey, Canfield, Ohio, September 4, 1829. Comments on the political news contained in Clay's letter to him of August 6 in a manner reflecting and supporting Clay's own opinions. Believes that since Clay's friends have captured control of the Kentucky General Assembly, they should pass "one, or more resolutions expressive of the confidence they have in You personally," and in the "measures You have so long advocated"; but doubts "the propriety of making any nomination this winter either in this State [Ohio] or in Kentucky." Fears that a majority in the Ohio legislature will favor Jackson even though there "never has been a time, (and I trust never will be,) when a majority of the inhabitants of this State have really thought that Gen Jackson was fit for the Office he holds."

Thinks it "a remarkable fact" that when a man "became soured" on his neighbor, family, or church he was "sure to support Gen Jackson, the better to satisfy his revenge—" Explains further: "The [William H.] Crawford party supported him [Andrew Jackson] to be revenged on You, because You did not aid them by the weight of Your influences. The [John C.] Calhoun party supported him, because they supposed that it would insure the election of Mr Calhoun after four Years—Mr [Martin] Van Buren and his friends supported him, because Mr [John Q.] Adams did not send Mr Van Buren to England, and he was sure of being rewarded if Gen Jackson was elected. [Mordecai M.] Noah and a host of other Editors supported him, because Mr Adams did not purchase them up—And altho but little is said in favor, of Gen Jackson, the public mind is not settled as to any measures to be adopted here after. The Jackson party not having had a majority in our Legislature, the leaders will use all their exertions to obtain a majority this fall, in order to fill some important appointments in the Supreme Court. Our friends are comparatively supine and inactive. If however we shall be able to carry a majority, it will be a very small one and too small to have much influence abroad. My opinion is, that time should be given for Mr Calhoun and Mr Van Buren to strive for the mastery, before any public demonstration is made. Judge [John] McLean's influence here is very considerable, and whatever may be his own feelings, many of his friends profess to support the present administration."

As for choosing a vice presidential candidate for the 1832 campaign, argues that if it is to be a Pennsylvanian, Henry Baldwin of Pittsburgh would make a stronger candidate than Richard Rush, especially "among those who control the lower classes of people." Were McLean to run for that office "it would settle the question" so far as Ohio is concerned. Does not think Samuel L. Southard would be a propitious choice, since "It is to be hoped that New Jersey will be invulnerable against the Jackson fever the second time" without having to put Southard on the ticket to assure that result. Has heard the name of Governor Samuel Bell of New Hampshire mentioned as a possible New England vice presidential candidate, but notes that Bell is "not in favor of internal improvements, or rather, he denies, that the general government has the power, to construct them—"

Concludes with the observation that the tariff is not being collected in Charleston, S.C., by the customs officers there and that this evasion of the law should become known. "There is no doubt but the manufactures of the country are going down—" ALS. DLC-HC (DNA, M212, R3). In the autumn election for the Ohio legislature, the Jacksonians won control of the senate by a margin of 21 to 15 but were out-numbered in the house 40 to 32. *Niles' Register* (November 7, 1829), 37:165. For Samuel Bell, see *DAB*.

To FRANCIS T. BROOKE
Lexington, September 5, 1829

I recd. both your favors of the 11h. July and 4h. Ulto. to which I should have sooner replied but for my absence from home, and that I did not suppose there was any urgency in my transmitting a reply.

On public affairs I have but little to say, in addition to what you will find in the public prints. The result of our Elections to the legislature of K. gives a decided majority, beyond all doubt, to our friends in both of its branches. The people of this State would tomorrow give a different decision from what they did in November last, upon the same state of the question on which they then acted, that is a contest between the same parties. The manner in which the power of patronage has been exercised has dissatisfied thousands of those who voted for Jackson. There is a large class of his supporters who now avow that their opposition was to Mr. Adams and not to me. The same distinction is taken in other Western States. I have every reason to be satisfied with the state of things in Kentucky. Whether any measure, in relation to myself, will be adopted at the next Session of our Legislature, and if any what its character may be, will depend upon intervening events, and upon consultation among my friends after they assemble at the seat of Government.

I hardly know what to say about your land near Madisonville. It would afford me much pleasure to render you any assistance in my power, but I am afraid to assume any direction about it lest I should not be able to do what might be necessary. The land is remote from me, and it would be as difficult for me to attend to the tenanting or processioning of it, as it would be for you to perform the same operations on a tract of land in Franklin [Va.], or Pittsylvania [Va.]. I have great confidence in [Robert] Triplett, and I think when you hear from him he will account satisfactorily for his silence. My personal acquaintance in that quarter is very limited. I shall set out, in a few days, on a trip to Russellville, and perhaps I may meet with some one, during the performance of it, who may give me useful information in regard to your land. And I will bear the subject in mind, so as to make enquiries when opportunities shall occur. But I must advise that you would rely more particularly on some one residing nearer the land than I do.

If it has no intruder upon it, you are in no danger. But if there be any person settled on it claiming under an adverse title, it may be necessary for you to adopt measures, by bringing suit or otherwise, to prevent the operation of the

Law of this State commonly called the 7 years limitation law.[1] According to that law, a peaceable & undisturbed possession during seven years, under a title derived from the State, protects the occupant against any out standing adverse claim. I need not tell you that the validity of the Law is controverted; but it is wise not to be obliged to depend upon that plea exclusively. . . .

ALS. KyU. Printed in Colton, *Clay Correspondence*, 4:242-43.   1. William Littell and Jacob Swigert, *Digest of the Statute Law of Kentucky* (Frankfort, Ky., 1822), 2:721-22.

From Joseph Ficklin, Lexington, September 5, 1829. Submits, in an enclosure, an itemized list of Clay's account with the Lexington post office for the quarter July 1 to September 30, 1829. The list shows that Clay subscribed by mail to the following newspapers, which came to him postage due: Washington *Daily National Intelligencer*; Washington *Daily National Journal*; a "Hagerstown [Md.] paper [Mail]"; Lowell *Massachusetts Journal*; Boston *Sentinel*; *New Hampshire Sentinel*; Natchez (Miss.) *Ariel*; Cincinnati *Daily Gazette*; Columbus (Ohio) *Gazette*; a "Martinsburgh [*sic*] V[a]. paper [Martinsburg (W. Va.) *Gazette*]"; a "Stubenville [*sic*] [Ohio] paper [*Western Herald and Steubenville Gazette*]"; Richmond (Va.) *Constitutional Whig*; a "Knoxville paper [*American Whig and Knoxville Enquirer*]"; Trenton (N.J.) *True American*; Hamilton (Ohio) *Intelligencer*; Hartford, Conn. *American Mercury*; *Niles' Register*; Providence (R.I.) *Subaltern*; and the "Georgetown [Ky.] *Centinel* [*sic, American Sentinel*]." ALS. DLC-TJC (DNA, M212, R13).

A similar account for the period April 6 to July 1, 1829, includes, in addition, Frankfort *Kentuckian*, Frankfort *Commentator*, and Louisville *Focus*. *Ibid.* (R16).

From John L. Bridges, Harrodsburg, Ky., September 6, 1829. Reports that after conversations with local "new court, relief and Jackson men" it has been decided to have a large barbecue at Harrodsburg in mid-October at which it is hoped Clay will speak. Notes that a "committee composed principally of Jackson men, will address you on the Subject and request your company." Remarks that it is important that you "give us one of your best" speeches on this particular occasion. ALS. DLC-HC (DNA, M212, R3).

In a letter to Bridges dated September 12, not found, Clay accepted the invitation. Bridges wrote Clay on September 16 thanking him for his acceptance and setting October 16 as the date of the event. He informed Clay that this was not to be a Jackson or anti-Jackson rally. Instead, it was to be a pro-American System event which was being sponsored by "warm and zelous friends of both Genl. Jackson and Mr. Adams in the recent struggle." While emphasizing that the gathering was designed to have a bipartisan flavor, "your reflecting friends here have no doubt but that the proposed meeting will greatly advance your interest in this quarter—you have many new made friends in this Section, and unless I am mistaken there are now many on the 'anxious Seats'—" *Ibid.* Addressed to Clay at Bowling Green, Ky.

A public exchange of invitation and acceptance then followed. On September 29, Bridges wrote Clay formally extending the invitation. He noted that while "a majority of us voted for General Jackson at the last November election," others interested in having Clay speak included partisans of both Jackson and Adams, men who were united "in support of that System of policy emphatically denominated the 'American System.'" Copy. Printed in Lexington *Kentucky Reporter*, November 18, 1829.

Clay replied on October 6, formally accepting the invitation, and remarking that it would be a pleasure to address friends of the American System. He added: "Although it was my misfortune to differ from a majority of you, in the choice of the present Chief Magistrate of the Union, it was my anxious desire, after he was constitutionally elected, that his administration should be conducted on such principles as I could approve. If hitherto I have not, in all instances, found this to be the case, I indulge the hope that the future developements of its policy may be of a character to admit of my hearty, though humble support. Most earnestly do I wish this, in reference to the preservation of the

American System, with regard to the policy of which I have the happiness to coincide in opinion with you." *Ibid.*

For a summary of Clay's Harrodsburg speech of October 16, 1829, see *ibid.* In the course of this address, said the Lexington *Kentucky Reporter*, Clay "drew a fine picture of the practical operation of the American system—vindicated his own character against the calumny of his enemies; paid a manly tribute to the talents, integrity, industry, impartiality, forbearance and devoted habits of business of the late president [John Q. Adams]. He spoke with moderation and forbearance of the present administration, hoped that the country would prosper under its management, and that it would be supported in all its just measures."

From JOSIAH S. JOHNSTON   Washington, September 6, 1829

[Comments at length on his trip to Boston to attend commencement exercises at Harvard, the social activities related thereto, and the political views of various people with whom he talked in Massachusetts and on his way back to Washington. In conversations with Governor Levi Lincoln he learned that the Jackson administration had lost whatever appeal it had initially had in New England. Continues:]

He [Lincoln] Consider[e]d the fate of the admn. as settled in N. England. & that Mr. Clay was every where looked—to as the man Capable of restoring the Government—He said the Van Buren men as far as he had learnt in N. England, were opposed to Genl. Jacksons Continuance a second term—They said they understood that he had given what was equal to a pledge, not to Serve longer than four years. . . .

He desired to know how & When you would be brought out in Nomination   I told him you Would be at a proper time put in nomination, but I was not informed When or Where—that better information Would be had after the Ky Elections—I thought it very probable, the Legislature of Kentucky, would at the Next or the Session after put you in Nomination—But it would be impossible to Controul the Legislatures of all the states—they might act of their own accord & Without Concert—I s[ai]d I did not think it very important. Mr. Clay is now Considerd by every body & by both parties as a Candidate & he Would not have the power to withdraw himself—The public attention is drawn upon him now More intensely than upon any Man at any former period—He is the Candidate by Common assent & by a Will higher than the Will of State Legislatures—The Nomination of the [Ky.] Legislature will have the effect in Case of doubt to assure the other States of their Support—but the opinion of the N. England States is Well Known abroad as if there Was an express declaration of the Legislature. I told him I thought You would Carry six Western States in addition to the four of Mr. Adams.[1] That a Legislative declaration from these States Would be desirable, at as early a period as it Could be obtain[e]d—without any risque as an assurance for the Northern States, that they might rally with Confidence upon you—The Govr. said he had intentionally abstain[e]d from any topic of that Nature in his Messages—I promised to give him information.—The Nominations in the West will afford the best evidence of your strength but nothing Must be hazzarded, by a premature attempt—There must be great discretion & Caution—time will bring all things right—If Kentucky will redeem herself, by a magnanimous Course, her example will be felt & followed but it will be better to wait a year than to incur the risque of a failure or even a doubtful issue—You

95

are on the spot to regulate all that. The Govr. asked me What Course would be persued Next Winter—Which I explain[e]d as far as I knew & particularly my own views. . . .

Maine is safe—You have seen the manifesto put forth there—it has been published in the journal I think.[2] At Providence I saw Mr. [Asher] Robbins & Mr. [Nehemiah R.] Knight. They have just terminated a very interesting Contest, but in a very triumphant Manner for Burgess [*sic*, Tristam Burges] & [Dutee J.] Pearce & our friends—[3]The N. England States & the friends of the Tarif[f] look[e]d with some anxiety to the Conflict   The Jackson Men had the folly to attempt to avail themselves of the Manufacturing distress to Create a party, in opposition to the Tarif—The period was propitious—& Considerable alarm Was felt—but the triumph was Compleat—Duff Green had been there & no doubt the plan Was organized—I send you some of the publications that grew out of the occasion—

[Concludes with details of his journey on to Washington via New York and Trenton. Reports that Washington "looks like the City of the dead." Mentions in a postscript that the "Article in the Monthly Magazine Boston on Mr. Clay is from the pen of [Daniel] Webster it is clear [and] strong . . . [and] will [be] republished in all the papers."][4]

AL. InU.   1. Reference obscure.   2. A convention of Clay and Adams supporters in Maine met and adopted an address which condemned the Jackson administration, accusing it of unconstitutional actions and calling on all good men to raise their voices against such action. Louisville *Public Advertiser*, Sept. 5, 1829.   3. Robbins and Knight were senators from Rhode Island; Burges and Pearce were reelected to Congress from that state. *Niles' Register* (Nov. 14, 1829), 37:181.   4. This laudatory sketch of Clay's life, entitled "Mr. Clay," appeared in the *American Monthly Magazine* (August, 1829), 1:341-46 and was reprinted in the Washington *Daily National Journal*, Sept. 16, 1829.

From S. Newton Dexter, Whitesborough, N.Y., September 9, 1829. Sends Clay, on behalf of the stockholders of Oriskany Manufacturing Company, a piece of broadcloth. "Knowing the interest you feel in behalf of the manufacturers of this country," would like to be able to supply an encouraging account of the company's progress, but "This I cannot do." Continues: "We certainly cannot sustain ourselves unless we receive all the protection we are fairly entitled to under the last Tariff. A remedy should be found against the gross frauds practised at some of our principal Custom Houses, and the 'dollar minimum' we think should be stricken out." Hopes "that the nation may one day see what are its true interests, and who are its real friends." Copy. Printed in *Niles' Register* (December 5, 1829), 37:229-30.

Clay replied on October 28, 1829, thanking Dexter and the stockholders for the cloth which "would bear advantageous comparison with the best piece of French broad cloth." The pleasure in receiving it, however, "is not so lively as it would have been, if their establishment and the other woollen manufactories of the United States were in a flourishing condition." Adds: "If existing laws were fairly executed, facilities to foreigners in the sale of their merchandise subjected to proper restrictions, the dollar minimum repealed, and the raw wool not produced in our country were allowed to be imported at a moderate duty, I have no doubt that our woollen manufactories would immediately revive and prosper. I sincerely wish that the next session of Congress may not terminate without the adoption of some, if not all, of these measures." *Ibid.*; also Washington *Daily National Journal*, December 2, 1829. For the "dollar minimum" problem, see Brown to Clay, October 23, 1829.

To CHARLES HAMMOND   Lexington, September 9, 1829
I wrote you a letter three or four weeks ago [August 12] of a confidential nature, just before I left home for the Olympian Springs, and as I have not heard of

your receiving it I entertain some fear that it may not have reached you. How is your P. Office? Is the P.M. worthy of confidence?

Your paragraph[1] purporting that no nomination will be made this winter, and hinting at the possibility of Mr. McL. [John McLean] being brought out, has produced much agitation among friends. What effect it has had among opponents I cannot tell. I have received several letters about it, and I have seen various articles in friendly papers concerning it. Mr. [Philip R.] Fendall writes: "Some anxiety has arisen in Maryland from an article of Mr. Hammond announcing most positively that you will not be nominated in the West next Winter. . . . . . . I was utterly astonished at it . . . I took it for granted that he had some good, however incomprehensible at this distance, reason for it. Some think that he is seriously turning his attention to Mr. McLean, but it cannot be true. . . . .

"On the point of nomination it is obvious that the sooner it can be prudently made, the sooner that organization will take place which, in the state to which the Jackson party has reduced the public mind, is essential to the triumph of good principles. Mr Hammond may rest assured that a *Western pledge* to procrastinate the nomination too long would be as bad as a premature nomination."

Mr. [John] Sergeant writes: "A legislative nomination at the next Session in Kentucky is very desirable. The next best thing is such an expression of confidence and willingness to support you, as is spoken of. If it would make any considerable difference in the vote, I should incline to take the latter. If not the former, as evincing a more determined purpose, which always has influence. The *en avant* system is felt from its own momentum. My impression is that the time has come for beginning it."

I send you these extracts that you may give them such weight as they deserve. I hope you will not, for a moment imagine, that my confidence in you has been weakened in the smallest degree. It is full, entire, and unimpaired.

On the subject of a nomination, I do not feel that I am a competent judge. I know (and I presume that you have learnt the same thing from Genl. [Joseph] Vance) that our Eastern friends in Congress expressed a strong wish last winter for early Western demonstrations. They still entertain it. My own impression was and yet is that it is best to hold ourselves free to act or not next winter under all the intervening lights that may arise; and to put ourselves in a position to act if contingencies should seem to make it advisable. Several important ones may occur, such as the President's message being in open hostility to the Tariff &c. I have received satisfactory information that he will do so.[2] The purpose may be changed, but I believe it now exists.

Kentucky stands on peculiar ground, in regard to myself. I am a Citizen of the State. An exparte trial of me before her Senate took place.[3] The result of our Congressional elections, from various local causes, is not as favorable as could have been wished. These united considerations might render it proper that K. should act in one of the modes suggested by Mr. Sergeant, although no other State should make a movement. My opinion is, on the state of things now existing, and excluding the consideration of contingencies that may hereafter arise, that it would be best for this State to adopt the latter of Mr. S's suggestions. That measure I think would unite the greatest number of votes, and would be equivalent or nearly so to the other.

If these ideas strike you as having weight, would it not be advisable to insert an article qualifying some what the universality and the positive character of your former paragraph? You might say, for example, that whilst the Western States generally might forbear to act on the question, Kentucky might feel herself called upon, from peculiar circumstances, to express her confidence in and attachment to Mr. C. She cannot be expected to regard with indifference the malignant attacks, so perse[v]eringly continued, upon his character. Having through her Senate taken up the investigation of the Bargain story she owes it to herself and to him to express her discredit of that calumny, which she has never done &c &c &c. If she remains silent, she might be supposed to be acquiescent in the story. Now that the contest is over, the public mind calm, and admitting of a deliberate examination of the past, and Mr. C. in private life, an expression of her opinion might be made with propriety &c &c —

I shall leave home tomorrow on an excursion to Russellville, which will occupy me about three weeks. I should be glad to hear from you on my return —

ALS. InU. 1. Hammond's editorial stated that "the friends of Henry Clay, have no intention of nominating him for the Presidency NEXT WINTER," and suggested that "Another man, even another Western man, may more effectually concentrate their suffrages." Cincinnati *Daily Gazette*, August 12, 1829; reprinted in Lexington *Kentucky Gazette*, Sept. 11, 1829. 2. For Jackson's Dec. 1829, speech to Congress, see *MPP*, 2:442-62. The speech was anti-tariff. 3. See 7:54.

From JOSIAH S. JOHNSTON   Washington, September 9, 1829

I have been four days in this City & a more dull & desolate place I never saw — *I do* not Know Who are most to be pitied, those Who are removed or those Who live in perpetual dread of it   They say there is a perfect system of espionage — that every thing is Carried to the Capitol — that in Consequence all are suspicious — afraid to speak & afraid to be seen together — I have seen the President, who appears in good health, but not one of his Cabinet. I have not been able to learn any thing of the relations of Men here — all here is secrecy & Mystery — The [Washington *United States*] Telegraph last ev[en]ing, took some notice of some articles in the Boston paper, Which he ascribes to Mr. [Henry] Orne, Who is of the party of [Theodore, Jr.] Lyman [John P.] Boyd &C — These papers reflect upon Duff Green — [1] He threatens to Come out with the Correspondence — I was told *in Confidence* that Green Said that that party had offer[e]d him $20,000 to favor their views — You may look therefore to the progress of this affair — They are no doubt a Corrupt set, Who thought it fair to employ all necessary Means to obtain office —

Duff still maintains the ear of the General & his independence — We still speak, about McKinney & Dickins neither of Whom can be dispensed with — [2] He appears to hold a high & independent Course   They are all tired of him & disgusted with him but they Cannot get Clear of him — & some say he will set up an independent press, & go against such Members of the Cabinet as he can not govern.

An affair is now in agitation here Which promises some Amusement — It is much Whispered about, but the exact details can not be given — It appears as Well as I can learn, that Mr. [John N.] Campbell the Presbitiren Minister — has spoke to some of his Clerical Brethern about a Certain Lady — [3] Among others to a Notorius Jacksonian Preacher Mr. Eli [*sic*, Ezra Stiles Ely] — Who has Written the General [Jackson] on the subject — [4] Mr. Campbell Was called on by Mr. E[ly]. He Mr C. required the presence of a third person & Col. [Nathan] Towson was called — He repeated what he had said & what he had heard — The General sent for him — He repeated what he had said & refused to make any denial or explanation or apology—The General said he would be prosecuted   He replied, that that was what desired—that the truth would appear—since that E.[5] has not been at his office, but is said to be engaged in the development of the affair—has been to several persons at Alexandria—Mr. Eli has arrived from Phila. last night—& the General is determin[e]d to investigate the affair—Mr. C. is very firm, & fearless, has many friends—& will go with them through the investigation   It is s[ai]d. the Genl. has told Mr. Campbell that he was a Liar—They have left his church—Eaton[6] must be Wretched—This is about to lead to a Curious state of things—Mr. C. is strong & the Clergy will stand by him—Is it not strange that they should fix this upon Mr. C[ampbell]—When it has been a town talk so long? When neither [Samuel D.] Inghams or [John] Branchs or [John M.] Berrians [sic, Berrien] families will associate with him [Eaton]? & When the ladies of his [Jackson] own House receive him only by Compulsion?—& When Towson gave him the information, before E[aton]. was appointed. This is a private affair & not to be talked of yet—a few days will bring some thing to light. The Genl. will never give her [Peggy O'neale Eaton] up, & E[aton] will hold [on] as long as the Genl. holds to him—But it [will] be a Curious investigation—[7]

ALS. DLC-TJC (DNA, M212, R13).   1. Orne was publishing a series of essays, signed "Columbus," in the Boston *Bulletin* attacking Duff Green and others allied with the Boston *Statesman*. Green replied in the Washington *United States Telegraph* on Sept. 8, 1829: "I have read . . . the publications which have issued from the pen of Col. Orne. . . . The manner in which he has referred to the 'Jackson Republican party,' and to me, by name leaves no other alternative than the publication of so much of my private correspondence with himself, Gen. Lyman and Doctor Wm. Ingall, as will expose the *true* character of the 'Jackson Republican party' now called, and as is necessary to my vindication against his calumnies." For fuller discussion, see Darling, *Political Changes In Massachusetts*, 63-71; and Washington *Daily National Journal*, Oct. 31, 1829.   2. Possibly a reference to Asbury Dickins and Samuel McKean. Blake to Clay, April 9, 1829.   3. Mrs. John H. (Margaret O'neale Timberlake) Eaton.   4. For the roles of the Rev. Messrs. Campbell and Ely in the growing Peggy Eaton affair, see Marquis James, *Andrew Jackson, Portrait of a President* (Indianapolis, 1937), 210-13.   5. It is unclear whether he refers to John Eaton or to Ely.   6. Last four letters of "Eaton" struck through.   7. For its outcome, see James, *Jackson*, 213.

From SAMUEL L. SOUTHARD   Trenton, N.J., September 12, 1829

Yours of the 9th of Aug. reached me, a few days ago, after a very long journey, but apparently in sound condition.

I rejoice with you, in the result of your election for the State Legislature.—I hope the majority will be found to be a "practical" one—. The two propositions seem to me so nearly equal, both in their character & results, that either may be taken. If there be any difference between them, it is favor of the resolution & against an absolute nomination. But, one of them ought to be adopted. A rallying point is necessary—It should be speedily provided—This opinion is the result of my own reflections, & of communications which I have had with others, on whose Judgments I rely. Would not Ohio, or some of the other States to the West, unite with Kentucky? If a movement be made, it should be strong & decisive.

In the Eastern states there will be no serious difficulty—No one can calculate on New York—nor for the present, is there any certainty of N. Jersey—I mean as to the coming election—we cannot rouse our people to exertion yet—but of the final vote, I have no doubt. It is very possible for the enemy to obtain a majority in the next Legislature—but not such a majority as will do much harm—[1]not one that can be managed for their purposes.

So far as I hear, you are the only object — There is in this State a good feeling, and it increases —

Will Judge [John] McLean be an obstacle in the West? We are afraid of trouble from him.

Mr. [Josiah S.] Johnson [*sic*, Johnston] passed thro' here, to Washington a few days ago, leaving a note for me & promising me a visit on his return — He says he has much to tell me — & I desire greatly to see him.

The movements of [Thomas] Ritchie indicate clearly that Van Buren is his man — but if I am correctly informed, he will have great difficulty, in bringing the state to his mode of thinking. The [Va. Constitutional] Convention in October will do great good.

My confident expectation is, that Genl. J[ackson]. will not live thro' his Term — his health is very bad & I regret it — Mr. C. [John C. Calhoun] will be Pres[iden]t before the people elect him to the office.

I have a late letter from Govr. [James] Barbour — he will be here before long & promises me to stop a day or two. He has been quite "in his element" — L. L. D. at the end of his name, & put there with such a sound of trumpets, must have gratified him — [2]

A letter from Genl. Lafayette lies before me — He expresses distress at the rumor which had reached him of your having fallen in a Duel — [3]tho' he says they do not give credit to it — He is very well. — I have recd. a letter from your son Henry [Clay, Jr.] — we were disappointed in not seeing him but hope to be more fortunate at some future time.

Mrs S. has been & continues to be a good deal unwell. She is in bed. We all unite in affectionate remembrances to you, Mrs Clay & all your children.

ALS. DLC-HC (DNA, M212, R3). Letter marked "(Confidential)." 1. In the October election in New Jersey, the Jacksonians carried both houses of the state legislature by wide margins. *Niles' Register* (Oct. 24, 1829), 37:132. In the 1832 presidential election Jackson carried the state by a plurality of 360. *Presidential Elections Since 1789* (Washington, 1975), 66. 2. Before he returned home in the autumn of 1829, Oxford University awarded Barbour the D.C.L. degree. *DAB*. 3. With John Pope.

From Thomas H. Blake, Terre Haute, September 13, 1829. Reports that elections for the state legislature in Indiana are over and that while "In some parts of the State a Jackson excitement was got up & brought to bear upon the election . . . in the general no attempt of the sort was openly avowed." Announces that he himself was elected to the lower house of the general assembly, where there is "a bare majority of Jackson men of the old stamp; who, between you & Jackson might (tho' doubtful) go for him, but he being out of the way would go for you against the World." Notes that in the state senate Clay has a "decided majority, which in joint ballot secures you the majority of the Legislature." Believes that Clay has a chance to receive a presidential nomination from the Indiana General Assembly "next winter," although there would be "*some risk* in the *attempt*" because "uninstructed as we are in the views of the great body of your friends, we are at a stand, not knowing what to prepare for, what to anticipate or how we are to act in unison." Comments that there "appears to be a strange medley in the politicks of Kentucky, — the majority of the Legislature being of your friends, and in Congress an encrease of Jackson men, and it is a state of things to be regretted." Calls Clay's attention to an editorial in the Cincinnati *Gazette* of August 12 [Clay to Hammond, August 12; September 9, 1829], "on the subject of your nomination by the [Ky.] Legislature," in which the editor, Charles Hammond, "as if speaking with authority, disclaims the intention of your friends to nominate you next winter, and intimates the possibility that another Western man may be finally supported." Presumes that person is John McLean. Informs Clay that "Neither your New England interest nor the small interest you have in Pennsylvania which is notwithstanding powerful, could be got to support Mr. McLean but as a choice of evils." Says he himself could not support McLean "under any circumstances." Concludes with the request that he be told "what course your friends intend to pursue in Kentucky, and what course they desire your friends here to pursue." ALS. DLC-HC (DNA, M212, R3). In the August 3, 1829, elections for the state legislature, the Anti-Jacksonians retained control of the senate while the Jacksonians won control of the house for the first time. See Indiana *Journal*, December 8, 1829, and David Kreuger, "Party Development in Indiana, 1800-1832," Ph.D. dissertation, University of Kentucky, 1974, pp. 227-28. The Indiana legislature did not nominate Clay in the winter of 1829-30.

Russellville Speech, September 17, 1829. In an unsigned letter to the editor of the Providence (R.I.) *Advertiser*, dated Nashville, October 2, 1829, the writer reports having heard Clay's speech in Russellville on September 17. Says that Clay spoke for over an hour to a gathering of nearly 3,000, "including 200 ladies," saying in part that it was still the "honest sentiment of his heart" that the people had made the wrong choice at the last presidential election and that he himself saw "no reason to change the sentiments by which he was actuated when he gave his vote in the last Presidential contest." Without attacking the administration, vindicates himself from the aspersions cast upon his character by the president and his partisans. Also focuses on the question of the tariff and its "importance not only to the Eastern States, but the whole nation." Summary, printed in Washington *Daily National Journal*, October 29, 1829; reprinted from Providence *Advertiser*. No manuscript text of Clay's Russellville speech has been found. Following his remarks at Russellville, Clay went to Elkton, Ky., "where he was received by 2,500 of his fellow citizens," and then traveled to Hopkinsville "where 3 to 5,000 were assembled."

On May 3, 1829, Walter Jones *et al.* had extended the invitation to Clay to speak in Russellville. Copy. Printed in Lexington *Kentucky Reporter*, June 17, 1829.

Clay replied on May 13, 1829, declining the invitation "for the present" due to "the occurence of unexpected circumstances." Promises to come "towards the close of the summer" at which time his visit could not be misinterpreted as an attempt to affect the results of the August election. *Ibid.*

From "ALEXIS DE SARCY" N.P., September 17, 1829

I[1] have a thousand things to say, many of them should be said quickly, yet must it be deferred untill *we meet*; what there is of most importance to be said, may require commentary and illustrations, may give rise to questions beyond my power to anticipate; and besides much that I would say *cannot* be written; *must not* be committed to the hazard of either the Post Office or private conveyance. Success may depend on Secrecy as much as upon judgment vigilance and industry.

May it not be necessary to recall Mr. [William B.] Rochester from Guatamala [*sic*, Guatemala]?[2] think of this—that is provided you are sure of Rochester when here.—New York is a most important point, and nothing should be left undone which can either secure or neutralise it. Rochester is said to be nearly strong enough to hold Van Buren in check, if so his presence is indispensable—they are leaders in the same party, and I know not whether you have another in that party of equal potency with Rochester. In a contest against Calhoun & Van Buren my opinion is that you would succeed; in a contest with Jackson I think differently and hence the necessity of keeping him out of the field. I am confident the party entertain the same opinions with myself on this subject and hence the effort to continue J[ackson]. another term by which time is gained for harmonizing conflicting interests, and to profit by every contingency that may be turned to account once more therefore, I repeat, let your presses disseminate far and wide the opinion that J. *cannot be a Candidate*, unless by a sacrifice of all his candor the candor of his friends and the forfeiture of pledges solemnly made to the American People that he would not under any circumstances serve a second term — I am not so silly as to suppose that this will deter the party from the adventure, but you will perceive the advantage to be made from it in the event that you are *compelled* to run against J.   I know that it may be employed with powerful effect in such a Contest; as you shall hear when we meet.

Calhoun cannot by any effort within his power obtain the Vote of either Pennsyla. Georgia, Alaba. Mississi. or Louisiana, and I think you have a better chance for these Votes than V. B. [Van Buren] except of Georgia, in that State prejudices are very strong against you, and every, topic *is urged*, has been, and will continue to be employed to render you — odious to that community — nothing but a reaction of public opinion on the subject of the tariff can redeem you there.

Every effort should be made to separate Pennsyla. &c N. York from J. and I greatly mistake if the next Session of Congress does not afford facilities for such an event — Be ready to profit by every contingency which the next six months may present you. The Presidt. cannot, will not, nay he dare not desert the South, and during the heat of the Contest between the friends and enemies of the Tariff the manufacturing States will have abundant proof unless I greatly err that no reliance can be placed on the Admn.

The Presidt. feels confident that should he sustain the Eastern or Manufacturing policy, he would lose in Virga. No. Cara. So. Carola. Georga. Alabama Louisa. Mississi. without gaining any thing in N. York — he prefers therefore hazarding Pennsyla. relying on [Samuel D.] Ingham [George] Wolf &ca &ca. to suffering the defection of the whole South — I think however that next winter will prove it wanting a decision and energy as a Statesman although abundant in these qualities as a Warrior, and by this very defect I look to see him lose South & East by trimming between both — mark me! he will trim, be you watchful, be you ready, and much may be done; all your friends should be prepared, be on the alert, and seize every favorable event as it is developed for advancing your interest — for depressing the Adversary which is the same thing. I shall be on the spot, and so far as one individual can go, will not lose the occasion for rendering service — When we meet, remind me to tell you of Van Buren, you shall hear of what you would little expect. It is said you will visit Louisiana & Mississi. in the spring if you do so, it should not be sooner than April else I may miss seeing you which is all important to ulterior operations, untill feby. perhaps March shall be on *my tour*, and by the latter month, may be in Louisville or Cincinnati where we must have an interview and consultation — if it be decided that Judge [John] McLean must be the Candidate, I will not desert the cause,[3] although I shall give *you* up reluctantly, and the more so, as I consider you the strongest *every way*. Do not commit me *to any one in any way* — our correspondence is confidential and sacred, and my *most important* services can be rendered only whilst I remain in secret — whilst I so remain, my access to Cabinet secrets is free and certain; discover me, and the avenue is immediately closed.

102

A gentleman takes charge of this who will deliver it personally if you are in the South of Kentucky as reported, if you are not he will drop it in some Post Office there. The bearer knows nothing of me.

Don't fail to be ready with the protest and manifests by the Kentucky Legislature — be sure that they are skillfully framed; temperate but energetic and pointed — decorous but keen and pungent, as language can make them. — I find most, nay nearly all, the J. men agreeing with me that he cannot with propriety be a Candidate again — and that if he is, he deserves to be abandoned. — This is my text, and so far I am successful in laying the foundation for future operations,

ALS. DLC-HC (DNA, M212, R3). Enclosed in an envelope postmarked Sept. 21, which was addressed to Maj. John Tilford, president of Lexington Office, Bank of the United States, with the request: "Deliver the enclosed to its address." Entrusted to unknown bearer with the instructions outlined in paragraph six of the letter itself. Not finding Clay in "the South of Kentucky," the bearer posted it in Russellville, Ky., on Nov. 5, 1829.   1. The identity of "Alexis de Sarcy," an assumed name, is not known. He had written Clay on Sept. 6 informing him that he had important information to communicate and telling him he would soon "hear from me under cover to some friend in Lexington. In that dispatch you will learn the mode of communicating with me." ALS. DLC-HC (DNA, M212, R3). On Feb. 11, 1830, de Sarcy again wrote Clay (see below). The tone of the letter, postmarked in Huntsville, Ala., Feb. 12, as well as a notation on it (probably by Calvin Colton), indicates that he was well known to Clay.   2. Reference obscure, because Rochester had already returned to the United States. See 7:473.   3. Word "you" struck through and "the cause" substituted.

From HENRY CLAY, JR.

West Point, N.Y., September 18, 1829

I recd your favour of the 3d inst.   I am glad to be able to write in answer to a portion of it that I am not only satisfied about West Point but in fact am so well persuaded that advantages closely connected with my future welfare may result from the continuation of my Academic course that nothing would now induce me to leave this place — My dear father your kindness & indulgence has convinced me that I have greatly erred and that I cannot too soon ask your forgiveness of my offence — When I wished to act in direct opposition to your decided advice by not returning to West Point, my unwillingness to return did not arise from any obstinacy of opinion as to the utility of the Course of this School, but merely from a sanguineneses of success which so often leads young men to suppose that they are as competent to contend against the difficulties of the law at 18 years of age as they will be at any future time   However all this has passed by and I am now completely submissive — You tell me that you wish me to receive your opinions, not as commands, but as advice — Yet I must consider them as commands doubly binding for they proceed from one so vastly my superior in all respects and to whom I am under such great obligations that the mere intimation of an opinion will be sufficient to govern my conduct.

I have to study very hard, with the exception of about two hours and a half in which time we take our meals, I am in the Recitation rooms or drawing Acady or am studying from 5 o clock in the morning until 9½ at night — I am a little apprehensive that my eyesight will be injured — However I shall take precautions against it — If you have time I should be delighted to hear from you frequently. . . .

ALS. Henry Clay Memorial Foundation, Lexington, Ky. Printed in Colton, *Clay Correspondence*, 4:241-42.

From William L. Brent, Georgetown, D.C., September 19, 1829. Reports on the politics of "this part of our Country." Believes Maryland will give "a good account of herself at the October elections" for the U.S. House even though "for a time the publications in [Charles] Hammond's Cincinnati paper [*Daily Gazette*] startled our friends [Blake to Clay, September 13, 1829]." Calls particular attention to three races: William Price, "a warm friend of yours," of Hagerstown vs. "that ungrateful fellow" [Michael] Sprigg; Dr. [Benedict J.] Semmes vs. [John C.] Weems; and "a decided friend of yours" vs. E[phraim]. K. Wilson, "from the eastern shore." Is convinced that "should we succeed in these *three* elections there will be a large majority of the members in Congress from Maryland opposed to the present administration." Feels confident that the Maryland state legislature "will be decidedly opposed to Genl Jackson & his party and ready to adopt any measure which may be deemed prudent and expedient by our party."

In his conversations with the "heads of the different Departments" in Washington he has discovered "that they all believe *no other* Candidate than Genl Jackson could successfully oppose you for the next Presidency—" Notes, further, that Martin Van Buren "in my presence never speaks against you and I think at heart, he hates Calhoun. . . . In such men I have no confidence, but should not be astonished to find him going against the present 'powers' if all do not unite to worship him—He certainly is playing a deep game."

Relates at length the story of the role of clergymen John N. Campbell and Ezra Stiles Ely in the growing social isolation of Peggy O'neale Eaton [Johnston to Clay, September 9, 1829] and President Jackson's opinion of them. Comments: "it is disgraceful to the nation to have such goings on!—What a scene for the cabinet of our Country to be engaged in!" Compares the moral conduct of Mrs. Eaton with that of H[enry] Lee of Virginia. Has been told that Catherine Murray (Mrs. Richard) Rush and her sister, Anna Murray Mason, the wife of General John T. Mason, "and all their families visit and receive visits from Mrs Eaton—I give these things to you in confidence, only to shew You what kind of beings there are in this world."

Asks Clay to assist in building up the subscription list of the Washington *Daily National Journal* in the West. "That paper has stood by us in all times and under all circumstances and we owe it much. . . . we ought to rally upon one paper and give it strength for next winter—[Joseph] Gales & [William W.] Seaton wait for the wind and the current we cannot confide in them—He who is not for us in every thing in these times is at heart against us—It will not do to let them Know that we Suspect them, but at this moment when every exertion ought to be made, it is difficult to get them to publish any thing—!"

Warns Clay to write him only at Piscataway in Prince Georges County, Md., rather than at Washington or Georgetown, because "I have no confidence in the Postoffice and believe your letters would be opened." Notes that this letter will be mailed to Clay from Hagerstown, Md. ALS. DLC-HC (DNA, M212, R3). Letter marked "(Confidential)." In Maryland district 2 (Anne Arundel and Prince Georges counties), Semmes defeated Weems. In district 4 (Washington, Frederick, and Allegheny counties) Sprigg defeated Price. In district 8 (Somerset and Worcester counties) Wilson was reelected, unopposed. In the state elections the Anti-Jacksonians defeated the Jacksonians 40-39 in house of delegates seats; however, the Jacksonians controlled the senate, 11-4. See *Niles' Register* (October 17, 1829), 37:122. For the scandal involving Henry Lee and his wife's sister, see Douglas S. Freeman, *R. E. Lee, A Biography* (New York, 1947), 1:98, and Claude Bowers, *The Party Battles of the Jackson Period* (New York, 1922), 82-83.

Hopkinsville Speech, September 21, 1829. After thanking the people for their cordiality and friendship, explains the motives for his acceptance of their invitation—"a desire to vindicate his character from the foul aspersions which had been cast upon him," and a desire to explain the policies of the previous administration "which had been denounced as wild and visionary projects." Explaining the reasons he voted for Adams rather than Jackson in 1824, notes that his opinions "of General Jackson had been frankly expressed in his speech on the Seminole War—that he deemed him unfit for civil rule—"

Discusses the accomplishments and policies of the Adams administration—the public debt was diminished, the Navy and forts improved, and commercial interests enlarged. Observes that the failure to open trade with the British West Indies resulted from Britain's contemptuous rejection of a U.S. proposal for mutual reciprocity in that trade. Explains that the failure of the Panama Mission resulted from intrigues carried on by the Latin American Republics themselves, but that "the grand object of the mission was the promotion of commerce."

Referring to "the calumny and detraction" which had been used against him, asks "why . . . was this unceasing torrent of abuse and vituperation poured upon his devoted head? Why should they now, that he was in retirement and private life, continue to annoy his domestic comfort and peace, by their unabated fury of attack?—he had no army marching to the city to drive the public functionaries from their seats—but, says he, the reason is, Mordecai the Jew still sits at the King's gate."

Speaks of the American System, saying that the tariff and internal improvements are "the best means of securing political independence and domestic security." Warns, however, that "Southern demagogues" threaten to "resist and subvert" the American System "by physical force." Summary printed in Washington *Daily National Journal,* October 31, 1829; also Lexington *Kentucky Reporter,* October 14, 1829. No manuscript text of Clay's remarks have been found. The speech, delivered at 11:00 a.m., was said to have been heard by "at least 4,000 persons." The "Mordecai the Jew" reference could be taken to refer to Mordecai M. Noah.

From Joniah Whitaker *et al.,* Providence, R.I., September 21, 1829. Send Clay specimens of four types of combs made at their factory, on "a carved Tortoise shell, made expressly for Mrs. Clay." Note that their company, the "Clayville Comb Factory," while "yet in infancy," employs 80 "hands" and annually produces $60,000 worth of combs for sale in the U.S. Note, further, that their "raw materials consisting principally of Horn," are imported in the amount of $22,000, a sum on which they pay a 15 percent ad valorem duty. Bring this information to Clay's attention and send him the sample combs "as a tribute of respect to Your private worth and important public Services," and because he is the "fast friend and able and zealous advocate of the American System." LS. DLC-HC (DNA, M212, R3) Letter also signed by Oliver Taylor, Peter G. Taylor, and William Easter. Clayville is in present-day Providence County, Rhode Island.

From Edward Bates, St. Louis, September 23, 1829. Invites Clay to visit Missouri in order to greet his many political friends there. "I am not singular in supposing that your presence in this State for a short time, would encourage & sustain your friends, confirm the waverings, and draw over many from the ranks of your enemies. Let it not be objected that your visit here would draw upon you the malicious virulence of your enemies. That storm has spent its force; but if it had not, it is impossible for you to avoid it, unless you retire to a cell, & abandon the world forever. You cannot now move from one county to another, without encountering the abuse of those whose slanders spring from their fears." ALS. DLC-HC (DNA, M212, R3).

From Christopher Hughes, Brussels, September 23, 1829. Assures Clay of his continuing affection and loyalty and comments at length on his own many qualities of character and intelligence and on his disappointment in losing his job when Jackson replaced Adams. Says he knows very little about the political issues that divide people at home. "I have never studied them." Thinks of himself "as an officer in foreign service" obliged to follow the instructions of his superiors in the State Department or resign if those instructions do not comply with his judgment or conscience. Reminds Clay "how heartily I cooperated with *ye all,* in sustaining the objects & march of our foreign policy" during the Adams administration. Comments at length on the many virtues of John

Quincy Adams, who thinks so highly of him [Hughes], and who recently advised him to "make Friends with disappointment, and wait for calmer times. Think of me always as your Friend."

Blames his removal from office by the Jacksonians on Albert Gallatin's hostile "interference" when the new administration was considering continuing him in his post and when the Senate was debating his reappointment in the period December, 1828-February, 1829. "*God damn Him*, for a false old Traitor. . . . his undermining, his snake like society deprives me of my fortune, by first deposing me of my fame. . . . He assailed me in my profession & in the delicate points of talents, competency & fitness for office, he desported & defamed me . . . & if I ever forgive him, why I'll be d___nd." Reveals that he learned of Gallatin's hypocritical opposition to him from his father-in-law, U.S. Senator Samuel Smith of Maryland, who wrote to him on January 2, 1829, that "Gallatin is talked of, and to his interference, I am persuaded, you owe the present opposition." Concludes with a vigorous attack on the character and competence of his replacement in Brussels, William Pitt Preble. ALS. DLC-HC (DNA, M212, R3).

On October 20 Hughes wrote Clay that he had left the "foregoing unfinished on my table . . . for a month" while debating whether to send it. Admits that "there is more ardor than dignity, in its terms & temper," but has decided to send it anyway. Asks Clay, however, "to *burn* it, after you shall have read it." Resumes his attack on Gallatin's "treachery . . . for I know, that he said, in drawing Rooms at Washington when my name Was before the Senate, that I was not fit to be a minister." Thanks Clay for his "kindly & honourable testimony in my behalf at that time." Boasts that from "one end of Europe to another" his reputation "places me in the first class of diplomatists." Vows that if the Jackson administration offers him a job, as they say they will, he will not take it at the chargé d'affaires rank, because clearly he deserves to be a minister. Informs Clay that he and Adams should have sent him to Brussels in the rank of minister in 1826 and that their "motives for not doing it" had never been satisfactorily explained. *Ibid*.

From Anonymous, Little Falls, N.Y., September 25, 1829. Informs Clay that he has many friends "in this quarter" who are "anxious to behold the great champion of the American System, and the eloquent advocate of the 'Rights of Man—'" Explains to him that if he intends to visit the springs in New York State during the summer of 1830, he should, for political reasons, travel there by way of the central sections of New York and Pennsylvania. ALS. DLC-HC (DNA, M212, R3).

From William L. Brent, Georgetown, D.C., October 2, 1829. Informs Clay of a "resolution adopted at a meeting of yr friends last evening in Washington City, which will explain the nature of the association—without expressing any wish or making any nomination, (which would be very improper)." Explains that "the real object is to unite yr friends and prepare for action wherever necessary—The object also is to sustain the [Washington *Daily National*] Journal which is upon the eve of stopping for want of funds." Thinks it is important that "your friends in the *West* ought to make a nomination as early as possible this winter as the people are anxious for it in the middle and Eastern states—If not done we have to fear a division—already M'Clean [*sic*, John McLean] . . . and others we spoke of—" Reminds Clay that Jackson's early nomination by the Tennessee legislature in 1825 had helped him. Concludes with the observation that the Maryland elections on October 5 will go well, and that the Jackson party is showing signs of stress. Indeed, "it is said [John] Tyler of Virginia declares he will not vote for many of the opponents made by Genl Jackson,—If so, it will be a glorious thing—" ALS. DLC-HC (DNA, M212, R3). The resolution passed by Clay's Washington friends has not been found. The Washington *Daily National Journal* did not cease publication until January 23, 1832.

From PETER B. PORTER   Black Rock, N.Y., October 2, 1829

I ought to have written you, many months ago, but, during the forepart of the season, my time was, so much engrossed by private avocations & on superintending the construction of our harbour, that I was obliged to neglect my distant friend, until this neglect became itself—as I presume you have some times experienced.—the cause of its continuance

I write now, merely to say that our annual elections for members of the State Legislature,[1] commenced yesterday, and to apprise you that their result, whatever it may be, will afford no indication of the sentiments of the people of this state on the subject of the next presidential contest. The general opinion among the friends of the late Administration throughout the State seems to have been that we ought not, for a while at least, to attempt an organised opposition to the present one—as the effects of doing so, would be to foster a spirit of animosity against ourselves, and, at the same time, to repress the hostilities which are growing up between the different sections of the opposite party. So general has been the sentiment in favour of this neutral course that I doubt whether there are half a dozen counties in the State, where a ticket has been formed based on the political distractions, which marked the last presidential election. Another inducement to this neutral course at *present*, in this state has been produced by the "Morgan excitement"[2] which, with pure Jacksonism, or love of office (par nobile patrium) appear to be the only stimulating influences that operate upon the election. From their two factions, in opposition to each other, most of our tickets, are formed. Those of our friends who are disposed to take a part in the contest, divide between these two fractions—but most men of honor & principle keep aloof from both.

Situated as I have been, I have had an opportunity during the summer & fall, to see Gentlemen from almost every part of the Union—and I take great pleasure in assuring you that, so far as I have been able to ascertain the public sentiment from their representatives of it, our political friends, almost unanimously,—and even most of our enemies who have the candour to avow their real sentiments—concur in believing, that your chances for the station, three years hence, is decidedly superior to that of any other Candidate—not only of our own party, but of the whole field. I take it for granted that New England, will go throughout & strongly for you—and this alone will give you I think, more strength, than any other candidate can now calculate upon with certainty. As to New York (I speak of the state at large & not of the city,) you have a vast, & continually increasing, number of zealous & most respectable friends, and there is not a doubt but that, a most decided majority of our most respectable, up right & wealthy population is with you—But we have, unfortunately, a great many Irishmen, and a great many time-serving politicians. My honest opinion is that, as a candidate for the presidency, you stand much higher in the confidence & affections of the people of this State, than any other Individual, and that, if it shall appear, as the election approaches, that your chances elsewhere is good, you will unquestionably receive the vote of the State. But if a contrary impression prevail, it is possible that the fate of the election may be decided by these office seekers, of whom we have too many, and who are governed by no other principle than that of being on the strongest side. No calculations can, I presume be made, at present on the course of Pennsylvania, which is as likely, perhaps, three years hence, to go for you as for any other candidate. with the state of public sentiment in the Western & Southern States, you are much better acquainted than myself.

I beg you not to fail to make timely arrangements for visiting us next summer. a leisurely journey from Niagara to Albany & the Springs, along the [Erie] canal, & through our rich commercial & manufacturing Towns, will present so many interesting objects to a patriot as can be found in any equal distance in the U States, & make you better acquainted with an immense number of our enterprising & intelligent citizens, whom I hope you will be as much gratified to meet, as I know they will be delighted in seeing, & offering invitations & distinction to you.

Mrs P. & myself were much relieved, on learning by the papers received yesterday, that Mr & Mrs [James] Brown had arrived at New York. From the accounts we had received how persons lately arrived from Europe, we had reason [to believe] that Mrs B. would never again have the happiness to see her native land — But as the papers say nothing of her indisposition, we flatter ourselves at the belief that, if not yet entirely restored, her health is not so deplorable as her friends had cause to expect on her arrival if, indeed, she arrived at all.

ALS. DLC-HC (DNA, M212, R3).   1. In nine N.Y. senate seats contested, the Jacksonians won eight, bringing their strength to 26 of the 32-member body. In the N.Y. house races, the Jacksonians captured 92 of the 128 seats. Louisville *Public Advertiser*, Dec. 1, 1829; *Niles' Register* (Nov. 7, 1829), 37:164, 177.   2. See 7:400-401.

To **HEZEKIAH NILES**   Lexington, October 4, 1829

You have anticipated me. I intended long since to have *first* written to you, but your agreeable favor of the 24h. inst. just recd. has preceded the execution of my purpose.[1]

Your account of your visit to New England has greatly interested me. Your observations upon the character of its people are in perfect coincidence with my own. When I visited them in 1817, I was astonished at the unjust prejudices prevailing at the South against them, and I returned full of admiration and esteem for them, and of gratitude too for their kind and hospitable treatment of me. There is not a better, more moral and religious, or more enterprizing and industrious people upon earth than the descendants of the pilgrims.

I regret extremely to learn the discouraging state of our Manufactures, which you describe, and of which I have received corresponding intelligence. On the point, respecting which you consult me, that is, what is best to be done in their behalf at the next Session of Congress, I will give you my opinion with much pleasure. This opinion is of course expressed in ignorance of the actual measures which may be attempted to injure them, by the party of the present Administration. Those measures, if I knew them, might have the effect of some modification of my present judgment.

I think our policy, under existing circumstances, should be limited to two general objects:

1st. To maintain all that has been heretofore done in support of the Tariff. And

2dly. To give effect — complete effect — to existing laws by supplemental enactments.

As to the first. If you allow any breach in the existing system, that is any repeal or reduction of duties now imposed, you endanger the whole. The consequence of such modifications would be to produce combinations between those whose parts of the Union might be affected by such repeal or reduction, and those who are opposed to all protection. I know that the Tariff of 1828, in some of its provisions, bears hard upon Navigation; but then it is very favorable, or, which is the same thing, is believed to be so, to the West. The West will be the great point of struggle between the two parties. At present the support of the West to the Tariff (including K.) is strong ardent and sincere; but it results more from a conviction of the general utility of the policy, than from any local interest which the West *now* has in its maintenance.

Under the second head.   I would recommend the passage of laws to enforce the system as it now exists; to detect and prevent frauds; and to regulate auctions.[2]

It strikes me that it would not be politic to attempt at the next Session more than I have suggested. Should we successfully resist the attacks of the adversary, and maintain our present ground, that alone will give some moral encouragement. It will be seen that the policy of the Nation is firmly settled, and our Manufactures will take fresh courage. If the auxiliary laws, mentioned under the second head, can also be passed, a great deal will have been accomplished.

I have not time to enlarge. You must fill up the sketch.

I have just returned from an extensive excursion through the Southern part of our State; and I can answer, with full & entire confidence, for the hearty support of this State to the American System, at present. An overwhelming majority of the people are with us, and so our members of Congress will be obliged to vote. But several of them (including both our Senators)[3] are not true to the faith, and want only a pretext to abandon us. Any reduction of duties benefiting the West (which are principally those on Hemp, Cotton bagging, Iron and Spirituous Liquors) would furnish that pretext.

Our friends have a decided majority in both branches of our General Assembly. I think it probable that they will pass resolutions approving of the American System and Internal Improvements, and deprecating any abandonment of the policy.

From what I can learn, they will do nothing, in regard to myself, that you or other friends can deem indiscreet. Something I believe they will do. But, unless events hereafter happening shall otherwise recommend, they will make no nomination. Such events may possibly occur; but if they do not, they will probably restrict themselves to some expressions of confidence, attachment &c.

In respect to opposition to the present Admon, I think we ought not to go ahead, if I may use that Steamboat term, but that it ought to be pari passu with *cause* of opposition. If we are silent, when patriotic duty urges us to speak out, our silence will be construed into acquiescence; and this presumed acquiescence will discourage both our friends & the better part of our opponents willing to come to us. To prevent that discouragement, and to preserve and augment our strength we must raise a banner.

But I concur with you in thinking that what may be proper for my friends may not be proper for me. I wished to have concluded my meeting large masses of my fellow Citizens by that which took place [May 16, 1829] at Fowler's garden; but I have found it impossible to decline all. They have placed, in some instances, their invitations upon such ground as to leave me no alternative. I have declined many more than I have accepted. In all my late addresses I have confined myself either to a defence of the prominent measures of the late Admon and myself, or to a consideration of the American System and Internal Improvements. They have been well received by both parties and I persuade myself have done some good.

I have the [*Niles'*] Register from the 1st. to the 34h. Volume inclusive, with the exception of the 31st. I wish you to send me that and all you publish after the 34h and tell me how I shall remit you the price.

I am glad to hear that my little namesake[4] has passed the difficult process of teething. God bless and preserve him!

Do not be surprized if you see, without naming you, an extract from your letter published respecting your tour to New England. If I publish it, no body will be committed, and I shall do it to effect good. . . . P. S. Give my best respects to Mr. [Matthew] Carey when you see him; and you are at liberty to shew this letter in confidence to him or other discreet friends.

ALS. MeHi. Letter marked "(Confidential)."   1. Letter of Sept. 24 not found; but likely it included a solicitation of the political views Clay expresses herein.   2. For the auction problem, see John Bach McMaster, *A History of the People of the United States, From the Revolution to the Civil War* (New York, 1908), 4:341-46.   3. John Rowan and George M. Bibb.   4. See 7:544-45.

From David L. Child, Boston, October 5, 1829. Reports "a most extraordinary & distressing" situation in the economy of "this part of the country." Explains: "All suffer from the stagnation of business & the general shock which credit has received, but none half so much as the manufacturers. They have nearly without except[ion] made a dead loss of *50 per cent* on their investments." Believes that losses in Boston alone will total $15,000,000. Blames the problem on "the mad spirit of competition" and asks Clay for "an article or two from your pen" on possible remedies, because no "man can separate so well as you that wh[ich] is essential & inherent in the system from that which is accidental & temporary." ALS. DLC-HC (DNA, M212, R3). For an explanation of the depression in cotton and woolen textiles, as well as the effect of tariff legislation on that industry, see Albert S. Bolles, *The Financial History of the United States From 1789 to 1860* (3rd ed., New York, 1891), 368-412.

To JOSIAH S. JOHNSTON   Lexington, October 5, 1829
I received with great thankfulness your several interesting communications from Northampton [Mass.], which shall be returned as you desire. I have also recd. your last favor, without date, from Washington. I have perused with great attention these several letters. The contents of some of them are highly curious.

I envy you your pleasures at Boston. How much should I have been delighted, if I could have shared them with yourself and Mrs. J.

I have just returned from my dreaded tour to the Southern part of this State. I went as far as Hopkinsville. Mr. and Mrs. [James] Erwin and four or five ladies from Mississippi accompanied me to Russellville — From that point they proceeded to Nashville. The tour was full of gratification. Every sort of enthusiastic demonstration of friendship and attachment, on the part of the people, was made towards me. Barbacues, Dinners, Balls &c &c. without number. I have been really in danger of that gout, with which I have been threatened by some of the Jackson party. And tell Mrs. J. that if I had a younger heart that also would have been in danger amidst the blaze of beauty in the State of Green River. I thought the men and women too would devour me. I devoured many of their good dishes at their numerous festivals.

In spite of all my prudence, which nobody I am sure will question, I was forced to speak often and long. At Russellville and Hopkinsville I spoke upwards of three hours together to at least 3000 persons at each place.[1] My addresses were never better received by all parties, nor were ever more satisfactory to myself.

Things could not be expected to be more favorable in K. than they are at this time. I entertain not a particle of doubt of there being at this moment a decided majority for me against all and every person whatever.

From what I learn, the Legislature will do something at the next Session to testify its regard to me. What that will be may depend on subsequent events. But something will be done. Should things remain pretty much as they now are, it may not, and, I think, ought not to, be a nomination. We ought not to take upon ourselves the responsibility of a premature agitation of a certain question. Still, events at Washington may possibly occur early in the winter to render necessary and to justify that measure. I think our friends may place all reliance on Kentucky and on the discretion of the next G. Assembly.

Present me affectionately to Mrs. J. whose leisure I hope will permit her often to write me during your abode at Washington.

ALS. PHi. Printed in Colton, *Clay Correspondence*, 4:243-44.   1. See Russellville Speech, Sept. 17, 1829; and Hopkinsville Speech, Sept. 21, 1829.

To CHARLES HAMMOND   Lexington, October 7, 1829

Your favor of the 27h. Ulto. has been duly received, and perused with great interest. I regret that you should have delayed answering my letters to which it replies under any persuasion that I was dissatisfied. Of your friendly purposes and motives I never can doubt, and I have said that, in the strongest terms, in answer to various letters which I have received from friends calling for explanations of the article of the 12h. August.[1] It is very possible that you were right in both parts of that article; but the doubts which I entertained of it grew out of my belief that it might deceive our friends. So far as relates to the Judge [John McLean], it was a russe de guerre; but as such it was liable to be misunderstood and was generally misunderstood by friends as well perhaps as by opponents. If its motive had been generally known among our friends (which was impracticable) none would have been deceived. As to the other member of the paragraph, intimating that no nomination would be made in the West, upon the supposition of the state of your Legislature which you anticipate is to be apprehended, it was politic and prudent in regard to Ohio. But, then, in Kentucky there is a more propitious condition of the Legislature. Here, if a nomination, were expedient it might be practicable; but the article tended to discouragement here, where stimulus might be wanted. I do not myself believe upon the state of things, as it now exists, that a nomination is the preferable measure even in Kentucky. On the other hand, I do not think it would be wise now to decide absolutely against it, and thereby preclude all intervening contingencies. I think where we can we should keep the game in our own hands, without shewing them. As to what the adversary says or may say we ought not to mind that. He will denounce before hand the thing he most fears, render it unpopular if he can, and frighten us from it. That is the course of his policy. If we say we will not do what he wishes us not to do we say the very thing most agreeable to him. If, as you fear, there may be a state of parties in your Legislature rendering any friendly measure impracticable then there may be policy in our taking credit for not doing before hand what we could not do. I do not believe however that the article has done any mischief and I should be sorry that your should retain any unpleasant feeling about it. I ought to add that I never saw the piece signed B in the [Lexington *Ketucky*]

Reporter until it was published.[2] I understand it was the production of Mr. Robert Breckenridge [*sic*, Breckinridge].

I am happy to tell you that the views which prevail here, as to what our Legislature ought to do, if things remain pretty much as they are, coincide entirely with yours. I understand it to be in contemplation to propose

1st. Some friendly expressions of attachment confidence &c —

2 A firm conviction of the wisdom of the policy of Internal Improvements and the Tariff.

3. A disapproval of the principle of recent removals.[3]

4. Something on the principles lately avowed in our Indian relations[4]

5 And probably some thing in regard to the Public lands, disapproving of their surrender &c —[5]

Most if not all of these measures will be considered. And I find that most of them are suggested in your letter. How would the two last do in your State [Ohio]? It is very desirable that the two States should act in unison as far as they can.

I returned a few days ago from Hopkinsville, which was the limit of my trip to the South. I did not go on to the den of the Lion in his absence. Vast crowds flocked around me in all the towns, and frequently on the Highways. At Hopkinsville and Russellville each there was about 3000 persons. The demonstrations of friendly attachment were enthusiastic. My addresses were well received by both parties and gave no dissatisfaction. With that at Hopkinsville I was better satisfied than with any popular address I ever made. Hundreds attended me from Tennessee. Upon the whole my excursion, which was reluctantly undertaken, I think did much good. In my late addresses, I avoided topics of direct attack, and limited myself to defence of the late admon or of myself or of certain great measures. I have yet one more, and I sincerely hope it may be the last, of these public meetings on my hands. It is to be at Harrodsburg on the 16h. instant.

ALS. InU. 1. Clay to Hammond, August 12; Sept. 9, 1829. 2. "B" argued that there were two distinct political parties — one favoring internal improvements and a protective tariff and one opposed. He believed the Hammond editorial was intended to test the mood of Ohio about one of its own "distinguished" citizens who might supplant Clay as the opponent of the Anti-Tariff party. Such an occurrence, he concluded, "is out of the question. . . . The man designated by almost the entire national Republican party East, West and South, as its candidate, is long ago marked out by the fears and malice of his foes, the unshaken confidence of his friends, and the energies of his own noble genius. That man it is needless to say is Henry Clay." Lexington *Kentucky Reporter*, Sept. 9, 1829. 3. Reference is to the Jackson administration's policy of removing from public office its political opponents and replacing them with its supporters. 4. On March 23, 1829, in his "Talk to the Creek Indians," Jackson promised that "Beyond the great river Mississippi . . . your Father has provided a country large enough for all of you, and he advises you to remove to it. . . . You will be treated with kindness, and the land will be yours forever." Washington *Daily National Journal*, August 3, 1829. On April 18, Secretary of War John Eaton in an "Address to the Delegation of the Cherokees" maintained that the Indians have never been independent of the laws of the states in which they reside and that the federal government has no right to stop a state from exercising its authority over them. Washington *Daily National Journal*, August 3, 1829. For more on Jackson's Indian removal policy see Francis Paul Prucha, *American Indian Policy in the Formative Years* (Cambridge, Mass., 1962), 213-77; Michael P. Rogin, *Fathers and Children: Andrew Jackson and the Subjugation of the American Indian* (New York, 1975), 212-48. 5. A movement had begun as early as 1826 for the federal government to cede to the states the public lands lying within their boundaries. A resolution that the Committee on the Public Lands inquire into this matter was proposed in the Senate on Dec. 20, 1827, and defeated on April 22, 1828. See *Register of Debates*, 20 Cong., 1 Sess., 15, 675. An effort continued, however, to bring about an alliance of the South and West on the principles of the public land cessions and opposition to the tariff. See further, Magdalen Eichert, "John C. Calhoun's Land Policy of Cession," *SCHM* (Oct., 1954), 55:198-209.

To JOSIAH S. JOHNSTON   Lexington, October 8, 1829

Will you think of the suggestion contained in the enclosed letter, from a very worthy and intelligent friend,[1] formerly in Congress, and send it to [Hezekiah] Niles or some other competent person to act upon, if you do not disapprove it?

I have nothing new to send you from this quarter — In K. and I believe generally in the West we have every reason for encouragement.

I shall go to the last (I most sincerely hope) of the public Barbacues in this State next week. That is in Mercer, to which I am invited by a majority of Jackson men. You know Mercer is the centre of our State and Tom. Moore's head quarters. If my address should satisfy me as well as those did at Russellville and Hopkinsville, it will do good.

ALS. PHi. Printed in Colton, *Clay Correspondence*, 4:245.   1. Letter not found; sender not identified.

To THOMAS SPEED   Lexington, October 8, 1829

Just at the moment of my departure from home on my tour to the Southern part of our State I recd. your favor under date the 22d. August at Orleans.[1] My tour was full of personal gratification and I think was attended with good.

Your suggestion as to the utility of employing the instrument of Almanacs to disseminate true views of the policy of the Tariff is worthy of adoption. I will communicate it where I hope it will receive attention. What think you of the project of forming societies at the principal points of the State (of which Bardstown would be a most important one) to promote that policy? The only doubt I should have is whether there is sufficient excitement to get up those Societies and render them attractive and interesting. If the contemplated attack on the Tariff should be seriously made that desideratum would be suplied. Such societies might discuss the general question; its particular bearings on our Country; and the results of experience here as well as elsewhere. They might circulate information, statistical facts &c &c

Throughout the Green river Country, I should say, from what I heard and witnessed, the attachment to the American System is strong, ardent, and unshakable. I believe that thousands would there desert the Jackson standard sooner than that. Thousands are deserting that standard at any rate.

I am happy to assure you that the general complexion of my information, from all quarters, is highly encouraging. I know not whether I shall live to witness the overthrow of the most unprincipled combination that ever disgraced the councils of any Country; but I now feel full assurance that a few years will bring about that overthrow whether I shall live to witness it or not.

Will you be at Frankfort the coming winter? I should be very glad to meet you there about the middle of December if convenient to you.

I have accepted an invitation to a public Barbacue in Mercer, the last I think that I shall attend, at least for a season. It is signed by a majority of gentlemen who voted for Jackson and is to take place on the 16h. inst. unless the day should be altered.

ALS. NhD.   1. Not found; but see Clay to Speed, Nov. 13, 1829.

From Francis T. Brooke, Richmond, Va., October 11, 1829. Reports on the proceedings of the Virginia constitutional convention [7:575-76], "the hostile feelings" of the convention members toward one another, and the fact that Littleton W. Tazewell has "managed the interest of [the] east but clumsily." Explains: "I allude to his [Tazewell's] proposition to take the present constitution as perfect until it was Shewn in what respects it was defective which he [illeg. word], by which the west were put into possession of the debateable ground—with respect to the Folks at Washington they are loosing ground There can be no doubt, in Virginia, this has alarmed their friends and increased their activity against you, the dificuty is to fix on another aspirant to the Presidency—and great [word missing] will be made, to prevail on the east to unite, with the South in a more restricted construction of the constitution of the US, and the hope is that by turning the attention of the people from persons to principle to build up the party again on that new ground, the politics of Virginia will depend on the Tariff question mainly, it is gaining popularity evidently hence the numerous essays in the papers against it." ALS. DLC-HC (DNA, M212, R3).

To JOSEPH VANCE   Lexington, October 11, 1829

An excursion to the Southern part of our State has delayed my acknowledgement of your favor of the 2d Ulto. That excursion was full of personal gratification, and I think did good, which was more than was expected by me when I undertook it.

I concur with you generally in the sentiments contained in your letter, as to the most expedient course to be pursued by us. I do not believe that much was ever gained by temporizing. I am sure, if any thing is to be gained in that way, it is not by *me*. At the same time I have the utmost confidence in the friends mentioned by you. With one of them (Mr. [Charles] H[ammond]. at Cincinnati) I have freely corresponded, on the news paper paragraph to which you allude.[1] It appears to me that our true course is to erect our standard temperately, but boldly & firmly, preserve our forces unbroken, and invite to it all who are worthy and who are disposed to unite with us in preserving our free institutions and our systems of policy. If we do not raise our standard, we discourage our own friends, and prevent those of the other party, who are disposed to unite with us, from coming to us. It is true that the effect of our erecting our standard may be to furnish cement to the other party; but, then, many of them will be influenced by reason, as well as by their own disappointments, and all these will come to us, if they see any hopes. We must never forget that the basis of our Government is popular intelligence. To that we should constantly appeal. It may some times fail, but its permanent failure would prove that we have nothing in our political institutions worth contending for.

In advising to this course, I do not mean to preclude the observance of precaution and of every dictate of prudence We ought not, for example, to make opposition without cause, nor to anticipate causes for it, without solid reasons. But when the *cause* exists, I think it mistaken policy (to say no more) that we should forbear, waiting for divisions in the ranks of our adversary. We should not, if thus Silent, perform our duty to our Country.

I may underrate the person [John McLean] whom our friends would conciliate; but I am quite sure they overrate him. I should be glad that his patriotic sense of duty should make him co-operate with us; but if he does not, I really should not think it of much importance. Of the body of which party has he now the confidence? And does he not now as heretofore endeavor to please both by giving words to one and deeds to the other?

I shall be glad often to hear from you, at Washington, and also before you go as to the result of your Elections.

Young C[harles]. Wickliffe was killed in a duel the day before yesterday, by [George J.] Trotter the present Editor of the [Lexington] K. Gazette.[2] The event has produced no excitement.

ALS. KyU.   1. Clay to Hammond, Sept. 9, 1829.   2. Wickliffe to Clay, March 15, 1829.

To ELISHA WHITTLESEY   Lexington, October 12, 1829

My absence on an excursion to the Southern part of our State has delayed my acknowledgement of your favor of the 8h. [sic, 4th] Ulto. for the sentiments and suggestions contained in which be pleased to accept my thanks. Our Legislature, from what I can learn, will do something. What it will be may, in some degree, depend upon contingencies. I think you may confidently anticipate upon expressions of opinion favorable to our great measures of policy. We have both the moral and numerical force in the General Assembly, and we will keep it in this State. I do not think you need apprehend any indiscreet resolutions. If nothing else be done in your Legislature it is desirable that it should express a firm adherence to the Tariff &c.

I regret the supiness among our friends, of which you speak. It appears to me that whilst we avail ourselves of, we ought not exclusively to rely on, the divisions of the foe. If we do not unfurl our banners, we discourage our friends. We do more; we offer no inducements to the reasonable and considerate of the other party to come to us. Despair will seize upon them and upon our friends. At the same time I would not advise indiscriminate nor indiscreet opposition. Assuming as the basis of our institutions, adequate intelligence among the people, for [s]elf Government, we ought to appeal to it, when there is just cause. If, by presenting ourselves in the seeming attitude of an organized opposition, we alarm and unite the other party, we at the same time point out to the patriotic among them the mode by which redress, if there be necessity for redress, can be obtained. Whilst general silence might lead to the conclusion of general acquiescence.

I shall be glad to hear from you whenever your convenience will admit of your writing; and particularly as to the composition of your next Legislature.

The young [Charles] Wickliffe who was acquitted in a criminal prosecution last Spring was killed in a duel the day before yesterday [sic, October 9] by the successor [George J. Trotter] of the Editor [Thomas R. Benning] of the [Lexington] K. Gazette, whom he slew. No excitement is produced by the event.

ALS. OClWHi.

To R. GIST   Lexington, October 13, 1829

I recd. your favor with the enclosure Your boy starts this morning with a Ewe and a ram lamb. We took much pains in the selection, and hope you will be pleased with them. The ewe is probably in lamb by a ram which I have, one half Saxon blood.

ALS. Courtesy of Mrs. John Stofer, Mt. Sterling, Ky. Addressed to "Capt. R. Gist near Mount Sterling," and carried there "By his servant." Gist is possibly Rezin H. Gist [1:552].

From Francis T. Brooke, Richmond, Va., October 19, 1829. On the question of whether it would be politic for the Kentucky legislature to nominate Clay for president: "I think your friends in the Legislature of Kentucky would do well to impress in as Strong terms as possible the confidence of your State in you as a Statesman and Patriot, it would tend to allay Suspicion which has been unwarrantably excited by your enemies[;] this I intend as a hint for your consideration — " As for the reaction to such a nomination in Virginia and the Southern states, "I find but one sentiment among your friends, they think it would be preciapiate."

Mentions that the state constitutional convention moves slowly and that James Madison's compromise solution to the deadlock over the reapportionment of seats "is not relished by either side." ALS. DLC-HC (DNA, M212, R3). Reformers wanted white population to determine representation in both houses of the legislature, white conservatives favored a basis for both houses determined by a combination of white population and direct taxes or federal numbers. Madison favored the white basis for one house but not for both. Ultimately a compromise proposed by William Fitzhugh Gordon was adopted, providing for a mixed representation with an arbitrary but equitable apportionment of representatives and senators to each of four sections of the state. Madison also proposed that future reapportionments should take place every ten years with the number of delegates not to exceed 150 and the number of senators 36. This proposal was adopted over the bitter opposition of reformers. See Ambler, *Sectionalism in Virginia*, 147, 148, 169-70; and Merrill D. Peterson (ed.), *Democracy Liberty and Property, The State Constitutional Conventions of the 1820's* (New York, 1966), 271-85.

From Jesse B. Harrison, Göttingen, Hanover, October 20, 1829. Reports on his European travels, noting that the Americans he met in Paris during a stay of seven weeks there did not much impress him. They have "a shameful ignorance of their own country, & either a frivolous inclination to waste time at cafés and other public places, or to imitate the travelling English in their extravagant taste & alien follies."

Assures Clay "that all the Liberals in Europe have been mortified at the late election of our President. In France the lovers of America freely express their condoling sentiments to us in conversation." On the other hand, calls attention to several flattering articles about President Jackson that have appeared in the French press, particularly a recent one by former U.S. consul in Paris, David B. Warden, in *Moniteur*. Concludes with lengthy descriptions of sights he has seen, interesting people he has met, and his plans for further sight-seeing before returning to Lynchburg, Va., in May, 1831. ALS. DLC-HC (DNA, M212, R3). For Warden, see *DAB*.

To JOHN Q. ADAMS   Frankfort, October 23, 1829

It has been some time since I had this pleasure. After the receipt of your letter [May 2, 1829] communicating a melancholy domestic event,[1] I forebore to write, being fully persuaded that time and reflection alone can heal such wounds. Your friends in this quarter, and none more than I, nevertheless sincerely sympathized with yourself and Mrs. Adams on the occasion.

I take great pleasure in offering you cordial felicitations on another domestic event, of a more pleasing and happy nature.[2]

Being here on business a letter struck my eye from Mr. Jefferson to the late Mr. Breckenridge [*sic*, John Breckinridge], published in the [Frankfort] Argus.[3] It fortifies very strongly your opinion of the necessity of an amendment of the Constitution to admit States into the Union, formed out of Louisiana. Not knowing that it might catch your attention, I transmit it enclosed.

Should you execute your purpose of replying to the Boston Federalists,[4] I pray you to forward me a Copy of the Reply. . . .

ALS. MHi.   1. Adams to Clay, May 2, 1829.   2. Probably Charles Francis Adams's marriage to Abby Brooks on Sept. 1, 1829. Marie B. Hecht, *John Quincy Adams* (New York, 1972), 299.   3. On August 12, 1803, Jefferson wrote John Breckinridge concerning the Louisiana Purchase, "I suppose they must then appeal to *the nation* for an additional article to the Constitution." See further, Lowell Harrison, *John Breckinridge, Jeffersonian Republican* (Louisville, 1969), 162-63.   4. Adams to Clay, April 21, 1829.

From Jonas Bond Brown, Boston, October 23, 1829. Informs Clay that the tariff act of 1828 was enacted "under circumstances of great political excitement, and of extraordinary and profligate purposes of party and personal aggrandizement." Explains that it was based on a plan gotten up in Congress by "political friends of the Middle States and the West, to frame such a Bill as it was Supposed could not receive the sanction of the East. When, on testing the question, Members from the East generally came to the Support of the Bill, the chagrin and disappointment of the South, broke out in an open charge of treachery against their political coudjutors of the Middle & Western States. It was ungrateful on the part of the gentlemen from the South, to make this charge against their political friends who contrived the Bill for I really believe it was their hope, and confident expectation that the East would go in a body against it, not So much because they were unwilling the measure itself should be adopted, as, for the Sake of political advantage, they were desirous it should be defeated by the vote of New England. Members from this Section of the Country did right in supporting this Bill, after attempting in vain, materially to amend it. It is true they gained but little, if any thing for themselves, while they gave much to the Middle and Western States, by voting for the duties on Iron, Hemp, Spirits & Molasses. They gave the people of those States a proof of their willingness to go far in support of the System, even where, in an estimate of relative advantages to the different Sections of the Country, they themselves were among those who shared the least. The East was deeply interested in the protection of the woollen Manufacturers."

Comments at length and in detail on the need for a higher level of tariff protection on manufactured woolen goods lest hard-pressed New England wool manufacturers be forced to "abandon their establishments." Notes that many of "our most industrious and enterprising manufacturers" have already gone under and that raw "wool bears So low a price, that the farmers are Killing off their sheep." Points out, therefore, that it is "the duty of the friends of the protecting System, to lay before Congress at the approaching Session, the condition of these two great branches of National industry, and So ask for efficient measures of protection against foreign competition, which is kept up by a System of fraud and false Swearing at the Custom House in New York, to an extent that baffles every attempt at Success, on the part of the American Manufacturers, however great may be his industry, capital and skill." Asks Clay to assist the woolen interests in their approach to Congress for adequate tariff protection, specifically for an amendment to section 2, paragraph 4 of the wool schedule of the 1828 tariff law that would remove "the one dollar minimum" requirement which "almost wholly" destroys the "protection sought by the manufacturers." Also asks for Clay's aid in ending the fraud in the customs house in New York that, because of the one dollar minimum, permits assessment variations in "the amount of duty secured on goods of like quality and value." Requests, in closing, that Clay inform him of the attitudes on these matters of the members of Kentucky's delegation in Congress. ALS. DLC-HC (DNA, M212, R3). For the "dollar minimum" clause [section 2, paragraphs 3-4], see 4 *U.S. Stat.*, 271. Jonas Bond Brown was a Boston merchant, textile manufacturer, and indefatigable advocate of the protective tariff. Charles M. Wiltse (ed.), *The Papers of Daniel Webster, Correspondence* (Hanover, New Hampshire, 1974, 1977), 2:302; 3:241.

From HENRY CLAY, JR. West Point, N.Y., October 24, 1829

I received your last letter which conveyed to me the intelligence of the death of Aunt Sophia [Grosch] Clay:[1] I had learned before the decease of her only daughter, What a shock this double calamity must have given Uncle Porter [Clay]: But I am sure he will sustain it with firmness; and Frederick I hope will conduct himself in such a manner as to afford him consolation hereafter—

Every thing goes on as usual at West P. Richard Shelby[2] about whom his father feels so much solicitude is getting on very well. He is at present in the 2d section of each of the branches of his year's course—

I myself am very much pleased indeed with the studies of my year and I now fully concur in your opinion that the knowledge acquired here will be useful to a man in whatever pursuit he may embark   The Chemistry, Philosophy, and civil Engineering will in all probability be eminently useful if I determine to reside in Kentucky after leaving here — The desire of improving the local conveniences of the State cannot I think subsid[e] until it is in some measure satiated: and certainly the want of public works such as improved roads — &c. is so palpable that the most ignorant must in time perceive it. The road from Maysville to Lexington is, I hope, the first of a series of roads to be constructed intersecting the state in different directions And if as I suppose the Legislature will engage in the undertaking A number of Engineers will be required and the consequent appointment of a chief Engineer — I would be very glad to be employed in the service of the state for a few years in the capacity of Engineer   I know that this office is a very responsible and a very honourable one: still I do not conceive it presumption in a graduate of the Military Academy to aspire to it, with a faint hope it is true, but yet, a hope of obtain'g it; particularly when we consider that his competitors would be men but little versed in the sciences pretaining to the art and with perhaps crude ideas deduced without reflection from practice only — My ideas concerning the practice of Law have very much changed of late — I had all along considered it as a kind of preparatory step to my engaging in politics; but I am now determined never to engage in politics since the late elections in Maryland[3] & several other States, but to make the Law my profession for life if I commence it at all. If I could obtain a competency in any profession in which I might indulge my taste for literature I think I should embrace it at once, and forget that I ever had the least ambition to gain the popular applause —

I have been considerably indisposed for the last week, owing, I believe to too close application but am now recoved.

Your letter is not answered so soon as it ought to be. I wrote a letter to you some time since but mislaid it and forgot it had not been carried to the office until today when I found it among papers where I had put it through mistake —

I would be very glad to hear from you frequently, advice on any subject on which you might think proper to write would be highly acceptable to me. . . .

ALS. Henry Clay Memorial Foundation, Lexington, Ky.   1. She died Sept. 28, 1829. For more information on the Clays, see Zachary F. Smith and Mary Rogers, *The Clay Family*. Louisville, 1899.   2. See 7:588.   3. Warfield to Clay, April 9, 1829.

From John W. Taylor, Ballston Spa, N.Y., October 26, 1829. Reports plans "to sustain ourselves" politically, "not only in Saratoga but in this Senatorial District" comprising the "nine northeastern counties of the State." Points out, however, that the "Anti masonic excitement is doing us considerable injury in Washington & Montgomery & some in this County [Saratoga]. If we fail it will be owing to that cause." ALS, draft. NHi. Letter sent also to John Q. Adams. In the New York congressional elections held on Nov. 2-6, 1829, the Jacksonians won 19 seats in the U.S. House while the Anti-Jacksonians won 15. In Washington and Montgomery counties Jacksonian candidates won, while in Saratoga County an Anti-Jacksonian was victorious. See *Niles' Register* (November 13, 20, 1830), 40:187, 202.

FromJOSIAH S. JOHNSTON   Philadelphia, October 27, 1829
It is about three weeks, since We left N. York, & We shall remain here until the 15 or 20h. of Novr. — We have heard to day of the safe arrival of Mr. & Mrs. [James] Brown at N. York & expect the pleasure to see them here very soon —

118

My own opinion is that the Course you suggest[1] is perfectly Correct with regard to the proceedings of your Legislature on the Nomination —

It will certainly be Wise to wait until the Meeting of Congress in order to ascertain the state of public opinion and the State of parties — of which no conjecture can be now formed —

It is now understood generally through the U States that you will be a Candidate — & perhaps it is not necessary to make any annunciation of the fact Until we can Concert some general Cooperation —

In my opinion New England stands ready to sustain you, Whenever it is necessary & she will not Change — Nothing has been lost there — Some declaration from the Legislature of Kentucky expressive of the opinion of the State with regard to you will have a good effect — But it will be judicious I think to have the nomination, when it is made, sustained by some of the other states.

I do not Know the Character of the Ohio Legislature, nor the state of parties there — It is of great importance, that that state should Cooperate — While I see no pressing necessity for the immediate Nomination, there is danger of a premature one — That is before the other states are ready — We have some thing to hope by delay

I confess I have no opinion that the Senate will display any independence or that they will take their stand against the power of the Executive — My experience of parties teaches me to believe they will Utterly disregard all principle & sanction every abuse — Yet there are Causes that may give a new turn to parties — & produce results that cannot be looked for While they hold together —

The Southern States or rather the Southern leaders are disappointed — they are Secretly dissatisfied   Excluded from all Confidence & all influence with this Admn. & deprived of all power & office under it they can have none of the ordinary Motives to support it — They must plan for the power it Confers, not like most of those Who now fill the offices for the emoluments it gives — They see themselves excluded for Eight years under the General if he succeeds — then if the party prevails, they have only half a chance of succeeding — That is it remains very doubtful, Whether, Calhoun or Van Buren or Some body else of the Same party may Succeed — It appears to Me they are effectually excluded & that those now on the Stage have very little Chance of Success — & they must See that their hopes are very distant & uncertain — They are Men of Ambition, eager & anxious for its gratification — They expected to have office & influence, to have Controul[e]d the Government & directed public opinion — How sadly they must be disappointed! Their respect for the President is greatly shaken — They feel Contempt for the Cabinet — They disapprove all the measures of the admn. — There is besides an ill Concealed jealousy between the parties of Calhoun & Van Buren — & there are moreover Among them personal difficulties & differences not easily reconciled   From all these there are some hopes, although faint, that some divisions may grow up during the Winter or appear or their Meeting, from Which a new state of things may arise — Nothing can hold them together but a common enemy — if let alone they Must divide — What motive can Calhoun & [Littleton W.] Tazewell & all the S. Carolina delegations have to hold up this full adm. — for 8 years, by which they exclude themselves? Yet it is Certain they will not Consent to be broken down as a party, although they may be willing to divide the party themselves & become the heads of a New party & become gradually so alienated & at length hostile by Collisions as to throw themselves onto our Scale —

It will be Well to Wait until the meeting of Congress — We May then have some Clue to judge of the future — At present every thing is uncertain.

You will be well informed at Washington — & will Know how to act upon it. —

The only hope is in the Senate, as to the people they are devoted Slaves of their leaders — You see in all the Elections, the Spirit of the party Continues to animate them — In Maryland, Where the parties have not changed, they succeed by exertion & zeal & Concert   In Jersey it is the same thing — It is the stimulus of Success, still operating — but I do not believe there is any change of opinion or any thing to discourage our hopes — Yet it is very important at a time When the Legislative nominations may exercise a very great influence over public opinion —

I fear the same Causes will produce the same effect in Ohio & else Where. — I have no doubt peace is made with Russia [and] Turkey although We have no Certain information. I have Recd. your letters of the 5.8 & 11 Ins. —

My letters are all returned —

William [Johnston] has just left us for Northampton [Mass.] & Mrs. Johnston is busy in Making arrangements for the Winter. . . .

ALS. DLC-TJC (DNA, M212, R13).   1. Clay to Johnston, Oct. 5, 1829.

From Thomas Patterson, Hagerstown, Md., October 30, 1829. Reports that the Jackson party carried the elections for the general assembly on October 5, although "I have not the least doubt that a considerable Majority of the people are against the present Administration of the Genl. government." Thinks the Jacksonites will make a "mighty exertion" to keep the Van Buren and Calhoun factions together as the 1832 election approaches. Laments that Tobias Watkins, "poor deluded man has given a prodigious weapon to our foes"; but believes that factionalism within the Jackson camp will keep the level of suspicion high within the administration. Thinks the time has come "to get the lower class to examine and understand the meaning of the American System, which is a very complicated subject which zealots will not stop to examine."

Discusses at length various political issues and personalities in the Hagerstown area, especially the struggle for control of the local post office. Criticizes Jackson's policy of proscription, but notes that he mutes his low opinion of the president around Hagerstown because "if I am turned out" of office "it will be very tough" given the fact "I have 7 helpless but very promising children." Believes he will be ousted from his position [Patterson to Clay, June 8, 1830] sooner or later, however. Remarks on the depression that has hit Hagerstown property values, blaming decreases of 25 to 30 percent on Jackson. Says a friend in Cannonsburg, Pa., has assured him that Clay would be the next president, and that "all west Penna. would ultimately go for you." Tells Clay he cannot risk signing his name to this letter — "it must be kept a secret." Reports in a postscript: "a report came here yesterday that your son had killed [George J.] Trotter in a duel. I hope not. and that no affair of the kind has taken place." AL. DLC-HC (DNA, M212, R3). For Trotter, see Wickliffe to Clay, March 15, 1829. The son involved in the false rumor could have been either Theodore Wythe Clay or Thomas Hart Clay. Both were home at the time.

To ALLEN TRIMBLE   Lexington, October 30, 1829

I send you herewith a letter about hemp.

You and Mr. [Charles] Hammond differ in respect to the character of your Legislature. He assigns a majority of[1] six in each branch to the Jackson party. How is this?

As to the subject about which you have done me the honor to consult me, I should think that in temperate language well considered, it would be expedient and have a very good tendency for you to express disapprobation

1st. of the principle which appears to have regulated the exercise of the power of patronage by the present Admon of the General Government, especially the removal of honest and capable officers for no other cause than the exercise of the common right of every freeman.

2dly. The appointment of so many Editors of newspapers, threatening as it does the purity and independence of the Press. and

3dly. The appointment of so many members of Congress equally menacing the purity and independence of the National Legislature.

And I also believe it would have a good tendency to express in strong terms your approbation of the policy of the American System and Internal Improvements; and your anxious hope that it may not be abandoned.

Govr. [Thomas] Metcalfe did me the honor to converse also with me on the same subject; and I think his message will embrace all the above points.[2]

Supposing things to remain as they now are, our Legislature will forbear to make any nomination, in all probability, and will limit itself to the expression of its opinion on the preceding topics.

I rejoice to hear of the Election of McArthur, Morrow, Corwin, Doherty[3] &c &c.

ALS. NjP. Letter marked "(Private and Confidential)." 1. Word "about," following "of," is struck through. 2. Annual Message to the Ky. General Assembly, Dec. 3, 1828. Text in Lexington *Kentucky Reporter*, Dec. 16, 1829. 3. These men were elected to the Ohio State Legislature in 1829. For Duncan McArthur, Jeremiah Morrow, and Thomas Corwin see *BDAC*; for William Doherty see Cincinnati *Advertiser*, Nov. 11, 1829.

From George Smith Houston, Dayton, Ohio, October 31, 1829. Reports that he still retains his office as postmaster, which is his "main dependence for support," but that the "Jacksonians have sent on petition after petition for my removal and the appointment of one of their own party in my place." Says that Elijah Haywood, a Jacksonian, examined the files of "the weekly Journal in Dayton" which he (Houston) formerly published, a paper which had advocated Clay's election to the presidency. Believes that Haywood wants him removed for having supported Clay. Fears that if Haywood is appointed second assistant postmaster general, replacing Dr. Phineas Bradley, he will surely be removed.

Condemns Jackson's "proscription system"; despairs that the republic will endure ("my prayer to God is to save my country"); and feels that throughout history military achievements have too great an influence on "the great body of the people." Thanks Clay for his "fearless undaunted course," thinks more of the people are beginning to "see and reflect on their delusion," and concludes: "Identified as you are with the American System, May almighty God preserve your life in health." ALS. DLC-HC (DNA, M212, R3). George Smith Houston was editor-in-chief of the Dayton *Watchman and Farmers' Mechanics Journal*, cashier of the Dayton Bank, and postmaster from 1821 until his death in 1831. Robert Steele, *Early Dayton* (Dayton, Ohio, 1896), 80. Dr. Bradley was removed as second assistant postmaster general and was replaced by Selah R. Hobbie, a member of Congress from N.Y. *Niles' Register* (October 10, 31, 1829), 37:99, 149.

From James Brown, New York, November 1, 1829. Comments on his voyage home from France and an invitation to a public dinner in his honor on November 6 from "respectable inhabitants of the city . . . without distinction of political parties" to whom he had shown personal and professional attention while serving as U.S. Minister in Paris. Will go to Philadelphia on November 7 where he and his wife will spend the winter. Informs Clay that "they say here that many are anxious to make you President. Are you not tired of the troubled ocean of politics or will you again launch into the busy strife. I hope my poor bark is once more safe in port and it is not my intention again to meddle with politics unless driven to it, by ill usage or persecution which I do not now apprehend." ALS. DLC-HC (DNA, M212, R3). Printed in *LHQ*, 24:1144.

From Daniel Mallory, New York, November 2, 1829. Remarks that he recently spoke with Louisiana Senator Josiah S. Johnston who advised him to write "fully and freely." Reports on a very recent visit to several of the New England states and has "cheering" news to relate. Specifically, "that there is scarcely a doubt but that nearly all the states north and east of this will join heartily in your nomination. The excitement in this subject in these sections of the country is much greater than I had supposed." States that "We can securely rely on Connecticut, Massachusetts, R. Island & Vermont," and feels that "no reasonable doubt can be entertained of the other two." Suggests that the "wish is very general" he visit New England next summer, but does not "consider a visit to them half so important or politic as a visit to New york," where "Thousands of people are anxious to see you, and among them are many leading and influential men." ALS. DLC-HC (DNA, M212, R3).

To JOHN HARE POWEL   Lexington, November 5, 1829
I have lately had leisure to peruse, and I have read with profit and pleasure, Hints for American Husbandmen,[1] published in 1827, and for a copy of which I was indebted to you. Do you continue still to breed the Improved Durham short horns? And what could I obtain a pair for, two years or three years old, the heifer in calf by a different bull from her mate, delivered in Baltimore in March next? I have, for ten years past, been raising from a stock of the Hereford Reds, which I imported from England. They are a good species, and very thrifty, but I am now satisfied that their great rivals, the race which you have been propagating, possesses the superiority.

As a brother grower of Stock, I should be glad to be informed what price could be commanded for a lot of Kentucky bred Mules of sixty in number, and of course now ready for service, if I were to send them to your market of Philadelphia?[2] I shall be obliged by any information, on this subject, you can communicate.

ALS. PPL-R. Addressed to Powel at "Powelton, near Philadelphia." For Powel, see *DAB* or *CAB*. 1. Pennsylvania Agricultural Society, *Hints for American Husbandmen, With Communications to the Pennsylvania Agricultural Society*. By Order of the Directors. Philadelphia, 1827.   2. Powel responded to Clay on Dec. 20, 1829: "I am much gratified by having the opportunity of showing my readiness to be *commanded* in sincere things, as well as *great*, by *the* man whom I am prepared to hail at last as 'Brother' in the *most important pursuit*." ALS. DLC-HC (DNA, M212, R4).

To ANDREW M. JANUARY &   Lexington, November 10, 1829
WILLIAM HUSTON, JR.
Mr. Rob. Scott sent a Rifle to your care addressed to the Honble James Clarke [*sic*, Clark], Washington City, by my direction. I hope it was received.[1] If not already forwarded, I wish it sent to the care of Mess Dobbins & Co. of Wheeling or some other house there to be expedited to its destination. Be pleased to inform me when it is received and forwarded, and to what house you may direct it. [Continues to Mr. January alone.]

You must not suppose, from the movement making in this quarter respecting the Turnpike road to Frankfort, that a deep interest is not felt in that from Maysville to this place.[2] At least for one I can truly avow that interest. I found, as you must have perceived when here, that public spirit, if not extinct, was very languid. It was desirable to awaken it. The road to Louisville united most opinions, and I supposed that if we could put in motion that to Frankfort the same public spirit that would engage on that object would soon apply itself to a cooperation in the completion of the Maysville road. What we want is to bring the advantages of roads finished in the McAdams [sic, macadam] method home to the senses of our fellow Citizens most of whom have never seen one. With that view I was willing to concur in the completion of a road in almost any direction. When one is made others will come on.

We do not know yet whether we shall fail or succeed with the road to Frankfort. I hope and believe we shall succeed. How have you found Mr. [Col. John S.] Williams as an Engineer? Is your road in such progress that he could be obtained, if he is approved of, for the Frankfort road?[3]

ALS. KyLoF. 1. Clay to Vaughan, June 18, 1829; Vaughan to Clay, July 1, 1829. 2. Clay to Henry Clay, Jr., Dec. 2, 1829. 3. Col. Williams was "a pioneer engineer" on the Maysville and Lexington turnpike. Collins, *History of Kentucky*, 1:62.

From WILLIAM L. BRENT
Louisville, November 11, 1829

I wrote to you a few days since from on Board a steam Boat and put my letter into the Post office at Cincinati [sic, Cincinnati], which you must have received. I would not trouble you with this letter in so short a time, if it were not to communicate to you the substance of a conversation I had with Judge [John] McLean at Cincinati the other day relative to Genl Jackson and his leading friends. Judge McLean introduced the subject to me in a few minutes after I called upon him at his own House and expressed very great dissatisfaction and disappointment with and at the course of the administration so far, observing that the proscription it had persued disgraced the nation and was calculated to destroy our Government and that no administration acting upon those principles could be or ought to be sustained by the american people. He remarked to me that it was contrary to the advice he had given Genl Jackson and contrary to the promises the General had made him when he left Washington City, but said he "the General has lost all the moral firmness he ever had, if he had any—" and indeed I am inclined to believe that he has much less independence of character than I supposed he had—." He spoke with great contempt of [Martin] Van Buren as a juggler in politics and a man not to be relied upon—He expressed great *personal* friendship for Mr [John C.] Calhoun, but expressed the opinion that his course had been such that he stood no chance for the Presidency and intimated that *politically* he was opposed to him—. In speaking of Genl Jackson, he said, the General certainly will not be weak enough to let the men who surround him persuade him to be a Candidate for the Presidency again. I told him that such was the belief at Washington City,—He replied to me they are mistaken, I am Satisfied that he will not offer and I should like to Know upon what Grounds they can support him after the frequent declarations made that he would Serve only for *four years*—I answered, I believe, the true reason to be, a fear that Mr Clay would be elected, for Genl Jackson aside, Mr Clay is certainly the choice of the people, and would succeed in opposition to any other person, this they know and to try and prevent his election, they will urge Genl Jackson to offer again—To this remark of mine Mr McClean [sic] observed. Such a reason would be like

123

many of those now urged upon the President, and without principle, other than that of holding offices — a better reason and a good one too must be given before they can bring the people to think with them, "No, General Jackson will not offer again" — I then asked him if he did not think that you could out-Poll the General in Ohio. — He said, I think not — Mr Clay has warm friends here, but I am inclined to think that upon this side of the River Ohio, General Jackson has more at present, what he *may have* hereafter and after his course is disclosed during the next Session of Congress I cannot say. — From all these things, I am well satisfied that Mr McLean is no friend to the reelection of Genl. Jackson, or to the election of Mr Van Buren or Calhoun — But from his caution as to you, I rather infer he looks "a head" perhaps for himself. His remarks as to you, were very respectful but I thought cautious — . As these things may give you some little insight into the feelings of certain Individuals and as to the probable course which may be persued, I have thought it best to confidentially state them to you as I think you ought to know as far as practicable the feelings of very distinguished men in the present state of things — . should Genl Jackson decline offering, I think the contest will be nothing. — If Van Buren be not their candidate, he will be with you, at least I think so. — If Van Buren be the Candidate McClean will be with you, and as to Calhoun he has no chance any where —

I leave this in the "Huntress" in the morning for New orleans and hope to reach "St. Martinsville" my residence in six days to which place please to write as often as inclination lets you — .

ALS. DLC-HC (DNA, M212, R3). Letter marked "(Confidential)."

To THOMAS SPEED   Lexington, November 13, 1829

Your favor of the 5h. inst. is received.[1] I know nothing of the origin of the Societies in Shelby and Woodford to which you refer. The first knowledge which I acquired of them, like yours, was derived through the News papers, and I have not yet seen the Shelbyville address. I observe another is proposed at Frankfort.[2] From all this I suspect some secret concert, and I confess also that I apprehend an inimical prompting. I concur with you entirely as to the impolitic tendency of some of the proceedings of these meetings and especially those of them which denounce the productions of sister states. It is against the foreign manufacturer and not the American that we should act. Nothing can be more erroneous than the supposition that the Tariff favors the large Capitalist and the large manufacturer to the prejudice of the small. The very reverse is true. And, in point of fact, during our deliberation in Congress, we constantly encountered opposition, or received but a cold support from the large companies. That of Waltham[3] (one of the largest Cotton factories in the U. States, and one of the richest) was always against it. Break down the tariff and what then is the condition of the small beginner? He has to contend with the Mammoth Companies of Europe. Against these our own Companies could possibly maintain some competition, when all the smaller establishments are swept away, as swept away they would be if the Tariff were repealed.

I shall endeavor to find out how these Societies have sprung up, and I should be very glad to contribute to prevent their bad effects.

I do not think that they involve any violation of the Constitution, provided no laws nor force should be employed. Any one or any number of individuals may enter into a resolution not to purchase the productions of another State or even another County in the same state. But they cannot inforce their resolution by law, nor by the bayonet without offending against the Constitution.

I shall be in Frankfort from about the 16h. of next month until the 22d., and I should be very happy to meet you there, if convenient.

ALS. NhD.   1. Not found, but see Clay to Speed, Oct. 8, 1829.   2. The "Address to the Farmers and Mechanics of Woodford County," which was presented in Versailles on Oct. 17, 1829, referred to and lauded the Shelbyville address. Specifically, the committee which wrote the address advocated the development of manufacturing in Kentucky so that finished goods would not have to be imported from other states or from foreign countries. "There are many considerations that favour our becoming the nursery of the mechanic arts," the authors of the address argued. Lexington *Kentucky Gazette*, Oct. 30, 1829.   3. See Caroline Ware, *The Early New England Cotton Manufactures* (Boston, 1931), 60-66.

To JOHN W. TAYLOR   Lexington, November 13, 1829

Your acceptable favor of the 26h. Ulto. has been received with its enclosure. I am glad to see that our old friends in your quarter are up and doing. I am waiting with anxiety to hear the result of your elections. I anticipate an unfavorable issue of them generally, but I shall not be discouraged by it. If all others were to give up the Republic, I would still hope. But its cause is not yet, thank God, even desperate. In the West things wear a brighter aspect than they did. In this State, all the branches of the Government are with us and so I think they will continue. In the elections of Ohio this fall we have at least made a drawn battle, if we have not won the victory. In Indiana parties are nearly balanced in the Legislature, one branch being for us and the other against us by a small majority.

The developements of the next Session must have a powerful influence on public sentiment. I think our friends ought 1st. to maintain firmly the ground which we have gained in relation to the present tariff. If they attempt to repeal any existing duty, laid for protection, no matter on what article, the seeds of fatal division will be sown. Harmony and concord, among the friends of the American System can only be preserved by an adherence to what has been done, although some of it has been ill done.

2dly. to attempt to correct frauds on the revenue

And 3dly. Some modification of the Auction System,[1] so as to restrict the facilities granted to the foreigner.

Whether and when and how these two later measures should be brought forward should be regulated by the ascertained strength of parties.

A great effort will be made to detach the West from the support of the Tariff. The people in this State and in all the States North of the Ohio are warm in their attachment to it. All our delegation but one member of the house will feel themselves constrained to vote for it. All but that one stand pledged to support it. But it is not to be disguised that many of the Jackson members only want a pretext to abandon the policy. Such a pretext would be furnished if the duties on Iron, Hemp, Cotton bagging, Spirits, Molasses and Lead (the only articles in the protection of which we are *directly* interested) should be reduced. Many of our farmers are now water rotting their hemp, which I trust will tend to lighten the burden of the existing duty upon our navigation.

I think calls on the Executive ought to be made for

1st. The number of removals, and the persons removed &c.

2. The number of Editors by name appointed and the offices to which they have been appointed.

3. The same as to members of the last or the present Congress.

4. The number of new offices created &c.

I would ask for no reasons. They may refuse the Calls. Well if they do, the public will make the proper inference.

I shall be happy to hear from you, and it will afford me pleasure at all times to communicate any suggestions which may occur to me.

Your own discretion will enable you to perceive that I write confidentially

ALS. NHi.   1. See Clay to Niles, Oct. 4, 1829.

From JOSIAH S. JOHNSTON   Philadelphia, November 14, 1829

We remain still at this place, reluctant to go to Washington, We shall defer our departure until the Last moment. I believe that all I have heretofore suggested will be found true in the sequel—The division of the Cabinet & of the party about [John] Eatons affair is matter of public notority—[1]Things remain as they were—You may rely upon What I have said of the division of the Cabinet—that is irreconsiliable & you may depend that Eaton does *not go out*—The General is resolved the [*sic*, to] retain him & to Carry him through—It remains to be seen how they will manage—[William T.] Barry & [Martin] Van Buren will go with the Genl. & Eaton—[John C.] Calhoun & all his friends will be in the other side—What I have said upon the jealousy of the rivals & their friends is true—It will be Curious to see it develope itself. The Southern Leaders see that they are prescribed effectually during the present administration & that in the mean time, their power is undermined & their influence distroyed—That they can expect no share of the power under the Jackson party either with the Present Executive or his Successor—What effect this is to produce on their Conduct, time only can disclose—I shall watch over the signs of the times & give you earliest information—Calhoun has no popularity to rely on among the people or the States—but they may have a decisive Weight in the party to which they belong in both Houses—They (his friends) have it completely in their power to make the Genl. & his Cabinet dependent on them   In the Senate they may controul his measures & limit his power—& they Consider they have all the talent of the H. of R.   It seems to me impossible that things can remain in this state—The power of the Govt. must be divided with these men or they will rebel—What is Calhoun to do? He Cannot be a Candidate again—Van Buren will not change with him—He will never waive his Claims in favor of V. Buren—We Must wait patiently for the gradual development of the Character & feelings of these parties—. They will have a fine opportunity of pulling their opposition upon great principles—& at the same time to shew the Admn. their dependence on them—

By the 1st of Jany We shall be able to give you some information

Barry has been here with his wife & Mrs. [John] Eaton he seems disposed to take this affair upon himself & I heard he had some words with [John] Branch in the presence of the President on this subject—He & Van Buren have identified themselves with Eaton & will go the Whole with the General—

We shall go to Washington about the 1 Dec.   You ought to think yourself very happy to be out of the Contest for one Winter—I hope you will restore your health—& be ready to come back to the Senate on the first vacancy—

Mr. [James] Brown is here in excellent health and accepts a public dinner here on thursday—He comes back very popular—He will make this place his residence—Mrs. Brown has better health than I expected—She has received company since her arrival—appears in good spirits—but is considerably changed—but I can tell you no more of her health than if I had not seen her Mr. Brown has improved in appearance—

You have seen the vote of this State for Governor—²Much of that is ascribed to the Secret influence of Anti-Masonry—Which continues to spread & will run over the U. States—

Govr. [James] Barbour has returned—I did not see him—He is very happy with his visit to Europe & returns in good spirits—

We have no News from Constantinople   There is nothing to oppose the ambition of the Conqueror [Russia], but England & France—

There will be peace—they will dictate the terms—The Black Sea will be opposed—Greece independent—Russia indemnified &C—The Emperor [Nicholas I] Cannot make War at so great a distance & at such expense with a powerful enemy in the rear & the English & French fleets in the Black Sea—

England is not willing to make war & France is not at ease at home. . . .

ALS. DLC-TJC (DNA, M212, R13).   1. Johnston to Clay, Sept. 9, 1829.   2. The election was held on Oct. 14. For results, see Sergeant to Clay, July 20, 1829.

Agreement Dissolving Partnership, Lexington, November 18, 1829. Robert Scott and Osborne Henley agree to dissolve, as of this date, the firm of Scott, Henley & Co. "engaged in the town of Lexington in the purchase and manufacture of Hemp." Henley surrenders to Clay and Scott all his interest in the firm, for which Clay and Scott pay him $2,758.33. Henley agrees to work for the firm until December 25, 1829, without further salary. Attached receipts show that payments to Henley were made on November 18 and December 9, 1829; and the final payment on May 1, 1830. ADS, signed by Clay, Scott, and Henley. KyLxT.

On this same day, November 18, 1829, an agreement between Clay and Scott was signed in which Clay bought out Scott's interest in the firm of Scott, Henley & Co. for $6,750 "(being the amount advanced to the said concern by the said Scott) six months from this date, with eighteen months interest thereon." Clay also assumed ownership and control of two large shipments of bagging and rope for which expected payment had not yet been received. Indeed, his arrangement with Scott was made contingent on his either receiving payment for these goods or physical repossession of them. Finally, "It is further understood and agreed between the parties that the said Clay is to pay the debts of Scott Henley &Co." ADS. DLC-TJC (DNA, M212, R16).

Also on this date, November 18, Clay borrowed $3,000 from Esther Montgomery (Mrs. James) Morrison subject to payment on 20 days notice. Endorsements show interest payments in November of 1831, 1832, 1834. Bond. ANS. *Ibid.*

To James Barbour, November 21, 1829. Welcomes him home from Europe. Notes that "We are looking with great anxiety to the results of your Convention [7:575-76]. Sees, in the state of American politics, "nothing in their condition to discourage the hope of a speedy restoration of the reign of reason and common sense." ALS. NN.

To John T. Edgar & Benjamin Mills, November 21, 1829. Acknowledges receipt of a letter of November 16 from the Board of Managers of the American Colonization Society of Kentucky asking him to deliver an address at the society's annual meeting on December 17. Accepts the invitation, "although a compliance with it will subject me to some inconvenience." Copy. Printed in Lexington *Kentucky Reporter*, December 9, 1829.

To James F. Conover, Cincinnati, November 22, 1829. Comments on Conover's idea of starting a new newspaper in Cincinnati. Points out that no newspaper can "permanently succeed which does not abstain from any violation of public decorum in its discussions, make truth its guide, and avoid personality," and that no place "in the Western Country is so important for diffusing intelligence to the people as Cincinnati." Says he will subscribe to Conover's paper, if it is launched, but cannot invest in it. Hopes there will be no "competition or collision" between Conover and Charles Hammond, editor of the Cincinnati *Daily Gazette*, since Clay has a great deal of confidence in and respect for Hammond's "talents." ALS. ViU. Conover [5:193] and Isaiah Thomas started the Cincinnati *American* in February, 1830. It was dedicated to promoting Clay's presidential candidacy in 1830-32. It ceased publication in May, 1832.

To PETER B. PORTER   Lexington, November 22, 1829

I have duly received your agreeable favor dated the 2d. Ulto. and post marked the 5h. instant. Like yourself I had intended long since to have written, and like you I had omitted it, principally because I had nothing to add to what the News papers would have informed you. I am highly gratified with the intelligence which you communicate, and of which I receive corroborations from other friends. I am anxiously looking for the general results of your elections, which may afford some indications of the future, altho' as our friends did not think it expedient to make a general struggle I do not anticipate any thing very favorable. Those of the City [N.Y.] have reached me and they are not bad. Our friends there are in high spirits. Mr. M[atthew]. L. Davis has opened a correspondence with me and keeps me well informed of movements in the City. Do you still think him worthy of confidence?

Altho' the issue of the elections this fall is not as good as we could have wished, throughout the Union, I see nothing in it to discourage. The late contest was too recent and the next too distant to admit of great exertions on our side. One party was flushed with recent victory, and the other, yet suffering from recent defeat, saw no object near at hand to justify an attempt to put forth their strength. The developements of the policy of the new administration which must be made at the approaching Session of Congress cannot fail to benefit our cause, whatever that policy may be.

In our Legislature we have a decided majority in both branches. But from what I hear I think no nomination will be made, because it is considered premature and impolitic. It would however probably be done, if our friends out of the State generally thought it advisable; but they are much divided, and I believe the major part of the most discreet of them are opposed to it. The Legislature will probably content itself with expressions of its dis approbation of the proscriptive system, of the appointment of Members of Congress Editors of News papers &c; and with some strong resolutions in favor of the Tariff and Internal Improvements.

I hear with much regret that the [Washington *Daily*] National Journal is laboring hard to maintain its existence, and that it is in danger of stopping for want of pecuniary support. I should regard its discontinuance as a misfortune to the Country; for it has been edited, since the commencement of the new administration, with uncommon ability. A project is on foot to purchase out Mr. [Peter] Force, and for that purpose to create a stock divided into about 100 shares of $100 each, and to place it on a solid foundation, principally under the care of Mr. [Philip R.] Fendall, in whose abilities and honor I have entire confidence.[1] Can any thing be done in your quarter to aid the scheme, by taking five or six of the shares?

I have been very much occupied since my return with farming and my other private affairs. And I am happy to tell you that I am daily improving their condition. My health too has been generally in such a state as not to be complained of. If I am spared a few years I hope to place my Estate on the most satisfactory footing; and if I should be cut off I have even now the consolation of knowing that I should leave my family independent.

My wish is to visit you next summer, but as something unexpected may occur to prevent it, I do not desire to excite expectations which may not be realized. I purpose going to Louisiana in January and remaining there during the month of February.

[William B.] Rochester I presume is near you. Be pleased to remember me to him. . . .

ALS. NBuHi. 1. This plan did not succeed. On the masthead of the Washington *Daily National Journal*, Feb. 2, 1830, Peter Force gave notice: "I have disposed of the establishment of the National Journal to Mr. GEORGE WATTERSON, of this city, (late Librarian of Congress) by whom it will be published hereafter."

To NICHOLAS BIDDLE   Lexington, November 28, 1829

My former relations to the Bank [of the United States] and the friendly interest which I still feel in its prosperity will, I trust, excuse the liberty I take in addressing you this letter.

The Bank is the largest proprietor of real estate in Lexington and Frankfort. No matter how that has happened such is the fact. It did not happen by the fault of the other proprietors of real estate in those towns. As a proprietor it is under the same obligations which appertain to all other proprietors to contribute towards those objects of improvement which conduce to the common prosperity of those places. We lately experienced a great calamity in Lexington, by the destruction of the principal edifice of the University, on the success of which the prosperity of Lexington greatly depends. The Bank has contributed nothing towards the alleviation of that misfortune.

We are now engaged in a most important object the accomplishment of which will greatly promote the prosperity of the above towns and enhance the value of property. It is the erection of a Turnpike road between them, after McAdam's [macadam] method.[1] Considered as a distinct thing, unconnected with the subsequent extension of the road, from one end towards Maysville, and from the other towards Louisville, it is highly consequential. Considered as a section of a more extensive road uniting Maysville and Louisville, through Lexington and Frankfort, its importance is still greater. There is no doubt that the whole road will be completed in a few years (they are now executing parts of it at both ends) if we are not defeated in our present purpose of making the contemplated section between Frankfort and Lexington.

Its cost will not, I think exceed $75.000. of which we have now about $60.000 subscribed. With less property in the two places than the Bank owns, I have subscribed $2000, and many others have subscribed in an equal proportion. The Bank owns two of the largest establishments in Frankfort, appropriated to Taverns, which will be more benefited than any other discription of property. If they belonged to private individuals of ordinary liberality there would not be subscribed by them less than $1500 for each establishment.

129

Will not the Bank subscribe some thing towards this interesting object? If a doubt be suggested of its power, it may be answered, that having legitimately acquired the property, they have the right to entrance its value. But at all events if they can not assume the character of a Stock holder in an incorporated Co. they can *give* a sum. And, as Turnpike Stock generally may be estimated as actually worth about one half of its nominal amount, they might present a sum equal to one half of what they would subscribe as a Stock holder.

I need not dwell upon the good effects of such an act, in removing prejudices and stimulating exertions. But I must say that very bad impressions will be made if the Bank declines doing any thing. The injury is not merely in the abstraction of the contribution of the Bank, but in the example. Why, other proprietors will say, do you call upon us to advance money to improve the value of the property of an immensely rich Corporation, which will do nothing!

I hope, my dear Sir, you will employ a portion of that eloquence which has been recently so handsomely exercised on a kindred object near you,[2] to prevail upon the Board to unite with us in executing the above work; and that I shall have the honor of shortly hearing from you that the proper authority has been conferred to grant or subscribe a sum worthy of the Bank of the U. States.[3]

ALS. Courtesy of Dr. Thomas D. Clark, Lexington, Ky. Biddle read this letter on Dec. 11 and referred it to the committee on the offices.   1. Named for John L. Macadam (1756-1836), a Scotch engineer.   2. On Oct. 17, 1829, Biddle made a speech at the opening of the Chesapeake and Delaware Canal. See Thomas P. Govan, *Nicholas Biddle, Nationalist and Public Banker* (Chicago, 1959), 102-3 which incorrectly dates this event as 1828; the canal did not open until 1829. The text of Biddle's speech was printed in the Lexington *Kentucky Reporter*, Nov. 11, 1829.   3. Biddle to Clay, Dec. 22, 1829.

To Nicholas Biddle, Philadelphia, November 28, 1829. Points out that James Harper, "the best of officers," cashier of the Lexington office of the Bank of the United States, recently experienced a reduction in salary followed later by a restoration to his original salary. Asks that since Harper "has a large and interesting family, and . . . is poor," he be paid the amount lost during this period of flux. ALS. NjHi. Letter marked "(Private.)" See Biddle to Clay, December 22, 1829.

From William C. C. Claiborne, Jr., New Orleans, November 28, 1829. Reports the death of "Uncle John Clay" [1:18] on November 19 while on board the steamboat *Plover* en route from St. Louis to New Orleans and that he was buried at Helena, in Arkansas Territory, near Memphis. "He went off like an infant without a pang or a struggle. Peace to his soul." Remarks that "My Uncle [Martin] Duralde" looks forward to a visit from Clay "this winter," but that if Clay wishes to come later Duralde will be "better prepared to receive" him, because "he is about building himself a fine house in a beautiful part of the City, which will be finished by next fall." Leaves the timing of the visit to Clay but asks that he "be good enough to tell us in your next, when we can positively expect you." Discusses his own plans to tour Europe in 1830. Comments on the news "that your friends at Washington have established a Committee, and are making efforts to extend the circulation of the [Washington *Daily*] National Journal. We will endeavour to assist them here in this laudable object." Concludes with the observation that "in spite of the Yellow fever," New Orleans "is very gay and crowded with people. Not a house vacant, and rent excessively high. We are daily and anxiously expecting the arrival of Mr. & Mrs. [James] Erwin." ALS. DLC-HC (DNA, M212, R4).

From Sidney Breese, Kaskaskia, Ill., November 30, 1829. Believes that the Jackson administration is heading for a "speedy downfal" and that Clay will soon "be called from your retirement to preside at the head of affairs." Speculates "that if the Jackson malcontents of the South attack, as they will, the Tariff, at this Coming session of Congress, Pennsylvania will break off, and she, with other Tariff states will rally around you. This event, in my humble judgment will take place — Either this, or Jackson will so identify himself with the Tariff and Internal Improvements, that a Candidate of Southern politics, either [Martin] Van Buren or [William H.] *Crawford* will take the field against him. Van Buren is strengthening himself all in his power. In this state, every office that has been Conferred, has been upon *his men* through [Elias K.] Kane of the Senate." ALS. DLC-HC (DNA, M212, R4).

From Francis T. Brooke, near Fredericksburg, Va., November 30, 1829. Comments on the proceedings of the constitutional convention at Richmond, especially the "bitter sarcasms of [John] R[andolph] and the dignified and cutting reply of [Chapman] Johnston [*sic*, Johnson]." Reports also that he and John H. Pleasants had gotten up a testimonial dinner to James Barbour, "much to the mortification of [Thomas] Ritchie & Co." ALS. DLC-HC (DNA, M212, R4). For the exchange between Chapman Johnson of Augusta County and John Randolph on November 24, 1829, see *Proceedings and Debates of the Virginia State Convention of 1829-30* (Richmond, 1830), 444-45.

From James Brown, Philadelphia, November 30, 1829. Regrets that he cannot honor Clay's request to borrow $20,000 from him at 6 percent. Explains in what enterprises he presently has his funds tied up. "I have however no doubt of the practicability of obtaining the loan on the terms and with the security you mention and had I the paper signed by Mr [Martin] Duralde and Mr Erving [*sic*, James Erwin] and yourself. I could negociate it for you. If my signature in addition to, or guarrantee of theirs should be wanting it shall be at your service."

Reports that he has no desire to re-enter public life. Realizes, however, that "You are younger and of a different temperament and will probably . . . pursue the phantom till the last moment of your existence."

Warns Clay that "The cause of the present administration if I may judge from what appears in the papers is gaining ground and unless General Jackson declines another election the party will probably remain united, and overcome all opposition. The small beckonings of discontent at Washington may serve for table chat but are of too little importance to have any great influence. Besides this the insurrectionary feeling is confined to the weaker sex, is somewhat ungenerous, and will be overcome by the energy of the husbands and the influence of time and reflexion." ALS. DLC-HC (DNA, M212, R4). Printed in *LHQ,* 24:1145-46.

To HENRY CLAY, JR.   Lexington, December 2, 1829
Your grandfather Watkins[1] died last wednesday night, after a short illness. I went to Woodford to see your grandmother, who is also very feeble, and I fear will soon follow him. I offered to take her to Ashland to reside with us but she prefered to live with your Aunt Blackburn,[2] where she now is. Perhaps it was the best arrangement.

Thomas [Hart Clay] started this day, with Mr. [John H.] Kerr to see my Illinois land near Terre Haute.[3] If he likes it he intends settling upon it, as Kerr proposes also to do. It is a fine piece of land and I think he cannot fail being pleased with it. But I confess I have very little confidence in Thomas's stability, and I shall be agreeably surprized if he becomes steady.

I observe what you say in your last letter [October 24], in regard to being employed by the State as an Engineer. Should you wish such a service, after you are fully qualified, I have no doubt you can obtain it. The spirit of Internal

Improvement seems to be awakening here. I have put it in motion by an attempt to construct a Turnpike road between Lexington and Frankfort, which I think will be made.[4]

But my opinion remains the same as to the propriety of your Studying Law when you leave the Point. That is my sincere and anxious wish, which will however be yielded to yours', if you have a contrary one.

We have had the most disagreeable fall I ever experienced Rain — rain — incessant rain. I hope the weather has been better with you. . . .

ALS. Henry Clay Memorial Foundation, Lexington, Ky.   1. Clay's step-father, Henry Watkins. On Dec. 4, 1829, ten days after her husband's death, Elizabeth Clay Watkins died at the age of 80.   2. Patsy Watkins (Mrs. William B.) Blackburn was Clay's half-sister. Col. Blackburn, her husband, was a lawyer residing in Versailles, Ky.   3. Clay's land lay on the Illinois side of the Wabash, in Edgar County, Ill., between Paris, Ill., and Clinton, Ind. In Dec., 1829, Clay put his son Thomas Hart Clay to work on this farm of 137 acres, called "Clay's Prairie." He subsequently supplied the place with seed, livestock, and other farm equipment. By mid-1833 the place had accumulated debt enough to cause Clay to sell off the animals, liquidate the operation, and bring son Thomas Hart back to Lexington. In the fall of 1836, however, he was still paying Illinois taxes on the land. Moore, Morton & Co. to Clay, Illinois Land Agency, Quincy, Sept. 5, 1836. ADS. DLC-TJC (DNA, M212, R18). Receipt, M.K. Alexander, Clerk, Oct. 24, 1836. *Ibid.*   4. The 1830s opened a period of rapid turnpike building. By 1838-39 several turnpike road companies operated out of Lexington, including the Lexington, Versailles & Frankfort Turnpike Co.   J. Winston Coleman, Jr., *The Squire's Sketches of Lexington* (Lexington, 1972), 40. Clay was active in the movement for macadamizing various streets and roads. On Oct. 30, 1829, a large public meeting held in Lexington endorsed a plan for the Lexington-Maysville Turnpike, the first macadamized road in the state. George W. Ranck, *History of Lexington Kentucky* (Cincinnati, 1872), 317.   For more on turnpike development in Kentucky, see Turner W. Allen, "The Turnpike System in Kentucky: A Review of State Road Policy in the Nineteenth Century," *FCHQ* (July, 1954), 28:239-59.

From Henry B. Bascom, Pittsburgh, December 4, 1829. States that he is traveling as general agent of the American Colonization Society "and am successful, in my efforts." Comments on Clay's political prospects: "I have lately *toured* & pretty extensively thro' N. York, where I find you have many friends — Pena. is *leaning* toward you — Ky is gradually becoming *sane*, & so of some other states —" Suggests "caution" on the "*Masonic* excitement" and "the question of the *Purchase of Texas*." Notes that the latter issue "is exciting much *alarm* in the non-slaveholding states — and if you *touch* it, the *contact* will *tell*, for or against you —" ALS. DLC-HC (DNA, M212, R4).

From WILLIAM L. BRENT   Steamboat "Facility," Ohio River, December 5, 1829

I am so far on my way to Louisiana and cannot pass through your state without writing to you. When I left Washington I calculated upon taking Lexington in my way, but being detained by bad roads I am compelled to relinquish that determination.

I feel much disappointed and in rather bad spirits at the result of the late elections in the western states and in Maryland & New Jersey,[1] in all of which we hoped for majorities opposed to the present administration. — As I have always thought, our friends ought now to see, that without union & discipline we will always be defeated. It was the case in Maryland the people could not be brought up to the *acting* point, for the want of an open avowed object, a *rallying point*. — The mere Idea of opposing Genl. Jackson would not and will not do, we must have an avowed object to support, a *Substitute* for him — Rely upon it, that, the Jacksonians manage things better, From the moment Mr Adams was elected they not only declared an opposition, but they named their Candidate, and having carried their choice, they do not rest there, but

132

they still keep their party together by holding out the Idea that Genl Jackson will be a candidate again, and their Committees and Sub-Committees are constantly in action — we *wait* for events to develope themselves and contingencies to occur, and they *act* for the moment. — In Maryland there is a large Majority opposed to Genl Jackson but the people say, why oppose him, if we have no other Candidate given us to rally upon — I have seen many friends since the elections in Maryland and N. jersey and upon the road as I travelled out to the West, and I find the opinion gaining ground very fast that, Your success in opposition to Genl Jackson would be doubtful but the Genl aside, Yr election would be certain — This proceeds alone from our party indirectly admitting it, by being afraid to act in opposition, and by the tame submission to his acts — Suppose You or Mr Adams had been President and introduced the abominable proscription that Genl Jackson has, do You believe that the opposition would have contended itself with a few Newspapers strictures? No! the people would have been roused and stimulated, by public meetings being called and the expression of feelings opposed to such a course, and it would have been right, — Why do we not act in the same way,! we want *energy* and union as a party, and our *fears* to attack, are defeating us, if they have not already done it. — I have represented these things, but my influence is too small to have any weight and I have always been replied to, that "*we ought to look to the West for our movements* —" so I think too, but our western friends upon this occasion certainly have not acted with their usual energy. —

There is another subject in which we manage the "canvass" most wretchedly. — From Mr Adam's election to this day, the object of the party has been to assail and destroy You in every way in their power — This object is never lost for a moment. not a column in their Newspapers is ever printed, which does not contain an attack upon you — Why is this done? Is it not to put You out of the way of Calhoun, or Van Buren. Does it not shew that You are the only person they fear and that they feel Your Superior claims before the people. Ought our party to rest under this constant attack, without meeting them with their own arms? why are Mr Calhoun & Mr Van Buren left without notice! Ought not our papers to keep up the same constant attacks upon these Gentlemen that they encourage against you? — In other times and in a different state of things, I would say no, but the people have been corrupted and demoralised by the System pursued by the present ruling party, and if we leave things to the result of their Judgment, I fear it will not do —

How will this "Masonic" question effect you?[2] I am sorry it has been got up — You are a mason and as such cannot oppose Your Society, besides it is *Intolerance* and not consistent with the principles of our free Government. I heard a friend of Yours say the other day "I prefer Mr Clay to any M[an in th]e union, but if he be a Mason, I am opposed to making him President" — are not our friends sorry to push this question? I am told that neither Van Buren or Judge McClean [*sic*, John McLean] are Masons, and I find the question so far working in their favor with some — . After the election of Genl Jackson, I should not be supprised at the elevation of any man — . It appears to me that if a man is to be proscribed because he is a Mason, he ought to be for his religion. — You know these things will make no difference with me, for *Masons* or *no Masons* You must be satisfied of the Sincerity with which I advocate Yr elevation to the Presidency — as the only event I wish from my heart to witness in this world, for the prosperity and happiness of our Country. In saying this too, You know how to appreciate my motive and to make proper allowances for the warmth of feeling of a friend.

I saw Genl [Peter B.] Porter in the City and he told me he intended to write to You, of course I need not say what he mentioned to me. — Excuse me, for what I am going to say. I know you estimate Genl Porter very highly and I would not say any thing against him — He may be your Sincere friend, but I believe he is a better friend to himself — Yr friends were much hurt at his calling and leaving his card at Genl Jacksons, and his *dining* with him — . after Genl Jackson's conduct towards Mr Adams and his Cabinet, and his avowed hostility to you and yr friends, assailing upon every occasion Your private characters, I do think, that no circumstance under Heaven, ought to have induced Genl Porter to have stooped to *leave his card* and *dine* with him — I would have suffered poverty and death sooner than have done such a thing — . Genl Porter observed to me, that he had left his Card with the President and in return had that moment received an invitation to dine and that he did not know whether He ought to accept it or not and asked my opinion — I replied to him "Sir, *You* ought never to have left a card for Genl. Jackson, there was your error, but having done it, the rules of gentlemanly politeness requires you to accept the invitation, if you cannot give a Satisfactory excuse, but I am truly sorry that *You* should have placed yourself in that situation." His reply was, "I have accounts to settle with the Department of War, and I thought it best policy to call upon the President" — . I feel hurt and mortified at his conduct — . How very differently he ought to have acted. — I name this to You, out of no ill will to Porter, but I think it my duty as Yr friend to communicate to you every thing that I think looks a little awry and in doing it I speak to you freely. Shall we See You in New orleans this winter? I trust and hope You will come — I think You ought. — If you do write to me in time beforehand, that I may be in N. orleans when you arrive — At all events write to me and direct to St. Martinsville, St. Martin, Louisiana.

I retir[e] to N. orleans at the meeting of our Legislature, and upon assertaining our strength I will try to get something done, expressive of our Confidence in You and approbation of Your political course, as well as some *resolution* disapproving the *persecution* You have undergone, and *disbelief* in the charges and a hope to see you at some proper time and soon elevated to the first office in the Country — write to me, if you think it best not to have it done — Between us every Confidence is to [be] placed, and I trust you will speak to me always without restraint, as I do to You. . . .

ALS. DLC-HC (DNA, M212, R4).   1. For results of the Maryland election, see Warfield to Clay, April 9, 1829; for New Jersey see Southard to Clay, Sept. 12, 1829.   2. See, 7:186-87.

From JOHN Q. ADAMS   Washington, December 11, 1829
On my return here from the North a few days Since I received your Letter of 23d. Octr written at Frankfort and enclosing the printed copy of Mr Jefferson's Letter to Mr Breckenridge [*sic*, John Breckinridge] of 12. Augt 1803.[1] It corresponds in opinion with his Letter to Mr [William] Dunbar of nearly the Same date which had been published before.[2]

The Sacrifice of principle, by Mr Jefferson, in Sanctioning The assumption by Congress of the power to do that which he thus acknowledges could rightfully be done only by an amendment to the Constitution, is destined to produce Consequences from which I turn my eyes.

I have written a reply to the Confederate Appeal of Mr [William B.] Giles's auxiliaries;[3] but have hitherto forborne to publish it — The friends to whom I have communicated it are not altogether agreed as to the expediency of its immediate publication, and I have cheerfully postponed it for the present   When published I Shall not fail of transmitting a copy of it to you —

I offer you my warm and Sincere thanks as well for your condolence as for your congratulations. I have had the pleasure this day of Seeing Mr Clarke [sic, James Clark], and of Learning from him the entire re-establishment of your health — I saw Mr [Samuel L.] Southard last Saturday at Philadelphia, and rejoiced at meeting him, quite recovered both in health and Spirits — Mr [James] Brown is also at Philadelphia; but my Stay there was so Short I did not See him. I heard that Mrs Brown's health was much improved. . . .

ALS. DLC-HC (DNA, M212, R4). 1. Clay to Adams, Oct. 23, 1829. 2. Paul L. Ford (ed.), *The Works of Thomas Jefferson* (New York, 1905), 10:19-20. 3. On Nov. 26, 1828, Harrison G. Otis *et al.* wrote Adams asking for specific evidence on his allegation that certain Massachusetts Federalists had conspired against the Union during the embargo crisis of 1807-8. Adams replied on Dec. 20, 1828, but refused to give specifics. The group responded on Jan. 28, 1829, in a letter headed "Appeal." See *Correspondence Between John Quincy Adams, Esquire, President of the United States, and Several Citizens of Massachusetts Concerning the Charge of a Design to Dissolve the Union Alleged to Have Existed in That State.* Boston, 1829. For Giles' involvement in this controversy see 7:516-17 and Charles Francis Adams (ed.), *Memoirs of John Quincy Adams* (Philadelphia, 1876); 8:121.

From Eliza [Mrs. Josiah S.] Johnston, Washington, December 12, 1829. Apologizes profusely for not having written sooner. Notes that she and her husband arrived in Washington from Philadelphia just in time for the convening of Congress. Continues: "I have been gratified to find many of my friends here, altho' much dispirited by the sad changes we hear from every one, that the party in power are in a most desirable state of confusion, differing openly with each other, some of them not speaking — the Ladies however with Mrs. [Emily] Donelson at their head, have determined to be very amiable & have called promptly upon all the Strangers in this popular movement, has made the best impression, I believe if you had consulted your own feelings on this subject, you would have recommended it to the Ladies of the last administration — I have not yet seen Mrs. [William T.] Barry, or Mrs. [John] Eaton, (they called together), I wish to spare the feelings of the latter as long as possible, as I fear I shall, be compelled in accordance with the arbitrary decrees of the society here, to leave her visit unreturned — I am sure you will not blame me, when I tell you that my sympathy has been excited for her, & her husband, women are the greatest persecutors of their own sex, quietly, or otherwise where Christian charity should incline us to forgiveness — perhaps I have taken a wrong view of the subject, it will however be of little consequence to the unfortunate person, if I never see her, or confess my feelings to the world —"

States, further: "The East room is now really furnished; for 9,000$ — the effect is well enough, it is gay, & will be handsome when well lit, but there is a glaring want of uniformity about it — the mirrors are splendid, but the curtains of common worsted, & so it is, through the whole apartment — they have given one very grand dinner, a few days before our arrival, the President had Mrs. [C.D.E.J. Bangeman] Huygens on his right, & Mrs. Eaton on the left, who was conducted to table by Mr. [Charles R.] Vaughen [sic, Vaughan], it is said to have gone off very well — Mr. [Daniel] Webster is to be married on Wednesday next to Miss [Caroline] LeRoy of N. York, he has at last made choice of a person whom his friends approve, she is a Lady of good manners, good appearance & suitable age (say thirty) he comes next week with the bridal party."

Discusses other current gossip, mentioning that James Brown "is expected this Eveg, to make a short visit to the President." Although Mrs. Brown is not well enough to accompany him "I found her in better health & having a better appearance that [sic, than] was expected her countenance bears the marks of having been a great sufferer, but her person is still full—Dr. [Philip] Physic gives her encouragement—"

Closes by urging Clay to "let them send you to the Senate next year," and by inquiring about his plans to visit New Orleans this winter. ALS. DLC-HC (DNA, M212, R4).

From JOSIAH S. JOHNSTON
Washington, December 12, 1829

We arrived here on the 2d. & took our old Lodgings—We have been absent near 9 nine months & have travelled about seven thousand miles without the slightest accident—

You have seen the Message,[1] Which has been looked for with so much interest.—You will know how to estimate it without any Commentary from me & you will find in the papers the usual remarks made by individuals upon it—it is clear he does not express the opinions of any party in this Country & by disclosing his own upon any Subject, he pleases one party while he offends the other—but I do not believe the party can be shaken by the declaration of any opinions—I think he is explicit with regard to the Tarif[f], he has put the Seal to that—If the South & especially Virginia have been influenced by principle, What pretense can they now have for sustaining him—What must S. Carolina say? What must [James, Jr.] Hamilton now think?

His Scruples about the Constitution & his attack on the Bank are intended as a Set off & a Salvo for the South—While the distribution of the revenue & the National Bank, will be as little acceptable to them as the acts they now Complain of—

With regard to the Indians, he has thrown his whole power into the Seat of Georgia—How Can 70 000 indians be removed & What must become of them if moved?—[2] If rotation is the true principle, & the Zeal of a New Man is better than the experience of an old officer every one should be turn[e]d out—& if 4 years is the proper period of Service, all his own ought to go out at the expiration of the term—

If every principle that is contested is Considered doubtful, & no doubtful power Can be experienced until the Constitution is Amended, The will of the Majority Must in every such Case yield to the Minority—We have not heard from the South, but I am prepared to hear them approve of it—as they have every thing else.—

But Sooner or Later We may expect a breach among them—when & how it will occur I cannot anticipate—

All that I have told you of the State of things here during the Summer is perfectly true. Van Buren has prepared himself to Succeed to the Jackson party to the exclusion of Calhoun   He has availed himself of the Case of the Lady [Peggy Eaton] to Commit himself with [John] Eaton & [William T.] Barry & through them to obtain the confidence of the President—This is the Nucleus of the Van Buren party & Calhoun is forever extinguished—Unless the President dies. Calhoun has just arrived & there are yet no indication of the Course they mean to pursue   Genl. Jackson intends to Continue for another term—Van Buren is to be successor to the party—Calhoun cannot be a Candidate again for the Vice Presidency—none of his friends can expect any portion of the power of this admn—It appears to me he is as effectually excluded Under the present arrangement, as well as all his friends, as we are—& the exclusion operates as efficiently on them as Proscription does on others. [Samuel D.] Ingham is Said to be his friend—but he has no weight in the Cabinet & all the app[ointmen]ts. in his Department [Treasury] have been made without any view to him—The Collectors have in every instance been Selected by the President—Ingham will eventually go with the party in his State [Pa.]—I cannot perceive what hope remains for him or his friends, or What motive he can have for adherence—The present affords an opportunity of breaking on principle—This system of Proscription, the power of removal the appt. of Editors—&c. His policy with regard to the Tarif, distribution of the public money, national Bank &C. &C. are good grounds of difference & consistently with their principles they cannot support his administration—But now is the time—before we act on the nominations to take their Stand—But I confess I have little hope, although they must break Sooner or Later

Calhoun has very little popularity to stand on but he has friends enough to give us the Controul in the Senate & to hold the admn. in check—& has besides Considerable talent in the House of R—

[Thomas] Ritchie is Wedded to Van Buren—I think the Majority of the Jackson Men in that State [Va.] will go with him—& perhaps N. C. & Georgia will do the same—so that with all their profestations of principle I doubt if they would Sustain any more, against Van Buren Who should ever avow all their principles—But the Cecession of Calhoun would in the present state of parties give us great strength   The succeeding week will throw more light on this subject & next Sunday I will write you fully—I think We shall have indications enough to judge by that time.

ALS. DLC-TJC (DNA, M212, R13).   1. *MPP*, 2:442-62.   2. Clay to Hammond, Oct. 7, 1829.

From John L. Bridges, Harrodsburg, Ky., December 13, 1829. Reports that Clay's visit to Harrodsburg [Bridges to Clay, September 6, 1829] "has had a Most happy effect, you now have warm friends in this County in the same individuals who has been hitherto your bitter opposers; you have nothing to fear in this quarter, your friends here will attend to your Interest—" Advises that a nomination of Clay for president by the present session of the Kentucky legislature would be premature, but "I have no doubt of its being adopted at the next session by an overwhelming majority—" Believes there should be resolutions adopted at this session in favor of the American System. ALS. DLC-HC (DNA, M212, R4).

From Thomas Patterson, Washington, December 13, 1829. Discusses the political situation in Washington, saying: "You have seen the Presidents message composed by the company. It is wondered here whether he would recognize a single section of it if shewn to him 10 days hence—If you have ever noticed the practice of quack doctors to run down others and praise themselves & their remedies you see it completely exemplified in the case of this message and its accompanying documents—I refer you to the extreme eloquence of Mr [John] Branch. Mr [John] Eaton is doing great things, if he manages the army a a [*sic*] few years, Buonapartes [*sic*, Napoleon Bonaparte] & Wellingtons war regulations will sink into fooleries—" Notes also that William T. Barry "rises into most conspicuous view the many abuses reformed" in the Post Office Department. Asks: "But where is John McLean will he calmly hear such a reprimand for his ill management of the Post Office. . . . he must come off the fence now or confess his faults . . . he was not your friend nor Mr Adams." Believes McLean "is rapidly losing his influence"; that Van Buren "is making rapid strides" and seems to be winning over William H. Crawford's supporters; and that John C. Calhoun who is "Thought to be the author of most of the President message" is "going down" and "no doubt will advise Jackson to go for another term unless he finds himself ready to proceed for himself at the close of the present 4 years."

Comments on his own endangered position as a clerk for the House of Representatives, saying that Matthew St. Clair Clarke, the chief clerk, was chosen "with the express view that he should make no change in the office—" Now an attempt is being made to remove Thomas Patterson himself, and "whether they will succeed or not a few days will determine—I this day got wind of this   I have mentioned it 12 or 15 friends of the late administration who seem to be very hot. Every man of them say they voted for Clarke on the express conviction that he would turn out no one. It will be tomorrow morning in the possession of every Adam & Clay man. They seem to be hot indeed. They say if Mathw turns out a man of us he is ruined forever. . . . I shall have to bear events but I had rather sweat than be a slave for the support of my large and helpless family—I must breast the storm which seems to be coming—If I am turned out I shall have to sacrifise my property this is the worst."

States his hope that "the tariff question will run high even this session—" Wonders what effect Jackson's denunciation of the Bank of the U.S. will have in the cities and commerical regions of the country. Mentions the Peggy Eaton affair, noting that Van Buren who "has no wife & will not fail to advantage even by this case or matter." Further, "Mrs Eaton I am told flatters up the old General in great stile and it runs down even to the hem of his garment like oil—" ALS. DLC-HC (DNA, M212, R4). For Jackson's message, see Johnston to Clay, December 12, 1829.

To GENTLEMEN OF THE COLONIZATION SOCIETY OF KENTUCKY

Frankfort, Ky., December 17, 1829

I most sincerely wish that the task of addressing you, on this occasion, had been assigned, by the Board of Managers, to some individual more competent than I am to explain and illustrate and enforce the claims of the Society to the friendly and favorable consideration of the public.[1] I yield to none in a thorough persuasion of the utility of the scheme of the Society, in a profound conviction of its practicability, and in an ardent desire for its complete success. But I am sensible that there are many others who could more happily than I can, throw around the subject those embellishments which are best calculated to secure attention, and engage the cordial and energetic co-operation of the community. — When the application was first made to me to deliever this address, I hesitated to comply with it, because I apprehended that my motives would be misconceived, and my language be misrepresented. Subsequent reflection determined me to adhere to the maxim of my whole life, to endeavor to render all the good in my power, without being restrained by the misconceptions to which I might expose myself. In entering upon the duty which has devolved upon me, I ask only the exercise of ordinary liberality in judging the imperfections which will doubtless mark its performance.

In surveying the United States of North America and their Territories, the beholder perceives, among their inhabitants, three separate and distinct races of men, originally appertaining to three different continents of the globe, each race varying from the others in color, physical properties, and moral and intellectual endowments. The European is the most numerous; and, as well from that fact, as from its far greater advance in civilization and in the arts, has the decided ascendency over the other two, giving the law to them, controling their condition, and responsible for their fate to the Great Father of all, and to the enlightened world. The next most numerous and most intelligent race, is that which sprung from Africa, the largest portion of which is held in bondage by their brethren, decendants of the European. The aborigines, or Indian race, are the least numerous, and, with the exception of some tribes, have but partially emerged from the state of barbarism in which they were found on the first discovery of America. Whence, or how they came hither, are speculations for the research of the curious, on which authentic history affords no certain light.

Their future fortunes or condition, form no part of the subject of this address. I shall, I hope, nevertheless be excused for the digression of dedicating a few passing observations to the interesting remnant of these primitive possessors of the new world. I have never been able to agree in the expediency of employing any extraordinary exertions to blend the white and colored races together, by the ceremony of marriage. There would be a motive for it if the Indians were equal or superior to their white brethren, in physical or intellectual powers. But the fact is believed to be otherwise. The mixture improves the Indian, but deteriorates the European element. Invariably it is remarked, that those of the mixed blood, among the Indians, are their superiors, in war, in council, and in the progress of the useful arts, whilst they remain in the rear of the pure white race still farther than they are in advance of the pure Indian. In those instances (chiefly among the French) during the progress of the settlement of this continent, in which the settlers have had most intercourse with the Indians, they have rather sunk to the level of their state, than contributed essentially to their civilization.

But if there be no adequate recommendation to the white race, of an union by intermarriage with the Indian, we are enjoined by every duty of religion, humanity and magnanimity to treat them with kindness and justice, and to recall them if we can, from their savage to a better condition. The United States stand charged with the fate of these poor children of the woods in the face of their common Maker, and in presence of the world. And, as certain as the guardian is answerable for the education of his infant ward, and the management of his estate, will they be responsible here and hereafter, for the manner in which they shall perform the duties of the high trust which is committed to their hands, by the force of circumstances. Hitherto, since the United States became an independent power among the nations of the earth, they have generally treated the Indians with justice, and performed towards them all the offices of humanity. Their policy, in this respect, was vindicated during the negotiations at Ghent, and the principles which guided them in their relations with the Indians, were then promulgated to all Christendom. On that occasion, their representatives, holding up their conduct in advantageous contrast with that of Great Britain, and the other powers of Europe, said: "From the rigor of this system, however, as practised by Great Britain and all the European powers in America, the humane and liberal policy of the United States has voluntarily relaxed. A celebrated writer on the laws of nations, to whose authority British jurists have taken particular satisfaction in appealing, after stating, in the most explicit manner, the legitimacy of colonial settlements in America, to the exclusion of all rights of uncivilized Indian tribes, has taken occasion to praise the first settlers of New-England, and the founder of Pennsylvania, in having purchased of the Indians the lands they resolved to cultivate, notwithstanding their being provided with a charter from their sovereign. It is this example which the United States, since they became, by their independence, the sovereigns of the territory, have adopted and organized into a *political system*. Under that system, the Indians residing within the United States are *so far independent*, that they live under *their own customs and not under the laws of the United States*; that their rights upon the lands where they inhabit or hunt, are *sacred* to them by boundaries defined in *amicable treaties* between the United States and themselves; and that whenever those boundaries are varied, it is also by *amicable and voluntary treaties*, by which they receive from the United States ample compensation for every right they have to the land ceded by them. They are so far dependent as not to have the right to dispose of their lands to any private person, nor to any power other than the United States, and to be under *their protection alone*, and not under that of any *other* power. Whether called subjects, or by whatever name designed, *such* is the relation between them and the United States. That relation is neither asserted now for the first time, nor did it originate with the treaty of Greenville. These principles have been *uniformly recognized* by the Indians themselves, not only by that treaty, but in *all the other previous as well as subsequent treaties* between them and the United States." Such was the solemn annunciation to the whole world, of the principles and of the system, regulating our relations with the Indians, as admitted by us and recognized by them. There can be no violation of either, to the disadvantage of the weaker party, which will not subject us, as a nation, to the just reproaches of all good men, and which may not bring down upon us the maledictions of a more exalted and powerful tribunal.

Whether the Indian portion of the inhabitants of the United States will survive, or become extinct, in the progress of population which the European race is rapidly making from the shores of the Atlantic to those of the Pacific ocean, *provided they are treated with justice and humanity*, is a problem of less importance. The two races are not promiscuously mingled together, but are generally separate and distinct communities. There is no danger to the whites or to their purity, from the power or from the vices of the Indians. The case is widely different with those who form the immediate object of this address.

The African part of our population, or their ancestors, were brought hither forcibly and by violence, in the prosecution of the most abominable traffic that ever disgraced the annals of the human race. They were chiefly procured, in their native country, as captives in war, taken, and subsequently sold by the conqueror as slaves to the slave trader. Sometimes the most atrocious practices of kidnapping were employed to obtain possession of the victims. Wars were frequent between numerous and barbarous neighboring tribes scattered along the coasts or stretched upon the margin of large rivers of Africa. These wars were often enkindled and prosecuted for no other object than to obtain a supply of subjects for this most shocking commerce. In these modes, husbands were torn from their wives, parents from their children, brethren from each other, and every tie cherished and respected among men, was violated. Upon the arrival, at the African coast, of the unfortunate beings thus reduced to slavery, they were embarked on board of ships carefully constructed and arranged to contain the greatest amount of human beings. Here they were ironed and fastened in parallel rows, and crowded together so closely, in loathsome holes, as not to have room for action or for breathing wholesome air. The great aim was to transport the greatest possible number, at the least possible charge, from their native land to the markets for which they were destined. The greediness of cupidity was frequently disappointed and punished in its purposes, by the loss of moieties of whole cargoes of the subjects of this infamous commerce, from want and suffering and disease on the voyage. How much happier were they who thus expired, than their miserable survivors!

These African slaves were brought to the continent of America, and the islands adjacent to it, and formed the parent stock of the race now amongst us. They were brought to the colonies now constituting the United States, under the sanction, and by the authority of British laws, which at an early period of our colonial existence, admitted and tolerated the trade. It is due to our colonial ancestors, to say, that they frequently and earnestly, but unsuccessfully remonstrated to the British Crown against the continuance of the practice. The introduction of slavery into this country is not, therefore, chargeable to them, but to a government in which they had no voice, and over which they had no control. It is equally due to our parent state to advert to the honorable fact, that in the midst of the Revolutionary war, when contending for her own independence and liberty, she evinced the sincerity of the spirit, in which those remonstrances had been addressed to the British throne, by denouncing, under the severest penalties, the further prosecution of the slave trade, within her jurisdiction. And I add, with great satisfaction, that the Congress of the United States passed an act, abolishing the trade as early as by their constitution it was authorized to do. On the second day of March, 1807, the act was passed, for which it was my happy lot to vote, the first section of which enacts, "that from and after the first day of January, 1808, it shall not be lawful to import or bring into the United States, or the territories thereof, from any foreign kingdom, place or country, any negro, mulatto or person of color, with intent to hold, sell or dispose of such negro, mulatto or person of color, as a slave, or to be held to service or labor." Thus terminated, we may hope forever, in the United States, a disgraceful traffic, which drew after it a train of enormities surpassing in magnitude, darkness and duration, any that ever sprang from any trade pushed by the enterprise or cupidity of man.

The United States, as a nation, are not responsible for the original introduction, or the subsequent continuance of the slave trade. Whenever, as has often happened, their character has been assailed, in foreign countries and by foreign writers, on account of the institution of slavery among us, the justness of that vindication has been admitted by the candid, which transfers to a foreign government the origin of the evil. Nor are the United States, as a sovereign power, responsible for the continuance of slavery within their limits, posterior to the establishment of their independence; because by neither the articles of confederation, nor by the present constitution, had they power to put an end to it by the adoption of any system of emancipation. But from that epoch the responsibility of the several states in which slavery was tolerated, commenced, and on them devolved the momentous duty of considering whether the evil of African slavery is incurable, or admits of a safe and practicable remedy. In performing it, they ought to reflect, that if when a given remedy is presented to their acceptance, instead of a due examination and deliberate consideration of it, they promptly reject it, and manifest an impatience whenever a suggestion is made of any plan to remove the evil, they will expose themselves to the reproach of yielding to the illusions of self-interest, and of insincerity in the professions which they so often make of a desire to get rid of slavery. It is a great misfortune, growing out of the actual condition of the several states, some being exempt and others liable to this evil, that they are too prone to misinterpret the views and wishes of each other in respect to

141

it. The North and the South and the West, when they understand each other well, must be each convinced, that no other desire is entertained towards the others by any one of them, than their welfare and prosperity. If the question were submitted, whether there should be either immediate or gradual emancipation of all the slaves in the United States, without their removal or colonization, painful as it is to express the opinion, I have no doubt that it would be unwise to emancipate them. For I believe, that the aggregate of the evils which would be engendered in society, upon the supposition of such general emancipation, and of the liberated slaves remaining promiscuously among us, would be greater than all the evils of slavery, great as they unquestionably are.

The several States of the Union were sensible of the responsibility which accrued to them on the establishment of the independence of the United States, in regard to the subject of slavery. And many of them, beginning at a period prior to the termination of the Revolutionary war, by successive and distinct acts of legislation, have effectually provided for the abolition of slavery within their respective jurisdictions. More than thirty years ago an attempt was made in this Commonwealth, to adopt a system of gradual emancipation, similar to that which the illustrious Franklin had mainly contributed to introduce in the year 1779, in the state founded by the benevolent Penn. And, among the acts of my life, which I look back to with most satisfaction, is, that of my having co-operated with other zealous and intelligent friends, to procure the establishment of that system in this State. We believed that the sum of good which would have been attained by the State of Kentucky, in a gradual emancipation of her slaves at that period, would have far transcended the aggregate of mischief which might have resulted to herself and the Union together, from the gradual liberation of them, and their dispersion and residence in the United States. We were overpowered by numbers, but submitted to the decision of the majority with the grace which the minority in a republic, should ever yield to such a decision. I have nevertheless never ceased, and never shall cease, to regret a decision, the effects of which have been to place us in the rear of our neighbors who are exempt from slavery, in the state of agriculture, the progress of manufactures, the advance of improvement, and the general prosperity of society.

Other states in which slavery exists, have not been unmindful of its evils, nor indifferent to an adequate remedy for their removal But most of them have hitherto reluctantly acquiesced in the continuance of these evils, because they thought they saw no practical scheme for their removal, which was free from insuperable objection and difficulty. Is there then really no *such* remedy? Must we endure perpetually all the undoubted mischiefs of the state of slavery, as it affects both the free and bond portions of the population of these States? Already the slaves may be estimated at two millions, and the free population at ten, the former being in the proportion of one to five of the latter. Their respective numbers will probably duplicate in periods of thirty-three years. In the year '63, the number of the whites will probably be twenty, and of the blacks four millions; in ninety-six, forty and eight, and in the year 1929, about a century, eighty and sixteen millions. What mind is sufficiently extensive in its reach, what nerves sufficiently strong, to contemplate this vast and progressive augmentation, without an awful foreboding of the tremendous consequences? If the two descriptions of population were equally spread and intermingled over the whole surface of the United States, their diffusion might diminish the danger of their action and corrupting influence upon each other. But this is not the state of the fact. The slaves of the United States are chiefly restricted to one quarter of the Union, which may be described with sufficient general accuracy, by a boundary beginning with the mouth of the Potomac river, extending to its head, thence to the Ohio river, and down it and the Mississippi to the Gulph of Mexico, and with that and the Atlantic ocean, and the Bay of Chesapeak to the beginning. Maryland, Delaware, Missouri, a part of Louisiana and Arkansas, compose the whole of the residue of the slave district of the United States. Within those limits all our slaves are concentrated, and, within a portion of them, irresistible causes tend inevitably to their further concentration. In one of the States, comprized within these limits, the slave stock had at the last census, the superiority in numbers, whilst in several others, the enumeration exhibits the two races in nearly equal proportions.

Time alone, which unveils every thing, permitted men to see, can disclose the consequences, now wrapt in futurity, of the state of things which I have slightly touched. But, without violating his prerogative, we may venture to catch, in anticipation, a glimpse of some of them.

The humanity of the slave states of the Union, has prompted them greatly to meliorate the condition of slaves. They are protected in all instances by just laws, from injury, extending to their lives, and in many, from cruelty applied to their persons. Public opinion has done even more than the laws in elevating their condition in the scale of human existence. In this State, as well as in others, they are treated with much kindness, and abundantly supplied with substantial food of meat and bread and vegetables, and comfortable clothing, whilst they are moderately tasked in labor. But still they are subject to many civil disabilities, and there is a vast space between them and the race of freemen. Our laws continue to regard them as property, and consequently as instruments of labor, bound to obey the mandate of others. As a mere labourer, the slave feels that he toils for his master and not himself; that the laws do not recognize his capacity to acquire and hold property, which depends altogether upon the pleasure of his proprietor; and that all the fruits of his exertions are reaped by others. He knows that, whether sick or well, in times of scarcity or abundance, his master is bound to provide for him by the all powerful influence of the motive of self interest. He is generally, therefore, indifferent to the adverse or prosperous fortunes of his master, being contented, if he can escape his displeasure or chastisement, by a careless and slovenly performance of his duties.

This is the state of the relation of master and slave, prescribed by the law of its nature and founded in the reason of things. There are undoubtedly many exceptions, in which the slave dedicates himself to his master with a zealous and generous devotion, and the master to the slave with a parental and affectionate attachment. But it is not my purpose to speak of those particular though endearing instances of mutual regard, but of the general state of the unfortunate relation.

That labour is best, if it can be commanded, in which the labourer knows that he will derive the profits of his industry, that his employment depends upon his diligence, and his reward upon his assiduity. He has then every motive to excite him to exertion and to animate him in perseverance. He knows that if he is treated badly, he can exchange his employer for one who will better estimate his service, that he does not entirely depend upon another's beck and nod, and that whatever he earns is *his*, to be distributed by himself as he pleases, among his wife and children and friends, or enjoyed by himself. He feels, in a word, that he is a free agent, with rights and privileges and sensibilities.

Wherever the option exists to employ, at an equal hire, free or slave labour, the former will be decidedly preferred, for the reasons already assigned. It is more capable, more diligent, more faithful, and, in every respect, worthy of more confidence. In the first settlement of some countries or communities, capital may be unable to command the free labor which it wants, and it may therefore purchase that of slaves. Such was, and yet is the condition of many parts of the United States. But there are others, and they are annually increasing in extent, in which the labour of freemen can be commanded at a rate quite as cheap as that of slaves, in States which tolerate slavery.

Although in particular States, or parts of States, the increase of the African portion of population would seem to be greater than that of the European stock, this fact is believed to be susceptible of an explanation, from the operation of causes of emigration, which would not assign to it greater prolific powers. On the contrary, all the enumerations of the people of the United States sustain clearly the position, that, contrasting the whole European race throughout the Union, with the whole of the African race, bond and free, also throughout the Union, the former multiplies faster than the latter. As time elapses, our numbers will augment, our deserts become peopled, and our country will become as densely populated as its agricultural, manufacturing and commercial faculties will admit. In proportion to the density of population, are the supply and the wages of labor. The demand for labor also increases with the augmentation of numbers, though probably not in the same proportion. Assuming our present population at twelve millions, when it shall be increased, as in about thirty years it will be, to twenty-four millions, we shall have double the amount of available labour that we can command at present. And there will consequently be a great, though probably not proportionate reduction in the wages of labour. As the supply of labourers increases, a competition will arise between, not only individuals, but classes for employment. The superior qualities which have been attributed to free labor, will ensure for that the preference, wherever the alternative is presented of engaging free or slave labour at an equal price. This competition and the preference for white labour, are believed to be already discernable in parts of Maryland, Virginia and Kentucky, and probably existed in Pennsylvania and other States north of Maryland, prior to the disappearance of slaves from among them. The march of the ascendency of free labour over slave, will proceed from the North to the South, gradually entering first the States nearest to the free region. Its progress would be more rapid, if it were not impeded by the check resulting from the repugnance of the white man to work among slaves, or where slavery is tolerated.

In proportion to the multiplication of the descendants of the European stock, and the consequent diminution of the value of slave labour, by the general diminution of wages, will there be an abatement in the force of motives to rear slaves. The master will not find an adequate indemnity in the price of the adult for the charges of maintaining and bringing up the offspring. His care and attention will relax; and he will be indifferent about incurring expenses when they are sick, and in providing for their general comfort, when he knows that he will not be ultimately compensated. There may not be numerous instances of positive violation of the duties of humanity, but every one knows the difference between a negligence, which is not criminal, and a watchful vigilance stimulated by interest, which allows no want to be unsupplied. The effect of this relaxed attention to the offspring, will be to reduce the rates of general increase of the slave portion of our population, whilst that of the other race, not subject to the same neglect, will increase and fill up the void. A still greater effect, from the diminution of the value of labor, will be that of voluntary emancipations; the master being now anxious to relieve himself from a burthen, without profit, by renouncing his right of property. One or two facts will illustrate some of these principles. Prior to the annexation of Louisiana to the United States the supply of slaves from Africa was abundant. The price of adults was generally about $100, a price less than the cost of raising an infant. Then it was believed that the climate of that province was unfavorable to the rearing of negro children, and comparatively few were raised. After the United States abolished the slave trade, the price of adults rose very considerably, greater attention was consequently bestowed on their children, and now no where is the African female more prolific than she is in Louisiana, and the climate of no one of the Southern States is supposed to be more favorable to rearing the offspring. The serfs of Russia possess a market value inferior to that of African slaves of the United States; and, although the Lord is not believed to be bound to provide for the support of his dependent, as the American master is for his slave, voluntary manumissions of the serf are very frequent, influenced in some degree no doubt by his inconsiderable value.

What has tended to sustain the price of slaves in the United States has been, that very fact of the acquisition of Louisiana, but especially the increasing demand for cotton, and the consequent increase of its cultivation. The price of cotton, a much more extensive object of culture than sugar cane, regulates the price of slaves as unerringly as any one subject whatever is regulated by any standard. As it rises in price, they rise; as it falls, they fall. But the multiplication of slaves, by natural causes, must soon be much greater than the increase of the demand for them, to say nothing of the progressive decline which has taken place, in that great Southern staple, within a few years, and which there is no reason to believe will be permanently arrested. Whenever the demand for the cultivation of sugar and cotton comes to be fully supplied, the price of slaves will begin to decline, and as that demand cannot possibly keep pace with the supply, the price will decline more and more. Farming agriculture cannot sustain it; for it is believed that no where in the farming portion of the United States would slave labor be generally employed, if the proprietor were not tempted to raise slaves by the high price of the Southern market, which keeps it up in his own.

Partial causes may retard the decline in the value of slaves. The tendencies of slaves is to crowd into those countries or districts, if not obstructed by the policy of States, where their labor is most profitably employed. This is the law of their nature, as it is the general law of all capital and labor. The slave trade has not yet been effectually stopt in the Island of Cuba. Whenever it is, as slaves can be there more profitably employed, on more valuable products than in the United States, and as the supply there is much below the demand which will arise out of the susceptibilities of the island for agricultural produce, they will arise in price much higher there than in the United States. If the laws do not forbid it, vast numbers will be exported to that island. And if they do prohibit it, many will be smuggled in, tempted by the high prices which they will bear.

But neither this, nor any other conceiveable cause, can for any length of time, check the fall in the value of slaves to which they are inevitably destined. We have seen that, as slaves diminish in price, the motive of the proprietors of them to rear the offspring will abate, that consequent neglect in providing for their wants will ensue, and consequent voluntary emancipation will take place. That adult slaves will, in process of time, sink in value even below a hundred dollars each, I have not a doubt. This result may not be brought about by the termination of the first period of their duplication, but that it will come, at some subsequent, and not distant period, I think perfectly clear. Whenever the price of the adult shall be less than the cost of raising him from infancy, what inducement will the proprietor of the parent have to incur that expense? In such a state of things, it will be in vain that the laws prohibit manumission. No laws can be enforced or will be respected, the effect of which is the ruin of those on whom they operate. In spite of all their penalties the liberation or abandonment of slaves will take place.

As the two races progressively multiply and augment the source of supply of labor, its wages will diminish, and the preference already noticed will be given of free to slave labor. But another effect will also arise. There will be not only a competition between the two races for employment, but a struggle, not perceptible perhaps to the superficial observer, for subsistence. In such a struggle the stronger and more powerful race will prevail. And as the law which regulates the state of population in any given community, is derived from the quantity of its subsistence, the further consequence would be an insensible decline in the increase of the weaker race. Pinched by want and neglected by their masters, who would regard them as a burthen, they would be stimulated to the commission of crimes, and especially those of a petty description.

When we consider the cruelty of the origin of negro slavery, its nature, the character of the free institutions of the whites, and the irresistible progress of public opinion, throughout America as well as in Europe, it is impossible not to anticipate frequent insurrections among the blacks in the United States. They are rational beings like ourselves, capable of feeling, of reflection and of judging of what naturally belongs to them as a portion of the human race. By the very condition of the relation which subsists between us, we are enemies of each other. They know well the wrongs which their ancestors suffered, at the hands of our ancestors, and the wrongs which they believe they continue to endure, although they may be unable to avenge them. They are kept in subjection only by the superior intelligence and superior power of the predominant race. Their brethren have been liberated in every part of the continent of America, except in the United States and the Brazils. I have just seen an act of the President of the Republic of the United Mexican States, dated no longer ago than the 15th of September last, by which the whole of them in that Republic have been emancipated. A great effort is now making in Great Britain, which tends to the same ultimate effect, in regard to the negro slaves of the British West Indies.

Happily for us no such insurrection can ever be attended with permanent success, as long as our Union endures. It would be speedily suppressed by the all powerful means of the United States, and it would be the madness of despair in the blacks that should attempt it. But if attempted in some parts of the United States, what shocking scenes of carnage, rapine, and lawless violence might not be perpetrated before the arrival at the theatre of action of a competent force to quell it! And, after it was put down, what other scenes of military rigor and bloody executions would not be indispensably necessary to punish the insurgents, and impress their whole race with the influence of a terrible example!

Of all the descriptions of our population, and of either portion of the African race, the free people of color are by far, as a class, the most corrupt, depraved and abandoned. There are many honorable exceptions among them, and I take pleasure in bearing testimony to some I know. It is not so much their fault, as the consequence of their anomalous condition. Place ourselves, place any men, in the like predicament, and similar effects would follow. They are not slaves, and yet they are not free. The laws, it is true, proclaim them free; but prejudices, more powerful than any laws, deny them the privileges of freemen. They occupy a middle station between the free white population, and the slaves of the United States, and the tendency of their habits is to corrupt both. They crowd our large cities, where those who will work can best procure suitable employment, and where those who addict themselves to vice can best practice and conceal their crimes. If the vicious habits and propensities of this class were not known to every man of attentive observation, they would be demonstrated by the unerring test of the census. According to the last enumeration of the inhabitants of the United States, it appeared that the rate of its annual increase was only about two and a half per cent. whilst that of the other classes was about three. No other adequate cause for this disproportion can be assigned, but that of the improvidence and vices of the class referred to. If previous enumerations exhibited different results, they were owing chiefly to the accession of numbers which it received by the acquisition of Louisiana, and the events of St. Domingo. But, if the reasoning which I have before employed be correct, this class is destined, by voluntary manumission or abandonment, to increase and ultimately perhaps to be more numerous in the United States, than their brethren in bondage, if there be no provision for their removal to another country.

Is there no remedy, I again ask, for the evils of which I have sketched a faint and imperfect picture? Is our posterity doomed to endure forever, not only all the ills flowing from the state of slavery, but all which arise from incongruous elements of population, separated from each other by invincible prejudices, and by natural causes? Whatever may be the character of the remedy proposed, we may confidently pronounce it inadequate, unless it provides efficaciously for the total and absolute separation, by an extensive space of water or of land, at least, of the white portion of our population from that which is free of the colored.

This brings me to the consideration of the particular scheme of the American Colonization Society, to which this is Auxiliary. That scheme does not owe the first conception of its design to any individuals, by whose agency the society was first constituted. Several of them, and especially the late Rev. Mr. Finley of New-Jersey, and Mr. Caldwell of the district of Columbia, were entitled to great praise for their spirited exertions in the formation and organization of the society. But the original conception of such a project is to be traced to a date long anterior to their laudable efforts on this subject. However difficult it might have been supposed to be in the execution, it was an obvious remedy, and the suggestion of it may be referred back to a period as remote as the Revolutionary War. The state of Virginia, always preeminent in works of benevolence, prior to the formation of the American Colonization Society, by two distinct acts of her Legislature, separated by intervals of time of sufficient length to imply full deliberation, expressed her approbation of the plan of colonization.

In considering the project of the American Colonization Soceity, our first enquiry should be into what it really is; then what it has done; and finally what it is capable of achieving. It is a voluntary association formed for benevolent purposes, as must be freely acknowledged by all, if they should even prove an experiment to be impracticable. Its aim is to transport to the Western shores of Africa, from the United States, all such free persons of color as choose voluntarily to go. From its origin, and throughout the whole period of its existence, it has constantly disclaimed all intention whatever of interfering in the smallest degree, with the rights of property, or the object of emancipation, gradual or immediate. It is not only without inclination, but it is without power, to make any such interference. It is not even a chartered or incorporated company; and it has no other foundation than that of Bible Societies, or any other christian or charitable unincorporated companies in our country. It knows that the subject of emancipation belongs exclusively to the several states, in which slavery is tolerated, and to individual proprietors of slaves in those states, under and according to their laws. It hopes indeed, (and I trust that there is nothing improper or offensive in the hope) that if it shall demonstrate the practicability of the successful removal to Africa, or free persons of color, with their own consent, the cause of emancipation, either by states or individuals, may be incidentally advanced. That hope is founded not only on the true interest of both races, of our population, but upon the assertion, so repeatedly made, that the great obstacle to emancipation arose out of the difficulty of a proper disposal of manumitted slaves. Its pecuniary means, applicable to the design of the institution, are voluntarily contributed by benevolent states or individuals. The states of Virginia and Maryland, besides numerous pious or generous persons, throughout the United States, have aided the society.

Such was the object of the American Colonization Society, organized at the City of Washington about thirteen years ago. Auxiliary institutions have been formed in various parts of the Union, to aid and co-operate with the parent association, which have limited their exertions chiefly to the transmission to the Treasurer of the Society, of such funds as they could collect by the voluntary contributions of benevolent and charitable individuals. The Auxiliary Society for the State of Kentucky, which I now address, was organized at the commencement of the present year.

The American Colonization Society, so constituted, with such objects and such means, shortly after its formation, went into operation. It transacts its business at home, principally through a Board of Managers, which, for the sake of convenience, is fixed in the Metropolis of the Union, and in Africa, through an agent abiding there and acting under instructions received from the Board. The Society has an annual session in the City of Washington, which is attended by its members, and by representatives from such of the auxiliary institutions as can conveniently depute them; at which sessions the Board of Managers makes a report of the general condition of the affairs of the society during the previous year.

It would be an inexcusable trespass upon your time, to enter into a minute narrative of all the transactions of the society from its commencement up to this time. Those who chose to examine them particularly, will find them recorded in the several reports of the Board of Managers, which, from time to time, have been published under its direction and authority. It will suffice at present, to say that one of the earliest acts of the society was to despatch a competent agent to Africa, to explore its coasts and the countries bordering upon them, and to select a suitable spot for the establishment of the contemplated colony. The society was eminently fortunate in the choice of its agent, as it has been generally in those whom it subsequently engaged in its service. A selection was finally made of a proper district of country, a purchase was effected of it from the native authorities, to which additions have been made as the growing wants of the colony, actual or anticipated, required. The country so acquired, upon terms as moderate as those on which the government of the Union extinguishes the Indian title to soil within the United States, embraces large tracts of fertile land, capable of yielding all the rich and varied products of the Tropics, possesses great commerical advantages, with an extent of sea coast from 150 to 200 miles, and enjoys a salubrious climate, well adapted to the negro constitution, and not so fatal to that of the whites as many thickly peopled parts of the United States.

Within that district of country, the society founded its colony, under the denomination of Liberia, established towns, laid off plantations for the colonists, and erected military works for their defence. Annually, and as often as the pecuniary circumstances of the society would admit, vessels from the ports of the U. States have been sent to Liberia, laden with emigrants and with utensils, provisions and other objects for their comfort. No difficulty has been experienced in obtaining as many colonists as the means of the society were competent to transport. They have been found, indeed, altogether inadequate to accommodate all who were willing and anxious to go. The rate of expense of transportation and subsistence during the voyage, per head, was greater in the earlier voyages. It was subsequently reduced to about $20, and is believed to be susceptible of considerable further reduction. The number of colonists, of both sexes, amounts now to about 1500.

The Colony, in the first periods of its existence, had some collisions with the native tribes, which rose to such a height as to break out in open war about four or five years ago. The war was conducted by the late gallant Reverend Mr. Ashmun, with singular good judgment and fortune, and was speedily brought to a successful close. It had the effect to impress upon the natives, a high idea of the skill, bravery and power of the colonists, and having since become better acquainted with them, perceiving the advantages of the colony, and gradually acquired a taste for its commerce and arts, no further misunderstanding with them is apprehended, and the colony is daily acquiring a salutary influence over them.

The colony has a government adequate to the protection of the rights of persons and property, and to the preservation of order. The agent of the society combines the functions of Governor, commander-in-chief, and highest judicial officer. The colonists share in the government, and elect various officers necessary to the administration. They appoint annually Boards or Committees of public works, of agriculture and of health, which are charged with the superintendance of those important interests. It has established schools for the instruction of youth, and erected houses of public worship, in which divine service is regularly performed. And it has a public library of twelve hundred volumes, and a printing press, which issues periodically a gazette. The colonists follow the mechanical arts, or agriculture, or commerce, as their inclinations or attainments prompt them. The land produces rice, casseda, coffee, potatoes, and all kinds of garden vegetables; and is capable of yielding sugar cane, indigo, in short, all the productions of the Tropics. It is rich, easily tilled, and yields two crops of many articles in the circle of a year. They carry on an advantageous commerce with the natives, by exchanges for ivory, gums, dye-stuffs, drugs and other articles of African origin; and with the United States, which is annually increasing, and which amounted last year to $60,000 in the produce of the colony, and in objects acquired by their traf[f]ic with the natives; receiving in return, such supplies of American and other manufactures as are best adapted to their wants.

Such is the present condition of the Colony, according to the latest intelligence. Here the society may pause, and with its pious and enlightened patrons and a generous public, look back with proud satisfaction, on the work, which, with the blessings of Providence, has so prospered. That in its progress, it has met with obstacles and experienced discouragements, is most true. What great human undertaking was ever exempt from them? Its misfortunes in Africa have been similar in character, though it is confidently believed, less in degree than those which generally attend the establishment of distant colonies, in foreign lands, amidst ignorant and untutored savages. A large portion of the deaths which have taken place, may be attributed to rash exposure, and other imprudencies, under an untried sun, and subject to the action of a strange climate. But the Colony can triumphantly exhibit its bills of mortality, in comparison with those of colonies, in their early foundation, on this or any other continent. And experience justifies the hope, that the instances of mortality will constantly diminish with the augmented population, means and strength of the Colony.

But at home, in the parent country, here in the United States, notwithstanding the concurrence of so many powerful motives recommending success to the exertions of the society, has it met with the most serious opposition and bitter denunciation. At one time it has been represented as a scheme to forge stronger and perpetual chains for the slaves among us. Then, that it had a covert aim to emancipate them all immediately, and throw them, with all their imperfections, loose upon society. Those who judged less unfavorably of the purposes of the institution, pronounced it a bright vision, impracticable in its means and Utopian in its end. There is unfortunately in every community, a class not small, who, devoid themselves of the energy necessary to achieve any noble enterprize, and affecting to penetrate with deeper sagacity into the projects of others, pronounce their ultimate failure, with self-complacency, and challenged by anticipation, the merit of prophetic wisdom. Unmoved by these erroneous and unfriendly views, the society, trusting to the vindication which time and truth never fail to bring, has proceeded steadily and perseveringly in its great work. It has not been deceived. It has every where found some generous patrons and ardent friends. The Legislatures of more than half the States of this enlightened Union, among which I am happy to be able to mention our own, have been pleased to express their approbation of the scheme. It has conciliated the cordial support of the pious clergy of every denomination in the United States. It has been countenanced and aided by that fair sex, which is ever prompt to contribute its exertions in works of charity and benevolence, because it always acts from the generous impulses of pure and uncorrupted hearts. And the society enrolls amongst its members and patrons, some of the most distinguished men of our country, in its Legislative, Executive and Judicial councils. We should be guilty of an unpardonable omission, if we did not on this occasion, mingle our regrets with those of the whole people of these States, on account of the lamented death of one of them, which has recently occurred. He was the President of the American Colonization Society from its origin and throughout the entire period of its existence. Like the Father of his country, his illustrious relative, whose name he bore and whose affection he enjoyed, he was mild and gentle, firm and patriotic. The Bench, of which he was an ornament, and the Bar of which he was the delight, feeling his great loss, deeply, share with us all in the grief which it produces.

The society presents to the American public no project of emancipation, no new chains for those who unhappily are now in bondage, no scheme that is impracticable. It has no power, and it seeks none. It employs no compulsion, and it desires to employ none. It addresses itself solely to the understanding; its revenue flows from spontaneous grants, and all its means and agents and objects are voluntary.

The society believes it is within the compass of reasonable exertions, to transport annually to the colony of Liberia, a number of free persons of colour, with their own voluntary consent, equal to the annual increase of all that class in the United States. That annual increase, estimated according to the return of the last census, from the parent stock of 233, 530, at a rate of augmentation of 2 ½ per cent. per annum, may be stated to be 6000. Estimating the whole expense of the voyage at $20 per head, the total cost of their transportation will be $120,000. Is this sum of such an appalling amount as to transcend the ability of the people of the United States? All admit the utility of the separation of the free people of colour from the residue of the population of the United States, if it be practicable. It is desirable for them, for the slaves of the United States and for the white race. Here invincible prejudices exclude them from the enjoyment of the society of the whites, and deny them all the advantages of freemen. The bar, the pulpit, and our legislative halls are shut to them, by the irresistible force of public sentiment. No talents however great, no piety however pure and devoted, no patriotism however ardent, can secure their admission. They constantly hear the accents, and behold the triumphs, of a liberty which here they can never enjoy. In all the walks of society, on every road which lies before others to honor and fame and glory, a moral incubus pursues and arrests them, paralyzing all the energies of the soul, and repressing every generous emotion of laudable ambition. Their condition is worse than the fabled Tantalus, who could never grasp the fruits and water which seemed within his reach. And when they die

"Memory o'er their tomb no trophies raise."

Why should such an unfortunate class desire to remain among us? Why should they not wish to go to the country of their forefathers, where, in the language of the eloquent Irish barrister, they would "stand redeemed, regenerated and disenthralled by the mighty genius of universal emancipation."

The vices of this class do not spring from any inherent depravity in their natural constitution, but from their unfortunate situation. Social intercourse is a want which we are prompted to gratify by all the properties of our nature. And as they cannot obtain it in the better circles of society, nor always among themselves, they resort to slaves and to the most debased and worthless of the whites. Corruption, and all the train of petty offences, are the consequences. Proprietors of slaves in whose neighborhood any free colored family is situated, know how infectious and pernicious this intercourse is. And the penal records of the tribunals, especially in the large cities, bear frightful testimony to the disproportionate number of crimes committed by the free people of color. The evil of their increase in those cities is so enormous as to call loudly for effective remedy. It has been so sensibly felt in a neighboring city (Cincinnati) as to require, in the opinion of the public authorities, the enforcement of the vigorous measure of expulsion of all who could not give guarantees of their good behaviour. Their congregation in our great capitals has given rise to a new crime, perpetrated by unprincipled whites, and of which persons of that unhappy colored race are the victims. A New-York paper of the 27th ult. but lately fell into my hands, in which I found the following articles: "Beware of kidnappers! It is *well understood* that there is at present in this city, a gang of kidnappers, busily engaged in their vocation of stealing colored children for the Southern market! It is believed that three or four have been stolen within as many days. A little negro boy came to this city from the country three or four days ago. Some strange white persons were very friendly to him, and yesterday morning he was mightily pleased that they had given him some new clothes. And the persons pretending thus to befriend him, entirely secured his confidence. This day he CANNOT be found. Nor can he be traced since seen with one of his new friends yesterday. There are suspicions of a foul nature, connected with some who serve the police in subordinate capacities. It is hinted that there may be those in some authority, not altogether ignorant of these diabolical practices. Let the public be on their guard." To which the editor of the paper from which this quotation is made, appends the following remarks: "It is still fresh in the memories of all, that a cargo or rather drove of negroes was made up from this city and Philadelphia, about the time that the emancipation of all the negroes in this state took place under our present constitution, and were taken through Virginia, the Carolinas, and Tennessee, and disposed of in the state of Mississippi. Some of those who were taken from Philadelphia were persons of intelligence, and after they had been driven through the country in chains, and disposed of by sale on the Mississippi, wrote back to their friends, and were rescued from bondage. The persons who were guilty of this abominable transaction are known, and now reside in the state of North Carolina, and very probably may be engaged in similar enterprises at the present time — at least there is reason to believe, that the system of kidnapping free persons of color from the Northern cities, has been carried on more extensively than the public are generally aware of."

Whilst the concurrence is unanimous as to the propriety of the separation of the free colored race, and their removal to some other country, if it be practicable, opinions are divided as to the most proper place of their destination. Some prefer Hayti, others to set apart a district beyond the Rocky Mountains, within the limits of the territory of the United States, whilst much the largest number concur in the superior advantages of the plan of the American Colonization Society. The society opposes no other scheme. All other projects, if they are executed, are perfectly compatible with its own, and it wishes them full success. The more drains the better for this portion of our population. It would only deprecate the result of a distraction of the public attention amidst a variety of proposals, and a consequent failure to concentrate the energies of the community on any one of them.

Hayti is objectionable as the sole place of their removal, on various accounts. It is too limited in its extent. Although a large island, containing considerable quantities of unseated land, it is incompetent as an assylum, during any great length of time, for the free persons of color of the United States. It possesses no advantage, either in the salubrity of its climate, or the fertility of its soil over the Western Coast of Africa. The productions of both countries are nearly the same. The expense of transportation to the one or to the other, is nearly the same. The emigrants would be in a state of dependence on the present inhabitants of the island, who have more intelligence and have made greater advances in civilization, and moreover possess all the power of the Government. They speak a different language. It should not be the policy of the United States, when they consider the predominant power of the island, and its vicinity to the Southern states, to add strength to it. And finally, Hayti is destitute of some of those high moral considerations which belong to the foundation of a colony in Africa.

The country West of the Rocky Mountains, is also objectionable on several grounds. The expense of transportation of emigrants to it, whether by sea or inland, would be incomparably greater than to Africa. They would be thrown in the midst of Indian tribes, to whom they are as incongruous as with the whites. Bloody and exterminating wars would be the certain consequence; and the United States would be bound to incur great expense in defending them and preserving peace. Finally, that wave of the European race which rose on the borders of the Atlantic, swept over the Alleghany Mountains, reached the Mississippi, and ascended the two great rivers which unite near St. Louis, will at no distant day pass the Rocky Mountains, and strike the Pacific, where it would again produce that very contact between discordant races which it is so desirable to avoid.

The society has demonstrated the practicability of planting a colony on the shores of Africa. Its exertions have been confined exclusively to the free colored people of the United States, and to those of them who are willing to go. It has neither purpose nor power to extend them to the larger portion of that race held in bondage. Throughout the whole period of its existence this disclaimer has been made, and incontestible facts establish its truth and sincerity. It is now repeated, in its behalf, that the spirit of misrepresentation may have no pretext for abusing the public ear. But, although its scheme is so restricted, the society is aware, and rejoices that the principle of African colonization, which it has developed, admits of wider scope and more extensive aplication, by those states and private individuals, who may have the power and the inclination to apply it.

The slave population of the United States, according to the last returns of their census, as was shown more in detail, on another occasion, increased in a ratio of about 46,000 per annum. It may perhaps, now be estimated at not less than 50,000. It was said on that occasion: "Let us suppose, for example, that the whole population at present of the U. States, is twelve millions, of which ten may be estimated of the Anglo Saxon, and two of the African race. If there could be annually transported from the United States, an amount of the African portion equal to the annual increase of the whole of that cast, whilst the European race should be left to multiply, we should find, at the termination of the period of duplication, whatever it may be, that the relative proportions would be as twenty to two. And if the process were continued, during a second term of duplication, the population would be as forty to two—one which would eradicate every cause of alarm or solicitude from the breasts of the most timid. But the transportation of Africans, by creating, to the extent to which it might be carried, a vacuum in society, would tend to accelerate the duplication of the European race, who, by all the laws of population, would fill up the void space." To transport to Africa fifty thousand persons, would cost one million of dollars upon the estimate before stated. One million of dollars applied annually, during a period of sixty or seventy years, would, at the end of it, so completely drain the United States of all that portion of their inhabitants, as not to leave many more than those few who are objects of curiosity in the countries of Europe. And is that sum, one tenth part of what the United States now annually appropriate, as a sinking fund, with out feeling it, and which will soon not be requisite to the extinction of the national debt, capable of producing any suffering or creating any impediment in the execution of other great social objects of the American communities? What a vast moral debt to Africa, to the world and to our common God, should we not discharge by the creation of a new sinking fund of such a paltry sum?

This estimate does not comprehend any indem[n]ity to the owners of slaves for their value, if they are to be purchased for the purpose of colonization. It is presumable that states or individuals, no longer restrained from the execution of their benevolent wish to contribute their endeavors to blot out this great stain upon the American name, by the consideration of the difficulty of a suitable provision for liberated slaves, when they perceive the plan of colonization in successful operation, will voluntarily manumit many for the purpose of their emigration. One of the latest numbers of the National Intelligencer, states the fact, that a recent offer has been made of 2000 slaves to the society, to be sent to Liberia, which the want of funds alone prevents its accepting. If the reasoning before employed, founded upon the decline in value of that description of property, be correct, many will be disposed, to emancipate from less disinterested motives. From some, or all of these sources, and from the free colored population, an amount may be annually obtained for the purposes of colonization, equal to the number of fifty-six thousand which has been supposed. As the work of colonization advances, the ability of the European race to promote it will increase, both from the augmentation of its numbers and of its wealth, and the relative diminution of the negro race. And, in the course of the progress of its execution, it will not be found a burthensome appropriation of some of the revenue of the people of the United States, to purchase slaves, if colonists cannot otherwise be obtained. Meanwhile it affords cause of the sincerest gratification, that in whatever extent the scheme of African colonization is executed, good is attained, without a solitary attendant evil.

I could not discuss the question of the extent of the respective powers of the various governments of the union, without enlarging this address, already too much prolonged, in a most unreasonable degree. That the aggregate of their total powers is fully adequate to the execution of the plan of colonization, in its greatest extent, is incontestible. How those powers have, in fact, been divided and distributed between the General and State Governments, is a question for themselves to decide after careful investigation and full deliberation. We may safely assume that there are some things which each system is competent to perform, towards the accomplishment of the great work. The General Government can treat with foreign powers for the security of the Colony, and with the Emperor of Morocco, or other African Princes or States for the acquisition of territory. It may provide in the Colony an asylum for natives of Africa introduced into the United States, in contravention of their laws, and for their support and protection, as it has done. And it may employ portions of our Navy, whilst engaged in practising to acquire the needful discipline and skill, or in proceeding to their appointed cruising stations, to transport emigrants from the United States to the Colony. Can a nobler service, in time of peace, be performed by the National flag, than that of transporting under its stars and stripes to the land of their ancestors, the sons of injured Africa, there to enjoy the blessings of our pure religion and a real liberty? It can employ the Colony as the best and most efficacious instrument of suppressing the infamous slave trade.

Any of the States may apply, in their proper spheres, the powers which they possess and the means at their command. They may remove restraints upon emancipation, imposed from a painful conviction that slavery, with all its undisputed ills, was better than manumission without removal. Such of them may as can, safely and justly, abolish slavery and follow the example of Pennsylvania, New-York and other States. Any of them can contribute some pecuniary aid to the object. And if an enlargement of the Constitutional powers of the General Government be necessary and expedient, they are competent to grant it.

I have thus, gentlemen, presented a faint and imperfect sketch of what was contemplated by the American Colonization Society, to which you form an auxiliary of what it has done, and of what the principle of African Colonization, which it has successfully illustrated, is susceptible, with due encouragement, and adequate means, in the hands of competent authority. We ought not to be disheartened by the little which has been accomplished in the brief space of thirteen years during which it has existed, or the magnitude and difficulties of the splendid undertaking which lies before us. In the execution of those vast schemes which affect the condition and happiness of large portions of the habitable globe, time is necessary, which may appear to us mortals of long duration, but which in the eyes of Providence, or in comparison with the periods of national existence, is short and fleeting. How long was it after Romulus and Remus laid the scanty foundations of their little state in the contracted limits of the Pininsula of Italy, before Imperial Rome burst forth, in all her astonishing splendour, the acknowledged mistress of the world? Ages passed away before Carthage and other colonies, in ancient times, shone out in all their commercial and military glory. Several centuries have now elapsed since our forefathers first began, in the morasses of James river and on the rock of Plymouth, the work of founding this republic, yet in its infancy. Eighteen hundred years have rolled over since the son of God, our blessed Redeemer, offered himself, on Mount Calvary, a voluntary sacrifice for the salvation of our species; and more than half of mankind continue to deny his divine mission and the truth of his sacred word.

We may boldly challenge the annals of human nature for the record of any human plan, for the melioration of the condition or advancement of the happiness of our race, which promised more unmixed good, or more comprehensive benificence, than that of African Colonization, if carried into full execution. Its benevolent purpose is not limited by the confines of one continent, nor to the prosperity of a solitary race, but embraces two of the largest quarters of the earth, and the peace and happiness of both of the descriptions of their present inhabitants, with the countless millions of their posterity who are to succeed. It appeals for aid and support to the friends of liberty here and every where. The Colonists, reared in the bosom of this Republic, with a perfect knowledge of all the blessings which freedom imparts, although they have not always been able themselves to share them, will carry a recollection of it to Africa, plant it there, and spread it over her boundless territory. And may we not indulge the hope, that in a period of time, not surpassing in duration, that of our own Colonial and National existence, we shall behold a confederation of Republican States on the western shores of Africa, like our own, with their Congress and annual Legislatures thundering forth in behalf of the rights of man, and making tyrants tremble on their thrones? It appeals for aid and support to the friends of civilization throughout the world. Africa, although a portion of it was among the first to emerge from barbarism, is now greatly in the rear of all the continents in knowledge, and in the arts and sciences. America owes to the old world a debt of gratitude for the possession of them. Can she discharge it in any more suitable manner than that of transplanting them on a part of its own soil, by means of its own sons, whose ancestors were torn by fraud and violence from their native home and thrown here into bondage? It powerfully appeals for support to patriotism and humanity. If we were to invoke the greatest blessing on earth, which Heaven, in its mercy, could now bestow on this nation, it would be the separation of the two most numerous races of its population and their comfortable establishment in distinct and distant countries. To say nothing of the greatest difficulty in the formation of our present happy Constitution, which arose out of this mixed condition of our people, nothing of the distracting Missouri question which was so threatening; nothing of others, springing from the same fruitful source, which yet agitate us, who can contemplate the future without the most awful apprehensions? Who, if this promiscuous residence of whites and blacks, of freemen and slaves, is forever to continue, can imagine the servile wars, the carnage and the crimes which will be its probable consequences, without shuddering with horror? It finally appeals emphatically for aid and support to the reverend clergy and sincere professors of our Holy Religion. If the project did not look beyond the happiness of the two races now in America, it would be entitled to their warmest encouragement. If it were confined to the removal only of the free colored population, it would deserve all their patronage. Within those restrictions how greatly would it not contribute to promote the cause of virtue and morality, and consequently religion! But it presents a much more extensive field — a field only limited by the confines of one of the largest quarters of the habitable globe — for religious and benevolent exertion. Throughout the entire existence of Christianity, it has been a favorable object of its ardent desciples and pious professors to diffuse its blessings by converting the Heathen. This duty is enjoined by its own sacred precepts, and prompted by considerations of humanity. All christendom is more or less employed on this subject at this moment, in some part or other of the earth. But it must, in candour be owned, that hitherto missionary efforts have not had a success corresponding in extent with the piety and benevolence of their aim, or with the amount of the means which have been applied. Some new and more efficacious mode of accomplishing the beneficent purpose must be devised, which, by concentrating energies and endeavors, and avoiding loss in their diffuse and uncombined application, shall ensure the attainment of more cheering results. The American Colonization Society, presents itself to the religious world as uniting those great advantages. Almost all Africa is in a state of the deepest ignorance and barbarism, and addicted to idolatry and superstition. It is destitute of the blessings, both of christianity and civilization. The Society is an instrument, which, under the guidance of Providence, with public assistance, is competent to spread the lights of both throughout its vast dominions. And the means are as simple as the end is grand and magnificent. They are to deviate from the practice of previous Missionary institutions, and employ as agents, some of the very brethren of the Heathen sought to be converted and brought within the pale of civilization. The Society proposes to send, not one or two pious members of christianity into a foreign land, among a different and perhaps a suspicious race, of another complexion, but to transport annually, for an indefinite numbers of years, in one view of its scheme, six thousand, in another, fifty-six thousand Missionaries, of the descendants of Africa itself, with the same interests, sympathies and constitutions of the natives, to communicate the benefits of our religion and of the arts. And this Colony of Missionaries, is to operate, not only by preaching the doctrines of truth and of revelation, which, however delightful to the ears of the faithful and intelligent, are not always comprehended by untutored savages, but also by works of occular demonstration. It will open forests, build towns, erect temples of public worship, and practically exhibit to the native sons of Africa, the beautiful moral spectacle and the superior advantages of our religious and social systems. In this unexagerated view of the subject, the Colony, compared with other Missionary plans, presents the force and grandeur of a noble Steamer, majestically ascending, and with ease subduing the current of the Mississippi, in comparison with the feeble and tottering canoe, moving slowly among the reeds that fringe its shores. It holds up the image of the resistless power of the Mississippi itself, rushing from the summits of the Rockey [sic] Mountains, and marking its deep and broad and rapid course through the heart of this continent, thousands of miles, to the Gulph of Mexico, in comparison with that of an obscure rivulet, winding its undiscernable way through dark and dense forests or luxurient prairies, in which it is quickly and forever lost.

Gentlemen of the Colonization Society of Kentucky! not one word need be added, in conclusion, to animate your perseverance or to stimulate your labors, in the humane cause which you have deliberately espoused. We have reason to believe that we have been hitherto favored, and shall continue to be blessed with the smiles of Providence. Confiding in his approving judgment, and conscious of the benevolence and purity of our intentions, we may fearlessly advance in our great work. And, when we shall, as soon we must, be translated from this into another form of existence, is the hope presumptuous, that we shall there behold the common Father of whites and of blacks, the great Ruler of the Universe, cast his All-seeing eye upon civilized and regenerated Africa, its cultivated fields, its coast studded with numerous cities, adorned with towering temples, dedicated to the pure religion of his redeeming Son; its far famed Niger, and other great rivers, lined with flourishing villages, and navigated with that wonderful power which American genius first successfully applied; and that, after dwelling with satisfaction upon the glorious spectable, he will deign to look with approbation upon us, His humble instruments, who have contributed to produce it?

Copy. KyDC. *An Address Delivered to the Colonization Society of Kentucky, at Frankfort, December 17, 1829, by the Hon. Henry Clay.* Frankfort, Ky., 1830.   1. On Dec. 18, 1829, Clay wrote from Frankfort to Thomas Metcalfe *et al.*, a committee appointed by the Kentucky Colonization Society, promising to supply a copy of his speech for publication. *Ibid.*

From James Barbour, Barboursville, Va., December 20, 1829. Reports that his "visit to Europe was one of universal gratification—and my return, however, otherwise intended was scarcely less so—" Continues: "I bestow now but little thought on politics—I fear the mania is far from being exhausted—Till it is all effort in vain—After what had been enacted at Washington by the removal of the faithful and the substitution in many instances of the most abandoned . . . and instead of a general indignation being expressed whole states actually going over to him—these are circumstances that fill me almost with despair—On my arrival in New York I was met with these onerous results—" Adds that he consulted with Daniel Webster and others as to whether it is "possible that the injustice done you was so deeply rooted in the public prejudice that another person against whom they had not been so successful in their wicked efforts, might be advantageously presented as a rallying point, being fully persuaded your patriotism would at once induce you to unite with us in that event—but I learned that with our Friends every where, you alone, promised anything like a successful opposition—" Notes that John C. Calhoun seems to have as many supporters in Virginia as Martin Van Buren, while "Your friends are as stedfast as you could wish but they are a minority of the State—perhaps however equal to either of the others. . . . I pray to God that something may occur to restore sobriety and reason once more in the land—" ALS. DLC-HC (DNA, M212, R4).

From Josiah S. Johnston, Washington, December [*ca.* 20], 1829. Believes "it is the intention" of Jackson to run again in 1832 and that a decision to do so is the "desire of his friends & those who hold office under him." The president will have to explain why he is abandoning his earlier pledges to serve but one term. This he can do by arguing the "necessity" of "preserving the Union of the party & in opposing your election—The object is therefore to make it appear that the opposition is Strong & United upon you—that you are still formidable—that the party cannot be united on any other man & that you Can beat any other man—& therefore the necessity of his maintaining his position." Speculates that Van Buren's friends will urge Jackson to retire because they think Van Buren can take the leadership of the Jackson party and "can successfully oppose you—" Urges Clay to put off a presidential nomination, "which the General desires," because "He would hold it dishonorable to withdraw in the face of such an opposition & necessity would be pleaded as a justification for his holding on—" Points out that it is to Clay's advantage to have Jackson retire from the political scene "because he is a much more formidable man than any one of the party—" Thinks that John C. Calhoun's situation within the Jackson administration is "certainly awkward." If Jackson steps down, Van Buren will head the party in 1832. The "only hope" of the Calhoun people, therefore, seems to lie in "the Generals death & the turn of V. B.'[s] fortune—" Sees Van Buren as the "strong man of the party" in that he can secure the support of the "Jackson Men" in the North and West as well as command that of New York, Virginia, Georgia, and "probably N. Carolina." Is "surprized that Calhoun does not see this," or realize that "Now is the time to take his Stand upon his Southern principles. . . . Although he has not much popularity, he Might hold the admn. in check & save the Constitution—& defeat Van Buren—He & his friends are not ready for So bold a movement," even though "Some of the Southern Jackson papers have expressed strong disapprobation" of the president's annual message to Congress. Feels Clay's best hope lies first in the "separation" of the Jackson party and next in the General's "withdrawal." Assures Clay that "our own party" is "entire & unbroken," and that "You May rely upon the United Strength of the party—" Reports that "all" of New England as well as New Jersey and Delaware "are safe." The issue will be decided in the West. "If the General withdraws I have great—entire Confidence—If he does not no one Can forsee what Scism & defection may arise—You have only to Stand Still—Keep your Mind at ease—preserve your health & Wait for events." ALS. DLC-TJC (DNA, M212, R13). Dating based on Johnston to Clay, December 12, 1829, which promised that "next Sunday I will write you fully."

From ROBERT P. LETCHER   Washington, December 21, 1829

I recd. your favor of the 7th. Inst yesterday. The $100 you request me to advance for you, shall be handed to Mr. Taylor,[1] the moment he makes himself known to me.

I had expected to have written you very soon after my arrival here, but have delayed doing so, until I could have a more satisfactory view of *things* as they are. And even *now*, I am by no means prepared to furnish you with any thing of much interest. But my speculations (such as they are) in reference to the political movements of the great men here, you shall have in sufficient abundance.

Van Buren is the first favorite at Court. He looks and acts, like one having authority, with assurances and promises of higher elivation. He has contrivd. to obtain the ascendency thro' [John] Eaton—With some adroitness, and a great deal of *meanness*, he has availed himself of many advantages, growing out of *that affair*,[2] with which you are fully acquainted. His object is to make the most of it. The Foreigners you know for their own purposes take sides with him; so does the President and [William T.] Barry.

[John] Branch and [Samuel D.] Ingham have taken a most decided stand on the other side, and will not be moved from their position. Barien [*sic*, John Berrien] having hauld. off it is said, is now, with Branch and Ingham. Branch and Eaton don't speak. I should not be at all surprized if Branch & Ing. both go overboard before the close of this Session. Indeed I have been told so, by a gentleman who ought to have a knowledge of the fact, and he spoke with great confidence.

The truth is, neither of them, has the slightest influence in the administration at present. Woodberry [*sic*, Levi Woodbury] it is believd. will be Branchs. successor, but to be no longer, *the friend of* [John C.] *Calhoun*. It is not know[n] who will take the place of Ing.[3]

Mr. Calhoun has made no demonstration of his views since his arrival at the City. Judging from his appearance, I should say, he considers every thing *lost*, tho' some few of his friends yet speak of his prospects as highly promising. I am myself very much inclined to the opinion that *he* will be withdrawn and some other Southern man put up. What would you think of [Langdon] Cheves? Such an idea is certainly in contemplation. Whether any arrangement of that sort, will be made is yet to be seen. The South is exceedingly dissatisfd. with the Message.[4] Jackson is destined to become odious in that quarter, as he will be almost every where else. My deliberate belief is, he will be the most unpopular president at the close of his administration that this nation ever had. I think *he* is disposed to run, again, from an impression that no one *but himself*, can make successful opposition agaist his ancient enemy. Such is the notion with which he is daily flatterd. But its all Fudge. They have no idea whatever of running him again, not the least in the worl[d]   It is now given out in speeches "that the Genl. will again offer if its necessary."

You may however rest perfectly assured that he will not be again a candidate. If I were not fearful of making my letter too tedious, I could give you many facts establishing the correctness of this assertion. One of itself is sufficient — Van Burens. leading friends say, it is impossible for him to be brought again, that he himself and his friends have given to the public too many pledges to the contrary

The fact is V. B. *feels* perfectly confident of success at this moment, and will not allow the opportunity to escape him. I never saw any man more flusd. with hope Or one more actively engaged in preparing for action. Virga. and Pena. are both claimd. by his friends.

Your friends pray for *that match race*, and have no more doubt of victory, than they have of their existence. They are firm and united, and seem to be more affectionate to each other, than brothers. It is believd. by many of them, that it would perhaps be the most judicious course, to have no expression from our Legislature in reference to *yourself*, or to the next presidential election. I have talkd. with most of your prudent friends particularly upon that point and altho' they reason somewhat differently, yet they all arrive at the same conclusion. Every one here seems to know how matters stand in Ky, as well as *we* did, before the meeting of Congress. Indeed I have not heard the first suggestion of a doubt as to the vote of that state, since I came here. I do not myself perceive any very strong reason, why there should be any movement by the Legislature. It will not add to the zeal or to the confidence of your friends in this quarter. Their zeal is now *very great*, but not greater than *their confidence*. You may probably entertain a different view of this matter, and no doubt will comprehend all its bearings much better than I can. I have given you the facts. The course to be adopted is left to yourself and to your friends in Ky.

Long as my letter is, I cannot omit to comply with my promise to Baron [Paul de] Krudener to say to you, he had it in charge from the Emperor Nicholas [I], to offer you the expression of his highest regard esteem and confidence, to which he beggd. me to add the strongest assurances of his own friendship, which he declard. would remain with him during life. All this was said with the most conclusive evidence of his sincerity. [P.S.] This letter is written very hastily and is only intended for yourself. . . .

AL. DLC-HC (DNA, M212, R4).   1. Probably Jonathan Taylor.   2. Johnston to Clay, Sept. 9, 1829.   3. For the extensive cabinet reorganization of April, 1831, see James, *Jackson*, 273-79.   4. Johnston to Clay, Dec. 12, 1829.

From Nicholas Biddle, Philadelphia, December 22, 1829. Responds to both of Clay's letters of November 28. Reports that the board of the Bank of the United States has voted a $1,750 salary adjustment to Mr. James Harper; also, that the bank will contribute $1,500 to the Lexington-Frankfort turnpike enterprise. "I hope you will think this satisfactory. I hope also that you will find the McAdams [macadam] road softer than the Adams road on which you were a little jolted during the last four years. A better road than the latter I suppose you think could not be." ALS. DLC-HC (DNA, M212, R4).

To HENRY CLAY, JR.   Lexington, December 23, 1829
My last letter [December 2] announced to you the death of your grandfather [Henry] Watkins. I have now the distressing task of communicating that of

my mother [Elizabeth Clay Watkins], which happened about ten days after, and that also of your uncle John [Clay] which occurred about the same time. He died on board a Steamer in descending the Mississippi.[1] It has th[us] pleased Providence to visit our family with severe aff[lict]ions.

Thomas [H. Clay], who went three weeks ago, to [see a] fine tract of land which I own near Terre Hau[te, Indiana, on] the Wabash, has not yet returned, nor hav[e] [word(s) missing] heard from him. I expect him in a few d[ays or at] least to hear from him.

In other respects the family remains pret[ty much as] when you left it. I intend to visit N. Orlea[ns] [word(s) missing] and expect to leave home for that object [about the] middle of next month. I believe I should no[t go after] the melancholy events above mentioned, but [for the] hope of deriving benefit to my health.

I delivered an Address to the K. Coloniz[ation So]ciety[2] last week, of which I will transmit you a copy when published by Mr. [Thomas] Smith, in whose hands it now is. . . .

ALS. Henry Clay Memorial Foundation, Lexington, Ky.   1. Claiborne to Clay, Nov. 28, 1829.   2. See Address, Dec. 17, 1829.

To **CHRISTOPHER HUGHES**   Lexington, December 25, 1829

Your favor of the 23d. Septr continued to the 20h. Oct. is just received. I need not say how much I was gratified with the friendly sentiments which it expresses towards me, nor that they are fully reciprocated. Among the circumstances which resulted from the late change of Administration, there was no one of an individual character that I so much regretted as that which concerned you. I had hoped that the fact of Genl. [Samuel] Smith being a member of the Senate, and of his connexion with the dominant party, and the fact of the interest which Louis McLane professed to you to feel in your behalf, would have secured the confirmation of your nomination. Such would have been the result if either or both of them had been sincere and zealous. I think you attribute too much to the agency of Mr. [Albert] Gallatin, in defeating your nomination. I know he was opposed to it for I argued with him in behalf on your competency, which he controverted. But I believe political causes more than his influence produced the result. It was thought necessary to win the State of Maine, if possible, and to reward Mr. Prebble [sic, William P. Preble]. Of Mr. Gallatin I think pretty much as you do; but his race is now nearly run, and he is beneath the feeling of resentment.

You think you ought to have been nominated[1] in 1826. As it regarded the public there was no urgency for it at that time. It would indeed have been a just reward of your long and faithful service; but that was a season when every thing was caught at for opposition. And we then had not the good reason for the measure which existed last winter, from the case of the arbitration. It is true the King of the Netherlands [William I] had set us the example of sending a minister to reside near our Government of a higher grade than you had; but the practice of our Government is not always regulated by the course which others pursue towards us. The mission too had then been not very long reduced. If however there had been a nomination at that time what security was there that those would not have proved false in the Senate, who did so in 1829?

I was lately in hope that you would be appointed M. P. [Minister Plenipotentiary] to Mexico; but I have just learnt that Col Anthony Butler is appointed Chargé d affaires to that Government. He is wholly incompetent, of desperate fortunes and bad character, and was a fugitive from civil justice both in this State and Mississippi. He actually fled or retired to Texas, from whence he did not emerge until lately, since the elevation of Genl. Jackson.

You must come home, conceal your chagrin, and keep up your spirits. I will tell you how you may get any employment abroad, within the gift of the President. Go directly to him, flatter him, and abuse me, and you will certainly succeed. I should be glad to see you a Candidate for Congress from Balto. where I think you could be elected. In Congress, if you are discreet, as I know you can be, you would make the same friendly impressions which you have done wherever you have been. These will enable you to take advantage of future events.

Your other friends will no doubt inform you of every thing relating to public affairs which I could communicate. As for myself, I am here retired, with a constantly diminishing relish for them. Indeed my state of health, which 'though generally better since I left Washington than it was there, is still such as gradually to wean me from public concerns. I am admonished also to think less of them, and of this world, by events occurring around and near me. In three weeks lately I lost my poor old mother [Elizabeth Clay Watkins], my elder brother [John] and my father in law [sic, step-father, Henry Watkins].

I intend to pass a portion of this winter with my only surviving daughter [Anne Brown Clay Erwin] at N. Orleans and my sons in law [James Erwin and Martin Duralde]. I shall leave home for that purpose in two or three weeks.

I hope, my dear Hughes, you will continue to write to me; for altho' you have found me a careless correspondent, I have ever perused your letters with the most lively satisfaction.

I lately [December 17] delivered an Address to the K. Colonization Society in Frankfort, which is now in the Press, and of which the partiality of the public has induced it to think too favorably. Should you visit England and see our old friend Lord Gambier, tell him that I intend to transmit him a Copy. . . .

ALS. MiU.   1. As U.S. minister to the Netherlands.

To JOSIAH S. JOHNSTON   Lexington, December 25, 1829

I recd. your obliging favor of the 12h. instant. I shall leave home for N. Orleans from the 16h. to the 20h. of next month, and I purpose remaining there until early in March. There will be time for a letter to reach me after you receive this, if you write by the next mail. Tell me how I can serve you whilst there, who is to be soothed, who to be won, to the support of your re-election.[1] Whatever I can do on that subject, with propriety, shall be done.

Will you do me the favor to place the enclosed letter to [Christopher] Hughes in a train for reaching him?[2] Poor fellow he has met with most unkind and unjust treatment. . . .

ALS. PHi. Printed in Colton, *Clay Correspondence*, 4:249.   1. Johnston was reelected to the Senate by the Louisiana legislature in Jan. of 1831, by the vote of 29 to 22 over his opponent, General John B. Dawson; 2 votes went to other candidates. *Niles' Register* (Jan. 29, 1831), 39:386. 2. Clay to Hughes, Dec. 25, 1829.

To HENRY CLAY, JR.   Lexington, December 26, 1829

Two letters from me which you must have received subsequent to the date of your's of the 12h. inst. will assure you, that you are not forgotten at Ashland, as you seem to apprehend. They bore melancholy tidings to you.[1] You are constantly in our recollections and affections, and form one of the strongest tyes to human life which I now feel. Your sister [Anne Brown Clay Erwin] is now, I presume, at New Orleans; and her transit thither from Tennessee has been most likely the cause of her not writing to you. Your mother and I have both lately suffered from bad colds. The rest of the family is well. I adhere to my purpose of visiting New Orleans; and in that case I shall not return until March.

On the question of the establishment of an American institute, respecting which you consult me, I have no doubt of the utility of such an establishment. The experience of other Countries demonstrates it, and the wants of our own require it. The only doubt about your project which I have is whether all the advantages of such an institution could be secured at West point. A large City in which many literary and learned men of leisure are congregated seems in the general to be the most eligible place for its location. If the Cadets remained permanently at the point, after their graduation, it would be a suitable place. Nevertheless the association there might be of essential service to the Cadets themselves, if they can command, from their regular studies, sufficient time to attend to it, and might also be of public utility. On that condition, I would earnestly advise you to connect yourself with it. There is a plan of Lyceums for the diffusion of information, I am told, now in successful operation in some of the Eastern State. Altho' they vary from the direct purposes of the contemplated institute, I consider all these modes of exciting emulation, and distributing useful knowledge, as worthy of warm approbation.

Have you received any letter from your uncle [James] Brown or written to him since his return to the U. States? He is probably able to communicate valuable information to you respecting the organization and operation of the French institute.[2] You are aware that he at present resides in Philadelphia.

Let me hear from you, my dear Son, at New Orleans. . . .

ALS. Henry Clay Memorial Foundation, Lexington, Ky. 1. Clay to Henry Clay, Jr., Dec. 2, 1829. 2. For the Institut de France, composed of five scholarly societies, the earliest of which dates to 1629, see "French Institutes," *Colliers Encyclopedia*.

From ROBERT P. LETCHER   Washington, December 26, 1829

This evening, I had the pleasure of dining with Mrs. [Josiah S.] Johnson [sic, Johnston], and she enjoined it upon me, under no less penality than the forfeiture of her high displeasure, in case of refusal, to write you this very night.

You know I have not the courage or the inclination to stand out against such dreadful consequences. To her then you are indebted for this short letter.

Time absence and Rivals, the three great enemies of womans. constancy, have made no inroad upon her affections. Her admiration for you, (I shall use no stronger expression) has not abated in the slightest degree. I have not the least hope of living long enough myself, to witness any change in her feelings, for if you were to die tomorrow, she would most certainly devote the residue of her life to grief and melancholy, so in any event I consider her lost now and forever.

Mr [Charles R.] Vaughan gave us a dinner yesterday in his his [sic] best style — I will not undertake to tell you who composed the party, or of what various dishes the dinner consisted — The latter I could not do, if I were to attempt it. This much however I can tell you, and that perhaps formed one inducement on her part for me to write, you, Mrs Johnson sat at the right hand

of Mr. Vaughan dressd. most eligantly, & played her part with the most be-
witching grace & dignity. During the entertainment, Mr. V. askd. Mr.
Johnson and myself to drink a glass of Champaign with him, & that he would
offer as a Toast, Henry Clay—The moment it was announced there was a
wonderful ratling of glasses all around the table, and I believe every one ladies
and gentlemen joined with great cheer. Poor Mrs. J. was so much elated at the
toast, and in so much of a hurry to drink it in due time, she seized upon a full
glass of Soturn, and drank it all, for Champaign.

V. Buren will be the candidate for the next Presidency. I have no sort of
doubt of it whatever. You will find, if I am not very much dece[iev]d. most of
our Jackson leaders in the West, on his side. I mean they will give up [John C.]
Calhoun. It is believd. by some Mr. Calhoun himself will fall in V. Burens ranks,
and in case of his success agree to be Secty. of State I know of no fact however
to justify this opinion. He see[ms] to be entirely quiet, or rather at a loss to
know what to do—hi[s] course seems to me to be a very obvious one, but I
doubt whether he will take the same view of it. Mr [Richard] Rush succeeded
in Holland in obtaining the Can[al] Loan of a million and a half at 5 per cent.[1]
I saw a letter from him this ev[en]ing announcing the fact. Mr. & Mrs [James]
Brown are still in the City—Th[e] latter I am told is in very bad health.

ALS. DLC-HC (DNA, M212, R4).   1. Rush represented investors in the Chesapeake and
Ohio Canal. *Niles' Register* (Jan. 23, 1830), 37:360.

From John Vance, Washington, December 28, 1829. Reports on his observations
since arriving in Washington. "When I first arrived at this place Mr Van Buren Was
certainlly the favorite of the Jackson party and he still retains the ear of the *Hero*,"
although "the *Knowing* ones begin to hint Slyly that he has been cunning overmuch and
that the result will in the end prove to be a decided Victory in favor of Calhoun who has
taken the other side of this momentous question [Peggy Eaton affair] that is like to
shake the Government to its center." Continues: "You may think this Very strange that
the admission of a certain Female into respectable Society at Washington should be
made the basis of political orthodoxy by one branch of the reigning party, and her rejection Equally So by the other, but strange as it may appear it is, no less Strange than
true, Mr Van Buren has been the friend of this unfortunate Lady and has made every
exertion to get her into Society, by this he has gained Mr, E[aton]. —and the President,
but the current of Female opposition could not be steme'd, and parties Even by Secr-
taris Ladies are got up in opposition and open defiance hurled at the Secrtary and his
Lady by leaving them off of the list of invitations. Such is the State of parties at
Washington, and what you and me, thought idle newpaper slang during the last Summer on this subject, does at this moment engross the principle part of the light talk at
Washington and has cost the President and his sage counscles more trouble than all the
other subjects brought before them during the present administration, not excepting
the paragraph in the Message relative to the Tariff on imported goods."

Reports on prospects for future success for Clay in other states: "The New England
people say that all is right in that quarter, with the exception of Maine and New Hampshire which may be considered doubtful. . . . Delaware is considered perfectly Safe.
New Jersey and Maryland doubtful. . . . The anti, masonic question is carrying all
before it in Pen[n]sylvania." Recommends that the Kentucky legislature "take no steps
relative to the succeeding Presidential Election, but that your name be Kept before the
american people through the medium of the Newspapers." Urges that "every exertion
. . . be made" to win the legislature at the next August election and that the legislature
then send Clay to the U.S. Senate. Predicts soon an open rupture between the Calhoun
and Van Buren forces and that the Van Buren faction will attempt to nominate him for

president and John McLean for vice president in 1832. ALS. DLC-HC (DNA, M212, R4). In 1832, Jackson carried the states of Maine, New Hampshire, New Jersey, and Pennsylvania, while Clay carried Delaware and Maryland. Samuel Rhea Gammon, Jr., *The Presidential Election of 1832* (Baltimore, 1922), 170. For Jackson's statement on the tariff in his first annual message, see *MPP*, 2:449-50.

To JOSIAH S. JOHNSTON   Lexington, December 31, 1829
Your favor of the [blank space] instant, under cover to Majr. [John] Tilford and franked by Judge Clarke [*sic*, James Clark], came safe to hand; and I thank you for the views and information which it communicates.

There is the best and most friendly disposition prevailing so far with our Legislature, at Frankfort. They are disposed to do any thing right and politic; but from what I learn I presume nothing will be done but to present an argumentative report in favor of the Tariff and Internal Improvements, in which will be embodied some friendly expressions concerning me. The Governor [Thomas Metcalfe] gets along without difficulty. Much good spirit exists in regard to the States doing something for its own improvement; but the great obstacle is the want of means and the want of union as to objects which be first undertaken.

I am busy in making preparations for my intended voyage to N. Orleans. I purpose leaving home in less than a fortnight, about the 12h. of next month. I regret to find that my expected visit there has already excited more expectation than I could have wished. I have heard nothing of Genl. [Stephen] V[an]. Rensselaer. I am afraid that the frightful state of our roads has deterred him from making his intended detour. I shall lament this the more because I think we might have arranged it to descend the river together. . . . P.S. Should you address me, as I hope you may, whilst I am at N. O. your letters put under cover to Nicholas Berthoud Esqr. Shipping port K. would quickly reach me.

ALS. PHi. Printed in Colton, *Clay Correspondence*, 4.249-50.

From Ann Garram *et al.*, Pittsburgh, January [n.d.], 1830. On behalf of "the females of this city" who have "publickly and actively, espoused the cause of justice . . . in behalf of the *Southern Indians*," ask Clay to represent these unfortunate and oppressed people if and when their claims to their homes and lands are brought to court. Inform him that they have chosen him for this important legal work because "We remember your exertions in favour of the South Americans, and of the Independence of the South American Republicks [2:853-60]—We have recently seen your masterly address [December 17, 1829] in behalf of the enslaved and degraded African; and we cherish with the most lively emotions, the recollection, of your efforts and your eloquence in the cause of the suffering *Greeks* [3:597-9, 603-14]." Point out, however, that "We do not offer to purchase your services by the tender or promise of pecuniary recompense, but the gratitude the blessing and the prayers of every feeling heart will reward you." LS. DLC-HC (DNA, M212, R4). Signed also by Margaret Bruce, Catherine S. Butler, and Prudence Lambdin.

To NICHOLAS BIDDLE   Lexington, January 2, 1830
If I had received a New years gift, it could not have afforded me more pleasure than the receipt yesterday, the first instant, of your letter of the 22d. Ultimo. The Bank, on both the subjects, (the affair of the road and the case of Mr. [James] Harper) has acted in the handsomest manner, creditably to its generosity and justice.[1] Mr. Harper is made very happy, and he well deserves to

be so. And I assure you that whenever I pass over the Road, after its completion, to Frankfort, I shall always recollect the liberal contribution of the B. of
the U. States. Nor shall I fail to realize the superior ease of travelling it than in
moving on another road intimated by you.

I congratulate you on the public disapprobation, so generally expressed,
of that part of the late message of the President, which affects your institution.[2]
On two points you have reason to be thankful for the notice which was taken of
you. It was premature; and, in the second place, the President brings forward
a contre projet,[3] a comparison of which with the existing Bank cannot fail to
redound to your advantage. Considering the prejudices, constitutional scruples &c. existing against you, a denunciation of the B. some years hence, *without presenting any substitute*, might have injured the institution. As it is, I think
the prospect of a renewal of the Charter better than if the President had remained silent.

ALS. PHi.   1. Clay to Biddle, Nov. 28, 1829; Biddle to Clay, Dec. 22, 1829.   2. *MPP*,
2:442-62.   3. The "contre projet" Jackson proposed was "whether a national one [bank],
founded upon the credit of the Government and its revenues, might not be devised which would
avoid all constitutional difficulties and at the same time secure all the advantages to the Government and country that were expected to result from the present bank." *Ibid.*, 462.

To EDWARD EVERETT   Lexington, January 3, 1830

I have taken the liberty of sending under cover to you a letter for a young
friend at Göttingen, Mr. [Jesse B.] Harrison,[1] which I hope you will excuse.
You will oblige me by forwarding it through some safe channel.

Congress appears as usual to have done but little yet. Will you not have a
storm about the Tariff? Or shall we all be disappointed in that respect?

I set out in about ten days for N. Orleans. I have been greatly disappointed in not seeing the Patroon.[2] I fear the frightful state of our roads has
deterred him from his contemplated visit to me.

ALS. MHi.   1. Below, this date.   2. For Stephen Van Rensselaer, see Martha J. Lamb,
History of the City of New York (New York, 1877), 2:411, 579, 594, 599, 600, 673-74, 693.

To JESSE B. HARRISON   Lexington, January 3, 1830

I received your letter of the 20h. October last, under date at Göttingen, and
perused its contents with much satisfaction. I am glad to perceive that you are
making such good use of your time in Europe. I am not surprized that you should
form so unfavorable an opinion of our Country men whom you met at Paris. I
was obliged to adopt a similar opinion of those whom I saw there in 1815. It is to
be regretted that so few of them who visit that captivating metropolis are able to
resist the temptations to indulgence which it presents. If I had known of your intention to visit Ghent, I could have furnished you with letters to some valuable
friends I have there; but I perceive that you did not stand in need of them, as you
were fortunately introduced to the Duke of Saxe-Weimar [Charles Frederick],
whose intellect and character, I think, you properly appreciate.

You, my dear Sir, who are capable of giving me advice, ask me to suggest
to you the proper objects of your study and research in the Northern States of
Europe. We are not likely to have very extensive commercial or diplomatic
connections with any of those Powers except the Emperor of Russia. There is
one point, to which I should like to see your attention directed, the practical in-
conveniences to which Germany is subjected by the divisions and subdivisions

of it into Independent States. Useful admonition may, I presume, be drawn from that fact, against the division of our own Union, the greatest misfortune which could befal our Country. Another subject which might usefully engage your attention is that of the condition of the Serfs of the North, with the view of reasoning upon it in relation to that of our African slaves. I touched upon this topic in a late Address [December 17, 1829] which I made to the K. Society of Colonization, of which I now transmit you a Copy. What is the value of Serfs? Is the Lord bound to provide for them, in any degree? Are any of them ever sold, separately from the soil to which they are attached? Are manumissions more frequent than they were formerly? Are they equally or more or less prolific than the residue of the population?

The state of German manufactures is also an object worthy of your enquiry. What is the degree of protection extended to them by Government? How is it enforced? Does one German State protect its own manufactures against the rival productions of another German State?

If your opportunities would admit of it, you could render an essential service to the Agriculture of the U.S. by a minute enquiry into the culture of Hemp, and the most approved modes of preparing and treating it. If you have any taste for that species of information, there is scarcely any subject on which you could write a book with more advantage. The best work extant is that of M. [Henri Louis] du Hamel du Monceau.[1] But that was written nearly a century ago, and great improvements have been since made. M. Marcandier,[2] a magistrate of Bruges, also wrote upon it, but I have never seen his work. There is a useful compilation in English, published about 20 years ago, by [Robert] Wissett, with an appendix by Lord Somerville.[3]

The great desideratum, in the preparation of that article is breaking it out with some machine which will save labor, after it is rotted. Many such machines have been tried without success. We still pursue most generally the old rude method of preparing it with a Brake which is worked by one man.

Your other friends no doubt keep you well informed as to the state of American politics. The public has not yet recovered from the disease of Jacksonism, but I think it is convalescent. His proscriptive system, under the delusive name of Reform, has opened the eyes of many. Others continue to be deceived by it. And I think his last message,[4] although it was distributed and received with much eclat, is likely to do the General lasting prejudice. There is much division and much acrimony among the members of his Cabinet. I learn that two of them ([John] Branch and [Samuel D.] Ingham) will probably be removed during the present Session of Congress.

It does not seem to be settled whether Jackson will be run again for the Presidency. He wishes it, and all the employées, for obvious reasons, wish it. He and they believe that he is the only man who can prevent the election of one that he would extremely dislike to see in the P. Chair. [Martin] Van Buren and his friends, meantime, protest against the General being again a Candidate. And he (V. B.) believes that he can be elected against any one but the General. My friends, perhaps from too much ardor and confidence, would be highly gratified with such a contest.

I have declined all public employment. My old district was anxious to return me to the H. of R. but I thought it better to remain in private life. I go next week to N. Orleans, where I intend passing a part of the Winter. P.S. I may authorize the publication of an extract from your letter; but if I do you shall not be committed.

ALS. DLC-HC (DNA, M212, R21). Addressed to Harrison to Göttingen, Hanover.   1. *A Practical Treatise of Husbandry.* . . . London, 1759.   2. *An Abstract of the Most Useful Parts of a Late Treatise on Hemp, Translated from the French.* . . . *Together With Some Observations upon the Prospect of Singular Advantage Which May Be Derived to Great Britain and Her Colonies from Their Early Adopting the Method Prescribed.* . . . Boston, 1766. A London edition was published in 1764. Marcandier's first edition in French is dated Paris, 1758.   3. *On the Cultivation and Preparation of Hemp.* . . . London, 1804; Wissett's later edition, with an appendix by Lord Somerville "on the most effectual means of producing a sufficiency of English grown Hemp," was titled *A Treatise on Hemp.* . . . London, 1808.   4. *MPP*, 2:442-62.

To WILLIAM BELL   Lexington, January 5, 1830

I have used in my family the patent bedsteads of Mr Wm. Bell of Lexington,[1] and have found them greatly superior to those in common use. Being constructed so that the posts are put together without screws, they are stronger and less liable to get out of order. They will hardly ever require any precaution to destroy bugs, as they afford no place of retreat to them.

Copy. Printed in Lexington *Kentucky Gazette*, Jan. 22, 1830. Quotation in advertisement of William Bell dated Jan. 18, 1830.   1. Bell was a plane maker whose shop was located on High Street in Lexington. See Julius P. B. MacCabe, *Directory of the City of Lexington . . . for 1838 & '39* (Lexington, 1838), 41.

To JOHN BRADFORD   Lexington, January 5, 1830

Expecting to be absent from Kentucky during some weeks, I do hereby resign my seat as a member of the Board of Trustees of Transylvania University, and request you to communicate my resignation to the Board.

ALS. KyLxT. Bradford was at this time chairman of the Board of Trustees of Transylvania University.

To DANIEL WEBSTER   Lexington, January 6, 1830

I offer you hearty congratulations on a late event which I hope, and have no doubt, will conduce to your happiness. The most favorable accounts of Mrs. W[ebster]. reach me from all quarters.[1] You have avoided an error too frequent, in second marriages, of a great disproportion in the ages of the parties. Rumor says that the late event is the prelude to another; that of your removal to New York.

I am about proceeding to N. Orleans where I purpose passing a portion of the winter with my daughter [Anne Brown Clay Erwin] and sons in law [James Erwin and Martin Duralde]. The effect of a Southern climate will be agreeable and I trust may prove beneficial to my health, which, tho' improved, still requires care. I shall be thus placed farther than ever from the scenes now passing at Washington. My correspondents there keep me pretty well informed of the actual state of things; but as yet no important movements appear to have been made in either branch of Congress. I am curious to know the issue of the nominations which, if not already, must be shortly sent in. One of the strangest, among them, from this quarter is that of Anthony Butler.[2] I had hoped that the appointment of Minister to Mexico, would have been conferred on C[hristopher]. Hughes, a most excellent fellow, and one of good capacity. But these are not the times in which such men are employed.

ALS. MBAt. Copy, printed in George T. Curtis, *Life of Daniel Webster*, 2 vols. (New York, 1870), 1:370. 1. Eliza Johnston to Clay, Dec. 12, 1829.   2. For Butler's appointment, see Robert V. Remini, *Andrew Jackson and the Course of American Freedom 1822-1832* (New York, 1981), 219-20, 289-90 and Clay to Hughes, Dec. 25, 1829.

To Anna Payne Cutts, January 9, 1830. Consoles her on Jackson's removal of her husband, Richard, as second comptroller of the U.S. Treasury. "For I assure you that amidst all the unpleasant occurrences since the 4h. of March, there is not one that has so much afflicted Mrs. Clay and myself as that of the dismission of Mr. Cutts." Announces that he is going to New Orleans next week but that Mrs. Clay will remain at Ashland. ALS. KyLoF. Mrs. Cutts was still in Washington at this time.

To Josiah S. Johnston, January 12, 1830. Reports that "your Alma Mater," Transylvania University, has petitioned the U.S. Congress for aid. Describes the school as "the first temple of Science erected in the wilds of the West," and asks Johnston to speak in favor of the application. ALS. PHi. Printed in Colton, *Clay Correspondence*, 4:251.

On the same day Clay also wrote Edward Everett asking that he too support Transylvania's petition. ALS. MHi. For Transylvania's petition see *Reports of Committees*, 21 Cong., 1 Sess., no. 308 and no. 138; and *House Exec. Doc.* 103, 25 Cong., 2 Sess., pp. 1-2. The latter, dated January 15, 1838, requested a donation of land.

From William Hawley, Washington, January 14, 1830. Thanks Clay for a copy of the speech he had given the Kentucky Colonization Society in Frankfort on December 17, 1829. Thinks it is an excellent statement, especially the "appropriate manner in which you have introduced the subject of Christianity & exhibited the powerful operation & extensive effects which would be produced by the successful accomplishment of the objects of the Society, in a religious point of view." ALS. DLC-HC (DNA, M212, R4).

From Josiah S. Johnston, Washington, January 19, 1830. Compliments Clay on his speech to the Kentucky Colonization Society on December 17, 1829, noting that it "is very able and has been generally read and extensively printed—Mr. [John Q.] Adams said it was your Strongest speech." Reports that the Senate will "debate the powers of the President"; and that the "parties stand as they did—no Union or seperation Every thing waits for the General [Jackson]—he will delay the determination [to run for a second term] as long as possible." Calls Clay's attention to a "supremely ridiculous message of the President to day about [Simon] Bolivar & Tom Moore." ALS. InU. For the Senate debates on the "executive powers of removal" see *Register of Debates*, 21 Cong., 1 Sess., 457-70, 385-96. For Jackson's message of January 19 see *MPP*, 2:466-67 which highly praises both Moore and Bolivar.

From JOSEPH E. SPRAGUE   Boston, January 20, 1830
Your friends here are making conitual enquiries about the things in the West and I suppose you feel a desire to know a little how they stand in the East—We are advised by your friends in Washington not to make any developement lest the hero of two wars should again be brought forward. They may be right, but it we wait too long Mr. Van Buren will get the saddle too firmly buckled to be losened—Much is said of their divisions but unfortunately we have no certain evidence of them—Mine own view would have placed you already at Washington and with a Senate so nearly poised I think you could have turned the ballanse. I may be however all wrong. I can only speak autheratively in regard to New England—The policy of the administration has lost them friends in every state but New Hampshire & Maine. Here I think we were never stronger. None of their appointments strengthen them—In Salem a Journey man Shoemaker [John Swasey] is Naval officer & in Ipswich a taylor [James H. Kendall] is Collecter. The Jackson party may possible show a few more votes because heretofore they have never got out half of their strength. I apprehend Vermont Rhode Island and Connecticut are equally Sound—I have a letter before me

from a cool and unimpatient gentleman from NH he says the Jackson party are losing ground there and he speaks confidently of an entire revolution there at the election in March next. Gen [Timothy] Upham the *reformed* Collector of Portsmouth will be the National Republican or *Clay* Candidate[1] he has consented to stand although it will not be publickaly known here for ten days— Maine is in a dreadful state the Senate are equally divided and the Jackson party will not yeild one inch so that the government must be disorganised or their views adopted—All this was the result of a most injudicious selection of candidate[s] for Governor, an obscure man who no one knew & whose character was open to the grossest impeachment—The candidate on the other side though undoubtedly Jackson was cunning & pretended to be of the contrary opinion—[2] I spent a week in November in Portland & our friends were confident that another year they should undo the mischief of this year. Does Mr [Daniel] Webster write you? I ask as there have been some curious reports in relation to him   I do not believe them however. He may however think of going to New York & giving up politics since his marriage with Miss LeeRoy [*sic*, Caroline LeRoy]. I think I know as much of New England as any man and I cannot doubt if the West gives us evidence that they will unite then we shall also Unite with them—Much anxiety is felt here about the course Judge [John] McLean is going to take—your friend Charles Hammond seems to have broken ground for him and Timothy Flint the Western Reviewer[3] when here a few months since, said all in Ohio, Jackson men and all were for McLean. I hope and trust you will not divide. I fear however that Mr Van Buren has learnt how the people may be corrupted and that our Constitution and our laws are a dead letter and our boasted liberties valueless. If we are to be hereafter a nation of office seekers our Country would be the last I should chose. [Word illeg.]   Turkey would be preferable to me

ALS. DLC-HC (DNA, M212, R4).   1. Matthew Harvey defeated Timothy Upham for governor of New Hampshire in March of 1830 by a margin of 23, 214 to 19,040. See Upham entry in *CAB* and *BDGUS*, 3:950.   2. In the September gubernatorial election in Maine, Samuel Emerson Smith defeated the incumbent governor, Jonathan G. Hunton 30,215 to 28,639. *BDGUS*, 2:600.   3. From May, 1827, to June, 1830, Flint edited in Cincinnati the *Western Monthly Review*. See *DAB*.

From JOSIAH S. JOHNSTON   Washington, January 26, 1830

Since I wrote you [January 19], nothing has occurred here to change the state of our affairs—The Idea gains ground that the General means to retire, although I believe there is no authority for the opinion, Coming directly or indirectly from him or any friend—The manner in Which Van Buren & Calhoun are marshalling their forces—& setting out their claims indicates they expect the succession will be open—They are both exerting themselves to gain an ascendency with the party—& I think it is clear that their claims & pretentions cannot be reconciled or Compromised   Van Buren had undoubtedly the advantage at the Commencement of the Session—but Calhoun has gained since— & their claims are more unsettled—Nothing will induce Mr. Calhoun to forego his rights. But I can say nothing of their strength or of their friends— because no indication is given—

I find every body possessed of the idea that the General will withdraw at a proper time & that Van Buren & Calhoun will contend—But who is the strongest in the South or how their merits will be settled no one knows—It it [*sic*, is] said there is to be a great meeting in Penna. to decide that question for that State—In that [Samuel D.] Ingham expects to marshall the party for Calhoun—how he will get along with his principles & opinions I know not. Van Buren it appears has no decided interest there—Your interest in Penna., as soon as the General withdraws & reason resumes her sway, will upon every principle be very strong—We must address ourselves to that people & appeal to their interests—Nothing but the desperate spirit of party & the power of party [word illeg.] Can prevent your Carrying the State—This must be the field of battle—In Competition with these two Candidates I do not fear the West—

[John] McLean of Ohio I understand has said *in Ohio* that if they would put by Mr. Clay he Could put down this admn.—& I have heard the same thing here—But it is not necessary to say he finds no hearers—He thinks Calhoun has no chance & that if he would retire he could be elected. &C. The two Virginia Senators have not arrived & we do not know Why—[1]nor When they will Come—They are aware how things stand in the Senate, they see perhaps they are more necessary than they have been thought to be—they may require to be sent-for & they may have no objection to the rejection of Certain persons &C—[George M.] Troup has gone home in Consequence of the death of the Governess of his children—& I do not know whether he will return—but he probably will in March   McKinly [*sic,* John McKinley] is Sick—[George M.] Bibb has been for several days—So that the majority is rather straighten[e]d—& they will not trust us with any thing—I think it probable we may reject all the printers—upon principle—[2]

[William] Smith of S.C. will vote with us entre nous—

We have had a very spirited & able debate in the Senate of which I will give you some account[3]

The journal is purchased & established—[4]

ALS. InU.   Addressed to Clay in New Orleans.   1. Littleton W. Tazwell and John Tyler were both members of the Virginia Constitutional Convention which did not adjourn until January 15.   2. Jackson had appointed several newspapermen, or "printers," to various positions. Henry Lee, James B. Gardner, Moses Dawson, Mordecai M. Noah, and Isaac Hill were not confirmed by the Senate. Amos Kendall's appointment as fourth auditor was, however, approved. U.S. Sen. *Journal,* 21 Cong., 1 Sess., 402-12, 423, 447, 457-58 and Bowers, *Party Battles of the Jackson Period,* 82-87. For Noah's subsequent renomination and confirmation, see Johnston to Clay, May 22, 1830. Smith voted against confirmation of any of the printers.   3. On Dec. 29, 1829, Sen. Samuel Foot of Connecticut introduced a resolution "That the Committee on Public Lands be instructed to inquire into the expediency of limiting for a certain period the sales of the public lands to such lands only as have heretofore been offered for sale, and are subject to entry at the minimum price." This resolution triggered wide-ranging debates which lasted from Dec. 29 until May 21, 1830, and which explored not only land policy but also sectional issues such as the tariff, internal improvements, and the constitutional and structural nature of the relationship of the individual states to the Union. *Register of Debates,* 21 Cong., 1 Sess., 3-452 *passim.* For the Webster-Hayne debate to which Johnston is probably referring, see Clay to Johnston, Feb. 27, 1830.   4. Probably a reference to the Washington *Daily National Journal* of which George Watterson became publisher on Feb. 3, 1830.

From JOSIAH S. JOHNSTON   Washington, February 2, 1830

The last week has been very interesting in the Cabinet. The report got into circulation that [John] Branch was to go out & the event was hourly expected—It seems that Branch & [John H.] Eaton are irreconcileable—& it is apparent they cannot long remain together in the Cabinet   The Course adopted by Branch with regard to Mrs. E[aton]. made the first breach, the discovery of the papers of [John B.] Timberlake which he Carried to the President & refused to return to Eaton made open War—[1]Eaton seems disposed to have him removed & he has great influence with the General still—I believe the President had determin[e]d to gratify him—but this produced a strong counter movement among the friends of Branch—& which after a great struggle has resulted in the restoration of Branch to his Dept.   It seems that the old divisions exist— Van Buren, Eaton [William T.] Barry—with the General—Branch [Samuel D.] Ingham [John M.] Berrian [*sic*, Berrien], all Calhouns friends &C on the other side to whom may be added the Ladies of the place—It is not known who interfered, for Branch—but it must have been a Strong & decided movement It was reported that Ingham & Berrian would go out if he did or that the same Causes would require their removal—From what I see I think a decided change must before six months take place   One party or the other must prevail—it is impossible for them to remain in this state—Eaton has the ascendency & the General will not give him up—Van Buren has his ear & Confidence—they will want Branch & Ingham out to produce harmony, & to distroy Calhouns influence yet they cannot remove these without a division in the party—& the moment that move is made, there will be an open rupture— The friends of these chiefs have exerted their utmost ability Since they met   It appears to me that Calhoun has gained very much on Van Buren—An effort will soon be made in Penna. by Ingham & his party to nominate Calhoun. It is very doubtful if it Can succeed—The parties are much broken up in that state—The opposition to Inghams party, our friends—the anti-masons—& Van Burens men will constitute a majority—.

For us it is perhaps better to have Calhoun succeed with the party, he can I think with his present principles unite only the South—The West, the North & the middle must go against him—

It seems to be believed the General will retire & that Calhoun will succeed—Van Buren is not in good health & I do not believe he can hold the office three years longer—

Movements are making every where among the party in favor of Calhoun especially in N. Hampshire—Yet in both Houses the party hold together—undivided & without the slightest disaffection—We have been the strongest during the Last week, but to day [John] Tyler Arrived, [Littleton W.] Tazewell will be here tomorrow & the Mississippi Senator [Robert H. Adams] this week—We shall make a great effort to reject the Printers—[2]but with what success I cannot say—Judge [William] Smith will go with us—others would be glad to if they dare—

[Thomas H.] Benton has Continued his speech until to day—[3]It is made up of materials gather[e]d from all the world   The object of his speech seems to be to make war on the North & to produce an Union between the South & West for the benefit of Calhoun—I think he is prepared to go for so much—& he is undoubtedly trying to build up a party for himself on this basis—which will wofully deceive him

I watch now for every motion—Our friends are perfectly decided—& firm—We have passed the Resolution for printing the documents by [Joseph] Gales & [William W.] Seaton, which would save them, but they are determined to defeat us, even by withholding the appropriation—but we must save the paper—[4]The [Washington *Daily National*] Journal is bought & under way—[5]

Mrs. Johnston joins me in kind regards to Mrs. [James] Erwin & desires to be remember[e]d to all her friends by you   I hope you see much of Judge [Alexander] Porter & his Sister   I need not recommend them to you—I hope you find our City [New Orleans] agreeable—You lose nothing by absence—&

gain health & pleasure—I refer you to the papers. . . . [P.S.] Present my respects to Genl [Stephen] Van Rensslear [sic, Rensselaer]—I have written in great haste—

ALS. InU.   1. For Branch's role in the Eaton affair and the related Timberlake papers matter, see Clyde N. Wilson, *The Papers of John C. Calhoun* (Columbia, S.C., 1978), 11:128-37, and Adams, *Memoirs of John Quincy Adams*, 8:179, 184, 197.   2. Johnston to Clay, Jan. 26, 1830. 3. Benton viewed Samuel A. Foot's resolution as part of a systematic attempt by the East to build up manufacturing at the expense of agriculture and charged that the resolution, if passed, would check emigration to the West. He suggested an alliance between the West and South. See *Register of Debates*, 21 Cong., 1 Sess., 22-27, 95-119.   4. For the resolution authorizing Gales & Seaton to publish the *American State Papers*, see *Register of Debates*, 21 Cong., 1 Sess., 94 and 2 Sess., 815-20; also William E. Ames, *A History of the National Intelligencer* (Chapel Hill, 1972), 173-76.   5. Johnston to Clay, Jan. 26, 1830.

From "ALEXIS DE SARCY"   [Huntsville, Ala.], February 11, 1830

It will not be in my power to meet you so soon as I expected, but you may rest satisfied that all goes well; be true to yourself, be discreet, and there is nothing to apprehend. Say nothing about Mr. Adams, nothing in allusion to him; the reasons assigned in your speech not long since, for accepting Office under him was injudicious;[1] it will be impracticable for me to be in Kentucky earlier than May or June[2]

[EXTRACT:]

You are reputed to possess judgment, tact, a deep and correct knowledge of the human character and a self possession that never falters; I am not disposed to controvert the opinion, yet I think if you are to be judged by the events of the last five years, your claim to these qualities must be denied: during that period you have committed errors so palpable and gross that no man so distinguished could have been betrayed into—it might be ungracious as well as unnecessary to notice all the blunders of that time, but you will permit me to mention one, that remarkable one, your defence of yourself against the charge of "bargain intrigue and management" had you avowed *a bargain* instead of denying explaining and defending. I am grossly mistaken in the character of the American People if you had not sustained your popularity at its highest flow. If instead of your letter to your Constituents [4:143-166] and all your other letters and speeches and sayings [6:1394-96; 7:339], and the sayings of all your friends, you had promptly declared that your vote for Mr. Adams was the result of a bargain, of a pledge on his part, to support the American System and internal improvements, whilst Gen. Jackson's silence, reserve, and affectation of offended dignity at being approached, left you the founder of the system and all its other friends in doubt as to the policy of his administration upon these subjects, that this consideration added to your other objections to the Genl. had decided your course upon that question, and that you accepted the depart[men]t. of State under the influence of the same motives, to aid in extending and supporting the system with a determination to resign and oppose the Administ[ratio]n. if Mr. Adams played false—that it was the operation of such considerations which induced you to disregard the recommendation of the Kentucky Legislature [3:901-92], and offer yourself a victim on the altar of your Country, as Gen. Jackson had himself done in declaring martial Law at N. Orleans: had you done this my life on it, the newspaper clamor would have hushed—that prolific theme been removed, and your adversaries confounded. It is over! how shall we repair the loss and correct the evil?[3]

173

It is to aid in this my services are now offered, how far they may be made efficient will depend much on yourself. It is my design to communicate to you facts from time to time, as relates to the views of the Cabinet, and the opinions as well as individual objects of its members; upon the correctness of these you may rely in full faith, nothing will be stated as fact, that does not exist beyond doubt, and upon which you may act with all the confidence that your own personal knowledge could give you. I shall occasionally add suggestions as to the course of policy yourself and friends should pursue, which may be taken for just so much as they seem to be worth.

The facts now to be communicated are—That Gen. Jackson *is to be Candidate* for another term;—that the Cabinet doubt as to the policy of supporting the tariff, [Samuel D.] Ingham standing alone as the advocate of the Tariff and internal improvement—The president fears the South notwithstanding all his *fearlessness*. [Henry] Baldwin of Pittsburgh is soured with the chieftain and malcontent with the Admin[istratio]n *you must win him.* James Ross of pittsburgh[4] is also wavering he adopts Baldwin's quarrel—He was disappointed by Ingham receiving the Treasury and himself nothing, and talks of promises *made him*, that have been disregarded; he is in the proper state to be operated upon. who have you to perform that work?—. The Court for the district of Columbia is to be *reformed*; the next Congress will pass a law *to amend and modify* the Judiciary system for the district, by this pretext the present law is to be repealed, the *Judges repealed* and a *new Court* (that name of bad omen) established: the present judges have offended incurably by what old hickory calls their "obstinacy in corruption," their refusal to pervert the law in Dr. [Tobias] Watkins cause. *The plan* for the next *political campaign is arranged*, it is artfully contrived and deeply laid, the work of two members of the Cabinet—the plan embraces *three great objects*, success in any *two* of which prostrates *you* now and forever—you must counterwork and defeat them or your political career is ended. I think it may be done, *I hope* it may be done. During next winter you shall *see me* and the plan, personally made known to you: it cannot be written, I cannot trust the communication to the post office, because to do so, if the letter get[s] into the hands of the Adminn. would disclose me as certainly, as the avowal of my name, and they shall not know me untill they feel me: during the last contest I was neutral, for this I am denounced, but they shall know that it is possible to make me act.

Your first object must be to secure Kentucky, it is the fulcrum upon which your political lever must rest; if you are weak at home or believed to be weak, you can have no influence abroad—You know Van Buren, and if you do, it is impossible but you must acknowledge that he is not a great man; he is a cunning man, a dextrous manager has secured an ascendancy in N. Y. and hence his reputation for greatness.—Can you not regain in Kentucky what you have lost? even with that I doubt whether you can beat old Hickory—without Kentucky your prospect is closed. The period is auspicious make the most of it; you have the present legislature, let their works tell. In my opinion you should not be nominated at the ensuing Session, it would be proclaimed immediately as a nomination merely for opposition; names always have had, always will have their effect, and an odious one should be avoided. If Jackson is not the Candidate you can always stand on equal ground with Van B. & Calhoun who will themselves be *bitterly hostile* depend on me; if Jackson is the Candidate, no other but yourself or [John] M[c]Lean will run against him, and it will be better that you are nominated late, as if merely for the purpose of enabling the people to rescue themselves from the imposition; in the meanwhile all the papers in your interest should begin now to reprobate the opinion that Jackson *can be a Candidate again* under any circumstances—his previous pledges, the pledges of his friends, that he would set the example of the Presidt. retiring at the end of 4 years should be repeated and re-iterated, and the holders of the contrary opinion treated as calumniators of the Presidt. —*he will be a Candidate* nevertheless, unless Van B. & Cal[hou]n can be harmonized. As a step towards uniting Keny. you must if possible conciliate the Pope family — John is discontented,and may be made completely disaffected; he is contemned at Washington considered of no weight, as a man utterly selfish, and kept ever vacillating on account of his apprehension of injuring self: Worden Pope is considered there as the only efficient man and perhaps rightly, but secure John and Worden will perhaps follow—Can't you make John Pope Ch[ief]. Justice of Kenty. with the reversion of [John] *Rowan's* [U.S. Senate] *seat in perspective*, and so secure him? Depend on me to secure the Pope's [*sic*] is worth an effort— I shall work up some materials to operate on Pope, but he must be nursed in Kenty. also. I think your next legislature should adopt a set of resolutions temperate but strongly expressive of their disapprobation of the *proscriptive course of the Adminn* and the *subsidizing the press*—they should also directly and strongly recommend and approbate the system of internal improvemt and the Admn. System, *instructing their Senators* and urging the Repts. to stand by the System to the last plank, this will serve to commit and pledge *the State*, and will be bringing matters back to their original position.[5] All this will be better than a nomination to the Presidency, and will be preparing the way for the nomn 12 months hence.[6] every state friendly to the same policy should follow the lead of Kenty. —Ohio especially. The manifesto and resolutions of your State should be drawn by one of your ablest writers, it should be keen, strong but temperate and decorous, displaying nothing of the violence or intemperance of party, but let it exhibit the character of a State paper, supporting principles and advocating a system of national policy rather than attacking one individual or recommending another, this latter effort will result from the *tendency* of the paper if well and ably digested and composed, and will be placing the matter upon the true ground it should be made to occupy, close the mouths of your enemies and afford the widest range to your friends: It cannot be necessary to urge your keeping Judge M[c]Lean right, he must be made useful in Ohio; his influence may perhaps be justly said to be confined to that State, for notwithstanding his correct administration of the Post Office department, and the occasional puffing he recd. you find his merits but little known or already forgotten beyond Washington City. it may be well to keep *the possibility* of himself being the Candidate still alive, but not so directly or prominently as to occasion offence or even indifference on the part of himself, and friends when he is put aside *as put aside he must be*, when the battle shall be really joined. The next Session of Congress will be the most tempestuous and violent of any assembled under the present Constitution—make the most of it; the period and the peculiar state of things may enable you to organise a *new party* or at least to take a *new name* which will be just as well: the Southerners or anti tariff are determined to press their policy to the extremest verge, and having the fire eater [George M.] Troup now amongst them may perhaps "stand to their arms" if argument fails. I am convinced that Jackson leans that way, but it is

175

not yet in my power to say positively; he is in truth severely beset with that subject, and it is the one which in my belief is to destroy him—he cannot satisfy both Pennsylva. and the South, and the question is with him—who shall be sacrificed so as to produce the least political loss? He is a bad manager in such things, and I shall not be surprised, if he displeases and loses both. In this dilemma Van Buren (who is the only one of the Cabinet *cunning* enough to help him) stands neuter for reasons you may readily perceive: [John] Branch & [John H.] Eaton with the Attorney Genl. [John M. Berrien] always anti tariff have completely neutralized [William T.] Barry and perhaps added him to their side   Van B. plays fast and loose, so that [Samuel D.] Ingham with his bull head stands alone, and cares in truth but little about the matter provided he was sure of another 4 years tenure with Hickory or any body else. The Presidents conduct to the Indians is fully reprobated Eastwardly, and quoted as a fair sample of his temper and true character when he dares display them—those who think correctly and are independent enough to speak freely, never hesitate to say, that at the head of an Army or to manage Indians each admitting if not requiring the exercise of the *Sic volo* character, is the only theatre for old Hickory. Let me give you one curious fact as I proceed, it is that the wiley Secretary of State [Van Buren] holds the Presidt. very cheap; and notwithstanding all his practised and habitual caution and discretion will sometimes let the secret out—when I see you, as see you I will if alive, you shall hear some strange and amusing incidents of these wise men of Gotham. The Secy. believes that he cannot be dispensed with, this may occasion confidence, and lead to more frankness than is habitual with him generally. I have travelled since July from N. York West & South as far as the Western part of Georgia, and shall continue through the whole of the South & West and *meet you* in Kentucky or Ohio during the winter on my way to Washington City & the East. In Virginia it might be hazarding too much to say that you were gaining fast, yet I state you the fact that from Winchester in the direction to Lynchburg and then up James River to the head of Roanoke I found but *one man* one solitary man, who expressed himself against you—this was singular and serves at least to prove, that although you have political adversaries throughout that section of Country, they must be less numerous than is proclaimed abroad, or how happens it, that I who talked politics with every body—whose business in making the long journey was and is to talk politics, found so few opposed to you. I am as cautious as possible on my journey and few are able to say decisively on which side I am, but under the character and affectation of neutrality I cut the deeper on my way I sow the seeds of disaffection deep and wide, and if they do not bud, blossom and ripen as rapidly as Aaron's rod, I have still the best hopes, and the fairest expectations that in due season fruit will be brought forth. The principles of modern warfare is to wage the contest in the enemies country, & experience has proved its advantages; in politics the principle is no less true, you must therefore keep up your correspondence and if possible add to your strength in Tennessee,   Col. [John] Williams and Genl. [John] Cocke are firm and will keep their retainers in the field: Carrol [*sic*, William Carroll] I think has sent in his adhesion, but Jackson and he hate each other so cordially, and feel that each is playing Mala grida so palpably, that but little will be necessary to produce discord again—you must set some agent of competent powers at that work, some of the Erwin's[7] perhaps, as they are all of them very intimate and confidential with Carrol. Two

176

of the members of Congress from Alabama are your friends as I am informed, [Clement C.] Clay and [Robert E. Bledsoe] Baylor: there is no doubt of the latter, you will at once see the propriety of cultivating them; Baylor is said to be a Nephew of Mr. [Jesse] Bledsoe of your State, look to that matter. I shall return by the way of Tennessee, Kenty. & Ohio in Feby or early in March and must see you, unless you disclaim my co-operation, for this purpose you will be apprised where to meet me and must not omit the conference, as I shall by that time have a mass of information that may be made useful. Treat my correspondence with all that delicacy and caution that belongs to the confidential communications of a friend. *Shew* my letters to no one[8] and use the facts sparingly and judiciously. you will of course understand the name subscribed to this letter an assumed one, I cannot trust the true one to the surveillance & espionage of the post office of the present time, as long as I remain concealed, it is impossible to prevent my obtaining a knowledge of cabinet secrets — expose me and you close all the avenues of information: this autograph betrays nothing even should the letter be intercepted. . . . [P.S.] Say in the [Lexington *Kentucky*] Reporter under the head "To Correspondents" [that] _◿_ is recd. the meeting shall be attended to—

ALS. DLC-HC (DNA, M212, R4). Partially printed in Colton, *Clay Correspondence*, 4:253. Postmarked at Huntsville, Ala., Feb. 12. At the bottom of this letter, in another hand, probably Calvin Colton's is written: "This note and the following extract from a long letter of bold advice, are written over an assumed name, Alexis de Sarcy, but the writer appears to have been well known to Mr. Clay, & a sort of Mentor. How he was entertained in this capacity, is not known." Nor is it known today whether the undated "following extract" was enclosed in "de Sarcy" to Clay, Feb. 11, 1830, or what its date of composition was.   1. Hopkinsville Speech, Sept. 21, 1829.   2. "de Sarcy" to Clay, Sept. 17, 1829.   3. Colton's printed version stops here.   4. See *BDAC*.   5. On Jan. 18, 1830, the Ky. house had passed a resolution, similar to that proposed by "de Sarcy," strongly endorsing the power of the federal government to levy a tariff and to support internal improvements. The resolution also condemned the doctrine of nullification. The Ky. senate passed the resolution on Jan. 23. Ky. H. of Reps., *Journal* . . . 1829-30, pp. 141-54, 254-57; Ky. Sen., *Journal* . . . 1829-30, pp. 253-67.   6. The Ky. legislature did not nominate Clay. On Sept. 13, 1830, it was decided at a meeting held in Winchester to hold a convention in Frankfort on Dec. 9 to nominate for president a candidate who would "secure the triumph of the American system and the union of the states, against the new and alarming doctrines of dissolution and nullification." The 290 delegates who met in Frankfort in December nominated Clay. *Nile's Register* (Oct. 2; Dec. 25, 1830), 39:90, 302.   7. Reference to Tennessee family connections of Clay's son-in-law, James Erwin.   8. Following phrase, "unless it be to Mr. [Charles] Hammond of Cincinnati," is struck through.

From James Riley, New Orleans, February 19, 1830. Charges that the nation under Andrew Jackson is pursuing "a crooked Machiavel[l]ian policy," and that Clay's "talents energies & exertions can alone save us." Reports that he lives in New York City where he had learned "last Summer" from "many of the Most respectable Gentlemen merchants & others of Charleston SC" that Clay's "many friends" in Charleston "longed to See you among them before the next Presidential Election — they Say it would have a powerful & electric effect." Regrets that illness has prevented his calling on Clay. ALS. DLC-HC (DNA, M212, R4). Addressed to Clay in New Orleans.

To JOSIAH S. JOHNSTON   New Orleans, February 27, 1830
Your several letters addressed to me in Kentucky and at this place have been received. Owing to the Ohio river being closed by ice, I did not receive the former as early as they would have reached me by land. That obstruction being now removed, and Boats daily arriving from Louisville, I shall receive the letters of my friends with more regularity, during the 10 or 12 days that I purpose yet to continue in this City. Except two short excursions to Mr. Soniots [*sic*,

Joseph Soniat du Fossat][1] and Mr. Milligans, I have not been out of the City and its immediate neighbourhood. I have been treated, throughout, with the greatest respect and attention. Some of the more prominent Jacksonians, especially those who are expecting office, keep at a distance; but all others, embracing many of that party, have been extremely civil. I have been invited to public dinners at Memphis, Vicksburg, Port Gibson, Natchez and Baton Rouge; but I have declined all, except that proposed at Natchez.

I have been often with your friend Judge [Alexander] Porter, who I think worthy of all the fine things you have said of him to me. I like him extremely and hope that our acquaintance will have impressed upon him towards me the same sentiments of esteem and friendship which I feel for him.

I shall expect eagerly Mr. [Daniel] Webster's second speech on Mr. [Samuel A.] Foot's resolution,[2] of which your letters and those of other friends have communicated such flattering accounts. The triumph which he enjoyed was a noble one. I fear his resolution agt. Duff Green was premature,[3] and dictated by a chafed and proud spirit, indignant at the vile misrepresentations of that execrable wretch. His 9h. Thermidor has not I fear yet arrived.

The short crop of the last year is much felt in this Country. I have been agreeably surprized to find the opinion in favor of the Tariff so general and so strong in this State. You must not be surprized to find yourself shortly instructed by the Legislature to support it.[4] From what I learn at least two thirds of the Legislature, if not more, are in favor of it; but they have great difficulty in collecting and keeping the members at Donaldsonville.

[Martin] Duralde has declined being a Candidate for Governor at a moment when they tell me his election would have been certain, if Roman had declined, and probable if he would not.[5] He did not wish to produce divisions among friends, and really cared nothing about the office. . . .

ALS. PHi. Printed in Colton, *Clay Correspondence*, 4:254-55.   1. See *LHQ* 7:308, 314.   2. For the Webster-Hayne debate, see *Register of Debates*, 21 Cong., 1 Sess., 31-93. Webster's second speech, in *ibid.*, 58-80, refuted the contention that the federal government was formed by a compact of the states and argued instead that it was formed by the people. It concluded with the famous quote: "Liberty *and* Union, now and forever, one and inseparable!"   3. See Claude M. Feuss, *Daniel Webster* (Boston, 1930), 1:385.   4. On March 6, 1830, Sebastian Hiriart wrote Clay, enclosing "the resolutions reported by the Joint Committee on the Tariff," and stating that these resolutions in favor of the tariff had passed unanimously in the Louisiana senate. He also predicts that they will pass the house by "a very large majority." ALS. PHi. Hiriart was a sugar planter of West Baton Rouge Parish who represented that parish as well as the Iberville Parish in the state senate in 1830. He was a native of Bayonne in southwestern France.   5. In the July 5, 1830, Louisiana gubernatorial election Armand Beauvais, a National Republican, received 1,502 votes; Andre B. Roman, also a National Republican, received 3,630; and William Hamilton, a Democrat Republican, received 2,730 votes. See *BDGUS*, 2:560-61.

From Josiah S. Johnston, Senate Chamber, Washington, March 4, 1830. Reports that the "debate proceeds — the question of Removal has been drawn into the debate — & Mr. [John M.] Clayton is now speaking very well to that question — besides the authorities which have been quoted — We have a very bold expression of [William B.] Giles opinions under Mr. Adams Admn." ALS. InU. For Clayton's comments on Jackson's removals from office see *Register of Debates*, 21 Cong., 1 Sess., 224-44 and for the Adams-Giles relationship see 7:516-17; and Adams to Clay, December 11, 1829.

To JOSIAH S. JOHNSTON   Steamboat *Caledonia*, near Baton Rouge, March 11, 1830

You will perceive, from the enclosed,[1] that my anticipation has been realized. You will now be at liberty to pursue your own Judgment, in relation to the great measure referred to.[2] On that subject, two grounds will naturally suggest themselves to you, as forming a justification for your future course. 1st the will of your Constituents and 2dly. that you will not assist in disturbing an *established* policy.

I expect to reach Natchez tomorrow morning. and I shall remain there until Sunday the 14h. when I shall ascend in the G. Washington.

All parties tell me that your re-election is safe. I think you were wise in declining being a Candidate for the office of Governor. [Andre Bienvenu] Roman, I believe, will be elected. I think it the interest of our friends to unite on him. There is a good prospect of our returning three friends to the H. of R. And yet I am not without fears that we may lose the majority in your Legislature.[3] The City of N. O. is the pivot; and it is extremely difficult there to animate our friends to proper exertion. It will be well for you to come here, after the close of Congress. . . .

ALS. PHi.   1. Probably Hiriart to Clay, March 6, 1830, in Clay to Johnston, Feb. 27, 1830. 2. *Ibid.*   3. In the July election, Clay supporters won a large majority of seats in the Louisiana state legislature. *Niles' Register* (August 7, 1830), 38:418-19.

SPEECH AT NATCHEZ

Natchez, Mississippi, March 13, 1830

After thanking his audience at length for the warmth and enthusiasm of their welcome, Clay "then adverted to that part of judge Turner's address, which spoke of Mr. Clay as the decided advocate of the late war. We cannot attempt to draw even the outlines of his observations, or to pourtray the feelings he discovered while depicting the part which Kentucky acted in the war; of the volunteers she sent forth to battle, of the deprivations she suffered, of the money expended, and of the blood that flowed from her sons in supporting the nation in the defence of her rights and independence. Yet what Mr. Clay said, no one can properly appreciate, even though we could give his own words, except those who heard him speak. The expression of his eye, his attitude and gestures, evinced how deeply the subject affected him—the people of Kentucky, he said, acted nobly throughout the whole contest; and whether in defeat or in victory, she still showed the determination to sustain the American character, and to maintain American independence—and it would be only to repeat, what was a common observation among the people of his state, to say, that their countrymen of Mississippi acted with a spirit during the war worthy the best days of the revolution.

In speaking of the invasion of Lousiana [*sic*], and of the battle of New Orleans, his feelings and his voice seemed to rise with the subject. We had a situation close to, and nearly in front of him; we fixed our eyes steadily upon him—there was a moral grandeur in his looks and his manners, and the encomiums he passed upon the hero who had achieved the victory, though said in a few words, were such as might be expected from a statesman so great in honor and so exalted in patriotism as Mr. Clay. He concluded this part of his speech by saying, that, although by the negotiations at Ghent, none of the objects for which the nation went to war were guarantied by the treaty of peace, yet they were secured to us by a power much stronger than any treaty stipulations could give—the influence of our arms, the resources and power of the republic, as brought forth and shown in the contest.

He now spoke of the apprehensions entertained by many, that the union would be dissolved; but he considered all apprehensions of this kind as arising more from our fears that such a misfortune should visit the country, than from any substantial reasons to justify them. Rumors, he said, had gone abroad ever since the adoption of the present constitution, that the republic would be dismembered. Whenever any important question arose in which the passions and prejudices of party, rather than the reason of the people, was brought to bear on the discussion, the cry would be heard, that the union would fall in the conflict; to-day, the disposition to separate would be charged on the west; to-morrow, against the north or the east: and then it would be returned back again to the south: but as long as I have lived, said Mr. Clay, amid the agitations and convulsions of different times, I have seen nothing to give me any serious fears that such an evil could befal us. First, the people were divided into democrats and federalists — then we had the funding system, and the bank of the United States — then came the Missouri question, and last the *tariff*. On this question, said Mr. Clay, his partial friend [Judge Edward Turner] had honored him with the appellation of the advocate of domestic industry. He was indeed, from conscientious convictions, the friend of that system of public policy, which has been called the American system — and *here*, among those who honestly differed with him on this question, he would be indulged, by this magnanimous people, in offering a few remarks on this subject.

It has been objected to this policy by a distinguished statesman in congress, that our country was too extended, the lands cheap and fertile, and our population too sparse to admit of the manufacturing system; that our people were physically incapable of that confined degree of labor, necessary to excellence in manufactures; but experience has surely disproved these positions. We are by nature inferior to no people, physically or mentally, and time has proved, and will continue to prove it. Mr. Clay said nothing particularly new on this subject — it was the clear, direct and striking manner in which he placed his observations, that made them come home to the understanding of all present.

He was aware that the people of this quarter of the union conscientiously believed that the tariff bore heavily on them; yet he felt, also well assured, from a retrospect of the past, that if the laws on this subject were even more severe in their operation than he believed them to be, this patriotic people would endure them patiently. Yes, if the independence of the country, the interests, and above all the *cause* of the union required heavy sacrifices, they would endure them. But whilst claiming no immunity from error, he felt the most sincere, the deepest conviction, that the tariff, so far from having proved injurious to the peculiar interests of this section of country, has been eminently beneficial. Mr. Clay asked to put two questions to those interested in your great staple — he would take the common operations of *sale* and of *purchase*; has the operation of the tariff lowered the price of what you sell? The price of every article must be regulated mainly by the demand; has then the consumption of cotton diminished since the tariff of 1824 or 1828? No, it has increased — greatly increased; and why? Because the protection extended by this policy has created a *new customer* in the American manufacturer, who takes 200,000 BALES, without having lessened the demand for the European market.

British merchants have found new markets for their cotton fabrics, and the competition, thus created, while it has reduced the price of the manufactured article, has increased the consumption of the raw material. Again, has the tariff increased the price of what you buy? Take the article of domestic

180

cottons for example — has not the American manufacturer, since the adoption of this system, afforded you a better article and at less price than before? Take a familiar instance, one in which having some personal interest he ought to be acquainted with — take the article manufactured in his own state, for the covering of your cotton bales; take any period, say six years before and six years since the tariff of 1824, has the average price of cotton bagging increased or diminished in that period? He thought he could appeal confidently to those around him for the reply. We afford you a better article than the European, and at a greatly reduced price. But, said Mr. Clay, I am permitting myself to be carried away by the subject; he would obtrude no longer on the indulgence of this generous people; I feel, said he, my inability to express my profound and heartfelt gratitude for the too flattering reception you have given me — and for the sentiments you have been pleased to honor me with, an humble individual in private life. He would ask permission to offer them a sentiment:

"The health and prosperity of the people of the state of Mississippi."

Copy. Printed in *Niles' Register* (April 17, 1830), 38:142-44. Reprinted from *The Natchez*, March 20, 1830. Delivered in the Mississippi Hotel to an audience exceeded only in size by that which "was in honor of general Lafayette." Judge Edward Turner of the Mississippi Supreme Court presided. *Niles' Register* regretted not being able to publish Clay's speech "as he delivered it," but felt that "what we have given, is, we believe, substantially correct, not essentially we think at variance with what he said." No manuscript version of the speech has been found. Printed also in the Washington *Daily National Journal*, April 10, 1830, and in the Lexington *Kentucky Reporter*, April 7, 1830. Minor variations are found in the latter version.

To James Erwin, Natchez, Mississippi, March 14, 1830. Asks Erwin to purchase for him a parcel of land of four or five acres situated on the river across from Baton Rouge. Says it is in the hands of the Bank of Louisiana and can be had either for $4,000 cash or for the same sum on one to four years credit at 9 percent. Prefers to buy it on credit "with *the liberty* of paying the principal, and ridding myself of the int. at any time I please." Reports that the public dinner he attended in Natchez "yesterday went off well. My whole reception has been full of gratification." ALS. NHi.

From JOSIAH S. JOHNSTON　　　　　　Washington, March 14, 1830

I have written you fully & frequently to N. Orleans — Where I hope you have had a pleasant time & a safe return — [Robert P.] Letcher writes you by this oppty., he is well informed, & will save me the necessity of much detail —

The Jackson party has been divided into the friends of Van Buren — Calhoun & the President — & all with different views, Latterly there has been a tendency to take sides with the two leaders, but this is kept quite secret — The parties present a curious spectacle — It appears as if the General & his friends had got into a false position — A Lady [Peggy Eaton] is Undoubtedly the point upon which the momentous affairs of this Country now turns — The General adheres to the Lady through evil report　his faithful Ministers of State [Van Buren] & of War [John Eaton] & of the P[ost]. office [William T. Barry] rally under her flag, with their adherents — The Vice President [Calhoun] Treasury [Samuel D. Ingham], Navy [John Branch] & Law [John M. Berrien] Depts. with many of the friends of General Jackson, & all their own partizans rally in the opposition — The General Was determin[e]d to have an Eaton Cabinet — but the peculiar state of parties, induced him to spare Branch for a time, as his removal would have been a signal of separation — It was necessary to carry the nominations through before the breach — as soon as that is done I think there will be some reform in the Cabinet —

Within the Last Week, plain intimations have been thrown out in the Senate, particularly by [Felix] Grundy that the General will be a Candidate again, but for What purpose I could not understand—but I have no idea that he will—He will not be able to get through this term—& if he Was he could not be elected—The opinion prevails extensively that he is incompetent, that his Admn. has been wretched so far—his party Cannot be kept together—

All things are Working to prepare the way for you as visibly as they did for the General—The idea of your Success is getting possession of the public mind you have only to stand Still—They are doing more for you than you Can do for yourself—Many individuals of the party are falling off—His patronage is exhausted—the disappointed begin to look in another direction—He has greatly abused his power & done no good—

Calhoun now has it in his power to hold the check over appts. but he is afraid to break ground, because he desires to keep the party together—I have had hopes that we should be able to reject the printers especially the Auditors, but things stand in so peculiar a state, that no Calculations can be made—If any of the Calhoun men vote agt. [Amos] Kendal[l] or [Isaac] Hill—& they are rejected—the War will break out—That will be the Signal for removing the Calhoun men from the Cabinet—All the Printers (appd.) are agt. Calhoun We must delay the nominations[1] as long as possible—They know how they stand & they are trembling for their fate—They say they will serve as clerks—

The debate has been interesting & you will read it with pleasure—it still goes on—

We Understand the General is much harrassed, that he is some times out of patience—He has a great deal to distract him, He has said—We Understand that the Senate mean to govern the Country—& there is no doubt he is dissatisfied with that body—I hope he may soon have more reason—I should be very glad to give some lands to the Transylvania University, but the vote on Fultons claim,[2] gives but little hope of the success of the bill—[3]

Mrs. Johnston is quite well & we Unite in kind regards to Mrs. Clay—Letcher will give you the news—[John] Pope is not satisfied with his share of the spoils—nor with his reception—He will go back to go With the people of Ky in the Next election—He will go for you—the effect of this will be good among his friends in Ky—& especially at Louisville—& will have influence every Where—

There is one point now of great importance & that the necessity of Union in the West—This idea must be inculcated every where—There is an attempt now on the part of [Thomas H.] Benton to Create prejudice agt. the north & Union with the South—& thus divide the West & Carry as many to Calhoun as possible—We must hold up the necessity for Union in the West—With this Scheme is connected the plan of running [John] McLean for Vice President—not yet fully disclosed—The plan of dividing the West Consists in Uniting Ky with Virga. & Tennessee with Carolina & exciting hostility & promoting a feeling of alienation towards the North in the states north of Ohio—

ALS. InU.   1. Johnston to Clay, Jan. 26, 1830.   2. The Senate on March 11 defeated a bill to pay a claim to the orphan children of steamboat builder Robert Fulton. *Register of Debates*, 21 Cong., 1 Sess., 247.   3. Clay to Johnston, Jan. 12, 1830.

From Martin Duralde, New Orleans, March 18, 1830. Reports that the resolutions concerning the tariff, which passed the state senate unanimously, also passed the lower chamber with but seven dissenting votes. Believes "unless a very great change should take place I have no doubt but that A.B. Roman will be elected Govr. of this State in July next." ALS. DLC-TJC (DNA, M212, R13). For the Louisiana gubernatorial election, see Clay to Johnston, February 27, 1830.

To [JOSIAH S. JOHNSTON] Frankfort, March 25, 1830

I reached this place this morning from Louisville. My passage from Natchez in the G. Washington comprehended all the agreeable circumstances. Nothing could surpass the warmth of my reception in Mississippi. Both parties attended the dinner and Ball [March 13] at Natchez, and they vied with each other in their testimonies of respect. I had the satisfaction to make the acquaintance of Dr's [Stephen] Duncan and [William Newton] Mercer[1] with both of whom I was much pleased.

I believe that I have not heretofore said to you that I found in Louisiana an unanimous and strong opposition to the acquisition of Texas. Your brother is disinclined to offer at the next election for the Legislature.[2] I endeavored to overcome his repugnance. I think he ought to be there where he might essentially serve you. He has an excellent standing in the House. Genl [Philemon] Thomas will beat [Eleazar W.] Ripley with ease for Congress if those two only offer.[3]

I have of course no news, for which we look to your quarter exclusively.

ALS. Courtesy of Dr. Thomas D. Clark, Lexington, Ky. Printed in Colton, *Clay Correspondence*, 4:256, with recipient incorrectly identified as Francis T. Brooke. 1. For Dr. Mercer, see Pierce Butler, *Laurel Hill and Later: The Record of a Teacher* (New Orleans, 1954), 5-6. 2. An asterisk has been placed before this sentence; a matching asterisk at the bottom of the page, written in a strange hand, is followed by an endorsement which reads: "His reference is to my father. J.S.J. Speaker of the La H of R 1830". The editors have concluded that the letter was written to Sen. Josiah Stoddard Johnston of Louisiana and that the brother referred to was John Harris Johnston who at the time was a member of the Louisiana house, though he was not its speaker. The endorsement, thus, was probably made at a later date by one of John Harris Johnston's sons who seems to have been confused about his father's position in the house. 3. For Thomas and Ripley, both Democrats, see *BDAC*. Thomas defeated Ripley by a majority of 111 votes. *Niles' Register* (August 7, 1830), 38:418.

To SAMUEL BARNES Lexington, March 29, 1830

My absence from home has delayed until this time the acknowledgement of your friendly letter of the 16h. Jan.

I saw, with much satisfaction, your engagement with the Chronicle.[1] I hope it may realize all the private advantages which you expected to derive from it. The public, I am sure, will profit by it. I needed no assurance, from any quarter, of your faithful adherence to the principles and to the cause which you had espoused. I thank God that there are some men yet to be found who are worthy of all reliance.

On the point, respecting which you have been pleased to consult me, my nomination, at this time, for the Presidency, I hardly know what to say. Of all men, I am the most unfit to decide that question. Whether I ought to be thought of for that office — above all, whether measures should be taken to secure my election to it, should depend upon the people or portions of the people. I am prepared to acquiesce in their will, whatever it may be. I learn, from all quarters, that those who have been pleased to turn their attention towards me, feel strong encouragement, and anticipate success with much confidence. They are the most competent judges to determine when and how my name shall be otherwise presented to the American public than it is at present. I suppose that particularly my friends in Congress would be able to command a better view of the field than I can; and with them I would recommend you to confer. There is no State that contains more highly valued friends, personal and political, than Maryland; and I feel a deep interest in all its movements. I regretted, in common with them, the result of the Election last fall; and I sincerely hope that a more favorable one may take place in the ensuing fall. It would be very discouraging if our friends should lose the U.S. Senator.[2]

Many of my friends, in various parts of the Union, have supposed that a certain degree of reserve on our part would lead to the developement of dissentions in the ranks of our opponents which would not appear if we were seen in corps and seen to be formidable. That policy is liable to objection that, if it exposes the weakness of one side, it tends also to the debility of the other by withdrawing the cement necessary to bind men together. At all events, I should think the period of the termination of the present Session of Congress would be long enough to await the effects of that policy. After that it seems to me that such movements might be made as to bring together those who think alike, and to encourage the Chiltons[3] of the other side. But these must be understood to be my private opinions subject to be overruled by the better judgments of my friends.

If I am right in them, I see no objection to the Chronicle at that time taking the stand which you intimate, not however as upon *authority* from *me*.

I think all the Western States, including Louisiana certainly, and Mississippi probably, may be counted upon. . . .

ALS. Courtesy of Mr. St. George L. Sioussat, Washington, D.C. Letter marked "(Confidential)."
1. Probably the Baltimore *Chronicle & Daily Marylander*.   2. The reference is likely to Ezekiel F. Chambers. *BDAC*.   3. Reference is to those who had opposed the Adams administration but who might, like Ky. Representative Thomas Chilton, switch and support Clay.

To HENRY CLAY, JR.   Lexington, March 29, 1830

I returned home from N. O. on the 26h.   I left your sister [Anne Brown Clay Erwin], Mr. [Martin] Duralde and our other friends there all well. You were often a theme of conversation, and your successful progress and persevering assiduity afford our friends there, as every where else, the greatest delight. I am often complimented on the high standing of my son, and I derive from it more satisfaction than I now should from any personal praise applied to myself.

I found your Mama quite cheerful and happy. She had passed the period of my absence with great tranquillity and with less trouble than ever during the winter. A new overseer that I had engaged (Mr. [William] Martin) has fulfilled all my hopes, and has put Ashland in a better condition than I ever saw it at this early season of the year. We have already ploughed almost the ground for the Crop of the present year.

I received your letter informing me of your honorable appointments to deliver the 4h. of July oration and the discourse on the contemplated Institute.[1] I am highly gratified to learn that such favorable opinions are entertained of you by your young associates; but I am almost afraid that you have over taxed yourself. In your Compositions attend more to the justness of the idea and sentiment which you wish to express than to the ornament of your language. The vice of our Countrymen, and especially the younger part, in composition, is a profuse use of epithets and metaphor. Let me advise you also not to consent to the publication of your productions, which you will be much urged to do. Reserve them for consideration at a future period of your life. A single [in]discreet sentiment or expression might occasion you bitter regrets.

I brought with me from N. O. your nephew H[enry]. C. Duralde, a fine sprightly boy, with whom we are all much pleased. H[enry]. C. Hart is also now here, and the Midshipman has become much improved. He does not promise to be large. Poor R[ichard]. Shelby occasioned his parents great pain until they were relieved by your letter.[2] They feel the warmest gratitude to you for your friendly interest in Richard.

I have good accounts from Thomas [H. Clay] at my prairie in Illinois. Theodore [W. Clay] is passing a part of his time in town.

I am glad to learn that you acquiesce in my opinion as to the utility of studying several years after you leave the Point. At the age of thirty you will be more than ever confirmed as to its propriety.

Your mother desires to be affectionately remembered to you. Indeed all of us are constantly thinking of you my dear Son as the pride and hope of your family.

ALS. Henry Clay Memorial Foundation, Lexington, Ky.   1. Clay to Henry Clay, Jr., Dec. 26, 1829.   2. Henry Clay, Jr., to Clay, Oct. 24, 1829.

To PHILIP R. FENDALL   Lexington, March 30, 1830

Your letter of the 25h. Jan. on the subject of my letter to [Simon] Bolivar reached me at N. Orleans and I postponed answering it until my return. I submit to your entire discretion the time and the manner of its publication, except that I should not wish that it should appear to be at my instance.[1] Perhaps you can somehow connect it with Genl. [William Henry] Harrison's return, without implicating him.

My visit below was attended with the highest gratification. I was as happy as one could be in the midst of his own dear connexions; and the delicate and respectful attentions every where shewn me could not have been surpassed When I attended the Legislature of Louisiana, the whole body, without concert, spontaneously rose and received me. At Natchez my reception was enthusiastic. Not an incident occurred at one of the largest public dinners that I ever assisted at, indoors, to mar the general satisfaction. I found myself there in the midst of equal numbers of both parties, with a Jackson man on my right and an Adams man on my left.

I shall be glad to hear fully from you soon. I hope the [Washington *Daily National*] Journal will do well under its new arrangement.[2] I think a special agent to solicit subscriptions would do well in the West and below.

ALS. NcD. Letter marked "(Confidential)."   1. Published in the Washington *Daily National Journal*, April 17, 1830, together with the Bolivar to Clay of Nov. 21, 1827. See 6:1298-99; 7:517-18.   2. Johnston to Clay, Jan. 26, 1830.

To Thomas Kell, Lexington, March 30, 1830. Remarks that he is pleased to learn from Kell that "my warm-hearted friends in Baltimore remain firm and steadfast in their attachment." Reports that his recent visit to Louisiana and Mississippi was "full of gratification." Copy. Printed in *MHM* (1910), 5:183-84.

From WILLIAM H. CRAWFORD   Wood Lawn [near Lexington, Ga.], March 31, 1830

I perceive by the news papers that your name, Mr Van Buiren's [*sic*, Van Buren] & Mr Calhoun's names are likely to be run for the next Presidency, in the event of General Jackson's not being a candidate. My friends are also solicitory that my name should be put in nomination. I do not profess to know much of public opinion, but I am very sure that if four names are run for the Presidency, no election will be made by the electoral Colleges. If your name Mr Van Bueren's & Mr Calhoun's name should be held up for that office, I am under the impression that Mr Van Bueren would be elected. For Giving you all the Western & South Western Votes; & Mr Calhoun the votes of South Carolina North Carolina and Pennsylvania which are all the votes that his most sanguine friends can claim for him, Mr Van Bueren would still have a majority of the colleges; unless you could divide the New England votes with him. This might happen for ought *I know*, but I do not expect it. In the first place I think it probable that Mr Adams interest in New England would not be concentrated upon you. 1st Because the men who would support Mr Adams from *principle*, would probably be opposed to *you*. Mr Adams and yourself are so different in *manners habits, sentiments* and *principles*, that it is not probable that you can be supported by the same men. Nothing but this discrepancy between you, could have given the vote of Ohio against Mr Adams in the late election. 2d In the election of 1824 almost every man of respectable standing in New England was against Mr Adams, yet he got every vote in those States by a majority of 5/6. My impression therefore is that you will not get a vote in New England. It is true Mr Van Buiren does not live in New England, but he lives near it, & you live a great way from it, & that circumstance will in all probability be decisive. It has occurred to me that if you are desirous of filling the Presidency, the most likely way of success, will be to avoid the contest for the next Presidency. If you do this & my name should be substituted for yours & receive your support, I presume there would be no doubt of my receiving the vote of the Western and South Western States. To this vote might be safely added that of Georgia N Carolina, Virginia & Delaware & perhaps Maryland. The aggregate would fall little short of a majority, & the remainder could hardly fail to be received from the States North & East of those mentioned. In the event of success, you would come again into the cabinet, & could hardly fail of success when I retired. Your union with Mr Adams has effectually destroyed your popularity in the Atlantic States South of the Chesapeake. I have even injured my own standing in this state by defending you against the charge of corrupt bargaining. If such is your standing in this state you can well imagine what it is in the other Southern Atlantic states. Do not suppose that I feel any solicitude upon the subject of this letter. I feel none; but supposing from what I have seen in the public papers that you may feel some, it occurred to me that the most certain mode of gratifying that feeling was to adopt the course which I have suggested. If you should be of a different opinion, let the matter rest wher[e] it is, & there will no harm have been done. On the contrary should you concur in the suggestion I have made, I shall be happy to hear from you as soon as leisure will permit. PS. It is possible that my friends at Washington may make the same suggestion to Mr Van Bueren. Should it be accepted, it is probable the same result would be effected as to myself, but I should rather it should take place with you.

ALS. DLC-HC (DNA, M212, R4). Endorsed on verso by Clay: "Never answered." For Clay's summary of this letter see Clay to Brooke, May 23, 1830, below, which is also printed in Colton, *Clay Correspondence*, 4:270-73.

It was a manouvre I think of Van Buren to present the General to the public again & withdraw himself—[1]to prevent Calhoun from carry off the party, to Unite them again—to obtain the advantage of yeilding the place & to throw upon Calhoun the odium of dividing the party—Calhoun is not withdrawn. The party is in great Confusion—It is very difficult to Cohere—It is difficult to hold them together—They have had several Night Caucusses—

It is said there are not more than 30 members in the House favorable to the Continuance of the Genl.

It is said to be the first object to hold together Until the nominations are passed—That done, I think the General will reform his Cabinet, He will have an exclusive Eaton Cabinet—that is a Van Buren Cabinet—The removal of [John] Branch [Samuel D.] Ingham & [John M.] Berrien, will be the signal of separation   The Calhoun flag will be raised—an effort has been made to Unite [John] McLean as vice President—It will be successful in my opinion— If the Calhoun men vote as they are secretly disposed to do against [Isaac] Hill & [Amos] Kendal[l] & they are rejected—[2]that will I think be the signal of Separation—& this is the difficulty now—If they hav[e] the independence to act, they will incur the hostility of the party of the Palace—They are not de- cided how to act & may be influenced by Circumstances that may occur every hour   The separation of Calhoun & Van Buren who is identified with Jackson is complete. It has been whisper[e]d that [John H.] Eaton will run with Van Buren as Vice President—We have discussed at length the power of the President to remove—

It is generally admitted that the President ex necessitat or as an implica- tion from the power of seeing the Laws executed may remove in Cases of necessity calling for the exercise of the power, that is where the du[e] execution of the Laws demands it—The President has abused it by Using it for political purposes—no one denies the purpose   The question is where is the remedy— We say in the negative preventive power of the Senate—The Calhoun men Say they would not exercise the power of removal for opinion sake & thereby pronounce a judgement upon the Course of proceedings—a virtual condem- nation of the principl[e]—the odium of which they will throw upon V. Buren   But then not to break with the party & escape the dilemma they say the Senate have nothing to do with the Correction of the error—They say he does it on his responsibility—That if he was impeachable they are the tryiers—If it is an assumption or abuse of power he must account to the peopl[e]—The whole thing then resolves itself into this   Must the Senate resist this violation—or must it have its Course   It is upon this pretense they vote for the nominations & thereby approve the whole Course—How Can he be impeached for nominations approved by the Senate? The Supervising & restraining power of the Senate is given up—

We hear these divisions of Calhoun & Van Buren are beginning to oper- ate among the peopl[e]—particularly in the West—I do not doubt that Prov- idence is working all things for good—I believe the party is are convinced that the President is a weak, incompetent old man—that his Cabinet is not much better—that he is under a strong influence of a few men, in whom the Country hav[e] no Confidence—I expect we shall find the officers in great Con- fusion—They are asking $100,000 now for the Post office—Several persons have told me that they have written you, from all our views you will know quite as much as we know & will make your own reflections—

ALS. InU. Internal evidence suggests this letter was written between Johnston's letter to Clay of March 14 and the one of April 13, 1830.   1. Johnston to Clay, April 13, 1830.   2. Johnston to Clay, Jan. 26, 1830; Clay to Watterson, May 8, 1830.

From John A. Quitman, Natchez, Mississippi, April 3, 1830. Assures Clay that he will send him some small magnolia trees, as per Clay's earlier request in the matter. Tried to get the plants to Clay before he left Natchez for Kentucky but failed. Comments on Clay's visit to Natchez: "You cd. not carry with you more friendly impressions towards our citizens, than you have left behind you towards yr.self. You may well consider yr. visit so fortunate to yr.self and to us. for I know that the circle of yr. friends has been extended." ALS. Ms-Ar. Written from "Monmouth," his plantation near Natchez.

To JOSIAH S. JOHNSTON   Lexington, April 6, 1830

I received your favor of the 14h. Ulto. transmitted through a friend. It discloses a state of public affairs at Washington both curious and mortifying. Your account and conclusions are substantially concurred in by other friends who write me. If the incompetency of the President could be manifested to the public I have no doubt with you that his re-election would be impracticable. But how is that to be done? How, especially, will that large portion of it which contributed to place him where he is be made to believe his unfitness? Particularly when majorities in both houses continue to support all, even his most exceptionable acts?

I say continue to support them; for I infer from what I have seen that the principle of removal, in its most odious form, has been sanctioned by the majority. What does the Senate believe will be thought of its dignity and independence, in after times, when it will sanction (as in the case of the Treasurer of the U.S)[1] the removal, without cause, of a high public officer whose appointment it only a few months before approved? Does it imagine that the miserable sophistry of that pliant tool Felix Grundy will justify it? According to him the Senate can not look beyond the mere question of fitness of the person nominated; the President acts upon his responsibility; and there is no remedy but in impeachment! Does he not see that he strips the body of one of its most important Constitutional functions, that of operating as a check upon the Executive? Does he not see that the Senate, after making itself a particeps with the President, in a dangerous and pernicious proceeding, will be a very unfit and unsafe tribunal to arraign him before for that identical proceeding?

The consequence, I fear, will be of this approbation in both houses of the worst acts of the President, that the Jackson portion of the public will be lulled into security and believe that all is right. In this point of view, I have thought it of much importance that where any great principle was involved (such as the appointment of Editors, or removals without cause) the Senate would shew itself worthy of the esteem which it once enjoyed by putting itself against the evils to be dreaded.

You perceive no effect at a distance from the state of things which you describe at Washington. Witness the result in New Hampshire.[2]

If Mr. Calhoun really intends to set himself up in opposition to Genl. Jackson, I should begin to think there was a prospect of some division that might lead to beneficial results.

Do not imagine, from any thing that I have said, that I at all despair of the Republic. I only fear that the day of soundness and sanity is more distant than you believe.

Mr. [Thomas] Chilton's last letter on the comparative expenditure of the two administrations, like his first, will do good.[3]

I shall not disappoint my friends in remaining still. I shall remain more than ever at Ashland, the occupations of which I relish more than ever.

[Martin] Duralde writes me [March 18] that the Tariff resolution which I informed you had passed the Senate of Louisiana unanimously has passed the House with only seven dissentients. I sent you a Copy of the resolution, which I hope you received

I heard nothing more after I wrote you of Waggerman's [sic] opposition to you.[4] I hope it will not take place. Our friends were very confident of your success; but you should go home after the Session. Duralde thinks [Andre B.] Roman will be elected Governor. . . .[5]

ALS. PHi. Printed in Colton, *Clay Correspondence*, 4:256-58.   1. William Clarke was removed as treasurer of the U.S. and replaced by John Campbell of Virginia. Richmond *Enquirer*, April 2, 1830.   2. The Jacksonians were victorious in New Hampshire, increasing their numbers in the state legislature and electing Matthew Harvey governor over Timothy Upham, 23,214 votes to 19,040. *Niles' Register* (March 20, 1830), 38:68, and *BDGUS*, 3:949-50.   3. In a letter to the editors of the Washington *Daily National Intelligencer*, dated March 9 and published the following day, Chilton announced his dissatisfaction with the Jackson administration and publicly switched his allegiance to Clay as the man "*preeminently* talented and qualified" for the presidency. In another letter, dated March 25 and addressed "Gentlemen," Chilton criticized the increased expenditures of the federal government under Jackson, comparing them with the expenditures of the Adams administration. Washington *Daily National Journal*, March 29, 1830.   4. George A. Waggaman, who was appointed secretary of state for Louisiana in 1830, did not run against Johnston for the Senate in 1830. For Waggaman see *NCAB*, 11:25; for Johnston's reelection see Clay to Johnston, Dec. 25, 1829.   5. Clay to Johnston, Feb. 27, 1830.

From James Brown, Philadelphia, April 7, 1830. Reports that "Every thing at Washington is carried on in a way which leaves us uncertain as to what will be the effect of present and past measures on the unpopularity of the administration—The Cabinet is said to be at sixes & sevens and will probably undergo some changes before or immediately after the *rising* of Congress   You perceive General Jackson is up for another term to the no small disappointment of certain persons. But you have friends at Washington who know more about these matters than myself and will doubtless keep you well informed. It is rumored that [John] McLean & Calhoun have been endeavoring to make some arrangement the particular[s] of which I have not heard. But there are so many of these loose rumors afloat and I go out so little since my *domestic* misfortunes that I cannot vouch for their truth—In fact my own opinion is and always has been that General J— —n will in a popular election succeed against any other single Candidate." ALS. DLC-HC (DNA, M212, R4). Printed in *LHQ*, 24:1147-48.

From Francis T. Brooke, near Fredericksburg, Va., April 8, 1830. Thinks Clay's recent trip to New Orleans "will be highly beneficial" to him politically. Remarks that "the course of the administration of which you no doubt are well informed and the divisions at Washington as to who will be run (as the phrase is) for the next Presidency has had great influence in Virginia though it has not mollified the temper of your adversaries they fear intensely that the division in their party as to Van Buyren & Calhoun will tire the people of both and that you will in consequence of it get the vote of Virginia and this is to them the most deplorable event that could happen." Reports that Daniel Webster remains loyal to the Clay cause although he has little political standing in the South.

Believes that the new state constitution produced by the constitutional convention at Richmond is "better than the old one in Some respects" and announces that he has "voted for it." Fears, however, "that our Western brethren will not be reconciled to it." Concludes that western Virginians "ought to have had the white basis in the House and the east ought to have been satisfied with the Federal numbers in the Senate, if Mr [James] Madison had not wasted his influence by delay and had come out with his plan in the first week of of [*sic*] the convention I have little doubt it would have prevailed, but he [James] Monroe and [John] Marshal[l] permitted their influence to evaporate and then the Knight of Roane Oak [*sic*, Roanoke: John Randolph] took the lead   he browbeat [Chapman] Johnson, and many others and carried a scheme of representation which is entirely arbitrary not having a single elementary principle in it." ALS. InU. Johnson was a leader of the reformers and Randolph was a prominent ultra-conservative; Madison, Monroe, and Marshall, though tending to vote with the conservatives, nevertheless, exerted a moderating influence on extremists of both sides. For the representation issue see Brooke to Clay, October 19, 1829, and *Proceedings and Debates of the Virginia State Convention, passim.*

To Edward Everett, April 10, 1830. Congratulates Everett on "the triumphant vindication of New England which the debate in the Senate has produced. Webster's Speech is above all praise [Clay to Johnston, February 27, 1830]. That of [John] Holmes, with the exception of one paragraph, is excellent, and I like its tone of sarcasm. Tell him that I recognize the same voice that dwelt on the public ear with so much pleasure during the War [of 1812]. These Speeches ought to be extensively circulated. Webster's seems to have been; and I have advised the publication of Holmess in this quarter. I anticipate a treat in those of [John M.] Clayton and our friend [Josiah S.] Johnston." ALS. MHi. Letter marked "(Confidential)." It is likely, but not certain, that Everett was the recipient of this letter. Webster's speech of January 26 was published under the title *Speech of Daniel Webster, in Reply to Mr. Hayne of South Carolina: The Resolution of Mr. Foot, of Connecticut, Relative to the Public Lands, Being Under Consideration. Delivered in the Senate, January 26, 1830.* New York, 1830. 72 pp.

For Holmes's speech, which defended New England against Benton's charge [Johnston to Clay, February 2, 1830] that she had followed a consistent policy of hostility to the West, see *Register of Debates*, 21 Cong., 1 Sess., 160-68; or *Speech of Mr. Holmes of Maine. Delivered in the Senate of the United States, February 18, 1830 on the Debate Which Arose Upon Mr. Foot's Resolution Relative to the Public Lands.* Washington, 1830. 24 pp. Clayton's speech of March 3-4 strongly opposed the doctrine of nullification, arguing that "we have no other direct resource . . . to save us from the horrors of anarchy, than the Supreme Court of the United States." He also maintained that the Senate should have the power to investigate removals from office, since its powers include the right to confirm appointments. See *Register of Debates*, 21 Cong., 1 Sess., 224-44. On March 30, Johnston, speaking as a westerner, defended New England against the charge of hostility to the West and denied that Benton spoke either for Louisiana or for the West as a whole. *Ibid.*, 277-81.

From William C. C. Claiborne, Jr., New Orleans, April 11, 1830. Reports that he has decided neither to commence the practice of law nor take a trip to Europe. Instead, he has determined to run for the lower chamber of the state legislature. Feels that the success of the slate of which he is a member turns on the success of Andre B. Roman's gubernatorial campaign. Believes that Roman's prospects in New Orleans and "throughout the State" are "somewhat doubtful, as Mr. [Armand] Beauvais will create a great division in the French votes. Our hope is in the divisions of the Jackson party, for if they were to unite upon one, they could elect him under present circumstances. Fortunately they are as yet more disunited than we are." Says that the Jacksonians, who call themselves "Democratic Republicans," have been unable as yet to convene a state nominating convention.

Reports that the "Stock to our Rail = Road was taken with much avidity, the project is fast going into execution, and excites a great deal of interest. An opening is already made through the Swamps to the Lake, of which we have a view from the Levee. I hope that your enterprize of the same nature in Kentucky will be pursued with at least equal promptitude and energy. —"

Informs Clay that if he wins a seat in the Louisiana legislature he will do the best he can there to support "your cause." ALS. DLC-HC (DNA, M212, R4). The railroad from New Orleans to Lake Ponchartrain was opened on April 23, 1831. *Niles' Register* (May 14, 1831), 40:181. On January 27, 1830, the Lexington & Ohio Railroad, later known as the Lexington-Frankfort Railroad, was incorporated by an act of the Kentucky legislature. The railroad was formally opened on August 1, 1832, after a mile and a half of construction; it was completed from Lexington to Frankfort in 1835. William H. Perrin, *History of Fayette County, Kentucky* (Chicago, 1882), 80-83. Claiborne was successful in his bid for a seat in the Louisiana House. Alcee Fortier, *A History of Louisiana*, 4 vols. (New York, 1904), 3:213.

From WILLIAM HENRY HARRISON

Near Maysville, Ky.,
April 11, 1830

I would have written to you immediately upon my arrival in the U.S. if I had not heard that you had gone on a visit to New Orleans, to inform you that I had forwarded your letter[1] to Genl. [Simon] Bolivar from Bogota & that I had received a note from him acknowing its reception and adding that there "was no answer" Herewith I send a pamphlet which I have lately published[2] in which you will find a letter addressed by me to the same distinguished Character to which also he did not think proper to reply. I could have inserted many interesting circumstances which I omitted from the fear of injuring persons who still remain subject to the power of the Columbian [*sic*, Colombian] Government.

ALS. DLC-HC (DNA, M212, R4). Published in Colton, *Clay Correspondence*, 4:258. Letter written on board steamboat *Telegraph*.   1. See 7:517-18.   2. Harrison's letter to Bolivar was published in his pamphlet, *Remarks of General Harrison, Late Envoy Extraordinary of Colombia, on Certain Charges Made Against Him By That Government*. Washington, 1830. In it he advised Bolivar to abandon his plans to establish a monarchy and instead to maintain a truly republican government. See also Dorothy Burne Goebel, *William Henry Harrison, A Political Biography* (Indianapolis, 1926), 282.

From JOSIAH S. JOHNSTON

Washington, April 13, 1830

I have just return[e]d from the Senate after a long Session — We have negatived [Isaac] Hill — which produces considerable Sensation in the City — I think we shall put a veto on the others — [Amos] Kendall particularly — The printers are in danger if we can hold all our friends together — [1]But we have one Uncertain man.[2] Kendall will not sleep until his fate is decided — Several minor characters among them have slipped through our fingers —

No changes have taken place — The President is now fairly in nomination — [3]This was necessary to stop the progress of Calhoun — [4]They saw dissention, division & defeat — I have believed the President, always intended to hold over, but meant to wait for some favorable pretext — such as your nomination or a division among his friends &c. — Van Buren found Calhoun gaining the ascendency rapidly, & therefore gave direction to the Courier — leaving Duff [Green] in the dark — The President will acquiesce with a reluctant grace — In the mean time Calhoun stands in an awkward position — He cannot wait 8 years, then to be beaten by Van Buren — He can not run again as Vice President — These two leaders & their friends are directly opposed — & personally hostile — they still seem disposed to act in Concert in Congress — I think something will ere long grow out of the proceedings in the Senate — If the General suspects any diriliction among the Calhoun men, he will reform his Cabinet — & set them at defiance —

We shall take some decisive measure with regard to you before we separate — & of which I will write you   I merely sat down to tell you of Hill & I am quite fatigued —

ALS. InU.   1. Johnston to Clay, Jan. 26, 1830.   2. Sen. William Hendricks of Indiana. Clay to Johnston, May 10, 1830.   3. On March 31 in Harrisburg, Pa., 56 members of the state legislature held a caucus and adopted resolutions approving the Jackson administration and proposing Jackson as a candidate for reelection. On April 13 in Albany, N.Y., the Democratic members of the legislature held a caucus and adopted similar resolutions. See McMaster, *A History of the People of the U.S.*, 6:116, and Washington *Daily National Journal*, April 13, 17, 1830. 4. The "Van Buren" part of the phrase "stop the progress of Calhoun-Van Buren" has been struck through.

To James Brown, Philadelphia, April 17, 1830. Responds to Brown's letter of April 7. Clay remarks that his recent trip to Louisiana and Mississippi was "full of gratification" and that when he unexpectedly attended a session of the Louisiana legislature "the whole body, without distinction of party (Speakers and all) rose to receive me." Reports also that he found "all my connexions" in New Orleans healthy and doing well. "[Martin] Duralde is now rich, and if he lives will become excessively opulent. [James] Erwin is also in great affluence, and has much capacity for business." Mentions that he and James Erwin had decided not to purchase a sugar plantation in Louisiana even though last year's poor crops had brought many such properties onto the market at "lower prices" than have "maintained for several past years. A general apprehension (in which I do not participate) prevails that the production will soon overtake the consumption of Sugar." Believes that "This fear has created a general disinclination to the acquisition of Texas. I believe they may suppress any solicitude on that head."

Informs Brown that Martin Duralde could have been elected governor of Louisiana "with great ease" had Andre B. Roman decided not to run and "with some struggle" if Roman continued in the race. But Duralde did not want to "divide friends, and therefore declined." Thinks, therefore, that Roman "will probably be elected. I think he ought to be. I heard several express regrets that you were not there that they might elect you." Remarks on the popularity of the protective tariff among Louisiana state legislators.

Reports that "Ashland never looked better than it does; and I never was so well satisfied with the state of my preparations for a good crop. I have, what is very rare, a capital overseer [William Martin]. I am getting a passion for rural occupations; and feel more and more as if I ought to abandon forever the strife of politics. I shall not be unhappy if a sense of public duty shall leave me free to pursue my present inclinations."

Notes, further, that his "friends at Washington keep me well advised as to all that is passing there, worth knowing. Their confidence is very great in the prostration of the present party, and the return of better times, and other men. They believe that the present incumbent [Jackson] is not more formidable than either of his Lieutenants. I should agree with them, if the incompetency which he exhibits was as well known every where as it is at Washn. As that it is impracticable, you may be right in your estimate of his strength." ALS. DLC-HC (DNA, M212, R4).

To James E. Welch, April 17, 1830. Thanks Welch for his "kind endeavor to vindicate me from the aspersions to which I have been exposed on account of my public conduct." Notes the warm reception he (Clay) received during his recent visit to Louisiana, and predicts that the American people will soon "come to right conclusions" about the Jackson administration. Copy. Printed in Colton, *Clay Correspondence*, 4:259.

From Christopher Hughes, Paris, April 18, 1830. Responds to Clay's letter of December 25, 1829. Extends sympathy for deaths in Clay's family, while hoping that Clay himself is well. Boasts at great length of his social popularity in Paris ("The very highest, & the *best*, welcome me to their intercourse") and of his social triumphs while serving as U.S. chargé in the Netherlands. Again criticizes the Jackson administration for having removed him from office and characterizes his successor, William Pitt Preble, as "one of the most narrowminded . . . inept, gawky Boobies, that ever yet, for the misfortune and ridicule of our country, has been sent abroad, vested with diplomatic & representative office." Claims that Preble has rendered himself and his nation ridiculous in the eyes of Europe. Reaffirms his "most devoted esteem, confidence, and admiration" for Clay. Remarks that French politics are at a crisis point. Predicts the dissolution of parliament, new elections that will strengthen the liberals, and the yielding of Charles X to the new situation in order to save his throne. ALS. DLC-HC (DNA, M212, R4). Following the elections of May 16, which produced a majority hostile to the monarchy, King Charles, on July 26, brought the press under rigid governmental control and dissolved the new parliament. In late July, Charles X was forcibly deposed and Louis Philippe was proclaimed constitutional monarch. See Paul H. Beik, *Louis Philippe and the July Monarchy*. Princeton, 1965.

From Daniel Webster, Washington, April 18, 1830. Reports that there may be a renomination of Isaac Hill as second comptroller, but that if Jackson decides not to submit his name to the Senate "I suppose Mr [Virgil] Maxcy, of Maryland, may likely be nominated to the place — " Believes that public opinion toward the Jackson administration is beginning to change in that "there certainly is far less complaint of the enormous abuse of the power of removal than I expected to see." Feels that "For my part, if there be no popular rebuke of this practice, I think it seriously endangers the continuance & well being of the govt. — We shall make a stand agt. the rest of the printers. — " Fears, however, that the anti-administration forces lack the votes to effect this stand successfully.

Remarks that the Jefferson Day Dinner of April 13 "was not only a failure, but has given great offence. . . . The object of those who originated the proceeding of the 13th [Senators Thomas H. Benton and Robert Y. Hayne] was to give a *state right anti Tariff* tone & character to the whole party. — It was to found the party on *Southern* principles, & such principles as should exclude, not only their avowed political opponents, but Mr. Van Buren's friends also — "

Is convinced that Jackson "means to be re elected" and "*has* meant so, all along." If he does become a candidate, "My own firm belief is, that if we were to let the Administration, this Session & the next, have their own way, & follow out their own principles, they would be so unpopular as that the Genl. could not possibly be re elected. I do not mean by this, that we should let them disturb the Tariff; or injure any other existing interest; still less, that we should, in the slightest degree, vote or act against our own principles. All these being safe, & all existing interests preserved, I still think if we leave to them to decide on *new* measures, of internal improvement &c, according to *their* own will, they will soon find what the sense of the people is. But I forbear further *talk* — " ALS. DLC-HC (DNA, M212, R4). Printed in Wiltse, *Webster Papers*, 3:58-59; printed in part in Colton, *Clay Correspondence*, 4:259-60. For the background of and events at the famous Jefferson Day Dinner at Brown's Indian Queen Hotel in Washington on April 13, see Bowers, *Party Battles of the Jackson Period*, 100-103; James, *Andrew Jackson*, 232-36; Charles M. Wiltse, *John C. Calhoun: Nullifier, 1829-1839* (Indianapolis, 1949), 67-71. For appointment of the printers see Johnston to Clay, January 26, 1830. Neither Hill nor Maxcy was appointed; James B. Thornton became second comptroller of the Treasury. *Biennial Register*, 1833, p. 13; and *NCAB*, 13:483. Later in 1830 Hill was elected to the U.S. Senate from New Hampshire, and Maxcy was appointed first solicitor of the Treasury.

To Francis T. Brooke, April 19, 1830. Remarks that his reception in Louisiana and Mississippi was warm and cordial and that he was well received by both Adams men and Jacksonians. Believes he can carry Louisiana in 1832 "against any one, and . . . Mississippi against anyone but Jackson." Sees Jackson rapidly losing his popularity in Mississippi. Reports that "My friends, prior to the recent nomination in Pennsa. [Johnston to Clay, April 13, 1830] were sanguine, extremely sanguine, of success. They represent great animosity as existing between the partizans of Calhoun and Van Buren, in so much that each party prefers me to the other; and that there are not thirty members of Congress who desire Jackson's re-election." Believes that if Virginia, Pennsylvania, and New York can unite on a common candidate, opposition "to that Candidate will be unavailing, in all probability. If there should be no such union, Jackson himself, or either of the two prominent members of his party, may be beaten."

Presumes that Virginia's new constitution will be approved. "It has incorporated in it some very exceptional elements of aristocracy. I should nevertheless vote for it, if I had a vote, as being with all its defects, preferable to the old Constitution."

Reports that each day he becomes more attached to rural life, that he could easily "renounce for ever the strife of public life," that Ashland is in "fine order," and that "I shall make a better farmer than Statesman." ALS. KyU. Printed in Colton, *Clay Correspondence*, 4:260-61. In April of 1830, the new Virginia constitution was ratified by a vote of 26,055 to 15,563. Peterson, *Democracy, Liberty, and Property*, 286.

To EDITOR, CINCINNATI AMERICAN

Lexington, *ca.*
April 22, 1830

I concur entirely with the American in the sentiments which it expresses on the 12th inst. upon the case of the dismissed officers.[1] Duelling in the abstract, is perfectly indefensible; and that particular duel was perhaps attended by aggravating circumstances. But the indignation which it excited by its unfortunate issue, ought not to blind us to the consequences of an arbitrary act of power, which falls with undue severity upon young gentlemen, who have only imitated repeated examples set by the very person who has inflicted the blow. It is obnoxious to the charge of being perfectly ex post facto. If there had been a previous rule promulgated to that effect, and they had knowingly violated it, their fate would have been merited. But they could have as little anticipated such a punishment, as the punishments which are applied by the codes of Russia and Turkey.

What will be the consequence to the army and the navy of a principle which is to restrain them from participation in any duel with private citizens? Will it not perpetually expose them to insults, when they can be offered with entire impunity? And will it not ultimately impair or destroy that lofty spirit and that high sense of honor, which are the best guarantees for their successfully combatting the enemies of the country?

Besides, the rule has no reciprocity. If the soldier is to be punished for fighting the citizen, the citizen ought to be punished for fighting the soldier. This view of the matter shows that if you wish to eradicate the vice of duelling, the axe must be laid at the root; the laws should be general; and public opinion should be corrected and enlightened so as to comprehend and detest the enormity of the evil. But according to the edict just issued from Washington, those only are to be punished for fighting, whose vocation is to fight.

Copy, extract. Printed in Cincinnati *American*, April 22, 1830. For Clay's authorship, see Clay to Fendall, April 30, 1830. The editor was James F. Conover.   1. Clay to Fendall, April 30, 1830.

From JOSIAH S. JOHNSTON Washington, April 28, 1830

My opinion of the intention of Genl. Jackson with regard to the Presidency, is not changed—He came here with the intention of not withdrawing his pretentions but of serving two terms—He meant to avail himself of any proper pretence that might occur, such as the division of his own party & your being a formidable candidate, to be held up again—

Van Buren & Calhoun however thought he meant to retire & began their operations with their friends in the different states—Calhoun began to obtain the ascendency & Van Buren found it necessary to put him down at once to preserve his own position & to gratify the General by falling in with his prevailing weakness to have him nominated again—This maintains him in power & in favor & places Calhoun in the necessity of acquiescing or of dividing the party—They stand now in this relation

The General does not like Calhoun or his friends or his principles—Van Buren is his favorite—He goes for the Tarif[f]—they against it—He is for the Union & against the Nullifying doctrine—They go for the Bank—he agt. it He & VB go for the proscription—they are against it in theory & practice— they are willing to avail themselves of the odium it excites, while they dare not oppose the nomination or resist him—Here they stand—acting together as a party, yet opposed in every object.

The friends of Calhoun are proscribed—& they feel it—how they will act we cannot say—He has not determin[e]d—he waits for events—Anti Masonry is extending itself through the N. Middle & W—It is very strong in N. York & Penna.—not a majority but capable of turning the scale—It is said Calhoun has had communications with *them*—[John] McLean of Ohio has courted them— They have made no selection—Their opposition is rather to Masonry than Masons—This new interest is to produce considerable effect in the election—

The Jefferson dinner[1] was an attempt to connect Calhoun & the Southern doctrines & the Anti Tarif & C with the name & popularity of the head [Jackson] of the Republican party The object Was Seen—The Generals toast[2] shews his understanding of the meeting & was quite intelligible to them as it is to all that reads it—

[Thomas H.] Benton is acting in concert with Calhoun & was the chief agent in getting up the dinner—His part of the play was to assail the North, excite prejudice in the West & to connect the Jackson interest in that quarter with the South—His speech[3] is well calculated to affect that object—I have thought it advisable to correct any impression he may make—I shall send you my remarks—[4]they are merely design[e]d to explain & Set right his charges agt. the North—I see by the Kentucky papers that he is Consider[e]d to have exposed the hostility of the North to the West—The explanation with regard to the defence of the Country—the navigation of the Mississippi, & the Lands might be published in the papers separately—to do away any improper impression he may have made—

I have made a speech[5] on the Nullifying doctrine & on the power of removal—which I will also send you. . . . [P.S.] The bill for subscription to the Maysville road passed to day—& it will pass in the Senate. [Robert P.] Letcher has managed it with great address

ALS. InU. 1. Webster to Clay, April 18, 1830. 2. "Our Union: It must be preserved."
3. Johnston to Clay, Feb. 2, 1830. 4. Clay to Everett, April 10, 1830. 5. On April 2

195

Johnston resumed his speech begun on March 30, making a strong argument that nullification would inevitably lead to disunion. *Register of Debates*, 21 Cong., 1 Sess., 284-302.

From James Brown, Philadelphia, April 29, 1830. Has heard it said that "some changes in the Cabinet will probably take place soon after the rising of Congress. I do not think so—" Remarks that Joel R. Poinsett is visiting in Philadelphia, will be honored with a public dinner on May 3, and is said to be in line for appointment as secretary of the navy or U.S. minister to Russia. Reports that the stock of the Bank of the United States has risen to 127½ "since the reports of the two Houses," and will continue to rise. ALS. DLC-TJC (DNA, M212, R10). First page of this letter not found. Poinsett did not reenter government service until 1837 when he became secretary of war under President Van Buren. McDuffie's April 13 report for the House Ways and Means Committee on the bank and Samuel Smith's report for the Senate Finance Committee of March 29 both defended the constitutionality of the institution and its necessity for regulating the nation's currency. See *Register of Debates*, 21 Cong., 1 Sess., Appendix, 98-133; Biddle to Clay, June 3, 1830; and Govan, *Nicholas Biddle*, 126-29.

From Josiah S. Johnston, Washington, April 29, 1830. Remarks that Thomas H. Benton's speech [Johnston to Clay, February 2, 1830] is being extensively circulated in the West to create prejudice there against the North and to prepare the West for an unnatural political union with the South. Promises to send Clay a "proof sheet of that part of my Speech [Clay to Everett, April 10, 1830] Which replies to the charges & which I think will put the History right." Reports that the separation between Van Buren and Calhoun is "wide and deep," as revealed in South Carolina Rep. George McDuffie's recent report on the Bank of the United States [Brown to Clay, April 29, 1830] and his speech against the tariff [Clay to Everett, May 6, 1830]. Points out that Calhoun "disavows proscription & says he goes farther than his friends—He says all the South is against it"; but that Calhoun "has not the Courage" to use the proscription issue against Van Buren. Notes that the "Nullifying doctrines" are disliked even in Virginia, and that "Southern Doctrines" on the tariff are "very much disapproved" in Pennsylvania and New York. Believes that McDuffie's speech against the tariff has "widened the breach" within the Pennsylvania congressional delegation. ALS. InU.

To Daniel Webster, April 29, 1830. Responds to Webster's letter of April 18, noting that "Your speeches, and particularly that in reply to Mr. [Robert Y.] Hayne, are the theme of praise from every tongue; and I have shared in the delight which all have felt." Believes, however, that it is "greatly to be regretted that the Senate has not better fulfilled its high duties incident to the power of appointment. It ought to have rejected all nominations made to supply persons dismissed for political cause; all to replace those whom they approved at the last session; most of the printers, and most of the members of Congress. If it has left undone some things which it ought to have done, we ought to be thankful for some of its rejections. Those of [Henry] Lee and [Isaac] Hill are especially entitled to the public gratitude; and I hope it will place us under a similar obligation for the rejection of [Amos] Kendall and [Mordecai M.] Noah." Feels that Jackson's patronage policy has produced a "great reaction in respect to the present administration," particularly in the "valley of the Mississippi." Notes, too, that he is aware of "the movements at Harrisburg and Albany [Clay to Conover, May 1, 1830]. The former, if we are rightly informed, was an abortion; and the latter may, I suppose, be considered as essentially Mr. V. B———'s. That Jackson will be again a candidate is highly probable. If he can unite in his support Virginia, Pennsylvania, and New York, opposition to his election will be vain. If either of those States can be detached from him, he may be beaten."

As for "the expediency of using my name in opposition to General Jackson," Clay wants it understood that "No personal or private considerations ought to have the smallest influence in its determination" since he has no objection to making "an honorable retreat from public life." Concludes: "After saying so much, it is scarcely necessary to add that I shall acquiesce — most cheerfully acquiesce — in whatever line of policy my friends may mark out at Washington. There are three courses: 1. Assuming that Jackson will be a candidate, to abandon all opposition to his reëlection; 2. To hoist our banner, and proclaim, prior to the close of the present session, our candidate; 3. To wait until the next session of Congress. I shall not discuss the advantages and disadvantages of each. My friends at Washington are more competent, from their superior information, and more impartial than I am, to compare and weigh them." Copy, text incomplete. Printed in Wiltse, *Webster Papers*, 3:62-64 from Curtis, *Life of Daniel Webster*, 1:374-76. Manuscript not found.

To Edward Everett, April 30, 1830. Concurs "fully" with Everett "as to the merits of Mr. [John M.] Claytons Speech." Assures him that "I have had no communication with the Anti Masons, other than that I received a visit last fall from a person (whose name even I have forgotten) representing himself as one of their agents. About the same time a Mr. Roberts also visited me, and I understood him to be a Masonic agent. I treated both with proper civility but entered into political engagements; of course, with neither. I understood, indeed, from both that their respective constituents were friendly disposed." ALS. MHi. In his speech on March 4, Clayton opposed the proposal to lower the selling price of public lands, argued against the nullification doctrine, and denounced Jackson's removal of officials from public office for partisan reasons as "hostile to the spirit of the constitution." Further, he proposed a provision "rendering any member of Congress ineligible to office under the General Government, during the term for which he was elected, and two years thereafter," except for judicial office. See also Clay to Everett, April 10, 1830.

To PHILIP R. FENDALL   Lexington, April 30, 1830

I have duly received your two favors of the 9h. and 11h. instant, and I have perused them with much satisfaction.

I am happy to find that the arrangement of the [Washington *Daily National*] Journal works well.[1] It is constantly gaining reputation, and I have no doubt, should it remain in its present hands, it will continue to deserve it. I think, on one subject, the press friendly to our cause has generally erred. I allude to the affair of the dismission of the Navy officers.[2] It was in my opinion a high handed and tyrannical act. The American at Cincinnati took, I think, correct ground as to that affair. I wrote to Mr. [James F.] Conover expressing my approbation of his course. Without my authority, but without any dissatisfaction on my part, he published an extract from my letter, which expresses my sentiments.[3] He did not use my name. His paper is well conducted. He writes me in great confidence as to Ohio and Indiana. Would it not be well to take some commendatory notice of his paper?

I observe that Jackson is considered as again a Candidate by the movements at Harrisburg and Albany.[4] Your true policy, it seems to me, is to regard those movements as Mr. V. Bs. denying that they are intended really to exhibit him as a Candidate, contending that it is impossible he should be, after repeated declarations to the contrary during the late Canvass, and considering his maladministration imbecility &c &c.

If he be really again a Candidate, the practicability of defeating him will depend upon detaching Virginia, Pennsa or New York from his support. Whatever may be the course which my friends may adopt at Washn. I shall cheerfully abide by it.

I am very anxious for the decision of my pauper case,[5] and I will thank you to urge our friend [Walter] Jones to have it tried at the May term. Its continuance leads to some insubordination among my servants here to whom it relates.

I shall be glad to hear from you whenever convenient. . . .

ALS. NcD. 1. Johnston to Clay, Jan. 26, 1830. 2. The participation of Lts. Edmund Byrne and Hampton Westcott, and Passed Midshipmen Charles H. Duryea and Charles G. Hunter in the duel between Hunter and civilian William Miller, Jr., of Philadelphia in which Miller was killed. Secretary of the Navy John Branch dismissed the four officers from the service. Washington *Daily National Journal*, April 3, 8, 20, 1830. 3. See Clay to Editor, Cincinnati *American*, April 22, 1830. 4. Johnston to Clay, April 13, 1830. 5. Probably a reference to the "Lotty" case. See 7:622-24; Clay to Dawson, July 8, 1829; Clay to Fendall, Sept. 10, 1830.

From Josiah S. Johnston, Washington, April 30, 1830. Sends the first part of his speech in reply to Thomas H. Benton's speech [Johnston to Clay, April 29, 1830]. Notes that the "fate" of the printers has been postponed to May 10. Claims that on this issue Senators Samuel Smith (Md.), Littleton W. Tazewell (Va.), and John Tyler (Va.) "are decidedly with us," whereas William Hendricks (Ind.) will "desert," since he is "a poor timid creature" who has been "operated on by some secret influence." Reports that Rep. Churchill C. Cambreleng (N.Y.) has introduced a bill that will "legislate away the tariff," will have "an excellent effect upon the people of Penna. & N. york," and will serve as an "excellent Counterpart of McDuffys [*sic*, George McDuffie] speech [Clay to Everett, May 6, 1830]." Concludes with the observation that "the *three men* [Smith, Tazewell, Tyler] are inflexible — every effort has been made — all the South are agt. the removals — No measure recommended by the President will Carry." Mentions that during the coming week the administration will make the "greatest exertions" to secure Senate approval of Amos Kendall's appointment. "I do not doubt that they would give any office in their Gift to Carry him." ALS. InU. Cambreleng introduced "a bill respecting the navigation laws and duties on imports" which would have expanded the policy of reciprocity. The bill was tabled on May 14 and was not called up again. *Register of Debates*, 21 Cong., 1 Sess., 863-65, 988-93. Kendall was confirmed by the Senate on May 10 with Vice President Calhoun breaking a 24-24 tie by voting in the affirmative. Hendricks and Smith voted for confirmation; Tazewell and Tyler voted against.

To JOSIAH S. JOHNSTON   Lexington, April 30, 1830
I received your favor of the 13h. inst. communicating the rejection of [Isaac] Hill, and your expectation that [Amos] Kendall will follow the same fate. This latter anticipation, from what others tell me, I apprehend has not been realized. I attach some consequence to the rejection of these men. Who is the uncertain Senator? Is he from Indiana?[1] If he be, it is to be attributed to his approaching election.[2] If my information from that State be correct he need not fear the issue, unless he proves treacherous to our cause.

I observe that you regard the movements at Harrisburg and Albany as putting Jackson in nomination.[3] They may bear that interpretation; but they are also susceptible of another. The terms in which the two Caucuss' express themselves do not necessarily import a presentation of Jackson as a Candidate. May the movements not be regarded as a stratagem of V.B. [Van Buren] to gain time, to disconcert his rival, to concentrate the Jackson party upon himself, and to come out at a suitable time as a Candidate? Ask Mr. [Daniel] Webster to shew you a letter which I wrote him a few days ago, stating a proposition[4] which I recently received from Mr. [William H.] Crawford,[5] and be pleased to regard that matter as strictly confidential, resting between you two. Mr. Crawford, supposing him to be in the secrets of

V.B. and his faction, does not appear on the 31st. of March to have expected that Jackson would be a Candidate.

You inform me that my friends contemplate taking some decisive measure in regard to me before they separate. I shall acquiesce in whatever decision they may make. If Jackson should be a Candidate, and can unite upon himself the three States of Virginia, Pennsa. and New York, opposition to him will be unavailing. If either of those States can be detached from his support, I think he can be beaten. Whether that be practicable or not you have better means and otherwise are more competent to judge than I am.

If it be deemed expedient to present my name as a Candidate the enquiry will arise where and how ought it to be first done? My impression is, that it had better be commenced in the West, and *quickly* followed in New England. The thought has occurred here of beginning in this State, immediately after the rise of Congress, by popular nominations in the various Counties. This it has been supposed would excite a spirit among the people that would secure in August the election of a friendly Legislature, which would afterwards exclude [John] Rowan and make next winter a more regular nomination at Frankfort. Should the purpose not be abandoned of opposing Jackson, think of this scheme, consult [Robert P.] Letcher, [James] Clark &c about it and write me as soon as convenient.

The disadvantage of delay if we mean to act is the uncertainty in which our friends among the great body of the people are left. Already I am frequently spoken to and some times have been written to to know if I am a Candidate. Of course, I give but one answer, which is that I shall never present myself as a Candidate.

ALS. PHi. Printed in Colton, *Clay Correspondence*, 4:264-65.   1. Johnston to Clay, April 13, 1830.   2. On Dec. 18, 1830, William Hendricks ("friendly to domestic manufactures, internal improvements and *Henry Clay*") was reelected on the fourth ballot to the U.S. Senate over Ratliff Boon, a Jacksonian, by a vote of 44 to 26, *Niles' Register* (Jan. 8, 1831), 39:384.   3. Johnston to Clay, April 13, 1830.   4. No Clay to Webster letter has been found that fits this date and content. However, Clay to Brooke, April 24, 1830, fits on both counts.   5. Crawford to Clay, March 31, 1830.

To JAMES F. CONOVER   Lexington, May 1, 1830

I have received your favor of the 22d. Ulto.   Altho' my view of the case of the dismissed officers[1] was not intended for publication, I have no objection to the use you made of it, supposing that it will not be known who is the author.

Altho' your paper [Cincinnati *American*] has not yet been patronized to the extent you expected in K. I am persuaded you will not ultimately be disappointed here, when your paper is more generally known.

[Discusses the possibility of a trip through the North, but has rejected the idea because the motive behind it will be imputed. Continues:]

The information which reaches me from all quarters but especially from Washington City, as to my future prospects, is in a high degree encouraging. My friends at the City write me in a spirit of the most perfect confidence of success. What effect will be produced by the recent movements at Harrisburg and Albany I do not know.[2] My opinion is that both policy and truth require our friends to insist that those movements are mere stratagems of Mr. V. Buren; that he saw Mr. Calhoun was about to snatch the South from him, after his assiduous courtship of it during the last eight or ten years, and to arrest his progress resorted to those expedients; that it is not contemplated by those who have the keeping and regulate the movements of Jackson ultimately to present him as a candidate; that such a step can not be taken without stamping all the professions and declarations, made during the late Canvass, with falsehood and perfidy; and that his notorious embicility and incompetency, as well as his maladministration, forbid indulging the idea that he will finally be a Candidate. &c &c.

I observe what your friendship for me has prompted you to suggest in respect to Judge [John] McLean. I have never wronged that gentleman. I felt, in common with the other friends of Mr. Adams, regret on account of the Judges course during the late Admon, but still I never did him any injustice. I have always been and yet am upon terms of civility with him. There is nothing on my part which would prevent my hearty co-operation with him in serving our Country, in any situations in which that Country might choose to place us. What more could I say? I was told several years ago by a mutual friend of his and mine, in his full confidence, now no more, that the cause of his coolness towards the late Administration, and towards me, was that we lived too near each other, and that I stood in his way. I am afraid that opinion was well founded; and that my success is deemed by him inconsistent with the scheme of his own advancement, which he has formed. I should be sorry, if this impression be erroneous, to have entertained it; but if it be well founded, you will perceive that his active support can not be anticipated.

The farce of the Jefferson dinner[3] at Washn. indicates the course of attack on the Tariff and Internal Improvements, which is meditated in future. It is to cry down all constructions of the Constitution; to cry up State rights; to make all Mr. Jeffersons opinions the articles of faith of the new Church; to hold out the notion of preserving the Union by conciliating the South, and to catch popularity by repealing Taxes &c. This latter course I predicted in a Speech which I made at Bards town [sic, Bardstown] last summer [July 30, 1829]. Well, it is fortunate that we know the plan of the Campaign of our opponents, and we ought now to prepare ours to defeat it. We ought to recommend the repeal of all taxes that can be dispensed with on objects which do not come in competition with native products. To contend that the sacrifice of our American System is to propitiate G. Britain as well as the South. That to surrend it to the South is to sacrifice the great principle that a majority ought to govern; and to sacrifice the interests of three fourths of the Union to those of the remaining fourth &c &c.

I believe I mentioned in my last to you that Louisiana has given in her adhesion to the Tariff.[4] Whilst I was there its Senate passed a resolution unanimously in favor of it, which its H. of R. has since concurred in, with only seven dissentients! . . .

ALS. ViU.   1. Clay to Fendall, April 30, 1830.   2. Johnston to Clay, April 13, 1830.
3. Webster to Clay, April 18, 1830.   4. Clay to Johnston, Feb. 27, 1830.

To JOHN S. WILLIAMS   Lexington, May 1, 1830
I have to thank you for a very great treat which you have afforded me by the perusal of the Review of Cambrelings [sic, Churchill C. Cambreleng] report,[1] which I duly received with your letter of the 14h. Ulto.   It is one of the best written publications which I have read for a long time; and exposes, with sound facts and argument, and in merited but gentlemanly irony the flimsy production of the little Hero of free trade [Cambreleng]. The friends of the

American System owe the author their most grateful acknowledgments. I hope he will keep a sharp pen ready to be used again, if necessary. There is n[o] danger of the Review not being extensively circulated

You are so near the seat of political informa[tion] that nothing which I could say would add to your stock of it. The Jefferson dinner shews that an arranged scheme of attack agt. the Tariff has been devised.[2] I think if the Author [John P. Kennedy] of the Review would take up the account of that dinner, toasts, speeches and all, as published in the [Washington *United States*] Telegraph he could make much use of it.

ALS. Courtesy of Joseph Logan Massie, Lexington, Ky. 1. Churchill C. Cambreleng, *Report of the Committee on the Commerce and Navigation of the United States*. Submitted to Congress, February 8, 1830. Washington and London, 1830; John Pendleton Kennedy, *A Review of Mr. Cambreleng's Report from the Committee of Commerce, in the House of Representatives, at the First Session of the Twenty First Congress*. By Mephistopheles. Baltimore, 1830. 2. Webster to Clay, April 18, 1830. For John P. Kennedy, see *DAB*.

To William Greene, Cincinnati, May 3, 1830. Declines an invitation to a public dinner to be given by the citizens of Cincinnati in honor of General William Henry Harrison. Cites "necessary business" as the reason he cannot attend, and expresses "my hearty wishes that all the hilarity anticipated from the entertainment may be fully realized." ALS. OHi.

To ADAM BEATTY   Lexington, May 4, 1830
[Comments on previous correspondence. Continues:]

There is not the smallest ground for the intimation which you have recd. of Mr. V[an]. B[uren]. being disposed to decline in favor of Mr. Calhoun. On the contrary there is the greatest animosity prevailing between those two rivals and their respective partizans. The late movements at Harrisburg and Albany[1] are well understood to have been prompted by Mr. V. B. to arrest the progress which Calhoun was making with the Jackson party. And I have no doubt that they are not to be taken as evidence that Jackson will ultimately be a Candidate.

My information from Washington from my friends evinces the most perfect confidence on their part, in the success of our cause. They believe, if I live, that I will be elected against *any Competitor*. Of one thing I am sure, that if they are right in being thus sanguine, success must essentially depend upon the character of the composition of our Legislature at the next Session. Hence the great importance of the approaching Election. I have heard nothing from your County [Mason] and Bracken and other adjacent Counties.[2] But I presume our friends are upon the alert as we know the other party to be.

It is impossible that any reception could have been more warm and cordial than that which was given me below.

I am very busy farming, to which I am becoming every day more and more attached.

ALS. Courtesy of Earl M. Ratzer, Highland Park, Ill. Printed with significant omissions in Colton, *Clay Correspondence*, 4:266. 1. Johnston to Clay, April 13, 1830. 2. In the Kentucky state election of August 2, 1830, John Chambers and James K. Marshall from Mason County and John Colglazer of Bracken County — all anti-Jacksonians — were elected to the Ky. House of Reps. Robert Taylor, an anti-Jacksonian, was elected to the state senate from Mason County, and James Parks, a Jackson supporter, was elected to the state senate from Nicholas and Bracken counties. Lexington *Kentucky Gazette*, August 13, 1830. The election produced an anti-Jackson majority of 18-20 in the house and the probability of either a party tie or an anti-Jackson majority of two in the senate. Lexington *Kentucky Reporter*, August 18, 1830.

From George W. Featherstonhaugh, Philadelphia, May 4, 1830. Explains that he and Baron Paul de Krudener (who has left Washington) are about to set out in six weeks time for a voyage to Europe. States: "I may never See you again, though I hope I shall. Wherever I am, I shall be most happy to see the Government of this Country in your hands. I have been long satisfied you are the Man America wants, and I now think with great Satisfaction, that she will call loudly upon you before two Years pass away. A great change is operating in the State of N York. Mr. Van Beurens [*sic*, Van Buren] political leaders are divided — in many cases permanently and bitterly. The working classes are withdrawing themselves altogether from the influence of their old leaders. This new concentration (eventually for good or evil) will find its interests assured by all the measures you have proposed for the protection of American industry. Mr Van Buren supposes himself to have acted adroitly, in avoiding to commit himself on the Subject of the Tariff and internal improvements, he has thus neglected to identify himself with great measures, or against them, and will have, in my opinion, to go to another Country, if he wishes to raise a Party based upon his personal merits. Besides he occupies the unenviable Situation of committing faults every day of his life, as must be the case where there are more Pigs than teats. The necessity of protecting American industry will be a public Creed in this Country ere long, and credit and honour, will be given, as they always are given in the long run, where they are due." ALS. DLC-HC (DNA, M212, R4). Partially printed in Colton, *Clay Correspondence*, 4:265-66.

To EDWARD EVERETT   Lexington, May 6, 1830

I have just recd. your favor of the 26h. Ulto.   I had intended this summer to visit Black rock, Saratoga, and New England. But I believe I shall decline it. I expect here my daughter [Anne Brown Clay Erwin] and some friends from Louisiana to pass some time with me, and that consideration together with the interest which I now, more than ever, take in my farms, and the various occupations to which they give rise, will keep me here. I am at the same time very grateful to yourself and other friends in New England for the desire to see me there. I reciprocate, cordially and sincerely, all their friendship; and I have no doubt, if circumstances admitted of my going there, that I should every where find warm hearts and kind treatment. There is not a spot in the Union that I should visit with more pleasure; and I should be distressed if I did not hope that I may have that satisfaction at some not distant day. Whenever I shall be able to realize it, I will not fail to embrace your friendly invitation.

I intended to ask you but forget whether I put the enquiry in my last letter, how the anti-Indian article found its way into the last number of the N. American reivew?[1]

I perceive by the last papers that Mr. [George] McDuffie has at length opened the whole subject of the Tariff.[2] Well; so much the better. The question was not to be avoided long, and I think our friends could not have met it at a more fortunate time. I presume you have read a capital little pamphlet reviewing Mr. [Churchill C.] Cambreleng's report.[3] Ask our friend Mr. [Josiah S.] Johnston how it happens that the adhesion of Louisiana to the Tariff,[4] which took place at the last Session of its Legislature, has been no where published in the Eastern papers. I have suspected him of concealing it from his Colleague [Edward Livingston], who certainly denounced the Tariff at a most unlucky moment,[5] in the Senate.

ALS. MHi. Printed in Colton, *Clay Correspondence*, 4:273, with the second paragraph and the last line of the final paragraph deleted.   1. "Documents and Proceedings Relating to the Formation and Progress of a Board in the City of New York, for the Emigration, Preservation, and Improvement of the Aborigines of America," *NAR* (Jan., 1830), 66:62-121.   2. For McDuffie's speech on the tariff, see *Register of Debates*, 21 Cong., 1 Sess., 842-62.   3. Clay to Williams, May 1, 1830.   4. Clay to Johnston, Feb. 27, 1830.   5. Livingston, in his speech of March 15, declared himself to be a convert to the free trade system and denounced the present tariff as "unwise, unequal, and oppressive" but not unconstitutional. *Register of Debates*, 21 Cong., 1 Sess., 247-72.

To Eveline Simpson, May 7, 1830. States that he has received "the pair of worsted socks which you did me the honor to present to me." Continues: "I thank you, most cordially, for this interesting testimonial of your favorable consideration of me, and for the friendly sentiments with which you have accompanied it. In finess and eveness of thread & neatness of appearance they excel any that I have ever seen. Mrs. Clay, who has supplied me many years with socks, wrought by her own hands from the best Merino wool, acknowledges the superiority of your's. I shall wear them with added pleasure from their being the production of one of my fair Country women. . . . Next to intellectual attainments, there is none, possessed by your sex, which more strongly recommend you to the regard of those among ours, who are worthy of your notice, than that of industry, with its usual concomitant, economy. That you may, in due time, meet with one, capable of justly appreciating your good qualities, and entitled, in return, to your warmest affection." ALS. Henry Clay Memorial Foundation, Lexington, Ky.

To GEORGE WATTERSON   Lexington, May 8, 1830

I duly received your favor of the 26h. Ulto. and was happy to find in it renewed assurances of your friendship and esteem, which I cordially reciprocate.

I heard with pleasure of the new foundation on which the [Washington *Daily National*] Journal has been placed and your connexion with it.[1] I considered the arrangement as a pledge for the continuance of the ability and zeal which it has displayed. Its reputation is continually increasing, and I have no doubt that ultimately its profits will reward the patriotic exertions of its conductors. I am sorry to hear however that, in the mean time, it is suffering for the want of some pecuniary aid; and I sincerely hope that the small sum which appears to be required will be obtained, through the agency of some of our friends, before the adjournment of Congress—Has any application been made by any one to Mr. James Brown of Philada.? He has the ability, if he possesses the inclination to contribute what is needed.

By this time the fate of [Amos] Kendall will be decided. I expect to hear of his confirmation, and that by the casting vote of the V. President [Calhoun], notwithstanding your opinion. Public decorum and public justice require his rejection, but I do not, I confess, anticipate it.[2]

I have read most of the Speeches which have reached me on Mr. [Samuel] Foots resolution.[3] I concur with you in thinking that our friends obtained an unquestioned victory. With regard to Mr. [Daniel] Webster, he has added greatly to his former high reputation. Other gentlemen (some for the first time) have presented themselves very advantageously to the public. From a remark in your letter, I think it proper to observe that I have entire confidence in Mr. Webster's zeal fidelity and devotion to our cause. There can be no mistake as to him. With respect to another person named by you (Col. [Thomas Hart] Benton) I do not believe there is the smallest ground at present for anticipating his return to a former attachment. All his recent movements plainly indicate his enlistment under the banner of Mr. Calhoun.

Your confidence in the overthrow of the present administration, I think, is well founded. At least, if it shall not be effected, it will be for the want of information among the body of the people as to the incompetency and tyrannical disposition of the Chief Magistrate.

I anticipate much good from the Anti-Tariff dinner lately given at Washington on Mr. Jefferson's birth day — from the withdrawal from it of the Pennsa. delegation — [4]and from the motion of Mr. [George] McDuffie to repeal the Tariffs, which is the natural consequence of the dinner.

The review of Mr. [Churchill C.] Cambreleng's report,[5] lately published at Balto., is the best controversial paper which I have seen for a long time; and I think it would be well to publish a new edition of it at Washn. to be circulated under the franks of the members. Be pleased to suggest this idea to some of our Congressional friends. . . .

ALS. DLC-George Watterson Papers (DNA, M212, R22).   1. Johnston to Clay, Jan. 26, 1830.   2. For Kendall's confirmation on May 10 as fourth auditor, see U.S. Sen., *Journal*, 21 Cong., 1 Sess., 457.   3. Clay to Johnston, Feb. 27, 1830.   4. Webster to Clay, April 18, 1830.   5. See Clay to Williams, May 1, 1830.

To JOSIAH S. JOHNSTON   Lexington, May 9, 1830

I recd. your favors of the 28h. and 29h. Ulto.   I do not think that the object of Col. [Thomas H.] Benton and Col [Robert Y.] Haynes [*sic*, Hayne] in detaching the West from N. England has been at all promoted by their Speeches on Foote's [*sic*, Samuel A. Foot] resolution.[1] It has been well understood, and I think has entirely failed. However extensively their Speeches have been circulated, they have not been so widely or so generally read as Mr. Webster's, and his triumph in that matter has been complete. Great aid has been afforded to him by the Speeches of Mr. [Peleg] Sprague and Mr. [John] Holmes. We are waiting anxiously however to see yours, and I hope you will not omit to send me the proof sheets promised by you.[2]

I am rejoiced at the passage in the H. of R. of the bill for the Maysville road, and I sincerely hope you are correct in your anticipation of the concurrence of the Senate.[3] The South will of course be opposed to it. If, as I hope, the N. England Senators, shall generally vote for it, there will be a fine commentary upon Col. Benton's text. We shall then be able practically to know who are our real friends. Give my respects to our friends from N.E. and tell them not to deprive us of the benefit of this weapon. The road, considered as a section of one extending from the Muskingum or the Scioto through K. & Tennessee to the gulf of Mexico is really of National importance. We see that N. England delegation well sustained the measure in the House; and we trust that similar support will be given to it by her Senators in the Senate.

I have much information from both ends of the State of N. York. It substantially corrorborates with the letter which you sent me. There seems to be perfect chaos in that State; and no one now can see what will come of it. If the friends of the late admon, the working mens party and the Anti Masons should unite they will compose a majority. Is it not probable that they will? The Anti Masons will bring out [Francis] Granger. I should think that the friends of the late Admon would support him against Throope [*sic*, Enos Thompson Throop] or [Erastus] Root, and even supposing those two parties only were to co-operate Granger would be elected.[4]

By the time of the close of the Tariff debate, which Mr. [George] McDuffie has, I suppose, precipitated, you will have a clearer view of the whole ground. Its effect cannot fail to widen the breach between the sections of the Jackson party.

I have entire confidence in the discretion of my friends as to the course which they may mark out. If Mr. Calhoun shou'd be announced as a Candidate, it will be clear. If not, the question will be as to the consequences of delay or immediate action. The first part of it (delay) involves a consideration of the discouragement or separation of our friends which might ensue; and, the second, the concentration of all the fragments of the Jackson party upon Jackson, which might be the result. I shall be glad to hear soon from you.

ALS. PHi. Printed in Colton, *Clay Correspondence*, 4:267-68.   1. Johnston to Clay, Feb. 2, 1830; Clay to Johnston, Feb. 27, 1830.   2. See Clay to Everett, April 10, 1830 for Holmes's speech and *Register of Debates*, 21 Cong., 1 Sess., 119-28, for Sprague's.   3. For passage of the Maysville Road bill in the House on April 29, see *Register of Debates*, 21 Cong., 1 Sess., 842 and in the Senate on May 15, see U.S. Sen. *Journal*, 21 Cong., 1 Sess., 306. Of the New England senators, only Samuel Foot of Connecticut voted against the bill.   4. In the November, 1830, gubernatorial election in New York the Democratic candidate Throop was elected over the Anti-Masonic candidate, Francis Granger, by a margin of 8,500 votes. *BDGUS*, 3:1076. Root had hoped to receive the Democratic nomination, but failed to do so. He was offered the Workingmen's party nomination but declined. *DAB*.

From FRANCIS T. BROOKE   Richmond, May 10, 1830

Yours of the 19h. ultimo I have received its contents are very cheering my information from Washington compares So far with yours   I think there can be little doubt that the Jackson party proper is very Small, and that the C[alhoun] & V[an] B[uren] partys are So exasperated with each other, that either (in most cases) would prefer you to its opponent, that Seems to have been foreseen by the V B party in Virginia and to avoid the consequences an effort is making to place the election of Presid[en]t on the Bank question by which it is believed that the C Party will be So Beaten, that it will prefer V B to you   this matter I think was Settled while V B was here in Winter, and this inference was drawn by myself from the facts which transpired while the two Champions at different times where and which I did not detail in my last letter — the interest of many of them has been lost In the Subsequent counts which are now known to many of them, without Some Such movement here C will be too Strong for V B in Virginia   he has been twice before the people and voted for as vice P[resident] — he belongs too to a Slaveholding State, against this V B has nothing to oppose, but his great dexterity as a partizan   there is no great public act on which to exalt him, as regards yourself your old friends will Stick to you and if the other two Should divide the majority of the State your minority will give you the plurality of votes, this I think would be the case now Supposing the Jackson party Split into two fragments but in the tide of time there is some reason to put more, both parties have been cajoling the Clay party, under the idea that it was passive, that time has gone by and in the last [Richmond] Enquirer you will see an attempt to revive the Bargain delusion, the proof of it is put on your letter to [Francis P.] Blair, I do not know if it would not be worth your while to get [Robert] Wickliff[e] &c to permit you to publish that Letter,[1] I See you are invited to N Y   ought you not to consider well before you decide to go, I learn from Washington that you are now Stronger in that State than V B — as to a union between it Penna & Virginia I do not see how that is possible the people must be more than ever deluded to bring it about, but of the probability of this you will have as correct information from Washington as myself — Though I Should much regret your retreat from the troubles of public life as a great loss [to] our distracted and misgoverned Country — I rejoice that you find in private life So many enjoiable resources, it is this in truth that qualifies you for State affairs much better than the mere partizan accomplishments of your opponents and will make the public Loss the greater—you will See that unless reelected I Shall go out of office under the amended constitution[2] personally I should rejoice at it, as I sure I Should live the longer and be more happy—but I do not believe that I am, to be told by the knight [John Randolph] of Roane Oak [Roanoke] that it is time to go to bed as a child yet—I think I shall have Some gratification in disappointing that expectation—I could Say much to you on this Subject, but I omit it. . . . [P.S.] you will See what use we are making of the letters of Algernon Sidney [sic, Sydney]—[3]an able vindication of your course of politics will follow them, are we not a little too soon in that—

ALS. DLC-HC (DNA, M212, R4).   1. See 4:9-11.   2. Under the new Virginia constitution "Judges of the Supreme Court of Appeals, of the General Court, and of the Superior Courts of Chancery, shall remain in office until the termination of the session of the first Legislature elected under this Constitution, and no longer." Judges of the supreme court and the superior courts would then be elected by "the joint vote of both Houses of the General Assembly." *Proceedings and Debates of the Va. State Convention of 1829-30*, 901.   3. See Benjamin Watkins Leigh, *The Letters of Algernon Sydney, in Defense of Civil Liberty and Against the Encroachments of Military Despotism, Written by an Eminent Citizen of Virginia, and First Published in the Richmond Enquirer in 1818-19. To which are added, in an appendix, the remarks of Mr. [Thomas] Ritchie as referred to by the author of "Algernon Sydney" in page 30 of this pamphlet. With an introduction by the present publisher*. Richmond, 1830, 65 pp.; and Washington *Daily National Journal*, April 30, 1830.

To JOSIAH S. JOHNSTON   Lexington, May 10, 1830

I received to-day your favor of the 30th ult., with the first part of the proof-sheets of your speech, which I have perused with much satisfaction. The editor of "The [Lexington *Kentucky*] Reporter" [Thomas Smith] promises to publish it in his next week's paper.[1] With the candid its views will be regarded as large and liberal, and its vindication complete.

I regret [William] Hendrick's course. It was not necessary to secure, but may endanger his re-election.[2] He was already distrusted in his State [Indiana], but was forgiven, or rather there was a disposition to overlook his course, in consideration of the circumstances under which he was placed. But if he votes for the printers, I think it probable he will be abandoned.[3]

I am very anxious, as you may well suppose, about the passage of the Maysville bill. I hope our New England friends will not desert us in that measure. Their support of it will be worth a thousand of [Thomas H.] Benton's speeches.

Copy. Printed in Colton, *Clay Correspondence*, 4:268.   1. Johnston's speech on Sen. Samuel A. Foot's resolution was published in the Lexington *Kentucky Reporter*, May 26; June 2, 9, 1830; see also Clay to Everett, April 10, 1830.   2. Clay to Johnston, April 30, 1830.   3. Johnston to Clay, Jan. 26, 1830. Hendricks voted for two of the printers—Amos Kendall and Mordecai Noah. U.S. Sen., *Journal*, 21 Cong., 1 Sess., 423, 447, 457-58, 469. Hendricks was re-elected to the U.S. Senate from Indiana in 1830.

From Boyd McNairy, Nashville, May 11, 1830. Mentions "in confidence" that the Governor of Tennessee, William Carroll, said "in a large company of strong Jackson men . . . that the Jackson party favored you more than all the men in the U. States, and as a personal friend no gentleman stood before you with him." Suggests that if it is "consistent with your views, I should like by some means or other you could renew your correspondence with him, if you feel a delicacy in doing so, through me you can effect it with perfect security—If we could get him openly with us, and I know there is strong predisposition that way, the state or a majority would be certain, (that is Jackson off the field) I am [a] very sanguine man, and probable govern[e]d it too much by my feelings,

but I fear not the contest or result between yourself V. B. or Calhoune [*sic*, Calhoun] —
All things would be certain if Carrolle [*sic*, Carroll] was with us. your friends must have
an independent intelligent gentleman as editor in Nashville, one who will tell the truth
fearless of consequences and he must have character — Your daughter Mrs. J[ames] erwin passed through Nashville some days ago well, Cant you pay her a visit next month,
how your friends in this state would rejoice to hear that you intended to visit us, and
your enemies I have no doubt a great many would be rendered neutral —" ALS. DLC-
HC (DNA, M212, R4).

From CHARLES R. VAUGHAN   Washington, May 13, 1830
I have procured for you from England a single Barrel Gun, and with a Percussion Lock, after having consulted with our friend [Robert P.] Letcher who
was of opinion that you would prefer it to the common Lock — you will find in
the case containing the Gun a plentiful supply of *percussion caps*. In consequence of Judge [James] Clark informing me, that an opportunity offered of
sending the Gun to you, I sent it yesterday to his Lodgings & I trust that it is
already on its' way to Kentucky — I only hope that you will be as well satisfied
with it, as I am with the excellent Rifle which you have presented to me,[1] &
which I am proud to have, as a memorial of your friendship.

It is expected that this Session of Congress will close on the 31st Inst, and I
shall take the opportunity of sending to Mrs. Clay the Lithographic Print of a
boy executed by the son [Charles John] of Christopher Hughes, by our friend
Mr Clark or Mr Letcher, & which has been due to her for so long a time. . . .

ALS. DLC-HC (DNA, M212, R4).   1. Clay to Vaughan, June 18, 1829.

From Porter Clay, May 14, 1830. Bill of sale, conveying "unto H. Clay all my right
and title to a negro man Lewis descended to the said H. Clay and myself from our
father John Clay and as the heirs of our brother John Clay." DS. DLC-TJC (DNA,
M212, R 17)

From ANNE BROWN CLAY ERWIN   Shelbyville, Tenn.
                                                                May 15, 1830
I hasten, my dear Father, to answer your kind letter of the 1st. and to assure
you that Mama and yourself cannot desire that we should be with you, more
than we both wish it; Mr [James] Erwin always spoke of our joining you early in
the summer, but his father being compelled to go to Georgia in a few days, he
now feels himself obliged to remain here until he returns, we shall Still be with
you the last of July or early in August, and I hope that we shall not then be
separated for a great while, as we shall be guided pretty much by your movements.

I am happy to hear that you have been so good as to purchase us a pair of
horses, as we are now without a good pair intending to purchase when we
should be in Lexington, as we shall not want them until then you will please
keep them for us. The poney you speak of has I presumed been raised on the
farm it will therefore be doubly prized by me — Mr Erwin wrote you I believe
that he had sold your horses, I enjoyed a great many good rides from them, as
we had just then purchased a servant who proved to be an excellent carriage
driver, besides being a very good boy in other respects.

Mr Erwin and his friend Mr Denton arrived on the 10th four or five days
earlier than I expected them; they were not so fortunate as I was in getting up
all the way by water, but they were detained at the mouth of Cumberland, and
then had a most tedious trip by land to Nashville.

I was a little surprised to see by the last papers Uncle Porter Clay['s] marriage, announced although I presume it was a very suitable match so far as age is concerned.[1]

My little children have grown very much since you saw them; Henry [Clay Erwin] now talks quite plain, and James [Erwin, Jr.] runs about every where and begins to say a few words; he is fattening so much since we have been here, that he is becoming quite a beauty, at least for his opportunities, not having any to inherit from either side of the house.

Father [Andrew] Erwin requested me to remember him affectionately to Mama and yourself. Mr Erwin joins me in love to all the family both in town and at home.

ALS. DLC-TJC (DNA, M212, R13). Printed in Colton, *Clay Correspondence*, 4:269-70. Postmarked "Mt. Reserve B. C. Ten." 1. Porter Clay had recently married Elizabeth Logan Hardin who was 48 and the widow of Sen. Mark D. Hardin. Collins, *History of Kentucky*, 1:89.

To GEORGE CORBIN WASHINGTON   Lexington, May 17, 1830

Although, as intimated in your obliging letter of the 3d. instant my friends at Washington have kept me pretty well informed as to passing events, I nevertheless received and perused your favor with much satisfaction. It communicated some things which I had not before heard; and it assured me of the continuance of a friendship, which I ever highly valued, and most cordially reciprocated.

The present state of public affairs is such as to fill every thinking man with the deepest solicitude. Nothing appears to be solid and safe. The Constitution, the Union, our foreign relations, our domestic policy, all are threatened, if not in danger. When we consider the Ironhearted proscription which prevails, by which nearly a moiety of the whole community is outlawed, and the public offices and honors are distributed, often amongst the most worthless, of the other moiety; the attempt to subsidize the press by lucrative appointments awarded profusely to the most profligate editors;[1] the persevering efforts to subvert the established policy of the Country, by which its industry has been protected, and the intercourse of its various parts facilitated; the attempt to establish a Mammoth paper bank to complete and seal the work of corruption; the stain upon the National character by the violation of the most solemn engagements with the Indians; the grave proposition to surrender (and that by the popular branch of the Legislature) the power of taxation into the hands of the President, to be exercised by proclamation founded upon an arrangement with any petty foreign power; and, finally, but worst of all, the nullifying doctrines of So. Carolina, leading, if sanctioned, as they are alleged to be by the President, to immediate disorder and disunion, surely there is enough to fill every patriot bosom with the most awful apprehensions. Any one feature of this faithful sketch is alarming; the whole picture is frightful. Your connexion, my dear Sir, with the illustrious founder of our Liberties, must increase your share of the grief in beholding the assaults upon the fair fabric erected by his paternal hands. But all, who are capable of sober reflection, must intensely feel the unhappy crisis of our affairs and the magnitude of the dangers impending over us.

It is of some personal consolation to me that I forewarned my Country men of some of the evils which afflict us. Others, far transcend, in enormity, any powers of prediction which I ever possessed.

It is of much greater consolation to learn from you that the public mind is becoming strongly impressed with the mischiefs which surround us; and that there is reason to hope that a competent remedy will be applied at no distant day.

I have seen also, with much satisfaction, that our friends in Congress are nobly opposing the terrible torrent which would sweep away if unresisted, every thing valuable to our institutions.

As far as my observation and information extend a Salutary reform is every where taking place in the popular feelings and judgement. It is retarded by the means which are still indefatigably employed to keep up the delusion, but it is nevertheless in successful progress. My own confidence in the exercise generally of good sense on the part of the people has never been destroyed. They have no interest in public affairs but that they should be rightfully administered. And, if sometimes they seem to countenance bad men and bad measures, it is because of the want of correct information. This they must ultimately acquire, through the press, by friendly intercourse and conversation or from experience.

I have been rejoiced with the passage in the H. of R of the bill for the Maysville road, both on its own account, and because, after the defeat of the Buffalo bill,[2] some assertion of the power of Internal improvements, in one form or another, seemed necessary. It was also highly gratifying to me to know that the merit of the measure is greatly to be attributed to our friend [Robert P.] Letcher. I find that his agency in that respect is generally understood and justly appreciated in this quarter.

I am extremely happy to learn from you that my friends in Maryland still cherish towards me their kind sentiments. Next to the Citizens of my own State, those of Maryland I have had most intercourse with, in consequence of my public service at Washington, the birth of my wife in that State, and the acquaintances which that circumstance produced. Should such a measure, as you hint at, be deemed expedient, there is no point in the Union, under the actual state of things, at which it could take place with more valuable effect. . . .[3]

ALS. NNPM. 1. Johnston to Clay, Jan. 26, 1830. 2. For passage of the Maysville Road bill, see Johnston to Clay, May 9, 1830; for the Buffalo and New Orleans Road bill, see *Register of Debates*, 21 Cong., 1 Sess., 637-82, 688-790. 3. Probably a reference to a nomination for the presidency by the Maryland legislature. See Johnston to Clay, May 26, 1830.

From Josiah S. Johnston, Washington, May 22, 1830. Predicts that Jackson will veto the Maysville Road bill, saying: "The President is now suspended on the horns of a dilemma — The Mayville road bill puts his principles & his professions to the test — He can no longer Conceal or disguise his Sentiments — He knows where he stands & is aware of all the consequences — The South expect him now to make good his pledges — I believe their adherence to him will depend on the issue & that he knows it — if he Signs the bill — it will afford them an opp[ortuni]ty to Seperate on principle, which they are quite disposed to do — In that event Calhoun will be brought out — The Southern members are generally for him, but [Thomas] Ritchie is for Van Buren — but he will acquiesce or he will be broken down —"

Notes also that Mordecai M. Noah has been renominated, that the Baltimore and Ohio Railroad bill was tabled, and that the "Indian bill will not be acted on before we know the Result of the Maysville [road] bill." ALS. InU. For the Maysville Road veto see Johnston to Clay, May 26, 1830. Noah was renominated for the office of surveyor and inspector of the port of New York on May 22, 1830, and was confirmed on May 28, 1830. U.S. Sen., *Journal*, 21 Cong., 1 Sess., 462, 469. The Baltimore and Ohio

Railroad bill did not pass until March 1, 1831. See *ibid.*, 38, 182; and *Register of Debates*, 21 Cong., 1 Sess., 830. The Indian bill which provided for removal of the Indians to lands west of the Mississippi River passed on May 26, 1830. *Ibid.*, 21 Cong., 1 Sess., 994, 1135.

To FRANCIS T. BROOKE   Lexington, May 23, 1830

Your favor of the 10h. inst. was safely conveyed to me through the friendly channel to which you committed it, and I have perused its contents with much interest. The project of Mr. V[an]. B[uren]. and his partisans in Virginia, of attaching that State to his support, upon the ground of an overthrow of the B.U.S., I should suppose was frustrated, for the present, by the events which have occurred at Washington, on that subject. The President's message,[1] in referring to it, committed two radical errors: 1st It was premature; and, in the second place, he brought forward a rival institution, far worse than the B.U.S. can be supposed to be by its most violent enemies. A comparison has been naturally made between the two institutions, and the result of it has been every where the same. The Reports of the two Commees. of Congress have been widely circulated,[2] and have confirmed the unfavorable impression which that part of the message produced, when it was first published. It is too soon yet to entertain much less decide on the question of the renewal of the charter. We have yet to acquire the experience of five years, which may bring about important developements. The National debt will, in the mean time, be paid, the duties reduced &c &c.

I have no intention of visiting the North or any other place this summer, with any political object. I am urgently solicited to go to almost every quarter of the Union. If I were to yield to these entreaties, I should be perpetually travelling. My own judgment is decided that I ought to go no where for any political purpose, but remain at home. Should I make an excursions this summer they will relate entirely to business or to my health.

I have recd. a most singular letter from Mr. [William H.] Crawford,[3] of which I beg however you will speak to no one, as I can not but think, from the nature of the proposal which it contains, indicates some want of self possession. He says, that he perceives from the papers, that Mr. Calhoun, V.B. and myself will be run for the Presidency; that his friends also think of bringing him forward; that no one Candidate would be elected, but that, if the contest be limited to the three first, Mr. V. B. would be finally elected by the H. of R; that I should not get a vote in New England, which would support Mr. V.B; and that all the South would go for Mr. Calhoun. Therefore he proposes that I should not be brought forward but support him, whereby he would get the votes of all the Western States which, with the aid of Virginia, No. Carolina, Georgia, Delaware, New Jersey and probably Maryland, and some few other votes, would Secure his election. Then, he says, I would of *course* come again into his Cabinet, and finally succeed him! He intimates that his friends may make a similar proposal to Mr. V. B., but he prefers that I should accede to it. He supposes that Genl Jackson will not be again a Candidate. I have not answered this most extraordinary letter which bears date the 31st. day of March last. I shall not answer it. I could not answer it in terms consistent with the friendship which I once bore to Mr. Crawford.

I think Mr. Calhoun has sealed his fate by his recent vote for [Amos] Kendall.[4] He had previously boasted to some of my friends that he had constantly

210

adhered to *principle*; that he would still pursue it; that he disapproved the system of proscription, and the appointment of Editors &c. Now it so happens that a finer opportunity could not have occurred to test the sincerity of these declarations. Kendall was a printer, and besides a man of infamous character. Yet Mr. Calhoun's casting vote saved him! I knew weeks before the nomination was decided that it depended upon Mr. Calhoun's vote; and knowing him as well as I do, I stated to some of my friends what the issue would be. It is remarkable that, weeks before the event, Kendall wrote to some of his Frankfort correspondents that if the Senate were full it would be equally divided, and that he would *get* Mr. Calhoun's vote. This fact ought to be generally known.

I perceive that your new Constitution is adopted.[5] I noticed the provision in relation to the Judiciary, both on account of the principle which it involves, and as it affected you. I most sincerely wish you may be re appointed; and considering the stability which has generally characterized your State I presume you will be. If you submit the question to the consideration of those who best know you they will be unanimous for your re-election. Twenty years hence it will be time enough to talk of old age, and its too frequent concomitants.

I have received several Copies of the new edition of Algernon Sidney [*sic,* Sydney] sent me by Mr. White.[6] I wish that the principles which they so eloquently illustrate and establish could be every where diffused. [Simon] Bolivar appears to be reading us a lesson on the same subject which ought not to be lost.[7] I hope you approved of my letter to him recently published.[8]

As to the other publication to which you refer I cannot so well judge as you can as to the most fit time of its appearance.[9] I should however think that it will not be too early, after the adjournment of Congress.

I cannot return this letter through the channel that you sent yours, for an obvious reason.

ALS. KyU. Printed in Colton, *Clay Correspondence,* 4:270-73 with minor variations in punctuation and capitalization.   1. For Jackson's "rival" bank suggestion, see his First Annual Message of Dec. 8, 1829. *MPP,* 2:462.   2. *House Reports,* 21 Cong., 1 Sess., no. 358; *Sen. Docs.,* 21 Cong., 1 Sess., no. 104.   3. Crawford to Clay, March 31, 1830.   4. Clay to Watterson, May 8, 1830. Vice President Calhoun broke a tie vote on Kendall's nomination as 4th auditor. U.S. Sen., *Journal,* 21 Cong., 1 Sess., 457.   5. See 7:575-76; and Peterson, *Democracy, Liberty and Property,* 438-43; Ambler, *Sectionalism in Virginia,* 171-72.   6. Brooke to Clay, May 10, 1830. 7. On Jan. 20, 1830, in a message to the Constituent Congress of the Republic of Colombia, which convened in Bogota on Jan. 27, Bolivar resigned as president of the republic and terminated his political career. He died on Dec. 17, 1830. Harold A. Bierck, Jr., ed., and Lewis Bertrand, trans., *Selected Writings of Bolivar,* 2 vols. (N.Y., Banco de Venezuela, 1951), 2:749-55. 8. Clay to Bolivar, Oct. 27, 1828 [7:517-18] had been published in the Washington *Daily National Journal,* April 17, 1830, and in *Niles' Register* (April 24, 1830), 38:173.   9. Reference obscure, but possibly having to do with his availability as a presidential candidate in 1832.

To GEORGE W. FEATHERSTONHAUGH

Lexington, May 23, 1830

I was extremely glad to be assured by your letter of the 4h. instant that I continued to enjoy your esteem and friendship, upon which I have ever placed very great value. I passed at N. Orleans some very pleasant days with our excellent friend Genl. V. Renselaer [*sic,* Stephen Van Rensselaer] and the account he gave you of my health and spirits was entirely correct. Since my return, the former has not been so good, but it has been sufficient to enable me to bestow constant attention upon my private affairs and to engage in usual occupations. I find great benefit as well as amusement in my agricultural pursuits. And, if the taste for them, which the last years experience has fostered shall continue to increase and strengthen, I shall be ready very soon to renounce for ever the strife and the cares of public life. But I never can cease to take a deep interest in the operations of our government, and especially in the success of that system to which both of us have devoted so much exertion. The political events of the last few years, in this Country, were of a discouraging tendency; but I never thought that they ought to extinguish our hopes of free government, or to dissuade us from the most strenuous efforts to sustain it. Man, in his individual and collective capacity, is some times wild and capricious, and I have thought that the election of Genl. Jackson ought to be regarded as an exception from the general good sense with which the American people have conducted their affairs.

This opinion derives countenance from the state of things which you describe as existing in N. York, of which corroborating information has reached me from other friends. In all parts of the Country there are symptoms of returning sobriety and discretion among the people. And I think there is much ground to hope that the error of the last P. election will be corrected in the next. Whether your friendly wishes, in respect to myself, will be then realized or not, it is perhaps too early at present to anticipate. They are not the less entitled to my thanks and gratitude.

I am sorry that you are going to leave us, but I hope, and infer from the tenor of your letter, that your absence will not be of long duration. I trust that you will in Europe continue to plead our cause, and make to the friends of liberty there the best apology you can for the late popular freak. On your return, can you not visit this Western world? It would delight me to meet you under my own roof.

You have made a most valuable acquaintance in Baron [Paul de] Krudener. He was my nearest neighbour in Washington, and all my intercourse with him, public and private, was ever friendly and agreeable. A faithful representative of the Emperor [Nicholas I], he was at the same time liberal in his views and a sincere friend of this Country. I regret his loss at Washington. But wherever he goes he will carry my warmest regard and my best wishes for his happiness and prosperity, and I beg you to tell him so. . . .

ALS. ViU.

From Peter B. Porter, Black Rock, N. Y., May 23, 1830. Urges Clay to undertake this summer his "long contemplated" visit to New York, noting that "politically speaking" the trip would produce the "happiest effects." Continues: "No one can calculate with certainty upon the politics of N York, but present indications are certainly favourable. For the past year the contest has been exclusively between the Jackson men & the Anti-Masons, until a short time since, when a New party began to rally in the city of New York under the banner of the 'Working Mens Party,' and is already spreading itself throughout the State. It will embrace most of the friends of the late administration, & particularly your friends, and will form a rendezvous for all those who detest & dispise Jacksonism & antimasonry. It promises well. It is impossible at present to say (if they know themselves) what course the Anti Masons will eventually take in the Presidential election. The most decent and discreet among them are desirous of supporting you; but in this they will be opposed by the more violent. Several of the more moderate and respectable men among them have recently applied to me confidentially to Know your views of masonry. I have told them that you are a Mason, but that like most other of the old and most intelligent Members, you are not disposed to rate very highly the present usefullness or importance of the Institution; although it might have been very usefull

212

once, before the other numerous & more efficient benevolent & charitable societies of the present day, had sprung up to perform the functions which were allotted to the craft in its earliest purest & best days; That therefore you, and many more respectable brothers had for a number of years past ceased to take any active part in the transactions of the Society—But, as an honourable man, you would never renounce (and they did not seem to expect or wish it) your obligations to the order."

Concludes with the further observation: "Do not suppose for a moment that I would urge you to speak (whatever you might think of it) disrespectfully of the Institution of Masonry—But if you could with propriety express to me in a private letter (with an understanding that I might shew it confidentially to some two or three of these gentlemen whose wishes I know are friendly) the views which, in our conversations, I have understood you to entertain on the subject of masonry it might be attended with good effects." ALS. DLC-HC (DNA, M212, R4); copy in OHi, dated May 8, 1830, with considerable variation. Porter's observations on the Workingmen's party, the Anti-Masonic movement, and Clay's relationship to Masonry have been edited out of Colton, *Clay Correspondence*, 4:270. For the Anti-Masonic party, see 7:186-87. The Workingmen's party, established in New York on April 23, 1829, is discussed in Edward Pessen, "The Workingmen's Movement of the Jacksonian Era," *MVHR* (December, 1956), 43:428-43, and "The Working Men's Party Revisited," *LH* (Fall, 1963), 4:203-26.

To HENRY CLAY, JR. Lexington, May 24, 1830

The period of the annual examination of the Cadets is approaching and I feel very anxious to know how you will acquit yourself. I had hoped to be able to visit you this summer, but I now fear it will not be in my power. You have another year to remain at West Point, and it will appear a very long one; but I hope you will command the fortitude necessary to carry you through it. Write me fully as to your feelings on that subject and consider me both as your friend and father. Your uncle [James] Brown will probably see you. He writes to me in terms of high praise of you.

Anne [Brown Clay Erwin] and Mr. [James] Erwin are now in Tennessee, near Shelbyville. I expect them here in a few weeks. Owing to her family condition[1] she has been compelled to abandon her Northern trip. They will remain some time with us. Tom [Thomas Hart Clay] is in Illinois on my Prairie, but I have very bad accounts of his habits. I despair of him. Theodore [W. Clay] is with us, and altho' he does not drink, he has other habits almost as bad. He has the most unfortunate temper that ever afflicted any person, and seems soured with all the world. Oh! my dear Son no language can describe to you the pain that I have suffered on account of these two boys. My hopes rest upon you and your two younger brothers [James Brown Clay and John Morrison Clay].

A young Mr. [Cary Harrison] Fry from near Danville has gone to West point. I promised his grandfather to give him a letter of introduction to you, but I was not at home when he passed through Lexington. His connexions are highly respectable, and I am told he is promising. I wish you would be attentive to him and treat him with kindness, as I hope you do all the young men from Kentucky.[2]

My friends at Washington write to me in the best spirits, and with great confidence as to our future success. Other informations also reach me from different points of the same encouraging kind. But I am getting so much attached to the pursuits on my farm—I consider life as so uncertain, and public affairs so full of vexation, that I have become more indifferent than I ever expected to be in regard to public life. . . .

ALS. Henry Clay Memorial Foundation, Lexington, Ky.   1. See 7:590-91.   2. Fry graduated from West Point on July 1, 1834. USMA, *Register*, 186.

To James Brown, Philadelphia, May 26, 1830. Asks Brown to purchase for him some "English Cattle" advertised for sale on June 16 by John Hare Powel. States: "I should be glad to get two bulls . . . from one to two years old, and two heifers from two to three. But I cannot afford to give for the four more than $300, that is averaging $75 a piece. If you can attend to this little commission, my friend Mr. [George W.] Featherstonhaugh, now in Philad[elphi]a, and who I presume is known to you, is an excellent judge of cattle and I am sure would accompany you to see and select them." ALS. KyU.

From Josiah S. Johnston, n.p., *ca.* May 26, 1830. States that the family of William Tudor are much distressed at his death [March 9, 1830]. At their request he is sending some of Tudor's letters to Clay. Suggests that Clay write them a letter of condolence "expressing an opinion of his character & talents. . . . Something that will do to preserve & to shew"; also, that he have the Lexington newspapers print something about Tudor's contributions and a notice of his death. "This is a tax you must pay—"

Mentions a letter from Henry Clay, Jr., which he received yesterday. "I am very much surprized at the ease & grace of his style—His letters bear the marks of Superior genius—"

Notes that [John] Randolph "is nominated to Russia with his approbation—" and that the administration has taken advantage of the absence of Littleton W. Tazewell from Washington to renominate Mordecai M. Noah [Johnston to Clay, May 22, 1830]. Continues: "Maryland is now put in a state of perfect organization—Our friends are determin[e]d to Carry the State & they will proportion their efforts to the importance of the object—They do not doubt of success—They seem to claim the honor of making the Nomination—If they Succeed as I think they will, your Annunciation can not come forward under better Auspices—The President still holds the maysville bills—You may judge of the difficulty & responsibility of his Situation—No one knows what he will do although they have had Several Cabinet Councils—The Case is very delicate & Critical—We Can do nothing until he decides—" ALS. InU. There is no mention of Tudor's death in the Lexington *Kentucky Reporter* or the Lexington *Kentucky Gazette* in May-September, 1830. Clay was nominated for president by the Maryland legislature on January 14, 1832. See *Niles' Register* (April 21, 1832), 42:150-51. For Randolph's appointment as minister to Russia, see U.S. Sen., *Journal*, 21 Cong., 1 Sess., 463, 465, and William C. Bruce, *John Randolph of Roanoke* (New York, 1922) 1:634-61. For Jackson's Maysville Road veto message of May 27, see *MPP*, 2:483-93.

From William C. C. Claiborne, Jr., New Orleans, May 28, 1830. Thanks Clay for the invitation to visit during the summer, and says he and his uncle, Martin Duralde, "intend starting in July." Mentions that his uncle is now electioneering for Andre B. Roman for governor of Louisiana. Continues: "The unhappy division in the French votes created by Mr. [Armand] Beauvais renders his election very uncertain, both being extremely anxious to attain their end, and as yet determined to hold on to the last. The Jacksonites are uniting upon [William S.] Hamilton, and speak confidently of his success. There is but little hope of getting Mr. Beauvais to retire, as his friends maintain that his chance is as good as Roman's. Mr. [David] Randall remains on the ranks merely as a tool to take away the votes of Lafourche [Parish] from Roman. I believe that our ticket for the Legislature will certainly prevail in the City." ALS. DLC-HC (DNA, M212, R4). For the Louisiana gubernatorial election see Clay to Johnston, February 27, 1830. For the Louisiana legislative elections which were favorable to the Clay cause, see Clay to Johnston, March 11, 1830. Edward D. White, also a Clay supporter, was elected to Congress from New Orleans.

To John A. Quitman, May 29, 1830. Thanks Quitman for sending some magnolias which were "this day received" in "remarkably" good condition. Adds that "I have just returned from transplanting them. . . . I hope that we shall some day or other have you to witness their prosperous growth in the grounds at Ashland." ALS. NcU. Addressed to Quitman at his estate, "Monmouth," near Natchez, Miss.

To CHARLES R. VAUGHAN   Lexington, May 29, 1830

I received your obliging letter of the 13h. inst. and the day after the case was delivered to me, containing the single barrel gun, with its accompanyments, all perfectly safe and well preserved.[1] Nothing of the kind, that I have seen, equals the neatness and beauty of the mechanical execution of the gun and its apparatus. I shall reserve it for my exclusive use, and it will, with many other agreeable recollections, constantly remind me of our friendly intercourse. My only fear is that you have incurred greater expence in the procurement of it than I was willing you should sustain.

You once promised me to visit us in Kentucky. I hope you have not abandoned that intention. It would afford me the sincerest gratification to have you under my roof, where if you would not find all the luxuries of your own house, you would meet a hearty and cordial welcome and whatever of comforts our young Country can supply. The best season to visit us is in the months of May and June. You would find the journey much less fatiguing than you imagine; and you might return by the Virginia mountains and Springs, which would recall to you some of the Asiatic scenes which you have witnessed.[2]

Johnny [John Morrison Clay] often speaks of you, and is proud of the attachment with which you honor him. He is making encouraging progress in his education. . . .

ALS. Codrington Library, All Soul's College, Oxford University, England.   1. Vaughan to Clay, July 1, 1829.   2. For Vaughan's early travels, see *DNB*.

From Daniel Webster, Washington, May 29, 1830. States that the "passage of the Indian Bill [Clay to Hammond, October 7, 1829] & the rejection of the Maysville Turnpike Bill [Johnston to Clay, May 26, 1830] have occasioned universal excitement. . . . There is more ill blood raised, I should think, than would easily be quieted again."

On whether or not a Clay presidential nomination should be made, advises "that a formal nomination here would not be *popular enough*, in its character & origin, to do good. It would be immediately proclaimed to be the act of your friends acting *at your instance*—It would excite jealousies, on the one hand, which are now fast dying away, &, on the other, check discontents & schisms among our opponents, from which much is now to be hoped.—Such is our view." Adds that he has refused to agree to Clay's nomination by the Massachusetts legislature, because "every body knows we are perfectly safe & strong in Massachusetts, & a nomination, then, would only raise the cry of *coalition revived*." Agrees that Maryland should be the first to nominate Clay.

Believes if Clay runs against Jackson, he will lose unless New York, Virginia, or Pennsylvania "can be detached from him. Of the three, I have, at present, most hope of N York, & least of Va." Thinks recent events have "*ensured* us Maryland, Ohio, Kentucky, & Indiana. This is one very good *breadth* South of it, I look for nothing but Louisiana, every thing north of it is worth a contest."

Continues: "On the whole, My Dear Sir, I think a crisis is coming, or rather *has arrived*. I think you cannot be kept back from the contests. The *people* will bring you out, *nolens volens—Let them do it*. I advise you, as you will be much watched, *to stay at home*; or, if you were to travel, visit your old friends in Va.—We should all be glad to see you, at the North, *but not now.* . . . . Parties must, now, necessarily, be sorted out, anew; — & the great ground of difference will be Tariff & Int. Improvements. — You are necessarily at the head of one party, & Gen. J. will be, if he is not already, identified with the other. The question will be put to the Country. Let the Country decide it — " ALS. DLC-HC (DNA, M212, R4). Printed in Wiltse, *Webster Papers*, 3:78-80. Of the states mentioned, Clay carried only Massachusetts, Maryland, and Kentucky in 1832.

From HENRY CLAY, JR.   West Point, N.Y., May 31, 1830

I merely have time to say to you that I have delivered the 1st of the addresses which I mentioned in a letter to you some time since.[1] I have been singularly fortunate

My pursuits in life are fixed — Never before did I derive such gratification as I have done from the expressions of the pleasure which my speech gave. To you & to you only would I dare to be thus frank. I fear the attention which I have given to my orations may be in some degree prejudicial to my studies.

However the examination is a week off — I propose to make up all losses, and to put in a claim to your approbation.

ALS. Henry Clay Memorial Foundation, Lexington, Ky.   1. Clay to Clay, Jr., March 29, 1830.

From John, Bishop of Charleston, Louisville, May 31, 1830. States that during the previous year he sought "to obtain by application to the President, the Several documents, in the office of the Secretary of State, respecting the application made by Rev. Messrs. [William] Harold & [John] Ryan then of Philadelphia, for protection against the order of their Superior . . . transferring them from the Mission of Philadelphia to that of Cincinnati." After obtaining the consent of President Jackson and Secretary of State Van Buren and receiving several documents, he found that the most important document — James Brown's report of his meeting with the Papal Nuncio in Paris — was not on file. Asks Clay's advice on how to proceed in securing this document, adding: "I feel that in making this application I owe it to you to state, that my object is to ascertain whether the late President [John Q. Adams] has not, perhaps unintentionally, interfered with the concerns of the Roman Catholic Church, in a manner which the constitution does not sanction. & if so, whether it is not my duty as a member of that church and a citizen of the United States, to take some steps, at least to guard against this interference being drawn with a precedent which might be seriously mischievous in it's consequences. I owe it to you to state with equal plainness, that so far as I can yet perceive, from the documents, & my enquiries, you have not laid yourself open to any charges, upon this ground."

Says that he plans to go to Bardstown for a few days and suggests that Clay write him there. ALS. DLC-HC (DNA, M212, R4). For the Harold and Ryan controversy, see 7:372-73.

To JOHN C. WRIGHT   Lexington, May 31, 1830

I duly received your favor of the 7h inst. which I perused with much satisfaction. As I *hope* to have the pleasure of seeing you at Columbus in July next, I will reserve for that occasion much of what I would otherwise now say. On the point of your offering for Congress[1] allow me now to remark that, if it would not be injurious to the interests of your family, I think it would be very gratifying to the friends of our cause every where to see you again in the H. of R. The election of no one, in any State, I am persuaded would afford them more pleasure; and nothing ought to prevent your being a Candidate, if there be a reasonable prospect of success, but the paramount duty you owe to your family.

The general results of the present Session of Congress are highly favorable to our cause. In the debate in the Senate on Mr [Samuel A.] Foot's resolution[2] our friends obtained a manifest advantage. The failure of the recommendations of the President;[3] the rejection of some of his nominations;[4] his wild project of a bank;[5] the Jefferson dinner;[6] the Indian subject;[7] the attack on the Tariff,[8] must all in their tendency aid us. Have you seen [John] Holmes's Speech on the resolution which he proposed calling for information of the cause of the removals?[9] It is well calculated for effect and deserves extensive circulation. The facts which he has brought forward of the number of removals, since the commencement of the present Constitution, and the contrast which they exhibit between the present and all former administrations must make a deep impression.

On the Tariff, I fear, our friends in Congress have suffered an advantage to be gained over them by allowing it to be attacked in detail. The reduction of the Salt tax has led to the passage of a bill in the H. of R. reducing the duty on molasses and allowing a drawback on its re-exportation in the form of spirits.[10] I am apprehensive that success in these two instances may lead to other attempts in particular articles, and that some of our friends dissatisfied by the reduction of the duties which has been thus may vote for further reductions. The true policy was to have considered every thing heretofore done towards protection as not to be changed, and to have resisted all change.

We have not yet heard whether the President has approved the Maysville appropriation.[11] If he gives it his veto, the effect will be very great in this State among even his friends. In that event, I should not be surprized at some violent manifestation of popular feeling. Whereas if he approves the bill, it will do him here but little good, as it is well known that our friends were chiefly instrumental in its passage.

ALS. ViU.   1. Wright [2:874], a "Henry Clay democrat," was defeated by John M. Goodenow. *Congressional Quarterly's Guide to U.S. Elections* (Washington, 1975), p. 551; *CAB; BDAC.* See also Clay to Greene, Oct. 30, 1830.   2. Johnston to Clay, Jan. 26, 1830. 3. *Ibid.*; Remini, *Andrew Jackson and the Course of American Freedom*, 230-34, 251-56.   4. *Ibid.*; 230-31; Johnston to Clay, Jan. 26, 1830.   5. Clay to Biddle, Jan. 2, 1830.   6. Webster to Clay, April 18, 1830.   7. Johnston to Clay, May 22, 1830; Clay to Hammond, Oct. 7, 1829.   8. *MPP*, 2:449-50; Johnston to Clay, Dec. 12, 1829.   9. Clay to Everett, April 10, 1830.   10. For the reduction of the duties on salt and molasses, see U.S. H. of Reps., *Journal*, 21 Cong., 1 Sess., 751, 753; U.S. Sen., *Journal*, 21 Cong., 1 Sess., 346, 357-58; 4 *U.S. Stat.*, 419.   11. Johnston to Clay, May 9, 1830.

From JOHN J. CRITTENDEN   Frankfort, June 1, 1830

Your letter of a few days ago, with its enclosures, was duly received, & will be attended to.

I think I am doing well in my canvass — I am quite industrious, & confident of my election — [1]I have passed the breakers without any damage — And to the questions put to me in the [Frankfort] Argus I have answered publicly in my speeches — that I *would not* pledge myself to vote for a Jackson man to the Senate of the U: States — that as to the rechartering the Bank of the U: States I would take five years more to think about it — And as to the next presidency that there was no man in the nation I would sooner vote for than H. Clay —

I feel great solicitude about the result of our August elections — J[ames]. T. Morehead is a candidate in Warren county, & E[phraim]. M. Ewing in Logan — This is very will [*sic*, well] — In Mercer county there is a capacity to do a great deal, & nothing is doing — From what I have heard I feel confident that if [Benjamin F.] Pleasants [Madison G.] Worthington & young Bridges (a son of the judge [John L. Bridges]) were candidates,[2] that the whole county might be carried. It is a great object to prevail on them to come out, & "hang their banners on the outward wall" — It must be done, & I have no means of doing it — Can you not in some way effect it? I know the delicacy of your situation, & that you have almost a fastidious disinclination to interfere on such subjects — But in common with all your friends you must feel an interest on the occasion, & I can not see any breach of the strictest propriety, in your expressing that interest to your friends, & uniting your exertions with theirs in giving to our State its proper political character & representation — Your own discretion will best direct the mode of your co-operation — But something ought to be done, & that immediately to induce the gentlemen before named to become candidates at once — And I think it an object of so much consequence as really to call for your interposition — The Quo modo is altogether for your consideration —

Jackson will reject (I *beleive* has *rejected*) the bill authering the subscription of $150,000 to the Maysville &c turnpike road — [3]And this while it furnishes a just subject of complaint, will afford a very happy occasion for those gentlemen to come out.

ALS. NcD.   1. On August 2, Crittenden was elected to the Ky. house of representatives from Franklin County by a majority of 14 votes over his opponent, Lewis Sanders, Jr. Lexington *Kentucky Reporter*, August 18, 1830. For Sanders, see Collins, *History of Kentucky*, 2:241.   2. Both Morehead and Ewing were elected. Pleasants, Worthington, and Bridges did not become candidates. In August, John A. Tomlinson and Robert B. McAfee, both Jacksonians, were elected to the Ky. house from Mercer County; and John B. Thomson, an anti-Jacksonian, was elected to the Ky. senate. Lexington *Kentucky Reporter*, August 18, 1830.   3. Johnston to Clay, May 26, 1830.

From NICHOLAS BIDDLE   Philadelphia, June 3, 1830

I send to you by this day's mail a copy of Mr. [George] McDuffie's & Genl. [Samuel] Smith's reports on the Bank & the currency which you will have the goodness to place on your shelves in token of my respectful remembrance. They realize I think the expectation with which your prophetic spirit consoled me on the first appearance of the document which they refute.[1]

Allow me now to reciprocate your good wishes on that occasion & to congratulate you on the fate of the Maysville Turnpike bill.[2]

ALS. DLC-HC (DNA, M212, R4). Copy in DLC-Nicholas Biddle Papers (DNA, M212, R20). 1. For the reports on the B.U.S., see Brown to Clay, April 29, 1830. The "document which they refute" is Jackson's First Annual Message (Dec. 1829) in which he charged that "a large portion of our fellow-citizens" question the constitutionality of the law creating the B.U.S., and that "it must be admitted by all that it has failed in the great end of establishing a uniform and sound currency." *MPP*, 2:462.   2. Johnston to Clay, May 9, 26, 1830.

From FRANCIS T. BROOKE   Richmond, June 4, 1830

I have this moment received your letter of the 23ed ultimo, your impression that the plan of bringing out Mr V[an] B[uren] in Virginia on the ground of his opposition to the B[ank] of US has been frustrated by Subsequent events at Washington is only in part correct, whatever impression has been made on the public mind by these events the effect upon all connected with State Banks Stil remains — the rival Bank recommended in the [President's annual] message[1] they were not afraid of, but though Mr V B when here was afraid to take the ground of opposition to the Tariff & Internal improvements, in his eagerness to overtake Mr C[alhoun], in the South you will perceive he has now, in advising him as to to [*sic*] the internal improvements & etc, in part taken that

ground, and to defeat Mr C in the South I Should not be Surprised if there should be an understanding ere long between Him & Mr [William H.] Crawford, who if his imbecility can be disproved will be Stronger than Mr C — but for his Supposed imbecility I think his extraordinary letter[2] ought to be made public, this though deserves much reflection, if he Should be brought out by his friends there will be no reason & tendency for him to withhold it, if he is of Sound mind it is a most flagitious act on his part — you will See in the [Richmond] Enquirer to day evidence of some alarm, the Editor [Thomas Ritchie] is endeavouring to revive the old Slander, I wish much that [Francis P.] Blair would publish your letter to him[3] I think your friends [Robert] Wickliff[e] &c ought to be reconciled to it, there is certainly nothing in it except Some remarks on them that can give you any concern, the effect of the [Maysville Road] veto will be great in Virginia, though the motive with which it is gotten up, will lessen it in some Degree and it may be doubted whether it will redeem the other acts of the administration a little time will Shew, it will operate differently in the East & the west — as to the publication of which I wrote, I fear it will not answer my expectations of it,[4] I shall see it probably in a few days.
. . .

ALS. DLC-HC (DNA, M212, R4). 1. Clay to Biddle, Jan. 2, 1830. 2. Crawford to Clay, March 31, 1830. 3. For Clay's letter to Blair, see 4:9-11. Ritchie charged that Clay "should not take the field again, without this Document in hand. . . . He will never clear himself of the charge of collusion & coalition with Mr. Adams, until he has the courage to publish the aforesaid letter." Richmond *Enquirer*, June 4, 1830. 4. Probably a reference to the "Algernon Sydney" article mentioned in Brooke to Clay, May 10, 1830.

From Josiah S. Johnston, Washington, June 5, 1830. Reports that he has seen Samuel L. Southard who "is Confident of New Jersey. . . . you will be Nominated in that State during the year —" Continues: "The rejection of the Maysville bill & the decided opposition to all internal improvements, has made a great sensation The question is fairly at issue — If he [Jackson] can be carried after that it will be decisive of that question for at least Seven years — I think it will have the effect in the West & in Maryland — The impression is now strongly made that that State is gone — but the party will try to rally again — You know What our hopes are in New York, every thing Seems to favor them — The Indian Question will be Used there & in Pennsylvania with great effect — The speeches will be Circulated extensively through both — the arrangements are made — We Must still look to Virginia — That great State is to undergo a great revolution — The present generation of politicians will give place to the new — They appear to be delighted with the [Maysville] Veto of the President, they are Lauding him to the skies — An impression has been made here among a few that a Compromize in Some form has been effected between the President, Calhoun & Van Buren — nothing determinate is Known — But no one Knows the purport of it —"
Adds that Jackson's hostility to Calhoun "may be ascribed to the part which rumor Said Mr. C. had in the question of Arrest for the Florida affair —" Believes, however, "it is mere Conjecture that that old affair has been Compromised —" Concludes with the observation that the "bill to Authorize the President to open the ports to Br[itish]. vessels is quite a stale trick — but it will serve us to Laugh at hereafter." ALS. InU. For Calhoun's role in the movement to censure Jackson for his actions in Florida during the Seminole War (1818), see James, *Jackson*, 236-39, 268-70. For the trade bill which passed the House on May 29 and the Senate on May 31, see U.S. H. of Reps., *Journal*, 21 Cong., 1 Sess., 743, 789; and U.S. Sen., *Journal*, 21 Cong., 1 Sess., 358. The Anglo-American trade restriction problem is treated in 3:729; 4:180, 417, 941-42; 5:632, 831-35.

From FRANCIS T. BROOKE   Richmond, June 6, 1830

Although I wrote you a hasty letter on the 4h I have thought it best to give you my reflections,   Since, on that extraordinary letter from Mr C — [1] I think it is impossible to doubt that it will be communicated to some of his friends and your silence be misinterpreted, would it not be better to answer it, in something like the following terms, that you have always thought that as the office was in the gift of the people, the people should be left to their own Selection, that you had so thought at the last election and acted upon that principle then, that you see no cause to change that opinion now, and therefore while you neither sought or refused the suffrages of the people it was your wish as it ever had been that the people should be left free to choose for themselves, — this would be sufficiently respectfull on the idia that he is non compos — and leave nothing to be inferred from the manner in which you treat the matter — excuse the liberty I take and put it to the account of the deep interest I take in whatever concerns you —

ALS. InU.   1. Crawford to Clay, March 31, 1830.

To Daniel Webster, June 7, 1830. Responds to Webster's letter of May 29. States that "The decision of my friends at Washington to stand still for the present, and to leave the first movement to Maryland was best," and that Webster is correct "in supposing considerations of policy to be opposed to a nomination at present in Massachusetts." Notes that the Maysville Road veto "has produced uncommon excitement in K." with many Jackson supporters, including those in Lexington, openly renouncing their faith. Adds: "We shall attack the Veto, by proposing an amendment of the Constitution" to allow a simple majority of both houses of Congress, rather than a two-thirds majority, to pass a measure over the president's veto. Predicts this proposal will put the Jacksonians "on the Aristocratic bench, and more than balance" Jackson's proposal in his December, 1829, annual message of a constitutional amendment that would remove all intermediate agency in the election of president and vice president, limit the president to one term of 4 to 6 years, and disqualify from appointive office the representatives in Congress whose votes may have determined the outcome of a presidential election [*MPP*, 2:448].

Advises Webster not to return to the House of Representatives. "You need make no change to advance your fame." Concludes: "To guard against the treachery of the P. Office, if you write me, put your letters under cover to James Harper (Lexington) To whom should I address mine?" ALS. NhHi. Full text printed in Wiltse, *Webster Papers*, 3:80-82.

To ADAM BEATTY   Lexington, June 8, 1830

We are all shocked and mortified by the rejection of the Maysville road and other events occurring at the close of the late Session. Meetings of the people are contemplated in several Counties[1] in this quarter to give expression to public sentiment and feelings. At these meetings it has been suggested that the public sentiment may be expressed, in terms of strong disapprobation of the act of the President. 2dy. in favor of Int. improvements. 3d. disapproving Mr. [George M.] Bibbs conduct and recommending to the legislature his recall. 4 Approbation of Mr. [Robert P.] Letcher. particularly and of the other members who voted with him. 5 Against the nullifying doctrines of the South. 6 agt. the re-election of Mr. [John] Rowan,[2] because he supports them, is opposed to Internal Im. and the tariff, in opinion, and has supported the most obnoxious nominations. 7. proposing an amendmt. to the Constitution, substituting a majority of all the members elected to Congress, instead of two thirds to pass a bill returned by the President. This is right I think, in principle. Your own reflections will suggest the immense advantages that we shall derive from supporting this amendment, whilst our opponents will oppose it.

It is thought by my friends that these public meetings will furnish suitable occasions for making a nomination for the next presidency and recommending to the next Legislature to Second and support it. They urge that this will be a popular measure, and not one of Caucus agency. That the nomination connects itself naturally with the question of Internal Imp. That the time has come. That Congress having adjourned no counteracting measure can be adopted by members of Congress at Washington. That other States look to K. for the first movement. That it will have good effect on the August elections. That it can do no harm, and may do much good &c. I think there is much force in these suggestions.

Will you have a meeting in Mason [County]? If you do, it will have beneficial consequences that there should be as many meetings as practicable in adjoining Counties. Let me hear from you. . . . P.S. My opinion is that, with prompt bold and decided action, much may be made of the events of the moment.

ALS. Courtesy of Earl M. Ratzer, Highland Park, Ill. Printed in Colton, *Clay Correspondence*, 4:276-77. Letter marked "(Confidential)." 1. These meetings were held in Fayette and Jessamine counties on June 21, 1830; in Woodford County on June 18; and in Mason County on July 3. Lexington *Kentucky Reporter*, June 16, 30; July 14, 1830. 2. Both of Kentucky's senators—Bibb and Rowan—supported Jackson's veto of the Maysville Road bill. Rowan, whose term expired in 1831, did not run again and Clay was elected to his seat on Nov. 9, 1831. The vote in the Ky. senate was: Clay 18, Richard M. Johnson 19, Worden Pope 1. In the Ky. house it was: Clay 55, Johnson 45. *Niles' Register* (Nov. 26, 1831), 41:237. Bibb's term did not expire until 1835. He, too, chose not to seek reelection and John J. Crittenden was chosen as his replacement. Ky. H. of Reps., *Journal* . . . 1834-1835, p. 107.

From Olof Wyk, Göteborg, Sweden, June 11, 1830. Thanks Clay for the hospitality and letters of introduction that made his extensive tour of the United States so pleasurable and educational. Reports that since returning home "a great many" Swedes who had known Clay have inquired of him. Sincerely hopes "that I shall in two years hence, have the great pleasure to congratulate you" on achieving the "Presidential Chair." ALS. DLC-HC (DNA, M212, R4).

From Robert P. Letcher, Lancaster, Ky., June 12, 1830. Says that he would be "very glad to hear all the news you have from Maryland & Pen[nsylvani]a," and predicts that "success must be enevitable, without some providential interposition." ALS. DLC-TJC (DNA, M212, R13).

To JAMES F. CONOVER   Lexington, June 13, 1830
I should not have deemed it necessary so early to acknowledge the receipt of your friendly letter of the 11h. Inst. but for the privilege which you have given me of writing to you on any subject, of which I mean now to avail myself.

They are going in this State to attack the [Maysville Road] Veto,[1] not to destroy but to qualify it. It is believed that a bare majority of all the Members elected to each house of Congress, instead of two thirds of a quorum, ought to be competent to pass a bill returned by the President; and that an amendment to that effect ought to be proposed to the Constitution. If a majority of both houses, after full deliberation, upon their own reasons, pass a bill; and again pass the same bill, after full consideration of the reasons of the president, in objection to it, they think that it ought to pass the bill. Such an amendment is comformable to the provisions of several of the State constitutions, and is in the spirit of our institutions. I believe such an amendment right or I would discountenance it. For we ought not, for party purposes, to support any great measure or any alteration of the Constitution which is wrong. The advantages, however, to our cause, in the prosecution of a proper and laudable object, form a collateral consideration, which may animate exertion. In this case they are manifest. We shall be contending against a principle which wears a monarchical aspect, whilst our opponents will be placed in the unpopular attitude of defending it.

If your judgment approves of this course, I submit to you the expediency of breaking ground on this subject.

Another idea has occurred to me, in regard to that most flagitious measure (the Indian bill)[2] which threatens to bring a foul and lasting stain upon the good faith, humanity and character of the Nation. This consequence can only be averted now in one way. The bill can only be carried into effect by treaties. These treaties must be ratified by the Senate, unless indeed their agency be dispensed with, which I hardly suppose will be attempted. Would it not be well to prepare the public mind to reject the treaties? They will probably teem with odious corruption. If such a course should be deemed advisable, the violation of treaties existing, the upsetting of our Indian System, as it has been established from the commencement of our Independence, the inhumanity of the Indian law, its enormous expence, its interference with internal improvements, ought all to be set forth in vivid and striking colors. If a favorable state of the public mind should be produced, public meetings of the people might be assembled, resolutions passed, and our members of Congress instructed &c.

If as I hope you are upon intimate terms with my friend Mr. [Charles] Hammond, be pleased to consult him as well as your partner [Isaiah Thomas], on the subject of this letter, and shew it to others.

ALS. ViU. Letter marked "(Confidential)."   1. Johnston to Clay, May 26, 1830; Clay to Beatty, June 8, 1830.   2. Clay to Hammond, Oct. 7, 1829; Johnston to Clay, May 22, 1830.

To PETER B. PORTER   Lexington, June 13, 1830
[In response to Porter's letter of May 23, points out that "several considerations, public and private," make it impossible for him to visit New York State this summer. Continues:]

So far as any visit of mine might have a political bearing, I think that effect wrong in principle. And my judgment also tells me that the good done in one place is more than counterbalanced by the evil in other places. My situation is different now from what it was during Mr. [John Q.] Adams's administration, but even then I never made any excursion for political effect. I was then no Candidate myself for any office. Now, although not formally announced as a Candidate, it is impossible that I should not regard myself in some sort as one, when I see and hear all around me. If these views were in opposition to those of my friends generally, I might perhaps yield them. But they accord with those of all who have communicated their opinions, and who are not influenced by their private wishes and personal friendship. I hope, my dear Sir, that you and Mrs. Porter will approve my decision.

222

I observe what you say on the subject of your local politics and of Anti masonry. It seems to me that I had better keep myself absolutely separated from and unconnected with either; and that no opinion or explanation should be communicated *as coming from me*. In regard to Masonry, I have heretofore freely expressed my feelings to you. I never was a bright mason. I never attached much importance to Masonry. In my youth I occasionally attended the Lodges prompted more by the social than the masonic principle. But I have long since ceased to attend the Lodges, and have not been a regular member of one for many years. I never made a difference in my life, in any private transaction, or on any public occasion, between those who belonged to the fraternity and those who did not. I never entered a lodge in Europe. I do not recollect ever communicating myself as a Mason to any man in my life. I believe Masonry practically does neither much good nor harm. After saying this much, I must add that I would not renounce or denounce Masonry to be made President of the U.S. not from any force of any obligation which I stand under to it, but from the force of a much higher obligation that of honor. Still, I do not think, my dear Sir, that such an explanation of my feelings as this would do any good, and I therefore request that you will not use it.

The rejection of the Maysville road bill, by the President, has produced great excitement here. It has sealed his fate in Kentucky, and I believe in all the West. Yet I regret his decision. I prefered the certain and present good to that which is future and contingent. I believe moreover that this act was not wanting to ensure his defeat, if a Candidate.

We shall attempt in this quarter an amendment of the Constitution to qualify the Veto, so as to declare that a bill which shall be again passed by a majority of *all* the members elected to both houses, shall become a law. I think such an amendment right. The advantages which supporting it will give us over our opponents, who will oppose it, must be manifest to you. If you approve it, I submit to you the propriety of putting it in motion *immediately* in your quarter.

My friends every where are animated by the highest confidence of success in our cause. Putting together all the information which I have received, I think their confidence well founded. They contemplate the first formal movement next winter at Annapolis.[1] *Perhaps* some important operations may in the mean time take place in this State.

I regret to tell you that the election of R[obert]. Breckenridge [*sic*] to the legislature, for a seat in which he is a Candidate, is far from certain,[2] on a most indefensible ground, that of his having petitioned Congress to abolish the Sunday mails! Altho' it is my opinion that they ought not to be stopt, it is absurd to urge against him such an objection for such an office. . . .

ALS. NBuHi.   1. Johnston to Clay, May 26, 1830.   2. Breckinridge withdrew from the contest, stating his reasons in a letter published in the Lexington *Kentucky Reporter*, August 4, 1830.

To NICHOLAS BIDDLE   Lexington, June 14, 1830

I received your friendly letter of the 3d instant transmitting copies of the two reports made to Congress in relation to the bank of the U.S.[1] These have not reached me yet, but as I had attentively read them, with much satisfaction, it will not be very important if they should not find their destination. Although I hope these documents will do much to avert or weaken the attack meditated on the B. of the U.S. You must not indulge the belief that it will escape assault. Unless I am deceived, by information, received from one of the most intelligent

Citizens of Virginia,[2] the plan was laid at Richmond during a visit made to that place by the Secy. of State [Martin Van Buren] last autumn, to make the destruction of the bank the basis of the next Presidential Election. The message of the President, and other indications, are the supposed consequences of that plan

I cannot accept your congratulations on the fate of the Maysville bill.[3] I most truly and sincerely regret it. I would have prefered its passage, with all the advantages which would have accrued, by that event, to the President, to its rejection with all the political effect against him, which may ensue. This last is likely to be great. Thousands have already renounced their faith. In the neighbouring town of Lexington he has scarcely any friends left, but a few leaders, where he possessed nearly a moiety of the population.

AL. DLC-Nicholas Biddle Papers (DNA, M212, R20).   1. Brown to Clay, April 29, 1830. 2. Brooke to Clay, May 10, 1830.   3. Johnston to Clay, May 26, 1830.

To JOSIAH S. JOHNSTON   Lexington, June 14, 1830
[Comments on where to address Johnston's mail. Continues:]

The decisions of the President, in respect to Internal Improvements,[1] have produced great effect, in this quarter of K. The larger number of all who supported Jackson in the circle of my immediate acquaintance, have left him. Few but desparate leaders remain to him.

Measures have been devised and are now in a train of execution to give expression to public sentiment. It is contemplated to disapprove of the exercise of the Veto,[2] the Indian bill[3] &c. and to propose an amendment to the Constitution requiring only a majority of both houses of Congress (of all elected to each) to pass a bill. returned by the President. I think such an amendment right, and I attach much importance to the discussions which it will provoke.

I saw [Robert P.] Letcher who gave me full information.

I shall not leave K. during the summer except to go to Columbus on professional business. . . .

[Comments on routine legal matter.]

ALS. PHi. Printed with some omissions in Colton, *Clay Correspondence*, 4:278. Addressed to Johnston in Louisville.   1. Johnston to Clay, May 26, 1830.   2. *Ibid.*   3. Johnston to Clay, May 22, 1830.

To FRANCIS T. BROOKE   Lexington, June 16, 1830
I received both your late favors of the 4h. and 6h. instant. In regard to Mr. Craword's [*sic*, William H. Crawford] strange letter,[1] I could not answer it, without violating the regard I once had for him, or the respect due to myself, and therefore I did not answer it. I think his proposal was insulting and derogatory. I do not apprehend that the injury to me, which you fear from my silence, can accrue. 1st Because he says in his letter: "Do not suppose that I feel any solicitude upon the subject of this letter. I feel none. But supposing from what I have seen in the public papers that you may feel some, it occured to me that the most certain mode of gratifying that feeling was to adopt the course which I have suggested. If you should be of a different opinion let the matter rest where it is, and there will no harm have been done. On the contrary should you concur in the suggestion I have made, I shall be happy to hear from you as soon as leisure will permit." This, you will agree, is a strong manifestation of sang froid and disinterestedness. But it also evinces that no

answer was expected, in the event of my disapproval of the proposal, which he seems to have anticipated as *possible*. In the second place, I have communicated the contents of the letter, in confidence, to a sufficient number to protect me against the presumption of any assent of mine, from my silence. Besides there will be no sort of evidence, direct or collateral, of such assent. It seems to me that where a base proposition is made, as I regard this, the most proper treatment of it is silent contempt.

As to publishing his letter, altho I feel no obligation of honor or of confidence which forbids it, I incline to think that under all circumstances it had better not be now done. Mr. C. is not nor likely to be formidable. His friends, 'though few of them are mine, are generally respectable. Their feelings would be affected. He has been high in public confidence. Ought that to be shewn as having been misplaced, especially as he may not be in his right mind?

In regard to [Francis P.] Blair's letter,[2] I took some time ago ago, public ground, from which I think I ought not to recede. I stated that I would not publish it, at the instance of Mr. Amos Kendall, but that it might be seen by any gentleman, and it was seen by many, and by him, 'though not of that number. The infamous story is now stale and cannot be revived even by Tho. Ritchie. I long since resolved to say nothing more to the public about it. I feared indeed that some portion of it may have considered me to have manifested too much sensitiveness concerning it. Such, I am sure, would be the judgment of many, if I were, in any form, again to present myself to the public respecting that matter.

Great sensation has been produced in this quarter about the Presidents course relative to Int. Improvements. Public meetings of the people in various places are about to be had, at which spirited resolves &c will be passed.[3] They mean to attack the [Maysville Road] Veto,[4] by proposing an amendment to the Constitution requiring only a majority of all elected to each branch of Congress, instead of two thirds of a house, to pass a returned bill. Su[c]h an amendt. I think right. If Congress pass a bill, on their own reasons, and again pass the same bill, after full consideration of the reasons of the President in opposition to it, the bill ought to be a law. The policy of proposing such an amendment, in the present condition of parties, is obvious. If our opponents agree to it, it will be adopted. If they oppose it, we shall get the weather gage of them.

Will you mention this matter to [John H.] Pleasants? As he and other of my friends in Virginia approve of the recent exercise of the Veto there may be some objection in espousing an amendment of the Constitution, which has been suggested by what we deem an abuse. But, if on principle, you should agree with us that the amendmt. is proper, it might be supported by you, without reference to the late exercise of power.

The desertions from the Jackson cause are numerous. He has lost the whole West, I verily believe.

ALS. KyU. Printed with the last two sentences deleted in Colton, *Clay Correspondence*, 4:278-80. 1. Crawford to Clay, March 31, 1830. 2. See 4:9-11. 3. Clay to Beatty, June 8, 1830. 4. Johnston to Clay, May 26, 1830.

To EDWARD EVERETT   Lexington, June 16, 1830
I recd. your obliging letter of the 18h. Ulto. I regret that the hope there expressed of defeating the Indian bill[1] was not realized. I have received and read

with much profit and satisfaction the Speech you delivered on the occasion. It is much sought after, and I am sorry that more copies were not sent here. But two, that I know of, have reached us and they have been in constant circulation. Mr. [Thomas] Smith will republish it[2] as soon as he can get rid of the mass of matter upon the all-engrossing topic of the day, the President's course on Internal Improvements. We shall find some compensation, for the loss of the Maysville road &c,[3] in the political effect, which is very great. It seals the fate of Jackson in all the West.

As to the Indian measure, I think our efforts should now be directed to the rejection of Treaties negotiated in pursuance of that abominable law, and to the withholding of appropriations to carry it into effect. With that end, its flagitious character, the disgrace which it would bring upon our name and nation, and its enormous expence should be spread fully before the people. We shall do much, I think, in this quarter. Public meetings of the people are getting up in various places at which spirited resolutions, on both the above subjects, will be adopted.[4] The inherent injustice of the Indian bill will be increased here, in consequence of the expence which it occasions being one of the pretexts for the course pursued in regard to Int. Improvements.

The Veto[5] will also be assailed here not for the purpose of destroying it but so to amend the Constitution as to require only a majority of all elected instead of two thirds of each House. Such an amendment is, in my opinion, proper; and if it be thought so with you, can you not aid us? The advantages which will accrue from the agitation of the question, in any contingency, are manifest, and will at once strike you.

I have concluded, after much consideration, that it is inexpedient for me to leave home this summer, except to go where business calls me. I should have been truly glad to have visited my friends at the North. My heart is with them. But, waiving the matter of personal inconvenience, I am convinced that the public effect would not be good. I hope you will make this decision acceptable in your circle of acquaintance.

Tell your brother [Alexander H. Everett], for Gods sake, to repair the mischief which was done by that very strange article in the Review relating to the removal of the Indians. . . .[6]

ALS. MHi. Printed in Colton, *Clay Correspondence*, 4:273-74.   1. Johnston to Clay, May 22, 1830.   2. Everett's speech has not been found in the Lexington *Kentucky Reporter* June-Dec., 1830. But for the text of his May 19 remarks against the Indian removal bill, see *Register of Debates*, 21 Cong., 1 Sess., 1058-79.   3. Johnston to Clay, May 9, 26, 1830.   4. Clay to Beatty, June 8, 1830; Clay to Speed, June 25, 1830.   5. Johnston to Clay, May 26, 1830.   6. Clay to Everett, May 6, 1830.

From James Brown, Philadelphia, June 17, 1830. Reports that he has been unable to purchase for Clay [Clay to Brown, May 26, 1830] the cattle from John Hare Powel for the price stipulated ($75 per head), as the cattle sold at prices ranging from $200 to $500 per head. Adds: "I am sorry I could not comply with your wishes."

States that he has had a favorable account of Henry Clay, Jr.'s examination at West Point — "He is second in his Class, and has labored hard to come out first, but the youth [Roswell Park] who precedes him has both speed and bottom and will not be overtaken —"

Turns to politics, commenting: "Mr [John] Eaton & his lady [Peggy] are here on their way to Tennessee by Buffaloe [*sic*, Buffalo] & the lake — The President will set out soon for Nashville by the most direct route. His object is said to be that of calling the Indian chiefs to the Hermitage and persuading them to remove — The measures of the last session have made some malcontents even in this steady state, but I think the disatisfaction has not descended to the mass and that the people will yet sustain the Administration—This however is but a loose opinion which cannot be much relied on as I do not mingle much in society or take any active part in politics. Mr [Isaac] Hills election to the Senate affords a proof of the unshaken attachment of New Hampshere [*sic*, Hampshire] to the present administration—Virginia North & South Carolina & Georgia will avail themselves of the Indian Bill and the rejection of the Internal improvements Bills & the repeal of the duties on Salt Tea and Coffee to deline [*sic*, decline] a nullification of the Tariff laws. Indeed the South will warmly support the President—In New York various movements and combinations are going on the objects of which are to me unintelligible—Much as I desire to see you & Mrs Clay, I am yet pleased that you have not travelled North. You would have subjected yourself to much newspaper abuse without promoting any one useful end—." ALS. DLC-TJC (DNA, M212, R10).

From Josiah S. Johnston, Maysville, Ky., June 20, 1830. Reports having been detained a week in Baltimore by fever. Traveled then to Wheeling and on to Maysville; hopes to reach New Orleans by July 1.

Continues: "Our friends separated at Washington with a full understanding, that you Would be the Candidate. & that that fact should be fully made known to the people—That there shall be a popular expression of opinion Simultaneously, in distant quarters of the Country, Which should distinctly point to you, as the only hope of the Country—I trust this will be fully realized—I have charged all our friends to write you on their return home—The public mind seems fully made up with regard to you—& you will present so formidable a front that they will be obliged to Unite & Concentrate all their forces—How the combination will be formed, I cannot say—I think although there is no evidence or disclosure, that a reconciliation is affected or attempted & that necessity will force it—The General was unfriendly to Calhoun & his interest & his friends were systematically postponed to those Van Buren   I think some explanation has been had—& that a reconciliation will grow out of it—The South were dissatisfied. & were meditating a Secession. They intended to erect the Standard of Anti Tarif—anti internal improvement—& bring out Calhoun. They Were not ready to seperate until all hope of restoration Was lost—Everything turn[e]d at this Crisis on the Presidents Course with regard to internal improvement—I have no doubt it was given to him distinctly to Understand that if he approved the bills the south would Secede—& leave him to his fate—I understood distinctly, that every thing rested on that—He has been forced into it—& the Condition is that Calhouns opposition is to be Withdrawn & that the South will support him—"

Adds that he has "no fear of Maryland," and in New Jersey "all is right." Predicts that the "Legislature of Maryland will announce you formally   They are impatient also in Massachusetts—Before the month of Feby you will be fully before the people—I wrote to Genl. [Peter B.] Porter with regard to plans of operation   he will know What to do in N. york—Judge [Ambrose] Spencer promised to write you on the prospects there on his return—I will try to sound Judge [John] McLean at Cincinnati—" ALS. InU.

From HENRY CLAY, JR.   West Point, N.Y., June 23, 1830
I have recd. your letter dated the 13th inst.   You express pleasure at the information, that my late address was well recd. To me, my father, it has been the source of much gratification: I almost feared to attempt the delivery of it; expectation was raised very high; I know not for what reason unless it was the name that I bear—All my friends tell me that it gave general satisfaction, and that it was not unworthy the son of Henry Clay, but that I cannot for a moment flatter myself to be true for with the disadvantages of no practice & no

candid criticism, under which the young men of this Academy must be placed, I do not suppose that I even did my *own* powers justice. I am at present preparing for the exercises of the 4th. July, and I earnestly hope that I shall acquit myself with credit.

In my last, I supposed at the time of writing it, that I had given you all the arguments for & against my leaving here, but after-reflection has suggested some other considerations that may be important, though they do not alter my own opinion as to the propriety of leaving the Academy — The first of these is the effect which a good example set by an elder brother may have on the younger — To carry an arduous undertaking through with credit to oneself is always useful in its influence by affording confidence, but it is particularly useful in inciting the younger members of a family to exertion. The last, is that to abandon such an undertaking as the one in which I am engaged, might appear badly to the world, as so many young men leave here from far different motives from those which I mentioned to you in my last.

My reasons for throwing their arguments out of the consideration are, that I expect by my future conduct at once to do away all the evil influences upon the minds of my younger brothers, that may be caused by my relinquishment of my present pursuits. And besides I shall expect to satisfy my friends by assiduity & attention to business.

I wish my dear father that you would write me your advice immediately. I am now in a state of suspense — I know that you will consider what I have written, a fair statement of the case, for I am now in my 20th. year, at an age when, at least, I should not be influenced by paltry considerations — No! my father I have permitted no disappointment or sudden elation to have the least weight with me; I have formed a cool & deliberate opinion & I hope I have expressed it without evasion or disguise.

I confess frankly that of the next year's studies, I shall take no interest in any but civil engineering & particularly architecture. & this can be learned, I am told in even shorter time than I mentioned to you — To you, my dear father, who have now at your own request the key to my opinions and to my feelings, I leave the decision; whatever it may be you may rest assured that it will be followed implicitly —

Mr [James] Shannon you know is on the board of Visitrs. I have been to see his family frequently & have been treated politely by all & even affectionately by the female part. I have acted upon the impression that sectional feelings & local politics should be forgotten away from home.

William Brand, with a large party of K'[entuck]ians. was here yesterday; among the rest were Mrs [Horace] Holley & Miss Brand.[1] They are going by Boston & the falls of N'[iagar]a to Ky — I have lately been appointed to the most responsible office in the corps, that of Adjutant —

I fear that the report of the Board of Visitors this year will not be so favourable as usual. Some of the most bitter enemies of the Academy are members of it; & Genl [Montfort] Stokes the acting President of the board, seems to labour under prejudices which the dismissal of a son[2] so frequently causes, 'though the sentence may have been just.

Aunt [Mrs. James] Brown has sent me word that she will perhaps visit W[est]. P[oint]. in July.

Give my aff-regards to my mother & the family. . . .

ALS. Henry Clay Memorial Foundation, Lexington, Ky. 1. Probably William Brand's sister Eliza, the only surviving daughter of Clay's friend John Brand. See Perrin, *History of Fayette County, Kentucky*, 566. 2. Montfort S. Stokes, Jr , of N.C., class of 1031. USMA, *Register*, 184.

From Asher Robbins, Newport, R.I., June 23, 1830. Sends a copy of his "speech upon [Samuel A.] Foot's resolution." Notes that it "was intended to aid in rescuing the constitution from the false glosses . . . put upon it" by Sen. John Rowan and others. Says that if "it contributes anything to that effect, I shall flatter myself with the pleasing idea, of having done something, in common with abler men toward putting down, what was fashionably called at Washington & elsewhere, the *nullifying doctrine*." ALS. DLC-HC (DNA, M212, R4). For Robbins's speech on May 30, 1830, see *Register of Debates*, 21 Cong., 1 Sess., 435-47; see also Johnston to Clay, January 26, 1830, and Clay to Robbins, August 23, 1830.

To HENRY CLAY, JR. Lexington, June 25, 1830

I received this day your letter of the 14h. inst. When you went to West Point I told you that if you remained there three years I would not insist upon your continuing longer. I now submit to your own exclusive decision the point of your staying the last year. I do this under a belief that you *now* are more competent to judge of that matter than I am. If I were to express an opinion, it would be altogether founded on the *use* you may make of your time upon your return home. If you abandon or relax your studies, and surrender yourself to the illusions too common to your age, I should think your quitting West Point will have been unfortunate.

Should you decide to resign, as I anticipate, I think it will be proper for you to observe the etiquette which belongs to that resolution, in reference to the Institution & the War Department.

I transmit herewith a check for $100 to be applied to such necessary uses as you may think proper. You ought not to pay more than ½ per Cent to get it discounted. If you want a further sum you may draw upon me for $100 at sight in addition.

I expect to be at Columbus in Ohio from the 12th. to the 20h. of July. Should you decide to resign and come home you may join me there and take a seat in my carriage with me to Ashland, or if you prefer it, you can pass directly from Wheeling down the river to Maysville.

ALS. Henry Clay Memorial Foundation, Lexington, Ky.

From John Sergeant, Philadelphia, June 25, 1830. Reports that the "political atmosphere seems to be unusually agitated just now, and if rational calculation were admissible, one might say that a purifying storm was approaching. But I am not sanguine. Perhaps the lesson of the last election has made too strong an impression upon me." Has reached a personal decision not to be a candidate for Congress again, because doing so "can be of no importance in its bearing upon public matters, while it would be a great and inconvenient private sacrifice." Believes, further, "that my coming forward now might rather do harm than good, by quickening old feelings, now in some degree dying away, & restoring, here, the former party lines, which are somewhat effaced."

Adds that the "current is at this time setting powerfully in your favor, if that be the right phrase for expressing the true state of the matter. It is more nearly this — there is a general and growing sense of the necessity of a change which can be effected only by placing you at the head of the government. If Jackson were out of the way, it would be irresistible. I do not know that the current will not be strong enough to sweep him off too. But the perversity which, in the face of so many unanswerable objections, put him into office, seems still to prevail pretty extensively, and actually to influence men who really wish he were out. His administration is absolutely odious, and yet there is an adherence to the man. It remains to be seen whether this will not yield to the conviction that his continuance must be destructive of every thing that is worthy to be cherished." States that "it is idle to talk about John McLean" for president as some are doing, because the "public eye is *fixed* upon you, and will not be diverted."

Continues: "The latest accounts we have from Washington tell us that Mr. Calhoun and Mr. Van Buren have come to an understanding. Genl. Jackson to go out at the end of his present term, Calhoun to be run for President, and V.B. for Vice Presd. I wish they would announce it. Let the field be once cleared of Jackson, and the rest will be easy, I think."

Concludes with the observation that the "country has now taken you up, and, whether you desire it or not, will make you a candidate. It may be that this state of things will require of you some reserve. . . . It may impose upon you the necessity of in some degree avoiding public occasions, carrying with them the appearance of exertions for yourself." ALS. InU.

To **THOMAS SPEED**   Lexington, June 25, 1830

I recd. your favor of the 16h. As you anticipated I recd. a letter from Bishop of England about a small diplomatic transaction that occured with the Popes Nuncio at Paris, during Mr. Adams's administration.[1] He avowed his object to be political, but expressly acquitted me of all blame in the affair. He can make nothing of it, nor of a civil answer which I wrote him.

There is much political movement in this quarter, public meetings, resolutions &c. relating to the Veto, Internal Improvments, the Indians, an amendt. to the Constitution limiting the Veto &c. You will have seen what was done in Lexn.[2] I was not present but learnt that every thing went off well. I think good, much good will result from those public proceedings. I approve of the amendmt. of the Constitution and your sagacity will at once perceive all the advantages which we shall derive from agitating the question. We ought not to lose the advantages which late acts of the admon have given to us. Prompt bold and spirited measures will secure them.

Intelligence from all quarters through members of Congress, letters, travellers &c. is highly encouraging. The old buck [Andrew Jackson] is mortally wounded. He will run awhile, make a shew of vigor and fall.

Mr. [John] Davis of Massachusetts has anticipated you in answering [George] McDuffie. He (Mr. D) has made one of the best speeches, which were delivered during the Session, and given McDuffie a Waterloo defeat. I am sure you will find it in your taste. It was very much in mine. He prostrated all McDs. positions[3] that imports are equivalent to export duties, that the South pays two thirds of the revenue, and that the *producer* and not the consumer pays the impost.

ALS. NhD.   1. John, Bishop of Charleston, to Clay, May 31, 1830; also 7:372-73.   2. At the meeting in Lexington, held on June 21, nine resolutions were adopted — condemning Jackson's stand on internal improvements and calling for a constitutional amendment allowing Congress to pass a bill over the president's veto by a simple majority vote in both houses; expressing "the strongest disapprobation" of the Indian bill; approving the actions of Kentucky's congressional delegation which contributed to the initial passage of the Maysville Road bill and disapproving the actions of Senators George M. Bibb and John Rowan on matters such as internal improvements, the tariff, and the Indian bill; proposing to nominate Clay for the presidency on the proper occasion and appointing a committee of correspondence to report the success of the meetings. Lexington *Kentucky Reporter*, June 23, 1830.   3. For McDuffie's speech see Clay to Everett, May 6, 1830; for Davis's speech see *Register of Debates*, 21 Cong., 1 Sess., 873-84.

To Joseph Blunt, Lexington, June 29, 1830. Acknowledges receipt of a copy of the *American Annual Register* [5:121]. Notes that "Of all the acts of the present Administration none will give you more pain to record than that relating to the Indians. It is producing great effect in the West, and I should think would have powerful influence in the North. That and other measures of the present Admon have lost it many friends, and cooled the ardor of many more. We share with you in the hope and belief that two years more will set every thing again to rights in our public affairs. Much will however depend upon the course of N. York." Points out, however, that he has "no intention of visiting" the North this summer. "So far as such a visit would have a political aspect (and I fear it would assume that in spite of my wishes) it would be wrong in principle and bad in policy." Takes out a subscription to the *Register*. ALS. Courtesy of J. Winston Coleman, Jr., Lexington, Ky.

To HENRY CLAY, JR.   Lexington, June 30, 1830

I was extremely delighted, my dear Son, to be informed by your letter of the 31st. Ulto. that you had delivered your first address and that it had been received in the most flattering and gratifying manner. I am eager to see it, and hope you will enable me to indulge my curiosity as soon as possible. You say nothing about the coming year. My advice to you is to remain until you close it. I assure you that it will not interfere with the purpose, which I rejoice to find, is now fixed as to your future pursuits. I had hoped to see you at West point, but I now fear that happiness will not be in my power. Public considerations restrain me from visiting places to which my heart and my feelings would carry me.

I have offered Theodore [W. Clay] the alternative of becoming a farmer and grazier or Cotton planter. He starts tomorrow to Indiana, Illinois and Missouri on an exploring expedition. I am anxious to see him settled and doing something. Poor Tom [Thomas Hart Clay], I fear, is irreclaimable. Bad accounts of him come to me from my Prairie [Illinois]. Both these sons have caused me inexpressible pain. But when I turn to you, my dear son, I find relief and consolation. On you my hopes are chiefly encentrd.

Ashland continues to look well. I have never had any crop so promising, or in such a satisfactory state. The farms—the garden—the grounds—my stock all look well and are now doing well.

Anne [Brown Clay Erwin] is in Tennessee. She will join us the last of July or early in August to stay, she says, a long time. I hope she will. The sole survivor of all my daughters, I feel on that account as well as for her excellent qualities, the greatest interest and affection in her.

On dit that Margaret Ross is to be married to young [James O.] Harrison. I wish you would never think of matrimony until you are thirty.

Your mama and the children [James Brown Clay and John Morrison Clay] unite with me in affectionate remembrance

ALS. Henry Clay Memorial Foundation, Lexington, Ky.

From HENRY CLAY, JR.   West Point, N.Y., July 4, 1830

The anniversary of the declaration of Independence was celebrated here on yesterday, from peculiar considerations—I again appeared before an audience of between 4 & 500, and was once more eminently successful. at the dinner given by the Corps, at which about 100 invited guests were present, the wit & eloquence of the sons of Kentucky were toasted with applause—But the toast of Mr. [Frederick] Skinner, the editor of the American farmer & Turf Register; "The Orator of the day, in the language of the turf, Blood will show itself" drew forth enthusiastic cheers—Do not accuse me, my father, of too broad an exhibition of vanity; I confess that I, in common with all my fellow-men, am subjected to that besetting sin of the human race; But I have thought that to you a candid expression of my sentiments would be far more acceptable than any affected air of indifference that I might force from my self-love.

You must know my object in accepting the honors conferred upon me even though prejudicial to my standing in my class. By the way I do not know that I have informed you that I am 3d in general merit for this year, If after the arguments that I have written to you, which were all that I could think of, you still think I had better remain here another year; there is not the smallest particle of doubt that I shall graduate 2d in general merit. My object in twice appearing before an audience at a time when even, with my class, minutes were invaluable, was simply to ascertain certainly my fitness for the law—To the attainment of my object I devoted all the faculties of my mind; and I am happy to be able to say to you I am now fully convinced—

Uncle [James] & Aunt [Ann Hart] Brown are in New York, I expect them up daily.

Remember me affectionately to our friends—Yesterday, in the pride of success & overwhelmed by compliments I was happy   to day, in perplexity and suspense in regard to my future life I am dejected. . . . P.S. I would be glad, if you can make it convenient, if you would send me $25.00 for the purpose of defraying expenses which my new office has rendered it necessary for me to incur.

ALS. Henry Clay Memorial Foundation, Lexington, Ky. Printed in Colton, *Clay Correspondence*, 4:280.

From Samuel B. Beach, New York, July 6, 1830. Inquires about Clay's health, comments on his own, and reports that in September he will take up residence in Richmond, Va. Assures Clay that "Politically, the *public health* is, every day, giving additional tokens of improvement—Rely upon it that I neither deceive you nor myself, when I tell you; that, in this state at, least, every successive week is affording new proof that the people are sick of the Military Idol whom their folly has set up, and of the 'little men' who are the officiating priests in his temple; and are anxious to embrace the first fair occasion for prostrating both. Three months since, I had not the most distant idea that it would be possible to rescue this state from the grasp of the 'Albany Regency.' Now, however, I feel a strong hope that such a result will be produced even as soon as the ensuing gubernatorial election; and quite confident that (if not sooner) it will be effected at the next Presidential election. Even candid Jacksonians begin to admit that the General's popularity is, in this state, sensibly on the decline; and the number is not small, within my personal knowledge, of such as were recently his active friends, but have now become either his covert or open opposers. Rely upon it, my dear Sir, that if the change in other parts of the Union has at all corresponded with what has, with the last six months, taken place in this State, Andrew Jackson could not be reelected, even if the election were to take place tomorrow.—and (as Napoleon said) 'revolutions never go backward.'" ALS. DLC-HC (DNA, M212, R4). For the New York gubernatorial election, see Clay to Johnston, May 9, 1830.

From JOHN SERGEANT   Philadelphia, July 7, 1830
Since writing you a few days ago, matters here have assumed a much more decidedly favorable appearance. One would be led to suppose Jacksonism to be,

as it ought to be, prostrate. At a large dinner in Southwark, where those who were formerly the friends of Jackson composed the company, he was not even named in the toasts. As President, he had not a toast to himself, but it runs thus "The President and Vice President of the U. States." In the upper part of the County, he was only toasted as President. In the City, there was an effort to form a comprehensive union. But it seems to have in a great measure failed. The *working people*, who had a dinner by themselves, did not toast him in any form. So much for the negative demonstrations.

Among the lower classes, especially the Irish, there has been some thing more positive. Jackson has been cursed more loudly and unanimously than any man ever was before. There is an absolute fury against him, as violent as that in his favor was a year ago. Signs of him have been taken down, and one of them burned. The hickory poles have disappeared. It is said, too, that he was hanged in effigy, and buried, upon the ground where Porter was hanged;[1] an instance of vulgar violence which no one can approve, but a decided symptom of change among those who formerly supported him, and upon whom he relied to sustain him in setting decency and justice at defiance.

The immediate cause of the excitement just mentioned is the pardon of Wilson and the execution of Porter. There was no reason for its discrimination, and it is deemed to have been weak and wicked. He ought, it is said, to have pardoned both or neither. There is, undoubtedly, a foundation of justice in the complaint, and if it has had the effect of convincing the people of what is certainly true — that the present administration is both weak and wicked — it has undoubtedly so far worked for the good of the Country.

But this excitement is itself rather the proof of a previous change, than of a change wrought by the cause which has immediately produced it. If he had done the same thing a year ago, I think it would have passed without disapprobation. The causes of this change of feeling are numerous. The silly attack upon the Bank of the U. States, the appointments, the renomination of worthless men, the rejection of the Maysville road bill, the virtual veto upon what is called the Light house bill, the appointment of Randolph,[2] &c have all had an effect to produce great dissatisfaction, and to extort a reluctant acknowledgment of incompetency. The discipline of party has hitherto kept men in their ranks. It remains to be seen whether it will do so any longer. Many of our friends (some who have only become such very lately) think it will not. I sincerely hope, and begin to believe, they are right.

A standard, however, must be raised to rally those who who [*sic*] are now simply in opposition. The time for this, will be the material question — I mean, here, for in other parts of the Country it is already up. Even here, if what I have heard be true, a beginning has been made. A Jackson sign was taken down in the Northern Liberties,[3] paid for, and burnt. A part of the arrangement, it is said, was, that a sign of you should be put up in its place, and the painter has it in hand.

Leaving these local matters, some of them of rather a mobbish nature, the general state of affairs seems to be this — If either of the three States, New York, Pennsylvania or Virginia, should give you her vote, you will be President, "a consummation devoutly to be wished" by every friend of our Country. Indications in the first (New York) are said to be strongly in your favor. Some of our friends maintain, that if you would come to the East by that route, it would be decisive. They have almost persuaded me to be of their opinion, and I wish you to take it into consideration. The question is a public, and not a personal one, and you, I am sure, will so consider it. If it should be practicable, and not inconsistent with your own judgment, you will still have it in your power to use the reserve mentioned in my last, to such extent as may seem proper.

I set out to morrow, with my family, on a tour to New York, Albany, Niagara and Buffalo. I hope to see Mrs. [Peter B.] Porter and congratulate her on the prospect of her prediction being verified. Should any thing occur worth mentioning, I will write to you.

I sincerely congratulate you upon the high standing of your son at West Point. . . . [P.S.] Mr. [Martin] Van buren was here last night on his way to N York. [Samuel D.] Ingham it is said will be here this evening. [John M.] Berrien has been in town several days. [John H.] Eaton is somewhere in the West, and [John] Branch, I believe, is not in Washington. The government is therefore left entirely to the underlings. For reforming pretenders, this is a little extraordinary, otherwise I should think no harm was done, as no hands can be worse than their own.

ALS. InU. 1. George Wilson and James Porter were charged and convicted of robbing a stagecoach which carried the mail between Reading and Harrisburg during the early morning of Dec. 6, 1830. President Jackson pardoned Wilson. Porter was hanged. For the story of the incident, see Samuel Hazard (ed.), *The Register of Pennsylvania Devoted To The Preservation Of Facts And Documents* . . . (Philadelphia, 1830), 5:312-17, 362-63. 2. Johnston to Clay, May 26, 1830. 3. An incorporated district northeast of the city district of Philadelphia. See *PMHB*, 45:385; and Michael Feldberg, *The Philadelphia Riots of 1844* (Westport, Conn., 1975), 11.

From Martin Ruter, Augusta, Ky., July 8, 1830. Informs Clay that the Rev. Mr. Henry B. Bascom, fund-raising agent for the American Colonization Society, is paid only his traveling expenses and "a very small compensation." Notes that the underpaid Bascom must contribute to the support of a "helpless" father. The problem is that Bascom "has been offered $1500-per annum by another benevolent institution, as a compensation for doing for another object what he is now doing for the Coloniz. Society; but refused it, preferring to do all in his power towards the colony at Liberia." Suggests that his personal remuneration be raised to 25 percent of "what he collects," and asks Clay to "hint" to the "proper officers of the Colonization Society" that such a financial arrangement would likely "secure a continuance" of Bascom's important services to the society. Concludes with the observation that Clay's political prospects seem to be improving. ALS. DLC-HC (DNA, M212, R4). For Ruter, a Methodist clergyman and president of Augusta College, Augusta, Ky., see *DAB*.

From HENRY CLAY, JR. West Point, N.Y., July 12, 1830

[Mentions visit of his uncle and aunt, Mr. and Mrs. James Brown, to West Point on July 6-7, their health and the fact that Brown, when asked, "gives it as his unqualified opinion that I ought not to leave the Academy." Continues:]

I explained to him the relations in which the officers of this post stand to the general government, their dependence on the executive for their situations and for extra emoluments. I told him also of the grasping ambition and the intrigues of him at the head of this Institution; as an instance of which, I pointed out to him the case of the present Secretary of War; Mr [John H.] Eaton came here with violent and avowed personal enmity to Col [Sylvanus] Thayer, but in consideration of the personal compliments of honour rendered to himself and the numerous attentions shown to his lady, he surrendered himself a victim to one more skilled in the detection of the weak points of attack which all men more or less leave exposed, and the methods of approach to even the most

234

repulsive—The tone of the Secretary's orders relating to the Academy has been entirely lost; formerly harsh & authoritative, they are now resigned and plainly indicate the subserviency of their author to the views and wishes of the master intriguer [Thayer]—But I am touching on a point on which I have been almost prohibited to speak—

Yet of a Superior who during Mr Adams supremacy was an Adams-man, but who now is a Jackson man, and who may to-morrow, should prospects change be a Clay-man I think I am justifiable in entertaining suspicion   Suspicion, do I say?—No! it is absolute certainty. I am a plain and well marked object of persecution! not of open palpable persecution but of that secret insidious kind which defies exposure—Do not suppose that I complain—To bear your name, to be your son would be to me indemnity a thousand times for the injuries that are inflicted upon me. But do not imagine that I have no friends here among the Officers. Some are my friends on your account and others I am proud to say I have made my friends by my own conduct. Captains [John L.] Gardner & [Ethan Allen] Hitchcock[1] have uniformly treated me with friendship. Captain Gardner is the enemy of the Secretary of War & conformably to the wishes of the Secretary he is an object of suspicion & aversion to the Superintendent of the Academy. By Capt. Hitchcock I have been appointed to the first office in the Corps of Cadets—Many of the young officers are warm friends of mine. But from the Academic Board who are immediately under the direction of Col. Thayer I expect not justice: But I do assuredly believe that distrust & persecution will be my lot as long as I remain here—You repose confidence, I doubt not, in the representations of Col Thayer—But it should be remembered that he belongs to the French school of Politicians. You understand me.

All that I have now mentioned to you I told uncle Brown, and still he advised me to remain here and to show myself superior to the obstacles which may be thrown in my way—I shall graduate 2d in my class, without a doubt, as Col Thayer told me the other evening. Then let me remain since my friends seem to desire it, & heaven grant that I may never oppose the ignorance and inexperience of youth to the advice springing from age experience & discrimination which my friends have so kindly tendered to me—

[Concludes with a statement of his affection for the Browns and his plan to visit them later in the summer at Ballston Springs, N.Y.]

ALS. Henry Clay Memorial Foundation, Lexington, Ky.   1. For Gardner, see *DAB*; for Hitchcock, see USMA, *Register*, 174.

To JOHN SLOANE   Columbus, Ohio, July 16, 1830

Among the agreeable anticipations which I made on coming here one was that I should see you. In that I have been disappointed, but I have the satisfaction to receive your favor of the 12h. inst.   I am glad to be put by you in possession of your view of the state of things in your quarter, altho' it is not very encouraging. In K[entucky]. I think we are authorized to conclude 1st. that the fever of Jacksonism is greatly abated generally; and 2dly. that many have openly and some covertly have renounced its faith. The beneficial effects we believe will be exhibited in our elections next month, as to the result of which we feel great confidence.[1]

In those parts of your State through which I have passed I should infer that similar effects have arisen, though perhaps not in the same degree. We shall see at your polls in the autumn.[2]

I learn that it is the purpose of my friends to present my name as a Candidate at the next P. election, unless circumstances not to be foreseen should prevent it. I think they have been right in avoiding to assume the responsibility of first agitating that question. This responsibility is attached to the other party, by the movements at Albany and Harrisburg.[3]

I have met many old and made many new friends here. Indeed my room has been the greater part of the period of my sojourn filled with Company. Our friends appear to be in excellent spirits; and generally express much confidence in the results of your elections. They consider the Jackson nomination of a Candidate for Governor[4] as having been made under circumstances not calculated to acquire for it much confidence; and they speak of its defeat with strong convictions.

It has been my purpose, during this journey, to avoid public entertainments; and yet at all the towns I am surrounded with large concourses of people, by all of whom I have been treated with great respect. I shall return next week by the way of the Yellow Springs and Cincinnati, and shall adhere to my purpose of declining invitations to public entertainments.[5]

ALS. MH.   1. Clay to Beatty, May 4, 1830.   2. In the Ohio elections held on Oct. 12, Clay supporters won 37 seats in the house to 35 for the Jacksonians, while the Jacksonians carried the senate 18 to 17. Cincinnati *Daily Gazette*, Oct. 18, 30, 1830.   3. Johnston to Clay, April 13, 1830.   4. The Jacksonian candidate, Robert Lucas, lost to the Clay candidate, Gen. Duncan McArthur. Cincinnati *Advertiser*, Oct. 20, 1830.   5. On July 26, 1830, writing from Yellow Springs, Ohio, to John Test *et al.*, Clay accepted an invitation to attend a public dinner at Lawrenceburg, Ind., on August 4. ALS. Courtesy of Maurice K. Gordon, Madisonville, Ky. On July 27, he told Joseph Vance in Urbana, Ohio that "They made me violate at Columbus my resolution to avoid public entertainments. The affair went off however admirably well, and I have no doubt that the local effect will be good. My only fear is how it will be regarded at a distance. I shall not again depart from my resolution, unless it be to yield to a very pressing invitation which I have recd. from Lawrenceburg." He also told Vance that he had received "an extremely cordial welcome at Springfield," Ohio, and that "wherever I have been the most hearty demonstrations accompany me." AL, signature removed. OHi. For other invitations to public dinners, see Milton Stapp *et al.* (Madison, Ind.) to Clay, July 31, 1830. ALS. DLC-HC (DNA, M212, R4).

To Adam Beatty, July 19, 1830. Reports that sentiment in Ohio with respect to the recent "popular movements in Kentucky" in support of Clay is that "they are very proper, must do good, and can do no harm." Argues that the "time is now passed" to leave the "other party to its own divisions," since it is apparent "that an opposition will be made to the re-election of its chief [Andrew Jackson]." Mentions "highly encouraging" political news from New York State, and the fact that he has seen many people from "all parts of this State" during his trip into Ohio. ALS. Courtesy of Earl M. Ratzer, Highland Park, Ill. Printed in Colton, *Clay Correspondence*, 4:280-81. Written from Columbus, Ohio.

From "The Fredonian," [Columbus, Ohio(?)], July 22, 1830. Raises the question of the nation's future, noting that "our affairs wear a sickly and a very gloomy aspect; our hopes hang on the Constitution of the country and the good sense of the people; and our fears arise from the dread of the conflicting passions and prejudices of the most angry and ill directed course pursued by a new set of politicians of this our day, now making a direct assault on the long established practices, usages, principles and institutions of the country." Announces that he will address future letters to Clay in the "public prints." Copy. Printed in Columbus *Ohio State Journal*, July 22, 1830.

From John Mercer, "Cedar Park," West River, Md., July 22, 1830. Reports on a political rally on July 4 "on Elkridge" of the "friends of the Union, the Constitution, Domestic Manufacturers & Internal Improvements, or in other Words, of your friends, both personal & political." The success of this meeting, together with "the clamorous voice of dissatisfaction which is now heard throughout our State," has induced the Jacksonians "to abandon the contest for our County [Anne Arundel]." Says that from the "best information I can obtain not a shadow of doubt remains of our recovering a complete ascendancy in the State at the next election." Reports that a similar meeting will be held on August 20 "at which some notice will be taken of the present state of things." Concludes with a detailed reply to Clay's inquiry of June 25 ("the subject of your letter") about establishing, stocking, and managing the game in the deer park. ALS. DLC-HC (DNA, M212, R4). For Cedar Park estate and Mercer, see J. Reaney Kelly, "Cedar Park, Its People and Its History," *MHM*, (March, 1963), 58:30-53.

After the 1829 election for the Maryland house of delegates, the Clay party held an edge of 40-39; but the Jacksonians still controlled the senate which was chosen every 5 years by an electoral college. It was not due for reelection until 1831. In 1830, the Clay party swept the house of delegates election by the margin of 64-16. The following year in the house they maintained their majority of more than 2 to 1 and also won a majority of the senatorial electors which allowed them to choose the entire state senate. See Mark H. Haller, "The Rise of the Jackson Party in Maryland, 1820-1829," *JSH* (August, 1962), 28:307-26.

SPEECH AT COLUMBUS, OHIO

July 22, 1830

Mr. Clay rose, and after having stated the unmixed purpose of his present visit to Columbus to have been to fulfil an old professional engagement, he remarked that prior to his departure from home, he had resolved to avoid attending any public entertainments, should he be honored with the offer of any. Acting in conformity with that resolution, he had already declined several; and he had, at first, determined to ask to be excused from accepting this.[1] But his wish in that respect had been overruled by the earnest persuasions of some of his friends among the mechanics, by the motive so honorable to their hearts, which had prompted them, of their own accord, to offer him this distinguished testimony, partly in consequence of incidents which had occurred here during his sojourn, and by the very high respect which he entertained for the mechanics and other laboring portions of the community. From no source could such a compliment, tendered to him, be more acceptable. To the mechanic and other arts, we are indebted for all the comforts and elegancies of human life. Without them, fields could not be cleared or tilled, cities built, or oceans navigated. The degree of their success and prosperity, always indicated the happiness, power and glory of nations. Mr. C. drew illustrations of this remark, from the condition of ancient and modern times.

Considerations like these had, at an early period of his public career, induced him to espouse the cause of protecting native industry. He traced the progress, and demonstrated the success of the system. If preserved and continued, he did not doubt that it would ultimately realize every hope and promise of its founders.

Connected with this system, he considered Internal Improvements. It had been indeed proclaimed, from high authority, that there existed no relation between them. If it were meant to assert merely the incorrectness of the imputation, that one system was fraudulently upheld in order to sustain the other, he agreed to the truth of the assertion. In no other sense, however, could it, he conceived, be correctly alleged that there was no connection between the two. They are intimately, and he hoped indissolubly united. Whilst at Washington the statement is put forth that the one system has no dependence upon, or relation to the other, an opinion directly the reverse is asserted at Charleston. There it is maintained by a Senator of the United States [Robert Y. Hayne] high in the confidence of the present Administration, and exerting a powerful influence in the control of its measures, that the Tariff and Internal Improvements are united; and exulting in the overthrow of Internal Improvements, produced by the Veto applied to the Maysville Turnpike,[2] that Senator predicts that the policy of protection will not long survive their death. Mr. C. hoped that his prediction will be as far from being fulfilled, as his recent Waterloo defeat, in the Senate of the Union will be memorable, when he attempted to subvert the fundamental principle of all Republics, that the majority ought to govern, and to substitute in its place the right of a minority, no larger than a single State, to nullify the deliberate legislative acts of the whole.

The object of the one system of policy, is to produce; of the other, to distribute. And of what avail will it be that the barns of the farmer are overflowing, and the shops and warehouses of the mechanic and manufacturer are filled with fabrics of their industry, skill and ingenuity, if there be no roads and canals to distribute them among the consumers? On the other hand, of what avail would roads and canals be, if we had not products to transport?

Of all parts of the Union, the West is most deeply interested in the prosecution of Internal Improvements. This resulted from its interior situation and remoteness from the Sea. Without them, the West could not participate in the expenditure of the vast revenues collected by the general government. Other sections of the Union want a Navy, fortifications, and all the train of improvements, breakwaters, lighthouses, &c. necessary to secure and invigorate the foreign and coasting trade. They ought to have them. The West has cheerfully co-operated in granting them; and he trusted, would continue to do so. But, in their turn, they ought to unite, for their own sakes, as well as for the West, in the establishment of a system which is useful to all, and indispensable to the prosperity of the Western country. He trusted that the West would never in any contingency, pause to calculate the value of this Union. Whatever might be the fate of Internal Improvements, that Union was of inestimable benefit. But it might well appeal to the justice, liberality and fraternal feelings of other portions of our common country, to sustain the only system of policy in which it had a direct and immediate interest.

Mr. Clay regretted a late unfavorable indication in respect to this important interest. He could not concur in the reasons assigned for the rejection of the Maysville bill. — He could not think of that measure without the deepest surprize, regret and mortification. No State in the Union had more zealously devoted itself to the cause of Internal Improvements than Kentucky. This it had done upon those broad, liberal and national considerations, which had ever guided the conduct of the people of that State in respect to the general government. Scarcely any State in the Union had enjoyed so little direct advantage from the exercises of the power by the General Government, as that State. Not one cent of the public treasure of the Union had ever been applied to the erection of any Road or Canal within its limits, except to that at Louisville, in which other States are much more interested than she is. Under such circumstances, to be selected as the first victim; to have a most important Road lying within that State, though a mere link of a much more extensive chain reaching into other States, singled out for the application of an extraordinary power: to be designated as the State, in regard to whose interests the

238

settled practice of the government, during a period of 25 years, must be over-turned and set aside—was, to say the least of it, very hard.

The present President, Mr. Clay did not doubt, had, with the most patri-otic intentions, when in the Senate of the United States voted for an appro-priation to a Canal, of only about 14 miles in extent, in the State of Delaware, uniting the waters of the Delaware and Chesapeake. That Canal was com-menced, and has been completed, by an incorporated Company. He presumed that the President gave it his support, because he thought the object was a national one. Mr. C. thought so too, and voted for it. But if it be national, that character cannot be derived from its length, but from the purposes and uses to which, in war as well as in peace, it might be applied. That is the true criterion; and if it be applied to the Maysville Road, Mr. C. must think that it ought to be considered as a national work, whether regarded by itself, or in connection with contemplated prolongations of it Northwestwardly and Southwestwardly.

The opponents of those systems of National policy have promulgated their plan of warfare. It is to attack in detail; to separate and destroy in succession. To overthrow Internal Improvements to-day; and then they boast the Tariff will not long survive their death. Upon the Tariff, they made a beginning at the last session. They reduced the duties on Salt and Molasses, and restored the drawback on Spirits distilled from Molasses. They have thus materially af-fected some of the few items in which the West had any direct interest.

Another important feature in their scheme of hostilities, is to attack and destroy, if possible, all those who are alleged or supposed to have had weight in laying the foundations of the American System. Hence, he had been pur-sued, persecuted and proscribed with a bitterness unexampled in the annals of Christian communities. They are very much mistaken who suppose that the calumnies which have been directed against him, and which have been con-tinued, with unabated fury, even after his retirement into private life, proceed from the election of Mr. Adams. They are very much mistaken who suppose that his opponents believe that he deviated from his duty, and violated the wishes of his constituents, in bestowing his suffrages upon that illustrious man. What! Can they be sincere in such a charge when those very consti-tuents, in the fall of 1828, upon the question between him and the present President being directly put to them, gave exactly the same vote for Mr Adams which they *alone* had empowered Mr. C. to give in February? No! No! It was not his participation in the election or Administration of Mr. Adams, that whetted the instruments of attack upon him; it was because he entertained cer-tain opinions as to the policy which it became this country to pursue.

His opponents did him, even in the motive of their violent assaults upon him, unintentionally too much honor. The existence and the preservation of the American System did not depend upon so frail a circumstances as his life. It sprang from a much higher, more important and more durable cause. It arose out of the wants and necessities of the nation and long, long after the short remnant of his days are spent, it will be borne and upheld upon the shoulders of a nation.

Why, if he has not correctly described the real cause of the continued at-tacks upon him, have they still been persevered in? He is now a private man, the humblest among the humble. He has no Army, no Navy, no power, no pa-tronage, no subsidized press, no official corps to offer its homage. He has nothing but the unbought affections of his countrymen. His opponents possess

239

all the honors and the offices, and the emoluments of government. Are all these unava[i]ling, *"whilst Mordecai the Jew stands at the King's gate?"*[3]

Copy. Reprinted in Cincinnati *American* of August 5, 1830, from an article in the Columbus *Ohio State Journal*, July 23, 1830. The address, in identical form, was also carried in the Washington *Daily National Journal* of August 5, 1830, reprinted from the *Ohio State Journal*. No manuscript version of the speech has been found. 1. The meeting at which Clay spoke was held at the Market Place. Some 350 to 400 people ("many of whom were Mechanics from this town") sat down to dinner at 2:00 p.m. The reporter present noted that Clay "used no notes" and left town without having had time to prepare a written version of his remarks for publication. This version, then, contains only "some idea of the principal points alluded to in the address" which "we have obtained from a friend" who made a "brief and imperfect outline of it" shortly after it was completed. The reporter noted also that "These are some of the topics as substantially touched by Mr. CLAY. There were many others of which we cannot undertake to give any account." Clay concluded with the toast: "COLUMBUS—It has the surest guaranty of its continued growth and prosperity, in the spirit, enterprise and respectability of its mechanics." 2. Johnston to Clay, May 9, 26, 1830. 3. For the invitation to Clay to speak, see Joseph Ridgway *et al.* to Clay (Columbus), July 19, 1830; for Clay's acceptance, see Clay to Ridgway *et al.* (Columbus), July 20, 1830. This exchange was published in the Washington *Daily National Journal*, August 5.

From PETER B. PORTER   New York, July 25, 1830

I received your favour of the 13th Ult. before I left home, but I did not *then* answer it, because I perceived by the Western papers, that you were about commencing a professional tour through the state of Ohio, which, I concluded, would consume several weeks. I regret very much that you have given up the idea of visiting the state of New York, not only because it deprives us of the personal gratification which we anticipated from it, but because, knowing that you would be received, every where, with cordiality, and even with enthusiasm, I had thought that the political effect would be highly favourable—I am aware however that the expediency of such a trip, presents a question, on both sides of which much may be urged. Your observations on the subject of Anti-Masonry entirely correspond with my own views, and are such as I expected.

The "signs" from every part of the union are highly propitious; and the manifestations of approbation & confidence which are every where shewing themselves in favour of "the Father of the American System" promise the most favourable results. The State of New York is at present, as it has often before been, a political chaos, and it is impossible to say what are the precise forces which will eventually emerge. It seems however to be pretty well ascertained that a decided majority of the people are opposed to the present administration bothe of the State and General government, but the great difficulty lies in combining the discordant materials of which this majority is composed so as to give them effect and more especially as regards the domestic policy of the state, about which there is a great diversity of opinions & views. In this city two thirds at least of the electors are in open hostility to the State Government, or, to what is called the *regency* of which V[an]. Buren is the head, & nearly the same proportion, secretly if not openly opposed to Jackson &c. I have been in town nearly a week and seen most of the leaders of the several sects. The great difficulty—and it will perhaps be insurmountable—is to select a candidate for Governor who will reconcile their discordant views; and *as regards this office*, it will probably be the policy of the old straight going republicans not to make any nomination but leave it to every one to vote either for [Francis] Granger, [Erastus] Root, or any other one as he may think proper. But great expectations are entertained that, by concert & union, tickets in opposition to the general admn may be formed & successfully carried. I have seen, in the course

240

of the week, Mr [William H.] Maynard[1] & Mr. [Thurlow] Weed, who are the two leading men of the Anti masonic party. They are extremely anxious that no candidate (other than Root, who will be brought on the course in some shape) should be put up to interfere with Granger, in which case they have great hopes that the latter will succeed. They inform us that their intention is, not to make a nomination at Philadelphia[2] but to go for you — a few weeks will test the sincerity of these professions. On the whole I think I may safely say to you that if the city of New York shall, at the fall election, go against the Jackson party, the *whole state* will follow next year — as *every* political revolution in the state, within my recollection, and there have been many, has commenced in this city.

I send you the first number of a political paper (The Age) just established in this city & devoted exclusively to your support. The Proprietor, Mr. Mallory,[3] an old democrat, is warmly & unalterably your friend & will make any sacrafice to sustain the great principles which have marked your political course. My only fear respecting it is that it may not have all the talent that could be desired — but he is promised assistance from our friends who, if not too long, are abundantly able to sustain it with credit.

I am here attending to the business of my accounts as Boundary Commissioner [2:162], the settlement of which I did not press under the late administration on account of the delicacy of the relation in which I stood to the Executive, and in regard to which the present admn are endeavoring to annoy me to the full extent of their ingenuity & power. I think however that I shall defeat their purpose. My trial will take place before the U.S. District Court at Albany on the 10th of August.[4] I will inform you of the result as I will also of any interesting occurrences which may take place in the interval, which I shall spend here, at Albany, and the springs.

ALS. InU.   1. For Maynard, a lawyer, see Jabez D. Hammond, *The History of Political Parties in the State of New York* . . . (Syracuse, 1852), 2:420-21.   2. The Anti-Masons met Sept. 11, 1830, in Philadelphia to hold a national convention. Francis Granger served as president of the convention which was attended by 96 members from 11 states. An "Address to the People" was agreed upon, and the convention adopted a report recommending a further convention on Sept. 26, 1831, in Baltimore to nominate candidates for president and vice president. See, further, Washington *Daily National Journal*, Sept. 15, 20, 1830, and William P. Vaughn, *The Antimasonic Party in the United States 1826-1843* (Lexington, Ky., 1983), 33, 54-55.   3. Possibly Daniel Mallory, later (1844) campaign biographer of Clay. The Cincinnati *American*, August 5, 1830, states that no. 1 of *The Age* was published by John M. Danforth. Only three copies of *The Age* are extant. The earliest — Sept. 18, 1830, located at The Huntington Library — states that it was published every Saturday evening by Jacob Acker at No. 8, Nassau Street, New York City. The two others, located at the Library of Congress and the New York Historical Society, are dated in 1831. In Sept., 1831, *The Age* merged with the New York *Evening Journal*. Washington *Daily National Intelligencer*, Sept. 21, 1831.   4. Porter's legal problem arose out of his accounts as a commissioner under Article VI of the Treaty of Ghent to determine the Northern boundary to the Lake of the Woods. See Porter to Clay, Oct. 6, 1830, for its resolution.

Speech at Yellow Springs, Ohio, July 27, 1830. According to a newspaper account, Clay spoke for 20 or 30 minutes to a dinner audience of about 200, some 30 to 40 of whom were women. These last Clay referred to as "the fairest and sweetest flowers in the bouquet of Life." That having been said, he then "took a manly and republican stand in favor of Internal Improvements, the American System, and the '*Union of the States.*' He alluded in eloquent and feeling terms to the persecutions of the poor Indians and gave some 'home thrusts' at the 'Nullifying System' of the Hotspurs of the South." He concluded with this toast: "THE UNION — Its laws paramount — Its bond unbroken but by the COMMON CONSENT of its members." Copy. Printed in Washington

Daily National Journal, August 7, 1830; reprinted from the Xenia (Ohio) *Backwoodsman*, July 29, 1830. No manuscript version of the speech has been found.

From Andrew Hunter, Charles Town, Jefferson County, Va., July 28, 1830. Condemns Andrew Jackson's policy of proscription, noting that he himself was dismissed "from a petty Clerkship" in the War Department "worth $800.00 a year" for having opposed the "shameful persecution and proscription of Col [James] Stubblefield," superintendent of the arsenal at Harpers Ferry, Va. Asks if an amusing anecdote in which Clay had skillfully pacified an irate constituent who opposed his support of the controversial Compensation Act of 1817 [2:171-72, 284-87] was true. Whether true or not, Hunter had written it up and had it published recently in the Harpers Ferry *Free Press*. Believes that "an overwhelming majority of us" in his "part of Virginia" support Clay for the presidency. ALS. DLC-HC (DNA, M212, R4).

From Nathan Sargent, New York, July 28, 1830. Sends Clay the "first and second numbers of a magazine, the publication of which I have lately commenced in this city." Knows that since Peter B. Porter has just written Clay [July 25] the political news of New York State, "I will only remark, that Mr. V.B [Van Buren] seems to be a good deal alarmed, as I think he has reason to be, for the fate of the [Albany] Regency — the working men's party, being composed of that class of men whom he has formerly flattered, cadjoled, and — used, is an enemy that will require all the cunning & management for which the world gives him credit, to conquer or controul — They will most assuredly carry the city elections next fall, against St. Tamany [*sic*, Tammany], unless they split among themselves." ALS. DLC-TJC (DNA, M212, R13). Sargent and Abraham Halsey founded the *Magazine of Useful and Entertaining Knowledge* in New York City which lasted for about one year, 1830-31. The first two numbers were called *Mechanics and Farmers' Magazine of Useful Knowledge.* Frank L. Mott, *A History of American Magazines, 1741-1850* (New York, 1930), 1:363.

From "The Fredonian," [Columbus, Ohio(?)], July 29, 1830. Refers to his letter of July 22 and states again that "The clouds which overcast our political atmosphere indicate a gathering storm." Calls attention to the "splendid Administration" of John Quincy Adams, "when new breath was breathed into our manufacturing establishments and they once more revived and stood up. But now I must confess, Sir, that I have my hopes and fears." Among the latter is the time "when the dark dispensations of revolt and insurrections may surround us." Copy. Printed in Columbus *Ohio State Journal*, July 29, 1830.

From Moses Dawson, Cincinnati, August 3, 1830. Announces that it is his intention to publish the enclosed article in his newspaper, the Cincinnati *Advertiser*, "to-morrow morning." Submits it to Clay today "in order that you may have as much time as possible both to consider the propriety of answering the proposition, and to prepare your answers, provided you think it expedient to notice them." Copy. Printed in Washington *United States Telegraph*, August 18, 1830. The enclosed article, printed in *ibid.*, criticized Clay for spending too much time in his speeches explaining his personal conduct and attacking Jackson's. Urges Clay to "waive those subjects entirely" and, instead, emphasize his views on the Bank of the United States and on the internal improvements issue.

Speech at Cincinnati, August 3, 1830. Defends the Bank of the United States as it is presently administered. Attacks President Jackson's conception of a national bank [Clay to Biddle, January 2, 1830], as outlined in his annual message to Congress on December 8, 1829. Thinks such a bank "would be an institution of a dangerous and alarming character; and that, fraught as it would be with the most corrupting tendencies, it might be made powerfully instrumental in overturning our liberties." As to whether or not the charter of the existing bank should be renewed in 1836, that "is a question of expediency to be decided by the then existing state of the country. . . . The question is premature." Explains and defends at length the American System, dismissing specific objections and arguments against it (mainly from critics associated with the American cotton and wool businesses), and noting that "to the laboring classes it is invaluable, since it increases and multiplies the demands for their industry, and gives them an option of employments." Concludes, further, "that, so far as the sale of the great southern staple is concerned, a greater quantity is sold and consumed, and consequently better prices are obtained, under the operation of the American system, than would be without it."

Asks why South Carolina's planters and "some of her politicians" attack the American System. "What is there in her condition which warrants their assertion, that she is oppressed by a government to which she stands in the mere relation of a colony? She is oppressed by a great reduction in the price of manufactured articles of consumption. She is oppressed by the advantage of two markets for the sale of her valuable staple, and for the purchase of objects required by her wants. She is oppressed by better prices for that staple than she could command if the system to which they object did not exist. She is oppressed by the option of purchasing cheaper and better articles, the produce of the hands of American freemen, instead of dearer and worse articles, the produce of the hands of British subjects. She is oppressed by the measures of a government in which she has had, for many years, a larger proportion of power and influence, at home and abroad, than any state in the whole union, in comparison with the population." In spite of this, South Carolina has embraced a doctrine [nullification] "as new as it would be alarming, if it were sustained by numbers in proportion to the zeal and fervid eloquence with which it is inculcated. I call it a novel doctrine." Points out that even during the controversy surrounding the Alien and Sedition Acts in 1798-1799, "No one contended that a *single* state possessed the power to annul the deliberate acts of the whole." On the other hand, "That the states *collectively* may interpose their authority to check the evils of federal usurpation, is manifest. They may dissolve the union. They may alter at pleasure the character of the constitution, by amendment; they may annul any acts purporting to have been passed in conformity to it, or they may, by their elections, change the functionaries to whom the administration of its powers is confided. But no one state, by itself, is competent to accomplish these objects. The power of a single state to annul an act of the whole, has been reserved for the discovery of some politicians in South Carolina." Argues that a state simply cannot nullify an act of Congress and "remain a member of the union." For "if one state can, by an act of its separate power, absolve itself from the obligations of a law of congress, and continue a part of the union, it could hardly be expected that any other state would render obedience to the same law. Either every other state would follow the nullifying example, or congress would feel itself constrained, by a sense of equal duty to all parts of the union, to repeal altogether the nullified law. Thus, the doctrine of South Carolina, although it nominally assumes to act for one state only, in effect, would be legislating for the whole union." Such a situation, if accepted, "would practically subject the unrepresented people of all other parts of the union to the arbitrary and despotic power of one state." The exercise of this "tremendous power claimed for South Carolina" cannot therefore be allowed. Indeed, "Under the South Carolina doctrine, if established, the consequence would be a dissolution of the union, immediate, inevitable, irresistible. There would be twenty-four chances to one against its continued existence." At the same time, threatened nullification of a tariff act is particularly difficult to understand since the protective tariff is so clearly constitutional and has been in operation since the beginning of the nation. If a tariff act can be nullified, "there is scarcely a statute in our code" that cannot similarly be overturned. As for threatening disunion over the tariff: "If the unhappy case should ever occur of a state being really desirous to separate itself from the union, it would present two questions. The first would be whether it had a right to withdraw, without the common consent of the members; and supposing, as I believe, no such right to exist, whether it would be expedient to yield consent. Although there may be power to prevent a secession, it might be deemed politic to allow it. It might be considered expedient to permit the refractory state to take the portion of goods that falleth to her, to suffer her to gather her all together, and to go off with her living. But, if a state should be willing, and allowed thus to depart and to renounce her future portion of the inheritance of this great, glorious and prosperous republic, she would speedily return." Is convinced, however, that talk of nullification and disunion over a tariff issue is mainly a political device to dismantle the entire American System piece by piece.

Attacks President Jackson's veto of the Maysville Road bill [Johnston to Clay, May 26, 1830] on narrow constitutional grounds and notes, for the record, that "the veto message is perfectly irreconcilable with the previous acts, votes, and opinions of gen. Jackson. It does not express *his* opinions, but those of his advisers and counsellors, especially those of his cabinet. If we look at the composition of that cabinet, we cannot doubt it." Remarks that he has heard it said, and "I believe it to be true," that while Jackson was considering the Maysville matter he was waited upon by "some of the gentlemen from the south" who informed him "that if he approved of that bill, the south would no longer approve of him, but oppose his administration." Says that as he reads and rereads the veto message he can think only of "diplomacy, and the name of Talleyrand" because the language is so artfully balanced on the subject of internal improvements that one might "extract from the message texts enough to support" almost any opinion. Proceeds to dissect Jackson's "piebald message" point by point. Argues specifically that the cost of the road to the Federal government would have little to do with retiring the public debt and maintains that the road itself would have been an important segment of an extensive national network. Moreover, "if the road facilitates, in a considerable degree, the transportation of the mail to a considerable portion of the union, and, at the same time, promotes internal commence among several states, and may tend to accelerate the movement of armies and the distribution of the munitions of war—it is of national consideration. Tested by this, the true rule, the Maysville road was undoubtedly national."

Complains that while Kentucky's representatives in Washington have consistently supported Federal appropriations for internal improvements, "Not one cent of the common treasure has been expended on any public road in that state." Charges, further, that Jackson's veto was aimed at "the measures of policy which I have espoused, against the system which I have labored to uphold." Assures his audience, however, that the principles of the American System will long outlive Henry Clay and that his political destruction will in no way reverse the tide. "Long, long after I am gone . . . the offspring of those measures shall remain."

Asks, in conclusion: "Why then am I thus pursued, my words perverted and distorted, my acts misrepresented? Why do more than a hundred presses daily point their cannon at me, and thunder forth their peals of abuse and detraction? . . . People of Ohio here assembled . . . ask yourselves, if I ought to be the unremitting object of perpetual calumny?" Copy. Printed in *Niles' Register* (August 3, 1830), 39:25-31. See also Johnston to Clay, May 26, 1830; and Daniel Drake to Clay, August 9, 1830. For the composition of this speech, see Clay to Greene, August 16, 1830.

Clay had received a letter of August 2, 1830, from Lyman Watson *et al.*, representing the mechanics and working men of Cincinnati, in which they invited him to a "Public Collation" in his honor on August 3. Copy. Printed in Cincinnati *American*, August 5, 1830. Clay replied the same day, accepting the invitation. *Ibid.*

From "The Fredonian," [Columbus, Ohio(?)], August 5, 1830. Refers to his letters of July 22 and 29. Asserts that Clay's political career has been "brilliant" and that "your enemies denied you the talents you possess as a Statesman until you passed the fiery ordeal of four years opposition and persecution." Says he heard Clay's "*maiden* Speech (so called)" in the Kentucky legislature in 1803 [1:123-24] and, that from that point on, Clay has demonstrated "consistency of character" and has been a "consistent man." Reviews Clay's constructive public career at the state, sectional, and national levels. Sees the nation moving toward barbarism and calls on Clay and builders like him "to guide our public concerns, and save us as a people, from sinking into ruin." Copy. Printed in Columbus *Ohio State Journal*, August 5, 1830.

From Samuel L. Southard, Trenton, N.J., August 8, 1830. Reports on the health and welfare of his wife and children, and on his busy law practice. As for politics, "I rejoice in the present aspect of politics — it does seem to me, as if the nation was about to be restored to correct opinions. You will, I hope, find justice & the people, safety. We shall have a severe struggle — and a doubtful one — the toils have been strongly laid in our State, & I fear we cannot break them soon eno' for the next Election — but we shall try. The effort will save us before the pres[identia]l Election comes on. One of the best symptoms is, that the Jackson papers here, have recently opened ferociously upon me — They would not do this, if they did not feel in some danger. I believe that your Election, depends in great measure on the anti-masonic excitement, being so directed that it shall not oppose you. It has great power in several of the States, and if it can be so governed, as not to thwart the views of your friends, all will be safe." ASL. InU. On September 26 the New Jersey legislature met and by majority vote in a joint session re-elected Peter D. Vroom, a Jacksonian, as governor. *BDGUS*, 3:1014-15 and *Niles' Register* (November 6, 1830) 39:171. Following the October legislative election in New Jersey, the Jacksonian majority on a joint house and senate ballot was reduced from 29 to 20. *Niles' Register* (October 23, 1830), 39:137-8. In the congressional election in New Jersey on December 28 & 29, all six National Republican candidates were elected. *Ibid.* (December 4, 1830; January 8, 1831), 39:241, 329. For the 1832 presidential election in New Jersy, see Vance to Clay, December 28, 1829.

From Daniel Drake, Cincinnati, August 9, 1830. Recommends that Clay not permit the publication and distribution of his Cincinnati speech of August 3, 1830. Explains: "On the various subjects embraced in it (with the exception of the S. Carolina doctrines,) your opinions have long since been made known to the American people, in speeches which will continue to be read for ages. Was this published, it would, by the enemies of yourself and of the system which you advocate (I might almost say, have originated) be referred to, as a new and inferior edition of what you had before given to the world. Inferior, because less extended and elaborated. Moreover, if divested of the personal allusions, the humour, & the sarcasm (all perfectly fair and just) which made it so piquant and palatable, it would be read with less interest than it was heard; while, if it were published with those aromatic garnishings, it would furnish fresh aliment to the presses which are arrayed against you and the system to which you are indissolubly bound." ALS. DLC-HC (DNA, M212, R4). The speech was published in *Niles' Register* (September 4, 1830), 39:25-32.

From WILLIAM B. LAWRENCE   New York, August 9, 1830

I have delayed expressing my acknowledgments for the polite attentions, which you were so kind as to extend to me during my late visit to Lexington, in hopes of being able to communicate something of interest from this section of the country. No decisive demonstration of public opinion has, as yet, been made in this state & of the measures likely to be taken preparatory to the autumnal elections you have no doubt received correct information. Perhaps, however, the result of my enquiries, in conjunction with the statements of other correspondents, may not be wholly useless in enabling our friends elsewhere to form an estimate of the political aspect of things here.

Sensible of the moral influence that would be produced throughout the Union by the defeat of Mr. Van Buren's party in New York and of the great danger that, numerically a minority, they might by their better organization prevail against opponents having in some respects distinct objects, it was deemed by many of our friends a matter of great moment that such arrangements should be made, as that the Anti-administration candidates, especially for Governor & Congress, might receive a combined support. As yet, however, the peculiar grounds on which the opposition in the Western part of this State rests, as well as some of the views of the "working mens," (who constitute a considerable portion of the Anti-Van Buren electors in this City, & the other large towns,) have presented obstacles which those, whose exertions are directed to an object of a far more general character, have not been able to overcome. But, should the Anti-Masonic Convention, the proceedings of which will reach you before this letter, be, according to the assurances of the leading men of the party, prudent & conciliatory, it is believed that Mr [Francis] Granger will be generally supported by the friends of the late administration and, if Genl. [Erastus] Root is not a candidate, by the workingmen. With the aid of the latter party Granger would certainly be elected. Much must, therefore, depend on the course adopted by the Jacksonians as to Genl. Root and the conduct that he himself in certain contingencies may think proper to pursue. He is the decided favourite of the ale-house politicians of both the old parties of the State. Strenuous efforts are making by these individuals to have him nominated at the regular convention at Herkimer.[1] Should Mr. Van Buren's friends find themselves obliged to yield to the popular demonstration, Genl. Root will with little doubt, be chosen by the people. In the event however of his being unsuccessful with his old associates, the working-men are confident that he will accept a nomination from them. If he yields to their request, a sufficient number of the Jackson party may desert the regular candidate to ensure Mr. Granger's election, an absolute majority not being required by our Constitution — This last result I deem, on the whole, the most probable.

What may be the effect of Genl. Root's nomination at Herkimer & election on the great cause now at issue before the country, cannot be so easily conjectured. It is evident that, if assented to by Mr Van Buren, it would only be as a jus alles & some of Genl. Root's supporters, with seeming confidence, declare, that his predilections as to a candidate for the next Presidency agree with our own. It is, however, to be remembered that his character can afford us no guaranty against the machinations of those by whom he will be surrounded & that the source of his nomination will almost impose an obligation of acting with the men with whom it is his boast to have hitherto uniformly cooperated.

I may here remark that great dissatisfaction is understood to exist among the former adherents of Govr. [DeWitt] Clinton, numbers of whom joined the opposition to the last administration from attachment to their leader. They have not received what they conceive to be a due share of attention from either the State or general government. on the contrary, some of them, who were previously in office, have been removed to make way for Mr. Van Buren's earlier friends. They have recently given, I am assured from respectable sources, pretty clear indications of an intention no longer to rally under the standard of our present rulers.

During my absence at the West some meetings were held of individuals opposed to the present administration and, besides a General Committee of

Vigilance, a committee of correspondence, of which John L. Lawrence (formerly Chargé in Sweden) is chairman, was formed. The views of these gentlemen are understood to be against the expedency of any distinct nomination of a Governor by your friends as such, but either hereafter to support Mr. Granger or, in case of there being three candidates, to allow the electors who rely on their recommendation to vote for Mr. Granger or Genl. Root at the same time, no efforts will be left untried as to Congress and the state legislature. Absence from the city during Genl. [Peter B.] Porter's recent visit prevented my renewing the acquaintance formed with him at Black Rock on my way home, but I am informed that the above course meets his approbation.

Whatever may be the difficulty of effecting, at this time, a cooperation among the different fractions of the opposition, it is believed that there will be no impediment to a union of the members elected by them to the legislature, especially as on a most important point the party is, I am convinced, of one opinion. There is, therefore, a reasonable chance of our being able to choose the Senator who will supply Mr. [Nathan] Sanford's place.[2] My journey through the western part of the State satisfied me that whatever influence the fervor of anti-masonry may have on the local elections, those among the party who regulate public opinion are not less decided in their attachment to the correct side in general politics. I have also conversed, since my return, with some of the organs of the working men's party and found them decidedly favourable to our Presidential candidate. They assured me that such were the general sentiments of the party, but, as there were still some Jackson-men among them, they deemed it expedient to defer any declaration till after the next state election. I will only add by way of explanation, that the committees &c. of the workingmen are, with few exceptions, mechanics or persons literally engaged in manual labour and that it is to the moderation & good sense of this class of society we, in the city of New York, must look for respectab[le] candidates, as we cannot yet venture to appear there under any other colours.

Of the congressional elections[3] a majority will be opposed to Genl. Jackson and Mr. Van Bu[ren] but in the city of New York such is the reputation of [Churchill C.] Cambreleng among the merchants that I fea[r] even the exertions of the working men will not to [sic] be able to assist him.[4] I should not, however, consider the vote for Congress as any indication of the one which two years hen[ce] will be given for Presidential electors. Many of the independent Voters, who are unconnected with party, will not support members of Congress favourable to high ta[xes] though they will be found on other grounds strenuous in their opposition to the presen[t] administration. Should, therefore, the opposition place on our ticket the avowed advo[cate] of protecting duties the result would not be a fair indication of your strength in this part of the State. Mr. John A. King will run for Congress from the adjoining district (Long Island) with a fair chance of being elected.[5]

Mr. Cambreleng told me, a few days ago that, by accounts received since the adjournm[ent] of Congress, Mr. [Louis] McLane still had hopes of success.[6] From other sources equally good I learn that every effort has failed. Mr. McLane has expressed a wish to return.[7] The claimants o[f] France have received no intimation of the progress of the negotiation in that country; [I] have, however, been indirectly informed that Mr. [William C.] Rives has not advanced one step in the business. . . .[8]

ALS. DLC-HC (DNA, M212, R4).   1. The Herkimer convention met on Sept. 8 and on the second ballot nominated Enos T. Throop for governor and Edward P. Livingston for lt. governor. *Niles' Register* (Sept. 18, 1830), 39:58-59.   2. William L. Marcy, a Jacksonian, replaced Nathan Sanford, a Clay supporter, as U.S. senator in 1831. The vote in caucus, which was tantamount to election, was Marcy 77, Erastus Root 15, and Sanford 6. *Ibid.* (Feb. 12, 1831), 39:427.   3. In the 21st Congress, Jacksonians held 18 of New York's house seats, while Clay supporters held 15; in the 22nd Congress, Jacksonians held 23 compared to 11 for Clay supporters. *Ibid.* (Nov. 13, 20, 1830), 39:187, 202.   4. In the New York City multi-seat congressional district C.C. Cambreleng, Gulian C. Verplanck, and Campbell P. White were the nominees of the "Regular Republican" or pro-Jackson ticket. Abraham R. Lawrence, A. Chandler, and T. R. Smith were the candidates of the so-called Clay Workingmen's party which comprised a variety of anti-Jackson groups and was endorsed by the Anti-Masons. Thomas Hertell, Isaac Pearce, and John Frazee were candidates for the Liberal Workingmen's or Frances ("Fanny") Wright tickets; and Thomas Skidmore, Alden Potter, and John Tuthill were the Agrarian or Poor Man's party (also called Skidmore party) nominees. In the November election the entire Regular Republican [Jackson] ticket was elected, garnering an average of about 10,000 votes to 7,000 for the Clay Workingmen's ticket, 2,000 for the Liberal Workingmen and 125 for the Agrarian ticket. New York *Evening Post*, Nov. 1, 8, 1830.   5. King, a Jacksonian, defeated the incumbent James Strong. *Ibid.*, Nov. 5, 1830.   6. Probably in arranging for the reentry of U.S. ships into the British West Indian trade. See 2:839; 3:729; 4:180, 417, 941-42; 5:632, 831-35; 6:316.   7. McLane sailed from Britain on July 1, 1831, and his successor, Martin Van Buren, arrived in London on Sept. 13. Beckles Willson, *America's Ambassadors to England (1785-1929)* (New York, 1929), 192-94.   8. Of negotiating a claims convention with France. See 2:846; 3:52-53, 312-13; 5:29-31; 6:113. The Convention Concerning Claims and Duties on Wines and Cottons was concluded by Rives on July 4, 1831. It was ratified Feb. 2, 1832, and proclaimed July 13, 1832. Clive Parry (ed.), *The Consolidated Treaty Series* (Dobbs Ferry, N.Y., 1969), 82:97-103.

From Robert W. Stoddard, Geneva, N.Y., August 9, 1830. Notes that "In a former letter I intimated that it was very probable that the Antimasons would be prevailed upon not to nominate a candidate for the Presidency at their Convention to be held in Phila, next month. I am now *satisfied* that the Antimasons of this State, with scarce an exception, will be opposed to making any such nomination at all." Believes also that Francis Granger "may be regarded as a friend of the American System." Reports that the Albany Regency is in a decline which Van Buren himself has been unable to halt, and that "Our next State election, which comes on this fall will be one of strangest sort that has ever occurred in New York since the declaration of independence. It affords this satisfactory evidence, that all parties & factions in the State, and we have enough of them, are united in one respect, however disunited they may be in every other—and that is to put down the Regency influence." Reports that there has been "a monstrous falling off of the friends of the Hero [Jackson]" in New York, and that there is little chance now that the Anti-Masons might support John C. Calhoun. Moreover, "The Antis are American System men—They will never go for one who is known to be opposed to that measure, or who is even equivocal with respect to it. They have had a forcible lesson set them by the Hero, who, during the last canvas was mightily taken with a 'judicious' tariff. They will not therefore be taken in again by hollow professions of that sort."

Remarks on the good political news from Louisiana and opines that "On the whole I think matters are looking pretty well every where, except in this State, where no one can tell how they look because they look every way. Order may grow out of our confusion. Much will depend upon how the City of New York goes—At present appearances seem to indicate a favourable change in that City—But from long acquaintance with the manner of conducting elections there, and of the means by which parties triumph in that City, I cannot undertake to say that implicit confidence ought to be placed in them—" ALS. DLC-HC (DNA, M212, R4). The election for members of the New York state assembly on November 1, 1830, returned 91 Republicans, 32 Anti-Masons, and 4 listed as Clay, Federal, or Workers. New York *Evening Post*, November 12, 1830. The Tammany ticket for all offices, state and local, was overwhelmingly successful in New York City. *Ibid.*, November 8, 1830. See also Clay to Johnston, May 9, 1830.

Stoddard was among the early lawyers in Geneva, N.Y.   George S. Conover (ed.), *History of Ontario County* (Syracuse, N.Y., 1893), 174.

From "The Fredonian," [Columbus, Ohio(?)], August 12, 1830. Comments on the structure of the federal government and argues that a major factor holding the "National Confederation" together is and has been internal improvements—"Roads, Canals, Steamboats, and machinery." Argues, further, that "a confederated republic like ours requires that our public men should be philosophers and statesmen, and not mere grabbing politicians and *office hunters*." Asks that the "Good Lord deliver us" from those in power today. Copy. Printed in Columbus *Ohio State Journal*, August 12, 1830.

From Christopher Hughes, Stockholm, Sweden, August 12, 1830. Remarks that he last wrote Clay from Paris, "a short while before the late wonderful revolution, which so completely changed the face and order of things in France [Hughes to Clay, April 18, 1830.]" Comments on the immediate influence of the revolution in Italy, some of the German states, Poland, and Belgium. Notes the related fall of Lord Wellington's Tory cabinet and the coming to power of Earl Grey and a Whig cabinet committed to the redistribution of seats in Parliament and the extension of the franchise. Describes these events as a "*a Revolution*, achieved by the People of England, without battle or bloodshed. . . . Reform became inevitable, *certain*, after the passage of the Catholic Relief [Emancipation] Bill." Claims he knew all this was coming because of his personal connections with England's "wisest and oldest Statesmen" and a "long tête à tête conversation" with Lord Wellington "as far back as March 1830." Is convinced that "Parl. Reform . . . was powerfully accelerated by the events in France," and that the "whole of Europe in fact, has been agitated and stirred up by the July Revolution at Paris; and terror has been carried to the hearts of Tyrants." Attributes the fact that Europe has recently remained at peace to the Polish insurrection and to "the diversion and occupation" it gave to counter-revolutionary Russian aims in Belgium and France. Without the Poles, "all Europe would have been, long since, in a blaze," a fact to which Lafayette called attention in remarks in the French Chamber.

Comments on the social life of the Swedish court and on the political attitudes found among the people. "The *Nation* has shown great sympathy with the Poles; the *Royalty* . . . unwisely shew sympathy on 'tother side." Reasserts his "devoted & unalterable attachment" to Clay. Discusses at length the activities, education, and artistic talents of his 13-year-old son, Charles. ALS. DLC-HC (DNA, M212, R4).

To ALEXANDER H. EVERETT   Lexington, August 14, 1830
Your letter of the 10h. Ulto. is received informing me of your having been placed by the Legislative Convention of Massachusetts at the head of the central Comee. of correspondence &c. and requesting a direct correspondence with me. It will afford me great pleasure to comply with your request; but at the same time I must say that the opinions of my friends are much more competent than mine, to advise or direct the general operations to promote the success of our cause. My duty perhaps is one of passiveness and neutrality of action, 'though that may be impossible as to feeling.

Whilst I am inexpressibly gratified with the friendly sentiments towards me which prevail in Massachusetts and throughout New England, I think it was politic in your General Assembly to forbear, at its late Session, to make any nomination. Under all existing circumstances, I am inclined to believe, that it is better that Massachusetts and New England generally should rather follow than take the lead in a formal nomination. Yet I believe the time for Legislative action will have arrived at the approaching winter Sessions. Hitherto it was wisest, perhaps, on the part of our friends, to forbear, to allow the public mind and feelings to sober down, and to throw the responsibility of commencing the agitation of the next Presidential election upon our opponents. All this has been accomplished. Henceforward, our flag should be unfurled, and we should march to the victory, which awaits us, with a prompt, fearless, and confident, step.

Our general election has just terminated. We shall have a majority on joint ballot in the Legislature composed in both houses of 138 members, of not less than 12 and possibly 18.[1] We ought to have had at least thirty. But, in four of our strongest Counties owing to collisions among friends, injudicious selections of Candidates, the impossibility of making the presidential election bear on the elections, and local causes, we lost, by small majorities, five. In other Counties also, owing to some of these causes, we lost where we ought to have gained. Notwithstanding, the general result of all the elections is highly cheering and favorable. It demonstrates a great decline of the Jackson cause and a proportionate increase of ours. It proves that now, on collateral elections, there is a majority of five thousand against our adversaries; and if the direct question had been before the people it would not have been less than from ten to fifteen thousand. [John] Rowan's defeat is certain, and the election of a friend will take place.[2]

The first returns from Indiana[3] and Missouri,[4] whose elections were on the same day of ours, are coming in, and if those which follow are equally good, they exhibit still more encouraging results than the Kentucky election. Louisiana is all that we could wish it.[5] We have not yet heard from Illinois.[6] The elections in Ohio[7] take place in October, and we count with much confidence upon success there.

Upon the whole and judging from existing data, I think that the States of Ohio, Kentucky, Indiana, Illinois, Missouri and Louisiana may be counted upon in all human probability. I believe that we shall hold the Hero a skuffle even in Tennessee and Mississippi; and the signs in Virginia[8] are such as to justify our calculating on that State with quite as much confidence as Jackson can.

I regretted the article in the N[orth]. A[merican]. review on the Indian Subject;[9] and I should rejoice to see its injurious effect done away. Taking the Union throughout, I am inclined to think that the policy of the present administration, in reference to that question, operates more powerfully against it than any other single subject.

I understand that a Comee. raised in Lexington will shortly address a circular on our late Elections. Mean time be pleased to shew this confidentially to your brother [Edward], Mr. [Daniel] Webster and any other friends.

ALS. MHi. Marked "(Confidential)."   1. Clay to Beatty, May 4, 1830.   2. Clay to Beatty, June 8, 1830.   3. In Indiana, Clay supporters won 33 seats in the house to 28 for the Jacksonians, and in the senate 18 to 5 for the Jacksonians. *Niles' Register* (Sept. 11, 1830), 39:55.   4. Clay supporters won a majority in the Missouri legislature of at least 7 and possibly 10. *Ibid.*   5. Clay to Johnston, March 11, 1830.   6. In the Illinois gubernatorial race John Reynolds, a Democratic-Republican, was elected over William Kinney, a Jacksonian-Democrat, by a vote of 12,837 to 8,938. Although both were friendly to Jackson, Clay followers supported Reynolds who favored the tariff and internal improvements. Results of the election for the legislature were so mixed that it was impossible immediately to tell which party was victorious. In January, 1831, however, the state legislature chose two Jacksonians as U.S. senators, indicating that the Jacksonians controlled the legislature. See Washington *Daily National Journal*, Sept. 14, 1830; *Niles' Register* (Sept. 11, 1830; Jan. 8, 1831), 39:55, 333; *BDGUS*, 1:367-68.   7. Clay to Sloane, July 16, 1830.   8. In Tennessee, William Carroll was reelected governor with no opposition in 1831, while five Democrats, one Whig, and one whose party was unknown were elected to Congress. *BDGUS*, 4:1469, and *Niles' Register*

(August 27, 1831), 40:449. Mississippi did not elect state legislators in 1830, but in the U.S. House race a Jacksonian, Franklin Plummer, was elected with 4,148 votes or 35 percent of the total number of votes in a 6-man race. The National Republican candidate John H. Norton, was fourth with 1,398 votes. See Edwin Miles, *Jacksonian Democracy in Mississippi* (Chapel Hill, 1960), 29-32; *Niles' Register* (Sept. 25, 1830), 39:74. Since Virginia's political parties were aligned more on the basis of sectionalism within the state and the states' rights issue generally than on divisions based on national parties or candidates, it is difficult to determine the party make-up of the legislature which was chosen in Oct., 1830. A correspondent of the Winchester (Va.) *Republican*, however, estimated that the house of delegates was composed of 68 Calhoun men, 50 Jackson men, and 48 Clay men. Washington *Daily National Intelligencer*, April 20, 1831. In Jan., 1831, John Floyd, a states' rights advocate, was unanimously elected governor by the legislature. *Niles' Register* (Feb. 19, 1831), 39:443. For the outcome of the 1832 presidential election in these states, see Sergeant to Clay, June 27, 1831. 9. Clay to Everett, May 6, 1830.

To JAMES F. CONOVER   Lexington, August 16, 1830

I have transmitted to Mr. [William] Greene, Chairman of the Comee. &c. a Sketch of my Speech delivered [August 3] at Cincinnati. On the question of the propriety of its publication, I have addressed a letter to my friend Dr. [Daniel] Drake,[1] to which I refer you. Altho stript of the advantages of oral delivery, I think the strength of the argument has been improved. But I submit it to my friends to decide whether it shall be published or not, being ready to acquiesce in their decision cheerfully, whatever it may be. Should their decision be against its publication, I hope you will be able to make some apology to the public which may be deemed sufficient.

The news from Indiana,[2] Illinois,[3] and Missouri,[4] so far as it has reached me, is highly encouraging. It affords grounds to conclude that far more than I expected has been accomplished. . . .

ALS. ViU.   1. Drake to Clay, August 9, 1830.   2. Clay to Everett, August 14, 1830.
3. *Ibid.*   4. *Ibid.*

To WILLIAM GREENE   Lexington, August 16, 1830

According to the promise which I made, prior to my departure from Cincinnati, I transmit, herewith, the Speech which I delivered there [August 3]. It embodies substantially all I said on that occasion, 'though some of the ideas and arguments are spread out to a greater extent, and it may contain a few not then expressed, but which were uttered by me at other places.

I have written to Dr. [Daniel] Drake and beg you to peruse my letter to him on the subject of the Speech.[1] My opinion remains that it may be productive of more good than harm, if published. But this opinion is not to be put in competition with that of my friends, to whose decision for or against the publication I cheerfully submit. . . .

ALS. OHi.   1. See Clay to Conover, this date.

From Baron Paul de Krudener, Philadelphia, August 16, 1830. Announces that Emperor Nicholas I has approved his [de Krudener] departure from the United States. "Having notified my departure to Mr. Van Buren and considering myself now as a mere traveller and Spectator, I feel no remorse in expressing to you my decided partiality, and my hope, of seeing the Presidential Chair and the Federal government, restored by you to their former dignity." ALS. DLC-HC (DNA, M212, R4). Printed in Colton, *Clay Correspondence*, 4:281-82.

From Robert Wickliffe, Jr., Lexington, August 16, 1830. Reports that the trustees of Transylvania University are considering erecting a building to be called Morrison Hall

[5:185]. Wants to know what amount of James Morrison's estate is in Clay's hands, to what extent and in what amount can this money be made available to pay for the building, whether all the specific legacies in Morrison's will have been paid, and whether the provisions in the will for Mrs. Morrison have been satisfactorily arranged. Asks also if the debts and claims on the estate have been paid, and requests that Clay provide the trustees with a statement of the land (and its probable value) that Morrison had held or claimed in Kentucky and other states at the time of his death. ALS. KyLxT. For Morrison's will, particularly the bequests to Mrs. Morrison and Transylvania, see 3:496, 507-8; 7:28. The complete will is in Fayette County Will Book, F 61-70.

To Francis T. Brooke, August 17, 1830. Doubts that a letter purportedly written by Thomas Jefferson to "some Manufacturer in Massachusetts," published recently in the Providence (R.I.) *Literary Subaltern,* by its editor, Sylvester S. Southworth, is genuine. This because it uses the term "American system, the first application of which, within my recollection, to the Tariff, was made by myself, in my published speech on that subject in 1824 [3:701], posterior to the date of the letter." Thinks that in publishing the letter, Southworth acted "improperly" and with "intemperate zeal." Asks what he should do about it.

Notes also that "about three years ago" the late Col. Thomas M. Randolph had "attributed to Mr. Jefferson some very disparaging opinions of me, and published them [6:974]." These were inaccurate. Soon after the statements appeared, Randolph's son, Thomas Jefferson Randolph, wrote Clay to set the record straight. "I could make no use of it during the life of the father, for obvious reasons." But after the father's death, the son gave Clay "permission to use it as I pleased." Asks Brooke how best now to get young Randolph's letter before the public, since "I observe that the statement of Col. R. is again relied upon to obviate the effect of the Southworth letter. . . . The publication of this letter will destroy the effect of Col. R. statement, & prove that Mr. Jefferson entertained friendly sentiments."

Concludes with observations on state-wide elections in Kentucky, Indiana, Illinois, and Missouri in language virtually identical with that employed in other letters of this date. ALS. KyU. Printed in Colton, *Clay Correspondence,* 4:482-84. See Brooke to Clay, Sept. 9, 1830; also Merrill D. Peterson, *The Jeffersonain Image in the American Mind* (New York, 1960), 25-26.

To Philip R. Fendall, August 17, 1830. Reports that the "proofs of the progress of our cause have been of late very strong." Believes that "The plan of conducting the [Washington *Daily National*] Journal, by putting into it numerous extracts from other papers, appears to me highly judicous. The facts or arguments contained in those extracts produce all the effect which they would do if they were contained in original articles whilst the extracts themselves are *evidence* of public opinion at all the points from which they are taken." Asks that if Daniel Mallory, "a stedfast friend," publishes another edition of his (Clay's) speeches, Fendall assist him in enlarging the collection by supplementing the original speeches with those he has since given at Noble's Inn, Lexington [July 12, 1827], Fowler's Garden, Lexington [May 16, 1829], Frankfort [December 17, 1829], Baltimore [May 13, 1829], Washington [March 7, 1829], and Cincinnati [August 3, 1830]. Reports that "Mr. Pierce [*sic*] (who is now in Lexington)" is writing a "Biographical account of me, which although I did not desire it, I did not feel at liberty to oppose." Hopes Mallory will find the Pierce sketch sufficient to his needs.

Comments on the political situation: "Our elections in Kentucky have just terminate[d]. We have secured a majority on joint ballot in the Legislature not less than 12 and which may amount to 18. But for the operation of local causes, unfortunate divisions among candidates of our party, and the difficulty of making the Presidential question every where bear, our majority would not have been less than thirty. The result, however, shows that there is a majority now not less than five thousand against Jackson, and it would have been from ten to fifteen, if the direct question had been before the people. [John] Rowan will *certainly* be permitted to remain at home. As far as we have received returns from Missouri, Indiana and Illinois, those States have done better than our own [Clay to Everett, August 14, 1830]. [David] Barton's re-election is considered certain."

Concludes with a personal request: "The decision of the pauper cause in my favor against my woman Lotty [7:622-24, 631-33], renders it expedient that I should get her at home. She is I believe in Mr. [Martin] Van Buren's service. Will you do me the favor to look her out, and tell her that I wish her to return. She ought to have means to bring herself home, as she has been receiving her own here for the last eighteen months; but if she wants money for that purpose I will thank you to apply to Mr. R[ichard]. Smith to advance her the necessary sum. If she shews any perverse or refractory disposition be pleased to have her imprisoned until I can hear of it, and give the necessary directions." ALS. KyLoF. See also Clay to Beatty, May 4, 1830, for results of the 1830 general assembly elections in Kentucky; and Clay to Johnston, August, 26, 1829, for a comparison of the 1830 race with the 1829 state canvass, the results of which had been more favorable to the Clay forces. Sen. David Barton of Missouri was replaced by Alexander Buckner. *Congressional Quarterly's Guide to U.S. Elections* (Washington, 1975), 469; and *Niles' Register* (December 25, 1830; January 8, 1831) 39:302, 334. "Mr. Pierce" is probably a reference to George D. Prentice who published *Biography of Henry Clay*. New York, 1831. There are apparently no extant copies of the first edition of Mallory's *The Life and Speeches of the Hon. Henry Clay. . . .* 2nd ed., New York, 1843. Here he is possibly referring to Mallory's, *A Biography of Henry Clay, the Senator from Kentucky . . . Containing a Complete Report of All His Speeches*. New York, n.d.

Clay's comments on the political scene in Kentucky, Missouri, Indiana, and Illinois are repeated in almost identical language in a "confidential" letter of this same date to John W. Taylor in Ballston, N.Y. ALS. NHi. Also repeated in a similar letter to Joseph Vance of this date. ALS. KyU.

From "The Fredonian," [Columbus, Ohio(?)], August 19, 1830. Refers to his preceding letters [July 22, 29; August 5, 12, 1830]. Laments the rise of the spirit of party and asks, "Whither, Sir, has the spirit of liberty fled?" Comments on the abuses of the Jackson administration. "When I now think of it, I tremble for my country! I say, Sir, then, that our present struggle is for liberty and national independence. I regard the present contest of our country, to be one between the people and their rulers. . . . the demagogues of our *degenerate* day." Believes, however, that "good may grow out of evil, by affording future generations a beacon to be held long in remembrance; and the future historians will point to the statesman and say, 'there lies the rock on which your national ship, made its first wreck — avoid it and pass by!'" Copy. Printed in Columbus *Ohio State Journal*, August 19, 1830.

From William Greene, Cincinnati, August 19, 1830. In response to Clay's letter of August 16, has held conferences with some of Clay's supporters on the question of publishing his Cincinnati speech of August 3. The "very strong [re]vision" suggested by "our excellent friend," Dr. Daniel Drake [Drake to Clay, August 9, 1830], was not sustained, and "the speech goes this night to the press without a single dissenting voice —" It will appear in Charles Hammond's Cincinnati *Daily Gazette* and James F. Conover's Cincinnati *American* on Monday, August 23. On politics in general, "this Jackson business, — certain[ly] in this Western country — is getting to be an up hill work — Of one thing I feel abundantly assured; let the *excitement* of the last three years ever get down & it will be exceeding[ly] difficult to get it up again — I cannot help thinking that there are thousands who are held to the [Jac]kson ranks merely by pride of opinion, & [wh]o only want an apology to desert, to make them ours — Another year — and still *another*—and we cannot fail—unless we yield the theory of public virtue & intelligence as the basis of our system—we cannot fail, I say, to see wondrous changes in the complexion of the public mind—" ALS. DLC-HC (DNA, M212, R4).

From Andrew Swift, Chillicothe, Ohio, August 20, 1830. Sends Clay a hat made in his Chillicothe factory as a "small token of the very high respect I entertain for your early constant and able exertions in favour of domes[tic] industry." ALS. DLC-TJC (DNA, M212, R10).

On September 2, 1830, Clay wrote Swift, thanking him for the hat which "is a fine specimen of the excellence of your manufacture" and which "fits me exactly." Copy. Printed in Cincinnati *American*, September 27, 1830.

From John L. Lawrence, New York, August 21, 1830. Remarks that the "last advices from Kentucky have dissipated the gloom produced among some of our friends by the prior accounts." Argues, however, that political circumstances in Kentucky "point imperatively to the necessity of a *general* organization, as essential to Success in the great contest which is in prospect.—" Points out that a national party organization built on distinct principles must be created before it is too late. "We have lost, at least for a Season, much Strength which a bold and manly course would have secured to us." Gives as an example the aggressiveness of the Anti-Masons ("these miserable fanatics") in New York State. Wonders if it is not now "too late for your friends to make arrangements to nominate a candidate of their own for Governor"; but notes that the Workingmen's party "may probably give us a candidate whom we can Support, and who will bring out all our votes on the Congressional & Legislative elections."

Concludes: "The aspect of the times seems to shew the absolute necessity of a general organization of our forces throughout the Union. It is essential that we give System to our future operations—that we prevent individual claims from clashing with the general interests—that we break up the factions which are fraudulently trading on our capital—and present the party before the Nation, in that attitude, which its actual force and its honest pretensions entitle it to assume. How is this to be effected?—Either by a movement of our friends in Congress, or by the recommendation of some central Committee of one of the Western States. The latter would be preferable, because it would operate more rapidly Silently, and therefore effectually. A circular should b[e] addressed to confidential & active friends in different [parts of] each State, who Should Set the machine [in motio]n in their own particular neighborhood. [In the tr]ain of Such a measure, would follow, the esta[blish]ment of general & official committees of Supervision and correspondence, in every State District County & town; mutual communication and co-operation would give vigurus confidence and effect to our efforts;—and the real opponents of our present misrule, knowing where to attach themselves to make their power felt, would no longer Seek Strange leaders, or be deluded by the devices of the enemy." ALS. DLC-HC (DNA, M212, R4).

To Edward Everett, August 22, 1830. Repeats, almost verbatim, the political news of Kentucky, Missouri, Indiana, and Illinois contained in his August 17 letter to Phillip R. Fendall. Adds that Ohio will do "equally well," and that the "proceedings in Maine appear to me judicious." Concludes: "From all that I can gather, the Antimasons are disposed to support me—rather, I should say, their Leaders. Mr. [Richard] Rush will not accept their nomination of him, if one should be tendered. He will do what he can to give them a right direction. Of what they may however certainly do at Philada. I am not able to say. I think, if the candidate should be Jackson, they will not support him. If any other, their weight could hardly ensure his election. I persevere in keeping unmixed with that strife." ALS. MHi. Written from Olympian Springs, Ky.

To JEREMIAH EVARTS   Olympian Springs, Ky., August 23, 1830
[Thanks him for his letter of January 22, 1830 (not found) which was apparently mislaid until "a few days past." Continues:]

I enter heartily into all your[1] feelings and sympathies on the subject of that letter; and the paragraph in my [December 17, 1829] Colonization Speech, to which you refer, was intended to indicate my opinions. I read, with great satisfaction, the numbers of William Penn,[2] and thank you for the copy of them which you transmitted to me; as well as for the Missionary Herald,[3] for which I did not before know to whom I was indebted.

The condition of the Indian question is very much varied since the date of your letter; and it is now too late to promote its particular object, that of a memorial to Congress in behalf of the aborigines. At any time, considering my relations to the President, and to the public, I should have doubted the propriety of a formal discourse on their subject from me. But since the publication of the able debates in both houses of Congress, in which their rights are so fully vindicated, and their wrongs so eloquently depicted, it would be altogether unnecessary, if it were not otherwise objectionable. Now, I think, the best thing to be done is, to defeat the execution of a bill, the passage of which could not be prevented. With that view, I think, an extensive circulation of those debates is advisable, and also of an address recently published from the Indians to the people of the U. States, in which their injuries are so feelingly described. It would also aid their cause very much, if the religious bodies, throughout the Union, would espouse it. The female sex is generally on their side, and a co-operation between that and the Clergy would have powerful, if not decisive influence.

I had hoped to have seen before now an article in the N. A. Review counteracting the effect of a previous article injudiously admitted into that work.[4] Such a counter action is due to the public.

If the Indians remain firm and refuse to treat, I believe they will ultimately be successful. Public opinion is with them; justice is on their side; honor, humanity, the national character, and our Holy religion all plead for them. With such advocates they ought to prevail, and they will prevail, if their friends are not too inactive.

ALS. DLC-HC (DNA, M212, R21). Addressed to the Rev. Mr. Evarts in Boston, Mass.   1. For Evarts, a lawyer and philanthropist, see *DAB*.   2. Using the pseudonym, "William Penn," Evarts had written *Essays on the Present Crisis in the Condition of the American Indians*. Boston, 1829. 3. Evarts was editor of the *Missionary Herald*, the organ of the American Board of Commissioners for Foreign Missions, which was published in Charlestown, Mass.   4. Clay to Everett, May 6, 1830.

To Asher Robbins, Newport, R.I., August 23, 1830. Thanks him for the copy of the speech enclosed in his letter of June 23 and trusts that "it may contribute yet to rescue our Country from the foul stain which the execution of the Indian bill [Johnston to Clay, May 22, 1830] would bring upon us." Repeats the political news conveyed to Samuel L. Southard on this date, adding facetiously, that "You will be deprived of the pleasure of Mr. [John] Rowan's company in the Senate after the 4h. of March next." ALS. NHi. That part of Robbins's speech of May 20, 1830, touching specifically on the Indian removal bill is in *Register of Debates*, 21 Cong., 1 Sess., 443. Written from Olympian Springs, Ky.

To Samuel L. Southard, Trenton, N.J. August 23, 1830. Repeats the political news conveyed to Philip R. Fendall on August 17, changing only his view that the likely Clay forces majority in the next Kentucky General Assembly will be a minimum of 14 seats rather than 12. Continues: "I regret to hear from you that any doubt should exist as to New Jersey. Our friends ought to exert every nerve in your State. Success this fall will leave the task comparatively easy hereafter [Southard to Clay, August 8, 1830]."

Adds: "I have reason to believe that the leaders of Anti-Masonry will support me. I have endeavored to avoid at the same time mixing with that excitement. It is a delicate and difficult matter. I think we may safely assume that it will not support Jackson. That is the next best thing to its co-operation with my friends. Mr. [Richard] Rush writes me that he will exert himself to give it a right direction in Pennsylvania." ALS. NjP. Written from Olympian Springs, Ky.

To HENRY CLAY, JR.   Olympian Springs, Ky., August 24, 1830
Your letters of the 4h. and 12h. Ulto. reached Ashland during my absence in the State of Ohio, and I have brought them here with some hundreds of other letters to be among the first which I should answer. Your mother, James [Brown Clay], John [Morrison Clay], Henry C. Duralde and I came here to remain a few days. We expect to return on friday and to meet Anne [Brown Clay Erwin], Mr. [James] Erwin and Mr. [Martin] Duralde at Ashland.

Although I did not feel at liberty to oppose my opinion to your own, about your remaining at West point, I am truly rejoiced that you have concluded to pass the last year there. And now let me advise you to be content for the present, with the honors you have acquired, by the delivery of the two discourses which you have pronounced & not on any account suffer yourself to be prevailed upon to deliver another, *but devote yourself steadily and constantly* to the studies of the present year, recover the ground you have lost, and if possible win the first honor. We are too apt to divide our time and attention between a multitude of objects. There is no great success ever achieved without exclusive and persevering attention to a single one.

I have no communications with Col. [Sylvanus] Thayer. I am afraid that you entertain some prejudices against him. I think your account of his attentions to the Secy of War [John Eaton] only proved that he is a very polite man as all know who are acquainted with him. Politeness was especially due from him towards the head of that department with which the Academy is connected. If his courtesy has won the Secy may it not prove that he is easily operated upon? Does it necessarily demonstrate any change of principle in the Col? To all men we should be civil. But there is no incompatibility between the practice of the greatest urbanity and the most stedfast adherence to our principles.

There is one feeling against which, my dear son, I would anxiously caution you, since it is often founded in mistake and is a source of much unhappiness. It is a feeling of distrust which prompts us to believe too readily that the world, or some particular individuals, do not render justice to our pretensions. Depend upon it that, in the general, the world justly distributes its praise and censure.

You will at once comprehend that this suggestion is made in consequence of your supposition that you have not been entirely fairly dealt with by the Academic board. Perhaps you have not been. I do not pretend to decide that point, because I have not possession of all the facts and circumstances upon which alone one should venture to form a conclusive judgment. In the absence of positive proof, it must be admitted that the presumption against their disposition to do you injustice is very strong. Why should they? Whether in the first, second, or third rank, your attainments are creditable to the institution. Your competition is not with any young man, whose parents connexions would be likely to create a bias in his favor to your prejudice. The bias, if any existed, would be more likely the other way. Mr. Professor Davies[1] I am sure is your friend.

But if you have experienced any injustice, your Uncle [James] Brown's advice that you should rise above all obstacles was good. You have only now about nine months to remain, and these, I repeat, I would devote exclusively to my studies.

I am quite content that you changed the Check, and I hope you went to Ballston [N.Y.] as you intended. I am sure that you will make a proper use of the money.

Your mama joins me in affectionate remembrance to you.

A letter came from you to Ashland for your sister Anne, which was not sealed. You must be more careful in future with your despatches.

ALS. Henry Clay Memorial Foundation, Lexington, Ky. 1. For Charles Davies, see *CAB*, or Thomas Hamersly, *Complete Regular Army Register* (Washington, 1880), 394.

From Josiah S. Johnston, on the Ohio River, near Cincinnati, August 24, 1830. Says he has been delayed by low water on his trip back to Washington from New Orleans. Is sorry he is unable to visit Lexington, but must enter his son William in Harvard on September 1 and so must continue his journey east without pause.

Reports that political prospects "look well in the West." Continues: "The expression of public opinion is quite as Strong as could have been expected in so short a time — In the course of the year it will be decisively expressed — The whole West with the exception of Tennessee & Mississippi will go in a body, & the former with proper concert & exertions might be changed — To these may be added the five N. England states — Jersey Delaware & Maryland — We must turn our attention to the three Large states — In Louisiana the election is satisfactory." Thinks that Clay will be nominated by the Louisiana legislature since "you have a majority" there. Thinks also that "we are strong enough in the Legislature" of Mississippi to elect George Poindexter to the U.S. Senate seat recently vacated by Robert H. Adams. Believes that James C. Wilkins of Natchez "has lost his election & he will be a lost man — He turn[e]d demagogue & made every Sacrafize — All his personal friends are disgusted with his Course." Reports that the "election in Missouri is much more favorable than could have been anticipated — We must allow time for great changes. It is said confidently th[at] [David] B[ar]t[on] will be elected." Is pleased with developments in Indiana and "of Kentucky & Ohio I had no fear." As for Tennessee, maintains that if Gov. William Carroll would unite with John Williams and David Crockett, "call out all their friends, take the question of internal improvements & the Tarif . . . they may shake the state But he has not the courage." ALS. InU. Poindexter was appointed to fill the vacancy caused by the death of Sen. Adams on July 2, 1830, and was subsequently elected to the seat. For Williams, Crockett, Adams, Poindexter, and Barton, see *BDAC*. For Wilkins, a prominent Natchez merchant, banker, and planter, see John F. H. Claiborne *Mississippi . . .* (Jackson, Miss., 1880), 1:345-46, 352-53, and James, *Antebellum Natchez, passim*. Wilkins ran third in a race for the U.S. Congress which was won by Franklin E. Plummer. *Niles' Register* (September 11, 25, 1830), 39:55, 74.

From Hugh Mercer, Fredericksburg, Va., August 24, 1830. Comments on the national political scene, beginning with the observation that there is testimony "which is now constantly developing in many of the States of the strong dissatisfaction which prevails in relation to the courses of the present very weak & incompetent administration — The late news from Louisiana, Ken[tuck]y [Clay to Beatty, May 4, 1830; Clay to Johnston, March 11, 1830] & other States of the west is most cheering—the first Newspaper Statem[en]ts from Keny were extremely dispiriting—a letter from a valued & intelligent & influential f[rien]d—in Philad[elphi]a a week since, who is ardently in yr Interest, laments very much that your Cause should have failed in your own State, saying that it was acquiring Strength daily in that City & thro out the State of Pennsyl[vani]a—The acc[oun]ts since from Keny have dispelled the Gloom—Announced as you now are regularly as the Candidate for the next Presidency of the national Republican party & of the friends of the american System, the prospects for our Success are most cheering—Virginia I fear will remain, for some time at least immoveable—long enough perhaps to support the present Incumbent for another term—An Incubus broods over the mind of Va as a State upon this Subject, which is truly astonishing & deplorable—altho' you know you have many faithful friends & bodies of people who are so, in several quarters of it—Our general Ticket System is unfortunate for us—Let the issue of the next election be as it may, & against us, wh[ich] God grant may be otherwise for the Character & prosperity of our Country, I deem your having been regularly announced as the opposing Candidate to the present Incumbent as all important, & as a sure Guarantee to your being the *Successor* of General Jackson, when he shall retire either by the wishes & votes of the nation or voluntarily at the close of his eight years—"

Discusses at length a past legal case in which both men had had a financial interest, then concludes on another political note, viz: "Genl [James] Taylor tells me that some of your friends in the West, wish you to come to the Senate of the U.S., as you will doubtless have a decided majority in both houses of the Ky- legislature—Before the American people as you now are for the Presidency, this Step should be well weighed & considered—& my first impression is that you should not come to the Senate, tho' there may be reasons & strong reasons perhaps, why you should—you will be best able to decide, with the advice & views of distant friends—Genl. T- tells me that he saw Mr [Richard] Rush on his way here, & he was against it—& had written or would write you—" ALS. DLC-HC (DNA, M212, R4). Under the new Virginia constitution counties were grouped together into election districts. Each district chose a state senator, U.S. congressman, and a presidential elector. Tadahisa Kuroda, "The County Court System of Virginia From The Revolution to the Civil War," Ph.D. dissertation, Columbia University, 1970, p. 167.

From "The Fredonian," [Columbus, Ohio(?)], August 26, 1830. Links Clay and the "American System" to Thomas Jefferson, contending that "Mr Jefferson advocated this cause throughout his life." Identifies himself as having been born in Virginia; and recalls that he was residing in the "vacinity" of Fayette County when he first heard Clay speak in the Kentucky legislature in 1803, a speech that "advocated the same cause then [Fredonian to Clay, August 5, 1830]."

Remarks that had Clay been listened to "as early as 1799, Kentucky, Sir, would long ere this been wholly peopled by freemen, and the voice of a task master, nor the groan of a slave, would not now be heard in ALL *that land*. . . . The die is cast and these unhappy slave States can now only look to the American Colonization society for ultimate relief; and here too you stand prominent." At the same time, denies that Clay ever had any "political connexion" with Aaron Burr and that such a charge, dating from 1806, "is altogether too absurd to mention on an occasion like this." Concludes with the lengthy observation and hope that the voice of the American people will soon force Jackson from office and place the "administration of our national affairs" in "more skillful and judicious hands." Copy. Printed in Columbus *Ohio State Journal*, August 26, 1830. See also "Fredonian" to Clay, July 22, 29; August 5, 12, 19, 1830.

To PETER B. PORTER   Lexington, September 1, 1830
Your favor of the 25h. July has been duly received, and I have perused with much satisfaction the full account which it contains of the state of N. York

politics. Since then I have observed the nomination of Mr. [Francis] Granger.[1] Some of the resolutions adopted by the Anti Masonic Convention I learn have given offence by their exclusive character.[2]

In Kentucky our elections have secured us a majority in each branch of the Legislature and on joint ballot of not less than 14.[3] Owing to local causes, collisions among friends and the impossibility of making general politics bear on all the elections we were disappointed in five or six Counties, where we have decided majorities, and in consequence our majority in the Legislature is less by one half than it should have been. Mr. [John] Rowan will certainly be defeated;[4] and I have not a doubt that at *this* time there is a clear majority agt. Jackson in the State not less than ten thousand. I regret that, owing to the circumstances intimated in my last, Mr. Breckenridge [*sic*, Robert J. Breckinridge] was not elected.[5]

We have now a fair prospect of electing this winter a Senator from Ohio, Kentucky, Indiana, Illinois, Missouri and Louisiana.[6]

I hope you will keep me well advised as to the movements and events in N. York. . . .

ALS. NBuHi.   1. Clay to Johnston, May 9, 1830.   2. Porter to Clay, July 25, 1830. 3. Clay to Beatty, May 4, 1830.   4. Clay to Beatty, June 8, 1830.   5. Clay to Porter, June 13, 1830.   6. For the outcome of elections to the U.S. Senate in these states, see Clay to Conover, Oct. 31, 1830 (Ohio); Clay to Johnston, Nov. 1, 1830 (Ind.); Clay to Beatty, June 8, 1830 (Ky.); Niles to Clay, Oct. 28, 1830 (Ill.); Clay to Fendall, August 17, 1830 (Mo.); Clay to Johnston, Dec. 25, 1829 (La.).

To John Meany, Philadelphia, September 3, 1830. Thanks Meany for his letter of July 6. Continues: "The dissatisfaction produced by the pardon of [George] Wilson, of which I have seen various accounts, I should think would hardly lead to any permanent consequences. It may however co-operate with other causes to produce a sober and serious state of the public mind, which is all that is wanting to lead to any necessary correction in the administration of our public affairs." ALS. NNPM. See Sergeant to Clay, July 7, 1830, for Wilson's conviction as a mail robber.

From Josiah Randall, Philadelphia, September 3, 1830. Discusses the political situation in Pennsylvania, saying "hope is exhilirating tho' we cannot count — on success as certain. The political opponents of Genl Jackson in Penna., are beginning to move and after the State elections will make a simultaneous nomination throughout the State." Believes there is a "probability of having a Majority" opposed to Jackson in the U.S. House of Representatives during the next Congress. Continues: "I have the best information that Genl. J. has declared among his friends that he will give it up if he is not better supported in Congress. It will be remembered that Genl J. has never yet said he will run again; as far as I can learn. Only think of it. He has not the slightest chance of reelection without the vote of N. York, the most uncertain State in the Union. So uncertain is his position. Nor is this remarkable his overwhelming majority in 1828, was more specious than solid 30,000 votes, or even less, would, properly distributed, have elected Mr Adams. The next Electoral vote according to the precedent of 1812, will be under the new Census. Our gain in the west — will be greater than their gain in N.Y. & Pa & loss in the South, and we can reject — I am without a vote from N Y. Pa & Virga. You see I take the worst — view that can be taken. We must however have a General Electoral ticket in Maryland & Maine. It is suicidal to fritter away our votes, & all their middle & Southern States moving en masse." Adds that "Nothing but supineness can lose us the contest. . . . The Working Men in N.Y. will next Winter make a Nomination in opposition to Genl. J. & all opposed to the Regency of Albany will join it." ALS. DLC-HC (DNA, M212, R4). The Jacksonians continued their control in both houses during the Twenty-second Congress. *Notable Names in American History* (Clifton, N.J., 1973), 77-78. Pennsylvania supporters of Clay gathered in Harrisburg on May 29, 1832, for the Pennsylvania National Republican convention where they nominated him for president. *Niles' Register* (June 9, 1832), 42:273. The New York Workingmen's party did not make a presidential nomination during the winter of 1830-31, because the party virtually disintegrated after the fall, 1830 elections. Frank T. Carlton, "The Workingmen's Party of New York City: 1829-1831," *PSQ* (Sept., 1907), 22:401, 412-13.

From John Sergeant, Philadelphia, September 3, 1830. Mentions that "The enthusiastic affection that met you in Ohio" has strengthened Clay's position. Notes that "your labours . . . in your *retirement* seem to be greater than those of most men in office."

Discusses various state elections, saying: "The Jackson papers in this quarter persist in asserting that they have carried Kentucky; and the [Washington *United States*] Telegraph claims Louisiana too. They are evidently afraid of the truth, and keep up this misrepresentation for the purpose of influencing the coming elections in Maryland, Delaware and New Jersey. *They* are undoubtedly very material. Some of our friends have been making calculations and think it quite possible there may be a majority against Jackson in the next Congress. In that case, he would withdraw, I think, and then the result would be certain — The Anti Masons in Pennsylvania are generally opposed to Jackson. Of those from other quarters who will be here on the 11th., I believe a great majority are of the same mind. It is highly probable that there is a majority in your favor. I should be content if they would simply declare against the present administration. The rest would follow of course. Indeed, I think this would be better than their nominating you —"

Adds that New York is in confusion with the Workingmen nominating Erastus Root. Believes Van Buren's party may "adopt that nomination" and "associate themselves with the working men," because if they nominate Enos T. Throop, Francis Granger "will have a good chance of success, which might be fatal to V.B. —"

Believes that in Pennsylvania both the Anti-Masons and Clay's supporters overestimate their own strength. ALS. InU. For the Kentucky state election, see Clay to Beatty, May 4, 1830; for Maryland, see Mercer to Clay, July 22, 1830; for New Jersey, see Southard to Clay, August 8, 1830; for Louisiana, see Clay to Johnston, February 27; March 11, 1830; for Delaware, see Rodney to Clay, October 7, 1830.

From Charles S. Todd, "Stockdale," Shelby Co., Ky., September 7, 1830. Discusses the prospect of borrowing $1,000 from the James Morrison estate for the purpose of enlarging and improving his farm. Continues: "I congratulate you on the result of recent elections in the West; and cherish the hope that Ohio and N. York will make the 'reform' certain. The very interesting attentions you received in Ohio were truly gratifying to your friends. . . . The division in the discordant materials of the Jackson party proceeding from the Tariff question is likely to cause the real friends of the System to look to you as its champion. and I hope, very fervently, that the persecution you have encountered, not less than the soundness of the principles you have advocated so ably and so unweariedly, may place you in the Presidential chair." ALS. DLC-HC (DNA, M212, R4). For the Ohio state election see Clay to Sloane, July 16, 1830; for New York see Stoddard to Clay and Lawrence to Clay, both dated August 9, 1830, and Clay to Johnston, May 9, 1830.

From FRANCIS T. BROOKE Fredericksburg, Va., September 9, 1830. I have your letter of the 17h ultimo before me, I am much at a loss to contrive the publication of the letter from Mr. T[homas] J[efferson] Randolph to you without any reference to you which would be injurious — I Shall See him at Richm[on]d and will make the effort to prevail on him to take it on himself — Though I fear the character of the letter is Such that it will be very dificult to prevail on him, it would be a very important publication especially as the [Sylvester S.] Southworth letter is like to turn out to be a forgery—[1]The news from France has put every other topick out of the public mind—[2]was there ever any thing So Glorious you will oblige me much by giving me your Speculations on it, it is big with the most important events—I have received a letter from the committee of Fayette county[3] and I am really at a loss to answer its inquiries the people of Virg[ini]a are not prepared to decide on any Settled course as to the next Presidential election—but for the Tariff & internal improvement questions I have no doubt they would fix on you   I believe the west will So decide, and I have Some hopes a portion of the east, but your friends generally are averse from any present nomination of you, an ineffectual effort was made in Westmoreland[4] an account of which you have Seen in the papers, They do not believe that Genl Jackson is to be the canditate, and they therefore prefer waiting to see who will be the candidate before they encounter the fixt friends of the Genl, this I collect from various quarters, do me the favour to Say this to Mr [M.C.] Johnson the Secretary of the committee, you will have perceived that Some effort is making by the [Richmond] Enquirer &c to revive the influence or rather to increase the influence of the Knight of Roane Oak [John Randolph of Roanoke], this is to counteract yours[5]   events may put all this out of the question, which are not improbable—nothing would afford me more [re]al Gratification than to See your native State voting for you,   NB Do excuse this hasty Scrawl—

ALS. InU.   1. Clay to Brooke, August 17, 1830.   2. Hughes to Clay, April 18, 1830.
3. A group of Fayette County citizens met at the courthouse on June 21, 1830, and adopted a series of resolutions condemning Jackson's Maysville Road veto and his Indian removal policy, as well as the votes of Kentucky Senators John Rowan and George M. Bibb on these issues. A committee of correspondence was also appointed to "promote the success of the sentiments of this meeting . . . by all fair and honorable means in their power." See Washington *Daily National Journal*, July 1, 1830, for a complete text of the resolutions.   4. Friends of Clay met at Oak Grove, Westmoreland Co., Va., on July 29, 1830, to adopt resolutions in favor of Clay and to nominate him for president. Although they made the nomination, it may have been "ineffectual," because many Clay supporters were "indisposed" or otherwise unable to attend. *Ibid.*, August 4, 1830.   5. For pro-Randolph articles and editorials in the Richmond *Enquirer*, see the issues of June 29; July 2, 6; August 3, 1830.

To PHILIP R. FENDALL   Lexington, September 10, 1830

I received your favor of the 31t. Ulto.   I approve entirely of your order to the Marshall to imprison Lotty.[1] Her husband and children are here. Her refusal therefore to return home, when requested by me to do so through you, was unnatural towards them as it was disobedient to me. She has been her own mistress, upwards of 18 months, since I left her at Washington, in consequence of the groundless writ which she was prompted to bring against me for her freedom; and as that writ has been decided against her, and as her conduct has created insubordination among her relatives here, I think it high time to put a stop to it, which can be best done by her return to her duty. How shall I now get her, is the question? There are persons frequently bringing slaves from the district to this State, some one of whom might perhaps undertake to conduct her to Maysville, Louisville or Lexington, or some other point from which I could receive her. Or perhaps some opportunity might occur to send her from Alexandria [Va.] to N. Orleans, free from much expence, to my son in law Martin Duralde Esqr.   I should be content to receive her in either way.

But I cannot think of troubling you unnecessarily with this affair. Perhaps Mr. John Davis (if you would have the goodness to speak to him) would undertake to look out for some person coming to this quarter who would engage to bring her. In the mean time, be pleased to let her remain in jail and inform me what is necessary for me to do to meet the charges.

I was informed through the papers of your resignation of the [Washington *Daily National*] Journal, prior to the receipt of your letter. As it respects yourself and your future prospects, I do not regret it. The situation of Editor of a Journal, however respectable and extensive its circulation, appears to me to be far from desirable, if any thing better can be done. Among the Editors who have had most eminence and success in the U. States how few are there who have made a comfortable provision for themselves! By quitting the district and commencing the practice of the law in some suitable and respectable place, you will be in a position in which you may, I hope, find an adequate support for your family, and from which you may enter the political career, if circumstances should be favorable, with much more advantage than you could from the district.

On the point, respecting which you consult me, that is, a suitable place for you to establish yourself in the West,[2] I do not know that I can add much to the information which I have communicated to you in different conversations which I held with you, prior to my departure from Wash. Our most important Western towns are Cincinnati, Louisville and St Louis. There is I think least competition and most business in amount at Louisville. Our friend Frank. [Francis] Johnson has lately moved there. Should you think seriously of a settlement to the West, it would be best and wisest, before you make it, to visit and reconnoitre the various places. No letter can impart to you information so valuable as that which your own eyes could see and your own faculties collect. Should you come to the West, I hope you will immediately repair to my residence where we should be happy to see you, and which you might make a sort of head quarters, sallying out to different points worthy of examination, from time to time.

I am glad that the Journal continues on a footing of so much safety and respectability. Mr. [John] Agg, writes remarkably well, and displays much readiness and tact. The Journal has established a very high character; and it requires no ordinary ability and diligence to sustain it. These I think will be contributed by Mr Agg.

I have not yet heard from Mr. Comptroller [Joseph] Anderson, nor recd. the Copy of the laws which you left with him to be transmitted to me. Perhaps I shall hear from him in a few days.

In regard to political events, except the election in Ohio next month, the most important that are likely shortly to occur are the elections in Maryland, Pennsa. New York &c   Their results will enable us to judge more satisfactorily in regard to the future.[3] Should they correspond with those which have recently taken place in the Western States we shall have it in our power to look forward with great confidence.

ALS. NcD.   1. See 7:623-24; Clay to Dawson, July 8, 1829; Clay to Fendall, April 10, 1830. 2. Fendall apparently remained in the District of Columbia where he later served as district attorney and where he died in 1868. *CAB.*   3. For the outcomes of these four state elections, see, respectively, Clay to Sloane, July 16, 1830; Mercer to Clay, July 22, 1830; Clay to Conover, Oct. 31, 1830; and (for New York) Clay to Johnston, May 9, 1830, and Stoddard to Clay, August 9, 1830.

To NICHOLAS BIDDLE   Lexington, September 11, 1830

Majr [John] Tilford having mentioned to me that you were considering whether it was proper to apply at the ensuing Session of Congress, for a renewal of the charter of the B.U.S. and that you entertained some doubts on the subject, I had a conversation with him and Mr [James] Harper, which I informed them that they were at liberty to communicate to you. I added that, perhaps, I might address a letter to you on the same matter. A leisure hour allows me to fulfill that intention.

It may be assumed, as indisputable, that the renewal of the charter can never take place, as the Constitution now stands, against the opinion and wishes of the President of the U.S. for the time being. A bill, which should be rejected by him for that purpose, could never be subsequently passed by the constitutional Majority. There would always be found a sufficient number to defeat such a bill, after its return with the Presidents objections, among those who are opposed to the Bank on Constitutional grounds, those who, without being influenced by constitutional considerations, might be opposed to it upon the score of expediency, and those who would be operated upon by the influence of the Executive.

I think it may even be assumed that a bill to renew the Charter can not be carried through Congress, at any time, with a *neutral* executive. To ensure its passage the Presidents opinion's and those of at least a majority of his Cabinet must be *known* to be in favor of the renewal.

President Jackson, if I understand the paragraph in his message at the opening of the last Session of Congress, relating to the Bank, is opposed to it upon constitutional objections.[1] Other sources of information corroborate that fact. If he should act on that opinion, and reject a bill, presented for his approbation, it would be impossible to get it through Congress at the next Session against the Veto.

That a strong party, headed by Mr. V. Buren, some Virginia politicians and the Richmond Enquirer, intend, if practicable to make the Bank question the basis of the next Presidential election, I have, I believe, heretofore informed you. I now entertain no doubt of that purpose. I have seen many evidences of it. The Editors of certain papers have received their orders to that effect, and embrace every occasion to act in conformity with them. This fact cannot have escaped your observation.

If you apply at the next Session of Congress, you will play into the hands of that party. They will most probably, in the event of such application, postpone the question, until another Congress is elected. They will urge the long time that the Charter has yet to run; that therefore there is no necessity, to act at the next Session on the measure; and that public sentiment ought to be allowed to develope itself &c. These and other considerations will induce Congress, always disposed to procrastinate, to put off the question. In the mean time, the public press will be put in motion, every prejudice excited and appeals made to every passion. The question will incorporate itself with all our elections, and especially with that as to which there is so great a desire that it should be incorporated. It will be difficult, when Congress comes finally to decide the question, to obtain a majority against this accumulation of topics of opposition.

But suppose, at the next Session, on the contingency of your application for a renewal of the Charter, instead of postponing, Congress was to pass a bill for that object, and it should be presented to the President, what would he do with it? If, as I suppose, he would reject it, the question would be immediately, in consequence, refered to the people, and would inevitably mix itself with all our elections. It would probably become, after the next Session, and up to the time of the next Presidential election, the controlling question in American politics. The friends of the Bank would have to argue the question before the public against the official act of the President, and against the weight of his popularity.

You will say what ought the Corporation to do? I stated to the above gentlemen that, in my opinion, unless you had a satisfactory assurance that your application at the next Session would be successful, you had better not make it. If, contrary to my impressions, you could receive such an assurance from both departments of the Government, who would have to act on the case, *that* would present a different state of the question, and would justify the presentation of your petition.

If not made at the next Session, when should it be made? I think the Session immediately after the next Presidential election would be the most proper time. Then every thing will be fresh; the succeeding P election will be too remote to be shaping measures in reference to it; and there will be a disposition to afford the new administration the facilities in our fiscal affairs which the B. of the U.S. perhaps alone can render. But suppose Genl. Jackson should be again elected? If that should be the case, he will have probably less disposition than he now has to avail himself of any prejudices against the Bank. He will then have also less influence; for it may be truly asserted, at least as a general rule, that the President will have less popularity in his second than his first term And that I believe would emphatically be the fate of the present President. At all events, you will be in a better condition by abstaining from applying to renew the charter during his first term, than you would be in, if you were to make the application and it should be rejected. Upon the supposition of such a rejection, and that the question should be afterwards blended with the Presidential contest, and Genl. Jackson should be elected, his re-election would amount to something like a popular ratification of the previous rejection of the renewal of the charter of the Bank. Indeed, if there be an union of the Presidents negative of the Bank bill with the next P. election, and he should be relected, would it not be regarded as decisive against any Bank of the U.S. hereafter?

My opinion, upon the whole, then is, that it would be unwise to go to Congress without something like a positive assurance of success at the next Session; and that the Corporation, without displaying any solicitude in regard to the continuation of it's charter, had better persevere, in the able and faithful administration of its affairs, which it has of late years manifested, and go to Congress at the first moment of calm which shall succeed the approaching Presidential storm.

I hope I need say nothing by way of apology, to satisfy you of the friendly feelings which have prompted this letter; nor to impress you with the propriety of receiving it in the confidence with which it is written. . . .

ALS. DLC-Nicholas Biddle Papers (DNA, M212, R20). Letter marked "(Confidential)."
1. Clay to Biddle, Jan. 2, 1830.

From John Sergeant, Philadelphia, September 11, 1830. Concerning politics, remarks: "If the elections of Senators in the West should all go favorably, Jackson will be nearly in a minority in Senate. It is possible he may be in the same state in the House. In that case, he will be very likely to withdraw. I hope it may be so." Adds that "The Antimasonic convention assembled to day, about one hundred in number. They did nothing but organise their meeting." ALS. InU. For the Anti-Masonic convention of September, 1830, see Porter to Clay, July 25, 1830.

To Nicholas Biddle, Philadelphia, September 13, 1830. Urges the Bank of the United States to erect in Lexington "a suitable edifice for the accommodation of its office" there. "Such a step would shew that the Bank . . . was willing to share in the fortunes of the place. It would moreover shew that it had full confidence in the renewal of its charter." ALS. DLC-Nicholas Biddle Papers (DNA, M212, R20).

From HENRY CLAY, JR. West Point, N.Y., September 16, 1830

I have not received a letter from you for a long time, but I have known too well your many engagements to expect one from you. You were, no doubt, surprised at my change of opinion, in regard to the propriety of leaving West Point; & with reason. It really appears to me that the age at which I have arrived, is one of vacillation & perplexity: Daily my mind ranges over all the professions & occupations pursued by men; and as often it returns into itself with a feeling of abhorrence of many, & discontent with nearly all

One of two Professions I believe I shall ultimately select: either the practice of Law, or the *Army*. The army in itself presents no attraction whatever, other than that of a *certain* & an *independent* support: But it will afford me facilities of prosecuting Literary studies in Europe—By the by, I have lately formed a very serious intention of obtaining a furlough for 1 or 2 years, to be passed in Paris or some other European metropolis in private study. $800. per annum, the pay of a Lieutenant in the army, I hope will be quite sufficient for that purpose—

I am well aware that the advancement of a Literary man to distinction is slow and must be loudly called for by the merits of the candidate before it is awarded; still there is something so pleasing in Literary distinction, & even in the prosecution of Literary researches, that life would pass off smoothly, even should it not be distinguished by any brilliancy of genius—Europe too in her libraries, & in the lectures of her eminent scholars, will afford me the means of prosecuting the historical & literary enquiries, of which you were so kind as to sketch me a general outline. Unless the histories which you mentioned, & especially those of Greece & Rome, are to be found in the libraries of the Harvard & Virginia universities, I fear they can not be had in the United States— To each of these Universities I have written to ascertain the fact

I have been relieved from the office which I lately held in the Corps, that of Adjutant, to receive the Academic distinction of Teacher with an increase of pay of $10. per month. I am much pleased with my new situation, for, although I have to spend 2 hours of each day with the 2 sections of the 4" class, entrusted to my care; my time is more at my disposal than it was before: I am relieved from all military duty and am invested with a number of little privileges which would appear insignificant to a stranger, but which are of material importance to me, such as keeping a light after 10 o'clock &c. Besides my regular course in the Institution, I am reading Latin, which I had almost entirely forgotten, & taking a course of French Literature. I sleep but 5 hours: the rest of the 24, with the exception of time for meals and about an

hour for exercise, I am engaged in study & recitation—I have suffered no unpleasant effects yet: Should it be too much for my health, I will give up the
course of French—

Uncle [James] & Aunt [Ann Hart] Brown were with me for a week during
the encampment. I am delighted with him—His mind, his liberal sentiments,
his erudition, his excellent feelings, his conciliatory simplicity of manners—all,
elicit the warmest esteem & affection, I have received from him the kindest advice & much instruction

I would be glad to hear your opinion as to what course I should pursue immediately after graduating.

Have you & my mother ever thought of sending James [Brown Clay] &
John [Morrison Clay] to Northampton or some other Northern school? It
would appear to me that nothing could be more serviceable to them—It is
however on my part a mere suggestion, for you must know what is best for
them better than I do.

You have no doubt heard ere this of the [revolution in] France—It is now
the only subject of convers[ation] everywhere—Mr [William] Wirt has engaged himself in the cause of the Cherokees a peculiarly beautiful field for the
display of talents of the order & class which he possesses—[1]

I receive but very few letters from home. When Anne [Brown Clay Erwin]
arrives, I shall expect them oftener—Though I have not written to her often of
late, I am sure she has formed excuses for me in her own mind better than I
can make—

ALS. Henry Clay Memorial Foundation, Lexington, Ky.   1. Wirt wrote a pro-Cherokee
pamphlet, titled *An Opinion on the Claims for Improvements, by the State of Georgia on the Cherokee Nation,
Under the Treaties of 1817 & 1828.* Baltimore, 1830. The pamphlet was published in *Niles' Register*
(Sept. 25, 1830), 39:31-88.

From Hezekiah Niles, Baltimore, September 17, 1830. Thinks "there is entire harmony among us all" in Maryland "except in one county." Continues: "I am entirely satisfied that if the people of this state were left free to go to the polls and express their own
sentiments we should have at least two thirds of our house of delegates. But there is a
terrible system of electioneering here. Whiskey flows like water; & money abounds,
very much for real *bribery*, in the presentation of coats, hats, boots &c. in the nearly
balanced counties. The federal & state officers are most busy and they 'bleed' freely,
especially the latter—some giving as much as one half of their whole earnings the present year, that they may have office in the next! It is 'neck or nothing' with them, & they
well know it. Our means are limited—&, if disposed to fight the enemy with his own
weapons, we have them not at command. The baseness of the press is also much
against us. No matter how cleanly a lie may be proved against them, they will not 'admit' it. . . . . It is no matter how often you put a falsehood down—it will be up and repeated as if founded on the Gospel! If we shall ultimately succeed against a degree of
profligacy that has no parallel, much credit will be due to the intelligence and virtue of
the people, and I shall think better of mankind than I have latterly done. But it would
rather appear that the *hurrah* is subsiding at least with us. The great thing is how to get
our friends into action. So far as I can judge there is a considerable change in the feelings
of the *laboring classes*. If they would read & think, a *reformation* would be easily effected."

Admits that there is "a majority of 7 in the [state] senate *against* us which must be
got over." Notes that Col. William Stewart "has again sacrificed" himself, at Niles's urging, and will run in Baltimore. He "is a mechanic" and "a great favorite with the people.
I think he is the strongest man in Balt. party being disregarded." Believes Stewart will
win, and "that will, indeed, be a victory!"

Adds: "I like the signs in New York very well. The regency party is certainly in a bad way. I hate the anti-masonic excitement, but [Francis] Granger is a warm friend of the tariff, & otherwise with us, & I hope that he will be supported. The great cause is, with me, like Aaron's rod. It swallows up all other considerations. Pennsylvania is much agitated. New Jersey is sound again; and I feel now satisfied of getting the whole west. Tennessee excepted — this season. We shall also have the entire cast in the *great struggle*."

Compliments Clay on his speech at Cincinnati [August 3, 1830], saying that it "has accomplished much good." Expects Clay to be in Washington next winter [Clay to Beatty, June 8, 1830], where, he believes, "new organizations of parties may happen."

Continues on September 18. Notes that "Our accounts from Maine are not pleasant — but do not render success hopeless." Despite "alarming accounts from little Delaware," feels "satisfied with our prospects there" since talking to "A gentleman zealous & intelligent" from there.

Reports that "Mr. Dupont has ordered 1000 copies of the pamphlet 'Politics for Farmers,' which I send you herewith. Many thousands have been printed. I think it will do good, in opening the eyes of the blind. I am much pleased with the reception that has been given to the essay. It is pretty high seasoned, but the times require it. The enemy is much displeased with it, & thats a good sign." ALS. DLC-HC (DNA, M212, R4). Stewart was defeated for a seat in the Maryland general assembly by Dr. John Spear Nicholas, a Jacksonian, by 4,278 to 4,105. Washington *Daily National Journal*, October 6, 1830. For Stewart (also spelled Steuart), see J. Thomas Scharf, *The Chronicles of Baltimore* . . . (Baltimore, 1874), 295-96, 314, 377-78, 418, 428. For the outcome of 1830 state elections in Maryland, New York, Pennsylvania, New Jersey, Tennessee, Maine, and Delaware, see, respectively, Mercer to Clay, July 22, 1830; Clay to Johnston, May 9, 1830, and Stoddard to Clay, August 9, 1830; Clay to Conover, October 31, 1830; Southard to Clay, August 8, 1830; Clay to Everett, August 14, 1830; Everett to Clay, October 29, 1830; and Rodney to Clay, October 7, 1830. Dupont is probably Eleuthere Irenee Dupont (*DAB*). "Politics for Farmers" had been published initially in *Niles' Register* (September 11, 1830), 39:50-55. The pamphlet version, an attempt to explain the American System to "farmers and other working classes," argued in part that because of domestic manufactures, sustained as they were by protective tariffs, farmers paid less for the articles they purchased.

From Josiah S. Johnston, Philadelphia, September 20, 1830. Reports his arrival in Philadelphia on September 1. Continues: "The Anti-Mason-Convention [Porter to Clay, July 25, 1830] have finished their work and adjourn[e]d — The[y] have made several reports, that are quite interesting, & which you will see published — They were a very intelligent & able body of Men — they manifested great zeal & spoke with feeling & effect. It is clear they have at this time no settled opinion with regard to their political Course — Some are undoubtedly devoted to the object of suppressing masonry, believing it a dangerous institution & they would sacrifize all other Considerations — They are for maintaining themselves independent of all parties — & having a Candidate who is not only, not a mason, but a real anti mason — The others who are not quite so zealous, know that they cannot yet stand alone — & that they must first unite their power so as to concentrate it & wield it with the greatest effect. They have certainly as yet no Unity of object & it is doubtful whether they can be brought to unite — They manifested great diversity of opinion about men — Having belonged to different parties, they have not lost their personal or political predilictions or prejudices — The greater number & especially those of N. york were favorable to you, but Were very prudent some of the others accused them of having a political object & of a design to favor your views — Which they were of Course compelled to disclaim — The real & Zealous anti masons were in favor of a Candidate of their own. . . . a Resolution was introduced for the nomination of an anti masonic Candidate, it was found that would not do — because they had not agreed on the man, & it was probable no man would accept the nomination unless he was already before the public – & besides this would not have accorded with the political views of the individuals of the Convention "anti masonic" Was stricken out – & then referred to a committee appd. by [Francis] Granger, Who reported – & it was finally agreed to make a nomination by the Convention to meet at Baltimore next sept. – & so the whole affair has ended. I doubt Whether they will ever agree on a nomination or agree to be bound by it – There are a few honest fellows who look only to the suppression of the order, but there are more political men among them than they are aware of. It was the object of the few among them friendly to the present admn. to defeat your nomination. Their first plan was to accuse them of having political, not anti masonic objects – then to manifest a disagreement of opinion – & finally to nominate [Daniel] Webster or [John] McLean as a foil to you – "

Discusses New York politics where the Anti-Masons, by Granger's estimate, are "90,000 strong . . . & gaining strength." Believes that a majority of Anti-Masons "are from our ranks." The plan, then, is to support Granger for governor [Clay to Johnston, May 9, 1830] and thus defeat the Bucktails or Van Buren party. Notes that "This will bring about a good understanding & Unite us in the Presidential election – [Erastus] Root will decline the nomination of the working men – & they will then probably divide or separate – & in that event We shall get our full share – " Contends that New York is crucial because the Jackson party is counting on it; therefore, "We *ought to concentrate* our *force there – "*

Adds that he is "sure that an attack is to be made in detail upon the Tarif – " and that "Sugar will be the first touched – " It "will be represented as a heavy burthen upon the poor, as an enormous bounty upon the rich capitalists. . . . It must be our duty to make Common cause – & to defend every interest," because "Each interest will be separately attack[e]d – " However, "The reduction of the duty on Molasses [Clay to Wright, May 31, 1830] was not injurious to us, & Was highly benificial to the trade of the country – The drawback on Rum, will restore that branch of trade, which was lost by the increased duty – I mean to make a small publication on this subject as well as on Salt & Sugar – " ALS. InU.

To GEORGE WATTERSON   Lexington, September 20, 1830

I recd. your favor of the 8h. inst. I had been previously informed by Mr. [Richard Smith] Coxe of the institution of the Committee which you describe.[1] Its active exertions will, without doubt, be productive of much good. In respect to your request of information from me, as to the condition of the West, I am perhaps, not the most impartial person to communicate it. Prone to regard things in the most favorable light, my mind may be biased in a case where possibly individual interest may have an unconscious influence. If I am not deceived, there would be but little doubt of the issue of a contest in the West (including Tennessee and Mississippi as well as Louisiana) to which Genl. Jackson is not a party. If he should be the competitor, I think he would lose Ohio, Kentucky, Indiana, Illinois, Missouri & Louisiana.[2] This opinion, in relation to all those States, except Ohio, is justified by the result of recent elections,[3] which, although not in every instance perfectly conclusive, indicates sufficiently strong the general tendency of public sentiment, to warrant it. Ohio will shortly by her elections, enable us to draw more satisfactory conclusions in regard to her disposition.

Peculiar causes affect the state of public opinion in Kentucky, the principal of which is the nearly equal division of the State, some years ago, into two parties [3:902], one for and the other opposed to the relief of debtors from their obligations to their creditors. The relief party, having been finally defeated, hoisted the Jackson flag, and uniting the popularity of the General with the unpopularity of Mr. [John Q.] Adams, succeeded in carrying the State for the former. But that party has been constantly on the decline, and the acts of the present administration have affected materially the popularity of the General. Still there is a difficulty in prevailing upon the people to govern themselves, in respect to the election of members to the State Legislature exclusively by their views of general politics. This difficulty will diminish as the period of the P. election approaches. I am satisfied that even at this time, if there were a direct question put to the people of this State between Genl. J. and myself there would be a majority against him not less then ten thousand.

Owing to the above cause, to divisions among our friends in some of the Counties, and to the operation of local questions, our majority in the next Legislature is not as great as it otherwise would have been. It is however not less than 14 on joint ballot. Pledges are claimed by the other side from some of our friends. There is much misrepresentation on this subject. Several of the members who are alleged to be under such pledges have in the public prints disclaimed them. In the instances where they were made, they amounted to nothing more than a declaration, during the canvass, that the candidate would vote according to *instructions*. But whether any instructions will, in fact, be given or not is uncertain. Most probably they will not be. Besides, some of the Jackson members are also under pledges to vote with the other party. Four or five of them represent Counties decidedly opposed to Jackson; and if instructions were attempted, they probably would also be instructed. It may therefore be assumed that the pledges and instructions will neutralize each other. No doubt is entertained that Mr. [John] Rowan[4] will be defeated, and that a Senator will be sent in his place opposed to the administration. Nothing but corruption can prevent that result.

I need not hint at the propriety of considering my name as confidential in this communication.

ALS. DLC-HC (DNA, M212, R22). Addressed to Watterson in Washington.   1. A large assembly of mechanics and other "friends of the American System, Internal Improvements, and HENRY CLAY" assembled in Washington, D.C., for a July 4 celebration. Washington *Daily National Journal*, July 7, 1830. Coxe gave the oration which was published as a pamphlet, *Address Delivered by Richard S. Coxe, Before the Mechanics and Other Citizens of the City of Washington, Friends of Henry Clay, on Monday, July 5, 1830*. Washington, 1830, 15 pp.   2. In the presidential canvass of 1832, Jackson carried all of these eight states except Kentucky.   3. For the Kentucky state election, see Clay to Beatty, May 4, 1830; for state elections in Indiana, Illinois, and Missouri, see Clay to Everett, August 14, 1830; for Louisiana, see Clay to Johnston, Feb. 27; March 11, 1830; and for Ohio, see Clay to Sloane, July 16, 1830; for the outcome of state elections in Mississippi and Tennessee, see Clay to Everett, August 14, 1830.   4. Clay to Beatty, June 8, 1830.

To JAMES MADISON   Lexington, September 22, 1830

Supposing you might not otherwise see it, I take the liberty of transmitting to you a copy of a Speech which I recently delivered to a public meeting at Cincinnati.[1] I do this for the purpose of inviting your attention to that part of it which relates to events in 1798-9, their motives and objects.[2] As you bore so conspicuous a part in them, no one can so well judge whether the view which I have presented be correct or not.

Late intelligence from Charleston justifies the hope that the contemplated measures of violence in So. Carolina will be arrested by the best of all remedies, a majority of the people themselves of that State.[3]

Mrs. Clay unites with me in presenting respectful regards to Mrs. Madison; to which I add assurances of my constant and profound esteem for yourself

ALS. KyU.   1. Speech at Cincinnati, August 3, 1830.   2. Reference is to the Alien and Sedition Acts controversy of 1798-1799 which resulted in the Kentucky and Virginia Resolutions; also to the theoretical relationship of South Carolina's doctrine of nullification to those resolutions.   3. Clay to Everett, August 20, 1831; Clay to Davis, March 10, 1832; Stoddard to Clay, Nov. 12, 1832.

From James Brown, Philadelphia, September 24, 1830. States that he and his wife spent two weeks with Henry Clay, Jr., while in New York and that he advised Henry to finish his course at West Point. "It gives me great pleasure to assure you that his standing is excellent with his instructors and his fellow students and that he is, in short, everything you could wish."

Comments that the French revolution [Hughes to Clay, April 18, 1830] "has terminated to the entire satisfaction of the friends of freedom and will be followed by important consequences. . . . I would at any time cheerfully have given a years Salary had it arrived before I left Paris." Feels that it will add to the popularity of William C. Rives, the new American minister in Paris, and that it may add "to the popularity of the [Jackson] administration." England, also, may be disposed to yield "more on the subject of the Colonial trade [Lawrence to Clay, August 9, 1830] in order to put aside . . . all causes of difference with the United States—"

Mentions that the "Antimasonic Convention has adjourned after having prepared several addresses to the people of the United States touching the dangerous influence of Masonry [Porter to Clay, July 25, 1830]. The meeting was respectable in numbers and talents and conducted its proceedings with singular moderation and good order—They have stated their capacity to bring ninety thousand votes forward in N York at the next election for Governor but this statement is thought by some to be greatly exaggerated. They are however very powerful as well in New York as in Pennsylvania and are believed to be rapidly increasing. A Resolution passed before they adjourned that they would meet at Baltimore in Septr 1831 to nominate Candidates for President and Vice President—It is believed, that Freemasons will be excluded from this nomination. I did not learn whether the majority were for or against the administration—Its standing was not alluded to as far as I followed their debates." Believes that the "Van Buren Candidate [Enos T. Throop] will be elected [governor] in New York [Clay to Johnston, May 9, 1830]," and that "the temper of this State seems to remain favorable to the administration—"

Asks if the result of the Kentucky election [Clay to Beatty, May 4, 1830] is "a symptom of declining interest in the west" in the American System. "May not the West be induced, in consequence of the opposition of some of the Representatives of N York and Pennsya. to internal improvements, to join the South and repeal the duties? I ask this with a view to the duty on sugar as I would sell out if we should lose the advantage of the Tariff—" ALS. DLC-TJC (DNA, M212, R10).

From Richard Rush, York, Pa., September 25, 1830. Reports that he has just returned from a trip, during which he "had much conversation with anti-masons. At Harrisburg, especially, I fell in with several, just from the convention, at Philadelphia [Porter to Clay, July 25, 1830]. I understand that the proper committee of that body, mean to unite to you. Now, my dear dear Sir, I do fervently trust, that you will feel yourself able to give them a satisfactory answer, though you may formerly have been, and for aught I know may still be, a mason. I go into no particulars upon this subject. Anti-masonry means, in effect, anti-Jacksonism. Think then what a great public good it may become the means of achieving, and consequently what a call its cause makes upon true patriotism under the present circumstances of our misruled country. Pray then, for your country's sake, let me implore you to conciliate this interest as far as your judgement, feelings, and principles will allow." Emphasizes that the Anti-Masons "look to you with anxiety and hope," and concludes "let me fervently hope, that you will feel yourself free so to unite to the committee, should you be addressed." ALS. DLC-HC (DNA, M212, R4). Letter marked "private."

To PETER B. PORTER   Lexington, September 28, 1830

Mrs. [Margaret Wilson] Warfield, the widow of Dr. Walter Warfied [*sic*] formerly of Lexington, a highly respectable lady has lost a valuable negro man, who, she has reason to believe, has made his escape towards Canada, and will probably engage as a servant on board some of the Steamers that navigate Lake Erie, a business with which he has some acquaintance. Both Dr. Warfield and his lady were well known to Mrs Porter. As she has no acquaintance, in the neighbourhood of the Lake, she has applied to me to recommend some friend to her. I take pleasure, in consequence, of requesting for her your friendly offices. I have advised her to transmit to you a power of attorney with testimonials of the identity of her slave and her property in him. You will render a very great kindness to a most estimable lady by assisting her in the recovery of her slave. . . .

ALS. NBuHi.

From Celestine Laveau Trudeau [Mrs. James] Wilkinson, Cincinnati, September 29, 1830. States that "having nothing to do at Lexington," she returned to Cincinnati "to take more enquirings, about the establishment that I wish to settle in this country." Adds: "I have determined to establish here my academy and I hope dear sir that you will do me the favor to patronize my establishment." Encloses "several of my prospectuses, allso a copy of a letter received from Francfort [*sic*, Frankfort] about my land business. . . . Will you have the goodness to advice me what I have to do on this subject." ALS. DLC-HC (DNA, M212, R4). Endorsed on verso by Clay: "Mrs. Wilkinson." A notice for Mrs. Wilkinson's academy for girls appeared in the Cincinnati *American*, September 27, 1830. Celestine Laveau Trudeau was the second wife of General James Wilkinson.

From "The Fredonian," [Columbus, Ohio(?)], September 30, 1830. Identifies this as his seventh and probably final "epistle to you." Points out that the people of Ohio have long admired Andrew Jackson as a military man but are beginning to have grave reservations about him as president. Demands that "the *measures* of the present Administration" be investigated. Charges that Jackson's veto ("or if more properly expressed . . . his nullification") of the Maysville Road bill [Johnston to Clay, May 26, 1830] clearly shows his hostility to internal improvements, even though he claims to favor such improvements. Says he is amazed to discover that the patriotic, intelligent, and talented editors of the Washington *Daily National Intelligencer* did not seem to know "that what is now styled the 'American System,' had been so called and named by Mr. Jefferson." Develops at length the argument that Thomas Jefferson was the father of the American System.

Notes that the "disaffection of the South is one of the strange events of the present age," especially since the South in 1828 "succeeded in the election of a President to meet her own views on every point." Believes that a critical period is "fast approaching, as to South Carolina and Georgia, when . . . in attempting the nullification of the laws of the United States," it is increasingly becoming in those states a question of whether, in the words of John Randolph, 'the negro runs away from his master, or the master from the negro.'" Thinks Jackson has been presented with a "fine opportunity" to deal effectively with this "hot bed of treasonable designs" against which William Drayton and others have "buckled on the national *armour*."

Comments on the disarray within Jackson's cabinet [Letcher to Clay, December 21, 1829] and predicts that the "crisis will soon arrive when a scape-goat must be made; and we do humbly trust that he will carry away the *sins* and *pollutions* of the *party*."

Says in conclusion that he supported Clay for the presidency in 1824 and Adams in 1828. Adds: "I see that Col. Wm. Drayton, of Charleston, S.C., has been recommended in the [Washington *Daily*] *National Intelligencer*, by 'a Virginia Farmer,' as a suitable person, as a candidate to be taken up by Mr. Clay's friends for the Vice-Presidency." Strongly endorses this idea. Copy. Printed in Columbus *Ohio State Journal*, September 30, 1830. The other six letters in this series were published on July 22, 29; August 5, 12, 19, 26, 1830.

To HAMILTON COUNTY (OHIO) AGRICULTURAL SOCIETY

Lexington, October, 1830

Having promised you some account of the method of culturing and preparing hemp in this state, I now proceed to redeem it. I shall endeavor to describe the general practice of the cultivators, without noticing all the deviations of particular individuals.

The district of country in which the plant is most extensively cultivated, is the Elkhorn region, around and near Lexington, which derives its name from a stream discharging itself into the Kentucky river, whose branches are supposed to resemble the horns of an Elk. It is also produced in considerable quantities in the counties of Jefferson, Shelby, Mercer, Madison, Clarke [*sic*, Clark] , Bourbon and Mason. The soil of that region is a rich, deep vegetable loam, free from sand and with but little grit. It lies on a bed of clay, interspersed with small fragments of iron ore, and this clay in its turn reposes on a mass of limestone lying many feet in depth in horizontal strata. The general surface of the country is gently undulating. The rich land, (and there is but little that is not rich,) in this whole region, is well adapted to the growth of hemp, where it has not been too much exhausted by injudicious tillage. The lands which produce it best, are those which are fresh, or which have lain sometime in grass or clover. Manuring is not yet much practised. Clover is used in lieu of it. Lands which remain in clover four or five years without being too constantly and closely grazed, recover their virgin fertility. The character of the soil in the other counties above mentioned, does not vary materially from that in the Elkhorn district.

The preparation of the ground, for sowing the seed, is by the plough and horses, until the clods are all sufficiently pulverized or dissolved, and the surface of the field is rendered even and smooth. It should be as carefully prepared as if it were designed for flax. This most important point, too often neglected, cannot be attended to too much. Scarcely any other crop better rewards diligence and careful husbandry. Fall or winter ploughing is practised with advantage—it is indispensable in old meadows, or old pasture grounds intended for producing hemp.

Plants for seed are ordinarily reared, in a place distinct from that in which they are cultivated for the lint. In this respect, the usage is different from that which is understood to prevail in Europe. The seeds which are intended to reproduce seeds for the crop of the next year, are sowed in drills about four feet apart. When they are grown sufficiently to distinguish between the male and female stalks, the former are pulled and thrown away, and the latter are thinned, leaving the stalks separated seven or eight inches from each other. This operation is usually performed in the blooming season, when the sexual character of the plants is easily discernible; the male alone blossoming, and, when agitated, throwing off farina, a yellow dust or flour which falls and colors the ground, or any object that comes in contact with it. A few of the male plants had better be left, scattered through the drill, until the farina is completely discharged, for an obvious reason. Between the drills a plough is run sufficiently often to keep the ground free from weeds and grass; and between the stalks in each drill the hoe is employed for the same object. The seed plants are generally cut after the first smart frost, between the 25th September and middle of October, and carried to a barn or stackyard, where the seeds are easily detached by the common thrail. They should be gathered after a slight, but before a severe, frost; and, as they fall out very easily, it is advisable to haul the plants on a sled, and, if convenient, when they are wet. If transported on a cart or wagon, a sheet should be spread to catch the seeds as they shatter out. After the seeds are separated, the stalks which bore them being too large, coarse, and harsh, to produce lint, are usually thrown away: they may be profitably employed in making charcoal for the use of powder mills. In Europe, where the male and female plants are promiscuously grown together in the same field, both for seeds and for lint, the male stalks are first gathered, and the female suffered to remain growing until the seeds are ripe, when they are also gathered, the seeds secured and lint obtained, after the rotting, from both descriptions.

After the seeds are threshed out, it is advisable to spread them on a floor to cure properly and prevent their rotting, before they are finally put away for use the next Spring. Seeds are not generally used, unless they were secured the fall previous to their being sown, as it is believed they will not vegetate, if older; but it has been ascertained that, when they are properly cured and kept dry, they will come up after the first year. It is important to prevent them from heating, which destroys the vegetating property, and for that purpose they should be thinly spread on a sheltered floor.

The seeds — whether to re-produce seeds only, or the lint — are sowed about the same time. Opinions vary as to the best period. It depends a good deal upon the season. The plant is very tender when it first shoots up, and is affected by frost. Some have sowed as early as the first of April; but it is generally agreed, that all the month of May, and about the 10th of it especially, is the most favorable time. An experienced and successful hemp-grower, in the neighborhood of Lexington, being asked the best time to sow hemp, answered, immediately before a rain. — And undoubtedly it is very fortunate to have a moderate rain directly after sowing.

When the object is to make a crop of hemp, the seeds are sown broadcast. The usual quantity is a bushel and a half to the acre; but here again the farmers differ, some using two bushels or even two and a half. Much depends on the strength and fertility of the soil, and the care with which it has been prepared, as well as the season. To these causes may be ascribed the diversity of opinion and practice. The ground can only sustain and nourish a certain quantity of plants; and if that limit be passed, the surplus will be smothered in the growth. When the seeds are sown, they are ploughed or harrowed in; ploughing is best in old ground, as it avoids the injurious effect of a beating rain, and the consequent baking of the earth. It would be also beneficial, subsequently to roll the ground with a heavy roller.

After the seeds are sown, the labors of the cultivator are suspended, until the plants are ripe, and in a state to be gathered — every thing in the intermediate time being left to the operations of nature. If the season be favorable until the plants are sufficiently high to shade the ground, (which they will do in a few weeks, at six or eight inches height,) there will be a strong probability of a good crop. When they attain that height, but few articles sustain the effect of bad seasons better than hemp.

It is generally ripe and ready to be gathered about the middle of August, varying according to the time of sowing. Some sow at different periods, in

273

order that the crop may not all ripen at the same time, and that a press of labor, in rearing it, may be thus avoided. The maturity of the plant is determined, by the evaporation of the farina, already noticed, and the leaves of the plant exhibiting a yellowish hue: it is then generally supposed to be ripe, but it is safest to wait a few days longer. Very little attentive observation will enable any one to judge when it is fully ripe. In that respect it is a very accommodating crop; for if gathered a little too soon, the lint is not materially injured, and it will wait the leisure of the farmer some ten days or a fortnight after it is entirely ripe.

Two modes of gathering the plants are practised; one by pulling them up by the roots, an easy operation with an able bodied man; and the other by cutting them about two inches (the nearer the better) above the surface of the ground. Each mode has its partisans, and I have pursued both. From a quarter to a third of an acre, is the common task of an average laborer, whether the one or the other mode is practised. The objections to pulling are, that the plants with their roots remaining connected with them, are not afterwards so easily handled in the several operations which they must undergo; that all parts of the plant do not rot equally and alike, when exposed to the dew and rain; and, finally, that before you put them to the Brake, when the root should be separated from the stalk, the root drags off with it some of the lint. The objection to cutting is, that you lose two or three inches of the best part of the plant nearest the root. Pulling, being the ancient method, is most generally practised. I prefer, upon the whole, cutting — and I believe the number who prefer it is yearly increasing. When pulled, it is done with the hand, which is better for the protection of an old leather glove. The laborer catches twenty or thirty plants together, with both hands, and, by a sudden jerk, draws them up, without much difficulty. The operation of cutting is performed with a knife, often made out of an old scythe, resembling a sickle, though not quite so long, but broader. This knife is applied much in the same way as the sickle, except that the laborer stoops more.

Whether pulled or cut, the plants are carefully laid on the ground, the evener the better, to cure — which they do in two or three days, in dry weather. A light rain falling on them whilst lying down, is thought by some to be beneficial, inasmuch as the leaves, of which they should be deprived, may be then easier shaken off or detached. When cured, the plants are set up in the field in which they were produced, in shocks of convenient size, the roots or but ends resting on the ground, and the tops united above by a band made of the plants themselves. Previous to putting them up in shocks, most cultivators tie the plants in small hand bundles of such a size as that each can be conveniently held in one hand. Before the shocks are formed, the leaves of the plants should be rapidly knocked off with a rough paddle or hooked stick. Some suffer the plants to remain in these shocks until the plants are spread down to be rotted. Others, again, collect the shocks together as soon as they can command leisure, (and it is clearly best) and form them into stacks. A few farmers permit these stacks to remain over a whole year, before the plants are exposed to be rotted. I have frequently done it with advantage, and have at this time two crops in stacks. By remaining that period in stacks, the plants go through a sweat, or some other process, that improves very much the appearance, and, I believe, the quality of the lint, and this improvement fully compensates the loss of time in bringing it to market. The lint has a soft texture and a lively hue, resembling water rotted hemp; and I once sold a box of it in the Baltimore market at the price of Russia hemp. In every other respect, the plants are treated as if they were not kept over a year.

The method of dew-rotting is that which is generally practised in Kentucky. The lint so prepared is not so good for many purposes, and especially for the rigging of ships, as when the plants have been rotted by immersion in water, or, as it is generally termed, water-rotted. The greater value, and consequently higher price, of the article, prepared in the latter way, has induced more and more of our farmers every year to adopt it; and, if that prejudice were subdued, which every American production unfortunately encounters, when it is first introduced and comes in competition with a rival European commodity, I think it probable that, in a few years, we should be able to dispense altogether with foreign hemp. The obstacles, which prevent the general practice of water-rotting, are, the want of water at the best season for the operation, which is the month of September; a repugnance to the change of an old habit; and a persuasion which has some foundation, that handling the plants, after their submersion in water during that month is injurious to health. The first and last of these obstacles would be removed by water-rotting early in the winter, or in the spring. The only difference in the operation, performed at those seasons and in the month of September, would be, that the plants would have to remain longer in soak before they were sufficiently rotted.

The plants are usually spread down to be dew-rotted, from the middle of October to the middle of December. A farmer who has a large crop on hand, puts them down at different times for his convenience in handling and dressing them. Autumnal rotting is more apt to give the lint a dark and unsightly color, than winter rotting. The best ground to expose the plants upon is meadow or grass land, but they are not unfrequently spread over the same field on which they grew. The length of time that they ought to remain exposed, depends upon the degree of moisture and the temperature of the weather that prevail. In a very wet and warm spell five or six weeks may be long enough. Whether they have been sufficiently rotted or not is determined by experiment. A handful is taken and broken by the hand or applied to the brake, when it can be easily ascertained, by the facility with which the lint can be detatched from the stalk, if it be properly rotted. If the plants remain on the ground too long, the fibres lose some of their strength, though a few days longer than necessary, in cold weather, will not do any injury. If they are taken up too soon, that is before the lint can be easily separated from the woody part of the stalk, it is harsh, and the process of breaking is difficult and troublesome. Snow-rotting, that is when the plants, being spread out, remain long enough to rot, (which however requires a greater length of time,) bleaches the lint, improves the quality, and makes it nearly as valuable as if it had been water-rotted.

After the operation of rotting is performed, the plants are again collected together, put in shocks or stacks, or, which is still better, put under a shed or some covering. When it is designed to brake and dress them immediately, they are frequently set up against some neighboring fence. The best period for breaking and dressing is in the month of February and March, and the best sort of weather, frosty nights and clear thawing days. The brake cannot be used advantageously in wet or moist weather. It is almost invariably used in this state out of doors and without any cover, and to assist its operation, the laborer often makes a large fire near it, which serves the double purpose of drying the plants and warming himself. It could not be used in damp weather in a house, without a kiln or some other means of drying the stalks.

The brake in general use, is the same hand brake which was originally introduced, and has been always employed here, resembling, though longer, than the common flax brake. It is so well known as to render a particular description of it, perhaps, unnecessary. It is a rough contrivance, set upon four legs abut two and a half feet high. The brake consists of two jaws with slits in each, the lower jaw fixed and immoveable, and the upper one moveable, so that it may be lifted up by means of a handle inserted into a head or block at the front end of it. The lower jaw has three slats or teeth made of tough white oak, and the upper two, arranged horizontally about six inches apart in the rear, and gradually approaching to about two inches in front, and in such manner that the slats of the upper jaw play between those of the lower. These slats are about six or seven feet in length, six inches in depth, and about two inches in thickness in their lower edges; they are placed edgeways, rounded a little in their upper edges which are sharper than those below. The laborer takes his stand by the side of the brake, and grasping in his left hand as many of the stalks as he can conveniently hold, with his right hand he seizes the handle in the head of the upper jaw, which he lifts, and throwing the handful of stalks between the jaws, repeatedly strikes them by lifting and throwing down the upper jaw. These successive strokes break the woody or reedy part of the stalks into small pieces or shoes, which fall off during the process. He assists their disengagement by striking the handful against a stake, or with a small wooden paddle, until the lint or bark is entirely clean, and completely separated from the woody particles.

After the above operation is performed, the hemp may be scutched to soften it, and to strengthen the threads. That process however is not thought to be profitable, and is not therefore generally performed by the grower, but is left to the manufacturer, as well as that of beating and heckling it. Scutching is done, by the laborer taking in his left hand a handful of the lint and grasping it firmly, then laying the middle of it upon a semi-circular notch of a perpendicular board of the scutching frame, and striking with the edge of the scutch that part of the lint which hangs down on the board. After giving it repeated strokes, he shakes the handful of lint, replaces it on the notch, and continues to strike and turn all parts of it, until it is sufficiently cleansed, and the fibres appear to be even and straight.

The usual daily task of an able bodied hand at the brake is eighty pounds weight, but there is a great difference not only in the state of the weather, and the condition of the stalks, produced by the greater or less degree in which they have been rotted, but in the dexterity with which the brake is employed. Some hands have been known to break from one hundred and fifty to two hundred pounds per day. The laborer ties up in one common bundle the work of one day, and in this state it is taken to market and sold. From what has been mentioned, it may be inferred, as the fact is, that the hemp of some growers is in a much better condition than that of others. When it has been carelessly handled or not sufficiently cleansed, a deduction is made from the price by the purchaser. It is chiefly bought in our villages, and manufactured into cotton bagging, bales, and other kinds of untarred cordage. The price is not uniform. The extrcmes have been as low as three, and as high as eight dollars, for the long hundred — the customary mode of selling it. The most general price, during a term of many years, has been from four to five dollars. At five dollars it compensates well the labor of the grower, and is considered more profitable than any thing else the farmer has cultivated.

The most heavy labor in the culture of hemp, is pulling or cutting it, when ripe, and breaking it, when rotted. This labor can easily be performed by men. Various attempts have been made to improve the process of breaking, which is the severest work in the preparation of hemp. A newly invented machine was erected for that purpose on my farm six or eight years ago, to dress hemp by dispensing with rotting altogether, similar in structure to one which was exhibited about the same time at Columbus, during the sitting of the Ohio Legislature. It was worked by horse power, and detached the lint tolerably well, producing a very fine looking article, equalling in appearance Russia Hemp. A ton of it was sold to the Navy department, which was manufactured into rigging for the ship of the line, the North Carolina, prior to her making a voyage of three years in the Mediterranean. Upon her return, the cordage was examined and analyzed; and, although its exterior looked very well, it was found, on opening it, to be decayed, and affected somewhat like the dry rot in wood. I considered the experiment decisive; and it is now believed that the process of water or dew-rotting is absolutely necessary, either before or after the hemp has been to the brake. There is a sappy or glutinous property of which it should be divested, and that is the only process that has been hitherto generally and successfully employed, to divest it.

An ingenious and enterprizing gentleman in the neighborhood of Lexington, has been, ever since the erection of the above mentioned machine, trying various experiments, by altering and improving it, to produce one more perfect, which might be beneficially employed on rotted hemp, to diminish the labors of the brake. He mentioned the other day that all of them had failed; that he had returned to the old hand brake, and that he was convinced that it answered the purpose better than any substitute with which he was acquainted. I observe Mr. H. L. Barnum[1] has recently advertised a machine, which he has constructed for breaking and dressing hemp and flax, which can be procured at the establishment of Mr. Smith,[2] in Cincinnati. I most cordially wish him success; but the number of failures which I have witnessed, during a period of thirty years, in the attempts to supercede manual labor by the substitution of that of machines, induces me to fear that it will be long before this desideratum is attained.

The quantity of nett hemp produced to the acre, is from six hundred to a thousand weight, varying according to the fertility and preparation of the soil, and the state of the season. It is said that the quantity which any field will produce, may be anticipated by the average height of the plants throughout the field. Thus—if the plants will average eight feet in height, the acre will yield eight hundred weight of hemp, each foot in height corresponding to a hundred weight of the lint.

Hemp exhausts the soil slowly, if at all. An old and successful cultivator told me that he had taken thirteen or fourteen successive crops from the same field, and that the last was the best. That was probably, however, owing to a concurrence of favorable circumstances. Nothing cleanses and prepares the earth better for the other crops (especially for small grain or grasses) than hemp. It eradicates all weeds, and when it is taken off, leaves the field not only clean, but smooth and even.

The rich lands of Ohio, Indiana and Illinois, are, I have no doubt, generally well adapted to the cultivation of this valuable plant; and those states enjoy some advantages for the cultivation of it, which this does not possess. Their streams do not dry up as much as ours, and they could consequently employ better than we can, the agency of water, in the preparation of it. Their projected canals, when completed, will admit of its being carried to the Atlantic capitals at less expense in the transportation than we can send it. On the other hand, the unfortunate state of slavery among us, gives us, at present, probably a more certain command of labor than those states have.

Copy. Printed in *The Western Agriculturist and Practical Farmer's Guide* (Cincinnati, 1830), 226-36.   1. A description of Barnum's machine is in *ibid.*, 344-45. Barnum also wrote a number of books including *The American Farrier; Containing a Minute Account of the Formation of Every Part of the Horse.* . . . . Cincinnati, 1832; and *Family Receipts, or, Practical Guide for the Husbandman and Housewife.* . . . . Cincinnati, 1831.   2. Probably the firm of Smith and Mason (William S. and Daniel M.), iron and steel commission merchants, located on Front, between Main and Walnut, Cincinnati.

From Peter B. Porter, Black Rock, N.Y., October 6, 1830. Comments on the political situation in New York State: "This cursed anti masonry embarrasses every thing, and defeats all attempts at systematic operation against the common enemy. Of one thing however I can reassure you, which is, that *you personally, as well as the leading measures of policy which you have so powerfully & conspicuously advocated*, are visibly and *rapidly* gaining ground in every part of our State; and I am now much inclined to believe that, if we had, two months ago, started a Candidate for Governor under the banner of Clay & the American System, we should have succeded. But the experiment would have been attended with some hazard as we must have come in conflict with the antimasons (who are formidable in numbers) and perhaps alienated them from our cause which we think they will eventually support. It was therefore deemed most prudent on the whole to continue, this year, the same neutral course that was adopted the last, making no nomination ourselves, but suffering the war to rage between the [Albany] Regency, the Working Men & the Anti Masons. A very large proportion of our friends will give a silent but efficient support to [Francis] Granger, (whose chance of success is very fair) but there are some who hold Antimasonry in such utter detestation, that they will vote for [Erastus] Root, or even [Enos] Throop, in preference of Granger."

Assures Clay that Root will decline the nomination for governor by the Workingmen's party and that "His feelings, which he does not hesitate to express, are evidently & strongly against the Regency, and friendly toward Granger, whom he will secretly support, unless he should be brought over to the Regency (which is more than probable) by the promise to make him U.S. senator, or give him some other office, in which case he will come out in favour of the Herkimer nomination."

Concludes that "On the whole, looking to the next Presidential Election, I think our prospects extremely flattering, and that in the course of the ensuing year we shall be able to raise a triumphant standard."

Discusses at length the "Maneuvers of the present Executive in relation to my accounts as a commissioner under the Treaty of Ghent." The problem turns on "the *rate* of salary which I was authorised by law to charge during different periods of the Commission." Remarks that under "the special direction" of Jackson a "balance of $9,500 was produced against me" by the Treasury Department. Attempts to work out the problem legally, "by an amicable suit" in the U.S. Supreme Court failed. At this point the president, in collusion with Van Buren, authorized a "'warrant of Distress' or Execution, against my property & person for the collection of the balance reported." To this Porter responded by filing a bill of complaint against the United States in the U.S. District Court for the District of Columbia. The trial which followed produced a *"judgment in my favour.* . . . The effect of this opinion is to create a balance of about $300 in my favour, & for which I shall not fail to *dun* the Secretary of State, at proper intervals until it is paid." ALS. DLC-HC (DNA, M212, R4). Printed in Colton, *Clay Correspondence*, 1:284. For the gubernatorial race in New York State, see Clay to Johnston, May 9, 1830.

From Thomas M. Rodney, Wilmington, October 7, 1830. Reports the "total defeat of the Jackson party" in Delaware, a victory "far beyond the most sanguine expectations of the warmest of our party." The anti-Jacksonians even elected a member of Congress, John J. Milligan, over "one of the most popular men in the State." ALS. DLC-HC (DNA, M212, R4). Milligan defeated Henry M. Ridgely, former U.S. senator, by the vote of 4,267 to 3,833. *Guide to U.S. Elections*, 554. In the Delaware legislature the National Republicans held a majority of 18 on joint ballot. *Niles' Register* (October 16, 1830), 39:121. *BDAC* spells it "Ridgeley."

From Mathew Carey, Philadelphia, October 9, 1830. Sends Clay copies of two of his recent essays in which "I have placed in a point of view, wholly new, unless I am mistaken, the advantages & disadvantages of disunion. How far you or other statesmen may agree with me, I cannot pretend to decide. Be that, however, as it may, I feel the fullest confidence in my doctrine — & had I the casting vote on opposition (a guarantee of peace for a century being secured — perhaps I might say half a century) I would give it in the affirmative. This is not a hasty opinion formed on this issue of the occasion — It has grown upon me from year to year; ever since 1820, when the wishes of the Country for protection were defeated by Southern votes." Admits that his "fears are greatly beyond those of most of my friends," but points out that "It rarely happens that such a state of excitement takes place, headed and guided by such talented & influential men as [Robert Y.] Hayne, [James] Hamilton, [George] M[c]Duffie, [Dr. Thomas] Cooper, &c without a convulsion. They have gone too far to recede."

Adds: "I congratulate you on your favourable prospects, which are improving from day to day. A change has taken place in this State to a great extent but I am fearful not enough to redeem Pennsylvania." Concludes: "I have been greatly indisposed for five weeks — been physicked, bled, blistered, cuffed & leeched   But I am now in a state of convalescence." ALS. DLC-HC (DNA, M212, R4). In 1820, Southern leaders had opposed a protective tariff bill and brought about its defeat. See Frank W. Taussig, *The Tariff History of the United States* (New York, 1888), 72-75. For Carey's nine essays, titled "The New Olive Branch Series," written under the pseudonym "Hamilton," see Washington *Daily National Intelligencer*, August 5, 9, 23, 30; September 13, 27; October 5, 13, 16, 1830. The series was ascribed to Carey in the *Intelligencer* of August 16, 1830.

From James Madison, "Montpelier," Orange County, Va., October 9, 1830. Thanks Clay for having sent him a copy of his Cincinnati speech [August 3]. "Without concurring in every thing that is said," he feels that the "rescue of the Resolutions of Kentucky in [17]89 & 99. from the misconstruction of them, was very a propos; that authority being particularly relied on, as an Aegis to the Nullifying doctrine; which notwithstanding its hideous aspect, & fatal tendency, has captivated so many honest minds." Calls attention to his recent letter "vindicating the proceedings of Virginia" during the Alien and Sedition controversy and tells Clay it is being published in the *North American Review* for October, 1830 [Everett to Clay, October 29, 1830]. ALS. DLC-HC (DNA, M212, R4). Printed in Colton, *Clay Correspondence*, 4:284-85. See Madison to Everett, August, 1830, in "Speeches Made in the Senate of the United States, On Occasion of the Resolution Offered by Mr. Foot, On the Subject of Public Lands . . . ," *NAR* (October, 1830), 537-38; also printed in *Letters And Other Writings of James Madison* (Philadelphia, 1865), 4:95-106. In this letter, Madison spelled out his views of the nullification doctrine.

From George W. Spottswood, Charleston, Va. (W. Va.), October 13, 1830. Says that he cannot support his family on the income from a tavern in Charleston and that he is thinking of relocating in Louisville or Cincinnati. Asks Clay's advice and assistance. Reports having received a letter from "a *Jackson* man" who related that President Jackson "had but little attention paid him in Charlottesville" when lately he visited there. Dr. Robert M. Patterson invited him to dinner at the university, "but he recd. no invite from the Citizens," and therefore "he supped at the public Table with the Boarders, & Travellers, (very condescending indeed)." ALS. DLC-TJC (DNA, M212, R13). For Patterson, see Philip A. Bruce, *History of the University of Virginia 1819-1919* (New York, 1920), 2:163-64.

From Henry Gibson, Richmond, Va., October 15, 1830. At the request of Lewis L. Barnes, sends Clay a snuff box, made by Barnes ("a youthful and worthy mechanic of this city"), as an "acknowledgement of your valuable services as the firm supporter of the Manufacturing interests of the United States." Lauds Clay at length and hopes that he will be president. ALS. DLC-TJC (DNA, M212, R10).

Clay utilized this gesture to write young Barnes on December 2, 1830, thanking him for the snuff box and pointing out in general terms the wisdom of the American System which, "like our gallant navy" will "conquer the public favor." Copy. Printed in *Niles' Register* (February 12, 1831), 39:428-29, reprinted from the Richmond *Constitutional Whig*.

From Henry Baldwin, Philadelphia, October 16, 1830. Introduces Mr. [James Reid] Lambdin,"a young artist of great genius and promise," who goes to Lexington "principally for the purpose of taking your likness." Probably intends the picture for his "Museum" in Pittsburgh. Asks Clay to assist Lambdin. ALS. DLC-HC (DNA, M212, R4). For Lambdin, see *DAB*.

From Josiah S. Johnston, Philadelphia, October 19, 1830. Reports the "sudden & unexpected death" of Mrs. James (Ann Hart) Brown at 11:00 a.m. today. "The disease which has proved so instantaniously fatal, Was Water in the chest, which has been gradually increasing & rendering her respiration more difficult. The Collection of water burst & extinguished life in a moment." Says funeral arrangements have been made and that news of her death has "made a great sensation" in Philadelphia. Concludes: "I have been with Mr. Brown this evening & he is more Composed." ALS. DLC-TJC (DNA, M212, R13). Printed in Colton, *Clay Correspondence*, 4:285.

To MATHEW CAREY   Lexington, October 25, 1830

I was sorry to learn by your letter of the 9h. inst. that you had been indisposed, and sincerely hope that this will find your health restored. It ought to be if there is in any virtue in a variety of remedies, to which you seem to have resorted.

The mail was less faithful in conveying the papers which you did me the favor to transmit; but I presume I shall have the pleasure of perusing them in the Journals, which appear eagerly to copy most of your productions.

If the painful alternative shall arise of coercing the State of So. Carolina into obedience to the laws of the Union, or expelling her from the family, as a quarrelsome, peevish and troublesome member, I am not sure that the branch which you seem disposed to embrace would not be most expedient. If she were separated, and proper laws were enacted by Congress towards her as a foreign people, she would very soon feel the pernicious consequences of her present folly, and knock at our door to be admitted again. On the other hand, if she provoke a civil war, and the General Government should exert its energies to quell the insurrection, I have no doubt that the final issue of the struggle would add strength and permanency to the Union. In neither branch of the alternative, therefore, do I perceive any other cause of regret than such as must always be felt for a deluded and misguided people.

I am inclined to think that no evil but perhaps good will grow out of a treatment of the question, in the public prints, which assumes that it will be for the interest of the other members of the Confederacy to let her go peaceably. But can you, the author of the Olive branch, the constant friend of Union consistently expouse such a course?

ALS. ICN.

From James Brown, Philadelphia, October 28, 1830. Discourses at length on the many virtues of his recently deceased wife, Ann Hart Brown. "The blow has crushed me into the earth." Thinks that he will soon follow her into eternal life. Encloses a copy of her will and asks Clay for advice and assistance on probating it under current Louisiana law. Mentions possible claims against his own estate and remarks that "I wish every thing so arranged that our two families may have nothing remaining in such a state as to disturb their harmony after Mrs. [Thomas, Sr.] Harts and my deaths—" Considers sailing to New Orleans in late November to attend to his business and legal affairs if "my health will permit me to embark. . . . I am too rhumatic and weak to bear the motion of the stage." ALS. DLC-HC (DNA, M212, R4). Printed in *LHQ*, 24:1148-52.

Sometime in early November, 1830, Clay wrote to the judge of probate for St. Charles Parish, La., one Jean Marie Morel Guiramand. He informed the judge that "Mrs. Nancy Brown" had died and that he was executor of her will. He also enclosed a copy of her will and asked that an inventory of her property in Louisiana, owned in common with her husband, be prepared. Clay to Guiramand, n.d. Copy. DLC-TJC (DNA, M212, R17).

From Hezekiah Niles, Baltimore, October 28, 1830. Reports on the outcome of the recent Maryland state elections. "The revolution in this state, like that in France, astounded the best informed of the actors in it. It was the result of the most pleasant political co-operations that I ever knew [Mercer to Clay, July 22, 1830]. All things worked in harmony. . . . We all went together, and what seems almost a *dangerous* ascendancy has been obtained. The greatness of the majority, will call the wisest counsels into requisition." Says that he has been urged to take a seat on the governor's council, but that his "private business and straightened circumstances" makes that impossible. Thinks, too, that such partisan service "could have a strong tendency to lessen the general influence of my paper [*Niles' Register*], as to those great principles on which the coming presidential election must be made to hinge. The power of my press, because of its consistency, I do think, is second to that of no other in the union, & I cannot consent to put it at hazard."

As for the coming presidential election: "The more immediate, as well as at present most important subject now before us is, as to the propriety of calling a convention to nominate a president, &c. and the manner of instituting that convention. The whole anti Jackson party in many cases has but one opinion as to the person—we are unanimous; but the *reasons* for that opinion are various, & partially adverse. . . . If a nomination is made without a statement of those *broad principles* on which all nominations should be supported, we run the risk of offending friends at home, whose character and talent deserve our courtesy & command our respect: if made without reference to those principles, the effect must be limitted, and the proceeding leave room for an unprofitable controversy, with our opponents. Thus we are in 'a straight betwixt two.' I am in favor of meeting the whole question fully and fairly."

Believes the Anti-Jackson party might have carried Baltimore city in the state election "could I have inspired our friends with half the confidence that I had in their strength." Elsewhere, "New York is, as usual, in a queer state. The result is just as *uncertain* as the 'Maysville Message' of the president — a beautiful specimen of Van Burenism. But finally, I have no fear that that state will go for the American system, and its friends. Pennsylvania too, is shaken. I feel a deep interest — [in] the affairs of *Illinois* & *Missouri*, at the present moment. The election of *three* senators is at stake."

Remarks in a postscript that "Your little namesake [Henry Clay Niles] is the finest fellow in Baltimore! And almost every day, taught by his mother, 'hurrahs for Cay [*sic*, Clay].'" ALS. DLC-HC (DNA, M212, R4). For the Missouri senatorial election, see Clay to Fendall, August 17, 1830. In Illinois, Elias K. Kane, a Jacksonian, was re-elected to the U.S. Senate by an almost unanimous vote while John M. Robinson (*BDAC*), also a Jacksonian, was chosen to fill the seat vacated by the death of John McLean. David J. Baker had been appointed by the Illinois governor after McLean's death and served from November 12, 1830, to December 11, 1830. *Niles' Register* (January 8, 1831), 39:333; Washington *Daily National Journal*, December 29, 1830; and *Guide to U.S. Elections*, 462.

From Alexander H. Everett, Boston, October 29, 1830. Thanks Clay for his letter of August 14 which he shared with his brother, Edward Everett, Daniel Webster, and "several other confidential friends." Agrees with Clay's viewpoints therein expressed. Reports that the results of the state elections in Maine on September 13 had been disappointing. Blames this on two factors: the Maysville "veto Message, which produced so much effect in the Middle and Western States, had none whatever in Maine, where it did not affect any sectional interest" and the "West India question . . . which has taken a turn rather favorable to the Administration, — is considered, whether justly or not, as more interesting to Maine than to any other State."

Discusses various campaigns for the U.S. House in Massachusetts. Notes that John Quincy Adams is running for Congress and "will probably be elected," although he decided to run "without consultation with his friends and their opinions are divided as to the policy of it"; also, that Everett's brother, Edward, is running for reelection "without opposition." Further, he himself has declined being a candidate for Congress, in opposition to Nathan Appleton, for fear of splitting the vote of "our friends." Has since supported and campaigned for Appleton who should win by a "large majority."

Calls Clay's attention to the current issue of the *North American Review*, particularly the article ("able and satisfactory though not quite so pointed as might have been wished") by Jeremiah Evarts on the Indians; also the piece by Edward Everett on nullification. As for the latter, "Mr. [James] Madisons letter, appended to it, is a highly interesting document and will have great weight through the country [Madison to Clay, October 9, 1830]." Reports that the January, 1831, issue of the *Review* will contain an article by himself on the protective tariff that will "endeavour to expose the sophistry and blunders" of Churchill C. Cambreleng's views of the tariff [Clay to Williams, May 1, 1830], as well as an article on the Bank of the United States by Mr. George Bancroft of Round Hill School. ALS. DLC-HC (DNA, M212, R4). For Appleton, see *BDAC*; for Bancroft and Evarts, see *DAB*. For the Maine gubernatorial election, see Sprague to Clay, January 20, 1830. Jacksonians controlled the Maine senate by a majority of 4 and the Maine house by a majority of 25. *Niles' Register* (October 2, 1832), 39:90. In Massachusetts, John Q. Adams defeated his opponents by winning 1,811 votes to 378 for Arad Thompson and 327 for William Baylies. *Guide to U.S. Elections*, 554. Edward Everett received 2,175 votes to 427 for James Russell. Appleton defeated his opponent, Henry Lee, 3,341 to 2,475. *Ibid.* For Evarts's article see "Removal of the Indians, Speeches on the Indian Bill. . . ." *NAR*, 31:396-441; for Edward Everett's, see "The Debate In the Senate . . . Speeches Made . . . On Occasion of the Resolution Offered by Mr. Foot, on the Subject of the Public Lands . . . ," *ibid.*, 462-546; for A.H. Everett's see "American System, Report from the Committee on Commerce. . . . A Review of Mr. Cambreleng's Report . . . ," *ibid.*, 32:127-73. For Bancroft's, "Bank of the United States . . . Report of the Committee of Ways and Means . . . as Relates to the Bank of the United States," see *ibid.*, 21-63.

To William Greene, October 30, 1830. Believes that the "election of a majority of the [Ohio] Legislature, of [Thomas] Corwin, of Stansberry [*sic*, William Stanbery] and of the Governor [Duncan McArthur], and the exhibition of such a majority in your fair City [Cincinnati] are points on which we may rest with much satisfaction." Feels that the "general aspect of affairs is encouraging," but that in Ohio as well as in Kentucky "some plan or scheme of future concert and co-operation of a character essentially popular" is needed. Reports that such a goal will be "a main object of the Frankfort Convention." ALS. OHi. For the Ohio state elections, see Clay to Sloane, July 16, 1830. William Stanbery is in *BDAC*. The Frankfort convention is discussed in Clay to Conover, October 31, 1830. Both Corwin and Stanbery were elected to the U.S. House of Representatives. Corwin defeated his opponent, James Shields (*BDAC*), by a majority of 600-700 votes. *Niles' Register*, (October 23, 1830), 39:138. Stanbery ("after a violent opposition . . . re-elected by a large majority over Mr. McLean") had switched from being a Jacksonian Democrat in the Twenty-first Congress to being anti-administration in the Twenty-second Congress. Overall, five Jacksonians were elected to Congress from Ohio together with nine anti-administration candidates. *Ibid.* (October 30, 1830), 154.

From WILLIAM B. LAWRENCE   New York, October 30, 1830
I took the liberty last summer [August 9] of giving you a summary, as far as I was then capable of making one, of the then aspect of our political affairs in this State. The nomination of General [Erastus] Root by the workingmen & his subsequent declension & return to the old party have been sufficiently announced in the papers. The embarrassments, which the zeal of the Anti-masons have occasioned, still continue; but your friends have endeavoured and are still exerting themselves to effect every thing that, under existing circumstances, can be accomplished.

The "Workingmen," who form a large mass of the opposition in this City & the other large towns are composed of two parties, one of which is carried away by all the extravagances of [Robert Dale] Owen and his associates.[1] The other consisted originally of the rank and file of the late Administration party and of a very considerable secession from the Jackson ranks, growing out of State politics.   With this latter party our friends have deemed it advisable to connect themselves, believing it the only feasible means, at this time, of laying the foundation for future efforts & as this City sends *eleven* out of one *hundred & twenty eight* members to the State assembly, its delegation will probably hold the balance of power between the present dominant party & the Anti-Masons. It was considered very important that we should have one or two members of some consideration in the State legislature in whom full confidence could be reposed & as my friends believed that I could be more useful at Albany than elsewhere, I waived in favor of Mr. A[braham]. R. Lawrence,[2] (one of the late Appraisers of this port & brother of J[ohn]. L. Lawrence) any prospects that I might have had of being preferred for Congress & accepted a nomination on the assembly ticket. I fear the chances are against our success,[3] but the efficient men of the party are extremely confident. New York City has 25,000 electors, thousands of whom are liable to be moved by sudden excitements. The Indian question will bear very hard on our present delegation to Congress & if we carry one part of our ticket, we shall probably succeed with the Assembly.[4] Mr. [Peter] Stagg, who was removed from the office of Surveyor [of the Port] to make room for Mr. M[ordecai]. Noah will undoubtedly be elected Register — the most lucrative office in the City.[5]

Should I be chosen to the assembly, I shall have associated with one Mr. R[ichard]. R. Ward, a lawyer of respectability, whose zeal in the cause is no less strong than my own. Our colleagues are men of respectability, who have heretofore had various predilections as to the prominent men of our country, but are united in hostility to Mr V. Buren, between whom & Genl. Jackson they make a distinction. They will, however, I trust be induced to vote correctly, should there be an occasion for their acting. We shall not be able to do so well for Mr [Francis] Granger as for the local candidates, owing to the many masons, who will, on no consideration, aid the Anti-Masonic cause. Many of them, indeed, entertain the same apprehensions, which I last summer took the liberty of expressing to you that the success of Anti-Masonry might operate unfavourably on the Presidential election. Taking, however, the whole state into view, the prospects of Mr. Granger are good, though no calculations on the result can with confidence be made.[6]

I write you, in great haste, almost on the eve of the election to assure you that you have a strong hold on the affections of a very large portion of our fellow-citizens & that if the friends to whom I have referred are chosen, there can be little doubt of the ultimate result in this City, which always has exercised great influence on the politics of the State.

ALS. DLC-HC (DNA, M212, R4).   1. Jerome Mushkat, *Tammany, The Evolution of a Political Machine 1789-1865* (Syracuse, N.Y., 1971), 122-24.   2. Lawrence to Clay, August 9, 1830. 3. In New York City, four groups ran candidates for the 11 assembly seats allotted to that district — the Tammany Hall Regulars, the North American Clay Workingmen, the Sentinel (Liberal) Workingmen, and the Agrarians. Lawrence ran on the Clay Workingmen's ticket, receiving 7,611 votes. All of the Tammany ticket won by an average of about 3,000 votes over their nearest competitors, the Clay Workingmen. New York *Evening Post*, Nov. 6, 8, 1830.   4. Stoddard to Clay, August 9, 1830.   5. For the duties of the office of register (or clerk) see Chancellor Kent (ed.), *The Charter of the City of New-York* . . . (New York, 1836), 126, 129, 167. Gilbert Coutant won that office with 10,059 votes to 7,905 for Peter Stagg, 2,165 for E.A. Byram, and 472 for Thomas Tripler. Noah was not a candidate for it. New York *Evening Post*, Nov. 8, 1830.   6. Clay to Johnston, May 9, 1830.

To HENRY CLAY, JR.   Lexington, October 31, 1830

The pressure of my correspondence and other engagements must be my apology for not writing you more frequently. You are however constantly in my hopes and thoughts — the more so perhaps because my regret and disappointment are so great in respect to your elder brothers [Thomas Hart Clay and Theodore W. Clay]. They are now both here, and I see nothing in the future respecting either of them, to mitigate the mortifications of the past. Theodore, after passing several months at St. Louis, consuming his money and time uselessly, has returned to commit fresh indiscretions at home. On the subject of a certain young lady he is, we all begin to fear, quite deranged. He seems to be doomed to misery and to render wretched all around him. Tom has been, during two or three months abode at home, in two debauches, and the last threatened his life. He is now well, and preparing to return to the Prairie [Illinois], from which I shall be in constant dread of hearing of other imprudencies.

I turn from these painful sons with pleasure to Anne [Brown Clay Erwin] who has been with us, with Mr [James] Erwin and the children, near two months.

She is one of the few sources which I have of real happiness. About a week ago she brought me a grand daughter, a fine-child, whom she purposes to give the name of your mother [Lucretia]. She will yet remain some weeks with us and, what affords me inexpressible satisfaction, there is a prospect of her permanent residence near me. Mr Erwin has made a conditional purchase of the farm of the late Genl [George] Trotter [Jr.], lying between Ashland and town, on which he intends to reside, if the purchase should not be defeated.

James [Brown Clay] has entered with credit the Freshman class of Transylvania and John [Morrison Clay] will shortly go into the preparatory department or to Mr. Peers.[1] I should be extremely glad, in conformity with your opinion, to send them both to Northampton, but the expence and the distance are too great.[2]

Whatever relates to your present comfort and future destiny interests me greatly. I am happy to hear that by your promotions in the Academy you are now placed in a condition of comparative ease. My advice to you still is to persevere during the seven months that remain, and direct all your energies to the prosecution of your present studies so as to emerge from the Academy with the highest attainable honor. You have now an established character, and many more eyes than you imagine are anxiously gazing upon you. This I know even better than you do. You are often a subject of the letters I receive.

After you have completed your course, obtain your commission if they will give it you, and avail yourself of the usual furlough to travel as suggested in your letter to your mother, and then return home, where we will deliberately discuss and you will decide on your future destination. My wishes on that subject are fully known to you. But I desire the ultimate decision to be made by yourself, after full consideration. Let me know in time what sum you will want to make your contemplated tour.

You will have heard of the death of your Aunt [Ann Hart] Brown. We are all greatly afflicted by it, altho' we long had too much reason to expect it. Her habits and pleasures were so interwoven with those of your uncle [James Brown] that the loss to him will be irreparable.

W. [C. C.] Claiborne [Jr.] is now with us, and he continues to be the same correct and manly youth that he has always shewn himself to be. He leaves in a few days to proceed to the State of Louisiana to take his seat as a member of the Legislature, from the City of N. Orleans. Few men at so early an age have met with such an honorable distinction.

I am making several improvements at Ashland. I have moved to the centre of the farm the Horsemill, which is undergoing a thorough repair. I am also building of brick a new conical ice house. I have got the farm in fine order, but the present Crop is very short, owing to the drought.

I will not trouble you with politics further than to say that the prospects are encouraging. Much may however depend on the result of the N. York elections, which you will know before this reaches you. You have the friendly salutations of the whole family. . . .

ALS. Henry Clay Memorial Foundation, Lexington, Ky.   1. The Rev. Benjamin O. Peers, an Episcopal clergyman, ran the Eclectic Institute in Lexington at this time. He was later (1833-1835) acting president of Transylvania University. Robert Peter, *Transylvania University: Its Origin, Rise, Decline, and Fall.* Filson Club Publications No. 11 (Louisville, 1896), 160-61; D. Lynn Koch Moore, "Benjamin Orr Peers and the Beginnings of the Public School Movement in Kentucky, 1826 to 1842," Ed.D. dissertation, University of Kentucky, 1981, *passim.*   2. Probably a reference to the Round Hill School founded by George Bancroft and Joseph Cogswell.

See Lawrence E. Wikander *et al.* (eds.), *The Northampton Book . . . A New England Town 1654-1954* (Northampton, Mass., 1954), 189-90.

To JAMES F. CONOVER   Lexington, October 31, 1830

I feel a lively interest in the success of the [Cincinnati] American and particularly that it should be better encouraged in Kentucky than it has been. The proposed Convention in K. will take effect, on the 9h. of December next at Frankfort.[1] It will probably be attended by several hundred of our most respectable Citizens, besides others who will be attracted to the place by curiosity. A nomination is, I think, the least important object of that Convention. It will bring together influential and intelligent men from all parts of the State, and the reciprocal exchange of feeling and sentiment, and the friendly intercourse which will take place cannot fail to be productive of the best consequences. It will probably adopt or recommend some plan of concert and co-operation in future, within the State, which may prevent here after collisions among friends in the canvass for elections. The movement is emphatically one of the people, and is therefore free from the objection which lies to the acting of the members of the Legislature, chosen for another and different purpose.

If you could place in some active hands your subscription paper to be presented to the members of that Convention, when assembled, I cannot but believe that many subscribers would be obtained. For obvious reasons, I shall not be at the Convention, nor if I were there, would it be proper in me to circulate a subscription paper.

The final issue of your Elections,[2] I perceive, 'though highly favorable, does not realize all the hopes inspired by the results which were first known. It must, notwithstanding, be regarded as a most cheering triumph. Even Pennsa. is not without encouraging indications.[3] We want only perserverance and confidence to achieve a glorious victory.

The elections of this summer and fall presented, I consider the turning point. That point has been gained, and henceforward the current of our fortunes will roll on unimpeded, if we do not sink in apathy or yield to despair.

Who will be your Senator?[4]

ALS. ViU.   1. In Dec., 1830, James Garrard was elected president of the convention and John Payne and David Irving were chosen as secretaries. On the second day, Dec. 10, the convention adopted 17 resolutions supporting the American System, recommending Clay as a candidate for president, and appointing twelve delegates to attend any national convention which may be called "by the friends of our principles, previous to the next presidential election." For a full text of the resolutions, see Washington *Daily National Journal*, Dec. 23, 1830. See also "de Sarcy" to Clay, Feb. 11, 1830.   2. Clay to Sloane, July 16, 1830; Clay to Greene, Oct. 30, 1830.   3. The party system was highly factionalized in Pennsylvania; hence, it is difficult to determine the party affiliations of members of the state legislature. The Anti-Masonic party, on which Clay seemed to be depending, did well in winning 4 of 33 seats in the state senate and 27 of 100 in the house. Cincinnati *Advertiser*, Nov. 5, 1830; and Harrisburg *Chronicle*, Oct. 18, 25, 1830. For slightly different numbers, see Vaughn, *The Antimasonic Party in the United States*, 93-94. For a discussion of the confused political conditions in Pennsylvania on the state and local level in the years before the election of 1832, see Philip S. Klein, *Pennsylvania Politics 1817-1832, A Game Without Rules* (Philadelphia, 1940), 324-52.   4. In Ohio, Thomas Ewing, a Clay supporter, was elected to the U.S. Senate over Micajah Williams, a Jacksonian, by a margin of 54 to 51. Jacob Burnet, the incumbent, declined to run for reelection. *Niles' Register* (Jan. 8, 1831), 39:335. For Ewing, see *DAB* and *BDAC*.

To JOSIAH S. JOHNSTON   Lexington, November 1, 1830

[Discusses recent death of Mrs. James Brown. Continues:]

I have recd. a confidential communication that Senator [Isaac D.] Barnard [Pa.] has renounced Jacksonism, and, at a time, which he may deem suitable, will exhibit evidence of his renunciation. I put you in possession of the fact that, if true, you may not be unapprized of it. Should it prove correct, the change may neutralize the loss of [William] Marks [Pa.] which I suppose is inevitable. We shall gain, I think, one Senator in K[entucky]; and there being now two to elect in Illinois ([John] McLean is dead) if we are in good luck we shall gain at least one there. On the other hand, I fear, from all that has reached me, [David] Barton [Mo.] may not be re-elected. Ohio will re-elect [Jacob] Burnet or some other friend. Indiana will re-elect [William] Hendricks (I hope reformed) or some less equivocal friend.[1] On these data you can estimate the probable state of the Senate.[2]

Should the elections to the Legislature terminate favorably in N. York (as some friends calculate) you may possibly get a friendly Senator there.[3] Of that you will be able to judge by the time this letter reaches you.

Upon the whole (let the issue of the N. York election be what it may) I think the campaign of this year has not closed discouragingly. Great faults have been committed, but they are not exclusively confined to our side. In this State, the proposed [Frankfort] Convention[4] will take effect, and one of its best results will, I hope, be to [guard against future *faux pas*. . . .]

AL. PHi. Final sentence of manuscript mutilated and illegible. For the final five words printed here, see Colton, *Clay Correspondence*, 4:286.   1. William Marks, Democrat of Pittsburgh, was defeated by William Wilkins, Democrat and Anti-Mason, also of Pittsburgh. For the results of other U.S. Senate elections mentioned here, see Clay to Beatty, June 8, 1830 (Ky.); Niles to Clay, Oct. 28, 1830 (Ill.); Clay to Fendall, August 17, 1830 (Mo. — Barton's defeat); Clay to Conover, Oct. 31, 1830 (Ohio); for Hendricks's reelection, see Clay to Johnston, April 30, 1830. Sen. John McLean of Illinois had died on October 14, 1830.   2. Although it is impossible to determine the exact party line-up in the 22nd Congress, given the state of flux of the political parties in 1830, it is clear that the Jacksonians controlled both houses. See *Guide to U.S. Elections*, 457-81, 554-55.   3. Stoddard to Clay, August 9, 1830; Lawrence to Clay, August 9, 1830. 4. "de Sarcy" to Clay, Feb. 11, 1830.

From NICHOLAS BIDDLE   Philadelphia, November 3, 1830

I have purposely delayed answering your favor of the 11th of Sepr, until I could speak with some degree of confidence as to the course which will be adopted in reference to the subject of it. In the meantime I have read repeatedly & with renewed interest all your remarks proceeding as I know they do from one who with ample materials of information & great sagacity in employing them gives the result of his, reflections with a sincere desire to serve the institution. For this in any event you will accept my grateful thanks.

After keeping the subject long under advisement, in order to observe the latest development of facts, I am now satisfied that it would be inexpedient to apply at present for the renewal of the [Bank] charter. My belief is from all that I have seen & read & heard, that there is at this moment a majority of both Houses of Congress favorable to a renewal, and moreover that the President would not reject the bill. The temptation is therefore great to take advantage of a propitious state of feeling like thus. But then the hazard is not to be disguised. A great mass of those who if they were obliged to vote at all would vote favorably will prefer not voting if it can be avoided, and the dread of responsibility, the love of postponement, & the vis inertia inherent in all legislative bodies would combine to put off the question during the approaching short session. To pass both houses & be rejected by the President — to be rejected in either house, to be postponed in either house, to be brought forward in any shape & not be finally & favorably acted upon, are degrees of evil but the mildest of them a great evil, much to be deplored & to be avoided if possible. My impression then is that nothing but a certainty of success should induce an application now. To this I am the more inclined because time is operating in favor of the Bank by removing prejudices & diffusing a general conviction of its utility

Having made up my own mind on the subject I am gratified that this, whi[ch] is the first expression I have made of this opinion, should be communicated to you whose views have so largely influenced my own. It will always afford me great pleasure to receive the benefit of your further suggestions on this or any other subject. . . .

ALS. DLC-HC (DNA, M212, R4). Printed in Colton, *Clay Correspondence*, 4:287

From JOSIAH S. JOHNSTON   Philadelphia, November 5, 1830
I intimated to you about the close of the Session, that some exclaircisement had taken place between the President & Vice President [Calhoun], relative to the old affair in the Cabinet, about his occupation of Florida — I now learn that a recent correspondence has taken place which has resulted in an open rupture It is known that [James A.] Hamilton [of] N. York obtain[e]d a letter from [William H.] Crawford through [John] Forsythe, which has explained the affair & set the truth in proper light — This led to the Correspondence, in which the Vice Pt. does not deny the part he took — complains of the unkindness of seeking evidence from his bitterest enemies &C — The parties are entirely at issue — [1] It can not be concealed that there is now a state of hostility existing in the Cabinet, between the friends of Calhoun & Van Buren that is very difficult to repress — & which greatly embarrasses the Administration —

There has been a serious difficulty about the late adjudication of the Mail Contracts, in which there are charges of injustice agt. the P.M. General [William T. Barry] & of improper & corrupt conduct in the office — [2] Mr. B was here during the Last week & recived information that the Malcontents had appealed to the President & that Berrian [*sic*, John M. Berrien] had espoused their Cause — He Barry said their object was to remove him from the office in order to place the controul of it, in the hands of a Calhoun man — This shews the jealousy & suspicion & distrust existing among them — I had also an opportunity of seeing the feelings of Barry towards Berrian You may see it also in the [Washington *United States*] Telegraph, in its tone towards Van Buren — There are reports in Circulation, from high authority, that some great change is about to take place in the Cabinet, but no one seems to know when it will occur — I think some thing is in Contemplation — The President is in a difficult position — He cannot safely caste off Calhouns friends — & they Cannot act together harmoniously — Duff [Green] continues to preach Union & good faith — because he is aware of the danger of his situation by the division of the party —

A proposition has been made to me to put out Duff, evidently with a view to put in a Van Buren man — We shall hear the proposition — see who is the man & then determine — It would produce a real scism in the party — I would make some sacrafize to put him down —

We have succeeded in Boston — Mr. Webster spoke an hour & half at the Ward meeting — & 3 ½ hours at the main Caucus when they adjd. to the next even[in]g The speech is said to be equal to the one of Last Winter — chiefly upon the Tarif—The audience was very Numerous—[3]Mr. [John Q.] Adams is elected—[4]He told me in my late visit to Boston, that Mr. Crawford had written to him about the affair in the Cabinet to which he had replied fully—This Letter is no doubt intended for Genl. Jackson—.

I have seen a letter from the Genl. in which he expresses his opinion strongly agt. the Nullifiers & says he is surprized there should be any doubt about the opinions of Mr. Van Buren—

They have a difficult question to settle about the Vice Presidency—They will not agree to let Calhoun run again—I think [Louis] McLane is to come home & take a place in the Cabinet, as a Coadjutor of V Buren, but we can not say in whose place—

It is said [John] Randolph has left St. Petersburg—[5]I hope he has—It will be quite in character—

We have News to day 8 days late—Belgium will be independent—[6]Things had gone on well in Paris but the discussions are free & violent—[7]the Clubs will be troublesome—The Ministry is not popular The National Guard is rapidly organizing throughout France—but with such a people, with the liberty of speech & of the press, divided into different parties, there will be violent debate & tremendous struggles—The flame will be lighted up over all Europe—

We have great hope of the election of [Francis] Granger—[8]but we can form no opinion now—Every thing has been done to effect it, with a full knowledge of the powerful effect it would produce on the main Contest—They have beaten us in the City—[9]

I do not see how the two parties can get through this Winter without hostility—Calhouns relation to the President & Secretary [Van Buren]—& the position of their friends is very delicate & Critical—The division in the Cabinet is irreconcilable—The first stroke that is made among them will be the signal of revolt

ALS. InU.   1. Bowers, *Party Battles of the Jackson Period*, 103-6, 110-15.   2. *Ibid.*, 183, 371-76.   3. Possibly a reference to the meeting of the National Republican caucus at Faneuil Hall on Oct. 21, 1830, called to consider the upcoming congressional election. Webster spoke briefly, promising a lengthier speech when the meeting resumed on the Saturday evening preceding the election. Boston *Daily Evening Transcript*, Oct. 22, 1830.   4. Everett to Clay, Oct. 29, 1830.   5. Johnston to Clay, May 26, 1830.   6. For the Belgian revolution, see Crane Brinton *et al.*, *A History of Civilization*, 2 vols. (Englewood Cliffs, N.J., 1967), 2:160-61.   7. Hughes to Clay, April 18, 1830.   8. Clay to Johnston, May 9, 1830.   9. Stoddard to Clay, August 9, 1830; Lawrence to Clay, August 9; Oct. 30, 1830.

To Josiah S. Johnston, Philadelphia, November 7, 1830. Reports that William C. C. Claiborne, Jr., has today departed Lexington for New Orleans determined "to do whatever he could to support your re-election." Also, that Midshipman Henry C. Hart, six months out of the U.S. Navy, but "anxious to return to it," is now in Lexington. Asks Johnston to assist in arranging Hart's reappointment. Discusses a legal case he is handling, dealing with a land survey problem in Louisiana. Says he intends going to New Orleans about December 15 to 20, "where it is my resolution to remain in great retirement until some time in February." ALS. PHi. Hart returned to the Navy, serving in the Pacific from 1831 to 1834. He resigned from the service on December 29, 1834. Clay was his legal guardian. Fayette County, Guardians' Bonds, Bk. 3 (1823-1835), p. 313.

From WILLIAM B. LAWRENCE   New York, November 8, 1830
I wrote to you on the eve of the election [October 30] to state our intended plan of operations, particularly for this City. Of the reelection of Mr. Van

Buren's Lieutenant [Enos Throop] & the defeat of the opposition [Francis Granger] you will have heard through the public papers. But, although matters have eventuated, both here and in the state at large, differently from the sanguine expectations of many of our friends, we did the best that we could, in the extremely embarrassing state of our politics; and we have scrupulously avoided bringing your name directly into a contest, from whence defeat was too likely to result. We have truly had difficulties of every kind to contend with. Not only did the Anti-Masons put forth their peculiar views, which were represented to be of the most persecuting & inquisitorial character, and refuse to allow the candidates for Governor & Lieutenant Governor[1] to be nominated by a general Convention of the opposition; but each of the other subordinate parties, into which the opposition was divided, placed, *in evidence*, principles, that drove from our ranks bodies of men, who would most zealously have co-operated in the great object of defeating the present administration. In Albany and the neighbouring counties, your friends were distinctly called on to resist Granger, as his success would, it was said, inevitably exalt Anti-Masonry and lead to a Presidential nomination. The influence, indeed, of Genl. [Stephen] Van Rensselaer, one of your warmest well wishers, was by this means used to draw out his numerous tenants against the candidates of the opposition and, when the Governor of one party is voted for, it is difficult to make the mass of the electors discriminate as to inferior nominations. A misapprehension of the character of the Workingmen's party under which name the opposition [to Jacksonism] rallied in New York, Albany &c., and its being confounded with the partisans of [Robert Dale] Owen & Miss [Frances] Wright, (who assumed the same title, though nothing can be more dissimilar than their principles,)[2] may also, perhaps, have lost us some votes in the higher classes of society. But, as universal suffrage prevails with us, the ballots which we gained from those practical mechanics and workingmen, who cannot yet be made to go openly against Jackson more than counterbalance the votes of those timid friends, who were foolish enough to be persuaded by the administration prints that Chief Justice [Ambrose] Spencer (the workingmen's candidate for Congress at Albany,) Mr. A[braham]. R. Lawrence, Mr. R[ichard]. R. Ward, myself and other men of property and education were in favor of agrarianism.[3]

On the other hand, the Jacksonians are fully drilled according to the system, which I remember your mentioning that Mr. Van Buren had once explained to you, and as they have regular nominations for their only watchwords, they are ever led astray by any differences respecting principles of public policy.

If we only looked to this part of the State, the election returns would be rather flattering than otherwise. Instead of the majorities, which they had in 1828, of 6 or 7000, Cambreling [*sic*, Churchill C. Cambreleng] & his associates have succeeded by 3000 votes & the highest on one assembly ticket is but 1800 behind the lowest Jackson candidate in a vote of 21 or 22,000.[4] The large majorities against Granger in Albany, Rensselaer[5] &c. have been accounted for on grounds unconnected with the popularity of the present administration. I cannot, however, dissemble that there is one subject to which I have alluded, that fills my mind with apprehension as to our political fate in this as well as some of the neighbouring states. I have already spoken of the unpopularity, which the support of an Anti-Masonic Governor [Granger] attached to our cause and since I commenced this letter, I have had a visit from a leading man of that party, (Mr. Henry Dana Ward, the Editor of the Anti-Masonic Review

&c,)[6] who more than realizes the fears which, on other occasions, I have taken the liberty to intimate respecting the future course of these fanatics. Though, at the late election, at least *7000* out of the *8000* votes, which the candidates for Govr & Lt. Govr. received in this City, as well as nearly all those that were given for Granger, East of Cayuga [County], were derived from Clay men, Mr Ward distinctly informed me that the Anti-Masonic party could not support our candidate for President, that they would nominate another individual for that office & that if we would advocate him, they would be obliged for our assistance, but that otherwise they would proceed without us!! He further intimated that Mr. [John C.] Calhoun was the person whom he had in view, as being the candidate most likely to break into the Jackson ranks, though on that point the party was not fully decided.

In thus stating to you what was mentioned to me by my visitor I violate no confidence, for I expressly told him that I should make you acquainted with the communication. With the nature of my answer as well as of those of other of our friends with whom Mr. W[ard]. has thought proper to confer, it cannot be necessary to trouble you. We have nailed your colours to the mast. But what are we to do with this demon of Anti-Masonry, which seems destined to blast the fairest prospects of putting down a proscribing & corrupt administration? With a union of all opposed to Genl. Jackson our entire triumph in this State, the electors being chosen by general ticket, would be certain; separated from the Anti-Masons we must be a minority. It was this view of the case that reconciled many of our friends to the support of Granger. We not only had the implied pledge as to his concurrence with us in our Presidential candidate, but if he had been chosen, a sufficient number of members of the legislature belonging to our party would also have been elected, to hold an effectual balance between the Anti-Masons & the Jacksonians.

It has been suggested that by aiding the anti-masons to wrest this State from Jackson, even in favor of a third person, the success of our candidate in the H. of Rep. might be secured.[7] But to attempt to act again in concert with them would disgust our best friends, & recent experience has shown that it is impracticable to induce the people to enter into so complex an arrangement. It is possible that we may through the Workingmen, who are nothing daunted by recent events, carry the Corporation elections in the Spring[8] against the friends of the Administration & this, in ordinary circumstances would greatly contribute towards changing the complexion of the coun[try] but the fanaticism of the Anti-Masons puts all calculation at defiance   To shew the little dependence to be placed on them, it may be observed tha[t] while we were hazarding every thing for Granger, they lost us Luther Brad[ish][9] who was supported as a member of Congress from the Northern part of the State, by setting up a third candidate and, in the same way, they have given us a Jackson Representative as successor to Mr. [Henry R.] Storrs.[10]

Under present circumstances, I must confess the prospects here are no[t] flattering, but you may rely on having zealous & steadfast friends, disposed to take advantage of any favorable circumstances that may aris[e] & to follow any suggestions that may be made by the candidate of their choice. [P.S.] Novr. 9. Mr. H. D. Ward has just called again on me & showed me a series of resolutions passed by the Exec. Committees of the Anti-Masons last evg., but not intended for publication, in which they State; 1. That the recent electi[on] has shown that that party cannot directly support Mr. Clay. 2. That they reco[m]mend to the Delegates who are to meet at Baltimore next Septr. to make a distinct nomination of Prest.[11] & to their newspapers in this State to abstain from attacking Mr Clay, with a view of conciliating his friends. 3. That the line of Anti-Masy. be so extended as to include such masons as no longer attend lodges & deny the authority & force of masonic obligations, though they may not have formally renounced. Mr. W. seemed more conciliatory than yesterday, & disposed to qualify his former remarks, but said nothing that in my judgment materially affects the preceding statement.

ALS. DLC-HC (DNA, M212, R4).   1. Samuel Stevens ran for lieutenant governor with Granger, and Edward P. Livingston ran with Throop.   2. Porter to Clay, May 23, 1830; Lawrence to Clay, August 9; Oct. 30, 1830.   3. Lawrence to Clay, August 9, 1830.   4. Lawrence's figures are basically accurate. See *ibid.*   5. The majority for Throop in Albany County was 938 and in Rensselaer County 1,980. New York *Evening Post*, Nov. 8, 1830.   6. For Ward, see *DAB*. For the *Anti-Masonic Review, and Magazine*, see *ibid.*, and *The National Union Catalog Pre-1956 Imprints* (Chicago, 1979), 18:47.   7. Apparently a reference to the National Republican prospects for success in the 1832 U.S. congressional election in New York City. In the at-large election in that district in 1832 the entire Jacksonian slate—Cornelius Lawrence, Campbell White, Dudley Selden, and Churchill C. Cambreleng—were victorious over the National Republican slate of David Ogden, Herbert Van Wagenen, Jonathan Thompson, and George Talman. *Guide to U.S. Elections*, 558.   8. The corporation elections of April, 1831, resulted in the election of the Anti-Tammany (anti-Jackson) ticket in 9 of 14 wards. New York *Evening Post*, April 13, 14, 15, 1831; and *Niles' Register* (April 23, 1831), 40:130.   9. Bradish was defeated by William Hogan, a Jacksonian, by the vote of 3,621 to 1,843 with the third candidate, Thomas Gilson, receiving 1,434. *Guide to U.S. Elections*, 554.   10. Storrs did not seek reelection. In that district, Simon Dexter was defeated 5,498 to 3,850 by Samuel Beardsley, a Jacksonian Democrat. *Ibid.*, 554.   11. Porter to Clay, July 25, 1830.

To HEZEKIAH NILES   Lexington, November 8, 1830

I received your favor of the 28h. Ulto. and prior to the receipt of this you ought to have received an acknowledgment from me of your previous letter. As you anticipated, many friends communicated to me the gratifying issue of your elections.[1] I rejoice heartily with you all. Your position is that of the centre, and I hope, in the coming contest, that our opponents will find themselves in a similar condition with the commander of an Army, whose centre has been broken.

The great consideration will be to maintain the ground which you have so nobly won. You will have some difficulties and even your great success will tend to increase them. I think you are right in declining a seat in your Council, the acceptance of which would impair the value of that neutral and impartial attitude, as respects the mere strife of party, which the [*Niles'*] Register has hitherto held.

On other points, to which you have invited my attention, I venture any suggestions with doubt and diffidence. In the general no one, at a distance, is so well qualified to judge of the expediency of any given movement as a Citizen of the State where it is to be made.

As between a nomination of a President by the Legislature or by a Convention, I think the preference belongs to the latter. It is essentially a proceeding of the people; and as they have been pleased to take up this matter, against the present encumbent, it had better continue in their hands. A convention brings together respectable Citizens from all parts of the State, commits them, pleases them. They form acquaintances, exchange opinions and sentiments, catch and infuse animation and enthusiasm, and return with a spirit of union and concert. We experienced a signal benefit from the Convention which nominated [Thomas] Metcalfe.[2] It secured his election. Considerations like these have induced the Convention which is to meet at Frankfort on the 9h.

proximo. Where the attendance of members may be inconvenient, members of the Legislature might be nominated, unless it be deemed best, as I think it would, that it meet in Balto.

To a Legislative nomination, besides other objections there is that of the members not being elected for such a purpose.

I am aware of the state of public opinion in Maryland in regard to the Tariff, and especially of the difference between the Eastern and Western shore. But I should suppose that, in any address of the Convention, it would not be difficult so to frame it as to urge strongly those points on which all are agreed and in a more guarded but satisfactory manner such as involved any difference of opinion; taking care not to abandon any principle.

I think Maryland is generally looked to among our friends for some movement. Such an impression was conveyed by the members of Congress to their constituents after the last Session.

On the subject of the exercise of the patronage of the government of Maryland, it seems to me clear that restoration of the officers who have been displaced on political grounds by the present State administration should be the general rule, subject to exceptions of those who were incompetent or unworthy. After that, new appointments should perhaps be generally made from friends, and from new converts to our cause. Policy and principle both recommend some encouragement to the latter class. If notwithstanding their change we proscribe them, they will relapse into Jacksonism. On this ground I have thought the re-election of Stansbury [sic, William Stanbery] in Ohio,[3] which was mainly by our friends, was highly expedient.

The election of [David] Barton is far from certain.[4] It depends on divisions among the other party. In Illinois we have hopes of one Senator at least.[5] In this State, I adhere to the opinion that we shall send an opponent of the present administration. I have been strongly urged to go;[6] but I have a repugnance almost inconquerable, founded upon both my feelings and my deliberate judgment. It could only be overcome by one contingency which I sincerely hope may [not] arise.

With my best wishes for your family, not forgetting my little namesake. . . .

ALS. PHC. 1. Mercer to Clay, July 22, 1830. 2. For the Adams-Clay convention held in Frankfort in 1827, see 6:1120-23. 3. Clay to Greene, Oct. 30, 1830. 4. Clay to Fendall, August 17, 1830. 5. Niles to Clay, Oct. 28, 1830. 6. Clay to Beatty, June 8, 1830.

From Peter B. Porter, Black Rock, N.Y., November 8, 1830. Reports Enos Throop's victory over Francis Granger for governor [Clay to Johnston, May 9, 1830]. Comments: "Although my *personal* feelings were strongly in favour of Granger, I am inclined to believe that, in a *national* point of view, and as regards its bearing on our general politics, the success of the anti masonic Candidate [Granger] was more to be depricated than is that of the Jackson man [Throop]. My fears, for some time past, have been — and they were greatly increased by the course adopted by the Philadelphia Convention [Porter to Clay, July 25, 1830] — that in the event of Granger's success, and other favourable indications in N. York & Pennsylvania, it was the calculation of the anti masons to bring forward a Candidate of their own — say John McLean — for the presidency; and trust to the aid of the weakest of the two existing national parties. The loss of N. York, added to their other recent defeats, would have prostrated the hopes of the Jackson men, while it would have encouraged the confidence of the antimasons; and I have no doubt that the former, who hate & fear *you* more than any other man, would have readily proffered such a coalition, & voted for McLean, if for no other purpose than defeating you. The result of our election, lessens, with each party, the inducements to such a combination."

Informs Clay that in three or four months "the friends of Internal Improvements and of the Tariff, intend to hold a state convention, for the purpose of organising a new party founded on national & reasonable principles, instead of the disgusting trash which has distinguished our late elections." ALS. InU. Letter marked "(Confidential)."

From ROBERT W. STODDARD

Geneva, N.Y., November 8, 1830

We are down in this State. Our friends at the east & north have behaved strangely indeed. After every demonstration that could be made of the intire party of Anti Masonics, in favour of the American System, Gen [Stephen] Van Rensselaer, Abraham Van Vectin,[1] with many others avowedly opposed to the Jackson interest, gave their influence decidedly, openly and vigorously on the side of the [Albany] Regency.[2] The natural consequence of this course is seen by the result of the election in favour of the Regency by a Small Majority of between 7 & 10 thousand. Ulterior effects cannot be mistaken—A Majority of the Voters west of Cayuga Lake approaching to twenty thousand, reposing implicit confidence that the Clay party in the other sections of the State would unite with them in overthrowing the Regency, have been grossly deceived—nay more—untill a little before the election, continued to receive assurances that they would be supported manfully by the Clay party, have the mortification of seeing, at an important moment, at a crisis the most favourable to their success, a most important part of that party, with its most influential leaders at his [sic, its] head go over in a body to the Regency!! How Gen. Van Rensselaer & Mr Van Vectin justify their course I neither know nor care—I wash my hands of them forever—So will the people of the west—They could not but know—they did know, that we here, were almost to a Man American system men—That we were not Anti Masons of the proscribing order—that we, by mixing freely with them not only gave tone to their politics but served to restrain their virulence—After all this, ou[r] friends at the East & North left us & went over to the enemy—Such is our situation—Looking at the consequences as they present themselves to me, I see nothing but the absolute prostration of our party in the State—The Anti Masons feel that they have been basely deserted in their utmost need & will never unite to us again.

Of those Dutchmen at Albany, & along the River, I have but a sorry opinion at the best—They are stupid, selfish—narrow-minded in every thing— They have property that gives their leaders an influence—To their paltry views we may ascribe not only this mortifying defeat, but the still more grievous calamity of having this great State consigned to the Jackson interest forever—

There cannot be any apology for keeping on the mask as long as those gentlemen did—If they really saw any reas[on] for preferring the Regency to the Anti Masonic party, why did they not let it be known in season—why suffer us at the west to remain under the delusion that we were acting not only with them but in accordance with their sentiments—Two evils presented themselves—To all appearanc[es] the Clay party throughout the State believed the Antimasons to be the least of the two—But at the very eve of the election they deserted us & came out in favour of the enemy—leaving us the most ridiculous plight immaginable.

Such   Sir is the result—I am mortified. In haste and with unabated respect. . . .

ALS. DLC-HC (DNA, M212, R4).   1. *DAB* and *CAB*.   2. Clay's friends in New York State had attempted to form an alliance with the Anti-Masons in 1830 and generally supported Anti-Mason nominations at the state level. A number of them, however, apparently fearing the growing Anti-Masonic strength and hoping to prevent it from leading to a presidential nomination for the 1832 election, broke away at the last moment and voted for the candidates of the Albany Regency, thereby ensuring the Regency a victor. For instance, on Nov. 8, 1830, the Washington *Daily National Journal* noted that Stephen Van Rensselaer had voted against the Anti-Masonic party and had carried the county with him. This action caused a serious split in N.Y. between Clay's friends and the Anti-Masons. See Clay to Lawrence, Nov. 21, 1830; Johnston to Clay, Nov. 24; Dec. 29, 1830; Lawrence to Clay, Dec. 2, 1830; and Vaughn, *The Antimasonic Party in the United States*, 38-39.

From James Strong, Hudson. N.Y., November 9, 1830. Announces that he decided not to stand again for Congress and that John King, a Jacksonian who is "for the Tariff," has been elected in his stead. Assures Clay that he is popular in this section of New York, but that "Anti Masonry has ruined us" here. Reports that Van Buren's party has carried New York, "by what majority is not yet ascertained."

Continues: "Should the West strongly sustain you — I have no doubt of your having the support of this state — The only fear is, the division, and distraction, which Anti masonry may make. I hope they will not hold a national Convention, as proposed — Or, if they do — that they will have good sense enough not to nominate a Candidate for the presidency — If they are wise enough to be silent, untill the Candidates are in the field, and then silently make their selection between them, they can, things remaining as they now are, decide the election."

Concludes: "I hope and expect to see you President — and Daniel Webster Secretary of State — And [alth]o' I may not be at Washington to greet you — yet I feel that I could then sleep in quiet — and that the interest and honor of my country would be protected and maintained —" ALS. DLC-HC (DNA, M212, R4).

To WILLIAM GREENE   Lexington, November 11, 1830

I duly recd. your favor of the 4h. inst. and perused with much interest your observations on the result of your late elections,[1] and the causes which influenced it. They coincide very much with my own, and with information communicated by other friends.

In regard to an immediate organization in your State [Ohio] with a view to future operations, that must depend, as it ought to depend, on yourselves exclusively. I may venture however two or three suggestions, witht. I trust any improper interference. In the general, system, that is organization, will prevail in any nearly equal division of the public. Enthusiasm may supply the want of it some times, as in the late revolution at Paris and perhaps at some of your elections; but these exceptions do not destroy the rule. The modification of the system is another but subordinate question. It may be inexpedient to adopt an odious name, such as Caucus, but the *thing* should exist. It may be even politic *systematically* to combat a Caucus. Your letter admits that you suffered, in the late Governor's election, for the want of organization. If you had had some Commee of correspondence (names are unessential, except when they have been rendered unpopular) would the people of any County, in your State, have been ignorant of the fact, as stated by you, that [Duncan] McArthur was the Candidate opposed to the administration? After all, was he not, in fact, brought out by a *sort* of Caucus? What else do you call the meeting at Columbus in July?[2] Perhaps, it may be said, it was a casual meeting of gentlemen. Be it so. Then these casual meetings of gentlemen, if they are often enough, are all-sufficient, let them have what name they may. If you decide upon a

295

system of concert and co-operation, the late campaign being now over, I suppose it is not material that it should instantly be done in reference to the next.

I have the most perfect confidence with you in our friend [Charles] Hammond. And still I think his notice of the K. [Frankfort] Convention was gratuitous and impolitic.[3] If the contemplated nomination had been the sole object of it, there would have been more ground for his objection. But it has other aims and will accomplish it is hoped much good. It brings respectable men together from all parts of the State; they exchange opinions and feelings, catch and infuse enthusiasm; and return home with plans and with the spirit of union. They are moreover flattered and committed by their appointments. A convention elected [Thomas] Metcalfe.[4] That is an acknowledged fact.

Then there was a general tone of discouragement in Mr. Hammonds article, underrating our strength on one side, and overrating that of our opponents on the other. What I confess too I felt very much was an intimation that Kentucky had been or was dictating to Ohio. At no time, that I know of, was this true. Certainly not in the case of the Convention, which was purely a measure of K. origin and for K. use. And this intimation to come from one in another State, who was objecting to the very interference of which he was giving a specimen! But enough of this. I repeat, that my confidence in the principles, fidelity and ability of Mr. H., is unshaken. . . .

ALS. OHi. Letter marked "(Confidential)."   1. Clay to Sloane, July 16, 1830.   2. The Washington *Daily National Intelligencer* on August 6, 1830, noted that McArthur had been requested to give his consent to be a candidate for governor, but he had stated that there were some already in the race who held the same principles as he. Clay may be referring to this approach to McArthur or perhaps to a public meeting of citizens "friendly to Internal Improvements and Domestic Manufactures" which met in Columbus on August 31, 1830, and drew up a ticket, nominating McArthur for governor, and making other nominations. Columbus *Ohio State Journal*, Sept. 2, 1830.   3. In his editorial, Hammond had expressed regret that the Frankfort convention had been called, saying that it was premature, since from a tactical standpoint no nomination should be made for at least a year. In the meantime, Hammond argued, those who voted for Jackson in 1828 but who were now disillusioned with him, and yet also disliked Clay, may be forced by "the measures of the present ruling powers" to support Clay. Hammond also stated in a subsequent defense of the editorial that the recent Kentucky elections had produced a "chilling" effect on Clay's friends everywhere and that it could not be removed by the bustle of a convention. Both the editorial and defense are in the Nashville *Republican & State Gazette*, Oct. 2, 1830. See Clay to Conover, Oct. 31, 1830, for the Frankfort convention.   4. See 6:1120-23.

To WILLIAM CREIGHTON, JR.   Lexington, November 14, 1830
I return you the letter of Mr. [Ambrose] Spencer with the perusal of which you have favored me. When you see him I request you to assure him of my cordial regard. Although I have not the advantage of his personal acquaintance, his character for high attainments, stern integrity and inflexible patriotism has been long known to me. I regret extremely to have heard of the loss of his election.[1]   The unfortunate divisions in N. York have produced, I apprehend, results which I long since feared would proceed from that state of things. The dread of Anti Masonry has driven many of our friends to the support of a cause which they condemned only a little less.[2]   I think they were unwise, but they had the exclusive right to judge for themselves.

ALS. KyU.   1. Gerrit Lansing, a Jacksonian, defeated Ambrose Spencer, the Clay candidate, for a congressional seat from New York's 10th district by a vote of 3,684 to 3,274. *Guide to U.S. Elections*, 554.   2. Clay to Johnston, May 9, 1830; Stoddard to Clay, Nov. 8, 1830.

To JOSIAH S. JOHNSTON   Lexington, November 14, 1830
The same information communicated to you, and which is contained in your letter of the 5h. inst. respecting the rupture between two high officers [Jackson

and Calhoun], has come to me from Nashville, pretty directly. I think therefore it may be presumed true. I should not be surprized if Jackson should denounce the Nullifiers in his next message and mount that Hobby to regain his popularity. But what will what can the V. President do? South Carolina is rather too contracted a position for him to start from. Besides, he is not very secure in that. It appears to me that V.B. has completely out-manouvered him.

In regard to the attempt to turn out Duff [Green], I can supply you with some facts which may throw light on the object. [Francis P.] Blair of the K. [Frankfort] Argus [of Western America] is now on his way to Washington, with his family, to set up a new paper.[1] And it is highly probable that the alternatives which the Jackson party means to offer you are Duff or Blair! Will not their division admit of our friends appointing some respectable Editor? If not I think it will be most expedient for them to present such an Editor and adhere to him to the last, without mixing in the contest between the above two.

The divisions in N. York have lead, I presume, to the issue which might have been anticipated—the triumph of the Jackson party in all the Elections.

I believe I mentioned to you in a former letter that [George] Poindexter dined with me, and that he talks like an independent man who felt that he was denounced and was resolved to cling to principle.

ALS. PHi. Printed in Colton, *Clay Correspondence*, 4:288. Addressed to Johnston in Philadelphia.
1. Blair was brought to Washington to establish *The Globe*, because Green's loyalty to Calhoun made him suspect to the Jacksonians as the growing break between Jackson and Calhoun became more apparent. The two editors did not openly declare their opposition to each other until early 1831. See, further, William E. Smith, *The Francis Preston Blair Family in Politics* (New York, 1933), 1:56-61, 68-76; and Elbert B. Smith, *Francis Preston Blair* (New York, 1980), 40-41.

From Samuel L. Southard, Trenton, November 14, 1830. Reports that he has been seriously ill and confined to bed for more than six weeks. Notes that while recent state elections in the West, Maryland [Mercer to Clay, July 22, 1830], and Delaware [Rodney to Clay, October 7, 1830] "give sincere pleasure to those who love their Country," the outcome of those in Maine [Everett to Clay, October 29, 1830], New York [Clay to Johnston, May 9, 1830; Stoddard to Clay, August 9, 1830], and New Jersey [Southard to Clay, August 8, 1830] "is not so good—still I see in them no cause to despair." Complains that in New Jersey "local causes of an agitating nature governed the results irresistably in some of the Counties—Canals, railroads—Judiciary bills and other subjects," to the exclusion of the "Gen question." Thinks "We shall have a better chance I hope at the Congressional Election which takes place in December, and which is general throughout the State—We have a decided majority if we can bring the voters to the polls—"

Says that there has been much pressure on him in New Jersey to run for Congress but that he has not consented and probably will not. "Going to Congress will occasion a sacrifice of one third to one half of my present income."

Concludes: "The Election in New York has mortified altho it has not much dissapointed me—The Anti Masonic question is not strong enough to carry any one state in the union, altho it is strong enough if properly directed to destroy either of the parties—It presents I think now, as I thought when I formerly wrote to you [August 8, 1830], the greatest danger and difficulty in the way of those who seek a real and honest *reform* in the concerns of government—What will be the effect of our friend Mr [John Q.] Adams' going to Congress [Everett to Clay, October 29, 1830]? I take it for granted you do not mean to go to the Senate [Clay to Beatty, June 8, 1830]. . . . Your true policy now is to remain as quiet and retired as possible—You can not I think add to your strength by appearing actively before the public—Will [John J.] Crittenden be Elected to the Senate—" LS, written by an amanuensis. InU. Samuel Southard did not run for Congress, but his brother, Isaac, was elected to the Twenty-second Congress as a "Clay Democrat" (*BDAC*), defeating Isaac Pierson, the incumbent. *Niles Register* (January 8, 1831), 39:329.

From HENRY CLAY, JR. West Point, N.Y., November 16, 1830

I am really distressed & mortified at the account which you give of my brothers [Thomas Hart Clay and Theodore Wythe Clay]. I had hoped that they had long since reformed; and I am now so much surprised & disappointed that I know not what expectations to form of the future. I cannot conceive what attractions dissipation and its votaries can offer to men of enlightened intellects; when the pursuits of the refined & liberal studies lay open before them. However many of the brilliant characters that history displays have torn themselves from the haunts of pleasure and folly, to live in the memory of mankind: And Plutarch even thinks that real greatness must be in a measure the work of previous folly & experience; or as he has it, that the truly great men must have undergone numerous changes & fermentations, like good wine in its process of purification. This I confess, is weak, & in its general application, fallacious reasoning, still it furnishes a slight foundation for a hope that Theodore & Tom may yet change their course of life and apply their talents to their appropriate uses.

I rejoice with you that there is a prospect of Anne's [Brown Clay Erwin] living near Ashland. I am extremely anxious that Mr [James] Erwin's purchase may not be defeated.[1]

I am happy to learn that Wm [C.C.] Claiborne [Jr.] is [a] member of the L'a Legislature from New Orleans. He has always had my esteem and I have desired nothing, more than his success in his enterprises.

You have no doubt heard the unfavorable results of the New York elections   I shall not therefore mention them.[2]

You mention that you are making improvements on Ashland. If there could be obtained a sheet of water in front of the house, it would furnish the finest relief to the eye that I know of And with some other improvements would make Ashland equal to any country-seat that I have seen.

I am at present much taken up with composition and eloquence. I am now writing an oration for my own improvement, which I shall beg you to criticize for me when I arrive at home: The design of it is similar to that of Cicero for Cluentius; And the narrative and arguments are taken from the only oration I ever heard you deliver, than of the 4 of July before the last,[3]   I fear that your's made too great an impression upon me; for in writing your arguments I fall into a language very like your own in that case, — though inferior.

On my return home, if I should make my contemplated tour, would it be inconvenient for you to give me letters of introduction to the following gentlemen, Mr [John Q.] Adams, Mr [Daniel] Webster & [Edward or Alexander H.] Everett, Mr [Jared] Sparks, Chief Justice [John] Marshall & Mr [James] Madison? I am already acquainted in New York, Philadelphia & Baltimore & should therefore need none to those cities.

You speak of my decision in regard to my future life — I sincerely wish that it had been already made. There are so many considerations to encumber the selection that I almost dispair of making a judicious one, and indeed am beginning to decline making one at all. I am pretty sure that on the next vacancy, should I suggest a wish to have the office, Genl [Winfield] Scott would make me his aid. And really that is a much better situation than that of a mere county-court lawyer.[1]

Your opinion, whatever it may be, will govern me entirely. I think that the compositions and speeches, which I shall bring with me will enable you to judge of the character of my mind. And I am sure you will tell me candidly without any fear of hurting my vanity, whether you think that with study and perseverance I would be able to attain to the first rank at the Bar. Any other would not satisfy me, and I should prefer the army.

If I do remain in the army, I will turn my attention during peace to Literature; and the better to prepare myself will go to Europe for 2 or 3 years on my pay. It is very easy to get a furlough for that purpose, Such tours have constantly met the approbation of the Secretaries of War.

Remember me affectionately to my mother & the Boys And all our friends

ALS. Henry Clay Memorial Foundation, Lexington, Ky.   1. Clay to Henry Clay, Jr., Oct. 31, 1830.   2. Clay to Johnston, May 9, 1830; Stoddard to Clay, August 9, 1830.   3. A July 4 speech by Clay for 1829 has not been found.   4. Young Clay received no such desirable appointment and resigned from the army shortly after his graduation in 1831.

From John Foster, Jr., South Scituate, Mass., November 17, 1830. Announces that his county, "by an almost unanimous vote," has elected John Q. Adams to Congress [Everett to Clay, October 29, 1830]. Reports that the voters laid "aside peculiar party prejudices" and elected "the *best Man*," an attitude in New England that also "extends to *you*." Is certain that Clay is the one person "left in whom a majority of the States will unite, for the redemption of our national — our Republican character." Cites the crushing of the Polish Revolution (a "lamentable scene lately acted in Russia") as an example of America's need for "one of the ablest Statesman which our Country can produce," to be brought forward so as "to redeem, at least in that quarter, our national character." Asserts that "the present administration" is "unequal" to such a task. Promises that he will use "every means in my power . . . through the medium of the press," to "secure the Presidency" to Clay. ALS. DLC-HC (DNA, M212, R4). For the obituary of John Foster, a South Scituate attorney, who died in 1848 at age 80, see *NEHGR,* 3:102.

From James Brown, Philadelphia, November 18, 1830. Relates at length his continuing grief over his wife's death, and instructs Clay not to go to New Orleans solely on account of legal problems associated with her will [Brown to Clay, October 28, 1830]. Continues: "I know nothing about politics generally and still less if possible about the state of party in New York — It is said however by your friends here that had a few days more elapsed before the last election the result would have been different   It is said a union was rapidly going on between the Antimasons and Masons and that this would have been soon so extensive as to have ensured the election — Mr. [Josiah S.] Johnston has written to [Francis] Granger on this subject as I have heard, and hopes that the Masons who have been too tenacious of a secret society which has no longer any secrets, will join their opponents on general and interesting questions — For my own part I wonder how any one can wish now to be a Candidate for the office of P[resident]. and sincerely wish you could avoid coming before t[he peo]ple. You have had enough of honors, and God knows enough of abuse, and with your interesting family might enjoy all the happiness of which our frail nature is susceptible in retirement — Besides I have always believed that the present incumbent would be re elected although he may have lost some of his popularity." ALS. DLC-HC (DNA, M212, R4).

To WILLIAM B. LAWRENCE   Lexington, November 21, 1830

I received your favor of the 8th inst. as I did that written on the eve of your election, for both of which I thank you. The result of your elections, in regard to the choice of members of Congress and of your State Legislature, has excited surprise and regret.[1] At this distance, and without the advantage of full local information, it is difficult to form an accurate judgment as to the true cause of that result. What therefore I shall say, on that subject, is just as things strike me without intending to convey reproach, or to indicate what ought to be done, if any thing, in future, respecting which my friends, in whose zeal and fidelity I have full confidence, are most competent to decide.

It occurs to me that the main cause of that result is the perfect system and organization on one side, or rather by two parties, and the want of it by the third. The Regency and the Antimasons were both organized; our friends were not. The consequence was that both of the former parties went to the polls with their forces marshalled and with objects in view, whilst our friends repaired to them, helter skelter, leaving things to take what course they might. The effect was, the total want of concert among them; in some places, and in the same place, some voting for one ticket, & some for another, and some not at all. The want of a candidate for the office of Governor, I take it, has led to the losses we have sustained in the members of Congress and of the Legislature. For when there are but two rival candidates, a vast number of the voters will look only at the head of the ticket, not caring to trouble themselves about the subordinate offices, the candidates for which are associated on the same ticket with the head. Thus, I presume, that in many instances our friends, who were opposed to the Anti-Masonic Candidate for Governor [Francis Granger] voted for his competitor [Enos Throop], although upon his ticket there were other Candidates whom they did not prefer for their respective offices. How otherwise are we to account for the issue of the elections in Rensellaer [sic, Rensselaer], Saratoga, Albany &c &c? It seems to me it would have been wiser either that our friends should have had a candidate of their own for Governor, or if that were inadvisable, that they should have met in Convention and resolved, as a party, to support the Anti Masonic Candidate.[2] In the first case they would have acted with the perfect concert; in the latter with more than they did, and probably, at least, with sufficient to have elected Mr Granger

I fear that both of the other parties have come out of the election stronger, and we weaker than before. The Regency have achieved another victory, when defeat was beleived to await them. This will add moral strength to them, and they will be regarded as invincible. On the other hand, the Anti Masons have made an exhibition of powerfull force greater than they ever before presented. This will encourage them to persevere. They will not give you credit for the aid you gave them. They will count hereafter upon your hatred to the Regency obliging you to give them similar aid or that they will derive collateral support from other popular dissentions, of which there is always a number. By not acting as a party, either in presenting a Candidate or in resolving to support Mr. Granger, we, in effect, acknowledged our weakness; and we have totally failed to attain the object, as I understood, of that forbearance, that is to secure a majority of the members of Congress and of the Legislature. The grounds of my fear that we will henceforward be weaker are 1t our failure to act in corps. 2 the strenghth exhibited by the other two parties, and 3d the impression that many of our friends have been absorbed and will henceforward act with the other two parties.

What is to be expected from the Antimasons you have learnt from Mr [Henry Dana] Ward, who told you that they could not support me, and would nominate a Candidate of their own. The leaders of that party are undoubtedly aiming at political power, whilst the great mass of it is actuated honestly by the sole motive of pulling down Masonry, which they beleive to be a great evil. It would be perfectly consistent with the object of the leaders to support any Candidate for the Presidency, Mason or AntiMason, whose election they could secure. But the difficulty with those leaders, in supporting a Candidate who was a Mason, would be that they could not carry with them the body of their party. They must, therefore, if they nominate any Candidate nominate an Anti-Mason. They may not, and I think it most probable they will not, nominate any Candidate, but leave their friends to vote as they please, as ours did at the late election in New York.

It is of the nature of all minorities, however split up into parties, to coalesce against the party in power. Accordingly we see that, in the Western reserve in Ohio, and I believe also in Vermont, the Anti Masonic party and the Jackson party being, in both those places, in the minority, acted in concert.

By connecting ourselves, in any degree, with the Anti Masons, we catch all the odium which attaches to that party, without any compensating benefit. To carry their purposes they will hold out hopes to us, conciliate us, perhaps many of the leaders sincerely wish to aid us; but I apprehend, when the trial comes, we shall find ourselves wofully disappointed in any efficient aid rendered to us by them, *as a party*.

What then ought our friends in N. York to do? That must depend upon themselves, and any suggestions of mine are only intended for your consideration.

We are opposed to a wicked, passionate and corrupt Administration, which we belcive menaces the best interests of the Country, and even the stability of our institutions. We are for principles, for liberty, for the Constitution, for the Union. Let us then march directly to our object. It is the manly course. Let us hoist our banner and rally our friends and organize them for systematic action. Let us make the calculation which the Antimasons make, that is that those who hate the Admin and the Regency more than they do us will come to us and not go to them. If there be any sincerity in the professions of the Antimasons they will support us, rather than our opponents. This they will probably generally do in your State, if they have no Candidate of their own. It will be easier for the leaders to persuade their party of the inexpediency of nominating any Candidate for the Presidency, and thus allow them to pursue the bent of their own inclinations in regard to the other candidates, than to prevail on them to agree to the formal nomination of a Candidate who was of the Mason order.

Had I been in N. York I should have voted for Granger for these reasons. He is the best man of the two Candidates. Antimasonry never can be general throughout the U.S. Jacksonism is. It is better to suffer a partial evil than a general one. Antimasonry is more controlable than Jacksonism. From its very nature Antimasonry will soon burn out. The Regency never will until it is put out. Many of our friends took a different view of the matter, and I regret it. I would ask them if they had not rather have an Antimasonic Governor of N. York, with the Administration of the general government according to their wishes, than the Regency dominant at Albany and Jacksonism at Washington, with the Anti Masons down? If Granger had been elected, I should have regarded the defeat of Jackson as certain. As it is, he may be defeated, but it will only be by vigorous, persevering and *united* exertions.

The effect of our friends running no candi[d]ate for Governor, coupled with the defeat of Granger, is discouraging in *other* States. More discouraging than if there had been three Candidates, and the Regency had then prevailed, *provided the agregate of the votes for the two unsuccessful Candidates would have been greater than that for the Regency Candidate*, which I take it would certainly have been the case. For then, our friends would have *hoped* for an ultimate union of the defeated parties; and this hope would have animated their efforts in other States.

Be pleased to make my best regards to Mr [Joseph] Blunt, to whom as well as to C[harles]. King Esq. you may shew confidentially this letter. Say to Mr Blunt that I received his obliging letter.

Copy. NBuHi. See Clay to Porter, below, this date, which identifies Clay as the author of this letter. Letter marked "(Confidential)."   1. Clay to Johnston, May 9, 1830; Stoddard to Clay, August 9, 1830.   2. Stoddard to Clay, Nov. 8, 1830.

To PETER B. PORTER   Lexington, November 21, 1830

I recd. your last letter, communicating the result of your election, and the preceding one. I transmit you enclosed a copy of a letter which I have addressed to Mr. W. B. Lawrence[1] as best conveying what I think of N. York politics past and present. In Mr. Lawrence's letter [November 8] to which mine is an answer he says: "Mr. Henry Dana Ward (Editor of the Antimasonic review) distinctly informed me that the Anti Masonic party could not support our Candidate for President; that they would nominate another individual for that office; and that if we would advocate him, they would be obliged to us for our assistance, but that otherwise they would proceed without us." In a P.S. he adds: "Mr. H. D Ward has just called again on me and shewed me a series of resolutions passed by the Executive Committee of the Antimasons last evening, but not intended for publication, in which they state 1st. That the recent election has shewn that that party cannot directly support Mr. Clay. 2. That they recommend to the Delegates who are to meet at Balto. next Septr. to make a distinct nomination of President and to their newspapers in this State to abstain from attacking Mr. Clay with a view of conciliating his friends. 3 That the line of Anti-masonry be so extended as to include such masons as no longer attend lodges and deny the authority and force of masonic obligations, though they may not have formally renounced."

The best state of things in N.Y. for our friends two years hence would be this: that the Anti. Masons should have a Candidate for Governor but no candidate for Electors; that our friends, being previously fully organized, should have a ticket for Electors, but no Candidate for Governor. Then the two parties would naturally unite. But if both parties should present two separate and entire tickets both would probably be defeated, unless in the mean time one or the other should acquire such additional strength as would enable it to succeed.

Perhaps the delay which has taken place in the organization of our friends may tend now to unite them with more zeal and animation.

I still hope that we shall succeed in most of the Senatorial Elections in the West. If we fail, our failure will have been produced chiefly by the inauspicious result of the N.Y. elections.

I expect to go with Mrs. Clay to N. Orleans this winter. My purpose is to live there in great retirement whilst we stay. Mrs. [James] Brown's death, of which you will have heard, will serve to enable us to execute that wish. . . .

ALS. NBuHi. Letter marked "(Confidential)." 1. Above, this date; see also, below, Porter to Clay, Dec. 10, 1830.

To JOHN M. BAILHACHE   Lexington, November 24, 1830

I received your favor of the 18th inst., communicating a very full and satisfactory account of your late election,[1] and of the causes which led to its results. Upon the whole, we have much reason to be satisfied with those results, although we may regret that our friends in the reserve did not bestir themselves more. On the subject of the operation of Anti-Masonry on the interests of our cause, respecting which you request my views, I will explain them very frankly.

The leaders of Anti-Masonry are in the pursuit of power; the great body of their party are endeavoring to remove what they honestly believe to be a great evil. The former would desire power, without regard to the means of acquiring it; the latter seek it only as an instrument of effecting their paramount object. To accomplish this object they believe, and their leaders industriously inculcate the belief, that a change of the administration of the actual Government (whether general or State) is necessary. Hence, in the Western reserve, and in Vermont, where our friends are in the majority, the Anti-Masons connected themselves with the Jacksonians to get hold of the Government, and to dispossess those who possessed it. For the same reason, in New York and Pennsylvania, when the Jackson party was in power, the Anti-Masons sought a coalition with our friends. If this coalition was not complete, and if the Anti-Masons did not succeed, it was not their fault.

I think it may be assumed that whenever Anti-Masonry is in the minority, it will seek a connection with any other party, which, in the same place, is also in the minority. This will account for the various and apparently conflicting directions which it takes. It is only an apparent inconsistency, for the object every where is the same, the acquisition of power.

In this respect, Anti-Masonry does not differ from any other party, for the natural tendency of all the divisions of a minority, is to cohesion. This will generally take place unless it is counteracted by some stronger feeling or sentiment than that of hatred to those in power, as was the case with a portion of our friends in the late New York election.

I do not know that it is to be regretted that the Anti-Masons did not succeed in Pennsylvania and New York. If they had been successful, they would probably have brought out an Anti-Masonic candidate for President. Still, if I had been in New York, with a right to vote, I should have given my suffrage to [Francis] Granger. I will not now trouble you with the reasons.

I regret that the failure of Mr. Granger is so well ascertained to have been, because our friends about Albany, and in the river counties, would not concentrate on him.[2] Unless this circumstance should produce an alienation between our friends and the Anti-Masons, I should think we will ultimately obtain their support, for the following reasons:

1. It is in conformity with the general nature of minorities, already noticed, that they should vote with us, if they have no candidate of their own party.

2. They agree with us as to the American System.

3. They have been violently assailed in New York by the Regency.

4. They believe that, although I am a Mason, that I have no bigotry, and that I have no very great ardor for the institution.

5. General Jackson has, as they think, persecuted them, which they believe I should not do, as most certainly I should not.

I can hardly believe that they will now present a Presidential candidate, although they still talk about it. Immediately after the election in New York, Mr. [Henry Dana] Ward (the editor of the "Anti-Masonic Review") told a friend of mine [William B. Lawrence] that they could not support me, and would present a candidate of their own, etc. The next day he called on that same friend, and informed him that the Executive Committee of the Anti-Masons had resolved, 1st. That the late election in New York had shown that they could not directly support me: 2d. That it be recommended to the convention at Baltimore, to nominate an Anti-Masonic candidate; and 3d. That the papers of the party in New York, be advised to abstain from attacking me, and to conciliate my friends.[3]

If there be an Anti-Masonic candidate, I am inclined to think that it would operate in Pennsylvania and New York, more against General Jackson than me, should we both be the candidates, while in your State, it would operate more against me than him. In that contingency, should our friends in New York and Pennsylvania unite with the Anti-Masonic party, Jackson would probably lose one or both of those States, in either of which cases I think he would be defeated.

What I think not unlikely, is, that this time two years hence, the Anti-Masonic party will present in New York a candidate for Governor, without any electors for President and Vice-President, and that our friends will offer these, without any candidate for Governor.[4] Upon that supposition, if there be concert between the two parties, each would succeed in its object. I do not know that any such arrangement has ever been thought of. None such has ever been suggested to me, and I infer it only from the natural operation of causes.

I am inclined to think, upon the whole, that a conciliatory course on our part, toward the Anti-Masons, is wisest. There is no occasion for our friends to attack them. Let us leave that to the Jackson party.

We shall have some trouble about a Senator, though I yet think we shall succeed in the election of a friend. I have been pressed of late to offer.[5] Mr. Adams' example[6] is quoted. But both my feelings and judgment are strongly opposed to my return to Congress. Nothing but a contingency, which I sincerely hope may not arise, would overcome them.

Copy. Printed in Colton, *Clay Correspondence*, 4:289-91.   1. Clay to Sloane, July 16, 1830; Clay to Greene, Oct. 30, 1830.   2. Stoddard to Clay, Nov. 8, 1830.   3. Lawrence to Clay, Nov. 8, 1830.   4. In the 1832 elections the Anti-Masons and the National Republicans in New York formed an Anti-Jackson coalition. The National Republicans supported the Anti-Mason candidates for governor and lieutenant governor, Francis Granger and Samuel Stevens. William L. Marcy, the Jacksonian candidate for governor, defeated Granger by the vote of 166,410 to 156,672. The Anti-Masons nominated presidential electors who were uncommitted, but since it was well known that the Anti-Masons preferred Clay to Jackson and that Wirt had no reasonable expectation of success, it was believed the Anti-Masonic strength would ultimately be thrown to Clay. The National Republicans did, in fact, endorse the Anti-Masonic presidential ticket. In the popular vote for president, Clay received 154,896 and Jackson 168,243; Jackson also received all 42 of New York's electoral votes. See Hammond, *The History of Political Parties in the State of New York*, 2:417-18; Joseph E. and Jessamine S. Kallenbach (eds.), *American State Governors 1776-1976* (Dobbs Ferry, N.Y., 1981), 1:419-26; and *Niles' Register* (Dec. 1, 1832), 43:213.   5. Clay to Beatty, June 8, 1830.   6. Everett to Clay, Oct. 29, 1830.

From JOSIAH S. JOHNSTON   Philadelphia, November 24, 1830

I shall obtain if possible the order from the land office on my Arrival & forward on [to] you immediatcly. I will pay attention to what you request about young [Henry Clay] Hart — [1]

We were Unable in so short a time to bring about a reconciliation in N. York[2] so that our masonic friends could vote for [Francis] Granger — We tried to affect a Union, which succeeded to a Certain extent,[3] but in the Counties, where we were the strongest the hostility against the anti masons, had become too violent   It was in fact the master passion — [Enos] Throop has 30,000 less than Van B. who had not a majority — [4] The event shews the weakness of the Regency & that Union alone is necessary to put down that party — I have address[e]d a letter to Granger, with all my views on the necessity of acting now together — & other means are employed to bring about this end — I have not heard from him — The question is fairly put to him & I will let you know the result — This Union will decide the vote of the State & this state will controul the national election — We shall put every engine in motion — upon this hangs the main question so important to us all & to the Country — [James] Strong is here, he says you will get the state — I understand you will have a popular nomination in N. york next week, which will be followed up through the State.[5] It is now time to act — I have not much Confidence in the Anti Masons, They have political & ambitious objects, they are difficult to manage. They have just power enough in N. york to settle the question & almost without a struggle — They are in great confusion in this State & they hang heavily on the admn — [Samuel D.] Ingham — with about 20 others were separated from the Republican party of the state & were the party that attempted to get up [John C.] Calhoun — He has contrived to impose himself upon the President as the leader of the Democratic party & as Secy of the Treasury wields the patronage of the Govt. for his own benifit & the advancement of his own friends — while the old friends of the President, his original supporters are treated with neglect. The Democratic party is extremely hostile to Ingham, & very much dissatisfied with his continuing in office & these views are now Urged strongly upon the President who finds himself in a very awkward situation — He in fact dare not touch Ingham or any friend of Calhoun   He would probably lose in that Case the majority of both Houses — & all the talent in debate —

He must therefore offend the real Democratic party of Penna. or he must reform his Cabinet — We must let this thing work   The President is not strong enough to throw off the Calhoun party — He will find it difficult to get along with Ingham who is a dead weight —

There appears some disposition among the Anti Masons of this state to bring out [John] McLean — & if the Democratic party here should come to an open rupture with the admn. which they will do reluctantly they will be inclined to bring out McLean also — That idea is merely suggested — Some thing very interesting will transpire among them during the winter — What it will be I can not tell

We are mere lookers on in Venice —

I am glad [Francis P.] Blair is Coming[6] — it will hasten the Crisis   I hope they will break at once — They may come to us — We cannot interfere with them — Let them quarrel —

I hope you will have a pleasant Winter & good health   We shall probably have an eventful one —

My own opinion is Calhoun will hold on as long as possible to the Jackson party—It will be difficult to shake him off—But if the President reforms the Cabinet, which he will scarcely venture to do, it will be a declaration of War—They cannot come to us, but they may then act so far with us as to hold the adm in check—

ALS. InU. 1. Clay to Johnston, Nov. 7, 1830. 2. Clay to Johnston, May 9, 1830; Stoddard to Clay, August 9, 1830. 3. Stoddard to Clay, Nov. 8, 1830. 4. Martin Van Buren had not received a majority of the votes cast for governor in 1828. He had received 136,794 votes to 106,444 for Smith Thompson and 33,345 for Solomon Southwick. In 1830, when Throop was elected over Granger by a majority of 8,500 votes out of a quarter million cast, he had received fewer votes than Van Buren, because the total number of votes cast was smaller. *BDGUS*, 3:1075-76; also, Washington *Daily National Journal*, Nov. 22, 1830. 5. Lawrence to Clay, Nov. 29, 1830; Porter to Clay, Dec. 10, 1830. 6. Clay to Johnston, Nov. 14, 1830.

From Josiah S. Randall, Philadelphia, November 24, 1830. Reports that the recent elections in Pennsylvania [Clay to Conover, October 31, 1830] "produced but one result—the defeat of the Anti Masonic party." Pronounces this a "good result." Believes that had the Anti-Masonic convention in Philadelphia in September decided to nominate a presidential candidate, the choice would have been between John McLean and Daniel Webster; and that McLean would probably have been the choice, with Webster being nominated for vice president. Continues: "I hope their defeat in Penna. & Ohio will induce them to give up the Convention at Baltimore in Septr. next, and that parties should recur to their original element in N. Y. and that upon the issue will depend the great results. Just at the moment when we could have put down the Regency party we are thwarted by the erection of the new party. I remonstrated with Mr [Francis] Granger but all to no purpose, he was infatuated in the success of their party and nothing but defeat would bring him to view this matter in a dispationate manner. What I would now desire is that our political friends in N. York shd. immediately organize themselves upon the ground of opposition to Genl. Jackson. Mr. Adams in 1828 was in a minority of only 3 or 4000, votes in the whole State and our position has since been abundantly improved." Is convinced, further, that "The next Presd. Election depends entirely on New York, all others are Subsidiary."

Concludes with the comment that "A grand subject has occupied our attention for sometime, the prospects of your coming to the Senate of the U States [Clay to Beatty, June 8, 1830]. I assume for a moment that you are willing to come. In your Votes you have nothing to fear, you have not like Genl. Jackson, pledges for and against the Tariff & Internal Impt. to redeem. *On no question are your Sentiments unknown*, and it will not [be] denied that your presence at Washn. would be desirable. What would Mr V Buren or Mr Calhoun be if they were at home instead of being at Washn. Add to this we are at Washn totally without concert or organisation and there is no one to look up to for advice or information I present these views for consideration." ALS. DLC-HC (DNA, M212, R4).

From William B. Lawrence, New York, November 29, 1830. Reports that Clay's friends in New York City "who have never yet publickly rallied as a distinct party," have called a general meeting at which "measures for a complete organization shall be adopted." Points out that by "taking this course, it has been conceived that we should be able to anticipate the anti-masons & induce them, if they are not desperate fanatics, from the utter hopelessness of carrying their own candidates, to support ours. at the same time, or, without their aid, nothing can be effected, every thing must be done to conciliate them. There is reason to believe that we shall be able to carry with us nearly all who supported the ticket of the Workingmen [Porter to Clay, May 25, 1830] & that we shall have accessions from persons, who were deceived as to the motives that governed that party or objected to an association with the anti-masons." Leading the Clay movement in New York City are David B. Ogden, Henry R. Storrs, Joseph Blunt, and himself.

Feels that "The late election has conclusively shown that neither the President nor Mr. V. Buren has a majority of the people of the State of New York. But, I am more & more convinced that a party to succeed in this State must adopt the tactics, by which the Jacksonians prevailed & go on the broad ground of opposition to the existing powers without putting *in evidence* any principles that may distract those, who might otherwise be made cordially to cooperate. We have just seen the effects of anti-masonry. Internal Improvements, however popular elsewhere, will not carry this State on account of the interest felt in the existing canals belonging to the public & private companies. In the interior the Tariff would be supported by a considerable majority but in this City & neighbouring Counties, embracing nearly one fourth of this State it would be sustained by a feeble minority & this is precisely the Section of country where Anti-masonry is almost unknown. We have, therefore, determined to avoid, as far as possible, all debateable ground & rest on the faults of the present administration—the personal merits of our candidate &c the great principle of upholding the Union, in opposition to the nullification doctrines of South Carolina, with which we shall endeavour to identify Genl. Jackson & his advisers."

In response to Clay's inquiries "about an individual of this place (M.L.D.) [Matthew L. Davis]," who "occasionally writes to you," warns that "he is not entitled to confidence" and that "his connection with any political party is calculated to do it material injury." ALS. DLC-HC (DNA, M212, R4). Encloses report of resolutions adopted at a "select meeting" on November 26. These called for "organizing a party in opposition to the present corrupt administration of the general government," scheduling a public meeting at Masonic Hall at an early date (at which Clay would be nominated for president of the United States), and forming a committee of "five persons from each Ward" who would organize "said general meeting" and preserve order at it when held. The Masonic Hall meeting was held on Monday evening, December 13. See, below, J. L. Lawrence to Clay, December 14, 1830.

From Thomas Rivers, Providence, R.I., November 29, 1830. Has forwarded to Clay a piece of blue satinet manufactured by the W. & D. D. Farnum Co. of Massachusetts. Speaking for the Farnums, and as the editor of *The Manufacturers and Farmers Journal* of Providence, informs Clay that "The Messrs. Farnums, in common with the Manufacturers of New England feel under many obligations to you, for your great & successful exertions in the cause of domestic industry and acknowledge that without the aid of your talents and patriotism, the 'American System' would, before this time, have been abandoned. As the father of that System, they have taken the liberty—to present you the Satinet in testimony of regard both for your private & public services—" ALS. DLC-TJC (DNA, M212, R10).

To JOHN W. TAYLOR   Lexington, November 30, 1830

I received your favor of the 8h. with a p.s. of the 15h. inst. and offer you my cordial congratulations on your re-election.[1] I wish I could extend them to the result of the whole of your elections in N. York;[2] but that I am prevented from doing by the unfortunate divisions which prevailed among those who thinking alike on general politics differed in respect to local questions. I perceive that, notwithstanding the triumph of our opponents, our friends are confident in the expression of the opinion that N. York will ultimately realize their hopes. One thing is certain that that cannot happen without more concert. I am surprized at the course of Col. [Samuel] Young, of whom I had been induced to entertain favorable sentiments.

Notwithstanding the inauspicious issue of the N. York elections the political aspect generally is encouraging. Here in the West we are now nearly united, and shall be entirely so before the P. election. Had things terminated better in N. York, our Senatorial elections in the West would have been more certain. We shall, I apprehend lose Mr. [David] Barton;[3] but on the other hand we shall get one, *possibly* two, friends in Illinois, & a friend in each of the States of Ohio, Indiana, Kentucky and Louisiana, if I am not deceived.[4]

You will have I presume a sharp though short Session. The demonstrations of public sentiment will I hope secure better treatment to the Indians. Should not an enquiry be instituted whether there be any necessity for further legislation to secure them in the possession of their territory, and in the privilege of self government?

ALS. NHi.   1. Taylor had won election to the U.S. House, receiving 2,597 votes to 2,350 for Samuel Young and 1,238 for David Garnsey. *Guide to U.S. Elections*, 554.   2. Clay to Johnston, May 9, 1830; Stoddard to Clay, August 9, 1830.   3. Clay to Fendall, August 17, 1830. 4. For the outcome of these U.S. Senate elections, see Niles to Clay, Oct. 28, 1830 (Ill.); Clay to Conover, Oct. 31, 1830 (Ohio); Clay to Johnston, Nov. 1, 1830 (Ind.); Clay to Beatty, June 8, 1830 (Ky.); Clay to Johnston, Dec. 25, 1829 (La.).

From John L. Lawrence, New York, December 2, 1830. Blames the disheartening outcome of the elections in New York State and New York City on the Anti-Masons. Specifically, "The loss of at least six members of Congress in this State, is attributable to the restlessness and disgust created by Anti-Masonic denunciation." Adds, however, that in New York City "thousands of votes were probably sacrificed to gain the three or four hundred whom the Anti Masons could contribute to our poll." Mentions the pending organization of a Clay party [Lawrence to Clay, November 29, 1830] in the city and the fact that "we shall boldly & explicitly avow our intentions in regard to the next Presidential election." The public meeting to launch the party and nominate Clay will take place "in less than a fortnight." ALS. DLC-HC (DNA, M212, R4).

To SAMUEL L. SOUTHARD   Lexington, December 2, 1830

I regret extremely to learn from your letter of the 14h. Ulto. that you have been indisposed and so seriously; but rejoice that you have recovered. The health of my family is not to be complained of. Our purpose at present is that Mrs. Clay John [Morrison Clay] and myself shall go in about two weeks to N. Orleans, and pass the winter there. Mrs. [James] Brown's death is one of the causes of this voyage, and it will enable us to be retired, which is my sincere desire.

I have no thought, certainly no wish, to go into the Senate, but on a contingency which I trust will not arise, that is that no friend could, and that I *certainly* could, be elected. Our belief yet is that Mr. [John J.] Crittenden will be chosen. Next week the Legislature meets and in the course of it the exact state of things will be ascertained.[1]

The N. Jersey election is very important on *several* accounts. It is not among the events that are impossible that the election of President may again devolve on the H. of R.   Whether that should be the case or not, the Tariff &c &c will undoubtedly come up. I should regret greatly the loss of that election.[2] Such a defeat, coming after our confident hopes of the State, and after the result of the N. Y. election, such as it is, would produce discouraging consequences. You could hardly be expected to allow your name to be used, at great sacrifice; and yet we should all be pleased to see you in the H. of R. Mr. [John Q.] Adams's election,[3] or rather his consent to be elected, excited surprize at first, but I think is followed by a feeling that, on principle there is no impropriety in it. I fear most on account of his own feelings and comfort. No harm, perhaps good, may accrue from it to the general cause. . . .

ALS. NjP. 1. Clay to Beatty, June 8, 1830. 2. Southard to Clay, August 8, 1830. 3. Everett to Clay, Oct. 29, 1830.

To PHILLIP R. FENDALL
Lexington, December 5, 1830

I recd. your letter respecting Lotty,[1] and am greatly obliged by your friendly attention to her unpleasant affair. She has safely reached N. Orleans and is now very penitent.

The political results of the year have so far been generally good. That of N. York was unexpected but I do not know that it is much to be regretted. I should have however been better pleased if [Francis] Granger had been elected, or if we had not lost so many members of the H. of R. If we succeed in the Congressional election of New Jersey we may upon the whole be very content.[2]

I go to N. Orleans in about a fortnight to pass the winter there. I shall return in March, and intend my sojourn there to be in great retirement. If you do not abandon your purpose of coming to the West, I shall expect to meet you here in the Spring.

ALS. KyU. 1. See 7:623-24; Clay to Fendall, Sept. 10, 1830. 2. Clay to Johnston, May 9, 1830; Stoddard to Clay, August 9, 1830; Southard to Clay, August 8, 1830.

From Richard Rush, York, Pa., December 8, 1830. Reports that the "popularity of the [Jackson] administration has been a little shaken with us, here and there; but it is still overwhelming. Hence I think, that to act and unite with a certain caution, is the most likely way to advance the great principles and objects before us." ALS. DLC-HC (DNA, M212, R4).

To HENRY CLAY, JR.
Lexington, December 9, 1830

Anne [Brown Clay Erwin] and Mr. [James] Erwin are still with us. They intend in a few days however to proceed to N. Orleans. And your mother and I, having also determined to pass a portion of the winter there, will either accompany them, or follow them a few days after. We purpose taking John [Morrison Clay] and H[enry]. C[lay]. Duralde with us. We expect to return early in March. The advantage we expect to derive from that more genial climate, some business connected with the death of your aunt [Ann Hart (Mrs. James)] Brown, and some other business are the motives of the voyage. That lamented event will enable us, I hope, to indulge our inclination to pass our sojourn in great retirement. We expect to meet your uncle [James] Brown below. By the laws of Louisiana, the wife is entitled to the disposition, upon her death, as she pleases, of one half of the Estate held by her husband. Your aunt availing herself of this privilege, has left her part (one fourth) of their Sugar plantation to Mr. Brown during his life, and after his death to her sisters and brothers or the descendents of such of them as are dead, in equal shares. And in the mean time she has left to her mother [Susannah Gray (Mrs. Thomas Hart, Sr.)] and her sister [Susannah "Susan" (Mrs. Samuel)] Price each $500 per annum. The arrangement has been entirely approved by your uncle, whose whole conduct in this affair has been characterized by great liberality. Mrs. Brown left me one of her Executors,[1] and altho' I am not aware of any thing at present which I shall have to do, that circumstance constitutes one of the motives of my voyage.

I have lately purchased 111 Acres of land, part of the tract which belonged to [John] McNairs Estate, adjoining Ashland.[2] This acquisition will give me more space to operate upon. A further small addition which I have in contemplation would make Ashland all that I wish it in respect to quantity of land.

I rejoice that the time which you will be absent from us is now not long and that it is daily diminishing. I hope you will continue, by your assidu[ity] and correct deportment, to merit the good opinion of those around you. Mr. Hitchcock[3] passed a part of a day with us, on his return to Alabam[a] and reported favorably. You will pursue your own inclination, after the expiration of your studies at West point, whether at once to take the tour you contemplate or to come to us first and afterwards perform it. Any letters of introduction or funds that you may want shall be freely supplied you.

I have no news. Our Legislature is in Session, and we daily look for some thing from Frankfort. The [Frankfort] Convention,[4] opposed to the present administration of the General Government, was also to meet there today. This winter will probably be an eventful one.

ALS. Henry Clay Memorial Foundation, Lexington, Ky. 1. On Feb. 3, 1831, Jean Marie Morel Guiramand, judge of probate, St. Charles Parish, La., named Clay as "executor of the last will and testament of the late Mrs. Nancy [Ann Hart] Brown of this parish," and authorized him "to collect the goods and effects which were of the said deceased and to make a just inventory thereof and all other lawful acts to do and perform as executor testamentary of the said last will and testament—" ADS. DLC-TJC (DNA, M212, R17). 2. Purchased from George W. and Elizabeth R. Morton, of Lexington, on Dec. 7, 1830, for $35 per acre. According to the deed, the tract measured "one hundred and eleven acres, three quarters of an acre and ten poles." DS, in Clay's hand. *Ibid.* 2. Ethan Allen Hitchcock, commandant of cadets, U.S.M.A., 1829-33. 4. "de Sarcy" to Clay, Feb. 11, 1830; Clay to Conover, Oct. 31, 1830.

From William Henry Russell, Frankfort, December 9, 1830. With regard to the pending election of a U.S. senator by the Kentucky state legislature, reports that since arriving in Frankfort he has "received from my county [Nicholas] the signatures of about four hundred of my constituents instructing me to vote for a Jackson senator," or be turned out of office. Says he cannot and will not do this, and that "I have worked myself up to a state of feeling that enables me for once to act the heroe (I will not contribute to the election of a Jackson Senator).—" Is certain that this "determination will cause me almost immediately to expatriate myself, for Nicholas will be by far too hot to me, I shall be placed in a most dreadfull situation, too unpleasant to remain in the neighborhood of men, who will regard me for the most virtuous & praiseworthy act of my life a traitor and deceiver.—Yes I will leave them." ALS. DLC-HC (DNA, M212, R4). Russell emigrated to Missouri in 1831.

From PETER B. PORTER   Black Rock, N.Y., December 10, 1830
We held a County meeting, last evening, at the Court House in Buffalo, of the friends of the *American System,* in compliance with a notice issued about a week ago in hand bills signed by 30 or 40 of our most respectable citizens. The meeting was large & animated. We passed resolutions with a preamble (drawn up, but I am afraid not very well, by myself) denouncing, in general & in detail, the whole course of the present administration; approbating the Tariff & Internal Improvts—and appointing six delegates (among whom are [William B.] Rochester & myself) to attend a State Convention of National Republs, which we recommend to be held at Albany on the 20th of January; and investing the convention with power either to nominate a candidate for the Presidency, themselves, or to appoint delegates to a national convention to be held at Washington, or elsewhere, for that purpose.[1]

The whole complexion of this meeting was cheering. It was a great object with us to draw the anti masons, as far as practicable, into our views, and as regards this county, I believe we shall entirely succeed. Many of the most respectable among them attended, and two of them were members with me of the Committee to draft Resolutions. [Oran] Follet, the Editor of the [Buffalo *Daily*] Journal, & whose dislike of Anti masonry was such as to induce him to sup port the whole Regency ticket at the late Election — [William A.] Carpenter, Editor of the (antimasonic) [Buffalo] Patriot,[2] & [Horace] Steele, Editor of the [Buffalo] Workingmens Bulletin,[3] were all present & zealous. The first was Secretary of the meeting. Besides publishing our proceedings in the papers we have ordered 1500 Copies to be struck off in Hand bills, which we shall distrib ute immediately through every part of the state, and also send some to our friends in Ohio, New Jersey, &c. They will probably be ready by tomorrow, when I will send one to you & two or three more to [John J.] Crittenden & other friends in your state.

In return for the friendly & in many respects just criticisms which you have made on our policy in this state, you will pardon me for saying that we have escaped one blunder which your friends in Kenty — the sticklers for *measures* & not *men* — have committed in calling a convention at Washington, for the purpose of nominating *Henry Clay* to the presidency.[4] It really appears to me to be not only repugnant to the spirit of our professions, but farcical, to send delegates all the way to Washington, to put in a vote for H.C. and, under no circumstances, for any other man. While we have avoided this error, there can be no question as to the individual to whom the spirit of our proceedings points. Indeed a Jackson man at Buffalo, and, what is rare, a flaming tariff man at the same time, came into our meeting last evening, & offered to vote for our resolutions if we would strike out the preamble which abused Jackson & recommended *you* for the presidency.

I have received your letter of the 21. Ult., inclosing the copy of one to Mr [William B.] Lawrence, and shall cheerfully attend to the many judicious hints they contain. You intimate an intention to spend the winter in New Orleans which I think may be of advantage to your health. But permit me to say to you that you must *absolutely* make your arrangements to pass through this state from Buffalo to N. York, or at least as far as Albany or Utica, in the course of next summer. Your design may be kept so secret that you will hardly be seen or heard of before you are on board a Steam Boat (and the [Steamboat *Henry*] *Clay* shall be in readiness for you) either at Sandusky or Cleveland. Be assured that it would be attended with the best consequences. But on this subject I will go more into particulars hereafter. . . .

ALS. InU. 1. For the National Republican convention at Albany, where Ambrose Spencer and thirty others were chosen to attend the national convention, see Dixon Ryan Fox, *The Decline of Aristocracy in the Politics of New York* (New York, 1919), 361. 2. H. Perry Smith, *History of the City of Buffalo and Erie County*, 2 vols. (Syracuse, 1884), 2:328. 3. *Ibid.*, 332. 4. A public meeting had been held in Jefferson County in November which had adopted a resolution instruct ing local delegates to the Frankfort convention to vote for delegates to the national convention who would be "friendly to the election of H. Clay." Lexington *Kentucky Reporter*, Nov. 10, 1830.

To JOHN L. LAWRENCE   Lexington, December 13, 1830
Your favor of the 2d inst. is recd. So far from feeling or expressing any dis approbation of the measures to which you refer, I am perfectly persuaded that without some such [organization] defeat awaits us in N. York at least in 1832. The issue of your elections demonstrates the efficacy of systematic effort on one side, and the fatal effects of the want of it on the other. There must be in formation, communication and concert of operation among those who think alike or they will be doomed to eternal defeat. Names are nothing, except that odious ones should be avoided, but it is *the system* which is needed.

Our [Frankfort] State Convention met last week in great numbers.[1] The elite of the State assembled and as far as I have yet heard their deliberations and proceedings were marked by harmony and vigor. They will produce great effect.

[David] Barton has lost his election, or rather he was not presented as a Candidate.[2] On the other hand the [Thomas H.] Benton candidate was defeated (Governor Miller) and I understand that a foe of proscription, and a friend of the Tariff, of Int. Imp. and of mine has been chosen.[3]

The election of a Senator in this State has not taken place. We have a decided majority in the Legislature, but some half a dozen of our friends have persuaded themselves or been persuaded by others that they are pledged, on the particular question of a Senator to vote for one of the Jackson party, whilst they are free on all other questions. The effect is that the contest will be close and is some what doubtful. Our friends however anticipate success. A few days will determine.

Before this letter reaches you I shall be on my way to N. Orleans, whither I go on private affairs exclusively.

ALS. ViU. Letter marked "(Confidential)." 1. "de Sarcy" to Clay, Feb. 11, 1830; Clay to Conover, Oct. 31, 1830. 2. Clay to Fendall, August 17, 1830. 3. Alexander Buckner defeated Governor John Miller for the U.S. Senate seat for which Barton did not offer. Miller had been elected governor of Missouri for a second term in 1828 and served until 1832. Clay to Fendall, August 17, 1830; Kallenbach, *American State Governors 1776-1976*, 1:340.

To DAVID LAWRENCE MORRIL   Lexington, December 13, 1830
[Thanks him for his letter of October 20 reporting that the Jacksonians in New Hampshire are beginning to understand that they have been mislead politically. Continues:]

What has surprized me is that one man and one press should have had so much influence in N. Hampshire, where you have such a mass of talents and information. And such a man![1]

I concur with you in thinking that the spirit of tyranny and oppression which has been manifested by our General government was not surpassed by that which produced the recent French revolution. It is a more vindictive spirit, and is less regardful of public decorum. There is a striking similitude too between the arts and means practised by the Polignac[2] administration in France and the Polignac administration at Washington. You will be convinced of this if you have read the Report of the Commee. raised to impeach the French ministers.[3] I hope Providence will deliver us from the one by means less bloody than those which he has permitted in the other case. If we do our duty, I entertain no doubt but that we shall have His smiles. . . .

AL, signature destroyed. Courtesy of J. Winston Coleman, Jr., Lexington, Ky. Addressed to Morril in Goffstown, N.H. 1. Reference not clear, but see 5:152-53, 692-93. 2. Hughes to Clay, April 18, 1830. 3. For the impeachment report against Polignac, the minister of foreign affairs, see Vincint Woodrow Beach, *Charles X of France* (Boulder, Colo., 1971), 321-27.

From John L. Lawrence, New York, December 14, 1830. Reports that the meeting in Masonic Hall to launch a Clay party [Lawrence to Clay, November 29, 1830] was held Monday evening, December 13. "Never was a more numerous, respectable & animated assemblage convened on a similar occasion." Rumored attempts to "interrupt our proceedings, were not ventured upon." ALS. DLC-HC (DNA, M212, R4). See also, Lawrence to Clay, December 2, 1830.

To Ralph R. Gurley, December 15, 1830. Regrets that he cannot attend the annual meeting of the American Colonization Society in Washington on January 17, 1831. Explains that he will be in New Orleans at the time, drawn there by "private interests and duties." ALS. DLC — Records of the American Colonization Society (DNA, M212, R20).

To Jesse Burton Harrison, December 15, 1830. Thanks him for his letter from Berlin, Germany, dated July 15. Assures him "that the existing administration is rapidly losing the public favor; and that the prospect of a restoration of our country to a better and sounder condition is bright and cheering." Copy. DLC-HC (DNA, M212, R4).

From F. H. Pettis, Washington, December 16, 1830. Informs Clay that he is looking for a newspaper editorship that would permit him to support Clay for the presidency, especially in "some state where there is a chance for a *victory* and not where the majority is already Anti-Jackson." Asks advice on this subject. Believes that to be elected, Clay must carry "all, or nearly all, of the Western and New-England states" and "one of the large ones, and that should be New York." Thinks that in his native Virginia there has been "a great change in your favor since last spring," but not enough to "give you a majority as early as '32."

Calls attention to President Jackson's recent annual message [*MPP*, 2:500-529], charging that it was written by Van Buren and submitted to "six to ten" cabinet meetings "before they could agree in what shape it should come." Reminds Clay that while Jackson is president of a majority of the American people, "he is not the President of a majority of the respectability & wealth of this nation."

Reports, in conclusion, that "A new paper (Jackson) has sprung up here within a few days past entitled 'The Globe [Clay to Johnston, November 14, 1830].' — A Jackson Member (supposing me to be with my *Brother* & the administration) stated to me that its object is to supplant Duff [Green] — that 'he is to be *killed*, and they mean to have the *honor* of doing it themselves.' — Great honor don't you think? — It is my opinion that Duff will lose the printing of both Houses — Our party will go against him to a man, and in the House a great many Jackson men will oppose him. he will scarcely get a vote from Pennsylvania, and many of the Jackson members from N. York will drop him." ALS. DLC-HC (DNA, M212, R4). "Not answered," Clay wrote on verso. Pettis's brother was Spencer D. Pettis, a Jacksonian Democrat from Missouri (*BDAC*). According to Richard P. Longaker, "Was Jackson's Kitchen Cabinet a Cabinet?" *MVHR* (June, 1957), 44:94-108, Amos Kendall and Martin Van Buren were the ones who assisted Jackson in writing the Second Annual Message. Clay supporters strongly criticized what they considered to be a didactic and preemptory tone of the message [Rush to Clay, December 22, 1830]. Duff Green did not lose the printing of either house. On February 1, 1831, the House elected him printer by a vote of 108 to 76 for Joseph Gales, Jr., and William W. Seaton, the nearest competitor, and on February 9, the Senate also chose him by 24 votes to 22 for Gales and Seaton; Francis P. Blair received 1 vote. *Niles' Register* (February 5, 12, 1831), 39:408, 437.

To ALLEN TRIMBLE   Lexington, December 18, 1830

I received your favor of the 11h. instant. I regret to learn that any doubt exists about the election of a friendly Senator.[1] In confidence, I should think it unfortunate that Genl. [William Henry] Harrison, after all that has lately occurred, should be elected.[2] Difficulties exist at Frankfort also about the election of a Friendly Senator, although we have a majority of 10 or 12. This is owing to the fact some five or six of our friends have considered themselves pledged on the particular question of a Senator to vote with the Jackson party. On all other questions they are free. Our friends are however in good spirits, and are confident of ultimate success in the choice of a friend.

I congratulate you on your message which is very well spoken of.[3] That of the President is all things to all men.[4] Its doctrines evidently favor the Antitariff and Nullification party; and if his councils are followed every item in the Tariff, one by one, will be repealed. On the subject of Int. Improvements he appears to have taken his stand to oppose them all. Destroy them and the Tariff, if we of the West were to imitate the example of South Carolina, and calculate the value of the Union, we should find it worth less to us than to her.

I leave home for N. Orleans the day after tomorrow. I should be glad to hear from you there.

Be pleased to give my respects to Genl. [Thomas C.] Flournoy and say to him that I am thankful for his last letters.

ALS. NjP. 1. Clay to Conover, Oct. 31, 1830. 2. Probably a reference to a controversy surrounding a toast Harrison gave at a dinner in his honor in May, 1830, at Cincinnati, a dinner which Clay declined to attend [Clay to Greene, May 3, 1830]. In the toast Harrison mentioned that General Anthony Wayne "was in truth the hero of two wars." On May 10, the Cincinnati *American* claimed that this remark was a "neat sarcasm" against Jackson who had falsely been referred to as "a hero of two wars." Subsequently the Cincinnati *Republican* printed a letter, signed "N," which said that Harrison had authorized a friend to say that the remark was not intended to allude to Jackson in any way, because many of Jackson's friends were at the dinner; further, to make a sarcastic remark would have been a breach of decorum. Harrison later wrote a letter to the Cincinnati *American* in which he stated that he had indeed authorized the "N" article in the *Republican* and in which he also called for an end to extreme partisanship. He avowed his friendship for some Jacksonians and said if that made him a "trimmer," as a Cincinnati *American* editorial had charged, then he would remain one. See, further, Cincinnati *American*, May 31; June 3, 10, 1830. Harrison had been suggested as a gubernatorial candidate in 1830, but the Clay people were instrumental in nominating and electing Duncan McArthur. In Jan., 1831, Harrison hoped to be elected U.S. senator by the Ohio legislature where the anti-Jackson men held a small majority. The Clay partisans, however, would not support him, so his strategy was to combine anti-Jackson and anti-Clay votes with those of the Jacksonians. This plan failed. Goebel, *William Henry Harrison*, 296. 3. Trimble's annual message on Dec. 8, 1830, had expressed his strong belief in "the necessity of a steady adherence to the American System and to the policy of Internal Improvements." Cincinnati *Advertiser*, Dec. 22, 1830. 4. Pettis to Clay, Dec. 16, 1830.

To Francis T. Brooke, December 20, 1830. Comments on the French Revolution, noting that "They have two dangers, the first in retaining a Bourbon on the throne, which they thought ought to be done to conciliate foreign powers, and the second the humane desire to screen the former ministers from punishment." Hopes, however, that "the work so gloriously begun will be happily consummated."

As for domestic political developments, argues that "The political events of the year, taken altogether, are not discouraging. Except in Maine and N. York they justify strong hopes of the future. And in N.Y. so far as the election of Governor was concerned it is far from certain that the issue should be regretted. In this State the Legislature has not yet appointed a Senator. Our friends are in good spirits and count upon success. But the vote will be a close one, owing to the fact that five or six members, opposed to the administration, believe themselves pledged to vote for a Jackson Senator. It is not impossible that no election will be made at this Session." ALS. KyU. Printed in full in Colton, *Clay Correspondence*, 4:291-92. For the elections in Maine, New York, and the Kentucky legislature, see Everett to Clay, October 29, 1830; Clay to Johnston, May 9, 1830; Stoddard to Clay, August 9, 1830; Clay to Beatty, June 8, 1830.

To Richard C. Langdon, December 20, 1830. Is delighted to learn that Langdon contemplates launching in Covington, Ky., a "new printing establishment, having in view the support of our principles." Assures him that there "will not be the least difficulty in your obtaining from the Legislature the privilege of publishing public notices from the Courts &c. It is a matter *of course* to grant it." Thinks, however, that the newspaper must be "actually commenced and in circulation" before application be made.

ALS. NbHi. The first issue of Langdon's paper, the *Farmer's Record and Covington Literary Journal*, appeared on May 20, 1831, making it Covington's first newspaper. Allen W. Smith (ed.), *Beginnings at "the Point": A Documentary History of Northern Kentucky and Environs, the Town of Covington in Particular, 1751-1834* (Park Hills, Ky., 1977), 87.

From Richard Rush, York, Pa., December 22, 1830. Believes the election of William Wilkins to the U.S. Senate [Clay to Johnston, November 1, 1830] "looks well for our cause." Continues: "Jacksonism has been so overwhelming in this state, and is still so strong, that we cannot hope to check it suddenly, or by means too violent; but I hope much from other and discreet courses, always keeping true to our great ends. An auspicious event has occurred I think, in the message of our governor [George Wolf]. If the right use be made of this document, it may and will do good. It contains so much that we can justifiably commend on points directly in the teeth of the Presidents message [Pettis to Clay, December 16, 1830], that by going with the former we may hope for an improved prospect of rendering the author of the latter, deservedly unpopular in the state. Once let Pennsylvania get her eyes open, and I need not add, that the reign of Jackson is over. In my opinion, his late message is the most replete with public danger; the most open to exception, by far, as to matter and manner, of any document that has ever issued from our government since its foundation. There are avowals in it, that would drive a king of France from his throne, and that would, undoubtedly, have cost John Quincy Adams an impeachment." ALS. DLC-HC (DNA, M212, R4). Gov. George Wolf in his annual message to the Pennsylvania legislature had strongly supported the constitutionality of the tariff and federal aid for internal improvements, stating that the people of Pennsylvania would not consent to abandon the tariff and that more extensive internal improvements were needed to give added value to those already in existence. See Harrisburg (Pa.) *Chronicle*, December 9, 1830, for the full text of Wolf's message. Jackson had stated in his Second Annual Message in December, 1830, that the tariff was constitutional but had called for its adjustment and had adamantly opposed, with minor exceptions, federal aid to internal improvements.

From HENRY CLAY, JR. West Point, N.Y., December 26, 1830
I have just learned with certainty by your letter that you & my mother are going to New Orleans. You will find there such a reunion of friends & relations, that I am sure you cannot fail to spend a very agreable winter. Would that I formed one of your party; but next to enjoying your society myself, is the pleasure I feel in knowing that you are reestablished in health & spirits and surrounded by your friends.

You desire me to continue in the course of conduct which I have hitherto pursued. You need not fear, my father, any relapse on my part into habits of dissipation for I have never yet discovered the boasted charms of the views of the profligate. In regard to study, An object has presented itself to my view & I eagerly pursue it. My perseverance and assiduity in this pursuit may perhaps be to my prejudice in others: but still I am willing to give up excellence in every other department of knowledge, to attain an honorable rank as a speaker. I am well aware that a general acquaintance with the whole circle of arts & sciences & in fact with every branch of human knowledge is isdensable to the accomplished orator; and this I shall endeavor to acquire without weakening or confusing my mind by too abstracted an attention to minutiae

I am glad that you are improving Ashland; I have a kind of filial affection for it which seems to increase with my years & distance from it.

You mentioned in your letter that I might follow my own inclination in the tour which I proposed some time ago. I suppose you alluded to my excursion through the northern States. In regard to the question whether I had better perform it before going home or return home & perform it afterwards? it seems to me that it will detain me so short a time that if I make the journey at all it will be as well to do it at once. As to funds I don't know that I shall want any. And I believe I mentioned to your in my last letter the persons to whom I would be glad to have letters of introduction. However I wish you would consult your own convenience entirely, & forget that I have asked you, if it should prove inconvenient, to give me letters.

From one of Anne's [Brown Clay Erwin] letters I believe that she mentioned to you a course which I marked out: I wrote it rather to show what might be my wishes did my situation in life permit my free consultation & pursuance of them, than what my desires are under present circumstances. I hope therefore, if you did read the letter which I wrote to Anne, that you will make the due abatement in the loftiness of the scheme suggested, and not believe me quite so extravagant as a hasty perusal of that letter would seem to justify—

Remember me very affectionately to all our friends who may be in New Orleans.

ALS. Henry Clay Memorial Foundation, Lexington, Ky. Printed in Colton, *Clay Correspondence*, 4:292. Colton misdates as December 20 and omits the first two sentences in paragraph 2 and all of paragraphs 4, 5, and 6. Addressed to Clay in New Orleans.

From Francis T. Brooke, near Fredericksburg, Va., December 28, 1830. Reports that there is a "favorable temper . . . respecting you" in Richmond but that "no open movement has or will be made, until it is Seen whether genl Jackson is to be in the field or one of his Substitutes." Believes, however, "we are Silently gaining ground in this State." Explains: "I think if matters go on as they are at Washington we may calculate on victory—a large portion of the West including the Valley and a portion of the Northern Neck, might be now counted on, it will be pretty dificult to Settle the pretensions of Messrs V B [Van Buren] and C— [Calhoun]   I think the latter will not easily be given up by his friends and it may be counted on that many of them will vote for you in preference to V B"

Warns Clay in closing: "I have lived in times when it would have been dishonorable to make the remark—and you will pardon me for making it to you, I do not believe that you are coming into the Senate, your Strongest position is at Ashland." ALS. InU.

From JOSIAH S. JOHNSTON   Washington, December 29, 1830
[Reports the political news from England and France, both of which have new ministries. Sees a "spirit of Revolution . . . abroad. It is at present a Civil Revolution, looking to reform"; but if reform does not go far enough, especially in England, "great danger of a revolution" exists. Continues:]

The Anti Masons in N. york you perceive appear to be very much excited against your Masonic friends & have declared their separation—They are also very hostile to the Regency—They intend to have a Candidate for the Presidency, & seek this difference as an apology for their Course—[1]They are in fact a political party, that they think will grow rapidly & obtain power, they hold together, not on account of their strength, but to obtain strength—they will present a Candidate, as they say in Consequence of the Conduct of the Masons in the late election—[2]They are very much Chagrined with the defeat, which is to be attributed to the hostility of our Masonic friends—I hope it will wear away, but the Jackson party are very much disposed to fan the flame & keep up the Excitement—I am in Correspondence with [Francis] Granger & every thing will be done to restore order & harmony—but at this time the difficulties are very great — With them we are the Strongest & Could Carry the state, without them we cannot — & divided there is reason to expect defeat to both — I shall Use every argument — There are some very strong as regards them — I think there would be no difficulty, if our Masonic friends could be brought to act wisely   The elections for the state, Congress & Presidency come on at the same time — a judicious distribution of the nominations in the State with our party & cordially supported, would bring them into the measure — But the fear is the masons will not consent to give the power of the state to the antimasons — If the Anti Masons erect their standard they will weaken us in Ohio & Vermont —

We have but one Course, to stand by our principles & the men of our principles — We can not turn to the right or left, stand or fall — The Anti Masons will try to get a man of sufficient Character & will aim to take him from our party, to detach a portion of our interest & they will go within north or west — We must maintain the integrity of our ranks —

We are progressing slowly with the impeachment,[3]   The House is doing nothing — The Tariff is safe for the present & until the payment of the debt — & that is far enough to look ahead in this age of Revolution —

We ought to have repealed Last Session the duties on all articles not made in the Country — It would then have reliev[e]d the people & postponed the debt —

The Presidents mode of arguing the power of Congress to protect domestic industry is quite new. . . .[4]

[Concludes with social news of the capital and the observation that "It is very dull here — no debate — no excitement — no parties — The spirit of the place is gone — The people are depressed — rents low, property dull & heavy."]

ALS. InU.   1. The Albany *Evening Journal*, a leading Anti-Masonic newspaper edited by Thurlow Weed, announced in December an irrevocable separation of the Anti-Masons from the Clay party. New York *Evening Post*, Dec. 22, 1830; Hammond, *History of Political Parties in the State of New York*, 2:337-38.   2. Stoddard to Clay, Nov. 8, 1830.   3. Judge James H. Peck of the U.S. District Court for Missouri was impeached by the House of Representatives for misdemeanors in office. A Senate Court of Impeachment acquitted him on Jan. 31, 1831, by a vote of 22-21. *Register of Debates*, 21 Cong., 1 Sess., 736; 21 Cong., 2 Sess., 46.   4. For Jackson's views of this matter, see *MPP*, 2:523-24.

From JOSIAH S. JOHNSTON   Washington, January 7, 1831

We held a meeting to night in which it was determin[e]d to hold a national Convention at Baltimore on the 2 monday of December — equal to the electors —[1]

The members are to communicate the fact to the proper persons in their respective states & recommend State Conventions to nominate you & appoint the Delegates —

There will be a Meeting in Connecticut on the 23d.[2] In which you will be nominated & an address made & recommendations of the same to the other States —

The Massachusetts Legislature will during the present month make a Similar Nomination & probably call a Convention, but if not they will Nam[e] the Delegates to the N[ationa]l. Convention —[3]The other States will follow the example   We shall as far as possibl[e] keep the ball moving — The Anti Masons are still hostile & seem determin[e]d to present a Candidate — That must have the effect to make Genl. Jackson lose N. york & Penna.

The election of Printer will take place tomorrow[4]   Immediately after that Calhouns publication will Come out, with all the Correspondence — It will be very interesting — His principal attack will I expect be directed agt.

[William H.] Crawford—but the Correspondence will develope the secret history of the whole affair—[5]What is to come of it we can not tell—A Separation seems inevitabl[e]   I should think this step would lead to an open rupture—Van Burens object is Certainly to Cut Away from Calhoun & [John] McLean—

There is a vague apprehension in the mind of the people, that som[e] great misfortune is impending over the Country— [P.S.] Burgess [sic, Tristam Burges] has finish[e]d his Speech upon the Minister *extraordinary* [John Randolph] *Near* th[e] Court of St. Petersburg—It is very Severe & quite able & eloquent. It will read well[6]

ALS. InU. Addressed to Clay at New Orleans.   1. Apparently a small, informal meeting not publicized in the newspapers at the time.   2. For Clay's nomination in Connecticut, see *Niles' Register* (April 16; June 18, 1831), 40:127, 279.   3. Clay was nominated unanimously by a "legislative political convention" of nearly 200 at the Massachusetts State House on February 17, 1831. *Niles' Register* (April 16, 1831), 40:126.   4. Pettis to Clay, Dec. 16, 1830.   5. For Calhoun's publication of correspondence concerning Jackson and the Seminole War, see Johnston to Clay, June 5, 1830, and Bowers, *Party Battles of the Jackson Period*, 103-6.   6. In his speech in the House, Burges advocated paying Randolph the $9,000 which had been promised him when he accepted the position as minister to Russia. Even though Randolph had remained at St. Petersburg only a few days, he had presented his credentials to the czar and the government was therefore liable for payment. Burges then attacked Jackson and Van Buren for making such a poor appointment at a time when Congress was not in session and the Senate could not consider the nomination. *Register of Debates*, 21 Cong., 2 Sess., 490-96; see also Johnston to Clay, May 26, 1830.

From SAMUEL L. SOUTHARD   Trenton, N.J., January 10, 1831

When I wrote you hastily a few evenings since,[1] I was misled by information—from one of the distant Counties—Our lowest candidate is not elected by so large a vote as I stated—but all are elected—and by an average over 2000. My brother is one of the members elect.[2] This election, we felt to be important in its general bearing at this time & we exerted ourselves accordin[g]ly. Our difficulty was not, in the number of our friends, but in bringing them out to the polls. They had become dispirited by defeats elsewhere & could not readily be induced to perceive the importance of exertion at this moment. Many of them are Friends, who dislike to go to elections or mingle in party struggles—and some of that sect had been misled by misrepresentations of which we were not aware until too late to correct them. The result however is gratifying & will be useful. We can, I think, at any time, give a majority against the Genl.—I was not able, from sickness to do all that I desired & the adversary exulted in the fact—but I think they feel in the result, that I was able to do something. We shall endeavor to keep matters right hereafter.

My health is still feeble & my professional & Official business burdensome. I cannot get time to be well—But do all that I can to regain the strength, which I had before my violent attack in the Fall.—

I am pained to hear doubts expressed as to the election of Senator in Kenty.[3] There ought not to be a failure in that matter—it would operate widely & injuriously.

What is to be done with Georgia?[4] Her madness has no limit.

I recd. a letter from our friend [Peter B.] Porter a few days ago—He is in good spirits again after his despondency at the Fall Elections. But there is great danger from the Anti M[asonic]. feeling—it will be difficult to manage it. We found it so—it came near defeating us. I have some curious matters to tell you in relation to my own correspondence with some of the Anti M. in N.Y. & P[a]. but I dare not trust them to the Mail, in a letter addressed to you.—

I saw my old father [Henry] just before I was taken sick — He still feels all his old attachment to you & ordered me when I wrote to repeat expressions of respect & good wishes — At 84, he was at the polls & did what age would permit him to do, in the good cause. He has within the last week recd. a blow in the death of my mother [Sarah Lewis], which I fear will bear him onward more rapidly to the grave than we could willingly see him carried forward. They were companions for more than 60 years. I intend to persuade him to spend the rest of his days with me if I can, & shall go to see him, as soon as my health & the weather will permit. . . . [P.S.] I have opened my letter to comply with the request of a friend to say something to you of a matter in which he feels an interest. The Presidency of your College at Lexington [Transylvania] is vacant by the appointment of Mr. [Alva] Woods to the Alabama Institution. I wish to recommend, as his Successor, the Revd Dr Frederick Beasley — formerly Prest of the Penna. University.[5] He is an Episcopal Clergyman, of high character for conduct & acquirement — a ripe & good scholar, much respected. May I beg your remembrance of him, when you act in the Appointment? You will find no difficulty in obtaining answers to any enquiries you may have a wish to make.

ALS. InU. Addressed to Clay in New Orleans.   1. On Jan. 1, 1831, Southard had written Clay that "We have succeeded with our whole ticket — the lowest by more than 1,000 votes." ALS. InU.   2. Isaac Southard, Samuel's brother, was elected to the U.S. House along with the entire slate of National Republican candidates in the New Jersey congressional election held on Dec. 28 & 29, 1830. The average majority of the victorious candidates was about 1,500 in the final tally. *Niles' Register* (Jan. 8, 1831), 39:329.   3. Clay to Beatty, June 8, 1830.   4. Johnston to Clay, Jan. 12, 1831.   5. Thomas Matthews, Charles Short, and John Lutz all served briefly as acting presidents of Transylvania after Woods's departure in the spring of 1831 to assume the presidency of the newly established University of Alabama. In Dec., 1832, Benjamin O. Peers assumed the presidency of Transylvania University. Wright, *Transylvania: Tutor to the West*, 127, 132.

From JAMES BROWN CLAY   Lexington, January 11, 1831

John [Morrison Clay] received your letter the day before yesterday, we were very glad to hear from you as we have not heard from any of our relations at [New] Orleans, neither has Mr [Thomas] Smith. John & I still remain pleased with Mr Pears [*sic*, Benjamin O. Peers], but not with his regulations, for I do not see why we should not be treated as well as the larger boys who are permitted to have fires, and go to bed and get up when the[y] please, whilst we smaller ones are kept studying untill 9 oclock and some times after and are obliged to get up by day break and study untill 8, however I will do my part as well as I can. I am getting on very well with my studies, far better than I did at colledge,[1] I had thought that the boys here were farther adva[n]ced than they really are for none of them are much farther than I am. Brother Theodore [Wythe Clay] was as well as usual on saturday, and I hope is entirely so. Grandmam [Susannah Hart] has been very unwell these 2 or 3 days but is getting better; Aunt [Susannah] Price and all the cousins came down from Paris the other day, I believe with the intention of spending the winter and I believe they are all well. Our money that mama was so kind to leave us is as much as we want but if you have no objections I should like to play on the flute, and I cannot get one unless you would let Mr Pears get me one, (I can play 2 or 3 tunes already). Every thing is going on well at the farm, and as far as I can see, Mr [William] Martin gets on very well with the negroes.

ALS. DLC-TJC (DNA, M212, R10). Erroneously addressed to Clay in "Washington City." 1.
James Brown Clay had earlier attended the prep department of Transylvania University, as well as
the school's freshman class. Clay to Henry Clay, Jr., April 19, 1829; October 31, 1830.

From Josiah S. Johnston, Washington, January 12, 1831. Reports that the "story of
the breach between the two highest officers [Jackson and Calhoun] is now in the
papers. . . . The denou[e]ment was delayed by the absence, no doubt intentional of
the V.P. — He did not call on the President, his friends with ill concealed feelings, accused V. Buren of instigating the quarrel and of pushing his claims too fast &C. . . .
The Admn. would be broken down if there was a Separation of [Samuel D.] Ingham &
Calhouns friends — Besides what hav[e] either Calhoun or V Buren to hope. When disconnected with the main party — They both Therefore hav[e] the highest interest in
adhering but with very different & certainly with hostile pretentions —"
Notes that the "friends of Calhoun began with some spirit" and that George
McDuffie "laid on the Table his manifestoe in the form of an Amendment to the Consti-
tution, Which was perfectly understood as intended to exclude — But We have not been
able to bring him to the point   It is delayed no doubt in expectation of a Compromise."
Adds: "It has been Said during the Week that Calhouns publication [Johnston to Clay,
January 11, 1831] was in the press — but it is evidently Suspended —"
Believes the separation between the Jackson and Calhoun forces may "hold the adm in
check in both Houses, but little strength would be added to us — We cannot Unite . . . in
the general measures of the Calhoun party — nor can they with us in ours."
Further: "It is my opinion the parties as now organized will continue to act together — That their object is to carry the principles of the Southern States into effect —
They design to strip the General Government of most of its powers, to bring it back to a
Confederation of *Sovereign* States — To take from the Supreme Court its means of preserving its authority & its jurisdiction — To repeal all the Tariff except for Revenue — to stop
the progress of internal improvements to prevent the renewal of the Bank &C   Whatever
views the President may express, (that are merely intended to amuse Penna.)   The
whole party N & South as well as West Unite in all these objects   The organization of the
party has that inevitabl[e] effect — See the votes of Maine N. Hampshire & New York on
the reduction of Sugar — You Wil[l] Se[e] they concur in every view of public policy with
the South — The same thing takes place in Tennessee & Kentucky — Every thing depends
now on the firmness of Pennsylvania   She, by her representatives, stil[l] adheres to her
principles. — Things are approaching a Crisis. Georgia will set the authority of the Court
at definace, the President will refuse his support — & thus the power of the Court wil[l] be
broken down — Georgia will take possession of the Indian lands — & they will be driven
out or Killed [Clay to Hammond, October 7, 1829]   It is impossibl[e] they can submit to
the intrusion of the Whites. We shall get along with the Tariff, until the public debt is
paid but then there wil[l] be a stand taken — It wil[l] be time enough then to provide for
the evils that may arise — We are upon the point of a Civil Revolution as great in its effect
upon this country, as those that have occurred in Europe — The Same question that existed in 1788-89 will now arise again — Shall this be a mere Confederacy of States or a
Union of the States — The object is to restore the Constitution to what the minority
design[e]d it should then be — To make a feeble Confederacy, with all the evils & defects
of the old one rather than a disunion — But if they fail in this object, it remains to be Seen
whether they will not resort to a Separation —"
Concludes: "What this Govt. is to be must depend very much on the next Presidential election — If the people consent to reelect [Jackson] — it will be a very decisive expression of opinion. He may then go on to effect a purpose which he knows well how to conceal now." ALS. InU. McDuffie had proposed a constitutional amendment to limit the
president of the U.S. to one term. On February 26, 1831, McDuffie failed in his attempt
to bring the resolution to a vote in the House. *Register of Debates*, 21 Cong., 2 Sess., 379,
820. For Georgia's defiance of the U.S. Supreme Court in the case of *Worcester* v. *Georgia*,
see Richard Morris (ed.), *Encyclopedia of American History* (New York, 1953), 171.

From JOHN MORRISON CLAY   Lexington, January 14, 1831

I heard from one of your letters that you; my mother, and Henry [Clay Duralde] were very well with the exception of bad colds, which I was very glad to hear. Grandmama [Susannah Hart] has been very sick but she is at present nearly well, with the exception of her all of my relations are very well. Cousin Lizar Marshal [*sic*][1] has come from Paris [Ky.], and she has brought all the children with her, the boys go to school to Mr [Benjamin O.] Peers. James [Brown Clay] received a letter from Sister Anne [Brown Clay Erwin], she and the children were very well, she stated in it that shea had not heard from Lexington since she had left here, she said that she had not heard whether my mother had gone to Washing[ton] or not. Mr [William] Martin, and Mrs [Sarah] Hall are very well and your farm is doing very well. I heard from the son of Mr [Thomas Edward] Boswell that Brother Theodore [Wythe Clay] is very well. Mr Peers school is doing very well. Mr Peers told me that he was going to write to sometime this week, and both myself and James are in high favour with Mr Peers. I am at present studying latin, French, Geography, writing, and I believe that I am going to study Arithmetic. Mr Peers has more boarders this session than he had last session, but he has not as many day schools. James is studying, French, Latin, and Algebra. But tell mama that I am studying, French with a real Frenchman by the name of Mr du Ford. That she may not fear of my loosing the pronunciation of the French.

ALS. DLC-TJC (DNA, M212, R13). Erroneously addressed to Clay at "Washington City."   1. Apparently a reference to Eliza Price (Mrs. Thomas A.) Marshall who was a granddaughter of Col. Thomas Hart and a niece of Lucretia Clay. W. M. Paxton, *The Marshall Family* (Baltimore, 1970), 185.

From Josiah S. Johnston, Washington, January 19, 1831. Reports that the Senate is "& still shall be during this month engaged with Judge Peck [Johnston to Clay, December 29, 1830]," but that the House of Representatives "regularly adjourn so that they have as little disposition to act as to debate—It appears to be a part of the policy to do nothing—To avoid discussion as well as disagreement." Notes that "We have been held in painful suspense by the events pending in Jersey—Ohio Kentucky &c—" because "every thing hung upon these elections, not only the Presidential elections but the Constitution & the whole policy of the Govt." Is relieved that the "vote of Jersey & Ohio has sustain[e]d us," while "that of Kentucky is a drawn battle." Fears, however, that the "Jackson Men except in Penna. have determin[e]d to go with the South, & if they get the power they will reduce us to a Confederacy." Predicts they will "tak[e] from the Government all general power over the States except the war power & taxation to the extent of the expences of the Govt."

States that consideration of a [National Republican] national convention to nominate a presidential candidate has been postponed, because "February was too Soon" and it was necessary "to take time for Consideration[.] In the mean time popular & State nominations are recommended."

Comments on the Jackson-Calhoun split, saying that "they can never unite personally" and that Jackson "is for Van Buren—& for his friends—He is personally against Calhoun & . . . is reconciled with [William H.] Crawford, Who will probably run as Vice President." Notes that Calhoun "is against Jackson secretly" but that his friends join Jackson "in all measures & in all debate" and will do so "Until they are driven off or agree to set themselves against the admn. openly." Believes they "cannot mend the breach, although they may prevent an open rupture & public disclosure." Adds that "McDuffy [*sic*, George McDuffie] has moved the *am*[endmen]*t*. with a view to exclude the President—This is perfectly Understood—The negociation has prevented his proceeding in it—It remains to be Seen What Course he will take—You will see by the [Washington] Glob[e] What are the views of the Ad[ministratio]n. upon the motion of this amendment—The Globe has certainly made a direct attack upon McDuffy—Which he will feel—I think it will be very difficult with such men & such elements to prevent an explosion—"

Concludes with a discussion of the tariff, noting that "Sugar is Safe for this Session—but Under the next Congress, who can say. . . . There is a Combination of all the Jackson party except Penna. to distroy the duty on Sugar—evidently concert[ed] to punish her—Every thing relating to the Tariff depends on Penna. she is yet firm—But she does not seem to perc[e]iv[e] yet the effect of Genl. Jacksons admn. upon the great interests of the Country, upon the Constitution & the Union itself." ALS. InU. For the Ohio elections, see Clay to Sloane, July 16, 1830; Clay to Conover, October 31, 1830; Clay to Greene, October 30, 1830. For the New Jersey election, see Southard to Clay, August 8, 1830. For the Kentucky attempts to elect a U.S. senator, see Clay to Beatty, June 8, 1830. For McDuffie's proposed amendment, see Johnston to Clay, January 12, 1831. A Washington *Globe* editorial on January 15, 1831, deplored the fact that McDuffie's amendment would limit the present incumbent to one term and suggested an alternate one which would render "every President *hereafter* ineligible for a second term" and which would give "the election of President to the people," while taking "it from the House of Representatives in the last resort."

To SUSAN (SUSANNAH) HART PRICE

New Orleans, January 28, 1831

Mr. [James] Brown yesterday handed to me $500 for you, and the same sum for your mother [Susannah Hart]. Supposing it would be agreeable to you, I delivered your money to Mr. [James] Erwin to be employed by him for your benefit in the same manner as he was to employ the sum you advanced to him before he left Lexington. Your mothers money I shall carry up with me and deliver to her. Mr. Brown continues to express himself in the same kind and generous manner towards the relations of his late wife [Ann Hart Brown]. He appears to be very much affected by his loss. I shall go up to his plantation next week to have the will proved.

Your sister [Lucretia Hart Clay] wishes James [Brown Clay] to tell Tom[1] to sow peas, early york cabbages and plant early potatoes by the first of March.

We reside with Mr. [Martin] Duralde at his place about two miles from the City, and are all tolerably well. Anne [Brown Clay Erwin] and Mr. Erwin stay in the City.

ALS. Courtesy of Eleanor Marshall Turner, Louisville, Ky. Endorsed "To be put in the P. Off. at Louisville," and postmarked "LOUIS[VILLE] FEB 18." 1. Probably a slave.

From JOSIAH S. JOHNSTON

Washington, February 10, 1831

The election of Printer[1] being over we expect the publication of Calhoun in a few days—[2]It is made up chiefly of Correspondence in which Crawford & Calhoun will be brought in collission—It is Said the Genl. is quite indignant at being menaced with the publication & there is no reconciliation in him—He appears to extend his hostility to all the Nullifyers—I think there will be a rupture with all that party—but of this more in a few days—

Calhoun cannot get back in to favor—It is Van B[uren] policy to cut him & [John] McLean off from the party—

I do not know what sort of exposition Calhoun will make, but his character depends much on the spirit with which he defends himself—

322

You may take it for granted that Calhoun is fixed in his determination of opposition to the admn. but of this I will write you more particularly in a day or two. [P.S.] [William] Hendrick[s] diserted us in the election of Printer or We should have Carried the election—we had one vote depending on his—which would have decided the question—

ALS. InU.   1. Pettis to Clay, Dec. 16, 1830.   2. Johnston to Clay, Jan. 7, 1831.

From JOHN L. LAWRENCE, New York, February 14, 1831. Refers to his December 14, 1830, letter. Encloses a Circular and a copy of the February 12 New York newspaper, *The Age*, which "will apprize you of our subsequent movements" since Clay's nomination for the presidency in New York City. Mentions that he has before him a letter "from a distinguished Senator at Washington" who writes that Clay's friends have never been "more united or more confident." Predicts that "if Mr. Clay cannot be elected no other man can." Notes that the "Same letter states that a Convention for the nomination of Prest. & V.P. will be held in Baltimore on the second Monday of December." ALS. DLC-HC (DNA, M212, R4). The enclosed circular, dated January 11, 1831, and signed by William H. Ireland, Joseph Hoxee, and Charles F. Green, gives notice that Henry Clay was nominated for president on December 13, 1830, at a "Meeting of Upwards of three thousand Citizens of New York" and that a general committee of 70 members and various ward-level committees, have been formed to achieve that goal. See Lawrence to Clay, November 29, 1830; Porter to Clay, December 10, 1830.

To SAMUEL L. SOUTHARD   New Orleans, February 14, 1831

I received your two obliging letters respecting the election in New Jersey,[1] the successful issue of which has every where had the happiest effect upon our friends. Indeed, upon that election probably hung the fate of the Tariff. I believe it is now secure.

I was inexpressibly mortified with the state of things in Kentucky,[2] the result altogether of accidental and local causes; for I entertain no doubt that we have a large majority in the State. And that such is the belief of our friends was demonstrated, during the last Session of the Legislature, by their offer and perfect willingness to have a general ticket for members to the H. of R. in Congress. The measure was not acceded to by the other party, and our friends thought it best not to incur the dissatisfaction generally produced by innovation. I am fully convinced that we shall have a decided and an available majority in the next Legislature.

You ask what is to be done with Georgia? What *will* be done I cannot say; what ought to be I do not doubt. The Constitution, treaties and laws ought to be faithfully and firmly executed.[3] If Georgia submits it is well. If she chooses to rebel, whilst we should regret her folly and its consequences, I have no doubt that she would be reduced to obedience, and that the final effect of the struggle would add strength to the Union.

In this State, every thing is as we could wish it. Owing to the inattention of our friends in some of the Parishes, a majority (small in amount) was returned to the Legislature of Jackson members;[4] but such have been the changes, since the election, among the members, that we have carried with ease all the Legislative elections. The attempt to repeal the duty on sugar, and the sales of some antient plantations for not complying with the formality of registering the titles, have goaded the people almost to madness.[5] I heard a man, who had prominently supported Jackson, say that the General could not now be elected a Constable.

I perceive, from the last papers, that he has graciously *permitted* himself to be again announced as a Candidate.[6] He will be beaten, if our friends do not allow their exertions to be paralized by a feeling of despair. We shall now probably have no third candidate, or, if we do, it will create a diversion prejudicial to him and not to us. The probability now is that the Antimasons will give us their support. Should they run in 1832 in N. York a Candidate for Governor and abstain from offering any ticket for electors; and our friends should abstain from presenting any candidate for Governor & content themselves with merely presenting Candidates for Electors, I should think, as a natural consequence, that an union would take place between them, and that both parties would succeed in their respective objects. If Jackson should lose New York, or Pennsylvania, or Virginia, he cannot be re-elected. His success depends upon the union of those three States, and that Union is more unlikely than his loss of some one of them.

I will not forget what you say in behalf of Dr. [Frederick] Beasley,[7] upon my return to Kentucky. As I am not however now a member of the Board of Trustees, which is alone authorized to make an appointment of President of Transylvania, I would advise your transmitting a recommendation directly to Robert Wickliffe Esq the Chairman of the Board.

I learn with deep regret that your health continues precarious. I trust that you will neglect no precaution to reestablish and preserve it. Your life is very important to our Country, in the coming events. . . . P. S. I learn indirectly that the correspondence between the President & V. P. [Calhoun] has been shewn to third persons;[8] and that the P. has lost much in dignity and temper, if not in the argument. I presume it will not be with-held much longer from the public.

ALS. NjP.   1. Southard to Clay, August 8, 1830.   2. Clay to Beatty, May 4, 1830. 3. Johnston to Clay, Jan. 12, 1831.   4. Clay to Johnston, March 11, 1830.   5. Clay to Unknown Recipient, Feb. 16, 1831.   6. On Jan. 22, 1831, Francis P. Blair announced in the Washington *Globe*: "We are permitted to say, that if it should be the will of the Nation to call on the President to serve a second term in the Chief Magistracy, he will not decline the summons." 7. Southard to Clay, Jan. 10, 1831.   8. Johnston to Clay, June 5, 1830; Jan. 7, 1831.

To UNKNOWN RECIPIENT, February 16, 1831. Reports finding upon his arrival in Louisiana "a general alarm pervading . . . in respect to the attack meditated upon the Tariff . . . which had been actually commenced in the H. of Representatives. The people of Louisiana . . . greatly attached to the Union, contemplate the success of that attack as involving their utter ruin." States that these people have convinced him of two propositions: "1st. That the repeal or reduction of the present duty on foreign sugar would totally disable them from continuing the culture of the Cane; and 2dly. that all parts of the Union would partake of the distress which would be certainly inflicted on them." Notes that "Most erroneous impressions prevail, in other parts of the Union, as to the profits upon Capital invested in Sugar plantations." Has been persuaded "from all I have seen and heard here, that Mr. Senator [Josiah S.] Johnston, in his late excellent letter to the Secy of the Treasury [Samuel D. Ingham], in assuming, as the average rate of profit upon Capital employed in the culture of S. Cane, from five to six per Cent. rather exceeds than falls short of the true standard. It is evident, then, that the Louisiana planter, if he were not protected by the existing duty, could not sustain a competition with the Sugars of foreign colonies." Contends that if manufacturers deserve protection, so do sugar planters, because the "seven or eight hundred Sugar plantations in Louisiana are, in fact . . . great Manufactories" which not only produce the raw material but also convert it into sugar and molasses. Moreover, these planters are "consumers of the objects of industry" of other parts of the country, "principally . . . Pennsylvania and the Western, middle and Northern States," where supplies of food, clothing, and farm implements are purchased. "Let us suppose the market for these various articles to be suddenly cut off, the inevitable consequence of the repeal of the duty upon Sugar, and . . . every part of the Union . . . would be deeply and sensibly affected by the destruction of the business of the Louisiana S. planter?"

Maintains also that the repeal of the sugar duty would not result in lower prices of sugar to consumers, because the "present low price of Sugar is attributable to the competition which has been produced between the West Indian and Louisiana planter." Repeal would, however, drive the Louisiana planter out of business, resulting in increased demand and higher prices for sugar from the West Indies. In addition, "If the cultivation of the Sugar Cane be abandoned, the labor now employed in it must be directed to some other object; and that object undoubtedly would be Cotton" which "is already produced in excessive quantity." This would be "most injuriously felt" in the cotton regions already suffering from over-production.

Turning to another subject of political interest in Louisiana, Clay notes that "Shortly after the session of Louisiana, an act of Congress required all the inhabitants to register their titles to land granted to them by the previous governments, and denounced, as a penalty for a neglect to comply with this law, that the proprietors should not be allowed to use their unregistered titles in any Court of justice. The object at which Congress aimed was a proper and legitimate object, it being to discriminate between the public domain and private property; but it may now be well doubted whether the means were not rigorously harsh and disproportionately severe. Many, from no disrespect whatever to the Legislature, but from a perfect confidence in the security of their titles, resulting from antient possession and complete grants, and strengthened by a positive stipulation in the treaty of cession, guarrenteeing their property, omitted to register their titles. Many, from ignorance of the Law, promulgated in a language not their own, also omitted to register their titles. An opinion has prevailed among the Bar that, in the case of perfect titles, the ceremony of registry was unnecessary. Notwithstanding this state of conscious security, the lands of many of the antient proprietors, who never dreamed of danger, have been thrown into the market. Sales have been actually made, in several instances, of plantations which have been in cultivation from fifty to 100 years; and the first knowledge of them which the unfortunate planters acquired was a notice, from the Speculator, not to remove, at their peril, any thing whatever from the plantation. A church even, long dedicated to public worship, has been actually sold! The interposition of the Executive has, I understand, been in vain invoked. I do hope that that of Congress, to which the Legislature has appealed, will be afforded, and that some efficacious remedy will be provided."

Suggests that "It may indeed be well questioned whether the act of Congress is not repugnant to that amendment of the Federal Constitution, which forbids a mans' property to be taken from him, without due process of law." Notes, further, that the lands most affected by this law comprise "the best and longest settled as well as the richest part of the State. And what aggravates the misfortune is that the omission to register has been chiefly on the part of the Creole planters, affording a strong presumption that it has proceeded from ignorance of the American laws and languages the American planters having most generally taken the precaution to comply with the law." Points out that despite this injustice, "neither the Legislature nor any public assembly has, for a moment, forgot its loyalty to the Union or its respect to the public authorities. We hear no menaces of violence, no charges of the oppression and tyranny of the majority, no threats to exercise the powers of nullification." AL, draft. Written from New Orleans. Printed in full in Colton, *Clay Correspondence*, 4:293-99.

Charles Haynes of Georgia had submitted a resolution in the House of Representatives calling for the Committee of Ways and Means to inquire into the expediency of reducing the duty on brown sugar. The House passed the resolution; subsequently the

Committee of Ways and Means reported a bill to reduce and equalize the duties on imports. The bill passed the House on July 10, 1832, but did not pass the Senate. *Register of Debates*, 21 Cong., 2 Sess., 455-66, 794-815, 828, 844; 22 Cong., 1 Sess., 1763-65, 3895.

On December 31, 1830, Sen. Josiah S. Johnston of Louisiana replied to interrogatories, dated July 1, 1830, which he had received in a circular from Secretary of the Treasury Samuel D. Ingham. In it, Johnston argued strongly for the necessity of the tariff for the survival of sugar production in Louisiana; he also pointed out the negative economic effects that would result if sugar production became unprofitable. In the long run, he maintained, ending the tariff on sugar would drive sugar planters out of business and make sugar prices higher. Letter printed in *House Exec. Doc.* 62, 21 Cong., 2 Sess., pp. 49-68.

Congress had passed an act on March 2, 1805 [8 *U.S. Stat.*, 324-29], providing that land titles in Louisiana claimed under French or Spanish grants made before October 1, 1800, were to be filed with the register of the U.S. land office. A board of land commissioners was given the power to decide in a summary manner on the authenticity of all claims. In effect, all landholders were required to come forward and prove the legitimacy of their claims. Persons who had made an actual settlement before December 20, 1803, with permission from the Spanish government, and who had actually cultivated the land were to be confirmed in their titles. On June 5, 1830, President Jackson proclaimed for sale nine fractional townships in the eastern district of Louisiana. About half of the tracts offered for sale consisted of lands held under Spanish titles. Though these comprised some of the most valuable land in the state, most had not been legally registered. Sales were held on the first Monday in November, 1830. Congress, however, passed an act [22 *U.S. Stat.*, 561-62, 903-11] in 1832 suspending further sales and allowing persons with claims to register and recover their property at any time before July 1, 1835. See also *American State Papers, Public Lands*, 6:290-91, 665-702; and Harry L. Coles, Jr., "A History of the Administration of Federal Land Policies and Land Tenure in Louisiana, 1803-1860," Ph.D. dissertation, Vanderbilt University, 1949, pp. 73-77, 136, *passim*.

From William Prentiss, Washington, February 22, 1831. Reports having become the proprietor of the Washington *Daily National Journal* by purchasing the interest of William Duncan, who on "account of his pecuniary resources," could not continue as publisher. States that when he considered "the bold and undeviatin[g] course that has been persued by the Journal . . . in your behalf — the necesity of such [a] paper at the seat of government — and the maney kindnesses bestowed on me," he "deemed it a duty under all hazzards to sustain that press so far as my pecuniary means would enable [me]." As a result, "I have advertised my stock of Jewelry watches silver ware for sale at auction — and shall appropriate my little all in advocating (through Mr [John] Agg who will continue to edit the paper) not only the vital principles of the true policy of this Government but the Election of Henry Clay (in doing the one we do the other)"

Notes that the *Journal* might have gone on as before "on its own credit, though nearly exausted at that time, but the evident want of confidence displayed in the countenance of your warm friends discouraged those who had been in the habit of extending credit to the Journal and the proprietors would have been compelled to have stoped the press—" States that since his purchase of the *Journal* on February 2, he has had "the manifest expression of good will from all your partizans & friends — but I do not expect one of them to come forward to offer any kind of pecuniary assistance." Asks Clay to use his influence to increase the circulation of the paper.

Believes the declaration of war between President Jackson and Vice President Calhoun [Johnston to Clay, January 7, 1830] makes Clay's election almost certain. Mentions that Sen. Littleton W. Tazewell of Virginia "made a strong speech today ag[t] the President & Secretary of State [Van Buren] in the Senate," and that there seems to be "a manifest disposition" in the Calhoun party "to take sides with us." Nevertheless, he looks on Calhoun "with[h a] very suspicious eye." Adds that Agg has published the Calhoun correspondence with Jackson in the *Journal* and will publish comments on the Jackson-Calhoun break appearing in *The Globe* ("the Government paper") and the Washington *United States Telegraph* ("the Calhoun paper").

Warns, further, that there "are rumers that [Daniel] Webste[r]s' Eye is directed toward the pre[s]idential chair — I drop this — in order that you may be on the elert." ALS. DLC-HC (DNA, M212, R4). Tazewell's speech questioned the president's authority to initiate a mission to Turkey during the congressional recess and thus without the advice and consent of the Senate. He argued that even if the president had this authority, he should have, at the beginning of the next session, sent to the Senate for approval the name of the person he had appointed during the recess. See *Register of Debates*, 21 Cong., 2 Sess., 217-18. Agg published the Jackson-Calhoun correspondence in the Washington *Daily National Journal* on February 21, 22, 1831, and the comments of *The Globe* and the *United States Telegraph* on February 24.

From Francis T. Brooke, Richmond, Va., March 6, 1831. Notes that since the open break ("the explosion at Washington") between Jackson and Calhoun, "you will have seen that Mr [William H.] Crawford does not mean longer to be on good terms with you. What else does he mean in his letter to Mr C[alhou]n by Speaking of the coalition between you and Mr A[dams]." Adds: "I did not hesitate on seeing that sentence in his letter to C[alhou]n to shew his letter to you of [February 4] 1828 in which he exculpated you from all blame in that matter — as to his last [March 31, 1830] letter to you, though I have shown it to [Daniel] Call [possibly Josiah S.] Johnston and a few others of your warm friends confidentially to prevent any improper inference from your silence I shall leave to you to expose it whenever you think proper."

Reports that the Van Buren party in Virginia has "fallen very much and the C[alhou]n party risen on its ruins." Believes that the Calhoun faction "will sooner come over to you that [*sic*, than] go back to V B as soon as the Jackson cement is dissolved by his folly." Asks Clay how he stands personally with Gov. John Floyd of Virginia. Says he will attend a proposed dinner for Calhoun if he "comes here as expected." Says also that "I begin to hope to live to see the morals of the governt of the U S regenerated and the States at peace with it." ALS. InU. Crawford had written Calhoun on October 2, 1830, that there had been "much less [sympathy] between Mr. [John Q.] Adams and myself than between him and you, at least before the coalition between him and Clay. In fact before that event my impression was, that from the time your name was put down for the Presidency you favoured the cause of Mr. Adams." For the full text of the letter, see Wilson, *Calhoun Papers*, 11:233-48. On his way home to South Carolina from Washington, Calhoun spent March 10 and 11 in Richmond where he attended dinners given by Governor John Floyd. *Ibid.*, 285.

To JOHN L. LAWRENCE   New Orleans, March 7, 1831
Your obliging favor of the 14h. Ulto. with its enclosure has been received. I see with pleasure that our friends in N. York are resolved to bring into operation a zeal and energy proportionate to the crisis in our public affairs. If there be union and cordial concert I do believe that we shall be able to rescue the Government from the dangers which are now impending over it. Information had reached me that there was ground to apprehend the disturbance of our harmony by divisions among ourselves. I am happy to be assured by you that there is no foundation for that apprehension. I was very unwilling to believe that any portion of our friends could be disposed to pursue a course so suicidal. We have every motive for concentration and united exertion. And altho' we need not conceal from ourselves the magnitude of the difficulties we

have to encounter, I firmly believe that they may be all overcome if we act like freemen and do not waste our strength in idle dissentions.

I consider the election of any particular individual to the Chief Magistracy so perfectly a consideration of secondary and subordinate consequence, compared to the great and patriotic object of preserving all that is valuable in our institutions, that I am entirely ready to surrender my pretensions, whatever they may be, to any one who can better unite our friends and hold out a more encouraging prospect of success. I express this sentiment not for effect, but as a sincere and genuine dictate of my heart. If the Convention should be held, which is contemplated at Philadelphia or Baltimore, would it not be better not to limit it to the nomination of any particular individual, but to place it upon the basis of certain great principles to be enumerated, and leave it to the free designation of such person as will best combine a hearty support of those principles?

Of the majority in this State our friends may be perfectly assured. It is now undoubted and daily encreasing. A gentleman, who had given to General Jackson a prominent and efficient support, at the last election, told me that he could not now be elected in Louisiana to the office of Constable. The changes pervade every class of society.

I shall leave this place in the course of the week and expect to reach home in all the month. I regret that I cannot coincide with some of my friends in the opinion they entertain of the policy and propriety of a visit to New York. If it were to do good with those with whom I might be brought into contact, I am apprehensive that the much larger portion of my fellow Citizens, whom I could not see, would condemn the step.

ALS. ViU. Letter marked "(Confidential)."

From James Madison, "Montpelier," Va., March 21, 1831. Recommends the Reverend Mr. Frederick Beasley for the vacant presidency of Transylvania University. Remarks that his "personal knowledge of Mr. B. is very slight, and that of his literary publications too much so, to admit of a compatent judgment of their merits." Suggests that Samuel L. Southard and Mahlon Dickerson would be better judges of Beasley's qualifications. ALI, draft. DLC-James Madison Papers (DNA, M212, R22). See Southard to Clay, January 10, 1831. Beasley, Dickerson, and Southard were all Princeton graduates.

From John L. Lawrence, New York, March 29, 1831. Refers to Clay's letter to him of March 7. Says, with reference to Clay's willingness to withdraw from consideration when the nominating convention meets: "In regard to your frank declaration of willingness to yield your own pretensions in favour of others, I must be equally frank in Saying, that to your numerous friends, here Such an avowal, publickly made, would not be acceptable." Continues: "Your own name has So long been identified with the maxims of government that are contending for Supremacy — has so long been the target for every arrow of the enemy — that all who are really desirous for the fight; look to you, and you alone, as the leader under whose guidance the victory is to be won. Any step, that should transfer the *bâton* to another, would be attributed to your despair of the cause, and be followed by the most fatal consequences." Believes, further, that the "enthusiasm created by Genl. Jacksons military achievement, and which operates so extensively towards his Support, despite of his manifest incapacity for his Station, must be counteracted by an equivalent zeal on our Side."

Reports that "our friends look with great anxiety to the next election [August 1, 1831]" in Kentucky [Webster to Clay, March 4, 1831], and that there are some "expectations of a Jackson triumph in that quarter."

Warns Clay, in closing "that an attack is in contemplation against [your] friend Mr. [Robert W.] Wickliffe, in relation to his agency [in the] affairs of a firm of which Mr. [Robert] Scott (I think) was a partner. I know no details, further than are above stated nor whether there are fair grounds for the suspicions which are entertained — but I have thought it adviseable to put him upon the alert to have his vouchers & statements in readiness for his defence, if indications at home should not contradict the anticipations here. . . . This part of my letter you must consider confidential, except So far as you may think proper to communicate it to him [Wickliffe]. My name is not to be used in connexion with the facts, which I have only from hearsay and at second hand." ALS. DLC-HC (DNA, M212, R4). A draft version, substantially identical in thrust and language, is in ViU. There is no evidence that the alleged Wickliffe-Scott indiscretion ever surfaced or became a political issue. See below, Clay to Lawrence, April 13, 1831; Wickliffe to Clay, April 30, 1831.

To HENRY CLAY, JR.   Louisville, March 31, 1831

We reached here this morning from N. Orleans.[1] Anne [Brown Clay Erwin] and her children are with us, proceeding to her new home near Ashland, the title to which Mr. [James] Erwin has secured.[2] He remained at N. Orleans, to follow us in five or six weeks. Our voyage has been quite agreeable. Your mother thinks her health has been benefited by passing the winter below, and mine has been not bad.

The time approaches when you will emerge from the Academy of West point. I rejoice at it, and I rejoice that you have remained there the whole term. I feel quite confident that you will never repent it hereafter. The time also approaches when you must finally decide the important question of your future pursuit in life. My wish is that you should devote yourself to the profession of law. Such has been always my desire. At the same time, I do not wish to control your own choice. Should you elect the profession of the law, you will enter on its studies at the most favorable period of life and with uncommon advantages. I wish you to study the Common law thoroughly, embracing all its branches, the Roman civil law, and the Public Law. You may commence, if you please, at Ashland, or wherever else you prefer. In the course of your studies, I wish you to pass a winter at N. Orleans, where you will have an opportunity of perfecting yourself in French, and witnessing the practice under the civil law.

In the mean time, and to afford further opportunity for Consideration and consultation, perhaps you had better obtain from the Department of War the commission which is generally granted to Cadets, and request the customary furlough. On that point, however, do as you please.

You have also in contemplation the tour of Quebec and the falls of Niagara, but had not decided when we last corresponded on that subject whether you would make it prior or subsequent to your return to Ashland. Let me know your wishes and purposes in that respect. *Perhaps*, if you postpone it until you come home, I may accompany you. I have such a wish but can not yet decide positively. In any event you will want money, and let me know what you will probably want.

Tom [Hart Clay], who has passed the winter at my Prairie in Illinois, has gone to N. Orleans on a Corn speculation. We passed him on the river without seeing him. Theodore [Wythe Clay] remained in Lexington, James [Brown Clay] at the [Transylvania] University, and John [Morrison Clay] is with us. H[enry]. C[lay]. Duralde is also returning with us. . . .

ALS. Henry Clay Memorial Foundation, Lexington, Ky. Addressed to young Clay at West Point, N.Y. with the instruction: "To be put into the P. Office at Philada." Postmarked, "PHIL 16 APR." 1. Ticket costs on the steamboat *Philadelphia*, New Orleans to Louisville, were: Clay and his wife, $35 ea.; Masters John Clay and Henry Clay Duralde, $17.50 ea.; two female servants, $17.50 ea.; sundries, $10. Total: $150. T.C. Twichell to Clay, March 31, 1831. Receipt. DS. DLC-HC (DNA, M212, R4). 2. Clay to Henry Clay, Jr., Oct. 31, 1830.

From HENRY CLAY, JR.   West Point, N.Y., April 3, 1831

In about 3 months now I shall complete my course at the Military Academy. In the retrospect of my academic labours I have much cause of gratification and perhaps some of regret. As an educated man I am much improved; for I feel my mind to be greatly enlarged and I have acquired habits of mental discipline which I am sure will be invaluable to me in whatever profession I may ultimately embark

In another place and under different circumstances I might have gained more knowledge of the world and made some acquirements which I now do not possess, but which are generally esteemed in one of my years. Yet I am well satisfied with the past. I am prepared to enter life with a character solidly formed and upon which no blemish has yet attached from any offences against propriety or duty. My information though not various nor brilliant is of such a nature as to be extensively employed: indeed I consider the sciences not so much as an end as a means and an instrument to be used in a variety of ways and in many different concerns of importance. Having such an advocate as Brougham[1] they must be of real intellectual utility even to the Statesman or member of the Bar.

But as you said to me in a former letter though the foundation of my education may already be laid the edifice is yet to be erected and adorned: in truth the design of the whole for good or for evil is yet to be determined — But without metaphor   If I am to leave the army not to engage in some scientific or practical pursuit I shall need so much preparation that it is almost discouraging to think of it. Besides the necessary details of professional knowledge, the studies of history and general literature though they are often deemed merely ornamental appear to me entirely indispensable to a person aspiring to an elevated station in his profession, whatever that may be — However all this we will discuss in Kentucky and if you will permit me, I will reverse your remark, and leave the ultimate decision not to my own immature judgment, but to your knowledge and experience.

Henry Hart has arrived in the East; he sent me word a short time since that he would soon visit West Point.

I do not expect to receive more than one or two letters from home before my departure from here, but I should be extremely [word missing] to hear from you, if you find it convenient to write. I have not yet learned how you have been pleased with your trip to the South but I suppose you & my mother must have been gratified. . . .

ALS. Henry Clay Memorial Foundation, Lexington, Ky. 1. For Henry Peter Brougham, Lord Chancellor of England, see *DNB*.

From DANIEL WEBSTER   Boston, April 4, 1831

It is a long time since I wrote you. This omision has happened, partly because I have had, at no time, much to say, and partly because what may as well be done tomorrow, is often neglected today. Even now; I have little to communicate & write mainly to cherish remembrances, & keep correspondence alive.

You have seen all that has transpired, at Washington, and in the Country, in the last four months. Your opinions & mine are not likely to be different, on any of those occurrences; and, probably the effect produced by them here, is very similar to that which they have also produced with you. Undoubtedly, the correspondence between the Prest. & vice President has lowered them both.[1] It shews feelings & objects so personal—so ambitious—I may even say so *factious*, in some or all the parties, that it creates no small degree of disgust. — As I came along home, I witnessed this result strongly, in Baltimore, Philadelphia, & New York.—I believe, & at this moment, a majority in each of those cities, would be glad of a change in men & measures.

Mr Johnstone [*sic*, Josiah S. Johnston] went west directly from Philadelphia, & could give you all the particulars, respecting the state of things there. I staid a week with Mrs Webster's friends in N York. You will see what publicly transpired. There is a great deal of good spirits in New York, but it is not, at present very well put in action. Great objects are, in some measure, lost in local division. They are canvassing for a City election, very warmly. I do not expect complete success to those opposed to the present State of things; but I have hopes of a great change, & such as shall give promise of a majority soon.[2] The influence & patronage of those in office, in the Corporation, is too great, I fear, to be overthrown by one effort. There is certainly a great disposition, in the City, to unbind itself from the fetters of Tammany. —

As to the State, I have no particular knowledge. The only distinct impression which I recd, was, that the Anti Masons were growing something more mild towards yourself—& giving a little more hope that they would not, themselves, make a nomination for the Presidency. —I think they will find such a nomination very difficult, if success should attend the Kentucky[3] & Mary land elections—[4]in Aug. & Septr. —I need not say to you how much depends on the first of these. If Ken: comes out strong, & decided, I am persuaded a very determined and active spirit will pervade every part of this Country; much beyond any thing yet experienced. —

It is an interesting inquiry, *whether Mr Calhoun will be put up for the Presidency.* If he should, would not both he & Genl Jackson be beaten, in Va & Pa.—& perhaps N. Carolina?—My own opinion, at present, is that Mr Calhoun *will not be brought forward*, unless, perhaps in S. Carolina, from the evident danger of utter overthrow, to which such a measure would expose the whole party. At the same time, I believe he is sanguine enough to make the attempt, if his friends would encourage it. —

I faithfully promised [Robert P.] Letcher that I would visit the West, this Spring. Tho' I have not yet abandoned this idea, my purpose is shaken a little by the advice of friends, here. They say, I could not go to Kentucky, at this moment; without exposing *myself*, & what is of more consequence, my *friends*, to invidious & odious remarks, which might have a bad effect on the public mind. I am quite unwilling to give up the jaunt; not knowing at what other period I may hope to be beyond the mountains. Nevertheless, if there be well founded doubts of the prudence of such a thing, it ought to be omitted. My purpose was to go to Ohio, Ken. & Missouri—but not down the Rive[r]

Our annual elections take place today. In a State having so many custom houses & Post offices, &c &c, the patronage of the Govt. will naturally produce some votes in its favor. But there is no general feeling favorable to the Administration. I suppose this State is as strong as any one in the Union. —

At your leisure, I shall hope to hear from you. I wish you could make Letcher or [James] Clark write. If anything occurs to either of them which friends here could be useful in, we should be very glad to hear from them. —

Notwithstanding appearances, do not despair of N. Hampshire. . . .[5]

[P.S.] Mar. [sic, April] 5. Tuesday. The Election returns,[6] which have come in this morning, shew a great falling off, even of the few Administration votes we had last year — [Levi] Lincoln & [Marcus] Morton are the opposing Candidates for Govr. — [Thomas L.] Winthrop & [Nathan] Willis for Lt. Govr. Morton & Willis the Jackson Candidates —

ALS. DLC-HC (DNA, M212, R4). Letter marked *"Private & Confidential."* Incorrectly dated "March" on manuscript. Printed in Wiltse, *Webster Correspondence*, 3:106-8.   1. Johnston to Clay, June 5, 1830.   2., Lawrence to Clay, Nov. 8, 1830.   3. In the Ky. general assembly elections of August 1-3, 1831, six Clay supporters and three Jacksonians were elected to the senate, giving Clay an overall majority of 21 to 17 in that body. In the Ky. house of reps., 56 Clay supporters were chosen to 44 for Jackson. Five Clay candidates and 7 Jacksonians were elected to the U.S. House. Cincinnati *American*, August 20, 1831; and *Niles' Register* (August 27, 1831), 40:449.   4. Mercer to Clay, July 22, 1830.   5. In the N.H. election, Jacksonians won the governorship, all congressional seats, and also controlled both houses of the state legislature. Ichabod Bartlett was elected governor over Samuel Dinsmore by a majority of about 4,200 out of 42,000 votes cast. Washington *Daily National Intelligencer*, March 16, 18, 1831.   6. In Massachusetts, Lincoln defeated Morton handily and National Republican candidates for state offices received about three-fourths of all the votes cast. *Ibid.*, April 9, 1831; and *Niles' Register* (April 16, 1831), 40:114.

From John B. Davis, Boston, April 5, 1831. Believes the end of "Jacksonian misrule" is near. Indeed, "Recent events at Washington afford most cheering encouragement to hope for such a result." Reports that annual elections in Massachusetts have ended [Webster to Clay, April 4, 1831], that Levi Lincoln has been reelected by an "increased majority," and that, "In Truth, we have no Jacksonism in Massachusetts." Says that the state legislative convention that nominated Clay for the presidency "was the largest and most spirited Convention I ever attended. . . . Regard for yourself and for Mr [Daniel] Webster is now the ruling passion with us here." ALS. DLC-HC (DNA, M212, R4).

To James Brown, April 8, 1831. Reports that he arrived back in Lexington from New Orleans on April 6. Comments on the weather and the health of their respective kin.

Concludes: "Mr. Senator [Josiah S.] Johnston will give you all the political news from Washington. He surprized me with one opinion which he expressed, that is, that Mr. Calhoun will be a candidate for the Presidency, and that he will probably obtain the vote of S. Carolina, No. Carolina and Virginia. I have not yet seen evidence sufficient to convince me of its correctness. All things are working well for our cause out of this State, and within it we have a fair prospect of securing majorities in the General Assembly, and in the H. of R. of the U.S.; but I forgot your aversion to politics, and will say no more on that odious topic." ALS. ViU. Addressed to Brown in New Orleans. For the general assembly and U.S. House elections in Kentucky, see Webster to Clay, April 4, 1831.

From George D. Prentice, Louisville, April 10, 1831. Contemplates writing an article on the expediency and constitutionality of the 25th section of the Judiciary Act of 1789 and asks Clay for his suggestions on the subject. Wants, "at the same time, to urge strongly upon the people of Kentucky the necessity of expressing, at the August Election, their disapprobation of the conduct of such of their Representatives as favored the repeal of that Section during the last session of Congress." Will send Clay copies of "the two Congressional reports upon the 25th Section." States that if Clay will write or assist in writing such an article, "I will publish the article in the [Louisville *Daily*] Journal, and distribute some thousands of it throughout the State and in pamphlet form. Some of our friends here are preparing pamphlets, and I have promised them my aid " ALS. DLC-HC (DNA, M212, R4). George Dennison Prentice (1802-1870), New England lawyer-turned journalist, was editor of the Louisville *Daily Journal* and in 1831 published a campaign biography of Clay (*Biography of Henry Clay*, Philadelphia, 1831). He had migrated to Kentucky in 1830. See *NCAB*, 3:121.

Section 25 of the Federal Judiciary Act of 1789 dealt with the jurisdiction and powers of the U.S. Supreme Court in certain specified situations. At issue was the right of the Court to declare federal and state laws unconstitutional, and the question of whether Congress had the right to withdraw from the Court powers it had earlier extended it. For the bill attempting to repeal or revise this section of the act, see *Register of Debates*, 21 Cong., 2 Sess., 532-35, 541-42. For the majority and minority reports on the subject from the House Committee on the Judiciary, see *House Reports*, 21 Cong., 2 Sess., no. 43; and *Register of Debates*, 21 Cong., 2 Sess., Appendix, 77. The House voted against considering the bill. Clay supporters in the Kentucky delegation voted with the majority to table the bill, while the Jacksonians in the delegation voted to take it up. *Register of Debates*, 21 Cong., 2 Sess., 542.

To JABEZ D. HAMMOND   Lexington, April 13, 1831

Upon my arrival at home from N. Orleans a few days ago I found your letter of the 13h. Ulto. and hasten, in compliance with your request, to transmit the enclosed letters,[1] which I hope may prove of some Service to yourself and Mr. Stewart.[2] I have not felt at liberty to offer you any to our ministers at London [Louis McLane] and Paris [William C. Rives]. I could have added one to G[eorge]. W[ashington]. Irving, but I presumed you were acquainted with him. I regret the necessity which exists for your visit to Europe, but you will make it at a most interesting crisis.

I regret to learn your opinion of the impracticability of Union among the opponents of the Administration in New York. On that union I am well assured depends the vote of the State.

As to the issue of the contest generally, it is perhaps yet too soon to hazard any opinion. If there should be no other parties to it than those now before the public, Genl. Jackson will be defeated, if he continues to lose during the next eighteen months in a ratio equal to his loss during the two years of his administration, and if his opponents exert themselves with zeal and confidence. Should Mr. Calhoun be a Candidate it will prejudice the General.

Wishing you an agreeable voyage to Europe, a safe return, and perfect restoration of your health. . . .

ALS. ViU.   1. One of which was Clay to Lafayette, April 13, 1831. It was a routine letter of introduction, in which Clay referred to Lafayette in passing as "the father of the liberty of France." ALS. NIC.   2. Probably Alvan Stewart (*DAB*), a well-known lawyer and author of a pamphlet which opposed Jackson on the tariff.

To JOHN L. LAWRENCE   Lexington, April 13, 1831

Your favor of the 29h. Ulto. has been received. I concur with you in thinking that there no longer exists any ground of apprehension of dissentions among our friends. I confess that I felt surprized and mortified that, at a period and in a state of things, requiring the greatest union cordiality and harmony among our friends, any thoughts should be entertained of creating divisions by presenting rival names from our ranks as Candidates for the Chief Magistracy. But I was not aware of the influence of either of those feelings in expressing the sentiment to you, that I was willing to retire from the contest, if there were another on whom the Country would be more likely to concentrate, in opposition to the present Chief Magistrate. That sentiment was dictated by a thorough conviction of the evils brought and likely to be brought upon the Nation by his misrule; and an anxious desire to avert them from my Country. It was not dictated by any unwillingness on my part to encounter the perils of a canvass, nor fears as to its successful termination. On the contrary, there is no danger which any man of honor ever dared meet, that I would not readily and cheerfully front to effect the deliverance of the Union. And, so far from entertaining fears as to the issue of the struggle, I have constantly believed, and yet think, that it will realize all our hopes, if the requisite zeal and confidence are employed in conducting it.

Nor was the sentiment prompted by any belief of my own that another's name could be advantageously substituted to mine. I believe, with you, that neither of the two gentlemen, mentioned by you,[1] for the reasons you state, would stand the smallest chance of success. But, altho' this was my opinion, I might be mistaken; and I felt, and yet feel, that I ought not to be in the slightest degree any impediment to a better choice of a Candidate, on whom the Country would be more likely to rally, if there be such an one, of which that Country, not I, ought to be the best, as it certainly is the most competent, judge. In other words, I did not, nor do I now think it right that I should seek my individual aggrandizement to the jeopardy of the safety of the great interests of the Country; but that I should be disposed of as might be deemed by our friends, generally, best for the security of those interests.

These were the feelings under which I expressed the sentiment to you. I communicated it to one or two others in the City of New York, the only point from which I received information by letter of the fact that the thoughts of some of our friends were turned towards another.

I recognize, in its fullest force, the obligation which I am under to dedicate the undivided energies of the remnant of my life to the service of my Country, if it wants it. It was under the influence of this principle of devotion that I expressed to you the sentiment in question. But I have never heretofore *forced* myself into public office, and never will hereafter seek to do it, against the public will, if I can ascertain it.

The considerations of attachments and enthusiasm, which you are pleased to think are connected with my name, are proper considerations for others to take and weigh, not for me to estimate.

In this State, our friends, I believe, are going to work in earnest; and, notwithstanding the contrary prediction of your Jackson informant at the City, are very confident of majorities both in the Legislature and in the H. of R. of the U.S. at the next August election.[2]

I will communicate to Mr. [Robert] Wickliffe the part of your letter relating to him,[3] for which I have no doubt he will be very thankful to you. . . . P.S. Will you be pleased to shew this letter confidentially to M[atthew]. L. Davis Esq, from whom I have this moment recd. a letter of similar import to your's?

ALS. ViU. Letter marked "(Confidential)." 1. Lawrence to Clay, March 29, 1831. No names were given by Lawrence, only descriptions, viz: "One of them, has of late years, undoubtedly done nobly — but errors of past times, not yet entirely forgiven, exclude the hope of producing it [nomination] as to him. The other is known only as a prudent performer of the duties of a comparatively subordinate station—and the uncertainty whether he is at this moment for us, or against us, puts all ardour in his behalf out of the question." 2. Webster to Clay, April 4, 1831; Clay to Brown, April 8, 1831. 3. Wickliffe to Clay, April 30, 1831.

From Richard Rush, York, Pa., April 14, 1831. Believes that the Clay cause is "prospering" in Pennsylvania, particularly during the past two months. Explains: "There have been state occurrences at the close of the late session of our legislature, certain taxes laid I chiefly mean, that threaten a revolution in opinion, some of the effects of which may lend material aid to other causes in withdrawing from him the vote of the state. Should the antimasons run a candidate and thus put three in the field, it will improve the prospect it is believed of the vote going for you, which god grant. Even should the antimasons carry their candidate, which I do not suppose possible, the ultimate effect, as we think, would still be favorable to you; so that, every how, the prospect looks fair."

As for the Anti-Masons, asks: "Is there no way, *my dear Sir*, in which, without doing violence to whatever opinions or feelings you may have as respects Masonry, or without offending that Institution, you could conciliate to a fair and reasonable extent the goodwill of antimasons, between this and September?" Is convinced that "With the direct aid of antimasons, we should carry your banner to a glorious victory, even if we do not without."

Sends Clay a newspaper containing an article by Rush, written over the pseudonym "Temple," one of a series which commented on British and American political affairs. The articles also occasionally provided Rush "a fit subject for merited satire upon our king [Jackson]." ALS. DLC-HC (DNA, M212, R4). For the Pennsylvania law taxing personal property one mill on the dollar, see Harrisburg *Chronicle*, March 21, 1831; and Klein, *Pennsylvania Politics*, 336-37. For Rush's "Temple" letters, see John Harvey Powell, *Richard Rush: Republican Diplomat* (Philadelphia, 1942), 229-30.

From Francis T. Brooke, near Fredericksburg, Va., April 17, 1831. Refers to his letter to Clay of March 6. Discusses the recent election of judges of the Court of Appeals (Supreme Court) of Virginia, the politics and personalities involved, and his own election to the court (though not to its presidency). Remarks that tactical bungling on the part of the Jacksonians resulted in Henry St. George Tucker having been elected president of the court. Indeed, "the running of him [Tucker] as a western judge lost me all my Clay friends in the Northwest."

Comments on John C. Calhoun's visit to Richmond. Believes that Gov. John Floyd of Virginia is "devoted" to Calhoun and will soon come out for him for the presidency. As for Clay's prospects in Virginia, "your friends will adhere to you with zeal and pertinacity—and if Jackson and Calhoun should both be run I think will give you the State, two thirds of those of the legislature who were not Clay men were Calhouns decided friends but they were afraid of their constitutents . . . [word obliterated in ms.] it is now very Clear that Jackson will owe his vote in the State to those who apparently follow and not to those who nominally lead them. [Thomas] Ritchie you find has admitted that you are too strong for V B [Van Buren] or C[alhoun]—this was to rally the Jackson party but it went too far for that object, and has had its influence on those who are always looking for majorities. I think it certain that there are many who will now vote for you in preference to Jackson, if they can not see that V B or C can be elected they will prefer you to Jackson—Ritchie has made an impression in the State that you have no respect for the constitution when any measure is popular, this has injured you. I think if you could have some inquiries made of you on that subject in your own State, that your answer to them would be of importance when published I wish on the receipt of this you would say what you intend as to Crawfords Letter [Crawford to Clay, March 31, 1830], and T J Randolphs [Clay to Brooke, August 17, 1830]—indeed I shall be glad to have all your views on these matters." ALS. InU. For Brooke's election to the court of appeals on April 11, 1831, an election necessitated by adoption of the new state constitution, see Richmond *Enquirer*, April 12, 1831; and Thomas R. Morris,

"The Virginia Supreme Court, An Institutional and Political Analysis," Ph.D. dissertation, University of Virginia, 1975, pp. 15-17, and Appendix C.; also, Clay to Brooke, April 24, 1831.

To HENRY CLAY, JR.   Lexington, April 20, 1831

I received your letter of the [April] 3d. and the one of previous date [March 31, 1831]. According to your request, I transmit enclosed a Check for three hundred dollars, of which I have no doubt you will make a proper use.[1]

The usual reports from the department of War of the conduct of Cadets are regularly received by me, and they assure me of your perseverance and success. I need not repeat the expression of the high gratification they afford me

When you join us at Ashland we will consider and decide the interesting question of your future pursuit in life. On that subject I wrote you a letter by Mr. Pope[2] on my way from New Orleans. My opinions there expressed remain the same, subject of course to re-examination.

Anne [Browne Clay Erwin] is busily occupied in preparing her house garden, and grounds attached to it, for Mr. [James] Erwin, whom she expects in about three weeks.[3] She takes great delight in the occupation, and they will have a delightful residence.

We have had, with the exception of three or four days of bad weather, a most agreeable April, and our fine Country looks charming. . . . P.S. Do you want the letters of introduction, about which you wrote to me formerly, or will you first return to Kentucky?[4]

ALS. Henry Clay Memorial Foundation, Lexington, Ky.   1. The most recent letter that has been found which requested money is that of Nov. 16, 1830.   2. Probably John Pope.   3. Clay to Henry Clay, Jr., Oct. 31, 1830.   4. Henry Clay, Jr., to Clay, Nov. 16, 1830.

To JOHN W. TREADWELL   Lexington, April 23, 1831

I recd. your[1] favor of the 15h. Ulto.   Far from considering you as having taken any unwarrantable liberty, I have perused its contents, and will communicate the information you desire, as far as I can, with pleasure.

I have been engaged in farming upwards of twenty years; but the business has had more of my personal attention during the two last years than at any former period. For about eighteen years, among other species of domestic animals, I have been rearing Merino Sheep, constantly breeding from full blooded rams, and frequently changing them. Other farmers in this neighbourhood have also been engaged in the same pursuit, but I know of none who has incurred as much expence and trouble as I have to keep up a stock of pure blood. The attention of the farmers has fluctuated according to the prices of wool, and the prospects of profit. My own has been less affected by it, as I have constantly believed that the day would arrive when the price of wool would reward the labor of producing it. But I have aimed not so much at the number as the purity of my flock, believing that when times got better I could enlarge it. There are no very large flocks within my knowledge in this quarter. I have about 130 full blooded, exclusive of lambs; and few of my acquaintances have so many. Most of us work up in our families some of the wool which we produce.

There is a better demand than usual this year for wool. I have had some applications for mine; but I have declined engaging it, partly in consequence of your letter. I sold my wool of full blooded quality last year at 35 Cents per lb. in the dirt, and it was intimated to me that I could get 37 Cents for it this year in the same state. I shall shear about the 10h. of May.

If you choose, I will send my wool to you, or to any agent of your's in Balto. or deliver it at Lexington, and take for it such price as you may deem it worth, upon inspection. My intention is to have it washed on the back, and, if I send it away, put up in bags. I am induced to make you this offer from the confidence inspired by your letter.

The expence of transmitting the article to Balto. by sea or by land is about the same. I suppose it would be cheaper to Boston to go by Sea.

I have no adequate idea of the quantity which could be purchased in this quarter; but I suppose with a diligent agent it would be considerable. Should you wish to employ an agent I would recommend to you Mr. Norman Porter,[2] an honest and respectable Citizen of Lexington, formerly from New England.

I am extremely happy to learn that you are doing well in the various branches of manufacturing in which you are engaged. On the point, respecting which you desire my opinion, the probability of a continuance of the policy of protection, it is difficult to form a very satisfactory opinion. I incline to believe, possibly because I wish, that it may be preserved, under all contingencies. Yet I cannot but fear, if Genl. Jackson should be re-elected, that it will be abandoned. So many have, during the last two years, modified or renounced their opinions on this and other subjects to suit what is conjectured to be his, that we ought not to be surprized, in the event supposed, if he should be able to carry a majority into his views, which I take to be adverse to the Tariff. Then, the public debt will probably be paid off in about three years more, and that will furnish an occasion for attacking the Tariff, which its opponents will not fail to improve. It would perhaps upon the whole safest to consider the policy unsettled and liable to be affected materially, one way or the other, by political events not very distant.

I do not know that I shall want any quantity of the articles myself that you manufacture, that would form an object to you to supply them. I have no doubt that you might dispose of large quantities of them for the Western consumption. I would recommend the houses of [Vallerian] Allain, Perrault and Allain of New Orleans, and [Chapman] Coleman and [Ardavan] Loughery of Louisville as worthy of all confidence. I know the members of both well. I concur with you entirely in the sentiment of the utility of cultivating and extending intercourse between our respective portions of the Union.

Requesting you to communicate my respectful Compliments to Messrs [Nathaniel] Silsbee and [Benjamin W.] Crowninshield. . . . P. S. I shall have from 100 to 120 fleeces of full blooded wool to dispose of.

ALS. KyU.   1. John W. Treadwell was president of the Merchants Bank in Salem, Mass., a justice of the peace, director of two insurance companies and of the Salem Laboratory Company, and a member of the East India Marine Society. *Salem Directory, 1837*, 120, 139; and *NEQ*, 6:451. 2. Norman Porter was a Lexington businessman who in 1834 was named to the first board of directors of the Bank of Kentucky and in 1838 was a hardware merchant with the firm of Porter and Butler at 2 W. Main Street & Cheapside, Lexington. Perrin, *History of Fayette County Kentucky*, 289; and MacCabe, *Directory of the City of Lexington . . . 1838 & '39*, 63.

To FRANCIS T. BROOKE   Lexington, April 24, 1831

Upon my return home from New Orleans, I found here your two favors of the 28th December last, and 6th ult. Although I met a vast accumulation of correspondence and of business, I should have immediately answered your letters but, to tell the truth, for my desire to see the issue of the elections in your Legislature.[1] My anxious looks were directed toward Richmond, on account of yourself especially, and other friends. The papers have at length brought the intelligence I desired, and I offer you my cordial congratulations on your election,[2] which, under all circumstances, is as honorable as I hope it will prove satisfactory to you. You are not, I remark again, appointed President of the Court, but, considering every thing, I do not think you should be mortified or even regret that the choice and the responsibility have fallen on a younger man [Henry St. George Tucker].[3] It would have given me inexpressible pain if I could have believed that your friendship to me, which has been of such long duration, and such great value, had affected you injuriously.

Important events at home and abroad have happened since I last wrote you. These changes in Europe are so rapid[4] that we have scarcely time to speculate on one before it is succeeded and supplanted by another. You will have heard probably by the time this letter reaches you, the decision of the question of a general war in Europe. I regret that such a war now seems to me almost inevitable. That regret will be diminished if we can remain at peace. But if there should be a general war, embracing England, she will make every endeavor to involve us in it. Such a purpose was openly avowed to me by men high in authority, when I was in England, on the contingency supposed.

Among the incidents at home, the correspondence between the President and Van Buren, is perhaps the most important occurrence during the late session of Congress.[5] I think it lowers them both, although confining our consideration to the parties to the controversy, Mr. Calhoun must be allowed to have obtained the advantage.

What course he may take in respect to the next election I am uninformed. From the knowledge I possess of his character and disposition, I believe he will be regulated altogether by his estimate of the probability of successful opposition to Jackson. If he thinks he can be defeated by himself or another, he will oppose his re-election directly or collaterally, according to circumstances. If he believes he can be defeated by no one, he will support his re-election make a merit of a magnanimous sacrifice of his sense of his wrongs, and endeavor to enlist the gratitude and sympathies of the Jackson party to elevate himself hereafter. In any event, we can not fail to profit by the controversy.

Mr. [William H.] Crawford's conduct, in respect to myself, surprised me. That he should, at the very period of holding such language toward me as he did in his letters, have been addressing letters to others containing the most improper expressions, betrays great duplicity. But, after his letter to me of March, in the last year,[6] ought we to be surprised at any thing he may do? I have never written to him since I received the letter, nor do I desire any correspondence with him again. I shall not, however, permit the publication of his letter of March. I could only be justified by some public good, and I see none that it would accomplish. The public feeling of Louisiana in regard to the President is all that we could desire. Not a doubt can be entertained of the vote of that State by any one acquainted with it. There have been numerous changes, and some of very influential individuals. In Kentucky, both parties are preparing for a vigorous campaign. Our friends are confident of carrying majorities both in the General Assembly and in the House of Representatives.[7] I was so greatly mortified with the issue of our last August election, that I am unwilling either to indulge or inspire hopes.[8] I can not, however, but believe that nothing but a corrupt and most extensive use of money can defeat us. Of that there is some reason to fear.

As to the issue of the contest generally, my opinion remains the same that it has been for the last eighteen months. If Jackson loses either New York, Pennsylvania, or Virginia, he will be defeated. If he unites the votes of all three of those States, he will succeed. And I have generally supposed that the degrees of probability of loss to him of those States were in the order in which I have placed them. If I am right, he is most certain of Virginia.[9] Of course I am unable to estimate the effect upon her of recent transactions, especially the correspondence and votes of your Senators [Littleton W. Tazewell and John Tyler]

The movement in Phila. is strong and encouraging. It remains to be seen whether it will be seconded in other parts of the state. I am afraid it will be. In N. York some progress has been made towards effecting an union of the various parties opposed to the present administration, but the problem is yet to be solved whether such an union can be accomplished.

The whole case presents one encouraging view. Jackson has lost, is losing, and must continue to lose. If the ratio of his loss hereafter, shall equal what it has been in the two last years he will be defeated.

I am much pressed to visit the north this summer; and although my judgement is opposed to any journey having a political object, or which might be construed into such an object, I have been some what shaken in my resolution by the great anxiety manifested. But I believe I shall resist it and remain in Kentucky, where (will you believe it?) I am likely to make an excellent farmer. I am almost tempted to believe, that I have heretofore been altogether mistaken in my capacity, and that I have, though late, found out the vocation best suited to it.

I recd. from our friend [Daniel] Call a very kind letter; and I have to request that you will ask him to consider this equally intended for his eye and your own. It has been a long time since I heard from him, but I see nobody from Richmond of whom I do not enquire about him; and I learn from all, that he retains generally his good spirits, and his attachments with great constancy; of mine to him and you I pray you both to be fully persuaded.

Copy. Printed in Colton, *Clay Correspondence*, 4:262-63. The first six paragraphs are found also in DLC-HC (DNA, M212, R4) and the last five paragraphs are in DLC-TJC (DNA, M212, R13). They are not, with the exception of the R13 paragraphs, in Clay's hand, and they incorporate minor variations in spelling, paragraphing, and abbreviating. Colton incorrectly dates this letter as April 24, 1830. 1. For judges of the Va. Supreme Court. 2. Brooke to Clay, April 17, 1831. 3. *Ibid.* 4. Changes related to revolutionary and independence movements in Belgium. See Johnston to Clay, Nov. 5, 1830. 5. Correspondence relating to Van Buren's resignation as secretary of state. John Spencer Bassett (ed.), *Correspondence of Andrew Jackson*, 7 vols. (Washington, 1926-35), 4:260-63. 6. Crawford to Clay, March 31, 1830. 7. Webster to Clay, April 4, 1831. 8. Clay to Beatty, May 4, 1830. 9. The DLC-TJC version ends at this point.

From William F. Dunnica, Jefferson City, Mo., April 26, 1831. In response to Clay's inquiries, announces that "I will take charge of your Lands in this State and give you my assurances that they shall be strictly attended to for the compensation of 25 cents for each tract per annum. . . . I can pay all taxes at this place." Notes that taxes for 1830 on "Your Lands in the counties of Ray and Randolph" have not yet been paid. On the other hand, taxes on land in St. Francois County owned by the late James Morrison, of whose estate Clay is administrator, have been paid. Comments on tax status of other Missouri lands in the Morrison estate. ALS. DLC-TJC (DNA, M212, R12). Dunnica served as an assistant in the Missouri state auditor's office.

To JOHN SLOANE   Lexington, April 29, 1831

I received your friendly letter of the 20h. inst. and was very happy to learn that you were doing well and enjoying health. I hope that your office¹ is profitable, and that the day is not distant when you may be transfered to some more extended and useful theatre. The exhibition of symptoms indicative of the return of the nation to reason and sobriety is very encouraging; and unless we are greatly deceived we are not doomed to more than about two years more of the present misrule.

The controversy between the P. [Jackson] and V. P. [Calhoun] lowers them both altho. limiting the question to themselves the latter has obtained the advantage. But what must be thought of the V. P. supporting a man whom he knew so well as he did Jackson? And of whose military conduct he thought so unfavorably?² And that too because the election of Mr. Adams was a violation of a *fundamental* principle! The principle violated was in not electing the man who was returned to the H. with most votes. Yet we find Mr. Calhoun combining with the party of Mr. Crawford who, by voting for the candidate having the smallest vote, most violated that fundamental principle!³ And what ought the public to think of Mr. Calhoun, who, in his interview with [James A.] Hamilton, to say the least, suppressed the truth, to benefit the election of Jackson, and then refused to allow his name to be used as authority?⁴

I receive your suggestions about the expediency of a tour and the mode of conducting it in the most respectful and friendly spirit. I am strongly urged by others to make the same tour,⁵ and if I make any excursion it will be in that direction, and I concur entirely with you in the expediency of avoiding public entertainments. But I must frankly own that I doubt both the propriety and policy of such a movement. I will say nothing on the first point; but, as to the other, would it not be deemed and condemned as electioneering by all parts of the Country which I should not visit, and all persons whom I did not see? And how few could I see! There the district suggested is precisely that in which Anti Masonry most rages. This is the most difficult and uncertain interest in the existing contest. Every word, every act of mine would be scanned and scrutinized. And the smallest countenance, real or imaginary, given by me to one of the two principles, would expose me to denunciation from the antagonist principle. Recollect how the contest raged between the two parties last autumn in N. York. Recollect the consequences of an indiscreet expression of Mr. Adams, in which he declared that he never would be a mason.⁶ I incline to think that I had better keep at a distance from the theatre of controversy and preserve myself free from and unmixt in it.

I have a letter from a valued and disconcerning friend at Richmond [Francis T. Brooke] who had passed two evenings with Calhoun at the Governor's [John Floyd], who is a decided friend of the V. P. My correspondent thinks that the V. P. will be a candidate for the Presidency; that that will create such a diversion from the Jackson party, that the vote of the State will be given to me; and that my friends in that State are resolved to adhere to me in every contingency.⁷

For my own part, I do not believe the V. P. has the moral firmness to break from the Jackson party, unless he persuades himself it will be defeated. In that case, he will woo us. But if he deem it invulnerable, he will affect to smother his wrongs and seek to engage the sympathies and gratitude of the Jackson party in his future elevation.

340

I think the National Convention ought to progress. It is not necessary for any purpose of nomination, except of a candidate for the V. P. but it is immensely important in securing concert, exciting animation, and forming acquaintance, and establishing correspondence. And it is of vast importance that Ohio should be represented in it, and engage with zeal.[8]

Louisiana is perfectly sure; and nothing, I believe, but most extensive bribery and corruption can prevent our success in K. in both the Legislature and the H. of R.[9] We have strong hopes of [Richard A.] Buckner becoming a Candidate.[10] [Robert P.] Letcher has consented again to run.[11]

ALS. MH. 1. Clerk of the court of common pleas in Wayne County, Ohio. 2. Johnston to Clay, June 5, 1830; Jan. 7, 1831. 3. Reference obscure. 4. In Feb., 1828, Calhoun and Hamilton had met at Washington. At this meeting Hamilton had inquired whether at any meeting of Monroe's cabinet in 1818 anyone had suggested the propriety of arresting Jackson for his actions in Florida during the Seminole War. Calhoun allegedly replied to Hamilton that such a course "was not thought of—much less discussed." Hamilton then wrote Calhoun on Feb. 25, 1828, attempting to confirm Calhoun's statement in order to prepare for "an apprehended attack" against Jackson in the 1828 presidential campaign. Calhoun replied on March 2, 1828, pleading the necessity for confidentiality between president and cabinet and stating that "I decline the introduction of my name, in any shape, as connected with what passed in the Cabinet." Wilson, *Calhoun Papers*, 10:354-57. 5. A campaign swing through the North, particularly New York State. 6. Adams made the statement during the 1828 presidential campaign that he "never was, and never shall be a Freemason." See Charles McCarthy, "Anti-Masonic Party," *American Historical Association Report 1902*, 1:381, published in *House Docs.*, 57 Cong., 2 Sess., 1902-3., no. 461, pp. 367-574. 7. Brooke to Clay, April 17, 1831. 8. Ohio sent a delegation of 18 to the convention. Gammon, *Presidential Campaign of 1832*, 64. 9. Webster to Clay, April 4, 1831. 10. Instead of running for Congress, Buckner ran for governor and lost. 11. He won.

From William Price, Hagerstown, Md., April 30, 1831. Reports that "In September [*sic*, October 3] next we choose the electors of our State Senate, and as that body is elected for five years, and secures to the party prevailing the contest of the state for that entire period, we consider it by far the most important of all our contests for the coming year [Mercer to Clay, July 22, 1830]. To this struggle we shall devote our entire and undivided strength, and you must not be surprised if you hear of us, — in this District I mean — withdrawing from the congressional canvass entirely. Indeed in regard to our member of congress, we have less reason than heretofore, to hazard a contest. Mr. [Michael C.] Sprigg, who is again a candidate, has supported our principles in congress and has moreover declared himself opposed to the reelection of Genl Jackson. If, as is now probable, he will be opposed by a decided Jackson man, he must as the contest waxes warmer, become, with his personal friends, completely identified with us; and we shall do as well perhaps to support and elect Sprigg, as to bring out one of our own party — myself for instance — and have been beaten."

Is more concerned about the political situation in Kentucky. Feels, moreover, that the outcome of the presidential election of 1832 turns on the result of Kentucky state elections in 1831 [Webster to Clay, April 4, 1831]. States: "Should we carry Kentucky, by a vote sufficient to put all question as to the ultimate decision at rest, Ohio will follow as a matter of course; and with the certainty of Kentucky and Ohio on our side, N York will perceive that with her rests the decision of the contest; and I believe that it is only necessary to satisfy N York, that her vote if given against Jackson will not be *thrown away*, to give confidence and an object to our friends in that state, and to ensure her vote in our favour. This calculation, as you perceive begins with Kentucky, and depends upon her." Believes, however, that Clay should not personally take "a prominent part in any of the measures that give expression to the will of the people."

Calls Clay's attention to the dissolution [Letcher to Clay, December 21, 1829] of Jackson's cabinet ("the *scatterment* at Washington"), and wonders what "Mr. Calhoun and his friends" will now do. Concludes: "I pray sincerely that all those elements of discord may work out in the end, the good of our common country." ALS. DLC-HC

(DNA, M212, R4). In the October election Sprigg lost to Francis Thomas by the margin of 4,452 to 3,872 votes. Both were Jacksonians. *Guide to U.S. Elections*, 556. Overall in the U.S. House elections in Maryland, five Clay men and four Jacksonians were elected. *Niles' Register* (October 8, 1831), 41:101.

From Robert Wickliffe, Lexington, April 30, 1831. Thanks Clay for letting him see the letter of John L. Lawrence to Clay, of March 29, 1831, and asks Clay to thank Lawrence for his courtesy. Remarks that although he is "totally at a loss to conjecture as to the individual at Town [New York] from whence the insinuations have been made relative to himself that he is now & at all times, will be prepared to defeat the vile purpose, Let it display itself, from whence, or where it may." ALS. DLC-HC (DNA, M212, R4).

To FRANCIS T. BROOKE   Lexington, May 1, 1831

Prior to the receipt of your favor of the 17h. Ulto. I had written you a long letter which I hope will safely reach you. I infer from your last a determination to accept your recent appointment. I think you ought to accept it, and I should regret that you did not. Under all circumstances it was an honorable testimony. I share with Mess. [Chapman] Johnson and [Benjamin W.] Leigh in their disappointment in not getting Mr. [Robert] Stanard on the bench; and I concur with them in the superiority which they assign to him over his successful competitor.[1]

We live in an age of revolution. Who could have imagined such a cleansing of the Augean stable at Washington? A change, almost total, of the Cabinet. Did you ever read such a letter as Mr. V.Bs?[2] It is perfectly characteristic of the man — a labored effort to conceal the true motives, and to assign assumed ones, for his resignation, under the evident hope of profiting by the latter. The "delicate step," I apprehend has been taken, because, foreseeing the gathering storm, he wished early to secure safe refuge. Whether that will be on his farm or at London we shall see.[3] Mean time, our cause cannot fail to be benefited by the measure. It is a broad confession of the incompetency of the Presidents chosen advisers, no matter from what cause, to carry on the business of the Government. It is a full admission of that unfitness of those advisers, for their respective stations, which the whole Country felt when they were first selected. And if, as I presume, [Samuel D.] Ingham and [John] Branch were dismissed, or compelled to resign, further dissentions must be sown in a party on the verge of dissolution.

Nor can the injury to his cause be repaired by any successors to the vacant places whom the President may call around him — certainly not by those whom rumor designates. Edward Livingston, to be secretary of State — a recorded defaulter to an enormous amount — the reviler of Jefferson, whom he pursued, in his retirement, with a malicious and vexatious suit — a man notoriously destitute of all principle.[4] Louis McLane to be Secy of the Treasury — a man who glories in his federalism, to be appointed by *the* Republican party. One whose degrading supplications at the Court of London for a worthless privilege must have disgusted every man who was not insensible to the honor and dignity of his Country.[5] &c &c.

I expressed in my former letter [April 24] my conjectures as to the course of Mr. Calhoun. Late events tending to shew the great probability of the defeat of Jackson may now determine him to take bolder and firmer ground against the President. The occurrence at Washington is certainly not intended or calculated to subserve Mr. C. The rumored successors will all be adverse to him. I understand that Judge [Daniel] Smith was one of the advisers of the P. in respect to the recent change, and *he* will advise nothing which can promote Mr. Calhoun's views. Thus situated the V.P. may declare, or cause himself to be declared, a Candidate, or aid, without such declaration, any and every opposition to the President. Unless I am deceived as to his strength, he will not be a Candidate himself, but will push forward, most probably, Judge [John] McLean. I observe a hint of such a purpose, on the part of his friends, in the [Richmond *Constitutional*] Whig. I long since learnt that there was (what shall I call it? a bargain?) between the Judge and Mr. C. an *understanding* that he of the two was to be supported who could command the greatest probability of success. My opinion of the condition of the Judge [McLean] has long been that he would not be at all formidable as a competitor of mine, although he might, if he were capable of sincere and open support, be highly serviceable in promoting our success. He can only become formidable in two contingencies 1st. that he shall be taken up by the Anti Masons and 2dly. that Jackson despairing of success shall retire from the contest. The concurrence of both is necessary. The first (which is quite possible) will not avail him. It might lose Jackson, should he continue a Candidate, the votes both of N. York and Pennsa. and secure them to our friends.

I observe what you state, as to the impression, in regard to my Constitutional principles, which Mr. [Thomas] Ritchie has made on the Virginia public; but I cannot concur with you, as to the utility, at this time, of any publication about them, from myself, in any form. If I am not now understood by the public, nothing that I could say, during the pendency of a warm canvass, would make me intelligible. And I must submit to any misconception of me which may unfortunately prevail. I need not say to you that my Constitutional doctrines are those of the epoch of 1798. I am against all power not delegated or not necessary and proper to execute what is delegated. I hold to the principles of Mr. [James] Madison as promulgated through the Virginia Legislature.[6] I was with Mr. Madison then, I am with him now. I am against all nullification, all new lights in politics, if not religion. Applying the very principles of Mr. Madisons famous interpretation of the Constitution, in the Virginia address, I find in the Constitution the power to protect our industry, and to improve our Country by objects of a National character. I have never altered any Constitutional opinion which I ever entertained and publicly expressed but that, in relation to the Bank, and the experience of the last war changed mine and almost every other person's who had been against the power of chartering it. Such are my views, but I will not consent to any publication of them, under existing circumstances, if I were sure even of achieving a conversion of my old friend Ritchie, who, by the bye, knows them perfectly well.

I adhere to my opinion that there is no sufficient public reason, *at this time*, for publishing Mr. [William H.] Crawford's letter.[7] I should be glad that that of Mr. T[homas]. J[efferson]. Randolph could be published,[8] without any direct agency of mine, but if it cannot be so published, I must acquiesce.

What am I to do with perpetual importunities to visit the North &c &c? My judgment is against all and every excursion for, or which might be fairly construed to have in view, mere political effect. But I should like to be fortified or corrected by the opinion of yourself and other Virginia friends.

343

ALS. KyU. Printed in Colton, *Clay Correspondence*, 4:299-301.   1. Brooke to Clay, April 17, 1831; Clay to Brooke, April 24, 1831.   2. Van Buren's letter of resignation as secretary of state. See Bassett, *Jackson Correspondence*, 4:260-63.   3. Jackson had appointed Van Buren U.S. minister to Great Britain while the U.S. Senate was recessed. When the Senate again met, it voted, on Jan. 25, 1832, to reject the nomination. James, *Andrew Jackson*, 275, 294-96.   4. Edward Livingston's highly publicized financial problems as U.S. district attorney in New York City during Jefferson's first administration, the resulting tension that developed between the two men before and after Livingston's removal to New Orleans in 1803, and the subsequent Livingston suit against Jefferson stemming from the so-called "Batture Controversy," are discussed in detail in the article on Livingston in the *DAB*.   5. Refers to the negotiations McLane conducted with the British concerning the West Indian trade. See John Munroe, *Louis McLane: Federalist and Jacksonian* (New Brunswick, N.J., 1973), 272-79.   6. For Madison's famous Virginia Resolutions of Dec. 24, 1798, see Merrill Peterson (ed.), *James Madison* (New York, 1974), 223.   7. Crawford to Clay, March 31, 1830.   8. Clay to Brooke, August 17, 1830.

To THOMAS SPEED   Lexington, May 1, 1831

I recd. your favor of the 26h. Ulto. and was a good deal surprized with its contents. I have never understood that Mr. R[obert]. W[ickliffe]. had prior to his visit to your quarter expressed similar sentiments to those communicated to you, and I think they may be safely traced to his brother [Charles A. Wickliffe]. He is for Calhoun, and that circumstance is operating much to his prejudice among the Jackson men, as I understand, in Jefferson [County]. He would no doubt be glad to be relieved from the difficulty in which he finds himself involved by support and countenance from our friends.

In my opinion we ought to stand or fall upon our principles; and make no compromise or surrender of them. As to Mr. Calhoun and his friends, their principles are directly opposed to ours. There should not, therefore, be any arrangement, understanding or engagements of any sort with them. You see the first step, proposed by Mr. Wickliffe, in the concern of which he speaks, is that we should abstain from condemning nullification—that is in effect that we should connive at disunion, if not approve of it! We have seen in the heterogeneous party of Jackson enough of the consequences of uniting men with antagonist principles. But we are to make this Union with South Carolina or rather a party in So. Carolina (by the bye, a party which I believe will 'ere long be there in the minority) which has denounced Kentucky, and even resolved not to purchase her productions![1] It would indeed be a monstrous union.

No, my dear Sir, let us march onward, straight forward, with our principles uncompromised and untarnished. Every day almost brings us some favorable demonstration, and if we are firm, resolute and united, I verily believe we shall prevail.

If the friends of Mr. Calhoun choose themselves to attack the common foe, let them do it with their own means and in their own way, without any committment to *them* of our friends. Each party may move on upon its own line of attack. Mr. Calhoun may possibly create a diversion favorable to us. Should he be able to get one or more of the Southern States he will undoubtedly aid us. And all this may take place without the odium of any combination or sacrifice of principle on our part. In this view of the matter, it may be politic in our friends to abstain from unnecessary attack on Mr. Calhoun. Indeed *so far as relates to his personal controversy with Jackson*, I think he has been wronged, and justice as well as policy prompts that he should, to that extent at least, be sustained.

As to the overture stated by Mr. R. W. (and which he no doubt learnt from his brother) to have been made by So. Carolina to Ohio to give the latter State the V. P. in consideration of its support of Mr. Calhoun for the Presidency, my life upon it, no such scheme will ever be sanctioned by the people of Ohio. They are too virtuous and intelligent thus to be bought. That such an overture has been, or may be, made is quite possible, but it will be spurned by the people.

I have long understood that there was an understanding between the V. P. and Judge [John] McLean to club their respective interests, and push him for the Presidency who was strongest. And you must have remarked in a late Whig[2] that the friends of Mr. Calhoun in Virginia were silently urging the pretensions of the Judge. I should not be surprized if that were to be the game that they would finally play every where.

Let us persevere in support of our great principles. As for myself, I am ready, at any moment, without costing me an effort, to retire in behalf of any Man who can better unite all the friends of those principles.

I regret to hear that you have a serious and dangerous collision in your Senatorial election. I trust that it will be accommodated. If Mr. B[enjamin]. H[ardin]. be the bold and fearless champion of our principles, which I have supposed him to be he ought to offer for the H. of R.   He can be elected agt. M[r]. C[harles]. A. W[ickliffe].[3]

ALS. NhD. Letter marked "(Confidential)."   1. At public meetings held throughout South Carolina in the summer and fall of 1828, the nullifiers resolved to purchase no protected goods from the North and to stop trade with Kentucky and neighboring states until the Tariff Act of 1828 was repealed. David Houston, *A Critical Study of Nullification in South Carolina* (Cambridge, Mass., 1896), 71.   2. Probably the Richmond (Va.) *Constitutional Whig*.   3. Clay was probably referring to the hotly-contested congressional race between Charles A. Wickliffe and Charles M. Thruston. Wickliffe, a Jacksonian, won the election by the narrow margin of 393 votes. In the state senatorial race, Benjamin Hardin, a Clay supporter, defeated Stillwell Heady by 323 out of 2,649 votes cast. Hardin did not run for the U.S. House until 1833, at which time he was elected. Bardstown *Herald*, August 10, 17, 1831.

To BARNETT SHORB & CO.   Lexington, May 3, 1831

I postponed answering your obliging letter of the 22d March last,[1] borne by Mr. Stephens, until the fate of the articles also committed to his care for my use was certainly ascertained. After various narrow escapes, from accidents unfortunately occurring, I believe, to several steam boats, I have the pleasure to inform you that I yesterday safely received them, consisting of a Spade, Shovel, Axe, Hoe, and Carving Knife and Fork. They are all excellent of their kinds, and do great credit to the partisans by whom they were made. I beg your acceptance of my grateful thanks for them, for the friendly spirit which prompted you to tender them, and for the flattering terms in which they are conveyed. Their value is much enhanced, in my view, as you justly anticipated, by the fact that every particle of these utensils, from the ore to the last finish, is the produce of American soil, skill, and labor. The successful manufacture of steel at Pittsburgh was a desideratum, and I am happy to perceive, from the specimen in these articles, that the quality of it, as far as I can judge, realizes every wish.

You are right in supposing that I derive very great satisfaction from witnessing the prosperity of Pittsburgh, and the complete success of our American System. Never had the friends of any great measure of national policy more cause to rejoice, never were the predictions of the foes of any such measure more fully refuted, than in the instance of the triumph of that system. It was objected to it, that it would dry up the sources of the public revenue. The revenue has been increased. It was said that our foreign commerce would be destroyed. Our foreign commerce has been greatly nourish[ed] and extended by its operation, changing only some of its subjects. It was urged that it would impair our marine. Our navigation, and especially the most valuable part of it, has been rapidly extended. It was reproached with comprehending enormous burthens to consumers by obliging them to purchase worse, and at dearer prices, articles of American origin, than similar articles of foreign manufacture. Almost every protected article has been greatly reduced in price, and, in some instances, so much that the cost of the article scarcely equals the duty of protection. It is in vain that the opponents of the system seek, by subtle and ingenious solutions, to account for this gratifying fact, itself falsifies their predictions, and it is worth a thousand hairsplitting theories. Finally, it was urged that the system would be a fruitful source of vice, and immorality, and depravity. It has rescued from impending ruin, thousands who, for want of employment, would have been lost, to society, and has filled their abodes with comfort, abundance, and happiness. It has saved and made virtuous members of the community, thousands, of both sexes, who, but for its existence, would have become victims to vice, indolence, and dissipation; and I sincerely believe that every part of our common country has been benefited by it. . . .

Copy. Printed in Frankfort (Ky.) *Commentator*, May 24, 1831. 1. Barnett Shorb & Co., of Pittsburgh wrote Clay on March 22, 1831, announcing that the tools, "made by Messrs. Packard & Estep of this place, from steel of our own manufacture," were being sent to him. Thank Clay for his patriotic support of domestic manufacture. Mention in postscript that "The Carving Knife and Fork were manufactured by Mr. E.L. Loscy." *Ibid.*

From Richard Rush, York, Pa., May 6, 1831. Refers to his letter of April 14 and raises again the question of Clay's handling of the Anti-Masons in Pennsylvania. Suggests "that if you could by any possibility feel free to throw out something, no matter how little, on this topick, as for example, that the Institution might be dispensed with, or any more word in your own form and manner to that effect, or something like it, without at all attacking the body, I believe that it would have the happiest effect on all our public prospects and welfare. I leave you of course to your own better judgement on this subject, but cannot avoid renewing my suggestion." ALS. DLC-HC (DNA, M212, R4).

From HENRY CLAY, JR.   West Point, N.Y., May 7, 1831
I have received your very kind letter transmitting to me 300 Dols. The intimation contained in your letter of a previous date, determined me at once, and conclusively, to return to Lexington immediately after my graduation: should I be permitted to travel with you, I shall esteem it an important favour; and one which will conduce, I hope, as much to my advantage, as to my delight.

On the subject of my future destination in life, my own opinion has frequently wavered; but I have always expected to leave it at last to your better judgment to decide for me. I will offer at this time but two suggestions, which may assist you in forming your decision. Whenever I am depressed by disappointments, or disagreeable reflections; when I long for ease and pleasure, even though it should be accompanied by obscurity and insignificance; I lean to the Army. But again whenever I am fired by ambition, when I elevate my thoughts to a survey of the eminence of your standing, and reflect upon the duty which I owe to you, to improve the inheritance of respectability and public regard which has descended to me with your name; my imaginary resort is immediately to the Forum. I will converse with you fully on all the subjects connected with the selection of my profession, when I arrive in Ky; and if you will oblige me, my dear Father, by relieving me of the responsibity of a choice; I will promise you sincerely to do all in my power to ratify the propriety of the choice, by my success. I am now constantly troubled with the fear that your hopes of my developments will far overrate and surpass the realities of my actual intellectual resources. Genius is not imbibed from the earth; but rather falls from the clouds upon a few, very few, favoured individuals; and descinds in no regular line of succession. I trust then that you will not entertain any hopes concerning me that may not be gratified by the persevering exertion of a moderate intellect. This I will promise. As to genius I may, or I may not have it; for few are willing before trial in their favourite pursuit, to confess themselves utterly devoid of it. . . .

ALS. Henry Clay Memorial Foundation, Lexington, Ky.

From Hugh Mercer, Fredericksburg, Va., May 9, 1831. Congratulates Clay on his nomination for the presidency "in several of the states" and assures him that his "Cause . . . is gaining Strength daily thro'out all her borders." Continues: "The Dissolution of the late Cabinet, is an expiring effort — to sustain the administration — but it will not avail Genl J — & mr van Buren — many think that the Genl will not hold out until the end of his present term & will resign also — It is impossible to decide with any certainty as to the course of a man, who is so entirely disqualified from want of Capacity, information Temper, &c for the dignified & vastly responsible station he fills as the Chief magistrate of an enlightened & great Nation — if his course depends on his own will — I am decidedly of the opinion that the Resignations of the Cabinet, if Cabinet it can be called, is the Result of the Scheme & whole plan of mr V.B — to save himself if he can from the total loss of confidence with the American People — He must sink, never to rise again, upon the coming in of a new administration of the Government — I always regarded him as unprincipled, & a most dangerous man to our Country — events prove the correctness of my judgment — "

Has heard from a friend in Pennsylvania that Jackson is rapidly losing ground there and that his nomination by the Pennsylvania legislature for another term [Johnston to Clay, April 13, 1830] "was brought about by some juggling management on the part of the Genl's Secy, Mr D [Andrew J. Donelson] — if the Newspapers speak truly — to which the Pres[iden]t must have been privy — It is impossible, that any admin can ever get along by such shuffling &c — "

Discusses at length some personal legal and financial matters being handled for him by Clay and John J. Crittenden. Concludes with the observation that "I am now reading my Copy of your Biography, *to this period* — by [George D.] Prentice — just delivered me — " ALS. DLC-HC (DNA, M212, R4). Letter marked "(private)."

To NICHOLAS BIDDLE   Lexington, May 10, 1831

We have been such beggars, and successful beggars too, from the Bank [of the United States], in this quarter, that I hesitated about addressing this letter to you. But, as its object is not for any new instance of the kindness of the Bank, and only to enable it to fulfill a benevolent purpose, I hope I shall receive a favorable hearing

You will recollect that the Board appropriated $1500 to a McAdams [macadam] road which had been projected between Lexington and Frankfort.[1] That project was superseded by a more noble object — a Rail road from Lexn. to Louisville passing by Frankfort, and your donation was not effectuated.[2] The R Road is about to be actually commenced, under flattering auspices. Mean time, a McAdams road from Maysville to Lexington was undertaken, and is now in considerable progress with a fair prospect of being completed in a few years,[3] in spite of all Veto's. When the Rail road and the McAdams road are both finished we shall strike the Ohio at two important points, greatly to the advantage of the whole Country, and especially to Lexington, Louisville and Maysville, and all intermediate towns.

Both of these improvements being contemporaneously undertaken, the Capital of the Country is most heavily taxed. The Maysville road particularly wants help, and, as we have manfully put our shoulders to the wheel, we call upon you for a little assistance. May we not then hope that you will direct the $1500, at least, to be diverted from the object, for which it was originally but now unnecessarily designed, to that of the Maysville road? All the considerations, (and stronger ones) which originally induced you to accede to our wishes so handsomely, recommend this diversion, as I think.

I know your abstinance from politics. Still it cannot be unacceptable to you to be informed that, unless we are overpowered by a free use of public money by the Jackson party in the Canvass, we shall I think certainly beat them in this State. We have a fair prospect, if we have a fair election, of returning eight or nine out of 12 members to the H. of R. and of electing a Senator.[4]

ALS. DLC-Nicholas Biddle Papers (DNA, M212, R20). 1. Biddle to Clay, Dec. 22, 1829. 2. The Lexington and Ohio Railroad Company was chartered on Jan. 27, 1830, and actual work began in early Feb. of 1832. The road to Frankfort was completed in 1835. William B. Graham, "Railroads in Kentucky Before 1860," M.A. thesis, University of Kentucky, 1931, pp. 13, 18, 20. 3. The Maysville Turnpike was chartered on Jan. 29, 1829, and the first phase completed in Nov. of 1830. It had first been chartered on Feb. 4, 1818, and renewed Jan. 22, 1827. After Jackson vetoed the Maysville Road bill [Johnston to Clay, May 26, 1830], Kentucky took stock and finished the road to Lexington. William H. Perrin, *History of Bourbon, Scott, Harrison and Nicholas Counties* (Chicago, 1882), 56. See also Clay to Henry Clay, Jr., Dec. 2, 1829. 4. Clay to Beatty, June 8, 1830; Webster to Clay, April 4, 1831; Clay to Brown, April 8, 1831.

From Richard Rush, York, Pa., May 11, 1831. Says that after mailing his letter to Clay of May 6, he received Clay's letter to him of April 26 "which answers all I have said about Antimasonry. I must believe that you are right, and acquiesce in your better judgement. I have heretofore urged upon Anti masons, your vote for Mr Adams, in preference to a Masonic candidate, as a proof that when your country is at stake, you throw masonry to the winds. I shall continue to do so, and I hope with advantage." ALS. DLC-HC (DNA, M212, R4).

To PETER B. PORTER   Lexington, May 14, 1831
Since I last had this pleasure many interesting political events have occurred — the meetings in N. York[1] and Philada —[2]the quarrel between the V. P. and P. — the recent election in N. Y.[3] and finally the total explosion of the Cabinet.[4] Public opinion is making, I think, a certain progress towards the final overthrow of this administration. The new Cabinet, if it be such as rumor indicates, will rather increase than retard it. The *positions* of the several members, their characters, their opposition to the Tariff must produce that effect.

Our prospects in K. are good. Nothing but a corrupt and profuse expenditure of public money in this State can prevent our obtaining two thirds of the delegation to the H. [of] R. and [a] Senator to the U.S.[5] In Louisiana, where I p[assed] last w[inter], no question exists, even among Jackson men, as to t[he] [v]ote of that State being in our favor.

I am anxious to hear from you, and especially on the point of Anti Masonry. Is it still obstinate and perverse? Will they make a nomination and of whom at Balto.?

My opinion is that I had better remain at home, and such is my inclination. Things are now doing well every where. Had they not be better left undisturbed by me?

Mrs. Porter, I understand, will visit us this summer. We shall be very happy to see her, and you too, if as I hope, you should accompany her. . . .

ALS. NBuHi.   1. Lawrence to Clay, Nov. 29, 1830; Porter to Clay, Feb. 10, 1830.   2. Porter to Clay, July 25, 1830.   3. Lawrence to Clay, Nov. 8, 1830.   4. Lawrence to Clay, Dec. 21, 1829.   5. Clay to Brown, April 8, 1831; Clay to Beatty, June 8, 1830.

From FRANCIS T. BROOKE   Richmond, May 15, 1831

I have received your letters of the 23d [*sic*, 24th] ultimo and of the 1st instant the interest you took in my reelection to the court of appeals could not be otherwise than very acceptable to me, and I can assure you I am now contented with the result, — the impression it was calculated to make out of the State, of the Jacksonism of the State is all that I regret about it,[1] your remarks upon the abdication at Wash[ing]ton will be verified,[2] in the results that will probably grow out of it,   V[an] B[uren]s retirement though wished for here has much perplexed the Calhoun party,   they are really at a loss what to do,   the impression grows stronger daily that in no event can he be elected is very perplexing — his locality and nullification doctrine some of his warmest friends think must defeat him, and the dificulty is to get back to Jackson,   If I am not much mistaken the Govr [John Floyd] will prefer to vote for you to that alternative I think there is no one more hostile to Jackson,   there is some impatience here and at Fred[ericksbur]g to make a movement in your behalf but I think it yet premature,   the public mind is visibly settling down in favour of you, and I think it best not to agitate it at present,   I approve of your judgment not to go to the north   Ashland I am sure is the strongest point in your line of defense or attack   if you think it of no importance to remain in your State in August a trip the [*sic*, to] our [White Sulphur] Springs would benefit your health and take off the imputation of electioneering in your own State, this I only suggest to you as I shall be at the court in Lewisburg in that month it would delight me to see you as it would also many of your friends from different points   but Kentuckey must not be neglected   the whole force of the government in every possible way will be imployed against you, and the issue is of great value, I saw your friend Judge Ewing[3] here this winter and he gave me flattering accounts of Ohio — it is not possible that the *Methodist* [John McLean] will aspire to the Presidency   it is only through him that Calhoun expect[s] any thing from the west, but he can not give him the the [*sic*] South, you need not fear the publication of Mr [William H.] Crawfords letter[4]   I said to you in my last that my friend [George M.] Troup told me that Calhoun tried to worm it out of [Robert P.] Letcher,   I did not hint to him that I had any knowledge of it,   I asked him if he knew any thing of the former letter to you from Mr C[5] he said he had not seen it — but learned that such a letter had been written,   I will see Mr T J R [Thomas Jefferson Randolph] this summer and get his second permission to publish some paragraphs of his letter,[6] I think towards the close of the year a movement will be made when simultaneously all these matters will come out — I have not seen yet a copy of your Biography by [George D.] Prentice,   some thing of use may be extracted from, it. . . .

ALS. InU.   1. Brooke to Clay, April 17, 1831.   2. That is, the dissolution of Jackson's cabinet. See Lawrence to Clay, Dec. 21, 1829.   3. The manuscript appears to read "Ewing," in which case it may refer to Clay's Ohio friend, Thomas Ewing. There is, however, no evidence that Thomas Ewing was ever a judge. 4. Crawford to Clay, March 31, 1831. 5. Possibly a reference to 7:76-77. 6. Clay to Brooke, August 17, 1830.

From George Robertson, Lancaster, Ky., May 16, 1831. Asks Clay's assistance in recovering his slave, "My boy Thornton," who was "lately taken forcibly from a Steam boat at [New] Orleans and is there imprisoned by Robert Oden on a pretext of claim by Oden's heirs." Asks Clay to ask one of his Louisiana friends to represent him legally in the matter. Explains legal background of his ownership of Thornton. ALS. DLC-HC (DNA, M212, R4).

From John Peck, Owingsville, Ky., May 18, 1831. Warns Clay, out of "a personal friendship for you," that from "a conversation I had this afternoon with *TDO* [Thomas Deye Owings] — and Knowing of a certain compromise that you are about to effectuate, I think it my duty to advise you, *in no event whatever,* to *part with any* of the [James] *Morrison Estate*; 'till you *See certain Documents* now in his *possession* — as it might implicate your *private fortune,* and in case of Death harras your heirs —" LS. DLC-TJC (DNA, M212, R13). Letter marked "(Confidential)." See 3:280-81, 379. W.C. Nicholas had held a note for £10,000 from Thomas D. Owings dated 1805. When Nicholas died in 1820 the note was purchased by Thomas Jefferson Randolph for James Morrison. Morrison died in 1823. In 1829, Clay, executor of the Morrison estate, sued Owings for the £10,000 and its accrued interest since 1805. The "certain documents" in the possession of Owings probably supported his contention that he had repaid Nicholas the £10,000 before his death. Legal papers relating to this issue are found in DLC-TJC (DNA, M212, R17).

To JOHN AGG   Lexington, May 20, 1831
[Explains that Agg's recent letter was delayed in the mails. Continues:]

I concur with you in thinking that, whether we regard the goodness of the cause of the American System, or the present flattering prospects of its final triumph, by the overthrow of the existing feeble corrupt and incompetent Administration, the friends of that system have every motive for renewed and energetic exertion. I am happy to learn that it is in contemplation to enlarge the [Washington *Daily National*] Journal, and to throw fresh vigor into its already able columns; but I regret extremely to hear that it is laboring under pecuniary difficulties. It has been decidedly the leading paper in supporting the principles of the Opposition, and has been conducted with unsurpassed ability and efficiency; and merits the most liberal patronage from all who desire to sustain our great measures of national policy or to rescue the government from a misrule which now threatens every thing most valuable in our institutions, not excepting the Union itself, the only guarranty of all of them. I should hope that you may confidently and successfully appeal to our friends every where, but especially to the friends of the American System, for countenance & support. I would gladly address some of them in different parts of the Union, in your behalf, if I were not unwilling to subject myself to the imputation of being impelled by the particular interest which I may be supposed to have in the existing contest. But you are at liberty to shew this letter confidentially to any friends who you may suppose will judge me more kindly and truly.

We have every reason to count upon a most signal triumph at our approaching Elections in August. I think we shall, in all human probability, return at least two thirds of the delegations to the H. of R. Indeed, at this time, there is not more than two Jackson Candidates for Congress safe in the State. Our prospects are equally good, in regard to the Legislature.[1] Nothing but a corrupt and profuse use of public money can disappoint our expectations, if that can.

Wishing you great success in the Journal and prosperity in every way. . . .

ALS. ViU.   1. Webster to Clay, April 4, 1831.

From Jesse D. Elliott, U.S.S. *Natchez*, Pensacola, Fla., May 22, 1831. Reports that on his recent cruise, "During my stay at Havana in February last I procured some tobacco seed of that variety of the plant from which the best Segars are made in Cuba — Understanding you are now engaged in agricultural pursuits I send you herewith a small bottle full of this seed, which I hope you will accept, also a few Beans which I request you to present with my respects to Mrs. Clay they are remarkable for the quickness of their growth, having a most luxuriant climbing vine, well suited for Bowers, windows &c." ALS. DLC-HC (DNA, M212, R4).

From Nicholas Biddle, Philadelphia, May 24, 1831. With reference to Clay's letter of May 10, reports that he is authorized to transfer $1,500 from the Lexington-Frankfort Turnpike project to the proposed Maysville-Lexington Road. Wants to know, however, the precise legal status of the company that had initially planned a "McAdams [macadam] road" from Lexington to Frankfort, an enterprise now abandoned in favor of a railroad linking Lexington to Frankfort to Louisville. Copy. DLC-Nicholas Biddle Papers (DNA, M212, R20).

From FRANCIS T. BROOKE

Near Fredericksburg, Va.,
May 26, 1831

I wrote you from Richmd an answer to your letter of the 1[s]t instant — before I left Richmond I had a long and interesting conversation with Go[v]r Floyed [*sic*, John Floyd] — the Calhoun party are much perplexed, to run him seems hopeless and to get back to Jackson is almost impossible after taking such open and Strong ground against him, though hints have been thrown out for a compromise with your freinds there is no possible ground for that, however opposed a part of Virginia may be to the American System, there is no portion of it that can hear of nullification without horror, on this State of things the prospects that Virginia will vote for you brightens daily — unless there should be some redeeming acts of the government, of which there is little expectation things must settle down as we wish them, I shall go to the University in a few days and will see Mr T J R [Thomas Jefferson Randolph] and if possible bring out his letter to you — [1]this is the more desirable as it will have a good effect in your State, or it might be postponed until a more decided demonstration of your strength is made here, I came on the stage from Richmd with a Doctor Drake from N Y[2] a very intelligent and genttlemanly man who assured me that there was the strongest hopes among your friends in that State that you would get its vote, the movements in Philadelphia have been flattering and there are indications in the State which promise well, we are anxious to see Inghams pamphlet, you will have seen Branches letter,[3] I wish if you have Livingston's Pamphlet published in 1810 you would send it to me, I do not mean his arguments on the Batture question, in the Spring Session of Congress of 1810 he gave it to me to read at Washington it was a bitter attack as well as I remember upon Mr Jefferson and extracts from it would be of use — [4]let me hear whether you have decided to remain at home or not. . . .

ALS. InU.   1. Clay to Brooke, August 17, 1831.   2. Probably Joseph Rodman Drake of New York. See Harold K. Hochschild, *Township 34: A History with Digression of an Adriondack Township in Hamilton County in the State of New York* (New York, 1952), 48-51.   3. No Ingham pamphlet as such has been found; but for the widely published letters of Ingham and Branch explaining to the public their version of the reasons for the dissolution of the Jackson cabinet, see McMaster, *History of the People of the U.S.*, 124-26.   4. Livingston had written a pamphlet titled *Address To the People of the United States On the Measures Pursued by the Executive With Respect to the Batture At New Orleans. . . .* New Orleans, 1808. Another aimed at Jefferson was titled *An Answer to Mr. Jefferson's Justification of His Conduct in the Case of the New Orleans Batture*. N.p., n.d. For the Batture controversy, see Clay to Brooke, May 1, 1831.

From George Lansdowne, Lexington, May 27, 1831. A bill of sale affirming that "I have this day sold and delivered to H. Clay a bay mare raised in Virginia with a blaze in her forehead and two or three white feet said to be got by Potomac, seven or eight years old." DS, in Clay's hand. Josephine Simpson Collection, Lexington, Ky.

To John W. Treadwell, May 27, 1831. Reports that "There has been a greedy demand for wool in Kentucky" and that he has been offered for his own [Merino] wool, "washed on the Sheep's back," 64¼ cents per pound. Has delivered 367 pounds at this price to Norman Porter, Treadwell's local purchasing agent. Notes that he is selling his "common wool, unwashed, at 33⅓ Cents per pound; and my neighbor, Genl. [James] Shelby sold his Merino Wool unwashed at 50 Cents per lb." Believes that the "continuance of these prices" will produce a "great increase of Sheep in a few years."

Concludes: "I rejoice in the prosperity of our manufactures in your quarter. The increase of those employed in the Cotton line, mentioned by you, is astonishingly great. But why should we not share with or supplant G.B. in the fifty five millions sheeting, which she annually manufactures? If any thing can conquer Southern prejudices, one would think it would be the very great extension of our establishments." ALS. MHi. Addressed to Treadwell in Salem, Mass. Sheeting is wool that has been combed.

From William C.C. Claiborne, Jr., Liverpool, May 28, 1831. Reports his safe arrival in England "after a long voyage of eight weeks." Comments on the sights he has seen in Liverpool and vicinity. Especially mentions that "There seems to be a very great excitement in this City on the subject of reform, and I have heard a revolution openly threatened, if it should not be granted by the next parliament. The King [William IV] has become very popular by the course he has pursued." Discusses a local political campaign for a seat in Parliament. ALS. DLC-HC (DNA, M212, R4). For the role of William IV in the coming of the Reform Act of 1832, see Philip Ziegler, *King William IV*. London, 1971.

From A.B. Roff, Cincinnati, May 31, 1831. Proudly presents Clay with copies of *The Farmer's Farrier* and *The Spy Unmasked*, "the materials, Engraving, Printing and Binding of which are *entirely* the products of *Western* Artists and Mechanics." ALS. DLC-HC (DNA, M212, R4). Roff, a Cincinnati bookseller and stationer, and partner in Roff & Hancock, auction and commission merchants, had published an edition of H.L. Barnum, *The Spy Unmasked; or, Memoirs of Enoch Crosby, Alias Harvey Birch. . . .* N.Y., 1828, and of *The Farmer's Farrier, Illustrating the Peculiar Nature & Characteristic of the Horse. . . .* Cincinnati, 1831. For the controversial Barnum book, see Tristram P. Coffin, *Uncertain Glory: Folklore and the American Revolution* (Detroit, Mich., 1971), 156-62.

To LEWIS WILLIAMS   Lexington, May 31, 1831
I recd. your favor of the 30h. Ulto and I thank you for the friendly suggestion of your opinion as to the expediency of my return to Congress. After much reflection, I brought myself to the conclusion that I had better remain in private

life. There has been no difficulty, at any time, to my being returned from my old district. The gentleman (Mr [Chilton] Allen) who is now a Candidate, and so far without opposition has repeatedly offered to decline in my favor. But I have thought Ashland was my best position, and that I ought here, in calmness and resignation, to leave events to their undisturbed course. So far their progress is highly encouraging. The incidents of the last Session, followed up by the unprecedented change of the whole Cabinet,[1] and the demonstrations of public sentiment in various ways, and in different States, authorize the confident expectation of the triumph of our cause

In this State the prospects generally are very flattering. Except Col. [Richard M.] Johnson, every Jackson member is in imminent danger of losing his election; whilst [John] Kincaid and [Thomas] Chilton, and our other friends it is believed will all be elected.[2] I shall be greatly disappointed if we do not return at least two thirds of the whole delegation. And our prospects of success in the Legislature are equally cheering.[3]

Who will the Jackson party run as V. P. — Mr. [William H.] Crawford? Mr. V[an] Buren? or [John] McLean of Ohio? I suppose the latter.

ALS. NcU.   1. Lawrence to Clay, Dec. 21, 1829.   2. Thomas Chilton was elected to the 22nd Congress; John Kincaid was not. Webster to Clay, April 4, 1831.   3. *Ibid.*

From RICHARD RUSH   York, Pa., June 1, 1831

[Acknowledges receipt of Clay's letter of May 21. Continues:]

To Mr [James] Clark, I had written a few days ago on the subject of antimasonry; also to Mr [Robert P.] Letcher. You will doubtless hear from one or the other, or both. To neither did I say that I had been in any correspondence with you. Under first impressions, I acquiesced, as you saw by my letter of the 11th of May, in your first intention not to take any step against Masonry, though greatly disappointed myself; but more reflection determined me to strive to obtain from you, through those friends, a reconsideration of your views, intending also to write to you again myself, as I now do. And, my dear Sir, let me entreat your re-consideration of them. If your *Masonic* principles stood in the way of this, I would be the last person in the world to ask it; but supposing[1] that you are really and wholly indifferent to masonry as such, as I have always indeed represented you to be, the question is merely one of expediency. It is a question, as I think, of what you owe to your great public principles, and to your whole country, over and above any thing that masonry can ever ask at your hands. The anti-masonic party, by the very principle of its existence, is becoming more formidable from season to season. In N. York, at the spring elections a couple of months ago, it swept entire counties,[2] till then not under its sway. It is in Vermont;[3] it is in New England; nobody can tell where it will stop. The Lockport trials[4] in February and March have done much towards giving it this new power, though the principle was deeply and surely at work before. In this state, it is very active, not indeed in Philadelphia, but in other parts. Should the gain of the party for 18 months to come, be equal to its gain for 18 months past, and the presumption is that it will be much greater, I do not for my part see how any candidate for the Presidency in 1832 can obtain a majority of the electoral votes, without its decided and avowed auxiliary support. That it will carry all N. York by that time,[5] those from whom I get my information, do not seem to doubt for a moment. They even declare that the state is anti-masonic at present, so great has been the gain of the party since last autumn. It seems to me that it is destined to produce most important results. If you were to gain its full confidence by *ceasing to be a mason*, above all, were you to do so under an admission of the mischiefs of the Institution, if this appears to you to be the case after all that has passed and is still passing in New York, there is nothing more clear in my belief, than that your triumphant election to the Presidency in 1832 would be secure, general Jackson, or any body, and every body, notwithstanding. Your great name with the nation would at once draw over such a host to the A. M. [Anti-Masonic] banner, as nothing could resist. The National Republicans would not, could not, give you up. It is impossible. A few indeed would, perhaps; let us say, certainly; the violent Masons; but the great body of the party would still hold on to you in [illeg. word]; and for every masonic vote that you lost, you would gain in Anti-masonic votes by that time, five-fold, ten fold. This is my firm conviction. Let it be remembered also, that, if you left the Institution, you would carry with you a vast body of the moderate masons, who cannot but see that it is losing ground, and who, like yourself, are not conscience bound to it. Individuals drop off from it every day, so that its course is now downward; for I do not believe that it makes up in new recruits. As to the injury that Mr [John Q.] Adams may have done himself in 1828, by the expression alluded to,[6] the times have changed totally. Anti-masonry was then an acorn. It is now a young oak, and growing. Will it be said that my letter has done this?[7] Delusive thought! I have no vanity in me to imagine it. The increased power of the party in N. York, and N. England, was shown by the spring elections, before ever my letter saw the light. The Lockport trials too had done this work. These are facts of record. That letter has been cordially received, enthusiastically it may be, by the antimasons, for they believe its principles to be just, as I do; and it has exerted the special ire of a *portion* of the masons; but the party, resting on its own broad and crescent principle, was up, long before I wrote, or thought of it.

I write to you without reserve my dear sir, because I ardently desire to see you triumph in all ways, and because I am deeply convinced in my own mind, that my suggestions open the surest path to your triumph. I am persuaded that you will give them the consideration they may claim on this score. Should your first judgement be against them all, as it probably will be, let me ask a fortnights pause, or double that time if you are still against them, before you announce that determination. I know your devotion to your country, and that that feeling will guide you now as always. The antimasons will put up a decided candidate of their own in September.[8] There will be no possibility of preventing this, or of their agreeing, I fear, upon you, *whilst a mason*, though you have so many ardent friends among them. You ought to be their candidate, and in my opinion would promote the highest interests of your country thereby. It may be said by some, that as things now stand, your country has a sufficient prospect of your services in the Presidency, without your taking any new step, and especially that of giving up masonry; but, in my belief, it would make that consummation sure, and this is what I so anxiously desire.

Until yesterday I could have said, that whilst my letter had been fiercely attacked in newspapers devoted to general Jackson, none engaged in your good cause, that I had heard of, had touched it in that spirit. But, yesterday I saw a Boston paper — the Courier — in which some body, under sheer masonic

354

anger, has fallen upon it, in a most foolish and most unwarrantable manner.[9] Whoever he is, he is a real foe to the best interests and hopes of the country, as I view them all.

ALS. DLC-HC (DNA, M212, R4). 1. Word "believing" struck through and "supposing" substituted. 2. Lawrence to Clay, Nov. 8, 1830. 3. In the gubernatorial election in Vermont in September, 1831, William A. Palmer was the Anti-Masonic candidate; Heman Allen, the National Republican candidate; and Ezra Meech, the Jackson candidate. Palmer received a plurality of the popular vote but not a majority, so the election was decided by the state legislature in which the Anti-Masons had a majority on joint ballot. Palmer was chosen by the legislature 114-36 over Allen. *BDGUS*, 4:1569; and *Niles' Register* (Oct. 22, 1831), 40:149. In the Vermont congressional election to fill the vacancy caused by the death of Rollin C. Mallary, several ballots were taken with various candidates before William Slade, an Anti-Mason, was chosen (4,614 votes) over Williams, a National Republican (3,815 votes), and White, the Jackson candidate (838 votes). *Niles' Register* (July 16, 1831), 40:342. 4. The trials of some of the conspirators who had allegedly abducted William Morgan were held in Lockport, N.Y., in February and March, 1831. None of the defendants was convicted. For further details, see Harriet A. Weed (ed.), *Autobiography of Thurlow Weed* (Boston, 1883), 1:286-95. 5. Clay to Bailhache, Nov. 24, 1830. 6. Clay to Sloane, April 29, 1831. 7. In April, 1831, newspapers published a public letter from four citizens of York, Pa., to Rush, asking his opinion of the Masonic Order and declaring their intention to publish his reply. Rush's reply heartily endorsed the Anti-Masonic revolt and condemned all secret societies. The letters were published in a pamphlet titled: *Highly Important and Interesting Correspondence. . . . Letter From the Anti-Masonic Committee of Correspondence of York County to the Hon. Richard Rush, and His Reply Upon the Subject of Masonry and Anti-Masonry*. West Chester, Pa., 1831. See also Powell, *Richard Rush*, 231; Vaughn, *The Antimasonic Party in the United States*, 57. 8. Clay to Brooke, June 23, 1831. 9. The Boston *Courier* editorial charged Rush with having become an Anti-Mason in order to obtain that party's presidential nomination, and said he had made the decision only after the Anti-Masonic party in New York decided it could not support Clay and would put up its own candidates. Reprinted in New York *Evening Post*, June 7, 1831.

From JAMES BROWN, Philadelphia, June 2, 1831. Discusses family matters concerning the death of his wife Ann Hart (Nancy) Brown and the disposal of her estate. Turning to politics, states: "Your friends here are active and sanguine. They believe that if you can obtain a respectable majority at the August election in your own state [Webster to Clay, April 4, 1831], that your election will be certain. They however all doubt of your success there and know that you will have to contend with many, and as some think, insurmountable difficulties. The majority they think wish the downfall of the admn. but some wish it on your behalf others to promote the Election of Calhoun, others of Webster, and a few of [John] M[c]Lean. The friends of all these would wish you put hors de combat in your own State (for they consider a defeat there as fatal to your hopes) and then each would hope that your supporters would join their ranks. This is what I hear. You know how little I interfere and how far aloof I stand from the means of information. My opinion as to the result is not changed. Jackson will take milder men into his Cabinet — They will adopt milder means of carrying on the Government, and he will have the mass on his side. The upper stratum of society seems to have changed, but the granite substratum, is in his favor, and is, in this State, immoveable — Such is my opinion — Take it for what it is worth —" ALS. DLC-HC (DNA, M212, R4). Printed also in *LHQ*, 24:1154.

To HEZEKIAH NILES
Lexington, June 3, 1831

I hasten to acknowledge the receipt of your favor dated at New York on the 22d Ulto. and to reply first to that part of it which relates to what you justly denominate your bold project.

The affect upon the character and utility of the [*Niles'*] Register by a transfer of it from Balto. to N. York would be favorable. It's principles belong to no peculiar latitude or position in our Country but pervade the whole. It's means of information and circulation would be greatly multiplied by being in N. York.[1]

The daily and semi weekly paper, if conducted upon the principles and with the temper and ability which have hitherto characterized the Register would be a powerful auxiliary to our cause, and might be decisive of the great question now pending. You would have an irresistible claim upon the liberality and patronage of our friends every where.

So far I can confidently speak. But on the points of the rupture, which must ensue, of your private and friendly relations in Balto—your pecuniary means to start and put forward—the state of your health &c. I am not competent to advise, and must therefore leave them to your exclusive consideration.

If your fame prosperity and happiness should be promoted by the change I should rejoice at it. I am sure that our Country and our cause would profit by it. But the fear of *my* friends suffering on my account has often inexpressibly afflicted me. And whenever I see a new project of a journal started, with which my fortunes are any way associated, the fear of injury to the pecuniary condition of the Undertaker counter balance the satisfaction which I derive from it.

Our prospects in K. continue to be most encouraging. We shall be more than ever disappointed if we do not succeed in August next in the election of two thirds of the delegation to the H. of R. and to the Legislature[2]

I lament extremely to hear of the dangerous illness of Mr. A. H. Schenck. Should the melancholy event which you feared be realized, along with my respects to his brother P[eter]. H. Schenck[3] (which be pleased to deliver in any contingency), do me the favor to communicate my sincere condolence.

The frauds on the revenue are truly provoking. I anxiously hope that the Convention of Manufacturers[4] will be able to detect and expose them, and to devise effective remedies for the future.

ALS. ViU.   1. Apparently Niles never made the contemplated move to New York City. 2. Webster to Clay, April 4, 1831.   3. For Abraham H. Schenck, who had died on June 1, see *BDAC*.   4. A convention of manufacturers (woolen) met at Clinton Hall in New York on May 18-20, 1831, to consider "alleged frauds on the revenue" perpetrated through violations of the tariff laws, especially the invoicing and entering of woolen goods at values much below their actual cost. This was a common practice used to avoid the two dollar and a half minimum and pay only the dollar minimum duty [Brown to Clay, Oct. 23, 1829]. For the proceedings and resolutions of the convention, see *Niles' Register* (June 4, 1831), 40:242-44. Peter H. Schenck participated prominently in the convention which also discussed forming a national association that would sustain the woolen industry "by united effort" against "foreign rivalry." Schenck started the first cotton factory in New York at Matteawan and, later, built a woolen factory. He was also one of the first directors of the Bank of the United States office at New York City. For Schenck, see William T. Bonner, *New York: The World's Metropolis, 1623-24—1923-24* . . . (New York, 1924), 711.

From Richard Rush, York, Pa., June 3, 1831. Reports that at an Anti-Masonic state convention in Harrisburg the previous week, an attempt was made "to get up a resolution *not* to nominate you for the Presidency at the Anti-masonic convention . . . in September; but it was thrown out by our friends." Adds, however, that he has "heard today, for the first time, that they would not find it possible to bring about your nomination at Baltimore in September [Porter to Clay, July 25, 1830] if you remained a mason, and that indeed a resolution passed to that effect; not with any mention of your name, but covering that principle." Concludes: "I write this as a supplement to my letter of the first instant [June 1], under renewed anxities that you may see the whole subject in the lights in which it so forcibly strikes me." ALS. DLC-HC (DNA, M212, R4). The Anti-Masonic convention met at Harrisburg on May 25 with sixty delegates, representing twenty-two counties, in attendance. See Harrisburg *Chronicle*, May 30, 1831; and *Niles' Register* (June 4, 1831), 40:237 for the proceedings.

To JOHN BARNEY
Lexington, June 4, 1831

I recd your favor of the 2Gh Ulto   We were much disappointed in not seeing you on your return to Balto.   Unfortunately the access to Lexington from the Ohio river is through bad roads, the difficulties of which prevent our friends from visiting us. We hope it will be otherwise when we get the McAdams [macadam] road to Maysville and the Rail road to Louisville completed.[1]

Mr and Mrs [James] Erwin are now my near neighbours enjoying their fine residence ["Woodlands"] adjoining mine and our charming climate. They will return in Novr. to N. Orleans and would be very happy in having the company of Mr. Patterson[2] & yourself. I hope you will both then visit us, on your way down. Whether I shall be able to go, as I wish, or not I cannot at present decide. I most certainly shall go if I can.

I thank you for the friendly expression of your opinion about my return to Congress.[3] It is a point about which there is much difference of opinion among my friends. Although there is no difficulty, as I believe, of my being returned to either House of Congress I must own that my own judgment has been constantly, and yet is opposed to such a step   I think, under existing circumstances, Ashland is my best position.

If we had not been so often heretofore mortified with the results of our K. elections,[4] in so much that we must have lost confidence with our distant friends, I would tell you of our cheering prospects. I will say that, if we do not in August elect two thirds of the delegation to the H. of R. and two thirds of the members of the General Assembly, I shall be more than ever disappointed.   . . .[5] [Endorsed in margin, not in Clay's hand:] "What shall I say to Prince Hal? when will we three meet again? Cant you accompany me to the White Sulphur next Sunday? May do"[6]

ALS. ICHi.   1. Clay to Biddle, May 10, 1831.   2. Possibly Joseph W. Patterson.   3. Clay to Beatty, June 8, 1830.   4. Clay to Beatty, May 4, 1830.   5. Webster to Clay, April 4, 1831. 6. Recipient of marginalia unknown.

To Adam Beatty, Washington, Ky., June 4, 1831. Extends condolences on the death of "our friend," Col. Nathaniel Rochester. Notes the rise in wool prices and reports that he sold common unwashed wool for 33 cents per pound and was "offered 62 for my merino, washed on the back of the sheep." Mentions that last summer a lame ram of his was left with a farmer in "your neighborhood." Asks Beatty to inquire after the animal. Copy. Printed in Colton, *Clay Correspondence*, 4:302. Rochester had died on May 17, 1831. *DAB*.

To FRANCIS T. BROOKE
Lexington, June 4, 1831

I reced. both of your favors of the 15th. ult. from Richmond and of the 26th. from St. Julien. I should be very happy to meet you in August at the White Sulphur Springs and Lewisburg.   but I believe I shall find it necessary to remain this summer in Kentucky. My private affairs require some portion of my time. I have several Executorships also to close, and I wish to avail myself of the leisure I can command this summer to settle them.

I regret that I have not a copy of the pamphlet of Mr. [Edward] Livingston to which you refer,[1] I will endeavour to procure one from N. Orleans. lately I have seen extracts from it, in which the author speaks very harshly of Mr. Jefferson.

Our prospects in K. as to the result of the August election continues very promising generally.[2] [Thomas] Chilton will be re-elected[3] by a great majority;

and I shall believ[e] we will have, at least eight out of the 12 members of Congress, there is much reason to hope that Mr [Charles A.] Wickliffe will be left at home.[4]

I should be very glad if you could obtain the consent of Mr. T[homas]. J[efferson]. R[andolph]. to the publication of the letter,[5] but I fear his apprehensions will lead him to withhold it.

Can you not when at Lewisburg extend your Journey this far? I should be delighted to see you here, and beg you will come, if it be possible.

Copy. DLC-TJC (DNA, M212, R13).   1. Brooke to Clay, May 26, 1831.   2. Webster to Clay, April 4, 1831.   3. Chilton lost to Albert G. Hawes by only 9 votes. Frankfort *Argus of Western America*, August 24, 1831.   4. Clay to Speed, May 1, 1831.   5. Clay to Brooke, August 17, 1830.

To JOHN GUNTER   Lexington, June 6, 1831

I received your letter of the 14th ult. describing the wrongs and sufferings of the Cherokee nation. Of these I had been previously well informed. In common with a large portion of the citizens of the United States, I regretted them, and felt the sincerest sympathy with you on account of them. I regretted them, not only because of their injustice, but because they inflicted a deep wound on the character of the American republic.

I had supposed that the principles which had uniformly governed our relations with the Cherokee and other Indian nations had been too long and too firmly established to be disturbed at this day. — They were proclaimed in the negotiation with Great Britain at Ghent, by the American commissioners who concluded the treaty of peace;[1] and having been one of those commissioners, I feel with more sensibility than most of my fellow citizens, any violation of those principles; for if we stated them incorrectly, we deceived Great Britain; and if our government acts in opposition to them, we deceived the world.

According to those principles, the Cherokee nation has the right to establish its own form of government, and to alter and amend it from time to time, according to its own sense of its own wants; to live under its own laws; to be exempt from the operation of the laws of the United States, or of any individual state; to claim the protection of the United States; and quietly to possess and enjoy its lands, subject to no other limitation than that, when sold, they can only be sold to the U. States. I consider the present administration of the government of the United States as having announced a system of policy in direct hostility with those principles, and thereby encouraging Georgia to usurp powers of legislation over the Cherokee nation which she does not of right possess.[2]

Such are my opinions, which are expressed at your request; but they are the opinions of a private individual, which can avail you nothing.

What ought the Cherokees to do in their present critical situation? is a most important question for their consideration. Without being able to advise them, I see very clearly what they ought not to do. They ought not to make war. They ought to bear every oppression, rather than fly to arms. The people of the United States are alone competent now to redress these wrongs; and it is to be hoped that they will, sooner or later, apply the competent remedy.

In communicating these opinions at your instance, I have done it with no intention that they should be published. A publication of them might do injury, and I therefore request that it be not made.

I feel very thankful for the friendly sentiments towards myself, which you have expressed, and offer my sincere wishes that your nation finally may obtain justice at the hands of the United States, and may become a civilized, Christian and prosperous community. . . .

Copy. Printed in *Niles' Register* (November 5, 1836), 51:150; copy also in DNA, RG75, Letters Received, 1838, no. C74. Gunter was an Indian from Gunter's Landing on the Tennessee River. See Thurman Wilkins, *Cherokee Tragedy: The Story of the Ridge Family and the Decimation of a People* (New York, 1970), 278; and Gary E. Moulton, *John Ross* (Athens, Ga., 1978), 72.   1. Article IX; Parry, *Treaty Series*, 63:429.   2. Clay to Hammond, Oct. 7, 1829.

From Alexander Porter, New Orleans, June 10, 1831. Comments on personal problems, including the death of his youngest daughter, Evelina. Continues: "We were perfectly astounded here at the intelligence of the dissolution of the Cabinet [Letcher to Clay, December 21, 1829]. I have no idea that Mr Van Burens resignation was voluntary. I think I know the President pretty well. He became uneasy at the general belief of his being governed by his secretary, and determined to get rid of him. He wished to shew the World, he could carry on the government himself. Blind men (it is an old saying) are jealous of, and easily vexed with those who lead them; and if the same opinion be as generally circulated, and as much believed in regard to [Edward] Livingstons influence on him, my life on it we will have another Secretary of State before the General goes out of office. — By the by. I notice in several of the newspapers friendly to you, an admission that the present Cabinet is superior to that which preceded it. — I do not see in what the superiority Consists. I question if [Louis] M[c]Lane be stronger than [Samuel] Ingham. [Levi] Woodbury I presume is very little better than [John] Branch. and Van Buren is certainly a wiser man than his successor. Livingston is eminently weak: fond of crooked ways, totally devoid of energy — and of an undecided character. I am surprised he has accepted the office. I do not suppose his appointment can pass through the Senate without an examination into the Causes which led to his dismissal from the office of District Attorney in New York [Brooke to Clay, May 26, 1831]. and how that matter will bear examination, and how he can bear the enquiry, — surpasses my comprehension. — "

Turns to Louisiana politics, commenting on prospective candidates for U.S. senator: "I do not think there is any, the slightest chance, of electing [James] Brown to the Senate, tho individually I should be well pleased to see him there. He is too great a Stranger to the generation which has grown up since he went away. [Dominique] Bouligny from other causes has still less chance. [George A.] Waggaman is a candidate — his politics you know. [Philemon] Thomas of Rapides is also one, on what side he is, I am not *very* sure, but I believe it is the *right* side. A Mr. [Henry] Carleton whom perhaps you never heard of, but who is a brotherinlaw of Mr Livingstons, offers himself as the Jackson representative. Whether the party will admit his claim is more than I can say, for I am not in their confidence. However if they have no greater weight of talent and character to present, (and I am not sure that they have,) they are certainly at a low ebb in Louisiana. It is impossible to say what will be the event, you know the Political Complexion of our Legislature. At this Moment I think Waggamans chance the best. We are aware of the importance of the election, and I hope and believe we will succeed. — "

Expresses the hope that "your friends in Kentucky will do their duty." Believes that "An importance has been given to this election [Webster to Clay, April 4, 1831], which I rather think fictitious, but this very circumstance make it in some measure of real importance." ALS. DLC-HC (DNA, M212, R4). For Livingston's dismissal, see Brooke to Clay, May 26, 1831. In the Louisiana senatorial election, held on November 15, Waggaman, a National Republican, was the winner over Henry Carleton, the Jackson candidate, by 32 votes to 30. *Niles' Register* (December 10, 1831), 41:267. In Jackson's new cabinet Edward Livingston replaced Van Buren as secretary of state; Louis McLane replaced Samuel D. Ingham as secretary of the treasury; Philip G. Randolph and Roger B. Taney were interim replacements for John H. Eaton as secretary of war until August 8, 1831, at which time Lewis Cass assumed that position; Roger B. Taney replaced John M. Berrien as attorney general; Levi Woodbury replaced John Branch as secretary of the navy; and William T. Barry remained as postmaster general.

From Francis T. Brooke, near Fredericksburg, Va., June 12, 1831. States that "as promised in my last I have seen Mr T[homas] J R[andolp]h his first objection to the publication of his letter to you, was that he did not recollect its contents and had kept no copy, on my Shewing him the copy of it, which I had about me, he requested that I would permit him to Shew it to his mother [Martha Jefferson Randolph] and that I would See her at his house, this I did, and held a long conversation with her — She apprehended that the publication of the letter would be improper as it reflected on her husband [Thomas M. Randolph] &c &c but had no objection to its being Stated that She and her family disagreed with Mr Randolph in his Statement of the opinions of her father [Thomas Jefferson], respecting you, her Son T J R did not appear but She Said he would write me in a few days — " Adds that he hopes the letter, or an extract, can be published before the August elections in Kentucky, and that Mrs R promised on parting that her Son Should write me a letter admitting that his fathers Statement of Mr Jeffersons opinions respecting you were incorrect & this I will get before the public in Some Shape or other — "

Notes also that "there has been a powerfull reaction upon Calhoun [Johnston to Clay, June 5, 1830; January 7, 1831], what his friends will do it is dificult to conjecture — it is I think impossible for all of them to return to Jackson   your Success (which I anticipate) in Kentuckey will have great effect on them." ALS. InU. For the Randolph letter, see Clay to Brooke, August 17, 1830; June 4, 1831; Brooke to Clay, May 15 and 26, 1831.

To EDWARD EVERETT   Lexington, June 12, 1831
Your favor of the 25h. April with a p.s. dated 21st. May has been received. Being quite sure of your friendly attachment I attributed your failure to write to me to the same cause which prevented my addressing you — the want of something interesting to communicate.

On the question of impeachment,[1] suggested by you, I entertain no doubt of the Presidents liability to it. But, at present, (what may be the state of the case hereafter we cannot now say) from the composition of the Senate, there is not the least prospect of such a prosecution being effectual. To attempt it, therefore, in the existing division of that body, would be unavailing, and, on that account, you would not be able to carry with you the judgment or the feelings of the public. Indeed there would be danger of exciting the sympathies of the people in behalf of a person, whom they have not yet altogether ceased to idolize. I think, in lieu of any formal proposition to impeach him, it would be better to embrace a suitable opportunity to assert and to prove him liable to impeachment and place the forbearance to attempt it upon the true ground.

As to the V. P. [Calhoun] and his friends, I think it best to avoid in *fact* and in appearance any co-operation with them. There can be no cordial co-operation between us. Our principles are diametrically opposite, and we ought to adhere to our principles, without bringing into Suspicion our sincere attachment to them. We may abstain from any attacks upon the V. P. & his friends as far as we can consistently with the proper support of our principles, and that should be the limit of any countenance extended by us to them. If they choose to attack the Administration let them march on their own line and conduct their own operations; and we on ours. In Congress, indeed, if they should be hostile to the President, you will necessarily find yourselves acting occasionally together. When that happens, I think our friends ought to take care to give no just ground for believing that they have compromised their principles, in the smallest degree.

But, in my opinion, whether the V. P. supports or opposes the re-election of the President, depends upon his (the V. P.s) estimate of the probable issue of the contest. If he believe Jackson will be re-elected, he will support him and place his support upon the ground of a magnanimous suppression of the sense of his own wrongs, and of an adherence to *principle* (a word which he will strongly emphasize) and he will thereby seek to establish upon the gratitude and justice of the Jackson party a claim in behalf of himself to the succession. If he believe that Jackson will be defeated, he will contribute what he can to his defeat, and thereby seek to secure future support from the Country.

I do not believe that the V. P. will be a candidate for the P. Already, I learn from Virginia, his friends, greatly excited and increased by the first appearance of the correspondence, are in despair of him. Some of them will come to us, some go back to Jackson, and some stand still. Our friends are in good hopes for us there.

In regard to the operation of Antimasonry upon the P. contest, we may assume, at present,

1st. That there will be an Antimasonic Candidate; and

2dly. That Antimasonry abounds most in the two States of Pennsa. and N. Y. both of which are indispensable to Genl J

Antimasonry does not exist South of the Potomac, nor in the Western States, except in the Northern parts of Ohio.

It was unfortunate in N. Y. last fall either that our friends gave Antimasonry so much, or that they did not give it more support.[2] By giving it so much, its apparent strength was greatly increased. By not giving it more our friends irreconcilably offended it.[3]

In the event of three tickets running, if we should not be strong enough, by ourselves, to carry either N. Y. or Pennsa. much will depend upon the course our friends may pursue. If they should cast their votes upon the Anti Masonic ticket in either State, they may thereby deprive Jackson of its vote. But I hope, by next fall twelve month, we may be able to carry both States. And before or by that time the Anti's may become convinced of the hopelessness of their cause.

[Richard] Rush, notwithstanding his late impassioned letter,[4] continues to write to me as to a friend in whose success he is extremely zealous. He is very desirous that I should make some declaration adverse to Masonry, which I have constantly declined.

We shall do well in this State.[5]

ALS. MHi.   1. There was no serious attempt to impeach Jackson at this time.   2. Clay to Johnston, May 9, 1830; Stoddard to Clay, August 9, 1830.   3. Stoddard to Clay, Nov. 8, 1830. 4. Rush to Clay, June 1, 1831.   5. Webster to Clay, April 4, 1831.

From William N. Pettit, Frankfort, June 12, 1831. Asks Clay, an "old friend" of his late father, for a $30 loan to assist him in entering "the grocery line." Reports that he is having a political gathering at his house, on July 9 "favourable to the Election of our candidate for congress." Hopes Clay can attend. ALS. DLC-HC (DNA, M212, R4). In this congressional district the Jackson candidate, Joseph LeCompte, defeated the Clay candidate, James Ford, by a majority of 367 out of 7,473 votes cast. Frankfort *Argus of Western America*, August 24, 1831.

From Richard Rush, York, Pa., June 12, 1831. Hopes that Clay is carefully considering "my suggestions on the anti masonic question." Sends Clay a newspaper "from the interior of New York" in which the editor writes that "the Lockport trials [Rush to Clay, June 1, 1831] brought him over to anti-masonry." Believes that "many more papers heretofore neutral, may be expected to follow in the same course." Claims "the run that my letters to the Anti-masonic committee has had" shows a willingness by the public to accept "plain sense and reasoning."

Argues that Anti-Masons in Pennsylvania are powerful and that in the nation as a whole they "far out-number" the Masons. Further, "I have a private letter from Mr [John Q.] Adams, now at Quincy, in which his opinions of the dangers of masonry from the predicament in which the Morgan case [7:186-87] and especially the Lockport trials, now places it, *go beyond mine*. He would be for putting an end to the Institution in this country, by stronger measures than any I intimate." ALS. DLC-HC (DNA, M212, R4).

From Thomas Patterson, Hagerstown, Md., June 13, 1831. Reports on the political situation in Washington and throughout Maryland. As for Jackson's presidential campaign: "I do feel decisively convinced that the Hero's cause is rapidly sinking—Indeed I begin to hope he will make a poor heat—I think he wishes he had not proposed himself a competitor—I believe his inveterate hatred to you is one of his strongest motives in proposing himself—but I suspect he must begin to fear a defeat which will be death— his diarhea will be brought on no doubt—" Remarks that a man from Pennsylvania had come to Hagerstown in early June to lecture on Anti-Masonry, "but here your friends at large set their faces against this disturbin[g] of our peace & mean not to have our ranks broken." Believes that the lecturer was "a [John] McLean man but McLean can do nothing in Mary[land]—he can never reach the point of his nervous ambition." Says that Clay's friends are working hard "to succeed in electing the Senate of Maryland for 5 years this will secure the state for 5 years." Comments on the personalities and political attitudes involved in the local campaign for senatorial electors [Mercer to Clay, July 22, 1830; Webster to Clay, April 4, 1831]. Announces that they will not run Michael Sprigg against Francis Thomas ("who is to be the Jackson candidate") for the U.S. House until Sprigg, a mild Jacksonian who "is veering," comes out "decided for you. . . . If he comes out decisively for you we will not put forth our man—but run Sprigg." If, however, Sprigg continues to remain "silent or non commital," and we bring out our own man, "Thomas will be elected [Price to Clay, April 30, 1831]."

Believes that Baltimore, Philadelphia, and New York City will all go for Clay in 1832 and their states along with them. Mentions that John Sergeant of Pennsylvania has been "active" in Clay's behalf. Indeed, Sergeant "hesitates not to say that the hopes of our country are centered in you."

Advises Clay that Pennsylvania congressmen Joseph Hemphill and Joel B. Sutherland, both Jackson Democrats, are now leaning away from the president and toward Clay. "I do know that no man in Congress more despised Jackson last session than him [Hemphill]—"

Concludes with the observation that "If Kentucky does well at her coming elections [Clay to Beatty, June 8, 1830; Webster to Clay, April 4, 1831]—publick opinion here is that all is safe—" AL. DLC-HC (DNA, M212, R4). For Hemphill and Sutherland, see *BDAC*. For the outcome of the Sprigg-Thomas election, see Price to Clay, April 30, 1831.

To JOHN MEANY   Lexington, June 14, 1831

I received your favor of the 4h. inst. and I believe all your previous communications, for which I thank you.

In respect to the approaching Elections in Kentucky,[1] as they are now near at hand, I am the more unwilling to hazard any conjecture, because of our previous disappointments. Our distant friends ought to be content only with practical results. But I will say that we shall be more than ever mortified if our friends do not return a large majority to the Legislature and to Congress. Nothing, I think, can possibly prevent that issue but a very large expenditure of money by our opponents, raised out of this State. Our friends are generally united, zealous and confident of victory. And they are fully apprized of the importance every where attached to the Kentucky elections.

ALS. ViU. Addressed to Capt. Meany [5:1034] in Philadelphia.   1. Webster to Clay, April 4, 1831.

From Nicholas Biddle, Philadelphia, June 17, 1831. Deed of sale. In his capacity as president of the Bank of the United States, sells to Clay, for $7,000, a town lot situated on Main Street in Lexington, "opposite the Court house," said property having come into the possession of the bank through a mortgage foreclosure on December 14, 1824. DS. Henry Clay Memorial Foundation, Lexington, Ky. Recorded in Book no. 7, p. 227, in office of James C. Rodes, clerk of Fayette County Court, on October 8, 1831.

To Trustees of Transylvania University, Lexington, June 20, 1831. As executor of the will of James Morrison, approves the construction plans for the proposed edifice to be called Morrison Hall, and transmits a deed for the two lots on which the building is to be situated. ALS. KyLxT.

In an undated letter to Clay, Alva Woods, president of the university, submitted his own plan for the building, saying: "This rough plan I have drawn merely for the purpose of giving intelligibly the dimensions of the rooms on the ground floor. I suppose the building is to be two stories high; & that the Chapel will embrace the two stories. In the second story, over the Library, two recitation rooms might be placed. In the 2d. story, over the Philosophical Apparatus Room, & Philosophical Lecture Room, there might be two other recitation rooms. The plan here proposed gives a building of the same width with the one burnt; but not so long by 24 or 25 feet. May not such a building be erected for the money which the Trustees have in hand?" *Ibid.* Body of letter preceded by a floor-plan sketch of the building.

From HENRY CLAY, JR.   West Point, N.Y., June 21, 1831
I have favorable news to give you in regard to myself: I have finished my examination and have graduated 2nd; and in the *Engineer* Corps. You know that it is the highest honour conferred upon graduates to be admitted into the Engineers; and one not often conferred upon the heads of classes.

Genl [Winfield] Scott is President of the Board for this year; You know he is your warm friend & consequently mine. I have received from him many manifestations of the kindest attention to my intrests. He wishes me to be stationed in New York, should I remain in the army. If you should advise me so to do, I shall be employed on the fortifications of New York Bay & Harbor: In the mean time I deem it proper to say that my talents remain the same as before this honor and I believe I may say my inclinations also.

I shall be with you probably by the 10th of July; when I hope to make a journey in your company. On my way home I shall stop a day or two in Trenton with Mr [Samuel L.] Southard & probably 3 or 4 days with Uncle [James] Brown in Philadelphia where I have many acquaintances among your friends. My route will be through Virginia; by the springs, and Charlottesville directly home.

I shall leave here tomorrow at 3 P.M. for New York. . . .

ALS. Henry Clay Memorial Foundation, Lexington, Ky. Printed in Colton, *Clay Correspondence,* 4:303.

From **William F. Peterson,** New York, June 22, 1831. Pleads with Clay to visit New York City and state to rally his supporters against "this Hydra headed monster that now rules this nation." Adds: "There has been & is now a deep game playing by those who ought to be Your friends or at any rate are opposed to Genl. Jackson & nothing but Your Personal presence here can set these things straight—" Remarks that he is writing this letter at the urging of George Sullivan [5:398], "a strong ardent & sincere friend of yours," and hopes that Clay will let "no considerations deter You—" ALS. DLC-HC (DNA, M212, R4). Peterson, a resident of Wheeling, Va., is otherwise unidentifiable.

To FRANCIS T. BROOKE   Lexington, June 23, 1831

I received your favor of the 12h. inst. I believe I have answered all your previous favors, altho' my last at the date of your's had not, I suppose, reached you. In that I informed you that I could not visit Lewisburg. It would have afforded me very great satisfaction to have been able to visit it, on account of yourself and other friends whom I should have met there or at the Springs; but it will not be in my power. Can you not come here, when you will, at Lewisburg, have penetrated so far to the West? I assure you that we would give you a warm and cordial reception, if you would visit us; and I hope you will be able and inclined to do so.

I am sorry to have troubled you with Mr. T.J.R. [Thomas Jefferson Randolph] and his letter.[1] Certainly their prudence is much to be admired. As it is but a small affair, I beg you to desist in the pursuit of it, if you encounter any further obstacles. I am not insensible to the value of the good opinion of his grandfather [Thomas Jefferson], as I desire indeed to deser[v]e and possess that of all men. His father [Thomas M. Randolph] bore evidence, which was widely promulgated, of an unfavorable opinion entertained of me by his grandfather. He voluntarily contradicted it in a private letter to me. During his fathers' life time, from considerations of delicacy, I did not desire the publication of the contradiction. After his death, he expressly permitted it. If he now refuses the publication, and chooses to allow his fathers' erroneous testimony to stand unrefuted, I must, without repining, acquiesce in the decision.

I had formed of Mr. T[homas]. W. White the same opinion which you express. But he writes me very often letters full of zeal and professions of attachment, devotion &c. Some times he delivers messages from you and other friends. I write him occasionally civil but brief letters. What else can I do with him? I should be glad to be relieved from his correspondence; but really I cannot treat with total neglect or unkindness any one who professes so much good will.

Our flattering prospects in K. daily increase, instead of declining.[2] And letters which reach me from all quarters of the Union (the four Southern Atlantic States excepted) exhibit a tone of the greatest confidence. Antimasonry seems to be the only difficulty now in the way of *certain* success both in Pennsa. and N. York. I have been urged, entreated, importuned to make some declaration, short of renunciation of Masonry, which would satisfy the Anti's. But I have hitherto declined all interference on that subject. Whilst I do not, and never did, care about Masonry, I shall abstain from making myself any party to that strife. I tell them that Masonry, or Anti Masonry, has legitimately, in my opinion, nothing to do with politics. That I never acted, in public or private life, under any Masonic influence. That I have long since ceased to be a member of any lodge. That I voted for Mr. [John Q.] Adams, no mason, against Genl. Jackson, a mason &c—

Mr. [Richard] Rush, among others, has urged me to make some declaration. Notwithstanding his late impassioned address,[3] he is firm in his devotion to our cause, and I think is worthy of all confidence. I do not believe that he would accept of a nomination for the Presidency from the Anti's. Nor that he would allow of any use of his name prejudicial to me

How will Anti Masonry finally operate is an important question. They may and probably will make a nomination at Balto. in Septr. of some person who is not a mason.[4] They cannot nominate Calhoun, on account of his political principles. They *will not* nominate V. Buren. If they nominate Rush, I think he will not accept the nomination. It is said that Judge [John] McLean will not. [Francis] Granger, they intend to run as Govr. of N. York.

If they do make a nomination, which shall be accepted, I think they will, before the next Spring, discover how hopeless it is, and abandon it virtually if not formally.

Upon the whole, I do not apprehend ultimately any serious mischief from it. . . . P. S. Mr. Waggerman [*sic*, George A. Waggaman], a friend, will be elected in Lousiana to supply the place of [Edward] Livingston.[5]

ALS. KyU. Printed in Colton, *Clay Correspondence*, 4:303-4.   1. Clay to Brooke, August 17, 1830.   2. Webster to Clay, April 4, 1831.   3. Rush to Clay, June 1, 1831.   4. Meeting in Baltimore on Sept. 12, 1831, the Anti-Masons nominated William Wirt (Md.), a Mason, for president and Amos Ellmaker (Pa.) for vice president. John McLean was also considered by the convention for the presidential nomination. No platform was adopted. See Thomas McKee, *The National Conventions and Platforms of All Political Parties* (New York, 1971), 30-31; Vaughn, *The Antimasonic Party in the United States*, 60-61. For Ellmaker, see *BDAC*; for Wirt, see *DAB*.   5. Alexander Porter to Clay, June 10, 1831.

From Stephen Van Rensselaer, Albany, N.Y., June 23, 1831. Comments that the changes in Jackson's cabinet have "confounded the supporters of the Administration Mr V Buren has arrived here & will endeavor to reconcile all by explanations his powers are great in manageing his party & his personal friends are numerous & influential—his absence from the country [Clay to Brooke, May 1, 1831] will diminish his power—I fear from my observations to the South that our Union is in danger I had no idea of the violence of the Planters, they are deluded by the ambitious leaders—I will not however despair of the republic I trust in an over ruling Providence—they we may transmit to our Posterity unimpaired our free institutions notwithstanding the Demegogu[es] of the day—" ALS. DLC-HC (DNA, M212, R4).

From Josiah Randall, Philadelphia, June 24, 1831. Sees a sharp increase in enthusiasm for Clay in the Philadelphia area and believes that if the Anti-Masons can be brought over "I still have hopes of Penna. I begin to think it cannot go for Jackson." Explains: "The political divisions in Genl J.'s Cabinet [Lawrence to Clay, December 21, 1829], you are aware, have their origin in divisions that have existed in Penna. The [Samuel D.] Ingham party in Penna. being a branch of the Calhoun party at Washn. The Jackson party are divided into 2 sections   The originals and the Calhoun party. The leaders of both are equally disgusted with Jackson and would abandon him, at once if they could do it with safety, but they fear the people. I have now in my possession an original document: signed by 100 original Jackson men in this Dist, comprising all their leaders, addressed to Genl J. asking him to comply with his pledge not to be a candidate for more than one term. I have shewn it to Mr [John] Sergeant alone." Believes that "this portion of the Jackson party will I think come into our views and ultimately unite with us." Indeed, these same people, "founders of the Jackson Club" in Pennsylvania, suggested to Randall that if they got no satisfaction from Jackson in the matter he (Randall) could assist their cause by publicly renouncing both Jackson and

Clay, and by designating a native Pennsylvanian as an alternate candidate. They mentioned John Sergeant as the alternate because they believed he can carry Pennsylvania. Randall affirms that he rejected this proposition "without even consulting Mr Sargt. & it dropped," and that Sergeant later "approved of the answer I had given."

Reports that "Mr Ingham has been here for two days, most of our friends went to see him & encouraged him, he says Jackson was the cause of the recent female disgraceful drama [Johnston to Clay, September 9, 1829], that [John] Eaton was governed by him [Jackson] only he wanted the courage to go as far as J[ackson]. wished. He is bitter beyond all example and his friends in that Dist. & the adjoining Counties will stand by him. Their leading friends have said they will wait and see whom to rally round, Calhoun they would prefer but they consider it impracticable and they still incline to [John] McLean who while he has no positive strength, is becoming formidable by being obnoxious to none of the parties, capable of being the Anti-M[asoni]c Candidate, tho' in my opinion preferable only to Jackson or V Buren. The Calhoun party will go against Jackson, but I do not think in Penna they will go for us."

Asserts that "The anti-Masonic party are the chief shield of Genl J." and that "I do sincere[ly] believe that there are many more in the Anti-Mas[oni]c ranks who keep up the excitement merely to defeat us. In Penna. they ha[ve] not 10,000, votes without us."

At the same time, warns Clay that the political situation in Kentucky is very serious. "You cannot conceive our anxiety abt. Kentucky. I have great faith but I still feel intensely anxious about it [Webster to Clay, April 4, 1831]. The Ingham people here say it will go for us tho' they say it is what they least desire, making their calculations that a defeat there will induce us to come to a third candidate, in which, I fervently hope they will be entirely mistaken. One more matter of grave importance. Nothing now is more probable than that the Election may come to the House. We cannot have 12 States without Missouri or Illinois, & yet I hear our friends are not running a Candidate in either State, tho' in Missouri there are, I am told, two Jackson Cands. for Congress. This is miserable management & may be finally most destructive to us. I beg leave to call the serious attention of our friends to this matter."

Concludes with an historical note on the Bank of the United States: "A curious fact was mentioned to me by N[icholas]. Biddle yesterday, for which he did not with his name given publicly as the authority, there are now filed among the archives of the Bank U. S. two Memorials one from Albany for a Branch bank there, signed by V Buren & the other from Nashville signed by Genl J. for a branch there. It is true these Memorials were signed some years ago, but that does not alter the State of the Case as they affect to consider the Bank fro[m] the beginning unconstitutional." ALS. DLC-HC (DNA, M212, R4).

In the Illinois race for the U.S. House, apparently none of the four candidates — Joseph Duncan, Sidney Breese, Edward Coles, or Alexander Field — was a Clay supporter. Duncan, the winner, was a Jackson Democrat. *Guide to U.S. Elections*, 556. In Missouri, Spencer D. Pettis, the Jackson candidate, defeated David Barton, the National Republican candidate, in the regular election for the U.S. House. Before Pettis could take office, he was killed by Thomas Biddle in a duel. At a special election in November, General William Ashley, a friend of the American System, defeated Robert Wells who was the Jackson candidate. *Niles' Register* (November 26, 1831), 40: 237-38. For Ashley, see *BDAC*.

For Jackson's application for a branch of the Bank of the United States in Nashville, see James, *Andrew Jackson*, 253-55; for Van Buren's application for a branch in Albany, see Govan, *Nicholas Biddle*, 111. These applications occurred in 1826 and 1827.

To ADAM BEATTY   Lexington, June 25, 1831
[Discusses legal and financial business. Continues:]

The same anxiety displayed by our friend Mr. [William B.] Rochester, as evinced in the extract from his letter which you were good enough to send me, in regard to the pending Kentucky elections,[1] pervades our friends throughout the Union. And I do believe that, if they should result, as we hope and believe they might be made to result, the Presidential contest would, in effect, be decided. My information as to our prospects in the State is highly flattering. Still no energy or exertion ought to be spared that can be thrown into the Canvass. I concur with you fully in the efficiency of the plan suggested by you for bringing out the voters, and hope you will have it carried into effect in your quarter. Such a proceeding is contemplated here, and it will be also suggested to the Central Committee.

We cannot tell, at this distance of time and theatre, how the Antimasonic excitement will result.[2] Should they make a nomination in Sept. their first difficulty will be to prevail on any prominent person to accept. I am quite sure, from the tenor of recent letters from Mr. [Richard] Rush to me, that he will not. I have *heard* that Mr. McLane [*sic*, John McLean] would not. They cannot nominate [John C.] Calhoun, without utter ruin to themselves. But if they should succeed in getting some prominent person to stand, I think before one year they wd. discover the hopelessness of the effort, and perceive that perseverance might be highly injurious. As between Jackson and me, I have every reason to count upon their preference.

ALS. Courtesy of Earl M. Ratzer, Highland Park, Ill. Printed in Colton, *Clay Correspondence*, 4:305.   1. Webster to Clay, April 4, 1831.   2. Clay to Brooke, June 23, 1831.

From JOHN SERGEANT   Philadelphia, June 27, 1831

I have nothing very particular to say, and suppose you have letters enough to read and to answer, but I cannot forego the opportunity by your son of expressing my continued respect and regard. The papers will keep you informed of what is going on, and among other things will disclose to you the increased probability that you will be called upon to take charge of the vessel of State. We rejoice here in the hope that the military experiment is drawing to such a close as will be permanently beneficial. Pennsylvania is in great commotion. In this part of the State there is a vast change. Indeed, the Jackson party seems to be in great danger of dissolution. I do not know how far the same feeling has penetrated. We shall be plagued by the Anti masons. I think, however, we shall be able to bear them down. Mr. [Richard] Rush has taken a step which most of his friends consider very injudicious.[1] I have had some correspondence with him, and believe his motives to have been good. I was glad to learn from his letters that you had resisted every effort to induce you to change your position. This, too, is the general feeling of your friends. I have a word to say to you about writing letters, and I will say it frankly. As the prospect brightens, you will be more and more assailed, and especially by those least entitled to confidence, in the hope of magnifying themselves in your estimation, and still more of availing themselves of the fact of receiving a letter from you to increase their importance at home. Two of your letters (not exactly to that description of persons) have been more shown about here lately than they ought to have been. It is not only *what* you write, but also to *whom* you write, that becomes material. My notion is (you will judge of it) that henceforward your position, as the candidate of a large portion of the people of the U. States, not only relieves you from the burthen of writing, but also requires that as to the generality of those who may desire to be your correspondents you should communicate with them (if it all) only in the most general terms. Pardon the freedom of this suggestion. I would not venture it, but that I am in the way of hearing many things which you will not hear—Washington has become what it might be expected to become under such a chief. It is a mortifying and disgusting subject. Still, I am glad that the depth and foulness of the disease have been made so manifest that the people of the United States may [be] forced to see what is the only remedy. If they will shut their eyes upon it, there is an end of our hopes, and an end too of the experiment of Republican Govt. —I am persuaded now that Mr. Calhoun is to be a candidate if he can any where get a nomination. His Carolina friends are very bitter against the Administration. Georgia for the present seems to be satisfied with being aided to rob the Cherokees, and N. Carolina to abide by Jackson. Virginia is in a ferment. There is a probabity that it will settle down into three parties. If so, we shall be stronger than either of the others. Maryland is becoming stronger & stronger— So is Delaware, and so is New Jersey. New York, as usual, is a riddle. The Antimasons are very strong, and under the influence of a bad spirit. The Eastern States (except N.H.) are with us. If the Kentucky elections should go strongly in our favor,[2] Pennsa. will probably also be with us, and then Jacksonism is—as it ought to be—prostrate. It is quite within the compass of possibility that Jackson may not have a single State, except Tennessee.[3] There is no moral tie in the case, such as held us together in 1829. On the contrary there is mutual distrust, contempt and animosity throughout their ranks, from top to bottom, and nine out of ten would hail with joy any event that would liberate them from their association and enable them to act according to their free will and judgment. There will be earnest efforts made to induce Jackson to withdraw. I am not sure that it is to be desired. If he should, however, I hope he will employ Van Buren to write his letter—Poor [John] Eaton is crazed. [Samuel D.] Ingham is not much better. He is mad with rage. [John M.] Berrien too must be in a great passion. [John] Branch is more supple than we had supposed. He bends a little to the storm—Van Buren has lived for two years upon what you left provided for him in the Department, and having exhausted *that*, had nothing left. He could not have met Congress again, and he knew it from what occurred at the end of the last session. So he skulked away, leaving every thing in disorder, for which he is to be rewarded by the mission to England, if he dare accept it under the terror of what the Senate may have to say when his nomination comes before that body.[4]

I have rambled further than I intended, and to little purpose. For some weeks past I have been disabled for all exertion by a tedious indisposition which kept me in my bed. Now that I am recovering, my greatest pleasure is in learning how well every thing has been going on. Our Country will yet be saved,

ALS. InU. Letter carried by Henry Clay, Jr., to his father.   1. Rush to Clay, June 1, 1831. 2. Webster to Clay, April 4, 1831.   3. In the 1832 presidential election, the electoral votes of the following states went for Andrew Jackson: Maine, New Hampshire, New York, New Jersey, Pennsylvania, Virginia, North Carolina, Georgia, Alabama, Mississippi, Louisiana, Tennessee, Ohio, Indiana, Illinois, Missouri; for Henry Clay: Massachusetts, Rhode Island, Connecticut, Delaware, Kentucky; for William Wirt: Vermont; for John Floyd: South Carolina. Maryland's electoral votes were divided between Clay and Jackson, five to three with two votes not cast. The electoral and popular totals were: Jackson, 219 (687,502); Clay, 49 (530,189); Wirt, 7 [*ca.* 100,000); Floyd, 11 (no popular). Van Buren was elected vice president, over John Sergeant, by 189 to 49. Pennsylvania gave its 30 vice presidential votes to native son. Sen. William Wilkins. See Gammon, *The Presidential Campaign of 1832*, 153-54, 170; and Morris, *Encyclopedia of American History* (1953), 174.   4. Clay to Brooke, May 1, 1831.

From Josiah S. Johnston, Belize, British Honduras, *ca.* July 1, 1831. Reports that he is on board the ship *Chester,* bound for Philadelphia, that during his visit to New Orleans he "disposed of a Considerable part of my property & placed the proceeds at interest," so that he can "Now devote myself entirely to my public duties." Believes that George A. Waggaman will win the U.S. Senate election in Louisiana [Porter to Clay, June 10, 1831]. Remarks, however, that "everything depends on Success" in Kentucky [Webster to Clay, April 4, 1831]. Explains: "The Country is in a very anomalous state — Jackson is now in a minority, & may be defeated — The peopl[e] will look to Kentucky with hope & Confidence — I pray that that State may see their true interests & that they the people may rally to save the Country — The loss of Ky. will be very disheartening I do not know what may be the effect; you will be abl[e] to form a Correct estimate of the West after the elections — You must look to your position & the Country — The Administration can be broken down as easily as it has been broken up — They hav[e] done every thing to affect it, more than I expected — You must look to this first great object. . . . We must put down this party, & these principles & restore the Constitution & the Country — "

Believes that Duff Green is turning against the Jackson administration. Further, "The south will eventually decide agt. Genl Jackson. . . . The friends of Calhoun will do anything to defeat him. . . . The idea of incompetence is gaining ground — The people see a feeble & distracted admn. of affairs — a want of fixed principles — shameful disagreements & a disgraceful disruption among the members [Lawrence to Clay, December 21, 1829] — In fin[e] the whole Govt has resolved itself into the design of forcing Mrs. [John] E[aton] into good society [Johnston to Clay, September 9, 1829], or electing Van Buren successor & the defeat & disgrace of Calhoun. The peopl[e] will see this — but they are Unwilling to acknowledge that they hav[e] been deceived — " Nevertheless, "the revolution of opinion is Certain, however Late."

Concludes: "I think the Tariff after the payment of the public debt may be modified so as to be acceptabl[e] to the south — I think there is ground to stand on there — They will be delighted with an assurance, that would justify their acquiescence & let them out of the scrape — They will seize on any pretext to be Let off — We must make the modifications not they — taking the duty off articles not made in the Country, will suffice — They will be Content." ALS. InU.

From WILLIAM PRENTISS   Washington, July 1, 1831

It is with pleasure I embrace the present opportunity of presenting to you my grateful acknowledgement of your kind favors to Mr [John] Agg and myself — the high estimation you have there expressed in favor of the [Washington *Daily*] National Journal has greately compensated me for the hazard (in a pecuniary point of view) of keeping the National Journal in existence — Mr Agg left Our City the latter part of May — in order to premote the circulation of Our paper — He attended the Convention at Albany — [1]and spent some time in New York — he obtained many subscribers — in the city of New York — he is now in Philadelphia — and has already Sent me more than 100 Subscribers from that City — we have encreased our circulation more than 300 during the past month — and if we can surmount our pecuniary difficulties — during the present summer & ensuing fall — we can then get on without any kind of difficulty — during Mr Agg's absence Mr Richd. S Coxe has been very attentive to our Editorial department — We published in this days paper a communication to the President over the signature of Curtius — from the pen of Mr Griffith — the brother in law of R S Coxe — [2]you will find it well worthy your perusal — you have heard of the Many explosions we have had here among the powers that be — Judge [Henry] Baldwin has been on here and made disclosure to the President — respecting the scheme of Van Beurin [sic, Van Buren] & [Louis] McLane — [3]the former being anxious — to have a seat at the court of St. James — wrote on to McLean that the period had arrived when he [Van Buren] could without difficulty be Elevated to the Vice Presidency — that the difficulty that ex[isted] between the President & Calhoun had placed Calhoun entierly out of the question and that there was no individual attached to the party could command as great a support as himself — but that it would be assencial that he should be here during the Canvass and in case he should like to run as a candidate — he had it in his power to place him at the head of the Treasury — Mr V Beuren informed Mr McL that the Cabinet was composed of such discirdent materials that he could desolve it without any kind of difficulty — by opperating a little on [John] Eaton — he would have no difficulty with the president — Mr McLean was much delighted with his prospects — and expressed the delight he would derive from Mr V. B — *disinteredness* — in a lengthy Letter — On the reciept of this letter Mr V B had no difficulty in opperating on Mr Eaton — he spoke to him very feelingly respecting the contemptuous maner which him & his family were treated by Messrs [Samuel D.] Ingham [John] Branch & [John M.] Berian [sic, Berrien] — and then told him there was no method of getting them out of the Cabinet — without sacrificing their own situations — and that unless they did, the Presidents reElection would be very doubtful — and that if Mr E[aton] would resign he [Van Buren] would allso resign immediately and then the President could have an excuse for removing the others — if they would not resign   Mr Eaton was much delighted with the plan and expressed his greatful acknowledgment for his kind disinterestedness — Mr. V. B. then went to the President informed him of the dilema that Branch Ingham & Berean were placing his administration and that unless his Cabinet were composed of of [sic] different materials — that his party would be come very much weakened — and that Mr Eaton & himself saw the necesity of such a course and in order to secure him from any kind of sensure had come for the purpose of tendering their resignation — and that it was assencial that he should accept them and submit them to the other members of the Cabinet — stating the necesity of forming a Cabinet "proper". and if they should not instantly resign he would then be perfically justifiable in removing them — the President was delighted with this new evidence of V B '*disinteredness*' — accepted their resignations — and soon effected the disolution of the Cabinet — the President then applied to V. B. for advise in creating a Cabinet "proper" — The first he sighted was E[dward] Livingston to fill the department of State and after Eulegising him very highly concluded by stating that he knew of no individual in every way so competent — but there was great difficulty in selecting a Competent individual to the Treasury — had "you" appointed McLean to the Treasury in the first instance he would have reflected honor on the Administration — and he knew of no individual unless he would recall him — the President had little difficulty in believing every word V. B. communicated to him, and instantly sent off for M. L. [McLane] — But the President met with another difficulty — who will fill the vacancy occationed by M L — Mr V B told him that he was ever ready to make any kind of sacrifice to premote his happiness & interest — and that if he could not find any person more competent than himself he would accept it — consequently the President requested him to make his arrangements for his departure — But what a sad disapointment — When Mr Baldwin and some other friends of the Gen informed him of the correspondence and the manner in which V. B. was using him to premote his own agrandisement the President become outrageous and swore by the Eternal that he would disapoint the Dambd Scoundrals—that McL should come home but should never enter the Treasury—that Van B should never see the Court of St James by his act—he left here the day after Mr Baldwin's departure for Old Point Comfort [Va.]—where he is at present—

Mr. Brown is at my elbow and requests me to present his respects and esteem to you he says he shall derive more than Ordinary pleasure from a shake of your hand up in the Capitol Yard on the 4th March 1833

please have us furnished with any and every news from Ky—

ALS. DLC-HC (DNA, M212, R4). By "Politeness of H. Clay Jun Esq." 1. The National Republican convention convened at Albany on May 25, 1831. It reconvened on June 4, to hear reports of the committees appointed at the previous meeting. New York *Evening Post*, June 7, 1831. 2. The son of Judge William Griffith of New Jersey (*DAB*), possibly John T. Griffith. See *Daughter's of the American Revolution Lineage Book* (Washington, D.C., 1896—), 1914, 108:117. 3. U.S. minister to Great Britain. Properly spelled here, Prentiss misspells McLane's name as "McLean" throughout the rest of the letter. Not to be confused with John McLean.

To RICHARD B. JONES   Lexington, July 5, 1831

I have received your friendly letter of the 24h. Ulto. and thank you for the proofs of esteem which it contains. I should be extremely happy to be able to avail myself of your obliging invitation to visit you after our Elections; but my private occupations will not allow me that satisfaction. I am very much engrossed with my farms. In this tract ["Ashland"] I have upwards of 500 acres and in another near it about 300 more. I work about fifteen hands, cultivate upwards of 200 acres of Indian Corn; 120 acres of other grains, and have upwards of a hundred head of horses & mules, upwards of 100 head of Cattle &c &c. You see then that I have my hands full.

I am greatly obliged by your kind offer of Stock. It so happens that I purchased several years ago a Jack and Jenny imported by Commodore [John] Rogers [*sic*, Rodgers] in the [U.S.S.] North Carolina.[1] They have proved very fine. Both are large, young, well formed, of good color and excellent breeders. I have lately purchased in partnership the best, as I am informed, of the Arabian horses brought out by Mr. [Charles] Rhind[2] last year; and I imported about 13 years ago from England some Cattle of the Hereford Reds, many of the produce of which I still have. So that, you see, I am pretty well supplied with Stock of all kinds.

Nevertheless, if the Jack of Commodore [William M.] Crane be fine, and you can purchase him at a price not exceeding $350, I will take one half of him, and you can retain the other, and if you will send him out (say in the month of September) I will do the best I can with him on our joint account. Good Jacks are in demand here. I have refused $500 for mine, and could probably get more. Vast numbers of mules are raised in this part of K. for the Southern market. Should you determine to purchase and send the Jack if your two young Durham bulls are of undoubted blood and good appearance, they might be sent with the Jack, and would sell here well. It would be advisable to send their pedigree with them. If you decide to send them, I will do the best I can for you with them. I should like to have one myself to cross with my Herefords. A man might be employed with you at 12 or 15$ per month to take charge of the Jack & Bulls, and proceeding early in Septr. by Washington in your State [Pa.], & Zanesville & Chillicothe in Ohio, and by Maysville in this

State, he could get here at a very trifling expence. I will remit my part of the price of the Jack as soon as you inform me of your having made the purchase on our joint account.

Have you any of the genuine Dray breed[3] of mares in your neighborhood, and what can young ones (three or four years old) be purchased for? I have supposed that they would cross well with the Jack.

I quit the preceding for the less pleasing theme of politics. Our friends in K. are zealous and marching forward as if they were confident and deserving of victory next month.[4]

The recent scandalous events at Washington must arouse the Country. From the original formation of the Cabinet to its final exit the confidence of the people has been more and more alienated, until it has almost entirely been destroyed.[5] *You* and *I* are not disappointed. A thorough knowledge of the character of Genl. Jackson enabled me to foresee some such events.

I rejoice to hear from you that Pennsa. begins to awake from her delusion. She owes much to the Union. She brought the present Chief Magistrate upon it, and ought *she* not to remove him?

Greatly obliged by your kind offer to communicate passing occurrences, I nevertheless will not tax you with that trouble. The papers, of which they send me every mail, large masses, inform me of every thing when I look into them. . . .

ALS. DNA, RG59, A. and R., 1861-1869, Folder on R.B. Jones. Addressed to Jones at Brookfield, near Philadelphia, Pa.   1. Rodgers to Clay, April 24, 1829.   2. Charles Rhind, while serving as an American official in Constantinople, was given four Arabian horses by the Sultan of the Ottoman Empire when he was preparing to return home. *House Reports*, 21 Cong., 2 Sess., no. 107.   3. A heavy draft horse such as a Clydesdale or Percheron.   4. Webster to Clay, April 4, 1831.   5. Lawrence to Clay, Dec. 21, 1829.

From John L. Lawrence, New York, July 13, 1831. Reports that the convention held in Albany in May and June [Prentiss to Clay, July 1, 1831] was characterized by "unanimity" and "zeal," even though the attendance was "not so large as was desirable." Says that Clay's decision not to renounce or denounce the Masonic Order for political gain "is both proper & politic." Concludes: "All eyes are directed to Kentucky. Her election, if its results should meet our hopes, will have a wonderful effect in this quarter." Urges Clay "to hasten the returns from those remote counties to Lexington, so as to inform us earlier, than the slow collections of the public press usually do, of the fruits of the campaign." ALS. DLC-HC (DNA, M212, R4).

From Thomas Patterson, Hagerstown, Md., July 13, 1831. Remarks that "all eyes seem to be upon the coming election" in Kentucky on August 1, and that "if it comes out hansomely . . . it is thought it will decide Jackson's fate [Webster to Clay, April 4, 1831]." Reports that in Maryland on September 5 "we elect two Senatorial electors . . . who are to appoint our next Senate consisting of 15 members for 5 years . . . success in this effort will be of immense consequence to us in our Octr general election as well as upon the next Presidential election." Hopes that the good news of Kentucky's election on August 1 can be widely circulated in Maryland before September 5. "It will have great influence in establishing the politics of this State if you can send us decisively favorable news." Discusses personalities and politics of local races for senatorial electors and the U.S. House [Price to Clay, April 30, 1831].

Mentions also that John Sergeant has been working hard for the Clay cause in Pennsylvania, where he has "great personal influence . . . even among Jackson men." Continues: " I think S[amuel]. D. Ingham is receiving the just pay for his bargain & sale story [4:63] of which he was the main author & propagator—I say lay on for although I am confident he will injure Jackson in Pennsyl[vani]a—yet he is an ill given black hearted man without one grain of magnanimity or honesty — Although [John] Eaton has acted a most ridiculas & even crazy part he is a far better man than Ingham — I am astonished that Mr [Richard] Rush should have acted so silly [Rush to Clay, June 1, 1831] I respected him much but he has blown himself sky high — I am no Mason but opposed to persecution — and shall never believe that thousands of Masons with whom I have had intercourse, associations and dealings — for 30 years would be guilty of [word illeg.] charges until mine own eyes shall [see] them, that there are bad men & [z]ealots & ignorant in all classes or associations both political and religious that would commit any degree of crime & then say they were doing God's service I have no doubt — That Mr Rush should take such a step as he has lately done I am astonished — as to him & John McLean they can do nothing — give me moderation but decision — McLean has none of the latter — but nervous ambition possesses him —"

Concludes by saying "do adopt measures to enable us to ring your Kentucky successes into the ears of every man in this State in all the Month of August first taking care to obtain them — If [Charles A.] Wickliff[e] is beat it will be deemed here a decisive sign [Clay to Speed, May 1, 1831] — we dont calculate much on it." AL. DLC-HC (DNA, M212, R4).

From Henry Jones, New Orleans, July 15, 1831. Remarks that "The political Horizon in this quarter grows brighter — your friends confirmed in their attachments — your opponents wavering in theirs a State of things promoted in no small degree by the late Cabinet explosion — courage perseverance and prudence are all indispensible — and with these your success is certain." ALS. DLC-HC (DNA, M212, R4).

To Adam Beatty, Washington, Ky., July 17, 1831. Had hoped to see "our friend" William B. Rochester when he visits Beatty's house; but since that is "impracticable," asks Beatty to tell Rochester "that I shall consider it unkind if he does not visit me."

Concludes: "I daily receive masses of the most encouraging information from almost every quarter of the Union. The defeat of Genl. Jackson seems to be deemed certain, especially if the approaching elections in K. terminate favorably [Webster to Clay, April 4, 1831]. On this point also the intelligence which reaches me is good. Nothing but previous disappointments in this State appear to create any distrust. Our friends seem resolved to repair former disasters, and to achieve a signal victory. God grant it. Give my best regards to Rochester." ALS. Courtesy of Earl M. Ratzer, Highland Park, Ill.

To FRANCIS T. BROOKE   Lexington, July 18, 1831

According to the wish expressed in your letter of the 2d. inst. duly recd. I transmit a Copy of Mr. [Thomas Jefferson] Randolph's letter to me.[1] I have another from him, written subsequent to his father's death, on which however I have not been able to lay my hands, in which he expresses his consent to my publication of the letter now sent. Notwithstanding, if there be any objection now existing to its publication, on his part, I do not desire it to be done.

I have been much importuned to make some declaration in regard to Masonry (not a formal renunciation or denunciation) which would conciliate and satisfy the Anti Masons.[2] I have declined to do so, and shall not depart from this resolution. I think it best not to touch the subject. Principle and policy are both opposed to my meddling with it. At the same time, I believe it would be politic to leave the Jackson party exclusively to abuse the Anti's.

Information has reached me, in which I confide, that about 100 of the most prominent Jacksonians in and about Philada. have addressed the Hero and requested him not to run again. He had not answered them, at my last dates.[3]

The confidence of our friends in the successful issue of our Elections is unabated; but as they are near at hand we shall soon know.[4]

ALS. KyU. Printed in Colton, *Clay Correspondence*, 4:305-6.   1. Clay to Brooke, August 17, 1830.   2. Rush to Clay, May 11; June 1, 3, 1831.   3. Randall to Clay, June 24, 1831. 4. Webster to Clay, April 4, 1831.

From William F. Peterson, Boston, July 18, 1831. Has learned recently, while visiting in New York City, that Daniel Webster and "his imediate & strong friends, disregardless (as I conceve) of all national considerations, were determined to advance his personal interests & views in preference to Yours & that the Webster Dinner in New York was got up expresly for that purpose." Warns Clay that Webster's recent journeys to New York City, New Hampshire, Saratoga Springs, and Niagara Falls are political in character and that "public sentiments on the 4th. of July & private conversations with many in this city [Boston] & elsewhere" further reveal his intentions. Urges Clay to protect himself politically by at least visiting Niagara Falls and Saratoga. Points out that New Englanders highly favorable to Clay are beginning to ask why there are "no public demonstrations" for him, why there is "no exciting cause" to engage their political attention. Concludes: "In my opinion *Your presence & Your presence alone can do it* and something decissive ought to be done. *there is no time to loose—* You might visit the Falls & Springs as Mr W is doing, & by that time, You could decide with more certainty the policy of advancing further East or not." ALS. DLC-HC (DNA, M212, R4). The dinner given for Webster on March 24, 1831, at the City Hotel in New York City was ostensibly to honor him for defending the U.S. Constitution in the Webster-Hayne debate [Clay to Johnston, February 27, 1830]; but there were those who believed it was designed to test the political water regarding the possibility of Webster's becoming a presidential candidate. See New York *Evening Post*, March 25, 1831; and Irving H. Bartlett, *Daniel Webster* (New York, 1978), 127.

On September 12, George Eustis, writing from Boston, assured Clay that there was nothing to the stories of Webster's presidential ambitions, that such accounts were Jacksonian ploys "to divide and keep asunder the interests which oppose them," and that "The A.M. [Anti-Mason] nomination has been offered him & declined without hesitation or reserve." Reports that Clay's friends in New England "are anxious to see you in the Senate next session." ALS. DLC-HC (DNA, M212, R4). There is no corroborative evidence that Webster was offered the Anti-Masonic nomination for the 1832 presidential contest; however, in preparation for the 1836 presidential election, a meeting of the Anti-Masons in the Massachusetts legislature nominated him on January 10, 1833. McCarthy, "The Antimasonic Party," 535-36.

To JOSIAH S. JOHNSTON   Harrodsburg, Ky., July 23, 1831
In passing through Lexington from my residence yesterday, to this place, where I propose passing a few days, I received your favor dated at the Balize [*sic*, Belize],[1] and sincerely hope that this letter may find you safe in port. I should have written you before, as at Louisville I intimated I would do, but you appeared to be in such constant motion in Louisiana, that I did not know how to take you on the wing.

Of the events at Washington, which have occurred since I saw you, I need say but little. Every one, fond of his Country, must have seen them with mortification and regret.[2] The only consolation deducible from them is, that they may contribute to dispel the delusion which placed those in power who have occasioned them.

You request, and I take pleasure in communicating, my views of the policy which ought to be observed by the Genl. Governt, in respect to the Tariff, after the payment of the public debt.

1. I think the *principle* of protection, both in theory and its practical application, must be preserved.

2. That as the wants of the Government, supposing the continuance of peace, will not then require more than about twelve millions of dollars, duties of import ought to be reduced or totally repealed, upon articles of foreign growth, not competing with the productions of domestic industry, to such an amount as will leave the revenue at about that sum. This I believe can be effected without touching any of the leading or essential articles, which are now protected.

3. As to Internal Improvements, I never would lay one cent of tax or duty for their promotion; but, from time to time, as surpluses of revenue accumulate, they should be applied to the object of their promotion.

4. The renewal of the Charter of the B[ank]. of the U. States with any modifications which may have been suggested by experience.

These are the general principles. Details are unnecessary. You will at once see their application. You will also perceive the expediency of your considering this communication confedential. The Country is at present so much excited, on most of the above subjects, that neither party is prepared impartially to consider any proposition which does not comprehend all it asks, in whatever spirit of extravagance. Any publication of my views would probably expose me to misconception with both parties. And I do not think, on the other hand, that during the contest now existing, any opinions of mine should be put forth, which might be construed into an appeal, on my part, to the public for its suffrage.

I think we are authorized from all that is now before us, to anticipate confidently Genl. Jacksons defeat. The question of who will be his successor may be more doubtful. The probabilities are strongly with us. It seems to me that nothing can disappoint the hopes of our friends but Antimasonry. If that party should nominate a Candidate at Balto. and *adhere* to him they may prevent any election by the Colleges, and possibly may lead to the Election of the present encumbent. I believe they will make a nomination of an Anti mason. The wish of many of them, I understand, has been to make such a nomination, and, then, that the person designated should decline. Accordingly an application was made to Judge McLane [*sic*, John McLean] to sound him, and to the surprize of the party he has expressed, it is said, a willingness to accept the nomination! This has produced embarrassment. Whether they will now nominate the Judge, or some person not so accommodating, remains to be seen. Should they nominate Mr. [Richard] Rush, I presume he would decline.

This gentleman has written me several letters, since the publication of his famous address,[3] in all of which he has expressed the strongest sentiments of attachment and friendship to me. His main object in them was to prevail upon me to make some declaration against Masonry, which would satisfy and conciliate the Anti's. I was opposed to it, both upon principle and policy. I was opposed, not exclusively upon Masonic, but also upon other grounds. I think we ought not to admit the right of mixing Masonry or Anti Masonry, or any other Society, whether literary, benevolent, or religious, with politics. I concluded, and so informed Mr. Rush, not to touch the subject but to stand still. Reflection since has confirmed my resolution.

Should the Anti's make a nomination, as supposed, in Septr. of an Antimason for the Presidency, it will be an interesting question what course our friends ought to take in relation to it in N. York and Pennsa. I submit some observations.

I think our friends erred in N. York last autumn, in not hoisting their own colors. The consequence was that, as a party, they acted with no concert, neither with the Antis nor the Regency, exclusively, but with both. They got the gratitude of neither. What is more, the Anti's were more embittered by the loss of some 15 or 20 thousand of our friends than they were gratified by their gain of upwards of 60.000 of them.[4] And they claimed these Sixty thousand as a clear addition to their own ranks—as in fact so many Anti's. The further consequence was to exhibit a great nominal increase of Anti Masonry since the election of the previous year. This apparent augmentation has had the effect of extending the Anti Masonic principle to other States which had been before almost exempt from it. If last fall Anti Masonry had in N. York been restricted to its own legitimate numbers, it would now be much less formidable there or any where else than it is.

We are taught by past errors what to do in future. That, I think, ought to be done this fall which was omitted the last, our standard should be raised, whatever may be the number, small or great, flocking to it. There may then be in N.Y. and P. three distinct tickets. These consequences will ensue 1st. that the Anti Masons will be reduced to their proper numbers, and be taught by the reduction moderation. 2dly. that the Jackson party may be the strongest of the three. 3dly. by union that the Jackson party may be defeated, and that, by division between the Antis and the N. Republicans, the Jackson party may succeed. And if the canvass should be conducted, in a conciliatory manner by our friends towards the Antis (which policy evidently enjoins), this final consequence next fall may follow, that they (the Anti's) will then come to our support.

The policy of the Antis is to *force* us into their support. Our's should be to win them to ours. Taking the Union at large we are certainly the stronger party. Taking any single State in the Union (N. York, Pennsa. Vermont for example) we are the stronger party. Upon the laws of gravitation we ought to draw them to us instead of being drawn to them. They and we agree as to every thing that the Genl Govt. can or ought to do. We differ only about Masonry respecting which the Genl. Government has nothing to do. In what part of the Federal Constitution can they find any warrant or authority to put down masonry? If they, by a pursuit of the delusive object which, as it respects Federal politics, they are prosecuting, should endanger the safety or occasion the loss of great practical principles, they will incur a great responsibility and an overwhelming odium.

I would not abuse them; I would not even attack them. I would leave that to the Jackson party.

Such are my general views on this perplexing question.

We are on the eve of our great K. contest. I think we shall achieve a signal victory. As to the Legislature we can not fail. But such is the arrangement of the Congressional Districts & so nicely are many of them balanced that we may be deceived as to some.[5] Yet I believe we shall gain at least seven or eight out of the twelve. Prodigious efforts, seconded by a vast expenditure of money, are making from Washington; and if we fail it will be because the power of corruption is superior to the power of truth. . . . P.S. I am rejoiced to learn that you have made a satisfactory arrangement of your private affairs.[6]

ALS. PHi. Printed in part in Colton, *Clay Correspondence*, 4:306-9.   1. Johnston to Clay, *ca.* July 1, 1831.   2. Lawrence to Clay, Dec. 21, 1829; Porter to Clay, June 10, 1831.   3. Rush

to Clay, June 1, 1831.   4. Johnston to Clay, May 9, 1830; Stoddard to Clay, Nov. 8, 1830.
5. Webster to Clay, April 4, 1831.   6. Johnston to Clay, *ca.* July 1, 1831.

To JESSE BURTON HARRISON   Harrodsburg, Ky., July 24, 1831

I avail myself of the leisure afforded, by passing a few days, at this watering situation, to acknowledge the receipt of your favor of the 25h. Ulto. and to tender my congratulations on your safe return from Europe. Since you left our Country, many events, highly important, have occurred at home and abroad. The spirit of all of them is favorable to the cause of improvement. I am rejoiced that England is likely to accomplish her great measure of reform, without the danger of civil commotion. It appears to me to be consonant to the true genius of her Constitution, and to be imperiously demanded by changes, effected by the progess of civilization. May it realize all the good anticipated!

At home too our prospects, gloomy enough when you left us, have become bright and cheering. I think there is now every reason to hope that we shall get rid of mad and incompetent rulers by the regular action of our free systems. The subject of the Tariff, to which you refer, will remain to be adjusted. If the moderate opponents of it would come out and separate themselves from those who, on account of its existence, are threatening the Union, I do believe that, after the payment of the public debt, such an arrangement might be made as ought to be satisfactory. This arrangement would, of course, be founded upon the basis of preserving the principle of protection in all cases where it would be needed, and of dispensing with taxes, on all foreign articles, not coming in competition with those of domestic origin, to an extent sufficient to reduce the Revenue to a limit corresponding with an economical administration of the Government. As to Internal Improvements, I have never thought that a cent of duty ought to be specifically laid for the purpose of their promotion; but as, in any proper adjustment of the Tariff, surpluses must occasionally accumulate, these I think should be applied to that object.

I scarcely need say that this expression of opinion is intended for your own eye only. Independent of the danger of misconception, I do not think that at this moment I should be placed in any posture, in which I might be supposed to solicit public suffrage.

You cannot dedicate your life to a profession nobler than that of the Law. But does Lynchburg present a suitable theatre for you? I should doubt it.

We are on the eve of our August Elections. Both parties feel or at least profess confidence in their issue.[1] That of the Administration is making prodigious efforts from without as well as within the State. I think our friends will triumph; but if they do not it will be because the power of corruption is superior to the power of truth.

ALS. DLC-HC (DNA, M212, R21). Addressed to Harrison in Lynchburg, Va.   1. Webster to Clay, April 4, 1831.

To GEORGE CORBIN WASHINGTON   Harrodsburg, Ky., July 24, 1831

I embrace the occasion of my retreat, for a few days, to this watering place, to thank you for your obliging letter of the 11h. I am rejoiced to learn that our friends in Maryland are so well prepared for their contests this fall, and that they are animated by such confident hopes of victory.[1] Ten days more, and our struggle in Kentucky will be over. Prodigious efforts, on both sides, have been, and will continue to be, made. Those of our opponents have been seconded by all the power, and I fear some of the money, of Government. Still we believe we shall gain a signal truimph. I think we cannot fail in securing a decided and a great majority in the Legislature. Owing to the arrangements of the Congressional districts, some of them are very nicely balanced, and our majority in the H. of R. of the U. States may not be as great as our aggregate majority throughout the State, or it may be greater. We must not be surprized at either event. I shall only be surprized if we do not obtain a majority both in the H. of R. and in the General Assembly.[2] [Robert P.] Letcher, I think, will be re-elected with ease, altho' his opponent also is a friend.

On the events at Washington every friend of his Country would gladly through [*sic*] a veil so that foreign eyes, at least, should not reach them. The only consolation deducible from them is that they may open the eyes of our fellow Citizens. If they do not I too shall begin to despair of the Republic.

Should we not be disappointed in the issue of our K. Elections means will be adopted to spread intelligence of them as rapidly as practicable. But, with you, we have abundant reason to distrust the fidelity of the Mail.

I am desirous of purchasing, for my own use, three or four young negro men between 17 and 21. Having obtained some from Montgomery [County], with whom I am well pleased, I should like to get them there. Could you assist me in obtaining them, and at what price? I should of course have to send for them, and I should like to do so in Septr.

ALS. MeHi. Addressed to Washington at Green Hill, near Rockville, Md.   1. Mercer to Clay, July 22, 1830; Webster to Clay, April 4, 1831.   2. *Ibid.*

To THOMAS I. WHARTON   Harrodsburg, Ky., July 25, 1831

I avail myself of the leisure afforded by a short retreat to this watering place to acknowledge the receipt of your favor of the 5h.   I join you heartily in felicitations on the improved prospects of public affairs. The demonstrations in your fair City [Philadelphia] have had considerable agency in producing them; but, more than all other causes, the incompetency and shameful scenes at Washington have contributed.

I think there exists now much reason to anticipate the defeat of Genl. Jackson. The current is running decidedly with us and against him. Without calculating the changes which in all probability will take place against him, in the next fifteen months, there is now a majority of the people of the U. States adverse to his re-election, if the parts of that majority could be brought to act in unison. You ask what is my opinion of anti masonry, or rather of the influence which it is likely to exert in our cause. We may assume, that there is a coincidence between the N[ational]. Republicans and the Anti's, generally in respect to the measures of government; & that as a party the N. R. are the most numerous and powerful not only throughout the Union, but in *every* State of the Union. I think, therefore, that as minorities generally combine against the dominant party, it is fair to conclude that ultimately there will be co-operation between the two parties. In the mean time, the Anti's will probably make a nomination at Balto. of an Anti Masonic Candidate.[1] Many of them will make it under the hope that he will decline. And he will either decline, or, in the course of next winter or Spring, he will be virtually deserted, from its being discovered that his Election is hopeless.

But to produce the co-operation supposed it strikes me to be expedient 1st. That the N. Republicans should, in Pennsa. and N. York, at the approaching autumnal elections, hoist their separate banner, whatever may be the number rallying under it. and 2dly. that they should abstain from abusing or attacking the Anti's, leaving that invidious office to the Jackson party. By acting with the Anti's, under their flag, the N.Rs. would be considered as Anti masons, and would, by apparently augmenting them, increase their power and confidence. By separating from them, the Anti's would either come to them, and thereby increase the power and confidence of the N.Rs., or if they continued to act as a distinct party, their numbers (the Anti's) would be greatly diminished, and it would be demonstrated that they could do nothing without co-operation with their brethren. This state of things would probably lead to an union next fall twelve month.

A powerful appeal might be addressed to the Anti's to dissuade them from struggling to obtain possession of the Federal Governmt. from the consideration that the Constitution absolutely contains no delegation of authority to put down or interfere with Masonry, any more than it does to put down Temperance, Sunday school or any other benevolent or charitable institution.

Next week will decide our K. Elections. The period is so near that I will not attempt to anticipate the result further than to say that we shall be greatly disappointed, if we do not achieve a signal victory.[2]

ALS. NHi.   1. Clay to Brooke, July 25, 1831.   2. Webster to Clay, April 4, 1831.

To JOHN QUINCY ADAMS   Lexington, July 26, 1831

There has been a long interval since I had the pleasure of addressing you, and now I write more for the purpose of manifesting my continued respect and attachment than from the interest of any thing I have to say or to communicate. In that interval many important events have occurred in Europe and America. After having more than any other man contributed to the downfall of the Bourbons, and the establishment of a free dynasty, our good friend Lafayette seems to have, some how, incurred its displeasure, and retired to private life. I wish his active spirit could be reconciled to the repose necessary to his age, if not to his fame.

In England, they appear to be likely, with less difficulty than was apprehended, to succeed in a genuine reform. The pleasure which it must inspire in the bosoms of liberal men, would be greater, if it were not to be feared that it will increase the already enormous power of that monarchy.

At home many highly important events attract our deepest attention. Among these, one of the latest seems hardly to be referrable to the ordinary dispensations of Providence. The death [July 4, 1831] of Mr. [James] Monroe, on the same fourth of July which had been doubly consecrated by the memorable deaths [July 4, 1826] of your father and Mr. Jefferson, would seem to indicate a renewed purpose of an Overruling Providence to make a deep and durable impression on our Countrymen. Such a death, I think, furnishes a juster occasion for congratulation than condolence. Hereafter it will be very unfashionable for any Citizen, who has filled the office of C. Magistrate, to make his final exit on any other day. And, then, on every fifth of July you may be assured of another year's existence. That *your* fourth may be far distant I most sincerely wish.

The incidents at Washington are worse than our worst anticipations. For the sake of the honor and character of our Country it is desirable that an impenetrable veil could be thrown over them. There is no mitigation of them in any effects which they may contribute to produce. It will be long before the wound in the National dignity, which they have inflicted, can be healed.

Have you read the numbers of X.Y. on the Colonial negotiation? Or rather are they not from your own pen? Whoever may be the author, he has rendered, with distinguished ability, a most important public service.[1] If Mess V. Buren and McLean [*sic*, Louis McLane] were to live a patriarchal age, they would, to their latest braths, feel the sting of the just castigation which they have received.

The public mind appears to be slowly in some places and rapidly in others recovering from late delusions. In this State, owing to the operation of auxiliary local causes, the progress of convalescence is least visible. It is however going on even here, and we anticipate, with confidence, cheering proofs of it in the results of Elections next week. . . .

ALS. MHi-Adams Papers.   1. The X.Y. articles, written by Edward Ingersoll, traced the history of negotiations on the British West Indies trade and sharply criticized McLane's attitude in dealing with the British, accusing him of exhibiting a deficiency of national pride by "begging" to the British. The articles were published in the Philadelphia *United States Gazette*, June 14, 17, 21, 23, 24, 27, 30; July 5, 12, 15, 22, 1831. They were published in pamphlet form under the title, *Review of the Late Negociation and Arrangement, Respecting the West India Trade; Being the Letters Which Appeared in the United States Gazette, Signed X.Y., in the Summer of 1831, Now First Collected, With An Appendix*. Philadelphia, 1831. See also Clay to Everett, August 20, 1831.

From James Brown, Philadelphia, July 29, 1831. Reports that the outcome of the August 1 elections in Kentucky will be crucial [Webster to Clay, April 4, 1831]. Indeed, "All parties here look to the result there as settling the question whether you are to be left out or held up as a candidate. It is said here that the late devellopements have made many changes particularly in the higher ranks of society unfavorable to the Administration, but I cannot learn that the changes are decidedly in your favor—Some wish that the New Candidate should have *once* been a Jackson Man believing that in that event he would be more indulgent to their former and present opinions. I doubt whether any very extensive change of *popular* opinion has yet taken place in this steady State. My notions are formed on the conduct of the leaders many of whom speak freely as I am told in private against the measures of Administration and yet avow themselves its friends in all public assemblies—"

Believes, further, that Richard M. Johnson's letter to Francis P. Blair had placed Johnson in an "unpleasant position" even though, like his letter to John M. Berrien, it was "intended to be confidential." Nevertheless, Brown is convinced that President Jackson's new cabinet [Porter to Clay, June 10, 1831] "is composed of men of discretion and talents and may perhaps give a wiser direction to public measures."

Concludes with comments on the drop of sugar prices in Louisiana ("The Planters must have better prices or all the new Plantations will go down") and Clay's health. "Prepare yourself to bear defeat—and make up your mind to perform the duties and relish the enjoyments of domestic life." ALS. DLC-HC (DNA, M212, R4). Printed in full in *LHQ*, 24:1156-57. The issue surrounding the Johnson to Blair and Berrien letters concerns a clear conflict of testimony between Johnson and John Berrien as to whether Jackson had specifically required members of his cabinet and their families to associate with Peggy [Mrs. John] Eaton. Duff Green's Washington *United States Telegraph* charged Jackson had; Blair's Washington *Globe* denied the charge. Johnson also denied that Jackson had laid down such a requirement, while Berrien affirmed that he had. The latter exchange became known as the "Berrien Correspondence." John C. Fitzpatrick (ed.), *The Autobiography of Martin Van Buren* (New York, 1969), 356-60; Washington *Daily National Intelligencer*, July 23, 1831.

To JOSEPH GALES, JR.   Lexington, August 2, 1831

Judging from the present state of political matters, it appears to me that nothing can prevent the overthrow of the Administration but the operation of Anti Masonry. Should the current, now running so strong in our favor, continue to swell even that cause may prove insufficient, should it be adverse, to defeat us. I have been almost importuned to make some declaration which would satisfy or conciliate the Anti Masons. Although perfectly indifferent to Masonry, to which, for many years, I have only borne a nominal relation, I have constantly declined to make any such declaration. I shall adhere to that resolution. I would do it upon grounds totally independent of all Masonic obligations. I would not subject my motives to the imputation which such a declaration would justly authorize.

But I cannot admit that either Anti Masonry or Masonry should be rightfully mixed up with Federal politics. What have they to do with either? What could a Masonic or an Anti Masonic President constitutionally do to promote the views or objects of either association? In what part of the Constitution is the power to be found which would justify a President to put down Masonry, to sustain it, or to put down or sustain Anti Masonry? The Sunday school, or Missionary or temperance or Colonization Societies might each as well attempt to elect a President upon the distinct ground of his attachment to one of those institutions.

The immediate object of my addressing you, however, is to recall your recollection to the circumstances attending a proposition of a Mr Richards,[1] formerly of the Treasury Dept. made some years ago to establish a Grand Lodge of the U.S. I remember that both you[2] and I, upon his urgent solicitation, attended informally some meetings upon that subject. I was adverse to the scheme, and by way of getting rid of it, submitted a proposal to refer it to the several Grand Lodges of the States. These, I was persuaded, would reject it, and I believe they did unanimously reject it, and there it ended [3:177-81].

I think our friends should say as little as possible on this disturbing topic. They should leave to the Jackson party the office of attacking and abusing Anti Masonry; and, as we generally agree with the Anti's as to the propriety of preserving certain great measures of National policy, our course should be to win them, by appeals to their reason and patriotism, to a cooperation with us. But I have thought that some suitable opportunity might, in the performance of your Editorial labors, offer itself to you to contradict the report of my having favored the establishment of a Grand Lodge of the U.S. No one could do it with more propriety than you. No one could devise a better mode of accomplishing the object. It may not be necessary, and of that also you will be a competent judge.

I am inclined to think that at the Elections *this* fall our friends, in the States, where Anti Masonry abounds, would do best to separate from them, or rather set up their own tickets in favor of the American System &c. and leave it to the option and the responsibility of the Anti's to join them or not. By pursuing this course they will counteract the policy of the Anti's which in N. Y. and Pennsa. has been to *force* our friends to join them. These consequences may follow   1s[t]. that both parties will be defeated   2. that by union they would have succeeded; and   3dly. that they will unite next fall twelvemonth.

What did we gain by the support given by our friends to Mr. [Francis] Granger last fall?[3] The 15 or 20 thousand of our friends, who would not vote with them, alienated them far more than they were conciliated by the 50 or 60 thousand votes which our friends gave them.[4] Indeed they have counted these last as so many Anti Masons, and are trading now upon this borrowed but unacknowledged Capital. And whilst reproaches are lavishly made for what they did not get, they have never had the gratitude to own the effective aid which they did receive.

We are in the second day of our Elections, but, of course, have heard but little beyond this Congressional district. That little as well as what has so far been manifested here is highly favorable.[5] In Lexington and its neighbourhood wonderful changes have been made beneficial to us. Mr. Clarke's [sic, James Clark] successor [Chilton Allan] will be elected by a majority not less than 1000.[6]

If the [John M.] Berrien correspondence[7] had reached K. a few days sooner there would have been probably an absolute route of the Jackson party. . . .

ALS. ICHi. Letter marked "(Confidential)." 1. Probably George H. Richards of Connecticut. *Biennial Register*, 1825, p. 17. 2. Gales was not associated with Clay in this. It was William W. Seaton. See 3:178, and Gales to Clay, August 27, 1831. 3. Johnston to Clay, May 9, 1830. 4. Stoddard to Clay, Nov. 8, 1830. 5. Webster to Clay, April 4, 1831. 6. Clark did not run for reelection. Chilton Allan defeated James Shannon by a majority of 1,350 votes. Bardstown *Herald*, August 10, 1831. 7. Brown to Clay, July 29, 1831.

From JOSIAH S. JOHNSTON   Philadelphia, August 2, 1831

I arriv[e]d after a very pleasant passage on the 23d. but I found nothing very interesting in the political world except the disruption of the Cabinet—[1]& the disclosures and disagreements of its members—which would be quite amusing, if they were not disgraceful to the Country—But mortifying as they are, I could not wish it otherwise—Some thing like this was necessary to dissolve a connexion, between two parties that had no Unity of principle or of object—to break the spell by which the people were bound—It is I trust one of the ways by which Providence designs to make them work out their distruction—They have done every thing we could have desired & more than we could have hoped—The Calhoun party are separated from the President, there is a great deal of ill concealed hostility towards him—There is throughout the country a general belief of his incompetency, as well as disgust at his whole course—There is a most anxious desire on the part of his friends that he should retire—Great Changes have taken place in every quarter—

He will go out of office with as little credit & popularity & as little claim to any just fame as any man who has or may fill the place—His friends are heartily tired of him—He has deceiv[e]d & disappointed all parties—But how to get clear of him—He is obstinate & will not resign—He must be met—The greater number must look to you—& do look to you as the only hope—That hope is Strong & daily increasing—

We are looking with intense interest to the events now in progress in your state—

I have myself the greatest confidence of Success in the pending Contest, but our friends look with apprehensions in proportion to the deep interest they take in the event—The Kentucky elections engross the public attention—If we carry the state, it will revive their hopes & infuse into our friends a new spirit—The Contest will then fairly begin—& then every effort will be made to obtain a final triumph—[2]

If the state is lost, which I do not anticipate it will disappoint & discourage our friends extremely — They will not know what to do — They have no prediliction for any other person — no desire to continue the contest — most of them will determine to vote for you in any event — to do right & trust to providence — Calhoun & his friends seem bent upon his distruction — They have disqualified themselves by the folly & violence of their course — [John] McLean has no party out of Ohio — He has no hold upon the public mind — He cannot run with either party — As to the Anti Masons they can have no Candidate either of Character or Weight & they will effectually disappoint & distroy the hopes & claims of any man that relies upon them   They might do great good or great mischief as a make weight in the scale — Their voice might be decisive in the Contest in Penna. & N. york   But in my opinion, they will even there produce a heavy drawback, by turning our masonic friends against us —

Although I feel bound to the Country to exert myself to put down bad men & bad principles, yet if you cannot be carried, it appears to me a hopeless & unprofitable contest — & I can look no farther — & will not until we see the result — The loss of Kentucky will throw us into great Confusion, we have so many timid, doubting friends that we shall be much distracted — The public mind is prepared to be thrown into confusion, on the loss of the state not that it is essential, but on account of the moral influence it will exert —

The Anti Masons are to meet in Sept. they will not nominate you & I fear it would have a fatal influence if they did. Their nomination will distroy any man & I doubt if they can find any man who will accept — They have been talking of Calhoun, McLean, [Richard M.] Johnson Webster &C. This only shows the distraction & division of the party — They do not know what to do — They will not they say, & how can they? nominate a mason — The body of the people will not recognize a party on such principles — Mr. [Alexander H.] Everitt [sic, Everett] writes me that they propose to dissolve the Lodges in the north — but this will do no good — I have not seen Mr. [Richard] Rushs letter,[3] but the public opinion is much against it —

In this City the change of opinion is decisive — The exposé of [Stephen] Simpson[4] is only the expression of many here & else where — We expect more amusement from Washington — & it may wind up in a Tragedy — [John H.] Eaton threatens Duff [Green] — I leave in a few days for N. york — perhaps Saratoga — I shall be absent three weeks. . . . [P.S.] God send you a safe deliverance.

ALS. InU.   1. Lawrence to Clay, Dec. 21, 1829; Porter to Clay, June 10, 1831.   2. Webster to Clay, April 4, 1831.   3. Rush to Clay, June 1, 1831.   4. In July of 1831, Stephen Simpson and five others who had been "original Jackson men" of Philadelphia published a long letter denouncing the president and declaring the withdrawal of their support from him. They began to gather signatures supporting their stance, but were unable to attain their goal of 6,000. Simpson's newspaper, the Philadelphia *Columbian Observer*, had formerly been a leading Jackson paper. Simpson, as well as the other original signers of the letter, was said to have turned against Jackson because he had failed to receive a desired appointment from the administration. Klein, *Pennsylvania Politics*, 121, 345-46. The complete text of the letter appears in the Cincinnati *American*, August 6, 1831. See also, New York *Evening Post*, July 29, 1831; Washington *Daily National Intelligencer*, July 25, 1831; Palmer to Clay, August 6, 1831.

To JAMES F. CONOVER   Lexington, August 3, 1831.

I recd. your favor of the 1st. inst.   The occurrences at Washington have followed in such rapid succession that we have hardly time to contemplate each by itself. Their effect must be the same on all regulated minds; — one of deep regret and surprize. We can Generally find compensation, for the degradation which they bring upon our institutions, in the corrective to which they must assurdly lead the people. Some evidence of the disposition to apply it is furnished in the Elections now going on in this State. Great changes have been exhibited in this Congressional district; and Mr. [Chilton] Allan, the Candidate on our side to succeed Judge Clarke [*sic*, James Clark], it is ascertained will be elected by a very large majority.[1]

The Antimasonic excitement, to which you refer, is likely to be troublesome; but we cannot yet predict how it will operate. I had heard that Judge [John] M[c]Lean would probably be nominated at Balto. next month, and that he would accept the nomination. In this it seems, from your statement, I have been misinformed. Agreeing with you that they will most likely bring forward a Candidate, I am altogether unable to anticipate who it will be.

I have determined, from the first, not to mix myself in that controversy. I have done nothing to make myself, in any way, a party to it. Nor shall I. I have been urged, to the point of importunity, to make some declaration adverse to Masonry, which would satisfy and conciliate the Anti Masons. Although perfectly indifferent to Masonry, I have declined making any such declaration. I cannot admit the propriety of blending either Masonry or Anti Masonry with Federal Politics. What has the General Govt. to do with either? What part of the Constitution authorizes it to discountenance either? It has no more power to put down either than it has to interfere with any of the literary, benevolent or religious associations of the Country.

I do not think that we ought to be diverted by Anti Masonry, from the direct steady and perservering pursuit of the great object of sustaining vital measures of Nat. policy, and of pulling down the present scandalous Administration. Mean time, it may be politic to leave to our adversaries the invidious office of abusing and attacking Anti Masons. They (the Antis) would in N. York and Pennsa. *force* our friends into their ranks. Our purpose should be, by friendly appeals to their reason and their patriotism, to win them to ours, seeing that we agree in all that the Federal Government *can* do and only differ about what it *cannot* do.

I have not heard from Mr. [Charles] Hammond for a long time. Doubt's are entertained by some about his fidelity. I do not myself distrust him. I believe him perfectly honest. Altho' I differ from him as to the expediency of a representation of Ohio in the Balto. Convention,[2] I can fully appreciate those local considerations, and struggles about Caucus's, which have carried him to a different conclusion. It some times occurs that things are proposed, to which we cannot exactly consent, but are forced along afterwards by uncontrollable circumstances. Perhaps such is the case of the Balto. Convention. Originally its policy might have been doubted, but it has gone too far to stop. And it would have been very unfortunate if Ohio had held back, without being represented in it. I think, too, much good may issue out of it. The sympathies, exchanges of local information, excitement of enthusiasm, to which it may lead, must be beneficial. . . .

[Concludes with comments on Conover's professional prospects.]

ALS. ViU.   1. Clay to Gales, August 2, 1831.   2. Of the National Republicans on Dec. 12, 1831. See Clay to Conover, Oct. 9, 1831.

From William F. Peterson, Francestown, N.H., August 3, 1831. Quotes from a letter from "our mutual friend in New York" (unnamed) to the point that Clay must visit New

York State to help counteract the "Anti masonic spirit" there. Reports that Anti-Masonry is also on the rise in Boston, but has "little or no foothold" in New Hampshire or Maine; in Vermont and Connecticut it has "considerable" appeal, "but it is denounced by the lead[ing] Jackson papers in the rankest Terms." Reports that the Jacksonians in New Hampshire have begun "the Campaign by issuing some Monthly sheets or papers . . . at 50 cts pr. annum."

Concludes with an expression of his "anxiety" as "to the result of the Ky [Webster to Clay, April 4, 1831] & other elections," noting too that "The late dev[el]opements of the late pitiful Cabinet [Lawrence to Clay, December 21, 1829; Porter to Clay, June 10, 1831] will also & has had an effect & a very Considerable one—It has set some of them quarrelling & turned others with disgust—" ALS. DLC-HC (DNA, M212, R4).

From Salvator Pinistri, Georgetown, D.C., August 3, 1831. Reminds Clay of his continuing effort to persuade the government to improve the acoustics in the U.S. House chamber, and also to build a national "Temple of Liberty" in Washington. Reports that his petitions to congress to accomplish these projects have been unsuccessful, because "I am well known to be not a Jackson man." Says he will wait until the presidential election is over, and Clay elected, before again pursuing the matter. Hopes Clay will be elected "for sake of our Country." ALS. DLC-HC (DNA, M212, R4).

From Daniel Palmer, West Philadelphia, Pa., August 6, 1831. Says that "From this day I consider you the President of the United States"; and promises that he will do all in his power to help make Clay the president. Claims he has been "totally Deceived" by the Jackson administration. Claims also that his opinions of various candidates "has . . . weight among about 13.000 constituents of mine in the city and counties of New York & Philad." Reports that while he had once been one of Jackson's "warmest Supporters," he and his neighbor, Stephen Simpson, "are together with Thousands of our friends withdrawn from the future support of Genl. Jackson." Encloses a "petition" already "signed by over 5000" and likely to include thousands more. Reminds Clay that they had seen one another "frequently" in Washington, that he is "Poor," and that he needs "any influence Mr. Clay may feel disposed to render me." ALS. DLC-TJC (DNA, M212, R13). Palmer, like Simpson, was a disappointed office seeker, but he was not one of the original six who signed the letter (or petition). See Johnston to Clay, August 2, 1831.

To FRANCIS T. BROOKE   Olympian Springs, Ky., August 15, 1831

I avail myself of the conveyance afforded by a passing traveller to drop you a few lines, in respect to our recent elections.

I have not seen all the returns; but the results of enough are ascertained to enable me to say that we shall certainly have the majority in the Legislature, and consequently will elect the U. States Senator. As to the members of the H. of R., we have heard of the election of five of our friends. There are opposite rumors as to the Sixth. If he be elected the parties will probably stand 6 and 6.[1] Two years ago they were ten to two.

The most extraordinary efforts have been made by the General Government to carry the election; and there is reason to believe that, in some instances, highly improper means have been employed. For example, in the County of Floyed [sic, Floyd], composing a part of the district from which I now write, where in the contest between [Henry] Daniel and [David] Trimble, the vote was nearly equally divided, Daniel obtained a majority of upwards of

300 votes out of 6 or 700.[2] That County is in the Mountains of Sandy, the most Eastern County of the State. It is almost inaccessible. Yet an Engenier of the U.S. arrived there from Philada in seven days, on the 27h. Ulto. just four days before the election, upon a service of reconnoissance, to effect objects of internal improvement. It is strongly suspected that he used some very efficacious *instruments*.[3] In every other County of the District, Daniel lost, upon the vote between him and Trimble, or the parties, in the recent contest, received respectively about the same support that was given on that occasion. But in Floyd Daniel got the majority which has been stated. That extraordinary majority is believed to be the result of extraordinary causes.[4]

Upon the whole, the issue of our late elections ought perhaps to be deemed satisfactory. These conclusions may be certainly drawn from it:

1st. That there is a large majority of the people opposed to Jackson.

2. That in every contested election, where we have succeeded, our majorities, since the last election have greatly increased, and where our opponents have prevailed, their majorities are greatly diminished. Mr. [Charles A.] Wickliffe is brought down from 1500 to about 200.[5] He would have been beaten, if many of our friends in the County in which he resides[6] had not voted for him, from local or private considerations. Daniel is brought down from 1200 to a little upwards of 200.

3. The City of Louisville, heretofore represented by a Jackson member of the Legislature,[7] gave upwards of 500 majority against Wickliffe, and upwards of 300 against the Jackson candidate for the Legislature.[8]

4. Our majority in a single Congressional district will of itself neutralize the majorities for the Jackson party in every other Congressional district in the State. In two other districts, our majorities would also effect the same neutralization.

5. Instances were frequent of leading Jackson men abandoning the party and voting our whole ticket. In Lexington, where that party has hitherto been strong, it is now totally prostrate from that and other causes. In Louisville, the Chairman of the Jackson Convention at Frankfort,[9] went to the polls and voted our whole ticket, declaring that Jackson was an embicile. Other leaders there, as well as elsewhere, gave a similar vote.

If the [John M.] Berrien Correspondence[10] had reached K. in time to be circulated throughout the State, prior to the election, there would not have been more than two or three Jackson members elected to Congress.

I conclude, therefore, that the late election affords decisive evidence that K. will not here after support Genl. Jackson.

I have not time to write on other topics. . . . P.S. My health is good, and I am here feasting upon Venison, in the greatest quantity and perfection.

AL. KyU. Postmarked, Lexington, Ky., August 26. Printed with paragraphs 5-9 and 11 omitted in Colton, *Clay Correspondence*, 4:309-10. 1. Webster to Clay, April 4, 1831. 2. Clay confuses the names of the candidates. In Floyd County Henry Daniel, the Jackson candidate, narrowly defeated Amos Davis, the Clay candidate. Bardstown *Herald*, August 10, 1831. 3. Word "improvements" struck through and "*instruments*" substituted. 4. Word "means" struck through and "causes" substituted. 5. Clay to Speed, May 1, 1831. 6. Nelson County. 7. James Guthrie. 8. John B. Bland. 9. Probably Gen. Robert Breckinridge. 10. Brown to Clay, July 29, 1831.

From Daniel Mallory, New York, August 17, 1831. Announces that he has relinquished *The Age* "into more experienced and abler hands." Charges that "It is, however, much to be regreted that there has not been sufficient spirit among those of our party who possess ample means to have improved its appearance and circulation long since. The arrangements and negotiations are still going on to make it daily, and I most devoutly hope and believe it will be accomplished, as it is the only *real* Clay paper we have here."

Reports that Clay's "Cause is progressing rapidly" in New York State, citing Rensselaer County as an example. There the Albany Regency won by 1,900 votes in the November 1830 state elections ("in consequence of the anti masonic interference"); now by a "moderate calculation," there is likely a majority of 500 to 800 "in favour of the Nat. R. [National Republicans] and that principally of the *Clay Stamp*." Adds that former Jacksonians are "now engaged in advocating the cause of Mr. Clay; particularly in the counties of Washington & Saratoga."

Informs Clay that he has gone to work as a collector of statistics for Redwood Fisher, formerly of Philadelphia, who has just commenced publishing a daily paper called the New York *American Advocate*. "Mr Fisher you know. It is hardly necessary to say he is your fast friend. It will not be the policy of the paper, at least for the present, to openly advocate your personal interests, but we trust to serve you eventually as effectively as if it appeared as your Champion"

Asks for "any [infor]mation touching your prospects in the Western States. Will Indiana go right?" ALS. DLC-HC (DNA, M212, R4).

Jackson carried Rensselaer County, N.Y., in the 1832 presidential election by 840 votes and New York State by 168,497 votes to 154,896 for Clay, giving Jackson a plurality of 13,601. *Congressional Quarterly's Presidential Elections Since 1789* (Washington, 1975), 66. Fisher's New York *American Advocate and Journal* eventually became the New York *Journal and Advertiser*. Henry Simpson, *The Lives of Eminent Philadelphians*. Philadelphia, 1859.

To **EDWARD EVERETT**   Lexington, August 20, 1831

Our elections have terminated less favorably than we had hoped and believed, but perhaps as much so as ought to have been expected, considering the means, some of them highly improper, of all sorts which the General Government brought to bear upon them. These are the results:

1st. We have elected 55 and our opponents 45 of the 100 members composing our H. of R. Our success in the few elections of the Senate that took place this year was in a greater proportion. We shall have ten members, on joint ballot, of a majority; and shall *certainly* elect a friend to the U. States Senate.[1] Our opponents concede to us the majority, although they endeavor to whittle it down below what it really is.

◦ 2dly. The Jackson party has elected eight and we four members to the H. of R. This disproportion has been owing 1st. to the organization of our Congressional districts and 2dly. to the extraordinary exertions of the Federal Executive. Our districts contain from six to seven thousand voters. In five of the districts which have elected Jackson members the aggregate majority given to the whole was about 1000, which is less than the majority (1300) given in this single district to Judge Clarke's [*sic*, James Clark] successor. [Thomas] Chilton lost his election by nine votes only out of near 8000. [Nathan] Gaither was reelected by about 100, and [Charles A.] Wickliffe, [Henry] Daniel and [Joseph] Lecompte by about 300 each. Many of our friends would not vote for [John] Kincaid and Chilton, because they had been Jackson men, whilst their convertion augmented the zeal of the Jackson party against them. Gaither was reelected, because our friends would not heartily unite on his opponent.[2]

3. It is demonstrated clearly by the late election that there is a majority, and not a small one, against Jackson, and consequently that he cannot obtain

the vote of this State. It is proven 1st. by the election of members to the popular branch of our Legislature and 2dly. by the majorities given in the Congressional elections. In the district of [Robert P.] Letcher alone (who is re-elected) we have a majority that will counterbalance all the majorities of all the Jackson districts in this State. In that district we had another friend competing with Letcher.[3]

The new members that we send, Allen [sic, Chilton Allan] in place of Clarke, [Thomas A.] Marshall for [N.D.] Coleman, and [Christopher] Tompkins for [Joel] Yancey, are highly respectable, and will be an acquisition to the H. of R.[4]

In Indiana we have lost the three Congressional elections by running two Candidates on our side to one; but we have gained the Governor, Lieut. Governor and Legislature by considerable majorities. Such at least is the latest intelligence.[5]

In Illinois [Joseph] Duncan is re-elected. And in Missouri [Spencer D.] Pettis. [David] Barton would not leave St. Louis. And Pettis' majority was swelled by an attack made by Majr. [Thomas] Biddle upon him.[6]

The [John] Berrien correspondence did not reach the West in time to affect our elections.[7]

Louisville, which hitherto had been for Jackson, has gone against him now by a very large majority. In that place, Genl. Breckenridge [sic, Robert Breckinridge] (the Chairman of the Jackson Convention) his nephew, Judge Purtle [sic, Henry Pirtle] and others have changed. In Lexington the principal Jackson leaders have changed; and throughout the State many changes have been made, as is evinced by the diminished majorities given to those who have been elected on his side.

I recd. your favor of the 5h. inst.

Circumstances would now seem to indicate that the V.P. [Calhoun] will be a Candidate. I learn that he will be nominated by the Anti Masons next month, and that he will accept their nomination. I can hardly yet believe that they will venture on such a step, as it would, I think, break them down in the Tariff States. The V.P.s exposition of his views on Nullification &c.[8] has not yet reached me. My opinion now is that he will be a Candidate, if he can get a nomination in Virginia. Should my name be withdrawn, he certainly would be; but he would stand no chance, in that contingency, to obtain the Western vote.

Depend upon it that the dissolution of the Masonic Lodges would not conciliate the Anti Masons. They go for power, and their object is to monopolize it, or rather to limit the sphere of selection, by excluding all Masons. If you were to dissolve, they would claim that as evidence of the criminality of Masonry, and continue their proscriptions of all Masons.

It is not true that I was in favor of a National Grand Lodge. I was opposed to it. [Joseph, Jr.] Gales knows all about it, and I would rather that any thing to be said on that subject, if there by any thing, should come from him and not me.[9]

There is one view of this matter that I think may be urged with effect upon rational Anti masons. What has the Genl. Govt. to do with Masonry or Anti Masonry? What *constitutional* power? The States may abolish masonry, by prohibiting Lodges and oaths. Let them contend then for power where it can be used, and forbear to struggle for it where it cannot be.

I think V.B. ought to be rejected.[10] Such a measure would cripple him and weaken the Administration. If there were no other ground of opposition to him, I would vote against his being sent to *England* for having given such an instruction as he did to Mr. McLean [*sic*, Louis McLane], on the Colonial question.[11] As to his being capable of doing more mischief at home than abroad, there is nothing in it. Detain him in N. York with the mark of the Senate's rejection on him, and he will be powerless.

Will you do me the favor to communicate to your brother [Alexander H. Everett], Webster & others, without publication, such parts of this letter, particularly relating to the Elections, as may render it unnecessary for me to trouble them with letters?

ALS. MHi. 1. Clay underestimated his party's majority in the state legislature. See Clay to Beatty, June 8, 1830; Webster to Clay, April 4, 1831. 2. For Chilton Allan's election to James Clark's old seat, see Clay to Gales, August 2, 1831; for Thomas Chilton's defeat, see Clay to Brooke, June 4, 1831; for Wickliffe's reelection, see Clay to Speed, May 1, 1831; for Daniel's election, see Clay to Brooke, August 15, 1831. Nathan Gaither was reelected over Samuel Brents by a majority of 166 votes. Lexington *Kentucky Reporter*, Sept. 7, 1831. Joseph Lecompte defeated James Ford by a majority of 367 votes. *Ibid.* John Adair defeated John Kincaid by 3,925 votes to 3,225. *Ibid.*, August 24, 1831. 3. In the fourth district Robert P. Letcher defeated Daniel Garrard by 3,787 votes to 3,306. *Ibid.* 4. In the second district Thomas A. Marshall defeated N. D. Coleman by a majority of 592 votes. *Ibid.*, August 10, 1831. In the tenth district Christopher Tompkins defeated Joel Yancey by 3,704 votes to 3,527. *Ibid.*, August 17, 1831. 5. Noah Noble, the Clay candidate for governor, won with 23,745 votes to 20,984 for James G. Read, the Jackson candidate, and 6,890 for Milton Stapp, an independent. David Wallace, Noble's running-mate, was elected lieutenant governor over Smiley, the Jackson candidate, and Gregory, an independent, by approximately the same margins as in the governor's race. In the congressional elections Ratliff Boon, a Jacksonian, was elected in the first district over John Law, the Clay candidate, by the vote of 11,281 to 10,905; in the second district John Carr, a Jacksonian, was elected in a six-way race over his nearest opponent William W. Wick, the Clay candidate, by 4,855 votes to 4,610; in the third district Jonathan McCarthy, the Jackson candidate, defeated two Clay candidates by the vote of 6,243 to 5,289 for Oliver H. Smith and 3,107 for John Test. In the state legislature the Clay forces won 22 senate seats to 8 for the Jacksonians and controlled the house by a margin of 41 to 34. Washington *Daily National Journal*, Sept. 29, 1831. For slightly varying election returns, see David Krueger, "Party Development in Indiana, 1800-1832," Ph.D. dissertation, University of Kentucky, 1974, p. 241; and Dorothy Riker and Gayle Thornbrough, *Indiana Election Returns, 1816-1851* (Indiana Historical Bureau, 1960), 85-86; for returns giving substantially lower figures, see Adam Leonard, "Personal Politics In Indiana 1816-1840," *IMH* (Sept., 1923), 19:257-61. 6. Randall to Clay, June 24, 1831. 7. Brown to Clay, July 29, 1831. 8. Calhoun's "Fort Hill Address," written July 26, 1831, and first published in the Pendleton (S.C.) *Messenger* on August 3, 1831. Published also in *Opinions of the Vice President of the United States, on the Relation of the States and the General Government*. Charleston, 1831; and in Wilson, *Calhoun Papers*, 11:413-40. See also Wiltse, *John C. Calhoun*, 2:113-16. 9. Clay to Gales, August 2, 1831; and 3:177-81. 10. Clay to Brooke, May 1, 1831. 11. Van Buren had instructed the U.S. minister to Britain, Louis McLane, to request from Britain the same terms on the West Indies trade which they had offered in 1825. He blamed the Adams administration for the delay in accepting the 1825 proposals [4:179-81; 5:630-32] and instructed McLane to accept a settlement based on statutory law, if this method was preferred by the British, rather than insisting on a treaty as the previous administration had done. See further, Munroe, *Louis McLane*, 264-66; Benns, *The American Struggle for the British West India Carrying Trade*, 186-87.

To JOSIAH S. JOHNSTON   Lexington, August 20, 1831

[Repeats verbatim the first nine paragraphs of his letter to Edward Everett of this date. Continues:]

I have been disappointed & mortified with the issue of our elections in the West. It is true that it is not such as to deprive us of reasonable hope; but it must diminish our confidence. Three points will now require to be considered: — 1. Shall the house of representatives party[1] persevere with my name? — 2. Shall it abandon all opposition to the re-election of Jackson? — 3. Shall it substitute another name to mine, & whose? — As to the first, I am personally indifferent; or rather I should say, I am willing to consent to the total withdrawment of my name. I am not sure that the second is not the wiser course. We cannot support Mr. Calhoun. We ought not to support Judge [John] McLean. Mr. Webster cannot now be elected.

I received your favor of the 2d. — I had previously written you a long letter, which I hope is received. I agree with you, that a dissolution of the Masonic lodges would not conciliate the anti-masons. The best ground to take with the rational portion of them, is that the federal government has no constitutional power over the subject. Let them limit themselves, then, to an endeavor to acquire power where it can be legitimately used. I am informed their wish is to nominate a person who will decline, & then leave them at liberty to support me, but there are so many Jackson ingredients in this composition that is very uncertain what they may do. Next month will throw light on the whole subject.[2] We had better wait to get it.

LS and ALS. Part written by an amanuensis, part by Clay. DLC-HC (DNA, M212, R4). Copy in PHi. DLC document endorsed, not in Clay's hand, "Results of elections in West — unfavorable — What is to be done?" 1. National Republican party. 2. The Anti-Masonic nominating convention met in Baltimore on Sept. 26. See Clay to Brooke, June 23, 1831.

To THOMAS SPEED   Lexington, August 23, 1831
[Refers to earlier correspondence, not found, in which Speed mentioned the issue of the emancipation of slaves in Kentucky. Comments:]

My general opinion on the matter is entirely coincident with your's; but I doubt the utility of stirring it at this time in K. I fear the public mind is not yet ripe for gradual emancipation. The tendency of all things, in England, and in America is at the same time favorable. The serious entertainment of the question of abolishing slavery in the West Indies; the melioration of the condition of slaves in America; the repeal of harsh and cruel laws against Slaves and their crimes; the operations of the Colonization Society; the increase of liberalism, all promote the cause of abolition ultimate[ly.] A premature agitation of the question in K. might throw us back instead of carrying us forward. Such briefly are my general views.

I have perused the letter which you sketched to Mr. [Charles] Hammond. The argument addressed to him would have been good, if your anticipations of the K. elections had been realized. Unfortunately those for Congress have turned out to be against us, and those for the Legislature have fallen far short of our expectations.[1] I must frankly say to you that, in consequence of this issue of them, present prospects are very much against us. If my Eastern friends now think that they can do better with the name of any other friend than mine, or if they think that the contest against Jackson is hopeless, I am prepared to acquiesce. I believe he would have been beaten, if our elections had terminated differently. Their result will surprize, afflict and discourage our friends. They will say, since K. has not thought proper, by decisive testimony, to give evidence of her disposition to support her own fellow citizen, why should we attempt to sustain him? They will extend their disgust of K. to the Candidate residing within her limits, and they may look around for some one who can at least bring to his support his own State. I am as ready now as ever to sacrifice every thing — life itself if necessary, to the rescue of our Country from the shocking and disgraceful misrule at Washington. But what can I do? If the people of my own State, and of the Union, will sanction and approve it, my wishes and my exertions would be altogether vain.

I am afraid that we have an impracticable party in our State. There is so much of individual ambition on our side, so much of jealousy, so much of indifference, so many collisions among friends, so little of that pure, Roman, straightforward patriotism, that I fear we cannot get along. Do not imagine that I have conceived any disgust, or suddenly yielded to the impulses of despondency. My feelings are of a far different kind—feelings of grief, and painful regret at the prospect of my Country.

We could have prevailed in five of the Congressional districts which we have lost, if there had existed that disinterested co-operation which the crisis demanded. In your's—that is in Nelson County—something must be wrong when our opponent obtained the majority, where we are supposed to have it by three or four hundred.[2] What it is I know not. Gaither's district, and Chiltons, and Lecomptes and Daniel's were lost for the want of co-operation and proper exertion.[3]

Our cause every where out of the State was progressing with the most decided and cheering manifestations. Our friends were looking forward, in the greatest confidence—a confidence inspired by communications from K., to our achievement of a great victory here. What must be their feelings—what the reaction, when they come to learn the truth?

ALS. NhD.   1. Webster to Clay, April 4, 1831.   2. For Wickliffe's defeat of Thurston in Nelson County, see Clay to Speed, May 1, 1831.   3. For Chilton's district, see Clay to Brooke, June 4, 1831; for Daniel's district, see Clay to Brooke, August 15, 1831; for Gaither's and Lecompte's districts, see Clay to Everett, August 20, 1831.

To James Brown, Philadelphia, August 24, 1831. Responds to Brown's letter of July 29. Thinks Brown's "advice, in respect to public life is good," and that if he, Clay, "could devise a proper and honorable mode, of withdrawing my name from public notice, I would instantly do it. The embarrassment arises out of fear of placing one's friends in an unpleasant and perplexing situation." As for the recent elections in Kentucky, reports that they have resulted "in a majority to the Jackson party in Congress, and a majority to the opposition in the Legislature—a drawn battle [Webster to Clay, April 4, 1831]. The former result is attributed to the interference of the General Government, to the organization of the Congressional districts &c. It is believed that the aggregate vote of the State exhibits a majority against Jackson. From whatever causes this result has been produced, its present, if not permanent effect, in other parts of the Union, must be great. If it should lead to the substitution to which I have already alluded, I shall be greatly relieved."

Remarks that he is considering placing his son, James Brown Clay, in a New York or Philadelphia "Counting House." Asks: "Could you aid us in effecting it, with any of your mercantile acquaintances?" Reports that he may go to Illinois in October "to visit a stock farm on which Thomas [Hart Clay] is established."

Concludes: "Our Crops are fine, especially our great Staple, Corn. I am pleased with the occupation, and the prospect of the profits of farming; but Mrs. Clay's repugnance to the cares of a Country life may induce us, possibly, to go to town." ALS. ViU.

To JAMES F. CONOVER   Lexington, August 26, 1831
I received your favor of the 24h. inst.   It gave me no surprize to learn that several of my prominent friends at Cincinnati were extremely discouraged by the issue of our Congressional elections, and were entertaining the project of substituting some other name to mine, as a Candidate for the Presidency. I have felt intense mortification at that issue, and have shared with them in their regrets and discouragement. As to the measure of bringing forward some

other name more likely than mine to oppose, with success, the re-election of Genl. Jackson, I should most cordially agree to such an arrangement, and even urge it, if such a substitute can be found with the approbation of our friends generally. I think, however, that we ought to avoid doing any thing rash or precipitate, and that whatever may be finally determined upon, should be in concert, and co-operation with the great body of the party with which we are associated, at least as far as may be practicable. From the first, and throughout the Canvass, I have been at all times prepared, so far as depends upon me, to yield any pretension whatever that I may be supposed to have, in behalf of any individual who, possessing our principles, can better unite the opposition to the Administration. This personal disposition has been strengthened by the recent elections in K. I feel that a Candidate who cannot carry forward, no matter from what cause, the *certain* support of his own State,[1] cannot justly call upon Hercules to assist him. My friends are very confident, and I believe, that I should get the vote of this State against Jackson; but I agree that such evidence of it has not been furnished, in the Congressional elections, as ought to satisfy those who reside in other States.

In the actual posture of affairs three points may be considered 1st. Whether all opposition to the re-election of Genl. Jackson shall be abandoned as hopeless and unavailing? 2dy. Whether the N. Republican party shall adhere to me as their Candidate? Or, thirdly, shall select another and who as a substitute? I mean rather to state than discuss these questions. The first I presume will find few in the affirmative. The two last I think resolve themselves into the single enquiry whether a person can be selected of our party, or of any party, who will combine greater strength than can be concentrated in my support. For obvious reasons, I am not an impartial if competent person to make this enquiry.

With respect to Chief Justice [John] Marshall, I should be delighted to see him instead of Jackson in the P[residential]. office. But we must not indulge wishes that are impracticable. Would he consent to serve, or, rather, to have his name presented as a Candidate? Can he be elected? Can he get the vote of *his* State? If the Vote of K. be deemed very essential, can *he* get *that*?

I should think it unwise that any step should be taken by a portion of our friends, without some consultation with the residue of them. Such a consultation is not merely due to them, in strict justice, but it is at the same time the safest course for all. In regard to myself, if it be deemed proper that my name should be withdrawn, how that object is to be accomplished is a proper subject of enquiry. There is no difficulty, if the body of our friends act. A manifestation of their wish that it should be withdrawn, of itself, with draws it. But if *I* am to act *how* am I to act? It could hardly be expected that I should address a note to the Editor of a Newspaper, as a County Candidate would address the Sheriff, requesting that no poll may be opened for me.

My opinion is that we had better wait awhile. By doing so events near at hand will develope themselves, and we shall have time to learn the views of our friends in the Eastern States. In regard to Anti Masonry, which possibly *may* exercise such a Material influence on the Presidential election, we shall know next month who will be nominated, and shortly after whether the nomination will be accepted. I presume that they will hardly *now* nominate Mr. Calhoun. His late exposition has nullified him.[2] Will they nominate, Mr. [Richard]

Rush, Mr. [Francis] Granger, Mr. [John] McLean? We shall see, and we had better see, before we adopt a definitive resolution.

Whatever our party does, I hope it will be careful in the preservation of its principles. It is far better to deserve success, without obtaining it, than to obtain it without deserving it. In the final resolution of the party, respecting a Candidate, my acquicesience may be certainly counted upon, as well as my hearty co-operation. And as far as my example and my advice can go they shall not be wanting. If, at the Balto. Convention,[3] or in any other equivalent mode, there be a manifestation of its wishes, I presume the party would generally unite in them; but, if without such a consultation, at Cincinnati, or at any other point a step should be taken compromitting the cause, the consequences cannot be anticipated.

After all, we should not despair, certainly not of the Republic, if we do of our Candidate. No great object has ever been attained without perseverance, energy, and occasional reverses. Do you think that our opponents are free from embarrassments? I remember that, prior to the election of Mr. [James] Monroe, the hope of that event was at one time given up and abandoned. We know notwithstanding the final result. Do not understand me as citing that case to stimulate adherence to myself. I am more and more indifferent to *personal* success. A few years retirement from public life have given me some taste for the enjoyment of private, or, like other men of advancing years, I am less ambitious of the toils and cares of elevated public station, or, perhaps my *own* indifference grows out of the lessened prospect of ultimate triumph. Be it what it may, I express myself truly and sincerely when I say, my only anxiety now is [to] do nothing of which my friends can reproach me. My duties and obligations to them being fulfilled, I should be ready, for ever, to remain in a private condition.

If you deem it of any importance, this letter may be shewn in strict confidence to any discreet friend, although I have neither revised nor copied it.

ALS. ViU. Designated "in strict confidence" in final paragraph.   1. Webster to Clay, April 4, 1831.   2. Clay to Everett, August 20, 1831.   3. Of the National Republican party, held in Baltimore on Dec. 12, 1831. See Clay to Conover, Oct. 9, 1831.

From JOSIAH S. JOHNSTON   New York, August 26, 1831

We return[e]d last evening from an excursion to Saratoga, Cattskill [*sic*, Catskill] — Albany &C —

I was induced to make this trip to escape for a short time from the heat of the City, to indulge William[1] with a little recreation during his vacation & especially to see & converse with the people of the State upon political matters —

I found Anti Masonry gaining ground & every where making the impression that it would finally carry the State & perhaps finally overrun the N. England states — This is to be ascribed chiefly to the Cause you mention — [2]but there are various other Causes — Their strength brings them proselytes & these give them Confidence — Until they are not only disposed to obtain the ascendency in the north & middle States, but determin[e]d to become a national party, founded on exclusive masonic grounds

I was informed from the best Sources that they had determin[e]d to nominate [John] McLean & that he had consented to Serve — This was spoken of at Albany without reserve & with confidence — Their object in this State is to break down the Regency — in which they expect our friends will concur — They say they cannot nominate you or any adhering mason—that they are openly hostile to the party of V. Buren in this state & to the administration—that they will do all they can to break down both—They say it is Settled that they will have a Candidate—that in that event, it must come into the House—& that General Jackson will then have thirteen or fourteen States—To wit Maine, N. Ham Shire [*sic*, New Hampshire], N. York—Penna. Virga. N.C. Georgia Alibama [*sic*, Alabama], Missi. Misso. Tenne. Illinois, Inda. & Kentucky—[3]

They Seem determin[e]d to succeed upon Masonic grounds or to lose all upon it—to make no arrangement or Compromise—Their hopes of success are founded upon the belief, that you cannot be elected without them—That the returns from Kentucky[4] will induce your friends & all those opposed to the Admn to unite with them—& that with our assistance they Can Succeed— These are the principles upon which they are now acting

The Convention will meet in September there will be a diversity of opinion among them—[5]It will be difficult to Unite so many persons of different parties—from different States & interests—It will be difficult to bind a party by a nomination & it will be extremely difficult to find any man willing to accept it—

But they will act with the full belief that if they nominate McLean, he will be Unobjectionabl[e] that we shall prefer him to the Present incumbent—& that these considerations will induce him to accept & that the Convention in December[6] will unite in their nomination—It seems to be a question whether they will yield to us or We to them—I still hope they may act more wisely, or that they may fail to make a nomination or to obtain an acceptance—& that they will finally act with us—

We have but one course to persue & that is firmly to adhere—to you & the Cause—Let what will Come—I shall Urge this upon all the editors & upon all our friends—We must stand or fall together—I approve of your determination to say nothing about masonry—I am opposed to making it a National party or Connecting it with political matters—The Anti Masons of all parties—& of every Sect with all kinds of political principles, unite not in reference to the affairs of the Country—or of the Government but merely to put down masonry & to proscribe masons They Select a Candidate, not whom they would choose (if they could agree) but whom they can get without regard to his character, Claims, principles or talents—& then call upon the peopl[e] of the Country to support him—

We must adhere firmly to our Cause as well as principles—Wait for events—We must preserve this tone in the papers—I write to the [Washington *Daily National*] Intelligencer & to Boston—I will See our friends here—& in Phila. Let us see what the convention will bring forth—& leave all with our Convention of Decr—

I hav[e] heard to day that the Anti Masons hav[e] Upon being told that we *could* not support Mr. McLean, asked if there was *any other man* whom they Could nominate, who would be acceptable to us—They are in a Quandary—I do not believe they can get any man of character to accept. They would willingly take Mr. [John Q.] Adams—or any body to Succeed—. [Richard] Rush began an enthusiast & has ended a fanatick—I understood from his letter[7] he had your Cause at heart, but he has now become an exclusive Anti Mason—I wrote him a letter in reply to his, which I apprehend he will not like—

He has distroyd himself, without doing any harm to us — Mr. Adams it is said will not accept a nomination —

The result in Ky is such as to enable us to adhere, although it is not what we desired — The Anti Masons, will Labor to make the impression, that you Cannot be elected & that the only way to break down the admn. is to Unite with them — & that they will Select an unexceptionabl[e] Candidate — This is well Calculated for the times but I trust we shall hold our friends together —

We can only say to them that we can do nothing & say nothing on the subject — I trust McLean will put them flat by a refusal. . . .

ALS. InU.   1. His son, William Stoddard Johnston, now about 15 years old.   2. Clay to Johnston, July 23, 1831.   3. Sergeant to Clay, June 27, 1831.   4. Webster to Clay, April 4, 1831.   5. Clay to Brooke, June 23, 1831.   6. National Republican convention in Baltimore on Dec. 12, 1831. See Clay to Conover, Oct. 9, 1831.   7. Rush to Clay, June 1, 1831.

From Joseph Gales, Jr., Washington, August 27, 1831. Informs Clay that his suggestion [Clay to Gales, August 2, 1831] concerning their roles in attempting to form a Masonic Grand Lodge [3:177-81] in March 1822 has been cautiously treated in the Washington *Daily National Intelligencer* of August 24. Considers it a subject of "the most delicate and unmanageable nature." Explains further: "I knew all the facts alluded to by you, but not because I was with you at the Meeting. It was Mr. [William W.] Seaton. I am not a Mason, though not fool enough to be an Anti-Mason. . . . Mr. [Richard] Rush, I fear is deranged: there is no other way of accounting for his course [Rush to Clay, June 1, 1831], consistently with his personal integrity."

Concludes: "Your Congressional Election has rather disappointed us [Webster to Clay, April 4, 1831]. It is intimated by some of your Ky. friends that you ought to come to the Senate [Clay to Beatty, June 8, 1830]. I incline to think so, if only to counteract [John] McLean's manoeuvres. I am proud of your confidence, & always happy to hear of and from you." ALS. DLC-HC (DNA, M212, R4).

From William Pawling, Harrodsburg, Ky., August 31, 1831. Reports that "There's a secret talk here among some of the prominent Jackson men, that you are to be a candidate for the senate [Clay to Beatty, June 8, 1830] & that they will suffer you to come out & then beat you with Ben Hardin — I do not know whether they have such a scheme in contemplation or whether they have started the rumour to deter you from being a candidate — I thought I would apprise you of the rumour, so that if you should become a candidate, that might not be mislead or deceived." ALS. DLC-HC (DNA, M212, R4). Pawling graduated from Transylvania Medical School in 1834.

With William Dunlop, n.p., n.d., [Lexington, fall of 1831]. Clay leases to Dunlop, for the period December 25, 1831, to March 1, 1833, and for the sum of $225, his farm in Fayette County, on Winchester Road, "adjoining the lands of John Price and Robert Wickliffe." Excluded until February 1, 1832, is a 50-acre field which Clay reserves to himself "for the purpose of feeding the crop raised this year on the said farm to his Stock." ADS, signed by Clay and Dunlop. KyLxT.

From Josiah S. Johnston, Philadelphia, September 1, 1831. Asserts that "The elections in Kentucky although not as favorable as we expected, are yet favorable. I consider it a triumph — You have a decided majority of the Legislature, which affords a clear expression of the public opinion, and evidence of a Change of Opinion in that state   The Legislature will give a Senator, which Under all Circumstances is a very important Consideration. We shall adhere to you. — " Dismisses the presidential pretensions of Calhoun, who "has nullified himself even in the South," and John McLean, who "cannot unite our friends." Assures Clay that "no others are thought of," and that "if you cannot be elected — no one can." The only other potential victor over Jackson would be someone who could unite the Clay and Calhoun followings with the Anti-Masons — "which seems impossible." Urges Clay to "stand firm" until the results of the nominating conventions are known. Believes, moreover, that if Clay could unite his group with the Anti-Masons, "I believe an opposition to the Present admn. would rise up in the South that would create a powerful diversion — But we must wait for events — It may be the decree of Providence that the Genl. shall rule over us — & if it must be let it be. you are wise not to set your affections upon things so Uncertain — " ALS. InU.

From James A. Watson *et al.*, Hanover, Ind., September 2, 1831. State that they have been appointed by an Anti-Mason meeting in Hanover to ascertain Clay's views on Masonry. Explain: "What may be your sentiments on this subject, we know not. By some it is affirmed that you are now a Mason of the highest order, and a zealous supporter of the institution; and, by others, that though you were once a Mason, you have of late abandoned the society, and now are opposed to the institution; so that we have been unable as yet to ascertain with certainty your sentiments on the subject. As we are again shortly to be called upon to choose a man to preside over the councils of our nation . . . it will then be our duty and privilege to raise our humble but independent voice in favor of him whom we may deem most worthy of our suffrage." Copy. Printed in Frankfort *Commentator*, November 22, 1831. Clipping in MHi-Adams Papers. Also signed by Noble Butler and James H. Thomson.

Clay responded from Lexington on October 8, 1831, pointing out that whatever his sentiments on Masonry and Anti-Masonry might be, they have no relevance to the great national issues now before the people or his own fitness to perform the duties of any public office. Nor does "a solitary provision" in the Constitution convey "the slightest authority to the general government to interfere one way or the other, with either Masonry or Anti-masonry." Concludes: "Entertaining these views, I have constantly refused to make myself a party to the unhappy contest, raging, distant from me, in other parts of the Union, between Masons and Anti-Masons." Copy. Printed in Washington *Daily National Journal*, November 29, 1831, from Lexington *Kentucky Reporter*. No manuscript version has been found.

From Henry A.S. Dearborn, Roxbury, Mass., September 3, 1831. Reports that "a number of your most influential friends" in Massachusetts urge him to return to the U.S. Senate where "Your presence will be a trust." Continues: "Not only the great interests of the country require your services, but your fellow citizens, who claim you as their candidate, can not be so well subserved, as by your being in Washington. We hope that no motives of delicacy will restrain you. The times are portentious, & there is no man in the land, who can do so much, to restore confidence, in the stability of the republic." ALS. DLC-HC (DNA, M212, R4). Printed in Colton, *Clay Correspondence*, 4:310-11. Dearborn [4:670-71] seconded the nomination of Clay at the National Republican convention in Baltimore on December 12, 1831. Thomas A. Clay, *Henry Clay* (Phila., 1910), 190.

From Francis T. Brooke, near Fredericksburg, Va., September 4, 1831. Believes that the newspaper accounts of the state elections in Kentucky [Webster to Clay, April 4, 1831] on August 1 were "so much exagerated at first by your papers, that our opponents have converted a victory on our part into an apparent defeat — which has too much cooled the expectations of your friends in Virga Your view of the result, though, which I had published in the Fredg paper, as an extract of a letter from a highly intelligent citizen of Kentucky [*sic*] has revived them in this quarter—"

Reports that Thomas Jefferson Randolph will write Clay a letter "on the subject of his grandfathers [Thomas Jefferson] opinions of you [Clay to Brooke, August 17, 1830]."

Notes that the state elections in Virginia have gone better than expected and that "we shall be pretty Strong in the house of delegates this winter, so much so as I hope to defeat a Jackson Caucus." Remarks, on the other hand, that "there is some diversity of opinion among your friends as to sending members to the [National Republican] Baltimore convention, I have had some question myself as to its effect, the people of Virga have great jealousy of self created bodies, but meetings will be held shortly, one in Fredg in the course of this month."

Concludes: "You have seen the deep tragedy which has been acted in the county of Southhampton, it has made a strong impression in the State, and is a melancholy commentary on nullification, in that respect it will do some good, though it presents a horrible aspect in others." ALS. InU.

Based on an analysis of scarce data, depending in large measure on the subsequent December, 1831 vote for speaker of the house of delegates, an election in which Linn Banks of Madison County defeated James Gholson of Brunswick County by the decisive margin of 86 to 36, it would appear that Clay and Calhoun partisans in Virginia functioned as an anti-Jackson front in the August state canvass. The number of seats each faction won cannot, however, be determined. Lynchburg *Virginian*, August 22, 25, 1831; Richmond *Enquirer*, December 6, 1831; Ambler, *Sectionalism in Virginia*, pp. 204-5. For similar results in the 1830 elections to the house of delegates, see Clay to Everett, August 14, 1830.

For the famous Nat Turner rebellion of August 13-23, 1831, see Stephen B. Oates, *The Fires of Jubilee: Nat Turner's Fierce Rebellion* (New York, 1974), *passim*; and for the debate on the status of slavery in Virginia in the 1831-32 session of the legislature, see Joseph C. Robert, *The Road from Monticello: A Study of the Virginia Slavery Debate of 1832* (Durham, N.C., 1941), *passim*.

From John Quincy Adams, Quincy, Mass., September 7, 1831. Thanks Clay for his letter of July 26. Refers to two speeches he has recently given on the "doctrine of *Nullification*," copies of both of which he has sent Clay. Points out that in both orations "you will have seen that among the States which I have charged with directly asserting or imprudently giving countenance to it [nullification] is your beloved State of Kentucky, as well as my own Massachusetts—I believe we are even indebted to Kentucky for the *word*."

Lectures Clay on the correct meaning of the Constitution, as he understands it, beginning with the basic proposition "that in our country *all* the powers of Government that can lawfully be exercised emanate from the People, it follows as a necessary consequence that neither the General Government, nor the State Governments can lawfully interfere with the appropriate functions of each other, nor exercise any authority or power not delegated to them by the People—*The State* is the Creation of the People—" Develops this theme in historical and legal detail, and at considerable length, arriving at the preliminary conclusion that the "doctrine of Calhoun and his squad at this day, all assert or countenance a right of *interposition* by the *States*, against Acts of Congress, which I find nowhere delegated to the States."

As for nullification, "The doctrine in all its parts is so adverse to my convictions, that I can view it in no other light than as *organized civil War*. That it has the Sanction of high and venerable names makes it but the more portentous of evil to the Union. . . . It is the odious nature of the question that it can be settled only at the Cannon's Mouth. The South Carolina nullifiers appear determined to come to that point, and I hear our *Sober* friend Langdon Cheves has made up his mind that the Union must be dissolved for incompatibility of interests between North and South—What shall we do with these Heroes?" ALS. DLC-HC (DNA, M212, R4). Printed in Colton, *Clay Correspondence*, 4:311-14; also in MHi-Adams Papers, Letterbook, no. 11, p. 204 (MR150).

To **THOMAS METCALFE**   Lexington, September 9, 1831

[Thanks him for recent correspondence and friendly sentiments. Continues:]

I am not surprized at the effect produced on Genl. [Duncan] McArthur by the result of our Congressional elections.[1] A similar effect will be produced every where. The first impression will be whether some other name than mine cannot be selected to unite all the opposition to Genl. Jackson. Perhaps such a name can be found; and if it can be it ought to be substituted to mine. Such is my undissembled feeling. At the same time, I must add that I doubt whether such a substitute can be found; but as self-interest may unconsciously bias me, others, not I, ought to decide that question. Fortunately, I think, it is not necessary *now* to decide it.

Nothing would be more indiscreet than for a portion of our friends to decide the question without consulting with them generally. The object should be general concert, and that can never be secured without general consultation. It is clear therefore to me that we ought to refer the question to the Balto. Convention in Decr. This course is absolutely due to our friends throughout the Union.

I think Genl. McArthur is mistaken in supposing that Mr. [John Q.] Adams will be nominated by the Anti Jackson party at Balto. this month.[2] My information is not direct, but it is such as induces me to believe that he will be neither nominated nor, if he were, would he accept the nomination.

Mr. [John] McLean I believe will be nominated, and late indications induce me to think that the Judge will accept the nomination. Supposing that to be the case, if *all* our friends would unite on him, he might possibly be elected. But would they unite? I think not. Recollect the Governor's election in N. York last fall, in which thousands of the N. Republicans prefered the Jackson Candidate to the Anti Masonic.[3]

I do not think that you and I could support the Anti-Masonic Candidate. What are the principles of that party? Exclusive, proscriptive, tyrannical. An Anti Masonic President for Jackson would be a mere exchange of one tyranny for another; of an exhausted volcano for a new volcano with a burning eruption just bursting forth. Elect an antimasonic President, and a new process of reform would begin by turning out all official encumbents who were not Anti Masons, and shutting the doors of office to all who did not belong to that party. And all this would take place when the Genl. Government, by the Constitution, has absolutely not a particle of power in respect to Masonry or Anti Masonry. Thousands would say we had better retain yet a little longer the tyrant that we know and understand than place in power a new and unknown tyrant, of indefinite duration.

Of the two parties the N. Republican and the Anti Masonic, the former is undoubtedly most numerous, and least sectional. Why should it give way to the weaker and the sectional party?

At all events, I do not think that we at present ought to hold any communication with the Anti Masonic Convention at Balto. Let them meet, make their nomination, and let the person nominated decide whether he will accept or not. And in Decr. next let our Convention decide with all the lights then before it. If a man can be found to accept the Anti Masonic nomination, as such, I am deceived if it do not prostrate him.

Allow me to say one word on a Call of the Legislature. I think you can be fully justified to convene it the last Monday in Octr. or the first in Novr. The called Session would then be converted into the ordinary Session and terminate at Xmas. All our friends that I have conversed with on this subject approve the measure. Mr J[ohn]. Chambers among others has communicated to me his wishes to that effect.

ALS. Courtesy of W. Richard Metcalfe, Georgia Institute of Technology, Atlanta, Ga. 1. Webster to Clay, April 4, 1831. 2. That is, the Anti-Masonic party; Clay to Brooke, June 23, 1831. 3. Clay to Johnston, May 9, 1830; Stoddard to Clay, Nov. 8, 1830.

From John Binns, Philadelphia, September 10, 1831. Given the less than triumphant results of the state elections in Kentucky on August 1 [Webster to Clay, April 4, 1831], proposes the following scheme to reinvigorate Clay's presidential candidacy: That John J. Crittenden, who expects to be elected U.S. Senator by the Kentucky General Assembly when it meets in November, be persuaded, as a patriotic gesture, to step aside in Clay's favor; that the general assembly elect Clay as U.S. Senator, the news of this decision being calculated to reach "the Atlantic States before the assembling of the Baltimore Convention" of the National Republicans in December [Clay to Conover, October 9, 1831]; but that Clay decline this honor in a letter to the general assembly in which he would "put before the country some of those sound principles & policy which appertain to his public life and which he can do in such manner as to make a deep and valuable impression." All this will indicate that Henry Clay continues "to be the favorite Son of Kentucky."

Concludes with the observation "that Jackson is on very ticklish ground in Pennsa. Every change and every combination must be against him. There never was a time when it was more difficult to foretell the Presidential vote of Penna. that at this time. If we can, as I hope we shall get up a zealous enthusiasm, in favor of Mr Clay I entertain a tolerably confident expectation we shall carry the State for him. The Anti Masonic question is embarrassing, yet it may be managed so as to aid us essentially." ALS. DLC-HC (DNA, M212, R4).

To JESSE BURTON HARRISON   Lexington, September 11, 1831

I have recd. your favor of the 28h. Ulto. requesting my opinion as to a suitable place to establish yourself, in your profession, West of the Mountains. There is some difficulty in advising, on such a subject, without knowing whether you mean to dedicate yourself exclusively to the Law, or to combine with its practice present or ultimate views to politics. The observations which I will make may be applied to both.

The elements of successful professional income are population and wealth. Where both are united, in a great degree, there is consequently much business and great demand for members of the profession. A poor but highly dense population may supply adequate professional employment, as a great accumulation of wealth, with a sparse population, may also do. The objection to Lynchburg, I should think, is that neither of these elements exists in sufficient degree. The same objection applies to Natchez, where however there is more wealth. The society is very good in that City, there is not much Serious competition in the profession, but the practice is very laborious, requiring excursions from 50 to 150 miles.

If I were to make a selection for myself I should think of Columbus and Cincinnati in Ohio, Louisville and N. Orleans. Columbus offers greater political and fewer pecuniary advantages than either. It will in 15 or 20 years contain a population of 10 or 12 thousand, now it has about 2 or 3. It is finely situated on a high bank of the Scioto, is surrounded by a rich and fertile Country, and is the permanent seat of Government. Society there is plain but respectable. A man who would establish himself there, live economically and industriously, throw his surplus gains into town property, and persevere 15 or 20 years would find himself rich, and, if he had a popular turn, might secure any political elevation which the State affords.

Cincinnati is the most rising City of the West, is much better than Columbus for business, society and enjoyment, and is not much inferior as a political location. There is however a numerous bar at that place, and professional services I believe are not very highly rewarded.

There is less competition at Louisville, which is, next to Cincinnati, the Western City that is most rapidly encreasing. A greater amount of business is probably transacted at the former than the latter place. It is in fewer hands, and I believe that professional services are much better paid there. There are several respectable members of the Bar at Louisville but not one who is first rate. It was formerly unhealthy but is otherwise now. Society is pretty good. The character of the population is more decidedly commercial than that of Cincinnati.

There is a numerous, though I do not think generally, a very talented Bar at N. Orleans. [Etienne] Mazureau, among the French Lawyers, and Grimes [sic][1] among the American stand at its head. Both are eminent. The former would be regarded so at the Court of Cassation.[2] Neither is popular. Neither possesses the public confidence in their pecuniary transactions. There are other Lawyers in N. O. who make more money, but none occasionally obtain such high fees. In a single case, including his fees and commissions, Mazureau some time ago received $19.000. Business is immense at N. Orleans, and it is rapidly encreasing, and must inevitably encrease   The repeal of the duty on sugar would give Louisiana a severe shock, but the business of N.O. would still augment. Your knowledge of French and Spanish would be of great advantage to you. They are almost indispensible. Some times, to obviate the inconvenience of a want of them, a connexion is formed between a French and an American Lawyer; but all partnerships are bad and unequal.

N. Orleans has the air, manners, language and fashions of an European Continental City. Society upon the whole is very good, and you may have any sort, gay or grave, American, Creole, or Foreign, learned or unlearned, commercial or professional, black, white, yellow or red.

Twelve years ago I had a thought of going to that City,[3] and they offered to guarranty a practice of $18.000 per annum, and I believe I could have made it. Should I not have done better than to have been the greater part of the intervening time running the guantlet of politics? Last winter, my opinion was asked professionally upon a novel case of insurance. I gave it, and a check was handed to me for $500 with a promise of $500 more, if it should be settled according to my opinion. It has been since compromised on that basis.

The Courts are generally shut the sickly months, so that you could come to the West or go to the North, as unquestionably you ought to do, if you go there, during their continuance.

Practice is very simple. The flummery of special pleading is entirely dispensed with. Every man's complaint or defense is stated just as it is, without any regard to technical forms.

Upon the whole, I think if I had your youth and attainments I should go to N. O. and, if I did not, to Louisville.

But, my dear Sir, your own eye and your own observation should decide alone for you. You ought to reconnoitre and judge for yourself. Should you determine to do so, I hope I may have the pleasure of seeing you here. My son in law and daughter [James and Anne Brown Clay Erwin] pass their winters at N. O. and their summer at their residence adjoining mine ["Woodlands"]. They, together with my son Henry [Clay, Jr.], now engaged in the study of the law, will go in November to that City. They would be glad to meet or go with you there.[4]

Louisiana does not, I need hardly remark, offer such advantages for high political elevation, as several other States.

ALS. DLC-Burton Harrison Papers (DNA, M212, R21). Addressed to Harrison in Lynchburg, Va.   1. For John Randolph Grymes, see *CAB*.   2. The Supreme Court of France, in Paris.   3. On May 5, 1819, the New Orleans *Courier* reported Clay's arrival in New Orleans "a few days ago." It was probably during this visit that Clay considered relocating in that city. See, 2:689-94.   4. On Nov. 12, 1831, Clay wrote Harrison a letter which was hand carried by Henry Clay, Jr. In it, he introduced his son, who was also en route to New Orleans, and enclosed for Harrison several letters of introduction to friends in New Orleans. Copy. DLC-HC (DNA, M212, R4). On Nov. 20, Clay again wrote to Harrison, addressing the letter to New Orleans. He repeated the information in his letter of Nov. 12 and hoped that Harrison and young Clay would meet. ALS. *Ibid.*

From Josiah Randall, Philadelphia, September 13, 1831. Laments outcome of state elections in Kentucky [Webster to Clay, April 4,1831]. Believes the Clay cause in Indiana "is still worse. Minorities in general unite & Majorities divide but we invert the rule." Urges Clay to make no bargains with the supporters of John C. Calhoun or John McLean. "To submit to them is ridiculous. Neither by themselves can count on a single Electoral vote or State College in the Union. I would like to gratify them if we could in the Vice Prest. but no further." Concludes: "By the bye are you prepared to make concessions to the South. *I* hope for the sake of the Union you are. Our friends here wish you to come to the Senate [Clay to Beatty, June 8, 1830]. On this subject—there is but one opinion. If we carry Missouri your presence in relation to Illinois may be conclusive [Randall to Clay, June 24, 1831]. The Election I fear will come to the House. I despair of uniting in N.Y. City—but in the support of the electoral Anti-M. ticket. [Richard] Rush, who never had any political stability, is acting under the Governt. of Mr [John Q.] Adams   Of Mr Adams alienation you need entertain no doubt. I have complete evidence of the mortifying fact—" ALS. DLC-HC (DNA, M212, R4). For the Indiana state elections, see Clay to Everett, August 20, 1831.

With Elisha I. Winter, September 14, 1831. An agreement in which Clay sells six town lots, which included the Tammany Mills property, to the Lexington and Ohio Railroad Company [Clay to Biddle, May 10, 1831] for $5,000 payable on September 10, 1833. The company agrees to pay Clay "legal interest" on this sum from September 10, 1831, to September 10, 1833. DS. Courtesy of Louisville & Nashville Railroad Co. Winter was president of the company.

On November 15, 1831, this agreement was redrawn to reflect the sale of three additional town lots, (thus making a total of nine) for the sum of $5,400. Stipulations regarding financing remained as written in the September 14 agreement. Clay's wife, Lucretia, joined him in signing this latter document. ADS. *Ibid.*

To Peter B. Atwood, Greensburg, Ky., September 15, 1831. Thanks Atwood for his letter respecting the purchase of an interest in the horse Stamboul. The horse has not arrived, thus no decision on how the matter will be handled has been made. Does not want to sell an interest in the animal to someone living too far from Lexington, "rendering it inconvenient to send mares of my own and my friends." Explains that "The terms I propose are that the purchaser pay $1000 for a third of the horse, and for his trouble and expence in keeping him that he have one half of his earnings. The price considering what he cost Mr. Berryman and me may seem large, but, in consequence of circumstances, he was sacrificed, and we bought a great bargain. We shall also be at considerable expence in his subsequent keeping, after the sale, and in bringing him to this State. If he should, as I fondly hope, prove equal to some of the celebrated Arabian horses in England, he will be a fortune to his owners." ALS. Courtesy of Egbert V. Taylor, Greensburg, Ky. The Berryman reference is to Edwin Upshur Berryman [5:538], Lexington merchant.

On November 17, 1831, Berryman and Clay sold to Buckner H. Payne a one-third interest in Stamboul for $1,000. The agreement stipulated that "The said Payne is to keep the said Horse the ensuing year, at his own proper cost and charges, and free from any expence whatever to the said Berryman and Clay; and he is to receive, also at his own proper cost and expence, all mares sent to be put to the said horse, during the seasons in the said year. The price of the season to the said horse of a mare is hereby fixed at twenty five dollars. . . . Mr. Payne is to be at liberty to allow any number of mares of extraordinary blood and promise not exceeding Six to go to Stamboul gratis, which mares and their owners he is to designate, upon future settlement. The expence of advertizing Stamboul, and of getting an engraving descriptive of him, if it be deemed necessary, is to be common to all the partners." ADS, in Clay's hand, signed by Clay and Payne and by James G. McKinney, witness to the transaction. Josephine Simpson Collection, Lexington, Ky.

On December 29, 1831, Berryman sold his third interest in Stamboul to Ben Keiningham of Paris, Ky. Endorsement on verso of *ibid.*

On October 3, 1832, Keiningham's name was substituted for Berryman's in the Clay-Berryman-Payne agreement (above). Endorsement on verso of *ibid.*

To HENRY A.S. DEARBORN   Lexington, September 15, 1831

The opinion entertained by yourself and other friends in Massachusetts, as communicated in your friendly letter of the 3d. instant, of the expediency of my going to the Senate, is thankfully received and will be duly considered.[1] Our Legislature, by a call of the Governor, is to meet on the first monday in November for the express purpose of appointing a Senator. I have been strongly urged by friends, within and without the State, to consent to go; but I must own that I have a great repugnance, from various causes, to the service. And yet I am willing to believe that my presence at Washington might be attended with some advantages, I would hope, to the public, if not to myself. It will be time enough to make a positive decision when the Legislature meets. Should I conclude to go, it will be in deference to public sentiment, and the wishes of my friends.

The defeat of Jackson is easy with hearty co-operation between all who are opposed to his re-election. Without that it will be difficult if not impracticable. I believe it may be effected by cordial union and constant firmness on the part of the N[ational]. Republicans. But if there be any one who thinks that another name can be advantageously substituted to mine, as our Candidate, I am ready cheerfully to acquiesce in the substitution, with the general consent of our friends. These observations are made in consequence of your suggestion that "there will be many Richmonds in the field." I know that is not your wish, and that you abide by the nomination so often repeated by the people of the Candidate of the N. R. party.

ALS. Courtesy of Justin G. Turner, Hollywood, California. Addressed to Dearborn at Roxbury, Mass.   1. Clay to Beatty, June 6, 1830.

From Peter B. Porter, Black Rock, N.Y., September 15, 1831. Thanks Clay for his letter of condolence for the recent death of his wife [Letitia Breckinridge Porter]. Discusses his own health. Comments on the political situation: "You will perceive by the

Buffalo Journal of yesterday (a copy of which I will put into the mail for you with this letter) that Judge [William B.] Rochester & myself have been taking a bold step, as regards *you* as well as ourselves, on the subject of masonry. That the effect of this exposé, so far as it may have any, will be salutory in the northern & middle states, and including, I think, Ohio, I can have no doubt — But how it will affect the south & the west I do not pretend to conjecture. The Jackson masons in this state will probably clamor about it, and endeavour to make it the subject of criticism & ridicule — But all of our honest masons, who have no political object to subserve, would be heartily glad to see this miserable institution which is only a nursery of fools & mad men, sent to the tomb of the Capulets. What we have done has been in haste, but not with out reflection. It will be in time for the Baltimore Convention, and may furnish an additional argument for the use of those members, of whom there are many, that are extremely desirous, if they can muster courage enough to attempt it, to prevent any nomination being made [Clay to Brooke, June 23, 1831]." ALS. KyU.

On September 10, 1831, H.B. Potter *et al.* had written to Porter and Rochester, asking their opinions on closing the Masonic lodges and also asking "what you may know of Mr. Clay's opinion on the same subject." Porter replied on September 12 that he believed it to be their "patriotic duty . . . to give up your charter at once and forever." Rochester wrote on September 13, concurring with Porter. The same day Porter and Rochester together replied, stating what they considered to be Clay's views on the subject [Clay to Gales, August 2, 1831], viz: masonry was no longer useful and should be abandoned. Noting that they had not been authorized by Clay to make a statement, they added that "the delicacy of his feelings . . . would forbid his doing any act that might be construed into an effort, on his part, to advance his well earned popularity by indirect means." Copy. Printed in Washington *Daily National Journal*, October 7, 1831.

To JOHN W. TREADWELL   Lexington, September 15, 1831
I received your favor of the 31st. Ulto. with a check for $39:11. being the bal. for my wool. I am perfectly satisfied & obliged by the disposition you made of it. I think it quite likely that it was not sufficiently washed, as it was my first experiment.[1] I hope we shall do better hereafter.

I have been aware, and regretted, that the Tariff of 28[2] assessed an extravagent duty on low price wools of foreign production not coming into competition with those of our own Country. That matter ought to be remedied whenever a modification takes place of the existing tariff. Our friends should even turn their attention to the tariff with a view to its adjustment on the paymt. of the public debt. The basis, I hope, will be adopted of preserving the principle of protection unimpaired with a repeal or reduction of duties on articles not competing with American productions or manufactures to an extent about equal to the Sinking fund.

I shall avail myself perhaps of your kind permission to introduce my friends to you.

ALS. MH.   1. Clay to Treadwell, April 23, 1831.   2. See 6:876-77; 7:101-2.

From Samuel L. Southard, Trenton, N.J., September 18, 1831. Reports his recovery from an attack of "inflammatory rheumatism" which reduced him "almost to a Skeleton." Comments on the national political scene: "The recent election in Kentucky [Webster to Clay, April 4, 1831], has somewhat disappointed our friends in this quarter — for myself, altho' I should have delighted in a more favorable result, yet the change since the previous elections, are as much as could reasonably be expected upon

403

any calculation which I could make. Is not the State perfectly secure against the Genl—?
. . . How wretchedly the opponents of the Genl. managed matters in Indiana. Will our friends always want policy? But is not that state safe on genl. vote? Is Missouri [Randall to Clay, June 24, 1831] quite gone forever?—Tell me frankly what are your prospects, in *all* the West?—"

Assumes that the National Republican convention in Baltimore will nominate Clay and reports that he has been appointed a delegate from New Jersey. Comments at length on the "danger" of the Anti-Mason campaign, concluding: "The strength of the A.M. as a party, is not, of itself, alone, sufficient to carry any one State—but they have strength eno', if withdrawn from your friends, to endanger more than one. My present impression is that they will nominate Judge [John] McLean—I also think that Calhoun will run, & will probably take Vir—N.C—S.C. & Alaba—perhaps more. If he do, the quadrangular war must bring you all to the Bar of the House. There I persuade myself the Genl. cannot succeed—"

Believes, further, that the Anti-Masons in New York State will not support Clay because General Stephen Van Rensselaer "and other masons, your friends," had not supported Francis Granger's gubernatorial candidacy in 1830 [Clay to Johnston, May 9, 1830; Stoddard to Clay, November 8, 1830]. Feels that the Anti-Masons in New Jersey "will give us some trouble—still I believe we can prevail." Calls Clay's attention to a meeting in Orange, Essex County, N.J. [July 30, 1831], in which Clay was nominated for president with Southard as his running mate: "That was one of the strongest meetings, in point of character & influence, ever held in our State, & spoke the sentiments of the party in the State, as I am induced to believe—but our delegates to Balto. will do whatever is the genl. will."

Thinks that Richard Rush's attack on Masonry [Rush to Clay, June 1, 1831] was unwise, and "If his views prevail, much injury will be done your cause." Promises to write Clay again on these matters after the results of the Anti-Masonic convention in Baltimore [Clay to Brooke, June 23, 1831] on September 26 are known. Remarks in passing that the possibility of his own nomination for vice president by the Anti-Masons has been mentioned, but he cannot believe he can "come up to their standard [said facetiously]."

Urges Clay to run for the U.S. Senate [Clay to Beatty, June 8, 1830], noting that his presence in Washington "would be useful to the cause of correct principles—and there has seldom been a time when there was more necessity for all the talent & virtue which could be commanded—Nullification—Tariff—Internal Improvement. & many other questions & principles demand the guardianship of those who have capacity & influence to guide to a right decision." ALS. InU. For the Orange, N.J., nomination of Clay and Southard, see Trenton *New Jersey Journal*, July 26, 1831. Clay supporters in Indiana had not been able to agree on a single candidate in any of the congressional districts; hence, by fielding more than one candidate, they had split their votes and handed all the congressional seats to the Jacksonians. See Everett to Clay, August 20, 1831.

From John Sloane, Wooster, Ohio, September 24, 1831. Rather than "cavil with our friends in Kentucky because they were not more successful in the late election [Webster to Clay, April 4, 1831] we are rejoiced that things are as well as they are and think it ominous of a return to a better state of feeling." Notes that after the state elections [on October 11] delegates will be chosen to represent Ohio at the National Republican convention in Baltimore. Comments on Charles Hammond's "erratick" and "exotic" political course. "I regret extremely the course he has adopted but that is of no avail: he is strong in argument but a perfect child as to policy."

Approves Clay's running for the U.S. Senate [Clay to Beatty, June 8, 1830]. Reports that the Anti-Mason convention will soon produce its nominee [Clay to Brooke, June 23, 1831]. "Judge [John] McLean is spoken of by some as a candidate but it is almost exclusively among our enemies." ALS. MH. Hammond had opposed bringing Clay's name out early for the presidential nomination and had hinted that another person might better unite the forces opposed to Jackson. He also opposed the Frankfort convention and the Baltimore convention. See, Clay to Hammond, September 9; October 7, 1829; Clay to Greene, November 11, 1830; Clay to Conover, August 3, 1831.

To **EDGAR SNOWDEN**   Lexington, September 25, 1831

I received your favor of the 14th inst with the number of the [Alexandria] Gazette containing an account of the proceedings of the Citizens of Alexandria in regard to the Presidential election.[1] They afforded me very great gratification and excited grateful feelings for the friendly and favorite notice which they were pleased to take of me. I was happy to see that they had resolved to be represented at the Balto Convention,[2] an assembly which cannot fail from its respectablility and numbers, to exert a powerful influence on the public mind.

I have attentively examined that part of the preamble to which you have invited my attention. The greatest difficulty in making any concession to the South at this time, in respect to the Tariff, arises out of the violence of So Carolina. It is to be feared that advantage would be taken of such a concession hereafter by other States pursuing the exceptionable example of the threat of nullification[3] to extort from the general government measures in opposition to the general welfare.

Nevertheless the approach of the period of the extension of the National debt[4] renders it necessary to make a considerable modification of the existing tariff;[5] and I think Congress ought to enter upon the duty of modifying it without regard to the impotent menaces of South Carolina. And I believe that a modification may be made which would satisfy the *moderate* portion of our Southern fellow citizens, without endangering our Manufacturing establishments.

Three principles, it seems to me, ought to govern in a new arrangement of the Tariff: 1st To repeal or reduce duties to the amount of the ten millions annually appropriated to the sinking fund which will no longer be wanted after the debt is paid. 2nd to preserve the policy of protection unimpaired in its application to essential articles of Manufacture. And Consequently, in the third place, to make the repeal or reduction of duties operate exclusively on objects which do not come into competion with the productions of American agriculture or the fabrics of American manufacture.

Such are the general principles which I would carry into the consideration of the question. I communicate them for your information and not for publication. Any publication authorized by me, at the present time, would be liable to the interpretation of being a solicitation of Southern suffrages, and might also be prejudicial in the other section of the Union. Some fit occasion cannot fail to occur, in the course of the insuing winter, to present my views to the public myself.

The opinion I expressed at Cincinnati,[6] and which the Richmond Enquirer has perverted, was not in the smallest degree opposed to the above views. That opinion was that it would be unwise in the friends of the American System to allow its enemies to attack and undermine it in detail.

ALS. Courtesy of R. C. Ballard Thruston and The Filson Club, Louisville, Ky.   1. Snowden at this time was editor and proprietor of the Alexandria (Va.) Gazette.   2. Clay to Conover, Oct. 9, 1831.   3. Stoddard to Clay, Nov. 12, 1832.   4. Clay probably meant to write the word "retirement" instead of "extension." For some of the problems and politics involved in disposing of an expected surplus in the treasury, see Bray Hammond, *Banks and Politics in America* (Princeton, 1957), 451-55.   5. Webster to Clay, Jan 8, 1832.   6. On August 3, 1830.

From Josiah S. Johnston, Philadelphia, September 26, 1831. Reports, confidentially, that John McLean has been offered the Anti-Masonic nomination and has declined it, because "He says the person who can successfully contend with the President must be able to unite all the elements of the opposition." Describes the mood of the Anti-Masons, whose convention convenes today: "It appears to me they all become fanatic or like all new converts manifest an extraordinary degree of Zeal—They break at once from all political ties & associations—declare that anti masonry is the paramount interest of the Country to which all things must bend & engage in a furious Crusade against the whole order—& publish a ban of proscription against all its members—I believe if the masons run-mad too, they will put on the spirit of martyrdom & we shall have a bitter malignant persecuting war between them." Remarks that they are "going to Baltimore to nominate McLean"; and explains: "I do not know whether they are ignorant of his withdrawal or whether it is a Settled determination to nominate him notwithstanding [Clay to Brooke, June 23, 1831]."

Reports that the political news from New York is good, that John Sergeant and Samuel L. Southard are firm in Clay's cause, and that "Mr. Webster has taken an occasion to explain himself and to do away any suspicions of his disloyalty." On the other hand, "Anti Masonry is still gaining ground in the North & threatens to over run the whole Country north of Maryland—It places our Northern friends in an awkward position—If they attempt to resist the torrent, they may be overwhelmed & Carried away—It seems very probable it will bear down our friends—many think masonry not worth contending for & not worth preserving & who would be glad if the masons would give it up, who will not give up the N. republican party—or desert us & who think it ought not to be a National party—" Mentions also that Alexander H. Everett, Peter B. Porter, and William B. Rochester all recommend the closing of the Masonic lodges to improve Clay's political prospects in New York State [Porter to Clay, September 15, 1831].

Notes that Chief Justice John Marshall's "withdrawal from a political Nomination" is desirable since "We cannot Sustain the Court if the judges mingle in political affairs." Notes, too, that Marshall's poor health may soon require surgery and were he to die, Philip Barbour would "certainly" be appointed to the Supreme Court and William Johnson would be promoted to chief justice. "Then with another Judge [John McLean] a Candidate for the Presidency—with [Henry] Baldwin who I fear is a mere political judge—what would the Supreme Court be worth—"

Concludes that "the freetrade Convention [Brown to Clay, October 2, 1831] begins to assemble," and that the South Carolinians "will be very Ultra—& will be a small minority—It will come to a debate & they will disagree as much in principle & degree as they differ from the friends of the Amn. System—I think the Tariff may be satisfactorily modified—I mean to Satisfy Virginia & N. Carolina—Nothing will Satisfy the Nullifiers—but free trade—the President—or disunion—" ALS. InU.

As the presidential campaign progressed and Clay's chance of defeating Jackson seemed to diminish, Webster was suggested by some as a substitute candidate. Indeed, Webster explored carefully the possibility that he might supplant Clay as the party's nominee. To that end, he wrote to friends who had suggested such a course, arguing that while he had little hope that Clay could succeed, neither did he believe any other candidate could do better. For further details, see Norman D. Brown, *Daniel Webster And The Politics of Availability* (Athens, Ga., 1969), 8-11; Wiltse, *Webster Papers*, 3:119-20, 134-35; and Bartlett, *Daniel Webster*, 127.

Chief Justice John Marshall was also proposed by some as a presidential candidate, but he shunned all political overtures. On September 8, 1831, he wrote a letter declining even to serve on an Anti-Jackson central committee in Virginia, because the propriety of his public office, as well as his personal preference, forbade it. *Niles' Register* (September 24, 1831), 41:70. When he was approached by several Anti-Masons and asked to be their candidate, he declined that also. Gammon, *The Presidential Campaign of 1832*, 49. In October, 1831, Dr. Philip S. Physick operated on Marshall in Philadelphia for a stone in the bladder. Marshall recovered and continued to serve as chief justice until his death in 1835. Roger B. Taney was then appointed chief justice in 1836; Philip

P. Barbour was also appointed to the court that same year. Albert Beveridge, *The Life of John Marshall* (New York, 1919), 4:520.

From Henry Shaw, Boston, *ca.* September 27, 1831. Argues that "there is but one opinion on the course your [Kentucky] Legislature ought to take. . . . Indeed there is but one way by which the State can repel the Idea, that the late Elections hav[e] gone wrong [Webster to Clay, April 4, 1831]—we would all give up the 4 Members of C[ongress]. for one Senator—that being the Sentiment can you longer doubt—consent to come to W[ashingto]n. & we will *try* to *keep your there—*"

Encloses a letter to himself (Shaw) from Alexander H. Everett, dated September 25, 1831, in which Everett comments on the pessimism that spread among Clay followers after the results of the Kentucky state elections on August 1 were known. Notes that he has inserted in a forthcoming issue of the *North American Review* a notice of George D. Prentice's *Biography of Henry Clay,* "which I think or rather hope will help the cause a little and which—coming out at this moment—will serve to satisfy our friends throughout the Union—if they had any doubt before—that our course is fixed." ALS. DLC-HC (DNA, M212, R4). A review of Prentice's biography of Clay was published in the *NAR,* (1831), 33:351-96.

From Boyd McNairy, Nashville, September 28, 1831. Reports that "The strongest wish of your friends in this quarter is that you should be elected Senator—It is not your interest alone we look to, but our country also, and the condition of our public affairs at present requires the best heads and the most patriotic hearts to avert the impending danger—Your enemies will continue to abuse you, but let them, nothing can or will stop them—You must not be surprised if you hear of [John] Eaton being our next Senator, I am told from good Authority orders have been issued from the City—At present [Felix] Grundy is opposed by a warm and personal friend of mine Colo. [Ephraim] Foster—and if the election can be brought on he will certainly defeat him—They have certainly become tired of Grundy as I believe, indeed I have no doubt Old [John] Overton and other Jackson men of the same grade will try and keep off the elections, hoping that in one year that Eaton can be elected—If the election is brought on your friends will try & make Foster defeat Grundy, he is also a strong Jackson man, but he is a gentleman, and I cant say that of Grundy." In a postcript dated September 29, adds: "I think you may rely upon it, that the election will be put off. So that Eaton will die." ALS. DLC-HC (DNA, M212, R4). The Tennessee legislature tried and failed to put together a majority to elect a U.S. senator both at the 1831 regular session and at the 1832 special session. At the end of the session in 1833, after 55 ballots, Ephraim H. Foster withdrew as a candidate and Felix Grundy was elected. See Brian H. Walton, "A Matter of Timing: Elections to the United States Senate in Tennessee Before the Civil War," *THQ* (Summer, 1972), 31:134; and Thomas P. Abernethy, *From Frontier to Plantation in Tennessee* (Chapel Hill, 1932), 296.

From JOSIAH S. JOHNSTON Philadelphia, September 30, 1831
The Anti Masonic convention[1] thrown into confusion & altogether unprepared for such a Contingency, have nominated Mr. [William] Wirt as the last chance—They have tried every body else—& he is the only one willing to put himself upon such a Cast—I have not seen his acceptance I am convinced he cannot hav[e] made engagements with them—& that as far as his influence will go he will do all he can to Unite the elements of Opposition They may yet come back to us & we must treat them as if they would—

If he has made pledges to proscribe masons, he can not under any Circumstances receiv[e] favor from Us—If he has not then what hav[e] the party gain[e]d but a political purpose which probably lies at the bottom of the affair.

He has mistaken the path of ambition if not of duty & honor in deserting us & betraying our Cause—& he will receive his reward if he does not bring back the party to us—

You will be astonished when I tell you that on the 27th a letter was receiv[e]d here from him (*dated 30th*) speaking of our party our prospects—our [National Republican] Convention & anti masonry & Mr. [John Q.] Adams & Mr. [Richard] Rush Utterly at variance & inconsistent with the Course he has persued   He was then as anti-anti Masonic as any of us & agreed perfectly with us upon that question—[2]

He writes to [Samuel L.] Southard,[3] speculating upon the means of defeating the election of Jackson—Calculates the Chances—alludes to our Convention—& what is to be done &C. tells Southard he must prepare the address &C &C

He says of Rush, that he had written him a very Candid letter, which Mr. Rush did not like—& return[e]d him a husky answer—He says his Rushs Last letter is devoted to answering the objections in his letter.[4] Of Mr. Adams he says although a very honest man, we may expect something *wild* of him.

The letter is remarkable—I must try to get a sketch   It will be a very amusing thing if he becomes a devoted Anti Mason.

Mr. Adams is quite as wild & mad as Rush   He is an Anti Mason—[5]but like [John] McLean saw it a hopeless Chance to carry us.—

Wirt will take from us as little as any other man they could have selected—He will try to get back—

Our friends stand fast—They are excessively disgusted with Wirts extraordinary Conduct—but it does not change our position—or our Confidence—

The Convention met to day & after considerable debate on the mode of electing a President they adjoun[e]d[6]   Indeed the election involves a great principle shall he be chosen by the consolidation or the state principle—If the latter by them as equal Sovereign States or According to representation in Congress—or according to free population.—This preliminary principle, will run through their deliberations & their Votes—Some wish to discuss the Constitutionality others to avoid it—S. Carolina is pretty hot Virga. moderate Penna. & N. York cold—They will differ essentially upon every question

ALS. InU.   1. Clay to Brooke, June 23, 1831.   2. For Wirt's shift of political course, see McCarthy, "The Antimasonic Party," 531-35.   3. The Wirt-Southard correspondence on this point is discussed in Michael Birkner, "Politics, Law, and Enterprise in Jacksonian America: The Career of Samuel L. Southard, 1787-1842," Ph.D. dissertation, Princeton University, 1981, pp. 202-3.   4. Although the specific correspondence referred to has not been found, two letters from Wirt, dated Oct. 3 and Oct. 6, 1831, are included in Anthony M. Brescia (ed.), *The Letters and Papers of Richard Rush*, Series I, items 9928 and 9929. These letters indicate that the subject under discussion was Wirt's judgment in accepting the Anti-Masonic nomination.   5. Clay to Sloane, April 29, 1831.   6. The Free Trade or Anti-Tariff convention. See Brown to Clay, Oct. 2, 1831.

To SAMUEL L. SOUTHARD   Lexington, September 30, 1831

I regretted to learn by your favor of the 18h. inst. that you had been so seriously indisposed. I hope the convalescence which it also communicates is complete; and that you will use every precaution to preserve and establish your health. It is important not only to your family but to your Country.

We were mortified and disappointed with the issue of our Congressional elections in K.[1] It was owing to a reluctance of our people to change; to interference of the Genl. Government; and in one or two instances to bad arrangements of our friends. But the result of all the K. elections, for the Legislature as well as for Congress, proves Jackson to be in the minority And I am confident that our majority would have been much greater if the direct question of the P. Election had been submitted. We feel perfectly assured of a favorable decision, whenever the vote is taken on that question.

You ask our prospects in the West. I think Ohio, Kentucky, Indiana and Louisiana may be certainly counted on. Beyond them, although we have hopes of Missouri and Illinois, there is no certainty.[2]

I agree with you that the Anti Masonic party, altho' incapable of electing a Candidate of their own, hold the balance in their hands, if they act in a body. What will be their final course I am unable to predict. I presume they have made a nomination at Balto. of Mr. [John] McLean of Ohio; and I imagine he will decline it.[3] I have heard that he would, 'tho not from himself. I think he will, because an acceptance of the nomination would prostrate him. If he, or whoever shall be nominated, should decline, matters will be brought to the issue which I have had reason to believe some of the leaders desired, and then they will support me. Mr. [Richard] Rush's course is exceedingly strange, and I lament it both on his and my account. I am afraid he has done himself irreparable injury.[4] He sought most urgently to induce me to make some declaration which would conciliate or satisfy the Anti Masons. I declined. He renewed his entreaty again, and I respectfully but decisively declined again. It would have ruined me politically. It would have been such a direct solicitation for suffrages that I must have incurred the contempt of all parties, and I should have felt that I richly deserved it. There were many reasons against the act.

Whatever the States may do to put down Masonry, the G. Government can do nothing. The Constitution gives it no power over the subject. The Antis have hitherto proceeded upon the principle of *forcing* our party to join them. That is impracticable. If the question were brought to the point of taking an Anti Masonic Candidate, with all his exclusive principles, proscription &c. or re-electing Andw. Jackson, thousands of our friends would embrace the latter alternative. They would say we had better continue the old tyrant than elect a new one—better stick to the old volcano, than open a new one. He can burn but four years longer, but no one can tell how long the eruptions of the new one would endure nor how far they would spread.

I care not a straw for Masonry. I never did. It never influenced my conduct in public or private life, but I will not say so to the public at this time. I regret that my friends [Peter B.] Porter and [William B.] Rochester have published any thing about me, on that subject. Their motives were friendly, but I would not have advised the publication, if I had been previously consulted, which I was not.[5]

You say the Balto. Convention in Decr. will nominate me. My wish is that, without regard to my feelings, they should nominate that individual of our friends who has the best prospect of defeating Jackson. That should be the great object to which every minor consideration ought to yield. I am not sufficiently unbiased to say whether I am that individual or not.

I do not see any thing like a concentration of public sentiment on any person for the V. Presidency. At Pittsburg[h], you see they recommend Mr. [William] Wirt.[6] All appear willing to leave it to the Convention, and I have no doubt that he whom it shall designate will meet the wishes of our friends. I shall be most happy if the Convention shall nominate you. As you are no Mason, such a nomination might be agreeable to the Antis' as I am sure it would be to our friends generally. I think you ought to go to the Convention, if you can without too much sacrifice. I do not think that you ought to be restrained by the possibility of your nomination. Spencer,[7] Wirt and perhaps others whose names have been mentioned in connection with that office will be there.

There is a remarkable degree of concurrence among my friends, in and out of the State, as to the expediency of my going to the Senate,[8] and I am not aware of any difficulty at home. [John J.] Crittenden would offer no impediment. But I have great repugnance to the service, and have not yet, brought myself to say that I will accept the seat. I shall think of the matter and decide when our Legislature meets, which is called for November.

Mrs. Clay unites with me in affectionate regards to Mrs. Southard and your family. Be pleased to present mine also to my young friend Miss Virginia,[9] and tell her that I am greatly obliged by the kind interest which she takes in what concerns me. I have her's also much at heart. Tell her that unless an exceedingly clever fellow offers himself not to change her name until I see her, which I hope will not be a great while.

Henry [Clay, Jr.] fully intended to call on you and stay a day or two. He so wrote to me. Something prevented it—His intention is to quit the Army and study law. He will pass the ensuing winter at N. Orleans, whither I purpose going myself, if my destiny does not lead me in some other direction. . . . P.S. Are we to regret Taliaferro's defeat?[10] If the Anti Masons nominate you, and put the nomination upon exclusive ground don't accept.

ALS. NjP. 1. Webster to Clay, April 4, 1831. 2. Sergeant to Clay, June 27, 1831. 3. Clay to Brooke, June 23, 1831. 4. Rush to Clay, June 1, 1831. 5. Porter to Clay, Sept. 15, 1831. 6. The Pittsburgh convention of August 27, 1831, passed resolutions recommending Clay for president and Wirt for vice president and also naming delegates to the National Republican convention in December. Washington *Daily National Journal*, Sept. 7, 1831. 7. Probably John C. Spencer who served as president of the Anti-Masonic convention. 8. Clay to Beatty, June 8, 1830. For Crittenden's role in the election of Clay to the U.S. Senate, see Kirwan, *Crittenden*, 90-91; see also, Worsley to Clay, Oct. 22, 1831. 9. Southard's daughter. 10. John Taliaferro of Fredericksburg, Va., was defeated by John M. Patton, his townsman, for reelection to the U.S. House, 22nd Congress. For both men, see *BDAC*.

From James Brown, Philadelphia, October 2, 1831. States that he is "happy to find [Clay to Brown, August 24, 1831] that you bear what I always predicted, with suitable resolution, and I even hope that the loss of the Presidency would eventuate . . . in the gain of more substantial advantages than can be expected in the palace at Washington."

Notes that "The nomination of your friend [William] Wirt [Clay to Brooke, June 23, 1831] has astonished every one here, not less than the Antimasonic frenzy of [John Q.] Adams and [Richard] Rush. It is not improbable that this strange excitement may carry with it Vermont Massachusetts New Jersey and even Pennsylvania. Some think that Virginia may also vote for Mr Wirt [Sergeant to Clay, June 27, 1831]—The leading Virginians who are members of the Anti Tariff [Free Trade] Convention would prefer Calhoun could they believe that his Nullification doctrines could be rendered palatable in that State." Continues: "The [Free Trade] Convention has appointed [James] Barbour to preside and a Committee of two members from each State has been raised to prepare Materials for discussion. Some persons think that much dissention may grow out of the proceedings of this meeting—The delegates from the South wish to discuss the question of the constitutionality of the Tariff. The Northern members are opposed to raising the question. Forty members from Virginia are in attendance."

Reports that he has made inquiries about a position "in a Commercial House to place your Son [James Brown Clay]." States that "Few Merchants here are doing business here on an extensive scale," but that Gen. Winfield Scott has suggested that a place might be obtained for James "in some large importing house at New York." Suggests Clay write his "old friend" John Jacob Astor who could probably help on the matter. Mentions that Gen. Scott expects Henry Clay, Jr., "to return and study law in New York."

Concludes: "Many persons here have expressed a curiosity to know whether you wished to enter the Senate. The next winter it is said will be one of much agitation in that body as it is believed to be nearly equally divided for and against the Administration. In times like the present I see but few inducements if you study your interest or comfort to become a Member of Congress." ALS. DLC-HC (DNA, M212, R4). Published in *LHQ*, 24:1158. The anti-tariff or free trade convention met in Philadelphia September 30 to October 7, 1831. Delegates from 14 states met to discuss their grievances against the existing tariff structure and to memorialize Congress. Among the prominent Virginians present were James Barbour, Burwell Bassett, James M. Gainett, John W. Jones, and George C. Dromgoole. Washington *Daily National Journal*, October 3, 4, 5, 6, 8, 10, 11, 1831. Not to be confused with the Friends of the Protective Tariff (or Friends of American Industry), led by Joseph Hemphill and Mathew Carey, who met in Philadelphia on September 26 and nominated 32 delegates to attend the tariff convention [Davis to Clay, November 2, 1831] scheduled for New York City on October 26, 1831. Washington *Daily National Journal*, September 29, 1831.

From Henry A.S. Dearborn, Roxbury, Mass., October 2, 1831. Urges Clay to return to the U.S. Senate, because "all your numerous friends in this section of the Union" anxiously desire that "you should yield your personal objections, for the good of the country." Continues: "It requires the powerful influence, of the patriotic, intelligent, virtuous & honest, to check the mad & ruinous course of an ignorant & unprincipled administration. The republic is in a fearful condition, & nothing can save it from ruin, but the powerful cooperation of our ablest & best men." Believes, further, that "A spirit of proscription & persecution has been evinced, which rivals in baseness & extravagance, the worst ebulitions, in the worst periods of the French revolution."

Predicts that "there will be a revulsion" against Anti-Masonry, a fanatic faction "as odius and contempable, as it is unchristian, irrational & wicked." It will, "Like witchcraft . . . rage for a season & then the deluded fools will look back with astonishment, & ask how they became such dupes."

Argues also that any National Republican candidate other than Clay is "out of the question." Concludes: "*We have nailed our colours to the mast*, & will gain the victory, by a glorious conflict, or *go down* with honor. There must be no hesitation — no doubts, — no want of confidence in success. The victory is *sure*, if we do our duty. We have a cause which would inspire the dead to action, and a general spirit of determined, united & energetic cooperation must pervade the whole Union. there is no time to be lost. . . . The Convention, in December, must speak in a voice, that shall electrify the nation & send dismay into the ranks of the enemy; and whether, few or many lead on the opposing forces, the national republicans will know but *one leader, one champion*, & Henry Clay is the man." ALS. DLC-HC (DNA, M212, R4).

From John Sergeant, Philadelphia, October 3, 1831. Writes that "Nothing could have been more unexpected" than the nomination of William Wirt by the Anti-Masonic convention at Baltimore [Clay to Brooke, June 23, 1831]. States: "Few things could have given me more uncomfortable feelings. I have not yet got the better of them sufficiently to speak of the matter with any patience. In the first instance, some of our friends were disposed to believe that Mr. W. was working for us, and that in one way or other his nomination was to be made to help the cause. All such speculations are now at an end. He has been working for himself, under the influence probably (self love being an egregious flatterer) of the same foolish notion which was entertained by A.M's, that *we* should be obliged to support him. If so, he has made a great mistake, and that mistake will make him more than ridiculous." Predicts that Wirt will get no support, except from the Anti-Masons "and even *that* a little weakened by the part he and they have acted." Believes that Calhoun's supporters, "(Duff Green included)," will attempt to convince Clay's friends that "if we all unite cordially in favor of Mr. Wirt, Jackson will be turned out" and that "we cannot otherwise succeed." Continues: "The President [John C. Spencer of N.Y.] of the A. M. Convention called upon me, on his way home, and laboured for a long time in that strain. I endeavoured to undeceive him, by giving him plainly to understand that I had long since made up my mind and saw no reason to change it, and that I firmly believed our friends generally would come to the same conclusion — I went even so far as to say (and I said it sincerely and still adhere to it) that if from any cause whatever we should be deprived of the candidate of our choice, I would withdraw from the whole affair and occupy myself with my own concerns — Such is in fact the only position I am capable of taking. It is the only one that is consistent with integrity of purpose, and with that duty which men associated as a party owe to one another — The injury we receive from this nomination is chiefly, if not solely, in the persevering determination it exhibits on the part of the A. M's. The sooner it is met by a corresponding determination on our part, the better, for until this is some how made manifest, the conclusion will be that we may give way, but they will not, and, that being the case, we shall suffer all the evil consequences of an impression that we are finally to yield, that is to say, that our cause is hopeless. We must let them know that our flag is nailed. I hope some opportunity for doing so, will soon occur. We shall have it, at the Convention in Baltimore, at all events, unless, indeed, treachery should find its way into that body, and Jacksonism, having manoeuvred under the cloak of Anti Masonry, should now assume the garb of National Republicanism." Concludes by entreating Clay to "Come to the Senate." ALS. InU.

To FRANCIS T. BROOKE   Lexington, October 4, 1831

I was rejoiced to learn by your letter of the 4h. ulto. that both your health and spirits were good. I hope they have so continued and may long remain.

I have received no letter from Mr. [Thomas Jefferson] Randolph lately. I do not think it worth while longer to press him on a point which he evidently evades.[1]

It appears to me to be right that I should put you in possession of at least a brief outline of the policy which I think adapted to the present state of our Country. This I do not for the purpose of publication, but that you may have the means of correcting any error that may fall in your way as to my real opinions. Such a correction might also, if necessary, be made in the [Richmond *Constitutional*] Whig, not however to be done at my instance, nor upon my authority.

I agree with Mr. [John C.] Calhoun that the next Session of Congress is a suitable time for such a modification of the Tariff as is called for by the near approach of the payment of the public debt. The modification may be prospective, to take effect on the happening of that event, or if there be any particular article the duty on which is burthensome, there might as to that duty be an immediate reduction or abolition. There is a great advantage to merchants as well as consumers to have adequate notice of a change in the existing tariff. The Executive too might avail itself of the contemplated and distant alteration to secure, in consideration of it, more favorable terms of Commercial Intercourse with Foreign powers.

There ought, I think, to be a dispensation with duties to an amount, after the paymt. of the public debt, equal to the sinking fund of ten millions which are annually appropriated to that object. This should be effected by an abolition or reduction of duties on articles not coming into compctition with the produce of our Agriculture or the fabrics of our manufacturers. In other words,

412

I think the principle of protection should be preserved unimpaired, in its application to our domestic industry; but, at the same time that no more revenue should be collected than is necessary to an economical administration. Laws ought to be passed to enforce a strict execution of the Tariff, by detecting and punishing all evasions. An arrangement of the Tariff upon the principles stated would be in conformity with what was always formerly admitted by Southern statesmen, that is that protection might be incidentally afforded in the collection of Revenue.

I have no idea of the propriety of laying or continuing duties for the purpose of accumulating surpluses. And as to the doctrine of distributing any such surpluses among the several states, I think there is not the slightest authority for it in the Constitution. The general government can no more devolve upon the States the duty of discharging any one of its own powers, than the States can delegate to the General Government, without an amendment of the Constitution, the duty of local or municipal legislation.

In regard to Internal Improvements, I never have thought or contended that a single cent of duty ought to be laid or *continued* for their promotion. I believe the power is possessed by the General Government. In any prudent adjustment of the Tariff, to produce a revenue, say of twelve millions, sound policy requires that a deficit should be guarded against, by laying duties enough. In some years, owing to the fluctuations of commerce, there may be a surplus, which might not be wanted. Such an occasional surplus I would apply to the purpose of Int. Improvements.

But the great resource on which I think we should rely for that object, after the payment of the public debt, is the proceeds of the sales of the public lands.[2] There is an obvious fitness in such an appropriation. And I think that a more liberal application to the Western States ought to be made of this fund than to the others for two reasons 1st. that the public domain is there situated, and improvements in that quarter have a tendency to enhance the value of the unsold residue. 2dly. As a sort of counter-balance to the expenditure on a Navy and Fortifications, which are for the more immediate benefit of the Maritime frontier. It is true that each part of the Union is concerned in the safety and prosperity of every other part. But this interest is sometimes only indirect. The Maritime States would have quite as much of this indirect interest in Internal Improvements made, under the authority of the Genl. Govt. in the West, as the Western States would have in Eastern fortifications and a Navy. But I would leave the consideration of what is due to the Western States, from the above views, to the enlightened sense of Congress.

I think the Charter of the Bank of the U.S. ought to be renewed upon equitable conditions. I am perfectly willing to abide by the reasons which I assigned for a change of my opinion (the only change of opinion I ever made on any great political question) relative to that institution, and which are to be found in my published speeches [1:527].

I have thus hastily sketched my views of the policy which is applicable to the present condition of our Country. I repeat that they are not intended for publication, nor, for reasons, which will readily occur to you, do I wish any Copy of this letter given to any one, for any purpose.

The doings of the Anti Masonic Convention at Balto. have not yet reached us.[3] From all I have heard, I presume Mr. [John] McLean of Ohio has been nominated. I do not believe that he has the moral courage to accept the nomination. But, to quote from your neighbour, nous verrons. If the alternative be between Andw. Jackson, and an Anti Masonic Candidate, with his exclusive proscriptive principles, I should be embarrassed in the choice. I am not sure that the old tyranny is not better than a new one. That can endure, at the farthest, only four or five years more, whilst the latter might be of indefinite duration. The one is an exhausted volcano, the other would be the bursting of a new eruption spreading no one can tell to what extent, nor how long it would last.

I believe that either Mr. McLean will not accept, or if he does that he will be ultimately abandoned from the impracticability of his election, in which case the great body of the Anti Masons will support me not because they love me, but because they hate Jackson more, and because there is greater coincidence between their political principles and mine.

You suggest the propriety of publishing an extract from a letter you addressed to me, disclaiming any wish for a Federal appointment in any contingency.[4] I have seen nothing which questions your disinterestedness; and therefore why make the publication? Might such a publication not be deemed a gratuitous and unnecessary display? I request your reconsideration.

I am glad that Virginia resolves to be represented in the Balto. Convention.[5] Whatever doubts originally might have existed about the policy of that movement it has now proceeded too far to be abandoned. And it is therefore desirable that there should be a full & respectable assembly.

I am strongly urged to go to the Senate; and I am now considering whether I can subdue my repugnance to the service.[6]

ALS. KyU. Printed in Colton, *Clay Correspondence*, 4:314-17. 1. Clay to Brooke, August 17, 1830. 2. For Clay's position on the distribution of the proceeds from the sale of public lands, see Glyndon G. Van Deusen, *The Life of Henry Clay* (Boston, 1937), 252-55. 3. Clay to Brooke, June 23, 1831. 4. Reference in Brooke to Clay, March 6, 1831, omitted by editors. 5. Clay to Conover, Oct. 9, 1831. 6. Clay to Beatty, June 8, 1830.

To JOHN SLOANE   Lexington, October 4, 1831

I recd. your agreeable favor of the 24h. Ulto. which breathes a spirit of perseverance and cheerfulness quite exhilerating in comparison with the despondence to which some have yielded themselves. Our friends in K. generally did the best they could, and if the result of the elections fell short of the hopes and wishes which prevailed out of the State, it was also short of ours' and occassioned us much mortification as well as disappointment. Except in the Congressional elections, we were however successful. We shall have a friendly Senator, and the issue of all the elections demonstrated that we have the majority.[1] I am urged by friends in and out of the State, with a remarkable degree of unanimity, to go to the Senate. Mr. [John J.] Crittenden would offer no impediment. But I have great repugnance to the service, and am considering whether I can subdue it. I shall decide definitively when the Legislature meets in Novr.[2]

Mr. Jno. McLean, I take it for granted, has been nominated at Balto. by the Anti-Masonic Convention.[3] I think we may anticipate either that he will not accept the nomination or that, if he does, he will be finally abandoned, from the utter hopelessness of his election. This latter consequence will be insured and accelerated by firmness on the part of the N. Republicans. I have no doubt that the Antis' have calculated that they would force us to join them by our presumed dislike of Jackson. When they are undeceived in that particular they will be more reasonable. I really should feel some embarrassment in a choice between Andw. Jackson, and an Anti Masonic Candidate, with his exclusive proscriptive principles. I should fear that it would be a mere exchange of tyrannies, with this difference that the old one is a volcano, nearly exhausted, and that the new one might prove to be a fresh volcano enabling a stream of political lava, for an indefinite duration of time, and of boundless extent. Good policy however recommends that we should continue to treat the Antis' kindly and leave to the Jackson party the office of abusing them. We should address friendly remonstrances to them, and ask what Constitutional power has the Federal Govt. in regard to Masonry or Anti Masonry? Will they expose it to a continued danger of misrule, or vital points, respecting which it *can* act, for the sake of an attempt to introduce into the Presidential Chair an Anti Masonic, who could not act in furtherance of his views?

[Discusses his positions on the extinction of the public debt, tariff readjustment, internal improvements, the handling of expected Treasury surpluses, and the Bank of the United States in terms similar to those used in Clay to Brooke of the same date. Continues:]

These views are confidentially communicated for an exchange of opinions and not for any eye but your own. I ought to add that the charter of the B. of the U. S. should, in my opinion, be renewed, on equitable conditions; and perhaps the bonus[4] might also be appropriated to Int. Improvements.

Since I commenced this letter, I have recd. intelligence that Mr. McLean declines the Anti Masonic nomination. His moral courage failed him I presume; for I think it pretty evident that he has been wooing that party.

Mr. [Josiah S.] Johnston writes me from Philada.[5] that our friends are every where firm, and resolved, at all hazards, to adhere. He says indeed that they are enthusiastic.

ALS. MH.   1. Webster to Clay, April 4, 1831.   2. Clay to Beatty, June 8, 1830.   3. Clay to Biddle, June 23, 1831.   4. Treasury surplus.   5. Johnston to Clay, Sept. 30, 1831.

From Edwin Upshur Berryman, New York, October 5, 1831. Reports having made "the necessary arrangements for sending out our Horse Stamboul [Clay to Atwood, September 15, 1831]" from Long Island to Kentucky "in four or five days." Believes it "will prove a first rate stock Horse but I do not think that his general appearance will strike you as any thing remarkably fine—" Continues: "You can recommend him as a *sure foal gettor*, as I permitted two of my friends to foal their Mares to him free of expense & they both proved with foal. I would recommend the Sale of part of him or even the whole provided it can be done to advantage—I think $2,000 for the whole or in the Same proportion for part of him would be a good price as I could send you a Horse of much finer appearance, that I think would do better in Kenty. The Horse I allude to is Sir Lovel. His appearance is very fine. Seven years old, blood Bay full Sixteen hands high, got by Duroc the Sire of Eclipse, & his dam Light Infantry the best blood of the country—His reputation as a running Horse is equal to that of any other Horse we have had, having beaten the celebrated racers Ariel & Arietta—He is owned by Jno H. Coster Esqr who I think would take $3500. his price is $4,000   Mr Coster would prefer Selling one half of him to Some gentleman in Kty who would see that he was well taken care of."

Hopes to visit Lexington in November and provide "news from your friends The *National Republicans* in N York. They are *determined* not to desert the good cause under *any circumstances* short of your express wishes on the Subject." ALS. Josephine Simpson Collection, Lexington, Ky.

415

From Daniel Webster, Boston, October 5, 1831. Reports that "some considerable regret was felt in this quarter" about the results of the Kentucky election [Webster to Clay, April 4, 1831], but that now "a general satisfaction . . . prevails, & all think that Kentucky has . . . declared ag[ains]t. the present Administration" by a certain, if not great, majority. Expresses his "gratitude to the good men of Kentucky, for the firmness with which they have breasted the storm."

Observes that Clay "must be aware . . . of the strong drive manifested in many parts of the Country, that you should come into the Senate." States: "I should rejoice, personally, to meet you in the Senate [Clay to Beatty, June 8, 1830]. I am equally sincere in saying that the *cause* would, under present circumstances be materially benefitted by your presence there. I know nothing so likely to be useful. Every thing valuable in the Govt. is to be fought for, & we need your arm, in the fight. At the same time, My Dear Sir, I would not, even thus privately & confidentially to you, say any thing not consistent with delicacy & friendship for Mr. [John J.] Crittenden; for whose character I have great regard. . . . Wd. to God, we could have you both at this crisis, in the public Councils!"

Notes that the next session of Congress will be "arduous" and "interesting." Adds that "Every thing is to be attacked. An array is preparing, much more formidable than has ever yet assaulted what we think the leading & important public interests. Not only the Tariff, but the Constitution itself, in its elementary & fundamental provisions, will be assailed with talent, vigor, & union. Every thing is to be debated, as if nothing had ever been settled." ALS. DLC-HC (DNA, M212, R4). Printed in Wiltse, *Webster Papers*, 3:128-30; and Colton, *Clay Correspondence*, 4:317-19.

To Nathaniel F. Williams, Baltimore, October 5, 1831. Applauds Williams's "spirit of firmness and cheerfulness" in the National Republican cause. Continues: "The calculation of the Antimasons has been to force our party to support their Candidate. By early demonstrations that they will be disappointed in that calculation, I think in the end the major part of them would come to us. To promote this object, the door should be left open to them, and consequently they should be treated kindly, but at the same time with a firm indication that we did not mean to run away from all the great interests of the Country, now in peril, after Anti Masonry." ALS. MCM.

From John L. Lawrence, New York, October 6, 1831. States that he has "abstained hitherto" from writing Clay about "the propriety of your coming to the Senate [Clay to Beatty, June 8, 1830]." Argues that "Circumstances have now however arisen, which make it, I think, indispensable, that you should soon be at Washington and if your appearance there as a Senator be deemed unadviseable, the calls of professional business, which would arise in case of your willingness to proceed to the Capital, should not be disregarded." Reports that rumors have circulated "that you would retire from the Presidential contest," and these have "excited considerable feeling among many of our friends, and much uncertainty among others." Believes that "To aid the course of events—to encourage ardour, and repress despondency—it is necessary I think that you should be at that point of the Union where our friends may have ready and frequent communication with you—where the honest and sincere may look for an index of their course—and where the means are at hand of effectively putting down the lie of one day, with the truth of the next. Had such been heretofore your position, the miserable intrigues which have by turns disgusted us by their folly, or provoked us by their insolence, would have been unknown or abortive." ALS. DLC-HC (DNA, M212, R4).

From Josiah S. Johnston, Philadelphia, October 8, 1831. Gives assurance "that the Anti Masonic nomination [Clay to Brooke, June 23, 1831] has produced little effect upon our party—We shall adhere as firmly as before—" Finds William Wirt's acceptance of the nomination to be "as extraordinary as his miraculous conversion [to Anti-Masonry]." States that "There is a great degree of delicasy in the papers towards Mr. Wirt, but he cannot fail to hear from private Sources & he will soon learn from public ones that treachery in politicks is nearly allied to treachery in war & will receive the same reward—I had myself seen the letters referred to by Mr. Wirt which he had written to his friends   they present his Conduct in no enviable light   He has disuaded his own friends from accepting the nomination—ridiculed Mr. [Richard] Rush & Mr. [John Q.] Adams & that not four days before the acceptance. . . . He Was the only man they could get   he was the only one who had the weakness and the folly to catch at that desperate chance   I do not know that it will operate injuriously to us, by the aid of our friends they may take N. york & Penna. from Jackson—but we shall adhere under all Circumstances—our friends are firm at Boston & N. york—"

Mentions that Jackson "has been sick but he will not die." Fears for Chief Justice John Marshall who is also ill [Johnston to Clay, September 26, 1831], because "Much indeed depends on his life—"

Concludes: "The [Anti-Tariff] Convention [Brown to Clay, October 2, 1831] has adjourned after making an address which you will read—The ring leaders in S. Carolina I believe are bent on Revolution—a fierce struggle is now going on—If [James] Hamilton gets a majority of the Legislature, there is no doubt—& We shall have a petite guerre between the young & the old chief [Jackson]   We must repeal the duties upon all articles not made in the Country & bring the others down to the protecting point—" ALS. InU.

To JAMES F. CONOVER   Lexington, October 9, 1831
I recd. your favor of the 6h. inst.   The acceptance of Mr. [William] Wirt of the Anti Masonic nomination has excited as much surprize at Lexington and with me as it has done at Cincinnati.[1] I had supposed when it was offered to him that he would seize the occasion to give it some turn favorable to the cause to which he was supposed to be zealously attached. Up to the 26h. of September his name is particularly mentioned in letters which I recd. from Philada. as being firmly decided and cordially united with us. But I suppose the ex-Attorney General found, in the magnitude of the fee presented to his acceptance, sufficient motives to silence all scruples as to the goodness of one cause, which he was called upon to expouse, and for the desertion of another to which he stood pledged by the highest considerations of honor.

A friend [Josiah S. Johnston] possessing my greatest confidence writes me from Philada. under date the 30h. Septr. a letter from which I make the following extracts. "The Anti Masonic Convention, thrown into confusion, and altogether unprepared for such a contingency, have nominated Mr. Wirt as the last chance. They have tried every body else and he is the only one willing to put himself upon such a cast. . . . He has mistaken the path of ambition if not of duty and honor [in deserting us & betraying our Cause],[2] and he will receive his reward if he does not bring back the party to us. You will be astonished when I tell you that on the 27th. a letter was received here from him (*dated 30h*) speaking of our party, our prospects, our Convention, and Anti Masonry, and Mr. [John Q.] Adams and Mr. [Richard] Rush utterly at variance and inconsistent with the course he has pursued. We [*sic*, he] was then as Anti-Anti-Masonic as any of us and agreed perfectly with us upon that question. He writes to [Samuel L.] Southard, speculating upon the means of defeating [the election of][3] Jackson—calculates the chances—alludes to our

417

[National Republican] Convention and what is to be done &c tells Southard he must prepare the Address &c.

"He says of Rush that he had written him a very candid letter, which Mr. Rush did not like and returned him a very husky answer. . . . Of Mr. Adams he says although a very honest man, we may expect some thing wild of him. The letter is remarkable, I must try to get a sketch. [It will be a very amusing thing if he becomes a devoted Anti-Mason.]⁴

"Mr. Adams is quite as wild and mad as Rush. He is an Anti Mason but like [John] McLean saw it was a hopeless chance to carry us.

"Wirt will take from us as little as any other man they could have selected. He will try to get back. Our friends stand fast. They are excessively disgusted with Wirts extraordinary conduct, but it does not change our position or our confidence."⁵

But without dwelling further on this strange event, I agree, that the essential enquiry is what are to be its effects—what ought to be done in the present circumstances?

More than ever now is manifest the wisdom of the Balto. Convention which is to assemble in Decr.⁶ I think we should now exert every energy to make it numerous, powerful and respectable; and that we should all abide by its decision. And in the mean time that there ought to be a forebearance to attack Anti Masonry or Mr. Wirt. This forebearance is advisable from two considerations 1st. Possibly the convention may think it politic to nominate him; but 2dly. if not it is prudent to leave the door open to his party and him to unite with us.

Exceptionable as I must think Mr. Wirts conduct has been, I would gladly see an union upon him, if it could certainly secure the defeat of Jackson. But is such an union practicable? Will the People of the U. States consent to make Anti Masonry the basis of a P. Election? These are questions for the consideration of the Balto. Convention.

Your article⁷ in Mr. [Charles] Hammond's paper [Cincinnati *Daily Gazette*] was most seasonable and exhilarating. It has been extensively circulated, more so than any article of a similar kind

ALS. ViU. 1. Clay to Brooke, June 23, 1831. 2. Information in brackets supplied from Johnston to Clay, Sept. 30, 1831. 3. *Ibid.* 4. *Ibid.* 5. Clay corrected and smoothed Johnston's punctuation and capitalization throughout this quotation. The two ellipses are Clay's. See *ibid.* 6. The National Republican convention met in Baltimore on Dec. 12-16, 1831. The convention chose James Barbour as its president and elected four vice presidents and two secretaries. It then proceeded to nominate Henry Clay for president of the United States and John Sergeant for vice president. See McKee, *The National Conventions and Platforms* . . . , 28-30. 7. Probably a reference to a letter of Conover of June 15, 1831, published in the Cincinnati *Daily Gazette* on June 16, expanding the reasons for his physical attack on the editor of the Cincinnati *Advertiser and Ohio Phoenix* a few days earlier. While he was editor of the Cincinnati *American*, he felt it was his duty to endure without comment the libelous attacks of the *Advertiser's* editorials, he said. But despite the fact that he had not worked for the *American* for five months, the attacks had continued. The previous Saturday's *Advertiser* carried an article accusing him of still having a concern in the editorial direction of the *American* and "falsely charging upon me . . . . a gross immorality, which, if true, ought to exclude me from respectable society." On Monday Conover had encountered the editor of the *Advertiser* and had inflicted "personal chastisement" on him. Charged with assault, Conover maintained that he was willing to abide by the verdict of an impartial jury.

From Rice Garland, Opelousas, La., October 11, 1831. Reports that "Since the result of the elections in your State [Webster to Clay, April 4, 1831] have been known your friends in this quarter have looked with the most intense interest for the effects it was like to have upon other sections of the Country. Here we have never wavered, and we are glad to see that no bad effects are likely to result in any other quarter—Many have been disappointed, but none have been induced to abandon the cause. We are taught by it, the necessity of greater unanimity and more decided exertion. So long as there is hope left us, your *friends* in this section are determined to stand by you, and they are numerous and influential. The change in public opinion in the Western part of this State is very great. Many supporters of the Administration are gradually withdrawing, and many more are becoming cool and indifferent. . . . I know many individuals who in 1828 were the warmest supporters of Genl. Jackson, that now openly oppose his re-election, whilst among those who were then his opponents there is not one, who is not so now."

States that Judge [Henry A.] Bullard will represent this congressional district [third] at the National Republican convention in Baltimore and that Josiah S. Johnston and James Brown "will be requested to attend as Delegates from the State generally." Notes that the Louisiana legislature will convene on November 14 and will shortly thereafter choose a senator to replace Edward Livingston [Porter to Clay, June 10, 1831]. Predicts that "the election of Judge [George A.] Waggaman is nearly certain." Informs Clay that it is "the desire of all" of his "most intelligent friends from different sections of the State" that he consent to being elected to the U.S. Senate [Clay to Beatty, June 8, 1830]. Louisiana "has interests of great magnitude at stake, and her people feel that on you they can rely to aid her Representatives in the National Councils in advocating and sustaining those interests." Believes that "Mr [John J.] Crittenden would willingly withdraw the claims he may have, when he learns it is the general wish of your friends and political supporters, that you should be elected." Promises that "at the polls in November 1832 we shall give the most decided proofs of our determination to support the principles upon which we think our National safety and prosperity rests, and the man who advocates them. My humble efforts shall be exerted to the utmost in the cause, which I sincerely hope may be successful." ALS. DLC-HC (DNA, M212, R4). Johnston and Bullard both served as delegates to the National Republican convention; Brown did not. Cincinnati *American*, December 23, 1831.

From John Sloane, Wooster, Ohio, October 15, 1831. Expresses surprise at the result of the Anti-Masonic convention at Baltimore [Clay to Brooke, June 23, 1831]. "As this result was never anticipated by any one, it is not easy to conjecture what may be its bearing on the Presidential election." Believes it is too soon to tell whether or not William Wirt "will continue a candidate, regardless of prospects, & probable consequences." Notes that "as regards our own course there is no cause for hesitating: we are upon principle opposed to the miserable misrule under which the country is suffering; and in justice to our principles; we are bound to make all the opposition in our power." Adds: "If . . . we should leave him [Jackson] to be elected without opposition, other than that of Anti-Masonry and Nullification, it will do much towards handing his name down to future generations, as a man of such commanding qualifications, and unquestioned integrity, that his most active enemies cowered before the brilliancy of his Administration, and left him to enjoy the public suffrage a second time without opposition. Should we thus act, we should be culpable as accessories in deceiving those who are to come after us, in a matter of incalculable importance to the cause of Republican government in all time to come."

Advises Clay that he should take a seat in the U.S. Senate where he could best communicate to the public his views "of the policy proper to be pursued in the event of the complete extinguishment of the public debt." Predicts that when the debt is paid, there will be a "clamour of the opponents of protection" and that "it would seem proper that they should be met in advance by a system suited to the new state of things." Advocates either the reduction or repeal of duties "on all articles which come not in competition with our home production." Believes that "To this branch of the policy I can see no ground for objection, on the part of the friends of the American System, except so far as it may have a bearing on internal improvements."

Confesses that "internal improvements by the general government has to my mind not been without its embarrassment." Because of this, "I would then say let the revenue be so established, as to be certain of a sufficient sum to meet all necessary demands, under any and all circumstances; and occasionally there would of consequence be a surplus, to which I would add the whole proceeds of the Public Lands and whatever might arise from the Bank of the United States, which ought to be rechartered. This I would say ought to be set apart as a fund for internal improvement."

Mentions his doubts as to the honesty and sincerity of those "who composed the Free Trade Convention, lately assembled at Philadelphia [Brown to Clay, October 2, 1831]." States that "I cannot believe these men actuated by a wish to promote the general public good, any more than I can that Mr Calhouns present Nullification doctrines are the honest convictions of his mind." Says he has heard he will be appointed as a delegate to the National Republican convention in Baltimore and, if so, he will attend. ALS. DLC-HC (DNA, M212, R4). Draft, in MH with some minor mechanical variations. Sloane was a delegate to the National Republican convention. Cincinnati *American*, December 23, 1831.

From Citizens of Vincennes, Indiana, October 18, 1831. Invite Clay to a public dinner in his honor when he passes through Vincennes. Copy. Printed in *Niles' Register* (November 19, 1831), 41:226; and Lexington *Observer*, November 4, 1831.

On the same day, October 18, Clay replied, declining the invitation on the grounds that "From the period my name was presented, by a convention in Kentucky [Clay to Conover, October 31, 1830], to the public consideration, for a high office, I have not accepted, nor, whilst it remains thus before the public, shall I accept, any public entertainment tendered on my own account." Explains, further: "During the late administration, and for some time after its close, I occasionally attended public dinners for the double purpose of meeting my fellow citizens at the festive board, and of vindicating my character there, which had been unjustly reproached. But although it was my duty and my right to defend myself, those occasions were never sought, never prompted, nor always embraced by me. If there be any who are not convinced that great injustice was done me, I must regret it, but I can do no more to undeceive them." *Ibid.*

From "TIMOTHY PICKERING"   Boston, October 22, 1831
Will you permit an ardent political friend to address you upon a subject of the highest importance.

You are already aware that the hon. Wm. Wirt has been nominated by a very respectable convention at Baltimore for the high office of President of the United States.[1] You are aware that at the election of J. Q. Adams you was accused of bargain and corruption[2]

You may be aware also that no respectable man of good information. does now believe it.

You recollect that you stated your conviction of Gen. Jacksons inability. and notorious incompetency to fill that high station and put your character and motives upon the issue.[3]

You are aware that the present organization renders your election impossible   You are aware that the sentiments of *Mr. Wirt* upon the great and important points of our domestick Policy are in unison with your own.

Now. Sir. since your own election is impossible would it not be the greatest benefit which you could not possibly confer upon your country to retire from the contest and let all your forces be brought over to Mr. Wirts side. and thus by securing his election you would be the means of delivering the country from the domination of the present weak and imbecil[e] administration.

Please to accept these remarks from a constant political friend.

420

ALS. DLC-HC (DNA, M212, R4). Printed in Colton, *Clay Correspondence*, 4:319. The name of the correspondent was a pseudonym; Timothy Pickering had died in 1829. 1. Clay to Brooke, June 23, 1831. 2. See 4:48, 52-55. 3. See 4:45-46, 152.

From William W. Worsley, Louisville, October 22, 1831. Reports that Thomas Crittenden has been in Louisville recently, and that "he expressed himself with much warmth on the subject of your friends having proposed you as a candidate for the Senate of the U. States [Clay to Beatty, June 8, 1830]; that the idea was first started in Lexington, insinuating thereby that you had some agency in the matter; that his brother [John J. Crittenden] had been *trampled on by you*, &c &c. So far as the [Louisville] Focus has had any agency in proposing you for the Senate, I can with truth say, that we have had no communication with a single individual on the subject. . . . I am told that Mr. Crittenden stated that his brother would not *now* be a candidate for the Senate, no matter what your determination might be. I had heretofore understood that Mr. J. J. Crittenden himself had pressed you to become a candidate, and was therefore much surprised to find that his friends felt aggrieved by your friends advocating the measure. Knowing that you entertain a high regard for Mr. J. J. Crittenden, both political and personal, I thought it advisable that you should at once be put in possession of the facts beforementioned." ALS. DLC-HC (DNA, M212, R4). Addressed to Clay in Terre Haute, Indiana. Note at bottom, not in Worsley's hand, reads: "Seen by none but your son T[homas] H[art] Clay."

From Asher Robbins, Newport, R.I., October 25, 1831. Reports that several of Clay's "leading friends" have requested him to urge Clay to "come into the Senate of the U.S. [Clay to Beatty, June 8, 1830]." States that "Recent events have made them doubly anxious for this object; I allude to the conventions at Baltimore [Clay to Brooke, June 23, 1831] and—Philadelphia [Brown to Clay, October 2, 1831]." Adds that "They have also become alarmed at the danger of the approaching crisis. They see that a collected and mighty effort is—preparing to be made at the approaching Session of Congress, to overthrow your system of national Policy; and they would count upon you, were you to be in the Senate, as a host in it's defence; and would confidently rely on it's safety in that Body. I pray God we may not be disappointed of your delegation to a seat there." ALS. DLC-HC (DNA, M212, R4).

From James Caldwell, White Sulphur Springs, Va., October 26, 1831. States that he is "glad to see from different quarters you are called on again to serve your Country in its councils." Adds that "your predicksions of the managers of this administration has been compleatly verrified and there is now a great field open for you there has been during the past season a great many of your old friends as well as oponents at this place." Remarks that Francis T. Brooke, Dabney Carr, John McLean, and William Wirt had all been recent visitors to the spa. Reports that "in a conversation with Mr. Wirt he [Wirt] exspressed great friendship for you, I think him a good man he has been a good friend of mine in his professional duties but he said during the conversation that McLeane [*sic*, McLean] told him you had no chance at all—I answered that McLeane and Calhoun would give that Idea as wide a spead as possible in order to divide your interest, from the nomination that has lately taken place at Balto. [Clay to Brooke, June 23, 1831] there wags the tail, it is not hard to tell who will be the dupe (it may have the effect to divide your interest) I hope your Legislature will look to you & also that you will serve them & your Country."

Mentions that his son W. B. Caldwell and H. Y. Erskine have been appointed as delegates to the National Republican convention in December [Clay to Conover, October 9, 1831]. Warns that "intrigue from all quarters and in every shape will be at that Balto. convention it is hard to tell who is sincerely a mans friend in these times." ALS. DLC-HC (DNA, M212, R4).

From E.U. Brown *et al.*, Terre Haute, Ind., October 28, 1831. Thank Clay for visiting Terre Haute and assure him that "we cannot forget the benefits which you have rendered the west, whilst engaged in the national councils, both in congress and the cabinet." Assure him that even if the coming presidential election goes against him, they will still admire his ready sense of patriotism. Copy. Printed in *Niles' Register* (December 3, 1831), 41:261; also in Washington *Daily National Journal*, November 29, 1831, with letter incorrectly dated October 12, 1831.

Clay responded to this communication on the same day, October 28, thanking Brown and his committee members for their sentiments and pointing out to them the importance to Terre Haute of the national road: "In this remote point, more than eight hundred miles from the capitol of the union, it is impossible not to recognise the cementing tendency of the national road, which, in the progress of its construction, has already reached your town, and passed on still farther west. Who can be on any part of this great road without feeling that its physical connection increases much the strength of the moral and political ties which happily bind us together? We have only to persevere in our American System, relieving consumption, after the payment of the public debt, as much as possible consistently with an economical administration of the government, without impairing the principle of protection, to be assured of continued prosperity." *Ibid.*

From Thomas Jenifer, Pittsburgh, October 30, 1831. States that "your frinds in Baltimore and indeed throughout Maryland are looking with anxiety to the meeting of your Legislature, and are undecided both in their wishes and opinions that you should come to the Senate of the U. States [Clay to Beatty, June 8, 1830]. They believe that your presence at Wash[i]ngton the coming Winter also important—The State of Md. is evry day more and more disgusted with the developments of the present administration and are equally anxious that you should be placed in the most favourable aspect notwithstanding the *Anti-Masonic Nomination* [Clay to Brooke, June 23, 1831] concerning the object of which there is such diversity of opinion." ALS. DLC-HC (DNA, M212, R4). The correspondent is probably Daniel of St. Thomas Jenifer of Maryland, brother of Daniel Jenifer (*BDAC*).

To John Ewing, October 31, 1831. Expresses regret for having disappointed "those of my fellow Citizens of your neighborhood [Vincennes] who wished to have seen me." Explains that bad roads compelled him to abandon his contemplated visit to Indianapolis, while "my desire to reach home speedily" induced him to by-pass Vincennes. Adds that his "conviction remains strong as to the expediency of a full representation at the Balto. Convention [Clay to Conover, October 9, 1831]." ALS. In.

From Matthew L. Davis, New York, November 2, 1831. Reports that about 500 delegates from 13 states attended the tariff convention in New York City. Says that during the convention (on October 27) he met with Josiah Randall of Philadelphia and that they decided to take advantage of the presence of so many Clay friends and supporters in the city by calling an informal meeting of some of them "for the purpose of interchanging opinions on the present aspect of our affairs." A preliminary meeting was therefore held on Friday evening, October 28. It was attended by men from New York, Pennsylvania, Delaware, Maryland, and Virginia—17 in number. This group voted to call a second meeting for the following evening, October 29, which was attended by "between 45 and 50 persons." It reconvened on Monday evening, October 31, and continued the discussions. "I never witnessed more zeal, more ardor, or more unanimity," Davis affirms. The questions addressed were these: "1st Has the Jackson party, recently, lost or gained in your State! 2d Are the Anti Masonic party increasing, and in what ratio! 3d What effect, probably, will the nomination of Mr [William] Wirt produce? 4. What would be the effect of an attempt to unite the friends of Mr Clay, on Mr. Wirt, or any other candidate?"

As for the answers to these questions, "All seemed to agree That the Jackson party were losing ground; That the Anti Masonic party, except in New York and Vermont, were not gaining, and in Some States were losing; That the nomination of Mr. Wirt when first announced, had astounded our friends, and, therefore, had created a momentary embarrassment. But, in every instance they had recovered from that embarrassment; and that indignation at, and abhorrence of the selfish policy which it evinced, had taken its place; and That an effort to rally the National Republicans, on any Candidate, but Mr Clay, was certain, and inevitable ruin; and that no member of the Baltimore Convention could, for one moment, listen to the name of any other individual, without disgrace and infamy, accompanying him to his home. A number of the delegates were in the room, and five or six, from various States, expressed the same sentiment"

It was the opinion of the conferees that there was little or no hope for the Clay National Republicans in New Hampshire and Maine; that New York would probably go for Jackson; that Pennsylvania and Virginia were probably safe; and that Massachusetts, Connecticut, Rhode Island, Delaware, Vermont, New Jersey, and Maryland were clearly safe. Explains, in part: "It was stated by gentlemen from Vermont, that the Anti Masons in that state, were National Republicans. . . . New York, *I say*, all in the wind, and lost, but Peter R. Livingston Expressed a very different opinion, and others present, belonging to the state, think with him. . . . Maryland considered perfectly safe, but I confess I am at a loss, to understand how that can be. Mr. [Hezekiah] Niles insisted upon it, that the nomination of Mr. Wirt could do us no injury. He added, that Mr. Wirt, during the past week, had sent in a written resignation of his Seat, as a delegate to the Baltimore Convention; and that he (Niles) would be appointed in his place"

Believes that these conferences "will prove beneficial" in that "They will . . . enable, directly and indirectly two or three hundred delegates to convey to their respective districts, of their several States, the sentiments, feelings and opinions of the National Republicans in the [tariff] Convention. They will tend to harmonize, if there existed any diversity of opinion, (which I doubt), among the delegates to the Baltimore Convention."

Concludes with these political recommendations and observations: "In my opinion, the most important political move that can now be made, is to secure an early application, during the next session of Congress, of the United States bank, for a renewal of their Charter. It will in all, probability, pass, in a satisfactory form, and will place the president in a situation to *act* on this subject. The friends of the bank think he will sign the Charter. I attach much consequence, therefore, to the question coming before the president during the session, so as to have the bill *returned*. . . . Our election commences on Monday. We shall be beaten, I think, by a greater majority, than last year. The Anti Masons in this city will not make a ticket; and I think, from a desire to make the national party appear small, will privately vote the Jackson ticket. . . . I hope my next from you will announce; that you have been chosen to the Senate of the United States." ALS. DLC-HC (DNA, M212, R4). The tariff convention met in New York City on October 26-31, 1831. The 400 to 500 delegates represented 13 states. Their business emphasized the effects of the existing tariff on the nation's economy and foreign trade, presented the burden of the convention's discussions to the public, and memorialized Congress. Prominent at the convention were William Wilkins (Pa.), James Talmadge (N.Y.), Joseph Kent (Md.), George Blake (Mass.), Robert Tillotson (N.Y.), and Joseph H. Pierce (N.H.). See Brown to Clay, October 2, 1831. At the November 7 election for the New York general assembly 24 Jacksonian senators were chosen and 8 Anti-Masons; no Clay supporters were elected to the body. In the house race, 95 Jacksonians were elected, 26 Anti-Masons, 3 National Republicans, and 4 "doubtful." New York *Evening Post*, November 19, 1831; Washington *Daily National Journal*, November 1, 1831.

With John & Ann Rowan, Lexington, November 5, 1831. Purchases from the Rowans for $2,000 two town lots in Louisville, both fronting on Monroe Street. DS, in Clay's hand. DLC-TJC (DNA, M212, R17).

To WILLIAM GREENE   Lexington, November 14, 1831

Your favor of the 31st. Ulto. reached here prior to my return from Illinois, and hence the delay in acknowledging it.

A late event rendering it probable that we may meet on our way to the Eastern Cities, I will now say less than I otherwise would do. An union of the N.R. party with the Anti Masonic, by the former nominating the Candidate of the latter is not practicable if desirable, and I am not sure that it would be desirable if it were practicable. If Mr. [William] Wirt stood on any other ground, he might make a competent President; standing on that of Anti-Masonry, I should fear his administration, notwithstanding all his protestations and disclaimers. But it is my deliberate opinion that if the Balto. Convention in Decr.[1] were to nominate Mr. Wirt he would not get one State in the Union, unless it be Vermont. The mass of our friends could not be made to comprehend the expediency of putting aside all our principles, and adopting those of the new sect. Then, to what ridicule should we not justly expose ourselves! I have not time to pursue these suggestions.

It may be a question worthy of consideration whether your Convention shall make any nomination. I am not prepared to decide that question. But, if after a comparison of testimony from all parts of the Union at Balto. it shall be evident to the Convention that they cannot elect their Candidate whoever he may be, why nominate? May our principles not be better sustained by repressing all endeavors to elect a Candidate of our party than by the hopeless attempt, if hopeless it shall then appear to be? This is an enquiry worthy of being made.

For the present, all that is certain, I think, is that it is wise to meet and deliberate in the proposed Convention. I am happy to find that you are a member, and one resolved to go. Every day some new fact may arise to throw light and give hope as to the future. The result of the N. York Election;[2] that of the Pennsa.[3] election, not yet certainly known to me; the Presidents message[4] &c &c. all may prove important.

I write you in strict confidence. You must be aware, in the existing posture of affairs, how much it is necessary for me to be guarded. Whilst I attach but little importance to any opinion I entertain, in respect to the Presidential question, others might be disposed greatly to magnify it. . . .

ALS. OHi.   1. Clay to Conover, Oct. 9,1831.   2. Davis to Clay, Nov. 2, 1831.   3. Clay to Sloane, Nov. 14, 1831.   4. Third Annual Message, Dec. 6, 1831. *MPP*, 2:544-58.

To JOHN SLOANE   Lexington, November 14, 1831

I am extremely happy to find, from your letter of the 15h. Ulto., recd. since my recent return from Illinois, that a perfect coincidence exists between us on the public affairs of which it treats.

You will have seen that I am sent to the Senate, whither I shall go with no anticipated satisfaction.[1]

Should the late elections in N. York[2] & Pennsa[3] have been decidedly against our Cause (of which I have not yet heard) will you consider whether at the Balto. Convention, of which I am glad to see you are to be a member, it may not be expedient to avoid a nomination at all, of any one?[4] Between Wirt, *as an Anti Masonic Candidate*, and Jackson our friends would be greatly embarassed; and I am inclined to believe that Wirt would not get one State in the Union, in such a contest, unless it be Vermont.

424

The question is, if the Balto. Convention should not nominate, or if their nominee should decline, whether our principles would be probably better supported?

These are suggestions not decided opinions.

ALS. MH.   1. Clay to Beatty, June 8, 1830. On Nov. 14, Clay's election as U.S. senator on Nov. 10 was certified by Ky. Governor Thomas Metcalfe. DS. DNA, RG45, 11B-B2.   2. Davis to Clay, Nov. 2, 1831.   3. In the 1831 state elections in Pennsylvania, 22 Jacksonians, 4 Clay supporters, and 7 Anti-Masons were elected to the state senate; 74 Jacksonians, 4 Clay supporters, and 24 Anti-Masons were elected to the house. Harrisburg *Chronicle*, Oct. 24, 1831. 4. Clay to Conover, Oct. 9, 1831.

To James F. Conover, Cincinnati, November 16, 1831. Says he accepted a U.S. Senate seat only "from a sense of public duty and in conformity with the almost unanimous wishes of my friends. I go to my post however with no anticipations of pleasure from occupying it." Concludes with the presidential political observation that "all idea of concentration on Mr. [William] Wirt is vain and idle. If he and Jackson should be the only Candidates, there will, I believe be concentration, but it will be on Jackson." ALS. ViU.

To John J. Crittenden, Frankfort, Ky., November 20, 1831. Asks Crittenden to represent him in a suit being brought against him as executor of the James Morrison estate. Remarks that he leaves for Washington "with anticipations of a much less agreeable Session than I sincerely hope you may have in Frankfort," and hopes Crittenden will write often. ALS. DLC-John J. Crittenden Papers (DNA, M212, R20).

From James Brown Clay, Lexington, November 30, 1831. Hopes that his father's trip to Washington went well. Reports that he and his brother, John Morrison Clay, have been in Lexington over a week. Remarks that he thinks Mr. Benjamin O. Peers [Clay to Henry Clay, Jr., October 31, 1830] "one of the finest men I know." Relays Ashland farm news and Lexington social news. Sends love to "You and mama especially to little Henry [Clay Duralde]." ALS. DLC-TJC (DNA, M212, R10).

From Thomas I. Wharton, Philadelphia, December 1, 1831. Congratulates Clay on his election to the U.S. Senate [Clay to Beatty, June 8, 1830]. Criticizes Robert Walsh, Jr.'s, "political aberrations & other manifold sins" when his Philadelphia *National Gazette* compared Clay's "return to Washington with Napoleon's return to Elba." Adds: "I trust the result will be the same & that the old imbecile [Andrew Jackson] who fills the chair of state will experience the fate of Louis 18th." Discusses the coming election of a Speaker of the House of Representatives. Since we cannot hope to elect "one of our thorough friends . . . we must choose between an *out & out* Jackson man & one who is so only in name and who is with us in heart & feeling & in every thing that regards principles & measures." Recommends Rep. Joel Barlow Sutherland of Pennsylvania for the speakership, because he is "a warm friend of Mr. [Samuel D.] Ingham & a determined enemy of [John] Eaton, [William B.] Lewis &c." ALS. DLC-HC (DNA, M212, R4). For Sutherland, a Jackson Democrat who turned Whig in 1836, see *BDAC*. Rep. Andrew Stevenson (Va.) was reelected Speaker of the House in the 22nd Congress.

From James Brown, Philadelphia, December 2, 1831. Discusses his plans to depart from New York for New Orleans by sea on December 8, a voyage "postponed by the marriage of my Niece [Susan Brown]" to a young Philadelphia lawyer. Comments on his poor health, which he diagnoses as "a disease of the heart which must be fatal." ALS. DLC-HC (DNA, M212, R4). Printed in *LHQ*, 24: 1160-61. For the marriage of Susan Catherine Brown to Charles Ingersoll, see Clay to Ingersoll, June 11, 1835.

From Henry C. Carey, Philadelphia, December 3, 1831. Encloses "a short article" concerning a gradual reduction of the tariff. Believes "that the adoption of the suggestion it contains" would "give security to the manufacturing interest" and also "would satisfy so large a portion of the South, as would put an end to opposition — or at least to danger —" A law that would "gradually bring us back to the old system of revenue" would be acceptable to "some of the warmest opponents of the Tariff policy."

Congratulates Clay on his election to the Senate [Clay to Beatty, June 8, 1830] and says that no other man has "it so much in his power to heal the dissensions between the North & the South." ALS. DLC-HC (DNA, M212, R4).

From James G. McKinney, Lexington, December 3, 1831. Reports that "the note for Stamboul [Berryman to Clay, October 5, 1831] has been received by me." Turning to politics, he advises Clay "to court the Jackson boys as much as possible — and dont abuse old *Jackson*." He would not give such advice "was it not that it will have its good effect." ALS. DLC-HC (DNA, M212, R4).

From James Morrison, Maysville, Ky., December 3, 1831. Encloses extended comments on the details of a proposed new charter for the Bank of the United States and remarks that a copy has also been sent to the editor of the Maysville *Eagle* "under the name of Mercator." Informs Clay that while in Philadelphia in early September, 1831, he had written a "short note" urging the establishment of "A Peoples Bank," but no newspaper there would publish it.

Morrison's enclosure proposes a "Mother Bank" located in Philadelphia or New York, chartered by Congress for 50 years, with branching privileges in each state. Capital stock in the amount of $50 million would be sold as follows: "Counties in every State to be enumerated and the free white male inhabitants above the age of Twenty One to have the Privelege of becoming Stockholders, let the Stock be subscribed Simultaneously throughout the States in Shares of fifty dolla[rs] each duly apportioned agreeably to the inhabitants in a County for Each and Every Share of Stock So Subscribed one fourth part to be paid in Gold or Silver to Sworn Commissioners whose duty It Shall be to affix their Seal on the Same which Shall not be broken Untill after the Expiration of ten days — this Step it is believed Will prevent Monopolerers from taking an Excess of Stock. It is Sugested that the Congress of the United States take fifteen Million or More in Subscribed Stock which they Shall not have the power to transfer With the limited privilege of Chosing one half the Directors only"

Other details of the internal organization and administration of the proposed bank are also presented and discussed (no foreigner would be allowed to buy stock), as well as suggestions on how best to phase out the existing national bank. Believes that the stock of the new bank will rise 50 percent in value, "particularly if Congress Should Grant A Charter for fifty years." Suggests, further, that stock not privately subscribed might be purchased by the states.

Concludes: "Again Money is power and to prevent Its Misuse as far as is Consistant the votes of Stockholders whether a Body Corporate or Individual Shall not Exceed the power of Twenty Shares which may Counteract any preponderating Effect that might be desired from a greater privilege   the object in Sealing the Gold or Silver With Sworn Commissioners is to prevent Its Subserving the Double purpose of taking Stock twice or a hundred times." L, signed by Morrison. DLC-HC (DNA, M212, R4). Morrison, a wealthy Maysville merchant, active also in banking and realty circles there, died of cholera in 1832.

From HENRY CLAY, JR.   New Orleans, December 7, 1831

Since I last wrote to you, I have received two letters from Ashland; both were directed to Louisville, but I recd only one of them in that city; the other reached me in New Orleans. I find much difficulty in answering them: Several letters have been written in answer; but I am dissatisfied with all of them, and in truth with myself too. I shall, therefore, tear them to pieces, surrender at discretion and submit to the penalty which I am sure you will impose, entire reformation.

I have been in this city nearly two weeks; and Anne [Brown Clay Erwin] has not yet arrived. She has however been in Mobile for some days, and I expect her here very soon. I am still in a hotel, the same in which Anne will remain during the winter. Mr. [Martin] Duralde has invited me to reside with him at a house which he is building near his saw-mill. I think I shall accept his invitation.

I am pleased with New Orleans, but abhor its climate: the atmosphere is filled with a humidity that pierces the body through and through. I have been confined to the house for some time since my arrival by sickness and the inclemency of the weather; but I am now nearly well, and the skies are brightening into smiles. This letter will reach you in Washington in the midst of the most important session of Congress since the first under the Constitution. Your time I know will be much occupied by Public business, for, though many refuse to give you the credit, yet all rely upon your prudence and wisdom, in the dernier resort, for the safe guidance of the ship of State. You will, I hope, transmit to me all that is interesting. The people among whom I am, seem to me to be not a reading people; I shall therefore receive but scanty supplies of information unless you furnish them.

I am sorry that I disagree with you in regard to the time proper for my appearance at the New Orleans Bar. I am inclined to believe that now is the flood-tide of my prosperity.

I have a character, I find, among the citizens for industry, which I fear, might be lost even by the appearance of indolence, which a law student must have; at this moment your friends here are so zealous and warm that your name is almost the certificate of my prosperity; The old lawyers too are over-burdened with fees, and not remarkable for grace of speech & above all other considerations, New Orleans is a very expensive city and I would by no means be willing to impose upon you the charge of much longer maintaining me. I think therefore that by next winter I shall be ready to appear at the Bar. The present winter, I shall devote as you recommend to civil law, French & Spanish and the next summer to common law, after which I may continue my historical and legal studies, for, as in all other cities I shall probably be for some months, Mr Duralde says years, without business. I am not yet in a law-office: I dislike very much Mr [George] Eustis' tragical air; however, I shall probably study with him. Had I a library of my own, I should prefer much to study in my room. The lawyers, from what I learn, pay no attention whatever to their pupils, further than recommending and lending books, and Eustis has much business to attend to.

In regard to my expenses, I am sorry to say that I am not economical. I neither drink, nor gamble and my other habits are not worse, perhaps, better, than those of most young men of my age: But should I exceed, not what your indulgence, but your judgment dictates, for God's sake, let me know it at once, and put a stop to my career. To me it appears that this is the period of my life when an expenditure of what means I can, in justice, use, is most necessary—But my judgment is very fallible; and especially now and upon such a subject.

Aunt [Julie Duralde] Clay is a most amiable lady; I am already very much attached to her. My little nephew [Martin Duralde III] too is a fine boy and will be an intelligent man

I came down the river with young [Jesse Burton] Harrison   He is a very excellent person and well educated. He will commence the practice here almost immediately.

Several dinners have been given me by your friends and I have met with great attention. But my sheet is full. Give my love to my mother & Henry [Clay Duralde] . . . [P.S.] Anne arrived the morning after I wrote this letter. She, Mr [James] Erwin, & their children [Henry C.; James, Jr.; Andrew; Lucretia] were all well. I believe she is now writing to you.

ALS. Henry Clay Memorial Foundation, Lexington, Ky.

From John L. Lawrence, New York, December 7, 1831. Congratulates Clay on his safe arrival at Washington and says the "favourable effects" of his "going thither" are "already manifest." Believes that at the Baltimore convention next week [Clay to Conover, October 9, 1831] "there will . . . be but one sentiment as to the Presidential candidate." Notes that the vice presidential nominee "is not yet decisively indicated," but if Daniel Webster will agree, "it is probable that he may be selected." Regrets he has been unable to accept a position as a delegate to the convention, but his brother, Abraham R. Lawrence, will be a delegate and will visit Clay in Washington after the convention adjourns.

Notes that the president's Third Annual Message [*MPP*, 2:544-58] arrived in New York from Washington in fifteen hours. "It affords another proof of the variety of the Presidents style; and of his conviction that consistency between profession and practice, is but the badge of a novice—" ALS. DLC-HC (DNA, M212, R4).

From ANNE BROWN CLAY ERWIN
New Orleans, December 8, 1831

I wrote Mama last from Caha[w]ba not being certain whether she would go to Washington or not, I addressed my letter to Lexington so that you will probably receive this one before that, we went on board of the boat a few hours after I wrote and had a very pleasant passage of 2 days to Mobile where we remained a week with our friends. We left there on the 4th expecting to be here in 24 hours but owing to the Steam boat's being badly managed we were two days and 3 nights in coming, we had a most comfortless time and on arriving here found our friends very anxious about us as there was a report that we were lost. I was delighted at finding Henry [Clay, Jr.] here, he has not been very well for a day or two past but is in good spirits and appears to be very much pleased with the prospects of settling here, all of our friends have been very kind and attentive to him, old Mr [Stephen] Henderson gave him a dinner at which he invited some of the oldest gentlemen in the City to meet him, this was intended of course as a great compliment to his understanding. We found our rooms that Mr [James] Erwin had engaged last spring ready for us, and I think we shall be quite pleasantly situated   I am as yet the only lady in the house but as we have a private table I shall prefer it, as I must necessarily be a greater belle there being no competition in the case, and you know my dear Father too well for me to diguise the fact that all ladies like the attention of gentlemen. I have not as yet had time to see any of my friends except Aunt [Julie Duralde] Clay, the weather for the last 2 weeks has been detestable. Judge [Alexander] Porter called this morning to see us, he appears to be in

428

good health but is of course very dejected; his daughter [Anne] will remain in the City this winter with Mrs Judge [George] Matthews and will spend next summer with me in Kentucky.

We have Mr Denton boarding with us and several other gentlemen with whom Mr E[rwin]. is intimate which will make it very pleasant. Mr [Martin] Duralde is now building a house at his Saw Mill where he intends to live he insists upon Henry's going with him, I shall not advise him either to go or stay, of course if I were to consult my own gratification I should prefer him to remain where he is, but I think it best for him to choose for himself. Mr Duralde feels obliged to live entirely at his Mill as he is no longer a partner; Mr Donette has been obliged to abscond owing to a most disgraceful and inhuman act, it was no less than the murder of one of their negroes he died very soon after having been unmercifully whipped and as Donette would have been sued he thought it wise to get off as soon as possible, this affair of course mortified Mr Duralde very much, it was even reported here that he had forged Mr Duralde's name for a large amount of money but this fortunately was not the case the fact itself was bad enough without any exaggeration.

Mr [James] Erwin is in very fine spirits about his last year's speculations, he finds he could realize a still greater profit than he expected he could when he came here, I shall leave it to him however to write you all about it as I have no doubt he will do so.

Little [Martin III] Duralde is in very good health and has grown very much; he goes to school and as I want the boys to learn French this winter I shall send them both to the same school. The baby [Lucretia Hart Erwin] grows almost too fast and is running about every where. I hope, my dear Father, you will not be so entirely absorbed in politics but that you will find time to write us frequently. Present me affectionately to all those persons who remember me in Washington, and give Mr Erwin's love as well as mine to Mama

ALS. DLC-TJC (DNA, M212, R13).

From Hezekiah Niles, Baltimore, December 8, 1831. States "I send you 25 copies of the N.Y. Address" which "I wish . . . sent to your friends, especially in Mississippi." Asks Clay to frank them. ALS. DLC-HC (DNA, M212, R4). The address of the New York Convention of the Friends of American Industry, held on October 26, is in *Niles' Register* (November 12, 1831), 41:204-16. See also Davis to Clay, November 2, 1831.

To FRANCIS T. BROOKE
Washington, December 9, 1831

I have recd. your favor of the 7h. inst. That to which it refers was not received by me until after my return from Illinois and after my election to the Senate.[1] As this latter event brought me nearer to you I concluded to postpone writing until I reached this City, and even now I have nothing material to communicate which the papers do not present. Parties have not yet exhibited their respective strength; nor, except the Election of Speaker,[2] has there been any occasion for its display. In that instance there was evidently no concert between those opposed to the Administration; and such a concert I apprehend to be extremely difficult, if not impracticable. You will have seen from the message and the Reports of the Secy of the Treasury [Louis McLane] and his colleagues[3] that the entire policy of the Government, in relation to every one of the great interests of the Country, is proposed to be changed. Was there ever a wilder scheme than that respecting the public lands?[4]

The impression here is that the Balto. Convention will make a nomination of me.[5] I wish I could add that the impression was more favorable than it is as to the success of such a nomination. Some thing however may turn up (and that must be our encouraging hope) to give a brighter aspect to our affairs.

I shall be glad to receive the *long* letter promised in your last. . . .

ALS. KyU. Printed in Colton, *Clay Correspondence*, 4:321.   1. Clay to Beatty, June 8, 1830. 2. Andrew Stevenson of Virginia, a Democrat, was elected Speaker. *BDAC*.   3. Clay to Southard, Dec. 12, 1831.   4. McLane proposed selling all the public lands to the states in which they lay and distributing the proceeds of the sale to all the states. See Munroe, *Louis McLane*, 310-12.   5. Clay to Conover, Oct. 9, 1831.

To James Barbour, December 10, 1831. Notes that "I must have been entirely regardless of passing events, if I had not observed that my name has been repeatedly mentioned as being likely to be brought before the [National Republican] Convention, and that, in some instances, delegates have been instructed by their constituents to yield support to it, as a Candidate for the Presidency." Feels that "any restriction upon the perfect freedom of deliberation and decision of the Convention [Clay to Conover, October 9, 1831], is inexpedient." Advocates that the convention should make "a comparative estimate of the many citizens of the United States who are competent to discharge the duties of Chief Magistrate" and select "from among them that one, who, possessing the requisite principles, would probably unite, to the greatest extent, the public confidence and the public support" in order to rescue "the Executive Government of the Union from the misrule which threatens to subvert established institutions and systems of policy, long and deservedly cherished, and to bring disgrace and ruin upon the country." Promises that if the convention chooses "any individual other than myself, it shall have, not only my hearty acquiescence and concurrence, but my cordial and zealous cooperation." Asks Barbour to communicate this sentiment to the convention if its members do put his name in nomination. Copy. Printed in the Washington *Daily National Journal*, December 15, 1831.

From Samuel L. Southard, Trenton, N.J., December 10, 1831. Reports that the "severity of the weather & the state of my health prevent me from attending the Balto. Convention, which I very much regret." Adds that "N.J. will be fully represented there and, I believe, unanimous in the course to be taken." Notes that "My friend [William] Wirt, whom . . . I love & esteem, cannot take such a hold on our people as to get along—He has taken one false step—injurious, I fear, to all [Clay to Southard, December 12, 1831]." ALS. InU. Wirt's "false step" was probably his acceptance of the Anti-Masonic nomination [Clay to Brooke, June 23, 1831].

From Thomas Speed, Nelson County, Ky., December 10, 1831. Discusses a Revolutionary War claims case and asks Clay's assistance in resolving it. Asks that in his reply, Clay also add "a brief sketch of your views as to 'the prospect before us,' relative to the American System and its friends & supporters. . . . The plans & designs of the enemies of that system will to some extent ha[ve] been developed—the hopes and expectations of its friends will be known to you—the Baltimore Convention [Clay to Conover, October 9, 1831] will have set." ALS. DLC-HC (DNA, M212, R4).

From Josiah S. Johnston, Baltimore, December 11, 1831. Reports that "bad weather & the closing the navigation" has delayed the arrival of many at the National Republican convention [Clay to Conover, October 9, 1831], but "150 are on the spot & the others are expected—" Assures him that the New York and Pennsylvania delegations will be "nearly full," and the convention "will be very respectable in numbers & character." Reports that the delegates are all agreed that "they can have nothing to do with anti masonry or with Mr. Wirt [Clay to Brooke, June 23, 1831]—That you are the only man who can hold them & the party together—" Adds that "It is vain to talk of not nominating or of you withdrawing, they have never thought of it, & will not deliberate upon it—Such a step could not now be taken, either by You or the Convention It would produce a tremendous explosion—We must deliberate on what is best & you must acquiesce. . . . We cannot withdraw from the contest—nor can you . . . if we are lost let us all go together—" Advises Clay "to go on in the Senate & act as if you were not a Candidate—act freely & without reserve—boldly & without reference to consequences—" ALS. InU.

From Josiah S. Johnston, Baltimore, December 12, 1831. Reports that "We met this morning & organized the Convention," and predicts there will be 200 delegates in attendance "before the vote." Outlines the schedule for the convention. Emphasizes that the only course "is to nominate you—& to fight the battle out—It would be impossible to make a retrograde movement. . . . you must submit to what we think is proper to be done for the Cause & the Country—I think we shall take [John] Sergeant for Vice President in that event, we ought to make [James] Barbour President & Govr. [Allen] Trimble & Genl. [Peter B.] Porter Vice Presidents . . . of the Convention so as to divide the honors &c." ALS. InU. For the officers and nomination of the convention, see Clay to Conover, October 9, 1831.

From John Sergeant, Baltimore, December 12, 1831. Reports that since arriving for the National Republican convention [Clay to Conover, October 9, 1831], he has conversed "extensively with our friends . . . from all parts of the Union." Has found them to be of "one mind, without exception—to make a nomination, and to nominate you." The only doubt that has been entertained was upon the proposition that "under existing circumstances, it would not be as well to abstain from nominating and give up the contest." This, however, has been rejected, as "we are all of opinion that this course is not open to us—" Notes that he can "readily perceive how much it would contribute to your case, perhaps to your advantage" not to be nominated, but "it appears to me that you have nothing to do but acquiesce." Continues: "Personal feelings are to be sacrificed, it is true; but you have been so long the property of the public, that I do not think you can now deny them the right to dispose of you, especially where the great interests of our Country are at stake. . . . Whether you succeed or fail, you will have no cause of self reproach." ALS. InU.

To SAMUEL L. SOUTHARD   Washington, December 12, 1831
Prior to the receipt of your favor of the 10h. inst I had heard with regret that the state of your health would not admit of your attendance at the Balto. Convention;[1] but I am happy to learn from yourself that it is improving. Mrs. Clay and my grandson H[enry]. C[lay]. Duralde constitute the whole portion of my family here. My son Henry [Clay, Jr.] passes the winter at N. Orleans with his sister [Anne Brown Clay Erwin]. Mrs. Clay and I would be delighted to see you and Mrs. Southard and Miss Virginia [Southard] here. Can you not come to us in the Spring?

[William] Wirt has taken a very false step which, with you, I fear will benefit no one. [Richard] Rush is mad.[2] On the other hand it is very gratifying to find that you, [Peter B.] Porter, and [James] Barbour are faithful to our cause. As for Mr. [John Q.] Adams, though honest, Wirt says we may expect wild things of him. I have not yet seen him, 'though I promptly called on him.

The President and Secy [of the Treasury] have marked out a great quantity of business for Congress, but not with perfect coincidence between themselves. The Secy. has some dashing projects.[3]

From what I learn there will be entire unanimity at Balto. and I sincerely hope their deliberations may produce the good effects you anticipate. . . .

ALS. NjP.   1. Clay to Conover, Oct. 9, 1831.   2. See Southard to Clay, Dec. 10, 1831, for Wirt's "false step"; reference to Rush apparently refers to his support for the Anti-Masonic cause. Powell, *Richard Rush*, 232.   3. Louis McLane's "Report on the Treasury [*House Exec. Doc.* 3, 22 Cong., 1 Sess., pp. 5-8]" proposed a plan for paying the national debt by March 3, 1833. Included in his proposal was the government sale of its stock in the Bank of the United States, renewal of the bank's charter "at the proper time," a reduction of the tariff to the level needed for revenue, and sale of the public lands "to the states in which they lay and then distributing the proceeds at one swoop to all the states." Munroe, *Louis McLane*, 310-13. By contrast, Jackson's Third Annual Message of Dec. 6, 1831 [*MPP*, 2:544-58], also called for a lower tariff, but cautioned that the reduction should take place only as soon as "a just regard . . . to the preservation of the large capital invested in establishments of domestic industry, will permit." He differed even more with McLane on the public lands, advocating their sale to settlers "in limited parcels, at a price barely sufficient to reimburse the United States the expense of the present system." *House Exec. Doc.* 2, 22 Cong., 1 Sess., pp. 8-11. Further, Jackson's opposition to the B.U.S. had been evident since his First Annual Message [*MPP*, 2:462].

To PETER R. LIVINGSTON *et al.*   Washington, December 13, 1831

I have the honor to acknowledge the receipt of the note which, as a Committee of the Convention of National Republican delegates, now assembled in Baltimore, you addressed to me,[1] stating that I had been this day unanimously nominated by the Convention as a Candidate for the office of President of the U. States.

This manifestation of the confidence of a body, so distinguished, is received, gentlemen, with lively sensibility and profound gratitude. Although I should have been glad, if the Convention had designated some Citizen of the U. States, more competent than myself to be the instrument of accomplishing the patriotic objects which they have in view, I do not feel at liberty to decline their nomination. With my respectful and cordial acknowledgments, you will be pleased to communicate to the Convention my acceptance of their nomination, with the assurance that, whatever may be the event of it, our Common Country shall ever find me faithful to the Union and the Constitution, & to the principles of public liberty, and to those great measures of National policy which have made us a people, prosperous, respected and powerful.

Accept gentlemen of my thanks for the friendly manner in which you have conveyed the act and sentiments of the Convention.

ALS. MiU-C.   1. On the same day, Dec. 13, Peter R. Livingston *et al.* had written Clay from Baltimore, notifying him that they had been appointed as "a committee, by the National Republican Delegates, now assembled in this city, to announce that you were, this day, unanimously nominated as a candidate for the office of President of the United States." Copy. Printed in Columbus *Ohio State Journal*, Dec. 24, 1831.

From William Prentiss, Washington, December 13, 1831. Reports that he has just received a letter from John Agg, written from the National Republican convention, detailing the election of officers for the convention and the unanimous nomination of Clay for president [Clay to Conover, October 9, 1831]. ALS. DLC-HC (DNA, M212, R4).

To Nicholas Biddle, December 15, 1831. Discusses in detail financial and legal problems still pending concerning his (Clay's) property transactions in Louisville and Lexington in 1808-13.

Continues: "Have you come to any decision about an application to Congress at this Session for the renewal of your [Bank] Charter [Clay to Brown, December 18, 1831; Webster to Clay, January 8, 1832]? The friends of the Bank here, with whom I have conversed, seem to expect the application to be made. The course of the President, in the event of the passage of a bill, seems to be a matter of doubt and speculation. My own belief is that, if *now* called upon he would not negative the bill; but that if he should be re-elected the event might and probably would be different." ALS. DLC-Nicholas Biddle Papers (DNA, M212, R20).

From Francis T. Brooke, Richmond, December 15, 1831. States that we are "anxiously waiting for the proceedings of the Baltimore convention [Clay to Conover, October 9, 1831]." States that "the Calhoun party here has almost entirely disappeared since the last Session, and we want some new impulse to decide what it will do, the Gov [John Floyd] who may be said to be the leader I am persuaded can never go back to Jackson, so with many others, but to unite the discordant materials of the opposition here as at Washington, will be very difficult, if the Govr could have been prevailed on to leave out of his message his attack on the Tariff which I really at one time had some expectation he would do, as he professed great inclination not to offend the Clay party there would have been more ground to hope he would come over to that party." Adds that he has just heard of Clay's nomination at the Baltimore convention "which has given great pleasure to your friends here." ALS. InU. For Floyd's 1832 annual message, which argued that the tariff was unconstitutional, see Richmond *Enquirer*, December 8, 1832.

From Alexander Naismith, Louisville, December 15, 1831. Reminds Clay that he had once promised "in Lexington When you Went to Congress that you Wood See the old sholder" would receive justice. Continues: "Sir I have bin A penesor" since 1815 "While you was at Gent [*sic*, Ghent]. . . . I have bin drawing my pay up to sept. 1828." Asks Clay's help in restoring the pension with back-pay to "A pore Soldher cripeld and pore by my cuntrey." ALS. DLC-TJC (DNA, M212, R13).

On January 2, 1832, Clay wrote to Secretary of War Lewis Cass inquiring whether Naismith, "a pensioner . . . has been struck off or remains on the roll"; if so, for what reason was he removed and could the case be opened for reconsideration. ALS. NN.

From James Brown, Philadelphia, December 16, 1831. Reports having had a bout of influenza, as well as a severe fall, which may prevent his traveling to New Orleans this winter. Inquires if James Erwin would be able to renew some notes for him at a New Orleans bank. Turning to politics, states: "I see you are in for the Presidential race. I fear the choice of the Vice President [John Sergeant] will not give much weight to the cause in this State although it has fallen on an able and worthy man. I hear that he is not very popular in this State." ALS. DLC-HC (DNA, M212, R4).

From HENRY CLAY, JR.   New Orleans, December 16, 1831
Though I wrote the last letter, yet as you perhaps feel some anxiety concerning me, I think it proper again to address you, at the risk of depriving you of time which may be invaluable. Nothing new has occurred in regard to my situation. I am still in a hotel studying Law under the direction of Judge [Alexander] Porter who has been so kind as to recommend and lend me the Institutes of Justinian as translated by [Thomas] Cooper the Nullifier. I shall probably go to Mr [Martin] Duralde's next week   His house is not yet finished.

Anne [Brown Clay Erwin] & Mr [James] Erwin & the Children[1] are all well. I am greatly disappointed in Mr [George] Eustis and have declined studying with him. I am somewhat disappointed too with my prospects at the Bar. I had formed I fear, an erroneous conception of the New Orleans Bar. I had supposed that an active lawyer might make a fortune in the period of ten years and then retire to a free state. But I find that the fees of L'a lawyers have been greatly overrated; that if the income be greater, the expenditures are also greater than elsewhere, and in fine that the Bar in New Orleans is like the Bar every where else. Still, I believe it the best Location for me, and that I shall make my permanent residence here, if I can.

William [C.C.] Claiborne [Jr.] has not yet arrived; but he is expected very soon.

I have not heard lately from Uncle [James] Brown He and Gen'l [Stephen] Van Rensselaer are both expected. A Gen'l Parker[2] is at present living in the same room with me. He was Adjutant General during the War & seems to be well-acquainted with you.

Mr [George A.] Waggaman will no doubt give you all the political news of the city. . . .

ALS. Henry Clay Memorial Foundation, Lexington, Ky.   1. Henry Clay; James, Jr.; Andrew Eugene; and Lucretia Hart Erwin.   2. Probably Daniel Parker [4:616].

To JAMES BROWN   Washington, December 18, 1831
[Expresses regret for Brown's injuries, sustained in a fall (Brown to Clay, December 16, 1831), and recommends postponement on his contemplated trip to New Orleans. Assures him that James Erwin will be most willing and competent to take care of Brown's business there. Continues:]

Mr. [John] Sergeant's nomination is thought here to have been the best that could have been made.[1] What the result will be of the proceedings at Balto. time alone will disclose.[2] You saw, from my letter to Mr. [James] Barbour,[3] that I was perfectly willing to yield my pretensions to those of any other person whom the Convention might select.

I have seen Mr. Calhoun several times, but have had no political conversation with him. What will be the course of himself and his friends has not been indicated, at least to me. From what I learn, he will not be a Candidate. An intention to the South existed to bring him out last September, but his Expose on nullification defeated the design.[4] In the event of the President approving a bill to recharter the Bank [of the U.S.] (which I think he will do, if it be passed at this Session, and not otherwise)[5] it has been suggested that [Littleton W.] Tazewell will be brought out as the Southern Candidate for President. . . .

ALS. ViU.   1. Sergeant had been nominated for vice president by the National Republican convention on Dec. 12.   2. Clay to Conover, Oct. 9, 1831.   3. Clay to Barbour, Dec. 10, 1831.   4. Clay to Everett, August 20, 1831.   5. Jackson vetoed the measure on July 10, 1832. See MPP, 2:576-91; also, Webster to Clay, Jan. 8, 1832.

From Horton Howard, Columbus, Ohio, December 19, 1831. Believes that sentiment for Clay in Ohio "has undergone a substantial improvement." Warns Clay that now that he is in Washington "to be at all times on thy guard," because "I have no doubt that attempts will be made in many ways, to get thee out of the way." Cautions him not to be provoked into a duel.

Asks Clay's assistance in the petition to the Senate of John H. Harrison of Greenville, S.C., a state legislator and "a most decided friend of the Union in opposition to the Nullifying doctrines of the south." ALS. DLC-HC (DNA, M212, R4). Printed in Colton, Clay Correspondence, 4:321-22. For Harrison's legal problems with the U.S. government, see U.S. Scn., Journal, 22 Cong., 1 Sess., 22, 39; Sen Docs., 22 Cong., 1 Sess., no. 8, pp. 1-2; U.S. H. of Reps., Journal, 22 Cong., 1 Sess., 119, 1151, 1193.

Remark in Senate, December 19, 1831. Asks that memorials from merchants in New York, Philadelphia, and Pittsburgh requesting a "further reduction of the duties on teas"—requests that had been deemed "inexpedient . . . at this time" by the Committee on Finance—be taken off the table and considered by the Senate. Such action is "due to the merchant, to the consumer, and to the important interests of the country." *Register of Debates*, 21 Cong., 1 Sess., 5. See also Comment in Senate, December 20, 1831.

From Leslie Combs, Philadelphia, December 20, 1831. States that "I shall, today, send some forty or fifty of the X. Y. & Z [*sic*, X.Y.] pamphlets in relation to the Colonial treaty [Clay to Adams, July 26, 1831], to some of my acquaintances in Congress." Adds: "Our friends here seem highly delighted with our proceedings at Baltimore [Clay to Conover, October 9, 1831]—We have planted our Standard on a granite rock & I for one, sink or swim—live or die, am prepared to fight under it to the last—But *we must triumph*—" ALS. DLC-HC (DNA, M212, R4).

Comment in Senate, December 20, 1831. Speaking to the question of possible reductions of the duties on tea on January 1, 1832, argues that such reductions should not be considered "without examining the great and important question of the tariff in general." Notes, further, that the reduction of tea duties, opposed by Secretary of the Treasury Louis McLane because of the need to eliminate the public debt at an early date, would have little or no impact on discharging that debt by March 4, 1833, the date chosen by the secretary. Concludes with the observation that while he is "decidedly in favor of a substantial preservation of the system of protection," he is "ready to concur in any measure of relief to the country not inconsistent with it." He does not think "that the object of paying off the whole public debt by a precise day in the year 1833, ought to delay, for one moment, the repeal of duties on objects not falling within the scope of that system." *Register of Debates*, 22 Cong., 1 Sess., 15-16.

From Nicholas Biddle, Philadelphia, December 22, 1831. Responds to questions [Clay to Biddle, December 15, 1831] concerning Clay's financial and legal problems. Turning to politics, states that "nothing is yet decided" concerning the application of the Bank of the United States for a renewal of the charter [Clay to Brown, December 18, 1831]. Congratulates Clay "on your return to the Senate," and adds that "few things have given me more pleasure than this vigorous rebound of an elastic spirit whom pressure has neither bent nor broken." ALS. DLC-HC (DNA, M212, R4). Copy in DLC-Nicholas Biddle Papers (DNA, M212, R20).

To HENRY CLAY, JR.   Washington, December 23, 1831

I have this day recd. your letter of the 7h. inst. from which I have much satisfaction in perceiving that your reflections upon what passed in K. immediately preceding your departure to N. O. have brought you to right conclusions. In respect to yourself I have no wish but what is connected with your prosperity and success, and I will add that your success is the strongest desire that binds me to this world. As to the time of your commencing your profession, it has been far from my view to limit it by days and months. What I wish is that when you *do* commence it, you may begin with a preparation, by study and research, which shall make you what I want to see you, respectable and eminent. Without such preparation, whatever advantages the state of the Bar and of Business may present, you cannot embrace them.

On politics, the papers will inform you of all that I can communicate. I have sent you some documents & will send you more.

Your mother is well, and joins me in love to you to Anne [Brown Clay Erwin], Mr. [James] Erwin, Mr. [Martin] Duralde, & Mrs. [Julie Duralde] Clay.

ALS. Henry Clay Memorial Foundation, Lexington, Ky.

To BENJAMIN GRATZ
Washington, December 24, 1831

An idea has been suggested of allowing a drawback to the amt. of the duty, or a part of it, on all Cottonbagging exported from the U. States, whether *American* or Foreign.[1] It strikes me that its operation would be in the nature of a bounty to our manufacturers, and consequently would not be prejudicial to them. It is very different from limiting the allowance of drawback to the foreign article which would be equivalent to a repeal of the duty.

Consult some of our most intelligent men, and let me know what is thought of the above idea. P.S. I wish you would send me an estimate of all the Bagging manufactured in K.

ALS. KyU. Letter marked "(Confidential)." 1. Clay spoke again to this issue in his Senate speech on the tariff on Jan. 11, 1832. *Register of Debates*, 22 Cong., 1 Sess., 72-73. But in the tariff act of July 14, 1832, no special provision was made for drawbacks on exported cottonbagging. On the tariff on cottonbagging in general, see U.S. H. of Reps., *Journal*, 22 Cong., 1 Sess., 1005, 1126; and *Register of Debates*, 22 Cong., 1 Sess., 3887-88.

From Christopher Hughes, Stockholm, December 24, 1831. Reminds Clay that "At this hour, Seventeen Years ago, we were at Ghent, and it was the moment of the consummation of *your* labours; that gave peace to our country." Regrets, however, that "my news from home, (received only on yesterday:) do not leave the slightest hope of your success in the Presidential election." Assures Clay that "You are not the less dear, the less loved, the less venerated by me, and by thousands of others who know you, on this account! as for myself, I declare to you honestly, that the public error, on this great question, gives a new spring to my private affection for you." Believes that until the election of John Q. Adams, Clay was "the choice, the boast, the favoured of our Nation." Expresses his disillusion with public life and wonders at "the motive that hurries happy, honourable, clever men into this career of turmoil and illusion." Asks, "though you certainly have gained the gratifying reward of great celebrity, fame & applause, yet, what has been the price, at which, this reward has been sought and gained?" Is certain the sacrifices of public life are "over-proportioned" to the joy of successes, "glorious and gratifying as they may have been at the moment." Complains that after 18 years in the service of the United States, he will never be able to look forward to an annual salary in excess of $2,000. ALS. DLC-HC (DNA, M212, R4).

From John Smith, Freedom, Me., December 24, 1831. Writes that he has "Read with much intrest your reply" to a letter "by an Antimasonic committee of Ind. [Clay to Citizens of Vincennes, October 18, 1831]" requesting Clay's views on Anti-Masonry. Believes if the Anti-Masons "should succeede in electing a president," it would be equivalent to seeing "the inquisition established." Notes that "your sentiments exactly correspond with my own," and that "after our present president has retired," he will be among "the first to suport you." ALS. DLC-TJC (DNA, M212, R10).

To FRANCIS T. BROOKE
Washington, December 25, 1831

With the compliments of the Season, I acknowledge the receipt of your favor of the 15h. inst. Here, we have nothing new. Opinions are in a progress of formation, on the leading measures of the Session. That of the Tariff will be the most difficult and agitating. I fear that there will be no agreement among parties either as to the amount of the reduction of the revenue, or the objects on which it shall be effected. The ultra's of South Carolina are very wrong headed on the latter point. They appear to be bent on the destruction of the system of protection, or on their own destruction.

The Executive is playing a deep game to avoid at this Session the responsibility of any decision on the Bank [of the U.S.] question. It is not yet ascertained whether the Bank, by forbearing to apply for a renewal of their Charter, will or will not conform to the wishes of the President. I think they will act very unwisely if they do not apply.[1]

You say the Calhoun party has almost disappeared at Richmond. Judging from the number of the members of the G. Assembly who attended the late Caucus,[2] I should suppose all parties but that of Jackson had disappeared in Virginia. I see the [Richmond *Constitutional*] Whig has repeatedly admitted that the N. Republican party is in the minority. I suppose it is so, but is it politic to make such a admission? Will such an admission secure either additional strength or any credit even for candor? Is it consistent with the purpose of making a struggle, if that be designed in Virginia? . . .

ALS. KyU. Printed in Colton, *Clay Correspondence*, 4:322-23.   1. Clay to Brown, Dec. 18, 1831.   2. A legislative convention, or caucus, had been held on Dec. 17, 1832, for the purpose of organizing their support for Jackson. Ninety-two of the 134 members of Virginia's general assembly and 22 of 32 state senators announced their intention of helping to form the Jackson ticket. After debate, the convention decided not to nominate a vice presidential candidate. Richmond *Enquirer*, Dec. 20, 1832. For subsequent conventions attempting to nominate a candidate for vice president, see Brooke to Clay, Feb. 9, 1832.

To HENRY CLAY, JR.   Washington, December 25, 1831

Enclosed I sent a letter addressed to you.

I have received a letter from Anne [Brown Clay Erwin], and am happy to find that she writes in her usual good spirits. She tells me of Mr. [Martin] Duralde's friendly offer that you should reside with him. On that point, you will be the best judge. You will find a residence with him loansome, but it may be favorable to diligent study. But consult exclusively your own feelings.

Mr. [James] Erwin will supply you with money, and get the draft I gave you discounted if necessary.

Make my respects to Judge [Alexander] Porter and Mr [George] Eustis.

ALS. Henry Clay Memorial Foundation, Lexington, Ky.

To ANNE BROWN CLAY ERWIN   Washington, December 25, 1831

We were very glad to learn from your letter of the 8h. inst this morning received that you had got safely to N. Orleans and were comfortably lodged. Our journey to this place was throughout very cold the winter having set in the day after we left home, and it conti[n]ues up to this time with uncommon severity. There have been already eight or ten falls of snow. We have taken lodgings in a very good house near the General post office. Mr. [Thomas A.] Marshall and Mr. [Daniel] Jenifer[1] of Maryland and our family compose at present the Mess, and there is not room for more than one other person.

We have been called on by all the heads of departments, foreign ministers &c. I have every reason to be satisfied with the attentions which have been paid us. The greater part of the Balto. Convention,[2] after its adjournment, came here and visited me in crowds. Indeed I have been almost overwhelmed with company. We took on the road very bad colds, from which we have not yet recovered. Several enquiries have been made about you, with great interest.

I am truly mortified with the incident which you related about Mr. Donnet.[3] It must have given much pain to Mr. [Martin] Duralde, and, by devolving the whole business of his Saw Mill establishment upon him, must give him full and not very agreeable occupation.

We hear frequently from home, where every thing goes on well. John [Morrison Clay] writes us that Mrs. [Caroline Milton] Watkins had been very ill but was getting better. In other respects, matters were as you could wish them at your place.

I am happy to hear both from you and Henry [Clay, Jr.] that he is well pleased with N. Orleans. I hope he will throw off that recluse disposition which he some times evinced, and without neglecting his studies, or mixing in the dissipations of society, freely partake of its rational enjoyments. He must decide for himself on Mr. Duralde's friendly proposal.[4]

I will not annoy you with politics, on which I know not that I could add any thing to what is contained in the News papers. The nominations at Baltimore have given fresh animation to our friends, and inspired them with strong hopes.[5]

Your uncle [James] Brown has met with an accident,[6] in falling which without being serious will confine him some time. He has postponed going to N. O. until Feby. and I think it doubtful whether he will go at all. He wrote me that he wished to entrust some business to Mr. [James] Erwin.

We brought H[enry]. C[lay]. Duralde with us, and he is in good health. Your mother has undertaken to instruct him.

Your mother wishes you to bring up with you in the Spring a dress of the wide Bombazine,[7] from which she and you got dresses last winter, as she cannot get any so good.

Give our love to Mr. Erwin, and kiss the children.

ALS. NcD.   1. See *BDAC*.   2. Clay to Conover, Oct. 9, 1831.   3. Erwin to Clay, Dec. 8, 1831.   4. Henry Clay, Jr., to Clay, Dec. 7, 1831.   5. Clay to Conover, Oct. 9, 1831. 6. Brown to Clay, Dec. 16, 1831.   7. A silk and cotton dress fabric.

To WILLIAM GREENE   Washington, December 26, 1831

I was extremely sorry to learn by your letter of the 29h. Ulto. that a serious domestic affliction would prevent your attendance at Balto. But as the principles which you would have carried there prevailed, with great unanimity, your presence was not so important. You will have seen the proceedings of the Convention before this reaches you, which appear to have given great satisfaction to our friends generally.[1]

The opinions of members of Congress, on the various important measures which are likely to come up this Session, being in a progress of formation, I cannot venture to conjecture even final results. It is not yet ascertained whether the Bank will apply for a renewal of their Charter. The President is believed to be very anxious that they should not make an application at the present Session. . . .[2]

ALS. OCHP.   1. Clay to Conover, Oct. 9, 1831.   2. Clay to Brown, Dec. 18, 1831; Webster to Clay, Jan. 1, 1832.

From Hugh Mercer, Fredericksburg, Va., December 26, 1831. Recommends John Lewis of Spotsylvania County "as a Candidate for the Presidency of the Transylvania University." Praises highly the preparatory school Lewis now operates and which his own son [Hugh W.] attended before going to West Point. "I have heard him more than once say, that in the instruction of youth consisted his highest enjoyment & Happiness —" ALS. KyLxT. For the choice of a new president for Transylvania University, see Southard to Clay, January 10, 1831. For John Lewis, who moved from Spotsylvania County, Va., to Georgetown, Ky., in 1832, see Albert Johannsen, *The House of Beadel & Adams and its Dime and Nickel Novels: The Story of a Vanished Literature* (Norman, Okla., 1950), 181-82.

From Thomas Smith, Lexington, December 27, 1831. Remarks that the "unanimity and zeal" of the Baltimore convention [Clay to Conover, October 9, 1831] have "revived" his spirits. Continues: "The proceedings at Frankfort have not been so fortunate. Judge [James] Clark was much dissatisfied, and some of his friends following his example, seem disposed to disseminate disheartening opinions as to the result. I doubt whether the strongest man has been selected, but he is certainly a better choice than Clark would have been. We are perfectly sensible of the great importance of the August election in reference to the Electoral election, — your friends here are resolved not for one moment to entertain a doubt as to the result. We will elect the Governor & Lt Govr. by triumphant majorities." Estimates that "we have at present more than 5000 majority in the State, and will give more than that in August." Adds that Robert P. Letcher "must work hard, — for his district is infested —" Notes that "The Governor [Thomas Metcalfe] was greatly harrassed by the applicants for the vacant Judgeship . . . and it does not seem to me that he extricated himself like a general." His choice was John Chambers, but he ended by nominating "a man [Charles M. Cunningham] who was the choice of nobody, except [Benjamin] Hardin and [James] Guthrie." Notes also that the race for mayor of Lexington "begins to excite apprehensions for the result — [Daniel] Bradford on one side — C[harlton]. Hunt, [James E.] Davis & [Stephen] Chipley on the other — but we do not intend to elect a Jackson mayor. Hunt or Davis will back out, and then we must make the other beat Chipley and Bradford." ALS. DLC-HC (DNA, M212, R4). At a National Republican meeting in Frankfort on December 20, 1831, Richard A. Buckner was nominated for governor and James T. Morehead for lieutenant governor. The Jacksonians nominated John Breathitt for governor and Benjamin Taylor for lieutenant governor. In the August election, Breathitt defeated Buckner 40,681 to 39,421, while Morehead defeated Taylor 40,046 to 37,452. Frankfort *Argus of Western America*, December 21, 1831; also Clift, "Kentucky Votes, 1792-1894," 312, 318. In the general assembly elections in Kentucky in 1832, Clay supporters won 60 seats in the house and 22 seats in the senate to 40 in the house and 16 in the senate for Jacksonians. Lexington *Observer & Kentucky Reporter*, August 30, 1832. Governor Metcalfe had appointed Cunningham to replace Henry Pirtle as circuit and general court judge in Louisville. Frankfort *Argus of Western America*, February 1, 1832. In the Lexington mayoral race, Charlton Hunt defeated Daniel Bradford by 326 votes to 321. *Ibid.*, January 18, 1832.

Comment in Senate, December 30, 1831. Opposes the bill to abolish the duty on alum salt and questions to what committee to refer it. States the importance of protective tariffs to U.S. industry and agriculture with particular reference to the salt tariff and American salt production. *Register of Debates*, 22 Cong., 1 Sess., 32-33, 35, 40-41.

From John Bond Trevor, Philadelphia, December 31, 1831. States that John T. Sullivan has been nominated by the president as a director of the Bank of the United States. Recommends him highly. Notes, however, that some officials of the Bank of Pennsylvania, where Sullivan had served as a director, were prejudiced against him, and that John Sergeant, a Bank of the U.S. director, has written to Daniel Webster and others to block Sullivan's confirmation by the Senate. Informs Clay that Sullivan "was with us in the last Presidential election," and that his belated conversion to Jacksonism has not been a deep one.

439

As for Pennsylvania politics, remarks that "We have nothing interesting here at present and are waiting with anxiety for movements and developements at Washington which shall prove favorable to our cause. At a private meeting of several of our friends a few evenings ago a Committee was appointed to take measures for calling a town meeting to approve of the proceedings of the Baltimore Convention [Clay to Conover, October 9,1831], and notwithstanding the coldness of the weather I hope we shall on that occasion manifest a warmth of feeling worthy of the cause we have espoused." Believes also that the "mantle of Jacksonism begins to set more loosely upon the shoulders of a majority of the members of our Penn[sylvani]a legislature." ALS. DLC-HC (DNA, M212, R4). John T. Sullivan's nomination was approved by unanimous consent of the Senate. U.S. Sen., *Journal*, 22 Cong., 1 Sess., 501.

Remark in Senate, January 5, 1832. Mentions the need to discuss a revised schedule of import duties, including the duty on Indian blankets, that would be "adapted to the wants of the country when the public debt should be discharged." *Register of Debates*, 22 Cong., 1 Sess., 53.

From William L. Stone, New York, January 5, 1832. Reports that the meeting "for submitting the proceedings of the Baltimore Convention [Clay to Conover, October 9, 1831] to the National Republican citizens of New York" was held last evening, and that, despite inclement weather, attendance was "highly respectable" with about 2,000 present. Remarks that "the long, loud, and oft-repeated bursts of applause" indicates that "a more fortunate selection of candidates could not have been made."

Adds in a postscript that Van Buren's nomination [Clay to Brooke, May 1, 1831] "*must* be rejected. . . . If he should be confirmed, by the votes of our friends in the Senate, the disappointment would be severe, and the discouragement too great for us to surmount." ALS. DLC-HC (DNA, M212, R4).

From Hezekiah Niles, Baltimore, January 6, 1832. Reports that "Things begin to look bright" since the stand Clay has taken in the Senate on the tariff [Webster to Clay, January 8, 1832]. Notes that he is also "*now* . . . satisfied that the anti masonic party will return, or come, to us—if treated as they should be—as the great majority are, though, as I think, mistaken, entirely honest." States that "It seems as if understood" in Baltimore that William Wirt "will soon decline being a candidate [Clay to Brooke, June 23, 1831]," and predicts that "we shall do better than the prospect a-head seemed to afford a hope of." Argues in closing that U.S. trade relations with Great Britain be introduced into the presidential campaign [Clay to Adams, July 26, 1831; Clay to Everett, August 20, 1831]. ALS. DLC-HC (DNA, M212, R4).

From John Denio, Albany, N.Y., January 7, 1832. Informs Clay that as "principal proprietor" of the Albany *Daily Morning Chronicle* he had, in 1828, "engaged heartily . . . in the cause and support of the Hon. J.Q. Adams . . . but when his opponents triumphed here, I lost all." Says that when the campaign was over "the friends of Mr. Adams became faint hearted and left me to suffer." Estimates that he lost about $5,000, "the whole of my 20 years earning," when the paper went under. Asks Clay, if he deems it proper, to notify Adams of his desperate financial situation. ALS. DLC-HC (DNA, M212, R4). Denio had engaged in the printing and bookselling business for 20 years in Greenfield, Mass., prior to moving to Albany in 1827. His wife was niece to Ezra Stiles, president of Yale College.

From ANNE BROWN CLAY ERWIN　　　　New Orleans, January 7, 1832
I today received your favour of the 23 Dec. and read it with more than ordinary pleasure as we had not heard a word from you since your arrival at

Washington, although we had been tantalized with a sight of your hand writing, as you had enclosed the Message both to Mr [James] Erwin & Henry [Clay, Jr.]. You have no doubt heard before this that [William C.C., Jr.] Claiborne has declined returning this winter, it is owing to his health which is much better than it was when he left here but he writes that his eyes are still so much affected that he thinks it prudent for him to remain at least another year. They have elected Mr [S.D.] Dixon to fill his place[1] he is a warm partizan of yours and was elected by one vote over Mr [Bernard de] Marigny, but the opposite party speak of contesting the election, it is not supposed however that they will succeed in turning Mr Dixon out so much for politics you see it is impossible to be the daughter of a politician without at least knowing what is going on.

We have been suffering here with the same influenza which appears to be prevailing at the North, the Creoles have felt it more than the Americans, indeed in some cases where the individuals were old it has proved fatal Mrs [Julie Duralde] Clay has been severely attacked she was confined to her bed for several days, and has not left the house for more than 2 weeks, I am glad to be able to say that she is much better now Mr [Martin] Duralde also has been quite sick with it but I beleive he is well enough now to go down to his Saw mill. Henry [Clay, Jr.] has commenced the Study of law under Judge [Alexander] Porters directions; he complains a little of the large folios he sends him, and thinks the Judge does not estimate his talents quite high enough when he supposes it will require 2 years of hard study to prepare him to commence the practice. The Judges family appears to be completely broken up since the death of Miss Eliza[2] he has taken lodgings in town and his daughter [Anne] is passing the winter with Mrs [George] Mathews; I have invited her to spend the ensuing summer with me and her father has promised that she should accompany us on our return to Kentucky. We have not heard a word from Lexington since the 27th Nov. the River being frozen up there is no communication at all between this and the *Western* country. The last letter I received was from James [Brown Clay] I was very gratified to find that he writes an uncommonly good letter for so young a boy.

I have been so fortunate as to find an infant school established here upon the same plan as those at the North where I send the boys [Henry Clay; James Jr.; and Andrew E.], they did not like to go much at first but by giving them a few sugar plums every day I hired them for the first week and they are now becoming interested in it; it is a very great relief to me to know that they are doing well and are out of mischief from 9 until 3 every day. Little Lucretia [Erwin] grows every day she is the most mischievous child of her age I ever saw, Aunt Lotty and her have at least a dozen quarrels of a day; I cannot thank my dear Mother enough for having spared Lotty to me, she is the best creature I ever saw and appears to be quite as much attached to the children as she ever was to yours. Tell Mama I shall certainly execute her commission with a great deal of pleasure, and if she can think of any thing else she wishes, you will have quite time to let me know, as we shall not leave this before the first of March; I have begun to make her the collection of baskets she wished me to get for her. The children all send a kiss to their dear grand parents as well as their love to Henry Duralde. Mr Erwin joins me in love both to Mama and yourself. If Uncle [James] Brown is with you you will remember us both affectionately to him; you will please say to him that Mr E. will [be] happy to render him any service in this country in his power.

ALS. DLC-TJC (DNA, M212, R10). Printed in Colton, *Clay Correspondence*, 4:323-24.   1. In the Louisiana house.   2. Porter to Clay, June 10, 1831.

From THEODORE W. CLAY   Hospital [Lexington], January 8, 1832
In my letter which I wrote last week I did not speak of getting out of this, I believe. I am, at a loss to know how I am to be released from this place;[1] And I begin to think that the time is wearing uselessly away. I have no expectation that in the press of business which must crowd upon you, time will be allowed you to answer my insipid, and useless letters, but I should suppose you could have more weight than any one else with those empowered to direct & superintend this institution.

Nor have I much hope that you will find it convenient, or consistent with your views, or that an opportunity may occur, in which you may aid me in my views of a place in some respectable commercial house in one of the large cities. Even should you not think proper to interfere in any way in my behalf, if I was at large & liberated from here so that I could engage in some thing to acquire the means to enable me to make my way to one of the commercial towns, altho' not under as good auspices as with an introduction from you., still I could get on, in some way or other. I have not the slightest mistrust about my habits or temperament; or that I could fulfil any reasonable expectation from industry, fidelity & perseverence. I know it is a tedious & at best a precarious undertaking, but I am young, my health is good, and I feel buoyant with hope, and as yet untried in the world, and of course not corroded with disappointedment and chagrin. Thanks to your liberality I have enjoyed the best means of education, & hope I am not devoid of a small portion of the learning of my time. I think, without more light, that the trial is worth making: I believe I could make my services at least equal to a competent support. A destitute, friendless young man, animated with the desire of bettering my condition, of respectibility & independence; unless all that is said, & written of the benefits of our institution be a deceptive here, I think I need hardly fear, bounded as are my desires by moderation, to obtain a competency at least.

I hope my education, if not sown upon the most fertile soil, is at least sufficient to point me out what is right, and to assign me my proper lot in society. And I trust that all obstacles from my own uncowardness, & perverseness of disposition are forever dissipated. This appears to me the most rational & feasible plan, in my present destitute condition; and you may perceive that altho bowed and prostrate as I am, my spirit is yet unbroken.

This town offers no inducement I think you will agree with me; and in the obvious propriety, of my seeking a new Theatre as the scene of my future exertions. Still if you or any friend would indicate to me now the same desirable object could be accomplished, it would not lay with me to present captious or fastidious objections. My greatest wish is, to simply earn my living, and enjoy a portion of the good things of this life.

They have just elected Charlton Hunt lord Mayor of the town.[2] I have no news to offer you; but that our friends are well as I feel myself to be; and not to be too pertinacious, anxiously desirous of having something to do.

Tender my love to Mother & accept my heartfelt congratulations of the season

ALS. DLC-TJC (DNA, M212, R14).   1. The Lunatic Asylum of Kentucky to which Theodore had been recently committed. On Oct. 3, 1831, Clerk of the Court of Fayette County, Thomas Bodley, ordered the sheriff of the county to "Summon and impannel Twelve good and lawful men of your bailiwick . . . to enquire and say, whether Theodore W. Clay is or is not a *Lunatic*," and, if so, when that "infirmity" commenced. This action stemmed from a complaint on Sept. 29, 1831, by John Brand [2:635] and his son, William Moses Brand [4:58], who had appeared before Oliver Keen, justice of the peace of Fayette County, and sworn that "they believe Theodore W. Clay Insane, & of unsound mind, & further that they consider the lives of themselves, & familys, in danger from said Theodore W. Clay, — provided he is not taken in custody & confined." Among the twelve men summoned to consider the insanity issue were such prominent Lexingtonians as Dr. Charles Caldwell [2:724-25], Col. Leslie Combs [1:396], Richard H. Chinn [1:707], Thomas Smith [1:452], Robert Wickliffe [1:82], John Postlethwait [1:134], and James E. Davis [1:833]. The decision of the panel was that Theodore W. Clay be confined to the local asylum for the insane. See *Commonwealth of Kentucky* v. *Theodore W. Clay* (Writ de Lunatico), Fayette County Circuit Court (Sept. 1831, term), file no. 746. See also Clay to Henry Clay, Jr., Oct. 31, 1830. For the hospital in which young Clay spent most of the rest of his life, see "Some Account of the Lunatic Asylum of Kentucky, With Remarks, Etc. By Samuel Theobald, M.D. Late Attending Physician of the Institution," *Transylvania Journal of Medicine* (Feb., 1830), 3:72-94. 2. Smith to Clay, Dec. 27, 1831.

From DANIEL WEBSTER
Washington, January 8, 1832

I have shewn these Resolutions[1] to Mr Selibee [*sic*, Nathaniel Silsbee], & Mr [Nathan] Appleton. We agree, that it will be well that they should be brought forward tomorrow, provided Genl. [Samuel] Smith reports no Bill, in the morning, from the Comee. on finance.

I would suggest that the word "all," in the first line of the first Resolution, might be advantageously left out. There may, perhaps, be some few articles, of high luxury, which it wd. be well to have taxed, tho' they do not come into competition with our own products.

We have not had an opportunity to consult Mr. [John] Davis.

The Bank, as perhaps you know, has decided to apply, immediately, for the renewal of its Charter. The Memorial, I believe, is in the City; & I presume it will make its appearance in the Senate tomorrow,[2] thro' the V. P. [Calhoun] — It will be best, will it not, to let the Administration Gentlemen give a disposition to it, for the present, such as suits them?

ALS. DLC-HC (DNA, M212, R5). 1. Clay had written Webster the same day, Jan. 8, enclosing resolutions he had prepared concerning the tariff "which with the concurrence of Mr. [Nathaniel] Silsbee, yourself, Mr. [John] Davis, I will offer tomorrow [*Register of Debates*, 22 Cong., 1 Sess., 55]." ALS. NhD. Printed in Wiltse, *Webster Papers*, 3:141. Clay's resolution of Jan. 9 looked toward lowering duties on certain imported articles not in competition with similar articles produced in the U.S. His major speeches on the tariff were delivered in the Senate on Jan. 11, 1832, and Feb. 2, 1832. *Register of Debates*, 22 Cong., 1 Sess., 66-75, 257-96. For the tariff act of 1832 (passed on July 14), see Taussig, *The Tariff History of the United States*, 109-10. 2. The B.U.S. "Memorial" for recharter, signed by Nicholas Biddle, president, was presented in the Senate on Jan. 9 by Sen. George M. Dallas (Pa.). It asked for an early renewal of the bank's charter, which was due to expire on March 4, 1836. *Register of Debates*, 22 Cong., 1 Sess., 53-55. It passed the Senate on June 11 by 28-20 votes and the House on July 3 by 107-85 votes. U.S. Sen., *Journal*, 22 Cong., 1 Sess., 345; U.S. H. of Reps., *Journal*, 22 Cong., 1 Sess., 1074. See also Clay to Brown, Dec. 18, 1831; Clay to Fendall, August 4, 1832; and Hammond, *Banks and Politics in America*, 382-86, 389-91.

From Peter B. Porter, New York, January 9, 1832. Reports that Van Buren's nomination excites "a great deal of interest & feeling in this state" and "the almost universal sentiment of our friends . . . is against his confirmation [Clay to Brooke, May 1, 1832]." Mentions that when he leaves New York City in "a day or two," he will "spend 3 or 4 weeks at Albany, Saratoga & that nieghbourhood from whence I may perhaps be able to furnish . . . some, political information, & form come conjecture as to the course the anti masons intend to pursue." Continues: "There will shortly be a split in the Jackson, or rather *Regency* ranks in this State. The [New York] Courier & Enquirer will come out against the Albany Regents, & support [Erastus] Root against [Enos] Throop, for Governor [Clay to Bailhache, November 24, 1830]. This demonstration however may be of no advantage to us, as each of the two factions will probably consider its success as dependent upon the zeal it can display, & the clamor it can raise in favour of the 'hero [Jackson].'"

Mentions that Gen. James Lynch of New York City is going to Washington "as an agent of the late Tariff Convention [Davis to Clay, November 2, 1831]" and "might be usefull in effecting . . . a compromise with the Southern members in relation to some parts of the Tariff."

Reports, in conclusion, that the "last news from New Jersey is of the most cheering nature, and our political prospects generally in the North are evidently brightening." ALS. InU. In the New Jersey legislative elections in October, 1831, 7 Clay men and 7 Jackson supporters were elected to the council, while in the assembly 26 Jacksonians and 24 Clay supporters were chosen. Jackson papers boasted that they had gained 1,900 popular votes, but Clay newspapers saw it as a victory for themselves, saying that the election signified a loss of 2,092 votes for Jackson. New York *Evening Post*, October 18, 1831; and Washington *Daily National Journal*, November 15, 1831.

Remark in Senate, January 9, 1832. Submits resolution lowering the duties on certain imported articles not in competition with similar articles produced in the U.S. Omits wines and silks. *Register of Debates*, 22 Cong., 1 Sess., 55. See Speech in Senate, January 11, 1832.

On this day Clay also supported a bill to build a military depot at New Orleans. Remarks not reported. *Ibid.*

From JOHN SERGEANT   Philadelphia, January 9, 1832

I did not receive 'till this morning your favor of the 6th inst — Before this gets to hand, you will probably be informed of the intentions of the Bank, by the *acts* of the Board. The truth is, no such design as has been attributed to them was ever entertained.[1] I left the Board on the 2d inst, my three years having expired. Up to that time, there was no wavering, and I am persuaded there has been none since. But it was thought prudent to reserve their opinions 'till the last moment, as well as to treat with respect the views of those friends who differed with them as to *time*. They had no notion of yielding the point, but they deemed it a duty of friendship to explain, before they acted, the grounds of their proceeding. This will be a key to what may have occurred to you as dilatory or suspicious.

You have every reason to be gratified with what occurred at Baltimore,[2] whatever may be the result. The whole convention was of one mind and one heart as to your nomination, and I never witnessed a tribute of respect & homage more spontaneous or more sincere. When you consider the composition of that body, its numbers, the numbers of those it represented, its moral worth, and general weight and respectability, and then consider that its voice was unanimous and earnest, you will find it difficult to suppose a more flattering testimonial than its nomination furnished.

Pennsylvania is in a ferment, and it is not easy to see what will be the result. Our friends will not meet in Convention 'till May,[3] by which time they will have a clear view of the horizon and be able to shape their course accordingly,

ALS. InU. Letter marked "(Private & confidential)." 1. On Jan. 6, 1832, Nicholas Biddle asked for and received approval of the B.U.S. board to lay before Congress an application for rechartering the bank. See Hammond, *Banks and Politics in America*, 385-86. See also, Clay to Brown, Dec. 18, 1831; Brown to Clay, Jan. 24, 1832; Webster to Clay, Jan 8. 1832. 2. Clay to Conover, Oct. 9, 1831. 3. Clay to Ketchum, May 15, 1832.

Remark in Senate, January 10, 1832. Asks that his resolution of the previous day on lowering certain import duties receive a hearing tomorrow. *Register of Debates*, 22 Cong., 1 Sess., 57.

Speech in Senate, January 11, 1832. Has no desire to discuss the "established policy of protection" since that policy "stands self-vindicated, in the general prosperity" of the nation [Webster to Clay, January 8, 1832]. But believes that given the "near approach of the entire extinction of the public debt," certain tariff adjustments downward are now called for. Traces the history of the gradual decline of the public debt. Claims that "By various acts, and more especially by the tariff of 1824—the abused tariff of 1824—the public coffers were amply replenished." But tariff reductions must be equitable to all groups of Americans. Hopes that once the public debt is extinguished the proceeds from future public land sales will in part be used for internal improvements [Comment in Senate, April 16, 1832; Speech in Senate, June 20, 1832]. "This is due to the American people, and emphatically due to the Western people." Explains the West's developmental needs and its positive attitudes favoring internal improvements, and argues that, given the general economic health of the nation, government subsidy of such improvements is in order. Considers various approaches to reducing tariffs, concluding that "the most equitable and reasonable" would be "To abolish and reduce the duties on unprotected articles, retaining and enforcing the faithful collection of those on the protected articles." Such an approach "extracts no sacrifice of principle from the opponent of the American system; it comprehends none on the part of its friends." Most importantly, it maintains the protective system. Discusses frauds and violations built into the existing tariff system. Suggests that this problem can best be addressed by shifting the locus of the valuation of a given commodity for ad valorem tariff purposes from the foreign port of its departure to the U.S. port of its arrival. This would prevent foreigners from effectively setting the duty to be paid. Also, the U.S. should reduce or abolish credits extended to foreign merchants which allow them to postpone the payment of duties. Estimates changes in total government receipts from all sources if his tariff philosophy is adopted. Mentions specific commodities on which the duties should be reduced and increased. Attacks Secretary of the Treasury Louis McLane's plan [Clay to Porter, May 1, 1832] to "reduce no part of the duties on the unprotected articles prior to March, 1833, and then to retain a considerable portion of them. And as to the protected class, he would make a gradual but prospective reduction of the duties. The effect of this would be to destroy the protecting system by a slow but certain poison." Explains how his own plan will still permit McLane to achieve his goal of extinguishing the public debt by March 4, 1833. Concludes: "Our common object should be to reduce the public revenue as to relieve the burdens of the people, if indeed the people of this country can be truly said to be burdened." *Register of Debates*, 22 Cong., 1 Sess., 66-75. Printed in Colton, *Clay Correspondence*, 5:416-28. See also Speech in Senate, February 2, 3, 6, 1832.

To PETER B. PORTER   Washington, January 14, 1832

I recd. your several favors from N. York. The Bank, you will have seen, has applied for a renewal of its Charter.[1] It is believed that there is a majority in each house in its favor, but it will be some time before reports will be made.

All the Secretaries have been approved by the Senate and the Secretary to our Minister to England. The Minister himself has not been approved, and the issue of his [Van Buren's] nomination is uncertain.[2] It will depend upon the course of a certain part of the Jackson Senators. I think there is a more prevalent opinion among our friends as to the expediency of his rejection than existed when you left us. Of its justice none of them ever doubted.

445

We are in the midst of a discussion that will involve the whole policy of the Tariff.[3]

ALS. NBuHi. Letter marked "(Confidential)." 1. Clay to Brown, Dec. 18, 1831; Webster to Clay, Jan. 8, 1832. 2. Clay to Brooke, May 1, 1831. 3. Webster to Clay, Jan. 8, 1832.

Comment in Senate, January 16, 1832. With reference to the debate on Robert Y. Haynes's amendment of this date to Clay's tariff bill in which he proposes the "gradual reduction of the present high duties on articles coming into competition with similar articles made or produced within the United States" after the public debt has been liquidated, asserts he will not be intimidated by menacing statements from Sen. John Forsyth of Georgia ("We . . . will fight from post to post, and die in the last ditch") against the entire protective principle. *Register of Debates*, 22 Cong., 1 Sess., 106-7. Haynes's strict tariff-for-revenue amendment and his supporting speech is in *ibid.*, 77-104.

To HENRY CLAY, JR. Washington, January 17, 1832

I was this moment very much delighted by being told by Judge [Josiah S.] Johnston that he has received a letter from Judge [Alexander] Porter in which he writes that you are pursuing your studies with the same ardor and perseverance as young men generally pursue pleasure. Such my dear Son is the course which will make your Country and me proud of you, and what is not less important, give you occasion to be proud of yourself.

I made a Speech[1] the other day of which I sent you a Copy. Quite as much has been said in its praise as it merits. I shall have to make another in a few days on which I am now exhausting all the intellectual labor which I can command.[2] If I should be able to fulfill my hopes I will send a Copy of it to Judge Porter and to you.

Your mother and I are both suffering under a very bad cold. The weather has become very fine, 'tho we can hardly expect it to continue.

We hear frequently from Ashland and our friends at Lexington. Things go on very well there generally.

I hope Mr. [James] Erwin supplies you with money, or will do it as you may want it.

Give my respects to Judge Porter and our love to Anne [Brown Clay Erwin] & family.

ALS. Henry Clay Memorial Foundation, Lexington, Ky. 1. Speech on Tariff, Jan. 11, 1832. 2. Speech on the nomination of Van Buren as minister to Great Britain, Jan. 25, 1832; or his Speech on the Tariff, Feb. 2, 1832.

From Hezekiah Niles, Baltimore, January 17, 1832. Says that Clay's speech in the Senate on the tariff on January 11 "is, in every respect, the master-speech that you ever delivered. . . . It is clear, comprehensive and concise." Believes also that "its brevity will give it the greatest cirulation that any thing of its kind ever received in the U. States. The small weekly papers can 'get it in'—which is a matter of much importance, and especially just now." Assures Clay that the political light "is dawning upon us." Argues that the tariff, the Van Buren nomination as U.S. minister to Great Britain [Clay to Brooke, May 1, 1831], and the recharter of the Bank of the United States [Clay to Brown, December 12, 1831; Webster to Clay, January 8, 1832] are issues that can be used effectively to beat Jackson. "Things *do* look well." Thinks that William Wirt will soon withdraw from the presidential race and that in so doing he "may have a mighty influence on events about to happen." ALS. DLC-HC (DNA, M212, R4).

Remark in Senate, January 18, 1832. Responds to a question relating to the selection of an arbiter under the Northeast Boundary Convention of September 29, 1827, with Great Britain [6:1100]. *Register of Debates*, 22 Cong., 1 Sess., 109.

From James Duane Doty, Lowville, N.Y., January 19, 1832. Charges that non-citizens of the Michigan Territory have been nominated for various offices, including that of governor. Complains that "This troop of foreign mercenaries is coming among us, either as political missionaries, or to receive their reward for services rendered in Genl. Jackson's last campaign." Asks that the U.S. Senate see to it that as Michigan's offices become vacant, they "be filled by its own citizens." ALS. DLC-HC (DNA, M212, R4). For Doty, see *BDAC*. George B. Porter of Pennsylvania had accepted the governorship of Michigan in August of 1831. Doty may also have been protesting his pending dismissal as an additional judge for the Michigan Territory. He was replaced by David Irwin of Virginia on January 31, 1832. Carter, *Territorial Papers*, 12:332, 425, 552.

To BRANTZ MAYER   Washington, January 21, 1832

I recd. your favor of the 18h. inst. with the address of the young men of the N. R. party in Balto. to their brethren in Maryland.[1] The patriotic sentiments which it contains do great credit to their hearts and their understandings, and, with you, I sincerely hope that they may be shared by the young men throughout the Union. For those which are personal to myself I am infinitely obliged.

A real crisis in our Republic has arrived, and the question which it involves is, whether the government shall be administered according to the principles of purity and moderation which governed all the Administrations prior to the present, or upon a system of corruption and proscription, embracing Congress, The Press, and the great body of the people, as far as they can be reached, and all official encumbents in the power of the Executive. If this system is to be established and perpetuated, our Government will deserve to be called by any name other than that of Republican.

I pray you to accept for yourself and the Comee. of which you are Chairman[2] assurances of my cordial esteem and regard.

ALS. NcD.   1. *Address of the Young Men of the National Republican Party, of the Fifth Congressional District, to the Young Men of the State of Maryland.* Baltimore, 1832.   2. For Mayer, a lawyer and later the founder of the Maryland Historical Society, see *CAB*.

From Henry A.S. Dearborn, Washington, January 22, 1832. In response to a request from Clay, submits figures for 1825, 1826, 1828, and 1829 showing for those years the amount of merchants, shipping tonnage registered in Charleston, S.C., and the total ship tonnage using the harbor there. While the figures show "an apparent falling off" of registered tonnage from 12,871 in 1828 to 7,842 in 1829 and total tonnage from 32,445 in 1828 to 13,074 (corrected to 18,786) in 1829, the declines can be explained as follows: the "death of vessels" and the sharp decline in shipbuilding in Charleston. At the same time, however, "Their exports have increased & if they have not more navigation, it is because others understand it better." Continues: "The business of ship building & navigation is better understood & can be more cheaply prosicuted in the northern states than in the extreme south & the tariff has nothing to do with it. The exports & imports are going on well & because Charleston does not participate is not owing to the tariff. Navigation is a different business from planting & Philadelphia N. York & N. England can do it best."

Promises he "will ascertain the imports & exports from & to Great Britain for as many years as possible, & give the results to you to morrow, if it is possible to achieve it from the books in the Capitol." ALS. DLC-HC (DNA, M212, R4). Dearborn, at this time, was a member of the House of the 22nd Congress. Clay incorporated his Charleston tonnage figures into his speech on the tariff in the Senate on February 2, 3, 6, 1832. *Register of Debates*, 22 Cong., 1 Sess., 266.

From James Brown, Philadelphia, January 24, 1832. Says he will try to visit Washington on his way home to New Orleans via Pittsburgh. Has heard that "Our crops . . . are very bad. I have only made three hundred hogsheads and yet, few [sugar] planters in the State have made as much."

Reports that "[Robert Y.] Haynes speech [January 16] is thought to be able and would strike dismay into the hearts of the tariff men did they not hope that you and Webster would fully answer it—Your last speech [January 11] gave very general satisfaction to your friends in this quarter as an opening speech but they wait impatiently impatiently [*sic*] for your great effort [Speech in Senate, February 2, 1832]."

Informs Clay that "The mass in this state are said to remain Jacksonmen the leaders are thought to be held to him by the mass—Will [William] Wirt continue as a Candidate? It is rumoured here that he will decline—If you negative Van Buren [Clay to Brooke, May 1, 1831] it will make a place for [George M.] Dallas or [William] Wilkins at London—But the [numero]us friends of Van think that his defeat [w]ould conduct him to the Presidency [Clay to Brooke, May 1, 1831; Clay to Porter, March 10, 1832]. Few here seem to think it would have that effect   I am so little of a politician and converse so little on the subject that I know not ho[w] it will then eventuate—"

Concludes with the observation that "I did not suppose the French treaty would [meet] with any opposition." ALS. DLC-HC (DNA, M212, R4). The Hayne speech of January 16 is found in *Register of Debates*, 22 Cong., 1 Sess., 77-104; Clay's "great effort" of February 2, 3, 6, is in *ibid.*, 256-96. For the Franco-American Commercial Convention approved unanimously by the Senate (signed July 4, 1831, ratified February 2, 1832), see Parry, *Treaty Series*, 82:97-103. For the legislative history of the spoliation claims crisis that grew out of France's noncompliance with the terms of the 1832 treaty, the subsequent reaction of the Senate Foreign Relations Committee to Jackson's bellicosity on the issue, and Clay's major speech on the issues that had resulted in the threat of war, see Remark in Senate, January 6, 1835, and Speech in Senate, January 14, 1835. It was not until February 22, 1836, that the president announced a successful conclusion to the controversy. The diplomatic history of the events that transpired before, during, and after the indemnities crisis is in Richard A. McLemore, *Franco-American Diplomatic Relations, 1816-1836* (Baton Rouge, La., 1941), 204, *passim*.

To EDITOR, WASHINGTON DAILY NATIONAL INTELLIGENCER [Gales & Seaton]   Washington, January 24, 1832

The Globe. — The Government paper is getting scurrilous, which is what no official paper ought ever to be. A more wicked attempt to injure the character of **Mr. Clay** has been rarely made than that contained in this Official yesterday (the 24th.)   The Globe had so promulgated the fact of the recent extraction of a bullet from the arm of General Jackson as to make the impression, that the wound had been acquired in the public service. Some other paper, adverting to the fact, had stated that the ball was received in a rencontre with the Messrs. Benton [1:820]. Now what had **Mr. Clay** to do with this affair? Nothing upon earth. But see how he has been lugged in. After alluding to an unfortunate affair [1:400] between that gentleman and a member of the Kentucky legislature [Humphrey Marshall], which happened twenty-three years ago, the Globe proceeds:

"He (Mr. Clay) was taken to a kind friend's house in the neighborhood of Louisville; he was treated with the utmost tenderness and courtesy by that friend's wife and family, and *while enjoying their hospitalities*, he amused himself, *it is said*, by winning the money of his kind host at brag. It is very *certain* that the generous hearted man who took him to his house was bereft of a large fortune by playing, and it is equally *certain* that Mr. Clay had a share of it."

Now we are well informed that there is not one word of truth in all this statement. **Mr. Clay** was not, on the occasion referred to, taken to a friend's house. He went to the tavern [5:587] of Mr. [John] Gwathmey, in Louisville, where he remained during his short confinement from the very slight wound which he had received. He did not win from his generous host at brag or any other game. It is not true that Mr. Clay obtained any share of a large fortune of which any one was bereft. The Editor [Francis P. Blair] of the Globe knows, or ought to know that Judge [Fortunatus] Cosby (although a Jackson man) the person alluded to, has under his own signature in the public papers contradicted this one. Yet, in contempt of all decency, if not of truth, he has revived it.

A more wanton unprovoked assault than this was never made on the personal character of any individual. It is one which, if it had the sanction of the Administration, would cover it with indelible disgrace.[1]

Copy. Printed in Washington *Daily National Intelligencer*, Jan. 25, 1832.   1. Transmitted in Clay to Joseph Gales, Jr., and William W. Seaton, Washington, Jan. 24, 1832. "Will you oblige me by publishing as editorial the enclosed article, either in its present form, or in such other as you may prefer? I vouch for the facts." ALS KyU

From David Milne, Philadelphia, January 24, 1832. Gives a lengthy comment on Clay's speech of January 11 on the tariff as a person who has had 25 years experience as an importer in England and Scotland, and who admits at the outset that "My views of the Tariff have always coincided in most respects with yours."

Discusses how best to eliminate the fraud inherent in an ad valorem duty system in which the valuation of a given commodity is determined by the foreign exporter rather than by American importers. Believes that "specific duties ought to be substituted for the advalorem." That failing, suggests that American importers or consignees should determine valuation by estimating the cost price of the commodity plus freight and insurance. Following this estimate, a sum would be "deposited in the hands of the Collector of Customs equivalent to the duties at that valuation, a Permit is then granted for their being landed, and such articles as can be safely and properly examined on the Quays along side of the Ship, are there opened, and if found to have been fairly entered, are passed, and such goods as require to be more minutely examined in a Warehouse, are sent to the Custom house for that purpose — If the Appraising Officer finds that they have been undervalued, he has it in his power to detain them, upon paying the Importer according to the Valuation at which they were entered, with the addition of Ten P. Cent as a Profit —"

Argues also that while Clay had "most properly directed the attention of the Senate to the present *Credit* allowed on duties," he had "said nothing as a substitute; as your idea seems to be only for lessening or shortening it — In my humble opinion the Credit system ought to be abolished in toto, and in lieu thereof the Bonding system ought to be adopted, but that only to a limited extent, or rather applicable only to certain description of goods and to particular ports of entry, with the privilege of transporting them from port to port without payment of duties, but still under Bond, or to be reshipped and transported to places beyond the U.S., which would save an immensity of trouble to all parties of shipping and drawing debentures —" Discusses the "evils attending the Crediting of duties," and explains at length how the bonding system began and developed in Britian. ALS. DLC-HC (DNA, M212, R4).

Comment in Senate, January 25, 1832. Urges Senate to get on with the business of the tariff. Suggests to Sen. John Tyler of Virginia, who opposes the protective tariff, that "finding himself in so small a minority" he should "come over to the right side." *Register of Debates*, 22 Cong., 1 Sess., 176, 178.

Speech in Senate, January 25, 1832. Opposes the nomination of Martin Van Buren as U.S. minister to Great Britain [Clay to Brooke, May 1, 1831]. Bases his opposition mainly on the grounds that the policy of Jackson and Van Buren on Anglo-American trade in the British colonies, principally in the British West Indies, was one that was "prostrating and degrading the American eagle before the British lion"; also, that Jackson had exceeded his authority in nominating Van Buren while the Senate was in recess. *Register of Debates*, 22 Cong., 1 Sess., Appendix, 1310, 1320-26. Printed in Colton, *Clay Correspondence*, 5:429-36, with minor variations in punctuation and capitalization. It was in response to Clay's remarks on this day that Sen. William L. Marcy of N.Y. made his celebrated observation on patronage politics, viz: "the politicians of the United States. . . . see nothing wrong in the rule, that to the victor belong the spoils of the enemy," a policy that is "practised by his [Mr. **Clay's**] own political friends" in Kentucky. *Register of Debates*, 22 Cong., 1 Sess., Appendix, 1325.

From William J. Mayo, Paris, Ill., January 26, 1832. Congratulates Clay on his unanimous nomination by the Baltimore convention [Clay to Conover, October 9, 1831] and hopes he will triumph over the "military chieftain." Heard from Thomas Hart Clay a few days ago. He was well, but "I shou[l]d rejoice if he would be a little more temperate. and am well pleased with him in every thing else." ALS. DLC-HC (DNA, M212, R4). It is not certain that this William J. Mayo was the former county clerk of Floyd County, Ky. [1:829] or what business relationship he had with Thomas Hart Clay, who was at this time farming his father's land just west of the Wabash River in eastern Illinois near Terre Haute, Ind.

To NORBORNE B. BEALL   Washington, January 27, 1832

A most scurrilous attack was made a few days ago[1] by the [Washington] Globe upon me, importing that after my affair with Mr. H[umphrey]. Marshall,[2] now more than 23 years ago, I was taken wounded to the house of a friend, and after being tenderly nursed by his wife and family won a large sum of him and contributed to his ruin. It was supposed that the friend alluded to was Judge [Fortunatus] Cosby, and a prompt and preemptory contradiction of the tale was immediately made in the [Washington *Daily National*] Intellr.[3] Whereupon the Globe[4] asserted that not Judge Cosby but another friend was meant whose name, if required, would be given privately to the Editors [Gales and Seaton] of the Intellr.   It was required, and to my astonishment yours' was surrendered. A copy of [Francis P.] Blair's letter to the Editors of the Intellr. is enclosed.[5] This new version of the calumny has been contradicted, and I do not know that it is necessary for you to take any notice of it. I was carried, as you know to Mr. [John] Gwathmeys, where I remained until my wound healed. You and I, in our youthful days, have had some frolics but I should be sorry to believe that *I* ever contributed to any serious misfortune on your part.

We have rejected V. Buren,[6] and our friends are in high spirits. I think when you see the debate you will be satisfied with the grounds on which we have placed his rejection. The Bank question — the Tariff &c. will all come up.[7] If our friends do their duty every where we shall defeat old Hickory. [William] Wirt is now here, and I think will some how get out of the scrape in which he is.[8]

450

ALS. KyLoF. 1. Clay to Gales & Seaton, Jan. 24, 1832. 2. See 1:400. 3. On Jan. 25, 1832, in an editorial written by Clay. See Clay to Gales & Seaton, Jan. 24, 1832. 4. Jan. 26, 1832. 5. The *Intelligencer* did not publish Blair's letter to Gales and Seaton identifying Beall; but on Jan. 28, 1832, an editorial appeared in the *Intelligencer* which stated that the *Globe* had privately supplied the name and that the *Globe*'s charge against Clay "is destitute of all foundation whatever." 6. Clay to Brooke, May 1, 1831. 7. Clay to Brown, Dec. 18, 1831; Webster to Clay, Jan. 8, 1832. 8. Clay to Brooke, June 23, 1831.

From HENRY CLAY, JR.   New Orleans, January 27, 1832

In the last letter which you wrote to me [January 17], you wished me, if I understood your words, to draw upon Mr [James] Erwin for money instead of using the order you gave me on Allain Perrault & Allain   I accordingly received from Mr Erwin on the 13h. of January, the sum of $100.00. He has in his hands idle money of yours, which he thinks I had better use than that which is drawing interest.

Anne [Brown Clay Erwin] thinks of returning to Kentucky in February or early in March. Mr Erwin will probably return to New Orleans to remain till May or June. When may we expect you? I suppose you will not be able to leave Washington much before June.

I am still in the Hotel in which Anne is. Mr [Martin] Duralde has been unwell with the influenza, and has just gone below: I have not yet determined whether I shall go with him or not.

Your friends in this quarter are looking with interest to all your movements in the Senate.

Anne intends having at her house next summer several of her young friends   Mr Erwins' sister, a daughter of J[ohn]. P. Erwin, a little boy, a son of one of Mr Erwin's brothers, and Miss [Anne] Porter, the daughter of the Judge [Alexander Porter].

I have often thought of reminding you of a promise which you made to me when I was at West Point to permit me to go to Europe. If it be convenient I should like to go in the Spring. My health, I hope would be improved by it; my mind and manners certainly would. but could you afford it. I know not. Anne thinks you would be able to gratify me without a sacrifice. But you know best, and will tell me; and that will decide the matter. I was anxious to commence the practice next winter in this city. But Judge Porter agrees with you & disagrees with me as to the propriety of doing so. He thinks that History Literature & a thorough course of law should first be diligently attended to. He mentioned two or three years as the term of preparation   You know that I have long cherished the desire to visit Europe. I have looked to the visit as the completion of my course of elementary studies, as that which will finally perfect the little scientific knowledge that I have acquired, enlarge my mind and mature my taste: this time seems to me the most convenient that I can select. I am now entirely unincumbered and I think in other respects better prepared for the voyage than I shall be at any future time.

But let me entreat of you, that you will not yield to my instances if it do not meet your approbation.

I would be glad to hear from you early. Aunt [Julie Duralde] Clay is just recovering from a fever. Anne & Mr Erwin and their children [James, Jr.; Henry Clay; Andrew Eugene; Lucretia Hart] are in uncommonly good health & spirits   Mr Erwin as usual seems to be prosperous in his business

William [C.C.] Claiborne [Jr.] I suppose you know, has res[i]gn[e]d his seat in the Legislature, & is now, I believe, in Italy.

Give my love to Mama & Henry [Clay Duralde]. John [Morrison Clay] wrote to me from Lexington a very good letter indeed, well composed & well written. He & James [Brown Clay] seem to be well contented at Mr [Benjamin O.] Peer's.[1] Martin Duralde [III] is a very fine boy; manly & intelligent.

I am told that Paris is a cheaper city than New Orleans. I do not know: you can tell me.

Excuse this letter; it was written without care or previous reflexion; just in the shape in which the ideas presented themselves. . . .

ALS. Henry Clay Memorial Foundation, Lexington, Ky.   1. Clay to Henry Clay, Jr., Oct. 31, 1830.

From Leslie Combs, Lexington, January 27, 1832. Comments on Clay's speech on the tariff on January 11: "You have made a very Sensible speech on your proposition to take off certain duties & reduce others — You occupied the true ground on every point you made & did it with becoming temper — I regret the Southrons are crazy, but let them fret; *you* must not quarrel with them — You occupy higher ground than any of them & must look down upon them & sooth them, not *yourself* play the gladiator — That would do for me if I were in Congress — as I am not, others must do it — *Your* course must be above all partisan warfare & God will speed you — It must be for the Union, the whole Union & nothing but the Union. —"

Reports that the Bank of the United States now charges ½ to 1 percent brokerage on bills "between *Lexington* and *Louisville*." Thinks this excessive, that the maximum between banks so close together should not exceed ¼ percent, and that regardless of distance the brokerage charge should not exceed 1 percent "as for instance between New Orleans & New York or Phila. — Indeed ½ would do very well for the highest rate of exchange." Concludes that this "may seem a small matter but it is one which has produced & is producing enemies to the Bank — I think some petitions will come on from here for a removal of the charter & the opinion of our Legislature may well be inferred from the fact that a charter was refused for a State Bank in our great Commercial city, (Louisville) last winter; — a large majority being of opinion that the branches of B.U.S. afforded capital enough & a better medium than any state institution possibly could. . . . Will you pass the Bank bill & will Jackson sign it? . . . P.S. If this is opened in the post office or does not reach you, I have adopted means to catch them —" ALS. DLC-HC (DNA, M212, R4). Printed in Colton, *Clay Correspondence*, 4:325.

Comment in Senate, January 27, 1832. Questions the utility of a proposed Senate investigation of the facts surrounding the manufacture of alum salt, because he objects to approaching the tariff issue in piecemeal fashion, article by article. *Register of Debates*, 22 Cong., 1 Sess., 182-83, 185-86.

From Joseph Howard, Tiffin, Ohio, January 27, 1832. Transmits the 1831 annual report of "our Canal Commissioners — by which it will be seen that one more link will shortly be completed in the great chain which I hope, when completed, will add greatly to the strength and perpetuity of our Union." Is sure Clay derives "great satisfaction" from being the "author of a System which but a few years ago existed only in theory." ALS. DLC-HC (DNA, M212, R4). Printed in Colton, *Clay Correspondence*, 4:325. Howard was a prominent politician of Seneca County, Ohio, who later (1834-35) served as a state senator. See F.E. Scobey and E.W. Doty, *The Biographical Annals of Ohio* (Springfield, Ohio, 1902), 287. The canal mentioned was the Ohio Canal between Portsmouth and Columbus. A celebration of its completion to Chillicothe took place on October 22, 1831. The canal was finally completed to Portsmouth in 1832.

On October 1, 1832, Duncan McArthur wrote Clay, inviting him to attend, on October 12, a celebration of the canal from Chillicothe to Portsmouth. LS. DLC-Duncan

McArthur Papers (DNA, M212, R22). See Francis P. Weisenberger, *The Passing of the Frontier, 1825-1850*, vol. 3 in *The History of the State of Ohio*, Carl Wittke (ed.) (Columbus, Ohio, 1941-44), 99; George Perkins, "The Ohio Canal: An Account of Its Completion to Chillicothe," in the *Ohio Archaeological and Historical Publications* (Columbus, 1926), 34:597-610.

To JOSEPH GALES & WILLIAM SEATON

Washington, January 28, 1832

Mr. Clay's respects to Mess. Gales and Seaton and he informs them that he has prepared a sketch of his *first* remarks in the Senate, on Mr. V. Bs. nomination,[1] making about nine pages similar to those which he sent them, on his resolution. They are at their service when they are ready for them

Mr. Clay suggests the expediency of some notice being taken of the article in the Globe,[2] respecting the alleged negotiation about Impressment, which may be interrupted by the rejection of the Minister.

Can any thing be more ridiculous than that the public may be prejudiced as to that *old* affair? We want no treaty Security, no negotiation about it. The best security is the thunder of our Cannon, and the valour of our Tars, to be applied to the very *first* instance hereafter when G.B. shall dare to impress an American Seaman.

AL. NN.   1. Speech in Senate, Jan. 25, 1832.   2. The article in the Washington *Globe* of Jan. 28, 1832, argued that Van Buren had been nominated and sent as minister to Britain to prevent the continuing impressment of American sailors. It charged also that Clay and Calhoun did not want Van Buren to receive sole credit for ending this long-standing diplomatic problem with Great Britain.

From Thomas Metcalfe, Frankfort, Ky., January 29, 1832. Remarks that Clay's Senate speech of January 11 on the tariff "has been received here by our friends with expressions of the most decided, entire & hearty approbation. It unquestionably contains the true policy: or rather lays down the true basis upon which to build the present & future policy of the Republic — the only policy under which we can expect to thrive & prosper as a Nation   Mr. [Robert Y.] Haynes speech [Brown to Clay, January 24, 1832] of four hours has not yet reached us. We look not only for an energetic speech from Mr Hayns [*sic*], but expect it to be tinctured with violence when he touches upon your views respecting *protection* & Internal improvement. . . . Upon the whole the debate on this subject and that upon the rechartering of the bank [Clay to Brown, December 18, 1831], excites great interest here,   It is believed that our political adversaries are a little dismayed. At any rate they speak in a tone somewhat subdued."

As for Kentucky state politics, "But little is said at this time about the approaching election of Governor & Lt Governor [Smith to Clay, December 27, 1831]. The little incidents occurring here at the time of the convention, which I hinted to you, encouraged the [John T.] Breathitt party exceedingly. But I think it is passing, or has passed off without leaving much — impression   It is I think hardly possible that such a man as [Richard H.] Buckner can fail to run up to the strength of the question —" ALS. DLC-HC (DNA, M212, R4).

From THEODORE W. CLAY   Lexington Hospital, January 30, 1832

I recieved your favour and the documents in 3 parcels and return you my sincere thanks.

This attention during the variety of engagements which must oppress you there, is as grateful as unexpected to me. I have executed your request to Dr Jordan[1] and he says he intended to have written to you.

I did not take occasion to express to you the extent of my gratitude for all your kindness to me, during I may well say the whole course of my life, and which I will now only allude to and leave you to imagine the rest, as you can much better do, than I can find language to explain; and for its greater generosity because of the unfortunate and helpless attitude in which I stand to society, and which my being here has for the *first* time apprised me of. The concern you and my good Mother feel for my welfare, and the disposition you express to lend me aid, in which I stand so much more in need now than ever I could have done in my life is just what I was secure in the belief you had. I need not stop to say that a prejudice perhaps natural and right, exists in Lex. among many towards me, and for which also perhaps I can account, and which I confess myself both unable and unwilling to undertake to stem, if I have the option. Such a footing of equality as I think myself entitled to, I think I am not mistaken it was fully communicated, to me in one way or another will not be awarded to me, among those whom I consider equals according to every principle of common sense, right reason, and the institutions of our Country; and any other must bring inevitable misery along with it. Retirement, and perhaps as much obscurity as is attainable would no doubt be the happiest state for me. The expense of living here I suppose is little; but if I had a situation such as I have before mentioned to you I am very confidently persuaded, I could obtain That object of cardinal importance; and also open as reasonably encouraging a prospect as my unhappy condition would admit. Personal independence is at all times, as far as is compatible with our nature, and laws, an object of duty, as well as choice, to an ingenuous mind, and I confess is now doubly so to me, from the reflexion that I have been so long a burthen without being able to requite your generosity or to exonerate you from it. I am at present not conscious that there exists any other necessity for my remaining here, but my want of a refuge or home elsewhere. In the event of my disappointment as to the situation I took occasion to allude to before; And which is more congenial owing to the state of my frame and health of body; the plan you suggested of going on your land for a while in Illinois has occurred me: of course merely residing there devoid of such a sum of money as would enable me to conduct the business with success & energy would be useless: but with some security in bank; or a small loan say of $2000 I could easily pay the interest, and make a handsome profit. This would make an retreat acceptable to me.

Indeed I feel that I have made such an *expiation* for my idleness & dissipation that rest is almost indispensable, as well as my due. I believe my library was taken home. I had a few little things which I hope are not lost. They will be of use to somebody. I think Dr Jordan informed me you were good enough to assume the little sums I owed in Lex. which with the one to Robert Scott of $395 & one of $100. are all I owe in the world of any kind: so that on that score I am quite unembarassed. I believe our friends are all well, tho' I seldom hear from them, & never see any but Thomas [Pindell] Hart. Please present my best love to Mother. . . . P.S. I would be glad if convenient, you would send me a copy of Elliott's [*sic*, Eliot's] Almanac for 1832.[2] I suppose it can be got easily.

ALS. DLC-TJC (DNA, M212, R14). 1. Dr. J.C. Jordan, a physician on the staff of the Lunatic Asylum of Kentucky. See also, Theodore W. Clay to Clay, Jan. 8, 1832. 2. *Eliot's Pocket Almanac and Annual Register of the Federal and State Governments for 1832.* . . . . Washington, 1832.

To James Herring, January 30, 1832. In response to Herring's inquiry, believes that "one of the best portraits of me" was made by the late Matthew Harris Jouett of Kentucky.

Thinks that it might be "somewhere" in New York City. It was once owned by Joseph Delaplaine [2:685]. Reports that "Another Western artist is now in this City to retouch a painting of me, when I can set to him, which promises well." Says he has no painting of himself in Washington which he can send to Herring. ALS. ViU. For Herring, a prominent artist, see *CAB*.

From John L. Lawrence, New York, January 30, 1832. Believes that recent events in the U.S. Senate have given "confidence and animation to our friends. It has affected them, as the capture of the Hessians did the dispirited whigs." In New York, "consternation" has visited the Jacksonians. "Already have they called a meeting in this City, to dissipate each other[s] fears by indulging in the language of denunciation." Further, wonders how it can be that Indiana, "which we have considered one of the most decided States in the Union," sends a Jacksonian delegation to the House of Representatives [Clay to Everett, August 20, 1831; Southard to Clay, September 18, 1832]. ALS. DLC-HC (DNA, M212, R4). Jackson carried New York City in the 1832 presidential election by a margin of 5,508 votes. New York *Evening Post*, November 9, 1832. For New York State, see Clay to Bailhache, November 24, 1830.

Remark in Senate, February 1, 1832. Asks reconsideration of a resolution, just passed, which requires the reporting of the names of holders of unclaimed dividends of the funded debt of the U.S., if such dividends have been due for more than two years. *Register of Debates*, 22 Cong, 1 Sess., 224-25.

From Peter B. Porter, Saratoga Springs, N.Y., February 2, 1832. Congratulates Clay on the "happy direction" of the Van Buren nomination issue [Clay to Brooke, May 1, 1831] and the bank recharter question [Clay to Brown, December 18, 1831]. Had feared that "the Jugglers at Washington would over reach the Directors and by threats or promises, or both, succeed in placing that institution in a situation which would deprive the numerous & intelligent body of men connected with it, of the fair exercise of their political rights. I am therefore thankfull to find that the Directors have, at length taken such ground that a regard to their own interests will compel them to give an open & manly support to their political friends. Every sort of trick & chicanery will doubtless be resorted to, to give the subject the go-by for the present Session; but I trust that the friends of the Bank have talent & tact & strength enough to carry the measure through & oblige the 'Hero' to meet it with his sanction or his *veto*."

Thinks, too, that the rejection of Van Buren's nomination is "one of the most auspicious events to our party & country that has happened since the commencement of the present administration." Believes that there are "not a few" Jackson men in New York who "secretly rejoice in the decision of the Senate."

Reports that several of the Anti-Mason leaders in New York "have lowered their tone exceedingly & are evidently willing to aid us in the Presidential election if they can devise the means, which I much doubt, of doing so without breaking up their party, the very existence of which as they, very truly, say, depends upon its being *exclusive*. They have even suggested some particular plans of co-operation." Hopes, therefore, that William Wirt will eventually withdraw from the race, because "If he were out of the way we might I think calculate with considerable confidence on the co-operation of most of the Anti Masons [Clay to Weed, April 14, 1832]." Concludes: "Please burn this." ALS. InU. Draft, dated February 1, 1832, in NBuHi.

Speech in Senate, February 2, 3, 6, 1832. Supports at length and in detail the protective tariff and related elements of the American System [Speech in Senate, January 11, 1832]—domestic manufactures and internal improvements—in response to a long speech [*Register of Debates*, 22 Cong., 1 Sess., 77-103] by Sen. Robert Y. Hayne, of S.C.

on January 16, 1832, attacking the protective tariff. *Register of Debates*, 22 Cong., 1 Sess., 257-96. Clay's counter-attack appeared in pamphlet form under the title, *Speech of Henry Clay in Defense of the American System; Delivered in the Senate of the United States, February 2, 3, and 6th, 1832*. Hartford, 1832, 25 pp. It was also printed in full in *Niles' Register* (March 3, 1832), 42:2-16, under the heading "Speech in Defense of the American System" and in Colton, *Clay Correspondence*, 5:437-86. See Niles to Clay, February 28, 1832; also Hayne to Clay, February 8, 1832.

On February 14, Clay purchased 50 printed copies of Hayne's speech for $3.50 and 100 copies of New Jersey Sen. Mahlon Dickerson's speech of January 23 for $4.00. *Ibid.*, 155-74. The latter supported Clay and the protective tariff. Clay to Elliot, February 14, 1832. ADS. DLC-TJC (DNA, M212, R17). For Dickerson, see *BDAC*.

From Edward P. Little, Boston, February 3, 1832. Writing as a member of the Massachusetts state legislature, informs Clay that he will work for his election "in this part of the Country" if he can answer two questions satisfactorily, viz: "1st hast thou been engaged in Dueling in one or more instances; 2d dost thou believe that to be the most honorable way of settling differences." Concludes that if this letter is not answered, "I shall take it for granted that thou approves of that Honrable practice." ALS. DLC-HC (DNA, M212, R4).

From Daniel Mallory, New York, February 3, 1832. Believes that the Senate is "entirely in the dark in relation to the Turkish treaty" and that an investigation of the instructions sent to the American commissioner should be undertaken. Remarks that the Turkish government has protested aspects of the treaty in "bold and indignant language," and that "The President has been weak enough to commit himself and the Government in a letter to the Sultan [Mahmud II]." ALS. DLC-HC (DNA, M212, R4). The American treaty commissioners were David Offley, David Rhind, and Commodore James Biddle, USN. Rhind, former U.S. chargé in Constantinople, also assisted the Turkish negotiators. For the treaty, signed May 7, 1830, ratified October 5, 1831, see Parry, *Treaty Series*, 81:1-17. For the treaty negotiations, including subsequent problems with translations, and with the Senate's rejection of a secret article concerning the building of Turkish warships in the United States, see Charles O. Paullin, *Diplomatic Negotiations of American Naval Officers* (Baltimore, 1912), 144-53; and *House Docs.*, 22 Cong., 1 Sess., no. 250, pp. 94-95.

From Hezekiah Niles, Baltimore, February 3, 1832. Has seen a notice of Clay's tariff speech of February 2 in yesterday's Washington *Daily National Intelligencer*. Believes that its "effect on the *public reason* must be powerful." Adds: "My opinion is, and I have some pretty good reasons for it, that even the *madness* of party cannot be rallied to the support of the *great rejected* [Jackson]. I shall feel humbled if — he is not now killed — & if he falls alone. Some of the party here call him *liar* & *traitor*. But how long this *honesty* will last, is yet to be seen." ALS. DLC-HC (DNA, M212, R4).

From HENRY CLAY, JR.   New Orleans, February 4, 1832
I have just received your letter of the 17th ultimo and a corrected copy of your speech [January 11] in the Senate. I am grateful to you for both. The address I think is one of the happiest efforts you ever made; and the letter assures me of your continued attachment. I know well that I have frequently erred, yet I believe that my heart is good; and I am sure that my affection for you is warm and unabated. It is indeed one of the greatest gratifications that I experience to receive from you these continued expressions of esteem and approbation. But I very much fear that Judge [Alexander] Porter's friendship for you, and

456

through you, for me, has overrated the exertions that I am making. I am not idle, but yet I do not apply myself so closely as I could wish to do

We have been in some expectation of seeing Uncle [James] Brown, but are now beginning to despair of his coming.

Judge [John] Rowan and family, and Mr [Isham] Talbott, who travelled with us to Vincennes, are all in the City.

No certain political demonstration has been made since I have been here.

In my last [January 27, 1832] I said something about going to Europe. You will not I hope, permit my remarks to bias your opinion.

Mr. [James] Erwin's success in speculations have far exceeded his anticipations. The operations of one year have secured him a handsome fortune. You mentioned in Kentucky among the plans which you had marked out for me, that of engaging in some manufacturing business, and devoting my leisure to study and politics. The same capital here, invested with judgment, by one well acquainted with the interests of the city, might be infinitely more productive: If you have any idle capital,[1] I could command the judgment of several in this city, among others Mr Erwin, who would be glad to serve me, and by whom such capital would be rendered more valuable far than that which draws even an interest of ten per cent, And with their judgment and knowledge of particular locations and the individual interests and relations of the city, together with what little care and attention I could bring, such an advantage might accrue as would be profitable to you and of deep interest to me.

You may suppose, perhaps, that I am too desirous of making money; but I can assure you, that it is my ambition which prompts me to endeavor to pursue your steps in political fame and as an Orator. No one who is poor in certain situations of life, can be independent; and the dependent politician is too often corrupt. It is then to place myself in an attitude of contempt towards the offers of corruption so profusely held out to political aspirants, that I should desire the possession of property.

It has been by an exertion that I have forced myself to write the above. I know your pecuniary difficulties, but I believe they are all in a course of adjustment. I have feared that perhaps your own debts called for all the Capital at your disposal and that I might perhaps be making to you an indelicate proposal. However, my feelings were in some measure calmed when I recollected that you had money loaned out at interest drawing but 10 per Cent, when by speculation in city property this interest at least would almost necessarily be secured. And perhaps much more which might be advantageous to both. I believe too that you know me too well to suppose that I could for a moment desire to disturb your peace of mind or the regular adjustment of your affairs. If [you] think then that our interest may be united without too much hazard, and if, indeed, your affairs permit of any hazard, though I think it will be very slight, I think that the application of a few thousand dollars might be well made in New Orleans City property: but if there be any objection in your view of the subject sufficient to outweigh the advantages, then do not let my feelings be any consideration whatever with you.

To give you some idea of the rise of property. Mr [William] Beal bought a lot last year for $15.000 and sold it a few days ago for $58.000. Mr. Erwin's property have had great accessions of value even since he has been down, and even on property which he buys today and sells tomorrow he sometimes realises large profits.

457

We are all in good health and spirits. Give my love to Mama and Henry and my respects to Mr & Mrs [Josiah S.] Johnston and Mr [Thomas A.] Marshall —

ALS. Henry Clay Memorial Foundation, Lexington, Ky.   1. The following phrase, "and should object to my going to Europe," is struck through.

From Samuel G. Mitchell, Indianapolis, February 4, 1832. Reports that the National Republicans of Indiana met on January 31 in the state senate chamber and chose an electoral ticket of Clay for president and John Sergeant for vice president. The meeting was attended by "a number of distinguished gentlemen from different parts of this State" as well as a number of Indiana legislators "favorable to our views." Names the seven electors and their two alternates. Says a central committee has been formed to fill vacancies in the electoral ticket should any occur. Names the five men on this committee. Adds: "This meeting meet, acted, and parted in perfect harmony. The selection of Mr. Sergeant by the Baltimore Convention [Clay to Conover, October 9, 1831] meet the unanimous wishes of the national republicans. Your friends remain firm and decided. And I beleve since the present Session in Congress, are on the increase in this State. But the enemies to the best interests of the union are growing more vigelent in their opisitton. The patronage of the present administration are exerted by the office holders. and they rely on *money* knowing *money is power*."

Assures Clay that Indiana favors internal improvements. Gives as evidence the fact that the state legislature which has just adjourned passed a Wabash Canal bill, a bridge bill linking Indiana and Kentucky at the falls of the Ohio, and five railroad charter bills, of which "three or four will pass this place." Also, that the Indiana lower house has recently passed a resolution requesting that branches of the Bank of the United States be located in the state. "We believ[e] the present Bank, gives us a sound circulating medium," he concludes. ALS. DLC-HC (DNA, M212, R4). Mitchell, the first physician in Indianapolis, had migrated there from Paris, Ky., in 1821. He died in 1837. Jacob Dunn, *History of Indianapolis*, 2 vols. (Chicago, 1910), 1:542.

From John Noel, Reeds Mill, Jackson County, Ohio, February 4, 1832. Thinks it a poor idea to reduce the tariff when government funds are so badly needed to finance coastal defense installations. Suggests, specifically, that major fortifications should be built on Cape Charles and Cape Henry, and on two man-made islands in Hampton Roads. Argues that these forts would deny to the British access to the Chesapeake Bay in future wars. Feels that such expenditures for defense would serve as part of Clay's "American System." Recounts at length the destruction and death wrought by the Royal Navy in the Chesapeake during the War of 1812. Asks that Clay pass this letter on to editors Joseph Gales and William W. Seaton for publication in the Washington *Daily National Intelligencer*. ALS., manuscript torn. DLC-TJC (DNA, M212, R10). Noel had served as a junior officer in the War of 1812. Heitman, *HRDUSA*, 749.

From Benjamin B. Howell, Washington, February 5, 1832. Submits to Clay a number of statistics on iron imports and the duties thereon, showing that the import duty on that commodity is about 35 percent rather than the 159 percent to 282 percent to 300 percent claimed by some. Suggests that Clay might want to include these corrective figures in his concluding remarks in the Senate tomorrow [Speech in Senate, February 2, 3, 6, 1832] on the tariff. ALS. DLC-HC (DNA, M212, R4). Clay did not use Howell's data. Benjamin B. Howell & Co. were Philadelphia merchants.

From William L. Stone, New York, February 5, 1832. Reports "that the attempts of Van Buren's friends here to create an excitement in consequence of his rejection [Clay to Brooke, May 1, 1831], has utterly failed. There is no mistake about it in this city. They could not drum up half the office-holders. The whole concern is discomfitted. Their efforts have been complete abortions. On the other hand, this act of the Senate has been received in New York, with great enthusiastic joy, by nine-tenths of all those whose good opinions are desirable." ALS. DLC-HC (DNA, M212, R4).

From Robert Y. Hayne, Washington, February 8, 1832. Responding to Clay's inquiry, reports that "having kept no memorandum on the subject," it is "impossible for me to give you the several corrections made by me during the delivery of your Speech [February 2, 1832]." Asks Clay, in turn, to reconsider in his own remarks Hayne's alleged reference to the Charleston *City Gazette*. Clay was about to cite that particular paper on the low price of cotton in the South when Hayne interrupted him and was quoted as saying that the paper was "not southern in its sentiments [*Register of Debates*, 22 Cong., 1 Sess., 285]." Asks that Clay correct that statement so as to "preclude the inference that I would use the influence of my station to impair the standing of any Paper known to be politically opposed to me and my friends." ALS. Courtesy of Morristown (N.J.)-Edison National Historical Park.

From FRANCIS T. BROOKE   Richmond, February 9, 1832

I have not written you for Sometime waiting until after the Jackson Caucus here which it was rumoured was to be held last night, but has I understand been postponed,[1] from what I learn it is doubtfull whether when it meets it will nominate Mr V B [Van Buren] as V P   I incline to think he will not be named but that the caucus will wait for the convention at Baltimore,[2] I heard a member of the legislature Say who is a Jackson man that the [Thomas] Ritchie party could not carry him in the caucus here, at present I rather wish he Should be nominated as I think the Calhoun party in that event (Some of them) would come over, there is a great desire here to see your reply[3] to Colol [Robert Y.] Hayne, and if it is published in pamphlet form which I presume it will,[4] Shall be obligated to you for Some of the copies, as Soon as they are out, we Shall probably have no caucus here but shall make out a Clay ticket,[5] this is not because there is any want of Zeal or numbers, but to avoid the general objection to Caucus   This is not yet Settled,

ALS. DLC-HC (DNA, M212, R4).   1. Two Jackson conventions, actually legislative caucuses, were held in Richmond. The first, on Feb. 29, 1832, met to select a vice-presidential candidate. Failing that, a second gathering was held on March 14-16, 1832. The latter chose a slate of Jackson electors but again could not agree on a vice-presidential candidate. Richmond *Enquirer*, March 1, 20, 1832.   2. For the details of the Democratic national nominating convention in Baltimore on May 21-23, 1832, which produced the nomination of Jackson and Van Buren, see Gammon, *The Presidential Campaign of 1832*, 96-104.   3. Speech in Senate, Feb. 2, 1832.   4. *Ibid.*   5. The National Republicans in Virginia decided not to nominate candidates by legislative caucus. Instead, they called for a more broadly based convention that convened at Staunton on July 16, 1832. The 90 delegates present, representing 17 out of the 21 state house of delegate districts, endorsed Clay and Sergeant and chose presidential electors. Henry Harrison Simms, *The Rise of the Whigs in Virginia 1824-1840* (Richmond, Va., 1929), 58-59.

From John L. Lawrence, New York, February 9, 1832. Informs Clay of an "assemblage last night," called to counter Jacksonian denunciations of the Senate vote on Van Buren's nomination as minister to Great Britain [Clay to Brooke, May 1, 1831]. It was, "notwithstanding the inclemency of the weather, the largest collection of our Citizens that I have ever known to be assembled *within doors*. The large Hall was literally crammed, as well as the gallery over the entrance, and numbers were obliged to go away in consequence of a want of the necessary space to accommodate them. Great animation prevailed, and when the nomination at Baltimore [Clay to Conover, October 9, 1831] was alluded to by one of the Speakers, a most gratifying exhibition was made of the feeling of the throng on that subject." Believes that "the proper Spirit is now fairly awakened, and that New York is not to be altogether despaired of when the Presidential canvass shall take place." ALS. DLC-HC (DNA, M212, R4). The meeting in support of the Senate's rejection of Van Buren's nomination was held in Masonic Hall on the evening of February 8. Washington *Daily National Intelligencer*, February 13, 1832; see also, Ketchum to Clay, February 12, 1832.

From HIRAM KETCHUM   New York, February 12, 1832

The rejection of Mr Van Beuren's [*sic*, Martin Van Buren] nomination by the Senate is, in my judgment,[1] the best point that has been made by the opposition, since the election of Genl Jackson; in this State I entertain a strong belief it will be more effectual in producing a union among the whole opposition, at least for a short time, than any other measure which has yet been agitated. The meeting of Citizens held to sustain the Senate, last Wednsday evg[2] was the largest I have ever known in this City, except the meetings occasionally held in the open air, and this too, notwithstanding the inclemency of the night, and the fact that the notice of the meeting was very short. You doubtless noticed, that two well known anti-masons acted conspicuous parts in this meeting;[3] this was not without design, and the gentlemen themselves, as well as our friends, are desirous that this example should be followed in other parts of the State, whereever meetings shall be held. My policy is to get the whole opposition in this State, to unite, during the present Session of Congress upon as many subjects of great public importance, as I can; hoping that when we have learned to act together upon some subjects, and have been unitedly brought to regard the re-election of Andrew Jackson as the greatest evil that can befall the country, we shall be unwilling by a separation, to make him again the President. To this end, with one or two others, I labored for several days, to get up the late meeting; the only difficulty in the way of this object was to get old and respectable citizens, who had long declined an active part in politics, to sign the call; this difficulty being overcome, all obstacles to the accomplishment of that gratifying, result which has followed, were removed.

The Indian Question[4] too has been pushed with a view of producing Union; this business has, at length been placed in the hands of a very small and efficient Committee, who have funds in hand, and will not fail to awaken as much attention to the subject, not only in this State, but all over the Union, as diligence and zeal can produce. A large number of young men, in this City, have engaged in this business; a memorial is prepared and now circulating praying Congress to enforce the treaties and law in favor of the Cherokees; this Memorial will be forwarded in two or three weeks, with as many names, appended to it as any that ever came from any one locality in the Country. It seems to me that these and all other subjects of great national importance, calculated to take hold of the feelings of the people at large should be pressed with all the zeal and energy that our party can put forth, especially in the States of New York, Pennsylvania & Vermont, for thus only will the people come to *forget*, that exciting topic, *Anti Masonry*.

In pursuance of this policy I would recommend that as much interest should be awakened as possible, among the friends of the tariff; as soon as the debate on your resolution is over, a very large edition of your speeches[5] upon it, carefully prepared by yourself should be published and scattered all over the three States I have mentioned; pains should be taken at Washington to have every man who can read furnished with the speech; I would recommend

that a large Pamphlet edition be published,[6] and, for more general distribution, that the Speeches be published entire in an *extra* of Niles Register,[7]
and sent to every man in the Country who would read them, and who can
pay two cents postage. The Pamphlet edition can circulate under the frank of
members of Congress. I have written [James] Lynch, now at Washington, to
this effect. The manufacturers owe it to their cause, they owe it to you as the
uniform friend and champion of that cause, to see this matter attended to
without delay. For this purpose I am aware that funds are required, and it is
proper that you should know, that on this article, you are under no obligations to the manufacturing interest in this part of the Country; the gentlemen
engaged in this department have been exceedingly niggardly in their contributions, and their exertions, for the support of your nomination, and I
have occasion to know that the friends of the protective system are not your
most efficient friends here. I wish you would talk with Lynch; and if the committee are not disposed at once, to undertake this publication, please let me
know and I will see what can be done among the manufacturers and domestic
dealers in this City. I believe *great* and *prompt* exertions, such as a few of your
friends here are disposed to make, may yet save New York, Pennsylvania,
and Vermont.

In this matter of Van Beuren's nomination, more of the old federalism of
the City has been around than on any other recent occasion; the ultra federalists are Jackson men, but the sound and most respectable portion of the old
stock is exceedingly opposed to the present administration. I believe that this
body of men though few in number, yet of great weight in the Community,
could, by a united effort, give to the National Republican candidates, the vote
of this State. Should the anti-masons make no nomination of Electors, and the
National Republican party make no nomination for Governor and Lieut:
Governor I believe both these parties might indulge a reasonable hope of success. Now I know of no body of men, except those referred to, whose influence, judiciously put forth, could place the parties upon this footing; if indeed
they could, It is my intention to make an effort, as soon as I shall think matters
are ripe for it, to call into action the secret influence, of these old federalists
between whom there subsists a bond of Union, which has never yet been sev-
ered. I have not yet communicated this intention to any person, but should
any thing be done the men whose influence would be most conducive to the
desired end are Chancellor [James] Kent, Genl [Stephen] Van Rensselaer,
and Abraham Van Vechten; if there be any way in which you can reach these
gentlemen, or either of them, by any civility, I would suggest your doing so.
Chancellor Kent is personally very well disposed towards you, and if, accompanying a copy of your Speech,[8] you should think proper to write him a letter
he would doubtless be flattered. George Griswold is well disposed, and since
his return has evinced it by a liberal pecuniary contribution to our party,
though he detests the tariff; he too would be flattered by a private letter accompanying a copy of yr Speech; John Horn too is a friend of yours, and getting to
be a tariff man; do not forget him

I would rather you would not speak of this projected movement with
federalists *even to our most intimate friends yet*. In closing I wish to say that Mr
Joseph Hoxie[9] will probably write you soon, you have doubtless seen his name
connected with the proceedings of our committees, I need only say you have
not a truer, a more efficient friend in the State

ALS. DLC-HC (DNA, M212, R4).   1. Clay to Brooke, May 1, 1831. Ketchum, a New York City attorney and Websterite, had been a delegate to the New York State National Republican convention in June, 1831. He was not, however, elected as a delegate to the party's national nominating convention in Baltimore on Dec. 12, 1831. New York *Evening Post*, June 4, 1831. 2. Lawrence to Clay, Feb. 9, 1832.   3. At least one "well known" Anti-Mason present at the meeting was Samuel Stevens, recently defeated Anti-Mason candidate for lt. governor of New York. Washington *Daily National Intelligencer*, Feb. 13, 1832. The *Intelligencer* of this date lists a number of prominent political figures who were present at the meeting.   4. Clay to Hammond, Oct. 7, 1829.   5. Speech in Senate, Jan. 11; Feb. 2, 1832. No such edition was published. 6. Speech in Senate, Feb. 2, 1832.   7. *Ibid.*   8. *Ibid.*   9. Hoxie (see *CAB*) had been elected vice president of the New York State National Republican convention [Prentiss to Clay, July 1, 1831] in June, 1831. New York *Evening Post*, June 4, 1831.

Comment in Senate, February 13, 1832. Delivers the report of the joint committee of the Senate and House, with accompanying correspondence and documents on arrangements for the celebration of "the centennial birthday of George Washington." Speaks also on the question of the disinterment and reburial of Washington's remains in a proper vault under the Capitol in Washington City [Clay to Bodley, February 14, 1832]. *Register of Debates*, 22 Cong., 1 Sess., 367-77.

To JOHN WESLEY HUNT   Washington, February 13, 1832

I have to thank you for your friendly letter respecting Theodore [W. Clay] of the 4h instant. His condition has been a cause of inexpressible regret and anxiety to us.[1] And I am happy to learn from you, as I have from others, that there is some improvement in his situation.

Dr. [J.C.] Jordan has mentioned to me that he thought exercise on horseback would be beneficial to him. I have left at Ashland a grey horse that he sometimes rode. Will you do me the favor to send for that horse or for Mr. [James] Erwins poney and have the one or the other kept, at my expence, at the Hospital for his use? Or, if you think another would better answer the purpose, purchase one, and draw on me for the amount? His saddle and bridle, I understand, are in the Garret at Ashland.

I have nothing to add to the News papers. Mr. Shannon has been appointed Chargé to Guatemala —[2] a mission which Mr. [John Q.] Adams did not think the public had any occasion for. Had I been in the Senate (which I was not) I should have objected to the mission, 'though perhaps not to the person nominated.

ALS. KyU.   1. Theodore W. Clay to Clay, Jan. 8, 1832.   2. James Shannon of Lexington, Ky., nominated as U.S. chargé d'affaires in Central America (Federation of the Centre of America, commonly called Guatemala) on Jan. 26, 1832, commissioned on Feb. 9, 1832, died before reaching his post. On April 12, 1832, Clay opposed an appropriation to sustain the mission. Adelaide R. Hasse, *Index to United States Documents Relating to Foreign Affairs, 1828-1861* (Washington, 1921), 1476, 1782; *Register of Debates*, 22 Cong., 1 Sess., 768, 771-74.

To THOMAS BODLEY   Washington, February 14, 1832

[Apologizes for not having written earlier, pleading "important duties" that have "crowded on me." Continues:]

I am happy to learn that the Convention went off so well. Of the objection which you mention as having been taken to Mr. [Richard A.] Buckner's nomination,[1] I have also been apprised from other quarters. We must rely on the proper feeling of our Fellow Citizens, to resist any attempt, to use your own language, "to make religious opinions a test for office."

Your account of the local [Lexington] election on the 7th. inst. discloses a division among our friends which is much to be regretted.[2] But I trust that the consequences of the election may, as it regards the by-laws and appointments of the new board, be as favorable as you anticipate.

We are still discussing the Tariff question in the Senate;[3] and it is difficult to conjecture, with any plausibility, when the vote will be taken. Yesterday both Houses passed Resolutions to remove the remains of [George] Washington to this City on the 22nd. inst.[4] The Resolutions were generally, though not without exceptions, opposed by the State Right men, and the Jackson men proper. . . .

LS. KyHi.   1. See Smith to Clay, Dec. 27, 1831. Buckner had been accused of being a petitioner in favor of stopping the Sunday mail. In a letter to Andrew Moore of Harrison County, Buckner denied the charge, saying "When that was a subject of discussion, and petitions were sent to Congress respecting it, I was not a member of any church, and took no interest whatever in it." Lexington *Observer & Kentucky Reporter*, Feb. 14, 1832.   2. Smith to Clay, Dec. 27, 1831. 3. Webster to Clay, Jan. 8, 1832.   4. Comment in Senate, Feb. 13, 1832.

From THOMAS METCALFE   Frankfort, February 14, 1832

I have received additional evidence this morning, of the unpatriotic, if not base subserviency of the followers of the Hero. The Secretary of State for the State of Tennessee[1] has forwarded to me certain Resolutions of the Legislature of that State[2] denying the right of Congress to make Internal Improvements in the States without their consent, or to subscribe stock to State Incorporations &c &c These resolutions do "most cordially approve the views & sentiments of Presdt. J[ackson] as expressed in his veto Message &c.["]

I have also recd. from the same quarter resolutions "instructing," "requesting" &c to use their exertions to have all the lands belonging to the U S sold as soon as the same can be reasonably done at *a graduated price* — the proceeds to be distributed to the several states & Territories for educating &c — These last were adopted on the *21st Dec.* Prompt work, after having snuffed the gale from head quarters. Now in all this I think I see the downward tendency of the Republic. There is no such thing as principle — no moral courage among the leading politicians: or rather among the miserable demagogues who continue to lead, and to mislead the people.

Many of the Tennessee Members of Congress signed the original application to Mr Barber [*sic*, James Barbour] to appt an Engineer to survey the route from Zanesville to Florence[3] (Gov Huston [*sic*, Sam Houston] among them), but it seems that the powerful reasoning of Vanburens [*sic*] veto[4] has convinced Tennessee of the erroneousness of her former professed principles. I refer to these things barely for the purpose of showing in part the ground upon which I have conducted my mind to the conclusion that the system of Internal improvement. — so far at least as the interior of the country may be directly concerned might as well be given up; and with it the Tariff must and will go. It will then be the policy of Kentucky to *take care of herself.* Her efforts must hereafter be made to reduce the duties to the lowest possible extent; to save herself from taxation for the benefit of other Internal improvement and Tariff States. in whose eyes She has found no sympathy; and of whose Justice she may well complain   This antisocial, narrow, contracted and selfish policy I deprecate as much as any one can do. It will operate as a most powerful check to the growing greatness & prosperity of the Republic. But by dissimilation, intrigues, and fraud this policy will be forced upon Kentucky.

From these premises you will see that I am pretty well prepared for the lowest possible reduction of duties, without much regard to the Tariff — not of choice but from necessity. In standing up *for* the Tariff Kentucky has acted a noble, a National and a *disinterested* part — I mean *sectionally* disinterested In her turn She receives nothing but insult & contuemely from those who are immediately benefited by that policy — Then let it go; and let us do the best we can, upon the little niggardly plan of each State scuffling out its own salvation against the competition of the world —

I received last evening the [Washington *Daily National*] Intelligencer of the 2nd Inst intimating that you would reply to Mr. [Robert Y.] Hayne that day[5] I am anxious to see your views as they are developed in that speech   The principle; or rather the right of Congress to impose protecting duties I know you cannot yield. But for one I care not how much of the expediency you may under existing circumstances surrender   I think you may go as far as our old friend J Q [Adams] will venture to go — at least without offence to Kentucky — Nothing new here.

ALS. DLC-HC (DNA, M212, R4).   1. Samuel G. Smith.   2. *Public Acts Passed at the Stated Session of the Nineteenth General Assembly of the State of Tennessee 1831* (Nashville, 1832), 137-38. 3. See 6:1150.   4. Clay to Brooke, May 1, 1831.   5. Speech in Senate, Feb. 2, 1832.

From Buckner H. Payne, Baltimore, February 14, 1832. Mentions his belief that Rep. George McDuffie of South Carolina is the son-in-law of Col. Richard Singleton of that state, owner of the mare "Clara Fisher." Asks Clay to inform McDuffie that he is willing to breed "Stamboul" to "Clara Fisher" until three colts are produced; and that this service for Singleton will be "free from any expence whatever to him." Adds, in a postscript, that "Prospects were pretty good for Stamboul when I left Kentucky." ALS. DLC-TJC (DNA, M212, R10). See Clay to Atwood, Sept. 15, 1831; Berryman to Clay, Oct. 5, 1831; also Fairfax Harrison, *The Roanoke Stud, 1795-1833* (Richmond, Va., 1930), 175.

Remark in Senate, February 14, 1832. Comments on the request of Congress to the relatives of George Washington to permit removal of the General's remains; speaks also on how Congress should handle invitations to the Washington family to attend a commemoration ceremony. *Register of Debates*, 22 Cong., 1 Sess., 390-91. Both the House and Senate approved a resolution to authorize the removal of Washington's remains from Mount Vernon for reinterment in the Capitol. U.S. Sen., *Journal*, 22 Cong., 1 Sess., 134. However, when Francis T. Brooke, John Floyd, and George Munford, all prominent Virginians, protested the proposed move, and John A. Washington and other family members refused their permission, the resolution was tabled, and Washington's body remained interred at Mount Vernon. *Ibid.*, 141; U.S. H. of Reps., *Journal*, 22 Cong., 1 Sess., 404-5.

Comment in Senate, February 15, 1832. Attests that the presiding officers of the two houses have been invested with the power to make all proper arrangements relating to the removal of George Washington's remains to Washington City [Remark in Senate, February 14, 1832]. *Register of Debates*, 22 Cong., 1 Sess., 391-92.

From "Patrick Henry," Washington, February 18, 1832. Suggests that Clay "*forthwith*" introduce a Resolution that the government purchase Mount Vernon, leave George Washington's remains buried there, and otherwise "use the property for some national purpose." ALS. DLC-HC (DNA, M212, R4). Printed in Colton, *Clay Correspondence*, 4:326. In 1858, the Mount Vernon Ladies' Association bought Mount Vernon from the Washington family, and it remains in their hands. Elswyth Thane, *Mount Vernon is Ours, the Story of its Preservation*. New York, 1966. The name "Patrick Henry" is apparently a pseudonym.

464

To FRANCIS T. BROOKE   Washington, February 21, 1832

I have been so constantly occupied that I have not been able to write you as much or as often as I wished. That terrible long speech of mine in the Senate, which gave me less trouble in its delivery than it has since occasioned me, is now in the hands of the printer, and being disposed of,[1] leaves me at leisure to say a few words.

Every thing is going on well. V. Buren, old Hickory and the whole crew will, I think, in due time be gotten rid of. The attempt to excite public sympathy in behalf of the little Magician [Van Buren][2] has totally failed; and I sincerely wish that he may be nominated as V. President.[3] That is exactly the point to which I wish to see matters brought. Do urge our Jackson friends (if there be any that you can approach) to nominate him on the 28h.   It will be so *consistent* that they should support him who is, or, at least, pretends to have been, for the Tariff, and oppose all others who are for it. You may rely upon it that his nomination will complete the work of Jackson's overthrow.

We have had various affairs here, of which the papers will give you some account. The most bitter of the opposition is the Calhoun element. I heard today that a South Carolina Governor is in correspondence with a Virginia Lieut. Governor — [4]Will our friend [John] Floyd on that occasion call out the Posse, as he was supposed by some here to have intended, to prevent the removal of the remains of Washington?[5]

ALS. KyU. Printed in Colton, *Clay Correspondence*, 4:326-27. Addressed to Brooke in Richmond, Va.   1. Speech in Senate, Feb. 2, 1832.   2. Clay to Brooke, May 1, 1831.   3. Brooke to Clay, Feb. 9, 1832.   4. Reference obscure.   5. Comment in Senate, Feb. 13, 1832.

To HENRY CLAY, JR.   Washington, February 21, 1832

I have been so engaged with the Senate, the Court, the Committees, and above all with the Tariff, my Speech upon it, and its subsequent preparation for the Press,[1] that I have been forced to neglect my correspondence, and among others yourself. I have this morning sent the last Sheets of the Speech to the Press, and it will be out in a few days. I will send you a Copy, when you will be able to judge if it has not been extravagantly praised.

I received your letter [January 27] communicating your wish to visit Europe this Spring, and I am gratified with your respectful reference of the propriety of your voyage to me. I do not wish to decide it, but, in that spirit of candor and affection towards you which has ever governed me, I will state my views. You have now seriously and profitably commenced the Study of the law. If you were to go at this time it would occasion a suspension of your Studies during the whole time of your absence. Had you not therefore better postpone your voyage until you have completed your course of study and undertake it between the termination of your labors as a student, and the commencement of the practice of your profession? I submit this view of the matter to your consideration, and would advice you to consult with Mr. [James] Erwin and my friend Judge [Alexander] Porter. If your own judgement, with or without that of theirs, prompts you to go, I yield my consent; and in that case this letter may be deemed a sufficient authority to Mr. Erwin to supply you with the requisite pecuniary means, and he can best advice in what way and in what form to take them.

Your uncle [James] Brown is here, and he thinks you had better postpone, for the present, your voyage. He is in good health. My own health and that of

465

your mother have been as usual. I find incessant work less exhausting to me than I had feared.

Our friends are in good spirits as to political affairs and prospects. Tomorrow there is to be a great dinner in honor of the day,[2] which I shall attend.

Give our love to Anne [Brown Clay Erwin] and tell her that I shall write her in a few days. Remember us also to your aunt [Julie Duralde] Clay to [Martin] Duralde, and to little Martin [Duralde III]. Tell them that Henry [Clay Duralde] had been generally well and is growing stouter.

ALS. Henry Clay Memorial Foundation, Lexington, Ky.   1. Speech in Senate, Feb. 2, 1832.
2. George Washington's centennial birthday.

Remark in Senate, February 21, 1832. To the question of how much cotton can be produced "per hand," Clay believes that "the average of the whole of the cotton-planting States . . . be equal to five bales." *Register of Debates*, 22 Cong., 1 Sess., 456.

From Robert W. Stoddard, Geneva, N.Y., February 21, 1832. Instructs Clay not to "heed the noise and violence" which comes from the Jackson camp in New York. "Take my word for it, the clamour proceeds wholly from those whose fortunes and hopes rest upon the success of Van Buren." Since the defeat of his nomination as U.S. minister to Great Britain [Clay to Brooke, May 1, 1831], Van Buren's "servile friends" have attempted "to arouse the people, on the ground of state pride, and to induce the belief that his rejection was an insult to N. York—Thus far they have been disappointed." Indeed, the "people at large" in New York "approve the Rejection." Believes, therefore, that Van Buren's forces, like Aaron Burr's before him, will desert him as his political "discomforture" grows. Asks that copies of Clay's response to Robert Y. Hayne on the tariff be sent to New York [Speech in Senate, February 2, 1832]. Concludes: "On the whole, I feel that the public sentiment is turning rapidly round in the state, and that the prospect of success here is better than I had any reason to believe it would be three months ago." ALS. DLC-HC (DNA, M212, R4).

From William H. Underwood, Gainesville, Ga., February 21, 1832. Asks for a dozen copies of Clay's "second speech on the tariff [February 2, 1832]" for distribution in Georgia, adding: "the rejection of Van Buren by the Senate [Clay to Brooke, May 1, 1831] will be sustained by a large majority in this State, but I do not believe it Can affect Jackson, his popularity here is so great that it appears to me that neither ignorance or turpitude in himself or his agents can in the least degree injure him, he permits Georgia to take possession of the Cherokee Country [Clay to Hammond, October 7, 1829] and that is sufficient to hold the people to him here; The Indian Country is settling now by a white populat[ion as rapi]dly as any new Country Whatever, How long Will Congress permit This Shameful Violation of the often pledged faith of the nation." ALS. DLC-HC (DNA, M212, R4). For Underwood, see *CAB*.

From JOHN J. CRITTENDEN   Frankfort, February 23, 1832
As you have disposed of Mr Van Buren's nomination & by this time, as I suppose, of your Tariff resolution,[1] you will have leisure, I hope, occasionally to write to me. My patience is none of the greatest, & has been already pretty severely tried by the total silence & neglect of all my Congressional acquaintances. Not one line have I received from Washington during your session.

The intelligence of Van Buren's nomination being rejected was received with general satisfaction by your political friends in the West, & so far as I can judge seems to produce but very little feeling even among the Jackson men—The

466

truth is that he has no popularity here, & few, very few, care any thing about him. The reasons upon which the Senate has rejected him are no less congenial to sound policy than they are to every sentiment of National pride & honor.

I have almost lost the hope of your being able to effect any amicable or satisfactory adjustment of the tarif—Could you not go a little further than your resolution & consent to a reduction of duties on such of our manufactures as are most firmly established? I am not conversant enough with the subject to decide, but I have supposed that our manufactories of coarse cottons would go on & flourish now without any protection from the Tarif, or at any rate with a diminished protection—If a reduction of the duties on imported cottons could be made without endangering our own establishments, it seems to me that such a measure would afford a most happy peace-offering at the present crisis—And furthermore that it would be perfectly consistent with the principle of the Tarif which, as I understand it, proposes by a temporary protection to bring our manufactures to such vigor & perfection as would enable them to stand un-aided against all competition. It would be a great triumph to our Tarif, if its friends could proclaim that it had already accomplished its great object in rela-tion to any branch of manufacture, & that to that extent the duties on importa-tion might be reduced if not abolished—Such a reduction as to cottons would in itself go far to conciliate the opponents of the Tarif, & would shew them how by its own operation & by degrees, they would be relieved from all its burthens real or imaginary. But I am going beyond my purpose, which was merely to offer a suggestion for your better reflection.

Is there any ground for the [rum]ours that have been circulated of any dissension or alienation between Mr [John Q.] Adams & yourself?[2]

Is it known whether [Henry] Daniel or [Chittenden] Lyon will support our friend [Richard A.] Buckner for the office of Governor? I have hoped that one or both of them would. Their support would be very important to him in the coming contest.[3]

Do write me a long letter, full of all the great doings at Washington, & giving me a full account of your prospects. . . . P. S. It is said that you & [George M.] Bibb have become reconciled—I hope it may be so.

ALS. NcD.   1. Clay to Brooke, May 1, 1831; Webster to Clay, Jan. 8, 1832.   2. Various newspapers had reported that the 1825 alliance between Clay and Adams had now dissolved because of disagreements on the tariff issue. Adams was quoted as saying that Clay's tariff "pro-position is inadmissible" and that the South should be given "substantial relief." Frankfort *Argus of Western America*, Feb. 8, 1832. See Munroe, *Louis McLane*, 341-50, for a more complete discussion of their differences.   3. Smith to Clay, Dec. 27, 1831.

From Peter B. Porter, Black Rock, N.Y., February 25, 1832. Reports that while recently in Albany "I had, while there, full & frequent conversations with most of the Anti masonic leaders of this State, as well as with our own friends, on the subject of the approaching election. The Anti masons, & particularly their leaders have lowered their tone very much, and it is perfectly obvious that they are willing to support an Electoral ticket that will vote for our President, provided we will support their Governor [Clay to Bailhache, November 24, 1830]—But the grand difficulty is in devising the means of ef-fecting this object without creating alarm & dispersion among their troops, and possibly too, among our own."

Continues: "They submitted to me in a manner not to be misunderstood, although not in direct terms, this proposition [Clay to Weed, April 14, 1832—That *they* would form an electoral ticket (and that our friends should be consulted, & participate, in its formation) to be composed of about equal numbers of anti masons, & national republicans or Clay men—who are neither anti masons nor belong to the masonic fraternity—to be called the Anti masonic ticket, but *all* of whom should vote for our Candidate—it being understood that Mr [William] Wirt is ready to decline on the slightest intimation from them to that effect. This overture is known to our friends at Albany, and the whole subject is under advisement between them and the principal Anti-masons at Albany." Is not convinced, however, that this arrangement will really work out.

Assures Clay, on the other hand, that "the rejection of V. Buren [Clay to Brooke, May 1, 1831] is the best *coup d'etat* that has been made by our party this winter" and that at least a third of the Jacksonians "*although obliged to cry out against it*, secretly rejoice that it has taken place."

Also assures him that his "project for the new Tariff [Webster to Clay, January 8, 1832]" has been "highly approved by every man in this part of the country who is capable of understanding it and has political independence enough to express his sentiments," and adds that "We are looking with much anxiety for your *great* speech [February 2, 1832] in answer to Mr [Robert Y.] Haynes & others, in which we expect to see the benefits of the protective system made plain to the comprehension of every farmer in the Country."

Hopes that Clay can get the bank recharter bill [Clay to Brown, December 18, 1831] through Congress "so as to oblige the President to act on it. He would rather see a Ghost enter the Palace than such a Bill; and if it should not cause his political, I am not sure that it would not his physical, death."

In conclusion, informs Clay of the successful termination of his legal and financial problems with the government [Porter to Clay, July 25, October 6, 1830]. ALS. InU. Letter marked "(Confidential)."

To HENRY CLAY, JR.   Washington, February 27, 1832

The day after I wrote you on the subject of your going to Europe, I received your letter of the 4h. inst. communicating your wish that I would advance you a sum of money to be employed, under the advice of Mr. [James] Erwin, in N. Orleans.

If you abandon or post pone for the present the voyage to Europe, I am willing that out of monies of mine in Mr. Erwins hands he may advance to you $2500 to be employed with his advice and for your exclusive benefit in the City of N. O. I could not both advance that sum, and the sum necessary to defray your expences if you went to Europe. Mr. Erwin may consider this letter as an authority to him to make the advance upon the condition above mentioned.

Nothing important has occurred here since my last. The debate in the Senate has not yet terminated. It will probably continue a week or two longer.

Give my love to Anne [Brown Clay Erwin], Mr. Erwin and their children [Henry C.; James, Jr.; Lucretia; and Andrew Eugene].

My Speech on the Tariff [February 2] will be forwarded by this mail.

ALS. Henry Clay Memorial Foundation, Lexington, Ky.

From HENRY CLAY, JR.   New Orleans, February 28, 1832

I am now living at Judge [Alexander] Porter's, on the coast. I found that in the city I was so much interrupted by the kindness of friends and acquaintance, that I could not devote that time to study which I desired. At the solicitation of the Judge, I therefore determined to spend in the country the few months that I shall be in Louisiana.

Judge Porter's residence, as you will recollect, is near the battle-ground, three or four miles from the city. He has an excellent library, and is himself a learned man in the law, animated with the best spirit of learning, that which applies useful maxims to the common wants of mankind.

The civil law begins to open before me. What I thought the study of a year, I perceive now would exhaust the energies of a lifetime. But I am determined, if ever I shall arrive at an independence of fortune, to carry what little talents and attainments I may possess to another tribunal than the bar of justice, the tribunal of public debate.

I am at present making all exertions to gain a knowledge of the law, and I have no reason, I think, to be dissatisfied with my progress. By the winter after next, I shall be able to come to the bar with a fair prospect of ultimate success.

Copy. Printed in Colton, *Clay Correspondence*, 4:327.

From JAMES BROWN CLAY   Lexington, February 28, 1832

It has been just one week since I received your letter, but I hope you will excuse me for not answering it, and I promise you I will not fail to answer your next immediatly. I was out at home ["Ashland"] last week and I believe every body was well, and all the stock are doing well. Mr [William] Martin has swapped South America for another horse and thinks he has made a good bargain, and I think so too if the horse is worth 75 dollars as he says he is. Tell mama that Johney [John Morrison Clay] has swapped his gun for a cow, and he seems very much pleased with with [*sic*] his bargain. Since the mayor [Charlton Hunt] has been elected[1] we have had no such quarrells as we used to have, and every body seems pleased with him. With your last letter you sent me Mr. [Robert Y.] Haynes speech with your next I wish you would send me your own.[2] We have not heard from New Orleans for some time and I feel afraid that the city is overflowed, as, Louisville was nearly. You must excuse me for the shortness of my letter as I feel rather sleepy. give my love to all the folks as little Henry[3] says I forgot to tell you that all our relations are well.

ALS. DLC-TJC (DNA, M212, R10).   1. Smith to Clay, Dec. 27, 1831.   2. Speech in Senate, Feb. 2, 1832.   3. Reference obscure.

From Hexekiah Niles, Baltimore, February 28, 1832. Thanks Clay "heartily" for the copy of his recent speech on the tariff [February 2, 1832] pointing out that "The array of argument and fact, I hold to be irresistible, and I think that its effect will be powerful." Continues: "It came just in good time for *me*. My next paper will commence a new volume, and be printed in a beautiful new type. I shall get. in the whole speech. The errors have been corrected. In page 29, the word *exerted* is again used for the word *excited*. It might as well be corrected, in the thousands of copies that, will yet be printed. By the newspaper press & otherwise, I suppose that more than 200,000 copies will yet be spread before the people. My committee in the N. Y. [word illeg.] will send several thousands *southwardly*. We have now the means of a large circulation in South Carolina, Georgia & Alabama — if aided by our friends. in Congress; and they well disposed to speed information, and this, is tricky, for the southern members will not do it." ALS. DLC-HC (DNA, M212, R4).

From Thomas McGiffin, Washington, Pa., March 1, 1832. Inquires about some "improved" livestock Clay was to send, and asks if several mares "be bought for you?"

Comments that "of all the parties that have ever yet existed . . . the Anti Masons are the most *stupid* and ruthless or the most profligate." Reports that at their Harrisburg convention [Rush to Clay, June 3, 1831] "9 out of 10 agreed . . . that the only probable chance of success for either [Anti-Masons and Jacksonians] depended on on [*sic*] union and concert—They [Jacksonians] do have the Governor [George Wolf] of this state & even the Electoral Ticket." Continues: "In what way we are now to act, is difficult to imagine, but one thing I am strongly inclined to go far with heart & soul—viz—cut *their Tails* off *as close as possible—drown them as so many rats*—If Wolfe [*sic*] & his party can by any means be disconnected from Jackson (as possibly may be by the Van Buren nomination for vice Presy—our support of him for Governor would be consistent as he supports our policy openly & manfully—From the highest to the lowest at Harrisburgh [*sic*, Harrisburg], they swear they will not support Van Beuren [*sic*, Van Buren]—" Suggests that at the May [29] convention at Harrisburg [Clay to Ketchum, May 15, 1832] "we ought to act *as one*—our power ought to be felt, otherwise it never will be respected or conciliated."

Reports that "we have not yet seen your *great* speech [February 2, 1832]." Asks about "the Tariff at this session." Assures Clay that "your course so far meets the entire approbation of your friends & commands the respect of your intelligent enemies." ALS. DLC-HC (DNA, M212, R4).

From Pleasant Matthews, Glasgow, Ky., March 4, 1832. Charges that the dismissal of himself and others from the post office is "evidence of the corruption of this Monarchal Administration; You will see that we were *cut down* solely because we are Your friends." Mentions that the National Republican candidate for governor, Richard Buckner, passed through a few days ago, "and I am sorry to inform You that several of Your friends in this County [Barren] say [they] will support [John] Breathitt," and the same is true in Logan and Green counties [Smith to Clay, December 27, 1831]. ALS. DLC-HC (DNA, M212, R4). For Matthews, postmaster in Glasgow, see Franklin Gorin, *The Times of Long Ago* (Louisville, 1929), 65.

From Samuel Martin, Campbell Station, Tenn., March 5, 1832. Encloses his plan for a national bank, and remarks: "if you believe public opinion will be against Jackson as his refusing to sign a bill to recharter the Old Bank you are mistaken [Clay to Brown, December 18, 1831]." Says he has "laboured thirteen years for my P[ost]. office plan," and that "my Bank plan is the ways & means the Dividends on the stock in the Old Bank ought to go to support the P. office." ALS. DLC-HC (DNA, M212, R4).

Remark in Senate, March 6, 1832. Asks Senate to postpone consideration of apportionment bill; withdraws suggestion; makes further remarks on the bill. *Register of Debates*, 22 Cong., 1 Sess., 513.

From James Barbour, Barboursville, Va., March 7, 1832. Remarks that Clay's tariff speech [February 2, 1832] "is the strongest view I have ever seen on the subject." Suggests "that if any . . . domestic articles will admit of a diminution without an injury, let it take place. Not because it is necessary or calculated to produce any effect (except in name and that is always to be looked for in political contests) but as furnishing ground for compromises and also for a retreat to the violent."

Mentions the Democratic caucus in Richmond [Brooke to Clay, February 9, 1832; Clay to Porter, March 10, 1832] saying, "discord appears in the ranks—[Thomas] Ritchie is in trouble and his Party—for meself I wish they may nominate Van [Buren]—he will be a dead weight to Jackson. Ritchie says Van is of the true faith except as to the Tariff—Now he voted originally for the erection of Gates on the Cumberland Road—the most frightful Monster to the Senate rights People. Reference to the Senate journal some ten or 12 years back will furnish the evidence—if to use the fact will be of any service—I am somewhat at a loss to judge on the best time to effect the choice of our Electors for Virg[ini]a Can you advise me on this point—" ALS. DLC-HC (DNA, M212, R4). For Van Buren's vote in 1822 in favor of "An act for the preservation and repair of the Cumberland Road," see U.S. Sen., *Journal*, 17 Cong., 1 Sess., 331, 378.

From James Pleasants, Goochland, Va., March 7, 1832. Asks that if Clay's "speech on the tariff [February 2, 1832] was printed in Pamphlet form," he be sent a copy. Remarks that the speech "appears to be a powerful defence of a system the constitutionality of which I have never doubted, but the expediency of pushing it far I have been led to call in question." Concludes that "in the Southern states, hundreds look with alarm almost at a friend of the tariff, who if you ask them what the tariff was, would not be able to answer you." ALS. DLC-HC (DNA, M212, R4).

To Richard B. Jones, Brookfield, Pa., March 8, 1832. Reports that he has engaged a friend [Thomas McGiffin] in Washington County, Pa., to procure several mares for him. Suggests, further, that if two bulls and a heifer "could be sent as far as Washn. County in your State, I could make an arrangement there to have them forwarded on to K." ALS. DNA, RG59, General Records of the State Dept., Appointment Papers, 1861-69.

On March 24, 1832, Clay wrote Jones declining the purchase of the cattle and two mares. *Ibid.*

From Harrison Gray Otis, Boston, March 8, 1832. Acknowledges receipt of Clay's tariff speech [February 2, 1832]. Remarks that the speech "calls the agricultural, & especially the mechanical class to look to the case as their own — The adversary has been too long permitted to present it [the tariff issue] as question between the great cotton and woolen monopolies, so called, and the people at large." Continues: "In a word I consider the Speech as a political manual . . . and were it the only one you had ever made, and the last you ever should make, it would be a rock to which you might securely moor your reputation." As to its political utility, adds: "Would to God, those to whom you have made your pathetic appeal would retrace their Steps — But they will not end I look forward to serious results — Compromise in the force of the term implies mutual concession, and requires the concurrence of two parties, — But So Carolina and her friends insist that whatever is done shall be predicated on a present or future renunciation of the protective element; otherwise say they, ruin awaits them — We know if it be abandoned our ruin is inevitable."

Encloses a speech he made last year, and remarks that he does so only "to indulge my vanity in proving to you in how many points it was my good fortune to entertain views similar to yours."

Thinks, too, that "There is another subject — that of slavery — which first or last must be looked full in the face." In this regard, suggests a plan for the recolonization of slaves. Proposes that the expense of recolonization "would be gradually incurred, and that no expense which could be requisite, in the present circumstances of the Country, should be considered inordinate — and though a long time would be requisite to *complete* the scheme, it might be commenced forthwith, or in another year — and its advantages would *begin* with the beginning —" Hopes that "some of our northern friends would take the lead in this matter for obvious reasons," but if they would not, asks Clay to do so. Believes that this plan would result in an "implied compact between the different sections of the Country to repay protection by protection — The North would say to the South 'Save our property & we will Save your lives.'" States that "unless this or some other resource . . . be adopted, I see nothing to prevent the two tribes from compelling the rest of Israel to repair to their 'tents.'" ALS. DLC-HC (DNA, M212, R4). Printed in Colton, *Clay Correspondence*, 4:328. Otis' speech was published as a pamphlet titled, *Mr. Otis's Speech to the Citizens of Boston On the Evening Preceding the Late Election, of Members of Congress.* Boston, 1830; also discussed in Samuel E. Morison, *The Life and Letters of Harrison Gray Otis* (Boston, 1913), 2:289-90.

At about this time, early March, 1832, James C. Dunn, publisher of the American Colonization Society's *African Repository and Colonial Journal*, gave a receipt for Clay's payment of $12 for the *Journal* from March 1826 to March 1832. ADS. DLC-TJC (DNA, M212, R17).

Remark in Senate, March 8, 1832. Asks why the Committee on Roads and Canals wants to be discharged from consideration of a petition asking for government aid in the construction of a railroad from Buffalo, New York, to the Mississippi River. *Register of Debates*, 22 Cong., 1 Sess., 515.

To JAMES BARBOUR

Washington, March 10, 1832

I recd. your favor of the 7h. inst. with a letter for Mr. [Richard] Rush which I have forwarded to him. I think if you will give the page of my Speech[1] to which you refer another perusal you will perceive that you have misconstrued it. I am, in that part of the Speech, considering the *cause* of the acknowledged reduction of prices of manufactured articles. The adversary contended that it proceeded from the reduction in the amt. of the produce of the mines, the transformation of armies in Europe into laborers, and improved machinery. I examine each of these alleged causes and endeavor to assign to it the proper agency which belongs to it in lowering prices. And I then proceed to shew that Competition, here and in Europe, each acting *within* itself and in collision with the other is the *main* cause of the very great diminution in the price of manufactured commodities since the passage of the Tariff of 1824.

We shall consider, or rather, I should say, are now considering whether some duties on protected articles may not be reduced,[2] without prejudice to the System, with the view of tranquillizing some of the opponents of the Tariff. With those who *admit* the principle of protection, some thing may be done. As to those who deny its constitutionality and its expediency I fear no impression is to be made. I believe that, without injury to the policy, some reductions and modifications may be made. But on this subject the time has not arrived, nor am I prepared, to speak definitively.

Our public affairs are evidently tending to a crisis. The consequences of the recent decision of the Supreme Court must be very great.[3] If it be resisted, and the President refuses to enforce it, there is a virtual dissolution of the Union. For it will be in vain to consider it as existing if a single State can put aside the Laws and treaties of the U.S. and when their authority is vindicated by a decision of the S. Court, the President will not perform his duty to enforce it. It is *reported* that he said to a Georgia member, since the decision, that he hoped Georgia would defend her rights!

The difficulties at Richmond with the Jackson party are not their only difficulties. You will have seen that the Great rejected [Van Buren], has been rejected at Harrisburg.[4] Old Smilie[5] used to say that the people would not *take* War and take taxes *together*. Pennsa. it seems will not take Jackson and V. Buren together, or rather will not take V. at all.

By the bye, you may not have heard the result of the movement attempted in this City in behalf of your gallant kinsman.[6] It had a most ridiculous and abortive issue. They had a difficulty in organizing the meeting. At length some workie was found to act as Charman. Whereupon a string of resolutions was proposed in behalf of Tecumseh. An individual rose and alleged that the proposer was not the author of the resolutions and demanded that the author should come forward in proper person. The Chairman decided that that was altogether indispensable; but the author would not appear. Some confusion ensued, and the meeting was dissolved, sine die.

ALS. NN. 1. Speech in Senate, Feb. 2, 1832. 2. Webster to Clay, Jan. 8, 1832. 3. Johnston to Clay, Jan. 12, 1831. 4. Clay to Porter, March 10, 1832. 5. Probably John

Smilie of Pa.; see *BDAC*.   6. Probably a facetious reference to Richard M. Johnson. A meeting, sponsored by the mechanics and workingmen, was held on March 6, 1832, in Washington to promote Johnson's candidacy for the vice presidency. Washington *Daily National Intelligencer*, March 6, 1832.

To MATTHEW L. DAVIS   Washington, March 10, 1832

I recd. your favor of the 23d. Ulto. from Albany, and thank you for the information which it contains. I recd. one of about the same date [February 25], from Genl. [Peter B.] Porter, who corroborates your statement as to the probable co-operation between two great parties.[1] On that point I should be glad to be kept informed.

The Bank,[2] the Indian question,[3] the Tariff,[4] the South Carolin[a] excitement[5] &c. &c. are evidently tending to a great crisis. All sorts of expedients will be resorted to for the purpose of procrastinating the decision on the Bank; and its issue may be regarded as doubtful. It is not known whether the President, in the event of the refusal of Georgia to abide by the decision of the Supreme Court, will exert the Executive powers of the Government or not. It is rumored that he will not, in which case there will be a virtual dissolution of the Government.

We shall have a long Session, probably running into June.

ALS. Courtesy of Dr. Thomas D. Clark, Lexington, Ky.   1. Clay to Weed, April 14, 1832. 2. Clay to Brown, Dec. 18, 1831; Webster to Clay, Jan. 8, 1832.   3. Johnston to Clay, Jan. 12, 1831.   4. Webster to Clay, Jan. 8, 1832.   5. Beginning in the fall of 1831, associations, which functioned as political clubs to rally nullification sentiment, were formed in virtually every South Carolina county. See William W. Freehling, *Prelude to Civil War, The Nullification Controversy in South Carolina, 1816-1836* (New York, 1965), 227-31.

To PETER B. PORTER   Washington, March 10, 1832

I was glad to learn by your favor of the 25h. Ulto. from Black Rock that your health had improved. I sincerely hope it may be entirely re-established, and I pray you to take the best care of it.

I never doubted about the propriety or policy of the rejection of V[an]. B[uren]. and all my intelligence fully justifies the previous opinion which I had formed.[1] It has thrown the Jackson party into the greatest confusion. The effort to take him up as their candidate for V.P. has failed both at Harrisburg and Richmond. I think it is our policy that they should run him, but they will not.[2]

The scheme of co-operation between the Anti Masons and the N.R's which you describe appears to me to be reasonable and just; and I should think might be carried into effect; but of this you are the best judge. If such a scheme were adopted in N. York, her example would probably be followed in all the States in which Anti Masonry abounds. In this view of the matter, you will perceive that good might come of it, even if you should finally be defeated in N. York.

All sorts of expedients are resorted to by the Jackson party to procrastinate, for the present Session, a decision on the Bank question. A movement to that effect is now making in the H. of R.[3] I think we shall, in a day or two, have a bill reported in the Senate,[4] where we will attempt to pass it, without regard to what may be doing in the House. So that, in some way or other, I hope, during the Session, we shall present the case directly to the President.

The decision of the Supreme Court, on the Cherokee question, must be fraught with important consequences.[5] It is said that the President has avowed

473

his determination not to execute it, and even went so far as to express to a Georgia member of Congress, the hope that Georgia would defend her rights! If he does not execute it; if Georgia shall be allowed to trample upon the Laws of the U.S. and the decision of the Supreme Judicial tribunal, there is a virtual dissolution of the Union. Public affairs are evidently tending to a great crisis. They cannot remain as they are. The Country must be redeemed, or its ruin is inevitable.

I sent you a Copy of my Tariff Speech [February 2, 1832] and should like to know what you think of it. The resolution is not yet disposed of. I think it will pass and that the measure will be carried.[6] Such will undoubtedly be the result, unless Jackson politics should so far prevail with members of that party as to induce them to unite with Southern members to defeat it.

The case of [Joseph E.] Nourse, I was told, went off upon a want of jurisdiction;[7] but Mr. [John] Sergeant probably has given you a correct account of its effects, among which I sincerely hope may be that of your success in your contest with the Treasury. [8]

[Samuel L.] Southard is here, looking badly. He has come to argue before the Supreme Court the cause between your State & New Jersey.[9]

ALS. NBuHi. 1. Clay to Brooke, May 1, 1831. 2. The Harrisburg convention, held on March 5, 1832, had been called for the purpose of forestalling Van Buren's nomination for vice president. The Pennsylvanians, who associated Van Buren with New York's domination over their own state, nominated William Wilkins for vice president. In Virginia, a Democratic convention was called on March 14-16, 1832, in an attempt to line up the state for Van Buren despite the state's preference for James Barbour. Seeing that the opposition to Van Buren in the convention was too strong, they forced an adjournment. Two weeks later a legislative caucus in Virginia failed to agree on Van Buren and voted against making a vice presidential nomination. At the National Democratic convention in Baltimore on May 21-22, 1832, Van Buren was nominated on the first ballot with 208 votes. See Gammon, *The Presidential Campaign of 1832*, 95-102; and Brooke to Clay, Feb. 9, 1832. 3. A resolution was brought forward in the House and passed on March 14 to appoint a select committee to investigate the B.U.S. and report whether or not its charter had been violated. U.S. House of Reps., *Journal*, 22 Cong., 1 Sess., 487, 491. For the "Report" see Clay to Brooke, April 17, 1832. 4. On March 13, the bill to modify and continue "An Act to Incorporate the Subscribers to the Bank of the United States" was brought up and passed to a second reading. For the outcome of this bill, see Clay to Brown, Dec. 18, 1831; and Webster to Clay, Jan. 8, 1832. 5. Johnston to Clay, Jan. 12, 1831. 6. Speech in Senate, Feb. 2, 1832. 7. Jackson dismissed Joseph E. Nourse as register of the Treasury in 1829. Nourse brought suit against the federal government for past compensation. The case dragged on for years; finally, on April 19, 1856, the executors of Nourse's estate were awarded $2,827.32 to be paid by Congress. See *Niles' Register* (May 7, 1831), 40:166; Charles C. Nott and Smauel H. Huntington (eds.), *Cases Decided in the Court of Claims of the United States at the December Term for 1866* (Washington, 1868), 2:214-17. 8. Porter to Clay, Oct. 6, 1830. 9. Southard was arguing the case of *New Jersey* v. *New York*, a boundary dispute which resulted in a controversy over states rights. See Charles Warren, *The Supreme Court in United States History* (Boston, 1937), 1:770-73.

From Robert W. Stoddard, Geneva, N.Y., March 10, 1832. Acknowledges receipt of Clay's tariff speech [February 2, 1832] and plans "to have a new edition struck off" soon and given "a general and wide spread through our western Counties."

Reports that "a rupture has already taken place between the leaders of the Regency & our celebrated 'small light' Govr [Enos T. Throop]. They say he must & shall retire & the quandary is, who shall the '*party*' fix upon for a successor [Clay to Bailhache, November 24, 1830]. The present Lt. Govr. [Edward P.] Livingston, the Comptroler, Mr [Silas, Jr.] Wright & Gen [Erastus] Root are spoken of." Believes that the governor "will be but a feeble obstacle in the way of any Candidate which the prime movers of the machine may set up." Thinks Wright has the best chance for the nomination, "as matters now stand."

Suggests that Martin Van Buren "is too cunning and too much practised in the political schemes of this state not to perceive that as to the general government, his hopes are blown, and that he has no chance for retaining any share of political influence except it be here in this state." Believes Van Buren might therefore become a candidate for governor.

Reports that the Anti-Masons "talk of uniting the opposition," and that Francis Granger believes "it is idle to think of running Mr. [William] Wirt when there is not the slightest prospect of success." Suggests that Granger, who "talks too much," will support Clay. He says "Mr. C — — — is the man & he must be supported."

Assures Clay that with the support of the Anti-Masons, "together with the increasing dislike of the *People* to Van Buren," he is confident of success. Indeed, "I would sooner bet a hundred dollars that we carry New York, than I would fifty that it goes for Jackson." ALS. DLC-HC (DNA, M212, R4).

From Robert Wickliffe, Lexington, March 12, 1832. Upon reading Clay's speech on the tariff of February 2, 1832, remarks that "if any thing could be necessary to fire the American publick in favour of the Tarriff System your views ought to do it." Suggests that the South "must feel that they can only ruin themselves or their country by their course." Believes that "the Internal improvement question is the most people catching & the permanent argument for protection," and that "the Tarriff & internal improvements go down or rise together."

Asks how Georgia will "act on the Indian decision of the Supreme court." Also asks what Jackson will do concerning it [Johnston to Clay, January 12, 1831].

Discusses several farm-related matters, including sickness among his slaves and farming conditions in general. Is concerned with breeding Shakespeare with one of Clay's mares. Suggests that the mare "is rather under size to breed from Stamboul [Berryman to Clay, October 5, 1831]." ALS. DLC-HC (DNA, M212, R4).

From James Madison, "Montpelier," Va., March 13, 1832. Thanks Clay for sending a copy of his speech "In Defense of the American System &c [Speech in Senate, February 2, 1832]." Calls the speech "very able . . . very eloquent, and a very interesting one," which "If it does not establish all its positions in all thier extent, it demolishes not a few of those relied on by the opponents." Regrets, however, "that an effusion of personal feeling was, in one instance, admitted into the discussion." ALS. ICU. Printed in Colton, *Clay Correspondence*, 4:329.

Comment in Senate, March 14, 1832. Suggests that since the motion to recommit the apportionment bill to committee was passed, various instructions for its modification should be attached to it. *Register of Debates*, 22 Cong., 1 Sess., 559.

From George McClure, Bath, N.Y., March 14, 1832. Reports having "seen your remarks in the Senate on the Subject of Vanburen's [*sic*, Van Buren] rejection [Clay to Brooke, May 1, 1831]." Notes that it is no surprise "that Mr. V-B. should attempt as he has in his instructions [to Louis McLane], to sacrifice the honor of his country & Government to his party [Clay to Adams, July 26, 1831; Clay to Everett, August 20, 1831], knowing him as I do, to be governed in all his public acts with a single eye to party." He is, however, "really astonished that Jackson should be so simple as to avow that the degrading instructions to his minister [McLane] emanated from himself, when all who are acquainted with the little Magician know the contrary." Believes that the "rebuke" Van Buren "has lately met with [Clay to Porter, March 10, 1832] will prevent him from being Vice President, but not from being our next Governor [Clay to Bailhache, November 24, 1830], his *Regency troops* are too well drilled to leave his success for a moment doubtful."

Refers to the Supreme Court decision "in favour of the Georgia Indians [Johnston to Clay, January 12, 1831]" as "a most righteous decision, one that will try Jacksons patriotism & firmness, and which he is bound by his oath to carry into effect, but he will evade its execution if possible." Adds: "Your prospects in this state is not very flattering, unless the Anti Masons will unite with us, in that case it is believed we would carry the whole ticket, and I am of the opinion that if Mr. [William] Wirt would withdraw from the contest they would fall in." ALS. DLC-HC (DNA, M212, R4).

From Francis T. Brooke, Richmond, Va., March 15, 1832. States that "You will see by the [Richmond *Constitutional*] Whig the result of the caucus last night [Brooke to Clay, February 9, 1832; Clay to Porter, March 10, 1832]—it meets again tonight, it will probably nominate no V[ice] P[resident]." Asks "what will Georgia do with the Decision of the S[upreme]. C[ourt]. [Johnston to Clay, January 12, 1831]—" ALS. DLC-HC (DNA, M212, R4).

From William L. Stone, New York, March 15, 1832. Reminds Clay that while in Washington last December they had discussed "the extract of a letter, said to have been written by yourself, in favor of free Masonry, which first appeared in the Albany Daily Advertiser," and which has been made the "subject of malignant comment by Mr. [Benjamin Franklin] Hallett, late of Providence but now of Boston." Has learned, and Clay has previously confirmed, that Hallett has "in his possession a letter from you, explicitly denying the authenticity of the extract, and Hallett himself had admitted as much to me. . . . Nevertheless, with a degree of hardihood unparalleled *out* of the ranks of the Jackson party he persists in the repetition of the falsehood." States that "Soon after my return from Washington, Hallett having repeated the publication, I caused it to be contradicted in the Evening Journal, and likewise saw that in doing so, he received a good sound drubbing." Then, "This morning, on opening Hallett's paper [the Anti-Masonic Boston *Daily Advocate*], I found the enclosed article; and, as the last resort, in order to nail the base coinage to the counter, determined explicitly to contradict his statement, and mention the fact, as from yourself, of his having your own denial in his pocket, at the time he was again reporting the falsehood." Encloses a paragraph he has written on this subject and requests Clay's advice concerning its future publication. ALS. DLC-HC (DNA, M212, R4). On March 14, 1832, the Boston *Daily Advocate* reported that the Albany *Advertiser* had published an extract from one of Clay's letters which expressed the sentiment that Masonry "had done and must continue to do, more good that it is susceptible of doing harm."

From Unknown Author, Charleston, S.C., March 15, 1832. Presents a memorandum on cotton consumption and the tariff. Argues that South Carolina is "far more prosperous in 1832 than at any former period since the War [of 1812]," and that the steady growth of the consumption of cotton since 1819-1820 in both the U.S. and Great Britain has produced the competition for the superior American product that has kept the domestic price of the commodity rising. In 1819, the U.S. supplied 52 percent, or 70,000,000 lbs., of Britain's cotton imports of 123,000,000 lbs. In 1831, the U.S. supplied about 80 percent, or 213,121,300 lbs., of the 267,000,000 lbs. Britain imported. In 1816, the U.S. produced about 320,000 bales of cotton (at about 300 lbs. to the bale); in 1830, the U.S. produced 1,038,000 bales (at about 350 lbs. to the bale). These export and production growth rates have rendered "The Southern Country & especially So Carolina the richest in the world in proportion to territory and number of inhabitants." Concludes: "How can an equal proportion of the Tariff Tax be pd in the south where there is the least consumption even taking only the *white* population. — The blacks consume little of foreign production — what part of a *direct* tax should the Blacks pay compared with the white population in the north — supposing the expenses of government were raised by *direct* taxation? Compare it with what is now paid thro' the C[ustom]. House by their masters." D. DLC-HC (DNA, M212, R4). The figures given Clay here are a bit low. In 1819, Britain imported 149,739,820 lbs. of cotton; in 1831, 200,674,053 lbs. Edward Baines, *History of the Cotton Manufacture in Great Britain . . .*, 2nd ed. (London, 1966), 347. In 1816, the U.S. produced 439,716 bales of cotton compared to 1,069,444 in 1831. U.S. Department of Agriculture, Bureau of Statistics, *Cotton Crop of the United States 1790-1911*, by George K. Holmes, comp., (Washington, D.C., 1912), 6.

Comment in Senate, March 16, 1832. Moves to table the bill to exempt certain imported merchandise from the operation of the tariff law of 1828. *Register of Debates*, 22 Cong., 1 Sess., 590.

To FRANCIS T. BROOKE Washington, March 17, 1832

I recd. your favor of the 15th. I am sorry that I can give you no satisfactory information as to the course of Georgia in respect to the recent decision of the supreme court. It is *remoured* that the President has repeatedly said that he will not enforce it, and that he even went so far as to express his hope to a Georgia member of Congress that Georgia would support her rights.[1]

The Comee. of investigation into the conduct of the Bank[2] leave here on wednesday for Philadelphia. The impression now is that the Bank charter will pass at this session.[3] Mr. [John Q.] Adams being appointed one of the comee., took the occasion to be asked to be excused from serving on the Comee. of Manufactures, as its Chairman, whereupon the head was immediately knocked out of a barrel of oil, and the whole quantity poured on him by southern gentleman and other anti [ta]riffites. He was induced to postpone his motion.[4]

I have requested Mess. [Joseph] Gales & [William W.] Seaton to send fifty of my Speeches[5] to Mr. White.[6]

Copy. DLC-TJC (DNA, M212, R14). Printed in Colton, *Clay Correspondence*, 4:329. 1. Johnston to Clay, Jan. 12, 1831. 2. Clay to Porter, March 10, 1832; Clay to Brooke, April 17, 1832. 3. Clay to Brown, Dec. 18, 1831; Webster to Clay, Jan 8, 1832. 4. See *Register of Debates*, 22 Cong., 1 Sess., 2175-77, 2231. 5. Speech in Senate, Feb. 2, 1832. 6. Possibly Thomas W. White [5:184].

To HARRISON GRAY OTIS Washington, March 17, 1832

Altho' your kind consideration of the pressure of my numerous engagements prompted you to excuse my not answering your favor of the 8h. inst., I cannot deny myself the pleasure of acknowledging its receipt, together with the Copy of your Speech and the publication extracted from a Newspaper which accompanied it.[1] I have read them all with interest and attention. There is a remarkable coincidence, as you justly observe, between the train of your reflections, as indicated in that Speech, and my own as described in that of which I sent you a Copy.[2] Indeed, it is so remarkable that I am not sure, as your's was prior in time, that I shall not incur the charge of plagiarism. I might have profited very much by a previous perusal of your speech, but I did not possess that advantage until you obligingly placed it in my power. What will be the fate of the policy, to which they both relate, it is difficult to anticipate. I need not inform you that we have here two systems, one of politics or rather a personal system, and the other of measures; and that they sometimes come in conflict with each other. This state of things renders it impossible to estimate the degree of influence which they may mutually exert upon each other. But as I always endeavor to look forward to the best issue of any contest, I hope we shall be able substantially to preserve the American System.

The other subject to which your letter and the article in the [Boston] Courier relate is of the deepest importance. The resources of this Country, now that the public debt may be regarded as paid, would admit of the application of ten millions annually to the emancipation of slaves, without the amount being felt injuriously by any section or any interest. Such an appropriation might be made during a season of peace and suspended in a season of War. But such is the morbid feeling on this matter that I doubt whether the South would now receive the proposition much more kindly than they did that of the late Mr. R[ufus]. King.[3] I intimated, at an early period of the Session, a willingness to propose an amendment to the Constitution embracing a power to Congress to remove the free, and purchase the bond, people of color. The Southern Senator, to whom I communicated the disposition, has not been enabled by the state of feeling at home to assure me that it would be well received.

Public affairs are evidently tending to a crisis—not one of the numerous crises of Mr. [William B.] Giles—but a real *crisis*. May our Country come out of it, as hitherto it has emerged from every danger, without prejudice to our Union, our liberties, or our National character. P.S. I regretted that absence from the City, indisposition and other causes prevented my making the acquaintance of your son,[4] during his late sojourn here. I once or twice called at his lodgings (an obligation of which, by the bye, I am seldom able to acquit myself, in respect to those who do me the honor to call on me) and was not so fortunate as to find him within.

ALS. MHi.   1. Otis to Clay, March 8, 1832.   2. Speech in Senate, Feb. 2, 1832.   3. For King's speech on the Missouri Compromise and slavery, see *Register of Debates*, 15 Cong., 1 Sess., 372-73; also, Samuel Eliot Morison, *Harrison Gray Otis 1765-1848, The Urbane Federalist* (Boston, 1969), 426.   4. Either James William Otis, William Foster Otis, or George Harrison Otis. Morison, *The Life and Letters of Harrison Gray Otis*, 1:238.

Comment in Senate, March 19, 1832. States that since his tariff resolution of January 9 [Speech in Senate, January 11; February 2, 1832] was "merely the assertion of a great federal or general principle," it was unnecessary to enter into details "until a bill should be reported in conformity to that principle." *Register of Debates*, 22 Cong., 1 Sess., 592.

From Matthew L. Davis, Albany, N.Y., March 20, 1832. States that while in New York he "received, from Constantinople an interesting letter; and through another source, additional information, in regard to our National affairs in that quarter." Asks if Clay knows that the "treaty *ratified* by the Senate [Mallory to Clay, February 3, 1832], was pronounced by the Turkish Government, an *incorrect* translation; and they refused to recognise it as a true copy of the one they had negotiated." Adds that Commodore David Porter ratified "so far as his signature would go, the translation for which the Turks contended, and which, if there is any difference, has never been ratified, by the Senate." Wonders if the president knows this and if he has communicated it to the Senate. Also asks whether the president knows and has communicated to his constitutional advisers the fact that Commodore Porter has virtually reinstated the secret article of the treaty which was rejected by the Senate. Informs Clay that in "his *official capacity*," Porter has "given a *written pledge*, that he will afford the Turks the information and aid, the Secret article was intended to insure them." Indicates also that Porter has exceeded by about $14,000 the sum he was authorized to give the Turkish government as a gift. "Is this fact known? In what manner is the difference to be raised?" Asks Clay "whether you consider" these matters, "as I do, of sufficient importance, to raise the question of enquiry, before the Senate?" ALS. InU. Copy in OHi. Apparently, no inquiry was raised in the Senate on this issue.

From James W. Denny, Frankfort, March 20, 1832. Reports that the "prospect of our success in August is flattering & God grant that the people of this nation may be so far enlightened as to preserve their true interests when they come to the polls next fall. . . . I do not, think that things are managed *exactly* in the right way here, but it is our duty to acquiesce & by no dissension amongst ourselves to give the enemy aid or comfort—" ALS. DLC-HC (DNA, M212, R4). For the Kentucky elections, see Smith to Clay, December 27, 1831.

Comment in Senate, March 21, 1832. Believes it is not necessary to commit the bill that "remits the duties on certain paintings and furniture presented by two foreign potentates to the Catholic church at Bairdstown [*sic*, Bardstown], in Kentucky." Hopes that said bill will pass to a third reading [6:462-64]. Discusses bill. *Register of Debates*, 22 Cong., 1 Sess., 592-94.

Later this day, Clay explains the parliamentary procedure applicable to his tariff resolution of January 9, noting that the resolution is "still open to amendment." *Ibid.*, 595.

On April 9, 1832, the Bishop of Bardstown, Benedict Joseph Flaget, wrote Clay thanking him for his "steady and zealous" support of the bill which the Senate has passed. Informs Clay also that he has received a copy of his February 2, 1832, speech on the tariff which "was read by me with as much satisfactn. as the one you sent me seven or eight years ago [3:682-730] upon the same subject. May all the members of Congress feel about it what I feel myself." ALS. DLC-HC (DNA, M212, R4).

From John P. Kennedy, Baltimore, March 22, 1832. States that "Mr [William James] Hubard a young artist who has acquired great celebrity in this country for his small full-length protraits, and who is now successfully pursuing his profession in this city, is very anxious to obtain the favour of a few sittings from you; and, with that view, has asked me to communicate his wish to you." Notes that Hubard has done engravings of several people, including one of General Jackson which "is found decorating the walls of *the loyal* in many houses in Washington," and that "His object is to propagate your fame in the same way." ALS. DLC-TJC (DNA, M212, R10). Hubard did a portrait of Clay in 1832. Later that year, it was exhibited at the Pennsylvania Academy of Fine Arts. See *McClure's Magazine* (May-October, 1897), 9:939-40. For Hubard, see Mantle Fielding, *Directory of American Painters, Sculptors and Engravers* (Green Farms, Conn., 1926), 178.

From James Madison, "Montpelier," Va., March 22, 1832. Gives his opinion on the tariff, stating: "I know only that the Tariff in its present amount & form is a source of deep & extensive discontent; and I fear that without alleviations, separating the more moderate from the more violent opponents very serious effects are threatened. Of these the most formidable & not the least probable, would be a Southern Convention, the avowed object of some, and the unavowed object of others whose views are perhaps still more to be dreaded. The disastrous consequences of Disunion obvious to all would no doubt be a powerful check on its partizans: But such a Convention, characterized as it would be by selected talents, ardent zeal, & the confidence of those represented, would not be easily stopped in their air; especially, as many of the members tho' not carrying with them particular aspirations for the honors &c presented by ambition or a new Political Theatre, would find them germinating in such a hotbed." Expresses the hope that "some accommodating arrangements may be devised that will prove an immediate anodyne, and involve a lasting remedy to the Tariff discords." ALS. DLC-HC (DNA, M212, R4). Printed in *James Madison, Letters and Other Writings* . . . (Philadelphia, 1865), 4:216-17; and Colton, *Clay Correspondence*, 4:329-30.

Remark in Senate, March 22, 1832. Speaks in opposition to delaying amendments to the tariff bill which would address the question of precisely on "what protected articles a reduction could be made." Thinks that about as much as Congress can realistically accomplish this session is a reduction or abolition of duties on the unprotected articles in the amount of $7,000,000. *Register of Debates*, 22 Cong., 1 Sess., 607-8, 610.

From James Brown, Philadelphia, March 25, 1832. Explains that ill health has deterred him from traveling to New Orleans. Asks if Clay has heard from James Erwin.

Reports that the committee investigating the Bank of the United States [Clay to Porter, March 10, 1832; Clay to Brooke, April 17, 1832] "are now in Conclave and have resolved to accept no invitations until their business shall be finished. It is said that all is right in the Bank and the report must be favorable. I hope so because I consider the Institution a valuable one at this time." Adds: "I was at the Unitarian Meeting to day and coming out found the two sides of Locust Street lined with persons anxious to see Mr [John Q.] Adams on his leaving church, whether to have full proof of his connexion with that Heterodox sect, or to admire the former President and the only man who can now save from ruin our sinking nation, is matter of conjecture —" ALS. DLC-HC (DNA, M212, R4). Printed in *LHQ,* 24:1164.

From HENRY CLAY, JR.   Lexington, March 26, 1832

I am much obliged to you for the letter which I received just before my departure from New Orleans on the subject of my visit to Europe. I am convinced of the excellence of your advice, and heartily accede to your Conclusions. It would be better for me to cross the Atlantic after the termination of my legal studies which I hope to complete in a year or eighteen months. Whilst I was in the South I read Justinian's Institutes, Domat's [*sic*, Domot's] civil laws, many titles in the digests of Justinian, Sir William Jones on bailments, and I am now reading Pothier on obligations. I have yet to read several books of Pothier on separate title, Toullier's treatise 14 Vols and the codes.[1] I will then commence a course of common & commercial law, for you know English laws of evidence, English criminal jurisprudence and English maritime law are used in the courts of La. To render my legal education complete for La I shall then only have to study the adjudged cases, and the Statutes of La & the United States.

But besides Law I have to study history, the Latin & Spanish languages and the best models of oratory. All that is necessary I hope to accomplish by May 1833: When if you permit I would like to go to Europe: but if by remaining longer and commencing the practice of Law I shall be able to relieve you of the burden of my expenses I think I shall again desire to postpone my visit.

I am delighted to learn that uncle [James] Brown is in good health and has been so Kind as to express an opinion about my Voyage. There is no one, after yourself, whose advice on most subjects I would follow more implicitly.

Anne [Brown Clay Erwin] & family Miss [Anne] Porter and myself arrived here on the 23d instant after a delightful voyage. All our friends are well. James [Brown Clay] & John [Morrison Clay] are so much improved that I hope you will leave them at Mr [Benjamin O.] Peer's even after your return. I have not seen poor Theodore [Wythe Clay]. He is however, in the same situation as when you left.[2] Tell my mother that I understand he is comfortable and in good health. I shall visit Dr. [Benjamin Winslow] Dudley tomorrow and shall then be able to write you with more certainty if we should entertain hopes, or resign ourselves to the calamity which providence seems to have dispensed to us.

You will not leave Washington I suppose till June. I am pruning your Shrubbery, and putting your grounds in order. I hope to make Ashland more beautiful than it has been for several years. Tom[3] is doing very well in the garden, he is very industrious and I think his work will satisfy my mother on her return. I intend to have some posts & light railing substituted for the great stakes, for the grape vines to run on. At present the stakes do no essential service and only serve to deform the garden. My mother and yourself need not hasten your departure homewards on account of the grounds. As I have no experience in farming, I cannot write about the state of the farm.

I sleep at Anne's as Mr. [James] Erwin could not come up, and there is no one but Mr Hall (no gentleman I mean) in the house. I left Judge [Alexander] Porter's reluctantly but I considered it a duty to accompany Anne. It is now so late in the season that I cannot return to La.

I have not been for years in such spirits and health as I am at this moment: I am possessed of more strength and vigor than I ever had before.

Please send me such orders about Ashland as you think [necess]ary to prepare it for your return. Lexington will be [one word obliterated] I think by a great many of your southern friends. prop[erty] they say has risen here from ten to twenty per cent since the railroad was commenced.[4]

We left all well in New Orleans, but little [Martin III] Duralde, whose health was very delicate. . . .

ALS. Henry Clay Memorial Foundation, Lexington, Ky. 1. *Justinian's Institutes of the Roman Law. Corpus Juris Civilis. Institutianus. The Four Books of Justinians Institutes of the Roman Law.* London, various editions; Jean Domot, *The Civil Law in Its Natural Order. Translated from French by William Strahon.* . . . Boston, various editions; Sir William Jones, *An Essay On the Law of Bailments.* London, 1781; Robert Joseph Pothier, *A Treatise On the Law of Obligations, or Contracts.* Philadelphia, various editions; Charles Bonaventure Marie Toullier, *Le Droit Civil Français, Suivant l'Order du Code.* . . . Paris, various editions. 2. Theodore W. Clay to Clay, Jan. 8, 1832. 3. Probably a slave. 4. Clay to Biddle, May 10, 1832.

Comment in Senate, March 26, 1832. Opposes the resolution offered by Sen. [Peleg] Sprague of Maine that "calls for a list of the names of persons owning unclaimed dividends on public stocks." Mentions reasons for his opposition, mainly the personal privacy consideration. *Register of Debates*, 22 Cong., 1 Sess., 639-40.

Remark in Senate, March 27, 1832. Moves to consider the bill for the relief of certain importers of merchandise, without reference to the act of May 19, 1828. Also speaks briefly in favor of recommitting the apportionment bill [Clay to Weed, April 14, 1832]. *Register of Debates*, 22 Cong., 1 Sess., 640-41.

To FRANCIS T. BROOKE   Washington, March 28, 1832

You will have seen the disposition made on thursday last [March 22] of my resolution respecting the Tariff.[1] On that occasion some developements were made of a scheme which I have long since suspected—that certain portions of the South were disposed to purchase support to the An[ti] tariff doctrines by a total sacrifice of the public lands to States within which they are situated! A more stupendous, and a more flagitious project was never conceived. It will fail in its object, but it ought to be denounced. A majority of the Senate (composed of all the Anti Tariff Senators, and some of the Jackson-Tariff Senators) referred a resolution concerning the public lands to the Comee. of Manufactures.[2] Can you conceive a more incongruous association of subjects? There were two objects. The first I have suggested; the second was to affect me personally, by placing me in a situation in which I must report unfavorably to the Western and So. Western States which are desirous of possessing themselves of the public lands. I think I shall disappoint the design, by presenting such views of that great interest as will be sanctioned by the Nation.[3] Mean time, I should be glad if you would give some hints to our friend [John H.] Pleasants, and let him sound the tocsin. In Illinois there are about 40 millions of acres of public land, and about 150 or 160 thousand people. What think you of giving that large amt. of land to that comparatively small number of people? If it were nominally sold to them, it would in the end amount to a mere donation.

We have nothing new abt. the course of Georgia, and the President's intention as to the decision of the S. Ct.[4] The current opinion is that he will not enforce it.

We shall report in part in a day or two a bill limited to a repeal of duties on the unprotected class of foreign imports,[5] reserving for future report the other class, as to which however I do not anticipate that any thing can be done to satisfy So. Carolina.

ALS. KyU. Printed in Colton, *Clay Correspondence*, 4:330-31. Letter marked "(Confidential)." 1. Webster to Clay, Jan. 8, 1832.   2. The resolution, introduced by John M. Clayton of Delaware, required that "the Committee on Manufactures be instructed to inquire into the expediency of distributing the public lands, or the proceeds of the sales thereof, among the several States, on equitable principles." *Register of Debates*, 22 Cong., 1 Sess., 638.   3. For Clay's views on the bill and its outcome, see Comment in Senate, April 16, 1832.   4. Johnston to Clay, Jan. 12, 1831.   5. The bill was tabled. U.S. Sen., *Journal*, 22 Cong., 1 Sess., 218.

To JAMES BROWN   Washington, March 28, 1832

I was sorry to learn from your favor of the 25h. inst. that your old complaint still pursued you. I think you are wise in determining, at this period, to abandon your trip to N. Orleans. Anne [Brown Clay Erwin], with her children, and eschorted by Henry [Clay, Jr.], left there on the 10h. inst. for Kentucky, Mr. [James] Erwin remaining behind to attend to his business. From him I learn, that on the night of the 14h. or 13h. inst. he was robbed at his boarding house of his pocket book containing notes (promissory, which he had unfortunately indorsed to put into the Bank) fo the amt. of upwards of $20.000.   Another boarder was robbed at the same time of his pocket book. He immediately took the necessary measures to apprize the makers of the notes and the public of the robbery, and, from what Mr. [George A.] Waggerman [*sic*, Waggaman] tells me of the Laws of Louisiana, in such cases, I hope no injury will happen to him.

Mrs. [Susannah Gray] Hart and Mrs. [Susannah Hart] Price will feel greatly obliged for the remittance you have directed to be made to them.[1] My accounts from K. speak of them as enjoying good health.

Mrs. Clay and I would be happy to avail ourselves of your friendly invitation to visit you at Philada; but I fear it will not be in our power. As for myself, whenever I go from my abode, I become a State prisoner, and I love liberty in name, but more in fact.

I have nothing agreeable to communicate to you on politics. . . .

ALS. ViU.   1. Clay to Henry Clay, Jr., Dec. 9. 1830.

Comment in Senate, March 28, 1832. Presents memorial from numerous Kentucky citizens asking government aid to assist in colonizing free blacks on the coast of Africa. Hopes that the nation can someday rid itself of slavery, but notes that abolition is strictly a state matter, not to "be touched by the General Government." Thinks, however, that ridding the country of free blacks would be a "preliminary measure" that "all states" could embrace. Addresses the constitutional question as it is related both to abolition and colonization. Argues that abolition is patently unconstitutional; and suggests that the constitutionality of the power of Congress to apply the proceeds of public land sales to the costs of the colonization of free blacks is an open question. Assures his colleagues that no member of the American Colonization Society "had ever advocated the power of Congress, after removing the free blacks, to emancipate and remove the slaves." *Register of Debates*, 22 Cong., 1 Sess., 641-44. See Clay to Birney, September 16, 1834; Eaton, *Henry Clay*, 124.

To EDMUND H. TAYLOR   Washington, March 28, 1832

I recd. your favor of the 19h. with the Bank note for $10. enclosed. I have paid nine of it to Gales & Seaton, as requested by you, and transmit their receipt. I have sent to the persons named by you issues of my speech [of February 2],[1] and if necessary you must explain to them the cause of their being sent. The one dollar I must account for to you.

I will attend as much as I can to the Revolutionary matters suggested by you, and also to Mr. [Simon] Tripletts case.

Every thing here is uncertain — the Bank — the Tariff — the Georgia question &c.[2] Never have I seen any period of the Republic when all the future was wrapped in more doubt. I hope for the best and look for the worst. In this state of things, there is one duty of patriotism, and that is to exert ourselves to the last and to strive to save the Union, the Constitution and our Country. We may fail; but if we do, we shall at least have no cause of self-reproach, if we perform our duty firmly and fearlessly.

Kentucky may do a great deal. If *she* gives way, all is gone. All may be gone indeed, if she does her duty, but she will then have the consolation to reflect that she has stood firm.

ALS. KyHi.   1. Webster to Clay, Jan. 8, 1832; Speech in Senate, Feb. 2, 1832; Ketchum to Clay, Feb. 12, 1832.   2. Johnston to Clay, Jan. 12, 1831; Clay to Brown, Dec. 18, 1831; Webster to Clay, Jan. 8, 1832.

To LUKE TIERNAN   Washington, March 28, 1832

I recd. you favor of the 27h inst. with the two Copies of the interesting Maryland address,[1] which I have sent as you desired. If it be convenient to send me 20 more, I shall take pleasure in forwarding them to Kentucky.

The same calm in politics which you describe in Balto. prevails here, but it is that sort of calm which does not indicate repose and satisfaction, but painful foreboding and distressing uncertainty as to the future. As for myself, whatever may be the state of things, I pursue straightforward but one line, the line of duty and patriotism, as I can best discern it. Wherever and to whatever that leads me, I shall continue to march onward in it, trusting in Providence for a favorable issue.

When the Tariff memorial[2] is printed, I shall endeavor to recollect your request.

ALS. KyU.   1. Clay to Mayer, Jan. 21, 1832.   2. A memorial of a "Convention of Friends of Domestic Industry" which assembled at New York on Oct. 26-Nov. 1, 1831, was presented to the U.S. House of Representatives on March 26, 1832. U.S. H. of Reps., *Journal*, 22 Cong., 1 Sess., 535-36. See also Davis to Clay, Nov. 2, 1831.

From Francis T. Brooke, Richmond, Va., March 29, 1832. Reports having "a very interesting conversation yesterday" with Governor John Floyd. States that Floyd said he "Sorely regretted that he ever gave the certificate of a conversation held with you on the Subject of your intended vote for a President of the US not that it did not contain the truth, but that it was not called for, and was imprudent, and left others to infer from it, what was not true." Floyd, moreover, indicated he was sorry that the remarks Clay made about him "at General [Robert] Breckinridges Table Some time after" ever "came to his knowledge," because he was "compelled to notice the remarks in a manner that was very painfull to him."

Adds that before the Virginia legislature adjourned, "a Clay ticket was Silently made out," because it was thought best "not to irritate the other parties and thereby induce them to unite against us." Has learned from the governor that a Calhoun ticket will be made out, and "if so to defeat Jackson they must come over to us or we must go to them, in either way and only in one or the other can Jackson be defeated in Virginia." ALS. DLC-HC (DNA, M212, R6). Floyd's conversation with Clay in late 1824 is discussed in Charles H. Ambler, *The Life and Diary of John Floyd* (Richmond, Va., 1918), 79. Clay's remarks about Floyd at "Breckinridges Table" have not survived, although the time and place may have been the public dinner described in 4:406-7.

Comment in Senate, March 30, 1832. Discusses his tariff proposal [Speech in Senate, January 11; February 2, 1832] and the report on it made by the Committee on Manufactures. Says the "fate of the protecting system" is really the question before the Senate. Points out that the committee's bill reduces duties between five and six million dollars and that the debate on these necessary reductions should not now stall on the issue of how and to what extent further reductions might be made in the future. Adds: "It was not possible for the committee to frame such a bill as would answer the views of every Senator." Affirms that Sen. Thomas Hart Benton, a critic of the current tariff bill, does not necessarily speak for "the West! — the West!! — the West!!!" when he gives his and Missouri's views on "public lands and the protective system." Others are just as "entitled to speak the sentiments of the West." *Register of Debates*, 22 Cong., 1 Sess., 656-58, 670-72.

From Mathew Carey, Philadelphia, March 31, 1832. Sends Clay an essay which is "my last attempt to allay the storm that Southern violence has been engaged for years in preparing almost wholly unopposed   Whether any good effect will result from it, or not, I cannot pretend to decide. My fears greatly outweigh my hopes." Adds: "I might believe that the plan would succeed; were it not that I am persuaded that the leaders are determined on a secession — & have been for a long time — & that they only wait till the mass of the people can be united sufficiently to support them. This opinion is not taken up hastily, or on slender grounds. It results from a close examination of the proceedings in South Carolina for two or three years past. I am persuaded foreign influence has been at work there." ALS. DLC-HC (DNA, M212, R4). See Carey to Clay, October 9, 1830. Carey's plan, dated March 21, 1832, was to reduce all duties over 25 percent by one-tenth the average annually until they reached the 25 percent level, the level he considered non-protectionist. The idea came from Henry C. Carey. See Kenneth W. Rowe, *Mathew Carey: A Study in American Economic Development* (Baltimore, 1933), 103-4.

To FRANCIS T. BROOKE   Washington, April 1, 1832
I recd. your favor on the 29h. Ulto. communicating the tenor of a conversation with Govr. [John] Floyd. At the time that the Govr. appeared as a witness before the public to testify against me,[1] during the late administration, I was surprized and hurt, and thought he took a course utterly inconsistent with the friendly relations which had previously existed between us, to say nothing of the opposite views which he and I took of the matters to which his

testimony related. But whatever feelings were excited in my mind, at the time, have been long since thrown aside with a mass of analagous feeling awakened during an ardent and angry Presidential contest. My nature is such as to prompt me to forget these things, and I should be sorry if it were otherwise.

The clue to the motive which induced Govr. Floyd voluntarily to make that explanation I have discovered here, since I recd. your letter. A design exists on the part of Mr. Calhoun and his friends to have his name presented as a Candidate, provided they conceive that he will stand any chance of getting three or four Southern States; and provided, as the means of their accomplishing that object, our friends will co-operate in Virginia and South of it with his to give *him* their votes.[2] Mr. Calhoun had, at his instance, a conversation with a friend of mine, which was general and, understood by that friend to be, preliminary, to another which Duff Green subsequently sought with him. In the course of this latter, Duff explained fully the views and wishes of the Calhoun party. They are, that his name shall, in the course of the ensuing summer (say August) be presented as a Candidate; that if no ticket is run in Virginia by our friends, and if they will co-operate with his, he can obtain the vote of that State; that, with a fair prospect of receiving the vote Virginia, he will obtain those also of No. Carolina, Georgia and South Carolina, and *probably* Alabama and Mississippi; that the result would be to defeat the re-election of Genl. Jackson, and to devolve on the House the election; that there they suppose I would be elected; and that they would be satisfied with my election. Such is the general outline of their project, the *details* of which were communicated by Duff, after the previous general conversation with Mr. Calhoun. My friend presumed their intention was that he should communicate to me what passed, and he has accordingly communicated it. Duff stated that the success of the whole plan of the campaign, on their part, required that our friends should not present an Electoral ticket, and moreover should support theirs, in Virginia.

I have neither said, nor done any thing, in reply to all this to commit my friends or myself. I could not, without dishonor, have ventured upon any sort of commitment of them. They are in fact free, and so I wish them to remain, to act according to their own sense of propriety.

As to the project itself, I have supposed that Mr. Calhoun has too little capital any where out of So. Carolina to engraft upon; that it would be impracticable, if it were desirable, to induce our friends in Virginia to abandon all purpose of supporting a ticket on our side, and of co-operating in the support of one for Mr. Calhoun; that if such a concerted movement were made, it would be very probably defeated by the imputations which would be brought against it; and that the whole idea has sprung out of the desparate condition of Mr. Calhouns' political prospects. If there could be any movement to the South which would secure to Mr. Calhoun the vote of three or four Southern States, next to their being given to our cause, it would undoubtedly be the best thing that could happen for us. It would every where else stimulate our friends to the greatest exertions, by holding out the hope of certain success. It would break the power of Jacksonism, and discourage his friends in other States quite as much as it would animate ours!

Let me, my dear friend, hear from you on this matter; and particularly your view as the strength of the party of Mr. Calhoun in Virginia. Has it not relapsed into Jacksonism? Could it be brought forth again, in its original force, to the support of Mr. Calhoun? Supposing Mr. Calhoun not put forward as a Candidate, what course generally will his friends in Virginia pursue? Could our friends be prevailed upon to unite on a ticket for Mr. C — —n? Or, in the event of no ticket being put up for our cause, would they not divide between Jackson and Calhoun, the larger part probably going to Jackson? When do our friends contemplate bringing out the ticket which has been thought of for our side?[3]

How long will you remain at St. Julien? that is, when will you return to your official duties at Richmond?

If I am to judge of what I see, and hear, and know, there is a general persuasion in the public mind of the insecurity and danger in the existing state of the general Administration. That there is too much cause for that persuasion, I sincerely believe. The important enquiry is what ought to be done, what *can* be done? As for myself, I am ready to consent to any disposition that would rid the Country from impending perils, if any disposal of myself could contribute to that most desirable result. You are upon the *judgment* bench, and perhaps may there see, more calmly than we can, who are in the contending arena, what the good of our common Country, in the present crisis, really demands from her true and devoted sons, among whom, whatever to the contrary others may profess to think or say, *I* know none to be more sincerely and zealously attached than [myself.]

ALS. KyU. Printed in Colton, *Clay Correspondence*, 4:331-34. Letter marked "(Confidential)." 1. Brooke to Clay, March 29, 1832.   2. The Calhoun party in Virginia ultimately met in Charlottesville on June 12-14 and nominated Jackson and James Barbour for president and vice president. For the complicated maneuvering which led to this event, see Wiltse, *John C. Calhoun*, 2:106-8; and Gammon, *The Presidential Campaign of 1832*, 143-44.   3. The Clay party in Virginia formulated its ticket at a meeting in Staunton on July 16, 1832. *Niles' Register* (July 28, 1832), 42:387.

From ANNE BROWN CLAY ERWIN   Lexington, April 1, 1832

We returned home a week since in a hack from Louisville, the River being too low for boats to run, I found our friends all well, Mr [Thomas] Smith and the boys [John M. and James B. Clay] were waiting for me at my own house ["Woodlands"]; they have been out frequently since and appear to be very well and happy, John looks stronger and has a better color than I have ever seen him have.

I found my garden and the work generally very backward, owing to the young man's not being very energetic that Mr [James] Erwin left here, I astonished them all by rising at day light and having them at work before break fast and hope by a little industry to have our place looki[ng] quite in order before Mr Erwin returns. Seeing me so engaged has set Henry [Clay, Jr.] to work, he has commenced and [near]ly finished pruning the grounds and intends to have eve[ry] think [*sic*, thing] looking very clean and beautiful against you com[ing] out. I am delighted to see him so happy and occupied; he sle[eps] at my house and dines at home every day. You may tell M[ama] not to be uneasy about the garden for as usual it is more forward than any that I have seen, Tom is a most valuable [inden]ture, as to your stock &c I have not yet had time to enquire [abou]t them as I have been over but once or twice and I was [word illeg.] stealing shrubbery all the time I was there. Grand Ma [Susannah Hart] looks as well as I ever saw her and it is remarked by all of our friends that her spirits have generally been better than usual, I have no doubt that is because she has had a larger family than formerly and the children have served to keep her alive; Cousin Nannette [Price Smith] was complaining when I first came back but says that I have cured her already. Mr & Mrs [Waldemarde] Mentelle breakfasted with me this morning but they have learnt nothing new during my absence. Mrs [Caroline T. Milton] Watkins has been extremely ill but is now about as well as usual.

The children join me in sending their love to Mama & yourself, James [Erwin, Jr.] who was quite ill the week we left N. Orleans, already looks like a little Kentuckian.

ALS. Josephine Simpson Collection, Lexington, Ky.

Comment in Senate, April 2, 1832. Speaks on the amendment calling for increased appropriations for foreign and diplomatic intercourse and disputes the remark of Sen. William Marcy that the previous administration "effected no good for the country" with the money expended in foreign intercourse. Claims, to the contrary, that the Adams administration had concluded more treaties with foreign powers than had any preceding administration, perhaps more than "all of them together." *Register of Debates*, 22 Cong., 1 Sess., 684.

From Erastus T. Montague, Waltham, Va., April 4, 1832. Asserts that the "wealth and prosperity of our people," as well as the "very existence of republican institutions," now rest on Clay's shoulders. Believes that the nation is "now divided by two powerful parties—the one in favor of and the other opposed to the American System." The opponents of the System, mostly in the South, "have not failed to call in the aid of sectional prejudices." Feels that "no proposition for a compromise of the differences growing out of this difficult question will ever emanate from the south, and unless it shall come from the National republican party no arrangement can ever be effected." Clay must therefore, for patriotic reasons, take the lead in working for a tariff compromise. Notes, however, that Clay's tariff bill "now pending before the Senate . . . [Webster to Clay, January 8, 1832] presents no compromise. It sustains, to the full extent the *protective policy* without conceding a single point." Assures Clay that he says this even though he personally agrees with Clay's views on the tariff. Charges that the substitute offered in the Senate by Robert Y. Hayne [January 16, 1832] "is equally destitute of the mild spirit of concession" in that it "aims a deadly blow at all domestic industry and casts a withering li[ght] over the arts & sciences just budding into life in this western world." Suggests the following compromise between the Clay proposal and the Hayne counterproposal: "an ad valorem duty of 25. percentum upon all articles grown or manufactured in the United States and one of 10 percentum upon all other articles. . . . By this plan the produce & manufactures would concede 2/5 the amount of protection, by allowing just that amount of duty to be laid upon the unprotected articles, while the consumer would [word missing] 3/5 by permitting just that much to be added solely for protection   The manufacturer would thus receive a real protection of 25 percent while the actual bounty would be but 15. This I think would be a mutual concession—a just and equal compromise, whereas if your resolution, (as I understand it,) prevail the whole amount of duty would operate as a direct and actual bounty to the manufacturer."

Admits that if Clay were to support such a statesmanlike compromise, and thus harmonize conflicting sectional interests, "it would afford but little if any aid in forwarding your advances to that high station on which your friends are anxious to place you." Indeed, even if he were to "propose an entire abandonment of the protective policy," the South would still "continue to support the *Idol* as the friend of Southern principles and denounce you as their enemy." Asks, in conclusion, that Clay send him one or two copies of his February 2 speech on the tariff. ALS. DLC-HC (DNA, M212, R4). For Montague, who was subsequently auditor of the U.S. Treasury, see George William Montague, *History And Genealogy of Peter Montague . . . And His Descendants, 1621-1894* (Amherst, Mass., 1894), 191-92.

From Francis T. Brooke, near Fredericksburg, Va., April 5, 1832. Has just received Clay's letter of April 1 and believes "the project of the Calhoun party which it details" is "entirely impracticable in Virginia" and results only from "its desperate state everywhere." Notes "what an opportunity the [Calhoun] party lost in not bringing forward a resolution in the house of Delegates disapproving the vote of our Senators [John Tyler and Littleton W. Tazewell] in favour of V[an] B[uren] [Clay to Brooke, May 1, 1831]." Continues with the observation that the Calhoun party is very weak, because "nullification, has broken it down in Virginia—and though [John] Floyd spoke confidently of a ticket I doubt much whether it will make out one, if it is tried it will be found very dificult to bring the Clay party to vote for Calhoun—I would myself vote for Calhoun before Jackson but there are many of our party who would not, yet I think if we cannot do better it will be well to try the project, when we see their ticket we shall be better able to judge. . . . my impression is that we shall run our ticket and most of the Calhoun party must in their own defence come over to us—" Adds, in conclusion, that Thomas Ritchie has assured him that unless Van Buren comes "over to the Virginia school he would not support him." ALS. DLC-HC (DNA, M212, R4). Ritchie eventually threw his support to Van Buren for vice president. Charles H. Ambler, *Thomas Ritchie, A Study in Virginia Politics* (Richmond, 1913), 147.

From R.S. Browning, Rome, Italy, April 5, 1832. Is visiting Rome and comments upon ancient history. Compares Clay to Cicero and suggests that "the Republicans of the U. States" reward "your virtue and talents with the first gift of the Nation." ALS. DLC-TJC (DNA, M212, R10). Printed in Colton, *Clay Correspondence*, 4:334.

Remark in Senate, April 6, 1832. Offers resolution seeking information from the secretary of the treasury on his correspondence with collectors of the revenue pertaining to their interpretation of the laws determining duties on foreign imports. *Register of Debates*, 22 Cong., 1 Sess., 710.

To HENRY CLAY, JR.   Washington, April 7, 1832

The cheerful tone pervading your letter of the 26h. Ulto, just received, has given me great pleasure. I anxiously desire your happiness and success in life. It is indeed one of the strongest feelings which reconciles me to existence. I hope you will continue to cultivate your present temper of mind.

The course of study which you have pursued the past winter, and which you have marked out for the future, appears to me to be very judicious. You were very fortunate in winning the friendship of Judge [Alexander] Porter, who writes to me in highly flattering terms about you.

I am glad that you have taken an interest in the grounds and garden at Ashland. I had heretofore always regretted that none of my sons would take such an interest and that they seemed to regard themselves as strangers in their fathers home. What you propose as to the grape vines is very proper and what I intended. Mr. [Adam] Long will make whatever frames you may direct. I had intended to have all the dead trees and shrubs cut out and removed from the shrubbery, and should be thankful if you could have it done. I sent some superior water melon seed to Mr. [William] Martin which should be planted; and we should desire Tom[1] to plant some Cantelopes also. For water melons and potatoes the same piece of ground, between the shrubbery and garden might be used that was last year. Mr. Martin must have more force than necessary to work the farm, and can spare you some when necessary. I hope you will prevent any Stock from running on the grounds about the house, unless it be some favorite young calves. I should be glad to know how my Jacks, and especially the yearling, have got through the winter, as well as the other Stock. Tell Mr. Martin that the Stock should be allowed to graze the Rye fields until the 20h. of this month. I wish them kept off the Woodland pasture as much as possible, to give it a chance, for once. It has been heretofore fed too soon and too close.

Give our love to Anne [Brown Clay Erwin], and tell her that I wrote her a short letter a few days ago. I wish you would also call and see your grandmother [Susannah Hart] and Aunt [Susan] Price and give our love to them. It will be painful to you to visit Theodore [W. Clay], but is it not a duty?[2]

ALS. Henry Clay Memorial Foundation, Lexington, Ky.   1. Probably a slave.   2. Theodore W. Clay to Clay, Jan. 8, 1832.

To Francis T. Brooke, near Fredericksburg, Va., April 9, 1832. Asks for an invitation to Brooke's estate, St. Julien, for a few days of rest. Mentions that he is "wearied and exhausted . . . by public business" and would prefer being received "*incognito.*" Copy. Printed in Colton, *Clay Correspondence,* 4:335.

From HENRY CLAY, JR.   Lexington, April 9, 1832

I have lately been engaged in pruning and cleaning your shubbery and in the ardour of my zeal have met with a misfortune in injuring one of my eyes: It has prevented me from studying, as I was afraid of using one eye until the recovery of the other. When I commenced, Ashland was very much out of order, but it is now nearly cleaned, and I hope you will find it improved by my labours. I have removed 30 or 40 loads of dead trees from the grounds and am now engaged in the removal of 15 or 20 more of stones, sticks &c. The house too is once more in pretty good order; but I write principally to tell you that it is very damp and quite out of repair. If you feel disposed to give any orders about it, I will attend with great pleasure to the execution of them. A man will be here in a few days, expert in stuccoing. You spoke of having the house covered with a coating of stucco: If you still feel so inclined, you can now have it done with more than ordinary facility. It will certainly very much improve its appearance, and might otherwise benefit it in rendering it less damp. The windows[,] window shutters, and the interior need much attention   I do not believe, however, that it could all be finished before your return.

Your farm and stock look to me in good order, Mr [William] Martin will commence planting corn in a day or two   Stamboul is now at Ashland,[1] and will remain there for a day or two. He is much improved since you saw him. Mr. Martin does not know how to dispose of your three best mares when they have colts and wished me to mention it. He has himself written to you several letters which he says you have not received. Will you allow me to tell him to put the Wickliffe mare to Stamboul.

Theodore [W. Clay] visited me to day at Ashland with Mr [J.C.] Jordan who attends him.[2] He looks better than I ever saw him before: But let us not be too sanguine of his recovery; And really we have ample reason for satisfaction and consolation in his present situation   The necessity of placing him where he is was certainly a melancholy affliction for us all; but it has long existed, and he is now in better health than he has been for a long time; and if ultimate recovery be in the train of human events, he is now in the way of attaining it. Let us then be resigned to our destiny, the more especially as my unfortunate brother is under a better regulation than ordinary for the promotion of his own welfare and for the happiness of his friends

Anne [Brown Clay Erwin] is in excellent health, very industrious about her garden and grounds and has the prospect of spending a happy summer.

When will you reach home? I suppose [n]ot until late in June.

James [Brown Clay] & John [Morrison Clay] and all send their love

ALS. Henry Clay Memorial Foundation, Lexington, Ky.　　1. Berryman to Clay, Oct. 5, 1831. 2. Theodore W. Clay to Clay, Jan. 8, 1832.

From Francisco de Paula Santander, Washington, April 10, 1832. Says he regrets leaving Washington without reassuring Clay of his "recognition of your efforts toward the American cause. We Colombians maintain the happy certitude that you will under all circumstances be the courageous advocate of independence, liberty, and order in all the new American states." Hopes that Clay will be advanced to "the premier position" in his homeland. ALS, in French. DLC-HC (DNA, M212, R4).

On June 4, 1832, Santander wrote Clay from New York announcing that he had been elected president of New Granada and would soon be leaving for Cartagena. Hopes that as president [5:225] he will be able to devote himself "to the reestablishment of public order, to concord, to union, and to the strengthening of liberal Institutions," but fears that "the ignorance of the people" may still be "fatal to the consolidation of liberty." Thanks Clay again for his past firm and sincere advocacy of South American independence. *Ibid.* Both letters translated by Ingrid A. Hansen.

To Nicholas Biddle, Philadelphia, April 11, 1832. Encloses letter "shewing that the Road between Frankfort and Lexington (the Turnpike) is not likely to be constructed [Clay to Henry Clay, Jr., December 2, 1829]." Suggests that "the donation from the Bank of $1500" be directed instead to the Maysville and Lexington Turnpike. ALS. KyLoF.

From ANNE BROWN CLAY ERWIN　　　　　　Lexington, April 11, 1832
Your letter of the 11th March arrived in New Orleans the day after my departure and was only received by me this morning; my husband [James Erwin] writes me to answer you exactly as I think proper on [the] subject of the carriage, I have therefore to say that I approve of all that you have done, although the price is a high one, I think that ought not to be a consideration when we know that it is worth it, & Mr Erwin having made some pretty little speculations this winter I feel more disposed to indulge in a little extravagance. I thank you for your kindness in sending so far the trees for me, I hope Mr White will be fortunate enough to get them.

I have not a great deal of news to give you as I have been to town but once to see my grand Mother [Susannah Hart], our friends however are kind enough to come out very often, particularly Cousin Nannette [Price Smith] & Sidney Edmiston who have taken tea with me frequently. Henry [Clay, Jr.] suppose has given you all the news of the farm, he seems to be quite engaged in having things put in order, and has already improved the grounds very much by cutting out the dead trees limbs &c. he has also pruned your grape vines according to Mr [William] Prince's[1] most approved plan and is now having railings put up for them; he is very desirous to improve the house also, I think it would be advisable for you to direct him to have the dining room repaired as it looks very bad now, the paper is much more torn off than it was;

490

if Mama thinks proper he could order Mr [Charles A.] Potter to put the paper on it that he has, or I think if he could paint it again it would be much better, she could if she wishes it done write what color and any other directions she has to give and I promise her to see that they are fulfilled to the letter. I am afraid Mama is becoming home sick I hope though she will rest perfectly contented until you can come with her as I feel anxious for her to visit the Northern Cities if it is only for a few days before she returns; She need feel no uneasiness on my account as I have never been in better health in my life than I have enjoyed for the last six months. The boys [John M. and James B. Clay] come out generally to dine with me every day; they complain a little of the eating at Mr [Benjamin O.] Peers' but from their appearances they have not been starved; I never saw John look as fat as he does and James is constantly laughing at him for eating so much. John comes out every Saturday and stays until Sunday evening with us. I was at Ashland on Sunday. Miss [Sarah] Hall has already had the house cleaned & put in order, and every thing is going on as well as usual on the whole farm. The children join me in love to Mama & yourself.

ALS. Josephine Simpson Collection, Lexington, Ky. Addressed to Clay at Fredericksburg, Va. 1. See 6:279.

Remark in Senate, April 11, 1832. Objects to an amendment in the proposed appropriation bill providing $10,000 for indexing documents in the departments of State, Treasury, War, and Navy. States that it "had never, within his knowledge, taken five minutes to find any document." *Register of Debates*, 22 Cong., 1 Sess., 766-67.

Comment in Senate, April 12, 1832. Calls the attention of the Senate to an appropriation item proposed for the diplomatic service — the salary of a chargé d'affaires at Guatemala. Deems the position unnecessary because the country is in chaos and trade with it "too inconsiderable" to justify placing a U.S. diplomat there. Moves to strike from the bill the appropriation for the salary. *Register of Debates*, 22 Cong., 1 Sess., 768, 771-74. See Clay to Hunt, February 13, 1832.

To FRANCIS T. BROOKE   Washington, April 13, 1832

I have this moment recd. your favor of yesterday. Anxious to complete and present to the Senate an important Report on the Land subject,[1] I have postponed my excursion to St. Julien until the 19h. or 12h. [*sic*][2] inst. I will advise you on Wednesday next the day. [Robert P.] Letcher, and perhaps [Joseph] Vance will accompany me.

According to late information, we shall get N. York.[3]

ALS. NcD.   1. Comment in Senate, April 16, 1832.   2. Apparently Clay meant April 21 rather than 12.   3. Clay to Weed, April 14, 1832; Clay to Henry Clay, Jr., April 17, 1832.

Comment in Senate, April 13, 1832. Speaks on an appropriation for the outfit of a minister to France, on the history and use of the contingency fund in the Department of State's budget, and on the propriety and legality of a president's appointing diplomatic officers during recesses of the Senate. *Register of Debates*, 22 Cong., 1 Sess., 775-76, 778-79.

Later this day, moves to strike out of the appropriation bill the provision for a minister to the "new Power," that is Belgium. Says that the U.S. should have nothing to do with the "upstart King of Belgium [Leopold I], who was not seated on the throne by the will of the people, but by the act of a few sovereigns." Proclaims the virtues of economy in staffing diplomatic posts abroad. *Ibid.*, 781-83.

From **Lucius H. & J. Scott,** Terre Haute, Ind., April 13, 1832. Report, as per Clay's request, that they have advanced to his son, Thomas Hart Clay, "money to aid him in commencing his farming operations this Spring." Note also that "The Severity of the winter & general failure of crops" were such that he "would have found it utterly impossible to put in his crop without assistance." ALS. DLC-TJC (DNA, M212, R14).

To JOHN H. EWING Washington, April 14, 1832
[Discusses mares he may purchase from Ewing and details of their transport to Lexington. Continues:]

The position of our friends in Pennsa. as described by you is very important; and I am glad to learn that they feel it, and are resolved to make themselves felt. Measures of co-operation have been nearly matured in N. York between the Anti Masons and the N. Republicans (as I am informed) which will secure to our cause the support of that State.[1] The influence of those measures, when consummated, I should think, would reach to all the ramifications of Anti Masonry. The Anti Masons of N. York say that they must save the Republic, by putting down Jackson, and preserving our institutions; and that, without abandoning their peculiar principles, they must forbear, for the present, to insist upon their being carried into Federal politics. This is a reasonable and patriotic view on the matter.

I am glad to see our Washington [Pa.] Jackson fellow Citizens awakening to a sense of the dangers impending over the Tariff. They are real, and ought to excite alarm. The state of the case is, that Jackson *pretends* to be for the Tariff, whilst the great body of his party is open and violent against it. With the exception of Pennsa. Jacksonism and Opposition to the American System every where else are hand in hand.

They have been attempting to conciliate support to the Anti tariff principles by a sacrifice of the Public lands. I shall endeavor to disentangle the two subjects and shall shortly make a report with that view on the Public lands.[2] But I feel as if I were sitting upon a Volcano. There is no safety no certainty with the Jackson party; and as they are in the majority in both houses they can do as they please.

ALS. KyU. Addressed to Ewing in Washington, Pa.   1. Clay to Weed, April 14, 1832.   2. Comment in Senate, April 16, 1832.

To THURLOW WEED Washington, April 14, 1832
I received your favor of the 9th inst., as I did the previous ones, communicating the progress of measures to produce coöperation between the anti-Masons and the National Republicans in the State of New York. I most earnestly hope that such coöperation may be cordially produced, to the satisfaction of both parties. If it could be secured, and if, as the necessary consequence, the Jackson party could be defeated in New York, there is only wanting a perfect persuasion of that result, throughout the Union, to insure a signal overthrow of Jackson at the approaching election. You see, then, how important the movement is in your State.

And was there ever an occasion which should prompt true lovers of their country to more vigorous exertions? It is not merely some measures of public policy at hazard; but, I verily believe, the purity of the government and the existence of the Union are involved in the struggle. The party or parties, therefore, that shall save the country, in this its greatest peril, will deserve thanks, gratitude, and honor.

492

I am extremely happy to learn, as I have from several quarters, that Mr. [William H.] Maynard, for whose character and talents I have long entertained very high respect, has taken a course so decided and efficient in bringing about union and concert.[1] I regret that, having no acquaintance with him, I cannot express to him personally how much I have been gratified with his firm and patriotic conduct. It seems to me that if, by the efficient aid of anti-Masons, the dangers can be averted which now threaten the liberty, the institutions, and the union of our country, they will establish themselves strongly in the public confidence; they will evince the sincerity of the paramount article in their creed, which ought to be the paramount article in the earthly creed of all associations and of all men, — our country first, our country always.

Should the measures to which I refer be consummated, it seems to me that a convention, on the part of our friends, would be still desirable, some time or other during the summer, in order to insure harmony and unity of action.[2] With great deference, I think that was the error committed in your last canvass for Governor. There was no concert, no united exertions, among our friends.[3]

A scene, disgraceful to the place, occurred here yesterday. The ex-Governor of Tennessee, General [Sam] Houston, made a brutal attack upon a member of the House of Representatives from Ohio [William Stanbery], for words in debate,[4] thus realizing a prediction as to the consequences of Jackson's election made to me by Colonel [Thomas Hart] Benton eight years ago.[5] The papers will give you a detail of the affair, and of the proceedings of the House of Representatives.

I think the apportionment bill will be decided next week. . . .[6]

Copy. Printed in Thurlow Weed Barnes (ed.), *The Life of Thurlow Weed, Including His Autobiography and a Memoir*, 2 vols. (Boston, 1884), 2:42-43.   1. For more on the attempts to unify the Anti-Masons and National Republicans in New York, see Vaughn, *The Anti masonic Party in the United States*, 42-45; also, Clay to Porter, May 1, 1832.   2. Clay to Porter, May 1, 1832.   3. Stoddard to Clay, Nov. 8, 1830; Clay to Johnston, May 9, 1830.   4. For the details of Houston's attack on Stanbery, provoked by statements Stanbery made about Houston in the House of Representatives, see *Register of Debates*, 22 Cong., 1 Sess., 2321-22, 2512, 2571-73; and New York *Evening Post*, April 17, 1832.   5. In the debate on rechartering the Bank of the U.S., Clay "asserted that in the campaign of 1824 Benton had said many things derogatory to Jackson to the effect that the latter was a little better than a murderer, a cowardly braggart, and that dirks and pistols would be constantly in evidence if he [Jackson] were elected." Joseph Morgan Rogers, *Thomas H. Benton* (Philadelphia, 1905), 145.   6. The bill entitled "An act for the apportionment of representatives among the several States according to the fifth census" passed the House on Feb. 16, 1832, and the Senate on April 27, 1832. U.S. H. of Reps., *Journal*, 22 Cong., 1 Sess., 368; and U.S. Sen., *Journal*, 22 Cong., 1 Sess., 258.

From HENRY CLAY, JR.   Lexington, April 15, 1832

Though I wrote to you but a few days ago, yet as I have since received your letter of the 27th of February which was directed to me at New Orleans, I cannot refrain from expressing to you the pleasure which the reception of that letter has given me. As I am now in Kentucky I cannot use the authority you gave me to apply to my exclusive benefit the sum of $2500. of your monies in the hands of Mr [James] Erwin: But I assure you, I am as sensible of the favour as if I had enjoyed it: Had I remained in New Orleans I should have connected myself with the city and with business by a chain of interest for which I should have been deeply indebted to you; but now, I only remember your kindness as another evidence of your affection, and of your confidence in my discretion. Everything at Ashland is going on as you could wish. I believe you will find some improvement in the appearance of the shubbery and garden when you return. I found the house and grounds quite out of order, but I think they are now quite as clean as when you left Ky.

Most of your pecan trees have died, but in their place I have substituted some brought up by Anne [Brown Clay Erwin]. nearly all Mama's plants were killed by the severity of the winter, but Anne's liberality has again been my resource; I have filled most of the boxes with plants which Anne brought for Mama. Your firs and pines are all alive with one exception. I wrote to Louisville for twenty-five more but could not get them. I wished to form a cluster of ever-greens in the meadow before the house where Mr Foy once planted some. Could you get any of the Fringe[1] trees which grow between Washington and Baltimore? They would be a great embellishment both to Ashland and to the Woodlands.[2] What do you think of a thick grove of American forest trees, embracing all the varieties of evergreens & others on the ground where the cherry orchard once stood. I think it would be a beautiful ornament and a very interesting collection. There might be planted one or two trees of each species, for example one or two live oaks, magnolias, holleys, pines, crab-apples, large white-oaks, red do. &c &c. Many of the trees would have to be reared from the seed; but this itself would be a pleasant occupation, to watch their growth and to propagate them — But trees in every stage of their growth are beautiful; and though we might not live to behold the acorns which we ourselves have planted endure to be the patriarchs of the forest, yet the incipient shrubs might be the objects of a very pleasing attention which would well repay our labour; and others would possess the advantage of its magnificint growth and expansion which a timely foresight had taught us to anticipate.

I am getting very enthusiastic about hedges, if you will allow me I shall commence next fall the culture of thorn holley and crab-apple hedges and perhaps some other kinds. A nursery on a small scale might be soon formed and I think would repay the little expenditure that would be necessary —

In the mean time I am not remiss in my studies — All are well and send their love.

ALS. Henry Clay Memorial Foundation, Lexington, Ky. 1. An ornamental olive tree. 2. The Lexington estate of James and Anne Erwin.

Comment in Senate, April 16, 1832. Reports, as spokesman for the Committee on Manufactures, on the question of the distribution of the proceeds of the sales of public lands to the states, and submits the committee's bill to that end. Asks that the bill be ordered printed and copies be distributed to the public. *Register of Debates*, 22 Cong., 1 Sess., 785, 787-88, 790. For the report of the Committee on Manufactures, dated April 16, 1832, in which Clay's distribution plan is spelled out in detail, and the counter-report of the Committee on Public Lands, dated May 18, 1832, see *ibid.*, Appendix, 112-27. The report of the Committee on Manufactures was also printed as a pamphlet, entitled *Report On the Expediency of Reducing the Price of Public Lands, and of Ceding Them to the Seveal States Within Which They are Situated, on Reasonable Terms.* Washington, 1832. For Clay's main defense of his plan, see Speech in Senate, June 20, 1832, and notes thereto. The political and sectional ramifications of Clay's distribution proposal are discussed in Van Deusen, *The Life of Henry Clay*, 252-55.

Writing from York, Pa., on April 23, Richard Rush thanked Clay for having sent him a copy of his committee report on the public lands and remarked that "you have established in an irresistible manner all the main points of the policy you recommend." ALS. DLC-HC (DNA, M212, R4). Clay's bill passed on July 3, 1832, by a vote of 26 to 18. *Register of Debates*, 22 Cong., 1 Sess., 1174. The House did not act on it.

To FRANCIS T. BROOKE   Washington, April 17, 1832

I shall leave here on thursday next in the Steam boat for Fredericksburg, and reach St. Julien, if, I can, that evening. Gen. [Joseph] Vance and Mr. [Robert P.] Letcher will probaly accompany me. Mrs. Clay thinks she had better remain here with our grandson [Henry Clay Duralde] &c.

Mr. Mc. Duffie [*sic*, George McDuffie] of the Bank Comee. has returned from Phila. and the rest of the Comee. are expected this evening or to-morrow. It is understood that the Committee were not very harmonious, but it is not known what will be the character of their report.[1]

Copy. DLC-TJC (DNA, M212, R14). Printed in Colton, *Clay Correspondence*, 4:335.   1. By a majority of 4-3 the committee recommended that the bank not be rechartered. See Hammond, *Banks and Politics in America*, 393-404; and *Reports of Committees*, 22 Cong., 1 Sess., no. 460.

To HENRY CLAY, JR.   Washington, April 17, 1832

I recd. your favor of the 9h. inst, and it afforded me great satisfaction to perceive that you continued to take an interest in improvements at Ashland. As to rough casting the house, I have always wished to have it done, but before we definitively decide upon it, I would thank you to procure and transmit an estimate of the cost. Tell Mr. [William] Martin that I wish the Wickliffe mare put to Stamboul, the Arabian mare to Shakespear[e] and the Virginia mare to my neighbour Mr. Hunt's[1] Hunter horse. Tell him also that I hope he will have the lot between the old (wooden) stable and the Mill well prepared and sowed in Hemp, which I intend as a crop preparatory to putting it again in grass.

I am glad to hear that Theodore [W. Clay] looks well, but I seriously fear that he will never recover.[2] I wish you could reconcile it to your feelings occasionally to visit him.

There is a good prospect of co-operation between the Anti Masons & N. R. in N. York; and if [it] should be brought about cordially there is but little doubt of the defeat of Jackson.[3]

I yesterday made a Report, on the Public Lands, to the Senate, which has elicited very favorable commendation[4]

Congress will not I apprehend adjourn before the middle of June. Your mother joins me in love to you. PS. Will you get an estimate also of the expence of painting the outside of our house some light color?

ALS. Henry Clay Memorial Foundation, Lexington, Ky.   1. Possibly John M. Hunt, who owned land near Ashland. McCabe, *Directory of the City of Lexington and County of Fayette in 1838 & 1839*, 127.   2. Theodore W. Clay to Clay, Jan. 8, 1832.   3. Clay to Weed, April 14, 1832; an almost identical sentiment is expressed in Clay to Crittenden, April 15, 1832. ALS. DLC-John J. Crittenden Papers (DNA, M212, R20).   4. Comment in Senate, April 16, 1832.

Comment in Senate, April 17, 1832. Calls the attention of the Senate to the clause in the appropriation bill which makes appropriations for the salaries of two U.S. claims agents who reside in London and Paris. Says that while the jobs were useful in the Jefferson and early Madison administrations, they are now "mere sinecures." *Register of Debates*, 22 Cong., 1 Sess., 791-92.

Later this day, Clay votes in favor of a motion to strike out of the appropriations bill a provision for a minister to Colombia since that nation has split into three. *Ibid.*., 794.

To JAMES WOLCOTT   Washington, April 18, 1832

I have only time to acknowledge the receipt of your letter of the 14h. inst. and to add a few words. I regret that I can not inform you what is likely to be finally done with the Tariff.[1] We have a decided majority in both houses in favor of it, if men would act fearlessly upon their honest convictions. But the Jackson party, as a party, being against it, some of its friends, who belong to that party, on collateral questions, go against us, and in this way thwart and jeopard the cause. A movement, in regard to the public lands,[2] was made some time ago, looking to the use of them, as an instrument, to destroy the Tariff. I have made a report,[3] which you will shortly see, in which I have endeavored to separate the two subjects and to settle the question of the Public lands.

I consider every thing here involved in doubt and uncertainty. We must not despair, and hope for the best, but be, at the same time, prepared for the worst.

ALS. NcD. Addressed to Wolcott at 35 Cedar St., New York, N.Y.   1. Webster to Clay, Jan. 8, 1832.   2. Clay to Brooke, March 28, 1832.   3. Comment in Senate, April 16, 1832.

From HENRY CLAY, JR.   Lexington, April 22, 1832

I received yesterday a letter from you and one from Thomas [Hart Clay]; He writes me that he has not corn to plant, and desires us to send him the barrels from Ashland, in sacks;[1] which we have determined to do, believing that it will meet your approbation. The frost of last winter affected the germ of his corn, and all in that country, so that it will not come up; And he thinks that, from the neighbourhood of Louisville, no better than his own. This will account for his desiring particularly that grown at Ashland. It will be expensive to send it, but his loss would be much greater; and this, I suppose, may be a sufficient consideration for complying with his demand.

I have been out today to see poor Theodore [W. Clay]. It is indeed a duty to visit him, which nothing but his own opposing welfare could induce me to forego. I once thought his malady[2] of a transient nature, and that rest and tranquility would soon restore him. I was then unwilling to disturb the progress of his imagined recovery; But now that I am fully aware of the extent of our affliction, it will be an alleviation to visit him and render him all those attentions which may be offered by a brother. It is very painful to me, my dear father to tell you what Thomas Hart has asked me to do, that both your letters have produced the greatest excitement in Theodore; and that which was meant for a comfort, and a token of continued affection has been rather of disservice to him.

I assure you, my dear father, that it has only been from occular demonstration and the fullest conviction of its propriety that I have brought myself to mention this circumstance.

It will be a consolation to my mother to know that Theodore is entirely comfortable in regard to all his personal wants. We sent him a horse a week ago, which he rides sometimes, and he has even visited me once at Ashland.

When I arrived in Lexington a little challenge from Anne [Brown Clay Erwin] that she would make her place ["Woodlands"] more beautiful than Ashland induced me to attempt improvement; and I now find gardening so delightful an occupation that I continue it for amusement and recreation. I have also since I received your letter a new motive stronger than all the rest for my attention to the grounds, and which alone would more than repay it, that of pleasing you and my mother.

I have already had frames erected in the garden for grape vines and hops; by the by I have lately received from Mr Vandoren[3] a present for you of some grape-vine cuttings which I have planted according to directions. Anne, too, has supplied me with a few French grape-vines of a very fine description. The care which I have bestowed upon the shubbery I think will show for itself. I do not know whether you will be pleased with what I have done, but at least it has been my object to give you pleasure, and for that I am sure you will give me credit.

The water-melon and other seeds which you mentioned have been received.

Your Jacks are in fine order and the rest of your stock look as well as could be expected after the late severe season. In two weeks Mr [William] Martin will have finished planting corn, your clover-ground was twice broken, And he is making a good system of fencing; so that, I think the active operations of the farm have been pretty well conducted. We shall proceed immediately to release the woodland as far as it is possible from the stock now on it. The mules will be carried over to the [Nathaniel] Pettit farm and the other stock put upon the rye-fields as soon as the clover has become a little stronger which Mr Martin tells me is necessary for its vigorous growth: The season has been dry and the pond in the Morton woods has failed so that it is necessary to drive a part of the stock through the front woods to wa[ter.] I believe he will make every exertion to obey your com[mands]

He has had on the rye since the first of this month only the mares and colts and young cattle —

He is quite discontented with Dave,[4] who is an idle worthless fellow, full of tricks.

This I believe is a full report of the farm, as far as I could collect the materials to judge of it. I have very little experience myself and can, therefore, only obey orders.

Mr [James] Erwin has not yet arrived. Grandmama [Susannah Hart] is in very good health.

ALS. Henry Clay Memorial Foundation, Lexington, Ky.   1. The seed corn was sent. No sooner had Thomas planted it than the Sac and Fox Indians invaded the Paris, Ill., area, causing a "terrible state of alarm" and convincing Thomas he would "go out as a volunteer against black Hawk on the 2d call." Thomas H. Clay to Henry Clay, Jr. (Clay's Prairie, Ill.), May 23, 1832. ALS. Henry Clay Memorial Foundation, Lexington, Ky. For the background of the Black Hawk War, see Anthony F.C. Wallace, "Prelude to Disaster, The Course of Indian-White Relations Which Led to the Black Hawk War of 1832," in Ellen M. Whitney (ed.), *The Black Hawk War 1831-1832*, 2 vols. (Springfield, Ill., 1970), 1:1-51.   2. Theodore W. Clay to Clay, Jan. 8, 1832.   3. Probably Isaac or L. Halsey Van Doren who, together, ran Van Doren's Collegiate Institute for Young Ladies in Lexington.   4. Probably a slave [5:591].

From Peter B. Porter, Black Rock, N.Y., April 22, 1832. Apologizes for not having written earlier and suggests that "I have reason to believe that an arrangement will soon be concluded (if it be not already consummated) between our friends and the anti masons for running a joint Electoral Ticket [Clay to Weed, April 14, 1832], in conformity with a proposition which was discussed between us and the leading antimasons while I was at Albany last winter and which I believe I then communicated to you [Porter to Clay, February 25, 1832]. The proposition was that a ticket should be formed by a mutual agreement, to be composed of liberal & enlightened men, one half of whom should be anti masons to be taken from the anti masonic, or western, districts, and the other half national republicans but not professed masons. No pledges to be required from any of the Electors; it being however well understood that the anti masonic, as well as the other part of the ticket, will vote for you, if, by so doing, there is a reasonable chance of your succeeding: and it being also understood that in such case Mr [William] Wirt will decline at the proper time to effectuate the object. If this arrangement is or shall be amicably concluded, we shall have great reason to expect success in this State; and our anti masons will moreover, recommend a simular course to their friends in

Pennsylvania Ohio, Vermont &c. In return we will support [Francis] Granger & [Samuel] Stevens for the princepal State offices [Clay to Bailhache, November 24, 1830]. Remarks that the "zeal & talent displayed by our friends in Congress in exposing the corruptions & imbecility of the Administration deserve the gratitude of the country." Also discusses the split in the Regency party over "the Bank question," and suggests that Clay travel to New York, because such a visit, from a political standpoint, would be "productive of the best consequences." ALS. DLC-HC (DNA, M212, R4).

From Francis T. Brooke, near Fredericksburg, Va., April 23, 1832. Gives Clay suggestions on how best to take care of his health. Advocates that he use tobacco and wine only in moderation, and warns particularly against too much excitement, because "after high excitement from any cause there is invariably a consequent debility—which will always increase materially any predisposition to torpor and even paralysis, high excitement then from any cause ought to be avoided and especially from causes that always precede great debility—" Adds that the most "pernicious" excitement is that which results "from dwelling too much on the deplorable condition of our public affairs and on the relation in which you are placed in regard to them, it is the more dificult for you to look on them in the calm lights of a mild philosophy—but yet you ought to be satisfied with performing your duty and to leave the rest to others." ALS. DLC-HC (DNA, M212, R4). Printed in Colton, *Clay Correspondence*, 4:335-36.

Remark in Senate, April 23, 1832. Brands as "extraordinary" Secretary of State Edward Livingston's letter of April 21 to Sen. Samuel Smith, chairman of the Committee on Finance, stating that there is "at present" no vacancy in the office of minister to France; but that there will be a vacancy in October next since minister William C. Rives has asked for and has been granted permission to return home at that time. States that this letter has suddenly changed the circumstances of the request of providing at this time an outfit for a minister to France since earlier "we were given to understand that it was doubtful whether a successor to Mr. Rives would be sent out or not. We were told that he had applied for liberty to return; but we had no positive information whether leave would be given or not." Thinks Livingston's letter to Smith "an unconstitutional and unexampled interference with the rights of the Senate." *Register of Debates*, 22 Cong., 1 Sess., 825, 830.

From HENRY CLAY, JR.   Lexington, April 24, 1832
I wish to communicate the joyful intelligence that you are grandfather by a new title. Heaven, as if jealous of our fondness for Anne, has attempted to divide it by a new object of affection, but it will only give rise to a new source of feeling. Yesterday, between 2 and 3 P.M., Anne gave life and light to a fine daughter.

We shall be happy to introduce you when you come, to the youthful stranger. Mary is to be her name, and her aunt, Miss Mary Erwin her godmother.

I am now, for the first time for many years, enjoying the pleasures and scenes of a youthful spring in Kentucky. It is a charming country, and Ashland and the Woodlands have a thousand interests for me. I do not at all envy you your heated political atmosphere at Washington. I much prefer the serene happiness which the perusal of the elegant Thompson infuses,[1] while surrounded with the beauties which the season of bloom opens to the view.

When may we expect you? My mother, I suppose, will not precede you. I hope to show her when she comes, that Ashland has not fallen into bad hands. A little severity, which I used in the first place, and a continued exertion of energy, have introduced a system and regularity into the concerns of the place, which were much wanting when I came.

498

Copy. Printed in Colton, *Clay Correspondence*, 4:336-37.   1. Possibly a book by Benjamin Thompson. See *DAB*.

From John H. James, n.p. [Washington?], *ca.* April 24, 1832. Writes requesting a loan of $150, because "the long duration of my confinement here," and "the enormity of my expenses," as well as the rapidity with which "my nurse has become exhausted" have depleted his resources. Has discovered that a "letter on the Subject" to his father and brother did not reach Cincinnati until after they had departed for New Orleans. Turns to Clay, because "in your first visit to me, you bade me let you know if I needed any aid of the kind I now apply to you." ALS. DLC-TJC (DNA, M212, R10). Endorsed by Clay: "Advanced 24 Apl. 1832 by check on the Off. Bank U.S. at Washington the sum of $150 as requested." James was probably John H. James of Urbana, Ohio, who became a lawyer, banker, railroad builder, politician, editor, and writer. See Weisenburger, *The Passing of the Frontier*, 190, 279, 331, 345; William E. and Orphia D. Smith, *A Buckeye Titan*. Cincinnati, 1953; *OHQ,* 65:391-94; 68:34.

To FRANCIS T. BROOKE   Washington, April 26, 1832

I have received your affectionate letter of the 23d. inst; and the interest which it manifests in my health and prosperity has affected me sensibly. Among the many circumstances to disgust me with life and my fellow men, the warmth, fidelity and duration of your friendship have ever been a source of cheering satisfaction. You have described, I believe correctly, the true causes of my indisposition; and your advice is full of wisdom. Naturally ardent, perhaps too ardent, I can not avoid being too much excited and provoked by the scenes of tergiversation, hypocricy, degeneracy and corruption which are daily exhibited. I would fly from them, and renounce for ever public life, if I were not restrained by a sentiment of duty and of attachment to my friends. I shall endeavor to profit by your kindness, and to avoid as much as possible in future all causes of irritation. I have quit the use of tobacco, in one of the two forms to which I had been accustomed, and will gradually discontinue the other. I will also endeavor to moderate the interest excited by public affairs.

Since my return, I have felt (with the exception of one day) better. I wish I could have remained longer with you. Should I not feel my strength and health returning, I will make another excursion to Maryland or Philada.

Nothing material has transpired here. Our friends are acquiring daily more confidence, and the Jackson party are greatly alarmed. It was remarked to me this morning that they have become panic struck.

A report is anticipated from a bare majority of the B[ank]. Comee. recommending further investigation to be prosecuted in the recess.[1] There will probably be a counter report.

Two reports may be expected from the Secy of the Treasury [Louis McLane] and the Comee. of Manufactures next week on the Tariff, presenting different plans of modification.[2]

ALS. KyU. Printed in Colton, *Clay Correspondence*, 4:337-38.   1. For the committee's majority report, see Clay to Brooke, April 17, 1832. There apparently was no counter report.   2. For McLane's report, see Clay to Porter, May 1, 1832. The Committee on Manuactures recommended reduction of duties on non-competitive goods and the retention of duties on other items. See *Reports of Committees*, 22 Cong., 1 Sess., no. 481.

To PETER B. PORTER   Washington, April 26, 1832

It has been a long time since I heard directly from you. I have been kept advised, principally through our friend M.L.D. [Matthew L. Davis] of what is passing at Albany and in N. York. According to this information there seems to be a probability of co-operation between the A. Masons and the N. Republicans in your State, although it is attended with difficulties.[1] That co-operation is a point of great consequence, but probably, at last, is not likely to be secured by displaying too much eagerness to effect it. At a distance, it seems to me that our friends ought not to relax in their efforts at organization; that they should proceed to a Convention to be holden at some suitable time; and that on whatever they determine they will find it expedient to resolve to act in concert. For the want of such concert they failed to accomplish any thing at your last Governors' election.[2] It is only by union that they can make themselves felt and respected by each and all parties.

Genl. [Erastus] Root was here this evening and goes to N. York to-morrow or the next day, on a political errand. He says that there is a strong disposition to bring him out as a Candidate against [William L.] Marcy or who ever else may be the Regency Candidate; and that he does not mean to oppose or thwart that disposition. He hinted that possibly there might be a Jackson electoral ticket to run with [William] Wilkins, and with himself, in opposition to the Jackson Van Buren ticket; and that, in that contingency, our ticket might possibly prevail.[3] You know better than I what value these suggestions have. I am told that Marcy desires the nomination.

The tendency of things here is favorable to our cause. The sentiment of the total instability of the present state of public affairs is becoming stronger and stronger. Great dissatisfaction prevails with the Pennsylvanians both here and at home. The attack of the ex Govr. of Tennessee [Sam Houston] upon Stansberry [sic, William Stanbery]; the imprudent expressions of the President in regard to it;[4] the increasing discontent of the Calhoun party and their hopelessness of *their* success; the state of the Bank question, the Tariff &c &c are all working well for us. If the conviction could be impressed on the public mind that we shall obtain the support of N. York, there would be hardly a struggle.

I sent you my Land report[5] which, besides proposing an equitable arrangement of that interesting question, puts in the hands of my friends a powerful instrument.

The adjournment of Congress is altogether uncertain — No one yet thinks of the time of it.

ALS. NBuHi. Letter marked "(Confidential)."   1. Clay to Weed, April 14, 1832.   2. Clay to Johnston, May 9, 1830; Stoddard to Clay, Nov. 8, 1830.   3. Clay to Bailhache, Nov. 24, 1830.   4. Clay to Weed, April 14, 1832. Jackson was reported to have said to a friend that "after a few more examples of the same kind, members of Congress would learn to keep civil tongues in their heads." James Parton, *The Presidency of Andrew Jackson*. Ed. by Robert V. Remini (New York, 1967), 223.   5. Comment in Senate, April 16, 1832.

From Ambrose Spencer, New Albany, N.Y., April 28, 1832. Thanks Clay for sending a copy of his report on the public lands [Comment in Senate, April 16, 1832]. Discusses at length the reasons for his earlier support of and subsequent break with DeWitt Clinton.

Continues: "You must have been informed of the state of parties among us. I am entirely satisfied that our only hope of ditatching the vote of this State from Genl Jackson, is by the support by your friends of the Anti-Masonic ticket of Electors [Clay to Weed, April 14, 1832; Clay to Porter, May 1, 1832].   the Jackson party, should there be three tickets would succeed & give to Genl Jackson the electoral vote. The leading & intelligent men of the Anti-Masonic party, notwithstanding the offence your letter to the Anti-Masonic committee of Indiana [Clay to Citizens of Vincennes, October 18, 1831], gave them, are perfectly sensible that our institutions are in imminent peril, should Genl. Jackson be re-elected, & they believe that under your safeguard, the honor, the constitution & the integrity of the Union would be preserved. Yet they say they can not affirmatively support you an adhering Mason, without ruin to their cause & personal disgrace to themselves in regard to the principles they maintain—In my opinion we ought not to ask them to do any act which would alienate any considerable portion of their party which is made of all political parties—We want all their strength negatively—that is to say we want in the first place to elect electors who are opposed to Genl. Jackson on any account & having so far succeeded, if it shall be found absolutely necessary to prevent his election, we hope & expect that some means will be devised, enabling Mr. [William] Wirt with honor to retire from the contest, & in that way give the votes of the State to you. If however it shall appear that the House of Representatives would choose you in case of a non-election by the electoral colleges, this course may not be adopted. . . . In this State not withstanding the fact that our only hope of defeating the choice of Jackson electors depends on the support by the National republicans of the Anti-Masonic ticket, there are many professing to be your friends who in consequence of their Masonic attachments will not support an Anti-Masonic Ticket. Yet I say we must do without them."

Concludes with the observation that if Jackson is reelected the country is "doomed to national degradation, & to the ruin of all our most valuable institutions." ALS. DLC-HC (DNA, M212, R4).

From Felix Huston, Natchez, April 30, 1832. Writes to make some suggestions for arguments to use in favor of the tariff. States that "It cannot be urged too confidently that the Tariff is advantageous to the cotton growing states—" Points out that there is "good land enough in this state to produce 500,000 bales of cotton, which is one half the amt exported from the United States." Adds that "if the capital of the North was not diverted to some other channel, it would with certainty flow into the South, and the cotton growing business would be overdone." Argues also that "having two markets"—one at home and one abroad—is the second advantage of the tariff. Illustrates from his own experience how disastrous it would be for cotton producers to depend entirely upon exporting their cotton to the British market. Estimates that money he lost in the fall of 1830, because of civil disorders in London and a related drop in cotton prices in Britain, amounted to "more than the whole amt of increased prices I would have to pay on protected articles, for plantation use in 20 years—" Remarks that he "got mad at the idea that a petty little mob in London had the power to affect my interest so seriously." Maintains, moreover, that he would never have lost this money "if our own manufacturers consumed any thing like one half the amt of cotton we raise—" Contends, therefore, that his own study of the situation shows that "we can manufacture in the south," using slave labor. Reports that he himself has invested $12,000 in a company now considering such an endeavor.

Concludes that Clay is politically strong in "this county" and in "most of the river country—but the Pine Wood are too strong for us." ALS. DLC-HC (DNA, M212, R4). Jackson defeated Clay in the popular vote in Mississippi by 2,000 votes to 800. Gammon, *The Presidential Campaign of 1832*, 170.

To HENRY CLAY, JR. Washington, May 1, 1832

I recd. your two favors of the 15h. and 22d Ulto. and am highly gratified to find that you continue to take so lively an interest in all that concerns Ashland. I hope your attention to it will be unremitting until we return, and I doubt not that we shall find it improved under your management. The large dining room requires some reparation, that is the papering. I believe you would do well to have all the paper taken down, the cracks stopped, and the Wall again painted as it was formerly, or any other color that you and Anne [Brown Clay

Erwin] may think more agreeable. If you determine to do this, be particular as to the Painter you engage, and make your contract before hand—a precaution which is always best for both parties.

We are greatly grieved with the condition of your poor brother [Theodore W. Clay].[1] I fear, from what I hear, that he is incurable. I observe what you say about my letters to him, and I must cease to write to him. But I hope, my dear Son, that you will visit him as often as you can consistently with his tranquillity and your own feelings. Perhaps it would not be injurious to him occasionally to visit Ashland, but on that subject I know nothing that we can do better than to conform to the advice of his physicians.

You have said nothing to me in regard to money for your current expences. I hope you will never feel any diffidence or difficulty in communicating to me your wants and wishes.

I am very anxious about all my Stock, but especially in respect to my Asses. The young Jack was very promising when I left home, and I wish him to be kept in good plight, as well as the Jennies. When the Wickliffe mare has a colt I should like to hear what sort of a one it is.

Mr. [William] Martin's letter by Richard Pindell (who is here) has been delivered to me. I had just before written to him fully. I am glad to hear that he is attentive and industrious. You speak of Dave giving him trouble. I thought he had hired Dave out.

Tell Anne that Mr. [James] Erwin informs me that he will not leave N. Orleans until this day. I am sorry that they are long apart; but I hope he will safely arrive at the Woodlands about the time this letter reaches you. How fortunate you were to have escaped the dreadful disaster in the Brandywine![2]

It is very uncertain when Congress will adjourn. I should not be surprized if we were detained late in the next month. It is equally uncertain what will be done on any of the great questions before us.

Both your mother and myself have been unwell, but we are getting better.

ALS. Henry Clay Memorial Foundation, Lexington, Ky.   1. Theodore W. Clay to Clay, Jan. 8, 1832.   2. On April 9, 1832, the steamboat *Brandywine* caught fire off Memphis on her passage up the Mississippi River. About 75 of its nearly 200 passengers either died from the fire or drowned. *Niles' Register* (April 28, 1832), 42:153.

Comment in Senate, May 1, 1832. Calls attention to the "anomalous character" of the referral procedure by which the bill on the sale of public lands and the distribution of the revenue therefrom [Comment in Senate, April 16, 1832] is being handled. Argues that the chairman of the committee [Committee on Manufactures] reporting the bill should be given the usual opportunity to explain the measure before the Senate votes, without debate, on a motion to reassign the measure to still another committee [Committee on Public Lands] for further consideration. That this is not being done is a "course without precedent." Reviews why the bill was referred to the Committee on Manufactures in the first place and notes the "singular history" of this attempt to switch committees without there being "the presentment of a single objection to the details of the measure." *Register of Debates*, 22 Cong., 1 Sess., 870.

From Thomas G. McCulloh, Chambersburg, Pa., May 1, 1832. Warns Clay of "a design afloat" concerning the tariff. States that William Wilkins, suggested by some as a vice presidential running mate for Jackson, found himself "embarrassed by the uncompromising terms of our Resolution on the subject of the Tariff" which was passed by the Pennsylvania legislature. Consequently, Henry Baldwin "suggested certain modifications . . . which he alledged would satisfy Genl. Jackson." Chief among these was a "general reduction of duties to 25 pr ct. ad val." Adds that "after a careful examination" of the suggestions "we considered the whole plan . . . entirely falacious" and did not present them to the legislature. Explains that "we would not consent to yeild one inch, nor to hold out even the appearance of yeilding at all, on this subject. I am satisfied that this too is the feeling of 4/5ths. of the people of Pennsylvania. Abolish the tariff, break down our manufactures & the Union will be of little importance to us. We cannot, for the sake of gratifying the absurd pretensions of South Carolina, agree to sacrifice our own vital interests — and as the fiery politicians of that state insist on an absolute surrender of the very principle of protection, the universal sentiment in this country is, that no compromise ought to be made & that we may as *well try the question of the power of the Government now as at any other time*." Continues with the observation that "it is indeed the opinion of all classes & all parties" in Pennsylvania that the tariff on "those articles not coming in competition with our productions" should be reduced. In this, "we all agree with you in the proposed reduction."

Warns Clay that Mr. Baldwin's "recent conduct" has impaired "his political integrity." Concludes that Baldwin's "whole course for some time past seem to evince that he is deep in the plots & intrigues of the administration."

Adds in a postscript that Secretary of the Treasury Louis McLane's report [Clay to Southard, December 12, 1831] is worse than Mr. Baldwin's plan. Considers it "the first step towards the entire demolition of the protective system & consequently of manufactures." ALS. DLC-HC (DNA, M212, R4). The Pennsylvania legislature had unanimously adopted seven resolutions "protesting against any abandonment of the protective system and favoring the recharter of the national bank." Malcolm R. Eiselen, *The Rise of Pennsylvania Protectionsim* (Philadelphia, 1932), 108.

To PETER B. PORTER   Washington, May 1, 1832

I have recd. your favor of the 22d. Ulto.   Prior to its receipt I had addressed a letter to you which I hope will safely reach you. I am glad to learn that your health is improved, & sincerely hope that it may be perfectly re-established. On the subject of my visit to your State, I can not determine positively until my return to K. which depends upon the adjournment of Congress, and that is very uncertain. Should you make your contemplated visit to K. *possibly* we may meet there, in which event we can decide on the excursion I have so long talked of to N.Y.

Mr [Matthew L.] Davis has kept me well advised from Albany. But from the tenor of a letter which I yesterday heard read from Mr. [William] Maynard, I greatly fear that the co-operation between the Anti Masons and N. Republicans in N. York is far from certain.[1] If I understood him rightly, he thinks that the Candidates both for your State officers and Electors should be exclusively Anti-Masonic. Such a course would be fatal. The example would probably be followed in N. Jersey, Vermont and Ohio, and its effects there I need not state. The value of a co-operation in N.Y. which should not be confined exclusively to the interests of Anti Masonry would not be limited to that State, but would be felt in other States where Antimasonry exists. Whereas an *exclusive* ticket in N.Y. would work directly the other way.

Without meaning to advise our friends in N.Y., so much more competent than I am to decide what is best, it seems to me that a Convention of the N.R. party is highly desirable.[2] Whether there is or is not co-operation between the two parties, its expediency seems to me equally clear. If there is co-operation, *that* should be decided on in Convention, and it would every where influence our friends. If the N.R. party act separately, the Convention is indispensable.

The Secy of the Treasury [Louis McLane] has made a Report on the Tariff,[3] of which our friends must make good use, I should think, in your

State. It is utterly destructive of the interest of Woolens and Wool, and aims a severe blow at Salt. What will be here done on this subject is altogether uncertain. And it is very doubtful whether any thing will be done in regard to the Bank.[4] I have never seen a time when it was so difficult to anticipate results. Mean time, the Jackson party has become greatly alarmed, and our friends are more encouraged than they have ever been. If you could in N. York assure us of victory there, we should see the Jackson party speedily routed. The mere apprehension of an effective co-operation between the Antis and Nationals has contributed to produce the present dismay. P.S. [William B.] Rochester is here and will shortly see you.

ALS. NBuHi.   1. Clay to Weed, April 14, 1832.   2. The Anti-Masons held their convention at Utica on June 21, 1832, and the National Republicans held theirs at the same place on July 26. For their actions, see Clay to Bailhache, Nov. 24, 1830; and Vaughn, *The Antimasonic Party in the United States*, 42-45.   3. For details of McLane's "Tariff Report," submitted to the House Committee on Manufactures and supported by Rep. John Q. Adams, see Munroe, *Louis McLane*, 340-43.   4. Clay to Brown, Dec. 18, 1831; Webster to Clay, Jan. 8, 1832.

To Edmund H. Taylor, Frankfort, Ky., May 1, 1832. Reports that "Our friends entertain much stronger hopes than they have done heretofore as to our political prospects." ALS. KyHi.

From HENRY CLAY, JR.   Lexington, May 2, 1832

In my last [April 24] I informed you of the new accession to our family. Anne [Brown Clay Erwin] and her little daughter [Mary Erwin] are both in fine health, and gaining strength. —

You wished me in your last to get you estimates of painting and stuccoing the house at Ashland. Mr. [William] Shackelford informs me that he will do the stuccoing for 50 cents a square yard, which is the price that will be paid at the Bank. He of course will furnish the materials; perhaps, however, as we are out of town, we shall have to pay something for scaffolding: In town he furnishes that also. By a few estimates which I have made, there are not 650 square yards of surface, exclusive of windows and doors, in the wings and principal building of this house. I think then we may place the maximum cost at 350 dollars. Stuccoing ought to last for a great many years. A less expensive improvement would be to paint the house some light colour; but it would not be so durable. The painting I suppose might be done for $100.00. If you should determine to have it painted, how would you like a pearl colour, which would be nearly that of free-stone, but a little lighter? or a white tinged with the hue of straw? A still less expensive and less durable mode would be to wash the house some light colour, like the sides of Aunt Nelly's [Grosch Hart] house. I must confess that I think stuccoing, if it be well done, nearly as cheap in the aggregate, as any other mode, and much more satisfactory.

Mr [Thomas] Grant has money due you to the amount of upwards of a hundred dollars, which he is ready to pay, and upon which he, therefore, does not wish to be charged interest. There is also due from you to Mr Shackelford a debt of 100 or 150 dols, which he has desired me to mention to you. Probably one note would cancel the other.

The farm I believe is going on well. in ten days all the corn will be planted, and the hemp sown. Mr [William] Martin does not know how you desire the wool to be treated: whether washed on the back or not. The Wickliffe mare has a fine colt.

Please to send me if it be convenient, one of your reports on the public lands.[1] And Remember me to Mama and Henry [Clay Duralde] . . .

ALS. Henry Clay Memorial Foundation, Lexington, Ky.   1. Comment in Senate, April 16, 1832.

To PETER B. PORTER   Washington, May 3, 1832

I wrote you a few days ago, and intend now merely to communicate some additional reflections.

Without the N. Republicans organize, meet in Convention,[1] and act in concert, I am apprehensive that nothing will be done, in your State [New York]. Unless they pursue that course, their force will be wasted, and they will be absorbed at the polls by the other two contending parties. They will proceed, helter skelter, and will incur the displeasure if not contempt of both those parties. Let me make two suppositions.

1st. That there shall be a cordial and hearty co-operation proposed between them and the Anti Masons, by the presentation of a ticket nominated by the latter, half and half.[2] Then the Convention will be necessary to secure that co-operation. Without it the N.Rs. will be split up and divided.

2. That the Anti Masons should nominate an *exclusive* ticket, contrary to the hopes of some of our friends, but conformable to my apprehensions, founded upon recent information. On such a supposition, a ticket of N. Republicans will be indispensable. If such a ticket is formed, *and no Candidates for Governor &c.* be offered by you (which I think should be a part of the operation) what would be your attitude? The other two parties would each have its Candidates for Governor &c and for electors, and the N Rs. for Electors only. This party, in that situation, would be courted by both of the others for its suffrage in support of their Candidates for Governor. And as, I presume, both of them attach more importance to the possession of the Governor of the State, than to the choice of Electors, each would give support to your Electoral ticket, with the view of acquiring support, in turn, to its Candidate for Governor. In that way, I am persuaded, your ticket might prevail. As the Anti Masons must utterly despair of electing an Anti Masonic President, you would get most support from them. And whatever loss you might sustain among their fanatics would be more than counterbalanced by the gain from the Regency party. I am not sure that this plan of the campaign is not better than any arrangement with the Anti Masons. Such an arrangement will expose both parties to a certain degree of obloquy. Where as the course indicated would be manly, independent, and without any compromise of principles.[3]

In Pennsa. I understand that our friends are exactly at this time in the predicament suggested, in regard to N. York. They are admitted to hold the balance between the Jackson and the Anti Masonic party, and they are woo'd by both, and anticipate much from their position.

The Treasury Tariff[4] is giving deep dissatisfaction, especially in your State and in Pennsa. Some of your members have declared that they are off from the Jackson party, and great discontent prevails among all of them. The Secys [Louis McLane] plan sacrifices the American System, in some of its most important branches. It is a Southern judicious tariff.

When we shall adjourn is extremely uncertain.

ALS. NBuHi. Letter marked "(Confidential)."   1. Clay to Porter, May 1, 1832.   2. Clay to Weed, April 14, 1832.   3. Clay to Bailhache, Nov. 24, 1830; Clay to Porter, May 1, 1832. 4. Clay to Porter, May 1, 1832.

Comment in Senate, May 4, 1832. Urges his colleagues to speed up consideration of various important measures before the Senate and thus "quiet the disturbed feeling of the country." Lists the tariff bill and the public lands bill among these lagging concerns. Asks that those who oppose his own approach to the latter [Comment in Senate, April 16, 1832] at least bring forth an alternative which might be printed in the number "of 10,000, 20,000, any number," and circulated throughout the nation for discussion. *Register of Debates*, 22 Cong., 1 Sess., 883-84.

From Francis T. Brooke, Richmond, Va., May 5, 1832. Supposes that Clay will be unable to attend the races in Richmond. Informs him that "a Calhoun convention is getting up at Charlottesville" which is "what we wish and wait for, before bringing forth our ticket."

Reports that Richard K. Cralle, the editor of the Richmond *Jeffersonian*, "thinks there is no doubt of the union of the parties in N Y and that they will prevail." Continues: "he [Cralle] and the govr [John Floyd] look for a revolution in the Summer they are sure that S. Carolina will resist, and that as the President by his letter has said he will support the case and we shall have war." Adds that he thinks it is impossible. ALS. DLC-HC (DNA, M212, R4). Brooke apparently refers to a letter Jackson had written to the Unionists in South Carolina which had been read at the July 4, 1831, celebration. Although his language was oblique, the president clearly identified nullification with secession and indicated that he "would countenance no plan of disunion." Freehling, *Prelude to Civil War*, 224.

From John Marshall, Richmond, Va., May 7, 1832. Reports "the pleasure of receiving your report on the public lands [Comment in Senate, April 16, 1832]," which is a subject of "immense interest, and has long produced and is still producing great excitement." States that "My sentiments concur entirely with those contained in the report," and believes that it will "be approved by a great majority of Congress." Warns, however, that "Unanmity is not to be expected in any thing." ALS. DLC-HC (DNA, M212, R4). Printed in Colton, *Clay Correspondence*, 4:339.

From Thomas Metcalfe, Frankfort, Ky., May 7, 1832. Reports receiving a letter from Robert P. Letcher "in which he gave an opinion respecting the prospects ahead, more encouraging, than anything I had met with for some time." Letcher expresses "great confidence" that New York will go against Jackson, and believes if the Bank of the United States is defeated [Clay to Brown, December 18, 1831] and the Democratic national convention [Brooke to Clay, February 9, 1832] does not choose William Wilkins to run for vice president [Clay to Porter, March 10, 1832], Pennsylvania, too, will go against Jackson [Sergeant to Clay, June 23, 1831]. Adds that he conferred yesterday with [James G.] Dana who concurs with Letcher in believing that "Jackson can not be elected. . . . But he thinks [William] *Wirt* is to be the man." Notes that Dana takes "many anti-Masonic papers," is "perhaps the warmest & most zealous devotte to anti-masonry in Ky," and "his prejudices, his jealousies & hatred of Masonry, exceeds anything of the kind that I have met with." States also that Dana "shewed me [Charles] Hammonds paper recommending the *coalition* which is so much dreaded by the Jackson Papers (Viz) a united effort of the Calhoun & Clay parties, with the antimasons — which in the end is to result to the benefit of the latter."

Thanks Clay "for your excellent Report on the subject of the public lands [Comment in Senate, April 16, 1832]." Mentions that the "candidates for Gov & Lt Gov are in the field [Smith to Clay, December 27, 1831] — actively engaged   The Jackson men, speak in a tone less confident than at first of Breathetts [*sic*, John Breathitt] success." ALS. DLC-HC (DNA, M212, R4). On May 1, 1832, Hammond published in the Cincinnati *Daily Gazette* a lengthy editorial calling for a coalition of both Clay and Calhoun supporters with the Anti-Masons. Only in that way, he argued, could Jackson be defeated. He noted, further, that he had from the first opposed the National Republican convention in Baltimore which had apparently closed the door to a coalition. He believed, however, that Clay supporters could yet open negotiations for such a coalition and should consider uniting on the Anti-Masonic candidate, William Wirt. See also Cincinnati *Daily Gazette*, April 9, 1832.

Remark in Senate, May 8, 1832. Urges "prompt action" in the Senate on the three subjects on which Congress must certainly act before adjournment — the tariff, recharter of the Bank of the United States, and the public lands question. Notes that Congress has been in session "nearly six months" and "nothing" has been done. Suggests daily sessions of five or six hours, and "even" Saturday meetings if necessary. *Register of Debates*, 22 Cong., 1 Sess., 901.

To William S. Dallam, May 9, 1832. Writes that he "must defer until my return home deciding" whether or not to purchase "the Bledsoe farm." Thinks that "property appears to be rising," and believes Dallam can "do better with it than what you offer it to me for." ALS. NcD. The Bledsoe farm probably refers to a farm near Athens, Fayette County, Ky., which was purchased on June 16, 1824, by Simeon Bledsoe & Co. *RKHS*, 41: 307.

Speech in Senate, May 9, 1832. Following up on his May 1 comment on the referral procedures employed in considering the public lands bill, again condemns those procedures as being without precedent. Defends specific facts found in the report of the Committee on Manufactures, principally the amount of annual revenue to be derived from the sale of public lands under the proposed legislation. Argues that there are insufficient reasons to send the bill to the Committee on Public Lands for further analysis, unless its opponents simply want further to delay discussion of the issue. Demands that either the committee's bill, or "a different scheme if such should be offered," should be considered forthwith — "say next week." *Register of Debates*, 22 Cong., 1 Sess., 904-6.

To Robert Baird *et al.*, Washington, May 10, 1832. Thanks the journeymen of Mr. William Rankin's Hat Manufactory for the fur hat they presented him. Expresses gratification for this as a symbol of American manufacturing growth and independence. Expounds on the virtues of the American System. Copy. Printed in Lexington *Observer & Kentucky Reporter*, June 28, 1832.

From John M. Steuart *et al.*, Washington, May 10, 1832. Write as a committee appointed "by the National Republican Young Men now assembled in the city of Washington" to announce to Clay the resolutions passed by the convention giving their "unanimous concurrence" in his nomination for president and asking him when it will suit him to wait upon the convention. Copy. DLC-Duncan McArthur Papers (DNA, M212, R22). Also in *Proceedings of the National Republican Convention of Young Men, Which Assembled in the City of Washington May 7, 1832*. Washington, 1832.
    Clay replied the same day, stating that he would wait upon the convention tomorrow morning at 10 o'clock. *Ibid.*
    On the following day, May 11, 1832, the president of the National Republican Young Men [William Cost Johnson of Md.] extended to Clay "the respects, the gratitude, and the admiration of those that surround you," and predicted that "the CONSTITUTION and HENRY CLAY will be triumphant."
    Clay replied, thanking the convention for "the distinguished proofs . . . of your esteem and confidence." He then stated that next to liberty "what we want is a practical, efficient, and powerful Union — one that shall impartially enforce the laws towards all, whether individuals or communities, who are justly subject to their authority — a Union

which, if it shall ever be deemed necessary to chide one member of the Confederacy, for rash and intemperate expressions, threatening its disturbance, will snatch violated laws and treaties from beneath the feet of another member, and deliver free citizens of the United States from unjust and ignominious imprisonment. Gentlemen, it belongs to you, and the young men of your age, to decide whether these great blessings of Liberty and Union shall be defended and preserved. The responsibility which attaches to you is immense. . . . The eyes of all civilized nations are intensely gazing upon us; and it may be truly asserted that the fate of Liberty throughout the World, mainly depends upon the maintenance of American Liberty." *Ibid*. For William Cost Johnson, see *BDAC*.

From James Brown, Philadelphia, May 11, 1832. States: "I have long known Mr [Josiah S.] Johnston as one of your warmest friends and admirers   Have you not in the multiplicity of your occupations neglected to pay him & his lady your wonted attentions? A friend gave me a hint to that effect and begged me to suggest it to you. I am sure you esteem these excellent friends of us both and could not have intended to neglect them. Mr Johnston never mentioned the subject to me."

Reports that "Your report on the public lands [Comment in Senate, April 16, 1832] *seems* to find favor here and is generally acceptable." Hopes Congress will pass the bill rechartering the B.U.S. [Clay to Brown, December 18, 1831] and will "modify the Tariff [Webster to Clay, January 8, 1832] before you adjourn." Notes that the latter will be difficult, because South Carolina "will not be satisfied with any thing which the North can accept." Thinks North Carolina and Virginia will be "more reasonable" on the issue and "if satisfied would keep the South in check." ALS. DLC-HC (DNA, M212, R4). Printed in *LHQ*, 24:1165.

To HENRY CLAY, JR. Washington, May 11, 1832
I recd. your favor of the 2d. inst.   If you can engage Mr. [William] Shackleford to stucco the House at Ashland at a price not exceeding your estimate of $350 (including materials) I am willing and authorize you to have it done, if you please. Or if you prefer it, I consent that it may be painted either a pearl color or a white tinged with a straw hue, as you may think best. There is one consideration in favor of not going to any great expence at present, and that arises out of the pending contest. Should that be decided in my favor (of which there exists a better prospect now than at any preceding period) I may not want the house for some time and it will be unoccupied, unless there should be a change in your condition that might lead you to wish to occupy it.

Will you be good enough to tell Mr. [Thomas] Grant that any money he may deposit with the Bank of the U.S. at Lexington to my credit shall be deemed a payment of so much on account of his note to me. I forget what it is I owe Mr. Shackleford, and will thank you to ask him if he holds my note and for what amount. Any thing that I owe him I could send from this place. I have written to Mr. [William] Martin about my wool. I transmitted to you a Copy of my Land report.

My health is not very good and I am most anxious to be with you. But when I shall have that satisfaction is very uncertain.

ALS. Henry Clay Memorial Foundation, Lexington, Ky.

From HENRY CLAY, JR. Lexington, May 11, 1832
Your letter of the 1st of May has just been received. You mention some repairs of your house, which shall be attended to, to the best of my ability. The expense of stuccoing is greater than I supposed. You will remember that the estimate I

sent you excluded windows and doors. But I find that the whole surface is calculated, and the house is covered at the rate of 50 cents a square yard. The No of yards is about 1120. So that the expense instead of being $350. will be $560 or upwards. This expenditure would be so great that I do not know that painting would not be preferable. The more especially as the house wants window-shutters, steps, and many repairs in the interior; to prevent its having the appearance, were it well stuccoed on the exterior, of being a patch-work of ostentation. Besides, painting would be more easily done, and sooner completed: And again the oil would perhaps be a better safe guard against dampness than stucco.

Anne [Brown Clay Erwin] is in good health as well as her children. Mr [James] Erwin has not yet arrived, but he is expected next week.

Theodore [W. Clay] spent today with Anne and at Ashland. He is in good health.

You ask about your stock. It is in good order as far as I am able to judge. You[r] asses are well attended to. And your yearling Jack very large. The Wickliffe mare has a horse colt; but I have, not yet seen it. She had it on her way to Mount Sterling at Col Taylor's.[1]

You ask about my expenses. During my residence in L'a, I drew upon Mr Erwin for $500.00: Out of which sum I have remaining of my last draft about a hundred and fifty dollars, which will last me for some time in Kentucky where I have but few expenses.

Without being dissipated, I am more expensive in my habits than I ought to be. However, I hope before long to relieve you of the burden of my support. If nothing prevents, I hope to commence the practice of law in a small way next winter. If I fail, I should like to make the failure as soon as possible; so that I may turn my attention to something else. I do not expect to make much in the beginning. A mere support is all that I want. But if I perceive that I cannot make a competency in New Orleans in the period of 10 or 12 years, I believe that I did not find the city attractive enough to induce me to spend my life there.

But enough of myself—James [Brown Clay] and John [Morrison Clay] seem to be doing well where they are. James, though, has an idea that he is to be a farmer or a business man of some kind; and seems to forget that learning and education adorn and increase the pleasure of any station.

Perhaps this renders him less diligent than he would otherwise be.

There is here a great dearth of news. P.S. I suppose if you determine to have the house painted, you would like the out-houses done in the same manner. The window shutters too deform the house very much. Please to send me particular directions as to your wishes in every respect.

ALS. Henry Clay Memorial Foundation, Lexington, Ky.   1. Possibly Colby H. Taylor of Clark County, Ky.

Remark in Senate, May 11, 1832. Supports the pension claims of those "brave veterans" of the Revolutionary War, and denies that his advocacy of their cause has anything to do with the politics of the proposed tariff legislation. *Register of Debates*, 22 Cong., 1 Sess., 930. The pension bill passed the Senate on May 19, 1832, and the House on May 31. U.S. Sen., *Journal*, 22 Cong., 1 Sess., 288; U.S. H. of Reps., *Journal*, 22 Cong., 1 Sess., 820-22.

From Joseph Rogers Underwood, Frankfort, May 11, 1832. Remarks that "We have been much encouraged lately by flattering accounts of your political prospects received from various quarters." Adds that he looks "upon your cause as the cause of the country," and believes "all would be lost by Genl. Jackson's reelection." ALS. DLC-HC (DNA, M212, R4).

From Hiram Ketchum, New York, May 12, 1832. Assures Clay that the corresponding committee of New York City is "endeavouring to effect a thorough organization of our friends in every *County* of the State." Suggests that "it becomes more and more apparent, every day, that a union between the national republicans and anti-masons will defeat the Regency, but whether that union can be effected upon honorable terms to our party is yet doubtful, and will, I fear, continue so, until the Anti-Masonic Convention [Clay to Porter, May 1, 1832] has closed its labors in June. Our friends are laboring to effect a nomination at the Utica Convention, of an unpledged ticket, one half of which shall be composed of names satisfactory to the National Republicans, and the other half reasonable *Antis*, who may be expected to go right if by so doing they can prevent the re-election of Jackson. We can not hope for any thing better than this, and if this ticket be nominated it will require all the influence which we, aided by yourself, can wield to bring our friends to give a hearty support to the nomination, so great is the aversion of many of our friends to Anti-Masonry." Advises Clay to visit New York "should such a ticket be nominated."

Suggests that "our friends in Pennsylvania ought by no means to take a course hostile to Anti Masonry; if they do not mean to adopt the [William] Wirt ticket at the Convention [Clay to Ketchum, May 15, 1832] in this Month, they ought to adjourn to a day subsequent to the uniting of the Anti-Masonic Convention in this State, *this is exceedingly important*, otherwise all our efforts will be frustrated. You are doubtless aware that the Antis are divided, and that many of them are favourable to your election, and are now earnestly endeavouring to bring their party to give you in effect, the whole vote of this State, we ought to throw no obstacle in the way of our Allies."

Encloses a circular the corresponding committee of New York City is distributing and notes that they have persuaded Ambrose L. Jordan "to travel through the Counties in aid of our objects."

Reminds Clay of the political importance of Stephen Van Rensselaer and Abraham Van Vechten. Suggests that "if the Anti Masonic Electoral ticket shall be of the character we wish it to be these gentlemen . . . are the men whose public approval of it, will give it most currency among your masonic friends." States that Webster has promised to try to influence Van Vechten, and urges Clay to use his own influence with Van Rensselaer. ALS. DLC-HC (DNA, M212, R4). Jordan was a former N.Y. state senator from Columbia County.

From Peter B. Porter, Black Rock, N.Y., May 12, 1832. Reports that on the basis of many written communications and conversations he now feels confident that political cooperation between the National Republicans and Anti-Masons in New York can be effected. Mentions, however, that John C. Spencer, in a *"very singular* letter" recently received, does not share his optimism in the matter. Indeed, Spencer tells him flatly that the Anti-Masonic party can never be brought "to join their support to any [presidential] Elector who, it might be supposed, would join his vote for Mr Clay —" What this really means, Porter explains to Clay, is "that if we will deign to accept & support all their nominations, without requiring any equivalent, that the result *may* be favorable to our candidate. In short, I now understand their project and its true meaning to be, that we shall adopt passively & without enquiry their whole ticket, and, if successful, they having attained their object in regard in state offices, will then be in a situation to bargain advantageously for their presidential votes, as there will be no hope of turning them to any usefull account in the support of Mr [William] Wirt. To such a project I, individually, can never consent to submit, and I trust that our general committee, unless better advised that I am, will go on to call a N. R. State Convention [Clay to Porter,

510

May 1, 1832] for the purpose of nominating *our own* candidates for state offices as well as presidential electors."

Quotes from his answering letter to Spencer of "this date" that it was his understanding, from earlier conversations with Spencer, that "an amicable arrangement would be, if it had not already been, formed between our [Porter and Spencer] political friends [Clay to Weed, April 14, 1832], based, substantially on the proposition which was discussed between us, last winter at Albany and which was = assuming in the first place that the National Republicans would feel no difficulty in supporting, for the principal state offices, certain persons who were understood to be acceptable to the Anti Masonic party — That a joint electoral ticket should be formed to be comprised of some of our most liberal & enlightened men in different parts of the state, one half of whom should be anti masons, & the other half National Republicans, but not members of the Masonic fraternity — That no declarations or pledges should be required of any of the electers as to the person for whom they would vote, but to leave that question entirely to the discretion of each individual electer."

Tells Clay that he has also informed Spencer in this same letter that if the Anti-Masonic party cannot support any elector whose vote might be given for Clay, then "all idea of co-operation will, on our part . . . be at once & forever terminated. The National Republicans are surely not so abject in spirit, as to consent to aid in giving political ascendency to a party who hold them unworthy . . . of the confidence & employment of their country." Mentions, further, that in his letter to Spencer he has reported that his own talks with the Anti-Masons in New York have indicated "that they would *almost without exception* heartily rejoice" in the type of arrangement he had earlier outlined to Spencer. Finally, he has told Spencer that "if the great cause of our republic — and it is emphatically the cause of the whole human race — is to be sacrificed to the fastidious scruples & extraordinary levels of antimasonry — & extraordinary indeed they are, if such as might be inferred from your [Spencer's] letter — on you, and not on us, must rest the consequences."

Based on this exchange with Spencer, Porter recommends to Clay that the National Republicans in New York proceed to call a convention to nominate their own candidates. Does not believe that such an action will "endanger an eventual coalition with the antimasons, on the contrary I look upon it as the surest means of effecting that object." Notes in this regard, that he has today written "to Mr. [Jonathan] Thompson [4:548] the Chairman of our general Committee, urging anew the expediency of calling a convention without delay." Believes "If we go on resolutely as I trust we shall, in calling the convention & in nominating our own tickets, I do not dispair of some ultimate arrangements with the Anti-Masons." Copy. OHi.

To AMBROSE SPENCER   Washington, May 12, 1832

I recd. and perused with much satisfaction your letter of the 28h. Ulto.   With you, I have regretted that I have never been thrown into the way of making a personal acquaintance with you; but I have long known and respected your character, and, as a member of the profession of law, I have derived great profit from your judicial labors. The times are such as to remove all restraints among the well wishers of our common Country, and fully justify unreserved communications, if indeed there were not other considerations which fully warranted the letter with which you favored me.

It is useless to dwell much on the past. In a review of it, I concur with you in thinking that your illustrious connexion, Mr. [DeWitt] Clinton, committed an unfortunate error in lending his support to the election of Genl Jackson; and, had he been spared to us, I am persuaded he would, if now alive, be sensible of it, as I understand a great many of his friends are. He would have seen that the influence of his name would have been finally appropriated to the advancement of a man, the last, I am sure, in his estimation deserving it, and one who, with less claim, founded upon talents or services, is winding his way to the Chief Magistracy, regardless of all public principles, and of all purity in his means.

But it is better to survey our actual position and to look forward if we can to the future.

The reign of Jackson has been the reign of corruption & demoralization. My fears from his election were great, and they have been more than realized. He has put a pickaxe at the base of every pillar that supports every department and every valuable institution in the Country. And, if any of them can now be saved, it can only be by the most strenuous exertions of all who value their Government cordially uniting and putting their shoulders together to sustain its endangered columns.

The possible co-operation between the N.Rs. and Anti Masons in your State has thrown a stream of light upon the darkness which surrounds us. I have been advised, I presume correctly, of the measures adopted and in progress to bring about that co-operation.[1] I sincerely hope they may succeed, altho' fear and hope of that result alternate. The plan was so obvious, of concert, founded upon the basis of united support to the Candidates of the Anti Masons for State officers; and of the Candidates for Electors of the N.Rs. that I had supposed it would certainly be adopted. I know the difficulties, real or imaginary, which were alleged to exist; but I should have supposed, by patience perseverance and good temper, they might all have been overcome. The election of Mr. [William] Wirt is impossible. That all intelligent men must see. It is urged that, altho he may fail now, success at another election might be achieved. But, if by separate and exclusive action of the Anti Masons, they should lead to the re-election of Jackson, is it not worth considering whether there may ever be *another* election? Or if there should be whether the Government will then be in a state susceptible of restoration to its original purity?

The measure, I am told, in contemplation, is that of a ticket half and half (with such names as your's Chancellor [James] Kent's, Mr. [William] Woods &c &c) put forward under the auspices of the Anti Masons. A measure of that kind would out of N. York, under actual circumstances, I am induced to believe, be hailed with pleasure. It would animate our friends in other States, and might conduce to concert there between the same parties. But if the ticket is to be *exclusively* Anti Masonic, and *pledged* to the support of their Candidates, I should fear very bad consequences. The example of such an exclusive pledged ticket would probably be followed in Pennsa. Ohio, New Jersey & Vermont &c, and the effect you can well imagine. It would also dis spirit our friends every where.

I am sorry that any offence should have been taken at my letter to the Anti Masons of Indiana.[2] It was not so intended. I regretted that I had ever recd. the letter to which it was a reply. Having recd. it what was I to do? It was respectful in its terms. Suppose I had remained silent? Should I not have been accused of concealment, timidity &c? If I spoke out, what less could I have said? Sincerely believing that the Fed. Constitution has conferred no power which can be legitimately exerted in regard to Masonry, or Anti Masonry, I have expressed that opinion. I have asked, if I am mistaken, to be corrected; and I have asked to have the clause which *does* convey any power to be pointed out in the Constitution. If I have said nothing *for*, I have said nothing *against*

512

Anti Masonry. Neither have I said any thing for or against Masonry. I have said that I did not think either ought to be mixt with General politics, leaving Anti Masonry perfectly free to exert itself in the acquisition of power which it may constitutionally exercise.

Every thing here is uncertain. No one can tell the fate of the Bank, the Tariff, or the Public lands. All is wrapt in mystery.[3] The time even of our adjournment cannot be predicted.

The Young men's Convention has gone off in the best state.[4] They have created deep and powerful sensation.

ALS. PHi.   1. Clay to Weed, April 14, 1832.   2. Clay to Citizens of Vincennes, Ind., Oct. 18, 1831.   3. Word "uncertainty" struck through and "mystery" substituted.   4. Steuart to Clay, May 10, 1832.

To WILLIAM GREENE   Washington, May 15, 1832

I should long since have answered your favor of the 7h. April, if I had not been persuaded that I could add nothing material to the communications of the Public press. I agree with you as to the unhappy state of public affairs. Whilst the leading measures of Congress are suspended, or involved in doubt and uncertainty, from the state of public parties, we are living here in the midst of bullies and bludgeons. Immediately on the termination of the case of [Sam] Houston—[1]a termination sufficiently discreditable to the majority—Mr. Cook [sic, Eleutheros Cooke] of your State presented another, involving a breach of the privileges of the House. In less than half an hour after the House *refused* to enquire into it, Mr [Thomas D.] Arnold from Tennessee, on descending the steps leading up to the Western entrance of the Capital, was attacked by a man of the name of [Morgan A.] Heard, with a heavy bludgeon, and subsequently fired at with a pistol. Mr. Arnold defended himself, with great strength, courage and coolness, saved his own life, and got the better of the assailant. What or whether any thing will be done by the House remains to be seen.[2] Congress did not set to day in consequence of the death of Mr. [Jonathan] Hunt of Vermont.

It is perfectly impossible now to say what will be done with the Tariff—the Bank—the Public lands, or whether Congress will not adjourn without acting upon any of these subjects.

Measures are in successful progress in N. York to produce a co-operation between the Anti Masons and the N. Republicans; and confident anticipations are entertained that it will be completed, and that the Jackson party will be defeated in that State. The basis of the co-operation, it is understood here will be, that the Anti Ms. shall put forward an Electoral ticket, composed of half and half, and that both parties will support this ticket and support also the Anti Masonic Candidates for Governor &c. There are some difficulties with the co operating parties about settling upon this arrangement, but those who are best informed believe that they will all be finally obviated.[3]

In Pennsa. too movements are making and in contemplation which authorize strong hopes of that deluded state.[4] No doubt is entertained here that V. Buren will be nominated next week at Balto.[5] The week after the Legislature meets at Harrisburg, and it is believed that the nomination of Mr. V.B. will make a powerful impression, and lead to important consequences. In short, my dear Sir, at no time during the session of Congress, have our prospects looked fairer than they have done for the last 3 or 4 weeks. Judge then what were the surprize and regret produced among our friends here, at such a period, to witness the course of Mr [Charles] Hammond on your City![6]

ALS. OCHP. Letter marked "(Confidential)." Addressed to Greene in Cincinnati.   1. Clay to Weed, April 14, 1832.   2. For the details of Heard's attack on Arnold, see *Niles' Register* (May 19, 1832), 42:211.   3. Clay to Porter, May 1, 1832.   4. Clay to Ketchum, May 15, 1832. 5. Brooke to Clay, Feb. 9, 1832; Clay to Porter, March 10, 1832.   6. Metcalfe to Clay, May 7, 1832.

To HIRAM KETCHUM   Washington, May 15, 1832

I was very glad to learn from your favor of the 12h. inst. that the N. Republicans in N. Y. were resolved to organize, to meet in convention, and to act in concert.[1] Whilst every thing else may be uncertain, there can be not even a doubt as to the wisdom of that course, which will place you in a state of preparation for every event. Do you intend to co-operate with the A. Masons? Then you should meet in Convention and *resolve* to co-operate. In no other way can you secure that harmony among the N. Rs. indispensable to success. Will you be disposed to form an independent ticket? Then the meeting in Convention is absolutely necessary. The interests of the Anti Masons will be much more powerfully addressed by a party organized, and prepared for any emergency than by a party, divided, unorganized and liable to be individually impelled in every direction. Should the N.Rs. meet in Convention, make an electoral ticket of their own, and *abstain* from any nomination of State officers, it is far from certain whether that is not the very best posture for them, to secure afterwards the co-operation which is now in contemplation. After they shall have taken that position, as each of the two parties, contending for the State Executive, attaches more importance to securing that object than it does to the success in the Electoral ticket, both would come quickly and anxiously to the N.Rs. and solicit, upon any terms, their aid as to the State officers.

As so much has been said and done, in regard to co-operation between the Anti's & the N Rs., upon the basis of a ticket to be formed half and half, I think the work had probably better proceed and be completed. But if nothing had been done, and it were now an original question, I think it far from being very certain, whether the best course for the N. Rs. would not have been to proceed straight forward, formed an Electoral ticket of their own, put forward no candidate for Governor, and take the chance of success. On such a supposition, they would have been able to decide who should be Governor, and as the other two parties, in the progress of the canvass, would have become greatly incensed against each other, I am not sure that you would not have been able to have drawn votes from both of them sufficient to carry your ticket.

Foreseeing that any movement of the N. Rs. in Pennsa. adverse to the Anti Masons might have bad effect in N. York, prior to the receipt of your letter, I suggested that consideration to some friends in Pennsa, and also whether it would not be better for them to postpone until Septr. deciding whether they would nominate a Candidate for Govr. of their own or support one of the other two parties. . . .[2]

The papers will inform you of a great outrage attempted yesterday on Mr. [Thomas D.] Arnold of Tennessee, which his strength and courage enabled him successfully to repel.[3]

ALS. KyU. Letter marked "(Confidential)."   1. Clay to Porter, May 1, 1832.   2. The National Republican convention met in Harrisburg on May 29, 1832, elected officers, chose presidential electors, and appointed a standing committee of 15. Also passed was a resolution giving the standing committee power to reconvene the convention at any time "to transact such business as may be thought necessary to promote the success of the National Republican Party." Harrisburg *Chronicle,* June 4, 1832. Ultimately the National Republicans in Pennsylvania did not field a presidential ticket. Instead, they joined with the Anti-Masons, but received no commitments in return. Jackson handily carried the state. In the gubernatorial election George Wolf, a Calhoun Democrat, narrowly defeated the Anti-Masonic candidate, Joseph Ritner, by a vote of 91,144 to 88,072. Klein, *Pennsylvania Politics,* 348, 352; *BDGUS,* 3:1302-3; Vaughn, *The Antimasonic Party in the United States,* 95-98. 3. Clay to Greene, May 15, 1832.

To THOMAS METCALFE Washington, May 17, 1832

I rec'd your favor of the 7th. I should have written oftener to you and other friends but that I did not like to offer speculations instead of facts, and as to the latter I really possessed but few which the public wants; do not communicate. Within the last four or five weeks, however, our prospects, in the pending contest, have greatly improved, our friends have acquired much confidence, and our opponents are proportionally disposed. In New York, it is believed here, I may say by many of both parties, that Jackson will be defeated; and that we shall get the greater part, and in certain contingencies the whole vote. This result will be produced by a cooperation between the Anti Masons and the N. R. which is in progress and which it is thought will be consummated.[1] Jacksonism is shaking to its centre in Penn also,[2] and the nomination of V[an]. Buren at Pitts.[3] next week, which is confidently anticipated will complete its prostration there.

The Tariff—The Bank—the recent assaults upon members of Congress[4] etc, etc are all working favorably; and our friends speak now in a tone that is a token of final success.

I am utterly unable to inform you of the probable issue either of the Bank or Tariff question. We hope to propose the bill to recharter the bank, and there is no doubt of majorities in its favor in both houses, but some or other circumstances may produce a postponement.[5] As to the Tariff, I think we shall do something but what it will be I cannot predict. So far from any time being yet fixed for our adjournment, no one ventures to express an opinion as to the precise day. I shall not be surprised if it celebrates the 4th of July here. Some of our friends think the longer we remain the better; what is your opinion?

Mr [James G.] Dana no doubt thinks what he says in regard to Mr West's [*sic,* William Wirt] election; but nobody here entertains the remotest idea of such an event. As to Mr [Charles] Hammond, you have seen many proofs of his eccentricity. What movement has been made any where by the N. R. party that he says ought to make the first move, corresponding with his views?[6]

The young man's convention in this city went off in fine state and made a strong impression. Upwards of 300 assembled, and they have returned full of spirit and zeal.[7]

Copy. Courtesy of W. Richard Metcalfe. Letter marked "(confidential)." 1. Clay to Porter, May 1, 1832. 2. Clay to Ketchum, May 15, 1832. 3. Brooke to Clay, Feb. 9, 1832; Clay to Porter, March 10, 1832. 4. Clay to Weed, April 14, 1832; Clay to Greene, May 15, 1832. 5. Clay to Brown, Dec. 18, 1831; Webster to Clay, Jan. 8, 1832. 6. Metcalfe to Clay, May 7, 1832. 7. Steuart to Clay, May 10, 1832.

From NATHANIEL R. CLARKE, New Haven, Conn., May 18, 1832. Writes "to apprise you that the Legislature of this State now in Session in this City" has elected Nathan Smith to the U.S. Senate. In Smith's appointment "the friends of the 'American system' of internal improvements & above all the friends of Mr Clay have Secured an able advocate & one who will be true to them & their policy under all circumstances."

Reports that "Under the specious plea of democracy the Jackson party in this State hav[e] vainly attempted to Strengthen their ranks & diminish ours—Presses by the patronage of the Govt have been bought to Silence, or worse than Silence—old republicans calumniated & charged with federal amalgamation—Every Kennel has been made to disgorge & every unworthy artifice practised to corrupt & intimidate the weak & Sell the State to the enemy—but they hav[e] all been met, firmly met, & the good cause has triumphed." States that Clay's Connecticut friends have attempted to bring about "a defined division of the parties" with "friends of the administration on one *Side* & its opponent on the *other*."

Expresses the hope that Sen. Samuel A. Foote, whom Smith will replace, "will be remembered by his friends at home & that he will be called by the fre[e]men of his native state to some honorable station." States also that "patriots & good men look forward to your elevation as the only means of placing this great and once happy republic where it was before the days of Jacksonism, misrule, violence & corruption." ALS. DLC-HC (DNA, M212, R4). Clay carried Connecticut with 17,518 votes to 11,041 for Jackson, and 3,335 for Wirt. Gammon, *The Presidential Campaign of 1832*, 170. For Smith, see *BDAC*. Clark (or Clarke) was born in Boston, Mass., on July 16, 1792, and died on December 9, 1849. In 1840 he was judge of probate court in New Haven. See James M. Patten (ed.), *Patten's New Haven Directory for the Year 1840* (New Haven, 1840), 30; Donald L. Jacobus (ed.), *Families of Ancient New Haven* (Baltimore, 1974), 209.

From JOHN SERGEANT   Philadelphia, May 18, 1832

I duly received your favors of the 13th. and 15th. inst., the latter enclosing Mr. [Hiram] Ketchum's letter herewith returned.[1] Our difficulties in Pennsa. are very great, and do not seem to become less. On the contrary, the movements in New York rather increase them, as we are desirous to avoid every thing that may impede or disturb the plans of our friends in that State, being convinced that they are wise in themselves and entitled to our support. Mr. Ketchum has written several letters to Philada. of the same tenor with his communication to you. They have received, and will continue to receive, the greatest attention, and will have a decided influence in determining the course to be followed here. Our plan, I think, if Pennsa. stood alone, would be very different. But I am fully persuaded that every thing will be made to yield to the national object. What measures, in detail, the [Pennsylvania National Republican] Convention will adopt, I am not able to say.[2] We look every day for events, which if they should come in time, will probably lead to a postponement of the whole business of the Convention to a day in the latter part of the summer, so as to enable us to adapt its proceedings to the state of things which may then exist. If nothing should occur before the 29th., then it is very likely that the Convention will do very much as you suggest—In a few days, there may be more light upon the subject, in which case I will write you again.

Last night, the meeting was held for sending delegates to the Baltimore [Democratic] Convention.[3] It was feeble in numbers and weight, but sufficient, nevertheless, to bring on a state of hostility between the different sections of the party, which must end in submission on the part of the Anti Van Buren party, or in their taking open ground and coming to us. Submission by the V. Buren men is out of the question. It requires no more confidence to go on, than it did to begin, and as to both, they are backed by the powers at Washington—Anti Van Burenism I have regarded as rooted in Anti Jacksonism, being in fact a *mode* of opposition by those who are afraid to oppose more directly, but who, if encouraged, will at last break entirely loose. They are opposed to *Jacksonism* in all its shapes. What they have chiefly at heart is to be sure of the reelection of Govr. [George] Wolf. Pressed as they are by Anti Masonry, they cling to Jackson as essential to their security. If our friends could universally give their assurance of support to Govr. Wolf, I think it would finally win his party from Jackson, and I am even sanguine enough to believe it would give you the vote of the democracy of Pennsa. It is a fact, that the immediate adherents of Jackson, those who receive their orders from the underlings at Washington, are opposed to Wolf — they will go for [Joseph] Ritner, and, if he should be elected, I think they will proclaim it as a Jackson triumph — [4]Nor is this all. There is a strong political affinity between us and the Wolf party, already established. I have said they are opposed to Jacksonism. This is true in its fullest extent. They are supporting every thing, without exception, that we support, and they are doing so in the face of Jackson's known wishes to the contrary. It is owing to *them*, that Pennsa. maintains her present attitude upon all material points, and it is owing to her maintaining this attitude, that all the great interests of the Country have not been beaten down and trampled under the feet of Jackson. I cannot but regard it as important, in a National view, that they should be upheld. If they fall, I perceive no power in Pennsa. that can restrain the wildest fury of Jacksonism — Looking in this way at the matter, I have felt that we had reached a crisis of vast importance, and that the boldest measures were likely to be the most prudent and safe. Among them would be that of acknowledging our affinity with those who hold the same public principles with ourselves, frankly extending to them a helping hand, and having prepared them thus to give us their confidence, inviting them to renounce the only error we have now to impute to them, the abominable one of supporting Jackson. It might not succeed, entirely. We should certainly detach a great many: And, even if that hope too should be disappointed, I think we should keep the State right as to measures.

This is but a hint — it does not deserve the name of a sketch. I hope, however, it may answer the purpose of showing you something of the peculiarity of our position.

A very common opinion prevails, I find, like that you express, that my chance[5] is a good one. It would be odd if it were so, and would show the fallacy of calculations where so much depends upon accident. But I doubt its correctness. The struggle is yet to assume its final shape. Appearances now are not to be relied upon. It may be, that the whole of the forces, now seemingly discordant, will at the last be resolved into two great hostile masses, to be weighed against each other and the most weighty to prevail. If in the trial, I should happen to be elevated, I fear it will be because I am light and insignificant — a feather tossed up in the agitation of the elements,

ALS. InU.   1. Probably Ketchum to Clay, May 12, 1832.   2. Clay to Ketchum, May 15, 1832.   3. Brooke to Clay, Feb. 9, 1832.   4. Clay to Ketchum, May 15, 1832.   5. For election as vice president.

From HENRY CLAY, JR.   Lexington, May 19, 1832

Your letter of May 11th written in the Senate Chamber, conveys to me the authority to have your house at Ashland painted or stuccoed as I may think best, with a limit assigned to the expense of stuccoing. Many considerations induce me to prefer painting. As there is no competition, there will be much hazard of badly performed work, and enhanced prices. Oil will be a good preservative

517

against dampness, whereas the stucco-work would probably scale. If it be over stuccoed, the choice of alterations will hereafter be lost: But painting will last for several years, and will leave the option of further improvements. For these and other reasons, besides that weighty and sufficient one, that the true cost will far exceed the limit mentioned, I shall proceed immediately to have the house painted of a pearl color.

In the West there prevails a most unaccountable political lethargy. But I hope the details of Washington news personally rendered to the people, by their Representatives, may rouse our friends to action.

Anne [Brown Clay Erwin] and her children continue in excellent health. indeed Anne is perfectly well; and on your return, you and my mother, I am sure, will find a source of exquisite happiness in her fine disposition and invincible spirits.

I have lately commenced the common law. I am now reading with much interest the 1st Vol of Blackstones Commentaries. I did not finish the course of Civil Law which Judge [Alexander] Porter marked out for me. He wished me to read this summer 5 or 6 volumes of Pothiers seperate treatises, and 14 of Toullier's commentaries on the Napoleon Code, with the Civil Code and the Code of practice of L'a.[1] On my return to L'a he promised to mark out for me the important decisions of the Supreme Court of La. These studies, completed by that of the Statues of La, would give me in his opinion a sufficient elementary knowledge of the Civil Law. His was certainly good advice, but I have not the time nor the resolution to follow it. I have therefore commenced the common law, and intend if possible to get some idea of that and commercial law by next winter.

I know that I shall be but ill prepared to practice; but I hope to improve with years and increasing business. Besides, a little practice next winter would give me engagement and excitement which I much need, and would give a proper direction and greater vigor to my studies of the summer after. Perhaps too not a single case may be entrusted to my management for some years; and New Orleans is too expensive a city for me to linger in with a constantly disappointed hope of coming business. If you have time to bestow a thought on me and my studies, I would be obliged to you for some advice as to my proper course.

You seem to suppose that I anticipate a change in my condition that I am improving at Ashland. Far from it. I am becoming more and more determined never to change it. My own disposition and my pursuits, unless my present expectations be disappointed, are both opposed to it.

My only objects in attending to the farm and grounds at Ashland are present engagement on my own account, and on yours and my mother's, to render your residence more pleasant and satisfactory.

Mr [James] Erwin is expected in a few days. Your friends are well   P.S. [William] Shackleford will send you his account; I have not yet seen Mr [Thomas] Grant; but have asked Mr [Thomas] Smith to mention your order to him. I am obliged to you for the copy of your land report[2] which you sent me. In my opinion it is altogether your best piece of composition.   May 21st   Mr Erwin arrived last night.

ALS. Henry Clay Memorial Foundation, Lexington, Ky.   1. William Blackstone, *Commentaries On the Laws of England. . . . From the 18th London Edition. . . .* New York, 1832; Pothier, *A Treatise On the Law of Obligations, or Contracts*; Toullier, *Le Droit Civil Français, Suivant l'order du Code.* 2. Comment in Senate, April 16, 1832.

From Hiram Ketchum, New York, May 19, 1832. Reports an informal meeting attended by "a number of intelligent, and discreet friends from the interior of the State," including "a number of high Masons," whose purpose was to "concert measures proper to be pursued by the National Republican party, in reference to the November Election." States that those in attendance decided "that a Convention of our party should be called at the City of Albany, on a day hereaftre to be named [Clay to Porter, May 1, 1832]; that we should proceed at once by correspondence, and personal agency, to organize our friends in the several Counties." Also reports that they decided to hold the state National Republican convention after the Anti-Masonic convention [Clay to Porter, May 1, 1832].

States that "The language which in the meantime we hold to all the leaders of the Anti-Masonic party is, 'We trust you 'til the 21' June; if you make an electoral [ticket] which may be confidently relied upon, to defeat the re-election of Genl Jackson, or, in othre words, to give the whole vote of New York for Mr Clay, if that vote will elect him, your whole nomination for electors, for Governor, and Lieut Governor [Clay to Bailhache, November 24, 1830], shall receive a hearty support from us, but if not, we are prepared to take the field, and will certainly defeat that which you can alone hope to gain, the election of your Governor and, Lieut Governor."

Predicts "that the Anti-Masonic Convention will make a liberal electoral ticket, such an one as the whole opposition can honorably support, if this be not done, and the failure can not be ascribed to any steps of the N R party, public expectation will be disappointed; Anti-Masonry will, in popular judgment, be put in the wrong; a general opinion will come to prevail that if Anti-Masonry can make no sacrifises to save the Country, it is a thing so devilish that it ought to receive the reprobation of every honest man." Also suggests "that about that time Congress will adjourn . . . our friends in Congress . . . will deem it expedient to make an exposure of the actual dangers to which our Constitution and Union are exposed, in the form of an address to the American people."

Reminds Clay of the delicate political situation in Pennsylvania, emphasizing that when the National Republican convention meets in Harrisburg it should make no "step hostile to Anti-masonry [Sergeant to Clay, January 9, 1832; Clay to Ketchum, May 15, 1832]." ALS. DLC-HC (DNA, M212, R4). For a shorter, somewhat different version of this letter, see LS. KyLoF.

From Unknown Sender, New York, May 19, 1832. Reports on an informal meeting last night in which the strategy of the National Republicans in New York in the November presidential election was discussed. The meeting concluded that the National Republicans should call a state nominating convention [Clay to Porter, May 1, 1832], but not until after the Anti-Masons have held theirs [June 21, 1832]. If the Anti-Masonic convention should choose a Clay electoral ticket, the National Republicans would, in return, support Anti-Masonic candidates for governor and lieutenant governor [Clay to Bailhache, November 24, 1830]. Without such support, the Anti-Masonic gubernatorial candidates cannot win in New York. If the state Anti-Masonic convention does not endorse Clay, a National Republican convention will promptly be called [July 26, 1832]. Asserts that at last night's National Republican strategy meeting it was "particularly gratifying" to see a "number of high masons" who had voted against Francis Granger "at the last election [Clay to Johnston, May 9, 1830; Stoddard to Clay, November 8, 1830]." Points out to Clay that at about the time Congress adjourns the Congressional anti-Jacksonians should issue "an exposé to the American people, in the form of an Address, of the actual dangers to which our Constitution and union are exposed." Such a statement would "produce a great effect, and by many it will be expected." Calls attention to the political situation in Pennsylvania and urges Clay "to use *all your influence* to prevent the National republican convention at Harrisburgh [*sic,* Harrisburg] from taking a step hostile to Anti-masonry [Clay to Ketchum, May 15, 1832]." Explains:

"I care not about their making any movement in its favor, but let them do nothing, until our most difficult and delicate game is fairly played out, to defeat our anticipated Success. If I could, I would convey the idea to these *Antis* [Masons] that their Success in both New York, and Pennsylvania, depends entirely upon their pursuing a patriotic course in reference to the electoral ticket, in the former State. Let those of our friends who cordially hate the principle, of Anti-masonry, rest assured, that if by our movement in New York the National republican candidates shall be elected, that the days of the party for which they cherish such an aversion will certainly be numbered. —" ALS. KyLoF.

From THEODORE W. CLAY   Lexington, May 20, 1832

I wrote to you some weeks ago stating that I found myself unpleasantly situated here.[1] That at that time, so far from desiring to remove obstacles, or maladies if any existed in me observable to others, which I could not discover, they seemed inclined and anxious to increase them rather than to remove them. I have sometimes rode about and been seen by so many that it will rather be a wonder to many that I am not allowed to stay at Home, where I would be quiet and unmolested rather than in a Hospital. All who see me know that I am perfectly at my self. And I feel no reason why I should be subject to the will of others and not a free agent at least. My desires are lawful, and my conduct not in violation of any law, or the rights of any man. Why therefore I am thus restrained I cannot see, so long. No one has yet volunteered their friendly aid to me and I will not if I can chuse, be the slave of any man. I hope you will write to me what I had best do. The Commissioners[2] are John Brand, John W. Hunt Richard Higgins, Thomas D Hart, and Richard Ashton. I have written a respectful request to the Commissioners and they have given me no answer. And I have no reason to believe they will. I expect therefore that Justice will be done to me, and hope that it will speedily. Either with Thomas [Hart Clay], or any where—I might find employment, if you do not wish I should return a while to Ashland will suit me. So I get my liberty, and the peaceable enjoyment of the bounties of providence I shall be satisfied.

Give my love to Mother

ALS. DLC-TJC (DNA, M212, R10).   1. Theodore W. Clay to Clay, Jan. 8, 1832.   2. Of the Lunatic Asylum of Kentucky.

From A.R. Macey, Bowling Green, Ky., May 20, 1832. Notes that a new newspaper has been launched in Washington, D.C. [*The National Union*, J.A. Fell, editor], and asks Clay "if you you [*sic*] shall believe that the paper will likely [be per]manent & useful" to subscribe to it for him. Expresses the hope that "the honesty, virtue [&] patriotism of the country will be awakened & that [we] shall have at the ensuing contest an union [of] all the sound heads & pure hearts to put an [end] to these disgraceful scenes." Is pleased that Clay's Report on the Public Lands [Comment in Senate, April 16, 1832] "shares largely in the applauses of the . . . Country." Adds that "I [have] just read the speeches of [Peleg] Sprague & [John] Holmes upon [the] subject of the 'glorious' west India Trade Arrangement [Clay to Adams, July 26, 1831; Clay to Everett, August 20, 1831] they are well calculated to open the eyes of the multit[ude] to the tricks, degradation & delusions that [our] '[word illeg.] chief Magistrate & *able Negotiator*' is willing to practice upon the community, to sustain honors most shamefully acquired—A general circulation of those Speeches in [word illeg.] that & others of the like kind would subserve a [most] valuable purpose—For at this time the chief argument of [John] Breathitt in his public speeches in favor of the [word illeg.] of the 'Hero' is bottomed upon Jackson's success in making Treaties with England France, Denmark Turkey &c &c The former watchword 'Retrenchment & Reform' can no longer be used to gall & deceive the ignorant credulous & honest yeomanry — But I think I can safely say to you that our cause is safe in this State [Smith to Clay, December 27, 1831] — I discover a gradual falling from the ranks of your opponents & there is evidently among them a general apathy and indisposition to say any thing in behalf of the administration of Jackson whilst your friends are warm full of hope and enterprise." ALS. DLC-HC (DNA, M212, R4). For Jackson's treaties with Denmark, Turkey, and France see respectively, Parry, *Treaty Series*, 80: 463-71; 81:7-24; 82:91-103. In their speeches both Sprague and Holmes condemned Louis McLane's trade negotiations with the British. See *Register of Debates*, 22 Cong., 1 Sess., 24-26, 685-706. For the termination of the Anglo-American controversy over the so-called "Colonial" trade, see also Benns, *The American Struggle for British West India Carrying Trade*, 186-87.

From Robert Wickliffe, Lexington, May 20, 1832. Remarks that "We are as yet but; badly inform[e]d of the final result of the Bank Question [Clay to Brown, December 18, 1831]. In this place indeed, the whol[e] State, there is but one Sentiment & that is to rechartre nearly on the bases of the present charter I have just read Mr Adams's report [Clay to Brooke, April 17, 1832]. it is certainly most powerfull & most *caustic*. Indeed Its severity, howevre meritted, may injure it usefullness & yet I do not see how he could be more Temperate all things considered." Also reports that the "fatal apportionment *Bill* has disheartened some of our friends particularly in [Robert P.] Letchers District. I wish you would urge him to write & stir his friends every where to act for [Richard A.] Buckner & [James T.] Morehead [Smith to Clay, December 27, 1831]." ALS. DLC-HC (DNA, M212, R4). For the apportionment bill, see Clay to Weed, April 14, 1832. Wickliffe's dissatisfaction with it may have stemmed from the fact that Kentucky received only one additional representative (an increase from 12 representatives to 13) despite a 22 percent increase in population, from 564,317 in 1820 to 687,917 in 1830. Under the new apportionment act there was to be a ratio of one representative for every 47,700 persons; hence, Kentucky's ratio of one representative for every 52,917 was considered unfair. Collins, *History of Kentucky*, 1:29, 36, 369; 4 *U.S. Stat.*, 516.

Remark in Senate, May 21, 1832. Speaking to the proposition of a proposed public grant to bail out Columbian College in the District of Columbia, says he "would not vote to it a cent" unless there has lately been "a real reform, a radical change, in the management of this institution." *Register of Debates*, 22 Cong., 1 Sess., 938. The bill making a grant to Columbian College passed the Senate on May 22, 1832, and the House on July 14. U.S. Sen., *Journal*, 22 Cong., 1 Sess., 294; U.S.H. of Reps., *Journal*, 22 Cong., 1 Sess., 1181.

Remark in Senate, May 22, 1832. Hopes that the internal improvements bill from the House will be sent to the Committee on Commerce rather than to the Committee on Roads and Canals, which is "hostile to its objects." *Register of Debates*, 22 Cong., 1 Sess., 938.

Remark in Senate, May 24, 1832. Reiterates his plea of May 8 that the Senate act on either the tariff, the public lands issue, or the bank recharter bill "at once." *Register of Debates*, 22 Cong., 1 Sess., 953.

To HENRY CLAY, JR.   Washington, May 25, 1832
I recd. your favor postmarked the 13h. Prior to its receipt I had written to your fully in regard to the stuccoing or painting of the House at Ashland. Under all circumstances, I think it will be best to paint it, and if you concur the selection of the color is left to you.

When we shall get away from here is quite uncertain. I doubt whether it will be until some time in July. From a suggestion in Anne's [Brown Clay

Erwin] letter, this day recd., I have supposed you might like to come and join us here. We shall be very glad to see you, and if you have the least inclination to come I wish you to indulge it. You must indeed be very solitary at home, and a relaxation from your studies may be beneficial. You may even be necessary to us after the adjournment of Congress, especially if the Session should be protracted, as I apprehend.

The Bank question[1] has been begun in the Senate. When it will terminate is uncertain. We have then the Tariff,[2] the Public lands[3] &c to act upon.

ALS. Henry Clay Memorial Foundation, Lexington, Ky.   1. Clay to Brown, Dec. 18, 1831; Webster to Clay, Jan. 8, 1832.   2. *Ibid.*; Speech in Senate, Feb. 2, 1832.   3. Comment in Senate, April 16, 1832.

From John Sergeant, Philadelphia, May 25, 1832. Reports hearing from Hiram Ketchum who advises "us at once to nominate the *A*[nti]. *M*[asonic]. electoral ticket, and say nothing at present as to Governor [Clay to Ketchum, May 15, 1832]." Opposes this plan on the basis that "this would be a dissolution of the N. Republican party in Pennsa., and that it would at once give the State, with entire certainty, to Jackson, and probably to V[an]. Buren too. The probable result would be to carry [Joseph] Ritner for Govr., (as all the *genuine* Jackson men would support him against [George] Wolf) and the Jackson electoral ticket, which many of the A. M's would support as an equivalent for the support of their Governor." The "wildest Jacksonism" would thus "become the order of the day in Pennsa." Instead, "we ought to nominate an electoral ticket of our own, and support Wolf for Governor."

States that "You will probably think it strange that I should suppose Ritner may get the vote for Governor, and Jackson, for President." Explains: "The Jackson party in Pennsa. consists of two unequal parts. The smaller portion, backed and encouraged at Washington, and in immediate communication with the under Cabinet, are the Jackson men par excellence, being devoted body and soul to the cause. . . . These men are bitterly opposed to Wolf. . . . George Kremer is of this sect. The other, and far the larger portion . . . are the friends of Wolf, strongly attached to him, and governed chiefly, I might say entirely, by a view to his reelection. . . . They are either opposed to Jackson, or very weakly attached to him. They are truly attached to all the great interests of the State and the Union, as we understand them, and in principle are with us. . . . They suffer actual oppression from Jacksonism, and they dread even worse, but they are afraid to break loose, lest they might endanger Wolf." Notes that the "decisive combat" between these two groups "will be the Governor's election."

Moreover, both the "patent Jacksonmen" and the Anti-Masons "are bitterly opposed to Wolf." Believes that the "Presidential question will be no cause of discord between them. The A. Ms want the Governor; the Patents think that if they defeat Wolf, they will have the ascendancy, and can control the electoral election, either by making a new electoral ticket, or compelling the electors already named to stand by Jackson. . . . They will be helped by a great many of the A. M's."

Explains that "Upon all public questions, we agree with the Wolf party and judging him by his administration, we can support their candidate without violence to our feelings and principles. . . . They will not quarrel with us for supporting our National Candidates. . . . We cannot, by any course we may pursue, conciliate the Anti Masons, or hope to gain from them a single vote. They go on doggedly for Anti Masonry, and, I believe, are more opposed to us than they are to Jacksonism. . . . They will receive us as Antimasons, but in no other shape or way — The Wolf party are of a different description. We may, I think we certainly shall, gain from them, perhaps gain the whole of them, and give you the support of the democracy of the State — "

Argues that "Higher considerations" of "patriotism and love of Country" also dictate attempting to work with the Wolf party. "The Wolf party have hitherto opposes [*sic,* opposed] Jacksonism (I mean the will of Jackson) in all its attempts upon the Institutions and interests of the Nation. . . . Of how much importance this has been, you know better than I do. Ought we to join their opponents, and add our weight to the power already employed to crush them? . . . if the Wolf party succeed, they will at least keep Pennsa. in her position, and her support will be given to the best interests of the Nation. If they are over thrown, the torrent will roll through Pennsa. sweeping all before it."

Concludes that he is "painfully aware that my position exposed me to the suspicion of being influenced by views of my own," and that "the apprehension of such a misconstruction has been extremely oppressive, so much so that I seriously regretted being a candidate." ALS. InU.

To EDMUND H. TAYLOR   Washington, May 26, 1832
[Discusses financial transactions concerning the estate of James Morrison. Continues:]

Our friends are in high spirits as to political prospects. My own opinion is that they have greatly improved, and afford much ground to hope that we shall be successful. The nomination of V[an]. B[uren]. at Balto.[1] &c. it is believed will give the coup de grace to Jacksonism. Pennsa. is in great commotion, and much confidence is felt that she will burst forth from the delusion under which she has so long labored.

We have the Bank question[2] up in the Senate — The renewal will be carried in the Senate, and it is believed in the House also.

ALS. KyHi.   1. Brooke to Clay, Feb. 9, 1832.   2. Clay to Brown, Dec. 18, 1831; Webster to Clay, Jan. 8, 1832.

From Peter B. Porter, Black Rock, N.Y., May 27, 1832. Has been expecting "communications from our friends at the East, who manage the political concerns of the party." States that he "had become convinced. . . . that the views they express in regard to the Anti masons were correct, and that my friends in Albany had deceived me, or rather themselves, in supposing they were on the eve of concluding an arrangement with those ambitious politicians [Clay to Weed, April 14, 1832]."

Believes that John Spencer "would be more likely to thwart" an arrangement between the National Republicans and Anti-Masons "than any other man, excepting A[lbert]. H. Tracy, who . . . would be equally, if not more, determinnd to yield to any compromise in which he could not see some direct personal advantage to himself." Reports that he had "several interviews with Spencer, in the course of the winter . . . in which he expressed a most earnest desire for a friendly coalition, but always took care to qualify his desire for the compromise, with doubts as to its practicability." Informs Clay that he wrote Spencer about a month ago expressing "in general & guarded terms" his satisfaction "at having heard that such an arrangement was in progress among our respective friends in Albany."

Reports that upon receipt of Spencer's reply, he wrote Matthew L. Davis. Encloses an excerpt of that letter, in which he outlines Spencer's plan for the arrangement between the two parties in New York and his objections to it.

Mentions that he has also written Smith Thompson "the chair-man of our general committee, uging anew the expediency of calling a convention without delay." Suggests that "in calling the Convention & nominating our own tickets, I do not dispair of some ultimate arrangement with the anti masons." ALS. DLC-HC (DNA, M212, R4).

Remark in Senate, May 28, 1832. Presents petition from New York hair cloth manufacturers asking that certain duties not be lowered. Takes this opportunity to call the attention of the Senate to the "prosperous condition" of some U.S. manufacturers. Also urges his colleagues to exercise the "greatest caution" in regulating duties lest inadvertently they give "a fatal stroke to some branches of the arts." *Register of Debates*, 22 Cong., 1 Sess., 978-79.

Later this day, Clay notes the "failure of several banks" in Kentucky and states that the proposition to restrict the denominations of the notes of the rechartered Bank of the United States "would seriously affect the resources" of Kentucky and Kentuckians since "they had no bank of their own, and, by raising the notes of the bank above five dollars they would have to have recourse to notes of their neighboring States for their circulating medium, to transact their ordinary business and dealing." Is thus "opposed to a higher sum than ten dollars." *Ibid.*, 979-80.

From John Sergeant, Philadelphia, May 29, 1832. Regarding "the probable effect of our nomination [Clay to Ketchum, May 15, 1832] upon the fate of Govr. [George] Wolf," reports that "It is far from being clear to my mind that our espousing him may not afford a pretext for an opposition to him by the Jackson men and for their supporting either [Joseph] Ritner, or some candidate named by themselves. Neither is it clear that such an opposition might not be made available for his overthrown." Adds that this effect seems so likely that he has clearly presented to Wolf's friends "my views of the danger," and they have persisted "in earnestly desiring the steps to be taken, and say they have confidence in its results." Does not know how this nomination of Wolf will affect the National Republican presidential ticket, but "our condition will be no worse for it" even if it does not secure the desired support.

Mentions that he has heard nothing yet from Harrisburg [Clay to Ketchum, May 15, 1832], but that his "earnest injunction to the delegates has been, to deliberate carefully before they decide, and when they have come to a conclusion, to espouse it like one man."

Concludes: "What I alluded to in my last [May 25, 1832], as personal to myself, would not have occurred to me, but for the intimations (co[n]temporaneous or nearly so) in the Anti Masonic paper called the '[Philadelphia] Sun', and in [Stephen] Simpson's paper 'The [Philadelphia *Pennsylvania*] Whig', that the leaning to Wolf was in my favor. It might happen to be so. Not that there is any preference for me; but there is a preference for a Pennsa. candidate, which might (I do not know that it will) prove strong enough to counteract the efforts of Jacksonism in favor of Van Buren and give the vote to any Pennsylvanian, rather than to him. In these times, it would grieve me to incur the suspicion of want of faith towards our friends. As to our enemies, I care nothing what they say or think." ALS. InU.

From Matthew L. Davis, New York, May 30, 1832. Reports that he has just returned from a tour of northern New York, and "can not abandon the idea that the anti masons will make such a nomination as our friends may consistently support [Clay to Weed, April 14, 1832]. A large proportion of their electoral ticket will be, *nominally* anti masonic, but *really* national republicans." Yet because he knows "the self-delusion and fanaticism of those with whom we must act," he has "come to the conclusion, long since, that by a personal intercourse with the leaders of these men, we must produce the result at which we aim, or it can never be produced. I am for a Convention [Clay to Porter, May 1, 1832]. I am for announcing it in a few days, and for stating its objects; viz. to nominate Governor, lieut. Governor, and an Electoral Ticket [Clay to Bailhache, November 24, 1830], making no reference or allusion, in the call, to the Anti Masonic party." Recommends that this convention take place after the Anti-Masonic convention at Utica [Clay to Porter, May 1, 1832] on June 21 and the Jackson party convention at Herkimer on September 19. "If they shall have disappointed our *hopes*, we will have had time to deliberate, and to consult with each other as to the *policy* that ought to be adopted, under the *then* circumstances of the case." Continues: "On the other hand, if they shall have nominated such a ticket, as to meet the approbation of our party, they will require, and will have been allowed time to allay the discontents in their own ranks, which such a nomination will produce among them, to a greater or less extent. And we shall, by meeting after the 19th of Septemr, deprive the Herkimer Convention of the power of saying, that a Corrupt bargain has been *consummated*, by the two sections of the opposition having *formally* approved the same tickets."

Reports that he leaves tomorrow for the western part of New York, "where the Anti Masons are all powerful," and a majority of their leaders "would rather be *defeated* on a State & United States nomination, purely Anti Masonic, than succeed in a nomination of a mixed character — Because, in that district of territory, they can carry all their local or County nominations." Is not certain, therefore, that the Anti-Masons will make the desired nominations at the Utica convention, but "I am confident . . . that any other Course but the one which we have pursued for the last six months, and are yet pursuing, would have been ruinous." ALS. DLC-HC (DNA, M212, R4). At the September 19 Democratic party convention at Herkimer, William L. Marcy was nominated for governor and John Tracy for lieutenant governor. Presidental electors were also selected. Hammond, *History of Political Parties in the State of New York*, 2:423.

From John Sergeant, Philadelphia, May 30, 1832. Refers to a bill for the relief of Rebecca Smith (Mrs. Samuel) Blodget [7:477-78] which he had promised her he would mention to Clay. States that all he knows about the situation is that "Mrs. B. is an object of charity, and that she was once the object of universal admiration for her wit and beauty."

Reports in a postscript: "I have now a letter from Harrisburg [Clay to Ketchum, May 15, 1832], coming down to 8 P. M. yesterday — No thought of union with the Anti Masons — no thought of nominating a candidate of our own for Governor — whether to nominate Mr. [George] Wolf for support, still under consideration. If not nominated, it was thought he would be spoken favorably of, in the address. . . . I think we ought to go the whole length one way or the other, but mean to espouse whatever the Convention may do." ALS. InU.   On March 19, 1832, Rebecca Blodget's petition, "praying that her claim for arrears of her dower in the lots and building in the City of Washington, called the General Post Office, may be paid." The bill passed the Senate on June 4, 1832, and the House on July 13. U.S. Sen., *Journal*, 22 Cong., 1 Sess., 191, 268, 327; and U.S. H. of Reps., *Journal*, 22 Cong., 1 Sess., 1167.

Remark in Senate, May 31, 1832. Suggests that in the proposed tariff bill there be a provision to exempt from duty the iron bars used in railroad construction, since "in a few months, a supply could always be obtained from England." *Register of Debates*, 22 Cong., 1 Sess., 990-91.

From JOHN SERGEANT   Philadelphia, May 31, 1832

I have just seen a member of the Convention, who came from Harrisburg to day.[1] They have formed a strong electoral ticket — have made no nomination of Governor, and have appointed a standing committee, with authority to call the Convention together again; if they should think proper, either before or after the Governor's election. Very few of the members were for supporting [Joseph] Ritner — a majority were in favor of [George] Wolf — but there was not such unanimity as to make it prudent to take that step which many desired, of nominating him for the support of our friends. So the matter stands.

Van Buren (if I rightly interpret an article in the [Philadelphia] Inquirer this morning) is finally abandoned in Pennsa.[2] The argument seems to be that an attempt to form a ticket in his favour would endanger Jackson. And so, it certainly would, unless brought forward with strength enough to crush the advocates of the Jackson & [William] Wilkins ticket, which I think could not be. This retreat, however, is a symptom of fear among the Jackson people, which augurs well. The State is certainly much agitated, and it is quite possible may yet go against Jackson—Wolf will nevertheless be pressed by the combined force of the Anti Masons and the genuine Jackson men, and it will require all the skill of his friends to secure his reelection. They must look to us, and knowing this, especially if they should think the State ready for a change, they will perhaps be induced to make a demonstration against Jackson. This would carry our friends for Wolf, to a man, and would prove the reserve of the Convention to have been right.

A strong tariff resolution has been brought forward in the Legislature.[3] It is said to have been badly managed, and to have caused some debate. But it will pass, and will increase the excitement already prevailing on this subject. There is more *real* feeling about it than I had supposed.

The opposition to Van Buren must unavoidably draw a line in the Jackson party, wherever it extends, as it has already done here. I should suppose it must terminate in a separation. The opponents of V. B. are marked as not being real Jackson men, and they know that they will feel the weight of his (Jackson's) vengeance. Their only chance of safety is to deprive him of power. *That*, will be their aim. I believe it is already, to a greater extent than is generally believed. Here, their animosity is ready to break out. By the 4th. July I expect it will find audible utterance. In the mean time, our position is quite enviable. We are treated with respect by both the sections, and I think have the hearty wishes of the larger one for our success,

ALS. InU.   1. Clay to Ketchum, May 15, 1832.   2. Clay to Porter, March 10, 1832; Washington *Globe*, June 7, 1832.   3. McCulloh to Clay, May 1, 1832.

To FRANCIS T. BROOKE   Washington, June 2, 1832

I did not answer your last, because I had some hopes of seeing you here, and because I wished to be able to communicate to you something about the proceedings of the N.R. Convention at Harrisburg.[1] The inclosed letter from Mr. [John] Sergeant (which you can return after reading) will give you the latest information from that place. Other letters which I have received corroborate his views. The progress of the work of co-operation between the Anti-Masons and N.R.'s in New York continues,[2] and every day adds to our confidence that it will be secured, and that its result will be to deprive Jackson of the support of that State. It is an affair, however, of much delicacy and of no little difficulty, from the fanaticism of some, and the perverseness of others, of the Anti-Masons. The letter which you procured Governor [James] Barbour to write to [Robert S.] Rose has had good effect, and if he could repeat the anodyne it would not be amiss. [Samuel] Stevens (the Anti-Masonic candidate for Lieutenant-Governor in New York) was here a few days ago, and assured me that he was fully persuaded that we should succeed in New York. Lieutenant-Governor Pilcher [*sic*, Nathaniel Pitcher] (now a member of the House of Representatives from that State, and elected as a Jackson man) said to me, last evening, that he had no doubt of our success there.

We are going on with the Bank in the Senate,[3] and, I presume, will pass the bill on Monday or Tuesday. In the House of Representatives Mr. M'Duffie's Tariff bill[4] had only about forty-four supporters. No time of adjournment yet spoken of. L Hith, from Richmond, is here, and I am highly pleased with him.

Copy. Printed in Colton, *Clay Correspondence*, 4:339-40.   1. Clay to Ketchum, May 15, 1832.   2. Clay to Bailhache, Nov. 24, 1830; Clay to Porter May 1, 1832.   3. Clay to Brown, Dec. 18, 1831;

Webster to Clay, Jan. 8, 1832. 4. McDuffie's bill, introduced in the House on Feb. 8, 1832, called for duties to be slashed on the principal-protected articles to a 12 1/2 percent *ad valorem* level in a two-year period; everything else was to be admitted duty free. Debate on the tariff did not begin in the House until May 28; McDuffie's bill was laid aside on June 1 by a vote of 81 to 41. *Register of Debates*, 22 Cong., 1 Sess., 1763, 3119-70, 3190-3235, 3242; and Merril D. Peterson, *Olive Branch and Sword* (Baton Rouge, 1982), 23-33.

Comment in Senate, June 2, 1832. Denies that the Bank of the United States has ever taken part "in any political questions." Blames on the "newspapers . . . [and] demagogues of the country" the agitation of the proposition that the "premature" renewal of the bank charter was politically motivated. Does not believe the length of the bank's new charter will have anything to do with its interest in politics. Argues that the B.U.S. charter should be renewed for twenty years, rather than ten or fifteen — or the same length of time specified in the charters of "almost all" the numerous state banks. Discusses the constitutionality of the issuing of notes by branch offices of the bank. *Register of Debates*, 22 Cong., 1 Sess., 1018-19.

From John Sergeant, Philadelphia, Pa., June 2, 1832. Reports that the Pennsylvania house of representatives unanimously passed on June 1, 1832, "very strong Tariff resolutions, and also a strong resolution in favor of the Bank, declaring its 'speedy re-chartering' to be of vital importance to the public welfare." Is confident that the resolutions will also pass the state senate.

Views "the passage of these resolutions . . . as a demonstration more decided than any thing we have yet had," and thus anticipates the early "annihilation of Jacksonism in Pennsa."

Speculates that if "the Bank bill should pass," and Jackson vetoes it, "he will surely lose the State [Clay to Brown, December 18, 1831; Webster to Clay, January 8, 1832]." ALS. InU. Resolutions supporting the renewal of the bank charter and the protective tariff were unanimously passed by the state senate on June 5, 1832. Harrisburg *Chronicle,* June 11, 1832.

On June 1, 1832, Thomas G. McCulloh sent Clay a copy of the Pennsylvania resolutions. ALS. DLC-HC (DNA, M212, R4).

From Thomas Metcalfe, Frankfort, Ky., June 3, 1832. Discusses the outcome of the Democratic convention in Baltimore [Brooke to Clay, February 9, 1832]. Indicates that "the friends of our old friend R[ichard]. M. J[ohnson] are evidently greatly disappointed here." Suggests that "the skill of V[an] B[uren] & his friends will now be required to soothe the feelings of the friends of the patriotic colonel [Johnson] — perhaps the *War Dept* or something of this kind may do." Asks if it is "possible that Messrs [George M.] Bibb, [Charles] Wickliffe and [Henry] Daniel, will stick to the hero, [Jackson] with V[an]. B[uren]. upon his back [Clay to Porter, March 10, 1832]."

Comments upon gubernatorial campaign in Kentucky [Smith to Clay, December 27, 1831]. Mentions that Richard M. Buckner "makes a very favorable impression wherever he goes," but that "he has some prejudices to combat — his Presbyterianism &c."

Suggests that "the country has nothing to loose by a protracted Session [of Congress], the object of which is to adjust & settle" the problems of the bank, the tariff, the public lands, and "the Union; or at least the principles by which alone it is to be sustained." Adds that "our cause can not loose anything but may gain by it, and probably will gain much." ALS. DLC-HC (DNA, M212, R4). For Johnson's bid for the vice-presidency in 1832, see Leland W. Meyer, *The Life And Times of Colonel Richard M. Johnson of Kentucky* (New York, 1932), 398-401.

Remark in Senate, June 4, 1832. Opposes reducing from 6 percent to 5 percent the maximum interest rate which the Bank of the United States might be permitted to charge. *Register of Debates*, 22 Cong., 1 Sess., 1023.

Comment in Senate, June 6, 1832. Argues that the annual bonus to be paid to the government by the Bank of the United States, for the monopoly to be enjoyed by the rechartered bank in its handling of federal funds, might go as high as $200,000. Gives his reasons for suggesting this figure. *Register of Debates*, 22 Cong., 1 Sess., 1033, 1035.

From Hiram Ketchum, New York, June 6, 1832. Reports that "the time of calling a National Republican Convention [Clay to Porter, May 1, 1832] for this State . . . has been somewhat changed, and a Convention has been recommended by our General Committee." Notes that according to a conversation with Thurlow Weed of the Albany *Evening Journal*, "the prospects of Union, a *harmonious Union* [between National Republicans and Anti-Masons], upon all points, brighten." Warns, however, that nothing is "*certain* until after . . . the Anti-masonic Convention [Clay to Porter, May 1, 1832]." Adds that "from all the indications about us here the Anti-Masons are quite as eager for the Union as we are." Believes that "if the votes of New York will elect you President, they will be given for you. *I anxiously enquire will they be sufficient, according to fair and rational estimates?*" ALS. DLC-HC (DNA, M212, R4).

From Peter B. Porter, "Steam Boat Chippewa—Between Pittsburg and Wheeling," June 6, 1832. Reports that "the chance of a friendly & efficient coalition with the A[nti] Masons" in New York [Clay to Weed, April 14, 1832] "stands . . . much fairer than it did when I wrote you last." Believes that the Anti-Masons in the northern and western counties "appear very generally to be entirely willing & anxious to form an electoral ticket the whole of which will vote for you; and that the only objections to this course are to be found among the ambitious leaders of the party." Speculates that [Albert H.] Tracy "will strongly oppose any coalition to the last," but [John C.] Spencer will give in "when he shall become convinced . . . that we will neither follow nor unite without an equivalent." Continues: "I am sure that there is a common & fixed determination to nominate & support our own seperate tickets for State as well as federal officers, unless the AntiMasons will unite in supporting a ticket, one half of which at least, shall be composed of men distinctly & unhesitatingly avowing their determination to vote for you, and whose known sentiments & characters afford a sufficient pledge that they will do so." Reports that he has written Spencer and William Maynard to convince them "that the National Republicans throughout the State will have power & support . . . a ticket of their own unless their propositions for a joint ticket are promptly met [Clay to Porter, May 1, 1832]."

Speculates upon the date of the New York National Republican convention [Clay to Porter, May 1, 1832], and states that the date of the convention depends upon the actions of the Anti-Masons in New York. ALS. DLC-HC (DNA, M212, R4).

To SAMUEL L. SOUTHARD   Washington, June 6, 1832

I have this moment received your friendly letter of the 2d. inst. and assure you that it would afford us sincere pleasure to be able to spend some time under your hospitable roof. The principal difficulty in a Northern trip, on our return home, arises out of having a Carriage[,] horses &c. here which it would be inconvenient to take in that direction. Another, relates to the time of the adjournment of Congress, which is yet unfixed and uncertain.[1] If, as I now think is probable, we shall be thrown into July, my inclination is to return by N. Jersey New York &c. Should we resolve to do so, I will give you due notice. Mean time, I beg you to communicate our best regards to Mrs. Southard and Miss Virginia [Southard] and say to them that their kind wishes will have much influence with us.

I need say nothing to you about matters in N. Y. and Pennsa. as you are so near both of them. From this more distant point they look well—very well.

South of this place, the V. B-n [Van Buren] physic works badly. Those opposed to him from that quarter, who are in Congress, are confident that he can get no Southern support.

We are on the Bank,[2] the House the Tariff.[3] We shall pass the Bank bill. What will be done on the Tariff, God only knows.

ALS. NjP.   1. Congress adjourned on July 16, 1832.   2. Clay to Brown, Dec. 18, 1831; Webster to Clay, Jan. 8, 1832.   3. Webster to Clay, Jan. 8, 1832.

From Francis T. Brooke, near Fredericksburg, Va., June 7, 1832. Believes that "there is a stopping place in the public delusion which we must arrive at before the election," that "the distracted state of the mind of the public in Virginia . . . will settle down," and that "the persevering madness of the Richmd faction in pressing V[an] B[uren] on the people will end . . . in the overthrow of Jacksonism (god grant it)."

Informs Clay that he hopes "you will settle the Tariff question . . . the signing of that bill [Webster to Clay, January 8, 1831] will ruin Jackson, in the south, and be of no service to him elsewhere." ALS. DLC-HC (DNA, M212, R4).

From HENRY CLAY, JR.   Lexington, June 7, 1832

Your letters of the 25th and 29th May have both been received. You desire me to pursue my inclination to visit Washington: and in one of your letters [May 25, 1832] you intimate that I may be necessary to you. At present I am somewhat intent upon a little "affaire du coeur," which however I hope to arrange satisfactorily in less than a week. What would you say were I to present you another daughter? How changeable are our dispositions! how unfixed our determinations! — But yesterday, I was resolved upon a life of celibacy; today, I am almost equally resolved to propose a matrimonial union. Would it receive your sanction? That is a question that I have more than once propounded to myself; and which I am totally unable to answer. In all respects, the lady, Miss Julia Prather of Louisville, is worthy of being your daughter and my wife.[1] But again, another question occurs, will she consent? I must confess that it is uncertain. But a few words will clear up that affair

Tell my mother that the large dining room has been repaired, and looks so well that I could not resist the temptation of giving a party a few evenings to Miss Julia. It is painted of the original color and the cracks are stopped and smoothed.

In regard to your farm, your rye and wheat crops will be very fine your hemp is pretty good, some of your corn excellent, all very good.

We have lost the young colt of the Potowmac mare. It was foaled on one day, and died on the next. We have made a temporary disposal of Ulysses which I believe will please you. His mares of last season generally proved without foal; so that in this neighbourhood he was not in very good repute as a foal-getter. This has been the cause of but few mares (about 12 or 15) being put to him: two or three weeks since, it being near the end of his season, a Mr [Jacob] Embry, who had the Jack once before, came to me and informed me that his Jack had just died; leaving 40 odd mares engaged: And that if we chose, we might take them, he keeping the Jack and receiving half the profits. We made the proviso that all mares or Jennies that had already commenced their seasons should be entirely for our benefit. For all this we have his note and in it, I have secured to you the option of half the mules or half the season money; for he has engaged the mules at $20.00. Mr [William] Martin and myself, under existing circumstances both deemed these conditions highly favorable to you. I hope you will think them satisfactory. There is at present a great demand for mules. All your stock is in good order. We have borrowed a woodland pasture from [Robert] Wickliffe, near the far farm, so that we are enabled to release your front woods. We find great difficulty in procuring a suitable bull.

I am progressing with the painting &c of your house. I have on already the two first coats. One more will be added   All my improvements I hope will not cost more than $200.00, which I am sure, will be amply repaid you, in the increased satisfaction that you will have at Ashland.

You write inquiringly about Theodore [W. Clay]. His general health is better than I have known it to be for some years. You say that his letters to you are perfectly rational. Anne [Brown Clay Erwin] has not neglected him, nor have I. He spent a day with Anne and has passed 2 or three with me at Ashland. Like yourself I was beginning to believe that his mind was restored. But my dear Father let us not flatter ourselves. Theodore has not yet recovered his rationality on all subjects. I believe you do not doubt my affection for him. It is stronger now than it ever was before. He seems much attached to me. But I will first give you Dr Dudlys [sic, Benjamin W. Dudley] opinion and afterwards my own. According to that worthy man and excellent physician; Theodore is deranged upon two subjects, love and ambition. the first can only be cured by time, the second by humiliation. By humiliation he means that Theodore should be treated by all as an ordinary young man incapable of self direction   That no particular deference should be paid to his opinion or judgment that however much we may attend to his personal comfort; it should not appear. That no indulgences should be made the evidences of any particular respect. In fine that we should appear entirely indifferent to his opinion or his mind. He therefore thinks that Theodore has already had too much liberty in the use of a horse, and that we have done wrong in sending him the political periodicals, as it would seem to evince regard for his opinions. He thinks not only that Theodore is not recovered, but that it will be a long time before he can recover. He would establish his rationality, before he would permit him to go out into the world again, liable to all its changes and excitements, as firmly as his irrationality was established before. He would make him a sane man, and would make saneness habitual to him. He doubts, as I do, whether Theodore will ever be a useful member of society, for he has not been before. But to turn him now into the world, he thinks would be the destruction of all hopes of permanent recovery: And believes firmly that Theodore would not now even be an innocuous man in society.

The other day Theodore left the asylum and came to Ashland; he was with me a night and parts of two days: While he was there he convinced me that he was not restored. We were about to have a meeting of the commissioners, for the purpose of entrusting him with me until your return. But my own conviction and Dr Dudleys strenous asseveration persuaded me not to make the proposal. Theodore is again in the asylum, and I hope that all our friends, particularly you and my mother will so restrain your feelings as to permit him to remain there

He is certainly better there than any where else. His health is better and he appears more contented and happy than he has been for many years. our affliction and mortification should not impede his recovery. an ill directed affection might destroy him. And in truth, has not his conduct for many years

530

back, been a subject of much greater mortification and humiliation than his present situation?

But after all the humiliation and misfortune is in his insanity and not in his residence at the asylum, which is but the mode of his recovery. I write my opinions sincerely and frankly. disguise to you, a father; and from me a son and brother would be heartless. You must excuse, then, any terms that may have hurt your feelings. Affection for you and for Theodore have equally inspired my words

I have lately had a letter from Thomas [Hart Clay]. He writes that he will leave Clay's prairie for Lexington about the 15th of June. He is in expectation of being called out against Black-Hawk. . . . [2]

ALS. Henry Clay Memorial Foundation, Lexington, Ky.   1. For the Prather family, see Smith and Clay, *The Clay Family*, 178; J. Stoddard Johnston (ed.), *Memorial History of Louisville From its First Settlement to the Year 1896* (New York, 1896), 2:647-49.   2. Henry Clay, Jr., to Clay, April 22, 1832.

From William F. Dunnica, St. Louis, June 8, 1832. Informs Clay that his "Report upon the Public lands [Comment in Senate, April 16, 1832] does not meet the approbation of a majority of Our State. They have heretofore been so entirely devoted to [Thomas Hart] Benton's scheme that every thing that comes in opposition to his views are rejected." Concludes that Clay's plan is seen by his enemies "as a favorable scheme for the Eastern states." ALS. DLC-HC (DNA, M212, R4). For Benton's graduation plan for the public lands, which he had outlined as early as April 28, 1824, see Elbert B. Smith, *Magnificent Missourian* (New York, 1958), 88-91; and Bowers, *Party Battles of the Jackson Period*, 198-200.

Remark in Senate, June 8, 1832. Favors a free bridge and an aqueduct across the Potomac that would link Washington and Alexandria. *Register of Debates*, 22 Cong., 1 Sess., 1053. For discussion of the bridge, see Remark in Senate, June 11, 1832.

Later this day, Clay approves certain controlled uses of a facsimile of the president's signature in order to reduce the "unreasonable amount of mechanical labor . . . imposed on the Chief Magistrate, interfering with duties of an intellectual character." *Register of Debates*, 22 Cong., 1 Sess., 1053.

Remark in Senate, June 9, 1832. Chides the president for doing nothing in response to "the present state of our Northwestern frontier." Comments on this with particular reference to a Senate bill, amended by the House, authorizing the president to raise up to 1,100 mounted volunteer infantrymen for duty in that area. *Register of Debates*, 22 Cong., 1 Sess., 1071. The Black Hawk War had recently erupted in the Northwest. See Prucha, *American Indian Policy*, 181; and Henry Clay, Jr., to Clay, April 22, 1832.

From Fortunatus Sydnor, Lynchburg, Va., June 9, 1832. Asks Clay to give him "such information as you possess" on the current political situations in various states.

Reports that "our hopes in the 'Old Dominion' depend, entirely, upon the dissensions in *the Republican* Wigwam — of which, you know, Tom Ritchie is grand Sachem." Speculates that "there will be two electoral tickets form'd for Jackson. If the one intended for the Support of [James] Barbour's claims should about equally divide the strength of the party we may, very reasonably, calculate on a victory." Warns, however, that such a victory in Virginia against Jackson "will depend upon a very instable ground." ALS. DLC-HC (DNA, M212, R4). Sydnor was for many years cashier of the Virginia Bank in Lynchburg. See Margaret Couch Cabell, *Sketches and Recollections of Lynchburg* (Richmond, Va., 1858), 289-90.

To PETER B. PORTER
Washington, June 11, 1832

I recd. your favor written on board the Chippewa, as I did the preceding one. I sent you the [New York] Evening Journal of the 7h. containing a sort of Manifesto of our friends in the City of N.Y. It is carefully prepared and written in a conciliatory tone well calculated to unite the elements of Opposition in your State. My information from that quarter is very satisfactory. Mr. [Samuel] Stevens from the City of N.Y. was here a few day ago, and expressed to me the opinion that a hearty co-operation would be effected.[1] He told me also that Tracey [sic, Albert H. Tracy] had become more reasonable. Mr. Collier[2] has just returned from the City, and expresses a similar opinion, adding that J[ohn]. C. Spencer has also changed. I believe all the Anti Masons from N.Y. in Congress now heartily enter into the measure, and anticipate its successful issue. The 25h. July being fixed for the Convention of our friends at Utica will afford them an opportunity to be guided by the results of the previous Anti Masonic Convention.[3]

Whilst this favorable state of things exists in N. York, one not less favorable exists in Pennsa. The whole [George] Wolf Section of the Jackson party (believed to comprize a very large majority of the entire party) is thought to be on the eve of a total abandonment of Jackson, and prepared ultimately to come over to us. I have not time to detail all the circumstances that tend to establish the probability of such an event.[4] Our friends in Pennsa. (including Mr. [John] Sergeant) entertain strong hopes of it and much confidence in the success of our ticket.

Our friends here are in high spirits, and those of our opponents are proportionately depressed.

The uncertainty which still continues of the adjournment of Congress prevents my deciding on my route home. I do not believe we shall get off this month. We shall pass the Bank bill[5] in the Senate in a day or two by a majority of eight, if the body is full. I hope it will pass the House, as it will certainly, if its friends do not divide on its details. It is confidently asserted by those who ought to know that Jackson will put his veto on it.[6]

The fate of the Tariff remains in doubt.[7] But I think we shall preserve the principle of adequate protection, whatever else may be done.

ALS. NBuHi. 1. Clay to Weed, April 14, 1832. 2. Probably John Allen Collier. See *BDAC*. 3. Clay to Porter, May 1, 1832. 4. Sergeant to Clay, May 25, 29, 31, and June 2, 1832. 5. Clay to Brown, Dec. 18, 1831; Webster to Clay, Jan. 8, 1832. 6. Clay to Brown, Dec. 18, 1831. 7. Webster to Clay, Jan. 8, 1832.

Remark in Senate, June 11, 1832. Prefers not to comment "at this time" on the general "principles" of a pending proposal by Sen. Littleton W. Tazewell of Virginia to "repeal in part the duties on imports." Will wait until Tazewell presents his tariff bill. *Register of Debates*, 22 Cong., 1 Sess., 1073.

Later this day, Clay speaks on the question of financing a free bridge to be "built on the piers of" an aqueduct from Washington to Alexandria [Remark in Senate, June 8, 1832], a proposal supported also by Senators John Tyler (Va.) and Stephen D. Miller (S.C.). He congratulates those gentlemen on their "union with him on this question of internal improvement," and expresses "the hope that they would extend their new feelings beyond the District [of Columbia]." *Ibid.*, 1074.

At the end of the session, on July 14, 1832, Clay confesses that he felt "no slight solicitude of the subject of this bridge," partly because it was "the first subject on which he ever opened his mouth in this Senate [1:273]." He notes also that the destruction of the old bridge had "caused great inconvenience to the District, and to the transportation of the mail." *Ibid.*, 1296-97. By an act of Congress of February 5, 1808, the Washington Bridge Company was chartered to construct a bridge connecting Washington, D.C., and Alexandria, Va. See 2 *U.S. Stat.*, 457-61. The "Long Bridge" was completed in 1809 but was virtually destroyed by fire on October 29, 1813. In 1833, it was taken over by the government, reconstructed, and reopened as a street of Washington City. Mary G. Powell, *The History of Old Alexandria, Virginia From July 13, 1749 to May 24, 1861* (Richmond, Va., 1928), 233-34.

Comment in Senate, June 13, 1832. On the bill relating to French spoliations of American commerce prior to 1800, argues that U.S. claims on France are "equitable and just. . . . But there would be found to exist great difficulties in settling the amount to be paid." Opposes U.S. government absorption and payment of these claims "dollar for dollar"; but is willing to consider payment in part in year 1800 dollar values. *Register of Debates*, 22 Cong., 1 Sess., 1081-83. The bill on the French spoliation claims was voted down by the Senate on June 13, 1832. U.S. Sen., *Journal*, 22 Cong., 1 Sess., 31.

From CHARLES HAMMOND   Cincinnati, June 13, 1832

It is two years ago, in April last, since I addressed you a letter. I am well aware that, in this lapse of time your kind and confidential feelings toward me have undergone some change. This has induced no change of sentiment, on my part, toward you. Friends are often alienated in consequence of a repugnance, on either part to make the first advance towards explanation! Our cordial & friendly relations shall not be changed by a feeling of this kind — I have nothing to accuse myself with, and am conscious of no reason why I should not address you as a friend.

My life has been devoted to politics rather as a master passion, than from any yearning of the most honorable ambition. I have never wished or sought public employ, either for the pecuniary reward, or that of distinction. Though all ways an ardent actor, I felt myself a disinterested one, and have therefore, (not very modestly perhaps) claimed to be a more impartial Judge of surrounding prospects than others of equal experience. With much experience, without personal interest, totidis viribus opposed to Jackson and to his whole system of administering the government, as soon as that system was developed, I observed intensely, closely, carefully, and reflected earnestly on the best means of defeating his reelection. The result was a clear conviction that no rival candidate, and yourself especially, should be brought into the feild until the affairs of the country should have been understood as they would exist, in the Spring of 1832. To impress this Sentiment upon the public I made Some publications in the [Cincinnati *Daily*] Gazette, in August & September 1829 — [1]This gave great offence to some of your most devoted friends. When, in 1830, movements were made in Kentucky, which finally led to the Baltimore Convention, I again Ventured to express my disapprobation and was again rebuked in no very measured terms — [2]The result of the Kentucky elections of 1831, as I thought, furnished another proper occasion to press my views upon the party with which I considered myself associated. The assaults made upon me at Louisville & Lexington, by new papers established under the auspices of your particular friends provoked some retorts, of an unpleasant character,[3] and I must say to you, my wounded feelings found no balm in the perusal of a letter from you to Mr [James] Conover, in which my "*fidelity*" was gravely discussed,[4] as if I could owe any fidelity distinct from my own conscientious opinions respecting what was the true interests of the country: or as if I could be so much the subject of a party as to be held to conceal my own views and promulgate theirs in the public journal under my charge — I did not, however, permit my self to change my course, I entered under no banner, for I could not brook the terms of fealty which claimed to controul my judgement and silence my voice, at the Same time, unless I would consent to join a chorus to be set for me, by those who stood-forth, and put themselves up as leaders of the party with whom I proposed to act. At this time I was formally denounced in the [Washington *Daily*] National Journal,[5] and from thence I have been under the ban. Still I have steadily pursued the Same course, which led to leaving open the final adjustment of the measures to be taken to about this period. As the Gazette contained my views distinctly expressed or plainly indicated, I supposed that every number you received might be considered as a direct communication to yourself, authorising you, if you wished to do so, to make to me a communication of the lights in which you considered the Subjects presented or suggested. As you said nothing I drew the inference that you approved the movements that I condemned, — and consequently disapproved my publications. This gave me no offence: but furnished no inducement to write to you — Hence my Long Silence.

A large body of your original friends in Ohio have united in the views I have entertained and expressed. We have acted upon these views in different parts of the state, and we claim that by this policy we have so far saved Ohio. We have preserved our Judiciary & Executive and have sent [Thomas] Ewing and [Thomas] Corwin to Congress, at the least. We think that the most effectual mode of subserving the General cause is to take care of affairs in our own State, and that our brethren in other States instead of reading lectures to us, would do better to manage successfully affairs at home —

Before you receive this, you will probably hear from Columbus of some matters now in agitation there. The object is to form a *"coalition"* dont start at the word — with the anti Masons, to take the state from Jackson any how — To give as much as possible to you, not less than two thirds and perhaps all — One principal object of this letter is to request you to assure our common friends that we are not only hearty. in deposing Jackson, but Equally hearty in doing the best we can to sustain the December Nomination at Baltimore. They must allow us to be the best judges of what is the most proper course to take. If no coalition can be formed we shall take the feild in July, and leave nothing in honor unattempted to aid the cause of the Country —

There is difference of opinion amongst us as to the best mode of proceeding. How can it be other wise? Until the feild is set; and the battle in array counsel should be listened to, but in the combat the word of command alone should be heard.

I am a good deal encouraged of late here at home. The Jackson tone is lowered very much. Say to almost any Jackson man of intelligence — You have no heart for Jackson — You whip yourself into his support. You do not feel as you did in 1828 — He will not make admissions in terms: but there is seldom any heart in his negations of what is said — Many smile as though they felt themselves complimented — What party discipline may do, in such a state of feeling, none can conjecture. But there is nothing Very sanguine in making a favorable augury —

ALS. OHi.   1. Clay to Hammond, August 12; Sept. 9, 1829; see also William Henry Smith, *Charles Hammond* . . . (Chicago, 1885), 56-57.   2. Clay to Greene, Nov. 11, 1830.   3. For attacks on Hammond by the Lexington *Observer* and the Louisville *Journal*, see Hammond to Editor, Louisville *Public Advertiser*, Sept. 14, 1831; Sloane to Clay, Sept. 24, 1831.   4. Clay to Conover, August 3, 1831.   5. The Washington *Daily National Journal*, Sept. 22, 1831, condemned Hammond's alleged disloyalty to Clay's cause.

From THOMAS SPEED   Bardstown, Ky., June 13, 1832

I have read with great, & I may say a painful interest, the report of the Com. of the Senate on the public lands. I have for some time viewed this subject as one of dangerous influence, as to the harmony of the Union—perhaps to its peace. I did hope that the report of the Comtee. on Manufactures of the Senate,[1] was calculated, as I have no doubt it was designed, to give to the subject a direction, which would be at once permanent, satisfactory, and salutary—and I yet hope that that direction will not be affected by the other report in the minds of the disinterested. But unfortunately the new States are, or conceive that they are, directly interested—and others I fear are indirectly interested, that is by *keeping the subject open* for discussion, & electioneering—as is to be infered from the character of the report in the H. of Representatives.[2]

With the opinion of the *minority* of the Comtee. of Manufs. as to what should be the disposition of the proceeds of the Public lands, I heartily concur. The community of property in the domain has been, & yet is, a bond of union. When parceled out & sold to individuals for cultivation, the land itself, will come to its proper destiny—whilst the price, laid out in internal improvements, will preserve its character, & perpetuate its office of *bond of Union*—That is, if judiciously expended by the general government on rational objects—But when passed to the States, there is not, neither can be, any security for the manner of its expenditure—whilst even the temporary appropriations of it to the States, may beget in them the dangerous habit of looking to, & leaning on the genl Govt. for ordinary revenue.

One of the other objects of the Comtee., that of colonization,[3] meets also my unqualified assent. It was indeed, to speak on this point, that induced me to give you the trouble of this letter.

The sentiments of the "Comtee. on public lands" on the subject of colonization, affords a melancholy proof of the fatal tendency of error.[4] The danger to be apprehended from the increase of the free colored population—so apparent to calm & disinterested, & unprejudiced minds; The Comtee. say, should be left to the Slave-holding States—That if it is an evil, it is "a burthen which it is theirs to bear, & theirs to remove". The sentiment is as false in fact, as it would be unwise in practice. Though the evil originates with the Slaveholding States, it by no means follows that it is, or will be, confined to them. It is as natural, as it is assuredly common, for the free blacks to emigrate from the scenes, where their very color dooms them to an association with the most degraded portion of the human race. Hence their great numbers in the cities of the free States. And though in these situations, they are in fact less dangerous than if they remained in the Slave States, they form the nucleus of a population, which must inevitably become a nuisance, an annoyance, & ultimately dangerous. But even if the evil from their increase, were (as the sentiment of the Comtee. must suppose) confined to the Slave-States, the duty of the general govt. to provide against it, is not the less imprious resulting from the power "to provide for the common defence & general welfare".

535

There is a wreckless folly, & blindness, in the assumptions of the land Comtee. on the subjects of slavery & colonization, which seems to be the natural & ultimate result of an exemption from personal labor, by the coercion of involuntary servitude. & the consequent erroneous distinction between those who labor & those who do not — tending to a fatal infatuation. I have looked to see during this period of excitement, some bold clear-headed Northern Statesman, rise up & tell to these Southerns their own. To shew to them their real weakness — their arrogance, in using the language of menace to the Union — a union as necessary to them, as to the delicate female, is the arm of the husband to whom she is united. The forbearance of the North & East, can only result from a magnanimity which attends conscious superiority. It is a forbearance which excites my admiration. It is a State of feeling, from which if they are ever driven by the presumption of the south, the latter will have cause to mourn in a State of hopeless dependence.

Besides the habit of command, & of receiving servile obedience from their infancy, inspiring them with the desire to dictate, the Southerns, when they meet in national council, are deceived by their *show of strength*. There indeed, they appear in numbers rather proportioned to their real weakness, than their physical strength. Much has been said, & particularly of late, of the "concessions" & "compromises" made in forming the constitution — but this factitious power, in slave representation, is the only material "concession" that I can discover, except that of the equality of Representation in the Senate. And this, I verily believe was the greatest error committed in the formation of that instrument. The equivalent supposed at the time, of paying direct taxes in proportion to the representation, proves to be deceptious — as those taxes are only occasional, whilst the power is continual. But even if the power & the payment of taxes were of equal duration, the arrangement, or the agreement, was wrong in principle — it was selling power for sordid gold.

I know how apt we are to form opinions favorable to our own theories — perhaps it is oweing to this, that I think I have perceived the tendency of the error, of which I have spoken, to produce the present conflicts so threatening to our future harmony. Of one thing I feel assured, that if the South permit themselves through their infatuation to go so far, as to give to the free States a fair pretext for considering the constitutional compact as broken under no circumstances may they ever expect to enjoy again, that facticious power (so improvidently granted them in the Constitution) of representation for slaves.

But to return to the subject of colonization. I find myself an ultra-Colonizationist in regard to the power, & the duty, of appropriation for that object. I think it would be sound policy, not only to appropriate for the colonization of the free blacks — but also to pay a low price for such slaves as their masters would be willing to liberate for a reasonable compensation in land, on the terms of their being transported. Do not startle at the suggestion till I assign the reasons on which it is founded. By such a measure the Slave States would be benefited, by reducing the number of their Slaves, & thus lessening the danger from internal enemies, in case of future wars & commotions. The new States would be benefited, by an accelleration to their population — because most of those who accepted the terms would emigrate to those States. The free States generally, would find their advantage, in removing a population which sends a representation to the national councils, which hangs as an incubus on their prosperity. They would sanction the measure also from a higher consideration. They are devoted to the cause of freedom — and they would rejoice at the opportunity of confering its blessings on this portion of the human race, at the Small sacrifice of what it might require of their interest in the public domain, when it could be done without a sacrifice of the rights, or the property, of their slave-holding fellow citizens.

Another consideration of yet greater weight ought to animate all the States. It might prove the means of rendering this great Empire, the abode in fact, as it is now only in profession, of Liberty & of the equal rights of man.

The cost of effecting the object by means of the public Lands, would scarcely be felt. The Slaves we will suppose are 2,000,000 — Their average value say 250$. A much less price should be fixed for the government to pay say $150 — This would require but 300,000,000 of acres of land, if all were thus redeemed — leaving of the public domain according to its estimated amount, 790,000,000, & more. But knowing the reluctance with which the present race, & perhaps the next, would part with their Slaves, from their habits. There can be no doubt but that operation of the system would be for very many years exceeding Slow — so much so as that it could not be burdensome.

The power of the genl. Govt. to do so, resolves itself into the same as that which authorises the appropriation for colonization.

The evil of slavery, in both a moral, & political view, is I think the greatest that threatens or afflicts us as a nation. It lies in fact at the foundation, & while it lasts will continue to be the cause of fearful divisions amongst us — That great blessing, the rich inheritance of the public domain, seems in a fair way to be converted into a curse. How happy for the country would it be, if the threatened curse could be averted, & this great blessing enhanced, by making it the means of eradicating that greatest of evils.

I fear my suggestions will subject me to the imputation of extravagance — perhaps enthusiasm — but the cause must secure me from reproach. The suggestion, to be given to the public, I am sensible would not be suitable to the *present* excited State of feeling in a part of our Country — perhaps not suited to any period — Of this no one is better capable of judging than yourself —

Judge [Richard A.] Buckner addressed the people here on the 11th inst — Mr [James T.] Morehead about a fortnight before — both giving much satisfaction. There appears to be little excitement as yet on the subject of the election.[5] The Judge seems confident as to his own, & thinks the prospect favorable as to the presidential election.

May we not expect to hear from you on the prospects before us before you leave Washn. (if indeed you are to leave it at all this summer). I am extremely anxious to know how the standing of Mr [John Q.] Adams is towards you — whether friendly, indifferent, or inimical[6]

I will repeat my request for a copy of the Constitution of the Colonization society having an Auxiliary established here.[7]

ALS. DLC-HC (DNA, M212, R4). 1. Comment in Senate, April 16, 1832; "Report on Public Lands," *Register of Debates*, 22 Cong., 1 Sess., Appendix, 112-118, 120. 2. *House Reports*, 22 Cong., 1 Sess., no. 488 (Report of Committee on Public Lands, April 17, 1832). 3. "Report on Public Lands," *Register of Debates*, 22 Cong., 1 Sess., Appendix, 117. 4. Speed placed an asterisk here and at the bottom of the page added the following note: "That report I take to be the product of a Slave-holder — in principle so." 5. Smith to Clay, Dec. 27, 1831. 6. Crittenden to Clay, Feb. 23, 1832. 7. See 7:505.

From **"A Maine Man,"** Columbus, Ga., June 14, 1832. Suggests that Clay and Calhoun unite, for "to unite is the only way Jack[son]ism can be crushed." Asks Clay, "Should the Calhoun party unite and elect you, would you not be willing after one term to support him?" Mentions that Calhoun has been approached with the same plan. Assures Clay that it is the hope "of your supporters that something should be done to ensure your election." ALS. DLC-HC (DNA, M212, R4). Copy. InHi.

To **BRANTZ MAYER**   Washington, June 17, 1832

I recd. your favor of the 15h. intimating your purpose to compose a Memoir of Daniel Boone, and requesting me to indicate the best sources of information touching your subject.[1] I regret that I cannot give you a very satisfactory answer. I never personally knew Boone. When in 1797 I migrated to Kentucky, he had gone further West. Fond of roaming, and passionately addicted to the Hunter-life, he preferred the forest, where, by felling a tree, he could throw its lap into his Cabbin door. Kentucky therefore was too crowded for him, and he went where he could be in advance of the tide of emigration.

There was a series of numbers, written some seven or eight years ago, by the late Mr. J[ohn]. Bradford and published in the K[entucky]. Gazette at Lexington,[2] detailing early incidents connected with the first settlement of Kentucky. I read them rapidly as they were published, and believe you might gather from them some circumstances respecting Boone. I have not possession of the numbers; but I presume you could obtain a copy by application to Mr. D[aniel]. Bradford of Lexington. You are aware that [Gilbert] Imlay first and [Humphrey] Marshall, more recently, wrote Histories of Kentucky.[3] Neither of them is well written. The first is rare, and I really do not know where it can be procured. Imlay also wrote a bad novel,[4] the title of which I do not recollect. Marshall's history may be easily obtained in K. possibly in some of the Atlantic book stores.

But I presume the best repository of materials for your work is the family of Boone. The members of it are scattered from K. to Missouri. He was also connected with the Calloways, dispersed in the same manner. Mr. [Ratliff] Boone [*sic*, Boon] from Indiana of the H. of R. is a *distant* relative of Daniel, and perhaps could point to accurate sources of information. D. Boone was a native of North Carolina, where there may yet remain some traces of his early life.

Regretting that I can not be more useful to you, and wishing you great success in your undertaking. . . .[5]

ALS. ViU.   1. Mayer wrote Clay on June 15, 1832, asking for advice and assistance in writing a memoir of Daniel Boone which he hoped would result in introducing the West, "the most interesting portion of our Confederacy . . . to our fellow citizens." ALS. DLC-HC (DNA, M212, R4).   2. This series, in 66 installments, ran weekly in the Lexington *Kentucky Gazette* from August 25, 1826, through February 27, 1829.   3. Probably a reference to Imlay's, *A Topographical Description of the Western Territory of North America*. London, 1792. Humphrey Marshall's book was *History of Kentucky*. Frankfort, 1812.   4. Probably a reference to his novel, *The Emigrants*. London, 1793.   5. Although Mayer wrote a number of historical works, there is no evidence that he ever published anything concerning Daniel Boone or Kentucky.

Comment in Senate, June 18, 1832. Points out that consideration of the bill granting Missouri, Mississippi, and Louisiana 500,000 acres of public land each "for the purpose of internal improvement" be postponed until the pending bill [Comment in Senate, April 16, 1832; Speech in Senate, June 20, 1832] on the future disposal of public lands be decided, since both have the same goal. Condemns the "doctrine advanced elsewhere, that the new States had the right to all the lands within their limits, as the doctrine of those who would play demagogue. The public lands, when these States were created, were the property of the United States. They were, and are, the property of the whole community, purchased by common treasure and blood of all." *Register of Debates*, 22 Cong., 1 Sess., 1091-92. The bill was tabled.

From William L. Montague, Richmond, Va., June 18, 1832. Assures Clay that "you are gaining popularity in Virginia very fast and very many look forward with the fondest hopes of seeing you oust the Nest of Vultures that have been sitting in Public places already too long." Predicts that "you will get, if not the vote of our State a most respectable minority." Believes the tariff is the only issue keeping "Virginia from your ranks." Notes that while it is unlikely Virginia will ever support the tariff, "there are many who had rather you should be in [the] Presidential Chair than Genl. Jackson who is anything or nothing as it may suit his views, but oftener Nothing than what suits any but those who are his red hot partizans." Assures Clay that "you are not looked to now, as that great tariff Bug Bear and if you are, the storm is safer in the hands who raised it than he who cannot stear the vessel even in a calm."

Hopes to see Clay attend the political meeting at Hanover. Warns that Thomas Ritchie "will fire off his big gun at you"; however, assures Clay that "you will be honor[e]d and flattered to your souls good." ALS. DLC-HC (DNA, M212, R4).

On June 25, 1832, Francis T. Brooke wrote from Staunton, Va., to suggest that Clay not attend the meeting at Hanover for "in the wavering state of the public mind in Virginia a very little matter may have a bad effect." *Ibid.* For William L. Montague (1781-1839?), captain in the War of 1812, sometime member of the state legislature, see Montague, *History & Geneaogy of Peter Montague*, 103. There is no evidence that Clay attended a proposed testimonial dinner (see Richmond *Enquirer*, June 19, 22, 1832) in Hanover County, Va.

Speech in Senate, June 20, 1832. Thinks the decision to refer the public land bill to the Committee on Manufactures rather than to the Committee on Public Lands [Comment in Senate, April 16, 1832] "extraordinary" and "very unusual" since the members of the latter are "well acquainted with the subject" and "four out of five of them [W.R. King (Ala.), chairman; P. Ellis (Miss.); J.M. Robinson (Ill.); J. Holmes (Me.); R. Hanna (Ind.)] come from the new States." Referral to the Committee on Manufactures was "incongruous" because its members [M. Dickerson (N.J.), chairman; H. Clay (Ky.); S.D. Miller (S.C.); N.R. Knight (R.I.); H. Seymour (Vt.)] included "not a solitary Senator from the new States, and but one from any Western State." This especially embarrasses him because "I alone" among its members was thought to have "particular knowledge" of complex public lands issues. Believes, however, that the committee has done a good job given the circumstances; but complains that its unanimous report and the related bill it submitted to the whole Senate "were hardly read . . . before they were violently denounced." Nor were they considered by the Senate "before a proposition was made to refer the report to that very Committee on Public Lands, to which, in the first instance, I contended the subject ought to have been assigned." The result was that "The Committee on Public Lands . . . presented a report, and recommended a reduction of the price of the public lands immediately to one dollar per acre, and eventually to fifty cents per acre; and the grant to the new States of fifteen per cent. on the nett proceeds of the sales, instead of ten, as proposed by the Committee on Manufactures, and nothing to the old States." Launches into a defense of the report of the Committee on Manufactures and a criticism of the report of the Committee on Public Lands. Expounds at length on the importance to the nation and its future prosperity of the 1,080,000,000 acres of its public domain. Discusses in some detail the history of public land acquisition, administration, regulation, and divestiture at both the state and national levels, noting that much fraud and corruption have attended the sale and purchase processes. Sees the thoughtful disposal of the public domain as the key to the continued national expansion, population growth, internal improvement, agricultural development, and general prosperity in the transmontane west. Observes that "For fifty dollars, any poor man may purchase forty acres of first rate land; and for less than the wages of one year's labor, he may buy eighty acres." Mentions, too, that the federal government has been "liberal and generous" to the new states in its grants of public lands to them "for schools and for internal improvements." Fears the movement, led by Sen. Thomas Hart Benton, "to graduate the public lands, to reduce the price, and to cede the 'refuse' (a term which, I believe, originated with him) to the States within which they lie." Other politicians, "unwilling to be outdone," demand that the states take over all public lands within their boundaries. At the same time, asserts his conviction that if the federal government has "the power to cede the public lands to the new States, for particular purposes, and on prescribed conditions, its power must be unquestionable to make some reservations, for similar purposes, in behalf of the old States. Its power cannot be without limit as to the new States, and circumscribed and restricted as to the old. . . . It may grant to all, or it can grant to none." Traces the historical and constitutional origins of this proposition, and attacks the counter-proposition which argues in part that since "the new States have been admitted into the Union on the same footing and condition, in all respects, with the old, therefore they are entitled to all the waste lands embraced within their boundaries." Holds, further, that "The right of the Union to the public lands is incontestable. It ought not to be considered debatable." Criticizes in detail the recommendation of the Committee on Public Lands to reduce sharply the price of public lands, charging that such reductions will depress the price and value of all land, public and private, in the new states and territories. Adds that so-called "refuse lands" in those areas have remained unsold over the years not because they are "worthless," as claimed by some, but because too much public land has been thrown into the market as the result of political pressure on the government by the new states. To give away such land to transient settlers, or sell it to them for a pittance, or donate it free to the states, as proposed by the Committee on Public Lands, will only advantage land speculators and lead to a "great increase of price to actual settlers in a few years." Indeed, "It is a business, a very profitable business, at which fortunes are made in the new States, to purchase these refuse lands, and, without improving them, to sell them again at large advances." Advises that no changes now be made in the price of public lands or in the present control and administration of the public domain. Defends vigorously the plan brought forth by the Committee on Manufactures to distribute the proceeds from public land sales to all the states. Notes that "the General Government is absolutely embarrassed in providing against an enormous surplus in the treasury. Whilst this is the condition of the Federal Government, the States are in want of, and can most beneficially use, that very surplus with which we do not know what to do." Sees no constitutional difficulty in distributing the income from public land sales to the states, citing Article 4, Section 3 of the Constitution to the point. Also cites historical and legal precedents for granting funds to the several states for education, internal improvements, agricultural development, public buildings, the care of the deaf and dumb, and other good works. Points out that the plan of distribution proposed in the bill submitted by the Committee on Manufactures calls for dividing the net proceeds from public land sales among the states "according to their federal representative population, as ascertained by the last census; and it provides for new States that may hereafter be admitted into the Union. The basis of the distribution, therefore, is derived from the constitution itself, which has adopted the same rule, in respect to representation and direct taxes. None could be more just and equitable." Stresses the equity of the proposed distribution in that it "proposes to assign to the new States, besides the five per cent. stipulated for in their several compacts with the General Government, the further sum of ten per cent. upon the nett proceeds." Announces the sum "each of the seven new States [Ohio, La., Ind., Miss., Ill., Ala., Mo.]" would thus receive. Explains that the new states, "because they populate much faster than the old States," deserve more than the old states; and that "After the deduction shall have been made of the fifteen per cent. allotted to the new States, the residue is to be divided among the twenty-four States, old and new, composing the Union." Each state may decide for itself how to spend its money. "There is no compulsion in the choice." But the recommended areas of expenditure include education, internal improvements, the colonization of free Negroes in Africa, and the extinction of state debt. Urges special consideration of the colonization option. "The evil of a free black population is not restricted to particular States, but extends to, and is felt by all. It is not, therefore, the slave question, but totally distinct from and unconnected with it." Adds that the operation of the bill is limited to five years and that should war break out during that period the distribution of funds will cease. Concludes with the statement that the distribution of public land sales revenues will bind the states to the federal government, raise the moral and intellectual level of the people, facilitate social and commercial intercourse, and generally insure "national greatness." *Register of Debates*, 22 Cong., 1 Sess., 1096-1118. Printed in Colton, *Clay Correspondence*, 5:487-515, with minor variations in punctuation and paragraphing. On July 2, 1832, by a 27 to 20 vote, the Senate voted to split the difference in the distribution percentages to the seven new states proposed by Clay (10 + 5, or 15 percent) and by the Committee on Public Lands (15 + 5, or 20 percent). The compromise was set at 12 ½ + 5, or 17 ½ percent. *Register of Debates*, 22 Cong., 1 Sess., 1164-65; Remark in Senate, July 2, 1832. Also see Comment in Senate, April 16, 1832, and Speech in Senate, December 29, 1835. For the sectional and presidential political implications of this speech, viewed in conjunction with Clay's earlier speech of January 11, 1832, on the Tariff Bill of 1832, see Van Deusen, *The Life of Henry Clay*, 252-55. For Clay's persistent efforts and recurring arguments for the next four years to secure the distribution of public land sales receipts to the states, and the various arithmetic formulae and couplings of issues he devised to promote and regulate such distribution, see Speech in Senate, January 7, 1833; Clay to Wilde, April 27, 1833, footnotes 4 and 5; Speech in Senate, December 5, 1833; Remark in Senate, December 11, 1834; Speech in Senate, December 29, 1835; Speech in Senate, April 26, 1836; Comment in Senate, December 19, 1836.

From George W. Lay, Utica, N.Y., June 21, 1832. Reports that the result of the Anti-Masonic convention [Clay to Porter, May 1, 1832] in New York is "such as must prove entirely satisfactory to you." Assures Clay that "no resolutions were passed by the Convention except such as you would entirely approve of"; and notes that "the delegates are left entirely unshackled & unpledged." States that he and John Spencer "were assigned the preparing the address & resolutions," and adds that "there is not one single sentence to which you would not readily subscribe." Explains that arranging the address so that "the opponents of Jackson might be all persuaded, if not satisfied," while "leaving to the Electors a confiding & discretionary power to act as would . . . most conduce to the interest and welfare of the Nation," were tasks which "called for great discretion, discrimination & judgment."

Includes a list of the presidential electors nominated at the convention and comments that "the instances are very rare in the list of Electors nominated, that the individual is not entirely friendly to you & has never identified himself with the party nominating him." Believes that the fate of the Clay electoral ticket "depends entirely upon the sincerity of your friends in the middle & Southern Districts who if they play the Same game that defeated our candidate for Governor &c at the last election [Stoddard to Clay, November 8, 1830], will certainly blast all your prospects in this State." ALS. DLC-HC (DNA, M212, R4). For Lay, a Whig congressman from New York state from 1833-37, see *BDAC*.

To CHARLES HAMMOND   Washington, June 22, 1832
I recd. with pleasure your letter of the 13h. inst; and I shall answer it in the spirit of friendship and frankness in which it was written.

We differed, you will recollect, in the outset of this Administration, as to the principles on which it should be opposed. You thought we should lie still, do nothing, and leave it to crumble into pieces from its own want of cohesion. I thought that, being vicious in its origin, we should make bold determined and unsparing opposition, in every case in which there was ground for it. You were for relying on the weakness of the adversary; I, on the strength of our cause.

There was much to be said in behalf of each of these systems of policy — so much that no one who adopted one ought to have reproached him who prefered the other.

Perhaps each was best in particular places or States.

But this radical difference between us probably influenced our subsequent opinions.

That I have seen some things to regret — deeply to regret — in your paper [Cincinnati *Daily Gazette*] I must frankly own. Your dissatisfaction, but especially the manner of it, with the last K. election gave me pain.[1] Our friends there were disappointed and mortified. Why taunt them with their misfortunes? If their previous confidence had been too great, as the result shewed, it was not therefore insincere. In such a case, from friends oil and not vinegar might have been expected.

I thought your opposition to the Balto. Convention impolitic.[2]

Your late recommendation of the Anti Masonic Candidate seemed to me injudicous.[3] Undoubtedly if *all* the N. Republicans would heartily unite with *all* the Anti Masons, the union might effect the election of Mr. [William] Wirt. And most sincerely would I rejoice at his election, or that of any other fair man instead of the present encumbent. But could any one believe it possible that the N. Republicans could en masse be wheeled round, like a military corps, and at the command March forward place themselves under the banner of Mr. Wirt?

Why did not Col. [Edward] King of your City declare — have not many others of the N.R. party declared — a preference even for Jackson, bad as he is, rather than Mr. Wirt, under all the circumstances of the case?

An union between those two parties certainly is most desirable, if it can be effected. There ought to be less difficulty in the Anti Masons coming to us than there is in our going to them. Difficulties, undoubtedly, there are in both cases. We are the more numerous party; & the most extensive party, geographically considered. Both parties agree as to general politics. The N.R. party believes, on the only point which separates the two (Anti Masonry) that the Genl. Govt. has no constitutional power over the subject. The Anti Masons have not attempted even to shew such a power. They claim the right to use the ballot box as they please and they have undeniably such a right. But what further?

The time too of the appearance of your article was unfortunate, as I think. It was at the moment of consummation of a plan of cooperation between the two parties in N. York.[4] Whether it has had any effect on that plan or not I know not. But is there not reason to fear that, by exciting delusive hopes in Ohio, it may have contributed to the recent formation of an Anti Masonic ticket, which is understood here to have been put there in circulation?[5]

I have seen many Anti Masons here from the North, some of them highly intelligent. I have not seen one that entertains the smallest expectation of the election of Mr. Wirt. Most of them are with us and anxious for our success.

542

You say, I must have observed the course of your paper, and did not write you. True. But, my dear Sir, what right had I to attempt to control you? We differed on some points radically. That we both knew. I respected too much your estimate of your own independence (a quality which nobody can estimate too highly) to admit of the least interference on my part in the conduct of your journal.

One thing does surprise me; and that is your commentary upon an unfortunate word, as it seems, in my letter to Majr. [James] Conover. Certainly, in announcing my perfect confidence in your possession of a virtue, which I above most men ought highly to esteem, nothing could have been farther from my conception than that it should have been supposed I meant to cast a reflection.

But this review of the past is unprofitable and painful. It is not adverted to, with any unkind intention.

At this time our prospects are very bright. The Anti Masonic Convention met yesterday in N. York.[6] I have seen here Mr. [Samuel] Stevens (who will be their Candidate for Lieut Govr.) a member of the Convention, and many other Anti's. All these unite in the opinion, entertained also by our own friends, that there will be presented by the Convention such an Electoral ticket, composed of both parties, as can be supported by both parties. Should that be done, there is scarcely a doubt of the success of that ticket.[7]

In Pennsa. the [George] Wolf section of the Jackson party is secretly opposed to Jackson, and it is believed by Mr. [John] Sergeant and others will finally co-operate with our friends.[8]

Maine is revolutionized by the question of the. N E. boundary.[9]

A storm is getting up in Virginia and No. Carolina about the V. Presidency.[10]

Mr. Calhoun and others say So. Carolina will be neutral, and will not vote at all. As the majority there hates Jackson more than any one else my opinion is that they will give their vote in such manner as to defeat him, if it can be made to defeat him.[11]

ALS. InU.   1. Sloane to Clay, Sept. 24, 1831.   2. *Ibid.*; Clay to Conover, Oct. 9, 1831.
3. Metcalfe to Clay, May 7, 1832.   4. Clay to Weed, April 14, 1832; Clay to Porter, May 1, 1832.   5. The Anti-Masons in Ohio had held a convention and nominated a ticket on June 12, 1832. McCarthy, "Anti-Masonic Party," 1:528; Vaughn, *The Antimasonic Party in the United States,* 155-58.   6. Clay to Porter, May 1, 1832.   7. Rush to Clay, June 1, 1831.   8. Clay to Ketchum, May 15, 1832.   9. For an account of the new negotiations on the Northeastern boundary, see Henry S. Burrage, *Maine in the Northeastern Boundary Controversy* (Portland, Me., 1919), 201-11; see also, 6:1100-1101, 1272-74.   10. Brooke to Clay, Feb. 9, 1832; Clay to Porter, March 10, 1832. At the Democratic convention, North Carolina gave six of her votes to James Barbour for vice president and nine to Van Buren. Washington *Globe,* May 24, 1832.
11. All of South Carolina's electoral votes went to John Floyd of Virginia. Gammon, *The Presidential Campaign of 1832,* 170.

Remark in Senate, June 22, 1832. Successfully opposes an amendment to the internal improvements bill that would strike out an appropriation to improve navigation on the Cumberland River, especially near the important port of Nashville. Attempts unsuccessfully to amend the bill to improve further the navigation of the James River below Richmond, Va. *Register of Debates,* 22 Cong., 1 Sess., 1120, 1122-23.

To CHARLES PERROW   Washington, June 23, 1832
I have to acknowledge the receipt of your favor of the 18h. inst. and to thank you for the information which it contains.[1]

In the sentiments of regret for the [u]nhappy differences of opinion about the Tariff, and of desire that it should be amicably adjusted all ought to unite.

The difficulty is in finding some principles which can form the basis of a sa[tis]factory adjustment. It is evident that between those who conte[n]d for the policy of protection, in some form, and those who reject it in every form there can be no accommodation. Is there any medium? That is the problem to be solved, and a few days will determine it, so far as Congress at present can determine it.

Holding myself firmly to the power and to the policy of protection, I cannot consent to abandon it. But if any modification can be made, without impairing the value of protection, I should most readily concur in it. Ineffectual protection is as bad, if not worse, than no protection. It would cripple the manufacturer and injure the consumer.

A few days will decide whether a reconcilliation be practicable;[2] and I most earnestly wish that it may be effected.

Copy. KyU.   1. Perrow was a resident of Lovingston, Nelson County, Va.   2. Webster to Clay, Jan. 8, 1832.

From William L. Stone, New York, June 23, 1832. Sends Clay samples of cotton jean vestings, "printed with [colors] warranted to stand," from a merchant in New York City, in order that their quality and "actual cheapness be made known to the opponents of our Manufactures." Reports that the vesting sells for "only 16 ¾ cents per pattern, of ¾ ths of a yard for the first quality; and 15 ½ cents per ditto for the second." Also includes a piece of "American calico," pointing out that its cost is "only nineteen cents per yard." Suggests that another piece of the calico, along with its price, be presented to South Carolina Sen. Robert Y. Hayne "at some fitting moment." Affirms that the "exceedingly low price" of these articles provides the "most convincing argument against this southern heresy" of contending that "in all cases the consumer is obliged to pay for the protected article the whole amount of the duty, in addition to the intrinsic value of the article itself." ALS. DLC-HC (DNA, M212, R4).

From Lee White, Louisville, Ky., June 23, 1832. Suggests that there is little "excitement in this State upon the subject of politics . . . but it must not be inferred . . . that there is any abatement in the inter[est] felt or in the determination to do o[ur] duty when the time comes [at the] polls." Attributes the lack of excitement to "the fact that the errors and inconsis[tencies] of the dominant party have been m[ade] so plain that but few remain" who are willing to defend it. Assures Clay that "Kentucky will do her [d]uty."

Reports on a public meeting of former supporters of Jackson held in Louisville the previous evening. Informs Clay that resolutions "expressing the reasons of their form[er] support & present opposition, were unanimously adopted & will be published"; also reports that a resolution supporting the nominations of the National Republicans for president and vice president was passed with "'one small voice' only voting in the negative."

Concludes with complimentary remarks on Clay's report on the public lands [Comment in Senate, April 16, 1832] and hails the anticipated passage of the bill to recharter the bank [Webster to Clay, January 8, 1832]. ALS. DLC-HC (DNA, M212, R6). For a summary of the Louisville meeting and the resolutions, including one supporting Clay, see Lexington *Observer & Kentucky Reporter*, July 5, 19, 1832.

From Harrison Gray Otis, Boston, Mass., June 25, 1832. States that the tariff bill which has passed the committee will be "ruinous" to the woolen interest. Suggests that "If the 40Cent goods which are to be free, (almost) could be brot under the duty of 50prCent ad valorem; and the 40Cent provision be reduced to 30—and if the protection of 50 prCent could be extended to flannels & serges, they might struggle through." ALS. DLC-HC (DNA, M212, R4). See Taussig, *Tariff History of the United States*, 104-6.

544

Remark in Senate, June 25, 1832. Comments on news of Spain's abolition of discriminating duties on U.S. ships, conditional on similar treatment of Spanish vessels in American ports. Notes, however, that the Spanish do not include Cuba or other of their islands in the new arrangement, and warns that Spain would "soon monopolize" the trade with her islands unless the U.S. also insists on reciprocity there. *Register of Debates*, 22 Cong., 1 Sess., 1124.

Later this day, Clay supports a bill appointing a recorder for the General Land Office and providing a facsimile means of signing and issuing patents for public lands. Says the president spends too much of his valuable time signing patents, "instead of his being occupied with the great concerns of the country." *Ibid.*, 1125-26.

Still later this day, Clay supports an appropriation of $5,000 for a marble, full length pedestrian statue of Gen. George Washington to be placed in the rotunda of the Capitol. Laments the fact that Washington's remains cannot be moved to Washington [Comment in Senate, February 13, 1832; Remark in Senate, February 14, 1832], "the centre of the Union." *Ibid.*, 1127.

From Peter H. Schenck, New York, June 26, 1832. Comments upon John Q. Adams's version of the tariff bill [Clay to Porter, May 1, 1832], saying, "the bill of Mr. Adams had better be accepted . . . than to have the Subject again agitated at another Session." Believes that "the Woolen Manufacturers have not received as good a Protection as they will under this bill," and that "the greatest of all the advantages is the Cash duties" which "will put an immediate stop to the Gambling importations that flood the Country to raise Money for English Bankrupt Manufacturers." Continues: "I take it for granted that if this bill passes, the Tariff Question will be put to rest for some Years . . . that alone is of the greatest importance."

Assures Clay that "there are but few Men in the Country have more pecuniary interest at Stake than I have, or are more conversant with the Cause of the depression of our Manufacturers." Describes instances of fraud, detailing specific cases, and mentions other problems with the present tariff system. Suggests that many importers who engage in illegal schemes to realize profits of over 100 percent "are represented as being wealthy men, & respectable." ALS. DLC-HC (DNA, M212, R4).

On the following day, Schenck again wrote Clay to discuss Adams's version of the tariff bill. Comments upon the problems of the dollar minimum standard [Brown to Clay, October 23, 1829], and states that "the Manufacturers cannot sustain themselves during its continuance." Reiterates certain concerns with rates and fraud discussed in his letter of June 26, 1832. *Ibid.*

Remark in Senate, June 27, 1832. Opposes resolution permitting the assistant doorkeeper of the Senate to be a witness before a House committee. *Register of Debates*, 22 Cong., 1 Sess., 1128.

Later this day, Clay asks for support of a resolution requesting the president to designate a day of "general humiliation and prayer" that God in His mercy might "avert from our country the Asiatic scourge [cholera] which is now traversing and devastating other countries," or at least "meliorate the infection" should it be His will "to inflict this scourge upon our land." *Ibid.*, 1128-29. The Senate passed the resolution by a vote of 30 to 13 on June 28. *Ibid.*, 1132. The House of Representatives, on a motion by John Q. Adams, tabled the resolution on July 14, 1832. U.S. H. of Reps., *Journal*, 22 Cong., 1 Sess., 1182.

The first case of Asiatic cholera on the North American continent appeared in Canada in early June of 1832. It rapidly spread southward; by late June it was in New York City, by July in Norfolk and Philadelphia and by August in Natchez. It did not strike Lexington until the summer of 1833. At that time, it raged in the city for two weeks and caused about 350 deaths. Dudley Atkins (ed.), *Reports of Hospital Physicians, and Other Documents in Relation to the Epidemic Cholera of 1832* (New York, 1832), 8, 12;

University of Kentucky Library Associates, *Cholera in Lexington* (Lexington, 1963), *passim*. See also, Nancy D. Baird, "Asiatic Cholera's First Visit to Kentucky: A Study in Panic and Fear," *FCHQ* (July, 1974), 48:228-40; and Baird, "Asiatic Cholera: Kentucky's First Public Health Instructor," *FCHQ* (October, 1974), 48:327-41.

Still later this day, Clay speaks to a proposed amendment to the land bill [Comment in Senate, April 16, 1832; Speech in Senate, June 20, 1832] that would award to the seven new states an additional allowance of 15 percent of the income from public lands sales above and beyond the usual 5 percent each new state normally received when it entered the Union. Explains that the land bill reported by the Committee on Manufactures calls for an additional payment of 10 percent to the new states, whereas the bill reported by the Committee on Public Lands recommends 15 percent. Supports the 10 percent figure. *Register of Debates*, 22 Cong., 1 Sess., 1129.

Comment in Senate, June 28, 1832. Expands his observations of June 27 on the cholera menace, pointing out that to "implore Divine mercy" in such matters has been "the practice of all christian nations." Notes that the resolution is "recommendatory" rather than "obligatory" upon the president. Traces recent spread of the disease in Asia and Europe. Concludes: "A single word . . . as to myself. I am a member of no religious sect. I am not a professor of religion. I regret that I am not. I wish that I was, and I trust I shall be. But I have, and always have had, a profound respect for christianity, the religion of my fathers, and for its rites, its usages, and its observances. Among these, that which is proposed in the resolution before you has always commanded the respect of the good and devout; and I hope it will obtain the concurrence of the Senate." *Register of Debates*, 22 Cong., 1 Sess., 1130-31.

To FRANCIS T. BROOKE   Washington, June 29, 1832
It has been some time since I had the pleasure of addressing you. Since then every thing has gone on in N. York even *better* than I anticipated. The electoral ticket has been formed, satisfactory to our friends, which will be supported by them and the Anti Masons and which it is confidently believed *will be elected.*[1]

Pennsa. continues daily to exhibit signs of the most cheering character,[2] and there is great reason to *hope* that she is lost to Genl. Jackson.

A Tariff[3] has passed the H. of R. by a large majority. It will finally pass the Senate, with or without modifications. It is a law, which with some alterations, will be a very good measure of protection.

The Bank bill[4] will, I think, pass the Senate in a few days; and if Jackson is to be believed he will veto it.

Congress will adjourn on the 9h. or 16h. most probably on the latter day. Afterwards I believe I shall go to the White Sulphur Springs, but it may not be until the 1st. of Aug. that I shall reach them. I hope I shall find you there.

ALS. NcD. Printed in Colton, *Clay Correspondence*, 4:340.   1. Clay to Porter, May 1, 1832. 2. Clay to Ketchum, May 15, 1832.   3. Webster to Clay, Jan. 8, 1832.   4. *Ibid.*; Clay to Brown, Dec. 18, 1832.

Remark in Senate, June 29, 1832. Successfully moves to amend slightly a resolution to have the statistics in the House version of the tariff bill presented to the Senate in a particular mathematical format. *Register of Debates*, 22 Cong., 1 Sess., 1154-55.

To JAMES F. CONOVER   Washington, June 30, 1832.
I recd. your favor of the 11h. inst. and thank you for the information which it contains respecting public affairs in Ohio. Some things stated by you are to be regretted, but I yet hope all will go well with you. I see the Anti Masonic party

has formed an Electoral ticket in your State.[1] I presume it will hardly be pre-servered in. In N. York you will have seen that a cordial co-operation has been effected which promises the best result for our cause. It is confidently believed that the joint ticket will be elected by a large majority.[2] I trust that this example of harmony between two parties who think alike on National politics will have salutary effect every where. Much confidence is felt here that Pennsa. has left Jackson and that the N. R. party will obtain its vote. If, as rumor asserts will certainly be the case, Jackson should veto the Bank bill,[3] Pennsa. will beyond all doubt leave him. He will be put to the test on that measure in a few days.

The effect of late events has been such as to animate our friends with the highest hopes of success, and to depress our opponents in a like proportion. It is my deliberate opinion that we shall prevail in the pending contest.

We shall pass the Tariff in the Senate,[4] sent to us from the House, with some modifications. And I am not without hopes that the Land bill will also pass, as reported by the Comee of Manufactures.[5] If it should not pass, it will be from the want of time.

The adjournment of Congress has been fixed by the House at the 9h. but I think it will not be before the 16h.

ALS. ViU.   1. Clay to Hammond, June 22, 1832.   2. Clay to Porter, May 1, 1832.
3. Clay to Brown, Dec. 18, 1831.   4. Webster to Clay, Jan. 8, 1832.   5. Comment in Senate, April 16, 1832; Speech in Senate, June 20, 1832.

From Hiram Ketchum, New York, June 30, 1832. Reports on the proceedings of the New York Anti-Masonic convention [Clay to Porter, May 1, 1832]. Informs Clay that "the electors nominated are better than was expected." Believes that "more than one half of the persons named" are "avowed National republicans, who are not under any obligations express or implicd, from any promises or acts of theirs to vote for Mr [William] Wirt." Speculates that at least one half "of the persons named on that ticket [Anti-Masonic], will if elected, vote for you; and if Mr Wirt is out of the field every vote will be given for you, except perhaps, that of J[ohn] C Spencer."

Is not satisfied with the address of the convention, "so far as it indicates the course the electors are expected to pursue." Points out, however, that "this Convention had a difficult part to perform."

Suggests that if Clay believes Wirt will withdraw his candidacy, "the fact of such assurance ought to be made known extensively to confidential friends in this State." Is confident that although "great pains are required, great sacrifises of personal feeling must be made, private individuals, especially masons, must be labored with," your supporters "have it in their power to elect their ticket, by a handsome majority."

Recommends that Peter B. Porter be requested to use his influence in the western counties, and that Matthew L. Davis "return to N.Y. and do what he could for the Common Cause." Suggests that if Davis "will return here whatever of pecuniary compensation can be named for his servic[es] I will endeavor to procure."

Concludes with news on the possible date of the New York National Republican convention [Clay to Porter, May 1, 1832]. ALS. DLC-HC (DNA, M212, R4).

From Hugh Mercer, Fredericksburg, Va., June 30, 1832. Believes that prospects for success in Pennsylvania and New York are "very cheering." Speculates that if Clay is not successful in the present election, he will "*succeed* Genl J[ackso]n, should the vote of the Country place him again at the Head of the Government for another term of four years." Discusses Van Buren's bid for the vice presidency, and remarks that he has "an eye to the Successorship." Trusts, however, that his recall from Great Britain [Clay to

Brooke, May 1, 1831] will, "in all future time," undermine "the political Pretensions of this Person."

Reports to Clay that he "was much pleased to observe that your presence with the young men in Convention [Steuart to Clay, May 10, 1832], was carried into effect agreeably to their resolution."

Concludes with the observation that Clay has been invited to Hanover, Va. [Montague to Clay, June 18, 1832], and believes that he "would be invigorated" by such a visit. ALS. DLC-HC (DNA, M212, R4).

From Lucy L. Minor, Fredericksburg, Va., June 30, 1832. Thanks Clay for his prayer and fasting resolution [Remark in Senate, June 27, 1832]. Is thus certain he also appreciates the need for appointing chaplains to serve "our troops stationed on the Frontier — many of them so situated as never to hear the sound of the Gospel." Believes that through the influence of a chaplain, it could be shown "that the life of a Soldier is not inconsistant with that of a Christian." ALS. DLC-HC (DNA, M212, R4). Lucy L. Minor, a blind widow, was the mother of Lt. Charles L.C. Minor, a graduate of West Point in 1826, who died in the Indian Territory in 1833.

Remark in Senate, June 30, 1832. Opposes "indefinite postponement" [tabling] of the public lands bill [Comment in Senate, April 16, 1832]. *Register of Debates*, 22 Cong., 1 Sess., 1160.

From John Noel, Clinton Township, Jackson County, Ohio, July 1, 1832. Asks Clay to be more vigorous in denying that he had entered into a bargain with Adams in February, 1825, which had made him secretary of state. Thinks it might also be pointed out to the electorate than in its first three years the Jackson administration spent $10,000,000 more of the public money than had Adams in a comparable period. Urges Clay to "publish the truth" in these matters, but in language that those with "the weakest capacity may understand." Adds that "there is [a] goodly number that are ignorant . . . and blinded by prejudice in favor of the Hero." Asks also for full information on several controversial patronage issues, because "I mean and intend to do all I can to secure your election this fall." ALS. DLC-HC (DNA, M212, R4).

Remark in Senate, July 2, 1832. Opposes an amendment to the public lands bill increasing from 10 percent to 15 percent the public land sales receipts to be distributed to the seven new states [Speech in Senate, June 20, 1832; Remark in Senate, June 27, 1832]. Defends the 10 percent figure and the recommended uses of the monies — for colonization, internal improvements, and education — to be distributed to all the states. But after further discussion agrees to a compromise 12 ½ percent distribution percentage for the new states. Urges his colleagues to get on with the Senate's business so that the land bill as well as the tariff bill can come to a final vote before the session ends. *Register of Debates*, 22 Cong., 1 Sess., 1161-66.

Comment in Senate, July 3, 1832. Makes intermittent observations on various proposed amendments to the tariff bill. Points out that the bill might be rendered "more grammatical, but not more intelligible." Also states that South Carolina Sen. Robert Y. Hayne was in error when he charged that additional speeches against the tariff would be "in vain" because there was "an organized majority in Congress bound to carry the protective system." Argues that the tariff bill as amended was "better for the North, better for the South, and better for all the country." *Register of Debates*, 22 Cong., 1 Sess., 1174-80.

Comment in Senate, July 4, 1832. Supports appropriations for a breakwater at Lake Pontchartrain in Louisiana and for removing obstructions in the James River below

Richmond, Va. Chides President Jackson for supporting federal expenditures for local harbor development after having vetoed the equally local Maysville [Johnston to Clay, May 26, 1830] and Rockville Road bills. *Register of Debates*, 22 Cong., 1 Sess., 1181-84. For the Washington and Rockville Turnpike bill, see *Register of Debates*, 21 Cong., 1 Sess., 456, 1148; U.S. Sen., *Journal*, 21 Cong., 1 Sess., 356-57, 360, 381-83. For Jackson's veto message, see *MPP*, 2:293-94.

From John Connell, Philadelphia, July 4, 1832. States that he has "just returned from the great National Republican Dinner at Powelton, where about One Thousand of our fellow citizens were seated at the festive Board." Reports that "Influenced by one feeling, & animated by one hope, a spontaneous burst of applause succeeded every mention of your name." ALS. DLC-HC (DNA, M212, R4). The National Republican dinner was held at the estate of John Hare Powel near Philadelphia. Philadelphia *United States Gazette*, July 7, 1832.

From "A Daughter of Massachusetts," Washington, July 4, 1832. Writes "to offer you my sincere acknowledgment, for your recent [June 28] noble, and spirited avowal, of your belief of the Christian religion, and your reverence for its precepts; and I can assure you Sir, that a large majority of the daughters of the descendants of the Pilgrims unite with me in the same sentiment." ALS. DLC-HC (DNA, M212, R4). Printed in Colton, *Clay Correspondence*, 4:340. See Comment in Senate, June 28, 1832.

From Hezekiah Niles, Baltimore, July 4, 1832. States that "I shall send by this mail, addressed to Mr. [Mahlon] Dickerson, as chairman of the committee on manufactures, a memorial of the Central Committee of the *New York Convention* [Davis to Clay, November 11, 1831] concerning the tariff bill [Webster to Clay, January 8, 1832; Speech in Senate, February 2, 1832]." Notes that "this little effort is made to support *you. . . .* do with it what you think best." Continues: "I will not speak of the land bill [Speech in Senate, June 20, 1832; Clay to Niles, July 8, 1832], as I think. 'The bitter is bitter'—'roses have been gathered from thistles.' The bank too [Clay to Brown, December 18, 1831; Webster to Clay, January 8, 1832]! Our friends have, indeed, fought the 'good fight', nobly. And now the tariff bill amended as to woollens, canvas, slates, & some chemicals, &c. will, indeed, crown all in a *'blaze of glory!'* I thank you for what has been done. . . . All a-head looks beautiful. The tide has been turned, & the 'flood' is with us."

Reports that "We have gotten up an arrangement for Maryland. . . . & in spite of great discouragements, we shall do well." Concludes: "This has been a day of public prayer in Maryland [Remark in Senate, June 27, 1832]. My good & dear little wife attended Mr. [John P.H.] Henshaw's church — & said she heard a 'Clay sermon.' One of my friends was at Mr. [John] John's Church (also Episcopal) and says he heard an 'American System' sermon! Perhaps their own associations of ideas may have influenced their impressions. My wife is an 'entire' 'Clay man'—that is as much of a man as a gentle woman can be. Your little namesake often says, when I return home in the evening— 'Papa I've been a Clay boy, all day!' By this he means to say that he has been a good one." ALS. DLC-HC (DNA, M212, R4). Jackson defeated Clay 19,199 to 19,150 in Maryland and captured 3 of its electoral votes to 5 for Clay. Edward Stanwood, *A History of the Presidency* (New York, 1898), 164; Gammon, *The Presidential Campaign of 1832*, 170. For the memorial of the New York convention, see *Niles' Register* (March 31, 1832), 42:76; and *Memorial of the New York Convention, to the Congress of the United States. Presented March 26, 1832, and Referred to the Committee on Manufactures. . . .* Baltimore, 1832. For John Prentiss Kewley Henshaw, see *CAB*; for John Johns, see *DAB*.

From Louis B. C. Serurier, Washington, July 4, 1832. Writes because of his conviction that France and the United States share common economic interests. Notes specifically that "you could not cause irreparable damage to our great industry in Lyon, without suffering an immediate blow to the immense trade you do there with your cotton and labor." Suggests that it would be beneficial to improve trade with China by lowering the tariff on Chinese goods from 36 to 20 percent and on goods from France from 22 to 10 percent. Believes that in so doing "not a single interest would be hurt, neither in China (though we must see China as a rival) nor the United States nor in France." Promises, as French minister in Washington, that his nation would be willing to negotiate "on that which the United States can still want from us." Adds in a postscript: "I have been told that the administration would support whatever you proposed which would make article 19 [*sic*] the least damaging to our manufacture in Lyon." ALS, in French, trans. by Mrs. Siglinde Couch. DLC-HC (DNA, M212, R4). Reference to "article 19" is obscure; there was no article so numbered in the tariff acts of 1828, 1832, or 1833. The great industry in Lyon was silk and assorted textiles. John N. Tuppen, *Studies in Industrial Geography: France* (Kent, England, 1980), 137. The Tariff Act of 1828 had set a duty of 30 percent *ad valorem* on silk with an additional 5 percent to be levied after June 30, 1829. The Tariff Act of 1832 reduced the silk duty to 10 percent. In the Compromise Tariff Act of 1833, all goods from France and China were exempt from duties. 4 *U.S. Stat.*, 272, 588, 630.

From Samuel Meeker, Pittsburgh, July 5, 1832. Offers his political services and influence to Clay in the coming election, even though he also esteems Jackson highly and "should like to see you both Presidents." Inquires about his claim for part of the "large Sum of money advanced Genl James Wilkinson to Sustain the army in the alleged Burr conspiracy." Complains that the Committee on Claims has never read the "voluminous" papers and evidences in the case; remarks that he is near economic "ruin" as a result; and asks that a congressional "resolution be passed to advance me $20000.00 on the Claim." ALS. DLC-HC (DNA, M212, R4). For Meeker, see *PMHB*, 53:380. After receiving an unfavorable report from the House Committee of Claims, Meeker's petition for reimbursement for supplies furnished the U.S. Army in 1806-7 was read and laid on the table. U.S. H. of Reps., *Journal*, 21 Cong., 1 Sess., 99; *ibid.*, 22 Cong., 1 Sess., 477; *Reports of Committees*, 21 Cong., 1 Sess., no. 244.

Remark in Senate, July 5, 1832. Supports increase in duty on cotton bagging and the levy of a duty of ten cents per pound on tea imported from places west of the Cape of Good Hope or in foreign flag vessels. *Register of Debates*, 22 Cong., 1 Sess., 1186, 1190.

From Peter B. Porter, Black Rock, N.Y., July 6, 1832. Discusses his recent trip to Kentucky where he found that Clay's friends "appear to be in good spirits & confident of success in the approaching election." Regarding New York politics, states that "so far as I am acquainted with the men who compose the Anti Masonic Electoral Ticket, and I know about one third of them personally, they will if elected, vote for you, and from the whole complexion of the ticket, I have no doubt but that it was formed throughout with that intent. From partial conversations with some of my friends since my arrival and from some letters which I have received—written however before or about the time of the A-Masonic Convention [Clay to Porter, May 1, 1832]—I believe that their ticket will be adopted by *our* Convention, and, if so, receive the united support of the two parties." ALS. DLC-HC (DNA, M212, R4).

Remark in Senate, July 6, 1832. Supports an amendment to the tariff bill establishing a specific minimum duty of 35 percent on various grades of woolen cloth. Argues that such an amendment would benefit the South since the actual administration of a specific minimum duty is more precise, free of fraud, and efficient than is the administration of an ad valorem duty. Also, that the operation of this particular amendment "would be principally on the middle classes in the North and the East; so that the burden and the benefit would go together." *Register of Debates*, 22 Cong., 1 Sess., 1195.

On this same day, Clay also supported raising to 60 percent ad valorem the duty on all woolens to which the minimum did not apply. Pointed out "at some length" that an increasing number of farmers were entering the sheep-raising business and that he hoped "the sheep would not be made scapegoats." *Ibid.*, 1199.

Remark in Senate, July 7, 1832. Speaks and votes for an increase in the tariff on cotton bagging. States that he cannot vote for Sen. John Forsyth's motion to repeal all tariff legislation save the act of 1824, thus leaving the tariff question to the next session of Congress. Suggests to Forsyth that it would be better for him to "move an indefinite postponement of the bill [Webster to Clay, January 8, 1832; Speech in Senate, January 11; February 2, 1832]" as a "more parliamentary" approach to his goal. *Register of Debates*, 22 Cong., 1 Sess., 1202, 1204-5.

To HEZEKIAH NILES Washington, July 8, 1832
I recd. your favor of the 4h. inst. Mr. [Mahlon] Dickerson has not shewn me the memorial.[1] Perhaps he has forgotten to do so, in consequence of the rapid succession and absorbing interest of the events of the last week. Yesterday, by a vote of 31 to 15 the Tariff, as amended in the Senate was ordered to a third reading.[2] The improvements in the Senate were essential and cost us to obtain them extraordinary exertions. We failed in the Woolen minimum, by which the dollar grade would have been stricken out; but then we got the duty augmented from 50 to 57 per Cent. Carpenting [?] was preserved; the sugar duty; the Cotton bagging as *I* wished it; Slates, Chemicals &c &c &c. The pitiful duty of 1 Cent upon tea, by which in marking, weighing and certifying more would have been expended by the Treasury than received, and the ½ Cent on Coffee were expunged. The duty on wines and silks was lowered; French silk, upon the motion of [Littleton W.] Tazewell, supported by Forsythe [*sic*, John Forsyth] [Samuel] Smith &c, having been brought down to five per Cent.

Thus, my dear Sir, has every principle for which I contended at the commencement of the Session been substantially adopted. 1st. The principle of adequate protection, except, as in the case of Negro woolens, where it was voluntarily abandoned. 2 The reduction of duties has been placed principally on the unprotected articles. 3. The duty on wines and silks has been greatly reduced and that by the concurrence, and in the case of Silk at the instance of those who in the debate on my resolution declaimed against reducing duties on luxuries.

My land bill[3] was defeated in the House only for want of time and from party spirit.

The Session has indeed been one of a succession of glorious triumphs for the Country and our cause.

I am happy to hear that our friends in Maryland are preparing for battle Our prospects every where are bright and brightening The Veto of the Bank bill,[4] expected tomorrow, will I think finish the work.

My best respects to Mrs. Niles, and kiss my little namesake. . . .

ALS. DLC-HC (DNA, M212, R4). 1. Niles to Clay, July 4, 1832. 2. Webster to Clay, Jan. 8, 1832. For the Tariff Act of 1832, see 4 *U. S. Stat.*, 583-94. 3. Comment in Senate, April 16, 1832; Speech in Senate, June 20, 1832. 4. Clay to Brown, Dec. 18, 1831.

From Samuel L. Southard, Trenton, N.J., July 8, 1832. Asks for a copy of "your Speech on the Land question [Comment in Senate, April 16, 1832]" when it appears in pamphlet form. Adds that "we are anxiously waiting for the action of the Pres[iden]t" on the bank bill [Clay to Brown, December 18, 1831; Webster to Clay, January 8, 1832], and predicts "His *veto* [Clay to Fendall, August 4, 1832] will act severely against him."

Notes "We are a good deal anxious about the Cholera [Remark in Senate, June 27, 1832]—It is certainly in N. York to such an extent as to give just cause for alarm." ALS. InU. For the report of the Committee on Manufactures on the proposed land bill, see Comment in Senate, April 16, 1832.

Remark in Senate, July 9, 1832. Moves to postpone the date of adjournment from today, July 9, as resolved by the House, to July 16. *Register of Debates*, 22 Cong., 1 Sess., 1219.

Speech in Senate, July 10, 1832. Secret (Executive) Session: Discusses at length the historical background of the Northeast boundary controversy with Great Britain and the decision in 1827 to submit the issue to arbitration [6:1100-1101]. Recommends that the Senate reject the arbitral award handed down by King William I of the Netherlands. Does not believe that such rejection will lead to war with Britain. Advises reopening discussions with the British on the issue. *Register of Debates*, 22 Cong., 1 Sess., 1412-17. Printed in Colton, *Clay Correspondence*, 5:516-22. For the award and U.S. hostility to it, especially in Maine, see Samuel F. Bemis, *Diplomatic History of the United States* (New York, 1936), 256; Burrage, *Maine in the Northeastern Boundary Controversy*, 194-211; *Register of Debates*, 21 Cong., 1 Sess., 1394-98.

Remark in Senate, July 11, 1832. Approves a motion to form a joint House-Senate conference committee to reconcile differences in the tariff bills passed by the two chambers. *Register of Debates*, 22 Cong., 1 Sess., 1220-21.

Speech in Senate, July 12, 1832. Castigates President Jackson for having vetoed the bill rechartering the Bank of the United States on July 10 [Clay to Brown, December 18, 1831]. Charges that the veto "is an extraordinary power" which the members of the constitutional convention in 1787 did not expect "to be used in ordinary cases." Notes that Jackson has used the veto four times in three years, even though "The veto is hardly reconcilable with the genius of representative Government. It is totally irreconcilable with it, if it is to be frequently employed. . . . It is a feature of our Government borrowed from a prerogative of the British King." Asks: "Ought the opinion of one man overrule that of a legislative body twice deliberately expressed?" Resents the charge of the Jacksonians that the bill to recharter the B.U.S. was a premature agitation of the question "for electioneering purposes." Discusses and dismisses the objections to the B.U.S. given by the president in his veto message. Analyzes the vote on the recharter of the bank in 1811 and 1816 and explains his own vote against it in 1811 and for it in 1816. "A total change of circumstances" had occurred, "events of the utmost magnitude had intervened." Explains at length the economic harm Jackson's veto of the recharter bill will do in the West. Believes there are parts of the veto message "that ought to excite deep alarm; and that especially in which the President announces that each public officer may interpret the constitution as he pleases." Sees social chaos looming. Equates Jackson's veto with South Carolina's doctrine of nullification. "For what is the doctrine of the President but that of South Carolina applied throughout the Union?" Concludes with a listing of "some striking instances of discrepancy" in the veto message. *Register of Debates*, 22 Cong., 1 Sess., 1265-74. Printed in Colton, *Clay Correspondence*, 5:523-35. Colton incorrectly dates this speech July 10. For Jackson's veto message, see Clay to Fendall, August 4, 1832; and *MPP*, 2:576-91.

Later this day, Clay sharply questions one of the decisions of the House-Senate conference committee on the tariff bill. Asks why "Cotton bagging and sugar were given up [Remark in Senate, July 5, 1832]." Says he is distressed that the "interests of

Kentucky and Louisiana were . . . sacrificed." Complains, further, that the duties on sugar and cotton bagging were reduced in greater proportion than those on iron. Engages in testy exchanges with other members on whether personal, state, and sectional motives were indeed involved in forging the tariff bill. Remarks flatly: "If the gentleman [William Wilkins of Pa.] insinuates that I am actuated by any other motive than the public good, he has said that which is untrue." Notes that whatever the weaknesses of the final bill, it contains "a clear, distinct, and indisputable admission of the great principle of protection." At the same time, it reduces duties on articles not produced in the U.S. Hopes now that "we shall all go home in a better temper." *Register of Debates*, 22 Cong., 1 Sess., 1275-86.

Comment in Senate, July 13, 1832. Challenges Sen. Thomas H. Benton's remark that his (Clay's) speech of July 12 on Jackson's veto of the bank bill [Fendall to Clay, August 27, 1832] was "wanting in courtesy, indecorous, and disrespectful to the President." Denies this charge, repeating some of his objections to points in the president's veto message, particularly that having to do with the alleged "injurious effects" the bank has had on the prosperity of the West. Says, too, he will accept no instruction in etiquette and courtesy from a rough and rowdy character like the senator from Missouri, a brawling man who had once had a fist fight with Andrew Jackson [1:820]. The two men continue to exchange personal attacks and "atrocious" calumnies on each other's past behavior and veracity until called to order by the chairman. Both offer apologies to the Senate. "I was out of order," admits Benton, noting, too, that he and Jackson having fought like me, then made up like men. "I take the same opportunity to offer an apology [to the Senate]," remarks Clay, but "for the Senator from Missouri I have none." *Register of Debates*, 22 Cong., 1 Sess., 1293-96.

From John Meany, Philadelphia, July 14, 1832. With reference to Jackson's veto of the bill to recharter the Bank of the United States [Speech in Senate, July 12, 1832] reports: "I have great pleasure in Stating to you that the Veto has caused so great a sensation in our [City] that the Leaders of the Jackson party have joined the [a]lliance and have agreed to call a Town Meeting" tomorrow to discuss the issue. Notes that John Sergeant "appears Sanguine" concerning the presidential election in Pennsylvania. ALS. DLC-HC (DNA, M212, R4). Manuscript, barely legible, has been badly defaced by water. A "numerous meeting of the citizens of the city and county" of Philadelphia met and passed resolutions declaring their oppositon to Jackson's bank veto and to his reelection. It was also reported by a local newspaper that nearly every officer of the meeting had previously been "an earnest Jackson man." Philadelphia *United States Gazette*, July 18, 1832.

To SOLOMON ETTING   Washington, July 16, 1832

I regret extremely to perceive from your letter of yesterday,[1] that you have thought it possible that a remark of mine,[2] applied to a subordinate officer of the Customs, who was in attendance here, was liable to an unfavorable interpretation, in respect to the Jews generally. Nothing could have been further from my intention. The remark was intended to describe a person, and not to denounce a Nation. It was strictly, moreover, defensive. Some of my friends who were in the Senate had been attacked by Genl. [Robert Y.] Hayne, as I thought, rudely for the assistance which they had rendered about the Tariff.[3] In reply I said that they were not the only persons attending on that object, but that, on the other side, Moses Myers[4] (or Myers Moses, for I do not yet know his proper designation), had been summoned by the Secy of the Treasury [Louis McLane], and might be seen daily skipping about the house; and I proceeded to describe his person &c.

I judge of men not exclusively by their Nation, religion &c, but by their individual conduct. I have always had the happiness to enjoy the friendship of many Jews, among whom one of the [Benjamin] Gratzs' of Lexn. formerly of Philadelphia stands in the most intimate and friendly relations to me. But I cannot doubt that there are bad jews as well as bad christians and bad mahometans.

I hope my dear Sir that you will consider this letter perfectly satisfactory.

Copy. KyLxT. Printed in Walter H. Liebmann, "The Correspondence Between Solomon Etting and Henry Clay," *Publications of the American Jewish Historical Society* (1909), 17:81-82.   1. Etting had written on July 15, 1832, asking why Clay had used "the expression 'The Jew,' in debate in the Senate of the United States; evidently applying it as a reproachful designation of a man you considered obnoxious in character and conduct." Notes that "Several of the religious society to which I belong, myself included, feel both surprised and hurt" and consider the expression "illiberal." Concludes: "If therefore, you have no antipathy to the *people* of that religious society, I can readily believe you will have no objection to explain to me by a line, what induced the expression—" *Ibid.*   2. Comment in Senate, July 3, 1832.   3. Of 1832. See *ibid.*; and Webster to Clay, Jan. 8, 1832.   4. For Moses Myers and Solomon Etting, see Liebmann, "Correspondence Between Etting and Clay," 85-87.

From William McCaulley, Brandywine, New Wilmington, Del., June [*sic,* July] 16, 1832. Urges Clay to avoid "'an affair of honour' with the notorious [Thomas Hart] *Benton.*" Believes that "to be engaged with Benton . . . would be like fighting with a chimney-sweep," and that "in any conflict of the mind you are far his superior." Announces that Clay's duel with John Randolph remains "the greatest objection I have to you as candidate to the Presidency."

States that he also has "some objection to your *fasting & prayer Resolution* (of which, if you fight Benton, I shall begin to think you have not tak[en] the benefit)—all else so far as I have seen . . . and am able to judge I highly approve."

Assures Clay of his basic loyalty, however, by stating: "I have a son 23 months old this day, named 'Henry Clay.'" ALS. DLC-HC (DNA, M212, R10). For McCaulley, a well-known Wilmington businessman, see *DH* (April, 1968), 13:29. Clay introduced his resolution for prayer and fasting on June 27 [Remark in Senate, June 27, 1832]. The editors have concluded that McCaulley apparently erred in dating this letter June 16; it was likely written on July 16, 1832. For rumors of a duel between Clay and Benton, see William M. Meigs, *The Life of Thomas Hart Benton* (Philadelphia, 1904), 221.

To Whom It May Concern, July 16, 1832. Recommends "to the friendly offices of all good men" the 'Messrs. Audubons', father [John James] and son [John Woodhouse]," who are "engaged in the preparation and publication of a work on the Birds of the U. States." States that this work "has cost them great trouble labor and expence," and they "merit the partonage of the community, from their character, diligence, and the manner in which they have so far executed their design." ALS. MH. The study on which the Audubons were working was, *Ornithological Biography, or An Account of the Habits of the Birds of the United States of America.* . . . Edinburgh, 1831-49.

To FRANCIS T. BROOKE   Washington, July 20, 1832
I intend to take my departure from this City on monday next (the 23d) and hope to reach St. Julien[1] that evening. I design going from your house by Col. Wm. Bollings[2] in Goochland, and thence via Charlottesville or Lynchburg to the White Sulphur Springs. I do not think we can remain longer with you than tuesday, and I hope on our account, my dear Sir, you will not invite any company to St. Julien.

Nothing new, or at least nothing that will not keep new until I have the pleasure to meet you. . . .

ALS. KyU. Printed in Colton, *Clay Correspondence*, 4:341.   1. Brooke's estate near Fredericks-burg, Va.   2. Bolling was a descendent of the Indian Princess, Pocahontas. His home, "Bolling Hall," was located on the James River. John H. Gwathmey, *Twelve Virginia Counties: Where the Migration Began* (Richmond, Va., 1937), 232.

From HENRY CLAY, JR.   Lexington, July 21, 1832

I have at length arrived at Ashland after a very fatiguing journey. I stopped for some days at Louisville, but did not accomplish the purpose of my visit.[1] I found the family of Miss [Julia] P[rather]. preparing to go to the different springs in Ky by the way of Lexington. They are now in our little city. I think I shall not go to the Va Springs but remain in Ky.

The country is parched up by a most withering drought. The corn crops in this neighbourhood and for many miles around are almost destroyed. The crops of small grain have been unusually good. Hemp is very bad.

The Miss Erwins[2] are at Anne's [Brown Clay Erwin]   All are well

ALS. Henry Clay Memorial Foundation, Lexington, Ky.   1. Probably to propose marriage to Julia Prather. See Henry Clay, Jr., to Clay, June 7, 1832; Clay to Henry Clay, Jr., Oct. 23, 1832.   2. Probably Jane and Mary Ann Erwin.

To SAMUEL L. SOUTHARD   Washington, July 21, 1832

Several causes have determined us to abandon our purpose of going by Trenton. I regret their existence, whilst I feel that I ought to yield to their influence. Do make our peace with Mrs. Southard and Miss Virginia [Southard], to whom by way of some offering present our affectionate regards.

The Campaign is over, and I think we have won the Victory.[1] I leave here in full hope and confidence that Jackson will be defeated, with or without Pennsa. But I think that that State may be lossed to him if it be not gained to us.[2]

Here the rumor is that V. Buren will retire from the contest for the V. P.; that the weight of the admon will be thrown into the scale of [William] Wilkins; and that Van will return to the Dept. of State in the event of Jackson's re-election or before. I think all this probable. An immediate & advantageous use may be made of the arrangement.

Do believe yourself, and say to all our friends, that perseverance, in spite of occasional adverse circumstances (and such we must anticipate) will lead to success. Let us profit from the example of our adversaries, who never give up, but make defeat a new point for fresh exertions.

I shall stop at the White Sulphur Springs 'till the 20h. Augt. and shall be glad to hear from you there or any where else.

ALS. NjP.   1. Sergeant to Clay, June 27, 1831.   2. Clay to Ketchum, May 15, 1832; Clay to Southard, Oct. 23, 1832.

To Citizens of Hanover, Virginia, *ca.* July 28, 1832. Responds to an invitation to a public dinner from the citizens of his birthplace, saying that "Not having seen the spot that gave me birth for near forty years, it would afford me the sincerest satisfaction again to visit it, and to behold the scenes of my early youth; the humble parental roof which sheltered my brethren and me from cold and rain. . . . But, gentlemen, a visit to these endeared objects, at this time, in conformity with your invitation, would violate a rule which I have prescribed to myself." Cites his letter to the Citizens of Vincennes [October 18, 1831] stating that "whilst I continued before the public . . . as a candidate for its suffrage, I would not accept of any invitation, to a public entertainment proposed on my own account." Copy. Printed in *Niles' Register* (July 28, 1832), 42:387.

From Ambrose Spencer, "Near Albany," N.Y., July 28, 1832. Writes "to apprize you of the events" at the Utica convention [Clay to Porter, May 1, 1832]. Reports that "the convention, considering the busy time of year (it being harvest time), and the epidemic [cholera] prevailing in Albany & New York, was numerous beyond expectation; it consisted of a body of highly respectable & influential men; it was animated by one class & common feeling, the absolute necessity of sacrificing on the altar of patriotism all minor differences; & it was perfectly & I may say spontaneously unanimous in the opinion that the salvation of the Country & civil liberty required it of us to form a Union with, that numerous party, the anti-masons, in the support of the same candidates for Governor Lieut-Governor & Electors of President & Vice-President—accordingly we concurred with perfect unanimity in recommending to the national republicans of New York those tickets."

Adds that "altho' we dare only whisper it, that full one half of the electoral ticket are warmly for you. I have the *best ground* for saying that when our Electors meet, if they are convinced that it is necessary to prevent, the election of the *Barbarian*, to cast their whole votes for you, you will receive them." ALS. DLC-HC (DNA, M212, R4).

To JAMES CALDWELL
Staunton, Va., July 30, 1832

I reached this place yesterday evening on my return home, via the White Sulphur Springs, where I wish to stop with my family about a fortnight. The rumor is that you are over flowing and can take in no more. On the other hand, our friend Judge [Francis T.] Brooke (whom I left last wednesday, and who desires to be remembered to you) told me that you were reserving a Cabbin for me. I hope his information was correct. I shall leave here to day and I expect to arrive at the Warm Springs on tuesday night, on Wednesday night at Callahans [*sic*, Callaghan's],[1] and on thursday evening at the White Sulphur Springs. Will you have the goodness to drop me a line to meet me at Callahans' informing me of the prospect of accommodations? P.S. Supposing you would like to know who I have with me, I transmit this inventory: Mrs. Clay, a little grandson [Henry Clay Duralde] and myself compose the white members of our party. Then, we have four servants, two carriages, six horses, a Jack ass, and a Shepherds dog—a strange medley, is it not? I believe I shall send on one of the Carriages and a pair of horses a day or two after I reach you.[2]

ALS. ViHi. Printed in *VMHB* (October, 1947), 55:307-8, edited by Bernard Mayo. Caldwell's name is variantly spelled "Calwell." 1. Callaghan's Inn was located between present day Covington and Clifton Forge, Va. 2. Clay's board costs for a two week stay at White Sulphur Springs were: Mr. and Mrs. Clay, $32; young Duralde, $8; 2 servants, $16; 4 horses, $32. Total: $88. Bill dated August 16, 1832. DS. DLC-TJC (DNA, M212, R17).

From NICHOLAS BIDDLE
Philadelphia, August 1, 1832

You ask what is the effect of the veto.[1] My impression is that it is working as well as the friends of the Bank & of the country could desire. I have always deplored making the Bank a party question, but since the President will have it so, he must pay the penalty of his own rashness. As to the veto message[2] I am delighted with it. It has all the fury of a chained panther biting the bars of his cage. It is really a manifesto of anarchy—such as Marat or Robespierre might have issued to the mob of the faubourgh [*sic*, Faubourg] St Antoine: and my hope is that it will contribute to relieve the country from the dominion of these miserable people. You are destined to be the instrument of that deliverance, and at no period of your life has the country ever had a deeper stake in you. I wish you success most cordially because I believe the institutions of the Union are involved in it.

ALS. DLC-HC (DNA, M212, R4). Copy in DLC-Nicholas Biddle Papers (DNA, M212, R20). Printed in Colton, *Clay Correspondence*, 4:341. Letter marked "(private)." No. 1 of this date. Endorsed on verso by Clay: "N. Biddle Esq (with Mr. Sergeants opinion)." Enclosure not found. See below Biddle to Clay, no. 2 of this date. 1. Clay to Brown, Dec. 18, 1831; Webster to Clay, Jan. 8, 1832. 2. Clay to Fendall, August 4, 1832.

From NICHOLAS BIDDLE   Philadelphia, August 1, 1832

As it was necessary to consult the Counsel of the Bank [John Sergeant] before coming to any determination in regard to the subject which you had presented to the Board,[1] I was not able to give you any information about it previous to your leaving Washington—and now in the uncertainty as your stay at the [White Sulphur] Springs I have thought it best to write directly to Lexington.

Have the goodness to read Mr [John] Sergeant's views[2] & if you desire to communicate with Mr Shippen[3] he will be prepared for it by a letter which I will write today with a copy of Mr Sergeant's opinions.

ALS. DLC-HC (DNA, M212, R4). Letter marked "(private)." No. 2 of this date. Probably enclosed in Biddle to Clay, above, no. 1 of this date. 1. Possibly a reference to a $5,000 loan to Clay in 1832 extended him by a branch of the Bank of the United States. See Meigs, *Life of Thomas Hart Benton*, 274; Ralph C.H. Catterall, *The Second Bank of the United States* (Chicago, 1903), 388. 2. Probably of Jackson's veto of the bill to recharter the Second Bank of the United States. See Biddle to Clay, no. 1 of this date; and Speech in Senate, July 12, 1832. 3. Probably Edwin Shippen, cashier of the Louisville, Ky., branch of the Bank of the United States.

From JOHN SERGEANT   Philadelphia, August 3, 1832

Your favor of the 21st July was duly received, and Mr. Randall[1] has shown me your letter to him. Since then, I have a letter from our friend Genl. Chambers,[2] who has been detained at Washington by the confinement of Mrs. Chambers. He concurs in and enforces the views taken by you of the state of things in Pennsylvania. Recent occurrences have contributed to produce very generally the same opinions here. In fact, there is an irresistible tendency in that direction, too powerful to be controlled, if there were a disposition to control it. Such being the case, and harmony among our friends so desirable, the Committee appointed by the Convention have been summoned to meet at Harrisburg on the 11th. inst.[3] They will probably decide to reassemble the Convention, which may be accomplished in all August, and the Convention will decide—I presume they will recommend to go for [Joseph] Ritner.[4] The friends of Govr. [George] Wolf have brought things to this state by their own conduct. If he should lose his election (as it is thought he will) he must blame them.[5] They have acted a weak as well as a bad part, governed only by intense selfishness. They might have saved Wolf, and helped to save their Country, but their arithmetic had no sign for such a value. I hope the Country will be saved, notwithstanding. The prospect is certainly better, and improving. I have very strong hopes that we shall be able to take Pennsa., provided we can fairly consolidate the opposition. The Irish call, is a powerful one. Rather too much time has been allowed for conjuration of all sorts to be practised by the office holders. They are whining and canting to day about the impropriety of meetings of Irish.[6] But their efforts will be vain. The spirit is up, and they have not the power to lay it. Unhappily, a few of *our* regular croakers chime in with this strain, and the [cholera] epidemic which is among us, gives them some support. Still, I think the meeting will be a large one—Speaking of the epidemic—as yet, there is nothing in its character here to excite alarm. The cases to day are fewer than yesterday—the deaths, one less. I believe there is no more danger in the City, for those whose habits are tolerably good, than in any other part of the Country, and I rather incline to think (tho' our knowledge is almost too imperfect to found a theory) that there is risk in a change of residence. For the present, my intention is to remain where I am. My family is in health, and, happily, not much alarmed—I will write again in a few days. P.S. Genl. Chambers thought as you did about Van Buren and [William] Wilkins. The [Washington] Globe says, No. The matter is now made more complex by the rebellion of P[hilip]. P. Barbour, for so we must consider his contumacious determination to be a candidate.[7] Their troubles are thickening upon them.

ALS. DLC-HC (DNA, M212, R4).   1. Probably Josiah Randall.   2. Probably General Ezekiel F. Chambers. See *BDAC*.   3. Clay to Ketchum, May 15, 1832.   4. The Pennsylvania National Republican convention reassembled on August 22 and endorsed George Wolf for governor. Philadelphia *United States Gazette*, Sept. 7, 1832.   5. Clay to Ketchum, May 15, 1832. 6. A Meeting of the Irish Anti-Jacksonians was held in Philadelphia on August 6, 1832. This group supported Wolf for governor. Philadelphia *United States Gazette*, August 29, 1832.   7. Clay to Southard, July 21, 1832. For Barbour's vice presidential candidacy, see Simms, *The Rise of the Whigs in Virginia*, 52-53, 57-58.

To PHILLIP R. FENDALL
White Sulphur Springs, Va. (W. Va.),
August 4, 1832

I recd. your favor of the 28h. Ulto. and thank you for your kind attention to the publication of the Veto Speech.[1]

The news that has reached me from N. York and Pennsa. is very good; and that which I receive from K. is also very satisfactory. Still, I feel much solicitude as to the issue of our Governor's election,[2] from the causes which I stated to you.

We had an agreeable trip to this place, stopping by the way at Judge [Francis T.] Brookes, Govr. [James] Barbours, and Mr. [James] Madisons. The President [Jackson] and myself crossed each others tract and were near coming into contact but did not.

The proceedings of the Utica Convention[3] have arrived here, together with a letter from its President. They are highly satisfactory; and I hope we shall now soon hear of some definitive arrangement in Pennsa.[4]   P. S. We shall leave this place about the 16h. inst.

ALS. Courtesy of Dr. and Mrs. Raymond L. Roof, Paducah, Ky.   1. For Jackson's veto of the bank recharter bill on July 10, 1832, see *MPP*, 2:576-91; Speech in Senate, July 12, 1832. See also, Clay to Brown, Dec. 18, 1831; Webster to Clay, Jan. 24, 1832.   2. Smith to Clay, Dec. 27, 1831.   3. Clay to Porter, May 1, 1832.   4. Reference is to a possible alliance of Clay and Anti-Masonic supporters there. See Clay to Ketchum, May 15, 1832.

To JOHN MEANY
White Sulphur Springs, Va. (W. Va.),
August 4, 1832

I am greatly obliged by your friendly letter of the 29h. Ulto. with the accompanying papers, which were very acceptable. I must also now acknowledge the receipt of similar marks of your kind attention, during the late Session of Congress.

The demonstrations of public feeling and sentiment, recently made, are cheering and auspicious.[1] I believe the redemption of our Country from an arbitrary and weak administration is at hand. From the West the tidings that have reached me here are good. But, as we have so often been disappointed in Kentucky, we must await the resul[ts] of her elections which begin next Monday.[2]

I shall remain here about ten days longer and proceed home. Should the proceedings at the meeting of our Irish friends in Philada. take place in time to get here before my departure,[3] I should be glad to receive them.

ALS. Morristown (N.J.) Edison National Historical Park.   1. Connell to Clay, July 4, 1832; Meany to Clay, July 14, 1832; Sergeant to Clay, August 3, 1832.   2. Smith to Clay, Dec. 27, 1831.   3. Sergeant to Clay, August 3, 1832.

To FRANCIS T. BROOKE
White Sulphur Springs, Va. (W. Va.), August 5, 1832

We reached here safely on thursday last [August 2], and find a very great crowd. Two of your sons are here, and we saw the third at Staunton.[1] They are all well. I feel much better already and hope the water will completely eradicate the disease under which I was suffering at St. Julien.

The news that has reached me from N. York, Pennsa. and K. is all good. Most of it must have caught you eye. The union of the two parties in N.Y.[2] is now complete and success there may be regarded as certain. I transmit enclosed a letter from Judge [Ambrose] Spencer.[3] In Pennsa too matters are rapidly tending to a successful issue. My friends in that State write me from Philada. in great confidence. You will have seen an account of the Irish movement, to which I attach very great importance.[4] My information from K. is also satisfactory; but as the result of the Election,[5] which begins there to day, must be soon known, I will not undertake to anticipate it.

I am informed from Washington that the President has resolved to suspend the execution of the parts of the law passed at the last Session, relating to Internal improvements, to which he objects.[6] What think you of this high handed measure? What of his daring violation of the Constitution in re-appointing Gwin?[7] Is proud Virginia ready to bend her neck to these usurpations?

Speaking of your State, I do believe with proper exertions, it might be carried against Jackson.[8] The two parties exhibit at this time apathy and confidence on one side, and despondency on the other. If you would exchange for your despondency, zeal and concert, I am half persuaded that you would triumph. Your strength is greater than you are aware of. The weakness of the other side is greater than is believed. Let our friends organize throughout the State; let each County be divided into sections and let one or more members of your Comees. of Vigilance be designated in each to bring the voters to the polls, and I do incline to think that you would win the day. All this should be put in motion by some Central Comee. What would serve to animate our friends and to dis spirit our opponents is the high probability of success, whatever may happen to be the vote of Virginia.

We shall remain here until the 15h. . . .

ALS. KyU. Partially printed in Colton, *Clay Correspondence*, 4:341-42.   1. John, Robert, and Francis.   2. Clay to Bailhache, Nov. 24, 1830; Clay to Weed, April 14, 1832; Clay to Porter, May 1, 1832.   3. Brooke replied on August 10, 1832, urging Clay to make a similar communication to John H. Pleasants who would "make good use of it."Adds: "I shall do the best I can in this quarter, though the terrors of the Cholera [Remark in Senate, July 4, 1832] have nearly suspended every other feeling." ALS. DLC-HC (DNA, M212, R4).   4. Sergeant to Clay, August 3, 1832.   5. Smith to Clay, Dec. 27, 1831.   6. "An Act Making Apporpriations for Certain Internal Improvements for the Year 1832" passed the Senate on June 24, 1832, and the House on July 4. U.S. H. of Reps., *Journal*, 22 Cong., 1 Sess., 935, 1082, 1212. For the act see 4 *U.S. Stat.*, 551-57. Jackson had stated in his Fourth Annual Message [Clay to Brooke, Dec. 12, 1832] that he would approve only internal improvements "national in their character" and recommended to Congress that they refrain from approving such projects "except in relation to improvements already begun, unless they shall first procure from the States" a constitutional amendment to define the bounds of their power. U.S. Sen., *Journal*, 22 Cong., 2 Sess., 14-15. 7. On Oct. 3, 1831, during a congressional recess, Jackson appointed Samuel Gwin to the office of "Register of the Land Office at Mount Salus, in the State of Mississippi." The Senate subsequently rejected the nomination. On July 21, 1832, with Congress again in recess, Jackson once more appointed Gwin to the position. The Senate passed a resolution on Dec. 31, 1832, calling the president's reappointment of Gwin "a palpable violation of the constitution . . . and a dangerous usurpation of power" and declaring the office vacant since the adjournment of the Senate on July 16, 1832, "at which time the commission of said Gwin, granted by the President in the recess of the Senate in 1830, expired by its own limitation." U.S. Sen., *Journal*, 22 Cong., 2 Sess., Appendix, 279, 290.   8. Sergeant to Clay, June 27, 1831.

To HENRY CLAY, JR.
White Sulphur Springs, Va. (W. Va.),
August 5, 1832

Upon our arrival here on thursday last [August 2], I found your letter of the 21st. Ulto. which I was glad to receive, as I had not heard directly from you since you left Washington. As you do not say that your affair is off,[1] I presume it is only postponed until after the dog days.

The news that constantly reaches me here from N. York and Pennsa. through the public prints and through private letters is most cheering and satisfactory.[2] Should the issue of the K. election not be adverse,[3] I do believe the subsequent defeat of Jackson to be certain.

Tell Mr. [James] Erwin that we sent off his carriage the day before yesterday, under the care of a trusty Coachman, to proceed by Guyandotte and Maysville to Lexington. I gave orders to admit no person in the Carriage, and to move on leisurely.

We shall remain here about a fortnight. If you write, as I hope you will, direct your letters via Guyandotte, as I have reason to believe the stupid P. Masters would otherwise send them by Washington. Mention this also to Mr. Erwin and Mr. [Thomas] Smith.

Mr. [James] Caldwell has a young Pointer Dog for you, now a little lame. If he gets well, I will try and take him along with us. P.S. I wish you would employ the Coachman, when he arrives, in cleaning up the walks and grounds around the house

ALS. Henry Clay Memorial Foundation, Lexington, Ky.   1. Henry Clay, Jr., to Clay, June 7, 1832.   2. For encouraging reports from Pennsylvania, see Meany to Clay, July 14, 1832; Connell to Clay, July 4, 1832; Sergeant to Clay, August 3, 1832. For encouraging reports from New York, see Porter to Clay, July 6, 1832; Spencer to Clay, July 28, 1832.   3. Smith to Clay, Dec. 27, 1831.

From Edwin U. Berryman, New York, August 6, 1832. Reports that "Our political prospects in New York are brightening every day. Perhaps there never have been before in the space of six Months, so many different circumstances transpired to aid our cause. I am aware that we are too apt to think, that things will eventuate as we wish but predudices a side, we are *really* very *sanguine* of controlling the electoral ticket of New York in conjunction with the Antimasons [Clay to Bailhache, November 24, 1830; Clay to Porter, May 1, 1832]; Many of us are rather doubtful of the honesty of their intentions towards us, but in as much as we can do nothing without their aid, we must even make a merit of necessity & go with them." Notes that "great efforts have been made by the Jackson party in New York" and "that large amts of funds have been distributed throughout the State." Regrets that "we could not have rendered our friends some assistance," but "Our party here combining as they do Nationals, Workies & Antimasons are poor, and require all our energies to keep head with the opposition who hold the fat offices & who know that their time [in] office depends chiefly upon their liberality in advancing parts of their salaries —"

Recalls that last year he sold his part in "the Arabian horse Stamboul [Berryman to Clay, October 5, 1831]" without consulting Clay. Now, he has purchased Kocklani, another of the Arabians imported by Charles Rhind, and deems it "my duty to offer you one [thir]d of this Horse at cost say $200 [Berryman to Clay, October 30, 1832]." ALS. Courtesy of M.W. Anderson, Lexington, Ky.

From Henry Huntt, Washington, August 6, 1832. Reports that "we have the most flattering accounts every day from Pennsylvania." Has heard that "the most desponding *Clay men* some time ago are now in high spirits." Adds that the "administration party show great uneasiness. and are exerting every nerve to save themselves from sinking." ALS. DLC-HC (DNA, M212, R4).

From John Sergeant, Philadelphia, August 10, 1832. Reports that the state committee for the National Republicans will meet tomorrow at Harrisburg, and states: "They will consider whether it is expedient to reassemble the Convention [Sergeant to Clay, August 3, 1832], or what is best to be done. Our case is a complicated one." Details confusion among parties in making their nominations. Continues: "I hope, nevertheless, our Committee will be able to lay out a course for us. It is the more important because there is the same sort of difficulty to contend with in New Jersey and Ohio—"

Mentions that the cholera epidemic "seems to be spreading in all directions," and that "some have fled the City, and more will probably go as the cases increase in number." Adds that "Not a store or shop, as far as I know, has been closed, but a good deal of work is at a stand owing to the alarm among the mechanics and labourers." ALS. InU.

From Charles Hammond, Cincinnati, August 11, 1832. States that he was pleased "with the Spirit" of the letter he received from Clay [June 22, 1832], and agrees "that no good could result from discussing past matters." Notes that while "the results of the Kentucky election [Smith to Clay, December 27, 1831] are not So decisive as was hoped they would be, yet they are not So discouraging as it was feared they might be." Reports that "Our prospects in Ohio are not So promising as I could wish," because "In selecting candidates for Congress we have much division giving rise to rivalries and heart burnings of unfavorable omen." Continues: "Second & third rate men thrust themselves into the canvass by half dozens. I would not be Surprised if Cowin [*sic*, Thomas Corwin] [Joseph] Vance & [Samuel] Vinton are all of the present delegation that are returned. [Elisha] Whittlesey is endangered by Anti-Masonry—Indeed this is the rock upon which we are to be wrecked. Should we losse the Governor, of which I am fearful, we trust that our Anti Mason friends, Seeing the insignificance of their numbers and the unfortunate consequences will unite with us on the electoral ticket."

States that the "Veto [Clay to Brown, December 18, 1831; Webster to Clay, January 8, 1832] and other extravagant measures of the President have made no decided impression against him" in Ohio, but for the Jacksonians "apprehension Sits in the Seat of confidence, and this is worth a good deal, considering how high that confidence was a little while ago." Concludes: "To your Sanguine temperament this will appear like croaking. I shall rejoice as much as any man if it prove Such." ALS. OHi. In the gubernatorial race in Ohio, Robert Lucas, a Jacksonian, defeated the Anti-Jackson candidate, Darius Lyman, by a vote of 71,251 to 63,185. *BDGUS*, 3: 1199-1200. The Jacksonians won 7 congressional seats to 11 for the Anti-Jacksonians. *Niles' Register* (October 20, 1832), 43:118-19. The Jacksonians won 7 seats in the state senate to 11 for the Anti-Jacksonians and 30 seats in the state house of representatives to 40 for the Anti-Jacksonians. Cincinnati *Daily Advertiser*, November 2, 1832.

From Samuel L. Southard, Trenton, N.J., August 13, 1832. Discusses the cholera epidemic, then turns to politics and states that "so far as I can see, we have just grounds of hope" for success. Notes that the "prospects in Penna seem to improve rapidly — our danger there *now*, is, as it has been, from Antimasonry. In New York, I think we are safe — So, we are in N.J." Asks about the political situation in Kentucky and Ohio, saying "Our anxieties are directed to the West —" Adds: "I doubt whether V[an]. B[uren]. will go back to the State Dept. He succeeded so badly while there, that nothing but desperation can induce him to return." ALS. InU.

From Henry A.S. Dearborn, Roxbury, Mass., August 26, 1832. States that though ill from "the prevailing epidemick," he has made a trip to Portland. Reports that he was assured in Maine "that your friends would revolutionize the state." Notes that "Genl. Vance, one of the most influential leaders of the Jackson party, has come out, in an address to the people, denouncing the old tyrant [Jackson] in the most emphatic manner." Gives assurance that in Massachusetts "We are wide awake . . . & are mustering our forces for the autumnal campaign [Sergeant to Clay, June 27, 1831; Webster to Clay, October 22, 1832]." ALS. DLC-HC (DNA, M212, R5). For the outcome of the Maine state elections, held on September 10, 1832, see Dearborn to Clay, September 18, 1832. "Genl. Vance" is probably William Vance of Baring, Me., a large landowner, a member of the state legislature, and the man for whom Vanceboro, Me., was named. See Harold A. Davis, *An International Community on the St. Croix* (Orono, Me., 1950), 71-73; Ava H. Chadbourne, *Maine Place Names and the Peopling of Its Towns* (Portland, 1955), 359-60. For Vance's speech denouncing Jackson, see Kennebec *Journal*, August 3, 1832.

To NICHOLAS BIDDLE   Lexington, August 27, 1832

I recd. your private letter of the 1st. and sincerely hope that the overthrow, which you anticipate, of our present misguided rulers will be realized. Certainly I should be happy to be the instrument of accomplishing that patriotic service, but I should be glad of its consummation through any other agency.

I transmit under your cover a letter to Mr. [John] Sergeant, which, after perusing it, I will thank you to deliver to him. It contains a faithful account of our recent Elections.[1] Their result was certainly not satisfactory, in all respects, and yet I do believe that it will serve to invigorate exertions and render our triumph more sure in Novr. than if we had prevailed by a lean majority, in the Governor's Election. I still think that all our Western calculations will be fulfilled.

If the Speeches against the B. Veto[2] had reached the great body of the people, prior to our election, the result would have been widely different. Can not the same pen that prepared last year the review of [Thomas Hart] Benton's Speeches[3] be employed to make a similar review of the V[eto]. message? And cannot the same means be used to give such a document extensive circulation? Depend upon it, the most decided benefit would accrue from such a course. It is a common, sometimes fatal, error to suppose that the mass of the community is as well informed as the intelligent, respecting a given subject   It should be addressed as if it knew nothing about it, in plain, intelligible & forcible language. Such a paper is greatly needed.[4]

ALS. DLC-Nicholas Biddle Papers (DNA, M212, R20). Letter marked "(Private)." 1. Smith to Clay, Dec. 27, 1831. 2. Clay to Brown, Dec. 18, 1831; Webster to Clay, Jan. 8, 1832; Clay to Fendall, August 4, 1832; Speech in Senate, July 12, 1832. For the text of various Senate speeches against the bank veto, see *Register of Debates*, 22 Cong., 1 Sess., 1220-40, 1248-74, 1293-96. 3. Nicholas Biddle had written a "Reply to Benton," which was published in the Philadelphia *United States Gazette*, Feb. 26, 1831. Govan, *Nicholas Biddle*, 137-39. 4. Apparently Biddle did not agree to Clay's urging to write a review of the bank veto; however, a pamphlet on the subject was published anonymously in Philadelphia in 1832 under the title, *Review of the Veto*. . . . It was also alleged that numerous anonymous pamphlets and articles poured out of

Philadelphia "upon the order merely of Mr. Biddle." See Govan, *Nicholas Biddle*, 204; Carl B. Swisher, *Roger B. Taney* (New York, 1935), 205.

From Philip R. Fendall, Frederick, Md., August 27, 1832. States that he has learned while "on a short journey of health," that "a fine spirit prevails in this section of country in regard to the Presidential election." Reports that on Saturday evening he attended a public meeting at the courthouse where he heard Jackson's bank veto message [Clay to Brown, December 18, 1831; Clay to Fendall, August 4, 1832] "dissected . . . without mercy" and his "refusal to execute the Indian treaties and laws of the U. States" attacked. Notes that "Similar meetings are, I believe, held here once a fortnight, and frequently in other parts of the county."

Suggests that in view of the results of the Kentucky election for governor and lieutenant governor [Smith to Clay, December 27, 1831] "the National Republican Committee at Lexington or Frankfort . . . issue *immediately* an Address to the party at large setting forth the difference between the votes for [Richard A.] Buckner and [James T.] Morehead, showing why the latter should be regarded as the party test; insisting on our superiority in the Legislature . . . and taking such other views of the subject as may prevent the defeat of Mr. Buckner from operating injuriously on the general question."

Recalls that "Before you left Washington, I mentioned to you the unpleasan[t] position in which the publisher [J.A. Fell] of the [Washington] 'National Union' had placed me, and intimated my intention of writing a circular to some of the party in Congress who had contributed to establish it." Transmits copy of the circular and requests that Clay "after reading it, to forward to Mr. Marshall."

Adds in a postscript that Lewis P.W. Balch has recounted to him "an anecdote which Mr. [Thomas Hart] Benton had probably forgotten when he told the Senate that he and Jackson, after fighting like men, had 'made up like men, &c. [Comment in Senate, July 13, 1832].'" Balch said that he had talked to Benton in Washington in March, 1821, "(seven years after the fight)," and that in speaking of Jackson, Benton "proceeded to abuse [him] so vehemently that his face became inflamed with rage, and he seemed to have lost his senses." ALS. DLC-HC (DNA, M212, R5). For Jackson's attitude toward treaties with the Indians, see Prucha, *American Indian Policy*, 233-49, and Johnston to Clay, January 12, 1831. Before receiving Fendall's recommendation that the National Republicans issue a statement on the subject of Kentucky's gubernatorial election, the "Friends of Henry Clay" met in Lexington on August 28 and adopted resolutions stating that "the vote for the Gubernatorial candidate . . . is not a test of the strength of parties in Kentucky." Lexington *Observer & Kentucky Reporter*, August 30, 1832. The "Mr. Marshall" referred to is possibly Congressman Thomas A. Marshall. No circular has been found.

To CHARLES HAMMOND   Lexington, August 27, 1832
I recd. at the White Sulphur Springs the papers you had the goodness to send me, which were very acceptable, and your friendly letter of the 11h. instant. We reached home on the evening of the 24h. in time to witness the dissolution of Mrs. Clay's mother [Susannah Gray Hart], at a very advanced age; and to day we shall assist in the performance of the last melancholy office due to her remains. We have come home, therefore, to experience private distress and public mortification, growing out of the result of the late election.[1]

With respect to that result, you know, we Kentuckians are always ready with excuses, but in this instance I assure you that I believe they are well founded. The loss of our Governor is to be ascribed to various causes. The first and most important is, that Mr. [Richard A.] Buckner, though an excellent man, is a presbyterian, and against that sect there are deep rooted and inveterate prejudices. His great merits prevented the Convention who selected him as a candidate from sufficiently estimating the force of those prejudices. To this cause may be attributed the loss of, I think, three thousand votes. In [Robert P.] Letcher's district we lost from it about 1300 and in the Counties of Logan and Warren at least 700 more, whilst in all other parts of the State the influence of the objection was felt. These voters will be eager in November to efface the stigma of indifference to the cause which they are attached to.

2. A second cause of our defeat was the vast efforts and the corrupt means employed by the Administration from without as well as within the State to carry the election.

3. The third was an influx of Voters from Tennessee in several of the Counties bordering on that State. You know we have returns periodically made of all the Voters to regulate our Representation. Last year the returns were made; and in some of those border Counties the Jackson majorities given at the recent election were greater than the *whole* number of the voters according to those returns.

Such is the most unfavorable view of the late Governors' Election. On the other hand, there are some highly consoling circumstances. We have [sec]ured the election of our Lieut. Govr. [James T. Morehead] by upwards of 2500 votes; the election of 60 out of the 100 members composing our H. of R.; and in the Senate, where we were last year in the minority, a sufficient number of new members to give us 22 out of the 38, besides having the casting vote of the presiding officer. In the Northern part of the State, where alone any thing reached the body of the people, against the Bank Veto,[2] we have generally done extremely well In Fayette County, including Lexington, we have gained near four hundred votes;[3] and that County has given to our cause a larger majority than any other in the State.

Our partial defeat is working well in K. It has aroused our friends and will stimulate them to the greatest exertions. They have already commenced operations, and have devised plans which I think can not fail to lead to success. Indeed I believe that our triumph in November is more certain than if we had obtained only such a majority for our Governor as our Adversaries have secured.

I agree with you that there is nothing like that overwhelming opposition to the Administration any where manifested which its acts and measures ought to have excited. Still there are changes — great changes; and the prospect of our success is sufficient to animate us to the highest efforts. My information from N. York continues to be highly favorable. To use the very words of intelligent correspondents they consider N. York "as safe as Massachusetts." In Pennsa. too, altho' there is much confusion in the condition of parties there, we have some hopes. I lament the state of things in Ohio; and I trust that some means may be devised to reconcile the Anti Masons. Mr. [John] Sloan[e] from the Reserve left Washington last Spring with the best dispositions. Has he changed them? Could there not be some movement made among themselves, by which the portion favorable to our cause should publicly come out from the residue?[4] Could not the Anti Masons of N. York be induced to exercise their influence with their brethren of Ohio?

I do not know what has been the notice taken in the Gazette of our K. Elections. But if you could consistently with your own sense of propriety, present some such notice as I have sketched in the previous part of this letter it would have two good effects.[5] 1st. It would obtain from you more credit with the American public generally, in consequence of what you said last year about our Elections[6] & 2dly. It would be soothing and gratifying to the feelings of your K. political friends.

I shall remain at home generally until I return in the Fall to the City, and should be very glad both to see and hear from you.

ALS. InU. 1. Smith to Clay, Dec. 27, 1831. 2. Brown to Clay, Dec. 18, 1831; Webster to Clay, Jan. 8, 1832. 3. Fayette County gave 1,426 votes for Buckner for governor and 681 to Breathitt. For lieutenant governor, Morehead received 1,413 votes to 696 for Taylor. Frankfort *Argus of Western America*, August 23, 1832. 4. For the attempts made in Ohio to fuse the National Republican and Anti-Masonic parties, and their failure, see Weisenburger, *The History of Ohio*, 3:266-71; McCarthy, "The Anti-Masonic Party," 528-29; Richard P. McCormick, *The Second Party System* (Chapel Hill, 1966), 265-66. 5. On August 29, 1832, the Cincinnati *Daily Gazette* published a letter from an anonymous correspondent blaming Buckner's defeat on the dislike of Kentuckians for "*sectarianism*" and on Breathitt's personal popularity. The writer also claimed that over-all the election was a victory for the Clay forces who carried the office of lieutenant governor and won control of the state legislature. The following day, August 30, 1832, Hammond wrote in an editorial in the *Gazette* that he was "well satisfied" with the remarks of the previous day's correspondent and pointed out that he had maintained from the beginning that Buckner was an "injudicious" choice as nominee for governor. 6. Hammond to Clay, June 13, 1832.

To WILKINS TANNEHILL   Lexington, August 27, 1832

I was glad to perceive that you had transferred your Editorial labors from Nashville to a kinder soil at our commercial metropolis [Louisville]. I hope the change will prove beneficial to yourself as I am sure it will to the Kentucky public.

Be pleased to place me among the subscribers to your tri weekly paper,[1] for which I transmit enclosed five dollars, which I believe is its price.

ALS. THi. 1. For Tannehill, see *CAB*. He had edited the Nashville *Herald* which was the first newspaper in Tennessee to promote the political fortunes of Henry Clay. In Louisville, he edited the Louisville *Herald*. See also *RKHS*, 31:1.

To DANIEL WEBSTER   Lexington, August 27, 1832

Our Kentucky elections have terminated in the election of the Jackson Candidate for Governor [John Breathitt] by a majority of 1260* votes, the N. Republican Candidate for Lieut. Governor [James T. Morehead] by a majority of 2506* votes;[1] and in sixty* 60* [*sic*] out of the 100 members that compose our H. of Representatives, as well as in securing in the Senate, where the majority was against us last year, a majority of 22 out of the 38 members composing that body.

We have been so often mortified with the issue of elections in this State, that I do not know whether you will take any interest in the causes of our recent partial defeat. They were 1st the employment of extraordinary means by the Jackson party, within and without the State. On this point all their efforts were brought to bear; and every species of influence was exercised. The patronage and the means of that party were profusely used. 2dly An irruption of Tennessee voters who came to the polls in some of our border counties. Last year, official returns of all the voters, in all the Counties, were made to form a basis for the periodical adjustment of the ratio of our representation. In some of those border counties, at the recent election, I understand that the *Jackson majorities*, exceeded the whole number of the voters according to those retruns. But we should have been able to resist successfully the joint effect of both the above causes, if it had not been for a third, which operated most extensively. Our candidate [Richard A. Buckner] was a Presbyterian, and against that sect most deep rooted, and inveterate prejudices exist, the weight of which had not been sufficiently estimated when he was selected. Owing to this latter cause I believe we lost not less than probably three thousand votes.

But it is less important to dwell on the past and incurable event of our Governor's election than to look forward and provide against future disaster. The spirit of our friends is unbroken, their zeal is increased in warmth, and they are full of confidence of success in November. What is more encouraging, they are already engaged in the best plans to secure success. Far from being disheartened, their recent partial defeat, arouses them to exertion more vigorous than ever; and the exceptionable means employed by their opponents have fired their indignation. I think there is much reason to hope that the late event will lead to more certain success in November than if we had carried the election of the Governor by such a majority as the other side has obtained.

What is most absorbing of public attention at this time is the Bank Veto.[2] On that subject our opponents have been much more industrious in the circulation of documents, than the friends of the institution. The President's message and [Thomas H.] Benton's redomontade[3] have been scattered in countless thousands, and time enough to affect the election; whilst on the other side, but little reached us before the election, except Mr Clay's speech,[4] which had a limited circulation, as it arrived only at the moment of the election. A clear, intelligible, popular statement of the case, with a just account of the certain effects of the overthrow of the Bank is much needed.

I hope that our friends abroad will see in our election that the bad issue of it has been neutralized by the good; and that they will derive from it fresh motives to spare no exertions to save the Country. P.S. Whilst it would be indiscreet to publish this letter with my name, I request you to shew it to Mess. Dearborne [*sic*, Henry A.S. Dearborn] Everetts [Alexander and Edward Everett] or any other particular friends. Why has not your Speech on the Veto[5] been published at length?

LS, with dateline, postscript, superscription, and numerals of vote totals in first paragraph in Clay's hand. DLC-Daniel Webster Papers (DNA, M212, R22). Printed in Wiltse, *Webster Papers*, 3:188-89. Similar letters, with minor variations in language, but with personalized postscripts, all dated August 27 (save the one to Charles Miner, below), were written to the following: John Holmes (LS. MHi); postscript reads: "I need scarcely say that any publication of this letter with my *name* would be inexpedient." To Samuel L. Southard (LS. NjP); postscript reads in part: "We reached home two or three days ago finding Mrs. Clay's mother [Susannah Gray Hart] extremely ill, and she has since died." To Elisha Whittlesey (LS. OClWHi); postscript reads: "What are your prospects of re-election? Have you any opposition? What is the course of the Anti Masons in the reserve? Will they persevere in their separate tickets?" To Charles Miner, dated August 25 (LS. Wyoming Historical & Geological Society, Wilkes-Barre, Pa.); postscript reads: "Your own discretion will suggest to you the impropriety of the publication of this letter." A letter dated, August 26 to James Caldwell (ALS. ViHi) at White Sulphur Springs, Va. (W. Va.), conveys the same information and concludes: "Be pleased to . . . communicate the contents of this letter to . . . particular friends." 1. Smith to Clay, Dec. 27, 1831. 2. Clay to Brown, Dec. 18, 1831; Webster to Clay, Jan. 8, 1832; Clay to Fendall, August 4, 1832. 3. Clay to Fendall, August 4, 1832. For Benton's speech of July 13, 1832, see *Register of Debates*, 22 Cong., 1 Sess., 1293-95. 4. Speech in Senate, July 12, 1832. 5. For Webster's speech of July 11, 1832, see *Register of Debates*, 22 Cong., 1 Sess., 1221-65; published as *Speech in the Senate of the United States, on the President's Veto of the Bank Bill, July 11, 1832*. Boston, 1832.

To THOMAS HART CLAY   Lexington, August 28, 1832

We reached home on friday evening last [August 24] and found your grandmother [Susannah Gray Hart] lying at the point of death. She lingered speechless until sunday morning when she expired. Her death was hastened by an accidental fall that she recd. some weeks ago. Your mother and all of us have been much distressed, and we were particularly so because she was unable either to speak or to open her eyes.

The rest of our connexions are generally well. Mr. [James] Erwin Anne [Brown Clay Erwin] and their children are all well and at home. Henry [Clay, Jr.], James [Brown Clay] and John [Morrison Clay] and H[enry]. C. Duralde are with us.

I have not heard from you for some time. How is your Crop of Corn? Your ditching; has it realized expectations. Our crop of Corn and Hemp are both unpromising, but better than was expected some weeks ago. The corn has been much thrown down by a recent storm.

Do you intend to visit us this fall? We shall probably return to Washington in the month of November.

All the family unites with me in affectionate remembrance to you

ALS. DLC-HC (DNA, M212, R5).

From John L. Lawrence, New York, August 30, 1832. Reports that the "defeat of Mr. [Richard A.] Buckner [Smith to Clay, December 27, 1831], had a temporary effect among that portion of our friends, who prefer to look at the gloomy Side of the picture—and whom it has been So difficult for us, to cheer on, from the beginning. Their Spirits are however on the rally, and they will be brought ardently into the field at the proper time." Suggests that "our Western brethren" should follow the example of New York where "the most jarring personal feelings are made to yield to the furtherance of a great publick purpose." States that "With the chance which Indiana had of adding to our force in the Senate, and which Kentucky had of electing a patriotic governor, we should not have committed the errors they have been guilty of." Claims that "Our friends have the highest hopes of Success in this State, and Appearances seem to justify the expectations of the most Sanguine." Mentions that "several gentlemen, among whom I could not hesitate about enrolling myself," have wagered $2,000 on the result of the presidential election, and that the Jacksonians had responded to the challenge. ALS. DLC-HC (DNA, M212, R5). Following the elections for the state legislature in Indiana in August, 1832, the Jacksonians controlled the lower house by a majority of 3 to 5 votes while the National Republicans controlled the senate by a majority of about 12. *Niles' Register* (December 22, 1832), 43:267. In December, 1831, the Indiana legislature had elected Gen. John Tipton, a Jacksonian, to the U.S. Senate over Jesse L. Holman and several other candidates by a vote of 55 to 36 with 14 scattered. *Ibid.* (December 24, 1831), 41:297. For slightly variant figures on these elections, see Krueger, "Party Development in Indiana," 263.

From Peter B. Porter, Black Rock, N.Y., August 30, 1832. States that in his acceptance of the vice presidential nomination [Clay to Porter, March 10, 1832] Van Buren "has doubtless acted discreetly, as regards his own interests—for a retreat (which everyone would ascribe to sheer cowardice) would have sunk him lower in public estimation than a defeat, which I trust he is destined to meet." Is glad that Van Buren has not withdrawn from the contest, because "his withdrawing would have healed many wounds, and given it a strength & solidity which it cannot possess while he is so closely identified with the Hero."

Refers to the coalition between the Anti-Masons and National Republicans in New York [Clay to Bailhahe, November 24, 1830; Clay to Weed, April 14, 1832; Clay to Porter, May 1, 1832], saying: "Indeed I am very confident in the belief that we shall carry the whole Electoral ticket by a very handsome majority; and it is a ticket with which I think we ought to be satisfied. Something like, two thirds of the persons who compose it are are [*sic*] your decided political friends, and . . . in the state of things which we have reason to presume will be presented, they will doubtless all go together for you." Reports that Matthew L. Davis "is busily, & efficiently, employed in traversing every part of the State," and "has furnished himself with statistical, or numerical tables" which "furnish the data upon which he makes his calculations for the approaching election by which he gives us a majority of about 19,000." Admits "I have examined his tables & calculations with a good deal of attention, and, although I am not so sanguine as he is, my honest belief is that we will get a majority of 8 or 10 thousand." Mentions that some Jackson newspapers in the state have recently switched sides.

Comments that the Kentucky election [Smith to Clay, December 27, 1831] "furnishes, I think, incontestible evidence of the result of next fall's election." Continues: "There is great danger I think of Ohio, unless some compromise can be made with the Antimasons. A Mr. [William H.] Seward (an antimasonic member of our State Senate) was to have gone to Ohio before this time for the purpose of attempting such a compromise, but he has been taken sick & I fear will not be able to go. Whether they will supply his place by another antimason (and none other would be of any use) I know not. I trust however that our friends in Ohio will not fail to see & to do whatever may be necessary to ensure success to the great cause."

Urges Clay to stump upstate New York in September or October "as far as Syracuse or Utica." ALS. DLC-HC (DNA, M212, R5). For William Henry Seward, later a U.S. senator and secretary of state, see *BDAC*.

To JAMES CALDWELL   Lexington, Sepbember 2, 1832
[Discusses forwarding of letters for Richard Pindell which are in the post office at White Sulphur Springs, Va. Continues:]

Our friends in K. are in high spirits and making effective arrangements to secure a triumph in the Fall campaign.[1] We have not heard the issue of the Missouri election, except that Genl. [William Henry] Ashley has succeeded.[2] In Indiana[3] a majority of our friends are elected to the Legislature. . . .

ALS. ViHi. Printed in *VMHB* (Oct., 1947), 55:309.   1. Letcher to Clay, Oct. 30, 1832.
2. Clay to Dearborn, Sept. 6, 1832.   3. Lawrence to Clay, August 30, 1832.

From James Brown, Philadelphia, September 3, 1832. Expresses "feelings of the deepest sorrow" at the news of the death of his mother-in-law, Susannah Gray Hart [Clay to Thomas H. Clay, August 28, 1832]. "Alas how much . . . she resembled my dear Nancy [Ann Hart Brown] and how soon she has followed her [Brown to Clay, October 28, 1830]."

Turning to politics, states that opposition to the Jackson administration has been gaining in Pennsylvania "and would if united under one banner be strong." Notes, however, that the "lines of division are yet strongly marked and Masonry and Antimasonry continue to be violent antagonsts apparently incapable of amalgamation— The election of Breathit [*sic,* John T. Breathitt; Smith to Clay, December 27, 1831] has been a damper to the cause of the opposition in this state notwithstanding the explanations of the causes leading to that result [Clay to Webster, August 27, 1832]." ALS. DLC-HC (DNA, M212, R5). Printed in *LHQ*, 24:1166; and Colton, *Clay Correspondence*, 4:342-43.

To PHILIP R. FENDALL   Lexington, September 3, 1832
I recd. your favor of the 27h. ulto. transmitting a letter to Mr. Marshall which, according to your request, I have perused and sent to him. It exonerates you from all blame about the paper, and that is all that was necessary, as I apprehend it is now too late to render it of much service in the pending contest.[1]

Our friends in K. are far from being discouraged by their partial defeat in the recent Governors' election,[2] which may be traced to causes wholly unconnected with the P[residential]. question. They are full of confidence of success in Novr. and are taking efficient measures to secure it.

We reached home about ten days ago, finding Mrs. [Susannah Gray] Hart, the mother of Mrs. Clay lying extremely ill, and we had the misfortune to witness her dissolution the second day after our arrival. Our health is good, and Mrs. Clay joins me in respects to Mrs. Fendall. . . . P.S. Will you request Mess. G[ales]. & Seaton to send my [Washington *Daily National*] Intell[igence]r. to Lexington, as I apprehend it is forwarded to the W[hite]. S[ulphur]. Springs?

ALS. KyLoF.   1. Fendall to Clay, August 27, 1832.   2. Smith to Clay, Dec. 27, 1831.

From John Sergeant, Philadelphia, September 3, 1832. Reports that in Pennsylvania "The Kentucky gubernatorial election [Smith to Clay, December 27, 1831] is generally well understood," and "Our friends . . . are not at all discouraged by it." Believes that in the Pennsylvania gubernatorial election [Clay to Ketchum, May 15, 1832], the state will go for Joseph Ritner who will receive all the Anti-Masonic votes, and "the greater part of the National Republicans," as well as the votes of "many others who upon various grounds are opposed to [George] Wolf." Warns, however, that it is "not . . . entirely certain that the whole force which will support Ritner can be combined against Jackson." Notes that the Pennsylvania "Antimasons are obstinately bent upon following their own course" and will support "no electoral ticket but their own, and *that*, to vote for their own candidates, even tho' they should have no chance whatever of succeeding." States: "If they persist in this, there will be no way of taking the State from Jackson, but to vote their ticket. Such, is very likely to be the course."

Discusses prospects for the fall election in various states, remarking that William Maynard of New York was about to visit Ohio to attempt a union of the Anti-Masons and National Republicans when he was stricken with cholera [Remark in Senate, June 27, 1832]. Now his life is "despaired of." ALS. InU.

To ADAM BEATTY   Lexington, September 4, 1832

I recd. your favor of yesterday. The kind present of a barrel of wheat from our friend Mr. Child[1] will be very acceptable, and I am obliged by your promise to have it forwarded to me. I will have some ground carefully prepared to sow it in.

I am happy to hear of the good spirit prevailing among our friends in Mason. A similar one exists here, and generally as far as I can learn. If we could introduce every where an effective plan of organization, the State would go with us by at least 5000. I hope such a plan will be devised by the Convention[2] which is to meet on the 20h. and which ought to be composed of practical men.

ALS. MHi.   1. Probably David Lee Child.   2. The Kentucky National Republican convention met in Lexington on Sept. 20, 26, 27, 1832. Seventeen resolutions—endorsing internal improvements, a national bank, and Clay's land bill, among other things—were adopted by the approximately 400 men present. Lexington *Observer & Kentucky Reporter*, Oct. 4, 1832.

To HENRY A. S. DEARBORN   Lexington, September 6, 1832

I regretted to learn from your favor of the 26h. Ulto. that your health had been bad. I thought you did not look well during the latter part of our fatiguing Session, and I hope you will not fail to employ the vacation in re-establishing it.

The election of our Govr. terminated in favor of the Jackson Candidate [John Breathitt] by a small majority.[1] This was owing mainly to religious prejudices, the force of which had not been sufficiently estimated when he was selected as a Candidate. On the other hand, we elected the Lieut. Governor [James T. Morehead] by a larger majority, 60 of the 100 members of the H. of R. and in the Senate, where last year we were in the minority, we have now a decided majority, having turned out three Jackson Senators.[2] Still, the result of the Governor's Election is mortifying, and to be regretted especially on account of that class of our friends who are prone to look at the black side of the picture. Its' effect will be, I think, to render our triumph in Novr. more secure than if we had elected our Candidate by a lean majority. There are mingled feelings of mortification, State pride, and indignation, now at work, which cannot fail to lead to Success. A convention of the N.Rs. is to meet at Lexington on the 20h. inst.[3] which will adopt effective measures to carry the State.

In the States of Ohio, Indiana, Missouri and Louisiana our friends are in motion, and they assure me that their prospect of success is encouraging. From Missouri (on which I have not heretofore counted) Mr. Senator [Alexander] *Buckner*, since their election, writes me that the Veto[4] will not be sustained in that State; that [William Henry] Ashley has been re-elected;[5] and that my friends are in high hopes.

I sincerely hope that your anticipations as to Maine may be realized.[6] You will know the event by the time this letter reaches you; and I shall be glad to receive early intelligence of it. Prior to the receipt of your letter I had recd. the number of the Atlas containing *The Crisis* which had attracted my attention. I was much struck with it and advised our Editors here to re-publish it.[7]

Since our return home we have had the misfortune to lose Mrs. Clay's mother [Susannah Gray Hart], who was lying at the point of death on our arrival. Altho' she was in her Eighty sixth year, we feel much affected by the event. . . .

ALS. NjP.   1. Smith to Clay, Dec. 27, 1831.   2. Clay to Lawrence, Sept. 6, 1832.   3. Clay to Beatty, Sept. 4, 1832.   4. Clay to Brown, Dec. 18, 1831; Webster to Clay, Jan. 8, 1832.   5. In the Missouri gubernatorial election Daniel Dunklin, a Jacksonian, defeated John Bull, the anti-administration candidate, by a vote of 9,141 to 8,132 while Lilburn W. Boggs, also a Jacksonian, was elected lieutenant governor. *BDGUS*, 2:840. William H. Ashley, who called himself a Jackson man but whose policies resembled Clay's, was elected to Congress over Robert W. Wells, the true Jackson candidate, by 9,498 votes to 8,836. *Guide to U.S. Elections*, 558. In Nov., 1832, Thomas Hart Benton, a Democrat, was reelected to the U.S. Senate by a vote of 46 to 12 for National Republican Abraham J. Williams, his nearest opponent. William N. Chambers, *Old Bullion Benton, Senator from the New West* (Boston, 1956), 188.   6. Dearborn to Clay, August 26, 1832.   7. The Boston *Atlas*, August 21, 1832, published an article titled "The Crisis" which strongly attacked Jackson as "A CURSE TO THE COUNTRY" and endorsed the election of Henry Clay as president in order to end "the reign of terror."

To JOHN L. LAWRENCE
Lexington, September 6, 1832

I have duly received your favor of the 30h Ulto.   During the late Session of Congress I had the pleasure of receiving several letters from you, which, if I did not acknowledge, the omission proceeded from my numerous engagements, and which I hope you will excuse. I have much indulgence in this respect to ask of my friends.

The defeat of [Richard A.] Buckner[1] was very mortifying, and much to be regretted on account of its influence upon that class of our friends who are too prone to regard the unfavorable aspect of events. It resulted entirely from religious prejudices, which, it seems, had not been sufficiently appreciated in the selection of him as a Candidate. The other elections terminated very favorably. We have, for example, elected 60 of the 100 members composing the H. of R. and in the Senate, where last year, we were in the minority, We have now a majority of 22 out of the 38 members who constitute the body;[2] and the Lieut. Governor [James T. Morehead] who presides over it is also elected from the N. Republicans   Our friends are very confident of success in November, and feel more assured of it than if we had elected our Govr. by a small majority. A convention is to be held at Lexn. on the 20h. inst.[3] when those parts of the State not already organized will be placed under a system of organization. I do not entertain any doubts myself of success in November. The election of Electors comes on alone, without any disturbing cause, and it will present a simple question.

Our information also authorizes us to hope for success in Ohio, Indiana, Missouri and Louisiana. There will be a warm contest in some of those States, but our friends there believe that with proper exertions, which they promise to make, we must succeed.

I am happy to hear of the encouraging prospects in N. York. It will be expedient that whatever evidence of the probability of your success can be afforded, should be thrown into Ohio and Indiana.

I addressed a letter to Mr. Jonathan Thompson, Chairman of your Central Comee. on the subject of the Kentucky Election, which I hope he received.

ALS. ViU.   1. Smith to Clay, Dec. 27, 1831.   2. In the 1832 elections for the Ky. General Assembly, Clay supporters won 22 seats in the senate to 16 for the Jacksonians and carried the house 60 to 40. Lexington *Observer & Kentucky Reporter*, August 30, 1832.   3. Clay to Beatty, Sept. 4, 1832.

To JAMES F. CONOVER   Lexington, September 8, 1832

I regretted to learn from your obliging letter of the 27th. Ulto. that you had recently sustained a private affliction.[1] We can the better sympathize with as we have also experienced a similar misfortune. Mrs. Clay and myself reached home just in time to witness the death of her mother [Susannah Gray Hart]. It was a mitigation of our loss, which did not attend your's, that Mrs. Hart had attained a ripe old age.

I thank you for the interesting contents of your letter, in respect to the affairs of the public. The defeat of our Governor was mortifying.[2] Proceeding however as it did mainly from the force of religious prejudices, and accompanied as it was with other results of our Election which were gratifying, its bad effect will only be temporary out of the State, whilst it will serve to stimulate our friends to such exertions as cannot fail to lead to success in November. Accordingly our friends are every where on the alert and we confidently anticipate victory. If you could cause a few of the Extra's issued from the Cincinati papers to be sent to the Counties on Licking, opposite to you, they would have good effect. Some of our friends in N. Port [*sic*, Newport] would I presume undertake their distribution.

The division between the Anti Masons and N. Rs. in your State is to be regretted; but if it can not be healed before the election, I should think the Anti Masons would be absorbed, according to their individual predilections, by the two great contending parties. I can not imagine that many of them would persevere in the hopeless task of supporting their own tickets. Has there been any movement from the A. Ms. of N. Y. to reconcile those of Ohio to our cause? I should suppose that such a movement would be judicious.[3]

I am glad that the portion of our friends, among you, who were despairing, or cherishing other plans, have come back to us. Every thing should be done to soothe and encourage them, and no taunts or reproaches for the past should be employed. Both policy and justice urge the pursuit of this friendly and forbearing cause. We have not now time to wrangle, nor numbers to spare.

As to the issue of the P[residential]. Contest, I adhere to the opinion that Jackson will be defeated. From N. York my information, recd. from all quarters of the State, continues to assure me of the success of the Union ticket.[4] The agitations and divisions in Pennsa. do not allow us to see, with the same clearness, the probable result there; although I think they warrant a pretty confident belief that Jackson can not obtain the vote of that State. From Maine,[5] where our friends are in high hopes, we shall now hear very soon. South Carolina, I am fully persuaded, will not support Jackson; and altho her politics and mine are directly at variance, I do believe that in contingencies her vote will be given to our cause, in preference to Jackson. In Missouri,[6] our friends have taken courage and are in motion. I should have more confidence in Indiana, if they would adopt generally some system of organization to urge our friends to the Polls. Such a system is contemplated at the Convention,[7] which is to assemble at Lexington on the 20h., for this State.

I regret the perseverance of Judge [John] McLean[8] in the course which he pursues, both on his own and the public account. Entertaining the opinions which he does of the present Administration, one would think, that he would either be totally silent in regard to the issue of the P. Election, or contribute his exertion to avert what he deems a calamity.

ALS. ViU.   1. Reference obscure.   2. Smith to Clay, Dec. 27, 1831.   3. Clay to Hammond, August 27, 1832.   4. Clay to Weed, April 14, 1832; Clay to Porter, May 1, 1832. 5. Dearborn to Clay, August 26, 1832.   6. Clay to Dearborn, Sept. 6, 1832.   7. Clay to Beatty, Sept. 4, 1832.   8. For McLean's continuing hope that he himself might still become a compromise candidate in place of Wirt and Clay, thus uniting the anti-Jackson forces, see Francis P. Weisenburger, *The Life of John McLean, A Politician on the United States Supreme Court* (Columbus, Ohio, 1937), 79; Wilson, *Calhoun Papers*, 11:668.

To CHARLES JAMES FAULKNER   Lexington, September 8, 1832

I have the pleasure to acknowledge the reception of your letter of the 26h. of July last, delayed by my absence from home, communicating, by the instruction of the National Republican Convention of the State of Virginia,[1] recently assembled at Staunton, their unanimous concurrence in the resolutions adopted by the Baltimore & Washington Conventions, recommending me as a Candidate for the Presidency of the U. States.

This testimony of the favorable opinion of a deliberative body so distinguished as the Staunton Convention is received with sentiments of profound gratitude; and it is no slight addition to the estimate in which I hold it, that it proceeds from a State of which I have always satisfaction in recollecting that I was a native.

Having already announced my acceptance of the nomination made by the Baltimore Convention, it is now only necessary to add an expression of the gratification I derive from the concurrent resolution of the Staunton Convention; and to assure its members that I shall ever cherish a recollection of it with the highest esteem.

For the individual expressions of regard and friendship which are contained in your letter, I tender you also my cordial thanks. . . .[2]

ALS. KyU.   1. The National Republican convention in Virginia, which met at Staunton on July 23, 1832, chose Charles J. Faulkner as president, adopted a series of eight resolutions, and drew up an electoral ticket. Eighty-eight delegates were present. Richmond *Enquirer*, July 24, 1832. The "Address of the National Republican Convention Held in Staunton, Va." was published in *ibid.* on Sept. 18, 1832. For Faulkner, at this time a member of the Virginia house of delegates, see *BDAC*.   2. The phrase "cordial thanks" replaces "best respects" which is stricken through.

From William B. Rochester, Buffalo, N.Y., September 8, 1832. Reports his conviction that in the New York gubernatorial election [Clay to Bailhache, November 24, 1830; Clay to Porter, May 1, 1832], "[Francis] Granger will be elected by perhaps 10,000 maj." Says the "Jacksonians are evidently much alarmed" and have not been able to decide upon a candidate of their own, though "their wish is to meet Granger with a western man." Believes they will probably choose Jesse Buell [*DAB*], who will "be beaten by Granger & I shall be most egregiously mistaken if the vote on the electoral ticket do not exceed that of Granger." Adds "that were I a betting man, I would wage three to one upon it—" ALS. DLC-HC (DNA, M212, R5).

From Samuel L. Southard, Trenton, N.J., September 8, 1832. Reports that the Kentucky gubernatorial election [Smith to Clay, December 27, 1831] "disturbed us a great deal," but "will not do any material injury." Notes that the New Jersey "Legislative Election takes place on the 9 & 10 of Octr. & [is] deeply important," because "The joint Meeting will have to elect a Govr—Chief Justice—One & perhaps two Senators—a Clerk of the Sup: Court & several other important officers." States that the "Anti Masons have nominated an electoral ticket but no members of Congress & we hope to avoid any evil from that source." Believes that chances for success are good, in which case "Our friends assure me, that I shall be compelled to take either the office of Govr. Senr. or Ch: J[ustice]." Fears the "first will perhaps be insisted on," because "They say that my election to the off. of Govr—will tend to end all controversy here & secure the State hereafter." Asks if his presence in the Senate after the next session would be useful, and wants Clay's advice on what he should do. Adds that the "meeting to select members of Congress & Electors of P. & V.P. will be held on 16 Oct."ALS. DLC-HC (DNA, M212, R5). In the 1832 election for the state legislature in New Jersey, the National Republicans carried 8 out of 14 counties. On the joint state senate and assembly ballot, Clay supporters had a 42 to 22 majority over the Jacksonians. Lexington *Observer & Kentucky Reporter*, November 1, 1832. The legislature chose Southard for governor [Southard to Clay, November 3, 1832] and Joseph C. Hornblower [*DAB*] for chief justice. *BDGUS*, 3:1015 and *Niles' Register* (November 10, 1832), 43:171. In the 1832 presidential election in New Jersey, Jackson won 23,826 votes to 23,466 for Clay, and 468 for Wirt. Jacksonians narrowly won all six seats for the U.S. House. *Niles' Register* (December 1, 1832), 43:213.

From Josiah S. Johnston, Philadelphia, September 10, 1832. States that the result of the Kentucky state elections [Smith to Clay, December 27, 1831], "although not what we desired, is satisfactory & the impression is strongly made that that state is still safe." Notes that because the "strength of Genl Jackson depends much upon the idea of his invincibility, it is necessary to break this prestige—in order to let loose a great many men who are now held by the mere hopelessness of all opposition." Reports that "The impression daily gains ground that he will lose the election in the primary Colleges" due to the loss of New York and Pennsylvania. Hopes that before the election there will be "ample evidence that his power is broken in both," of these states, and this should be impressed "upon the people of the doubtful states of the West." Discusses the problem of the Anti-Masons and predicts "If those of N. York perceive that they can elect you by their own strength & terminate the Contest I think they will do it—"   Thinks it will be more difficult to convince the Anti-Masons in Pennsylvania. Predicts that if the Anti-Masons in New York and Pennsylvania support William Wirt instead of Clay, the presidential election will go to the House of Representatives. Contends that Wirt's "purpose

. . . is to defeat Genl. Jackson, and . . . He will I understand be ready to waive any pretentsions, & if it can be effectual to Urge the union of all the opposition." Believes that the Anti-Masons are a "very bigotted & impracticable set," but warns that "We must especially Unite cordially with them in N. York & Penna." ALS. InU.

To Charles H. List, September 10, 1832. Remarks that the "general prospects" of the coming presidential election "are cheering," and "Unless we are greatly disappointed in the issue of the Western Elections, Gen. Jackson's defeat is [inevi]table [Sergeant to Clay, June 27, 1831]." Concludes: "In this State our friends believe that success in November is more certain than if they had carried the Governor's Election [Smith to Clay, December 27, 1832] by a lean majority. Their loss of their Governor will operate as a stimulus to higher efforts." ALS. Courtesy of Justin G. Turner, Los Angeles, California. List has not been identified.

To ROBERT S. ROSE   Lexington, September 10, 1832
[Discusses a letter of recommendation he has previously received from Rose. Continues:]

I lately had an opportunity of passing a short time in Virginia with Mr. [James] Madison and Govr. [James] Barbour. Mr. Madison is feeble in health but his mind and memory are perfectly sound. He spoke with more freedom than usual on public affairs, and appeared to take a lively interest in passing events.

I rejoice to learn that there is an encouraging prospect of your State [New York] withdrawing its support from the present C. Magistrate of the U. States. In this State, our friends are confident of success in November; and their recent loss of their Governor,[1] from religious prejudices, has aroused them to more vigorous and systematic exertions that I think will ensure it.

ALS. ViU.   1. Smith to Clay, Dec. 27, 1831.

From Buckner H. Payne, Mt. Sterling, Ky., September 11, 1832. Informs Clay that he will see him in Lexington "one day next week" and will "bring with me the Books of Stamboul [Berryman to Clay, October 5, 1831] for the purpose of exhibiting the register of the mares served by him." Reports that Stamboul has earned "for seasons of mares which have been taken away nearly fifteen hundred Dollars." ALS. Josephine Simpson Collection, Lexington, Ky.

To SAMUEL L. SOUTHARD   Lexington, September 11, 1832
I addressed a letter to you communicating information respecting the issue of our Kentucky Election.[1] From subsequent intelligence I am perfectly satisfied that the loss of our Governor was attributable to inconquerable religious prejudices mainly; and that there is every reason to anticipate, with great confidence, success in November. We lost in five Counties that we know well, from the above cause, votes enough to have turned the scale — votes that we are perfectly satisfied will be given to us in the electoral election.[2] Our friends generally are greatly mortified at the result, highly incensed at the Jackson shouts of victory, and firmly resolved to achieve a triumph. Accordingly they are making the most vigorous and systematic arrangements. The operation of the Bank veto[3] is now beginning to be seriously felt. This is the season when we drive to the Atlantic and other markets vast numbers of horses, mules, cattle and hogs. The Bank was in the habit of aiding this traffic by supplying the means of driving them to market. Its suspension of purchasing drafts, founded upon sales contemplated of this description of property has subjected it to

considerable reduction of price, and the veto is in every body's mouth, and what is worse seriously felt in the purse.

I believe I omitted to acknowledge the receipt of your favor of the 13h. Ulto. You ask me what are the hopes in all the West? As to Kentucky, I have already said all that is necessary. In Ohio there are some difficulties with the Anti Masons, but measures are on foot to obviate them; and some of our best informed friends believe whether those measures are successful or not we shall carry the State. In Indiana there will be a warm and close struggle. I would not exchange chances with Jackson. In Missouri and Illinois, where until lately I had no hopes, our friends have taken courage; and do not despair of success, particularly in the former State. Louisiana is perfectly certain.

I have heard that some recent difficulties have sprung up in New Jersey.[4] What are they, and what is likely to be their influence?

Mr [John] Sergeant writes me that no doubt is entertained of the success of the Union ticket in N. York;[5] nor of [Joseph] Ritner's election in Pennsa.[6] altho' he speaks with less certainty as to the result of the subsequent choice of Electors in the latter State. Genl. [Peter B.] Porter and others also express entire confidence in regard to New York. . . .

ALS. NjP. 1. Smith to Clay, Dec. 23, 1831. 2. The Lexington *Observer & Kentucky Reporter* of August 23, 1832, attributed Buckner's defeat "solely to religious prejudices, and local feelings." It is not possible to determine the five counties to which Clay refers, because Clay carried twelve more counties for president than Buckner had carried for governor. *Ibid.*, August 30; Nov. 29, 1832. 3. Clay to Brown, Dec. 18, 1831; Webster to Clay, Jan. 8, 1832; Clay to Fendall, August 4, 1832. 4. Possibly a reference to problems with the Anti-Masons in New Jersey referred to in Southard to Clay, Dec. 1, 1832. 5. Clay to Porter, May 1, 1832. 6. Clay to Ketchum, May 15, 1832.

To JESSE BURTON HARRISON   Lexington, September 15, 1832

I duly recd. your favor of the 4th inst. I had heard at the White Sulphur Springs of your having been there, prior to my recent visit to them, and regretted very much that I had not the pleasure of meeting you. I am however much gratified to learn that you purpose passing through Kentucky in October, and I beg you not to neglect calling at Ashland. I should think that a week or two passed at Louisville and Lexington would enable you to make useful acquaintances among the men of business that might prove beneficial to you in your Professional pursuit at New Orleans.[1] There too you would have an opportunity of becoming better acquainted with Mr. [James] Erwin, whose summer residence adjoins my own, and who talks of going to N. Orleans towards the last of October. I feel no delicacy, and shall take much pleasure, in recommending to Mr. Erwin the performance of any friendly offices in his power towards you. I do not believe that he has much law business of his own, but he has a very extensive acquaintance in all the Southern and South Western States.

On the other point of your letter, my interposition to produce a Co-partnership between yourself and Mr. [George] Eustis, through Judge [Alexander] Porter, I feel some embarrassment. It is a matter in which I fear I could hardly interfere, without subjecting myself to some misapprehension. Supposing such a partnership desirable, I think you are probably mistaken as to the best agency to effect it. Unless I am misinformed, the relations between the Judge and Mr. Eustis are far from being of that friendly kind which you imagine. I am told indeed that they are directly and positively otherwise. Such is the belief of one, intimate with them both, on whose information I rely.

When I shall have the satisfaction of seeing you in October we will converse fully on these subjects, and I will communicate more freely with you in respect to those two gentlemen.

You appreciate justly the character of the population of N[ew]. O[rleans]. It is especially a place of business, and all are intently in the pursuit of wealth. Such a population is to be addressed, by a Professional man, through its interests. Satisfy it that the candidate for its patronage is a man of talents, and, what there is not of less importance, that he is industrious, punctual, and regular in his habits, and he will, sooner or latter, command public confidence, and a full share of public patronage. These essential qualities being possessed, whether employment is obtained more quickly or tardily, will depend upon address, pleasing manners and other collateral advantages.

I shall expect to receive the Pamphlet[2] which you are about to publish, from the perusal of which I anticipate much information, and gratification. Hoping I shall not be disappointed in seeing you in October. . . .

Copy. DLC-HC (DNA, M212, R5).   1. Harrison, a lawyer, settled in New Orleans and became secretary of the Historical Society of Louisiana in the mid-1830s. *LHQ*, 23:1044; Albert Fossier, *New Orleans the Glamour Period 1800-1843* (New Orleans, 1957), 243; *VMHB*, 80:320-21. 2. Probably a reference to the pamphlet, entitled *Review of the Slave Question . . . Showing That Slavery is the Essential Hindrance to the Prosperity of the Slave-Holding States. . . .* Richmond, 1833.

To WILLIAM H. TEAGARDEN   Lexington, September 15, 1832
[Discusses in detail the various provisions for land grants and pensions to soldiers of the American Revolution, and asserts that "I exerted myself to ensure the passage of the last Pension law."[1] Continues:]

The zeal you manifest to prevent the re-election of Genl. Jackson is worthy of your patriotism; and I am happy to assure you that it is my belief you are not working in a hopeless cause. It is my deliberate opinion, from all the information which has reached me, that the General will be defeated. I think he will *certainly* lose N. York and Ohio, and probably Pennsa.

You are better able to judge of your part of Kentucky[2] than I am; but if our friends there make exertions which are commensurate with the interests at stake, there can be no doubt of the issue. I believe North of the Kentucky will do better than it ever has done in any former election.

ALS. NcD.   1. 4 *U.S. Stat.*, 497.   2. Teagarden, who had formerly lived in Lexington and had studied medicine under Dr. Elisha Warfield, now lived on a farm near Hopkinsville. *RKHS* (April, 1942), 40:131.

From William F. Dunnica, St. Louis, September 17, 1832. Discusses Clay's tax receipts and methods which he may use to pay his current taxes. Turning to politics, notes that "Since your Report on the Public Land [Comment in Senate, April 16, 1832] . . . the reading part of Citizens have expressed themselves decidedly in favor of it." States also that "a great effort" will be made by this session of the Missouri legislature to unseat Sen. Thomas Hart Benton [Clay to Dearborn, September 6, 1832]. Continues: "Our Assembly is composed of 45 Hickory [Jackson] boys & 22 Clay. The plan contemplated, is to get 12 Jacksonites to settle upon some other one of their candidates amongst whom are 4 aspirant & then concentrate upon him. Of the Candidates there is [George F.] Strother, [Thomas H.] Benton, [Robert W.] Wells & [Thomas] Reynolds." ALS. DLC-TJC (DNA, M212, R14).

From Henry A.S. Dearborn, Roxbury, Mass., September 18, 1832. Expresses optimism as to the outcome of the presidential election. States: "In all quarters there is a glorious spirit bursting forth, which presages triumphant results. Confidence in their own strength, & zealous activity begin to be felt among the friends of the constitution. They can accomplish all that they hope if they are *sanguine of success*, & are *determined* to be *victorious*." Is especially encouraged by signs in New York and by the Maine state elections where "The result is so favorable, that our friends are confident of carrying their ticket for electors in November." Adds that the people "are Sanguine in the belief of a complete victory in the next struggle, for which this has been a good *premonitory sympton*."

Laments the death of Susannah Gray Hart [Clay to Thomas H. Clay, August 28, 1832]. ALS. DLC-HC (DNA, M212, R5). In the Maine gubernatorial election of 1832 incumbent Samuel E. Smith, a Jacksonian, defeated the Clay candidate, Daniel Goodenow, by a vote of 31,987 to 27,651. *BDGUS*, 2:600. In the state legislature in Maine, Jacksonians won approximately 97 seats in the house to 59 for Clay supporters, and also controlled the senate by 13 seats to 10. Kennebec *Journal*, September 28, 1832. In the presidential election, Jackson won all 10 of Maine's electoral votes, defeating Clay by a popular vote of 33,984 to 27,362. Gammon, *The Presidential Campaign of 1832*, 170; Lexington *Observer & Kentucky Reporter*, December 13, 1832.

From Elisha Whittlesey, Canfield, Ohio, September 19, 1832. Regrets the defeat of Richard A. Buckner for governor of Kentucky [Smith to Clay, December 27, 1831] "on account of its influence on doubtful states, still, I think the result of the election shows most clearly that Kentucky will not give her vote for Gen Jackson." States that he did not wish to be a candidate for Congress this year, so when the Anti-Masons nominated Judge Peter Hitchcock [*DAB*], Whittlesey recommended that the National Republicans also nominate him. They did so, but Hitchcock declined both nominations. Notes that the Anti-Masons "have lately nominated Thomas D. Webb," but the National Republicans "not being willing to support him, held a meeting and put me in nomination and I have consented to run." Believes that when the Jackson party holds its convention "tomorrow or next day," they will try to form a union with the Anti-Masons [Hammond to Clay, August 11, 1832; Clay to Hammond, August 27,1832] by nominating Webb. Adds that "The opposition to me is most violent," and "If the antimasons and Jacksonites unite they will carry the election." Considers a union doubtful, but also believes his own "election may be considered doubtful, tho my friends say not."

Complains that the "[Western] Reserve is in a state of distraction arising solely to the injudicious course pursued by the antimasons—They have been resolved not to yield any thing, however ruinous their course might be to the country." States that the Anti-Masons, with their "proscriptive courses, have disgusted a great many of our friends—and to retaliate on antimasonry—They have turned Jacksonites." Mentions that the "veto bank message [Clay to Brown, December 18, 1831; Webster to Clay, January 8, 1832; Clay to Fendall, August 4, 1832] contrary to all reasonable calculations, to a considerable extent is popular." Continues: "I am in hopes there will be but two tickets for the Presidential election, but there will be no union on any other tickets, and the Jackson party for causes adverted to, have undoubtedly gained strength, and so great are the dissentions between many of our friends and the antimasons, that the whole of our strength cannot be brot out on a union ticket. I have endeavored to reconcile the dissentions; but have not affected it to any considerable extent—I have no doubt three fifths of the antimasons in the district wish my election, and still individually, they dare not vote for me for fear of breaking up their party. They say they must adhere to 'principle.' This account is more gloomy than I ever expected to give of the northern part of the State. . . . Permit me to make a prediction. If the antimasonic, or union ticket, in New York, or in Pennsylvania, or in Ohio shall prevail, every antimasonic vote on either of them, will be given for Mr [William] Wirt—If the Election should go into the House of Representatives, every antimason will vote for Mr Wirt. The party is resolved to yield nothing. I shall be much surprised if my prediction fails." Concludes: "From what I can learn generally through the State, we shall probably have a majority in the next Congress." ALS. DLC-HC (DNA, M212, R5). Whittlesey handily won reelection with a vote of 4,281 to 2,980 for William Rayen, the Jackson candidate, and 1,997 for Thomas D. Webb, the Anti-Masonic candidate. Lexington *Observer & Kentucky Reporter*, October 25, 1832. For Rayen, see Harry R. Stevens, *The Early Jackson Party in Ohio* (Durham, N.C., 1957), 135; for Webb, see *Historical Collection of the Mahoning Valley . . .* (Youngstown, Ohio, 1876), 1:257. In the 23rd Congress the distribution of seats by party was roughly as follows — House: Democrat/Jacksonian-147, National Republican/Clay-60, Anti-Mason and other-53, [*sic*, 35]; Senate: Democrat/Jacksonian-20, National Republican/Clay-20, Other-8. Adapted from U.S. Bureau of Census (with cooperation of Social Science Research Council), *The Statistical History of the United States from Colonial Times to the Present.* Two volumes in one (Stamford, Conn., 1965), 691. The Anti-Mason figure is rendered incorrectly as 53 instead of 35. Glyndon G. Van Deusen, in *The Jacksonian Era, 1828-1848* (New York, 1959), 86, gives the breakdown in the House as: Democrat-147, National Republican-43, Anti-Mason-53 [*sic*, 35], Nullifiers-7, and States' Rights-10; Senate: Democrat-20, National Republican-20, Nullifiers-2, and States' Rights-6. Clay correctly interpreted the numbers to add up to a small Jacksonian working majority in the House and a small anti-Jacksonian majority in the Senate. Clay to Brown, December 10, 1833; Clay to Brooke, December 11, 1833. On the critical removal-of-deposits issue, for example, the key roll-calls in the House supported Jackson by a 12 to 15 vote majority. Clay to Tazewell, April 5, 1834. Conversely, the censure of Taney by the Senate was upheld 28 to 18; that of Jackson, 26 to 20. *Register of Debates*, 23 Cong., 1 Sess., 1187. See also, Bradley to Clay, October 16, 1832.

From John L. Lawrence, New York City, *ca.* September 21, 1832. Reports that "If matters . . . have not already been arranged" in Ohio, "we propose to send in some influential individuals to bring order out of the confusion there [Whittlesey to Clay, September 19, 1832]." States that in New York "we have the highest hopes notwithstanding the tremendous odds we have to fight against in the power & patronage of the govr." Mentions that "Our meeting of *young men* took place a few nights ago," and he has had "a cheering account of the numbers & spirit of the meeting." Adds that "Last night we had a most gratifying assemblage," and that "In drafting the resolutions, I took care that there should be no milk & water in them, but they were not one inch in advance of the temper of the meeting." ALS. DLC-HC (DNA, M212, R5). A meeting of "Young men opposed to the re-election of Andrew Jackson" met at Masonic Hall in New York City on September 18, 1832, with a thousand or more persons in attendance. Hiram Ketchum and Frederick Tallmadge both made speeches. Philadelphia *United States Gazette*, September 22, 1832; New York *Evening Post*, September 24, 1832.

From Unknown Author, Woodbury, Jefferson County, Va., September 28, 1832. Discusses whether or not the session of the Virginia state legislature should be postponed because of the advance of the cholera toward Richmond. States that newspaper accounts indicate the situation there is "pretty serious as there seems no demonstration any longer as to classes or situations in this desolating scourage." Adds that "as we can fit up our term of service without difficulty by pushing the commencement of the Court into the winter and its termination into the Spring I see no reason why we should expose ourselves and others to unnecessary hazard." L, incomplete. DLC-HC (DNA, M212, R5).

From JOSIAH S. JOHNSTON   Philadelphia, September 29, 1832
You will See by the papers that yesterday was signalized by a total defeat of the Jackson party in this City — [1] Against all the influence & all the exertions of the officers of General & State Governments, as well as of the Corporation — The

result exceeded all anticipations — Similar Changes may be looked for in other parts of the state, where the influence of the example will not be lost.

Francis Johnson is directed to publish 20 thousand Copies of the Review of the Veto[2] for Kentucky & Indiana — It will be published also in Lexington, Cincinnati & St. Louis. It will be well to have some Understanding with Johnson about the distribution.

But what is of the greatest moment & the Chief object of this letter, is to write to [Martin] Duralde to make a great effort in Louisiana Committees in N orleans should Correspond with every Parish in order to produce on[e] great United effort   I write about 30 letters to different places — Our friends in Ohio & Kentucky ought to Correspond freely with Indiana —

ALS. InU.   1. Clay to Davis, Oct. 6, 1832.   2. Clay to Biddle, August 27, 1832.

From Abbott Lawrence, Boston, October 4, 1832. States that "in consequence of the . . . Cholera," he has postponed "writing to you respecting obtaining a situation for your Son [James Brown Clay] in a mercantile establishment here." Now, however, the pestilence has diminished enough for the boy to be able to come with safety. Has learned today that James W. Paige & Co. will soon be seeking an apprentice. Notes that the "situation is a good one and I should be glad to have your Son placed there." If Paige cannot hire him, "I will endeavor to place him where he will obtain a good education." Indeed, he promises Clay to act "at all times as the friend and guardian of your Son, should you make up your mind to send him here." Also assures Clay that "there will be less risk in this city than in N York or almost any other City," because the "morals of our young men, I think generally very good and their habits better now than at any period since my remembrance." ALS. DLC-HC (DNA, M212, R5). James W. Paige & Co., of which Nathan Appleton was a partner, dealt in domestic goods. *Boston City Directory, 1837.* For young Clay's placement in a Boston commercial house, see Clay to Henry Clay, Jr., December 30, 1832. For Abbott Lawrence, see *NCAB,* 3:63-64.

From Francis T. Brooke, near Fredickburg, Va., October 6, 1832. Reports a rumor in Virginia that Clay had withdrawn from the presidential race. Attributes its origin to Duff Green, dismisses it, and promises that "we shall make great exertions in Virginia and something favorable may grow out of Division in the Jackson party as to the VP [Brooke to Clay, February 9, 1832]." Notes that the cholera is subsiding at Richmond, and he will go there in about ten days and will "learn more of the state of things in Virginia —" ALS. DLC-HC (DNA, M212, R5).

To MATTHEW L. DAVIS   Lexington, October 6, 1832
I recd. your obliging letter of the 15h. Ulto. with its valuable enclosure, for which I thank you.

In this State, our friends are in the best possible spirits, complete organization, and in the highest confidence of success. I never witnessed on any former occasion so much activity zeal and firm resolution to triumph in Novr. We cannot, I think, fail of success. Jacksons' late tour through our State has been turned with tremendous effect against him.[1]

From Indiana *all* my accounts speak of success in terms of the utmost confidence. More exertion is making in that State by our friends than on any former occasion.

Of Louisiana there is not a particle of doubt.

Even in Missouri and Illinois our friends have taken courage and do not despair.

I congratulate you on the events of the elections at Albany, Philada. and Pittsburg [*sic*] &c.[2] They justify strong hopes of the Empire and the Key States. God grant that they may be realized.

ALS. KyU.   1. Jackson traveled through Kentucky in early October enroute to Washington from Tennessee. On Oct. 7 he was honored at a barbecue in Lexington. Clay partisans charged him with electioneering in the state. Lexington *Observer & Kentucky Reporter*, Oct. 4, 11, 1832; Louisville *Public Advertiser*, Oct. 2, 15, 1832.   2. In the charter elections in Albany the anti-Jackson, anti-Regency group won 16 of 20 seats in the common council, carrying 4 out of the 5 wards in the city. Albany *Argus*, Sept. 26, 1832; Washington *Daily National Intelligencer*, Oct. 1, 1832; *Niles' Register* (Oct. 6, 1832), 43:83. In the election of city inspectors of the general elections for the city of Philadelphia, the anti-Jackson party prevailed in 13 of 15 wards with a vote of 4,331 to 2,811 for the Jacksonians. The vote in the county as a whole was similar. In Pittsburgh the anti-Jackson party received 808 votes to 647 for the Jacksonians. *Niles' Register* (Oct. 6, 1832), 43:84.

To JOSIAH S. JOHNSTON   Lexington, October 6, 1832

I recd. tonight your favor of the 29h. Ulto. as I did your previous one, which I postponed acknowledging until the return of the franking privilege.

The news from Albany, Philada. and Pittsburg [*sic*]is most cheering.[1] I trust that it is a prelude to the triumph of the Country and its Constitution in November.

In this State the best possible spirit prevails, and the best system of organization has been adopted. We have had three Conventions at Lexington and Russellville,[2] at which more than 1000 delegates were assembled. Every where our friends are excited. Jackson's recent Electioneering tour has fired their indignation;[3] and I entertain no doubt of our success in November. By appeals to the prominent individuals of our party, ample funds for all legitimate purposes of the Canvass have been procured. Farmers have promptly advanced their fiftys and hundreds of dollars. The State feels that every thing is at hazard on the issue of the Election. Men who never before took part in our Elections, or who had retired from the theatre of action, are amongst the most active of our friends. We shall not — we can not fail.

From Indiana[4] we have the most satisfactory accounts. Our friends there count with great confidence on success. You will hear from Ohio[5] nearly as soon as your receive this letter, and I am persuaded you will hear favorably. We do not altogether despair of Missouri and Illinois.[6] A fortunate issue of the Pennsa. elections[7] will exert a powerful influence on both those States.

I have this night written to [Martin] Duralde. The Review[8] is an admirable paper, and I am glad that measures are taken for its extensive circulation. It was much wanted. Who wrote it? My affectionate regards to Mrs. [Eliza Sibley] Johnston.

ALS. PHi. Copy in DLC-TJC (DNA, M212, R14).   1. Porter to Clay, Oct. 8, 1832.   2. The National Republican state convention met in Lexington on Sept. 20, and the Young Men's National Republican convention also met there on Sept. 25. The Green River convention met in Russellville on Sept. 27 "to collect and embody information upon the many exciting and interesting subjects appertaining to the election of President." Lexington *Observer & Kentucky Reporter*, Sept. 20; Oct. 4, 1832.   3. Clay to Davis, Oct. 6, 1832.   4. Lawrence to Clay, August 30, 1832; Clay to Lyman, Oct. 22, 1832.   5. Hammond to Clay, August 11, 1832; Clay to Brown, Oct. 23, 1832.   6. Clay to Dearborn, Sept. 6, 1832; Clay to Lyman, Oct. 22, 1832.   7. Clay to Ketchum, May 15, 1832; Clay to Davis, Oct. 6, 1832.   8. Clay to Biddle, August 27, 1832.

From Josiah S. Johnston, Philadelphia, October 8, 1832. States that "Tomorrow will decide the political character of the State," and predicts that "it will result in the overthrow of the party & the prostration of the power of Jacksonism." Reports that "a deep feeling of danger to the Country prevails in this Community," and "it begins to reach the class so long deluded—The working classes." Believes that although George Wolf is stronger than Jackson—"having [Samuel D.] Ingham & many others to adhere to him who have abandon[e]d the other"—Joseph Ritner will win the governorship [Clay to Ketchum, May 15, 1832]. Adds that in New York "I cannot doubt that the Hero [Jackson] & the Magician [Van Buren] will fall together [Clay to Bailhache, November 24, 1830]." ALS. InU. For the Pennsylvania legislative election on October 9, see Clay to Davis, October 6, 1832.

From Peter B. Porter, Black Rock, N.Y., October 8, 1832. Reports that "our political prospects in this State are admirable, & constantly improving," and "I feel now quite confident that we shall succeed, both in our gubernatorial & electoral tickets [Clay to Bailhache, November 24, 1830; Sergeant to Clay, June 27, 1831]." States that the "news of the favourable results of the charter elections in Albany [Clay to Davis, October 6, 1832], & the Inspector elections in Pennsylvania [*ibid.*], has had a most cheering effect." Mentions that Van Buren and Enos T. Throop, "or as they are jeeringly called 'The Jack O'Lantern' & 'The Small Light'—lately attempted an electioneering tour through the parts of this state," but when they heard of the result of the Albany election "or perhaps, of other not less favorable signs, they turned about and went home."

Notes that William B. Rochester "did not for a time behave in a manner entirely satisfactory to his political friends," at one time seeming to be willing to support Van Buren but not Jackson. Concludes: "Of late, however, he is much more decided," and has even offered to wager that Clay will defeat Jackson. AL, incomplete. InU. Draft, undated, and with slightly different phraseology, capitalization, etc., in OHi.

From Philip R. Fendall, Washington, October 9, 1832. Writes that "the Cholera has raged in this city with great severity," reportedly killing an average of thirty per day "for one period of 15 days." The disease "seems to be but little better understood either here or in every other part of the Union than it was at the beginning [Remark in Senate, June 27, 1832]."

States that the "defeat of the Regency at Albany [Clay to Davis, October 6, 1832], though intrinsically a small matter, is of great importance as a sign of the times in New York," because "It has broken the charm of invincibility, which has hitherto been so serviceable to that party, and encouraged the opposition all over the state." Believes that the Jackson men in Washington do not calculate on receiving New York's vote. Adds: "Taking New York from Jackson, and giving it to us, I can't see how he is to get 145 [electoral] votes, unless helped to them by the errors of his adversaries."

Laments the "imprudence" of the committee of the National Republican Young Men of Washington [Steuart to Clay, May 10, 1832] who have circulated "the prospectus of the Extra [Washington *United States*] Telegraph under their official recommendation." Believes the paper "ought undoubtedly to be aided, because it is endeavouring at least to weaken Jackson. But a formal sanction to it by any respectable organ of the National Republicans seems objectionable, and may hereafter be embarrassing." Explains that "Duff Greens game is not hard to be understood. He aims, should Jackson be defeated, at coming in again to the public printing with the winning party." Green, therefore, is working for William Wirt's election, "as he cannot hope for the support of your friends." Adds that Green supposedly entertains "serious thoughts of writing a letter" to Clay, asking him to step aside in favor of Wirt.

Concludes by asking Clay to write a letter to Nicholas Biddle supporting Fendall for the position of "Attorney to the Branch Bank of the U. States at this place." ALS. DLC-HC (DNA, M212, R5). No "Extra Telegraph" has been found, though one is mentioned in the Washington *United States Telegraph* of September 15, 1832.

From George W. Spotswood, Kanahawa (County) Court House, Va. (W. Va.), October 10, 1832. Reports that the "greatest and best [Jackson] made his appearance on Sunday [October 7] . . . and immediately hurried to the Prespeterian [*sic*, Presbyterian] Church, where he arrived just in time to receive the blessing." Later, "he was waited on by the very few Jackson men of the village and received their congratulations, others not belonging to his party waited on him more from curiosity, than otherwise and came away, better convinsed than ever . . . of his incompetency to fill the exalted station he now fills, which God grant he may be hurled from after the 4th. of march, not in the stile of Lucifer, for poor old man, he has suffered enough, and we ought to wish him peace & quietness, his few remaining days in private life." Relates that at dinner, those who dined with the president, "seazed with eagerness the carving Knife and would have fallen to work without regard to the sacred character of the God like man, 'but he who was born to command' (I am told) with a wave of the hand brought all to order, and in a most impressive manner pronounced a benediction." States that "several of my friends tried to prevail on me to pay my respects to the President, but I declined doing so, as I cannot reconcile it to my feelings to act the hipocrite." Complains of the "Dreadful . . . state of our Country," but believes "we have every reason to hope that the good sense of the people will not only consign to contempt and obscurity the present administration, but that it will also rebuke the audacious & parracidal effort to kindle the flames of cival war." ALS. DLC-HC (DNA, M212, R5). Jackson traveled through the western portion of Virginia on his way from Tennessee to Washington. Lynchburg *Virginian*, October 15, 1832; Washington *United States Telegraph*, October 9, 1832.

From Joseph Gales & William Seaton, Washington, October 12, 1832. Transmit "an Extra [Washington *Daily*] Nat. Intel[ligenc]er or two containing Mr [William] Russell's Letter, which we consider So important in its bearing that we Shall print & distribute at our own expense forty or fifty thousand copies of it." State that "We have nothing to fear now, we believe, but from the treason of pretended friends, Such as John McLean, John Bailey, & Co." LS. DLC-HC (DNA, M212, R5). Ohio Congressman William Russell, a former Jacksonian, had written a letter on September 21, 1832, "To the Electors of the 5th Congressional District," explaining his reasons for now opposing Jackson and arguing that all presidents should be limited to one term. Washington *Daily National Intelligencer*, October 9, 1832. The "treason" of John McLean and John Bailey was apparently their association with the Anti-Masonic movement. *BDAC*.

Clay replied on October 19, 1832, telling them that he had previously read the letter "and appreciate it as you do." Adds that his information "authorizes" the conclusion that Jackson has lost Pennsylvania and Ohio. ALS. NcD.

From Buckner H. Payne, Mt. Sterling, Ky., October 12, 1832. Sends list of the owners of 113 mares which Stamboul serviced during the season, at $25 each. This brings his gross earnings for that period to $2,825, less a refund charge to the owner of one mare that died and the lost income of $150 from six owners to whom no service charge was made. Net income was $2,650.

In regard to politics, states that "The boys are getting pretty warm—The passage of Gen. Jackson has aroused them, and I think we shall make his visit of very considerable advantage to the cause of the *Laws, Constitution* and *honesty.*" Notes that "Capt. [Henry] Daniel has prepared an address for his constituents, which takes the Gen. Mr. V.B. & the [Washington] Globe &c &c. into pretty rough keeping—it will be published in a few days." Adds in a postscript that "Col. [Aquilla] Young, the Jackson Senator from this district, who wields an immense influence with a certain Class of Jackson men, this day was immersed & joined the Baptist Church, and so he will be lost to them . . . for if he live up to his profession . . . he can't be high fellow with them any longer." ALS. Josephine Simpson Collection, Lexington, Ky. For Aquilla Young, see Collins, *History of Kentucky*, 2:632. Daniel's address, entitled "Circular to the People of the First Congressional District," asserted that the Washington *Globe* was established by those promoting the presidential ambitions of Martin Van Buren and that it received patronage in the sum of twenty to thirty thousand dollars a year from the departments of State, Navy, and the Post Office, as well as from the president. Lexington *Observer & Kentucky Reporter*, October 25, 1832.

From Elisha Whittlesey, Canfield, Ohio, October 12, 1832. Reports that "the election in this district . . . has resulted more favourably than I was led to fear when I wrote you [Whittlesey to Clay, September 19, 1832]" and that "there cannot exist I think, any doubt of my being reelected." Complains that the administration in Washington in the person of Elijah Hayward, commissioner of the General Land Office, the same Hayward "who only wanted 55 Additional Clerks last winter," has been flooding "this district" with pension promises and franked pro-Jackson campaign materials [Clay to Fendall, August 4, 1832]. Believes, nonetheless, that John Sloane has been reelected in the 15th District and that "the Western Reserve is Anti Jackson throughout, as to County and State offices [Hammond to Clay, August 11, 1832]." ALS. DLC-HC (DNA, M212, R5). For the cause of pension-claims favors as a Jackson party campaign device, see Washington *Globe* (Supplement), July 19, 1832.

From William A. Bradley, Washington, October 16, 1832. Reports that he has just been informed of "a most nefarious scheme" which "has been projected by certain leading Jacksonians, whose names I cannot learn." States that the scheme, which "may be the true cause of the [Bank of the U.S.] Veto [Clay to Brown, December 18, 1831; Webster to Clay, January 8, 1832]," calls for removal of the government deposits from the B.U.S., if Jackson is reelected, and their deposit in certain state banks "on the condition that loans are to be made to certain individuals to an immense Amount ($3.000.000 have been named)." Continues: "this sum is to be invested in *Western* property when it has reached the lowest point of the depression to be caused by the withdrawal of the deposits and consequent curtailments of the Bank of the U. States — When all this is done a Bank of the U. States is to be chartered to afford the rascals an opportunity to reap the profits of their villiany, which will be in the appreciation of the value of the property purchased." Mentions in closing that prospects for Clay's victory "on this side the Alleghany are very cheering" and that "even Virg[ini]a & N. Carolina may be hoped for [Sergeant to Clay, June 27, 1831]." ALS. DLC-HC (DNA, M212, R5).

For Jackson's proposal to remove government deposits from the B.U.S., his subsequent plan to place removed deposits in various state banks, and the movement in Congress and elsewhere to restore deposits so moved, see Hammond, *Banks and Politics in America*, 361; Munro, *Louis McLane*, 317-24, 335-39, 375-80; Govan, *Nicholas Biddle*, 236-59; Van Deusen, *The Life of Henry Clay*, 277-78. For Secretary of the Treasury Roger B. Taney's report to Congress, dated December 3, 1833, explaining the reasons for removing the deposits, see *Register of Debates*, 23 Cong., 1 Sess., Appendix, 59-68; Swisher, *Roger B. Taney*, 249-53. For Clay's principal speech attacking Jackson's proposal to remove the deposits and demanding the censure of Jackson and Taney, see Speech in Senate, December 26, 30, 31, 1833. Clay's role in the legislature history of the removal-censure issue in the Senate, and the subsequent vote there on March 28, 1834, to censure President Jackson and Secretary Taney, is in *ibid.*, 25, 27, 29, 30, 34, 36, 37, 51, 57-58, 94-95, 466, 477, 485, 492, 1172, 1187, 1813. For the legislative history of the issue in the House, where on June 13, 1834, the Senate resolution censuring Taney was tabled on motion of Rep. James K. Polk (Tenn.) by a vote of 114 to 101, see *Register of Debates*, 23 Cong., 1 Sess., 2170-79, 2867-70, 4467-68; Clay to Tazewell, April 5, 1834; Van Deusen, *The Life of Henry Clay*, 284. For Clay's unsuccessful attempt to censure Taney by joint resolution (it passed only the Senate), see *Register of Debates*, 23 Cong., 1 Sess., 1813, 1817-24, 1895-96. For House votes on April 4, 1834, on restoration of the deposits, recharter of the B.U.S., continuation of state banks as depositories for public monies, and the need to investigate the B.U.S. for administrative corruption and political chicanery, see Clay to Tazewell, April 5, 1834; and *Register of Debates*, 23 Cong., 1 Sess., 3473-77. The final Senate vote on the combined removal of deposits-Taney/Jackson censure issue is in *Register of Debates*, 23 Cong., 1 Sess., (March 28, 1834), 1187. For party and faction voting strength in the House and Senate in the 23rd Congress, see Whittlesey to Clay, September 19, 1832.

From Daniel Jenifer, Harris's Lot Post Office [Charles Co.], Md., October 16, 1832. Reports that "the Maryland Elections for Delegates to the Legislature" have "resulted in favour of the N. Repub: 54 to 26. But *Some Counties* in the State have carried their entire ticket for Jackson and but two others, Washington and Queen Ann[e], have indicated a preference." States that Maryland "as Districted for Presidential Electors, will in November give certainly *seven* [Sergeant to Clay, June 27, 1831], and our friends in the City of Baltimore are still sanguine as to their success there." Mentions having read of Jackson's visit "by accident, to Lexington [Clay to Davis, October 6, 1832]," and adds that he hopes the president "has not succeeded in converting you over to his '*judicious*' administration." ALS. DLC-HC (DNA, M212, R5). Jenifer's statistics on the make-up of the Maryland legislature are accurate. Washington County elected 4 Jackson men, while Queen Anne County elected 3 Jacksonians and 1 National Republican. Of Maryland's 10 electoral votes, 5 went for Clay, 3 for Jackson, and two were not cast. Jackson carried Baltimore city and county. Gammon, *The Presidential Campaign of 1832*, 170; Boston *Daily Advocate*, November 22; December 3, 1832.

To FRANCIS T. BROOKE   Lexington, October 18, 1832
[With reference to Brooke's letter of October 6, denies any intention whatever of withdrawing from the presidential race. Explains:]

I should not feel at liberty, upon my individual motion, to withdraw my name, even if circumstances rendered it expedient, at this period. I am in the hands of my friends, and should feel bound to consult them on such an important measure. But it would be strange if I were to adopt such a proceeding, at a moment when all the circumstances are decidedly favorable. I consider the defeat of Genl. Jackson as almost *certain*; and the probability of our success much greater than that of either the Genl. or Mr. [William] Wirt.

We are just receiving the returns from Ohio and Pennsa. I think [Darius] Lyman is elected in the former State, altho' it is not yet certainly ascertained.[1] If the Western reserve has gone, as a letter assures me it has,[2] he must be elected. [Joseph] Ritner too is elected or beaten by a small majority.[3] Our friends are perfectly confident of success in this State, and have adopted an effective system of organization, which will be executed with great zeal. We count also on Indiana, where our prospects are very flattering.

I did not write you after my return, because the papers would communicate all the information, on public affairs, which I possessed. We suffered, too, much by a private affliction, in the death of Mrs. Clay's mother [Susannah Gray Hart]. . . . P.S. You may hear that I am dead with the Cholera. I assure you upon my honor it is not true. We have as yet escaped that pestilence in Lexington 'though it is raging at Louisville and Cincinnati.[4]

ALS. NcD.   1. Hammond to Clay, August 11, 1832; Clay to Davis, Oct. 6, 1832.   2. Whittlesey to Clay, Oct. 12, 1832.   3. Clay to Ketchum, May 15, 1832.   4. Remark in Senate, June 27, 1832.

From Charles Kinsey, New Prospect, Bergen County, New Jersey, October 18, 1832. Reports that in the election in New Jersey, returns "give 43 Clay 21 Jackson in Joint meeting [Southard to Clay, September 8, 1832]." States that it is "an amusing scene" to go into the political circles of the Jacksonians and view the effect of the election "on the coun[te]nances and acts of different individuals on [so]me the settled gloom of despondency. in other[s] demoniac rage venting itself in furious denunciations whilst others pass it off with an hystercile grin." Adds that many of the most intelligent of both sides "consider the question in New York as decidedly ag[ain]st. the Chieftain [Jackson]." Asks for some indication about Clay's prospects for victory in the West. ALS. DLC-HC (DNA, M212, R5).

To JOHN HARE POWEL   Lexington, October 20, 1832

When I had the pleasure of seeing you at the City of Washington, you spoke to me of a Bull of your improved English Cattle which you were kind enough to say you were raising for me. I am about sending by W[illiam]. Martin, a person in my employment, a lot of Mules to Maryland, and he could very conveniently bring back with him a few Cattle. I am desirous of procuring a heifer of two or three years old, if possible in calf, of your celebrated Stock. Now, if Mr. Martin could obtain the pair, I know not any opportunity that would be so good to convey them to Lexington. Can you supply them? If you can I should esteem it a great obligation conferred on me, and would pay the price when informed of it. If they could be sent to Govr. [George] Howards farm (of course at my expence) on the road between Baltimore and Frederick City, it would add greatly to my accommodation. Mr. Martin will probably reach Maryland about the 15h. of November and leave it towards the last of the month.

You know, I presume, that we have a great many of the various races of English Cattle in K. but my confidence is greater in the superiority of your selections; altho.' some of our graziers affirm that ours are unsurpassed.

I have mentioned a heifer of two or three years old in calf, because if one younger were sent in company with the Bull, he would be sure to play some trick on the journey.

I offer you cordial congratulations on the results of your recent elections,[1] and on the existing prospect of the deliverance of our Country from the misrule of folly, passion, and despotism. P. S. Be pleased to write me by return mail. Mr. Martin can go to your farm, if it be inconvenient to send the cattle to Govr. Howards.

ALS. PHi.   1. Clay to Ketchum, May 15, 1832; Clay to Davis, Oct. 6, 1832.

To JOHN SLOANE   Lexington, October 20, 1832

From the returns which have reached us of your recent Election, I apprehend that the Election of Mr [Darius] Lyman has been defeated.[1] This unfortunate event has proceeded from causes, I think not difficult to comprehend; and as they will not operate so extensively, it is to be hoped in November, we may then look for better results. The issue of the Pennsylvania Election affords some consolation for the loss of yours.[2] In Kentucky, I entertain no doubt of success. Our friends are completely organized throughout the State, animated by the most determined zeal, and perfectly confident of a triumph.

Will you do me the favor, the moment the election is over in your County [Wayne], to send me by mail the state of the Poll, and also that of such other adjacent Counties as you can procure?[3] The Administration party being in possession of the P. office Department, information to our friends is suppressed by some of the P. Masters.

LS, written by an amanuensis, but apparently signed by Clay. MH. A slightly different version of this letter, with mainly minor variations in spelling and capitalization, is found in OClWHi. The name of Whittlesey as addressee has been supplied by an unknown person. This version is also LS, but is written and signed by an amanuensis. 1. Hammond to Clay, August 11, 1832. 2. Clay to Ketchum, May 15, 1832; Clay to Davis, Oct. 6, 1832. 3. In Sloane's home county of Wayne, Jackson won 2,195 votes to 973 for Clay. In neighboring Muskingum and Medina counties, Clay defeated Jackson 2,623 to 2,394 and 1,137 to 497, respectively. Cincinnati *Advertiser*, Nov. 21, 1832.

To SAMUEL P. LYMAN   Lexington, October 22, 1832

I have duly recd. your obliging letter of the 7h. inst. and thank you for the valuable information which it communicates. The prospects which it holds out of success in the Electoral election of your State [New York] are truly gratifying and encouraging. In combination with similar prospects in other States, a strong hope may now be entertained of the deliverance of our Country from abominable misrule. Pennsa seems to have shaken off the yoke; and here, in Kentucky, from the perfect system of organization which our friends have adopted, and the confidence animation and zeal which prevails among them, I have no doubts of a triumphant issue of our Novr election.[1] In Ohio too I think we shall succeed, altho' it is probable that your namesake has been defeated in the recent Governors' election.[2] If that has been the result of it (of which I have not yet certainly heard) it is attributable to the want of that full concert and co-operation, which you have happily secured in N. York, among those opposed to Jackson,[3] From Indiana the most favorable accounts are received; and our friends do not even despair of Illinois and Missouri.[4] Louisiana they have never doubted. . . .[5]

ALS. MiU. Samuel P. Lyman, a lawyer and business speculator from Utica, N.Y., was a close friend of both Thurlow Weed and Daniel Webster. See Weed, *Autobiography of Thurlow Weed*, 1:436-40 and Fuess, *Daniel Webster*, 2:365. 1. Letcher to Clay, Oct. 30, 1832. 2. Hammond to Clay, August 11, 1832. 3. Clay to Porter, May 1, 1832. 4. The presidential vote in Indiana was 13,000 for Jackson to 11,000 for Clay with Jackson winning all 9 electoral votes; in Illinois 5,000 for Jackson to 3,000 for Clay with Jackson winning all 5 electoral votes; in Missouri 6,000 for Jackson to 2,000 for Clay with Jackson winning all 4 electoral votes. Gammon, *The Presidential Campaign of 1832*, 170; Lexington *Observer & Kentucky Reproter*, Dec. 13, 1832. 5. Clay carried Louisiana and its 5 electoral votes by the popular vote of 3,546 to 1,954 for Jackson. *Ibid.*

From Daniel Webster, Boston, October 22, 1832. States that the first election returns from Pennsylvania "put us in very good spirits," but the "later returns from that state have not quite sustained that first impression [Clay to Davis, October 6, 1832]." Adds that, nevertheless, Pennsylvania is "better, than I had looked for," although "we are thrown sadly back by Ohio [Hammond to Clay, August 11, 1832]." Without "the dispiriting result in Ohio," believes Maine [Dearborn to Clay, September 18, 1832] and possibly New Hampshire could have been won. "As it is we do not entirely despair of Maine." Thinks the situation in New York [Clay to Bailhache, November 24, 1830] is favorable for the "Anti-Jackson ticket"; also, that "In our own State, we seem quite safe." Has heard a rumor that the Jacksonians and the Anti-Masons in the Massachusettts legislature "will unite, next January, to give my place to Mr. [John Q.] Adams." Says he can "hardly credit the possibility of any such union, & still less the possibility of his consent to an operation of that kind." Also, has "no reason to doubt . . . that the National Republicans will have a decisive majority, in the Legislature." ALS. ViU. Copy in InHi. Printed in Wiltse, *Webster Papers*, 3:193-94. For the outcome of the presidential election in those states mentioned, see Sergeant to Clay, June 27, 1831. In the Massachusetts election, Levi Lincoln, a National Republican, was reelected governor by a majority of about 4,500 over his opponent Marcus Morton. A "large majority" of those elected to the state house of representatives were National Republicans, while 31 of the 34 state senators belonged to that party. Webster subsequently was unanimously reelected as U.S. senator. Lexington *Observer & Kentucky Reporter*, December 6, 1832; *Niles' Register* (February 9, 1833), 43:385.

To JAMES BROWN   Lexington, October 23, 1832

[Discusses a court case Brown is appealing to the U.S. Supreme Court. Continues:]

My son Henry [Clay, Jr.] has recently married Miss [Julia] Prather of the City of Louisville, a young lady of good fortune, and, what is better, of amiable disposition, and cultivated mind. I went to the City to be present at the ceremony, and on my return was slightly indisposed with an ordinary complaint. As the cholera was there, you may probably hear that I caught the pestilence, and have been long since dead and buried. You are authorized to contradict, most positively, such a report if you should hear it, and to assert that I am now perfectly well, with the exception of a slight debility produced by medicine.

Mrs. [Anne Brown Clay] Erwins youngest child [Mary Erwin], an infant of four or five months old, which has been very feeble and delicate from its birth, is lying at the point of death. There is no hope of its recovery. The rest of our connexions, I believe, are all well. The cholera being on the Ohio river, with a strong probability of its reaching New Orleans, Anne will not probably go to that City this winter. Mr.[James] Erwin will go towards the middle or last of November.

The Ohio Election[1] has gone against us for the Governor by a majority of five or six thousand, owing, as it is said, to the want of arranging a proper concert between the Anti Masons and N. Republicans. The Congressional elections shew about an equal majority in our favor. So that it is still hoped and believed that the State will on friday week choose Anti Jackson Electors.[2]

In this State, I feel perfect assurance of success. Our friends are thoroughly organized, possessed of ample means for all legitimate purposes of the Canvass, raised within the State, and animated by the most determined zeal and confidence. We have not yet heard the final result in Pennsa. but I presume [George] Wolf has been elected by a small majority.[3] If N. York and Pennsa. go against Jackson, I think his defeat certain.

It has been some time since I heard from you. Have you abandoned your trip to N. Orleans? I should think, considering the prevalence of the Yellow fever there, with the prospect of its being followed by the Cholera, that it would be prudent for you not to undertake it.

ALS. ViU.   1. Hammond to Clay, August 11, 1832.   2. In the 1832 presidential election in Ohio, Jackson received all 21 electoral votes, winning 81,246 popular votes to 76,539 for Clay and 509 for the Anti-Masonic candidate, William Wirt. Gammon, *The Presidential Campaign of 1832*, 170; Lexington *Observer & Kentucky Reporter*, Dec. 13, 1832.   3. Clay to Ketchum, May 15, 1832.

To SAMUEL L. SOUTHARD   Lexington, October 23, 1832

I have recd. your two last favors communicating the result of the New Jersey election, on which I offer you cordial congratulations.[1] New Jersey has indeed done her duty and done it nobly. But you must not forget that we have a wary, resolute and reckless opponent, who will exert all his energies to recover the ground in Novr. which he lost in October. Your previous letter, in which you did me the honor to consult me as to the place you should accept,[2] was also recd. but my absence from home delayed my acknowledgment of it. I should prefer to see you in the Senate. If we fail in the Presidential election, your post there will be of immense importance. If we succeed, that position will not prevent any other arrangement by which the public may be availed of your services. Should you decide otherwise, I hope you will take care that we have from New Jersey some good and true man.

We shall succeed in the Electoral election of this State. I am sorry not to be able to speak with the same confidence of Ohio. They have lost the Candidate for Governor who was brought forward by the Anti Masonic party, and who was generally supported by our friends.[3] That unfortunate result I believe to have been owing 1st. to an exaggerated estimate of the Anti Masonic strength and 2d. to an insufficient appreciation of the difficulty, at a late period of the Canvass, of prevailing upon all of the N. Republicans to unite on the Anti Masonic Candidate. It was owing, in short, to a want of concert, and to a want of reciprocity between the two parties. The Anti Masons have, however, withdrawn their Electoral ticket; and as the Congressional returns[4] shew a majority of the State to be in our favor, our friends there hope and believe that they will yet carry our ticket.

I think we shall succeed in Indiana; and I do not despair of Missouri and Illinois. Of Louisiana we have never doubted.[5]

If we get New York and Pennsa. without Ohio, or New York and Ohio, without Pennsylvania, we are safe; but if we lose both Pennsa. and Ohio, even if we gain N. York, we must be defeated.[6] I hope our friends in Pennsa. will be fully aware of this state of things and that they will make corresponding exertions accordingly.

Let the worst happen, we shall carry a fresh infusion of vigor and power into Congress, and I hope be able there to check the mad career of the tyrant.

My family is suffering much with the illness of an infant grand daughter [Mary Erwin], the youngest child of Mrs. [Anne Brown Clay] Erwin. Delicate from its birth, it has lingered a long time and must expire in a few days.

On the other hand, we have another daughter by the marriage of my son Henry [Clay, Jr.] to Miss [Julia] Prather.[7] I think he has made a good choice, if, contrary to my wishes, he would marry; and his wife possesses what in Kentucky is deemed an ample fortune. . . .

ALS. NjP.   1. Southard to Clay, Sept. 8, 1832.   2. Southard to Clay, Sept. 8; Nov. 3, 1832.   3. Hammond to Clay, August 11, 1832.   4. *Ibid.*   5. Clay to Lyman, Oct. 22, 1832.   6. For the Ohio presidential election, see Clay to Brown, Oct. 23, 1832; for New York, Clay to Bailhache, Nov. 24, 1830. In Pennsylvania, where the National Republicans did not field a ticket, Jackson won all 30 electoral votes, and a popular vote margin of 90,983 to 66,716 for William Wirt, the Anti-Masonic candidate. Gammon, *The Presidential Campaign of 1832*, 170; Lexington *Observer & Kentucky Reporter*, Dec. 13, 1832.   7. Clay to Brown, Oct. 23, 1832.

From Philip R. Fendall, Washington, October 24, 1832. Reports that the appointment of Richard S. Coxe to the position of attorney for the Washington branch of the Bank of the United States was accomplished before Nicholas Biddle had time to receive Clay's recommendation of Fendall for the job [Fendall to Clay, October 9, 1832].

States that "Ohio has not done so well . . . as was expected [Hammond to Clay, August 11, 1832]." Believes, however, that with "the stimulating influence of the recent elections in Pennsylvania in bringing out our Ohio friends next month," there is barely any "reason to fear the result." Notes that "The Jackson men here . . . feel the late events in Pennsylvania [Clay to Ketchum, May 15, 1832; Clay to Davis, October 6,1832] as a Waterloo defeat." Adds that "Some of us here think that it is better for Wolfe [*sic*, George Wolf] to be elected by his small majority, than for [Joseph] Ritner to have been chosen." Continues: "The fact as it stands demonstrates the woful decline of Jacksonism in Pennsylvania, and surrounds the November election in that state with brilliant auspices," because the Anti-Masons might otherwise "have been disposed to play the dictator."

Mentions that "You probably saw enough last spring to satisfy you that the present [Jackson] Cabinet 'proper' is as completely subordinate as the last to the Cabinet 'improper.'" Gives an example in which Lewis Cass, secretary of war, hired George Forrest of Georgetown, D.C., as a clerk in his department, but when Forrest reported for work the next day, Cass told him that he could not have the job, because the "Chief Clerk, Mr. [John] Robb, had selected another person to fill it!" Explains that Robb "is a member of the Kitchen Cabinet," although he is "nominally a clergyman." ALS. DLC-HC (DNA, M212, R5). For Robb, see *Biennial Register*, 1833, 77. Forrest resided on West Street South, Georgetown, according to the 1834 city directory.

To ADAM BEATTY   Lexington, October 25, 1832

I recd. your favor of the 22d. inst. and am gratified to learn that you are so fully organized and have such flattering prospects. From all parts of this State our information is good—very good. I think we cannot possibly fail. The victory in Pennsa.[1] consoles us for the defeat in Ohio,[2] from which however they write me that they will efface tomorrow week the recent disgrace.

I have recd. and sowed the barrel of wheat, and I never saw any come up or look finer. Will you do me the favor to make my cordial acknowledgements to Mr. Childs[3] for it.

I have not recd. the Maysville Eagle containing the pieces to which you refer.[4] I presume however they will come to hand.

ALS. Courtesy of Earl M. Ratzer, Highland Park, Ill.   1. Clay to Ketchum, May 15, 1832; Clay to Davis, Oct. 6, 1832.   2. Hammond to Clay, August 11, 1832.   3. Possibly David Lee Child.   4. Reference obscure.

To UNKNOWN RECIPIENT[1]   Lexington, October 27, 1832

I recd. your fav[or] of the 19th inst. and [words illeg.] highly gratified by the continued confidence with which you speak of the success of the Anti Jackson ticket in N. York. In this State I entertain no doubt of success, and I believe notwithstanding the result of the recent election for Governor in Ohio,[2] that the vote of that State and also of Indiana will be adverse to Genl. Jackson. Should such be the case, and should Pennsylvania also be against him, there will be a large majority of the Electors opposed to his re election. This auspicious state of things may give rise to a possible collision between the Candidates of the N.R. party and the Antimasons; which ought to be prevented if it can be, and you are right in beginning to think that it deserves early consideration. It was however highly expedient to avoid the least agitation of that question whilst it might have any injurious influence on the election itself of Electors. And it affords much consolation to believe that, however much a collision, if it unfortunately should arise, may be decided, the paramount object will have been accomplished of ridding the Country of Jackson misrule, unless indeed the madness of contending parties should occasion the reelection of Genl. Jackson.

Hitherto almost all the concessions that have been made between the two parties (the N.R. and the Anti Masons) have proceeded from the former. Such has been the case in N. York,[3] Penna.[4] and Ohio,[5] in each of which the body of the N.R. party has supported, or it is expected will support the Anti Masonic Candidate for Govr. We have withdrawn our Electoral ticket in Penna.; and the N.R party agreed to support the A.M. ticket in your State. There has been no material concession from the A.M. party except it be their recent withdrawal in Ohio of their Electoral ticket; which under circumstances where certain defeat must have awaited them, they have done with not much grace. Their imaginations have greatly exaggerated their [word illeg.] [nu]mbers in Ohio, as the recent Governor's election demonstrates, in the [word illeg.] [Re]serve where alone Anti Masonry abounds in that State.

[The] first object, therefore, to which, in the event of a successful [issue of] the Electoral elections, the exertions of our friends should, it se[em]s to me, be directed, is to prevail upon the Anti Masons to withdraw Mr [William] Wirt, and concentrate their whole vote upon the National Republican Candidates. Mr Wirt himself, it is said, is well inclined to such a course; but I should doubt whether he has the boldness of resolution to adopt it, without some movement to that effect from the Anti Masons themselves. They ought therefore to be pressed on that point. And it seems to me there are conclusive reasons in favor of it.

In the first place, Mr Wirt has not been regarded by the Nation as the person who was, at this time, to be its President. Such an expectation has no where been entertained not seriously even by the Anti Masonic party itself. If he were to come in, under such circumstances (Jacksonism being down) his administration would be very uncomfortable, if not unsatisfactory.

2dly. If they persist in continuing him the question must go to the House; and in that event what prospect has Mr Wirt? There is not one representation from one State that is now understood to be in his favor. And, if the representations from the States, which may give him their electoral votes, should, on that account, vote for him, he would not get more than three States, with the possible addition of that of South Carolina. Let us indulge a possible supposition, that the Jackson party, abandoning their leader, should all unite on Mr Wirt in the House and secure his election. What then would be the propsects of an administration, the Chief of which had been elected under such circumstances? Would he not find himself under obligations to the Jackson party of the most inconvenient kind? Would he not totally alienate the N.R party? But I hardly believe such a combination to secure his election possible. Jackson out of the way, and the contest limited to Mr Wirt and myself, and I feel great confidence that I should receive the votes of Indiana, Missouri and Illinois and that of Kentucky, as I will presently shew will be for me, if we get the Electoral vote of this State, even against Jackson.

I have said that perseverance in holding out Mr Wirt as a Candidate must carry the election to the House, if there be a majority of Anti Jackson electors chosen. That assertion is founded upon the firm belief that my friends — at all events not a sufficient number of them will abandon me and vote for Mr Wirt, in the Electoral colleges, to secure his Election.

But if the object cannot be accom[plished] of prevailing on the Antimasons to withdraw Mr Wirt, the next [to whi]ch the strenuous exertions of our friends should be applied, is to [retai]n that portion of the Electoral vote of N. York which it has [been ex]pected all along would be bestowed on me, if the joint [ti]cket succeeded. If we are not greatly disappointed, that would place me ahead of the three Candidates returned to the House; and if I occupy that position, I have no fears of the ultimate result.

You do entertain fears; and this brings me to consider the probable issue of the Election if it should devolve upon the House. In the general, it may be assumed, that the Candidate having the plurality especially if it be a considerable plurality will be chosen. But you may say it was otherwise in the Election of Feb. 1825 [4:143-66]. Genl. Jackson constituted an exception from all rules. The experience however which has grown out of his defeat on that occasion, bad as he was, would now ensure the choice of the plurality-candidate. What that has been I need not now state. All timid men (and the majority of every house of Representatives may be presumed of that character) would be sure to take refuge under a vote for the highest Candidate. It is the most obvious course and that with which it is easiest to reconcile the people.

But you say that there is now in the H. of Representatives a majority of the States in favor of Jackson or, rather according to your estimate there are 10 for him, nine for me and five doubtful. You have not however sufficiently appreciated the effect of the influence upon the votes of members which will be produced by the particular course which their States may take. If for example, Indiana should, as we anticipate, give her Electoral vote for me, and the final Election devolves on the House, I think it highly probable her three members would vote then in conformity with the declared sense of the State.

Another view. If the election goes to the House, Jacksonism, if not annihilated, will be evidently on the decline. The charm will have been dispelled; his vincibility demonstrated. In that state of things, my word for it, there will be members enough disposed to avoid a sinking cause. What have they to gain by adhering to a declining party? What have they *not to lose* by lashing themselves to a dead or dying carcase? To the same States you have enumerated for me may now be added, I think, Kentucky. Messrs [Charles A.] Wickliffe and [Henry] D[anie]l have openly renounced the Administration,[6] and if the State [sh]ould vote for me I have no doubt that to the six members now [ad]verse to Jackson, others may be added who will follow their State. This will especially be the case, if, as is probable, the Legislature should give instructions on the subject. Illinois and Missouri, I have no doubt, would support me in the House against Mr Wirt if not against Jackson. I can hardly believe that if unfortunately, there should be a contest between him and me, that the votes of Virginia, North Carolina, Georgia, Alabama or Mississippi would be given to Mr Wirt.

You ask if any measures are in operation to produce a withdrawal of Mr Wirt? I am not aware of any. It has however confidently been believed that he would be withdrawn, in events which seem ahead; and this confidence has been inspired by his own declarations and those of his friends.

I have thus, my dear Sir, replied fully and frankly to your letter. After all, it must be left to the Country, at least to my friends, to decide what disposition they may think it expedient to make of me. For myself, I shall feel contented with any result by which I shall see that the Government of my Country is in safe hands

Copy. NBuHi. Letter not addressed. Letter marked "(Confidential)."   1. Said by the Buffalo Historical Society to be Peter B. Porter. The editors feel, however, that the letter's tone, its insistence on confidentiality, and the fact that no Porter to Clay exchange of October 19, 1832, has been found, indicates a recipient who was far less well-known personally to Clay.   2. Hammond to Clay, August 11, 1832.   3. Clay to Porter, May 1, 1832.   4. Clay to Ketchum, May 15, 1832.   5. For Anti-Mason, National Republican relations in Ohio see, Clay to Metcalfe,

May 7, 1832; Clay to Hammond, June 22, 1832; Hammond to Clay, August 11, 1832; Weisenburger, *History of the State of Ohio*, 3:263-71. 6. Wickliffe had made a speech in Bardstown on Oct. 6, condemning Jackson's bank veto and that part of the veto message in which the president proclaimed his right "to construe the Constitution as he 'understands' it." Daniel made a similar speech in Bath County the first week in October. Lexington *Observer & Kentucky Reporter*, Oct. 13, 23, 1832.

From Henry A. S. Dearborn, Roxbury, Mass., October 29, 1832. Reports that "To my utter astonishment, I was asked this morning, by Mr. Edward & Mr. Alexander Everett . . . whether it were not best to advise Mr. Clay to decline, in favor of [William] Wirt." States: "I replied that I had no doubt Mr. Clay would be chosen by the people, that the only doubt was as to what the electors of N. York & Penna, would do. As to the former I considered, that in good faith, they must go for Mr. Clay, as the national republicans had supported the anti mason candidates for Gov & Lieu. Gov. with such an understanding [Clay to Porter, May 1, 1832]; & as to Penna it would be the only state for Wirt & when he found that to be the case, he would decline in Mr. Clay's favor; that if the election came into the house I believed Clay would be chosen, as the members of Penna & N. York would be so far operated upon by the change of public sentiment, as to give the votes of those states to Clay." Says the Everetts consider "it certain you could not be chosen by the people or house, & that the only way of ejecting Jackson was by going for Wirt." Adds that he told them that Clay "had spent his whole life for the best interests of the country; that for eight years he had been constantly contending in the arena, as our chief champion; that to desert him now would be dishonest, dishonorable & ungrateful: that we should disappoint not only his friends in all parts of the Union, & especially in the west; that if any one was to decline it should be Wirt, & that I had always presumed he would, after the electors were chosen." States that he did everything possible "to discourage any such proposition from being made to you," but that Edward Everett said "that still he should probably write you [E. and A. Everett to Clay, October 29, 1832]." Concludes that "as to myself *my flag is nailed to the mast. . . .* I think we can shall & will triumph." ALS. DLC-HC (DNA, M212, R5).

On October 30, 1832, Dearborn wrote again, saying that he had gone to Boston "this morning to ascertain whether there was any defection among our friends." Reports that the only sentiment he found was one that "is decided, ardent & determined for Henry Clay. There is not another individual save those gentlemen that I can learn who has any other wish, or expectation, than that our selected candidate should be supported, *at all events*."

Urges Clay not to "yield to any suggestions from any quarter. If Wirt does not decline . . . *let the odium be on him.*" Adds: "Do not be deceived by any *friendly* advice. The country looks to *YOU*, for its salvation & be not deceived by any Judas. The prospect is not only bright but definite & clear, — the result is certain." Dearborn's electoral vote projections give Clay the following "Certain votes:" New York-42, Pa.-30, Ohio-21, Ky.-15, Mass.-14, Md.-7, Ind.-9, N.J.-8, Conn.-8, Vt.-7, La.-5, R.I.-3, Dela.-3 for a winning total of 172 with 10 from Maine, and 2 more from Maryland as "Probable" votes. Remarks that "I do not despair even of Virginia & South Carolina, & it is not impossible that Missouri may act right." Also comments: "J[ohn]. Q. A[dams]. you know, has all along been for Wirt. What *gratitude*. He is for himself & the devil take the hindmost." *Ibid.* Clay actually received 49 electoral votes in 1832. Jackson garnered 219. For the states carried by each, see Sergeant to Clay, June 27, 1831.

From EDWARD EVERETT &   Charleston, Mass., October 29, 1832
ALEXANDER H. EVERETT

The consciousness that we are known to you to have been, from the first, among your most decided & unwavering friends, induces us to make the present communication to you, on the aspect of the election. — The late letter of Mr [Richard] Rush to the Editor of the Antimasonic paper in Boston,[1] makes it *certain*, that the vote of Pennsylvania will be given to the Antimasonic Candidate. —It is equally certain, we presume, that without the vote of Pennsylvania, the National Republican ticket cannot prevail. —If then, that ticket is supported in the electoral colleges which are under the Control of our friends, One of two things is Certain, vizt. —either that Genl. Jackson, obtaining the majority, will be re-chosen, or that there will be no choice by the People, & that the designation will devolve on the House of R. —On the Other hand, if our friends in the Electoral colleges vote for Mr [William] Wirt, *he may be elected by the People.* —Two questions then present themselves, 1.° Is it expedient to produce this result (if practicable) & 2.° How can it be brought about? —

Knowing that you wish, in this great crisis, to hear the voice of Your friends, We beg leave to offer you our views on this subject, & to obviate the danger of miscarriage, we send you this letter, in duplicate, under cover to a friend in both cases. —

We deem it expedient to prevent the election from devolving on the House, for these reasons 1.° It is very probable, that Mr. W[irt]. will go there with a plurality over our ticket. This probability resting on Considerations as obvious to You, as to us, Need not be discussed. It would be very undesirable, as it seems to us, to take the risk of an election in the House, when we must go there with a Minority. —2.° And mainly, because with the present house of representatives, Genl. Jackson appears to us to have the better prospect. —At all events, the issue in that body must be regarded as highly doubtful, & the risk of the re-election of the present incumbent too great, to be unnecessarily assumed. —

As to the second question, how can the vote of our friends in the Electoral colleges be obtained for Mr Wirt, it is doubtful, whether it can be done, in any other way, than by the Influence of Your publicly withdrawing Your name. —Nothing else would probably convince the electors in some of the States, that the Course suggested was expedient, or that they were free to pursue it, even if it were. —And great dispatch would be required to give time for such a withdrawal to produce its effect, on some of the States, —Should Your own opinion of the measure coincide with ours.

We have been the more free to make known to You the view we take of this delicate subject, it being known to one of us, by direct communications with yourself last December,[2] that you were then of the Opinion, that it was expedient to withdraw your name, & desirous of doing so. —Since that time, the reasons urged by those of your friends, who dissuaded You, have in a good degree ceased to exist, & the possibility of success seems to be settled almost to demonstration, against Us. —Knowing that the thing you have least at heart, in this matter, is your individual aggrandizement, We have made this communication in the frankness of cordial attachment, & with a single eye to the salvation of the Country. . . . P.S. We beg leave to observe that these views meet the concurrence of our common friend J[oseph]. E. Sprague

ALS. DLC-HC (DNA, M212, R5).   1. Rush had written a letter on Oct. 19, 1832, to the editor of the Boston *Daily Advocate*, Benjamin Hallett, pointing out the growth of Anti-Masonry in the Pennsylvania legislature and predicting that the Anti-Masons will be working hard at the polls on behalf of their presidential electors. Boston *Daily Advocate*, Oct. 26, 1832.   2. Not found, but for Clay's sentiments, see Clay to Conover, August 26, 1831; and Clay to Barbour, Dec. 10, 1831.

From Edwin U. Berryman, New York, October 30, 1832. Reports that he has "been making a tour through Connecticut, Rhode Island & several other of the Eastern States."

Has noted in his travel a "scarcity of Jackson men." States that "We had last evening decidedly the largest Anti Jackson Meeting at Masonic Hall (in this city) I have ever witnessed." Has concluded from conversations "with Many of our leading politicians throughout the States" that "we shall carry the Electoral vote of this State & even that part of our candidates in *this city* the very *hot bed* of Tammany principles [Rush to Clay, June 1, 1831]." Is cheered also by news from Pennsylvania [Clay to Davis, October 6, 1832]; wonders, however, about "Ohio [Hammond to Clay, August 11, 1832], old Ohio, from whom we expected so much in the hour of Trial — will she desert her best friend, I cannot believe it! —"

Encloses the pedigree of the Arabian horse, Kocklani [Berryman to Clay, August 6, 1832], and concludes that "What ever arrangement or disposition you may make of him, will be perfectly satisfactory." ALS. Josephine Simpson Collection, Lexington, Ky. An "extremely large" meeting of the Anti-Jackson party had been held the previous evening in Masonic Hall in New York City and had made nominations for Congress and for the state assembly. New York *Daily Sentinel*, October 30, 1832.

From Henry Clay Hart, Valparaiso, on Board U.S. Frigate *Potomac*, October 30, 1832. Writes that his ship arrived in Valparaiso on October 24 "after a long but prosperous voyage around the world having sailed 37.000 miles since we left New York." States that he has "taken the liberty of drawing on you for the sum of one hundred and fifty dollars which I hope you will honor." Explains that he did this to help out "a young man on board, a great friend of mine, who was anxious to return home but had not the means of doing so." ALS. DLC-HC (DNA, M212, R5). With a note from Erskine Stansbury in favor of Henry C. Hart and endorsed by Hart to Henry Clay.

From Abbott Lawrence, Boston, October 30, 1832. States that he has had a conversation with Gen. Henry A.S. Dearborn who told him about the suggestion the Everetts had made [E. and A.H. Everett to Clay, October 29, 1832; Dearborn to Clay, October 29, 1832] for Clay to withdraw from the presidential race. Opposes such action, saying: "It is known to us here that Mr. John Q Adam's does not favor your election — and there is little doubt upon my mind that both the Everetts are in full communion with him. . . . there is I assure you but one sentiment in this State among a large majority of the Voters in relation to the candidate for the Presidency, You are the man on whom they have set their hearts — and whatever you may receive from Mr John Q Adams or any of his friends — I pray you not to consider such representations as emanating from sources entitled to credit, so far as relates to the people of this State." Concludes that if Clay considers withdrawing, it should not be until "after the Electors are chosen." ALS. DLC-HC (DNA, M212, R5).

From Robert P. Letcher, Lancaster, Ky., October 30, 1832. Reports that his "District will do its duty, handsomely, at the Novr. election." States that Rockcastle County is "organized . . . to my entire satisfaction," predicting that Jackson's votes there "will not exceed 75" and that Lincoln County will "give [Clay] a majority of 500." Also, Estill County "promises well, and . . . there is no call for any further efforts in that quarter." Adds that he would have gone "further in the Mountains in obedience to your wish, but I found it totally useless," because "Every body in that quarter is alive to the great importance of the contest, and is in the field, riding day & night. The truth is, they intend to give a large vote, and I know they wish to have the exclusive credit of it, and I am disposed to give it to them." Fears however, that the recent vote in Ohio [Hammond to Clay, August 11, 1832] may "have a bad effect . . . the other side of the mountains." ALS. DLC-HC (DNA, M212, R5). Clay garnered approximately 27,000 popular votes in Kentucky to 13,000 for Jackson, thereby gaining all 15 of the state's electoral votes. He defeated Jackson in Lincoln County by a margin of 768 votes to 340; in Estill 311 to 227; and in Rockcastle 328 to 63. In general, Clay carried most of central and eastern Kentucky, while Jackson carried most of the southern and western regions. See Gammon, *The Presidential Campaign of 1832*, 170; Lexington *Observer & Kentucky Reporter*, November 29; December 13, 1832.

To CHARLES P. DORMAN[1]   Lexington, November 3, 1832

I duly received your favor of the 16h. Ulto. communicating the wish of yourself and other friends that, on my way to Washington, I would pass by Lexington [Va.]. I feel greatly obliged by your friendly desire to see me, and assure you that I cordially reciprocate the sentiment.

I have not absolutely decided my route to the Cit[y] but think it will be either by Abingdon [Va.] or by Lewisburg [Va. (W. Va.)]. In either case, it will be quite convenient to pass by Lexington [Va.]; and should I take either of those routes, as is now probable, I will avail myself of the opportunity of exchanging friendly salutations with my friends in Lexington. I expect to leave home, in a private carriage, about the 20h. inst. and if I should be able to realize my wishes, in the contemplated visit, I will on the road apprize you of my purpose

Before this letter reaches you the fate of the P. Election, so far as it depends upon the choice of Electors, will have been decided. May the decision be such as will heal the wounds of our bleeding Country, inflicted by the folly & madness of a lawless Military Chieftain!

I have great hopes and strong confidence in the defeat of Genl. Jackson. If Pennsa. and N. York abandon him, his failure, I think is almost certain. Of my native State [Va.] I entertain but little hope. There will not have been time I fear to dispel the doubt [&] delusion (from Jacksonism, and from the [Thomas] Ritchie junto) under which a large portion of her population labors. We feel assured of a triumph in this State.

ALS. PP.   1. For Charles P. Dorman, a lawyer, editor, and for thirteen years a member of the Virginia assembly, see Oren F. Morton, *A History of Rockbridge County Virginia* (Staunton, Va., 1920), 249.

From Samuel L. Southard, Trenton, November 3, 1832. Writes that he has accepted the governorship of New Jersey, because "I could not avoid it — without serious injury to our friends & the cause." Adds that "On me they were all agreed — and an effort to elect another was likely to produce serious evils." Notes, however, that the legislature "left the appt. of Senator until next Session" when they will "if circumstances require it . . . be at liberty to place me there." Continues: "The Anti Masons in our State, will act well *now*, altho some of their leaders have done all the mischief they could. I think we are safe — but the struggle will be, beyond example — severe. — The results of the Election on friday, so far as we have heard from Penna are extremely favorable. Our prospects in N.Y. good." ALS. InU. Southard, who had been elected governor in October, 1832, served in that position until February 23, 1833, when he resigned to become U.S. senator. He served in the Senate from March 4, 1833, until his death in 1842. *BDAC.*

From James Brown, Philadelphia, November 5, 1832. Extends his best wishes to Henry Clay, Jr., and his new bride, Julia Prather Clay [Clay to Brown, October 23, 1832]. Turning to politics, states: "I sincerely hope . . . you may resume your seat in the Senate with a disposition to be satisfied with a place which I would have preferred to any within the reach of American ambition. You know that I have never for a moment doubted that General Jackson would be re elected. He will have a large majority in this State and I shall not be surprised should he be the choice of every State south of the Potomac and west of the Alleghany [Sergeant to Clay, June 27, 1831]. If I have proved more generally correct in my calculating than many of our active politicians, it may be accounted for by the fact that I derive my information almost exclusively from my knowledge of the American tendencies, my acquaintance with nearly all the prominent actors on the political theatre, and the perusal of the Journals; without entering into the busy scenes of active electioneering, by which my deliberate judgment might be warped, or conversing with eloquent and heated partizans who might inflame my imagination."

Comments that the "affairs of South Carolina rapidly approach their denouement. Nullification will be tried and the result will be either concession on the part of the Tariff States, or Secession from the Union on the part of South Carolina and perhaps all the Anti Tariff States, or an appeal to force. This last alternative will I think be resisted by all the States opposed to the Tariff, and would terminate in a division of the Union. Some leading Virginians who have visited this place protest against any attempt to use force against South Carolina, and intimate that the Ancient Dominion would endeavor by her physical force to prevent it." Adds that "Free trade is a favorite doctrine with a very considerable party in almost every State in the Union, and its friends will gain force and numbers when the question is made whether the duties shall be reduced, or the Union dissolved, or sustained by force."

Mentions also that the Bank of the United States "is decidedly unpopular in this State except in this city and in Pittsburg[h]." This fact "will be shown by the returns at the present election which will give an overwhelming majority for the President much of which may be considered as an approval of the veto message [Clay to Brown, December 18, 1831; Webster to Clay, January 8, 1832; Clay to Fendall, August 4, 1832]." ALS. DLC-HC (DNA, M212, R5). Printed in *LHQ*, 24:1167-69; and Colton, *Clay Correspondence*, 4:343.

From Charles S. Todd, "Stockdale," Shelby Co., Ky., November 5, 1832. Discusses his financial problems and asks for an extension on his notes [Todd to Clay, September 7, 1830]. Thanks Clay for "the kind condolence you offer on the recent afflictions we have sustained in our family," namely "the death of three children in one week." Adds that "we think now that they were our favorite children—a daughter nearly 10, just developing her powers and dispositions and two little boys. nearly 2 & 4—the elder resembling in a remarkable degree, the features, form and disposition of Col [Isaac] Shelby; the younger, bearing your name and indicating, as we fondly thought, promises of the genius of his illustrious prototype."

Comments that "This is the first day of a Contest involving greater interests to our country than at any period since 1798 & 1812." Adds: "I . . . fervently hope that full justice may be awarded to you. —Our party is at length aroused in this County. —our friends here think that the August Majority will be increased to not less than 500 probably 600. —Our Strength will be voted and we know that there have been a good many changes and that some will not vote who are yet reluctant to give up Jackson." ALS. DLC-HC (DNA, M212, R5). Todd's children were probably victims of the cholera epidemic [Remark in Senate, June 27, 1832] which struck Louisville in mid-October, 1832. Louisville *Public Advertiser*, October 13, 15, 1832. In the gubernatorial election in Shelby County in August, the Clay candidate, Richard A. Buckner, received 1,163 votes to 733 for John Breathitt, the Jacksonian. By contrast, Clay received 1,396 votes from that county in the presidential election, while Jackson received 758. Lexington *Observer & Kentucky Reporter*, August 20; November 29, 1832.

To FRANCIS T. BROOKE   Lexington, November 7, 1832
We are in the midst of our Election, this being the afternoon of the third day. From the returns already received, we are assured of a certain victory.[1] In every County we have heard from, there has been a favorable change, either in the reduction of previous Jackson majorities or in the augmentation of ours. So far as we have yet heard, every County visited by Genl. Jackson, during

his late tour of election and observation through our State,[2] has gone more against him than it had previously been.

From Ohio we have nothing yet decisive.[3] Putting together all accounts which have reached me the conclusion is, that, if the Anti-Masons in the Western reserve, have been faithful, we have succeeded; if treacherous, we are beaten.

The weather has been very unfavorable, and but for that cause, I should feel quite confident of Indiana.[4] If they have been as indifferent to its state as our friends in K. we have succeeded there.

We are unaware of the definitive issue in Pennsa.[5]

ALS. NcD.   1. Letcher to Clay, Oct. 30, 1832.   2. Clay to Davis, Oct. 6, 1832.   3. Clay to Brown, Oct. 23, 1832.   4. Clay to Lyman, Oct. 22, 1832.   5. Clay to Southard, Oct. 23, 1832.

To JOHN HARE POWEL   Lexington, November 7, 1832

According to the advice contained in your letter of the 30h. Ulto just received, I have directed Mr. [William] Martin to proceed to Powelton receive the pair of English Cattle and bring them to K.

He is a plain young man, without education, and his principal merit in his honest and industry. He has little or no judgment as to Stock; and I rely almost exclusively upon yours, which I beg you, my dear Sir, freely to exercise in the selection of a heifer. As formerly intimated, I should prefer one two or three years old, young in Calf, by one of your best bulls. The price whatever it may be shall be remitted to you as soon as I reach Washington and am informed of it.

We are in the midst of our Election, and have already received sufficient returns to assure us of success by a considerable majority.[1]

We have heard nothing decisive from Ohio, and of course not yet from your State [Pennsylvania].[2] May the result be auspicious to our hopes, and such as will bind up the wounds inflicted upon our Constitution and our Country by the made [*sic*, mad] acts of a *lawless Military Chieftain*!

ALS. Courtesy of Clay Myers, Salem, Oregon.   1. Letcher to Clay, Oct. 30, 1832.   2. Clay to Brown, Oct. 23, 1832; Clay to Southard, Oct. 23, 1832.

From ROBERT W. STODDARD   Geneva, N.Y., November 12, 1832

Defeat is again our lot in this State [New York]. Although I firmly believed, two months ago, that the Anti Masons of this state would support their own ticket,[1] still, strange as no doubt will appear to you, they basely deserted it & went almost in mass to the side of the enemy—never, since the rebellion in heaven, has there been a more perfect overthrow than we have met in this State. What are we now to expect? Will the people in their madness suffer this republic to go by the board? Will you men of the west, and those of the South fold your hands & patiently see the Constitution frittered away by the *detested* wretches who use Andrew Jackson for selfish purposes alone? Although I heartily concur in the reasons which induced the Senate to reject Martin Van Buren,[2] and that in doing so they only performed their duty, still had it been practicable to have overlooked that & continued him abroad, I sincerely believe we should have made a better fight. If those Nulifiers of South Carolina & Georgia proceed to an overt act, as I apprehend in their madness they will, the great man will sieze that occasion to write with his favourite red ink—If the

597

evils of such a conflict could be strictly confined to Jackson & Calhoun & their infuriated retainers, I confess I could [look] on with about the same indifference that the farmer did when [he s]aw the fight between the hawk & the snake: But Sir—I have read with attention the address of Mr. Webster to the meeting held in Worcester in Massachusetts,[3] and I dread the consequence of attempting to still [tha]t rebellious spirit by the *military*. Calhoun has been written to on [the] subject by a gentleman here at the west—[4]He disdains all intention on the part of the State to resort to force—He says no force will be used except by the United States, and in that case, the State will defend itself & call upon its Southern neighbours to sustain them—As nearly as I could collect the purport of his letter from the relation I had of its contents, it is this—The Convention will declare the tariff unconstitutional—The legislature will pass a law to prevent the collection of duties under the tariff & if any collection is attempted the officer will be proceeded against & cast into prison—he must then resort to a writ of error—if the law of S. Carolina is pronounced unconstitutional, the decree of the Supreme Court, as in the case of Georgia,[5] will be disregarded—The President will, as is supposed, interfere immediately & then the United States, not South Carolina, will begin the war, if war is to be had—It is understood by me, as contained in Calhouns letter, that the law to be passed by the Legislature of South Carolina is not to take effect untill after the rising of Congress next month, when it is supposed that the new Congress, having so many new members, will be frightened into a repeal of the tariff.[6] These are the substantial ideas I collected from what was said about Calhouns letter. I understood it was written to Vanderventer [*sic*, Christopher Van DeVenter] who resides not a great way from Buffaloe [*sic*, Buffalo]. As to abandoning the protecting tariff, it strikes me, that a measure of that sort is abandoning all—constitution, law & soveregnity—I know not how parties may stand after the 4th March next in both houses,[7] but I think the majority will be in favour of the protecting system & that there will be too much firmness among them to suffer the State of S. Carolina, nay all the South combined, to bully them out of it. If S. Carolina has calculated the value of the Union & wishes to retire from us an unprofitable sorcerer in the name of heaven let her take her leave peaceably & go her way; but to involve this happy Country in civil war on her account, or suffer her to bully the government into a repeal of its laws at her command is not to [be] born with—Although I could wish her to remain with us and like ourselves submit to the laws, yet if she is so mettlesome that she needs must go, let her go and find better friends if she can—But for Godsake do not repeal a section of the protecting law, rather increase protection than give the rebbels one inch—

ALS. DLC-HC (DNA, M212, R5). 1. Clay to Porter, May 1, 1832. 2. Clay to Brooke, May 1, 1831. 3. Webster spoke on Oct. 12, 1832, at the Massachusetts National Republican convention held in Worcester. His speech was subsequently published in the Boston *Weekly Messenger* and the Boston *Courier* on Oct. 18, and in the Washington *Daily National Intelligencer* on Oct. 23 and 25. See also Wiltse, *Webster Papers*, 3:192-93. 4. Reference obscure. 5. Johnston to Clay, Jan. 12, 1831. 6. For a detailed discussion of the nullification crisis, see William W. Freehling (ed.), *The Nullification Era, A Documentary Record*. New York, 1967; and *Prelude to Civil War*; also Wiltse, *John C. Calhoun*, 2:148-53. 7. Whittlesey to Clay, Sept. 19, 1832.

To DEMAS ADAMS   Lexington, November 15, 1832
[Discusses his lands in Ohio, including the taxes on them and a possible selling price for one tract. Continues:]

There can be no doubt that the issue of the Presidential Election is in favor of Genl. Jackson.[1] I sincerely wish that our Country may not have abundant cause deeply to regret the event. To me it is a source of great gratification that Kentucky has gone against him by a majority not less than 7000.[2]

ALS. Pioneer Museum, Colorado Springs, Colorado. Adams, who was born in New York, became a federal marshal for the United States District Court in Columbus, Ohio, in the 1840s. See Jacob H. Studer, *Columbus, Ohio: Its History, Resources, and Progress* (Washington, 1873), 30; *Biennial Register*, 1841, p. 198.　　1. Sergeant to Clay, June 27, 1831.　　2. Letcher to Clay, Oct. 30, 1832.

From John J. Crittenden, Frankfort, November 17, 1832. Urges Clay to "continue your service, in the Senate, for the next session, certainly & as much longer as your own inclination & the public service may require." Continues: "I am one of the last men, in Kentucky, who will wish for your resignation　I beg you not to believe, either that I repent of the *past* [Worsley to Clay, October 22, 1831] or, that I am looking forward to the *future* with any spirit of impatient ambition [Clay to Southard, September 30, 1831]. I am proud of what I have done, & not *restless* under its consequences." Copy. DLC-Crittenden Papers (DNA, M212, R20); and NcD.

To CHARLES HAMMOND　　　　　　Lexington, November 17, 1832
[Acknowledges Hammond's letter of November 6. Continues:]

The dark cloud which had been so long suspended over our devoted Country, instead of being dispelled, as we had fondly hoped it would be, has become more dense, more menacing more alarming. Whether we shall ever see light, and law and liberty again, is very questionable. Still we must go on to the last, with what spirit we can, to discharge our duty. It is under feelings of this kind that I expect, a week or two hence, to go to Washington. There I fear I shall be unable, either to do good or to prevent mischief.

Those who have labored to avert the result of the recent elections[1] have the consolation of clear consciences. I have the additional satisfaction of knowing that, in my own State, a majority, not less than about 7000, has manifested it's confidence and attachment towards me, and judged, as I think, rightly, of the existing administration.[2]

For your expressions of friendship and kindness, contained in your letter, I thank you, and assure you that they are fully reciprocated.

ALS. InU.　　1. Sergeant to Clay, June 27, 1831.　　2. Letcher to Clay, Oct. 30, 1832.

From Peter B. Porter, Black Rock, N.Y., November 22, 1832. Has delayed writing because "I was waiting to know the result of the elections, which had already taken place in Pa & Ohio [Clay to Southard, October 23, 1832; Clay to Brown, October 23, 1832]." Since he was then convinced "that we should succeed in N. York, Ohio & Kentucky [Sergeant to Clay, June 27, 1831; Letcher to Clay, June 27, 1831] I was quite willing to lose as it seemed probable we should, Pennsylvania; for it would at once have removed one of the serious embarrassments you anticipated [Clay to Ketchum, May 15, 1832] & which our success then would not have failed to produce. But almost simultaneously with the news of the loss of Pa came also the appalling information that Ohio & N. York [Lawrence to Clay, January 30, 1832; Clay to Bailhache, November 24, 1830] were also gone; thus rendering any further effort useless."

Informs Clay that "We are beaten, my dear Sir, 'horse foot &' but with a passing sigh which cannot be restrained, for the miserable infatuation of our country men, and for the certainty with which it forbodes the ultimate if not the immediate prostration of our liberties, we must bear it with what philosophy we can. So long as there is a hope

599

good men ought not to despair of the republic; & if it is to be redeemed, it must be done by the exertions of such men as yourself Webster & other kindred spirits who fortunately still have a voice in the counsels of the nation." Admits that he "was most woefully disappointed" in the election results in Ohio, particularly since in "this county [Erie] we gave a majority of more than 2600, which is 1100 more than has ever been given on any former occasion," and also because "We had a majority in each of the 9. counties which lie west of the Seneca River and . . . an aggragate majority of more than 12,000" in those counties. L, incomplete draft. NBuHi.

To HENRY CLAY, JR.   Lexington, November 24, 1832
I recd. last night your letter of the 21st. As it seems that I must go to Washington this winter, I have finally concluded to go a little earlier than I contemplated when you left us, and shall probably start on thursday or friday of next week. I shall go too by the public conveyances and by the Ohio river, if I can get up it. I need not say with what repugnant feelings I leave Kentucky.

Your observations on political affairs are just. The movement against nullification at Louisville[1] has no doubt been prompted from Washington; and if they would comprehend *all* nullification, our friends ought heartily to second the motion. But I can see no advantage in our taking part in proceedings agt S. Carolina heresy, whilst that of Georgia and the President remains triumphant.[2]

I hope, my dear Henry, that you will devote yourself assiduously to your studies; whether at Louisville or Lexington is not so material, provided you are diligent. You have a long and, I hope, a happy life before you; but you must never cease to reflect that whether happy or wretched depends mainly on yourself. You have all the external circumstances to cheer and animate you; and you have enjoyed advantages of education which few in our Country ever possessed.

According to my custom, on leaving home, for any length of time, I have made a Will which I have confided to the care of your mother. I have manifested my confidence in you by appointing you one of its Executors.

Your mother unites with me in affectionate regards to Julia [Prather Clay]. P.S. I wish you would enquire of Mr. McIlvaine[3] about a trunk of Thomas's [Hart Clay] which was sent to his care last Spring was a year [ago] from N. Orleans by Mr. [James] Erwin

ALS. Henry Clay Memorial Foundation, Lexington, Ky.   1. On Nov. 17, 1832, James Guthrie chaired a meeting in Louisville which adopted a series of resolutions condemning the doctrine of nullification. Louisville *Public Advertiser*, Nov. 19, 1832.   2. Johnston to Clay, Jan. 12, 1831. 3. B.R. McIlvaine & Co.

From John J. Crittenden, Frankfort, November 24, 1832. States that he has heard that Clay does "not intend going to Washington till about the 25th of the next month." Hopes, if this is true, that Clay will visit Frankfort [Clay to Crittenden, November 28, 1832]. Continues: "If I could see any way in which you could be the pacificator of the South, I should be impatient to see you off for Washington. But as things appear to me, I perceive no reason for your hurrying to the Senate. And should you remain at home till after the meeting of our Legislature, your friends here will expect a visit." ALS. NcD. The date of this letter might be read November 26, Crittenden's handwriting not being distinct on the "4" or "6."

From HENRY CLAY, JR.   Louisville, November 27, 1832
In regard to myself I am now perfectly happy. I am united to a lady[1] who possesses my entire love and veneration, and who returns me, in over-measure, the affection to which I am entitled. We are not rich, but it will be a source of

pleasurable occupation to become so. Like all young men of ambition and aspiring temperaments, the mere possibility of ill success keeps alive in me a thousand unnecessary and annoying fears. But I hope ere long to become settled in life, and then I shall begin in good earnest to mold my future destinies. In the meantime, I shall devote my principal energies to the law, and shall endeavor to compose my mind to a state of profitable study.

Whatever, my dear father, may have been my errors, I have always entertained for you the most unvarying filial attachment; and it shall always be my highest pleasure to endeavor to meet your wishes and commands.

Julia desires me to express her love to you all in the most tender and affectionate terms.

Copy. Printed in Colton, *Clay Correspondence*, 4:343-44.   1. Julia Prather Clay. Henry Clay, Jr., to Clay, June 7, 1832; Clay to Henry Clay, Jr., Oct. 23, 1832.

To JOHN J. CRITTENDEN   Lexington, November 28, 1832

I recd. your favor of the 24h. inst. as I had the previous one [November 17] to which it refers. Your views, in regard to your wishes on the subject of a service in the Senate, correspond with your character, and with my high estimate of it. I almost regret that your decision had not been different and such as to relieve me from a station which, I fear, will present no opportunity for any useful public service on my part.[1]

I had thought of not proceeding to Washn. until towards Xmas; but the dread of a winters journey, and the present good prospects of weather have induced me to proceed immediately. I shall therefore be deprived of all opportunity of seeing you and other friends at Frankfort. I wish you a pleasant Session, and that we may all live to see better days.

ALS. ViU. Copy in NcD.   1. Clay to Southard, Sept. 30, 1831; Worsley to Clay, Oct. 22, 1831.

From Samuel L. Southard, Trenton, N.J., December 1, 1832. Deplores the results of the presidential election [Sergeant to Clay, June 27, 1831], saying "I fear, that the Union & Govt are gone." States that the "recent elections, have greatly astonished me—Even in N.J. no one, of any party, who was well informed doubted a different result." Attributes the defeat to the "over confidence of our friends, who feared no danger—and the course of the Anti M[asons]—" Notes that "We were assured that they [Anti-Masons] would support our ticket, in preference to Genl. J's until the last moment—but the result shews that my early & constant fears respecting them, were well founded." Explains: "A little before our ticket was selected, they proposed that I should run on their Electoral ticket—select some of the others to run with me, & urge our friends to join, & every temptation which they could offer was presented—I refused—I could not—I ought not to have accepted their proposition. After this, one of them, avowed to me, their preference of Genl. J. to yourself—because your election might delay their ultimate success eight years, instead of four. It was then so late—so near the election, that I could make no movement to ward off the effects—Immediately on my refusal the[y] left my brother [Isaac] off their ticket—He had before that been a favorite with them. I thus destroyed him—but I could not help it—It was impossible for me to make the horrible sacrifice required of me. I have not the capacity fitted for such derelictions.—There is even now a large maj'y of our friends in this State—but they are of a class of people who will not go to the polls, unless they see an absolute necessity for it—& this they did not see—they felt secure—and they must bear the consequences. The genl. Election will exhibit most extraordinary results. The result of the Electoral Vote, will be most overwhelming—Yet the popular vote, thro'out the Union will be very close—the aggregate maj'y very small. And I believe it will be found, that the calculations of our friends, erred only where they relied too much on the A.M's."

Discusses his own position as governor [Southard to Clay, November 3, 1832] which he accepted at "a sacrifice of myself to my country." Mentions that "There are many who wish me to change my position to the Senate, in place of [Mahlon] Dickerson—under the belief that I can, in the present melancholy times, do more good to the country there, than where I now am. Whether this will be the wish of the Joint Meeting in Jany. I know not."

Asks Clay what is to be done with South Carolina [Stoddard to Clay, November 12, 1832]: "Do tell me your plan—prophesy for me." ALS. DLC-HC (DNA, M212, R5). Printed in Colton, *Clay Correspondence*, 4:344-45. Letter marked "(Confidential)." Isaac Southard lost a re-election bid for his U.S. House seat to William N. Shinn by a 24,363 to 23,310 vote. *Niles' Register* (December 1, 1832), 43:213.

To JAMES BROWN   Washington, December 9, 1832

I arrived here last night with my son James B. [Clay]   Mrs. Clay concluded to remain at home, as the Session was short and not likely to be a very agreeable one. The Cholera at N. O. delayed the departure of Mr. and Mrs. [James] Erwin from Kentucky for that City; but by this time they are on the river.

I have brought in James to place him in a mercantile establishment in Boston;[1] and I have some intention in a few days of accompanying him as far as Philada. on his way to Boston. I beg you will not mention the probability of my being in Philada. as I wish to avoid crowds and company as much as possible.

I can give you no news, as I have arrived too late to pick up any yet.

ALS. KyLxT.   1. Clay to Brown, August 24, 1831; Brown to Clay, Oct. 2, 1831.

To JAMES CALDWELL   Washington, December 9, 1832

Contrary to my intentions at one time, I came by the Ohio river and Wheeling to this place, instead of the W[hite]. S[ulphur]. Springs. The consequence is that I have been disappointed in meeting Mr [William] Martin, my overseer, who I suppose is returning by your place with a pair of English Cattle under his care for me.[1] Under that supposition, I take the liberty of transmitting for him the enclosed letter, which I request you will deliver, if he passes by you. If he does not *in two weeks* after you get the letter, be pleased to drop it in the P. Office.

I think I am entitled to your congratulations for our recent political defeat.[2] Jackson had so completely put every thing into disorder, that we should have found it very difficult to mend fences and repair his injuries. Besides, perhaps he and his brother nullifiers of So. Carolina[3] ought to settle matters themselves. . . .

ALS. ViHi. Printed in *VMHB* (Oct., 1947), 55:309-10.   1. Clay to Powel, Nov. 7, 1832.
2. Sergeant to Clay, June 27, 1831.   3. Stoddard to Clay, Nov. 12, 1832.

Comment in Senate, December 11, 1832. Will reintroduce tomorrow his bill "to appropriate, for a limited time, the proceeds arising from the sales of public lands." *Register of Debates*, 22 Cong., 2 Sess., 5. See Comment in Senate, April 16, 1832; Speech in Senate, June 20, 1832; and January 7, 1833.

To FRANCIS T. BROOKE   Washington, December 12, 1832

On my arrival here a few days ago, I found your favor of the 28h. Ulto.   Mrs.

Clay did not accompany me, but remained at home in consequence of the shortness of the Session and the apprehended bad state of the roads both in coming and returning.

It is useless to dwell on the issue of the P. election respecting which we were so greatly disappointed.[1] From whatever causes it proceeded, it is now irrevocable.

You ask what is to be done with nullification?[2] I must refer you to the Presidents proclamation. One short week produced the message and the Proclamation—[3]the former ultra, on the side of State rights—the latter ultra, on the side of Consolodation. How they can be reconciled, I must leave to our Virginia friends. As to the Proclamation, altho' there are good things in it, especially what relates to the Judiciary, there are some entirely too ultra for me, and which I cannot stomach. A proclamation ought to have been issued weeks ago, but I think it should have been a very different paper from the present, which I apprehend will irritate instead of allaying excited feeling.

Congress has not yet been called upon, and I sincerely hope it may not be necessary to call upon it, in this unfortunate affair. How is the proclamation recd. at Richmond?

I shall leave here tomorrow for a few days to accompany my fourth son [James Brown Clay] as far as Philada. on his way to N. England. . . .[4]

ALS. KyU. Printed in Colton, *Clay Correspondence*, 4:345 with minor variations in spelling and punctuation.   1. Sergeant to Clay, June 27, 1831.   2. Stoddard to Clay, Nov. 12, 1832.   3. Jackson's Fourth Annual Message on Dec. 4 indicated that southern pressure, particularly from South Carolina, had helped turn the president into a tariff reformer and had broadened the Jacksonian crusade against special privilege. It took a much softer tone toward those who opposed the tariff than did his "Proclamation to the People of South Carolina" of Dec. 10, 1832. The latter repudiated South Carolina's nullification and secession doctrines, asserting that the interests of the nation transcended those of the states. Freehling, *Prelude to Civil War*, 267; Glyndon G. Van Deusen, *The Rise and Decline of Jacksonian Democracy* (New York, 1970), 189-93. For Jackson's Fourth Annual Message, see *MPP*, 591-606.   4. Clay to Brown, Dec. 9, 1832; Clay to Henry Clay, Jr., Dec. 30, 1832.

Comment in Senate, December 12, 1832. Reintroduces and explains the recent legislative history of his bill to distribute to the states the revenue from public lands sales. *Register of Debates*, 22 Cong., 2 Sess., 6.   See Comment in Senate, December 11, 1832.

From ANNE BROWN CLAY ERWIN

Lexington,
December 13, 1832

I suppose by the time this reaches you that you will have arrived safely at Washington; we heard from you at Wheeling but not since; you have been seeing new faces & new things every day, whilst we have been going on in the same quiet routine, I will not say dull, that you left us in. The only change in our society is the arrival of Henry [Clay, Jr.] & Julia [Prather Clay] from L[ouisville].; they came a week since and are at Postlethwaits. They have been out frequently and we all spent a very pleasant day yesterday with Mama [Lucretia Hart Clay] who we found in good health & spirits. Theodore [W. Clay] went home the day after you left, and although Mama is now fully convinced that he is deranged, he has so far conducted himself quietly and she is much happier than if he were any where else.

Henry has recommenced the study of the law with increased energy, he is disgusted with the prospect of making a living at the bar in Kentucky and as a last determination which he does not intend to change, he is to go to N. Orleans in Febuary and at least open an office this winter preparatory to commencing business next year; this I think a wise course and I hope he will persevere in it. His health & spirits are both better than when he left us.

Nothing has occured worth noticing in the family except the very sudden death of Alfred Shelby who fell in a fit of Apoplexy and died a few hours after wards. Mrs M. Harrison[1] gave birth to a fine son on Saturday who I hope will not prove like his father a good *Jackson man.*

We are postively to leave on the 15th that is day after tomorrow, and we have every prospect of a quick and pleasant as the weather is fine and both Rivers in fine order. I leave the boys [Henry C.; James, Jr.; Andrew E.] with Mama. I expect they will occasion me to return very easily in the Spring.

Give my love to all those who may be so kind as to enquire for me, and particularly to James [Brown Clay], do my dear father, make him write me to N. Orleans if you cannot find time to do so yourself. Mr Denton begs to be respectfully remembered to you. Mr [James] Erwin & the children join me in love to you.

ALS. DLC-TJC (DNA, M212, R10). Printed in Colton, *Clay Correspondence*, 4:346. Mrs. Erwin dated this letter Dec. 15, 1832, an error revealed in the body of the letter.   1. Margaretta Ross Harrison, wife of James O. Harrison.

DRAFT PROPOSAL OF COMPROMISE TARIFF OF 1833
[Philadelphia, Mid-December, 1832]

Preamble recites, that differences of opinion have existed & continue to exist, as to the policy of protecting manufacturing industry, by duties on similar articles, when imported; that this difference is increased, so as to agitate public mind, & threaten serious disturbances; & it being desirable to settle differences &c. enact[s]

Sect. 1. existing laws to remain in force till Mar. 3. 1840 — then all to be repealed, & hereby are repealed.

S 2. until the 3d. of Mar. '40 no higher or other duties than those[1] now existing to be laid "And from and after the aforesaid day all duties collected upon any article or articles whatever of foreign importation shall be Equal, according to the value thereof, & solely for the purpose & with the intent of providing such revenue as may be necessary to an economical expenditure of the Govt. without regard to the protection or encouragement of any branch of domestic industry whatever"[2]

Copy. CSmH. Endorsed on separate sheet: "Mr. Clay's first project." Enclosed in Webster to Hiram Ketchum, Jan. 20, 1838, in Wiltse, *Webster Papers*, 4:263-64; see also Curtis, *Life of Daniel Webster*, 1:455-56; Curtis dates this document *ca.* Mid-Dec., 1832. *Ibid.*, 434. For Clay's presumed authorship of this document, which Webster later (1838) claimed to have copied verbatim from Clay's original version, see Peterson, *Olive Branch and Sword — The Compromise of 1833*, 52-54. See also Draft of Compromise Tariff Bill, *ca.* Feb. 11, 1833.   1. Word rendered as "shall" in Wiltse.   2. Clay's famous Compromise Tariff bill of 1833 was introduced in the Senate on Feb. 12, 1833, amended on Feb. 22, and passed on March 1, 1833, by the vote of 29 to 16. It was introduced in the House on Feb. 25, 1833, and passed on Feb. 26 by the vote of 119-85. See Van Deusen, *The Life of Henry Clay*, 264-70; Peterson, *Olive Branch and Sword*, 40-84; Curtis, *Life of Daniel Webster*, 1:434-56. For Clay's principal Senate speeches explaining and defending his proposal (Feb. 12 and 25, 1833), see *Register of Debates*, 22 Cong., 2 Sess., 462-82, 729-42.

HEZEKIAH NILES[1]
[Mid-December, 1832]

[For yourself.

I have reason to believe that a principal party in the south would gladly get back from the ground they have taken on the tariff — if they decently can.

A great effort will be made, on the part of the administration to *conciliate* there; but *you* should be the agent of that, if to be accomplished on just principles. I begin to believe, that something may be done to soothe the south, without materially affecting the protection of any great branch of our industry — the constitutional question being *waived*. I shall know more about this speedily, & shall then promptly see you. if the weather shall be such that I ought to venture from home — for though I am not sick, I cannot call myself well. You have shewn a disposition to meet on conciliatory principles; but my object is simply to suggest the facts, as they appear to me; thinking that I have good reasons for what I say.

AL, fragment. DLC-HC (DNA, M212, R6).   1. Although the surviving fragment of this letter is not signed, the editors have determined, by handwriting comparisons, that the author is Hezekiah Niles. Based on internal evidence, the date seems most likely to be shortly after the president's "Proclamation to South Carolina" on Dec. 10, 1832.

From William C.C. Claiborne, Jr., Paris, December 20, 1832. Writes that the "Americans in Paris among whom your friends are in a great majority, had been expecting the results of the Presidential contest [Sergeant to Clay, June 27, 1831] with the deepest interest. We have now heard enough to convince us that all is lost save honor. — It would have been the happiest day of my life, could I have heard that you had reached that station which you so highly deserve; but I endeavour to bear the dissappointment with the same philosophy which I have no doubt you exercise on the occasion."

Reports that he returned to Paris three months ago after "a very long and interesting voyage, which . . . extended as far as Russia." Of the political situation in Europe, states that the "news of the morning is that the Dutch Army is about to make a diversion by invading Belgium" which "would probably lead to a general war [Johnston to Clay, November 5, 1830]." ALS. DLC-HC (DNA, M212, R5).

From Francis T. Brooke, near Frederickburg, Va., December 25, 1832. Reports that in Richmond on the subject of nullification [Stoddard to Clay, November 12, 1832] "your former friends are much divided, as to what they wish you to do — Some of them wish you to come out a great State right man — others are anxious that you should not go the whole length of condemning everything in the proclamation [Clay to Brooke, December 12, 1832] but only that part which denies the right of a State to leave the Union and makes it treason to do so — holding also that there is a co-existing right in the Genl. Governmt to force S Carolina back by war, this I incline to think myself is the true course, this I infer is also the opinion of [William C.] Rives." States that "my impression is that the assembly will condemn S Carolina but I fear will at the same time also, so condemn the proclamation as to induce her, to persist in her course, this ought I think to be avoided if possible, [Thomas] Ritchie seems afraid that [John H.] Pleasants will cut his ground from under him, by putting *himself* at the head of the State right party, on the contrary his course in Virga. is well calculated to rally the broken ranks of Jackson." ALS. InU. Brooke correctly predicted the response of the Virginia legislature concerning nullification. See Robert Seager II, *And Tyler Too, A Biography of John & Julia Gardiner Tyler* (New York, 1963), 92, 568.

From John M. McConnell, Greenupsburg, Ky., December 27, 1832. Reports that it has been "confidently affirmed" to him "that you had an understanding with Mr. [John C.] Calhoun and the nullifiers [Stoddard to Clay, November 12, 1832] of the South & that you would during this winter come out & defend their doctrines." Adds: "Although I do not believe this story and certainly never would be influenced by it in words or actions until I had the irrefragable evidence of your own declarations and speeches upon the subject. Yet it has sunk deep in my mind and I must own has given me some uneasiness, lest the injustice done you by Genl. Jackson and his friends and that law of retaliation which is implanted in the breast of every man might superinduce you to give countenance to these doctrines or even to remain silent in regard to them. I do not wish to be understood that I desire you or any other of our friends to take upon you the task of leading the opposition to the nullifiers. That is the business of those who are at the head of affairs but I think it all important when the proper occasion shall present itself that you and every other friend of the American system should distinctly avow your opposition to the doctrines & the tendencies of the measures of the dominant party in South Carolina." Affirms that "Although the administration is radically wrong in many of its measures yet that could form no justification for an opposition to those in which it is manifestly right." States that "The true friends of good government in the main look up to you as the champion of its and their rights — Your situation therefore while it is enviable on the one hand is awfully responsible on the other. A mis-step on your part would demolish and Scatter the party who have ralied around the American System, the constitution and the Federal Judiciary. This result would to my mind endanger the Union and the liberty of the country."

Mentions that the National Republicans dislike three sections of the president's annual message [Clay to Brooke, December 12, 1832]: "The tariff, The bank & the public lands." However, "His proclamation against the nullifiers [Clay to Brooke, December 12, 1832] is popular with all men of all parties except that portion which anticipates a reduction of the tariff to a revenue standard." ALS. DLC-HC (DNA, M212, R5).

To HENRY CLAY, JR.   Philadelphia, December 30, 1832

I came here to accompany James [Brown Clay] on his way to Boston, and knowing that but little was likely to be done at Washington until the new year I have remained a few days longer than I intended. I shall return on wednesday. During my absence from Washn. my letters not having been sent to me I presume there are some there from you and others in K.   These I hope to receive on getting back.

James went on to Boston shortly after my arrival here He has entered the Commerical House of Mess. Grant and Severs [*sic*][1] on trial, and assures me that he will do all in his power to please them.

Our public affairs seem to be approaching a crisis. Still, I am inclined to think that South Carolina will yet pause, and postpone the execution of her Ordinance until she sees whether the Tariff will not be repealed.[2] Genl. Jackson seems bent on its destruction, and it will be difficult to sustain it against the means which will be employed to overthrow it.

During my sojourn here, I have been treated with the utmost hospitality, kindness and consideration.

John [M. Clay] writes me that you have finally resolved to go to N. Orleans. When do you go?

Give my love to Julia [Prather Clay]. P.S. Your uncle [James] Brown, with whom I stay, is very well, and in better spirits than I expected to find him. He speaks very kindly of you.

ALS. Henry Clay Memorial Foundation, Lexington, Ky.   1. Grant (Benjamin B.), Seaver (G.) & Co. (G.R. Dinsmoor & R. Barnett) dry goods was housed at 5 Liberty Square, Boston. *Boston City Directory*, 1837. Soon after young James B. Clay's employment by Grant & Seaver, Clay began shipping wool and bacon hams to the Boston firm on consignment. The shipments went by wagon from Lexington to January, Huston, & Co., in Maysville, Ky.; thence by steamboat to Knox & McKee Co., in Wheeling, Va. [W. Va.]; thence to Erskine & Echelberger & Co., in Baltimore via the wagons of the Baltimore and Wheeling Transportation Line Co., "with instructions to ship per first good packet to Boston to Messrs Grant Seaver & Co." January, Huston, & Co. to Clay, July 17, 1833 (two documents). ALS; and AD. DLC-TJC (DNA, M212, R17). Knox & McKee to Clay, July 20, 1833. ALS. *Ibid.* (R14).   2. Stoddard to Clay, Nov. 12, 1832.

From Edmund W. & Philip B. Hockaday, Winchester, Ky., January 1, 1833. State that they have "lately enclosed to you a bill" for Kocklanı which must "have miscarried." Adds that the "horse is in fine condition," and they "have written to Mr [Edwin U.] Berryman at New York advising as to the propriety of having the sum of $3000 insured on Kocklain [*sic*]—and having a handsome figure of the horse from the hand of some skilful artist." ALS. DLC-TJC (DNA, M212, R10). For Philip B. Hockaday, see Ronald V. Jackson *et al.* (eds.), *Kentucky 1830 Census Index* (Provo, Utah, 1976), 88; G. Glenn Clift, *Kentucky Obituaries 1787-1854* (Baltimore, 1977), 190.

To HENRY CLAY, JR.   Washington, January 3, 1832 [*sic*, 1833]
On my return from Philada. this morning by the way of Balto. I recd. your two favors of the 12h. and 23d. inst. [*sic*, ultimo]

I have formed no positive determination about resigning my Seat in the Senate, and it was therefore well enough for you to contradict the report or not as you pleased. My spirits were not good when I left home, nor are they very buoyant now; but political events were only *one* cause of them. I hope to regain them, and your success and happiness, my dear Son, would contribute not a little to the recovery of their tone. I have certainly, as you justly remark, much reason to look back, with satisfaction, upon my public life, 'tho' it has not been free from a full share of thorns.

As to the plan of your temporary settlement at N. Orleans, if it meets your own approbation that is much more important than mine. The plan which one forms for himself, after full deliberation, is much more likely to be satisfactory and successful than any which may be recommended by another. I have only the fear that your preparation may not be as thorough as it should be and that if you are not immediately successful you may be disposed to despond. With regard to a connexion with Col P.,[1] if it be practicable, you had better consult as to its expediency with Judge [Alexander] Porter, Mr. [James] Erwin and other friends.

In respect to your wife's [Julia Prather Clay] Estate, all that part of it which is personal, and which you may reduce into possession, during the coverture, is absolutely vested in you by law, in virtue of your marriage. A different rule holds as to her real estate. The fee simple of that remains on her and she cannot be divested of it but by deed executed by her and you, in conformity with the act of Assembly of Kentucky, regulating conveyances &c. If your death were to precede hers, she might after her survivorship dispose of it as she pleased, altho she might have had issue by you. If you survive her, and should have had any child by her, you would become tenant by the curtesy, that is you would be entitled to the use of it during your life and after your death it would pass to her heirs. If she left any children or child by you they would be entitled to it, and if they departed this life, during your existence, you would be then entitled to it as their heirs.

You have the power, with the consent of your wife to alienate any part of her real, provided it is conveyed in the manner required by the above mentd. act of Assembly.

Sometimes the husband to invest himself with the real estate of his wife joins her in conveying it to a third person in trust to be reconveyed to the husband. In this way Mr. R. Wickliffe is understood to have acquired the land of his present wife.[2]

I can give you no definitive opinion as to what will be done here. There is a general feeling of great instability in the present state of things. The Union is

607

not believed to be free from danger whatever course may be pursued. The Administration is urging a bill which may be regarded as a substantial repeal of the tariff; and I find the prevailing opinion is that it will pass the house, if not the Senate.[3] In that event we shall probably shift the theatre of discontent from the South to the North.

Give my love to Julia, to your mama and all the children.

ALS. Henry Clay Memorial Foundation, Lexington, Ky. 1. Possibly Daniel Parker, with whom Henry Clay, Jr., had shared a room in New Orleans. See Henry Clay, Jr., to Clay, Dec. 16, 1831. 2. Robert Wickliffe, Sr., had married his second wife, Mary O. Russell, in Oct., 1826. *RKHS*, 36:261. 3. The administration, or Verplanck bill, which provided for lowering the duties to a tariff for revenue only, was reported by the House Ways and Means Committee on Dec. 27, 1832. During discussion of the bill in the House on Feb. 25, Robert Letcher moved to strike out all of the Verplanck bill and substitute in its entirety Clay's compromise tariff bill which was then being debated in the Senate. Before adjourning, the House accepted Letcher's amendment, and passed Clay's bill the following day. See Draft Proposal, Mid-Dec., 1832; Speech in Senate, February 12, 1833; Remark in Senate, February 26, 1833; Munroe, *Louis McLane*, 368-75.

Comment in Senate, January 3, 1833. Speaks to Sen. George Poindexter's resolution of December 17, 1832, seeking to reduce by an aggregate of $6,000,000 the duties on various protected articles, but excluding such articles "essential to our national independence in time of war." Requests from the Treasury Department a list of "articles deemed essential to the national defence in time of war." Reports that "Before he recently left the city, he had, in conversation, expressed a wish to see the plan of the Treasury Department in a specific and responsible form for the reduction of the revenue, and particularily a specification of those articles which were considered . . . essential to national defense." Does not believe it appropriate, however, for the Senate to "call on the Executive or the head of a department for the projet of a bill." *Register of Debates*, 22 Cong., 2 Sess., 50-51. See also, Clay to Henry Clay, Jr., January 3, 1833.

To MADISON C. JOHNSON   Washington, January 4, 1833

I recd. your letter transmitting a statement of the amount paid by the University towards the Morrison College,[1] and a resolution of the Board requesting the payment of the interest upon $14.000.

In your former letter, the payment of the interest was demanded upon the ground of my contract. That ground is now shifted and it is requested upon the ground of the advances of the institution towards the erection of the College.

When that building was undertaken, I stated that I would advance towards its completion a specific sum, on a/c. of the residuary legacy; but that I could advance no more during the life of Mrs. [James] Morrison. I have advanced every dollar of that sum. I have done more. I have transferred to the University the Bridge Stock,[2] and put it in possession of the Maccoun house[3] and lot in Lexington.

I am now asked to advance more, what I never promised or contracted to pay, and what I have already stated to you I cannot pay consistently with my duties as Exor,[4] and with the just claims of others.

I regret to be obliged to adhere to this resolution. It would be much more agreeable to me to comply with the wishes of the Board if I could compatibly with a sense of duty.

ALS. KyLxT. 1. See 3:496. 2. Probably a reference to the bridge stock mentioned in Blanton and Dudley to Clay, May 15, 1829. Clay had written his brother, Porter Clay, on August 9, 1833, telling him "to call on Mr. H. Blanton and receive for me the dividends due on my Bridge Stock . . . and send me the amount." ALS. KyHi. 3. Probably the former home of James Maccoun, a Lexington merchant, who had built a house on Main Street, across from the court house. See William A. Leavy, "A Memoir of Lexington and Its Vicinity," ed. by Nina A Visscher, *RKHS* (April, 1942), 40·116, 125, 130; *ibid.* (Jan., April, Oct., 1943), 41:60-61, 120, 314, 319, 320.   4. Of the James Morrison estate.

To THOMAS HELM   Washington, January 5, 1833

I recd. your letter transmitting your Subscription for the [Washington *Daily National*] Intellr. and return a receipt enclosed.

I have yet some hopes that a Civil war will be avoided with So. Carolina. Her conduct has been rash and intemperate.

A bill to repeal the Tariff is before the House[1] and the prevailing opinion is that it will pass that body. We shall endeavor to arrest it in the Senate, with what success, time alone can disclose. How inconsistent is our President! Compare his messsage and his proclamation.[2] And whilst he would chastise South Carolina for opposing the Tariff,[3] the whole weight of the administration is exerted to destroy it. Whilst he wd. carry War into So. Carolina to vindicate the Laws he suffers Georgia to trample upon them with impunity.[4]

My best exertions will be employed to save the Union and to save also our Systems of policy.

ALS. Courtesy of Mrs. Henry Jackson, Sr., Danville, Ky.   1. Clay to Henry Clay, Jr., Jan. 3, 1833.   2. Clay to Brooke, Dec. 12, 1832.   3. Stoddard to Clay, Nov. 12, 1832.   4. Johnston to Clay, Jan. 12, 1831.

To JAMES CALDWELL   Washington, January 6, 1833

I recd your favor of the 31st Ulto.   Mr. [William] Martin returned by the Wheeling route, and will receive at home the letter which I forwarded to you.

You cannot, you say, contragulate me. I think you ought to congratulate me that I was *not* elected; for with the prospects before him, the President reposes on any other than a bed of roses.[1]

I think with you that the President has been the main cause of nullification.[2] By the encouragement he gave to Georgia,[3] he stimulated So. Carolina, which has constantly appealed to the successful example of her neighbours.

The proclamation has some sound principles in it mixt up with some ultra Consolodation doctrines. I have reserved any emphatic expression of my approbation of the good which it contains until I see that he acts in conformity with it. The message of the 4h. and the proclamation of the 11h. [*sic*, 10th] Dccr. arc as opposite as we are to the Antipodes.[4] Who can have confidence in any man that would put forth two such contradictory papers? Lord Chatham [William Pitt] said that confidence was a plant of slow growth. The seeds of mine are not yet sown.

The prevailing opinion is that the bill to repeal the Tariff will pass the House. Its fate in the Senate is not certain.[5] I shall do whatever I can to preserve our systems of policy, and should be most happy if I could contribute to the restoration of harmony. . . .

ALS. ViHi. Printed in *VMHB* (Oct., 1947), 55:310-11.   1. Clay to Caldwell, Dec. 9, 1832.   2. Stoddard to Clay, Dec. 12, 1832.   3. Johnston to Clay, Jan. 12, 1831.   4. Clay to Brooke, Dec. 12, 1832.   5. Clay to Henry Clay, Jr., Jan. 3, 1833.

Speech in Senate, January 7, 1833. Presents at length various arguments for the early distribution of the proceeds of the sales of public lands to the states, arguments similar to those employed in his distribution speech of June 20, 1832. Notes that the bill he is introducing in the present session, which has been sent to the Committee on Public Lands, is "identically the bill" which has already once passed the Senate. It proposes to set aside for the benefit of the new states 12 ½ percent "out of the aggregate proceeds, in addition to the five per cent. which was now allowed to them by compact, before any division took place among the States generally." It thus proposes to assign, in the first place 17 ½ percent to the new states, and "then to divide the whole of the residue among the twenty-four States." *Register of Debates*, 22 Cong., 2 Sess., 67-79. See Comment in Senate, April 16; December 11, 1832. Clay's public lands bill passed the Senate on January 25, 1833, by the vote of 24 to 20 and the House on March 1, by the vote of 96 to 40. Since Jackson did not sign the bill by March 3, the last day of the session, it was pocket vetoed. *Register of Debates*, 22 Cong., 2 Sess., 235, 1920-21. Not until December 4, 1833, did he issue a written veto message to the Senate explaining his objections to the measure. *MPP*, 3:56-69. See Van Deusen, *The Life of Henry Clay*, 252-55; Bowers, *Party Battles of the Jackson Period*, 197-200; also Speech in Senate, December 5, 1833.

From Oran Follett, Batavia, N.Y., January 10, 1833. Writes as one "personally unknown to you," suggesting that the National Republican party must demonstrate leadership in the nullification crisis [Stoddard to Clay, November 12, 1832]. Warns that Van Buren is taking advantage of the president's "late proclamation [Clay to Brooke, December 12, 1832]" to South Carolina. Predicts that Van Buren "will strive to place himself between the great parties of the *south* and the *north*, in the attitude of mediator, beckoning to each in turn by condemning the ultra doctrines of both." Adds that "Nullification, in its broad sense, will be condemned, to satisfy northern scruples — and, to soften the south, the principle of protection will be abandoned, and the tariff cut down so as to yield a revenue barely equal to the demands of the government."

Maintains that the National Republican party must devise "a rallying point . . . immediately" in order to meet this crisis. Believes "the National party must have a candidate, at least in prospective." Continues: "I will be plain with you in this communication. I feel the force of what I say, and none regrets the necessity deeper than I do, that compels me to say, you are not the man on whom the friends of the country can rely for the canvass of 1836. This is the secret conviction of the whole Nat. Repub. party, with, perhaps, a few exceptions. Your confidential friends and advisers in the last canvass, have to answer to the country for this — they compelled you to place yourself before the car of the political Moloch of the day, and you have been overwhelmed. I will not charge them with selfishness in this; but, certain it is, they erred in judgement, and to their indiscreet zeal is chargeable in a great degree the manifold evils that now threaten the country."

Contends that Van Buren has already made headway in converting some National Republicans, and cites William B. Rochester as an example. L, draft. OCHP.

To ROSWELL L. COLT[1]   Washington, January 11, 1833
I recd. in Philada. your favor communicating your views respecting the Tariff, for which I was greatly obliged.

I concur with you in thinking that one of the greatest evils under which we labor is the perpetual agitation of the question, and the consequent uncertainty as to all the interests concerned. I have been thinking of some mode of settling it which would give stability to the operations of Government, and quiet to the Country; but I have not yet finally determined whether I shall bring forward any proposition.

The fate of Mr. Verplank's [*sic*, Gulian C. Verplanck] bill is uncertain, 'though the prevailing opinion seems to be that it will pass. the H. of R.[2]

ALS. NjP.   1. See 5:252.   2. Clay to Henry Clay, Jr., Jan. 3, 1833.

To CHARLES J. FAULKNER　　　　Washington, January 11, 1833

Your favor of the 14h. ulto. reached this City during my absence from it at Philadelphia, and on my return I found that the subject to which it relates had taken such a course in your Legislature [Virginia]¹ as to render unnecessary any suggestions of mine, if I had any to offer that could have been useful to you, in the delicate and difficult task which you had to perform.

I thought when I first saw it, and still think, that the proclamation,² although an able and eloquent paper, containing many sound views and principles, was not calculated to allay, but to increase, the excitement on which it animadverted, and to extend it far beyond the infected State. Some of its doctrines, too, relating to the Sovereignty of the States, the election of President, the nature of the Representative office &c. appeared to me unsound. I thought and still believe that we have no security for an adherence to the good which is in it; and several circumstances have since transpired to shew that this apprehension is well founded. What confidence can any considerate man place in a C. Magistrate who shall have put forth two such opposite papers as the message of the 4h. and the proclamation of the 11h. [sic, 10th] of Decr.?³

As to the immediate question of your letter, the course which it becomes Virginia to pursue, in regard to the Ordinance, proclamation &c. it is one on which I should, even to you, speak with great diffidence. That course has probably been resolved on; and, if at any time my opinion would have had the smallest influence, it is now too late to exert it.

Generally it is a safe course in public affairs, when we do not see a very plainly marked way, to do nothing. The project of sending Commrs. to South Carolina appeared to me to be liable to the objection of involving you with her, if she took your advice, and against her, if she did not. Besides, what were they to do? To treat; to enter into any compact? That I believe was not contemplated. It was moreover calculated to draw upon you the invidious observation of other States. It seems to me, therefore, that the adoption of resolutions expressive of your sentiments was the most expedient manner of disposing of the subject, and that I understand you have probably done.

I wish I could communicate to you some definite and agreeable information from this place, but I cannot. We are all here, at least I am and those with whom I converse in a dense fog, and when and where light will break in upon us it is impossible to say. One day we are told the Tariff now before the House will pass,⁴ and that orders have been given both from Albany and the White house to that effect. The next we are assured there is no prospect of its passage, and that both the President and V. President elect are opposed to it. Scarcely any two members of the house, that you will meet, agree as to its fate. All that is certain is that if the President desires its passage, it will pass the House, if not the Senate also.

Meantime, we are assured from the North that the bill is fraught with utter ruin to that quarter of the Union; and that its enactment will be followed by scenes of tremendous distress.

After the opposition from the South to the proposition which I made at the last Session to limit the revenue of the Government to an economical expenditure and to them all the duties upon the protected articles, leaving those free which our Country does not produce, I almost despair of any amicable and permanent settlement of this question.

The Land bill is now before the Senate.[5] I think, or I should rather say, I hope, it will pass that body; and, in that event, there is some prospect of its getting through the House. But for the Tariff, and the operation of party feelings it would pass both houses, by large majorities.

ALS. KyLoF. Letter marked "(Confidential)." 1. Brooke to Clay, Dec. 25, 1832. 2. Clay to Brooke, Dec. 12, 1832. 3. *Ibid.* 4. Clay to Henry Clay, Jr., Jan. 3, 1833. 5. Speech in Senate, Jan. 7, 1833.

From PETER B. PORTER   Albany, N.Y., January 11, 1833

I recd. last evening, on my return from an excursion to Connecticut, your favors of the 29th ult. & 1st inst., for which I return you my thanks.

I write this merely to say that a rumor is in circulation here, & to which I understand Mr. Van Buren and his friends have taken particular pains to give currency, that you have "thrown yourself upon your reserved rights," formed a coalition with Mr. Calhoun, and are prepared to contest all the leading doctrines of the President's proclamation, & the message by which it was followed up.[1] In other words, that you will abandon your Northern friends and throw yourself upon the South.

I need not say to you that while those of your friends who know you well pay no attention to this gossip, there are some who, not having had the same opportunity to observe the uniformity and constancy of your political course, are much annoyed and distressed by it—For I can assure you that your political friends here, notwithstanding our late defeat, have lost nothing of their personal respect and attachment to you. These reports and the belief in them, have probably arisen from the circumstance of your having thus far kept yourself aloof (and in which I think you have acted wisely) from the quarrel between the Jackson and Calhoun parties.

The late scism (?) in the Jackson party here is far from being healed, & indeed every day thus far has given it additional rancour. I should not be surprised (although this perhaps is speculating rather too far ahead) if it were to result in the organization of a new party in this State, based on the tariff & other great interests of the country to the exclusion of personal favoritism (?) & supported by a strong press established at this place. If those who have made the demonstration against Van Buren and his friends, can be induced to go thus far, I should look to the Establishment of a great and powerful party for the formation of which abundant materials can be found among those who are sickened with the corruption & nuisance (?) of Van Burenism and Anti Masonry.

It seems (contrary to what I at first believed) that our new Senator elect [Nathaniel P. Tallmadge] was not Van Buren's favorite candidate.[2] Judge [Jacob] Sutherland was unquestionably the one whom he intended for that place; and to show him off as an Anti-Tariff man he was made the chairman of the [word illeg.] meeting at the Capital[;] Talmadge [*sic*] taking advantage of this circumstance announced *himself* a Tariff man, & to this declaration & the additional fact that the vote in caucus was taken by ballot, he probably owes his election. I have but a poor opinion of Talmadge but I think he will be inclined by his personal interest (for that will be his ruling star) to give a decided support to the Tariff.

Copy. OHi. 1. Clay to Brooke, Dec. 12, 1832; Stoddard to Clay, Nov. 12, 1832. 2. For Tallmadge's election, see Hammond, *History of Political Parties in the State of New York*, 2:432; and *Niles' Register* (Feb. 9, 1833), 43:386.

Remark in Senate, January 11, 1833. Objects to postponement of action on the bill to distribute to the states the proceeds from the sales of public lands. *Register of Debates*, 22 Cong., 2 Sess., 81. See Speech in Senate, January 7, 1833.

From Daniel Wells, Boston, January 11, 1833. Writes Clay in his capacity as chairman of a committee of the Massachusetts legislature, appointed to consider resolutions of the Tennessee legislature [Metcalfe to Clay, February 14, 1832] on the subject of the public lands. Asks Clay for relevant documents on the subject, pointing out that the motive behind the Massachusetts request is "to influence as far as practicable the action of Congress upon the subject." ALS. DLC-HC (DNA, M212, R5).

Comment in Senate, January 14, 1833. Presents a petition from Leonard Jones and Henry Banta of Kentucky for a public land grant, the land to be used "to extend and propagate their discovery" of the secret of eternal life. Reports that they represent themselves to be "subjects of endless life who [have] made important discoveries connected with the morals, religion, and external existence of man." Confesses "some doubts as to the propriety" of presenting this petition, but fears their "endless enmity" if he does not. *Register of Debates*, 22 Cong., 2 Sess., 98.

Later this day, Clay opposes discussion of bill to indemnify U.S. citizens "for spoliations committed on their commerce by the French prior to 1800" until the public lands bill [Speech in Senate, January 7, 1833] has been disposed of. *Ibid.*, 98-99. For the nagging and continuing French spoliations issue, see 3:154-55; 6:1013-14, 1193; also Brown to Clay, January 24, 1832; and Remark in Senate, January 6, 1835.

To John L. Gilliland, Brooklyn, N.Y., January 14, 1833. Thanks him for "the box containing the Specimens of your pressed glass ware." Informs him that the "whole policy" of tariff protection is "now in imminent danger," and that "the people alone can now save it." Does not believe that the recent election demonstrated popular opposition to the policy. ALS. ViU.

Remark in Senate, January 16, 1833. Complains of continuing delay in bringing the public lands bill to a vote. *Register of Debates*, 22 Cong., 2 Sess., 111-12. See Speech in Senate, January 7, 1833.

To FRANCIS T. BROOKE

Washington, January 17, 1833

I recd. your two last favors, and should have written to you before and oftun but that I really have had nothing interesting to communicate. As to politics, we have no fact, no future. After 44 years of existance under the present Constitution what single principle is fixed? The Bank? No. I[n]ternal Improvements! No. The Tariff? No. Who is to interpret the Constitution? No. We are as much afloat at sea as the day when the Constitution went into operation. There is nothing certain but that the *will* of Andw. Jackson is to govern; and that will fluctuates with the change of every pen which gives expression to it. As to the Tariff now pending, before the House,[1] whether it will pass or not in that body depends upon his commands.

I have been thinking of some settlement, of that question, but I have not entirely matured any plan; and if I had, I am not satisfied that it would be expedient to offer it. Any plan that I might offer would be instantly opposed because *I* offered it. Sometimes I have thought that, considering how I have been and still am treated by both parties (the Tariff and the Anti Tariff) I would leave them to fight it out as well as they can. The lingering hopes of my country prevail over these feelings of a just resentment, and my judgment tells me that disregarding them I ought to the last to endeavor to do what I can to preserve its molestations and re-establish confidence and concord. I shall act in conformity with this judgment, but I am far from being sanguine that I have the power to effect any thing.

You will have seen the late message. It is able and elaborate freer from passion than the proclamation but not more compatible with the doctrines which prevail at Richmond.[2]

Copy. DLC-TJC (DNA, M212, R14). Printed in Colton, *Clay Correspondence*, 4:345-46.   1. Clay to Henry Clay, Jr., Jan. 3, 1833.   2. Clay to Brooke, Dec. 12, 1832.

Remark in Senate, January 17, 1833. Opposes an amendment to the public lands bill proposed by Sen. George Poindexter of Mississippi that would gradually reduce the price of public lands remaining unsold for a specified period after being offered for sale, and for granting pre-emptions under certain circumstances. *Register of Debates*, 22 Cong., 2 Sess., 119. See Speech in Senate, June 20, 1832; January 7, 1833.

Remark in Senate, January 18, 1833. Opposes postponement of debate on public lands bill. *Register of Debates*, 22 Cong., 2 Sess., 122. See Speech in Senate, January 7, 1833.

From Peter B. Porter, Albany, N.Y., January 21, 1833. Writes that he is in Albany "to attend a trial before the U.S. district court in my old controversy with the Government, as commissioner under the Treaty of Ghent [Porter to Clay, October 6, 1830]." States that although he has won his case once in chancery and again in the circuit court, "A new suit has now been commenced . . . and . . . I am to have two jury trials each of which will become a subject of successive appeal to the Circuit & to the Supreme Court." Notes: "I have been somewhat surprised that Congress has not in some way noticed the enormous expences which have been & continue to be incurred by the present Administration in the reckless prosecutions of its political opponents, without the smallest prospect of success, and evidently with no other objects than to punish their enemies and feed the District Attorneys, Marshals & Clerks, with fees out of the public Crib."

Reports that "Van Buren's policy . . . is to sacrafice the North & propitiate the South, by an abandonment of the Tariff." Adds that it has been intimated that the New York legislature will "soon make a public expression of their opinion that the duties should be reduced to the revenue Standard &c &c in other words, that Verplanks [*sic*, Verplanck's] Bill [Clay to Henry Clay, Jr., January 3, 1833] should be passed." Has heard, however, that the "more wise ones" of the Democratic party, who perceive that the destruction of the tariff will lead to their political ruin, "are getting up a public meeting to be held at the Capitol on Wednesday next [January 23] to approve the proclamation [Clay to Brooke, December 12, 1832] and disapprove of Verplanks Bill." Says he has "no doubt but that the meeting will be very large & respectable, & I think it will have the affect to deter many of our Jackson Members of Congress from the support of Verplanks Bill." ALS. DLC-HC (DNA, M212, R5). The New York legislature issued a "Report of a Joint Committee of the Senate and Assembly," expressing the opinion that nullification was not only "unauthorised by the Constitution of the United States, but fatally repugnant to all objects for which it was framed." However, they also approved the expressed desire of the president to restore harmony and lower the tariff. Albany *Argus*, January 29; February 1, 1833. Another group of Democrats met on January 24, 1833, and adopted nine resolutions. These opposed nullification, supported the principles of the president's Proclamation to South Carolina of December 10, 1832, and called for a gradual reduction of the tariff but the retention of some discriminatory duties. *Ibid.*, January 26, 1833.

Remark in Senate, January 22, 1833. Favors scheduling debate on the Force bill, also called the Revenue Collection bill. *Register of Debates*, 22 Cong., 2 Sess., 174, 178. The Force bill passed the Senate on February 20, 1833, by a vote of 32 to 1 and the House on March 1 by a vote of 149 to 48. *Ibid.*, 688, 1903. For the history of this legislation, see Van Deusen, *The Life of Henry Clay*, 265-69, and *The Rise and Decline of Jacksonian Democracy*, 53-54, 198-99; Parton, *The Presidency of Andrew Jackson*, 305-6; Seager, *And Tyler Too*, 91-95; Peterson, *Olive Branch and Sword*, 78-79, 100.

Remark in Senate, January 23, 1833. Moves to adjourn if it is understood that the public lands issue will be taken up again tomorrow. *Register of Debates*, 22 Cong., 2 Sess., 208. For the public lands bill, see Speech in Senate, January 7, 1833.

To FRANCIS T. BROOKE
Washington, January 24, 1833

You mistook very much my feelings in supposing that the doubt which I some-times entertained of making any effort to rescue the Country from its present difficult situation proceeded from any spirit similar to that which actuated Coriolanus. That doubt sprang from the facts that there was an organized party ready ever to denounce any proposition that I could make because *I* made it; and that the other party (the Tariff party) contained many individuals, in whose views, the great interests, and even the peace of the Country, were sub-ordinate to the success of the dominant party to which they belong and to the success of the designated successor of the present C. Magistrate. It is mortify-ing — inexpressably disgusting, to find that considerations affecting an election now four years distant, influences the fate of great questions of immediate in-terest more than all the reasons and arguments which intimately appertain to those questions. If, for example, the Tariff now before the House[1] should be lost, its defeat will be owing to two causes   1st. the apprehension of Mr. V. Buren's friends that if it passes Mr. Calhoun will rise again as the successful vin-dicator of Southern rights: and 2dly. its passage might prevent the President from exercising certain vengeful passions which he wishes to gratify in South Carolina.[2] And, if it passes, its passage may be attributed to the desire of those same friends of Mr. V. B. to secure Southern votes. Whether it will pass or not; and if it does what will be its fate in the Senate remains altogether uncertain.

You ask me in your last letter if [John] Tyler is not a nullifer. I under-stand him to be opposed both to nullification and the proceedings of South Carolina. Will he be re-elected?[3] We feel here some solicitude on that point, being convinced that, under all circumstances, he would be far preferable to any other person that could be sent. I hope if you can say a proper word in his behalf you will do so.

ALS. NcD. Also in DLC-TJC (DNA, M212, R14). Printed in Colton, *Clay Correspondence*, 4:348, misdated as Jan. 23.   1. Clay to Henry Clay, Jr., Jan. 3, 1833.   2. Clay to Brooke, Dec. 12, 1832.   3. For Tyler's ambivalent views on nullification and his reelection to the U.S. Senate on Feb. 15, 1833, see Seager, *And Tyler Too*, 90-96; Chitwood, *John Tyler*, 112-23.

Remark in Senate, January 24, 1833. Opposes an amendment to section five of the public lands bill [Speech in Senate, January 7, 1833], introduced by Sen. Thomas Hart Benton of Missouri, that would grant to the other states named the same 1,600,000 acres of public land given to Ohio. *Register of Debates*, 22 Cong., 2 Sess., 230.

Comment in Senate, January 25, 1833. Opposes a motion by Sen. John C. Calhoun of South Carolina to postpone until December consideration of the public lands bill

[Speech in Senate, January 7, 1833], and reviews briefly arguments for speedy passage of the legislation. *Register of Debates*, 22 Cong., 2 Sess., 233-35. On this day Clay's public lands bill passed by a vote of 24 to 20.

To CHARLES J. FAULKNER   Washington, January 26, 1833

I have supposed that you might like to know the sentiments of our political friends in the Senate of the U. S. in regard to the re-election of Mr. [John] Tyler;[1] and have therefore taken the liberty to communicate them. There is I believe a general desire among them that he should be re-elected. We believe he is greatly to be prefered to any other person that you *could* at this time send from Virginia to the Senate. He is always manly and liberal in his course and never ill tempered or intolerant. Should he be re-elected we believe, in the new posture of public affairs, which is likely to result from the present extraordinary state of things, he will be on the side of the Union and correct governmt. In favor of State rights he is; but he is of the Virginia not South Carolina school. Entertaining these views there is not merely a preference for him but an anxious desire for his re-election.

ALS. KyU. Letter marked "(Confidential)."   1. Clay to Brooke, Jan. 24, 1833.

To JAMES BROWN   Washington, January 28, 1833

Prior to the receipt of your's of the 25h. inst I had written to you and presume you got my letter.

I do not know on what ground any one could have doubted my disposition to enforce the Laws of the U.S. in So. Carolina. Mr. [Robert] Walsh [Jr.][1] is resolved to misunderstand me. I said nothing equivocal. I said on the Contrary that I was for investing the Executive with all necessary and Constitutional power. I presume Mr. Walsh would not confer unnecessary or unconstitutional power. I have some repugnance to entrusting extensive Military means to the Executive because I have no confidence that he will not abuse them.

I recd. a letter from Mason Brown, and sent him to N. York some introductory letters.[2] He is a highly worthy and intelligent person.

[Discusses a legal case of Brown's pending in the Louisiana courts. Continues:]

Every thing here continues unsettled. The debate on the Enforcing act was begun to day,[3] and was preceded by some skirmishing in which Mr Calhoun I think suffered.

How the house will decide the Tariff[4] is quite uncertain.

ALS. KyLxT.   1. Editor, Philadelphia *National Gazette* [2:325].   2. Clay to James Kent, Jan. 24, 1833, is one such letter of introduction. ALS. NNC.   3. Force bill. Remark in Senate, Jan. 22, 1833.   4. Verplanck bill. Clay to Henry Clay, Jr., Jan. 3, 1833.

To PETER B. PORTER   Washington, January 29, 1833

I was sorry to learn from your letter of the 21st. inst. that you were still harassed with the suit brought by the Governmt. against you.[1] I had understood and hoped that it had been definitively settled in your favor. I have known, besides your's, other instances of very great annoyance to individuals in the commencement and prosecution of Government suits against them. There is more certainty in the existence of the grievance than in any practical measure which could be devised to remedy it.

The movement which you mention at Albany, respecting the Tariff, may contribute to the fall of Verplanks [*sic*, Verplanck's] bill,[2] which had been

616

previously tottering. It seems to me, however, that the Tariff, if not destroyed at this Session, will be sacrificed at the next. Jackson has decreed its subversion, and his partizans follow him wherever he goes. He has marked out two victims So. Carolina, and the Tariff and the only question with him is which shall be first immolated.

The debate commenced yesterday on the bill reported by the Judiciary Comee.[3] It will be violent. Much as I dislike giving additional powers to the President, as he is the C. Magistrate, I think we must confer on him all that are necessary to enforce the Laws.

You will have seen that the Land bill has again passed the Senate. Its fate in the House is uncertain.[4]

I shall be happy to hear from you whilst you are at Albany, or at any other time.

ALS. NBuHi.   1. Porter to Clay, Oct. 6, 1830.   2. Clay to Henry Clay, Jr., Jan. 3, 1833.
3. Force bill. Remark in Senate, Jan. 22, 1833.   4. Speech in Senate, Jan. 7, 1833.

To PETER B. PORTER   Washington, February 1, 1833

I was glad to learn from your favor of the 26h. inst. that you have again succeeded in your controversy with the Government.[1]

The return of defaulters has not yet been made. When it comes in, I will examine if you are included; and if you are transmit you a Copy of the list.

I believe that So. Carolina will postpone the operation of her ordinance[2] and the laws passed in conformity with it until after the *next* Session of Congress. When it is known here that the postponement has been or will be made, I should not be surprized if the Administration shd. postpone the enforcing bill now under consideration in the Senate;[3] and that, after that subject is thus disposed of, the whole weight of the Admon will be brought to bear upon the reduction of the revenue to the standard of the wants of the Governmt.   If we defeat this attempt (far from being certain) at this Session how can we prevent it at the next? My belief is that the Tariff is in imminent danger at the present or ensuing Session. The proceedings at Albany afford some but not decided encouragement.[4]

ALS. NBuHi.   1. Porter to Clay, Oct. 6, 1830.   2. Of nullification. See Stoddard to Clay,
Nov. 12, 1832.   3. Remark in Senate, Jan. 22, 1833.   4. Porter to Clay, Jan. 21, 1833.

To THOMAS ELLICOTT   Washington, February 2, 1833

I recd. your letter of this day and regret that it was not convenient to you to call on me prior to your departure from this City.

My belief is, that the Tariff is marked by the present administration for destruction, and that its object will be accomplished if some means are not soon devised to avert it, at the next Session. South Carolina will postpone the operation of her Ordinance[1] and laws passed in conformity with it until the end of the next Session. And, in the mean time, the whole weight of the Administration will be directed to the prostration of the Tariff. In the next Congress the Administration will be stronger in both branches than in the present.[2] I should not be surprised if the bill now under discussion in the Senate,[3] at the instance of the friends themselves of the Administration, will be postponed until the next Session.

Entertaining these apprehensions, the plan of temporary preservation of our Manufactures[4] which I communicated to you occurred to me. I shall be glad to receive from you any further views with which you may think proper to favor me. I should be extremely unwilling upon my own convictions, however strong, to make any movement which those more immediately concerned did not approve.

ALS. MdHi. Addressed to Ellicott in Baltimore. See 5:1003.   1. Stoddard to Clay, Nov. 12, 1832.   2. Whittlesey to Clay, Sept. 19, 1832.   3. Clay to Henry Clay, Jr., Jan. 3, 1833. 4. Draft Proposal, Mid-Dec., 1832.

From Charles Miner, Wilkes-Barre, Pa., February 4, 1833. Regrets that Clay did not win the election of 1832, but lauds him for having "met the result with a calmness which I could not command," and notes that he prays God to sustain Clay's health and public usefulness. ALS. DLC-HC (DNA, M212, R5).

To DANIEL WEBSTER   Washington, February 5, 1833
Disappointed in meeting you today in the Senate, I have to adopt this mode of requesting that you will join some of our friends at my lodging this evening between 7 and 8 oClock to confer on the same subject which engaged our consideration when we lately had a similar meeting. I hope it may suit your convenience to attend.

ALS. NhD. Printed in Wiltse, *Webster Papers*, 3:211.

From Charles Shaler, Pittsburgh, February 6, 1833. Laments the defeat of the National Republican party in the recent presidential contest, noting that "its coalition with Anti Masonry was its death warrant." Remarks that he does "not despair of the republic, but I do despair of its ever arising to that greatness & true glory that the American system policy would have brought it to." Believes that "henceforth the government must be in the hands of political intriguers who have nothing to do but to create factions in different States & then cast the administration into that scale that it wished to preponderate." Continues: "Patriotism is shipwrecked. National Republicanism is disgraced. . . . you alone stand in your original position and sustain the great cause to which your life has been devoted." Concludes that John Quincy Adams was "the rock on which we first split, he had neither the patriotism nor the honesty nor yet the talents that we attributed to him." ALS. DLC-HC (DNA, M212, R5).

From Allen Clapp, Philadelphia, February 7, 1833. Announces that the managers of the Pennsylvania Hospital, having two objects in mind, have agreed to sell Clay one of their two fine English heifers, "first to accommodate thee and secondly in being accessary of introducing so fine a breed of cattle in the State of Kentucky." Informs Clay he may have either the eldest heifer which has "a fine bull calf by her side two day[s] old," or a younger one, which was due to calve early in July. LS. DLC-TJC (DNA, M212, R14).

On February 18, Jilson Dove received $140 in advance from Clay to drive his cattle from Philadelphia to Kentucky. DS, in Clay's hand. *Ibid.* (R17).

On March 28 Dove, writing Clay from Washington, Pa., acknowledged receipt of $156.75 in payment for bringing Clay's "English Cattle" from Philadelphia and Hagerstown, Md., "to this place." *Ibid.*

Meanwhile, on February 21 Clapp had written Clay again from Philadelphia, telling him that Dove had left with the cattle and was taking the overland route. He enclosed the English pedigree of the cow "Nancy" which Clay had purchased, adding: "The Calf of Nancy which accompanies her, was got by '*Oliver*' the Bull now purchased by Mr. Clay." LS. *Ibid.*

On February 26 Clapp wrote, giving Clay the pedigree of the bull "Oliver." *Ibid.*

From NICHOLAS BIDDLE   Philadelphia, February 8, 1833

I send you a copy of the report of a Comite of the Bank, vindicating it from the charges preferred against it by the Executive.[1] I wish that you would examine it, and if as I hope, you may find in it a refutation of the calumnies of the kitchen cabinet & those whom the kitchen cabinet rules, I would then particularly ask your attention to this question, whether it would not be proper for Congress, as the guardians of the public character & credit of the country to rescue it from the imputations which have been cast upon it by the miserable people who fill or rather who occupy the executive offices. A declaration from the Treasury that the National Bank is unsafe because it has lent money to the Western people is calculated to prostrate the credit of the nation—[2]& I shall not be surprized if the Capitalists who have invested their funds in American stocks should throw back upon US these discredited funds. and instead of lending more should withdraw what they have lent already to a country which its own high officers represent as bankrupt. Such a movement in Congress would counteract this evil—& from no one could it come with more propriety & effect than from you & your political friends. It would have the collateral advantage too of placing the odium of their assault upon the Bank on the persons who ought to bear it, on the representatives of the Albany regency in the cabinet

ALS. DLC-HC (DNA, M212, R5). Letter marked "(private)."   1. In his Fourth Annual Message on Dec. 4, 1832, Jackson had questioned the solvency of the Bank of the United States and had recommended a congressional investigation of its practices. See *MPP*, 2:600. Secretary of the Treasury Louis McLane had previously appointed Henry Toland as a special agent to investigate the bank. Toland reported on Dec. 4, 1832, that there was no doubt that the bank was solvent and the public money deposited with it secure. See *House Exec. Doc.* 8, 22 Cong., 2 Sess., pp. 1-33. Jackson continued publicly and privately to maintain the reverse. McLane's treasury report of Dec. 5, 1832, likewise questioned the bank's stability. See *House Exec. Doc.* 3, 22 Cong., 2 Sess. Subsequently, the House Ways and Means Committee conducted an investigation. On Feb. 14, 1833, the Philadelphia *United States Gazette* published an extract of the "Report of the Bank of the United States to the Committee of Ways and Means." This report, as well as the "Report of the Committee on Banks in the House of Representatives of Pennsylvania" which was published in the *United States Gazette* on Feb. 8, 1833, exonerated the bank from any improprieties and applauded its stability. The majority report of the U.S. House Ways and Means Committee did likewise in its report on March 1, 1833; however, a minority of the committee, led by James K. Polk, issued a highly critical report. See *Reports of Committees*, 22 Cong., 2 Sess., no. 121; and Munroe, *Louis McLane*, 375-88.   2. McLane's Dec. 5 treasury report had questioned the stability of the B.U.S. based on its transactions "especially in its western branches." See *House Exec. Doc.* 3, 22 Cong., 2 Sess., pp. 13-14; and Govan, *Nicholas Biddle*, 214-22.

DRAFT COMPROMISE   Washington, *ca.*
TARIFF BILL   February 11, 1833[1]

Be it enacted &c.[2] that from and after the 30h [31] day of September [December] 1833, in all cases where duties imposed by laws now existing shall exceed twenty percent upon the value thereof, one tenth part of such excess shall be deducted; from and after the 30h [31] day of Septr. [December] 1835 another tenth part shall be deducted; from and after the 30h. [31] day of Sept. [December] 1837 another tenth part shall be deducted; from and after the 30h. [31] day of Sept. [December] 1839 another tenth part shall be deducted; and from and after the 30h. [31] day of Sept. [December] 1841 one half of the residu of such excess shall be deducted; and from and after the 30h. day of Sept. [June] 1842 the other half thereof shall be deducted.

And be it further enacted that so much of the second section of the act of the 14h day of July 1832 entitled "an act to alter and amend the several acts imposing duties on imports," as fixes the rate of duty on all milled and fulled

619

cloth; known by the name of plains, kerseys or kendal cottons of which wool is the only material, the value whereof does not exceed thirty five cents a square yard, at five per cent ad valorem, shall be and the same is hereby repealed. And the said article shall be subject to the same duty of fifty per cent as is provided by the said second section for other manufacturers of wool, which duty shall be liable to the same deductions as are prescribed herein by the preceding section.

And be it further enacted that until the 30h. day of Septr. [June] 1842 the duties on imports imposed by existing laws as modified by the act shall remain and continue to be collected. And from and after the day last aforesaid all duties upon imports shall be collected in ready money and laid for the purpose of raising such revenue as may be necessary to an economical administration of the Government; and, for that purpose, shall be equal upon all articles, subject to duty, according to the value thereof. And, until otherwise directed by law, from and after the said 30h. day of Septr. 1842, such duties shall be at the rate of twenty per cent ad valorem. And from and after that day all credits now allowed by law, in the payment of duties, shall be and hereby are abolished:[3] Provided that nothing herein contained shall be construed to prevent the passage of any law, in the event of War with any Foreign power, for imposing such duties as may be deemed by Congress necessary to the prosecution of such War.[4]

And be it further enacted that, in addition to the articles now exempted by the existing laws from the payment of duties, the following articles imported, from and after the 30h [31] day of Septr [December] 1833 and until the 30h day of Septr [June] 1842 shall also be admitted to entry free from duty, to wit. Bleached and unbleached linens, manufacturers of silk or of which silk shall be the component material of chief value, coming from this side of the Cape of Good Hope, and Worsted stuff goods, shawls and other manufacturers of silk and worsted.[5]

And be it further enacted that from and after the said 30h day of Septr [June] 1842 the following articles shall be admitted to entry free from duty to wit: Unmanufactured Cotton, Indigo, Quick Silver, Opium, Tin in plates and sheets, gum arabic, gum senegal, lack dye [sic, lac-dye], madder, madder root, nuts and berries used in dying, saffron, tumeric, woad or pastel, aloes, ambegris, Burgundy pitch, cochineal, cammomile [sic, camomile] flowers, correander [sic, coriander] seed, catsup, chalk, coculus indicus, horn plates for lanthorns [sic, lanterns], oxhorns, other horns and tips, India rubber, unmanufactured [sic, manufactured] ivory, juniper berries, musk, nuts of all kinds, oil of juniper, unmanufactured rattans and reeds, tortoise shell, tin foil, shellac, vegetables used principally in dying and composing dyes, weld, and all articles employed chiefly for dying, except, bichromate of potash, prussiate of potash, chromate of potash, and nitrate of lead, aquafortis and tartaric acids, and all other dying drugs and materials for comprising dyes.[6]

And be it further enacted that so much of any act as is inconsistent with this act shall be and the same is hereby repealed: Provided that nothing herein contained shall be so construed as to prevent the passage, prior or subsequent to the said 30h. day of Septr [June] 1842 of any act or acts, from time to time, that may be necessary to detect, prevent, or punish evasions of the duties on imports imposed by law.[7]

ALS. KyLoF. Undated endorsement by Thomas Ewing: "Original draft of the compromise bill of 1833 in the hand writing of Mr. Clay."   1. For the dating of this document, see Peterson, *Olive*

Branch and Sword—The Compromise of 1833, 66-67; and Remark in Senate, Feb. 11, 1833. The bill substantially in this form and language was formally introduced and initially defended in the Senate by Clay on Feb. 12, 1833. Speech in Senate, *Register of Debates*, 22 Cong., 2 Sess., 462-73, 480-82.   2. For the exact wording of the bill, as modified and finally enacted on March 2, 1833, see *Register of Debates*, 22 Cong., 2 Sess., Appendix, 10-11. Differences between the bill introduced and the legislation enacted are bracketed into the text or are herein noted.   3. The final version of the bill added in this paragraph the provision that after June 30, 1842, all duties required by law on goods, wares, and merchandise shall be assessed upon the value thereof at the port of entry under such regulations as may be prescribed by law.   4. This sentence does not appear in the bill as enacted.   5. Added to the free list in this category in the final version of the bill were table linens, linen napkins, and linen cambrics. Specifically excepted from this list was sewing silk.   6. Added to this list in the enacted bill were sulphur, crude saltpetre, grind stones, refined borax, and emory. Added to the exceptions to "all articles employed chiefly for dying" were alum and copperas. Deleted were unmanufactured cotton and "all other dying drugs and materials for comprising dyes." It was also stipulated that all imports on which the first section of the act may operate and all articles now admitted duty free or at a rate less than 20 percent ad valorem could, after June 30, 1842, be subject to duty up to 20 percent as shall be provided by law.   7. Added to this was the contingency provision that in the event of an excess or deficiency of revenue, or in order to prevent or punish evasions of duties, corrective legislation could be enacted prior to June 30, 1842. Such legislation could raise, up to 20 percent ad valorem, duties on items paying less than 20 percent under the tariff act of July 14, 1832. See, also, Van Deusen, *Jacksonian Era*, 76-78; Davis R. Dewey, *Financial History of the United States* (New York, 1903), 187-90.

Remark in Senate, February 11, 1833. Gives notice that he will tomorrow "introduce a bill [Draft Proposal, Mid-December, 1832] to modify the various acts imposing duties on imports." *Register of Debates*, 22 Cong., 2 Sess., 132.

Speech in Senate, February 12, 1833. Asserts that he seeks two objects in offering and supporting a tariff measure that would scale tariff schedules downward. The first is to preserve the principle of the protective tariff, the imminent repeal of which would be "productive of consequences calamitous indeed." The second is to stabilize tariff legislation by reversing a government approach to the tariff issue that has been "vacillating and uncertain." To accomplish these twin objects, "I propose to give protection to our manufactured articles, adequate protection, for a length of time"; time enough to secure tariff policy stability while simultaneously "allowing time for a gradual reduction on one side, and on the other proposing to reduce the rate of duties to that revenue standard for which the opponents of the system have so long contended." Outlines a scaled tariff reduction plan that over a period of nine and a half years would help protect certain manufactured items while gradually bringing all tariffs down to a 20 percent maximum levy by 1842. Notes that the 20 percent figure can be moved up or down by subsequent legislation as Congress, in the face of changing economic conditions, desires. Believes that the problem of the continued increase of surplus funds in the Treasury, a fact stimulating sentiment for the immediate adoption of a policy of tariff only for revenue, can be solved by the gradual reduction of tariff income under his proposed tariff legislation, together with passage of the pending bill that would authorize the distribution to the states of public land sales receipts [Comment in Senate, April 16, 1832; Speech in Senate, June 20, 1832; Speech in Senate, January 7, 1833]. If there are still surplus funds prior to 1842, they should be applied to internal improvements already commenced by the states with monies provided by the distribution of public land sales receipts. After 1842, new internal improvement enterprises should be paid for by funds from the land (distribution) bill. Asserts that it is not his object to unite the fates of his distribution bill and his tariff reduction bill, and believes that "partial as he might be to both . . . each should stand or fall upon its own intrinsic merits." Discusses at length specific duties on specific items and attempts to anticipate and parry various possible objections to the bill. To those who want a quicker erosion of the protective system he promises: "Now give us time; cease all fluctuations and agitations for nine years, and the manufacturers, in every branch, will sustain themselves against foreign competition. . . . It the tariff be overthrown, as may be its fate next session, the country will be plunged into extreme distress and agitation. I . . . want harmony. . . . I delight not in this perpetual turmoil. Let us have peace, and become once more united as a band of brothers." Emphasizes the importance of gradualness in reducing the tariff, pointing out that his nine and a half year plan can work if the opposition will but give it a chance. Urges national unity on the issue. Remarks in this regard that he has changed his mind on South Carolina's nullification policy. His first reaction was "a disposition to hurl defiance back again." But since his return to Washington [from Philadelphia on January 3] he has learned that South Carolina does not intend to use force to sustain nullification. "Her appeal was not to arms, but to another power; not to the sword but to the law. . . . Her purposes are all of a civil nature. . . . She disclaimed any intention of resorting to force, unless we should find it indispensable to execute the laws of the Union by applying force to her." Thinks, however, that South Carolina's action has been "rash, intemperate, and greatly in error," and notes that "not a voice beyond the single State of South Carolina had been heard in favor of the principle of nullification." Condemns nullification from a constitutional standpoint. Adds: "I am ready, for one, to give the tribunals and the Executive of the country, whether that Executive has or has not my confidence, the necessary measures of power and authority to execute the laws of the Union. But I would not go a hair's breadth further than what is necessary for those purposes." Cites previous examples of state defiance of federal authority that were solved peacefully. Observes that South Carolina has postponed her ordinance of nullification from February 1 to March 4. She "must perceive the embarrassments of her situation. She must be desirous . . . to remain in the Union." Certainly she cannot endure as an independent nation. To survive as such she must have armies, fleets, foreign missions, expensive government. In sum, "she must raise taxes [and] enact this very tariff, which [has] driven her out of the Union." Concludes that he wants neither to humiliate the South Carolinians nor engage in a civil war against them. Pictures the bloody horrors of civil war. Entreats and implores his colleagues to support his compromise tariff measure as an act of patriotism and thus "heal, before they are yet bleeding, the wounds of our distracted country." *Register of Debates*, 22 Cong., 2 Sess., 462-73. The bill itself is presented in *ibid.*, 480-82. Printed in Colton, *Clay Correspondence*, 5:536-50. See Draft Proposal, Mid-December, 1832; Draft Compromise Tariff Bill, *ca.* February 11, 1833; Stoddard to Clay, November 12, 1832; Remark in Senate, January 22, 1833.

From Reverdy Johnson, Baltimore, February 13, 1833. Congratulates Clay for having introduced the compromise tariff bill [Draft Proposal, Mid-December, 1832], noting that "nothing but a liberal spirit of compromise can save the [protective] system from almost immediate destruction" as well as avoid a struggle that might well destroy the Union. Remarks that Clay's plan will "save the manufacturers for the time, & in its consequence, (gradually brought about,) open the eyes of our Southern brethren to the manifold benefits of the system which they have so violently oppose[d]." Concludes: "I cannot but believe, that a few years of quiet & sober reflection will satisfy them that their present hostility to the prevailing policy, is the nearest creation of prejudice that was ever known, & that their true interests, like that of their northern Countrymen, is in protecting the nation & its industry against foreign restrictions. God grant that your efforts may prove successful." ALS. DLC-HC (DNA, M212, R5). Printed in Colton, *Clay Correspondence*, 4:349.

Remark in Senate, February 13, 1833. Expresses indifference as to which committee his compromise tariff bill [Speech in Senate, February 12, 1833] should be referred, but seconds a motion for forming a select committee [Clay to Brooke, February 14, 1833] to consider it. *Register of Debates*, 22 Cong., 2 Sess., 484.

To FRANCIS T. BROOKE   Washington, February 14, 1833

I had foreborne to communicate to you the plan of accommodation which I intended to submit, because altho' I had long since settled in my mind the principle of the plan, I had not finally arranged the details. That work was only completed a few days ago. You will see in the papers that I have presented it to the Senate in the shape of a Bill.[1] I was fully aware of all the personal consequences and personal risks to which I exposed myself, but "what is a public man worth who will not sacrifice himself if necessary for the good of his Country." The measure has been well recd.   Still every contrivance will be resorted to by the V. Buren men and by some of the Administration party to frustrate or defeat the project. That you know I anticipated. What will be the final issue of the plan I can not certainly say. I hope for success. We had a meeting this morning of the Comee. (with the constitution of which I am satisfied)[2] and things looked as well there as I expected. Webster & some other of the N England Senators will oppose the plan.[3]

ALS. DLC-TJC (DNA, M212, R14). Also, copy. Courtesy of Malcolm Stearns, Jr., Haddam, Conn. Printed in Colton, *Clay Correspondence*, 4:349-50.   1. Draft Proposal, Mid-December, 1832.   2. Clay's compromise tariff bill was referred on Feb. 13, 1833, to a Senate Select Committee composed of Clay, Calhoun, Webster, Felix Grundy, John M. Clayton, William C. Rives, and George M. Dallas. U.S. Sen., *Journal*, 22 Cong., 2 Sess., 175.   3. Webster voted against the bill. Among all New England senators, 6 voted for and 6 against the measure. *Register of Debates*, 22 Cong., 2 Sess., 809.

Remark in Senate, February 14, 1833. In the discussion of the Force bill [Revenue Collection bill], admits that South Carolina's acts against the United States in nullifying the tariff [Stoddard to Clay, November 12, 1832; Remark in Senate, January 22, 1833] were "much more offensive" than those of Virginia in *Cohens* v. *Virginia* [3:61-63] or of Ohio in its attack on the Bank of the United States [2:721-23; 3:646-47]. Believes that the idea of locating a U.S. custom house on board a vessel in South Carolina waters is "ludicrous." *Register of Debates*, 22 Cong., 2 Sess., 510, 518.

To NICHOLAS BIDDLE   Washington, February 16, 1833

I recd. your favor of the 8h and a Copy of the Report of the Bank Comee. The vindication which it contains of the conduct and condition of the Bank is clear and perfectly satisfactory. I hope means will be adopted to give the report wide circulation.

You will have seen that the bill to sell the B. Stock was rejected,[1] and rejected under unusual but very strong circumstances. The election of [Joseph] Gales and [William W.] Seaton as public printers,[2] in it self of no consequence, is highly important as *evidence*, considering their uniform and decided support of the Bank. If we had time, I should think it expedient to second those two events by other measures tending to favor the re-charter of the Bank at some future day. But situated as we now are here, I doubt whether it would be advisable to risk the ground we have won, by bringing forward any new proposition which there is neither time nor temper, perhaps, fully to consider. A sense of feeling and duty would prompt me, if a fit occasion were to present itself, to defend the Western people against the attack made upon them on account of the loans and accommodations obtained from the Bank.[3] Possibly such an occasion may yet offer.

I can hardly think it possible that this Administration, daring and unprincipled as it has been, will now venture upon such a measure as that of a transfer of the deposits.[4]

The fate of a compromise of the Tariff is very uncertain.[5] There is great division of opinion about each and all of the propositions looking to that end.

ALS. DLC-Nicholas Biddle Papers (DNA, M212, R20).   1. The bill to authorize the sale of the bank stock owned by the U.S. was introduced by James K. Polk. The House Ways and Means Committee reported it favorably on Feb. 13. The bill was quickly defeated, however, in the House by a vote of 102-91. *Register of Debates*, 22 Cong., 2 Sess., 1707, 1722. See also Munroe, *Louis McLane*, 379-80.   2. The House elected Gales & Seaton as public printers on the fourth ballot on Feb. 15, 1833. Gales & Seaton received 99 votes to 94 for Francis P. Blair and 4 scattered. *Register of Debates*, 22 Cong., 2 Sess., 1726.   3. Biddle to Clay, Feb. 8, 1833. 4. Bradley to Clay, Oct. 16, 1832.   5. Draft Proposal, Mid-Dec., 1833.

To PETER B. PORTER   Washington, February 16, 1833

I hasten to acknowledge your favor this day recd. of the 11h. inst. and to put you in the possession of my real views and motives in recent movements.

My opinions are totally unchanged as to the American System &c. But perceiving that by the treachery of persons in the North towards it, there was to be a total sacrifice of it at this Session by Verplancks bill[1] or at the next Session by some other bill, I have endeavored to bring forward a measure[2] that would 1st. protect the manufacturers for the present and gain time, with its chapter of accidents for them; and 2dly. would preserve the Union, prevent Civil war, and save us from the danger of entrusting to Andw. Jackson large armies &c. In the mean time I have not opposed but intend to support the bill before the Senate, with proper guards, to defeat Nullification[3] (against which no one can be more sincere than I am) and secure a due execution of the laws of the U. States. In short my desire and my efforts are to obtain stability and present security to our manufacturers, with the belief that when reason and good feelings once more return all will be done hereafter for them that they will require. Whether the measure which I have submitted will or will not be adopted is yet uncertain. The want of time may, nothing else I think will defeat it. The bill now pending before the Senate and for which I mean to vote will pass that body; but I should not be surprized if Congress adjourns without passing any act either enforcing or modifying the Tariff. You will remark however that the Virginia mission[4] is likely to lead to a postponement of the Ordinance[5] &c. beyond the next Session of Congress.

ALS. NBuHi.   1. Clay to Henry Clay, Jr., Jan. 3, 1833.   2. Draft Proposal, Mid-Dec., 1832.   3. Remark in Senate, Jan. 22, 1833.   4. Benjamin Watkins Leigh was sent by the Virginia legislature to South Carolina to inform the governor that Virginia was willing to mediate the nullification dispute. See Freehling, *Prelude to Civil War*, 290.   5. Stoddard to Clay, Nov. 12, 1832.

Remark in Senate, February 19, 1833. Announces that an amendment to his compromise tariff bill [Speech in Senate, February 12, 1833] will be offered dealing with the "valuation of goods" for tariff purposes, and will be so phrased as to "conciliate the conflicting opinions which have prevailed in reference to that point." *Register of Debates*, 22 Cong., 2 Sess., 601.

From JOHN M. CLAYTON   Washington, February 20, 1833

Prepare yourself fully for the debate tomorrow. We shall hear *a laboured* speech from our opponents.

Tomorrow will be the most eventful period of your eventful life. Your friends depend on your effort and I as one of them suggest to you *this thought*[:]

consider whether it be not your best course *to declare in your speech* on the bill that you are no candidate for the honours of office[1] — that you look only to the imperishable glory of preventing civil war and again uniting your distracted countrymen in the bonds of fraternal affection, while at the same time you ensure the continuation — the perpetuity of that great system with which your fame is identified. I advise this course at present. We have a yawning gulf in our Rome and it will never close till some patriot rides into it. This will stop the cry of coalition — save youself & your friends from calumny, and your country from ruin.

ALS. DLC-HC (DNA, M212, R5). 1. In his speech on the tariff on Feb. 25, 1833, Clay stated: "Pass this bill, tranquilize the country, restore confidence and affection in the Union; and I am willing to go home to Ashland, and renounce public service forever." *Register of Debates*, 22 Cong., 2 Sess., 742.

To Ralph R. Gurley, Washington, D.C., February 20, 1833. Says that Thomas Speed, president of the Bardstown, Ky., Colonization Society, wants to know if the "contribution" of that group has been received and whether a copy of the 1832 annual report of the American Colonization Society can be sent him. ALS. DLC-Records of the American Colonization Society (DNA, M212, R20).

On February 21, Gurley replied that the Bardstown "donation" had been received and that copies of the 1832 annual report would soon be available. ALS. NhD.

Comment in Senate, February 21, 1833. Opposes discontinuing the daily recess from 3:00 to 5:00 p.m., saying that he could not be present at these "evening sessions," because he found it "impossible to breathe the impure air of the Senate Chamber after dinner." Continues intermittently with an exposition of various amendments offered to his compromise tariff bill [Speech in Senate, February 12, 1833], especially with the issue of home valuation after 1842. Pursuant to his remark and promise of February 19, offers an amendment to his tariff bill requiring that after 1842 all duties would be "assessed on a valuation made at the port in which the goods are first imported." Thus would the principle of "home valuation," as distinct from "foreign valuation," be retained after the expiration of the Compromise Tariff of 1833, although future Congresses would be expected to write the principle into specific legislation if, as, and when they see fit. *Register of Debates*, 22 Cong., 2 Sess., 689-95, 699, 701. Clay's amendment was adopted, 26 to 16, on February 22. *Ibid.*, 716.

Comment in Senate, February 22, 1833. Discusses various aspects of his compromise tariff bill [Speech in Senate, February 12, 1833] and proposed amendments to it. Wonders whether it is reasonable to "take up and discuss a thousand difficulties" pertaining to the tariff that "may or may not arise" in the next ten years. Doubts that every conceivable contingency can be amended into his bill. *Register of Debates*, 22 Cong., 2 Sess., 710-11, 716-17.

Comment in Senate, February 23, 1833. Intermittently discusses aspects of his compromise tariff bill [Speech in Senate, February 12, 1833] and answers various objections to it raised by members. Mentions also, with reference to collecting the tariff in South Carolina, that the bill "for enforcing the collection of the revenue . . . met his entire approbation; and had he been present when the final vote was taken on its passage [Remark in Senate, January 22, 1833], he would have voted in its favor." Reminds his colleagues that the main object of his tariff bill "was not revenue but protection." *Register of Debates*, 22 Cong., 2 Sess., 718, 722-24, 726.

From Peter B. Porter, February 23, 1833. States that Clay's "views & motives in relation to the Tariff," as expressed in a recent letter, are "entirely satisfactory to your political friends here." Mentions that he has shown the letter not only to "two or three" friends, but also "to two of our most influential Jackson Tariff men, one of whom is Mr. [Benjamin] Knower, the President of the Farmers and Mechanics Bank, Father in law of our Governor [William L. Marcy], & one of the most influential politicians in the Jackson ranks." Knower, in fact, says that "his views accord precisely with yours" on the compromise tariff [Draft Proposal, Mid-December, 1832], because it secures "important protection to manufacturers for 6 or 8 years — and . . . he is willing to trust to the intelligence of the community at that time to adopt such measures as shall be found for its interests." Adds that "The break in the Jackson ranks here between Knower & his friends on the one side & Van Buren's friends on the other, appears to widen daily" and will probably "terminate in a permanent political separation." While this is a cheering prospect, fears, however, a schism in the Clay ranks as rumors circulate that there has been "a political alienation" between Clay and Daniel Webster. Urges Clay "to avoid, if possible, such an unhappy division." Remarks also that Clay's friends in New York "are equally glad that you intend to give your support to the Enforcing Bill [Remark in Senate, January 22, 1833] in such a shape (and we could ask for nothing more) as will enable the Executive effectually to meet & defeat the projects of Nullification [Stoddard to Clay, November 12, 1832]." Copy. OHi.

From W.R. Chaplain, Danville, Va., February 25, 1833. Reports that at a "large meeting" of the citizens of Danville, "in which men of every political party participated," resolutions were adopted supporting Clay's effort to secure compromise tariff legislation. Copy. Printed in *Niles' Register* (April 27, 1833), 44:137; reprinted from the Danville (Va.) *Reporter.*

On March 14, Clay replied from Washington, pointing out to Chaplain that he had little choice but to present a compromise tariff scheme [Draft Proposal, Mid-December, 1832; Speech in Senate, February 12, 1833] since it "appeared to me that the worst possible relations were getting up between the various parts of the country; that men in all sections of it were accustoming themselves to think and speak freely of a terrible event; that ultimate if not immediate civil war was seriously to be apprehended; and there was great danger, if we escaped that calamity, of the sudden overthrow of a system of policy which would have spread ruin far and near." *Ibid.*

Speech in Senate, February 25, 1833. Answers at length the objections of Sen. Daniel Webster of Massachusetts to various aspects of his compromise tariff bill [Draft Proposal, Mid-December, 1832; Speech in Senate, February 12, 1833], arguing particularly, and from history, that the bill does not "abandon or surrender the policy of protecting American industry." Covers again, in more detail, most of the arguments set forth in his speech of February 12, 1833. Says his bill is designed essentially to place the American System "on a better and safer foundation," and "to quiet the country." The controlling concern is to "preserve the manufacturing interest." For this reason, regrets that "Two States in New England, which have been in favor of the [American] system, have recently come out against it. Other States of the North and the East have shown a remarkable indifference to its preservation." Discusses again South Carolina's nullification policy and the horrible prospects of civil war; and urges that the tariff problem be solved before the end of the present session. Characterizes the president's Proclamation to the People of South Carolina on December 10, 1832, as "a paper of uncommon ability and eloquence, doing great credit, as a composition, to him who prepared it [Edward Livingston], and to him who signed it [Jackson]." But adds that "I think it contains some ultra doctrines, which no party in this country had ventured to assert." Observes, also, that both the force bill [Remark in Senate, January 22, 1833] and the compromise tariff bill ("the peace bill") ought to be passed. "The first will satisfy all who love order and law, and disapprove the inadmissible doctrine of nullification. The last will sooth those who love peace and concord, harmony and union." Charges that Webster "dislikes the measure, because it commands the concurrence of those who have . . . opposed . . . the tariff, and is approved by the gentleman from South Carolina [Mr. Calhoun] as well as by myself." Vehemently denies the charge that his motive in sponsoring the compromise tariff is his personal political ambition. Concludes: "Ambition! inordinate ambition! If I had thought of myself only, I should never have brought it forward. I know well the perils to which I expose myself; the risk of alienating faithful and valued friends, with but little prospect of making new ones . . . I have no desire for office, not even the highest . . . Pass this bill, tranquilize the country, restore confidence and affection in the Union; and I am willing to go home to Ashland, and renounce public service forever . . . Yes, I have ambition; but it is the ambition of being the humble instrument, in the hands of Providence, to reconcile a divided people, once more to revive concord and harmony in a distracted land." *Register of Debates,* 22 Cong., 2 Sess., 729-42. Printed in Colton, *Clay Correspondence,* 5:551-67.

Later in the same day, Clay moves that since the House of Representatives has "just now passed a bill, similar, if not identical, in its provisions to the one before the Senate [Speech in Senate, February 12, 1833]," and would present that bill to the Senate tomorrow for its sanction [Clay to Henry Clay, Jr., January 3, 1833], the Senate should adjourn for the day. Motion carried. *Register of Debates,* 22 Cong., 2 Sess., 749-50.

Remark in Senate, February 26, 1833. Sees no reason why the Senate need send to committee the compromise House tariff bill "(Mr. Clay's bill, which was introduced yesterday in the House, and passed today)" since "the same bill," had already been before a select Senate committee, and had been "sufficiently discussed." Suggests that the House bill [Clay to Henry Clay, Jr., January 3, 1833] be acted on "to-morrow or the next day." *Register of Debates,* 22 Cong., 2 Sess., 785. Clay's own tariff bill [Speech in Senate, February 12, 1833] "which was before the Senate when it adjourned yesterday, then came up as unfinished business, and was ordered to lie on the table." *Ibid.*

Comment in Senate, February 27, 1833. Assures his colleagues that the House bill modifying the tariff act of July 14, 1832 [Clay to Henry Clay, Jr., January 3, 1833], "corresponded word for word" to the compromise tariff bill [Speech in Senate, February 12, 1833] that has been before the Senate since February 12. Moves that it be reported to the Senate without further amendment. *Register of Debates*, 22 Cong., 2 Sess., 785-86.

From NICHOLAS BIDDLE

Philadelphia, February 28, 1833

I have a great deal to say—or rather to ask, about the manner in which you have been able to draw out the lightning from all the clouds which were towering over the country—but I will not trouble you now—and I only hope that you will come up when the Session is over, and talk into conviction all the doubters even my friend Mr [Robert] Walsh [Jr.] himself. The fact is, that for forty eight hours your friends held in their breath with anxiety till they saw you fairly across the chasm—and are proportionally gratified at seeing you on such a firm & commanding position. Of all this hereafter when you come to see us. What makes me write now is, that I think you may find an opportunity on Saturday or Sunday of saying a few words which may make a strong & favorable impression upon two large masses of the community whom I wish to see well disposed to you especially at the present moment—I mean the friends of the Bank & the Western States generally.

The fact is that there is a very great feeling of indignation in the West at the manner in which the western credit has been disparaged & the discontent it sharpened by the knowledge that these insinuations originate with the worthy chief Magistrate himself who had indulged in statements about the Branch Bank at Nashville which are entirely false.[1] This has exceedingly irritated his former friends there I received last night a strong letter from Mr [Joseph] Nichol the Prest of the Branch there — and this evening's mail brings me the enclosed letter from Mr Thos. H. Fletcher whom you know — now what I think would be very useful to all parties would be for you to introduce however briefly, a notice of the attack on the credit of the West — and of the course of the Bank. This from you would gratify many & would be specially opportune just now You will be at no loss for a fit occasion, as some financial matter comes up. Or if you prefer a more formal introduction the French indemnity[2] may furnish a fit topic The Secy of the Treasy [Louis McLane] in his letter to me on the 31st of October proposed to sell his bill on France. I advised him as exchange was falling to sell at once & offered a price — After nearly three months delay he again offers his bill & exchange having fallen, he received for it $8,484. less than the Bank had previously offered — making a loss of so much to the Claimants. There is a text. Have the goodness to return Mr Fletcher's letter. . . .

ALS. DLC-HC (DNA, M212, R5). Copy in DLC-Nicholas Biddle Papers (DNA, M212, R20). Printed in Colton, *Clay Correspondence*, 4:351, omitting second paragraph. Letter marked "(private)." 1. Jackson and Secretary of the Treasury Louis McLane had charged that the bank's western branches were engaging in unsound lending practices, thereby endangering the institution's solvency. Jackson, for example, had charged the Nashville branch with greatly overvaluing property it held as collateral for bank loans. See Biddle to Clay, Feb. 8, 1833; Govan, *Nicholas Biddle*, 216-22. 2. McLane had sold to the bank an order on the French government for the first installment of the indemnity payments arranged for in a recent treaty with France [Brown to Clay, Jan. 24, 1832], but he had hesitated to do business with the bank for so long that the exchange rate had fallen, costing the government more than $8,000. Munroe, *Louis McLane*, 379-82; Remark in Senate, Jan. 14, 1833.

To FRANCIS T. BROOKE   Washington, February 28, 1833

The compromise of the Tariff proposed by me is likely to be adopted with great eclat.[1] It has passed the House and will pass the Senate by a large majority. It will be popular every-where, even in the East. The eastern vote in the House has been given against it rather from policy than from any dislike of the measure.[2] Mr Webster and I came in conflict, and I have the satisfaction to tell you that he gained nothing. My friends flatter me, with my having completely triumphed. There is no permanent breach between us. I think he begins already to repent his course. As to the publication of my letter,[3] do as you please; but I think it hardly merits it. I shall go to the North or directly to the west immediately after the close of the Session. I regret that I cannot have the pleasure of seeing you. . . .

Copy. DLC-TJC (DNA, M212, R14). Printed in Colton, *Clay Correspondence*, 4:350-51 under incorrect date of Feb. 23. 1. Draft Proposal, Mid-Dec., 1832. 2. In the six New England states plus New York, New Jersey, Pennsylvania, and Delaware [i.e., "the eastern vote" as a whole], the compromise tariff, which finally passed the House 119 to 85 and the Senate 29 to 16, received 10 votes in favor and 10 opposed in the Senate; in the House, 27 votes were cast in its favor with 72 opposed and 7 not voting. *Register of Debates*, 22 Cong., 2 Sess., 809; U.S. H. of Reps., *Journal*, 22 Cong., 2 Sess., 428-29; Clay to Brooke, Feb. 14, 1833. 3. Reference obscure.

Speech in Senate, March 1, 1833. Speaks both to the compromise tariff bill [Speech in Senate, February 12, 1833] and the "enforcing bill" [Clay to Brooke, December 12, 1833; Remark in Senate, January 22, 1833], supporting both. Challenges Sen. John C. Calhoun's compact theory of the origin and scope of the Constitution as these two bills relate to it. *Register of Debates*, 22 Cong., 2 Sess., 807-8. Printed in Colton, *Clay Correspondence*, 5:568-69.

Late in the evening of this day he urged the passage of the public lands bill [Comment in Senate, April 16, 1832; Speech in Senate, June 20, 1832; Remark in Senate, January 7, 1833] prior to adjournment on the morrow and "in order that the Executive [Andrew Jackson] might have time to act upon the bill." *Register of Debates*, 22 Cong., 2 Sess., 809.

To JAMES BARBOUR   Washington, March 2, 1833

I thank you for your friendly invitation. If I returned through Virginia, I would with great pleasure avail myself of it, but I shall go back another route.[1]

Yesterday was perhaps the most important Congressional day that ever occurred; the Compromise bill, the Land bill and the Enforcing bill[2] having all passed during it. . . .[3]

ALS. NN.   1. Clay to Caldwell, March 12, 1833.   2. See Draft Proposal, Mid-December, 1832; Speech in Senate, Jan. 7, 1833; Remark in Senate, Jan. 22, 1833.   3. Clay placed in the mail a duplicate of this letter, dated March 3 [1833], remarking to Barbour that he was doing so, because he had "not entire confidence in the fidelity" of the U.S. Post Office. ALS. NN.

Comment in Senate, March 2, 1833. Explains what likely persuaded George Poindexter of Mississippi verbally to attack Daniel Webster of Massachusetts on the floor of the Senate on February 19 during the debate on the Force (Revenue Collection) bill. Assures his colleagues that Poindexter meant no personal harm or embarrassment to Webster and hopes the two men will patch up their momentary difference of opinion. *Register of Debates*, 22 Cong., 2 Sess., 810-11. For the Poindexter-Webster confrontation, which almost led to a duel, see *ibid.*, 655-56; and Fuess, *Daniel Webster*, 1:395.

Later this same day, Clay moves a vote of thanks to Sen. Hugh L. White of Tennessee for his able discharge of the duties of president *pro tempore* of the Senate during the 22nd Congress. *Register of Debates*, 22 Cong., 2 Sess., 812.

To James Maury Morris, Louisa Court House, Va., March 2, 1833. Asks if he is disposed to sell his lot on Poydras St. in New Orleans and, if so, at what price. ALS. ViU.

To DANIEL WEBSTER   Washington, March 2, 1833

Will you be at the Senate today? I wish much to see you here. I learnt with surprize and regret this morning that what passed the other day between you and Mr. [George] Poindexter is likely to be made the basis of a serious proceeding.[1] I think that ought to be prevented, and it can be prevented honorably to both parties. Do come here if you can.

ALS. NhD. Written in Senate Chamber.   1. See this date, Clay's Comment in Senate; for Poindexter's offensive remarks about Webster, see *Register of Debates*, 22 Cong., 2 Sess., 655-56.

To JAMES BROWN   Washington, March 3, 1833

I recd. your favor of the 1st.   I have this day addressed a letter to Philada. the ansr. to which will determine whether I go there or proceed directly to the West.[1] I prefer if I can the latter. Should I go to Your City, I will avail myself of your friendly invitation. I recd. a letter this day from Mr. [James] Erwin. He will return to K[entucky]. in April. I have no doubt that he has made satisfactory investments for you.

The Compromise bill[2] has passed, and will be well recd. throughout the Country. The Manufacturers will be content, and the politicians will find it best to acquiesce. Jackson pocketed the Land bill.[3] If he had applied the Veto and returned it, we would have passed it, I believe, by two thirds. No minister to England. [Edward] Livingston goes to France.[4]

ALS. KyU.   1. Writes Brown on March 14, reporting that he will not go to Philadelphia. Explains he has been detained in Washington by "the Court, by business and by indisposition." At this time Clay was representing John Minor before the U.S. Supreme Court in the case *Minor* v. *Tillotson*. Daniel Webster appeared for the defendant, Shurbal Tillotson. The case had been appealed from the U.S. District Court of the Eastern District of Louisiana on a writ of error in which a bill of exceptions was taken to the ruling of that court in rejecting certain evidence of plaintiff Minor in support of a land title. The Supreme Court reversed the district court and awarded the plaintiff a new trial. 7 Peters' 99-101.   2. Draft Proposal, Mid-Dec., 1832. 3. Speech in Senate, Jan. 7, 1833.   4. As U.S. Minister.

To NICHOLAS BIDDLE   Washington, March 4, 1833

I did not receive your favor of the 28h. Ulto. until Saturday evening [March 2] amidst the hurly burly scenes of a closing Session; so that really there was no fit occasion in saying the few words, suggested by you, and which I would have taken pleasure in expressing. We attempted to adjourn until Sunday, but our Presbyterian friends would not allow us. I regret all this the less because, on Saturday morning, as you will have seen, the Bank gained a complete triumph.[1] I do believe, if we had had two weeks more to go upon, we could have renewed the Charter, in spite of all Vetos. Don't despair; repose on recent victories for the present, circulate the Report of your Commee. &c. and I do hope that at the next Session or the Session after, the Charter will be renewed. I believe that we should have passed the Land bill by Constitutional majorities, if it had been returned, but the President pocketed it.[2]

My friends in Philada. could not have felt the intense anxiety about me which I did for a few days in regard to my measure. I thought I foresaw the current of feeling and events which would bear it through in triumph, and I have not been deceived. Its success is however attended with deep regret that it encountered the opposition of a highly valued friend. I wish you would say all you can to soothe him,[3] on his return. You hold a large flask of oil and know well how to pour it out. As for *your* friend Mr. W. [Robert Walsh, Jr.] (he is determined not to allow me to consider him *mine*) nothing that I can do seems right in his eyes; whilst others can do nothing wrong. I must be content with the approbation of every body else, at least of a very large majority of the community, which I fear not will be given.

I am not definitively resolved about going to Philada.   I shall be determined by an answer to a letter which I wrote yesterday.

The affair of the bills on France ought to be exposed.[4] Would it do at the next Session to call for the correspondence with the Bank?[5]

I return Mr. [Thomas H.] Fletchers letter.

ALS. DLC-Nicholas Biddle Papers (DNA, M212, R20).   1. For the "complete victory" of the pro-B.U.S. forces, see the exchange on, and action to table (by a 20 to 17 vote), the symbolic Additional Pension Agency bill. *Register of Debates*, 22 Cong., 2 Sess., 809-10; also, Bradley to Clay, Oct. 16, 1832.   2. Speech in Senate, Jan. 7, 1833.   3. Probably John Sergeant; see Clay to Johnston, March 15, 1833.   4. Biddle to Clay, Feb. 28, 1833.   5. On Dec. 10, 1834, a resolution was introduced in the House, directing the secretary of the treasury "to communicate to the House of Representatives . . . copies of the correspondence, not heretofore communicated, which has taken place between him and the president of the Bank of the United States on the subject of the branch drafts, and in relation to the claim made by the bank for damages, and the course pursued by that institution on account of the protest of the bill drawn on the French Government by the Treasury Department." The resolution passed on Dec. 11. *Register of Debates*, 23 Cong., 2 Sess., 6; U.S. H. of Reps., *Journal*, 23 Cong., 2 Sess., 69. For the response to this resolution, see *Register of Debates*, 23 Cong., 2 Sess., Appendix, 79-83.

To AUGUSTUS E. COHEN   Washington, March 4, 1833

I received and perused with great satisfaction your letter of the 22d. Feb. The measure[1] to which it relates, having received all the sanctions of the Constitution, is now the law of the land. I sincerely hope that it may produce the healing effects which it was intended to accomplish. As for myself, conscious of the purity of my motives, and knowing that I yielded to a high sense of duty towards all parts of the Country, I shall be most happy if the bill secures its beneficent purposes, whatever may be my own fate. Indifferent to this I do not affect to be, but if I know myself personal considerations are subordinate to those which belong to the Union, harmony and prosperity of our Confederacy.

Although I some times argue causes, I do not regard myself as a regular practitioner of the Law. It would not therefore be convenient for me to bestow those attentions which I should feel myself bound to render to you, if you were studying the law under my directions.

ALS. ViU. Cohen was a druggist, a notary public, and later was commissioner of deeds, living at 50 Broad Street in Charleston. He died on July 10, 1882, aged 72 years. Barnett A. Elzas, *The Old Jewish Cemeteries at Charleston, S. C.* (Charleston, 1903), 68.   1. Compromise Tariff bill. See Draft Proposal, Mid-Dec., 1832; Speech in Senate, February 12, 1833.

From William H. Garland *et al.*, Amherst, Va., March 6, 1833. Thank Clay for his "labors in settling those questions [tariff, nullilfication] which recently seemed about to shake our institutions to the centre," and for his patriotism in rising above "party spirit" in so doing. Copy. Printed in *Niles' Register* (April 27, 1833), 44:137; reprinted from the Lynchburg *Virginian*.

Clay responded from Washington on March 15, thanking them for their support of his labor for a compromise tariff. His tariff bill [Draft Proposal, Mid-December, 1832], he believed, was an "amicable settlement of a threatening question," and he but "an humble instrument in the hands of Providence, that had some agency in bringing it about." States, further, that the compromise tariff, "is founded on the principle of mutual concession" and "consults the interests, feeling and opinions of both parties, without affording to either just cause of exultation over the other." *Ibid.*

To FRANCIS T. BROOKE   Washington, March 11, 1833

At the date of your last you could not have recd. a letter which I had addressed to you at St. Julien. I shall leave here in a day or two, via Balto. Frederick & Wheeling to K. I have been detained by the Court.[1] I regret that I could not have seen you.

You ask how amity was restored between Mr. [John] Randolph and me. There was no explanation, no intervention. Observing him in the Senate one night, feeble, and looking as if he were not long for this world; and being myself engaged in a work of Peace, with corresponding feelings, I shook hands with him. The salutation was cordial on both sides.[2] I afterwards left a Card at his lodgings, where I understand he has been confined by sickness.

I heard to day that Livingston is to go to France, Barry to Spain, and Stevenson to England; and that McLane will be made Secy of State, Woodbury of the Treasury, Forsythe [*sic*] of the Navy, and Col. Wm. Wilkins P. M. General. Caring nothing about these arrangements, I vouch for nothing.[3]

You may like to know that there is no breach between Webster and me. We had some friendly passes, and there the matter ended. Since we have occasionally met on friendly terms. I *think* (of course I do not know) that if he had to go over again the work of the last few weeks he wd. have been for the compromise, which commands the approbation of a great majority.

ALS. KyU. Also in DLC-TJC (DNA, M212, R4); and Colton, *Clay Correspondence*, 4:351-52.
1. Clay to Brown, March 3, 1833.   2. See Van Deusen, *The Life of Henry Clay*, 270-71 for the
contest in which amity was restored.   3. Edward Livingston was appointed minister to
France, Cornelius P. Van Ness to Spain, and Andrew Stevenson to England—although he was
not confirmed until 1836. Louis McLane replaced Livingston as secretary of state, while Willaim
J. Duane replaced McLane as secretary of the treasury on May 26, 1833, and was subsequently
replaced himself by Roger B. Taney on Sept. 23, 1833. Levi Woodbury continued as secretary of
the navy until 1834 and Willaim T. Barry as postmaster general until 1835. In June of 1834, John
Forsyth became secretary of state. *Biennial Register*, 1833, p. 4.

From HENRY CLAY, JR.   New Orleans, March 11, 1833

This morning I stood my examination in open court before the Judge of the
Supreme Court, and I intend immediately to commence the practice. My visit
to Mobile and my examination and license there were entirely unnecessary. I
was admitted to an examination on the plea of residentship. I am full of hope
and energy, and loving the civil law as I do, I indulge a subdued confidence of
ultimate success. At all events, I shall continue the trial for two seasons after
the present.

Copy. Printed in Colton, *Clay Correspondence*, 4:352.

To JAMES CALDWELL   Washington, March 12, 1833

I recd. your favor of the 28h. Feb.   I shall return home by the Nat. road and
by Wheeling. I should have been glad at another Season to have gone by your
route, and conversed with you fully on the strange events of the last few
months. The measures which appeared to me necessary were all passed by
Congress; but Jackson pocketed one of them for future strife.[1] The Compromise of the Tariff[2] will be well received by a great majority. I shall get some
curses, but more blessings. I am content if they neutralize each other.

Ned Wyer[3] (the best authority I can quote) tells me today that [Andrew]
Stevenson is to go to England. . . .[4]

ALS. ViU. Printed in *VMHB* (October, 1947), 55:311-12.   1. The Public Land bill; Speech
in Senate, Jan. 7, 1833.   2. Draft Proposal, Mid-Dec., 1832.   3. Well known Washington
character and gossip. See also 1:867.   4. Clay to Brooke, March 11, 1833.

From John Marshall, Washington, March 12, 1833. Asks Clay to assist his nephew,
Marshall Jones, who has gone to New Orleans to begin a law practice, by mentioning
"him to some of your friends" there. Explains that Jones had to flee from Virginia when
a "personal rencontre with a young gentleman who had abused him wantonly and
grossly, terminated unfortunately in the death of his adversary," and that after visiting
Canada and Texas he had decided on "trying his fortune in New Orleans." ALS. DLC-
HC (DNA, M212, R5). For Charles Marshall Jones, the grandson of John Marshall's
brother William, see Paxton, *The Marshall Family*, 45, 255.

To James Kirke Paulding, March 13, 1833. Thanks him for "the volumes of your
work Westward Ho!" and promises to read it "a few days hence, when I shall be descending La belle Riviere in a Steam boat." Doubts that he will find anything about the west
in the book that will subject Paulding to criticism. Suspects that "if you have noticed
any of our Western pecularities, I am sure it is in a good natured and legitimate way."
Copy. Printed in Ralph M. Aderman (ed.) *The Letters of James Kirke Paulding* (Madison,
Wis., 1962), 131-32; apparently written to Paulding in New York City.

On April 6, Paulding, writing from New York, thanked Clay for his later letter
from Wheeling, Va. [W. Va.] (not found), which had praised "the general correctness"
of the book, noting that "It is always a dangerous undertaking to attempt to describe

what we have never seen. . . . You have however in a great measure relieved me from the [great] anxiety I felt." *Ibid.*, 130-31; also, ALS. DLC-HC [DNA, M212, R5). For Paulding, see DAB.

From Edwin Shelton, "Rural Plains," Hanover County, Va., March 13, 1833. Informs Clay that his (Shelton's) father-in-law, Capt. Peter Foster, died on March 11 leaving a will bequeathing $2,000 "to (your Lady) Mrs Clay." ALS. DLC-TJC (DNA, M212, R14). Apparently Foster was really Shelton's stepfather rather than his father-in-law. Mrs. Ann Shelton, the widow of John Shelton and the mother of Edwin Shelton, married Peter Foster on December 15, 1804. Edwin Shelton married Susan E. Oliver on September 4, 1827; and Peter Foster died of asthma at their home on March 11, 1833. *Hanover County Historical Society Bulletin* (November, 1977), 17:7; Genevieve Shelton Whittaker, *Some Notes on the Shelton Family of England and America* (St. Louis, 1927), 27; Richmond *Enquirer*, March 22, 1833. For Peter Foster's will, see *Hanover County Historical Society Bulletin* (November 1972), 7:5.

To JOSIAH S. JOHNSTON   Washington, March 15, 1833

You observe that your letter of the 13h. found me here. I had prior to its receipt sent you a Copy of my Speech, which is to be published by G[ales]. & Seaton in the order of the debate.[1] They have not published one word of the commendation of the Bill which has been put forth by other Editors. To preserve an attitude of impartiality they, in effect, make themselves partizans of those who opposed the measure. Do you think it necessary that I should revise the Speech which I made on the introduction of the bill?[2] That which was published for me was published without my seeing it.

I am sorry that Sageant [*sic*, John Sergeant] and [Horace] Binney[3] disapprove the measure, but I can't help it. I communicated it to them confidentially before I brought it forward, and they opposed no remonstrance. As for [Robert] Walsh [Jr.], he has but one God, and Mr. Webster is his prophet.

I hope you sent on my letter to [Abbott] Lawrence which I enclosed to you.[4] That part of the subject ought to be well understood among our friends.

I have been detained here by the most violent cold I ever had; but I hope to be off on sunday at farthest for the West. I cannot go now to Philada.   I gained my cause Minor agt. Tillottson.[5]

ALS. PHi. Printed in Colton, *Clay Correspondence*, 4:353-54; also in DLC-TJC (DNA, M212, R14). 1. The speech of Feb. 25 was printed in Gales & Seaton's *Register of Debates*, 22 Cong., 2 Sess., 729-42; and in Colton, *Clay Correspondence,* 5:551-67. On March 13, 1833, Clay paid Gales and Seaton the sum of $10 for "150 Copies speech on tariff." ADS. DLC-TJC (DNA, M212, R17). Published as a pamphlet, titled *Speech of Henry Clay, in the Senate of the United States, February 25, 1833, in Vindication of His Bill, Entitled "An Act to Modify the Act of 14th July, 1832, and All Other Acts Imposing Duties on Imports.*" N.P. [Washington], 1833.   2. His speech of Feb. 12 was printed in *Register of Debates*, 22 Cong., 2 Sess., 462-74, and in the Washington *Daily National Intelligencer*, Feb. 13, 1833. 3. See 3:371.   4. Lawrence to Clay, March 26, 1833.   5. Clay to Brown, March 3, 1833.

From Peleg Sprague, Boston, March 19, 1833. Reports that "public sentiment here has wonderfully changed in favour" of Clay's compromise tariff measure [Draft Proposal, Mid-December, 1832]. States that "It is now popular and becoming more & more so as it becomes better understood—" Continues: "In New York—I scarcely found an individual who did not approve—In Providence and in Boston there is yet some diversity of opinion among the *politicians*—but so far as I learn—*none* among the actual business men—engaged in manufacturin[g]. . . . They say—that they do not think fit to come out publicly in praise of the measure—because it might create uneasiness in the South—and generate a disposition to make further demands—and because it would carry a censure upon their delegation in Congress [Clay to Brooke, February 28, 1833]."

Adds that after talking with the leading government officials in Massachusetts, as well as many merchants and manufacturers, "I cannot doubt from their representations that the bill is *now* considered a good one—and will be *extremely* popular when fully understood—" Mentions that there has been a great deal of misunderstanding about the measure, because the debates have not been published and "every member of their [Massachusetts] delegation . . . voted against it—" One of the common errors he has found is the belief that "it relinquished the *principle of* protection after 1842" and that "the duties were to *be equal* on all articles—" Now carries a copy of the bill to prove this is untrue. Another "source of much prejudice from the beginning . . . is—that your course was adopted without consultation with your tariff friends—and operated as a surprise upon them all and particularly upon Mr W——[Webster]." Emphasizes that he has "taken the liberty every where and upon all occasions—to state the truth upon this point" and has informed everyone about "the conferences which were had—formal and informal—the propositions and suggestions which you submitted—and the remarks of Mr W—— [Webster]—and others." Believes when it is understood "*all* will be satisfied except a particular and I trust very *limited* class of politicians—who wished to carry matters to extremities with S. Car—and to see her *put down—prostrated* by force of arms, and with whom this feeling was paramount to any regard for the tariff—" ALS. DLC-HC (DNA, M212, R5). Printed, with minor variations in punctuation and capitalization, in Colton, *Clay Correspondence*, 4:354-56.

From NICHOLAS BIDDLE   Philadelphia, March 25, 1833

I duly received your last favor from Washington, & did not fail to bear in mind its interesting contents. It confirmed an opinion previously formed, confirmed by subsequent reflection, and since repeatedly declared, that it was of great importance to the country not to permit the difference of sentiment on the Tariff to produce any alienation between those who had hitherto acted in concert on all the other great public measures—and that more especially no estrangement should be allowed to grow up between the two most prominent leaders [Clay and Webster] who were opposed on that question. During the visit of our friend,[1] I was in habits of constant & confidential intercourse with him—In regard to the measure itself he retains all the opinions which he publicly expressed, but they are I think unaccompanied by any thing of an unkind or unfriendly feeling towards yourself, as you will perceive when the speech made on that occasion is published.[2] There was a strong disposition among many of his friends to give him a public dinner, but this I discouraged because I feared that it might oblige him to say more on that subject than it is prudent to express at the present time & because it would probably furnish an occasion for his less discreet friends to do & to say things excusable at a moment of excitement but which might afterwards be regretted. For such an exhibition I substituted a large meeting of gentlemen at my own house where his friends could have the pleasure of seeing him without imposing upon him the necessity of making any exposition of his views on any subject. I stated to him without reserve the share which I had taken in preventing a public dinner & my reasons for it in the propriety of which he entirely acquiesced. In short he has left us two days ago in a frame of mind entirely satisfactory—and your mutual friends seem to understand each other perfectly that there ought not to be and that there shall not be any alienation between you, however you may have differed on one measure of policy. For myself I entertain for him so sincere an attachment that I should have been greatly pained at a different result. These good dispositions will I doubt not be strengthened during the visit which he meditates to your country in the course of the spring, since no one can be insensible to the attractions of personal intercourse with you. . . .

ALS. DLC-HC (DNA, M212, R5). Printed in Colton, *Clay Correspondence*, 4:356-57. ALI. DLC-Nicholas Biddle Papers (DNA, M212, R20). Letter marked "(Private)." 1. Daniel Webster. See Clay to Biddle, April 10, 1833. Webster had stopped in Philadelphia, probably between March 21 and 23, on his way to New York City. Wiltse, *Webster Papers*, 3:225, 228. 2. Probably a reference to Webster's speech, published by Gales & Seaton under the title *Speech of Mr. Webster, in the Senate, in Reply to Mr. Calhoun's Speech, On the Bill, "Further to Provide for the Collection of Duties On Imports." Delivered on the 16th of February, 1833*. Washington, 1833.

From Abbott Lawrence, Boston, March 26, 1833. Reports that Clay's letter "of 13th Inst, with your speech upon the Tariff bill [Draft Proposal, Mid-December, 1832]" has "placed in my power the means of satisfying the minds of many prominent citizens among us, who had supposed the whole scheme was brought forward without the knowledge of your friends—" Those to whom he has shown it "are entirely satisfied with the purity of your motives, as well as your enlightened patriotism—" Continues: "The Newspaper presses are now silent here upon the subject, and will remain so—I know the Editors well and have taken some pains to place the whole subject upon the true ground. I had as you know strong objections to any concessions whatever, yet I am now well satisfied with the course the whole subject took in Congress—So are the people of this State. and of New England—Our interests have been greatly promoted by it. . . . I do not think there is the least unkind feeling toward you in New England—and I do not take I think too much upon myself, when I say you were never more popular than at the present moment—"

Predicts that in the next few years the American System, especially internal improvements, will bind the Union together "by ties stronger than all the constitutions that human wisdom could devise." ALS. DLC-HC (DNA, M212, R5). Printed, with minor changes in punctuation and capitalization and the deletion of the last two sentences and the postscript of the letter, in Colton, *Clay Correspondence*, 4:357-58.

From JAMES MADISON   "Montpelier," Va., April 2, 1833

Accept my acknowledgements for the copy of your Speech on the bill modifying the Tariff.[1] I need not repeat what is said by all, on the ability and advantages with which the Subject was handled. It has certainly had the effect of an Anodyne on the feverish excitement under which the public mind was laboring; & a relapse may happily not ensue. There is no certainty however that a surplus revenue will not revive the difficulty of adjusting an impost to the claims of the manufacturing and the feelings of the agricultural states. The effect of a reduction, including the protected articles, on the manufacturers is manifest: and a discrimination in their favor, will, besides the complaint of inequality, exhibit the protective principle, without disguise, to the protestors against its constitutionality. An alleviation of the difficulty may perhaps be found in such an apportionment of the tax on the protected articles most consumed in the South, & on the unprotected most consumed in the North, as will equalize the burden between them, and limit the advantage of the latter to the benefits, flowing from a location of the manufacturing Establishments.

May there not be a more important alleviation in Embris; an assimilation of the employment of labor, in the South, to its employment in the North. A difference and even a contrast in that respect, is at the bottom of the discords, which have prevailed; and would so continue, until the manufactures of the North, could without a bounty take the place of the foreign, in supplying the South; in which event, the source of discord would become a bond of interest;

and the difference of pursuits, more than equivalent to a similarity. In the mean time an advance towards the latter must have an alleviating tendency. And does not this advance present itself, in the certainty that unless agriculture can find new markets for its products, or new products for its markets, the rapid increase of slave labor, & the still more rapid increase of its fruits, must divert a large portion of it from the plough & the Hoe, to the loom & the workshop. When we can no longer convert our, flour, tobacco, cotton & rice into a supply of our habitual wants, from abroad, labour must be withdrawn from those articles and made to supply them at home.

It is painful to turn from anticipations of this sort, to the prospect opened by the torch of discord bequeathed by the Convention of S. Carolina,[2] to its country; by the insidious exhibitions of a permanent incompatibility and even hostility of interests between the South & the North; and by the contageous zeal in vindicating & varnishing the doctrines of Nullification & Secession; the tendency of all of which, whatever be the intention, is to create a disgust with the ·Union, and then to open the way out of it. We must oppose to this aspect of things a confidence, that as the gulf is approached, the deluded will recoil from its horrors, and that the deluders, if not themselves sufficiently startled, will be abandoned & overwhelmed by their followers.

As we were disappointed of the expected visit last fall, from yourself and Mrs. Clay, we hope the promise will not be forgotten when the next opportunity occurs. For the present Mrs. Madison joins in cordial regards, & all good wishes to you both.

LS, with final paragraph and signature in Madison's hand. DLC-HC (DNA, M212, R5). Printed in Colton, *Clay Correspondence*, 4:358-60; also in *James Madison, Letters and Other Writings*. Published by Order of Congress (Philadelphia, 1865), 4:567-68.   1. Draft Proposal, Mid-Dec., 1832; Speech in Senate, Feb. 12, 25, 1833; Clay to Johnston, March 15, 1833.   2. Stoddard to Clay, Nov. 12, 1832.

To NATHANIEL F. WILLIAMS   Lexington, April 9, 1833

I am very sorry that it is not in my power to send you the Copies you desire of my Tariff Speech, having disposed of every Copy I had prior to my departure from Washn. City.[1]

It affords me great pleasure to learn from all quarters that the measure to which you refer has given such general satisfaction. In K. there is scarcely a dissentient.

I returned about a week ago not very well; but the quiet and good nursing of Ashland will, I hope, soon restore me.

For the papers which you sent me I thank you.

ALS. KyU.   1. Clay to Johnston, March 15, 1833.

To NICHOLAS BIDDLE   Lexington, April 10, 1833

I received your favor of the 25h. Ulto. and perused its interesting contents with much satisfaction. Your friendly solicitude to prevent any estrangement between Mr. W. [Daniel Webster] and myself adds another to the many previous obligations under which you had placed me. I concur entirely with you in thinking that, on every account, such a change in the amicable relations between that gentleman and myself would be very unfortunate.

After the introduction of the Compromise bill,[1] it was manifest at Washington that a few of the Eastern friends of Mr. W., supposing that I had taken a step which would destroy me in the public estimation, indulged hopes that a new party could be formed, of which he might be the sole head. I thought that Mr. W. himself made an unprovoked and unnecessary allusion to me when, in describing the struggles of Mr. Calhoun in a Bog,[2] he stated that no friend could come to his relief without sharing in his embarrassment. Even the female part of the Audience understood to whom the allusion was directed. I need not say to you that I felt myself under no sort of obligation to Mr. Calhoun himself or to the State from which he came; that I had experienced nothing but unkindness from both; and that I have come under no engagement whatever with him in regard to the future. If So. Carolina had stood alone, or if she could have been kept separated from the rest of the South in the contest which I apprehended to be impending, I should not have presented the measure which I did.

On a subsequent occasion Mr. W. imputed to me, in a manner I thought unfriendly, an abandonment of the Protective policy. To that suggestion an immediate reply was made. And to his chief attack upon the bill itself a prompt answer was given, which you have seen in the public prints. Whatever momentary feelings were excited, during the progress of the measure, I assure you after it was carried that they entirely ceased; and all my sentiments of attachment to Mr. W. returned in their undiminished strength. I took several occasions to evince to him the state of my heart; and I was happy to believe that it was fully reciprocated by him. I assure you that on my part these feelings shall be constantly cherished.

You will have heard from him or others that the Compromise was not offered until after the fullest and freest conferences with him and others. Two distinct meetings at my quarters of 11 or 12 Senators (at the first of which he attended, and to the last he was summoned) took place, in which it was fully discussed and considered. At the last I interrogated each Senator individually, and I understood every one to agree substantially to the bill (for I had prepared a bill) except one, who finally voted for it. Several of those who had, as I supposed, assented to it voted against it.

I do not now think that the course of Mr. W. and other gentlemen from the East and North who voted with him, is to be regretted—certainly not, if the difference of opinion should produce, and it ought to produce, no alienation between friends. Many of them I know so voted, from considerations of policy, rather than from any positive objections to the bill. And the course which they pursued will probably tend to reconcile the South more strongly to a measure, in which it has got a nominal triumph, whilst all the substantial advantages have been secured to the Tariff States.

Mr. W. is to visit us in June. I hope he will not disappoint us. Every consideration is in favor of his coming, without a single opposing circumstance. He will find a warm and cordial reception.

I heard yesterday that you too would probably execute your long contemplated Western tour this Spring. I most anxiously wish you may; and it seems to me that there are considerations growing out of the Institution under your care which strongly recommend the journey. Come to us in May or June if possible. They are our best months, as they are every where, and I have a selfish view besides in desiring to see you at that time; it is that I purpose leaving home in July.

I returned not very well; but the quiet and good nursing at Ashland have already benefited me. In the midst of Arabian horses, English Cattle and

Maltese Asses, I think I shall recover much sooner than I should have done in the corrupt atmosphere of the Capital.

ALS. DLC-Nicholas Biddle Papers (DNA, M212, R20). 1. Draft Proposal, Mid-Dec., 1832; Speech in Senate, Feb. 12, 25, 1833. 2. Mentioned in Webster's speech of Feb. 16, 1833. *Register of Debates*, 22 Cong., 2 Sess., 553.

To JULIA PRATHER CLAY   Lexington, April 14, 1833

Upon my return home about a week ago, I found here your favor of the 3d. March, and intended last evening to have written to you and transmitted my letter under cover to your mother [Matilda Fontaine (Mrs. Thomas) Prather], when, to our agreeable surprize Henry [Clay, Jr.] arrived and informed us that you were at Louisville. We should have been happy if you had accompanied him; and hope as soon as you have given a reasonable portion of your time to your mother and relatives at Louisville you will come to us. You know this is the Season when Ashland looks most attractive.

Henry is thin, but his health otherwise appears sound. I am glad to observe that he is more weaned from Louisiana, and more attached to Kentucky. He even thinks of purchasing a farm in this neighbourhood, and we purpose this evening or tomorrow to go to look at one. We should be delighted to have you in our neighbourhood; and I think you might both be very happy here.

I had designed a long journey for Anne [Brown Clay Erwin] and yourself Mrs. [Lucretia] Clay, Henry [Jr.] and Mr. [James] Erwin this summer. It was to leave here early in July and go to Niagara, Quebec, Saratoga and Boston. But he has confirmed my apprehensions that you would not be in a travelling condition, and I fear Anne may be in a similar predicament. If you can't go (which I shall greatly regret) Mrs. Clay and I will have to leave you.

My health was not good after the adjournment of Congress. It has improved since, and I trust will be re-established by the quiet and good nursing of Ashland. That of Mrs. Clay and the rest of the family is good.

I wish you would write to Anne, if a letter will probably reach her prior to her departure from N.O. and tell her that her sons [Henry C.; James, Jr.; Andrew E.] are in excellent health, and that every thing goes on as well at the Woodlands as could be expected in the absence of the Master and Mistress.

Present us kindly to your Mother and relations. . . .

ALS. Henry Clay Memorial Foundation, Lexington, Ky. Addressed to Julia (Mrs. Henry Clay, Jr.) in Louisville, Ky.

To THOMAS HELM   Lexington, April 20, 1833

The Elections yet to take place of members to the H. of R. are very important and may have great influence on the public interests. Those of Kentucky should engage all our solicitude. I think that the re charter of the Bank of the U.S. is not to be despaired of, but the success of that measure will depend much upon the character of members to be chosen.

I regret to perceive that a division is likely to take place in your district among our friends. I consider the re-election of Mr. [Robert P.] Letcher is a point of the first importance.[1] No man in the H. of R. possesses any thing like the extent of personal influence that he does. That consideration, connected with his long experience, and his personal knowledge of men and measures, recommends him in the strongest manner to the people of your District. You have several gentlemen that would make highly respectable members. I mean to say nothing to disparage them, but only that I should regard Mr. Letcher's withdrawal from Congress as furnishing just occasion for deep regret.

I have thought that, whilst I am aware that it does not belong to me to interfere in your Election, I might without impropriety express these sentiments to you knowing that you would justly appreciate them.

ALS. Courtesy of Mrs. Henry Jackson, Sr., Danville, Ky. Letter marked "(Confidential)." 1. In the election on August 5, 1833, Letcher received 44 votes more than Moore. The sheriff of Lincoln County carried off the poll books of that county, an act which gave Letcher a majority of 149. Three of the five sheriffs in the district then signed the certificate of election in favor of Moore. Letcher contested the election. Each man presented himself to the U.S. House as the duly elected representative of Kentucky's fifth congressional district. After six months of investigation, the House declared that neither man qualified and called for a new election. The following August, 1834, Letcher defeated Moore in a second election by a majority of 270 votes. Collins, *History of Kentucky*, 1:38-39; Lexington *Observer & Kentucky Reporter*, Sept. 12; Dec. 4, 1833; June 25, 1834; *Register of Debates*, 23 Cong., 1 Sess., 2130-31, 2133, 2139, 2141, 2160, 3967, 4007, 4200, 4240, 4279, 4451, 4802.

To SAMUEL L. SOUTHARD   Lexington, April 22, 1833

I returned home not very well a few weeks ago. I hope the tranquillity and good nursing at Ashland will restore me. I recd your friendly letter of the 16h. Ulto. In behalf of the measure to which you refer, I can add nothing material to the Speech of which I sent you a Copy.[1] My great anxiety was as to its reception in the Eastern and Northern States. All my information abundantly assures me that it is acceptable there to the great body of the practical manufacturers. This is demonstrated by the conclusive fact that Stock in Companies has risen from 20 to 25 per Cent, in consequence of the passage of the bill. They have committed a new folly in So. Carolina by the impotent attempt to nullify the enforcing act.[2] It should be laughed at and not treated seriously. I presume that the desire to preserve the ascendancy to the dominant party will explain that and some other extravagant acts.

I regret to hear that you have been exposed to malignant attacks from the Jackson party. You must bear them with the same fortitude and philosophy which *you know* I have always exhibited under the influence of similar attacks. I think you are beyond the reach of their rage.

Had the Land bill passed,[3] I should certainly not have returned to Washn. The state of that measure creates some doubt whether it is not my duty to go back once more. I find also a strong motive for my return in the pleasure I should derive from meeting yourself, [Joseph] Kent and other friends in the Senate; but I have not yet positively decided what I shall do.

I shall go to the North this summer; and hope to meet you, at least in transitu, some where. . . .

ALS. NjP. 1. Probably his speech on his compromise tariff bill. See Clay to Johnston, March 15, 1833. 2. Remark in Senate, Jan. 22, 1833. 3. Comment in Senate, April 16, 1832; Speech in Senate, June 30, 1832; Jan. 7, 1833.

To Lafayette, Paris, April 27, 1833. Reports that "An anodine was given by the last Congress to our fellow Citizens of So. Carolina [Remark in Senate, January 22, 1833]. It has quitted, for the present, all our domestic troubles in that quarter; and I sincerely hope no others will arise to excite solicitude among the friends of liberty on either side of the Atlantic." ALS. NNPM.

To RICHARD HENRY WILDE   Lexington, April 27, 1833

I duly recd. your favor of the 13h. inst. communicating the adjustment of an important controversy, to which Mr. J[ames]. Erwin was a party. I am in the

639

daily expectation of his arrival, with my daughter [Anne Brown Clay Erwin], from N. Orleans, where they have been since last Decr. When he gets here I shall inform him of the successful issue of the suit,[1] which has afforded me great satisfaction.

I have perused with great attention and interest your observations on our public affairs. A large section of the Jackson party, headed by Mr. V. Buren, will attempt either to impress the North with the belief that its interest were injuriously affected by the Compromise of the Tariff,[2] made at the last session, or the South with the opinion that its interests were not sufficiently attended to. I think it most probable that that section will appeal to the South; whilst Jackson himself, who always follows the lead of his passions, provoked by the reception of his proclamation at the South, may possibly court the North. Perhaps we may find safety in this conflict of views. But, if it should not occur, and there shall be any serious endeavor to disturb the material terms of the adjustment of the Tariff, I shall rely greatly upon the good faith of yourself and other gentlemen at the South to unite in resisting it. I cannot but hope, should such an effort be made, that it will be in your power to give it a turn that will prevent any injurious operation upon you individually at home. The measure was proposed and adopted, and, I hope, will be adhered to, in good faith.

My belief is that the danger you apprehend from a surplus Revenue will not be realized. In the first place, the expenditures of the Government will be much greater than are generally anticipated. Are you aware that the unnecessary Indian War in which we were involved last summer[3] will cost from two to three million's of dollars? Such is my information. The amount was concealed from Congress, under the pretext that the accounts had not come in, or were not liquidated. And, in the second, you are aware that the act of the last Session makes a provision, which I think, if fairly executed, will guard sufficiently against the dreaded surplus.

But undoubtedly the passage of the Land Bill[4] would have afforded further security, and I think most desireable security, against the extraordinary inconvenience of a superabundant exchequer. There are so many, and such cogent, reasons in favor of that measure, that I have seen with surprize and deep regret the opposition it has encountered in the South. And I yet anxiously cherish the hope that, now the Tariff being settled, the opposition will cease. The passage of that single measure would go far to settle most of our difficulties. It would prevent the disturbance of the Tariff, supersede the exercise of the power of Internal improvements, and strip intrigue of its principal remaining instrument. Should I be in the next Congress I intend to propose a bill,[5] to take effect at the same time as that which was proposed in the bill of the last Session, that is, from the 31st. Decr. 1832. In the event of its passage, in that form, it will absorb all the proceeds of the Public Lands, during the current year; and of course will lessen any surplus, if there be any.

The currency is a most important interest which cannot too soon nor too earnestly engage public attention. The prospects of a renewal of the Charter of the U. States bank have decidedly improved within the last five months, and I do not despair of its being accomplished.[6] But between the Constitutional objections of a portion of Congress, and the perservering opposition of the Executive, it will I fear be very difficult to secure majorities of two thirds. There is a strong tendency too towards the establishment of local banks. It was successfully resisted in our Western Legislatures, during last winter; but it is to be feared, unless the Bank shall be shortly rechartered, it cannot be much longer opposed with success. I have thought that if Mr. [John C.] Calhoun would take up that subject at the next Session,[7] as he originally reported & sustained the present Charter, it might be of great advantage to the public, and to him individually; but not being in the habit of correspondence with him I cannot myself make the suggestion to him.

I feel most intensely for you, in respect to the agitation of the question of Emancipation in the British West Indies;[8] and the misfortune is that nothing can be done, with any probability of success. On principle, the danger is perhaps not sufficiently near or great to justify any interference from us. Such an interference, formally made, would be revolting to British pride, and perhaps might even accelerate Emancipation. It is no cause of War, and if it were possible to prevail upon the American people to engage in War, for such a cause, it would be a War in which we should have the sympathies of all the World against us.

Without this foreign ingredient in your Cup, Slavery had already made it sufficiently bitter. It lies at the bottom of many of the evils under which the Southern Atlantic States are suffering. Whilst you stand upon Constitutional ground, in protesting against the slightest interference of the Genl. Government with the institution of Slavery or the condition of its unfortunate subjects, it is perfectly manifest, I think, that you will have soon to alter materially the character of their labor. You will have either to find new products for it, or new markets for its present products.

I have written much more than I intended and much more than I am in the habit of writing. My apology is the interesting contents of your letter. I shall be happy some times to hear from you upon any subject, but especially on the point of the determination in your quarter to abide by the Compromise bill.

ALS. ViU. Letter marked "(Confidential)." For Wilde, see *BDAC*.   1. Reference obscure. 2. Draft Proposal, Mid-Dec., 1832.   3. Henry Clay, Jr., to Clay, April 22, 1832.   4. Speech in Senate, Jan. 7; Dec. 5, 1833.   5. Clay introduced his new land bill on Dec. 15, 1833, explaining, on Dec. 16, that it "was the same as that which passed at the last session . . . excepting the removal of the restriction of the States in the application of the proceeds." Nothing came of this bill. *Register of Debates*, 23 Cong., 1 Sess., 24, Appendix, 117. See also Benjamin H. Hibbard, *A History of the Public Land Policies* (New York, 1939), 177-84; Van Deusen, *The Life of Henry Clay*, 286-87.   6. On March 18, 1834, Webster had introduced a bill in the Senate in favor of recharter. This bill was tabled on March 26. *Register of Debates*, 23 Cong., 1 Sess., 984, 1145. See also Van Deusen, *The Life of Henry Clay*, 282-86; Hammond, *Banks and Politics in America*, 432-33; Govan, *Nicholas Biddle*, 263-66.   7. Calhoun addressed the subject on March 21, 1834, advocating a new and limited Bank of the United States which would be chartered for twelve years. *Register of Debates*, 23 Cong., 1 Sess., 1057-73; Wiltse, *John C. Calhoun: Nullifier*, 2:225-29.   8. Slaves in the British West Indies were freed in August, 1833. See Charles F. Mullett, *The British Empire* (New York, 1938), 721-25; George R. Mellor, *British Imperial Trusteeships*. London, n.d.

From Richard Ashton, Lexington, May 8, 1833. Receipt for $30 paid by Clay for a plot (Square 9, Lot 4) "for the purposes of the burial of free white persons" in the "new Episcopal Grave Yard" in Northeast Lexington and for the use of the "Vault in said Yard for the purpose of depositing his dead during the winter season." DS. DLC-TJC (DNA, M212, R10).

From Henry D. Steever, Philadelphia, May 10, 1833. Compliments Clay for his success in compromising the tariff issue and adds: "That you should have ventured the proposition you did, which seemed irreconcileable with those views of policy you had so ably and so successfully advocated—I regarded—as a proof that you preferred your

Country to any favorite *measure*." Assures him, further, that "The Manufacturers in this City as far as I can learn are satisfied with the operation of your bill. It was the best measure that could be proposed, and the only one that could have been adopted with any hope of peace." LS. DLC-HC (DNA, M212, R5). Steever was a Philadelphia accountant who did business on 9th Street. Desilver's *Philadelphia Directory and Stranger's Guide, for 1833* (Philadelphia, 1833), 208.

From George Woodward, Richmond, Mo., May 11, 1833. In response to an inquiry from Clay, explains how he might most conveniently pay the annual taxes on his lands in Ray and Chariton counties in Missouri. States his fee as Clay's possible agent in such matters, but is reluctant to estimate the value of Clay's property until he sees a description of each tract. Warns Clay of the problems with squatters on and disputed titles to Missouri lands. ALS. DLC-TJC (DNA, M212, R14).

To James Maury Morris, Louisa Court House, Va., May 19, 1833. Says he had earlier written Morris [March 2, 1833] about his lots in New Orleans "at the insistance of friends" and will "inform them of your determination to sell at auction." Adds in a postscript: "You remind me of some political predictions which you made at my house in Washn. I have an imperfect recollection of them. But I believe it is best to forget as much of the past, as we can. If others have found pleasure in contemplating the political condition of our Country, for the last few years, it is more than you and I have. Tell Mrs. M. that I am happy to have contributed to her pleasure by the reduction of the Tariff. As a good housekeeper she is however not to learn that the reduction of duties is not allways followed by the reduction of prices." ALS. ViU.

From JOHN SIBLEY   Natchitoches, La., May 22, 1833
Illy fitted as my mind is to write a letter, at this time, & painfull as the task is, I must in grief tell you that, J[osiah]. S. Johnston & his son William were last Sunday Morning on Board the Steam Boat Lioness on their way to make me a Visit, when about 35 Miles above Alexandria in Red River a large quantity of Powder in the hole of the Boat exploded & Blew the Boat to Atoms 15 or 16 Passengers were lost Amongst them our friend Johnston. William was blown off a distance, much hurt but not killed, is I hope safe with his uncle a few Miles below where the disaster happened, his wife [Eliza Sibley Johnston], my poor Child was left in Bad health in Philada. I Can now only command her to a merciful God, & implore your condolence to her, I will write you more particularly when I can.

ALS. DLC-TJC (DNA, M212, R14). Printed in Colton, *Clay Correspondence*, 4:360.

To James Heaton, Middletown, Ohio, May 28, 1833. Is pleased that Heaton [5:417] approved the tariff compromise bill [Draft Proposal, Mid-December, 1832]. Continues: "My convictions were very strong as to the propriety of that measure, and were fortified by frequent conferences with intelligent manufacturers, prior to its introduction. Nevertheless, I was aware that I exposed myself to much hazard by bringing it forward. If it had failed, I should have been condemned along with it, and when it was presented but few believed it would pass. It has since had a degree of success greatly exceeding my expectations." Concludes: "If another measure, to which I assign the highest importance, the Land bill [Speech in Senate, January 7, 1833], had become a Law, I should have retired from the Senate. I shall deliberate on the question whether it is my duty to return, and endeavor to bring that bill to a definitive issue. On that question I shall decide prior to the next Session." ALS. DLC-HC (DNA, M212, R21).

To JAMES MADISON   Lexington, May 28, 1833

I received in due course of the Mail your obliging letter of the 6h. Ulto. [*sic*, April 2] and was extremely happy in the inference, from observing one paragraph and the superscription in your hand writing, that your health was improved. Other accounts have also assured me of that agreeable fact. May it be fully re-established, and you long spared to us!

Your prediction as to the quieting effect, at least for the present, of the Compromise bill[1] seems to be realized. Should either of the contingencies mentioned in your letter arise we may hope that the Tariff will no longer create disturbances among us. The most probable of them is, that our Northern brethren will be able to supply most of the articles which they manufacture, without protection, as cheap as they can be brought from Europe. By 1842, I think that will be the case as to a great many fabrics. The single advantage, low wages, which Europe will at that time possess I hope will be countered balanced by advantages of other kinds, which we shall possess. Ultimately, but more distantly, the South will share in some branches of Manufactures.

I do not apprehend that any surplus that may accrue in the Revenue will create a necessity for disturbing the essential features of the Compromise. You are aware that the Act provides for the contingencies both of surplus and deficit. There is more reason to apprehend an attempt to modify it, from political considerations. Should such an attempt be made, with the view of lessening the amount of protection, I hope the good faith of the South will prompt it to oppose the attempt and to stand by the compromise.

The political malcontents in the South seem to have adopted a new theme to excite alarm and to disseminate sentiments unfriendly to the Union. And the measures which G. Britain appears to be resorting to, for the purpose of emancipating the slaves in the W. Indies,[2] may give some aid to the efforts of the [Washington *United States*] Telegraph, their organ, and other papers. I hope that the intelligence of the Country will perceive the object, and perceive also that there is not the slightest foundation for the alarm. I have never yet met with any Northern man who thought that Congress ought to interfere on the subject of the emancipation of the Slaves of the South further than to afford aid in accomplishing that object, *if the South desired it.*

Mrs. Clay and I are both thankful for the friendly recollection of Mrs. Madison and yourself, and for your kind invitation to visit Montpellier [*sic*, Montpelier]. We shall not fail to avail ourselves of it, should we ever be again near you. I have not yet decided to return to the Senate, and therefore do not know whether I shall ever visit your part of Virginia. If the Land bill had passed,[3] I should certainly not have returned; and I do not know whether I have not already done all that was encumbent upon me, in regard to that subject. The retention of that bill by the President was I have thought an unconstitutional act.[4] You have seen the question probably touched in the News papers. The consequence of withholding the bill, that is, as contended for, that it became a law, may not be so legitimate, but the failure to return it has appeared to me unauthorized by the Constitution. I know what a tax you must pay in your correspondence, and do not wish to augment it; but, if you should at any time favor me with a letter here after, I should be glad of one line expressing your opinion upon that Constitutional question.

I pray you to communicate the warm regards of Mrs. Clay and myself to Mrs. Madison. . . .

ALS. InU.   1. Draft Proposal, Mid-Dec., 1832.   2. Clay to Wilde, April 27, 1833.
3. Speech in Senate, Jan. 7, 1833.   4. *Ibid.*

To FRANCIS T. BROOKE   Lexington, May 30, 1833

I duly received your favor. I should have written to you before, but in this remote quarter we have rarely any thing interesting to communicate. Since my
return from Washington, I have been principally occupied with the operations
of my farm, which have more & more interest for me. There is a great difference, I think, between a farm employed in raising dead produce for market, &
one which is applied, as mine is, to the rearing of all kinds of live stock. I have
the Maltese Ass[e]s, the arabian horse, the Merino & Saxe Merino sheep, the
English Hereford & Durham cattle, the goat, the mule, & the hog. The progress of these animals from their infancy to maturity, presents a constantly
varying subject of interest, & I never go out of my house, without meeting with
some of them to engage agreeably my attention. Then, our fine green sward,
our natural parks, our beautiful undulating country, everywhere exhibiting
combinations of grass and trees, or luxuriant corps, all conspire to render home
delightful. Notwithstanding, I shall leave it early in July, to make a journey
which I have long desired to perform. I shall go through Ohio to lake Erie;
thence to Buffalo, Niagara, Montreal, Quebec, Saratoga, & towards
September, to Boston, where I have a young son [James Brown Clay] of 16.
The papers have attributed to me an intention of visiting New England, as if it
were the principal object of my excursion. It is the least important one, & I
should not go there but for the sake of my son. I intend travelling with as much
privacy as practicable, & absolutely to decline every species of public entertainment. I wished to have been accompanied by Mrs. Clay, & my son [Henry,
Jr.] & son in law [James Erwin], with their respective wives [Julia Prather Clay
and Anne Brown Clay Erwin]; but neither of the young ladies is in a travelling
condition, & my wife hesitates about going without either of them.

You perceive that the journey I have sketched will not admit of my having
the pleasure of meeting you at the White Sulphur Springs. I visit no place in the
summer with more gratification than that finest of all our mineral Springs; but I
have never seen the Falls of Niagara, & unless I avail myself of this summer to go
there, I shall probably never have another opportunity.

I have not decided whether I shall return to the Senate or not. If the land
bill had passed,[1] I certainly should not have gone again; & the condition in
which that measure has been left, creates the only doubt which I feel. But have
I not done all that was incumbent on me? Twice have I pressed the bill in the
senate, where it has twice passed, & once in the house. I regret most deeply
that the South, hitherto has opposed that measure. They will regret it some
day, if it fails; for the public lands will be lost to the country, without some
such measure is adopted. They will be used as an instrument to advance the
ambitious views of some presidential aspirant, by offering motives to the new
states to support him. Already they are attempted to be applied to that object;
for how otherwise can you account for the opposition of Mr. [Martin] Van
Buren's friends, in New York, to the land bill, & thus separating themselves
from the rest of the North, & evidently arraying themselves against the interest of their own State?

You tell me that Messrs. [Benjamin W.] Leigh &c., speak of me as a
candidate for the next presidency, & even think of having my name forthwith

announced. I am greatly obliged by their favorable opinion; but I really feel no disposition to enter again on an arduous & doubtful struggle for any office. I have seen no evidence of very favorable changes in respect to me, that are of an extent sufficient to justify the opinion, that a result of a new contest would take place different from former experiments. Nothing is so abhorrent to my feelings as to be placed in a position in which I should appear as a teasing suppliant for office. That of President is full of care & vexation.

One borne to it by the willing suffrages of a large majority of his countrymen, may get along well enough in it; but if it is to be obtained in a hard contest, by a lean majority, or by a decision of the house of representatives, between several Candidates, no one having a majority, it has no charms, at least none for me. I doubt very much whether any successful opposition can be made against Gen. Jackson's designated successor. The press, patronage, & party will probably carry him triumphantly through. I have borne the taunts of the Jackson party & principles long enough. The country has not thought proper to sustain my exertions. Distinguished men, who could not possibly have viewed things differently from me, have stood by with a cold indifference, without lending any helping hand. What can one man do alone against a host?

If I am asked, what I think of the present state of things, & of the future, upon the supposition of success on the part of the candidate referred to? I answer, bad enough, bad enough, God knows. But what can I do? — Have I heretofore ever ceased to warn the country against it? Worn out & exhausted in the service, why should I continue to sound the alarm, with no prospect of my being more heeded hereafter than heretofore? I want repose, I have reached a time of life when all men want it. I shall not neglect the duties which belong to one who has aimed to be a good citizen, & a patriot, even in retirement; but the country had better try other sentinels, not more devoted or zealous, but who may be more successful, than I have been.

Such, my dear sir, is the true state of my feelings. Your partiality & friendly wishes about me may not — your unbiased judgment must — approve them. . . .

Copy. DLC-TJC (DNA, M212, R14). Printed in Colton, *Clay Correspondence*, 4:360-63. 1. Speech in Senate, Jan. 7, 1833.

From UNKNOWN AUTHOR Petersburg, Va., May 31, 1833
The last speech which John Randolph of Roanoke ever delivered was at the late Jockey Club dinner of our New Market races, to a party of about 200 gentlemen.[1] Inter alios, he alluded to yourself somewhat thus; "I admire & respect such men (the old Federalists) "far more than such republicans as the Janus-faced Editor of the Richmond Enquirer,[2] who has contrived to keep in with every administration Save the short reign of John Adams the second, and then he kept an anchor out to windward for Henry Clay; (who by the way, gentlemen, is a much better man than Ritchie — Clay is a brave man.   he is a consistent man which [Thomas] Ritchie is not, an independent man and an honest man which Ritchie is not."

These remarks were responded to by the Company with rapturous applause; and I now communicate them to you (privately & incog:) because I like to impart pleasure to a generous mind & it must be some gratification to you to hear that these were the last public declarations of one of yr. most envenomed & distinguished political enemies & that they were uttered and applauded in a part of our Country which has been hitherto most decided in its opposition to you. I am, Dear Sir, with great admiration for your character personally & for yr. ardent patriotism,

ALS. DLC-HC (DNA, M212, R5). Printed in Colton, *Clay Correspondence*, 4:363, and attributed to J.W.P.   The letter is signed with initials which appear to read J.W.P.   1. For Randolph's speech at New Market, in Prince George County, Va., in May of 1833, see James G. Scott and Edward A. Wyatt, *Petersburg's Story: A History* (Petersburg, Va., 1960), 145-46.   2. Thomas Ritchie.

From JAMES MADISON   "Montpelier," Va., Early June, 1833
Your letter of May 28th: was duly received. In it you ask my opinion on the retention of the land bill[1] by the President.

It is obvious that the Constitution meant to allow the President an adequate time to consider the bills &c. presented to him, and to make his objections to them; and on the other hand that Congress should have time to consider and overrule the objections. A disregard on either side of what it owes to the other, must be an abuse, for which it would be responsible under the forms of the Constitution. An abuse on the part of the President, with a view sufficiently manifest, in a case of sufficient magnitude, to deprive Congress of the opportunity of overruling objections to their bills, might doubtless be a ground for impeachment. But nothing short of the signature of the President, or a lapse of ten days without a return of his objections, or an overruling of the objections by two thirds of each House of Congress, can give legal validity to a bill. In order to qualify [in the French sense of the term] the retention of the Land bill by the President, the first enquiry is whether a sufficient time was allowed him to decide on its merits; the next whether with a sufficient time to prepare his objections, he unnecessarily put it out of the power of Congress to decide on them. How far an anticipated passage of the Bill, ought to enter into the sufficiensy of the time for Executive deliberations, is another point for consideration. A minor one may be whether a silent retention or an assignment to Congress of the reasons for it, be the mode most suitable to such occasions.

I hope with you that the compromizing tariff will have a course and effect avoiding a renewal of the contest between the South and the North; and that a lapse of nine or ten years will enable the manufacturers to swim without the bladders which have supported them. Many considerations favor such a prospect. — They will be saved in future much of the expense in *fixtures*, which they had to encounter, and in many instances, unnecessarily incurred. — They will be continually improving in the management of their business — They will not fail to improve occasionally on the machinery abroad — The reduction of duties on imported articles consumed by them will be equivalent to a direct bounty — There will probably be an increasing cheapness of food from the increasing redundancy of agricultural labour — There will within the experimental period be an addition of four or five millions to our population, no part or little of which will be needed for agricultural labour; and which will consequently be an extensive fund of manufacturing recruits — The current experience makes it probable, that not less than fifty or sixty thousand or more of emigrants will annually reach the United States, a large portion of whom will have been trained to manufactures and be ready for that employment.

With respect to Virginia, it is quite probable from the progress already made in the Western culture of tobacco, and the rapid exhaustion of her virgin soil in which alone it can be cultivated with a chance of profit, that of the forty or fifty thousand labourers on tobacco the greater part will be released from that employment; and be applicable to that of manufactures. It is well known that the farming system requires much fewer hands than tobacco fields.

It is painful to observe the unceasing efforts to alarm the South by imputations against the North, of unconstitutional designs on the subject of the slaves. You are right, I have no doubt, in believing, that no such intermedling disposition exists in that Body of our Northern brethren. Their good faith is sufficiently guaranteed by the interest they have as merchants, as shipowners, and as manufacturers, in preserving a union with the slaveholding States. On the other hand what madness in the South, to look for greater safety in disunion. It would be worse than jumping out of the frying pan into the fire. It would be jumping into the fire from a fear of the frying pan. The danger from the alarm is that the pride and resentment excited by them may be an overmatch for the dictates of prudence; and favor the project of a Southern Convention insidiously revived, as promising by its counsels the best securities against grievances of every sort from the North.

The case of the Tariff² and Land bills cannot fail of an influence on the question of your return to the next Session of Congress. They are both closely connected with the public repose.

LS, with subscription and signature in Madison's hand. DLC-HC (DNA, M212, R5). Printed in Colton, *Clay Correspondence*, 4:364-66 with minor variations in capitalization and punctuation. 1. Speech in Senate, Jan. 7, 1833.   2. Draft Proposal, Mid-Dec., 1832.

From Peleg Sprague, Hallowell, Maine, June 2, 1833. Reports that "your compromise bill [Draft Proposal, Mid-December, 1832] meets the approbation of the great body of the reflecting and patriotic throughout New England—and that the more it is known—the more highly it is approved and the more justly the elevated motives of its author appreciated—I am anxious that it should be understood.—and that no erroneous or unfavorable impressions should be permitted to remain, either with respect to the manner of its introduction; in the character and purposes of the measure." As for politics, notes: "There is a dead calm in politics just now in Maine—but as our annual State elections will take place in September—we shall expect some more of agitation & interest in a few weeks—What is to be the course of political events here—no one can predict—The Jackson party are now strong—and the discipline of party seems to to [*sic*] be complete—but there is much disaffection in the ranks—the cord of discipline being drawn too tightly and the practice of proscription carried into effect upon their own members—has caused heart-burnings mournings & complaints and may break out in open rebellion—at all events—we trust that the yoke is not yet securely fixed upon the necks of all—even of the members of the party—" Adds, however, that "The President is expected to visit us—his tour will be very likely to gain him friends—or at least strengthen those that he had before—" ALS. DLC-HC (DNA, M212, R5). The trend in Maine in 1833 definitely favored the Democrats. In the election to fill the Senate seat formerly held by John Holmes, Ether Shepley, a Democrat, had been elected to the U.S. Senate against Mr. Greenleaf by a vote of 123 to 70. *Niles' Register* (February 9, 1833), 43:385. Later, in the gubernatorial election, Daniel Goodenow, the National Republican, was defeated by Robert P. Dunlap, a Democart, by the vote of 25,731 to 18,112, with Samuel E. Smith, a dissident Democrat, receiving 3,024. *BDGUS*, 2:410. In elections for the U.S. House, Rufus McIntire, Francis O.J. Smith, Edward Kavanagh,

Moses Mason, Joseph Hall, Leonard Jarvis, and Gorham Parks—all Democrats—were elected, along with George Evans, a National Republican. *Guide to U.S. Elections*, 560. Jackson planned to visit Maine on his New England tour during the summer of 1833, but illness forced him to cut the trip short and return to Washington before reaching Maine. Kennebec *Journal*, June 26; July 3, 10, 1833.

From Henry Clay, Jr., Louisville, June 3, 1833. Reports that from a division of property "relinquished" by his mother-in-law [Matilda Fontaine Prather], "we have had an accession of about $10.000; and perhaps our other property has risen some $5.000 more." Notes that real property values are rising rapidly in Louisville and that he is now reluctant to sell a five-acre lot valued at $5,000 in 1832. Instead of selling it, "to pay my debts in Lexington," he feels, instead, that "I could make myself comparatively very easy if I could borrow about $10.000 at the East at 5 or 6 per cent for 5 or 6 years. I should want immediately only enough to pay the Bank what I owe it; But I should want the certainty of getting the rest by next Spring. I could easily get from 20 to 25 per cent on the investment in warehouses on a river lot or rather on a lot adjoining a river lot but lying on a cross St.   I would therefore erect several warehouses which would enable me to lease out the remainder of the lot on much better terms. I believe that with your name I could get the money that I want. If you think it would be proper to lend me your assistance in this matter, and to send on the necessary papers to Philadelphia, for which place I shall start tomorrow morning (Tuesday) I will secure you by such mortgages as you would like on my return. My means of payment will be these. Our income from property here will then be about $3.000. Our relations will perhaps have paid us about what they owe us $5500. And in the time I have mentioned (5 or 6 years) the warehouses will pay for themselves." ALS. Henry Clay Memorial Foundation, Lexington, Ky.

From Peter B. Porter, Black Rock, N.Y., June 3, 1833. Recounts some of the details of Daniel Webster's visit to the Buffalo area on May 31-June 4, noting that he has had "some political conversation" with Webster since his arrival. Concludes that Webster's "general views I think are fair, & he speaks in the most friendly terms of you, although he is evidently a little wounded about the tariff question. He will not unite with the Anti Masons, and seems to be of the opinion that we ought for the present . . . lie still and wait the movement of the waters, & that we should keep united." Copy. OHi.

To HENRY CLAY, JR.   Lexington, June 7, 1833

I recd. your favor of the 2d. inst. and was highly gratified both with the account contained of your increasing prosperity, and the cheerful tone which pervaded your letter.

You are at liberty to use my name in endeavoring to effect a loan at Philada. or N. York, and for that purpose I transmit enclosed a power of Atto. I also enclose a letter of introduction to Mr. [Nicholas] Biddle. There is difficulty in obtaining a loan upon a security so distant, and it requires address to accomplish it. You may do well to consult with your uncle [James] Brown and Mr. Biddle.

We have been greatly afflicted in Lexington with the Cholera.[1] It unequivocally demonstrated itself on the evening of the third, and by that of the sixth upwards of fifty had died. Among these, I believe you know no one but Geo. Boswell and Andw. F. Price. The panic in the town was great and many have fled from the pestilence. No part of the white family at Ashland or at the Woodlands has been yet attacked. Among the blacks at both places there were two or three suspicious cases, but none have died.

I hear from you place[2] that every thing goes on well. Billy[3] has got a hand to assist him, and I have engaged another to come the tenth, and whom I shall send there if necessary.

Present my best regards to your Uncle Brown and tell him that it is a long time since I heard from him. P.S. Mr Thomas Smith lost his Cook by the Cholera. Mr. [Samuel] Redd lost three slaves. Old Mrs. [Judith Cary Bell Gist] Scott, the widow of Genl. [Charles] Scott, is dead or expected to die.

ALS. Henry Clay Memorial Foundation, Lexington, Ky.   1. Remark in Senate, June 27, 1832.   2. Henry Clay, Jr., owned 113 acres on Henry's Mill Road in Fayette County by 1838. MacCabe, *Directory of the City of Lexington . . . 1838 & '39*, 121.   3. A slave.

From William F. Dunnica, St. Louis, June 8, 1833. Notes his authorization from Clay to pay annual taxes due on his Missouri lands, thanks him for the list of lands he owns in Missouri, and assures him that "none of your lands contained in the list you furnished me, have ever been advertised" for taxes "since they have been in my charge." ALS. DLC-TJC (DNA, M212, R14).

From Robert P. Letcher, Lancaster, Ky., June 8, 1833. Asks Clay to repay his loan of $920, noting that "I charge no interest, & will receive none." Comments on the death of Josiah S. Johnston, "one of the best men in the world [Sibley to Clay, May 22, 1833]." Has heard that Lexington had 118 deaths from cholera from the morning of June 3 to the night of June 6 [Remark in Senate, June 27, 1832]; hopes "this account is exagerated greatly." Believes he will be elected to the U.S. House [Clay to Helm, April 20, 1832] if no other candidate announces; but feels that if James Harlan [6:295] remains in the race, Thomas P. Moore will announce and win, especially if he [Letcher] were to step aside in favor of Harlan. Is convinced, however, that "if [John] Adair runs, I can still be elected with ease. He avows himself for me, if he does not offer himself, but I suppose he means *if no Jackson man runs.*" ALS. DLC-HC (DNA, M212, R5).

From Daniel Webster, Columbus, Ohio, June 10, 1833. Reports experiencing long delays on his journey because of poor weather and roads; says he will be late reaching Lexington, if he gets there at all, and urges Clay not to wait there to entertain him if he has other obligations. Concludes: "I have heard only today the dreadful account about poor [Josiah S.] Johnston [Sibley to Clay, May 22, 1833]. It is inexpressibly shocking." ALS. DLC-HC (DNA, M212, R5).

To Julia Prather Clay, Louisville, June 13, 1833. Reports the spread of cholera in Lexington [Remark in Senate, June 27, 1832], noting that "its ravages there have been frightful. I will not dwell on the painful particulars but the pestilence has no where in the U. States, been more mortal than in our afflicted City, except N. Orleans." Adds, however, that "At the Woodlands and at Ashland we have been hitherto happily exempted from any losses. We have had, principally among our blacks, some suspicious cases, but they were relieved and we are not sure that any one of them was Cholera. The day before yesterday was very bad in town, and Anne [Brown Clay Erwin] got alarmed, and the whole family at the Woodlands came over and joined us. . . . I have endeavored to rally them, and they passed a very good night and have all risen this morning quite cheerful. The intelligence from the City last evening and this morning is that the disease has considerably abated." ALS. Henry Clay Memorial Foundation, Lexington, Ky.

To JOSEPH BERRY   Lexington, June 15, 1833
The existence of the cholera in the neighborhood and the cares and anxieties to which it has given rise, have delayed my acknowledgement of the receipt of

your letter of the 27th ulto., and now I can only briefly answer it. To do so fully would require a volume. Slavery may be considered in reference to the whole Union, and to the particular states. As to the first, I think the government of the United States possesses no constitutional power to touch the subject of emancipation in any way. It may grant such or similar limited aid, in the transportation of the African race after emancipation, as has been heretofore afforded to Africa or elsewhere. This restricts the question of emancipation to each state, where slavery exists, and confines the citizens of each state to the consideration of what might be proper for their own state.

Here in Kentucky slavery is in its most mitigated form. Still it is slavery; and for one, I should be willing now, as I was thirty-four years ago, to concur in the adoption of a system of gradual emancipation. But I doubt the expediency of agitating the question at the present time. It can only be effected, first, either by making compensation to the owners, or, second, by an amendment to the constitution. The resources of this state are inadequate to the first, and I doubt whether public sentiment is yet prepared for the second. And, after all, if we were to adopt the system here, while slavery existed in the other slave states, a great deal would remain to be done.

Meantime, a sensible progress, both in Europe and America, is making toward universal emancipation; and I think we had better leave to their full operation all the favorable concurring causes now existing than to make a premature and perhaps unsuccessful effort. Public opinion alone can bring about the abolition of slavery, and public opinion is on the march. We should wait in patience for its operation without attempting measures which might throw it back.

I believe it is now certain that Great Britain will emancipate the slaves in her West Indian dependencies.[1] That fact cannot fail to exert a powerful influence in both hemispheres. If subsequently it shall be demonstrated in these dependencies that they can be as well cultivated by the hands of freemen as those of slaves, slavery will be stripped of one of its most plausible supports.

In our country colonization continues, in my opinion, to meet public patronage. It is, I admit, a slow remedy, but it is to be remembered that slavery is a chronic disease, and I believe that in such maladies speedy recovery is not expected.

I write for your own satisfaction and not for publication. . . .

Copy. Printed in the Lexington (Ky.) *Leader*, February 14, 1906. Berry was a physician residing in Sharpsburg, Bath County, Ky.   1. Clay to Wilde, April 27, 1833.

To PETER B. PORTER   Lexington, June 16, 1833

I recd. your favor of the 4h.   Mr. [Daniel] Webster has not yet arriv[ed] among us, altho' I perceive that he is in Ohio. Owing to the prevalence of the Cholera at Lexington,[1] I doubt whether he will now visit us.

That terrible scourge has raged there with uncommon violence. Its mortality has been surpassed at no point in the U. States, N. Orleans perhaps excepted. The number of victims is not accurately known, but is supposed to exceed three hundred. Among them are Dr. [Joseph] Boswell, Genl [Thomas] Bodley and his son Breckenridge, Capt. [John] Postlethwait, a sister of Dr. [Thomas] Satterwhite &c. It has considerably abated in the City, but it still wears a frightful gloom. All the stores and shops are closed, the presses stopt, and no one moving in the streets except those concerned with the dead or the sick. It has reached the Country, but is less violent there. Happily I have met with no losses in my family, nor has Mr. [James] Erwin, my son in law. I have not heard that any have died at Cabels [sic] Dale.[7] We appear to have been in the midst of death; and the firmest hearts have felt appalled. It will be a long time before our Community can recover from its afflictions.

The uncertainty of life, inculcated by all the circumstances around us, makes one hesitate as to movements some weeks ahead. I still retain the intention, however, if I escape the Cholera, of executing my tour to the North. It will delay my departure some days; and I now hope to set out between the 10h. and 15h. July; but I will keep you advised fully as to the time.

You will have seen the account of a dreadful explosin of the Steamboat Lioness near Alexandria in Louisiana, and the sacrifice of about 15 lives, among them my lamented friend J[osiah]. S. Johnston.[3] This event has filled me with grief. He was among the truest and best of friends, and I shall never cease to deplore his untimely death.

ALS. NBuHi. 1. Remark in Senate, June 27, 1832. 2. Cabell's Dale was the Breckinridge family estate where Porter's children had lived since the death of their mother Letitia Breckinridge Porter. 3. Sibley to Clay, May 22, 1833.

To DANIEL WEBSTER   Lexington, June 17, 1833

The mail brought me today your letter of the 10h. from Columbus and also intelligence of your safe arrival at Cincinnati. I had been tracing in the papers your progress with much interest.

I regret extremely that you should find us, in so many places, suffering with Cholera. Its visit to Lexington has been frightful.[1] Its mortality there has been exceeded in degree at no other point in the U.S., New Orleans perhaps excepted. The Shops and Stores and principal Hotel have been all closed: The pestilence, within the two or three last days, has considerably declined, and, in a few more, will I think have disappeared. Happily, in a family of about sixty, we have as yet sustained no loss, and are not sure that we have had one case of genuine Cholera.

I shall be mortified and disappointed if you do not visit K[entucky]. and Lexington; but I hardly know how to advise you. You will certainly go to Louisville, where there is no danger. At that place, daily intelligence is recd. from Lexington, and you can hear whether there has been such an abatement of the Cholera as to enable you to visit us without hazard. I hope the state of things will admit of your coming, and I request that you and Mr. White[2] will come directly to Ashland, and any other gentleman, if there be any other in your party, where, judging from the past, you will be secure, if the disease should even continue to prevail at Lexington. It is not at Frankfort, the principal intermediate point, and where, as every where else, your visit has been anticipated with great pleasure.

As for myself, I shall not leave home for the North until between the 10h. and 15h. July, if I go at all.

Poor [Josiah S.] Johnstons untimely fate has filled me with grief. I fear Mr. White has not survived.[3]

Favor me with a line from Louisville as to your movements. . . . P.S. I write in duplicate to Louisville & Cincinnati.

ALS. DLC-Daniel Webster Papers (DNA, M212, R22). Printed in Wiltse, *Webster Correspondence*, 3:257.   1. Remark in Senate, June 27, 1832.   2. For Stephen White, a Boston merchant and close friend of Webster's, see Wiltse, *Webster Papers*, 3:57.   3. Edward Douglass White, a congressman from Louisiana (see *BDAC*), was severely injured, not killed, in the explosion of the steamboat *Lioness* on May 19. See also Sibley to Clay, May 22, 1833.

To JAMES BROWN   Lexington, June 18, 1833

Lexington has been visited by a most violent attack of the Cholera.[1] The pestilence made its first unequivocal appearance yesterday was a fortnight, and immediately entered rapidly on the work of death. The number of victims is not accurately known but it is supposed to be not less than 300. The shops were closed, the press stopt and the City almost abandoned   No one was seen moving in the streets, except those concerned with the dead the sick and the dying. Many of the inhabitants fled from the theatre of destruction. Of these many died in their places of refuge. Coffins to bury the dead were, in numberless cases, out of the question; and it was even difficult to procure the roughest constructed boxes. Some times several corp[s]es were enclosed in one box; and I have heard that, in some instances, the black and white were interred in the same common grave. Ten or a dozen dead bodies were some times in the grave yard waiting for graves.

Within a few days past the disease has considerably abated. It extended to the Country but was happily less fatal there. We have been fortunate in not losing one. We have had, chiefly among the slaves, a number of doubtful cases, but are not sure that there was one of genuine Cholera. Mr. [James] Erwin's family has been equally spared, as have been all our immediate connexions; but we are still not without painful apprehensions. Among the dead of your acquaintance are Genl. [Thomas] Bodley, Capt. [John] Postlethwait, Dr. [Joseph] Boswell, Andw. F. Price, Mrs. [Judith Cary Bell Gist] Scott, the widow of Govr. [Charles] Scott, &c. Most of the towns that we have heard from in the State have been affected, and some in as great a degree as our's.

You will have heard of the untimely fate of poor [Josiah S.] Johnston.[2] It has filled me with grief; and I shall never cease to deplore it.

Mr. Erwin informs me that he transacted your business below in a manner that he hopes will be perfectly satisfactory to you; and that he has written to you both from N[ew]. O[rleans]. & his residence.

Living in the midst of death, I feel the uncertainty of life, and the hazard with which one should talk of movements only a few weeks ahead; but if I am spared, I shall take my Northern trip in July.

ALS. KyLxT.   1. Remark in Senate, June 27, 1832.   2. Sibley to Clay, May 22, 1833.

To THOMAS SPEED   Lexington, June 19, 1833

I duly recd. your favor of the 2d.   About the time, the Cholera broke out at Lexn. and committed the most frightful ravages.[1] The accounts you will have heard are probably not exaggerated. Hitherto my family, and that of my Son in law, Mr. [James] Erwin, have escaped; but we are not without painful apprehensions that we may not continue to enjoy this exemption.

I regret the impracticability of an arrangement by which Mr [Benjamin] Hardin or Dr. [Burr] Harrison would decline.[2] As to the place of U.S. Senator, I have not positively decided whether I shall return or not. If I go back, it will be on account of the Land bill.[3] Had that been definitively decided I should not have returned.

There is too much reason to indulge in those feelings of despondence, on account of public affairs, which you entertain. But we must not forget that it is our duty to do what we can, and trust in Providence.

Undoubtedly the existence of Slavery has an unfavorable tendency on the Union. Still I do not think it incompatible with the preservation of the Union. The States in the South (Virginia and N. Carolina) which are most sound will not concur in a Southern Confederacy. The abolition of Slavery, which now seems certain, in the B[ritish]. W[est]. India islands⁴ will render our Slave States of the South more than ever dependent on the arm of the Union. That event too, with other concurring causes, will I think make large portions of the Southern people⁵ more reasonable in listening to schemes (such as the Colonization Society) which tend to meliorate the evil of the African element in our population. It is true, that with some it may have a contrary effect.

As to the Tariff,⁶ depend upon it, that the Northern manufacturers are generally perfectly satisfied with the Compromise. Of this I have the most conclusive evidence. Nor do I think, although it may be attempted, that its essential features will be disturbed. If they should not be, we have nine years of adequate protection. At the end of that time, many branches can sustain themselves with 20 per Cent. Should the measure of protection now or then be found insufficient, it is some consolation to reflect that those parts of the Union which enjoy most of its benefits have just cause of reproach against no one but themselves.

There was one motive with me for the measure of the last Session which, of course, I could not state in debate. It was this, that the Ultra Southern men were extremely unwilling that Jackson should have any credit in the adjustment of the controversy, and to prevent it were disposed to agree to much better terms for the manufacturers, if the measure originated with any other. This disposition I plainly saw and I availed myself of it. It is perfectly clear to me that, if nothing had been done at the last Session, the Admon would have carried at the approaching Session a measure much more injurious to the Manufacturers than the Compromise bill.

My belief is that the Compromise will be sustained. There may and probably will be a struggle, at the next Session, against it, proceeding from the partizans of Mr. V. Buren, but I think it will be upheld.

I fervently wish that you may escape the terrible scourge now sweeping so destructively over our land. . . .

ALS. NhD.   1. Remark in Senate, June 27, 1832.   2. After Harrison dropped out, Benjamin Hardin of Bardstown and Dr. Christopher A. Rudd of Washington County ended up being the candidates for the 7th congressional district seat in the U.S. House. Hardin, a National Republican who had been a member of the Kentucky senate since 1827, won by a vote of 2,826 to 2,610. Rudd had lived in Bardstown in 1816 when he married Ann Palmer, and he had been a member of the Kentucky senate since 1829. See G. Glenn Clift, *Kentucky Marriages, 1797-1865* (Baltimore, 1966), 16; Collins, *History of Kentucky*, 2:645, 749; *Guide to U.S. Elections*, 560.   3. Comment in Senate, Jan. 7; Dec. 5, 1833; Clay to Wilde, April 27, 1833.   4. Clay to Wilde, April 27, 1833.   5. Phrase "portion of the Union" struck through and "people" word substituted.   6. Draft Proposal, Mid-Dec., 1832; Speech in Senate, Feb. 12, 25, 1833.

From Daniel Webster, Chillicothe, Ohio, June 22, 1833. Announces that he has given up the Kentucky portion of his journey because "even tho' I felt no fear about personal safety" in the cholera epidemic [Remark in Senate, June 27, 1832], he did not relish visiting "those, whom I wished to see" in Kentucky either in a state of "alarm or in affliction." Hopes Clay will not give up his proposed visit to the North. ALS. ICU. Printed in Colton, *Clay Correspondence*, 4:336-37; and in Wiltse, *Webster Papers*, 3:258-59.

To JULIA PRATHER CLAY   Lexington, June 23, 1833

Thinking it possible that you may not have heard as late from Henry [Clay, Jr.] as the date of the enclosed, I transmit it to you. It appears that you may very soon expect him.

We continue at Ashland and at the Woodlands exempt from any serious case of Cholera.[1] It has also much abated in Lexn. altho' now and then a case occurs. Mean time, it has broken out at Paris and Lancaster with dreadful violence. At the former place 27 deaths occurred in a short time; and at the latter from 15 to 20. The whole village of Lancaster, horse foot and dragoon, with few exceptions, marched off. In one instance, the entire family deserted their house, leaving its head dead & unburied.

I am afraid that Louisville will hardly escape; and if you are in a movable condition, I wish on Henry's return that you would come to us, with Mrs. [Matilda Fontaine] Prather and any of the family that will join you. After it has totally disappeared from Lexn. (which we may now hope will be the case in a few days) it will, I think, be one of the safest places of refuge in the State.

ALS. Henry Clay Memorial Foundation, Lexington, Ky. Addressed to Mrs. Henry Clay, Jr., in Louisville.   1. Remark in Senate, June 27, 1832.

To PETER B. PORTER   Lexington, July 2, 1833

The Cholera continues to rage among us.[1] It has not even yet disappeared from Lexington, although it is now upwards of a month since it first broke out there. Yesterday there were several deaths. Among others a favorite servant of a niece of mine who was well in the morning & was in her grave before night.[2] It has committed terrible havoc among my friends and acquaintances. Captain [John] Postlethwait, Genl. [Thomas] Bodley, his son John Breckenridge, Dr. [Joseph] Boswell, and Andw. F. Price &c. &c. are among the dead. Near five hundred in Lexington alone have died. Mean time the Pestilence is sweeping most of our villages and is spreading in the Country. Its proportionate mortality has been as great on some of the farms as in Lexington. It is all around me. We have had a number of cases in my family which we feared would terminate in Cholera, but which were relieved. As late as yesterday we had two. Hitherto we have lost no one. But, considering that I have a family of about sixty, can I count upon this exemption continuing?

The loss of friends; the continuance of the scourge; the apprehensions that it might break out in my family, during my absence; and the risk of encountering it in the villages through which I might pass in Ohio and elsewhere, have determined me reluctantly to abandon this summer my contemplated journey. You can well conceive what would be my solicitude respecting my family, if I were distant from them, and how I should reproach myself if I were to lose any of them. The prompt attention which I have heretofore bestowed on the first indication of disease, has probably saved some who were sick; and it is possible that I may escape loss by similar attention. It seems to me therefore that both duty to my family and my personal safety enjoin my remaining here. I regret extremely both the cause and the effect; for I had promised myself much pleasure from a journey which I long have wished to perform and which I hope now is only postponed. Mr. Webster was compelled to abandon his visit to Kentucky. He returned after reaching Cincinnati.

The Cholera has, I think, been aggravated by the extraordinary wet spell of near two months continuance which we have had. The greater number of

654

days, during that period, have been rainy; and I never knew the earth so completely saturated with water as it has been and yet is. We have had no season
for harvest nor for making Hay. We shall lose a great portion of our small
grain, but our Corn Crop, which you know is our great staple, is very promising.

I have not spirits now to say one word on public affairs, about which I will
write you hereafter. . . .

ALS. NBuHi. 1. Remark in Senate, June 27, 1832. 2. Caroline, servant of Nanette Price
Smith. See Clay to Henry Clay, Jr., July 7, 1833.

To SAMUEL T. BEALL   Lexington, July 4, 1833

The abatement of the Cholera, which had raged so violently at Lexington, has
at length left us a little leisure to think of public affai[rs]. I have seen, with
much satisfaction, that the contest in your District is reduced to one on each
side, Mr. [Benjamin] Hardin, on that of the N. Republic[ans] and Dr.
[Christopher A.] Rudd of the Jackson party.[1] I know that the Doctor
profess[es] to be with us, but what are professions opposed to conduct? If
elected, by the uncontrollable force of circumstances, he must act with the
Jackson party, and ultimately will lend himself to the support of V. Buren. It
cannot be otherwise with one who has lost the confidence of his own party, and
has done all that he could to advance the interests of the other.

The next Congress will present many subjects of great importance to the
public, among which the Public Lands, the Bank, and the preservation unimpaired of the Tariff of the las[t] Session, stand pre-em[ine]nt. On all these subjects, the services of Mr. Hardin will be highly useful. He is admirably
qualified fo[r] the state of things at Washington, and I know of no one th[at]
we could send from this State more likely to promote the publ[ic] interests on
all those questions. On public grounds, therefore, so[lely,] I feel much
solicitude for his success.

Your friendship, which I highly value, will appreciate the motives of these
suggestions justly.

I sincerely hope that you may escape the horrible sco[urge] which has
scattered so many afflictions in our quarter.[2]

ALS. Courtesy of Dr. Robert M. Fort, Frankfort, Ky. For Beall, see 5:557-58. 1. Clay to
Speed, June 19, 1832. 2. Remark in Senate, June 27, 1832.

To William B. Calhoun et al., Springfield, Mass., July 5, 1833. Regrets that he cannot
accept their invitation to visit Springfield during a journey he had planned to make to
New England this summer. Explains that he has postponed his trip because of the
cholera epidemic in Lexington [Remark in Senate, June 27, 1832]. ALS. MS.

To THOMAS C. PATRICK   Lexington, July 5, 1833

I received your letter dated the 17h. and post marked the 25h. June communicating an account of the Sales of Stock &c at Terre Haute.[1] By this time, I suppose a man has called on you, for the Cattle not sold, agreeably to my directions.

I am anxious now to close the matter of Thomas's [Thomas Hart Clay]
debts and the Stock and farming utensils as soon as practicable; and I will
thank you to inform me what debts have been paid &c. It will be well, where
you can do it, to assign notes which you took at the sale, in payment of such
debts as you know to be just.

I wish also an account of the horses &c on hand and undisposed of, and of the Cattle you delivered to my order. I observe you did not sell Adventurer. How are his colts? Are they good? If you are satisfied, you may keep him for one half of what he earns until I otherwise direct. Did you sell any of the Colts of Kitty Clover, James's mare?

I am glad to hear of the good prospects of your Corn Crop. If you can always plant as early as you have done this year, there will be no danger of frost. Our Crop is also very promising. There has been great affliction at Lexington and in this neighbourhood with the Cholera.[2] More than four hundred have died in that City with it. Although I have near Sixty in family, hitherto we have been so far blessed as to have lost not one. But my apprehensions will not cease, until the Pestilence entirely disappears.

Let me hear from you as soon as you receive this letter.

ALS. InHi. Addressed to Patrick at "near Clinton, Indiana."   1. Porter Clay to Clay, July 21, 1833.   2. Remark in Senate, June 27, 1832.

To Henry Clay, Jr., Louisville, July 6, 1833. Reports that "Lexington is now almost entirely clear of Cholera [Remark in Senate, June 27, 1832]," and that the family of Anne Brown Clay Erwin, as well as his own, "continue healthy, and exempt from the Pestilence." ALS. Henry Clay Memorial Foundation, Lexington, Ky.

To JAMES BROWN   Lexington, July 7, 1833
I recd. your favor of the 28h. Ulto.   A few stragling cases of Cholera[1] only continue in Lexn.   Last monday Mr. Tho[mas]. Smith lost a female servant [Caroline], a favorite of Nanettes [Price Smith], and the second they have lost. On wednesday Mr. C[harlton]. Hunt lost his Cook, and some three or four other cases occurred during the week. The weather has been very fine for the last five or six days and I hope will contribute to extinguish the Pestilence. My family and that of Mr. [James] Erwin happily continue without any loss.

But the death of friends; the apprehension that the malady might break out in my family, in my absence; and the possibility of encountering it on my journey, have determined me to give up my contemplated trip to Niagara and the North.

Henry [Clay, Jr.] has returned to Louisville where Julia [Prather Clay] expects an increase of family this month. He is apprehensive that you might regard as unkind his failure to call on you, as you expected, prior to his departure from Philada; but he hurried away, in consequence of his great fears for his K[entucky]. connexions.

The abolition of Slavery, on which the British Governmt. appears to be resolved in the W. Indies,[2] will exert a moral influence on that institution in the U. States; but I do not apprehend any immediate effects from it. All have looked forward to some distant period when it would cease in the U. States; but I think it will not happen in our time. The emancipation of slaves in the W. Indies will induce the Southern Slaveholder to be more sensitive to the slightest disturbance of the question; and the influences in the North, which favor emancipation, are not those of interest, but of humanity or of fanaticism. The North is probably interested in the continuance of Southern slavery. At all events, it knows well the dangerous tendency of an attempt there to effect emancipation; and its leading politicians stand committed upon the subject.

ALS. ViU.   1. Remark in Senate, June 27, 1832.   2. Clay to Wilde, April 27, 1833.

To HENRY CLAY, JR.   Lexington, July 7, 1832

I was glad to learn from your letter of the 4h. that the health of Louisville and of your family and connexions continued good, and sincerely hope that it may remain so.

Our health here and at Mr. [James] Erwin's[1] also remains good. It is greatly improved in Lexington; but, now and then, a straggling case of Cholera occurs there.[2] On monday last Mr. T[homas]. Smith lost Caroline, a favorite servant of Nanette [Price Smith]. On wednesday Mr. C[harlton] Hunt lost his cook, and there have been one or two other deaths during the week. The weather is now dry, clear and fine, and I hope will contribute to the restoration of health.

It is now time to prepare for cutting your timothy, and you have said nothing to me about it. Our hands are so full here that I regret I cannot have it done for you. Mr. Erwin has engaged Genl [James] Shelby to have his meadow mowed, and he begins tomorrow.[3] If I can get him afterwards to cut your's I shall do so unless you otherwise direct. Your grass is wasting in your woods, and unless you have some stock to put there, I will send four or five head, if you have no objection. . . .

ALS. Henry Clay Memorial Foundation, Lexington, Ky.   1. "Woodlands," the Erwin summer home in Lexington.   2. Remark in Senate, June 27, 1832.   3. Clay to Henry Clay, Jr., July 14, 1833.

From Ralph Osborn, Columbus, Ohio, July 12, 1833. Says he will handle the payment of "something short of $5" of annual tax on Clay's land. Adds: "I regretted to hear that your Town suffered so severly from the Cholera [Remark in Senate, June 27, 1832]; from that solem warning I think the Inhabitants of every Town in our Country however remote from the seat of the disease, and however healthy in general such Town may be, ought to prepare by distance otherwise to meet; the same with resignation and fortitude and not flee from the place of its attack — our Town is healthy." ALS. DLC-TJC (DNA, M212, R14). For Osborn, see 2:723.

To HENRY CLAY, JR.   Lexington, July 14, 1833

The enclosed letter was recd. at the P. office for you.

Not hearing from you on the subject of your Hay, as I intimated in a former letter[1] I would do, I engaged ten mowers of Genl. [James] Shelby for two days at a dollar a piece. To these some of my own and of Mr. [James] Erwins were added. And the day before yesterday (friday morning) we began work. We left off last night, having cut both your lots, and stacked all in that which is next to the garden, and cocked all in the other lot so as to secure it from rain. There never were finer days for making hay, and your's is put in admirable order. After I have secured my own harvest, I will send some hands to assist Billy in completing the stacking.

Your mother, Anne [Brown Clay Erwin], Mr. Erwin and all the children, and Mrs. [Nanette Price] Smith &c. went with me to your place, where we dined the two days upon an excellent day [*sic*]. The meats were dressed at Ashland and Billy supplied us with a variety of excellent vegetables. We passed the time quite agreeably.

Your corn is clean and laid by, and the garden is in very good order. Billy is a very good faithful servant, and we all concluded that you had better purchase the family, altho' the price is high.

The Cholera[2] has, I believe, disappeared from Lexn.   Here and at the Woodlands all are well.   Our love to Julia [Prather Clay]

ALS. Henry Clay Memorial Foundation, Lexington, Ky.   1. Clay to Henry Clay, Jr., July 7, 1833.   2. Remark in Senate, June 27, 1832.

From Porter Clay, Frankfort, July 21, 1833. Reports that arrangements to sell off the cattle from Clay's farm near Paris, Illinois, have been made [Clay to Patrick, July 5, 1833], and that "I am fearfull you will not realize as much from your cattle as was anticapated." Says he is going out to Morgan County, Ill., in late August and while there "will transact any business for you in my Power." Believes that speculative opportunities in land abound in Morgan and Sangamon counties, and suggests Clay accompany him on his journey to "that country." Concludes: "amidst the ravages of the Awfull scourge [Remark in Senate, June 27, 1832] we should be thankfull we have been mercifully preserved, 15 deaths have taken place within one mile of our farm and on every side side [*sic*] some — yet not one of our family have had even the premonary symtoms this surely can be nothing else than a providential interposition in our behalf the family consists of 24 in number black & white the Lord grant you an equal instance of distinguishing favour and money I beg Jesus sake." ALS. DLC-TJC (DNA, M212, R10).

On July 24, 1833, Clay wrote John J. Hardin in Jacksonville, Morgan County, Ill., authorizing him to sell the cattle (two bulls, three cows, and two calves) at whatever they will bring. Adds that "I should be glad to invest the Cattle or their proceeds in good land in the neighbourhood of my brothers, or indeed any where in Morgan; and if it would facilitate the investment I would add five or six hundred dollars in Cash." ALS. ICHi. For Hardin, see *DAB* and *BDAC*.

On February 11, 1834, Clay again wrote Hardin, thanking him for having sold off the cattle and instructing him to invest the proceeds in a section or half-section of Morgan County, Ill., public land. Reports that the outcome of the struggle the anti-Jackson forces are making "for our Country" in Congress is "uncertain," because "In the House we fear there is a majority for sustaining the Executive [Whittlesey to Clay, September 19, 1832]." Wishes Hardin's father, Martin Davis Hardin (see *BDAC*), had lived to assist in the struggle. *Ibid.*

From Buckner H. Payne, Mt. Sterling, Ky., July 22, 1833. Reports that he and his wife have survived cholera attacks and notes that "Some parts [of] our county [Montgomery] are still suffering from the disease — The town is healthy [Remark in Senate, June 27, 1832]." Has learned that "Stamboul has served between 80 and ninety mares only this season inclusive of those that missed last season." Believes "that with his fall season, he will be able to obtain about 100 altogether, as we know of several mares which would have been to him but the Cholera, has prevented their being sent heretofore. His Colts are uncommonly fine, and such are the voluntary testimonials which have been received." Asks if it is Clay's intention definitely to have Stamboul stand "next season in Lexington." Asks also "whether any indulgence will be extended by the Branch Bank in Lexington to their debtors in consequence of the great stagnation of business by the prevailing epidemic — If you can give me any idea of the course the Bank may have resolved upon I will thank you —" ALS. Courtesy of M.W. Anderson, Lexington, Ky. No "indulgence" was extended to debtors by the bank as a consequence of the cholera epidemic. On the contrary, because of the necessity of making a payment in Europe on October 1, Biddle ordered a curtailment of loans throughout the B.U.S. system and directed the western and southern offices to refrain from all purchases and sales of exchange that did not concentrate funds in the Northeast where the payments would be made. Govan, *Nicholas Biddle*, 209-12.

To EDMUND H. PENDLETON   Lexington, July 22, 1833

I am desirous of procuring some full blooded Saxony Sheep, and as Dutchess [County] is celebrated for the number as well as the excellence of its Sheep, I take the liberty of addressing an inquiry to you. I should like to get 20 Saxony sheep, and will thank you to inform me if they can be procured in your County, at what prices and of whom? I understand that Mr. Davis[1] is the most successful of your farmers with Sheep, and perhaps he could supply them. I wish their genuiness to be indisputable.

We have been dreadfully scourged in K. with the Cholera.[2] My own family has been however signally blessed, as out of fifty or sixty, black and white, we have not lost one. The apprehension that we may be yet visited with the Pestilence has induced me to abandon the journey to the North which I contemplated this summer. . . .

ALS. NHi. Addressed to Pendleton in Hyde Park, Dutchess Co., N.Y. For Pendleton, see *BDAC.*   1. Probably John Livingston Davis, a farmer in eastern Dutchess County, where most of the county's sheep-raising was centered.   2. Remark in Senate, June 27, 1832.

To HENRY CLAY, JR.   Lexington, July 23, 1833

On my return from a visit to your place today, I received in town your agreeable letter of the 21st inst. containing intelligence which we were anxiously expecting. We most cordially felicitate you and our dear Julia [Prather Clay] on her safe delivery, and, not on that happy event merely, but that your first born should be a son.[1] And then, if we are to credit your account of him, so "noble a boy." We sincerely pray that they may both continue to do well, which we do not doubt they will, considering that they are in such good hands, and that the season of the year is so favorable to parturation. Tell Julia to make haste and get able to bring her prize here that we, as well as her Louisville friends, may have the satisfaction of seeing and caressing it. In regard to its name, I shall certainly feel flattered if mine is given to it, although I presume I should have to share the compliment with another. I should be most happy if the future fame of the new born should transcend any which his grandfather may have acquired.

I found all things looking well at your place. Billy was out in quest of turnip seed. Some of the walks were strewed with fruit. I have not yet been able to have the residue of your hay stacked up, owing to the pressure of my own harvest, a great part of which lies in the fields. I hope towards the last of this week that we shall be able to have your's, which has not suffered, permanently secured.

The health of all of us here and at the Woodlands continues good; and that of the town generally is excellent. In some neighbourhoods in the Country, the bloody flux has succeeded the Cholera,[2] and has proved fatal.

Give the love of your mother and myself to Julia, and kiss the little stranger for us.

ALS. Henry Clay Memorial Foundation, Lexington, Ky.   1. Henry Clay, III (1833-1862). 2. Remark in Senate, June 27, 1832.

To EDWARD EVERETT   Lexington, July 23, 1833

I duly recd. your letter of the 12h. inst. and feel grateful for the friendly solicitude concerning my health which it envinces. We have indeed had a terrible time of it at Lexington, and in other parts of K. with the Cholera.[1] The accounts which have reached you are probably not much exaggerated. But I have reason to be thankful for the signal exemption from loss with which we have been blessed. In a family of about sixty, white and black, we have had no death. And the connexions both of Mrs. Clay and myself have been generally equally fortunate. My daughter, Mrs. [Anne Brown Clay] Erwin, my nearest neighbour, has escaped the scourge with her entire family. And a letter from my brother [Porter Clay], received this day,[2] informs me that in his family, near Frankfort, consisting of about 24 there has not been a single death, nor even a case of premonitory symptoms, whilst they were dying all around him, as they were near me.

It was after the Pestilence had broken out that I received the distressing intelligence of the ultimely fate of our friend [Josiah S.] Johnston.[3] It filled me with grief. Great as I felt and deplored the loss of those around me, his struck deeper and gave me a more incurable wound. I can never cease to lament his fate, and the loss of an inestimable friend. The public has reason to regret being deprived of one of its most useful patriotic and honorable servants. And how will his unfortunate wife [Eliza Sibley Johnston] be able to sustain so heavy an affliction? The most indulgent of husbands, she must find the change in her condition insupportable.

The apprehension that the Cholera might visit my family in my absence determined me to abandon my Northern journey, from which I had anticipated so much satisfaction. I regret it extremely, but you will readily conceive how painful my situation would have been if, when distant from my residence, I had heard that it was here.

I am greatly obliged by the kind attentions of yourself and other friends to my little son [James Brown Clay].[4] I am sometimes afraid that he may be spoiled by the civilities which are showered upon him. . . .

ALS. MHi.   1. Remark in Senate, June 27, 1832.   2. Porter Clay to Clay, July 21, 1833.
3. Sibley to Clay, May 22, 1833.   4. Clay to Henry Clay, Jr., Dec. 30, 1832.

To FRANCIS T. BROOKE

Lexington, August 2, 1833

I duly recd. your favor of the 20h. Ulto. and take great pleasure in transmitting an account of the remedy most successfully applied in the treatment of the Cholera in Lexington.[1] I send you herewith a number of the Western Journal, which contains an article bringing into review almost all that has been written on the subject of the Scourge. The description and treatment of the disease by Mr. J. Kennedy (the first work reviewed) resemble most the appearance of it here, and accord best with the most approved practice.[2]

From all that I saw and heard about it here I have dawn these conclusions:

1st. That certain reliance can be placed upon no remedy after the disease has reached the state of collapse and cramps.

2. That prior to that state no sure reliance can be placed on any treatment which does not embrace the use of Calomel in moderate doses.

3. That if the disease commence, as it generally does, by a complaint in the bowels, Calomel, in doses of from 5 to 25 grains taken every hour or two, until the discharge from the bowels is checked may be relied upon with a high degree of certainty.

If there be considerable discharges from the bowels opium in the proportion of one grain to every ten of Calomel, or 15 or 20 grains of laudanum were advantageously given with the Calomel.

660

The use of emetics and bleeding was much controverted. I believe them both good in certain cases and they were both occasionally resorted to with benefit, 'though I think neither indispensable. In the early stages of the disease only, and when the disease has not assumed what Mr. Kennedy calls the rapid type, would it be advisable to employ the emetic. Epicac: Salt & mustard, and warm salt & water were all used. We had among our slaves a number of cases of violent pain in the abdomen which we feared might terminate in Cholera. In most of them we administered Salt & mustard in equal proportions (about a table spoonful of each forming a dose, which was however repeated until vomiting ensued) and after the operation, twenty grains of Calomel combined with 20 grains of Rhubarb. All of them were relieved. The same remedy with the same success was employed at Mr. [James] Erwin's, and at a Bagging factory in the City.

The attack made upon Dr. [Benjamin W.] Dudleys practice was in consequence of his use of the emetic, and I think was unfounded.

Some of our Physicians employed enormous doses of Calomel, but I believe with no advantage.

I send you a letter I recd. from Dr. [Boyd] McNairy containing an account of his practice, which I understand was very successful.

Most sincerely do I hope that you may not have occasion for the application of any remedy whatever to this terrible disease. It still rages with great violence in some parts of our State.

You seem to think that I despond as to our public affairs. If you mean that I have less confidence than I formerly entertained in the virtue and intelligence of the people, and in the stability of our institutions, I regret to be obliged to own it. Are we not governed now, and have we not been for some time past, pretty much by the will of one man [Andrew Jackson]? And do not large masses of the people, perhaps, a majority, seem disposed to follow him wherever he leads? Through all his inconsistencies? He does not, it is true, always govern positively, by enforcing the measures which he prefers; but he prevents those, altho' adopted by the representatives of the people, to which he is opposed, and although manifestly for their good, they acquiesce in or applaud whatever he does, and take sides with him against the Legislative authority. If that single man were an enlightened philosopher, and a true patriot, the popular sanction which is given to all his acts, however inconsistent and extravagant, might find some justification; but when we consider that he is ignorant, passionate, hypocritical, corrupt, and easily swayed by the baset men who surround him, what can we think of the popular approbation which he receives?

One thing only is wanted to complete the public degradation, and that is that he should name his successor. This he has done,[3] and there is much reason to believe that the people will ratify the nomination. Although that successor [Van Buren] may be now, in some places, unpopular, when we reflect that the whole patronage of the Government will for three years be directed to ensure his success; and that a system of organization exists in the largest State of the Union, wielding about 1/7h. of the whole Electoral vote, the probability of his final success must be admitted to be great. To these chances we have to add others. In the South, it is now pretty evident, that you are about to re-enact the scenes of 1824, when, under a romantic notion of adhering to your

Candidate, you threw away your votes upon Mr. [William H.] Crawford, a paralytic, although it was perfectly notorious that he stood no earthly chance of being elected. Now, under the erroneous idea that other parts of the Union contemplate an attack upon your Slave property, and with the purpose of adhering to what are called *your* principles, Mr. [John C.] Calhoun, or some body else, will be brought out and a great effort will be made to rally the South in his support. The contest will be between him and Mr. V.B. The latter aided by the dominant party in Virginia may secure that State. But it will so turn out that, whatever votes the Southern Candidate may get, will serve Mr. V.B. almost as effectually as if given directly to himself; because they will be so many abstracted from some other more formidable competitor. Thus, by the operation of the instruments now in full employment to secure his election, and by the divisions of those opposed to him, he will obtain the majority, or enter the H. of R. with a resistless plurality.

His election once secured, the corrupt means of preserving and perpetuating power, now in successful operation at Albany will be transfered to Washington. And then we shall have a state of things which will prepare the public mind, for a dissolution of the Union, to which, unfortunately, there is less aversion now than could be wished by those who love their Country.

I hope I may be deceived in these predictions, but I fear that I am not. Believing in them, you can not be surprized that, at the age of 56, and after the struggles which I have made to maintain the public liberty, and to avert the evils which now menace us, — struggles, I repeat, in which I have been too little sustained, — I should think seriously of a final retirement from the theatre of public life.

My daughter [Anne Brown Clay Erwin] was happy to find herself in your friendly recollection, and desires me to assure you of her cordially reciprocating your esteem. She is very happy, possessed of the affections of her husband [James], residing upon a beautiful place ["Woodlands"] adjoining mine, and enjoying affluence and every blessing. . . .

ALS. KyU. Copy in DLC-TJC (DNA, M212, R14); printed in Colton, *Clay Correspondence*, 4:367-70.   1. Remark in Senate, June 27, 1832.   2. James Kennedy, "Epidemic Cholera: An Eclectic, Miscellaneous and Clinical Review," *Western Journal of Medical and Physical Sciences* (April, May, June, 1833), 7:44-49. *The Western Journal* was edited by Dr. Daniel Drake in Cincinnati. For Dr. James Kennedy, a British surgeon who observed cholera in India, see *DNB*.   3. Brooke to Clay, Feb. 9, 1832; Clay to Porter, March 10, 1832.

To James Madison, "Montpelier," Orange County, Va., August 8, 1833. Strongly recommends Dr. Daniel Drake [3:448] for the professorship at the University of Virginia vacated by the resignation of Prof. Robley Dunglison. ALS. WM. Dr. Dunglison, a native of Glasgow, Scotland, taught anatomy at the University of Virginia. When he left Virginia to teach at the University of Maryland, he was succeeded by Alfred T. Magill, the son-in-law of Henry St. George Tucker. Bruce, *History of the University of Virginia*, 1:371; 2:172-73.

From William F. Dunnica, St. Louis, August 21, 1833. Explains to Clay the Missouri law pertaining to non-residents not having to register their Missouri lands for tax assessment purposes. Forwards receipt for tax [$2.18] paid on Clay's land in Cape Girardeau County, and notes that he has recently purchased 160 acres in Chariton County "agreeably to your request." ALS. DLC-TJC (DNA, M212, R14).

On September 14, 1833, Clay responded to this letter, pointing out that he was probably not the owner of the 640 acres in Cape Girardeau. "I expect it is one of several tracts which as Exor of Col. [James] Morrison I had bought at Sheriffs sale as the property of Mr. J[ames]. Morrison, and which I have since relinquished." Copy. KyU.

To James Brown, Philadelphia, September 8, 1833. Has heard from Dr. Nathaniel Chapman of Brown's "severe attack" on August 30 but hopes that all is now well. Announces that he will leave Lexington and "proceed directly to you in Philadelphia" as soon as Anne Brown Clay Erwin "is confined, which is expected in eight or ten days." ALS. ViU.

To Edmund H. Pendleton, Dutchess County, N.Y., September 9, 1833. Orders ten ewes and one ram of "pure Saxon blood" from the flock of Mr. Grove; says he will soon remit the price of $220, and points out that he will want the sheep delivered in Baltimore. Adds in postscript: "I will thank you to ask Mr. Grove, at my expence, to have a brand of C. put on the sheep—a precaution which may be necessary to guard against fraudulent exchanges on the road." ALS. NHi.

On September 21, 1833, Clay wrote Pendleton again, repeating the order, enclosing a check for $225 ("the excess of five dollars being to cover any little expences"), and asking that the sheep be "transported either by the Steamboats or by land or both as may be deemed best" to Baltimore by October 10 or 12. Concludes: "As a brother farmer, I hope you will excuse the trouble I have given you in this sheepish business." *Ibid.*

On October 15, 1833, Pendleton wrote Clay at the American Hotel, Broadway, New York, enclosing a bill of sale from Grove and noting that "The expenses of the Sheep, which include those of a man going to Albany & returning thence to New York & back to Dutchess County [N.Y.] are $17.75." ALS. Josephine Simpson Collection, Lexington, Ky.

On November 29, 1833, Clay paid Erskine, Eichelberger & Co. of Baltimore $91.21. This covered the wages of a shepherd, maintenance of the sheep on the road, and steamboat freight costs between Boston and Baltimore. Account and Receipt. DLC-TJC (DNA, M212, R17).

To Anne Brown Clay Erwin, Lexington, Ky., September 10, 1833. Conveys to his daughter for the sum of "five shillings" a parcel of land near Lexington, containing "one hundred and twenty five acres and fifteen perches," which he had purchased on May 2, 1833, from Fredcrick and Sally Montmollin [3:509]. Copy. Courtesy of Mrs. Jessie E. Anderson, Kansas City, Mo. Reproduced from Fayette County Deed Book 9, p. 188.

From Buckner H. Payne, Mt. Sterling, Ky., September 14, 1833. Reports that gentlemen in Mason County who intended to send "about 20 or 25 mares to Stamboul" were unable to do so because of the cholera outbreak [Remark in Senate, June 27, 1832] there. Asks to keep Stamboul until fall so that he can be sent up to Mason to stand at stud. Reports that the "payments this season, (originating from what Cause I can not say with certainty) have fallen so far short of what they did last Season, that I have never thought it worth while to pay over as yet the dividends, still hoping we may make such collections, as will at least be some little evidence of our faithfulness—" ALS. DLC-TJC (DNA, M212, R14).

To William Martin: Memorandum, Lexington, September 20, 1833. Detailed instructions to Clay's overseer on the management of "Ashland" for the coming eight months. Instructions include which fields to plant, when to plant them, and with what crops; which animals to wean and/or move to new pasturage; which animals and what farm produce to buy and sell; fields to be cleared; timber to be cut; and those of his slaves (six in number: named) to be hired out during the coming year, at an annual lease rate of $80 to $110 plus food and lodging. ADS. Courtesy of J. Winston Coleman, Jr. Printed in James F. Hopkins (ed.), "Henry Clay, Farmer and Stockman," *JSH* (February, 1949), 15:91-96. The memorandum occupies pp. 91-95.

To Christopher Hughes, Baltimore, September 24, 1833. Notes the safe arrival of Hughes back in the United States. Says he plans to be in Baltimore "in about three weeks" and looks forward to seeing him there. Explains that he is expecting "22 Saxon sheep" at Baltimore between the 5th and 12th of October [Clay to Pendleton, September 9, 1833], and asks Hughes to keep an eye on them. ALS. MiU-C.

To JAMES BROWN   Baltimore, October 8, 1833

With myself, Mrs. Clay, my son John [Morrison Clay], and Henry C. Duralde left home on the 26h. Ulto. I parted from them on the day before yesterday, this side of Cumberland [Md.], to accelerate my arrival here. They will join me here[1] the day after tomorrow, and it is our purpose to proceed on friday next to Philada.

I was rejoiced the day before I left home to receive a letter from Mr. Ingersoll[2] assuring me that your health was almost entirely re-established. I sincerely pray that the progress of your recovery may have been unchecked, and that we shall find you perfectly well.

Should our hopes about you be realized, we shall stop only a day or two in Philada. and proceed on to Boston. Otherwise we shall send for James [Brown Clay] to meet us in Philada.

I am happy to inform you that on my arrival here this morning I recd. a letter from Mr. [James] Erwin communicating that agreeable fact that my dear daughter [Anne Brown Clay Erwin] was delivered of a Son[3] on the morning of the 2d. inst.

ALS. ViU.   1. While in Baltimore the Clay party stayed at Barnum's hotel where their bill for the period Oct. 8 to 11, for the four whites and their two "servants," was $33.43 ¾. Account, dated Oct. 11, 1833. D. DLC-TJC (DNA, M212, R10).   2. Probably Charles Ingersoll. 3. This child, unnamed, was either stillborn or died quite soon after birth.

From John Trumbull, James Kent *et al.,* New York, October 11, 1833. Invite Clay to a public dinner when he reaches New York City. Copy. NHi.

Responding to Trumbull and Kent from Philadelphia on October 12, Clay declined the dinner invitation, but acknowledged his willingness to meet personally with any of New York's "inhabitants who may desire to see me." *Ibid.*

Similarly, while in Baltimore on October 9, he turned down an invitation to a public dinner there, remarking that he would be pleased to accept instead "any other less formal mode of social intercourse" with the citizens of Baltimore. Tiernan to Clay, October 8, 1833. Copy. Printed in Lexington *Observer & Kentucky Reporter,* October 24, 1833. Clay to Tiernan, October 9, 1833. *Ibid.*

Writing from Providence, R.I., on October 12, Joseph L. Tillinghast invited Clay to a public dinner there at which his advocacy of the "true system of American Policy" would especially be honored. ALS. RHi. Clay declined with thanks, noting that the prosperity of Providence could be attributed to American resources and skills "rather than dependence upon foreign supplies." Clay to Tillinghast, October 10 [*sic,* 18], 1833. Copy. Printed in Lexington *Observer & Kentucky Reporter,* November 7, 1833.

While in Providence, Clay was elected to honorary membership in the Philormenian Society of Brown University. Clay to Silas Bailey, October 21, 1833. AL. RPB.

Learning that Clay intended to visit Providence on October 19, Bradford Durfee *et al.,* wrote him from Fall River, Mass., on that date inviting him to attend a public dinner in Fall River, "the second Manufacturing village in business and population in the New-England states," and promising that "A Steam Boat will be in readiness to convey you to Fall River and back at any time you may designate." Copy. KyU. Clay answered Durfee on October 19, declining the Fall River invitation. ALS. *Ibid.*

On October 22, writing from Boston, Clay also declined an invitation from T.H. Perkins and others to attend a public dinner at Faneuil Hall there. He explained that he must adhere to his rule not to engage in such public political activities [Clay to Erwin, October 13, 1833]; but he noted that "as my sojourn here will be extended to a week or two, I shall, I trust, have many and various opportunities of mixing with my fellow Citizens of Boston, in an unreserved and social manner which best comports with my feelings and disposition." ALS. KyLoF.

Writing to Edward Everett from Boston on October 23, however, he agreed to visit with the citizens of nearby Charlestown, Mass., on October 28 and there join them in viewing "the spot where one of the most memorable battles for American liberty was gallantly fought." ALS. MHi. While in Boston, Clay also declined invitations to visit Portland, Maine, and Marblehead, Mass. Clay to J. Wingate, October 22, 1833. Copy. Printed in Lexington *Observer & Kentucky Reporter*, November 7, 1833. Clay to William B. Adams, October 30, 1833. Ibid.

On November 8, 1833, Clay declined an invitation from a committee of citizens of New Haven to visit that Connecticut city. *Ibid.*, November 21, 1833.

To JAMES ERWIN   Philadelphia, October 13, 1833

We arrived here last evening; and I found several letters from you (the last dated the 6h.) putting us much at ease about Anne [Brown Clay Erwin].[1] I think she has wisely decided against going to N. Orleans this winter, presuming as I do that she has stipulated for as short an absence from you as possible.

I am taken possession of, wherever I go, in spite of my remonstrances.[2] Here they met me on the Mary land shore, and crowds at the landing. Lodgings and every luxury are provided for us at public expence. Two Committees from New York, besides various others, are attending upon me. I decline all public dinners, but see in other modes all who call on me. We leave here on the morning of the 15h. intending to proceed to Boston, with as little delay as practicable, and return as soon as we can to this place.

We found Mr. [James] Brown entirely recovered from the attack, tho' feeble from the medicine which he took. He looks delicate, but otherwise well. His voice is clear. He observes a strict regimen, and if he can persevere in it may live yet some years.

The Saxon sheep will be at Balto. in a few days.[3] I think I shall purchase [John] Rodgers' Jack at $1000.[4] He is by far the largest I have ever seen, and he has a colt by him two years old much larger than Telemachus. . . .

ALS. NHi.   1. Clay to Brown, Oct. 8, 1833.   2. Trumbull to Clay, Oct. 11, 1833.   3. Clay to Pendleton, Sept. 9, 1833.   4. Reference obscure, but see Clay to Henry Clay, Jr., Dec. 1, 1833, and 6:1296; also, Rodgers to Clay, April 24, 1829; Clay to Jones, July 5, 1831. On Jan. 10, 1834, Lloyd Nicholas Rogers wrote Clay acknowledging receipt of $800 for "balance due for Warrior." ALS. DLC-TJC (DNA, M212, R10). For Rogers, a Baltimore lawyer, see *MHM*, 17:246; 44:190-99; and *NEHGR*, 16:365.

To John Howard Payne, New York, October 17, 1833. Assures him that while he has not yet been able to read the prospectus of Payne's "new Work," he can "safely, upon trust, subscribe to any work of which you are the author or editor." Concludes that "my name is freely at your service, if you deem it of the smallest use." ALS. NNPM. For John Howard Payne, actor, playwright, author of the song "Home Sweet Home," see *NCAB*, 2:347-48 and *DAB*. Payne had written *Prospectus of a New Periodical*. New York,

1833. The magazine was to be published in London and was to promote the advancement of the art, science, and belles lettres in the United States; however, no issue was ever published.

To Henry Shaw, [Probably Lanesborough, Mass.], November 3, 1833. Reports he and his family will return to Washington from Boston via Worcester, Hartford [Conn.], Springfield, Northampton, and Pittsfield. Hopes to see Shaw in Pittsfield. If the weather turns bad, however, he will go directly from Hartford to "New Haven and the Sound." ALS. NjP. Written in Boston.

On November 10, 1833, writing from Northampton, Mass., to John Pendleton Kennedy in Baltimore, Clay reports that he will proceed westward to Albany, then south to New York City and Baltimore. Asks that no public dinner be given him in Baltimore, as Kennedy had suggested. Says he is "almost entirely prostrated by the unceasing excitement of the scenes through which, for a month past, I have been passing." ALS. MdBP. See Trumbull to Clay, October 11, 1833.

From JOHN SCHOLEFIELD Philadelphia, November 13, 1833
[Asks if a group of Philadelphia "Manufacturers and Merchants" could honor Clay, "the Father of the American System," by greeting him in New York and escorting him to Philadelphia on his return trip to Washington. Continues:]

May I be permitted, Sir to embrace this opportunity for acquainting you with a little piece of history — partly secret — belonging to the present times? — About two weeks ago, Gen. Duff Green — alarmed at the notice you have recently attracted, and, as we understand, at an expression in your favor from the South — left Washington for New York, on a political mission. He commenced his operations at Baltimore:–got up a meeting of "Working Men," so called, at which John McLean was nominated as a candidate for the Presidency.[1] The scheme failed. His next attempt was in our city, where he also tried to operate on the same description of persons. At a very early stage of the business, we became acquainted with his designs, and measures were accordingly taken to frustrate them. We succeeded, and consequently he was defeated: he could not even get a meeting. He then went to Trenton, Newark and New York, for the same *avowed* purpose; and he was every where unsuccessful. Since that time, we have heard no more of him, except of his return home. — A few days ago, however, the partisans of Mr. McLean in this City, made another clandestine attmept; in a similar way, and for the same purpose; and again they have been defeated.

Now, Sir, in order to a right understanding of their movements, it is necessary to state, that the "Working Men," when well organised, constitute a considerable portion of the political strength of the city and county of Philadelphia. They have formerly been found quite available for party porpuses. At the present moment they are not very firmly bound together, not having recently moved in unison. It is evident that although many of their most influential men are decidedly of one party, they have among them political characters of every shade.

Such being the materials of which this class of our citizens are composed, a question presents itself as to the best mode of operating upon them, for the advantage of the public. The knowledge of one little secret, gives us a ready answer to the question. It is simply to make them of some consequence in the world — to give them an air of importance in the eyes of others. As a body, they are very ambitious to possess some weight in society. Let this feeling be gratified, and they are content. It is for these reasons that we apprehend they may some time or other, be induced to unite for evil as well as for good. And, in in [*sic*] order to prevent the former, we must endeavour to ensure the latter. As manufacturers & mechanics, in other words, as "working men", they have a deep interest at stake in the support of "the protective system". But, Sir, many of them do not perfectly understand it; nor, in this respect, is there any other way in which a favorable and lasting impression can possibly be made upon their minds, like that which would come from the lips of the *Father* of that system. Greatly therefore should I rejoice if by any means an opportunity co[u]ld consistently be embraced for doing so much go[od.] The benefit thus to be conferred on a great pu[bl]ic cause, would be incalculable — But m[ore] of this when we have the happiness to see you here. . . .

ALS. DLC-HC (DNA, M212, R5). Addressed to Clay in New York. Scholefield was a carpet manufacturer at 176 South, Philadelphia. Later he served as secretary of the St. George's Society, and president and vice president, respectively, of the Pennsylvania and the Philadelphia Societies for Promoting the Abolition of the Death Penalty. See *PMHB*, 68:49; 94:313; and *Desilver's Philadelphia, Pa., Directory, 1833*, 187.   1. For Green's activities in attempting to head-off Van Buren's nomination for the presidency in 1836 by promoting an alliance between John McLean and John C. Calhoun, see Weisenburger, *The Life of John McLean*, 83-84; Wilson, *Calhoun Papers*, 12:160-64.

To HENRY CLAY, JR.   Philadelphia, November 24, 1833

We have got so far back on our return from the East. The journey has at the same time been the most gratifying and exciting I have ever performed, as you may judge from the papers. They have loaded me with presents[1] and with all sorts of testimony of esteem. I have thought some times that I should be prostrated. But we are all living and tolerably well.

I congratulate most cordially on account of your late public discourse,[2] of which I have recd. the most flattering and agreeable information, accompanied by the expression of anxious desire that you should embark in professional life. . . .

ALS. Henry Clay Memorial Foundation, Lexington, Ky.   1. For example, see Clay to DuPont, Nov. 29, 1833.   2. On Nov. 5, 1833, Henry Clay, Jr., had delviered an oration of behalf of the Union Philosophical Society at the annual commencement of Transylvania University. Lexington *Observer & Kentucky Reporter*, Oct. 30; Nov. 7, 1833.

To Phillip R. Fendall, Washington, November 24, 1833. Writing from Philadelphia, asks Fendall to inquire about an apartment in Washington that will accommodate himself, his wife, "two little boys [John Morrison Clay; Henry Clay Duralde]" and "a servant" for the coming session. Suggests he ask first at the American Hotel, located at the head of Pennsylvania Ave., then at [John] Gadsby's National Hotel, also on Pennsylvania Ave., and also at Mrs. Thompson's, opposite Centre Market, where Webster had had an apartment. Requests that Fendall communicate the result of his inquiries to him at Baltimore which he expects to reach on the evening of November 28. Adds in a postscript: "I prefer a situation on the [Pennsylvania] Avenue between Mr. [Jesse] Brown's [Brown's Indian Queen Hotel] and the head of it." ALS. CtY. As it turned out, the Clays ended up at Mr. [Samuel] Ditty's house on C Street, which they shared with Rep. Thomas A. Marshall of Ky.   Perry M. Goldman & James S. Young (eds.), *The United States Congressional Directories, 1789-1840* (New York, 1973), 254-57, 266. See, also, Clay to Brown, December 10, 1833. Clay paid $75 monthly for the furnished Ditty house. Receipts, January 7; February 6, 1834. ADS. DLC-TJC (DNA, M212, R17).

Check, April 9, 1834. *Ibid.* Receipt, April 17, 1834. *Ibid.* To spruce up the house somewhat, Clay spent $82.50 for papering, painting, plastering, glazing, and minor interior repairs. Accounts and Receipts, March 10, 18, 20, 1834 (three separate items). ADS. DLC-TJC (DNA, M212, R17). Mrs. Thompson, Daniel Webster's former landlady, died on December 14, 1833. Wiltse, *Webster Papers*, 3:290.

To **THOMAS HART CLAY** Philadelphia, November 25, 1833

Your mother has shewn me several letters from you to her, which contain the most satisfactory information about Ashland, which I have recd. since I left home. I hope things have continued to go well there. Tell Mr. [William] Martin that I hope he will be very careful with the stock, and see that the winter provision of food is not wasted or misapplied.[1] I have sent a Jack Ass (that cost me $1000) and 22 Saxony sheep, and they ought to arrive abt. the time this letter does. I wish the Sheep housed every night or put somewhere so that the dogs cannot get to them, and the Jack well taken care of. I have purchased four other Jacks and a Jenny that are at Balto. by this time. I bought them in Boston.[2] And I have also purchased a bull & heifer calf of the Durham short horns from Genl. [Stephen] V[an]. Rensselaer, of the produce of Champion, his famous bull.[3] They are young, and will not go out until the Spring.

I hope every thing at the [James] Morrison farm[4] is well taken care of. Who stays there? I will write about it fully from Washington. Tell Mr. Martin that I have not heard from him since I left home. And tell Theodore [Wythe Clay] that I will write to him from the City. We leave here on Wednesday the 27h. and expect to reach Washn on Saturday or Sunday next.

ALS. KyU. 1. Clay to Martin, Sept. 20, 1833. 2. Clay to Pendleton, Sept. 9, 1833; Clay to Erwin, Oct. 13, 1833. The four Maltese jacks, three imported and one bred in Maine from imported stock, and the Maltese jenny, bred in Maine from imported stock, were together valued at $6,000. R.D. Shepherd to Reuben Davis, Boston, Nov. 14, 1833, in Josephine Simpson Collection, Lexington, Ky. 3. In 1823 Gen. Van Rennsselaer had imported from the herd of a Mr. Champion, the bull, Washington, and the cows, Pansy, Blaize, and Conquest. Washington and Pansy had several descendants whose produce were eventually distributed throughout the United States. The cattle Clay purchased were in all probability among those descendants. Lewis F. Allen, *History of the Short-Horn Cattle* (Buffalo, N.Y., 1872), 173. 4. Morrison's farm consisted of 250 acres located 2½ miles from Lexington and adjoining Clay's property. Lexington *Kentucky Reporter*, Jan. 8, 1821.

To E. I. DuPont, Wilmington, Del., November 29, 1833. Writing from Baltimore, Clay thanks him for the cattle he and [John] Connelly "had the goodness to present me (and for accepting which, considering their great value, I feel quite ashamed)." Suggests how they might best be shipped from Wilmington to Baltimore: "If they are travelled by land they ought not to come faster than 10 or 12 miles per day. But perhaps the Steam Boat will be the best conveyance." Insists on paying the cost of their transportation to Baltimore. ALS. DeGE. For DuPont, See *DAB*. Connelly had been a member of the board of directors of the Bank of the United States along with DuPont. See Govan, *Nicholas Biddle*, 80. The gift was of four full-blooded English cattle. See Clay to Henry Clay, Jr., Dec. 1, 1833.

Clay wrote DuPont again on December 9, 1833, pointing out his wish to bear the expense of transporting from Baltimore to Kentucky the gift cattle as well as "some other Cattle and some Jacks" of his that were already in Baltimore when the gift cattle arrived. "I wished them all sent out together." ALS. DeGE.

DuPont replied on December 11, 1833, regretting the delay in sending the cattle down to Baltimore. Says he will send the Holstein heifer tomorrow by steamboat. Reports that her mother's milk produced eleven and a half pounds of butter in one week. Wants to "procure you a bull also from her crossed with a Durham Bull." ALS, DLC-TJC (DNA, M212, R14).

On December 13, Clay thanked DuPont for sending the Holstein heifer along. Adds that if Connelly has also sent him the promised calf he will be able by December 16 "to start all my Stock from Balto (including those which have been there for some time on expences) to Ashland." ALS. DeGE.

On December 18, writing from Rossville, Baltimore County, Md., John Connelly apologized for delaying shipment of the bull calf, saying his earlier understanding was that at age 21 months, the animal was too young to sustain an overland trip to Kentucky until next spring. Now knowing Clay's wishes in the matter, he will ship the calf into Baltimore right away. ALS. DLC-TJC (DNA, M212, R14).

On December 28, Henry Thompson, agent for Clay in Baltimore, reported that "Your Calf is beginning to pick up, he eats Mangle Wortzle & Ruta baga turnips greedily." Encloses pedigree of Clay's heifer "Chloe," and bull calf "Clifton," citing the *American Farmer* (June 29, 1821), 3:112; (January 7, 1825), 6:332; and other data. ALS. DLC-TJC (DNA, M212, R14). See also, Clay to Thomas Hart Clay, November 25, 1833; Clay to Powel, December 17, 1833.

To HENRY CLAY, JR.   Washington, December 1, 1833

I arrived last evening and found here your favor of the 18h. Ulto. and I need not say that it afforded me inexprcssible satisfaction to learn from yourself that you, who are surrounded with so many circumstances to render you happy, are fully sensible of them and are enjoying them, as becomes you. I am very glad to hear that Julia [Prather Clay] is well, and that my dear little grandson [Henry Clay III] is stout and hearty. I wrote to both her and you from some of the points of my journey (though I forget where) and hope my letters were safely received. My journey has been full of excitement and has been every where attended with the most gratifying exhibition of respect and attachment. They have besides loaded me with presents to an extent and of a value that I felt sometimes ashamed to accept them.[1]

Your Sheep project is a good one, provided you will have a secure pound to put them in at night. Otherwise the dogs would destroy them. I have looked very much to the Sheep business to the north, and have some of my ideas changed about it. I am now satisfied that the best thing for us in K[entucky]. would be to raise ½ blooded sheep, that is to say the native ewes crossed by a Saxony ram or a Merino. Half blooded wool commands, and I think for a long time will command, a higher proportionate price than wool of the finest qualities. It now sells from 50 to 60 Cents, when Saxony will not average more [*sic*, than] 80. The half blooded sheep yields more and is more healthy than the fullblooded. You can buy Ewes of the common breed of the Country for about one dollar or a dollar & a quarter a piece. My Saxony sheep, that have, I hope, reached home by this time will have cost me upwards of thirty! If you determine to buy the Common Ewes, let them not be more than two or three years old & well selected. I will give you a Saxony ram, and you will thus be able at once to get the half-blooded. And in a few years, if the value of full blooded wool should rise, you can make your Sheep equal to full blooded, by using a Saxony ram.

I have four full blooded English Cattle given me,[2] and I have purchased three others, including a pair of full blooded Devons', the most beautiful of all the varieties of Stock.[3] Don't therefore go to any expence yourself, in the purchase of Cattle, as I shall be able in the Spring to supply you with some of the best.

I have also got four Jacks,[4] besides Warrior[5] already sent out.

I will now be able to correspond with you more regularly than I have done, and I hope to hear often from you.

My love to Julia, and request her to kiss Henry for me.

ALS. Henry Clay Memorial Foundation, Lexington, Ky.   1. Clay to DuPont, Nov. 29, 1833. 2. *Ibid.*   3. Erskine Eichelberger, Baltimore, arranged to have Clay's cattle driven west to Kentucky. They went first to Frederick, Md., on the Baltimore & Ohio Railroad, at a freight cost of $8.67; thence by road and drover [John O'Hara] to Wheeling at a cost of $145.47. Erskine Eichelberger to Clay, Feb. 18, 1834. ALS. DLC-TJC (DNA, M212, R17).   4. Clay to Pendleton, Sept. 9, 1833.   5. Clay to Erwin, Oct. 13, 1833.

Comment in Senate, December 2, 1833. Argues that Asher Robbins has the better claim to the Rhode Island seat being contested by Elisha R. Potter. *Register of Debates*, 23 Cong., 1 Sess., 2-4, 6-7. See also *Cong. Globe*, 23 Cong., 1 Sess., 1. Also delivers a eulogy to the late Sen. Josiah S. Johnston. *Register of Debates*, 23 Cong., 1 Sess., 11-12. In January, 1833, the Rhode Island legislature had chosen Asher Robbins, a Whig, to be U.S. senator, giving him 41 out of 78 votes. In November of that same year the newly elected assembly declared the previous election void and chose Elisha R. Potter, a Democrat, as senator. Both showed up in Washington when the 23rd Congress convened. After a lengthy investigation of the merits of the case, complete with a majority and minority report from the special committee appointed to resolve the matter, the Senate refused to seat Potter, the challenger. This allowed Robbins, the incumbent, to retain his seat. For the history of this contest, see *Register of Debates*, 23 Cong., 1 Sess., 2-15, 19, 804, 1230, 1252-57, 1813.

On this day, *The Congressional Globe*, edited, printed, and published in the offices of the Washington *Globe* by its Jacksonian editors, Francis P. Blair and John C. Rives, also began reporting the daily debates and activities of the Congress. It was supported by the Jackson administration. Not surprisingly, it came into immediate financial and political conflict with the *Register of Debates in Congress*, edited by anti-Jacksonians Joseph Gales and William W. Seaton, editors of the Washington *Daily National Intelligencer*. The Gales and Seaton *Register*, commenced in 1825, eventually lost this battle and was discontinued at the end of 1837. Ames, *A History of the National Intelligencer*, 153-55, 229-31; Smith, *Francis Preston Blair*, 48-49, 165-67. Hereafter, the citations to Clay's speeches, comments, and remarks in the Senate, and the quotations therefrom, are taken principally from the *Register of Debates*. Citations to the *Congressional Globe*, however, are also included, especially when the *Globe* prints Clay material not carried by the *Register*.

To Samuel Fleet, New York, December 4, 1833. Thanks him for sending "specimens of Sisal Hemp." Adds: "They look well, but I am not sufficiently acquainted with its properties, culture or produce to determine whether it could be advantageously introduced into our agriculture." Compliments Fleet on his skillful editorship of the *New York Farmer*, regrets that he is too busy to write for the magazine, and asks to become a subscriber. ALS. ViU. For Fleet, see Mott, *A History of American Magazines, 1741-1850*, 1:442.

Remark in Senate, December 4, 1833. Discusses procedures relating to the appointment of Senate committees when the vice president is absent; and on the importance, specifically, of appointing a select committee on contested elections to handle the Potter vs. Robbins issue without further delay [Comment in Senate, December 2, 1833]. *Register of Debates*, 23 Cong., 1 Sess., 13-14; *Cong. Globe*, 23 Cong., 1 Sess., 8.

To HENRY CLAY, JR.   Washington, December 5, 1833
The House of R. turned out the old Clerk,[1] and thereby exhibited a Jackson majority disposed to go all lengths. Whether they will be able to retain that

majority or not remains to be seen. In the Senate there are somewhat better indications, but there has been no fair trial of the strength of parties there yet.[2] I should not be surprized if Tom Moore is admitted to take the Oath and qualify as a member, leaving Mr. [Robert P.] Letcher to contest his seat afterwards.[3] They are trying to make a party question of it.

I wish you would ride over to Ashland occasionally and let me know how things go there. I fear from the tenor of the letters of Theodore [Wythe Clay] that his mind is more unsettled than ever[4]   And from Tom's [Thomas Hart Clay] recent silence I am apprehensive that he also has relapsed into his old habits.[5]

When you go over see what arrangements they have made for taking care of my Jack Ass Warrior[6] and for guarding my Saxony sheep against the dogs. Theodore writes me that [William] Martin is keeping constantly three or four head of stock. I wish with[ou]t giving offence to Martin you wd. ascertain that fact and what are our prospects for a plentiful supply of Winter provisions for my Stock and in what condition they are.

Give our love to Julia [Prather Clay] and kiss Henry [Clay III] for me

ALS. Henry Clay Memorial Foundation, Lexington, Ky.   1. Matthew St. Clair Clarke was replaced as clerk of the House by Walter S. Franklin by a vote of 117-110 on the third ballot. *Register of Debates*, 23 Cong., 1 Sess., 2137. John Q. Adams said there "never was a better Clerk" than Clarke and termed the dismissal "an act of heartless cruelty" and "a dark foreboding of what is to follow through the session." Adams, *Memoirs of John Quincy Adams*, 9:42-43.   2. Whittlesey to Clay, Sept. 19, 1832.   3. Clay to Helm, April 20, 1833.   4. Theodore W. Clay to Clay, Jan. 8, 1832.   5. For the range of his "old habits," see Wharton to Clay, March 6, 1829; Clay to Henry Clay, Jr., May 24, 1830; Henry Clay, Jr., to Clay, Nov. 16, 1830; Mayo to Clay, Jan. 26, 1832.   6. Clay to Erwin, Oct. 13, 1833.

Comment in Senate, December 5, 1833. Condemns President Jackson's pocket veto of the land bill on the final day (March 3, 1833) of the last session [Speech in Senate, January 7, 1833], charges him with hypocrisy in his dealings with Congress on the distribution issue over a two-year period, and announces that he will reintroduce on December 10 "a bill for the distribution of the proceeds of the sales of the public lands for a limited time, and for other purposes." *Register of Debates*, 23 Cong., 1 Sess., 14-15, 17-18. Printed in Colton, *Clay Correspondence*, 5:570-74, with minor variations in capitalization and punctuation. For Jackson's message of December 4, 1833, explaining his pocket veto of the land bill, see *Register of Debates*, 23 Cong., 1 Sess., Appendix, 77-82; *MPP*, 3:56-69; *Cong. Globe*, 23 Cong., 1 Sess., 9-12. See also Speech in Senate, June 20, 1832.

To Madison C. Johnson, Lexington, December 6, 1833. Maintains that under his contract with the trustees of Transylvania University, dated November, 1832, he cannot pay to them the annual interest on the $14,000 in his care as executor of the James Morrison estate. He can only incorporate the interest into the estate "on the first of January next, and so on until the Contract is changed." Informs Johnson that he cannot therefore "authorize you to draw for the interest, nor to pay it at Lexington." ALS. KyLxT.

The trustees had already disbursed some of "their own funds towards Completing Morrison College" and this was "a reason for Calling upon Mr. Clay for the interest upon the $14000." The board resolved that if he refused to "pay the Int[erest] under the authority of the act of the assembly of Decr. 22d. 1831 — he be notified to pay over the principal sum of 14000 Dols" to the institution. The board threatened to sue Clay to get either the accrued interest on the James Morrison bequest or the transfer of the entire corpus of the bequest to board control. Resolution of Board of Trustees, undated [ca. December, 1833]. D. *Ibid.* The "Act for the benefit of Transylvania University" of December 22, 1831, had been designed to facilitate the transfer of the residue of the Morrison legacy from Clay as executor to Transylvania University, eliminating in large part any potential liability Clay might have to suits by other heirs and enabling the university to utilize the funds. The act was a private bill in which the legislature itself acted as a probate court. Ky. Gen. Assy., *Acts* . . . 1831-1832, pp. 161-62.

From Peter B. Porter, Black Rock, N.Y., December 7, 1833. Thinks the current session of Congress will prove "not only more stormy, but more prophetic in developments of the future and final destinies of this Government, than any one that has preceded it since the formation of the Constitution." Hopes that "friends of the country" will be able to "arrest the reckless course of the tyrant who is daily abusing and insulting the generous people who have placed him in power." Believes that the situation, however, "will open a splendid field for the display of those great powers which all acknowledge you to possess." Offers his personal assistance to Clay in the collisions that lie ahead and notes that the primary issue will center on attacks on the Bank of the United States and on the person of Nicholas Biddle. Warns that in the unlikely event that the bank appears to command majority support in the Congress, "I should not be surprised, indeed I should expect, to see our little magician [Martin Van Buren] attempting to drive a bargain, the only aim of which would be to give them aid in procuring a charter [Clay to Wilde, April 27, 1833], in exchange for their assistance in his personal elevation." Would not be surprised if such a bargain required "the immediate removal of Mr. Biddle from office," a "displacement" that would be "offered as the inducement to and apology for Mr. V.'s change of sentiment." Adds: "One can hardly suppose so disreputable a course among the respectable directors of the institution—but it must be recollected that the god of a bank is money." Copy. OHi.

From Hezekiah Niles, Baltimore, December 9, 1833. Confesses his belief, as a "practical republican of the school of '98," that the continued existence of the "rights & liberties of this people," as well as "the preservation of their union" has devolved upon Clay. Warns him that "an attempt will be made to remove you by *brute* force," and that he faces future "contests with persons so polluted that their very touch is almost enough to make one lose his *caste* in society." Informs Clay that he now belongs "not . . . to yourself, or even to your family—you belong to the country, to all the world wherein just ideas or free government are cherished." ALS. DLC-HC (DNA, M212, R5).

Remark in Senate, December 9, 1833. Speaks on the historical background of the appointment of Senate committees and the role of the vice president in the appointment process. *Register of Debates*, 23 Cong., 1 Sess., 19, 22-23. Moves to table Sen. Thomas H. Benton's motion requiring the secretary of the treasury to reveal the amount of money deposited in the Bank of the United States. Wants to broaden the resolution to include "other banks as well." *Ibid.*, 19-20; *Cong. Globe*, 23 Cong., 1 Sess., 17.

To JAMES BROWN   Washington, December 10, 1833
We have not heard from you since we left Philada.   I hope you will be able occasionally to write a line of information as to your health, which I assure you I am most anxious to hear is re-established.

As a measure both of comfort and economy, we have taken a small furnished house in the rear of Gadsbys,[1] and I believe both will be promoted by it. The furniture is plain and we must make some additions to it, when it will correspond with our moderate views.

The Session has opened with an apparent majority in the house for, and in the Senate against the Admon, judging from what has passed in each.[2] In the House they made a victim of the Clerk,[3] and so far seem satisfied with his blood. In the Senate, we have as yet carried every measure against the party of the Admon. Today by a vote of 22 [*sic*] to 18 the Senate resumed the appointment of its own Committees.[4] We mean to use with great moderation the power thus acquired.

The defense of the Bank is thought here to be most able and triumphant.[5] It will require a microscope to find the Secy. of the Treasury [Roger B. Taney] after reading it.

Lucretia joins me in affectionate respects to you.

ALS. ViU.   1. Clay to Fendall, Nov. 24, 1833.   2. Whittlesey to Clay, Sept. 19, 1833. 3. Clay to Henry Clay, Jr., Dec. 5, 1833.   4. Remark in Senate, Dec. 4, 9, 10, 1833. The vote was 23 to 18.   5. Either a facetious reference to Taney's Treasury Report of Dec. 4, 1833, or possibly a reference to the "Report of a Committee of Directors of the Bank of the United States." See Govan, *Nicholas Biddle*, 249; Remark in Senate, Dec. 18, 1833; Clay to Biddle, Dec. 21, 1833.

Comment in Senate, December 10, 1833. Introduces a bill "to appropriate for a limited time the proceeds of the public lands, and granting lands to certain states [Speech in Senate, June 20, 1832]." Explains that the bill is "the same as that which passed at the last session [Speech in Senate, January 7, 1833]." *Register of Debates*, 23 Cong., 1 Sess., 24.

Moves that Secretary of the Treasury Roger B. Taney be required to report the name, location, capitalization, specie reserve, and general fiscal stability of the various banks into which the government deposits recently ordered to be removed from the Bank of the United States [Bradley to Clay, October 16, 1832] are to be placed. *Ibid.*, 24-25.

Asks that a document proported to be written by Jackson, dated September 18, 1833, and read by him "to the heads of the several departments," be made available to the Senate so that its genuineness might be ascertained. This document relates to the removal of deposits and includes the president's reasons for his removal decision [Comment in Senate, December 12, 1833]. *Ibid.*, 25-27.

Mentions revising the rules so that the Senate might once again appoint its own committees. *Ibid.*, 27-29. On this day, the Senate voted 23 to 18 to resume appointing its own committees. Clay voted with the majority. The Jacksonians were generally opposed. *Ibid.*, 29. For the events of this day, see also *Cong. Globe*, 23 Cong., 1 Sess., 18-20.

To Francis T. Brooke, December 11, 1833. Reports that his journey to New England was "full of gratification" and that he everywhere received "enthusiastic demonstrations of respect, attachment and confidence." Adds that "looking back on the scenes through which I passed, they seem to have resembled those of enchantment, more than real life." Believes that the session opens with a Jacksonian majority in the House but with a majority in the Senate against the administration [Whittlesey to Clay, September 19, 1832]. Mentions that in a vote yesterday on the Senate appointment of its own committees, the anti-Jacksonians had prevailed 22 [*sic*, 23] to 18 [Remark in Senate, December 9, 1833]. Notes that "We hope to reverse the majority in the House, and to strengthen it in the Senate, if we have no *desertions*." Mentions that he has recently addressed a long letter to John Floyd "in ansr. to a long letter I had recd. from him, on public affairs." ALS. KyU. Printed in Colton, *Clay Correspondence*, 4:371. Floyd recorded in his diary that the object of his letter was "to induce Mr. Clay to detatch himself from the Northern constructionists and to prevail upon him to unite with the States Rights party, and to prevail upon his friends in the Legislature of Kentucky to reaffirm their resolutions of 1798." Floyd now became "a sort of Clay man," going so far as to apologize in his diary for abuses he had made of Clay's confidences. Ambler, *The Life and Diary of John Floyd*, 117, 232.

Comment in Senate, December 11, 1833. Defends his insistence of the previous day that the executive document, dated September 18, 1833, dealing with the removal of deposits [Bradley to Clay, October 16, 1832; Comment in Senate, December 10, 12,

1833], be made available to the Senate. Questions its authorship and the motives and circumstances underlying its issuance. *Register of Debates*, 23 Cong., 1 Sess., 30-36.

Earlier in this day, Clay amends slightly the language of his resolution of December 10 ordering Secretary of the Treasury Roger B. Taney to report to the Senate the condition of the banks into which government deposits slated to be removed from the Bank of the United States would be placed. *Ibid.*, 29-30; *Cong. Globe*, 23 Cong., 1 Sess., 20-21.

To JOHN M. CLAYTON
Washington, December 12, 1833

Until today, we have gone on swimmingly in the Senate. On tuesday last this day was assigned to proceed to the appointmt. of Commees. by the Senate itself.[1] We came prepared with all our arrangement, and able to carry them, if all proved *faithful*.[2] To my surprize a motion was made by Mr. [Felix] Grundy and supported by *Mr.* [Daniel] *Webster* to postpone the appointment until monday next. And It was carried. If you are here, I believe we shall be safe, even if there be defection. For Gods sake then come to us. And do not let any thing keep you away.

ALS. DLC-John M. Clayton Papers (DNA, M212, R20).   1. Remark in Senate, Dec. 9, 1833.   2. Whittlesey to Clay, Sept. 19, 1832.

Comment in Senate, December 12, 1833. Insists that an official copy of Jackson's "state paper" of September 18, 1833 [Comment in Senate, December 10, 1833], on the removal of the deposits [Bradley to Clay, October 16, 1832] which has been "published to the world, with the sanction of the President," be submitted to the Senate so that it might there be evaluated for its genuineness and for the president's presumed authorship. Affirms that since the document has been printed in the newspapers, the issue of executive privilege — "intervention between the President and his confidential advisers" — does not pertain. *Register of Debates*, 23 Cong., 1 Sess., 37-38. On this day, Jackson, citing the constitutional basis of executive privilege, informed the Senate that he would not turn over the September 18, 1833, document as the Senate had demanded in its resolution of December 11. *Ibid.*, 37. See also *MPP*, 3:36.

Later on this same date, Clay urged his colleagues to put political maneuvering aside and get on with the election of Senate committees [Remark in Senate, December 9, 1833]. *Register of Debates*, 23 Cong., 1 Sess., 40-41; *Cong. Globe*, 23 Cong., 1 Sess., 23-24.

To JAMES COCHRAN
Washington, December 13, 1833

I should take great pleasure, in compliance with the request contained in your letter of the 1st. inst. in communicating the information desired, if I possessed any that was definite. The political complexion of either branch of Congress is far from being certain; and what would be the opinion of either, on any question of Internal improvement, I can not venture to predict. One thing is pretty certain, that if the Veto shall continue to be used, as it has been used, on such questions, that there is no chance of the passage of a bill for internal improvements against its exercise. As far as any indication has yet been given, the Session, opens with a majority for the Admon in the House, and against it in the Senate.[1]

The connexion of Lakes Erie and Ontario, by a Canal[2] on the American side, would be regarded by most men as a National object. Whether it would be so considered by President Jackson I am utterly unable to say.

If you should decide to come to Congress for aid in the accomplishment of that object, my opinion is that the application had better be made by petition, as numerously signed as possible. Even if it did not succeed, it would attract public attention to the work, and possibly might promote it hereafter.

ALS. CSmH. Addressed to Cochran in Oswego, For Cochran, see *BDAC*. 1. Whittlesey to Clay, Sept. 19, 1832. 2. The canal linking lakes Erie and Ontario is the Welland Canal, located on the Canadian side of the border. The first canal was opened in 1829 and gave access to the Niagara River. It was extended in 1833 and enlarged in the period 1871-87. Construction of the modern canal began in 1912. See *EB*.

To JAMES BROWN Washington, December 14, 1833

I regret to hear by your letter of the 16h. that your head remains a source of disquietude to you. I should think, and sincerely hope, that the treatment which you are observing may dissipate your apprehensions.

I am inclined to believe that the Force bill[1] will not produce the effect you anticipate, among the opponents to the Administration. Those who desire its repeal distinctly understand that we shall adhere to our principles. They ought not to persevere in a vain attempt, but if they do they will be defeated. On all other subjects they profess to be disposed to do right, and I hope will. The South is every day becoming more and more united in Opposition to this administration.

There is but one opinion here as to the Bank report,[2] and that is that it is an uncommonly able and most conclusive paper.

We were baulked on thursday about the appointment of Committees in the Senate. I yet am inclined to think that we shall on Monday do what is right.[3]

Dont trouble yourself to write me at any time when writing is uncomfortable to you. But I should be glad if some friend would let me know occasionally the state of your health.

I wish you could come down and see us, if there be no danger to your health. If you would give us a little notice, we could provide comfortably for you in the house which we have taken.

ALS. KyLxT. 1. Remark in Senate, Jan. 22, 1833. 2. Biddle to Clay, Feb. 8, 1833. 3. Remark in Senate, Dec. 9, 1833.

From Henry Clay, Jr., Lexington, December 14, 1833. Reports riding over to "Ashland" yesterday morning to see how things were going there. "I passed around the farm and every where I saw evidences of neglect. The fences in places are falling from the want of that constant attention which you know they require on a large stock farm. The winter provender has no doubt been neglected, but I think there is still enough to carry the stock through the winter. Corn is at present very high, 1 dollar and a half, and it will perhaps be higher. The winter however has heretofore been very mild so that but little provender has been used." Blames this situation on overseer William Martin, noting that "His neglect of the farm I suppose to arise from his frequent absence from it caused by attention to the milk concern and perhaps by his conn[ection] with petty traders in the neighborhood." Cautions against discharging Martin just yet "as the stock looks very well." Thinks the solution to the problem is "not to let Martin retain money in his hands as it will give him the means of trading and speculating to which he is but too prone." Complains, too, that "The hands have not worked as they would have done, had he been more with them."

Turns to "a very painful subject," viz: "Anne [Brown Clay Erwin] Mr [James] Erwin and the rest of the family, with the exception of myself determined from the great and apparent increase of Theodores malady [Theodore W. Clay to Clay, January 8, 1832] and from the positive risk and danger of his going at large that he ought to be again placed in the Hospital in this place. The commissioners have taken him once more under their protection. They applied to me to know if I consented to it. I told them that I should have nothing

675

to do in the matter but that as one nearly related but without any authority or desire to act, I had no objection. When he was placed in the Hospital I was applied to as his brother, the nearest relation present, to advance $50 for his bo[ard] and to give my bond for $500." Emphasizes that the decision to recommit Theodore was mainly his sister Anne's—"She placed him where he is"—since he had become too dangerous to have in the house. Notes that Theodore's health is poor, "his face pale and emaci[ated]," and his mind filled with "suspicions of plots and conspiracies." Concludes that "Anne has done right." Continues: "Let me say with a full knowledge of what I owe to you and to my mother, that we should allow the best physicians to operate with this most subtle and distressing disorder   When he was in the Hospital before, his health was reestablished and his mind certainly improved. Let us then curb our feelings and not destroy our brother and our child by mistimed affection. If the malady is a great affliction to us all and the most awfu[l] calamity to which a human being is subject, then let the remedies be applied with proportionate care. Let the wisest men and the most skilful in cures take our patient under their charge. I have every hope and others entertain hope also that Theodore will be eventually cured if left in the Hospital. His disorder from being confined to a few subjects has I think become more general and I hope unsettled. At all events we ought never to resign hope and the experience of mankind informs us that the living and discipline of a Hospital are the best remedies for the disease." Is convinced that Theodore has improved since his return to the hospital.

Concerning Thomas Hart Clay, "of whom you asked, I can say nothing good." Reports that he has been drinking heavily since Clay left Lexington and is quite "addicted" to liquor.

Concerning himself, remarks that he has purchased an additional 28 acres for his farm "at a little upwards of $50 per acre at one two & three years with interest," and has his eye on another parcel of about 11 acres. Anticipates procuring "a flock of about 400 hundre[d] sheep which I hope with the other resources of our place will yield us about $1000 per annum without trouble." Adds that his wife "has presided over her first dinner, in honor of J. J. Crittenden, a[nd] tomorrow sees the connexion at a small evening party. My son [Henry Clay III] is pronounced a remarkably fine specimen, and his fath[er] I assure you is one of the happiest of all men." Asks in a postscript that Clay send "A line now and then" on political events in Washington. ALS. DLC-HC (DNA, M212, R5). Part of letter obliterated. Printed in Colton, *Clay Correspondence*, 4:373-74.

John Headley replaced William Martin as manager of "Ashland" in 1835 at an annual salary of $450. Clay to Headley, November 12, 1835. DS, in Clay's hand. DLC-TJC (DNA, M212, R17).

To WILLIAM DUNLAP[1]   Washington, December 14, 1833

I regret extremely that my public engagments will not allow me time to communicate any thing valuable, respecting the ornamental artists in the West, according to the request contained in your letter of the 3d. inst.   You judge rightly in supposing me to take a lively interest in all that concerns them. If you could open a correspondence with some Western gentleman of more leisure than I possess (perhaps if you were to address my son H. Clay Junr. at Lexington) you might obtain the information you desire.

The three most eminent Kentucky painters were Jouitt [*sic*, Matthew Harris Jouett], [William Edward] West and [Chester] Harding.[2] West (who painted the portrait of Lord Byron, said to be the best) is yet I believe in Europe. Mr. Harding is in Boston. He is not a native of Kentucky; the other two are.

ALS. KyU.   1. For Dunlap—playwright, painter, historian—see *DAB*.   2. For Harding, who painted Clay and many other prominent men, see Collins, *History of Kentucky*, 1:170.

From AMBROSE SPENCER   Albany, N.Y., December 14, 1833

[Apologizes for intruding on Clay's time and speaks of the highly favorable impression he made during his recent visit to Albany. Continues:]

I rejoice to perceive strong symptoms of a majority in the Senate opposed to Genl. Jackson,[1] after all that body may be the conservator of the Union & constitution. Mr [John] Forsyth probably said truly, there were at least three parties there, but if two of them unite in restraining & thwarting the President in his mad career, they will deserve well of the Country. were I a member of your body, I would co-operate with any party or set of men, in setting bounds to the arbitrary, despotic & infamous course of that headstrong & ignorant man.

The informal message containing the Presidents reasons against your land bill is the most bare faced piece of sophistry I ever saw. He objects to the 12 & ½ per cent to the seven new states, because it is a violation of the equality of distribution, prescribed by two sessions, & yet he proposes after a few years to cede all the unsold lands to the states, within whose limits they are —[2]under the flimsy pretext that we are not to keep these Lands forever. I presume the 12 & ½ pr cent was given on the equitable principles, that the inhabitants have been the pioneers & have encountered great hardships & extra labour in making roads, bridges &c. whereby the residers of the lands have been greatly enhanced. But on what principle is it that the trustees of the national domain, shall not only renounce a sacred trust for the whole people, but expressly violate it. all the cessions were made not as donations, but as acts of justice, inasmuch as these crown lands, were acquired by the valour, blood & treasure of all america; and as to those ceded by France & Spain, a full consideration was paid out of the common treasury — a more wicked & mischievous project was never conceived, than this, & it will embolden the new states, before well inclined to seize on these common lands & appropriate them exclusively to themselves, in defiance of every principle of justice — in fact the President is on this, as on almost all other subjects ministering to the worst passions of the human mind — but I am talking to you on a subject you understand much better than myself—

I am aware that it is quite premature to think or speak of the next Presidential candidates, but it seems that *nolens volens* the Press will talk of it & consequently the public will think of it — in my opinion the national republicans, ought to keep themselves wholly uncommitted — unless a great change should take place in the public mind, & the prejudices of party be greatly abated the annunciation of any one of our distinguished friends, would have the effect to unite the whole Jackson phalanx on some one of their Leaders, & I think Mr. Van Buren would probably be that man — from present appearances the contest on the part of our adversaries will be between Van Buren, Judge [John] McLean, & Mr. [Lewis] Cass. I had no opportunity to obtain your opinion of the two latter, but I confess I feel strong repugnance to both of them. The question is not whether they are as unprincipled as Jackson, for I console myself with the belief that we under no circumstances can elect a worse, or more incompetent man — If we are driven to a choice between the three, which of them will be the least mischievous? McClea's [*sic*, McLean] judicial course, has been jesuitical & trimming, & it will be a strong objection to him, that he enters the arena with the robes of office on. As to Cass, I once thought well of him, but did he not write an article in the North American review, expressly to propitiate the favor of Jackson, chiming in with his crude notions that Georgia had a right to abrogate the laws &c. of the Cherokees & subject them to their jurisdiction? this was in July 1830.[3] Did he not write an Essay for the Globe reviewing Judge [John] Marshal[l]'s opinions in the case of the Missionaries, to prepare the public mind for the President's refusal to obey & carry into effect the mandate of the Court?[4] Is he not the one of the cabinet, who gave an oral opinion against removing the deposits, but saying if they were removed he would stand by the President?[5] If he has done all or any of these things, he is a fit instrument for a Tyrant, & I despise him. can you enlighten me on any of these matters, at a leisure moment?

I feel as I did when I saw you, most desponding at the prospect before us, & yet were I called to act, I would if possible nerve myself for the contest & fight the battle, on the last inch of ground left.

Excuse I pray you, my want of method. I write on just as I feel — We are all well; present my respects to Mrs. Clay & say to her Mrs. Spencer presents her respects & will long remember her with affection. [P.S.] Mrs. Dewitt Clinton told me she regretted very much you did not call on her. she has not one remaining prejudice against you & her husbands were conceived in error & even I doubt not produced by misrepresentation.

ALS. DLC-HC (DNA, M212, R5). Printed in Colton, *Clay Correspondence*, 4:372-73.   1. Whittlesey to Clay, Sept. 19, 1832.   2. For Jackson's objections to the 12½ percent provision in the land bill as an unconstitutional violation of the compacts by which the United States obtained its western lands, see *MPP*, 3:63-64. The president advocated that the price of the public lands "be reduced and graduated, and that after they have been offered for a certain number of years the refuse remaining unsold shall be abandoned to the States and the machinery of our land system entirely withdrawn." *Ibid.*, 68-69.   3. For Cass's article, see Anonymous, "Removal of the Indians," *NAR* (1830), 30:62-121; also, Andrew C. McLaughlin, *Lewis Cass* (Boston, 1891), 155-60.   4. For the case of *Worcester* v. *Georgia* — "the case of the missionaries" — see, Johnston to Clay, Jan. 12, 1831; also, McLaughlin, *Lewis Cass*, 158, for a discussion of the article in the Washington *Globe*.   5. Cass favored the Bank of the United States and opposed Jackson's removal of government deposits from it. On two occasions he offered his resignation because of this disagreement, but the president refused his offer. In general, Cass avoided comment on the issue. See Frank B. Woodford, *Lewis Cass: The Last Jeffersonian* (New Brunswick, N.J., 1950), 179.

To Daniel Jenifer, Harris's Lot, Md., December 15, 1833. Reports that "The Session opens with an apparent majority in the House for the Admon and against it in the Senate [Whittlesey to Clay, September 19, 1832]. We hope there may be a favorable change in the House, but that is uncertain. From the South our information is encouraging." ALS. DLC-Seth Barton Papers (DNA, M212, R20).

To FRANCIS T. BROOKE   Washington, December 16, 1833
I addressed a letter to you at Richmond, but understand that you are at St. Julien,[1] to which I direct this letter.

We were highly gratified today in the Senate. We carried the appointmt. of every Chairman of the Committees as we wished;[2] and, as far as we proceeded, every member of the several Committees, with one unimportant exception. There is a fair prospect of our having in the Senate a majority of 26 or 27.[3]

Whether it will be practicable to rescue the Government and Public Liberty from the impending dangers, which Jacksonism has created, depends, in my opinion, mainly upon the South; and the course of the South will be guided mainly by Virginia. Hence the very great importance of this State taking a patriotic direction. I understand that you are thought of for her C. Magistrate. I know the sacrifices you must make if you accept that station; but cannot *you* make them? "What is a public man worth who is not ready to sacrifice himself for his Country"? Depend upon it, that every thing for which you fought, or which you and I hold valuable, in public concerns, is in imminent hazard. By means of the Veto, the power *as exercised* of removal from office, the possession of the public treasury and the public patronage, the very existence of Liberty and the Government is, in my judgment, in peril.

I mean myself to open and push a vigorous campaign. It is the campaign of 1777.[4] I want aid—all the aid that can be given.[5] I mean (which will surprize you) to be very prudent; but very resolute. Can you not assist us?

ALS. KyU. Copy in DLC-TJC (DNA, M212, R14). Printed in Colton, *Clay Correspondence*, 4:375. 1. His estate near Fredericksburg, Va. 2. Remark in Senate, Dec. 9, 1833. 3. Whittlesey to Clay, Sept. 19, 1832. 4. He probably meant to write 1799, the date of the condemnation and rejection by Virginia and Kentucky of the Alien and Sedition Acts. See Speech in Senate, Dec. 26, 1833. 5. On the same day, Dec. 16, 1833, Clay wrote Leslie Combs that "Before us there is a great struggle—a contest for liberty and for the existence of the Government. . . . we want aid—all aid. . . . On Virginia (which beyond all doubt is fast getting right) and Kentucky now, as in 1799, hangs the destiny of the Republic." Copy. Printed in Louisville *Journal*, Jan. 8, 1861.

Remark in Senate, December 16, 1833. Suggests that the Senate elect the chairmen of each of its various standing committees prior to electing the other members of each. His suggestion prevailed. *Register of Debates*, 23 Cong., 1 Sess., 42. Clay was elected to the Committee on Public Lands. He was defeated for the chairmanship of the Committee on Manufactures by Theodore Frelinghuysen of N.J. by a vote of 23 to 16, with 6 votes scattered. *Ibid.*, 42-43. See Sergeant to Clay, December 18, 1833; Clay to Erwin, December 21, 1833; *Cong. Globe*, 23 Cong., 1 Sess., 33.

From William Woodbridge, Detroit, December 16, 1833. Encloses a document [not found] proporting to deal with a number of "horrid murders in a period of war [of 1812]." Among the perpetrators of this event, which is "deeply imprinted upon the minds of the early settlers here," was "the half breed Indian Caldwell . . . the same terrific monster, who took so prominent a part in the massacre at the Riviere aux Raisins." Asks whether an investigation of the allegations set forth in the document should be undertaken in the Senate. LS, draft. MiD-B. For the "Memorial of the Legislative Council of Michigan Territory" appealing for compensation for losses suffered in the "horrid murders" in the War of 1812, see *Sen. Docs.*, 23 Cong., 1 Sess., no. 176. For the massacre at the River Raisin, see G. Glenn Clift, *Remember The Raisin!* (Frankfort, Ky., 1961), *passim*. Captain Billy Caldwell was the son of a Shawnee mother and Col. William Caldwell, a Loyalist during the American Revolution. In 1812, Billy had been commissioned a captain in the British militia. *Ibid.*, 168-69.

To John Hare Powel, Philadelphia, December 17, 1833. Reports that when he was recently in Albany, he had "purchased a pair of full blooded Calves, descendants of the importation made by Genl. [Stephen] V[an]. Rensselaer [Clay to DuPont, November 29, 1833]." Asks if Powel is acquainted with that particular blood-line. ALS. PHi.

Remark in Senate, December 18, 1833. Submits resolution requiring Secretary of the Treasury Roger B. Taney to produce correspondence of William H. Crawford, dated February 13, 1817, dealing with the Bank of the United States; also, Taney's recent correspondence and reports having to do with the terms on which various state banks had agreed to receive government deposits were such funds removed from the B.U.S [Bradley to Clay, October 16, 1832]. Agrees to a postponement of the discussion of the removal of deposits until additional information of the subject comes to hand. *Register* *of Debates*, 23 Cong., 1 Sess., 44-45. In his report to Congress dated December 3, 1833, presented December 4, which sought to justify Jackson's removal of the deposits [*Register of Debates*, 23 Cong., 1 Sess., Appendix, 59-68], Taney had cited then Secretary of the Treasury Crawford's correspondence (in 1817) with the president of the Mechanics' Bank of New York advocating the removal of government funds from the B.U.S. and their deposit in state banks. Swisher, *Roger B. Taney*, 249-53. For Clay's main speech on the removal of deposits, see Speech in Senate, December 26, 1833.

From John Sergeant, Philadelphia, December 18, 1833. Says that his wife is sending the white china Mrs. Clay has ordered. Remarks that some of Clay's friends in Philadelphia became "agitated and anxious" when they learned that he was not chairman of a Senate committee this session [Remark in Senate, December 16, 1833], but understand the situation now that Clay has explained it [Clay to Sergeant, December 16, 1833]. Asks Clay to tell "our friend" Chilton Allan that he has read his speech of December 16, 1833, on the removal of the deposits [*Register of Debates*, 23 Cong., 1 Sess., 2183-86] "with great pleasure, and have heard it much commended by others, who were better judges and under no bias of personal regard." ALS. DLC-TJC (DNA, M212, R10). Endorsed by Clay: "With bill for China — sent a draft to him for $100 to pay for it 20h. [*sic*, 21] Decr. 1833."

The bill for $92, dated December 18, was for 124 pieces of "French White China" purchased from W.R. Kerr & Co., Philadelphia importers of china, glass, and queensware. D. *Ibid.* (R17).

Speech in Senate, December 19, 1833. Speaks in support of his resolution of December 18 [Remark in Senate, December 18, 1833]. Defends the solvency of the Bank of the United States. Charges that Secretary of the Treasury Roger B. Taney exceeded his authority, an authority belonging by law to Congress, when he approved the removal of government deposits from the B.U.S. [Bradley to Clay, October 16, 1832]. Condemns Taney's employment of the "old exploded doctrine of the general welfare in a most odious form" in defense of his act of removal. Maintains that former Secretary of the Treasury William H. Crawford never supported the principle that the secretary had the power or the right to transfer government funds from the B.U.S. to state banks. Concludes with a statement explaining his personal connection with the bank over the years. In this he denies that there had ever been a "dishonorable connexion" between himself and the institution or its officers. *Register of Debates*, 23 Cong., 1 Sess., 51-53. For Clay's principal speech attacking the proposed removal of deposits, see Speech in Senate, December 26, 1833.

Earlier this day, Clay supported a resolution calling for an investigation of the financial management of the U.S. Post Office by Postmaster General William T. Barry. *Register of Debates*, 23 Cong., 1 Sess., 47. See Speech in Senate, June 27, 1834. He also presented a petition from Schenectady, N.Y., asking the attention of Congress to the frequency of fires on steamboats. *Cong. Globe*, 23 Cong., 1 Sess., 42.

Additionally, on this day, Clay's motion of December 18 demanding information from Taney was also passed. Added to it by amendment of Sen. Thomas H. Benton was the requirement that the secretary also submit the "entire correspondence" between Crawford and the president of the B.U.S. during the first six months of 1819. Ibid., 42-43.

To NICHOLAS BIDDLE Washington, December 21, 1833
I mentioned to Mr [Horace] Binney that I thought it wd. be beneficial to obtain from the Bank in Philada. testimony to establish that the business transacted by the Exchange Comee: of the B. U. S. was usual and according to their custom.[1] I think so yet.

If the state of public opinion at Philad. should be such as to favor the operation, it would be well to have a general meeting of the people to memorialize Congress in favor of a restoration of the deposites.[2] Such an example might be followed elsewhere; and it would be more influential as it might be more general.

If the local Banks could be induced to concur in such a movement so much the better.

I think it would be expedient to obtain, at the general meeting of the Stockholders in Jan. an expression of their approbation of the conduct of the Board, and particularly of the expenditure which has been made in defending the Bank agt. unfounded attacks.[3]

We have before the Senate a nomination of the Govt. Directors.[4]

ALS. DLC-Nicholas Biddle Papers (DNA, M212, R20). Letter marked "(Confidential)." Endorsed by Clay: "Sent by J. S. to whom it came enclosed." J. S. was probably John Sergeant. Enclosed in Clay to Sergeant, Dec. 21, 1833, which has not been found. See Sergeant to Clay, Dec. 23, 1833.   1. The Exchange Committee had existed since the beginning of the B.U.S. and had responsibility for the purchases and sales of bills of exchange. Its transactions had always been reported to the board after they occurred, because in some instances in this phase of its operation the bank was a competitor with its mercantile directors. When John T. Sullivan was appointed as a government director in Jan., 1832, he leaked the substance of the board's discussions to Reuben Whitney who in turn informed Amos Kendall, a member of Jackson's "Kitchen Cabinet." As a result, Biddle began to refer all important matters to board committees from which Sullivan was excluded. At the same time, the powers of the Exchange Committee were expanded so it could make loans or discounts under the same conditions of secrecy. See Govan, *Nicholas Biddle*, 225, 230-31; Swisher, *Roger B. Taney*, 250-55. Horace Binney spoke for three days, beginning Jan. 7, in the House in defense of the bank. *Register of Debates*, 23 Cong., 1 Sess., Appendix, 2320-64.   2. Memorials related to the removal-restoration issue were received from Philadelphia on March 4, 7, 14, 19, 25, 26; June 19, 1834. See *Register of Debates*, 23 Cong., 1 Sess., Appendix, 802-4, 826-32, 958-59, 1006-7, 1141, 1145-67, 2036-37; and James Parton, *Life of Andrew Jackson*, 3 vols. (New York, 1860), 3:546.   3. Taney had severely criticized the expenditures of the bank in publishing documents in its own defense. See Hammond, *Banks and Politics in America*, 426-27. No evidence has been found indicating that the stockholders at their January meeting in 1834 took the action recommended by Clay; however, the private directors (those not appointed by the government) had previously addressed this criticism in detail in their "Report of a Committee of Directors of the Bank of the United States." *Register of Debates*, 23 Cong., 1 Sess., Appendix, 289-305.   4. On Dec. 17, 1833, Jackson nominated James A. Bayard, Peter Wager, Henry D. Gilpin, John T. Sullivan, and Hugh McElderry as government directors. The Senate approved Bayard on Jan. 21, 1834, and rejected the others on Feb. 27. On March 11, Jackson renominated those who had been rejected, at the same time stating that Bayard had refused the appointment. The Senate again rejected the nominees on May 1, 1834. *Ibid.*, Appendix, 309-16; or *MPP*, 3:41-48.

To JAMES ERWIN   Washington, December 21, 1833

From a letter from Anne [Brown Clay Erwin] recd. tonight, I find that this letter may reach you before you leave home. I transmit enclosed a letter to Mr. [William] Martin which explains itself.[1] If it be necessary, I will thank you to dismiss him and get another in his place. I should prefer a single man, but in that respect you will do the best you can. I am sorry to trouble you, but I know no one but you or Henry [Clay, Jr.] to whom I can address myself, and you are nearest to Ashland. Thomas [Hart Clay], I fear, has not sufficiently renounced his old habits;[2] but if he has, he might supply Martins place (if it be expedient to dismiss him) until a successor is obtained.

Waggerman [*sic*][3] has arrived. He wants Govr [James] Barbour's negroes and would go higher than $3000, but not to $5000 each. I wrote you abt them fully, and I hope you may be able [on reac]hing N. O. to make a good sale for him, if his Agent [should] arrive.

We have strong hopes of a decided majority in [the Sena]te[.] Suspicions were entertained of Webster, but they are disapp[earing.] I declined being at the head of any Committee in the Senat[e]⁴ [words illeg.] never stood better with my friends in that body. P.S. for my dear Anne—If Mr. Erwin has left you, be pleased to get Henry [to replace] him in the above agency as to Mr. Martin; and give [words illeg.]

We have just come this evening from dining with [words illeg.] Minister. Your mama [Lucretia Hart Clay] and Johnny [John Morrison Clay] were of the party. We [words illeg.] Mr [John Q.] Adams, Mr [Samuel L.] Southard, Mr [Daniel] Webster &c.

ALS, manuscript torn. NcD.   1. Henry Clay, Jr., to Clay, Dec. 14, 1832.   2. *Ibid.*
3. Sen. George A. Waggaman of La.   4. Remark in Senate, Dec. 16, 1833.

From John Sergeant, Philadelphia, December 21, 1833. Reports that "Our friends here are in high spirits, and delighted with what you are doing at Washington. You have given the Secretary [Roger B. Taney] a hard hit [Speech in Senate, December 19, 1833], such as, he deserved. I am glad to see too, that Mr. [Willie P.] Mangum has taken the field, upon ground that may probably bring him support in Virginia and N. Carolina, where Constitutional questions are in favor—The blows now should be multiplied as much as possible, showered upon the profligates, 'till their audacious effrontery gives way and exposes them as they are." ALS. DLC-TJC (DNA, M212, R14). On December 19, 1833, Sen. Mangum of N.C. had called for the appointment of a committee to study carefully the constitutional issues involved in the Senate's demand that President Jackson turn over to it a document on the removal of deposits question, dated September 18, 1833, and Jackson's refusal to do so on the constitutional grounds of executive privilege [Comment in Senate, December 10, 11, 12, 1833]. *Register of Debates,* 23 Cong., 1 Sess., 47-49.

From NICHOLAS BIDDLE   Philadelphia, December 23, 1833
The Govt. Directors¹ have behaved so ill & are so much disliked by all their colleagues that we hope you will reject them. They are nuisances on the Board—of no use whatever—the other Directors will not associate with them—nor serve with them on Committees—in short they are put into Conventry completely. I fear too if they are confirmed, they will be considered as having their conduct sanctioned by the Senate which would be very much to be deplore[d] in the present state of the question between the Kitchen Cabinet & the Bank.

I shall not fail to attend to your suggestion.

Copy. DLC-Nicholas Biddle Papers (DNA, M212, R20).   1. Clay to Biddle, Dec. 21, 1833.

Remark in Senate, December 23, 1833. Asks for postponement of consideration of the question of the legal power of a secretary of the treasury to remove government deposits from the Bank of the United States [Remark in Senate, December 18, 1833] until additional pertinent information on the issue comes to hand. *Register of Debates,* 23 Cong., 1 Sess., 57-58; *Cong. Globe,* 23 Cong., 1 Sess., 50.

From John Sergeant, Philadelphia, December 23, 1833. Acknowledges receipt of Clay's letter of December 21 [not found], enclosing a draft for $100 in payment for the china [Sergeant to Clay, December 18, 1833] and enclosing also "the letter for Mr. Biddle [Clay to Biddle, December 21, 1833], which was immediately handed to him." Discusses the problem of buying and shipping the china. Notes in postscript: "Mr. B[iddle]. will write to you." ALS. DLC-TJC (DNA, M212, R14).

Remark in Senate, December 24, 1833. Opposes resolution to adjourn until December 30, urging, as a reason, "the distressed condition of the country, and the necessity of prompt legislation, in order to relieve the public distresses." Motion defeated 18 to 17. *Register of Debates*, 23 Cong., 1 Sess., 58; *Cong. Globe*, 23 Cong., 1 Sess., 52.

To PETER B. PORTER

Washington, December 26, 1833

I recd. your obliging favor of the 7h. inst. and was highly pleased to find that you took such a lively interest in my Eastern tour.[1] Nothing could have been more gratifying to me; and indeed upon looking back on the scenes through which I passed they appear to me to resemble more those of magic and fairy life than real exhibitions.

We shall have an arduous if not agitated Session. You will have seen from my movements that I do not mean to spare this wicked administration. Today I delivered the first part of my speech on the Deposite question.[2] It was limited to an examination of the power exerted by the President over that subject. I said what I felt, and no one can feel more than I do. The Hall of the Senate was crowded to overflowing; and if I am to judge of the Speech by what has been said in its favor, I ought to be satisfied. That is much more than I expect will be the case at the White house and with the K. C.[3]

You talk of coming here. I shall be most delighted to see you. We want all the aid and advice from such men as *you* are. How happy I am to find myself sustained by and yet acting with such men as yourself [James] Barbour and [Samuel L.] Southard. Come if you can; but do not come from any apprehensions of personal danger to me. The scoundrels dare not approach me. Their assassination is of character, not of persons, where they fear any perils to themselves.

I do not think, from any thing that has yet occurred, that the Magician [Van Buren] will attempt to drive the bargain you anticipate with the Bank. I believe [Nicholas] Biddle and many who act with him are real patriots. You will have seen that the Regency men are the most subservient of the Collar gang.[4]

Your friend Macy[5] has been with me, and corresponded very well with your previous description of him. I should like to have seen more of him but his stay was short here and I was much engaged.

I must reserve for a future occasion every thing I have to say about a visit to the Great Lakes and the Falls. When we shall get from here, God only knows.

Should you go to K. in May I hope (tho' it is very doubtful) that I may see you there before you leave it. If you conclude to come here let me know it before hand.

ALS. NBuHi. 1. Trumbull to Clay, Oct. 11, 1833. 2. Speech in Senate, Dec. 26, 1833; Comment in Senate, Dec. 30, 1833. 3. Probably, Kitchen Cabinet. 4. "Collar gang" was a generic term of opprobrium used to describe those subservient to Jackson. An article taken from the Wabash (Ind.) *Mercury* and printed in the Kennebec (Me.) *Journal* described a collar man as one who "uses an argument not because it is correct, but because it is put into his mouth by the 'powers that be.' He adopts an idea, not because it is good of [*sic*, for] the country, but because it will be for the good of the party. He is a mere machine—he acts only as he is acted upon. The measures which he advocates to-day, if abandoned by the party, he would condemn to-morrow. . . . He is like one of the following sheep of a flock; so soon as he ascertains by the tinkle of the bell, that the bell-weather is in motion, he shakes his tail, cries baa! and is off in a canter." The term, for example, was applied to Richard Rush after his switch from the Anti-Masonic to the Jackson party. "An Anti-Jackson man—*A friend of the Bank*—a PENNSYLVANIAN, he turns in among the collar men, to pull down the Bank and to shout 'Hurra for Jackson.'" Lexington *Observer & Kentucky Reporter*, April 3, 1834, reprinted from the Baltimore *Patriot*. 5 Possibly John B. Macy who was born in Massachusetts, later resided in New York City, Buffalo, and Cincinnati. A founder of Toledo, Ohio, he also served as a congressman from Wisconsin in the

32nd and 33rd Congresses. While in Buffalo he was president of the Buffalo City Bank. See *BDAC*; also Samuel Welch, *Home History, Recollections of Buffalo* (Buffalo, 1891), 52, 97-98, 344; Rossiter Johnson (ed.), *The Twentieth Century Biographical Dictionary of Notable Americans*. . . . Boston, 1904.

Speech in Senate, December 26, 1833. At the outset of his three-day oration, which occupied all of December 26 and the greater part of December 30 and 31, Clay introduces two motions of censure. The first condemns Jackson for dismissing Secretary of the Treasury Louis McLane because he refused an order to remove the deposits, and for appointing Roger B. Taney as secretary of the treasury "to effect such removal, which has been done." In so doing, "the President has assumed the exercise of a power over the treasury of the United States, not granted to him by the constitution and laws, and dangerous to the liberties of the people." The second motion censures Taney for the "unsatisfactory and insufficient" reasons given by him for the removals, as he had explained the reasons for them in his communication to Congress of December 4, 1833 [Comment in Senate, December 30, 1833].

Launching into his address, Clay charges that President Jackson has commenced "a revolution, hitherto bloodless, but rapidly tending toward a total change in the pure republican character of the Government, and to the concentration of all power in the hands of one man." To demonstrate this contention, attacks Jackson's use of the veto, his summary removal of cabinet officers and other government officials who do not do his bidding, his cruel treatment of the Indians, his undermining of the integrity of the currency, his ambivalence and hypocrisy on the tariff issue, and his support and abandonment of internal improvements. Believes that within a few years under such confused and despotic leadership, "the Government will have been transformed into an elective monarchy — the worst of all forms of government." Maintains that the removal of deposits is nothing less than an attack on the last remaining power of Congress, "that over the purse." Develops this assertion at length with detailed references to early U.S. financial history, the origins of the Department of the Treasury under the Constitution, the previous history and current charter of the Bank of the United States, and the separation of governmental powers in general. Argues that, under the constitution and the relevant enabling legislation passed soon after the government went into operation, the secretary of the treasury is responsible to the Congress rather than to the president; thus the president has no constitutional power over the public treasury. Nor does the charter of the B.U.S. give the president power over public deposits. This power is given to the secretary of the treasury who then answers to Congress. "Thus is it evident that the President, neither by the act creating the Treasury Department, nor by the bank charter, has any power over the public treasury. Has he any by the constitution? None, none." Nor has Jackson somehow acquired such power by virtue of his reelection to the presidency. Charges that the president is even working to subvert the free press in the United States. Examines at length Taney's role in the removal of the deposits and denies flatly that the secretary's asserted power over the deposits is, in Taney's own words, "absolute, unconditional, and exclusive." Only Congress has this power. As for the change of locus of government deposits, that is, "the care and safe keeping of the public money," that duty Congress has devolved by law upon the treasurer of the United States. Evaluates Jackson's attack on the Bank of the United States, emphasizing the president's political motives in the matter and citing instances of his past ambivalence on the institution's proper role in the American economy. Claims that Jackson's victory in 1832 was no popular mandate to destroy the B.U.S. since the president had waffled on the issue. Defends the bank against Jackson's and Taney's recent assertions of its misconduct. Laments that public monies are being removed from the stable and well-managed B.U.S., chartered by the federal government, and placed in unstable, undercapitalized, and uncontrolled private local banks chartered only by the several states. Sees economic confusion ahead. Throughout his remarks, Clay repeatedly calls attention to the monarchial and tyrannical personality of President Jackson and

684

visualizes the imminent collapse of the republic. His conclusion, delivered to the "loud and repeated applause from the immense crowd which thronged the galleries and the lobbies," was that the "premonitory symptoms of despotism are upon us; and if Congress does not apply an instantaneous and effective remedy, the fatal collapse will soon come on, and we shall die—ignobly die—base, mean, abject slaves; the scorn and contempt of mankind; unpitied, unwept, unmourned!" At this point, "Loud and repeated applause from the immense crowd," caused the vice president to order the galleries cleared. *Register of Debates*, 23 Cong., 1 Sess., 58-94; *Cong. Globe*, 23 Cong., 1 Sess., 54-57, 65-67, 71-72. Printed in Colton, *Clay Correspondence*, 5:575-620 with minor variations in punctuation and capitalization. This was Clay's major speech on the removal of the deposits and the censure of Jackson and Taney. For its political implications, see Van Deusen, *The Life of Henry Clay*, 277-84; Bowers, *Party Battles of the Jackson Period*, 322-26, 330-37; Smith, *Magnificent Missourian*, 147-51; Govan, *Nicholas Biddle*, 247-52.

On March 28, 1834, following weeks of lengthy and acrimonious debate, the motion to censure Jackson was finally passed 26 to 20 by the Senate; that criticizing Taney's report of December 4, 1833, passed 28 to 18. *Register of Debates*, 23 Cong., 1 Sess., 1187; *Cong. Globe*, 23 Cong., 1 Sess., 271. The wording of the censure of Jackson had, by this time, changed to read: "Resolved: That the President, in the late executive proceedings in relation to the public revenue, has assumed upon himself authority and power not conferred by the constitution and laws, but in derogation of both." *Ibid.* For the legislative history of the restoration of deposits and censure issues in the House, see Bradley to Clay, October 16, 1832.

Comment in Senate, December 30, 1833. Labels "a most extraordinary and . . . unprecedented document," Secretary of the Treasury Roger B. Taney's "long communication" of December 4 [*Register of Debates*, 23 Cong., 1 Sess., Appendix, 59-68] in reply to the Senate's resolution of December 19 [Speech in Senate, December 19, 1833]. Charges that Taney's explanation contains misquotations and evasions. Notes that the Senate had asked him for information and gotten back an argument. Denies that Taney has the power (which he bases on an alleged precedent attributed to Secretary of the Treasury Crawford) to remove government deposits from the Bank of the United States. *Register of Debates* 23 Cong., 1 Sess., 94-96.

Remark in Senate, January 3, 1834. Moves that a private relief bill be tabled so that Sen. Thomas H. Benton might resume his remarks on the removal of the deposits [Bradley to Clay, October 16, 1832; Speech in Senate, December 26, 1833] issue. *Cong. Globe*, 23 Cong., 1 Sess., 77.

From PETER B. PORTER   Black Rock, N.Y., January 5, 1833
                                                        [*sic*, 1834]

I received, yesterday, your kind letter of the 26th ultimo; and the same mail that brought it, brought also the [Washington *Daily*] National Intelligencer, with the first part of your speech on the Deposits question.[1] I have read the speech, thus far, with great delight as well as with patriotic pride; and should its force and spirit be sustained in the second part, it will doubtless be put down as one of your noblest and most splendid efforts.

The people of this country appear to be perfectly spellbound. Lolling at their ease, in wealth and luxury, they seem to be entirely unconscious of the causes of their prosperity, and insensible to the dangers which threaten it; and if they are not awakened to a sense of their true situation by the bold and prophetic expostulations of yourself and copatriots, nothing short of the actual adversity which must soon follow (and which, if not the best, is always the most infallible instructor) can teach them practical wisdom. I confess I am not without hopes that your efforts may prove successful and save the country, without subjecting it to that last though surest of all remedies, which often destroys the value of what it is intended to preserve.

I am glad to see the question of the deposits progress so *moderately* in both houses; for I think you will constantly gain by delay, if not continued too long. Every day's discussion, aided by manifestations of public sentiment, and evidences of public distress, cannot, I think, fail to produce some effect on the Jackson men in Congress who have not abjured every sentiment of patriotism; and if you can succeed in gaining a majority of one only in the house of Representatives (the Senate I take it can be relied on) in favor of restoring the deposits, your good work will I think be accomplished. I have no doubt, knowing Gen'l Jackson's violence, that he will veto any bill or resolution you may send him for the removal of the deposits — but I think that this move would be much more likely to prostrate him and his administration than if he were to sanction it. After having acknowledged in a late public document (I think his manifesto to his Cabinet)[2] the appropriate and exclusive power of Congress over the public monies, and regretted that they had indiscreetly divested themselves of that power in their conduct with the Bank; and after this part of the contract has been satisfied and cancelled by the actual, and as he says, rightfull removal of the money from its vaults, with what force can his adherents justify his retaining the monies, and refusal to place them where the two houses of Congress may direct — whether in the Bank of the U. S. or elsewhere?

Should you not succeed in obtaining a resolution by both houses for the restoration of the deposits,[3] a very interesting question arises whether the Senate should not, by withholding appropriations or some other hostile act, meet the encroachments of the Executive. On this subject I rely, with perfect confidence, on the wisdom and patriotism of our friends in the Senate, and I have no doubt but they will be sustained in any move they may think proper to adopt.

You will have a delicate question to meet in the bill which Mr. Calhoun has presented to the Senate for the repeal of the *force act*,[4] on account of the probable sensitiveness of some of your friends in the Senate, and particularly Mr. Webster, on that subject. You did not, I think, vote for that Bill, although you expressed yourself, *under the then peculiar situation of the country*, as favoring its enactments. It seems to me that the law may now be repealed, by those who supported it, without any charge of inconsistency against, or grounds of dissatisfaction with them. The law, at the time of its passage, was acknowledged to give high military and discretionery powers to the President, and was justified only by the extraordinary posture of affairs at that time. But now, after the imaginary occasion of its passage is past, it would seem to be inexpedient as well as unnecessary to retain it in the Statute Book. But the strongest and most conclusive of all reasons for its repeal is, that the *present* Executive has, since its passage, shown himself wholly unworthy of such high discretionery power. This argument, indeed, in the present state of affairs, seems to me sufficient to sway and put at nought every other consideration — for Caesar has entered the house of Representatives and is now at the door of the Senate, and it behooves you to oppose every constitutional bar to his entrance.

You seem to apprehend no danger of Mr. V.B.'s driving a bargain with the Bank.[5] — I hope, and indeed I believe, you are correct — but my belief rests entirely on my good opinion of the general integrity of the gentlemen who form that Institution. I know Mr. Van Buren well, and I know of no man who can more readily smother and forego personal sentiments, or with less compunction, sacrifice principle for policy. I am aware that his tools are openly clamorous against the Bank on every question, and so has he been. But if he finds himself foiled in open warfare with it, its power will be too great to be disregarded, and I shall be much disappointed if he does not attempt to save or at least to maintain its influence by some secret and insidious alliance.

I presume you have become acquainted with Mr. Selden, from N. York, who has attracted considerable attention by the course he is taking in regard to the Bank;[6] and if you do not know him, I think you should, and show him some attentions. He is clever, and too independent for a N. York collar man.[7] He has great personal respect for you, and 2 or 3 years ago, when he had about resolved to abandon his party, he wished and I agreed to give him a letter of introduction to you. But his party, who suspected his fidelity, retained him by office and preferments and by giving to his father[8] (a worthy old man) the Agency of the Harbor and the Docks (in place of Maj. Marriner) and which will doubtless now be taken from him.

You will excuse anything in my letters which may have the appearance of a disposition to offer advice. I have no such intention. In my letters to you I throw out suggestions on the prevailing topics of the day because I presume it will be satisfactory to you to know the views, even of your most unimportant friends in the country in regard to the public measures in which you are taking so distinguished and effective a part.

The "Spy"[9] I perceive is still pouring out a stream of secret information. I did not know that he was in Washington this winter, but presume from his letters that he must be.

Copy. OHi. Misdated as January 5, 1833.   1. Speech in Senate, Dec. 26, 1833.   2. "Removal of the Pubic Deposits," read to the Cabinet Sept. 18, 1833. See *MPP*, 3:5-19.   3. Bradley to Clay, Oct. 16, 1832.   4. Calhoun introduced a bill to repeal the Force Act on Dec. 9, 1833. On April 9, 1834, he moved for consideration of the bill and addressed the Senate on its behalf. The bill was referred to the Committee on the Judiciary which never reported it. *Register of Debates*, 23 Cong., 1 Sess., 20, 57, 1266-81, 1287; Wilson, *Calhoun Papers*, 12:189; Remark in Senate, Jan. 22, 1833; Root to Clay, Jan. 12, 1834.   5. Porter to Clay, Dec. 7, 1833.   6. For Congressman Dudley Selden of New York, see *BDAC*. Selden argued in the House that in order for the question of removal of deposits to be settled quickly, it should be considered by the House as a Committee of the Whole rather than being referred to the Ways and Means Committee or a Select Committee. *Register of Debates*, 23 Cong., 1 Sess., 2186-89.   7. For the term "collar man," see Clay to Porter, Dec. 26, 1833.   8. For Joseph Dudley Selden (1764-1837) of Troy, N.Y., see Sophie Selden Rogers *et al.*, *Selden Ancestry, A Family History* (Oil City, Pa., n.d.), 134-35.   9. Reference obscure. But see "de Sarcy" to Clay, Sept. 17, 1829; Feb. 11, 1830.

Remark in Senate, January 9, 1834. Objects to a motion by Sen. William Wilkins (Pa.) to print 5,000 extra copies of a "second report of the Secretary of the Treasury [Roger B. Taney] (made a few days ago)" on the removal of government deposits from the Bank of the United States [Bradley to Clay, October 16, 1832; Speech in Senate, December 26, 1833]. *Register of Debates*, 23 Cong., 1 Sess., 199; *Cong. Globe*, 23 Cong. 1 Sess., 90. For Taney's report, dated December 30, 1833, see *Register of Debates*, 23 Cong., 1 Sess., Appendix, 90-101. It was also published as a pamphlet, titled *Report From the Secretary of the Treasury, in Reply to a Resolution of the Senate of the 19th Instant, Requiring Copies of Certain Correspondence Relative to the Removal of the Public Deposits, and Funds in the Bank of the United States. . . .* Washington, 1833.

Remark in Senate, January 10, 1834. Supports a resolution by Sen. Theodore Frelinghuyen (N.J.) asking Secretary of the Treasury Roger B. Taney for information on how the compromise tariff legislation of 1833 [Draft Proposal, Mid-December, 1832; Speech in Senate, February 12, 1833] is actually being interpreted by the Treasury Department and administered by the collectors. Expresses his "astonishment" at some of the interpretations said to be current with respect to calculations of the reduction of the ad valorem duty on cotton. *Register of Debates*, 23 Cong., 1 Sess., 200; *Cong. Globe*, 23 Cong., 1 Sess., 94. See Comment in Senate, January 13, 14, 1834.

From Alexander Gardiner, East Hampton, N.Y., January 11, 1834. Sends resolution "unanimously adopted by the members of the Philomathian Society" which thanks Clay "for securing to the rising generation that greatest of all blessings—human freedom." ALS. CtY.

Clay responded on February 3, 1834, thanking Gardiner and the other members of the society for their resolution and noting that in the hands of such American youth the "destinies" of the nation rest. *Ibid.* For Alexander Gardiner, brother of Julia Gardiner Tyler, President John Tyler's second wife, see Seager, *And Tyler Too, passim.*

From SAMUEL C. OWINGS   Baltimore, January 11, 1834
Your favour came duly to hand containing a Check for 18 50/100 $ being the Amt due me for the keeping of your Horses except my thanks for your prompt attention to my little bill which was very exceptiable at a time of such preshure for many and my hasty wish that you may suckseed in getting the Govament deposits restorde to the bank of the United States from wence they were removed and restore to the people there former facillity of getting Money

ALS. DLC-TJC (DNA, M212, R10). Endorsed by Clay: "Rect. for Livery Stable."

From Erastus Root, Delhi, N.Y., January 12, 1834. Praises Clay's speeches on the removal of deposits [Bradley to Clay, October 16, 1832; Speech in Senate, December 26, 1833]. Wonders if or when "the mad career" of the "military Chieftain" will ever be checked. Asks whether "Under the Constitution, *as now understood*," Secretary of the Treasury Roger B. Taney can be impeached for "High Crimes & Misdemeanors." Asks about Clay's stance on the repeal of the Force bill [Remark in Senate, January 22, 1833], recalling that "You was not present on the final passage of that odious bill, but I got the idea (I hope an erroneous one) that had you been present you might have voted for it. With the sword & the purse & that bill at his command an American Caesar [Jackson] might sink into comparative insignificance that puny whipster of a Caesar [Julius] whom you so eloquently described as swaying the fiscal destinies of Rome. A part of the most odious part of the force-bill I believe will expire with the present session, but the statute-book ought to be purged of that foul stain—" ALS. DLC-HC (DNA, M212, R5). The first and fifth sections of the Force bill were to expire automatically at the end of the first session of the 23rd Congress, which ended on June 30, 1834. The first section authorized the president to use land, naval, or militia forces to prevent the removal of detained vessels or cargo and/or to protect customs officials. The fifth section authorized the president to use military force, or any other means necessary, to suppress obstructions of the laws within any state. 2 *U.S. Stat.*, 632-35.

Comment in Senate, January 13, 1834. Continues his inquiry of January 10 [Remark in Senate, January 10, 1834] into the question of how Secretary of the Treasury Taney and his comptroller, Joseph Anderson, have been interpreting and applying the compromise tariff legislation of 1833, particularly with reference to levying the duty on cottons. Declares that errors have been made that have been admitted and asks the Committee on Manufactures to look into the situation. Explains how the recently legislated tariff reductions should be computed arithmetically. Moves that the Senate be shown the new instructions from Secretary Taney to the collectors of customs relating to the levying process. Hopes that these new instructions will "save our cotton manufacturers from the impending destruction." *Register of Debates*, 23 Cong., 1 Sess., 203-5; *Cong. Globe*, 23 Cong., 1 Sess., 97. For the valuation of dutiable goods at the port of entry, rather than at the port of departure, see Draft of Compromise Tariff Bill, February 11, 1833; Speech in Senate, February 12, 1833; Van Deusen, *Jacksonian Era*, 77.

Also on this day, Clay moved the following: "That the Committee on Finance be directed to inquire into the expediency of affording temporary relief to the community from the present pecuniary embarrassment, by prolonging the payment of revenue bonds, as they fall due, the obligors paying interest and giving satisfactory security." Not printed in the *Register of Debates* until January 14; see *ibid.*, 23 Cong., 1 Sess., 233.

To FRANCIS T. BROOKE — Washington, January 14, 1834

I recd. your favor of the 12h. That written by you early in December never came to hand, and I regret it. As to the repeal of the Force bill, there are parts of it which are permanent, and which in my judgment ought to remain, independent of and distinct from any excitement in So. Carolina. The two sections (the first and fifth) contain some provisions to which I objected on their passage.[1] If the repeal of them were asked, not on the ground of the truth of the principles of nullification, but as expedient since the necessity for them has passed by, to tranquillize the South, it might not be objectionable, altho', even in that view, those parts of the act expiring with the present Session,[2] by express limitation, there is no great utility in the repeal. But it is not asked on any other ground than that Nullification is right, and to that I cannot assent. If I could forget myself and my principles so much as to adopt those of nullification, it would prove my utter ruin as a public man. Nullification is every where in the minority but in So. C. In Kentucky it cannot hold up its head. And I think Mr Calhoun has been unfortunate in stirring this matter, which had better be left to sleep quietly.

What is doing in your Legislature about the deposites?[3] We want all aid here on that subject which can be given us from Richmond. What has been done there has been of immense service to us. Virginia is herself again, and has once more the power to rally around her standard the friends of freedom. But bold determined conduct on her part is necessary; and particularly on the subject of the Public treasury. If she now faulters or pulls back it would have been better that she should have never excited any hopes; for then we might have all sunk quietly into the abyss of despotism.

ALS. DLC-TJC (DNA, M212, R10). Letter marked "(Confidential)." 1. Root to Clay, Jan. 12, 1834. 2. *Ibid.* 3. A committee of the Virginia house of delegates voted 11 to 2 in disapproval of the removal of the federal government's deposits from the Bank of the United States and recommended that the B.U.S. continue to be the government's depository. *Niles' Register* (Jan. 4, 1834), 45:309. A group of citizens meeting in Richmond on Dec. 26, 1833, made the same recommendation. *Ibid.*, 312. Subsequently, the house of delegates passed six resolutions condemning the removal of deposits as usurpation of the constitution and urging Virginia's representatives in Congress "to adopt prompt and efficient measures to vindicate the constitution." *Ibid.* (Feb. 1, 1834), 45:388.

Comment in Senate, January 14, 1834. Defends his motion of the previous day, viz: that the Committee on Finance examine the "expediency of affording temporary relief to the community from the present pecuniary embarrassment, by prolonging the payment of revenue bonds [offered for the payment of duties], as they fall due, the obligors paying interest and giving satisfactory security." In this context, discusses the impact of the depression on the national economy and argues that the U.S. Treasury would still have the ability to handle its cash obligations if such bonds were simply renewed rather than paid off when due. "If there could be afforded any relief to the mercantile classes," he concludes, "some alleviation of the general distress would follow." *Register of Debates*, 23 Cong., 1 Sess., 223-28; *Cong. Globe*, 23 Cong., 1 Sess., 101. On this day, the Senate also received a memorial (not printed in the *Register* or *Cong. Globe*) from the "Sundry Importing Merchants of New York, Praying that Credits May Be Extended for Duties on Imports on Account of the Public Distress &c." On January 15, Clay offered a motion to consider relief for these merchants. The matter was referred to the Senate Finance Committee on February 19, 1834, and apparently died there. *Sen Docs.*, 23 Cong., 1 Sess., no. 99. See also Comment in Senate, February 19, 1834.

To JOHN PENDLETON KENNEDY   Washington, January 15, 1834
I recd. your favor. You will perceive from the papers that I lost no time in respect to the Treasury construction abt. the Cotton minimums;[1] and that the Secy. [Roger B. Taney] admits the error and throws the blame upon the Comptroller [Joseph Anderson]. He promises immediately by fresh instructions to correct the error. These we will call for, and watch him.[2]

The truth is the error was [John] McLean's and the Comptroller is made the Scape Goat. I believe with you it was a deep laid design.

ALS. MdBP.   1. Comment in Senate, Jan. 13, 1834.   2. On this same day, Clay wrote Messrs. Jackson, Carrington *et al.*, covering much the same ground. ALS. KyU.

Remark in Senate, January 15, 1834. Suggests that a motion to consider relief for the "Importing Merchants of New York [Comment in Senate, January 13, 14, 1834]" be tabled and agrees with Sen. George Poindexter (Miss.) that general discussion on the removal of deposits [Bradley to Clay, October 16, 1832; Speech in Senate, December 26, 1833] issue should proceed. *Register of Debates*, 23 Cong., 1 Sess., 252.

Clay also moved this day that certain papers, recently discovered, relating to a land claim, be sent to the relevant committee. *Cong. Globe*, 23 Cong., 1 Sess., 104.

Remark in Senate, January 16, 1834. Presents the claim of a Revolutionary War officer. *Cong. Globe*, 23 Cong., 1 Sess., 108.

To Henry Clay, Jr., Lexington, January 17, 1834. Complains that he has not had a letter from his son since that of December 14, 1833. Wants to be kept informed on what is happening at "Ashland." Discusses rents to be collected, notes coming due, and bills that need paying. ALS. Henry Clay Memorial Foundation, Lexington, Ky.

Remark in Senate, January 17, 1834. Opposes efforts to water down by amendment the wording of his resolution of January 13 [Comment in Senate, January 14, 1834], and urges that the discussion on the revenue bonds and the national depression be concluded on January 20. *Register of Debates*, 23 Cong., 1 Sess., 252, 259; *Cong. Globe*, 23 Cong., 1 Sess., 114.

To James Brown, Philadelphia, January 18, 1834. Sends a "corrected Copy of my Speech [Speech in Senate, December 26, 1833]; the first part of which had been published from the notes taken by the stenographers." Continues: "A reaction has however taken place to a limited extent against us, in consequence of the proceedings of certain State legislatures, and I now think that our final success in the House will depend upon the number and the influence of the popular meetings which are taking place throughout the Country." ALS. KyLxT. Clay's speech was published under the title, *Speech of the Hon. Henry Clay, on the Subject of the Removal of the Deposits; Delivered in the Senate of the United States, December 26, 30, 1833*. Washington, 1834. During 1834, the state legislature of New Jersey, New York, Ohio, Maine, and New Hampshire passed resolutions approving Jackson's position on the removal of deposits. Kentucky, Massachusetts, Connecticut, and Rhode Island passed resolutions opposing his actions. See *Niles' Register* (January 25, 1834), 45:370-71; (July 5, 1834), 46:195, 325, 335; and U.S. Sen., *Journal*, 23 Cong., 1 Sess., 124, 146, 178.

To JOHN D. DICKINSON

Washington, January 18, 1834

I received your favor of the 12h inst. and gave the letter to Dr Hunt [*sic*, Henry Huntt] which it enclosed the direction you desired.

The debate is still in progress in both houses on the deposite question.[1] I wish I was authorized to speak with more confidence as to a proper decision of it. We had evidently gained by the discussion, and had converted the majority, with which the Session opened for the Administration, in the house, into a minority or at least greatly diminished it.[2] But the resolutions of your Legislature of N Jersey and of that of Ohio[3] have produced a reaction against us, and, with some exceptions, members have returned to their first impressions. On the other hand, the proceedings of the Legislature and people of Virginia[4] have cheered and tended to sustain us. The effect of them however is not sufficient to counterbalance that of the other three states. The operation is only on the timid and wavering; but you know there are always enough of these to shift the majority from one side to the other. My opinion is that, unless the popular demonstration should be very powerful and general the Administration will maintain its majority in the house. Meetings of the people have and are taking place in several States; and should they continue, be very numerous, and embrace individuals of both parties we may finally prevail.

Tell Mrs. D[ickinson]. that we were at a very brilliant party a few evenings ago at her daughters[5] who I was glad to see look better than I expected to find her. . . .

ALS. KyLoF. 1. Bradley to Clay, Oct. 16, 1832; Speech in Senate, Dec. 26, 1833. 2. Whittlesey to Clay, Sept. 19, 1832. 3. Clay to Brown, Jan. 18, 1834. 4. Clay to Brooke, Jan. 14, 1834; Clay to Tazewell, Feb. 1, 1834. 5. See Hunt, *First Forty Years of Washington Society*, 344.

From Nicholas Biddle, Philadelphia, January 20, 1834. Discusses Clay's personal transactions with the Bank of the United States. Sees "difficulties which are coming upon the intercourse between the States in consequence of the disorders of the currency." Specifically calls attention to a rise in the rate of exchange from ½ or ¾ of 1 percent to 2½ percent. Remarks: "How far this is to proceed is uncertain—but it is manifest that the troubles are but beginning and unless you can succeed in your manly and patriotic efforts to drive these miserable people from the high places which they dishonor, there is a dark and dreary futurity approaching." Copy. DLC-Nicholas Biddle Papers, vol. 5, Supp. Roll 2.

From Nicholas Biddle, Philadelphia, January 23, 1834. Sends Clay copies of a correspondence with the War Department. Assures him that "there is not the slightest foundation for the claim advanced by the Executive" that there has been mismanagement of army pension funds deposited in the Bank of the United States. Copy. DLC-Nicholas Biddle Papers, vol. 5, Supp. Roll 2. For the army pension fund controversy see Comment in Senate, February 4, 1834.

To HENRY CLAY, JR.   Washington, January 23, 1834

I recd. your favor of the 14h. and was glad to perceive the cheerful & happy tone which pervades it. I approve entirely of what you have done in respect to Mr. [William] Martin, and hope you will continue your visits to Ashland.[1] I wish you would call on the lady who occupies the [Kentucky] Hotel and ask her to pay you the rent that is due. And I should like to know how my a/c. stands at the Bank. What premium is paid at Lexn. on Eastern checks?

You ask me the probable fate of the deposite question?[2] In the House I fear that the majority is against us. The caucus legislatures of N. York, N. Jersey and Ohio have strengthened the timid, and secured the wavering.[3] On the other hand, popular meetings are taking place every where, and our success in that house will depend upon the extent of the re-action among the people. Do you intend at Lexington to have a meeting? It might do good.

But if we lose in the House[4] (in the Senate we are safe) the immediate question, altho I shd. regret it, I would not yet despair. It will be the first act only in the drama. Others must follow, and I believe before the Session closes we will have the majority in both houses.

The distress in the Eastern Cities is intense. I am glad it has not reached you; but it will before next fall.

Our love to Julia [Prather Clay], and kisses for little Henry [Clay III].

ALS. Henry Clay Memorial Foundation, Lexington, Ky.   1. Henry Clay, Jr., to Clay, Dec. 14, 1833.   2. Bradley to Clay, Oct. 16, 1832; Clay to Tazewell, April 5, 1834.   3. Clay to Brown, Jan. 18, 1834.   4. Clay to Tazewell, April 5, 1834.

From William Sullivan, Boston, January 24, 1834. Thanks Clay for a copy of his speech opposing the removal of government deposits from the Bank of the United States [Speech in Senate, December 26, 1833; Clay to Brown, January 18, 1834]. Discusses the impact on the Boston economy of the depression caused by the removals. Observes: "We have arrived, I think with you, to the last stages of corrupt decline. We need only the servile guards, and a subservient judiciary, to close the career of the republic. Here, in the midst of plenty and prosperity, we are suddenly plunged into an artificial distress, more intolerable than the calamities which suppressed commerce, prostrate industry, and foreign war, produced. We discern no remedy. The delusion which governs a majority of the popular branch (as we understand here) and the determined perseverance of the Executive, bereave our community of all hope. I assure you, that in the last thirty five years, I never saw the intelligent men of our City so utterly despondent. . . . Where money can be had, it is at a rate between one and two per ct. a month — In fact business is comp[le]tely at a stand, and the attention of mercantile debtors is entirely absorbed in saving themselves from insolvency — though they are far from being bankrupt. — We look to such men as yourself to devise remedies." ALS. NHi. For Sullivan, a Boston lawyer and sometime member of the state legislature, see *CAB*.

To John R.D. Payne *et al.*, Lynchburg, Va., February 1, 1834. Thanks them for the resolutions passed at a January 9, 1834, meeting in Lynchburg and "For the distinguished notice which they have been pleased to take of my humble exertions against daring usurpation, and in defense of the constitution, the laws and the public faith." Feels that "If the country shall become convinced of the dangers impending over our liberties, I shall feel that my earnest and constant, but not always successful, endeavors, will not have been exerted altogether in vain." Adds that in Jackson's recent "seizure of the public purse [Bradley to Clay, October 16, 1832; Speech in Senate, December 26, 1833], doctrines have been advanced on the floors of the two Houses of Congress, which belong to the age of the British Stuarts. If these doctrines are sanctioned and maintained by the people, the supremacy of the Executive over every other department of the Government will be completely established." Copy. Printed in Lexington *Observer & Kentucky Reporter*, March 13, 1834. Payne, who at one time served as mayor of Lynchburg, was married to Susan Bryce. He later moved to Richmond, Va., where he died. *VMHB*, 24:315.

To LITTLETON W. TAZEWELL
Washington, February 1, 1834

I recd. your note with the highly interesting correspondence between yourself and Mr. [William J.] Duane. I read it with deep attention. It exposes a new and detestable[1] feature in the affair of the deposites.[2]

The doctrines by which that Executive measure is sustained are even more alarming than the measure itself. It is now contended that *all* Executive power is in the President; that he is to take care that *all* the laws are faithfully executed; that one will alone is to govern in that branch of the Government, to which all the Executive officers must conform; and that he has the power to remove, whenever he pleases.

Carried out into their consequences, these doctrines would prove that the Executive power is not to be sought in the Constitution, but in its inherent nature; and that the Executive of the U. States was Supreme, the two other branches of the Governmt being practically subordinate to it.

I should be glad, if you have leisure, to know your views of these doctrines; and particularly whether you believe that, by the Constitution, without reference to the recognition of the power of removal by the first Congress, the President possesses it; and whether he had *the power* to remove Mr. Duane, for declining to withdraw the deposites.

We are gaining ground; and I am not without hopes of final success in the H. of R. It will depend upon the amount of public opinion brought to act upon it. And in that respect the movements in Virginia have been of inestimable service.[3] In the Senate, we have never doubted.

ALS. KyU. Addressed to Tazewell in Norfolk, Va.   1. This word substituted for the word "dangerous" which was stricken.   2. Bradley to Clay, Oct. 16, 1832.   3. Clay to Brooke, Jan. 14, 1834.

From Nicholas Biddle, Philadelphia, February 2, 1834. Has learned from "our friend" Henry C. Carey that deposed Secretary of the Treasury William J. Duane had "some very interesting correspondence which he . . . was desirous of having published" if someone would but call upon him to do so. Asks Clay to make such a call if he thinks "the public interest would be promoted by it." Encloses (not found) a batch of letters which demonstrate the following: "The letter marked 1 . . . contains a passage to this effect—that if the Bank of the United States did not conduct itself in a manner that would be satisfactory the State Banks would be able to reserve its paper received for revenue, and break in succession every one of its Branches, showing that the design was entertained by the President of breaking the Bank. The letter marked 6, is considered by Mr Duane as the most important of the President's letters containing the most elaborate argument in favor of the proposed measure [Bradley to Clay, October 16, 1832]. The letter marked 7—was retained by the advice of a friend who told him it would inevitably occasion an explosion between him and the President. No 12. shows, I understand, that the President has stricken out from the instructions what related to an enquiry by the Agent into the effect on the Community of these measures, intimating that the President did not mean to ask or did not care to know what effects this would produce." Says that Duane does not wish to be summoned in person by the Senate, "but would readily give these papers when requested." Copy. DLC-Nicholas Biddle Papers, vol. 5, Supp. Roll 2. The Duane correspondence appeared, as reprinted from the Philadelphia papers, in the Washington *Daily National Intelligencer* in February and March of 1834.

To NICHOLAS BIDDLE
Washington, February 2, 1834

I transmit the enclosed just as I have recd. them. I wish you could accommodate, Mr. [Benjamin] Knower.[1] It may be done, I believe, with perfect safety. He is, you know, the father-in-law of Gov [William L.] Marcy and he belongs to that powerful interest in N. York (he is indeed the head of it) which is held by very loose bounds to the Regency The desired accommodation would have the best effects.

I recd. your letter respecting the Pension agency[2] The call for the correspondence *shall* be made. I thought it best to wait a few days.

My opinion is that no movement should be yet made towards a renewal of the Charter,[3] or the establishment of a New Bank. The Bank ought to be kept in the rear; the usurpation[4] in front. If we take up the Bank, we play into the adversarys hands. We realize his assertions that the only question is a renewal of the Charter. It is the usurpation which has convulsed the Country. If we put it by and take up the Bank, we may & probably would divide about the terms of the charter, and finally do nothing leaving things as they are. In the other course, the re charter will follow. The Country will take care of that. PS Be pleased to return to me Mr. Knower's letter and inform him directly of the fate of his application.

ALS. DLC-Nicholas Biddle Papers (DNA, M212, R20). Letter marked "(Confidential)."   1. For Knower see 5:144, and Mushkat, *Tammany*, 117-18, 135-36. The leading stockholder in the Farmers' and Mechanics' Bank of Albany (N.Y.), Knower was at this time facing bankruptcy. Govan, *Nicholas Biddle*, 151-56, 254.   2. See Comment in Senate, Feb. 4, 1834.   3. Clay to Wilde, April 27, 1833.   4. Removal of deposits. Bradley to Clay, Oct. 16, 1832; Speech in Senate, Dec. 26, 1834.

Remark in Senate, February 3, 1834. Speaks intermittently on the procedural dimensions of referring the December 4, 1833, report of Secretary of the Treasury Roger B. Taney on the removal of the deposits [Bradley to Clay, October 16, 1832] to the Committee on Finance without interrupting regular debate on the related larger issues involved. *Register of Debates*, 23 Cong., 1 Sess., 445-46, 448; *Cong. Globe*, 23 Cong., 1 Sess., 147. See also Remark in Senate, December 18, 1833; Speech in Senate, December 26, 1833.

To Robert Charles Winthrop, Boston, February 3, 1834. Sends him, as requested, a "corrected copy" of his speech in the Senate on the deposits question [Speech in Senate, December 26, 1833; Bradley to Clay, October 16, 1832]. Remarks: "The debate on the deposite question continues. Success in the House will depend upon the amount of public opinion brought to bear against the Executive measure." ALS. MHi. For Winthrop, a Boston lawyer and politician, see *BDAC*.

From Nicholas Biddle, Philadelphia, February 4, 1834. Acknowledges Clay's letter of February 2. Reports that the B.U.S. board today reviewed Clay's suggested accommodation for Benjamin Knower [Clay to Biddle, February 2, 1834] and "deemed it best not to discount. The sum is very large — the bills themselves not desirable at present — the time which they have to run is much beyond our present limits of purchasing." Concludes on a political note: "I coincide with you in opinion that the usurpation [Bradley to Clay, October 16, 1832; Speech in Senate, December 26, 1833] is the first object — the Bank the second — and that a force would be rallied upon the former which might not continue united on the latter. To obtain a vote restoring the deposits, is to break up the gang who govern the 'Government.' That should be the first purpose of every honest man among us. If that cannot be accomplished it is idle to talk about the constitution and the laws—there are no longer such things in existence. How far in the rear the recharter should be left, is a matter of which they on the spot can best judge, and that we must leave to the better judgment of you and friends like you in Washington." Copy. DLC-Nicholas Biddle Papers, vol. 5, Supp. Roll 2. Writes Clay again on February 5, 1834, referring to his "now having got through this New York embroglio" with respect to Knower. *Ibid.*

Comment in Senate, February 4, 1834. Responds to a message from Jackson to Congress, dated February 4, which attacks the Bank of the United States for the mismanagement of government Revolutionary War pension fund deposits in its care, and which encloses a report from Attorney General Benjamin F. Butler sustaining the president's view of this matter. Points out that Jackson is preparing to weaken the B.U.S. further by removing its legal obligation to pay American Revolutionary War pensions. Charges that all this is but further evidence of Jackson's continuing attack on the bank and lauds the B.U.S. for its resistance to the usurper. Asks for a Senate investigation of the situation. Remarks that he "can no longer respect the opinions of an Attorney General, or any other Executive officer," because Jackson "would instantaneously dismiss any officer who did not at once obey his behests." *Register of Debates*, 23 Cong., 1 Sess., 462-63; *Cong. Globe*, 23 Cong., 1 Sess., 151-52. Jackson and Secretary of the Treasury Roger B. Taney had ordered the B.U.S. to turn over these pension funds to agents appointed by the president. Nicholas Biddle flatly refused, on the grounds that the order was a flagrant violation of the law establishing the B.U.S. as the sole agent for the payment of the pensions. See Govan, *Nicholas Biddle*, 251; Woodford, *Lewis Cass*, 179-80.

Speech in Senate, February 5, 1834. Continues his attack on President Jackson's removal of the deposits [Bradley to Clay, October 16, 1832], Secretary Taney's role in the removal decision, attempts by the administration to manipulate pertinent documentary evidence, the president's dangerous "usurpation of power" in the matter, and both the illegality and unconstitutionality of the whole business. Charges, further, that the placement of government funds in "thirty or forty local, disconnected, and incompetent institutions" can only undermine the integrity of the currency issued by them. *Register of Debates*, 23 Cong., 1 Sess., 477-79. See also, Speech in Senate, December 26, 1833.

From James Brown, Philadelphia, February 6, 1834. Thanks Clay for having assisted him in a legal matter. Notes that "A fresh question seems to have been presented by the President respecting the Pension fund [Comment in Senate, February 4, 1834]," and wonders if Clay has been "indiscreet" in his attack on Attorney General Benjamin F. Butler [5:439] who, he has been informed, "is a gentleman of fine talents and unquestionable integrity." Reports that the "Jackson party" is holding "a large meeting as they say" tonight in a room of the District Court, but that "The names are not spoken of as standing very high as given in the list calling this meeting." Fears a split in the anti-Jackson forces in the U.S. Senate. ALS. DLC-HC (DNA, M212, R5). Printed in *LHQ*, 24:1169-70. The meeting in Philadelphia on February 6 passed resolutions commending Jackson for his veto of the Bank of the United States recharter bill [Clay to Wilde, April 27, 1833] and his removal of government deposits therefrom [Bradley to Clay, October 16, 1832]. The resolutions also endorsed his use of executive power. Washington *Globe*, February 11, 1834.

Remark in Senate, February 6, 1834. Attempts to smooth over a dangerously sharp personal exchange on the removal of deposits issue [Bradley to Clay, October 16, 1832] between Senators William Wilkins (Pa.) and Daniel Webster (Mass.). Succeeds. *Register of Debates*, 23 Cong., 1 Sess., 485.

Comment in Senate, February 7, 1834. Moves to take up his resolution to extend the time for the payment of revenue bonds [Comment in Senate, January 13, 14, 1834]. Speaks for his motion, noting the degree and extent of economic suffering abroad in the land. Argues that the purpose of his motion is to help alleviate the nation's economic distress. Calls particular attention to depressed conditions in the cotton textile and iron trades. *Register of Debates*, 23 Cong., 1 Sess., 492-94, 525.

On this same day, Clay praised a memorial signed by various "mechanics, manufacturers, laborers, and others" from New York City's second ward demanding the restoration of deposits [Bradley to Clay, October 16, 1832] and the recharter of the B.U.S. [Clay to Wilde, April 27, 1833] as means of relieving economic distress. *Ibid.*, 492; *Cong. Globe*, 23 Cong., 1 Sess., 160-62.

From George Tucker, Charlottesville, Va., February 8, 1834. Reports on political sentiment in Virginia: "The popularity of Genl. Jackson, taken in connection with the unpopularity of the Bank still maintains a nominal ascendancy in some parts of this state; among others in this county, but it is evidently in the wane, and every where some of his staunchest supporters have deserted him. I have lately heard from one of the leading members of the legislature that the states right party begin generally to take the same view of the re-charter of the Bank [Clay to Wilde, April 27, 1833] as I do, as the only effectual means of preventing that concentration of power & corrupt influence which the party aim at, whether they establish another bank, or distribute the public money among the state banks." Discusses at length the history, utility, and merits of metallic versus paper currencies, strongly favoring the latter. Defends the administrative decision of the B.U.S. gradually to call in some of its debts preparatory to winding up its business as a national institution. ALS. DLC-HC (DNA, M212, R5). Written from the University of Virginia. For Tucker, who held the chair of ethics at the University of Virginia, see Bruce, *History of the University of Virginia*, 2:19-24; and *BDAC*.

To FRANCIS T. BROOKE   Washington, February 10, 1834
I should have written you oftener, but for the best reason in the world, that I had really nothing to write that was interesting.

The debate on the deposits continues.[1] We are gaining both in public opinion and in number in the House of Representatives. We are probably still there in a minority,[2] although the majority is not large, and will melt away if the current of public opinion continues to mix with us.

I transmit you a letter in answer to one I received.[3] I wish you to read and deliver it, unless you think I had better not have it delivered. We are here so accustomed to vetos, that I voluntarily, you see, subject my letter to yours.

Our city is full of distress committees.[4] The more the better.

Copy. Printed in Colton, *Clay Correspondence*, 4:377.   1. Bradley to Clay, Oct. 16, 1832; Speech in Senate, Dec. 26, 1833.   2. Whittlesey to Clay, Sept. 19, 1832.   3. Reference obscure.   4. Usually organized to petition Congress for relief from the economic distress said to be caused by Jackson's removal of the deposits.

To SAMUEL BELL   Washington, February 11, 1834
In answer to the enquiry, contained in your[1] note of yesterday, whether the meteoric phenomenon, which appeared in New England, on the 11h [*sic*] of November last,[2] was observed at my residence in Kentucky, I have the satisfaction to state, that it was seen there, and as far as the Gulf of Mexico. We

696

have every reason to believe that there was no part of this Continent from which it was not discernible.

ALS. NcD.   1. For Samuel Bell of New Hampshire, see *BDAC*.   2. An unusual meteor shower occurred in the early morning of Nov. 13, 1833, and lasted about thirty minutes. *Niles' Register* (Nov. 16, 1833), 45:184.

To HENRY CLAY, JR.   Washington, February 11, 1834

I recd. your favor of the 30h. Ulto.   Mr. [Philip B.] Hockaday has offered me $1000 for the half of Warrior[1] which I retained. I have written to him that I would accept it, provided he deposited the amt. to my credit by the 20h. inst with the Lexn B[ranch] Bank   I hope therefore from that and other resources you will be able to meet my draft on you. If they shd. however fail draw on me for whatever deficiency may exist.

The deposite question[2] remains undecided. We have thought that we do not lose by delay. Great excitement prevails in the Eastern Cities, and strong impression has been undoubtedly made on members of the House. Still it is uncertain whether there does not continue to be a small majority in the House in favor of the Executive.

To day Judge [Thomas T.] Bouldin of Virginia expired in the H. of R. whilst announcing the death of his predecessor Mr. J[ohn]. Randolph![3]

Give our love to Julia [Prather Clay], and tell her that I have not now for a long time recd. a letter from her. We sent some of the Brussell cabbage seed to Anne [Brown Clay Erwin] to divide with Julia.

Kiss my dear grandchild [Henry Clay, III] for me.

ALS. Henry Clay Memorial Foundation, Lexington, Ky.   1. Clay to Erwin, Oct. 13, 1833. On Feb. 15, writing Clay from Winchester, Ky., Hockaday confirmed the $1,000 sale price, accepting Clay's condition that he be allowed to breed to Warrior, free of charge, three jennics this year and three next year. Asks Clay to negotiate for him $3,000 insurance on Kochlani and $1,500 on Warrior. ALS. Courtesy of M.W. Anderson, Lexington, Ky. For Kocklani, see Berryman to Clay, August 6; Oct. 30, 1832; and Hockaday to Clay, Jan. 1, 1833.   2. Bradley to Clay, Oct 16, 1832; Speech in Senate, Dec. 26, 1833.   3. *Register of Debates*, 23 Cong., 1 Sess., 2704-5. Randolph had died on May 24, 1833.

Remark in Senate, February 11, 1834. Supports a motion to print a memorial from a "committee of gentlemen" in Philadelphia blaming the depression and the "disordered state of the currency of the country" on the removal of the deposits [Bradley to Clay, October 16, 1832]. *Register of Debates*, 23 Cong., 1 Sess., 527; *Cong. Globe*, 23 Cong., 1 Sess., 169.

Speech in Senate, February 14, 1834. Speaks in defense of a motion by N.C. Sen. Willie P. Mangum to print and refer to committee a petition from citizens in Burke County, N.C., favoring the restoration of deposits in the B.U.S. [Bradley to Clay, October 16, 1832] so that the national depression and the currency-stability crisis might be resolved. Attacks the contention of pro-Jackson Sen. John Forsyth (Ga.) that such petitions simply lead to "long speeches" and "a great consumption of time, without the production of any proportionate advantage." Uses the occasion of Forsyth's remark to defend the B.U.S. and Nicholas Biddle and to launch a broad-ranging attack on the fiscal irresponsibility, administrative incompetence, and high-handed measures of the Jackson administration [Speech in Senate, December 26, 1833]. Specifically, attacks Sen. William Wilkins (Pa.) for his contention that economic distress in the nation has been produced by the "debate in this Senate." Charges that Wilkins also "ascribes all these terrible consequences to a speech which I had the honor of addressing to the Senate some weeks ago [probably Speech in Senate, December 26, 1833]." Chides those who blame the depression on "The bank, the bank, the bank!" Gives evidence of the depth and breadth of the depression which, he argues, the B.U.S. had no hand in bringing on save in being the victim of the president's dictatorial removal of government deposits. Asks: "And what are the remedies proposed by those in possession of the Government? None, none"; only "Idle, and visionary, and chimerical schemes" such as the proposal "to banish all paper from circulation, and to resort exclusively to hard money." Concludes that it is really not a question of bank or no bank. It is a question of the "predominance of the laws or the uncontrolled will of one man." Among those who are denouncing the existing B.U.S., it is also a question of where a United States bank should be located, Chestnut Street in Philadelphia or Wall Street in New York. "Bank or no bank! There is no such question now or hereafter likely to rise. All feel and own that a United States bank is indispensable." Explains once again his shift from an anti-B.U.S. stance in 1811 to a pro-B.U.S. position in 1816 [2:200-205], noting that the "experience of the war . . . had shown the necessity for the bank. The country could not get along without it." *Register of Debates*, 23 Cong., 1 Sess., 545-50, 554-56, 565. For the Mangum motion and Forsyth's remarks, see *ibid*, 529, 539.

From Peter B. Porter, Black Rock, N. Y., February 15, 1834. Discusses which of two "Jackson men" would be the lesser of evils as collector of the port at Lewiston, N.Y. Turning to national politics, remarks that the longer the removal and restoration of deposits [Bradley to Clay, October 16, 1832] debate is protracted, the greater will Clay's strength on the issue become. Hopes that a majority for restoration can be achieved in the House, if only by a single vote, because "There is no doubt the President would veto the resolution, but so outrageous an act (after his recent declaration that the control and disposition of the public monies belonged appropriately to Congress) would awaken the fears of every honest man, & would moreover place him so clearly in the wrong, as to justify the Senate in any measures they might adopt to arrest his course & bring him back to a sense of his duty."

Has read, "with great satisfaction," Sen. Samuel L. Southard's protracted speech [January 8, 1834] opposing the removal of deposits [*Register of Debates*, 23 Cong., 1 Sess., 143-98]. Is pleased, too, that "Mr. Webster has at length (as Jack Downing would say) got his dander up. His silent and noncommital course, at the commencement of the Session, added to the sly and pregnent intimations of our opponents that he was about to form a coalition with Jackson and Van Buren, had begun to alarm many of his friends in the East. I am glad too, that he has relinquished for the present, the intention which, in a moment of excitement he announced of bringing in a bill for the recharter of the Bank. Such a step at this time would have created a new question & greatly weakened your ground. If you succeed in the deposit question the other measure will follow almost of course." Copy. OHi. On February 5, 1834, Webster came out in support of Clay's resolution censuring Secretary of the Treasury Roger B. Taney for his removal of the deposits [Speech in Senate, December 26, 1833]. *Register of Debates*, 23 Cong., 1 Sess., 467. Not until March 18, 1834, did he submit a bill that would recharter [Clay to Wilde, April 27, 1833] the B.U.S. for a six-year period. *Ibid.*, 984-1005.

To Henry Clay, Jr., Lexington, February 17, 1834. Requests that he take care of some banking chores. Promises him "one of my Saxon Rams in the fall" and also "a portion of the flock." Reports "no decision yet" on the removal of deposits question [Bradley to Clay, October 16, 1832], and regrets to say that "your mother's health is not good. The derangement of her stomach is so great that she can take nothing in it, without injury." ALS. Henry Clay Memorial Foundation, Lexington, Ky.

Remark in Senate, February 17, 1834. Moves, without success, that there be printed 3,000 additional copies of the President's message of February 4 on the relationship between the pension fund and the Bank of the United States [Comment in Senate,

February 4, 1834]. *Register of Debates*, 23 Cong., 1 Sess., 573-74. The president's message is in *ibid.*, 461-62. The *Cong. Globe* of this date reports Clay's motion as calling for 6,000 copies. 23 Cong., 1 Sess., 179.

To Henry Clay, Jr., Lexington, February 19, 1834. Asks his son to take care of some financial details for him at the Lexington office of the B.U.S. Reports on national politics, viz: "The H. of R. yesterday by a vote of 116 to 112 sustained the previous question, by which Mr. [George] McDuffies instruction to the Comee. to report a restoration of the deposites was, for the present, put aside; but the same question will come up again in the House in another form. The above vote exhibits very nearly the state of parties in the House. Whether the Admon will be able to retain its present small majority there depends upon the continuance of the existing distress and the expression of public opinion. I still hope for ultimate success." ALS. Henry Clay Memorial Foundation, Lexington, Ky. The vote was on a motion by James K. Polk (Tenn.) to refer the December 3, 1833, report of Secretary of the Treasury Roger B. Taney on the removal of deposits [Bradley to Clay, October 16, 1832] to the House Committee of Ways and Means. McDuffie (S.C.) added to it the instruction that all public revenue "hereafter collected" by the Treasury Department be deposited in the B.U.S., as required by the charter of the bank. *Register of Debates*, 23 Cong., 1 Sess., 2735-38. The *Register* records the defeat of McDuffie's instruction as 115 to 112. See also, Remark in Senate, December 18, 1833.

Comment in Senate, February 19, 1834. Presents petition from New York citizens requesting legislation to prolong the payment of revenue bonds [Comment in Senate, January 14, 1834]. Speaks to the advantages of stretching out the bond payments as an anti-depression device and a hedge against personal bankruptcies. Wonders if the removal of government deposits from the B.U.S. [Bradley to Clay, October 16, 1832] has "incapacitated the Treasury from granting this necessary assistance to the merchants." *Register of Debates*, 23 Cong., 1 Sess., 612-13.

From Littleton W. Tazewell, Norfolk, Va., February 19, 1834. Answers Clay's letter of February 1, with special attention to the passages questioning whether "*all* Executive power is in the President," and whether the president "has the power to remove whenever he pleases." Says he first examined this question carefully in the Senate "many years ago, soon after I became a member of the Senate" and came then to "the conviction of my own mind, that all the executive power *created by the Federal Constitution*, was confided thereby to the President, to be exercised by him at his discretion, and upon his high responsibility, except in the cases of appointments and of Treaties, if indeed the latter may be considered as an executive power under this Constitution. In this opinion the majority of the Senate then concurred. Under this view of the subject, it seemed to me of little use to inquire, in regard to the power of removal from office, whether this was a substantive power, or one merely accessorial to the power of appointment. For, as it was already an executive power, if it was substantive power, it would then be embraced within the general grant of all executive power, which, by the Constitution is given to the President; and if it was but an accessorial power, it must follow its principal, and appertain to the same functionary, to whom the principal power of appointment was granted by the Constn.; in terms, altho' in the exercise of this power of appointment, he was required to consult his advisory council the Senate." Discusses at length his legal and constitutional reasons for this particular viewpoint. Continues: "it appeared to me manifestly absurd, to regard the President as responsible for the acts of subordinate agents, and yet to deny to him the uncontrolled power of supervising them, and of removing them from office whenever they had lost his confidence — While announcing these opinions, justice to myself requires of me to add, that in claiming for the President the exclusive right to all the executive power created by the Federal Constitution, I hold him accountable to Congress, to the People, and to the States, for every misuse of the discretionary power so granted to him."

Believes, further, "that all the powers of all our governments are derivative and not sovereign," and concludes with the observation that "I have never heard any so wild, as to claim for the President, any other executi[ve] powers, than such as are created by the Federal Constitution. Nor have I supposed that any could be so foolish, as to regard what is called executive power in Englan[d] or in any other country, as the measure and standard of such power here. The absurdity of such a pretension is so monstrous, that I cannot consider it as meriting any serious refutation. Once admit it to be true, and the Constitution woul[d] become a dead letter." ALS. DLC-HC (DNA, M212, R5). Printed in Colton, *Clay Correspondence*, 4:378-81. For Tazewell's speech of April 20, 1826, on the Panama Mission, in which he first set forth his views on executive power, see *Register of Debates*, 19 Cong., 1 Sess., 597-619.

To **WALTER DUN**   Washington, February 22, 1834
I recd. your favor of the 7h. inst.   I anticipate much satisfaction from viewing your English Cattle on my return home. Those which I recently sent out were some which had been given to me, and I consider them as a mere experiment. Your neighbor Mr. S. Smith and I have purchased a pair of Durhams from Genl. [Stephen] V[an]. Rennselaer; now from 6 to 8 months old that I think are surpassed by none that I have ever seen. I shall send them out in the Spring.

I agree with almost all you say about a Bank of the U.S. We can not do without one, and I think it ought to be restricted as to the amount of the notes it issues, that is that none should be less than 10. 20. or 25 dollars. But, unless the H. of R. is enlightened and instructed by public opinion, there is no prospect of a Bank at this Session.[1] Genl Jackson is resolved that there shall be none, and thinks that it is best to dispense with all banks and rely exclusively upon a metalic medium.

Your conclusion as to the amt. of protection necessary to our manufactures, from what Mr. Webster and I said, was not entirely correct. I believe that many of our Coarser cotton fabrics could sustain themselves without any protection. Our remarks related to the true construction of the Compromise act. My visit to the North last autumn[2] opened to me a view of the astonishing and successful progress of our manufactures, and that too in many branches entirely new.

Mr. [William C.] Rives resigned his seat in the Senate today, in consequence of instructions from the Virginia Legislature, respecting the deposites, adverse to his opinions.[3]

There is an increased intensity of distress to the North; and a serious apprehension is entertained of the general suspension of specie payments.

ALS. KyU. Addressed to Dun at "Dunduff," near Lexington, Ky.   1. Clay to Wilde, April 27, 1833.   2. Trumbull to Clay, Oct. 11, 1833.   3. For the resignation of Rives, see Seager, *And Tyler Too*, 100-101. He was replaced by Benjamin W. Leigh.

From Erskine Eichelberger & Co., Baltimore, February 22, 1834. Acknowledges receipt of Clay's payment [Clay to Henry Clay, Jr., December 1, 1833], and asks: "What are you going to do with that old reprobate in the white house will he be permitted to ruin the country with impunity, If you can get at him no other way *impeach* the old *scamp*." ALS. DLC-HC (DNA, M212, R5).

To James Brown, Philadelphia, February 25, 1834. Regrets learning of the recurrence of Brown's illness. Reports that restoration of the deposits [Bradley to Clay, October 16, 1832] "depends upon the People, and the demonstrations of their will. They can produce it." Does not think Sen. William C. Preston's speech has been or will be published. Mentions the resignation of Sen. William C. Rives [Clay to Dun, February 22, 1834] and the probable election of Benjamin W. Leigh to replace him [Clay to Leigh, August 24, 1835]. Asks Brown to assist Mr. Butler who is "writing the history of K." ALS. KyLxT. Preston's speech of January 23-24, 1834, in opposition to the removal of the deposits, is mentioned as having been delivered in *Register of Debates*, 23 Cong., 1 Sess., 337-38. The *Register* does not print his remarks. However, the *Cong. Globe*, 23 Cong., 1 Sess., 123, prints his remarks of January 23, omitting those of January 24. Mann Butler, *History of Kentucky, From Its Exploration and Settlement by the Whites, to the Close of the Northwestern Campaign, in 1813* was published in Louisville in 1834.

Remark in Senate, February 25, 1834. Notes that a petition from Troy, N.Y., to restore government deposits in the B.U.S. [Bradley to Clay, October 16, 1832] has been signed by "the great body of business men" as well as "men of all parties." Remarks that of Troy's 2,200 voters, 1,730 have signed this memorial. *Register of Debates*, 23 Cong., 1 Sess., 681. See Comment in Senate, March 11, 1834.

Comment in Senate, February 26, 1834. Remarks that a Berks County, Pa., remonstrance against the removal of deposits from the B.U.S. [Bradley to Clay, October 16, 1832] has been signed by 1,860 individuals, or far more than had voted against Jackson in Berks in 1828 or 1832. Concludes: "Gentlemen may be assured that this is no party struggle that now agitates the country. It is a question between the will of one man and that of twelve millions of people. It is a question between power — ruthless, relentless, inexorable power — on the one hand, and the strong, deepfelt sufferings of a vast community, on the other." *Register of Debates*, 23 Cong., 1 Sess., 718.

On this same day, Clay presents a memorial from Louisville, Ky., signed by nearly 1,000 people, "embracing individuals of both parties" and "almost the whole of the mercantile class," asking for relief from the severe economic distress caused by the removal of deposits. Uses this opportunity to deliver extensive comments on the damaging economic policies of the Jackson administration, especially in the area of money and banking. Reviews his earlier arguments in support of the B.U.S. and in opposition to the smaller and less stable banks into which government funds are to be placed. *Ibid.*, 719-24, 727, 733; see also *Cong. Globe*, 23 Cong., 1 Sess., 200. The *Globe's* version of Clay's comment includes a statement that he was aware of "the safety fund banking system of New York and the attempt by the President and Secretary of the Treasury, to introduce the same system among the deposit banks." He identifies the New York system, however, as insecure and dangerous and argues for rechartering the B.U.S. instead. For the N.Y. safety-fund banking system, see Lawrence to Clay, August 31, 1829; Porter to Clay, March 30, 1834.

Comment in Senate, February 27, 1834. Clarifies factual and substantive statements made in his remarks in the Senate on February 25 and 26. *Register of Debates*, 23 Cong., 1 Sess., 746-47.

Remark in Senate, February 28, 1834. Participates in a discussion "of nearly three hours" of Sen. George Poindexter's resolution of February 27 demanding that Secretary of the Treasury Roger B. Taney explain why and what public monies are to be removed from the Planter's Bank at Natchez and into what bank or banks such funds are to be placed. *Register of Debates*, 23 Cong., 1 Sess., 749-50. The actual debate on Poindexter's resolution, which passed, is not reported in the *Register of Debates*. The *Cong. Globe*, 23 Cong., 1 Sess., 209, however, carries a brief account of this discussion, during which Clay mediates a bitter personal exchange between Senators Poindexter and John Forsyth on the related issue of Taney's transfer to other banks, from the Planter's Bank at Natchez, the sum of $500,000 to pay for services having to do with the removal of the Creek Indians. Poindexter asserted that a Tennessee company as well as "nephews and other relatives" of President Jackson, were said to have profited by this transfer, a remark contested by Forsyth.

Remark in Senate, March 3, 1834. Asks that debate on the removal of deposits [Bradley to Clay, October 16, 1832] not be postponed; and that Sen. Isaac Hill (N.H.), who was entitled to the floor to speak on the issue, be given it. Hopes that debate on the question can be completed in "a few days." *Register of Debates*, 23 Cong., 1 Sess., 755.

Comment in Senate, March 4, 1834. Notes that the action of "several thousand" Philadelphia Jacksonians ("the pure, genuine, and unadulterated friends of General Jackson") who are opposed to the Bank of the United States, but are also remonstrating against the removal of the government deposits from it [Bradley to Clay, October 16, 1832], demonstrates the fact that the removal issue is "not a party question." Points out that these Jacksonians well understand the dangers of the proliferation of unstable state banks and the need for a national bank. *Register of Debates*, 23 Cong., 1 Sess., 802-3.

On this same day, Clay suggested postponing for one day further action on the disputed Rhode Island senatorial election [Comment in Senate, December 2, 1833]. *Ibid.*, 805-6; *Cong. Globe*, 23 Cong., 1 Sess., 214.

Remark in Senate, March 5, 1834. Discusses the procedures, mainly those involving due process [Remark in Senate, March 6, 1834], that might be employed by the Senate for finding out why such short notice had been given by the administration for the recent sales of public lands in Mississippi and Alabama. Notes that these particular lands had been purchased from the Choctaw and Creek tribes, and were thought by some to have been acquired fraudulently. *Register of Debates*, 23 Cong., 1 Sess., 818, 822. Sen. George Poindexter (Miss.), in the form of five resolutions, had asked for a Senate investigation of the circumstances surrounding these sales. Resolution 5 gave to the Senate Committee on Public Lands the "power to send for persons and papers, and to examine witnesses before them, on oath." *Ibid.*, 812; *Cong. Globe*, 23 Cong., 1 Sess., 216. All were passed. *Ibid.*, 217.

Remark in Senate, March 6, 1834. Interrupts the remarks of Sen. Silas Wright (N.Y.) on Sen. George Poindexter's fifth resolution dealing with an investigation of government land sales in Mississippi and Alabama [Remark in Senate, March 5, 1834]. Asks how depositions are to be taken from the officers of the companies that had been formed to speculate in former Choctaw and Creek lands without, in effect, accusing them of wrong-doing. *Cong. Globe*, 23 Cong., 1 Sess., 222.

From Samuel F. B. Morse, New York City, March 7, 1834. Asks to be included among the four artists who will be engaged to paint "the remaining four pictures in the Rotunda of the Capitol." Mentions his artistic training and background. Copy. Printed in Edward Lind Morse, *Samuel F. B. Morse, His Letters and Journals* (Boston and New York, 1914), 2:29. For Morse, see *DAB*. The four artists who were finally chosen were Henry Inman, John G. Chapman, Robert Walter Weir, and John Vanderlyn. Carleton Mabee, *The American Leonardo, A Life of Samuel F. B. Morse* (New York, 1944), 185.

Speech in Senate, March 7, 1834. Speaks to a memorial from 3,000 "building mechanics" of the city of Philadelphia, presented by Daniel Webster, calling attention to "the present distress of the country." Embraces the opportunity to blame the depression on the money and banking policy, "the fatal experiment," of President Jackson. Argues that only the restoration of the deposits [Bradley to Clay, October 16, 1832] can end the "heart-rending wretchedness of thousands of the working classes cast out of employment" and return the nation to prosperity. Urges Jackson to cast aside the "wicked counsels of unprincipled men around him" and restore the deposits. *Register of Debates*, 23 Cong., 1 Sess., 829-32. Printed in Colton, *Clay Correspondence*, 5:621-23.

On this same day, Clay suggests that a matter dealing with printing Senate documents be referred to committee for study. *Register of Debates*, 23 Cong., 1 Sess., 834.

Later this same day, Clay introduces, explains, and defends four resolutions designed to limit the president's power to remove public officials from office. They are: (1) under the Constitution, the president "is not invested with the power of removal from office at his pleasure"; (2) Congress, under the Constitution, is authorized "to prescribe the tenure, terms, and conditions, of all offices established by law, where the constitution itself has not affixed the tenure"; (3) the need for legislation providing that "removal from office shall not, in future, be made without the concurrence of the Senate" and, if removals are made when the Senate is not in session, such are to be considered provisional and be subject to Senate review when it convenes; (4) the need for legislation "requiring the concurrence of the Senate in the appointment of all deputy postmasters, under cetain restrictions." Taken together, these resolutions seek to place the power to remove public officials, including deputy postmasters, but excluding diplomatic appointees, in the hands of the Senate. These changes Clay deems necessary to curb the patronage abuses of "the present administration," which insists that "all persons employed in the Executive Department of the Government . . . are bound to conform to the will of the President, no matter how contrary to their own judgment that will may be." *Ibid.*, 834-36. Rough manuscript notes, in Clay's hand, from which these remarks and resolutions were fashioned, are in DLC-TJC (DNA, M212, R10). For the exact wording of the resolutions, see *Senate Docs.*, 23 Cong., 1 Sess., no. 155; also *Register of Debates*, 23 Cong., 1 Sess., 836; *Cong. Globe*, 23 Cong., 1 Sess., 220. See also, Comment in Senate, February 14, 1835.

To Francis T. Brooke, near Fredericksburg, Va., March 10, 1834. Says he has "really nothing of interest to communicate" since he almost daily expresses himself in the Senate on what he has to say on "public affairs." Speculates on what would happen if both the House and Senate rejected Secretary of the Treasury Roger B. Taney's reasons for having removed the deposits [Bradley to Clay, October 16, 1832; Remark in Senate, December 18, 1833]. Believes that "It would be conclusive, if the act of removing the public deposites was conditional, but it is a perfect, and performed act, before the reasons are communicated to Congress. I have always believed that if both houses concurred in pronouncing the insufficiency of those reasons, it would, without any further or other Legislative action, become the duty of the Secy. to restore them; and I have wished to be able to think that such wd. be his duty, if either house disagreed with him. But if one House agree, and the other disagree with him, is not the result a state of neutrality? We shall look to the issue of your approaching elections with very great anxiety." ALS. DLC-TJC (DNA, M212, R10). Printed in Colton, *Clay Correspondence*, 4:381-82. In January, 1834, the legislature of Virginia elected Littleton W. Tazewell, a states' rights advocate, as governor over his nearest opponent Ed. Watts, a National Republican, by a final vote of 85-53. The Jackson candidate, Peter V. Daniel, received only 2 votes on the last ballot. In the April, 1834, elections for the House of Delegates, Jacksonians won 50 seats to 84 for administration opponents; however, the Jacksonians still held a majority of 2 in the state senate. *Niles' Register* (January 11, 1834), 45:331; *ibid.* (May 3, 1834), 46:147.

On June 26, 1834, at a public dinner in Leesburg, Va., an excerpt was read of a letter from Clay expressing his regret at being unable to be present at the celebration of the recent elections which indicate "the probable success of the great principles of civil liberty." Copy, undated excerpt. Printed in Washington *Daily National Intelligencer*, July 9, 1834.

To JULIA PRATHER CLAY
Washington, March 10, 1834

I thought you had forgotten me, but your last letter is an assurance that I still hold a place in your friendly recollection. I was happy to learn from that, and from other sources, that both you and Henry [Clay, Jr.] have become much interested in the improvement of Maplewood.[1] Anne [Brown Clay Erwin] tells me a good deal of the embellishments actually made or in progress. You know that it was always a favorite of mine; and it is gratifying to the pride of opinion to find that you think of it as I have always done. It wants only water more conveniently situated to render it among the most desirable of residences. I am glad to learn that you expect soon your excellent mother [Matilda Fontaine Prather] with you. Besides the satisfaction you can not but feel in her company, her matured judgment will assist your's in many of the interesting concerns of your establishment. I wish we also could be with you, not for the sake of any instruction we could impart, but for the more selfish object of the happiness which we should derive, my dear daughter, from the company of yourself, your husband and your little boy [Henry Clay III].

When we shall be able to quit this City God only knows. No one can yet see even a distant termination of the Session.

James [Brown Clay] has become discontented with his mercantile pursui[ts][2] and I have consented, most reluctantly, to his return to us. We look for him daily. He now wishes to complete his education; and if he will really enter upon it, with ardor and zeal, I shall feel less regret in the change of his vocation.

Tell Henry that I have directed [William] Martin to supply him and Anne each with a bushel of the Foxite potatoes lately arrived at Ashland. They were a present to me from a friend in New Jersey. Tell him also to look at another Straw cutter, which has recently reached home. I thought well of it; and there is an additional which he can have if he likes it.

Mrs. [Lucretia] Clay's health, though yet feeble, is I think a little better. Exercise, and a strict regimen, which she now pursues, can only restore her. Mrs. [Thomas A.] Marshall continues with us, and adds to our social resources. All of us unite in warmest regards to you and to your mari [husband]. And I pray you to kiss my dear little namesake [Henry Clay III]. . . .

ALS. Henry Clay Memorial Foundation, Lexington, Ky. 1. Farm of Henry Clay, Jr., near Lexington. 2. Clay to Henry Clay, Jr., Dec. 30, 1832.

Remark in Senate, March 11, 1834. Corrects the number of signatures on a petition from Troy, N.Y., in favor of restoring the deposits [Bradley to Clay, October 16, 1832] that had been given the Senate on February 25 [Remark in Senate, February 25, 1834]. Says that "at least 400" of the 1,730 signers were "administration men," not the 100 earlier reported. *Register of Debates*, 23 Cong., 1 Sess., 860-62; *Cong. Globe*, 23 Cong., 1 Sess., 227.

From Edwin U. Berryman, March 13, 1834. Reports he is attemping to arrange insurance on Arabian horse Kocklani and jackass Warrior. Then comments on economic distress in New York City: "The pressure continues unabated in our city, & failures occur every day, indeed they are so numerous that they are passed over as an every day occurrence & forgotten except by the individual sufferers—God knows how long this state of affairs will continue, but we do not anticipate a change soon, & my own impression is that the worst has not yet come, nearly all the smaller houses have been obliged to obtain from their creditors extensions of time to meet their engagements—We are up & doing all that can be done to affect a change on our next charter election, We are sanguine of success—If we can effect nothing during the present excitement I think we may ever hereafter hold our peace—" Mentions in postscript that he has received $500 from Clay for his and J.H. Coster's share of "one-fourth part of the Arabian Horse Kocklani sold to the Messrs Hockadays [*sic*, Philip B. & Edmund W. Hockaday] for $750, the other three fourths of said Horse belonging to Messrs Clay, Coster, & myself." ALS. DLC-TJC (DNA, M212, R10). The New York City charter election of April 8-10, 1834, resulted in the Anti-Jacksonians—or "Whigs" as they were now being called—winning a majority of the council seats. The Jacksonian or Tammany candidate, Cornelius W. Lawrence, won the mayoral race over Gulian C. Verplanck, the Whig candidate, by a mere 171 votes out of some 35,000 votes cast. The major issue in the campaign was Jackson's attack on the Bank of the United States [Bradley to Clay, October 16, 1832]—the same issue which had caused Verplanck to leave the Jacksonians and become a Whig. The Whigs viewed the narrow margin of their defeat as a great victory and held a celebration at Castle Garden with thousands of people in attendance. Mushkat, *Tammany*, 154-56; Fox, *The Decline of Aristocracy in the Politics of New York*, 368-69. For John H. Coster, a merchant in New York City, see Bonner, *New York, The World's Metropolis*, 723.

To James Brown, Philadelphia, March 13, 1834. Reports that James Brown Clay has arrived in Washington from Boston. "I am much indebted for the kind interest you take in him and in his brothers." Is considering relocating James in Philadelphia and asks Brown's opinion of the idea. Discusses conditions relating to the sale of Brown's sugar plantation in Louisiana. Comments on his wife's stomach trouble. Concludes on a political note: "The majority, on the deposite question, in the House [Bradley to Clay, October 16, 1832; Clay to Tazewell, April 5, 1834] remains I fear unchanged. Nothing will change it but the demonstrations of popular opinion. If the Charter election in the City of N York should be decided against the Regency [Berryman to Clay, March 13, 1834], I shall count greatly upon its favorable influence at Washn." ALS. KyLxT.

Comment in Senate, March 17, 1834. Speaks to a memorial from the citizens of York County, Pa., favoring the removal of the deposits [Bradley to Clay, October 16, 1832] and opposing the recharter of the B.U.S. [Clay to Wilde, April 27, 1833]. Resists receiving such a memorial on the grounds, pointed out by Daniel Webster, William Preston, and others, that the petition had been rejected by two-thirds of the people present at the meeting where the issue had been debated and the memorial drawn up; also that it was defective factually. Points specifically to later erasures and insertions in the document, arguing that these changes compromised its character as a legitimate petition. *Register of Debates*, 23 Cong., 1 Sess., 969-70. The origin and character of the York County petition is developed in *ibid.*, 960-69. See also *Cong. Globe*, 23 Cong., 1 Sess., 244, 246-47.

To Henry Clay, Jr., Lexington, March 19, 1834. Thanks him for his check for $1,000. Asks him to pay Transylvania University $600 on April 1, "being the half year's interest on the twenty thousand dollars which I owe that institution." Continues: "James [Brown Clay] has returned and is now with us. He stated that, after a full trial, he did not like the mercantile business [Clay to Henry Clay, Jr., December 30, 1832]; and that he wished to complete his education. It was with great reluctance that I acceded to his wishes, but I thought it best to do so. Your mother's health is very bad. She is reduced to a mere skelton. Her disorder is in the stomach; and unless she gets relieved, as the warm weather approaches, I have serious apprehensions about her. We have had yet no direct vote in either house on the deposite question [Bradley to Clay, October 16, 1832]; but it is well understood that a majority in the H. of R. still exists in favor of the measure of the Executive. Give our love to Julia [Prather Clay] and kiss my little namesake [Henry Clay, III]." ALS. Henry Clay Memorial Foundation, Lexington, Ky. Clay's management of the James Morrison estate, as its sole executor, as well as its sometime debtor, can be traced in part in 3:425-26, 496, 507-8, 668, 735, 739-40, 774-75, 778, 882-83; 4:436, 565; 5:399, 941; 7:28, 29, 403, 414. See, also, Morrison, James (Morrison Estate), 7:675-76, 748; and Transylvania University, 7:685, 767; also Clay to Johnson, December 6, 1833.

Comment in Senate, March 21, 1834. Presents and reads two memorials praying for relief from the depression; one of these is from New York City and issigned by some 3,000 persons, mostly clerks and small businessmen; the other is signed by a "large number of traders" from ten of the Mississippi Valley states, Kentucky included, who "Happened lately to be in Philadelphia" for the purpose of "laying in their stock of goods for the season." *Register of Debates*, 23 Cong., 1 Sess., 1048-49; *Cong. Globe*, 23 Cong. 1 Sess., 254.

Remark in Senate, March 22, 1834. Complains that he too has a special order "locked up in the debates of the Senate" and hopes that another week would bring the issue to a close. *Cong. Globe*, 23 Cong., 1 Sess., 261. Likely a reference to his resolution censuring Taney and Jackson [Speech in Senate, December 26, 1833]. See Remark in Senate, March 28, 1834.

To FRANCIS T. BROOKE

Washington, March 23, 1834

I recd. your favor transmitting a copy of the address of the minority of your Legislature.[1] It did not strike me as possessing much ability, but on some points was very weak and vulnerable. I am not aware that any answer to it from this place will be attempted.

I recd. also your subsequent favor.

Things remain in Statu[s] quo here. There is a small but as yet inflexible majority sustaining the Executive in the House.[2] If the elections in Virginia[3] and the city of N. York[4] should be adv[e]rse to the Administration that majority proba[b]ly will be changed; but, in an opposite event, it may be increased. Mr V. Buren yesterday offered to bet me a suit of clothes upon each of the elections in the city of N. York and in your State. The Admn. party is very confident; and our friends are not without fears as to the issue of matters with you. It is with politics as with the currency. In certain states of both, a slight circumstances produces much effect. We were prepared here for the unfortunate result in [Thomas T.] Bouldins district.[5] It depressed our side and elevated the other far beyond what such an event would have done at any other time.

What are your real prospects? I should confide much in your judgement. Would you like to take up Van's bet?

I told him yesterday that if the people entertained the Admn. in its late measures, I should begin to feel that our experiment of free government had failed; that he would probaly be elected the successor of Jackson; that he would introduce a system of intrigue and corruption that would enable him to designate his successor; and that, after a few years of lingering and fretful existance we should end in a dissolution of the Union or in despotism. He laughed and remarked that I entertained morbid feelings. I replied, with good nature, that what I had said I deliberately and sincerely believed.

Copy. DLC-HC (DNA, M212, R5). Printed in Colton, *Clay Correspondence*, 4:382-83. 1. The report, "An Address to the People of Virginia," took a states' rights position in regard to a national bank, the tariff, and internal improvements. Richmond *Enquirer*, March 4, 1834. 2. Whittlesey to Clay, Sept. 19, 1832. 3. Clay to Brooke, March 10, 1834. 4. Berryman to Clay, March 13, 1834. 5. Thomas T. Bouldin, who held John Randolph's old seat in Congress, had died on the floor of the House on Feb. 11, 1834. His brother, J.W. Bouldin, a Jacksonian, ran against Randolph's half-brother, Nathaniel Beverley Tucker, and won. *Niles' Register* (March 22, 1834), 46:51.

To JOSEPH GALES   Washington, March 24, 1834

I recd. your note with the paragraph enclosed in it now returned.[1] There is no foundation for what it contains, as it respects me. I had no interview whatever with Mr. Calhoun as to his plan, prior to his presentation of it.[2] I had heard indistinctly that he had some plan in contemplation, but it is precise character I did not know until he disclosed it in his speech in the Senate.

It is idle to think of any thing being done towards a recharter of the Bank, until it is called for by popular demonstrations or the exercise of the elective franchise.

ALS. NN. Written in "S. Chamber." 1. Not found. 2. Calhoun presented his B.U.S. recharter plan [Clay to Wilde, April 27, 1833] to the Senate on March 21, 1834. *Register of Debates*, 23 Cong., 1 Sess., 1057-73; see also Wiltse, *John C. Calhoun*, 2:226-28.

Remark in Senate, March 24, 1834. Hopes that debate on Daniel Webster's bill introduced March 18, 1834, to recharter the B.U.S. for a six year period, can be concluded next week. *Register of Debates*, 23 Cong., 1 Sess., 1113. For Webster's bill, see Porter to Clay, February 15, 1834; and *Register of Debates*, 23 Cong., 1 Sess., 984-1005.

Later this day, Clay wondered whether the York County, Pa., memorial [Comment in Senate, March 17, 1834] supporting Jackson's attack on the B.U.S. was couched in "respectful language." Clay moved that it was not and should not be received; but the Senate voted to table his motion. *Ibid.*, 1115-16; *Cong. Globe*, 23 Cong., 1 Sess., 262.

Comment in Senate, March 25, 1834. Mentions the fact that the Bank of Maryland, located in Baltimore and chartered by the state of Maryland, had collapsed the previous day. Remarks further that the Union Bank of Maryland in Baltimore, selected by Secretary of the Treasury Roger B. Taney as one of the depository banks for public revenue, had suffered "an immense run" yesterday because of its close connection with the Bank of Maryland. It too was thought to be in serious trouble. Reports that Taney is said to be a major stockholder of Union Bank. Repeats the rumor that in the "last few days," U.S. Treasury drafts in the amount of $150,000 had been moved to Union Bank by the secretary in order to steady it. Moves that Taney be directed to furnish the Senate with a full report on the condition and ownership of Union Bank. *Register of Debates*, 23 Cong., 1 Sess., 1140-41; *Cong. Globe*, 23 Cong., 1 Sess., 264. Taney's detailed response of April 3 to Clay's allegations allayed suggestions of personal improbity in the matter. See *Register of Debates*, 23 Cong., 1 Sess., 1241-43; and Swisher, *Roger B. Taney*, 267-69.

Remark in Senate, March 26, 1834. Intends to say a "few words" more on the removal of deposits issue [Bradley to Clay, October 16, 1832], probably tomorrow, at which time he hopes that the discussion of the problem will close. *Register of Debates*, 23 Cong., 1 Sess., 1167.

Comment in Senate, March 27, 1834. Introduces and supports a Lexington-Fayette County, Ky., memorial, signed by some 1,200 persons of all occupations, calling attention to Jackson's usurpations and to impending economic distress in a region that is usually extremely prosperous. Remarks that the prices of hemp and corn in Lexington have fallen 20 percent since he left home in November, 1833, and that there are 6,000 "fat bullocks now remaining unsold," whereas "long before this time last year, there was scarcely one to be purchased." Concludes: "We are . . . not a complaining people. We think not so much of distress. Give us our laws—guaranty to us our constitution—and we will be content with almost any form of government." *Register of Debates*, 23 Cong., 1 Sess., 1170-71.

Speech in Senate, March 27-28, 1834. Clay's closing speech on the removal of deposits and the related censure question [Bradley to Clay, October 16, 1832; Speech in Senate, December 26, 1833], a debate which, he observes, has lasted three months, or "the longest period which had been occupied in a single debate in either house of Congress since the organization of the Government." Reviews the various arguments against Jackson, Taney, and the decision of the administration to remove the deposits that he and others have advanced since late December, 1833. Discusses at length the limited powers of the president under the constitution, and charges that Jackson has abused those powers in his removal of public officials [Speech in Senate, March 7, 1834]; hence, the need to censure him. Also defends the Bank of the United States and the need to recharter it. Concludes that the coming statewide elections in Virginia [Clay to Brooke, March 10, 1834] and Kentucky will be a test of his belief that "the intelligence and patriotism of the people" will soon "correct all these errors." Indeed, until Virginia and Kentucky have "sustained the present state of things," he would "never despair." *Register of Debates*, 23 Cong., 1 Sess., 1172-77. See also Clay to Tazewell, April 5, 1834; and *Cong. Globe*, 23 Cong., 1 Sess., 269-71. The final Senate vote on Clay's two resolutions of censure was cast on March 28, 1834. The censure of Secretary Taney passed 28 to 18; the censure of President Jackson passed 26 to 20. *Register of Debates*, 23 Cong., 1 Sess., 1187. The Kentucky elections in August, 1834, resulted in a victory for Clay supporters who won the state senate by a margin of 20 to 16 seats and the lower house by 73 to 17. Lexington *Observer & Kentucky Reporter*, August 20, 1834. In a special election for the U.S. House [Clay to Helm, April 20, 1833], Robert P. Letcher defeated Thomas P. Moore by the vote of 3,731 to 3,461. *Guide to U.S. Elections*, 562.

Remark in Senate, March 28, 1834. Slightly revises the wording of his resolution censuring Jackson [Speech in Senate, December 26, 1833]. Does this immediately preceding the Senate vote of 26 to 20 in favor of the resolution. *Register of Debates*, 23 Cong., 1 Sess., 1187; *Cong. Globe*, 23 Cong., 1 Sess., 271.

To Joseph H. Robertson *et al.*, Norfolk, Va., March 28, 1834. Declines with thanks their invitation to a public dinner in his honor. Discusses the act of Congress which established and organized the Department of the Treasury in 1789, noting that President Jackson and Secretary Taney violated that act when they decreed the removal of the deposits [Bradley to Clay, October 16, 1832]. Explains that the Treasury Department was carefully fashioned in such a manner as to provide within it "four distinct, independent and responsible checks, (the secretary, comptroller, register and treasurer), whose concurrence was necessary before a single dollar could be drawn from the treasury." Further, in none of the 24 states is the state treasurer under the direct control of the governor. Instead, in all states the treasurer, whether elected or appointed, "accounts directly to the legislature. . . . These are the doctrines of America and of every really free country." Concludes: "For the first time, in the history of our government, they are not controverted and others are advanced which tend to establish that union between the purse and the sword, with which the continuance of civil liberty is absolutely incompatible. It remains to be seen whether they will be approved by the people." Copy. Printed in *Niles' Register* (May 3, 1833), 46:166. Elections to the 24th Congress resulted in a distribution of seats roughly as follows: House. Democrat— 145, Whig and other—98; Senate: Democrat—27, Whig—25. Adapted from U.S. Bureau of Census, *The Statistical History of the United States From Colonial Times to the Present*, 691. See also Thomas B. Alexander, *Sectional Stress and Party Strength* (Nashville, 1967), 16. Both parties could argue that they had improved their situations over that in the 23rd Congress. Bowers, *Party Battles of the Jackson Period*, 365-66; Whittlesey to Clay, September 19, 1832.

From Peter B. Porter, Black Rock, N.Y., March 30, 1834. Says he plans to be in New York City in April 5-12 "during the charter election [Berryman to Clay, March 13, 1834], which I suspect from present indications will be the severest civil Conflict they have ever had. I am not without strong hopes of Success, but when I reflect that this election will probably decide the future political character of the State—that the Regency are fully aware of its immense importance to them, and will therefore spend, not tens but hundreds of thousands of the people's money in the struggle, and move heaven and Earth rather than be defeated, I confess I am not without some fears as to the result. As regards the candidates for the mayoralty whose general qualifications and popularity influence more or less the verdict, I think we have the advantage. I will advise you from day to day of the progress of the election." Reports that the people in western New York are beginning "to feel the pressure very heavily" of economic distress. Those in Erie County will probably soon send Congress a memorial with 4,000 or 5,000 signatures opposing the removal of the deposits [Bradley to Clay, October 16, 1832]. Concludes with a critical comment on New York State banking policy: "You have doubtless seen the proposition lately introduced into our Legislature by a message from the Governor [William Marcy], to borrow five millions of dollars on the credit of the State, to loan to the Safety Fund Banks [Lawrence to Clay, August 31, 1829]. From the manner in which the message was received and disposed of in the two houses, it is evident that the project has been fully understood and matured, and it will doubtless be adopted, unless time shall be given for protests by the people of the different parts of the State to reach them. This is not merely a 'tub thrown to the whale' in the hour of their distress, but it is a deliberate and daring outrageous(?) extension of the plan introduced by the Regency about five years ago, of uniting to the patronage of office, the whole public revenues & resources of the State for the purpose of controling its politics. They have already placed all the great public institutions, together with the money belonging to the Canal Fund (amounting to between $ 2 and 3 millions of dollars) in the hands of their partizans, and are now about to mortgage the credit of the State for the same purpose." Copy. OHi. The governor had sent a message to the legislature on March 22, 1834, recommending a loan of $5 or $6 million to the banks in the form of state stocks. Fox, *The Decline of Aristocracy in the Politics of New York*, 371. For the loan and canal fund, see also Hammond, *History of Political Parties in the State of New York*, 2·440-41, 3:119 20; Mushkat, *Tammany*, 155.

Remark in Senate, March 31, 1834. Moves to take up for consideration his resolution of March 25 asking Secretary of the Treasury Taney for information about the Union Bank of Maryland [Comment in Senate, March 25, 1834]. Now modifies this resolution which is agreed to as modified. *Register of Debates*, 23 Cong., 1 Sess., 1206.

Later this day, Clay attempts to explain what the absent Sen. Daniel Webster probably meant in a prior comment on economic distress in New York State, especially along the Erie Canal, when he earlier spoke to the Albany, N.Y., memorial opposing the removal of the deposits. *Ibid.* 1209; *Cong. Globe*, 23 Cong., 1 Sess., 278. For the Albany memorial, which Webster presented on March 28, see *Register of Debates*, 23 Cong., 1 Sess., 1177.

To JAMES BROWN   Washington, April 1, 1834

I thank you for the interest you so kindly take in James [Brown Clay]. We have concluded not to place him in Philada., and our present intention is to take him with us to K.   Mrs. Clays health continues feeble, and she will leave this City early in May for Ashland. James will accompany, and I shall *probably* also. Unless there should be a prospect of doing some thing here, I see no motive for remaining. There is well understood to be an inflexible majority in the House adverse to the opinions recently expressed by the Senate, in repsect to the public deposites.[1] That majority can only be operated upon by the people themselves. It is possible, should the result of the Virginia[2] and the N. York[3] elections, now near at hand, be favorable, the majority may be changed. In the contrary event it will be confirmed if not augmented. In the Senate our majority, on the resolutions which I offered, was as large as I ever expected.[4]

Mr. [James] Erwin writes me that the investments he has made for you are *perfectly safe*; and that he has sought rather absolute security than exorbitant interest, with doubtful security.

I have seen frequently Orlando [Brown]; and am happy to tell you that his associations, as far as I know or believe, are all of the best character.

ALS. KyLxT.   1. Bradley to Clay, Oct. 16, 1832; Speech in Senate, Dec. 26, 1833.   2. Clay to Brooke, March 10, 1834.   3. Berryman to Clay, March 13, 1834.   4. Speech in Senate, Dec. 26, 1833; Remark in Senate, March 28, 1834.

Remark in Senate, April 3, 1834. Moves that Roger B. Taney's April 3 report to the Senate on the Union Bank of Maryland [Comment in Senate, March 25, 1834], be printed. Says the public should know that Taney held 73 shares in that bank (par value, $5,475) when it was designated to receive deposits of public money; but points out that in fairness to Taney it should be noted that his stock in the institution had been purchased before he entered government service, and that he now holds 63 shares, having sold 10 shares in February, 1834, to pay a personal debt. *Register of Debates*, 23 Cong., 1 Sess., 1242-43.

Comment in Senate, April 4, 1834. Notes the fair and balanced manner in which the Senate to date has handled the Robbins vs. Potter case [Comment in Senate, December 2, 1833], and urges acceptance of the majority report on it. *Register of Debates*, 23 Cong., 1 Sess., 1253-54, 1256.

To LITTLETON W. TAZEWELL   Washington, April 5, 1834

Although your obliging answer of the 19h. Feb. to my previous letter did not require an immediate reply,[1] I beg you to excuse the delay which has arisen in transmitting one. Indeed I own you an apology for having given you the trouble of writing your letter. When I addressed you, it had escaped my recollection that you took part in the Debate in the Senate to which you refer, or rather the whole debate was not at that moment within my memory. If it had occurred to me, I might, by resorting to the files of the papers of the day, have acquired the information of your views which I desired to possess.

Since I wrote to you, I have offered certain resolutions to the Senate, respecting the Executive power of removal;[2] and in a speech not yet published, which I delivered last week to the Senate[3] I stated what appeared to me to be the true principles of the Constitution in respect to the power of the Executive branch of the Government. You have probably seen the resolutions.

On the occasion of the Speech, I contended that the clause in the Constitution, which declares that the Executive power shall be vested in a President, gives him no power whatever, but is a mere organic structure of the Executive functionary, the creation of a capacity to receive power; that the actual power conferred is to be found in parts of the Constitution subsequent to that clause, where they are expressly defined and enumerated; and that the true test in all cases is the same both for the Legislative and the Executive, that is, whether the power proposed to be executed is granted? is it proper and necessary to a granted power?

I further contended that Executive power may be granted by the constitution or created by law. That, in the former case, it is beyond the control of Congress; but in the latter, the Legislative authority which creates it, may define, limit and modify it, according to the Legislative view of the public interest. I give you the general course of the argument, without stating all the qualifications.

When the resolutions shall be taken up,[4] I shall explain myself fully on the subject of them. I will say now only, that I do not think the power of removal in general is necessarily incidental to any Executive power granted by the Constitution; and that, believing that the Constitution has failed to make any provision about it, express or implied, with the exception of the power of impeachment, it falls within the scope of the Legislative authority to regulate it, according to the public interests.

You will perceive, then, that there exists some difference in the opinions which we mutually entertain; but I concur, entirely, in the liberal sentiment, contained in your letter, that no diversity of views which we take on this or other subjects should affect the friendly relations which have so long subsisted between us; or I will add prevent our co-operation, in regard to measures, meeting with the concurrence of both of us, which may be adapted to the advancement of the interests of our Country.

The time has indeed arrived when such a co-operation among all real friends of the Union and of Liberty, should take place, or there will be a speedy termination perhaps of both. By the vote of the H. of R. yesterday, the recent alarming strides of the President, in regard to the Public treasury, are approved and sanctioned.[5] In spite of instructions and remonstrances from the districts of some of the members, they have voted with the Executive; and at present there is no prospect of Congress regaining its lawful custody of the Treasury, unless the President shall voluntarily loosen his grasp of it.

Our only hope is, that the elections in your State[6] and in the City of N. York[7] may exhibit, by their results, such evidence of popular disapprobation of the President's measures, as will make an impression on the House, which no considerations hitherto appealed to have produced. If that fail, nothing will probably remain for Congress but to adjourn and go home. We shall, prior to that event, have some Treasury scheme to regulate the relations between the Treasury department and the State banks, to which, for one, I can never give my support, since it would imply a ratification of what I believe to be an usurpation.

It will afford me pleasure to hear from you whenever your convenience may allow you to make me any communication. And I beg you to accept the hearty good wishes for the success of your administration of the Executive Government of Virginia[8] and for your health and prosperity. . . .

ALS. KyU.   1. Clay to Tazewell, Feb. 1, 1834; Tazewell to Clay, Feb. 19, 1834.   2. Speech in Senate, March 7, 1834.   3. Speech in Senate, March 27-28, 1834. It was not published in pamphlet form or in the Washington *Daily National Intelligencer*.   4. Clay's resolutions concerning the president's power to remove public officials [Speech in Senate, March 7, 1834] were taken up briefly on April 7, and again on May 8 at which time they were laid on the table. U.S. Sen., *Journal*, 23 Cong., 1 Sess., 253.   5. On April 4, 1834, House votes on the following resolutions had taken place: *Resolved*: That the Bank of the United States ought not to be rechartered — yea: 134, nay:82. *Resolved*: That the public deposits ought not to be restored to the Bank of the United States — yea:118, nay:103. *Resolved*: That the State banks ought to be continued as the places of deposite of the public money — yea:117, nay:105. *Resolved*: That the Bank of the United States should be investigated for possible violations of its charter in the areas of administrative corruption and mismanagement, illegal involvement in politics, and financial practices related to bringing on the current national economic depression — yea:175, nay:42. When Rep. Richard H. Wilde (Ga.), a Clay supporter, asked that a fifth resolution be considered, that of "declaring the reasons [for removal of the deposits] offered by the Secretary [Speech in Senate, Dec. 26, 1833] insufficient and unsatisfactory," Rep. James K. Polk (Tenn.) moved quickly to adjourn — yea:123, nay:70. *Register of Debates*, 23 Cong., 1 Sess., 3473-77.   6. Clay to Brooke, March 10, 1834. 7. Berryman to Clay, March 13, 1834.   8. Tazewell had been elected governor on Jan. 7, 1834.

Remark in Senate, April 7, 1834. Because several members are absent, he will postpone until April 21 his remarks on his resolutions to curb the president's power of removal and appointment [Speech in Senate, March 7, 1834]. *Register of Debates*, 23 Cong., 1 Sess., 1260. Other business occupied the Senate on April 21 and the resolutions were put over to May 8 [Clay to Tazewell, April 5, 1834].

To JOHN J. CRITTENDEN   Washington, April 8, 1834

You have found me more than usual, a bad correspondent during the present Session. You know me well enough to know that I have not failed to address you from want of inclination, but from want of any thing interesting to communicate. And even now I might remain silent if I were influenced solely by the matter of my letter; but I am induced to write to guard against any misconception from my silence.

The appointments of Monroe and Saunders[1] have been both approved. Your views and those of other friends as to the former had full weight

The H. of R. has a stern and inflexile 'though not very large majority in support of the Executive usurpations, as you will have seen from the papers.[2] This majority will be changed only by popular demonstrations or by the elective franchise. The Virginia elections[3] and the Charter election of the City of N. York[4] are now at hand, and their results are looked for by both parties with palpitating hearts. I think we shall succeed in Virginia, and obtain partial success in N. York; but a few days will now determine.

What are we now to do here? The Senate can yet do some negative good, altho for the want of the concurrence of the House it can perform no positive act of legislation. Our efforts therefore will be directed to preventive remedy.

The period of our adjournment is uncertain; but I am inclined to think it will be in the month of June.[5]

Orlando Brown is with us; and from a letter which he shewed me from you, I perceive you correspond with you [*sic*, him]. From him I have no doubt that you will learn things which strike his mind and [*sic*, as] interesting to you, but which escape my observation.

I have never seen party spirit in the house more shameless, or more determined to accomplish its purposes, without regard to means. I think it is even to be apprehended that they will give [Robert] Letchers seat to [Thomas P.] Moore.[6]

ALS. DLC-John J. Crittenden Papers (DNA, M212, R20). Written from "S Chamber." Copy, with substantial differences, in OHi.   1. Thomas B. Monroe was appointed judge of the U.S.

District Court for Kentucky in March, 1834, and held the office for twenty-seven years. See *Biographical Encyclopedia of Kentucky* (Cincinnati, 1878), 547-48. Lewis Saunders was appointed U.S. district attorney for Kentucky. *Biennial Register*, 1835, p. 159.   2. Whittlesey to Clay, Sept. 19, 1832.   3. Clay to Brooke, March 10, 1834.   4. Berryman to Clay, March 13, 1834.   5. The U.S. Senate adjourned on June 30, 1834, at 6:45 p.m.   6. Clay to Helm, April 20, 1833.

Remark in Senate, April 8, 1834. Suggests the order of taking up Senate business — reading of the *Journal*, followed by the call of the president of the Senate for petitions, then reports. *Register of Debates*, 23 Cong., 1 Sess., 1266.

Speech in Senate, April 9, 1834. Responds to Calhoun's speech supporting repeal of the Force Act [Remark in Senate, January 22, 1833]; this Calhoun undertook mainly by attacking the constitutionality of the protective tariff. Defends at length the constitutionality, practicality, and historical necessity of such tariffs. Says he has no objection to the repeal of the military part of the act but not its anti-nullification section. To nullification he "never could give his aid or consent." Argues, in the same breath, that "Sir, we have got . . . a nullification infinitely more dangerous, not in South Carolina, but in Washington, which threatens destruction to the liberties of the country, by an entire absorption of all the powers of the General Government in the hands of one man. The nullification of our Southern sister was by-gone. Was, this, then, the time for abstruce propositions and metaphysical discussions? It would be better to let them sleep, and for gentlemen to buckle on their armor to meet and avert the present and practical danger." Contends that his Compromise Tariff Act [Draft Proposal, Mid-December, 1832] has served to reduce sectional tensions and is pleased to know that it has "commanded" Calhoun's "approbation." *Register of Debates*, 23 Cong., 1 Sess., 1281-84. At the conclusion of his remarks, which shaded into a blistering personal attack on the contradictory policies and hypocrisies of President Jackson and his administration on the bank, tariff, internal improvement, and nullification issues, Clay moved to refer Calhoun's bill repealing the Force Act to the Judiciary Committee. There it died. See Wilson, *Calhoun Papers*, 12:187, 189, 277-98.

Comment in Senate, April 11, 1834. Suggests that the Senate compile and analyze all the memorials and petitions presented to the Congress dealing with the collapse of the nation's economy and how best to solve the problem. In this manner "the number, the class, or the genuineness of the signatures," pro and con, can be counted, evaluated, and authenticated. Guesses there have been 100,000 to 150,000 signatures against the removal of the deposits. *Register of Debates*, 23 Cong., 1 Sess., 1302-5. See Remark in Senate, April 29, 1834.

To PETER B. PORTER   Washington, April 11, 1834

I recd. your favor of the 30h Ulto. from Black Rock; and that of the 9h. inst. from N. York. I am rejoiced at the good prospects of the City election[1] and sincerely hope that its result may be auspicious. The losses and gains in the Virginia elections[2] will about neutralize each other. The members from that State are confident that the general result will not vary the complexion of the Legislature as exhibited at the last Session.

Unless the issue of pending elections should influence the House of R. we shall be able to effect nothing, I apprehend, for the relief of the Country at this Session. That issue, if it do not change the majority in the House may give more courage, which is wanted, to the majority in the Senate.

There is a project on foot of a Consultative meeting at N. York to bring out Mr. Webster as a Candidate for the Presidency.[3] I should think the Country would be fortunate with one at the head of its affairs so competent as he is to direct them; but we ought to be quite sure that he will combine more strength than any other Candidate of our party before he is resolved on.

Will you visit us?

ALS. NBuHi. 1. Berryman to Clay, March 13, 1834. 2. Clay to Brooke, March 10, 1834. 3. For Webster's growing hope of winning the 1836 presidential nomination, see Brown, *Daniel Webster and the Politics of Availability*, 69-104.

To Henry Clay, Jr., Lexington, April 13, 1834. Reports that Lucretia "is still feeble, and I fear not improving. . . . Her condition is such that unless she gets better in a few weeks, I fear she can not survive." Makes arrangements to lend his son "upwards of $3000" to meet a personal debt and pay the B.U.S. loan he had taken out recently to purchase land. Mentions his intention to invest $500 in "the Rail Road Co. [Clay to Biddle, May 10, 1831] if the state of my funds in Bank would admit of its payment." As for the future status of "Ashland" overseer William Martin [Henry Clay, Jr., to Clay, December 14, 1833], "it will be best not to dismiss him prior to my return. No one can settle with him so well as I can myself." Remarks that "Miss Prather" had visited with them in their Washington home for "ten or twelve days" and had departed last night for Lousiville. Concludes with the political observation that "The Tories in N. York [City] have succeeded in the election of [Cornelius] Lawrence by a majority of less than two hundred [Berryman to Clay, March 13, 1834]. We consider this a great triumph on the part of the Whigs." ALS. Henry Clay Memorial Foundation, Lexington, Ky.

"Miss Prather" was probably the sister of Julia Prather Clay, wife of Henry Clay, Jr. In an earlier letter to Nathaniel Pope, dated "Sunday" [*ca.* March 30, 1834], Clay insisted that Miss Prather stay in the Clay home when she arrived in Washington, even though "Mrs. Clay's health is still extremely feeble. Miss Prather was traveling from Kentucky to Washington in company with the Misses Pope and Oldham. Clay regretted that he and his wife did not have "room in our limited dwelling" to accommodate all three ladies. *Ibid.*

Speech in Senate, April 14, 1834. Presents memorials from Troy and Schenectady, N.Y., remonstrating against the removal of deposits from the Bank of the United States, praying for their restoration, and asking that the B.U.S. be rechartered [Bradley to Clay, October 16, 1832; Clay to Wilde, April 27, 1833]. Launches into a speech on the nation's economic distress, blaming it on the disastrous and dictatorial fiscal policies of President Jackson. Defends the B.U.S. against Jacksonian charges of corruption and mismanagement. Interprets the outcome of the charter elections in New York City [Berryman to Clay, March 13, 1834] as a great victory of "patriotic whigs." Continues: "It was a great victory. It must be so regarded in every respect. From a majority of more than six thousand, which the dominant party boasted a few months ago, if it retain any, it is a meager and spurious majority of less than two hundred. And the Whigs contended with such odds against them. A triple alliance of State placemen, corporation [city] placemen, and Federal placemen, amounting to about thirty-five hundred, and deriving, in the form of salaries, compensations, and allowances, ordinary and extra, from the public chests, the enormous sum, annually, of near one million of dollars. Marshalled, drilled, disciplined, commanded. The struggle was tremendous; but what can withstand the irresistible power of the Votaries of truth, liberty, and their country? It was an immortal triumph—a triumph of the constitution and the laws over usurpation here, and over clubs and bludgeons and violence there. . . . It was a brilliant and signal triumph of the whigs." Explains that those who oppose the usurpations of Andrew Jackson are rightfully called "whigs . . . a denomination which, according to all the analogy of history, is strictly correct. It deserves to be extended throughout the whole country." Compares America's Whigs with those Whigs in Britain who, in Parliament, had historically opposed the prerogatives of the king and the extension of royal executive powers. Asks: "And what is the present but the same contest in another form?" Calls for a united political front to save "the cause of the people, of the constitution, and of civil liberty" from the menace of Jackson, "a Chief Magistrate who is endeavoring to concentrate in his own person the whole powers of Government." *Register of Debates*, 23 Cong., 1 Sess., 1310-15. Printed in Colton, *Clay Correspondence*, 5:624-31, where it is misdated as March 14, 1834. It was in this speech that Clay first employed and defined the word "Whig" in U.S. political terms. See Clement Eaton, *Henry Clay and the Art of American Politics* (Boston, 1957), 113; also, Speech in Senate, May 21, 1834, in which Clay applied the term specifically to New York state political events. In the New York City charter elections of 1834 [Berryman to Clay, March 13, 1834] the word "Whig" first appeared on a ballot. Van Deusen, *Jacksonian Era*, 96.

To Henry Thompson, Baltimore, April 16, 1834. Asks Thompson to look after "a pair of calves from the famous stock of Genl. [Stephen] V[an]. Rensselaer of Albany" due soon to arrive in Baltimore. Expects a Kentucky drover to take charge of them there by May 1. Should the drover not arrive, asks Thompson to look for a suitable replacement. ALS. KyU.

To FRANCIS T. BROOKE   Washington, April 17, 1834
I leave here to-day for the Virginia Springs, on account of Mrs. Clay's health, which continues feeble and precarious. I shall return as soon as I can leave her with propriety. My own situation requires also relaxation. I feel very much prostrated. I hope I shall be able soon to return to my post with re-invigorated health.

We are very thankful for the kind invitation contained in your letter of the 13th, but the condition of Mrs. Clay at present, is such, that she would only be a burden at St. Julien, without being able to enjoy its pleasures. I transmitted to you at Richmond some letters from New York, communicating the issue of the great three days' contest.[1] It is felt by both parties here, as the precursor of the complete overthrow of Jacksonism.

We are still anxious about your elections, but feel confident of their being no variation from the last Legislature, in the aggregate result.[2]

The nullifiers are doing us no good here. You will have seen a badly-reported speech of mine, in answer to Mr. Calhoun.[3]

Copy. Printed in Colton, *Clay Correspondence*, 4:382.   1. Berryman to Clay, March 13, 1834. 2. Clay to Brooke, March 10, 1834.   3. Calhoun's speech in support of his bill to repeal the so-called Force Act [Remark in Senate, Jan. 22, 1833] was delivered on April 9, 1834. *Register of Debates*, 23 Cong., 1 Sess., 1266-81. For Clay's answer on that same day, see Speech in Senate, April 9, 1834.

From PHILIP S. PHYSICK   Philadelphia, April 19, 1834
Your letter dated the 16th instant containing one from Dr [*sic*, Henry Huntt] Hunt came to my hands this morning. I am happy to learn that Mrs Clay has experienced some relief since Dr Hunts first letter. As long as tender mutton and beef agree with her at breakfast and dinner they ought to be continued. Perhaps the crackers she obtains in Washington are made without butter in their composition and if so they may also be continued. The crackers made here almost all of them contain butter and such crackers often, after a few days use, disagree. If after some time the present breakfast ceases to suit, a trial may be made of eggs the yolks only to be taken. Two of these, poached, with a piece a stale crumb of good bread with a cup of black tea may constitute the breakfast   The Beef and mutton with crumb of stale bread may be taken for dinner but if she becomes tired of these a full grown pidgeon nicely stewed

would be found very tender and easy of digestion. Tripe are now in season and often agree extremely well. If Mrs Clay shd prefer either of these at breakfast she might take them instead of the eggs. Or she could take one of them with a cup of black tea for her supper. Under this course of diet it is very important to keep the bowels open. I have not been informed whether Mrs C. ever used for this purpose injections of warm water. One quart of warm water thrown into the bowels in the morning half an hour after breakfast in some persons answers the purpose very satisfactorily but if such injections are found inconvenient I know of no medicine more efficacious and at the same time strengthening than rhubarb taken in such doses at bedtime every night or every other night as may be found necessary to occasion a moderate effect the following morning   To relieve acidity of the stomach Mrs Clay has formerly used the alkaline solution made from fresh hickory ashes and soot. I very much prefer this solution to the carbonates of either soda or potass because it cannot add to the flatulent state of the bowels as the carbonates often do. In preparing the alkaline solution be careful to dilute it sufficiently with water to prevent it from excoriating the mouth or fauces. One tablespoonful of it may be taken about half an hour after each meal. — never on an empty stomach. — If this is found useful the dose may be gradually increased to half a wine glassful or more if acidity requires it. In some cases it is found beneficial to excite external inflammn over the stomach by the application of plasters composed of flour of mustard and water. A plaster of this sort seven inches long and five inches wide may be put on the pit of the stomach and may be kept on for fifteen or twenty minutes or until it excites inflammn of the skin to a moderate degree. It may be repeated every week or ten days. I have not been informed whether any of the preparations of iron have been prescribed & taken. If not, three grains of the *carbonate* of *iron* may be taken with each dose of rhubarb at bedtime. It is a question, as water appears to disagree so much, whether the mineral water to which Mrs Clay is going[1] will be proper & safe   No doubt the quantity taken at first should be small until she is able to determine how it agrees. — On going to a mineral Spring patients are often persuaded to take too much and are thereby injured. Dr Hunt has informed me that Mrs Clay sometimes took a glass of wine — He objected to its use and I think very properly. Perhaps if a stimulant is wanted occasionally a little weak gin and water may be tried — this very seldom becomes acid and in some instances suits very well. — Mrs Clay ought to chew her food very well and if her teeth are out of order they shd be attended to by a good Dentist — Moderate exercise every fine day will be found very beneficial. When the state of the weather forbids exercise or riding or walking[,] *friction* with a flesh brush or with coarse flannel over the whole body should be performed by an attendant so as not to allow Mrs C. to fatigue herself in doing it — The proper time for this operation is betw breakfast and dinner. . . .

ALS. DLC-HC (DNA, M212, R5). Addressed to Clay "at Warrenton (Fauquier Ct House) Virginia."   1. The springs near Warrenton were known as the Fauquier White Sulphur or Lee's Sulphur Springs. Perceval Reniers, *The Springs of Virginia* (Chapel Hill, 1941), 155-56.

Remark in Senate, April 21, 1834. Prefers not now to discuss Jackson's "supplementary message." *Register of Debates*, 23 Cong., 1 Sess., 1403.

On April 17, 1834, President Jackson had sent the Senate a long, detailed, printed letter (dated April 15), the so-called "President's Protest," which challenged his censure by the Senate [Bradley to Clay, October 16, 1832; Speech in Senate, December 26, 1833]. He labelled the censure an unconstitutional form of impeachment and insisted that he had no choice but to answer his detractors. He then proceeded to defend himself at length against the body of charges leveled against him by Clay and others. He concluded with the request that his protest be entered on the pages of the *Journal* of the Senate. *Ibid.*, 1317-36. No sooner was it read than Sen. George Poindexter (Miss.) moved "That this paper, sent to the Senate by the President of the United States, be not received." *Ibid.*, 1340.

On this day, April 21, 1834, Jackson sent the Senate his "Explanatory Message," also called his "Supplementary Message," in which he elaborated on various points made in his April 17 protest. *Ibid.*, 1393-94. After it was read, Sen. Poindexter moved, first, that like Jackson's protest of April 17, this presidential paper also not be received. He then moved that "the last message" be tabled. Following this, he offered four resolutions specifically attacking the constitutionality and arrogance of the president's protest of April 17. The fourth and last of these *"Resolved, therefore*, That the paper be not received by the Senate." *Ibid.*, 1394-95. Clay then moved to table Poindexter's motion not to receive the April 21 supplementary message "in order that the general discussion upon the President's [April 17] protest might be proceeded with." *Ibid.*, 1403. His motion produced a debate (*ibid.*, 1403-23), in which he himself complained that the printed protest from Jackson submitted on April 17, had corrections and alterations later penciled into it. These changes had been made on the morning of April 18, or after the paper had been printed, submitted, and first commented on in the Senate. It was merely "another instance of Executive encroachment," Clay charged. *Ibid.*, 1421. Jackson's "Protest" and "Explanatory" ("Supplementary") messages are printed in *MPP*, 3:69-94.

Remark in Senate, April 22, 1834. States that President Jackson's protest of April 17 need not be entered on the pages of the *Journal* of the Senate [Remark in Senate, April 21, 1834] in order to be discussed and voted on; nor should it be so entered. Sen. George Poindexter's resolutions on that point should be upheld. *Register of Debates*, 23 Cong., 1 Sess., 1433-34.

Comment in Senate, April 23, 1834. Speaks on memorials from New Jersey condemning "the conduct of the Executive in relation to the public Treasury." Argues that the submission of a memorial, "by the people themselves, acting in their primary and original character," is a much more democratic procedure than is the action of a state legislative body when it specifically instructs its senators and representatives in Congress to vote certain ways on particular national issues. Criticizes the legislature of New Jersey for having instructed Senators Theodore Frelinghuysen and Samuel L. Southard to uphold Jackson in his struggle with the Bank of the United States. Also criticizes the legislatures of Maine and Ohio in this context. Declares, further, that it is none of President Jackson's business how individual senators respond to instructions from their state legislatures. Says he has heard that Jackson has "stated to the brother of Napoleon, that he has made the Emperor of France his model." Reminds the president, however, that the "army and the navy, thank God, are sound and patriotic to the core. They will not allow themselves to be servile instruments of treason, usurpation, and the overthrow of civil liberty, if any such designs now exist." *Register of Debates*, 23 Cong., 1 Sess., 1434, 1436-39, 1447-48, 1450.

Later this day, Clay moved to amend Sen. John Forsyth's amendment to Sen. George Poindexter's resolution of April 21 that the Senate not receive Jackson's protest, submitted on April 17 [Remark in Senate, April 21, 1834]. Forsyth's amendment asked that the Senate receive the "President's Protest" as well as the "Explanatory Message" subsequently submitted by Jackson on April 21. Clay's three-part motion resolved first, that the assertion of presidential powers in Jackson's protest of April 10 [*sic*, 17] was "inconsistent with the constitution of the United States"; second, that while the Senate always stands ready to receive presidential messages of a constitutional sort, it cannot recognize "any right" of a president to make a formal protest against a Senate vote as being illegal or unconstitutional, and then request the Senate to enter such a protest on its journals; finally, that the "aforesaid protest is a breach of the privileges of the Senate, and that it be not entered on the Journal." In defending his amended resolutions, Clay made a constitutional and procedural distinction between receiving a proper presidential communication and entering on its journals one that is unconstitutional. *Ibid.*, 1450-53.

To HENRY CLAY, JR. Washington, April 24, 1834

[Discusses their mutual financial affairs in Lexington and authorizes his son to "pay the $500. to the Rail Road Co."[1] Continues:]

I left your mother at the Springs near Warrenton on sunday last.[2] She bore the journey better then I did. And James [Brown Clay] writes me on the 21st. that her strength was increasing. She will return here on the 2d. May and proceed a few days after to K.

I am rejoiced to hear that Theodore [W. Clay] is better.[3]

Great sensation has been produced here by the Presidents Protest.[4] We hope and believe that it puts the Seal to the overthrow of his party. No fears are entertained by our friends here of our being beaten in the Virginia Elections.[5] There will be variations, both ways, in particular Counties, but the aggregate result will not be essentially changed.

Have you any Sheep? I am concerned to hear of the loss in our Saxon Sheep. My love to Julia [Prather Clay]

ALS. Henry Clay Memorial Foundation, Lexington, Ky. 1. Clay to Biddle, May 10, 1831. 2. Physick to Clay, April 19, 1834. 3. Theodore W. Clay to Clay, Jan. 8, 1832. 4. Remark in Senate, April 21, 1834. 5. Clay to Brooke, March 10, 1834.

Legal Document, Lexington, April 24, 1834. Clay submits to the court a "List of Slaves belonging to the Estate of James Weir [1:188-89] dec[ease]d Including the Nine allotted to E[liza]. J[ane]. Weir in lieu of the H[ouse]. & lot on Mulberry St." AEI, by Clay. KyLxT. Eliza Jane Weir, an orphan of Dromore, Ireland, was one of the heirs of her great-uncle James Weir, a prosperous Lexington businessman who died on February 24, 1832. Frankfort *Commentator*, March 6, 1832. Clay became the legal guardian of her American property. See Fayette County Guardians' Book B: 284-85, 329-32; Fayette County Order Book 9:335, 10:397, 11:109; Fayette County Guardians' Bonds Book 6:19; William A. Leavy, *A Memoir of Lexington And Its Vicinity* (written 1875, published Lexington, 1944), 365-66.

On September 22, 1834, James Prenter wrote stating that he had sent "the necessary papers, authorizing you to act in the Managmt of the affairs of my Grandaughter Miss Weir at Kentuckey [*sic*]. Adds that "These documents have been authenticated in Every way Consistent with the form & practice of our Court of Chancery, & I have no doubt, will . . . be Considered quite Conclusive of my appointment as Guardian, & of my right to make the deputation I have had the Honor to do." LS. KyLxT.

James Stuart wrote on October 27, 1834, from "Liverpool Packet, Independence, off Sandy Hook" to say that in a few days he would send Clay "sundry documents, in the cause of the minor Weir." Notes that he was originally employed by James Prenter "to obtain on her behalf . . . the opinion of some professional gentn. in Ky, & I lost no time in having her case laid before you." Discusses legal problems arising from the contention of her uncles in Kentucky that she will forfeit the right to the property unless she comes to the United States to claim it, and that they should receive the property because James Weir allegedly owed them twenty years worth of wages. Concludes: "I know you will at once cause full justice to be done, realise the chattle property & remitt, as pointed out by Mr. P. through my agency, so that the education of the minor may

be ac[complished] while she is of proper age, and that she [may not] be longer a burthen to her G. father." ALS. *Ibid.*

On November 1, 1834, Stuart forwarded to Clay the documents mentioned in his
letter of October 27, "with the exception of the original appointment of Mr. Prenter, as
her Guardian . . . which is too heavy to be sent by post." *Ibid.*

Writing from Baltimore on November 24, 1834, Stuart acknowledged receipt "of
the papers in the case of the minor Weir and enclosing a copy of the report of the Commissioners and the decree of the Court of Chancery, as to the division of the Real estate
of the late Jas. Weir." Believes that "Although the division is not by any means such as
we wished, yet . . . we ought not to attempt to disturb the decree" provided "the price
of the five slaves . . . and also the rents as some may become due" are turned over to
Clay "without any delay." Adds that if "the Administrator will not pay to you promptly,
so as to get over to Ireland *Cash without* any *delay*, to educate & support the minor & pay
the heavy costs that has been incurred, I beg you to cause Such steps to be taken, as will
procure the sale and price of the Slaves, and the rents as the same become due, together
with the distributive share of the personal estate in the hands of the Adminr. forthwith.
Most persons value Landed estate above what it will sell for in Cash—not so much so
with Slaves. and I therefore apprehend, the Messrs. Weirs have obtained all that they
wanted in the division, by obtaining what is immeadiately productive." *Ibid.*

On April 8, 1835, Stuart wrote asking that money for Eliza Jane be sent to him
"immediately for her education & suppo[rt] and also to pay the costs incurred, in the
appointment of her guardian in Ireland." Adds that as soon as the money is received "I
will advance it to Mr. Prenter in Ireland." *Ibid.*

Eliza Jane wrote Clay on July 14, 1835, stating that she had at last been placed
"exclusively and finally under the protection of my dear Grandfather Prenter, who has
reared me tenderly, and educated me respectably since I was left an Orphan without
means of support." Offers Clay "my warmest thanks, for the kind interest which you
have taken in my affairs." *Ibid.* Her grandfather, James Prenter, wrote the same day
thanking Clay "for your condesention in acting for me as her guardian." Reports that he
has "been put to an immense expense by her father's relations here who have made attack after attack, both forcibly and legally, to take her from under my protection." Consequently, adds that "I would most Earnestly entreat that the chattel property should be
remitted *to me direct* as her legal Guardian, with as little delay as possible—." LS. *Ibid.*

On July 15, 1835, James Stuart wrote that the proceedings "taken by the Weir's, to
get old Mrs. Weir, the Minor's Grandmother, joined with Mr. Prenter in the Guardianship of Miss Weir" have failed, and "Mr. Prenter is to be sole guardian." Notes that
Prenter has placed Eliza Jane "at a highly respectable school in Belfast . . . and I presume she will get a good education there." States: "The representation that has been
made to you, that Mr. Prenter is not a good Character, is unwarrantable and unjust."
Explains: "The Minor's relatives, by both father & Mother, as far as known to me, are
all respectable, but since this property has fallen to her, the original bad feeling between
the two families have been revived, and Irish like, they have carried it to an extreme—."
Estimates that the money so far paid to Prenter from Eliza Jane's inheritance will not
cover the cost so far incurred, "but I do think, five hundred dollars per annum, will be
sufficient to pay her expenses until she comes of age." ALS. *Ibid.*

On September 15, 1835, Clay gave a guardian's bond of $15,000 in Fayette County
Court, obliging him to "well and truly pay . . . to Eliza Jane Weir . . . all such estate as
now is, or hereafter shall appear to be due from him to said orphan." James Erwin joined
Clay in signing the bond. DS. Fayette County Guardians' Bonds Book 4:19.

Also on September 15, James Prenter wrote from Dromore, Ireland, thanking
Clay for acting on behalf of Eliza Jane, and saying that "I feel satisfied from your high
standing in society that any obstacles thrown in her way will through your Influence be
Easily overcome." Explains his difficulties in fighting the Weirs in court for three and a
half years, noting that "Even the remittance which you so promptly obliged to be forwarded of £500 was not paid me but lodged in Court where it Must remain till November

next, and can then only be drawn out at considerable Expence." Adds that as to Eliza Jane's going to America, "I have left her entirely to her own wishes and feelings on the subject but am Inclined to think that at the present she would not like to separate from us with whom she has been Since an Infant and to tell you the truth it would be a great Crush to me in my old days to part with her." Encloses a statement of his granddaughter's expenses "for your Inspection and Consideration." ALS. KyLxT.

Eliza Jane wrote from Belfast on September 17, 1835, again thanking Clay for acting on her behalf. Although desiring "to attend to every wish and proposal of yours," feels she "could not at the present time, bear to part from all my dear friends here" in order to come to America. Regrets that "any person had attempted to impeach" the character of her grandfater but is relieved that "Mr. Stuart . . . has done away with so unjust a charge in his explanation to you." *Ibid.*

On October 24, 1835, James Stuart wrote from New York suggesting that "When funds come into your hands, I hope you can pay Mr. P[renter]. the amt. due him, and from July 1836, remit say $500 or one hundred pounds per annum for the minors education and support." Adds that he is sending the London *Morning Chronicle* of September 26 "that you may See the Municipal Reform Bill as it has passed." *Ibid.* For the English Municipal Corporation bill, passed September 9, 1835, see William L. Langer (ed.), *An Encyclopedia of World History*, 4th ed. (Boston, 1968), 658.

Stuart wrote on January 9, 1836, to inform Clay that he had transferred the $250 paid him by Clay to Prenter for Eliza Jane's support. Presumes the security Prenter has given in Ireland will "be found ample for the amt. that you are to pay, until she is of age." Hopes that "the Minor and her Grandfather will consent that she should emigrate to the U.S. soon." *Ibid.*

James Prenter wrote from Dromore, Ireland, on March 30, 1836, praising Clay for his success in otaining the legal guardianship in the United States of Eliza Jane. States that he has applied "towards Elizas Board Clothing and Education" the $250 received from Clay through James Stuart last January. Regrets that the court will not allow more than $500 per annum for her support and that it has "Refused to Remunerate me for the heavy Expense Incurred here by me occasioned by the unjust and unwarrantable proceedings of the Wiers [*sic*, Weir]." Asserts that Eliza Jane will not consider moving to the United States. *Ibid.*

Prenter again wrote on August 10, 1836, saying that Court of Chancery costs have more than swallowed up the money he has received. Begs Clay to "Send me a Remittance Including the Allowance of the Courts up to first of November, 1836" as soon as possible. *Ibid.*

Prenter reiterated in a letter of September 15, 1836, his need for money to pay Eliza Jane's board and tuition. Urges "please Say at what time or date your Court Allowed the 500 Dollars pr annum to Commence." *Ibid.*

On November 1, 1836, James Stuart wrote from New York, forwarding Prenter's letter. States that Prenter "is either far in advance" on expenditures for Eliza Jane "or her *board &c unpaid.*" *Ibid.*

Speech in Senate, April 25, 1834. Presents a memorial from Hanover, in York County, Pa., calling for the restoration of the deposits [Bradley to Clay, October 16, 1832], the rechartering of the Bank of the United States [Clay to Wilde, April 27, 1833], and a condemnation of the conduct of the governor of Pennsylvania [George Wolf] on these issues "as vacillating and time-serving." Clay also attacks Wolf's shift from a pro-B.U.S., sound currency stance to an anti-bank position, noting that he has abandoned those "Pennsylvania principles" which have long included internal improvements, the American System, and a national bank. Reports with pleasure that in his native Hanover County, Va., which Jackson had carried in 1828 and 1832 "by vast majorities," the Jackson party has been beaten soundly in the recent state elections [Clay to Brooke, March 10, 1834]. Asked by Sen. John Forsyth (Ga.) which of these two Hanovers "had the honor of giving birth to the Senator from Kentucky," Clay replied: "The place where that event happened, which enables me to stand before you, was between Black Tom's Slash and Hanover Court-House, or, to fix the spot more precisely, between the Merry Oaks and the Court-house, about half-way between them, and not very far from St. Paul's Church, at the vestry house of which I went to school several years." Concludes his remarks with the assertion of his right and duty to attack the actions of a state governor if it be necessary, and with renewed criticism of both Jackson's protest of his censure and his supplemental message [Remark in Senate, April 21, 1834]. *Register of Debates*, 23 Cong., 1 Sess., 1480-85.

Certificate, Washington, April 28, 1834. Certifying Clay's election as an honorary member of the Columbian Horticultural Society in the District of Columbia. DS, partially printed. DLC-George Watterston Papers (DNA, M212, R22).

On July 28, 1835, Clay wrote D.C. Wallace, accepting "with pleasure and gratitude" an appointment to honorary membership in the Hamilton County [Ohio] Agriculture Society. ALS. ICHi.

To JOHN PENDLETON KENNEDY   Washington, April 28, 1834

I recd. your favor of the 24h. inst. with the Balto. resolutions[1] which I perused with great satisfaction. They touched the marrow of the Protest; and have given us all inexpressible delight. Balto. is herself again.

I consider the Protest as the last stroke upon the last nail driven into the coffin of Jacksonism. I shall endeavor about the day after tomorrow to pay my respects to it.[2] Webster & Calhoun also mean to bestow on it their devoirs.[3] How cheering is it once more to behold light breaking in upon our deluded Country!

ALS. MdBP.   1. These stemmed from a Whig public meeting in Baltimore. They attacked arguments presented by Jackson in his protest [Remark in Senate, April 21, 1834] against Senate censure, and were laid before the Senate on May 1, 1834. *Register of Debates*, 23 Cong., 1 Sess., 1583-93; *Cong. Globe*, 23 Cong., 1 Sess., 355.   2. See Speech in Senate, April 30, 1834. 3. Calhoun spoke on May 6, 1834. *Register of Debates*, 23 Cong., 1 Sess., 1640-50. Webster spoke on May 7. *Ibid.*, 1663-90. See also *Cong. Globe*, 23 Cong., 1 Sess., 363, 368-69.

Remark in Senate, April 28, 1834. Challenges a memorial from the inhabitants of Huntingdon, Pa., which supports Jackson's policies toward the Bank of the United States, praises Sen. William C. Rives (Va.) for resigning his seat [Clay to Dun, February 22, 1834], and strongly implies that Clay is "a retained advocate of the bank." Clay "wished it to be distinctly understood, that for nearly ten years he had been in no connexion with the bank." *Register of Debates*, 23 Cong., 1 Sess., 1530-31; *Cong. Globe*, 23 Cong., 1 Sess., 349.

Later this day, Clay resolved that Secretary Taney be directed to report to the Senate the following: the gross amount of the proceeds from public lands sold in 1833; the number of acres sold in 1833, especially during the last quarter of the year; the amount received and number of acres sold in each state and territory; the manner in which the Treasury Department has calculated the amount and value of public land set aside in Ohio for public roads as provided in the 1802 federal compact with that then new state; and how similar allowances for roads have been determined by the department in other new states. *Register of Debates*, 23 Cong., 1 Sess., 1538; *Cong. Globe*, 23 Cong., 1 Sess., 350. See also, Speech in Senate, December 5, 1833.

Remark in Senate, April 29, 1834. Reports that 114,914 persons have signed memorials petitioning the government for relief from the economic distress occasioned by the Jackson's attack on the Bank of the United States, whereas 8,721 persons have "presented memorials of an opposite character." *Register of Debates*, 23 Cong., 1 Sess., 1541; *Cong. Globe*, 23 Cong., 1 Sess., 351. See also Comment in Senate, April 11, 1834.

Later this day, Clay speaks again to the Hanover, Pa., memorial [Speech in Senate, April 25, 1834] with particular reference to Gov. George Wolf's shift to a support of Jackson's position on the Bank of the United States. Attacks Wolf's lack of political constancy. Refers to the governor's "unexpected message" to the Pennsylvania legislature which "all parties" in Washington viewed as evidence that Wolf had "thrown his great weight into the scale of the President." Explains the shift in terms of Wolf's mistaken belief that the B.U.S. was hostile to Pennsylvania's negotiation of loans abroad to pay for proposed internal improvements. Notes that only three days before his message was "sent in," Wolf "avowed himself in favor of a re-charter of the Bank of the United States." *Register of Debates*, 23 Cong., 1 Sess., 1546-47. Wolf's message to the legislature of February 26, 1834, used ambiguous language which seemed to blame the B.U.S. rather than the government for the nation's financial crisis. See Govan, *Nicholas Biddle*, 257; Harrisburg *Chronicle*, February 27, 1834; Comment in Senate, May 1, 1834.

Speech in Senate, April 30, 1834. Clay's principal speech vigorously attacking the thrust, content, and constitutionality of Jackson's April 17 protest of his censure by the Senate [Remark in Senate, March 28; April 21, 1834], and of Sen. Felix Grundy's speech of April 29, 1834 [*Register of Debates*, 23 Cong., 1 Sess., 1547-59], in defense of the president. Also attacks Jackson personally. Thinks, for instance, that Jackson's head should be studied by phrenologists, such as Dr. Charles Caldwell [2:724-25] of Transylvania University, who would "find the organ of destructiveness prominently developed. Except an enormous fabric of Executive power for himself, the President has built up nothing, constructed nothing, and will leave no enduring monument of his administration. He goes for destruction, universal destruction; and it seems to be his greatest ambition to efface and obliterate every trace of the wisdom of his predecessors. He has displayed this remarkable trait throughut his whole life, whether in private walks or in the public service." Defends the Senate's judgment in and reasons for censuring Jackson, asserts the unconstitutionality of the president's protest, scores Jackson's argument that censure is an unconstitutional form of Senate impeachment, denies that the Senate maintains its journal for the convenience of President Jackson, and appeals to U.S. history to sustain his insistance that the president is a dangerous tyrant and that his protest of censure "is but a new form of the veto." Dismisses with contempt Sen. Grundy's argument that historical parallels to partisan attacks on Jackson can be found in the attempt of the Pennsylvania legislature to impeach Gov. Thomas McKean. Claims also that Jackson's contention that he is the "sole Executive; all other officers are his agents, and their duties are his duties" is "altogether a military idea, wholly incompatible with free government. I deny it absolutely. There exists no such responsibility to the President. All are responsible to the law, and to the law only, or not responsible at all." Points out that the president's April 21 supplement to his April 17 protest does "not let go one particle of the power claimed and asserted in the principal document." Asks, further: "What clause in the constitution gives him the power of removal?" Argues at length that Jackson has seized that power over the public purse clearly granted to Congress by the Constitution, a seizure that has plunged the nation into depression and one which reveals the president's policy of leading the United States "to a practical monarchy, in which, mocked with the forms of free government, we shall, in fact, have but one will, and that a unit." Concludes with the hope that the president's protest will turn out to be "the last stroke upon the last nail driven into the coffin — not of Jackson, may he live a thousand years! — but of Jacksonism." *Register of Debates*, 23 Cong., 1 Sess., 1550, 1559, 1564-81. For the attempts in the Pennsylvania legislature in 1806-8 to impeach Gov. Thomas McKean on trivial and absurd charges, see McKean entry in *DAB*.

Comment in Senate, May 1, 1834. Presents a memorial from Bald Eagle, Centre County, Pa., which condemns Jackson's bank policy and his protest of censure [Remark in Senate, April 21, 1834]. Believes it serves to "neutralize" a memorial from Easton, Northampton County, Pa., presented by Sen. Samuel McKean of Pa., supporting the president. Says the first is signed mostly by former Jacksonians while the latter is a produce of what its Easton signers call a "Democratic Republican, Jackson, Wolf meeting" there. Wonders what kind of peculiar coalition that could be. As for the shift in the stance of Gov. George Wolf of Pa. on the bank and removal of deposits questions, explains that in his message in December, 1832 [Remark in Senate, April 29, 1834], the governor seemed to regret Jackson's veto of the bill to recharter the Bank of the United States [Clay to Wilde, April 27, 1833; Speech in Senate, July 12, 1832; Clay to Brown, December 18, 1831] and had even suggested that a similar bill, if presented to the president, would receive his assent. *Register of Debates*, 23 Cong., 1 Sess., 1583-84. For Wolf's message to the Pennsylvania legislature on December 5, 1832, see Harrisburg *Chronicle*, December 6, 1832.

Later this same day, in response to a charge by Sen. Felix Grundy (Tenn.) that Clay himself had been inconsistent of the bank issue, Clay explained his own shift on the bank question back in 1816 [2:200-205]. "The experience of the war changed every body," he said, even Sen. Grundy, when serving in the House in 1814, had also supported the re-establishment of a national bank. *Register of Debates*, 23 Cong., 1 Sess., 1591-93; *Cong. Globe*, 23 Cong., 1 Sess., 355-56.

Comment in Senate, May 2, 1834. Presents to the Senate the report of its Committee on Public Lands on his bill [Speech in Senate, December 5, 1833] to distribute to the states the proceeds from the sale of public lands. Discusses also the reasons given by President Jackson for his belatedly written (December 4, 1834) veto of the 1833 land bill [Speech in Senate, January 7, 1833; Clay to Wilde, April 27, 1833; Speech in Senate, December 5, 1833]; moves for the printing of 5,000 extra copies of the committee report. Explains he would not ask for so many extra copies had not the president's December 4 veto message been heavily printed, and had not "we . . . on this side of the Senate" supported such a printing. Condemns the unconstitutionality and partisan political motivations of Jackson's silent pocket veto of the land bill passed on March 2, 1833, at the end of the previous session. Thinks this time, however, there are enough votes to override another veto. *Register of Debates*, 23 Cong., 1 Sess., 1599-1600, 1602-4, 1606; *Cong. Globe*, 23 Cong., 1 Sess., 358.

To JAMES BROWN
Washington, May 4, 1834

I recd. your favor on the 2d. Mrs. Clay returned this day from the Fauquier Springs,[1] and I am happy to inform you in health some what improved. She is however far from being well yet, and will remain only a few days here and proceed to the West, perhaps by the White Sulphur Springs.

Enough of the result of the Virginia Elections[2] is now certainly known to enable me to assure you that there is a most decided majority of members elected to the next Legislature, adverse to the Admin.

You will have seen that the Senate has again rejected the Bank directors, and that the Presidt. accompanied their renomination with a message[3] almost as extraordinary as the Protest.[4]

No talk of an adjournment.

ALS. KyLxT.   1. Physick to Clay, April 19, 1834.   2. Clay to Brooke, March 10, 1834.
3. Clay to Biddle, Dec. 21, 1833.   4. *Register of Debates*, 23 Cong., 1 Sess., 1317-36; Remark in Senate, April 21, 1834.

Remark in Senate, May 5, 1834. Objects to taking up any legislative business until the question of President Jackson's protest [Remark in Senate, April 21, 1834] of his censure by the Senate is disposed of. *Register of Debates*, 23 Cong., 1 Sess., 1613.

Later in the day Clay spoke again about the president's protest, asserting that the censure on March 28 was legal even though the Senate's resolution of censure might not have had a specific or immediate legislative purpose. *Ibid.*, 1638-39; *Cong. Globe*, 23 Cong., 1 Sess., 363.

From Henry Clay, Jr., Lexington, May 6, 1834. Discusses his own debts, his father's debts and assets, and his management of various collections and payments authorized by Clay. Informs his father that the Bank of the United States branch office in Lexington is currently charging ½ of 1 percent interest and a 1 percent discount on bills of exchange. Mentions that he has recently had to pay $58.52 on one such bill from Clay, adding: "They are becoming very particular in their operations; and they say they are not buying bills on the East which accounts for the discount. . . . They are not buying bills now, and seem unwilling even to take them in payment of debts." Reports that "We are getting up a State Convention &c &c for the 4th of July." ALS. Henry Clay Memorial Foundation, Lexington, Ky. For the continuing crisis and financial curtailments of the B.U.S., see Govan, *Nicholas Biddle*, 240, 245, 247, 271-72. Henry Clay, Jr., was a delegate to the Whig convention which met in Frankfort on July 4. Thomas Metcalfe was chosen president of the convention, while Chilton Allan made the principal address. Lexington *Observer & Kentucky Reporter*, July 9, 1834.

Remark in Senate, May 6, 1834. Discussion of a procedural matter during which Clay moves to table a resolution by John C. Calhoun amending slightly the language of Sen. George Poindexter's resolution that the Senate not receive President Jackson's protest of his censure by that body [Remark in Senate, April 21, 1834]. *Register of Debates*, 23 Cong., 1 Sess., 1661. For Poindexter's resolution of April 17, 1834, see *ibid.*, 1340; also *Cong. Globe*, 23 Cong., 1 Sess., 368.

To JAMES CALDWELL   Washington, May 7, 1834

Mrs. Clay is in bad health. She leves here tomorrow for Judge [Francis T.] Brooke's to which place I shall accompany her. On the 9h. she will take her departure from the Judges and I hope will reach the White Sulphur Springs about the 17h. inst.   She will remain with you about a fortnight and I hope, my dear friend, you and your good lady and family will take good care of her. She has used the water of Lee's Spring near Warrenton, she thinks with some benefit,[1] and we hope for more from your Water. She has with her my fourth son [James Brown Clay], and grandson H[enry]. C[lay]. Duralde her Carriage & four horses.

I have provided her with a sum which, accidents excepted, will be sufficient for her whole journey; but if there be any deficiency I must rely upon the deposites in your treasury.

I am happy to tell you that the Senate decided against the Protest to day by a vote of 27 to 16.[2]

ALS. ViHi. Printed in *VMHB* (October, 1947), 55:312.   1. Physick to Clay, April 19, 1834.
2. Remark in Senate, April 21, 1834; *Register of Debates*, 23 Cong., 1 Sess., 1711-12; *Cong. Globe*, 23 Cong., 1 Sess., 369. As if to celebrate his victory on the protest issue, Clay bought himself a "Gold patent watch" on this day at a cost of $107. J. Joseph to Clay, [Washington], May 7, 1834. DS. DLC-TJC (DNA, M212, R17).

From Alexander Coffin, Hudson, N.Y., May 12, 1834. Announces that he writes as a 94-year-old patriot who has recently despaired for the future of the republic because of

Jackson's "bold claims to lawless power." Thanks Clay for helping loose the president's "grasp of usurpation." Sends him in gratitude a cane "made from the Jaw bone of a Spermaceti whale, the head from a tooth of the same." ALS. DLC-HC (DNA, M212, R5). Printed in Colton, *Clay Correspondence*, 4:383-84.

On June 11, 1834, Clay wrote Coffin, thanking him for the cane and agreeing with his condemnation of Jacksonism. He concluded: "Like you, I have sometimes almost despaired of our Country. The delusion has been so long, so dark, so pervasive, that I have occasionally feared that it would survive me; but, I thank God, it is passing off rapidly, and I trust that both you and I may yet live to see many brighter and better days. What is now most to be regretted is the wound that has been inflicted upon the moral sense of the Community. What looseness of principle, what scandalous abuses, what disregard of moral and political rectitude have been quickened into life by the predominance of Jacksonism! It is worse than the Cholera, because it has been more universal, and will be more durable. The Cholera performs its terrible office, and its victims are consigned to the grave, leaving their survivors uncontaminated. But Jacksonism has poisoned the whole Community, the living as well as the dead." ALS. KyU.

To Samuel L. Southard, Trenton, N.J., May 12, 1834. Says nothing much has happened in the Senate this morning save, in executive session, discussion of the nomination of Judge Benjamin Tappan of Ohio as a U.S. district judge. Notes that Tappan's rejection has been unanimously recommended by the Judiciary Committee. ALS. NjP. The nomination of Tappan, a Democrat, was rejected by the Senate. See *DAB* and *BDAC*.

Comment in Senate, May 13, 1834. Refers to a public meeting in Adams County, Pa., on April 5, of "citizens of all parties, and among them a large body of the antimasonic party" which had condemned Jackson's policies toward the Bank of the United States. Presents examples of bank failures occasioned by the removal of deposits [Bradley to Clay, October 16, 1832; Speech in Senate, December 26, 1833]. *Register of Debates*, 23 Cong., 1 Sess., 1726.

Remark in Senate, May 14, 1834. Requests that a memorial from Columbiana County, Ohio, supporting Jackson's "cause" be read and sent on to committee, even though it refers to Clay as being "vindictive." Observes: "As the other side [is] the losing party, it would be very hard to deprive it of one of its last privileges—that of expressing itself with something like passion." *Register of Debates*, 23 Cong., 1 Sess., 1733-34.

Remark in Senate, May 15, 1834. Reports that 40,000 copies of President Jackson's April 17 protest of his censure by the Senate [Remark in Senate, April 21, 1834] have been printed "at the [*Congressional*] Globe office," and wonders "if it was done at the expense of the people of the United States." *Register of Debates*, 23 Cong., 1 Sess., 1743-44; *Cong. Globe*, 23 Cong., 1 Sess., 388.

From Anne Brown Clay Erwin, Lexington, May 16, [1834]. Thanks him for "approving of my conduct in those cases wherein I find it most difficult to act according to what I conceive to be my duty [Henry Clay, Jr., to Clay, December 14, 1833]." Is looking forward to her mother's early return home [Clay to Caldwell, May 7, 1834] and asks the best place to meet her on the road. Concludes: "I forgot to mention that Henry [Clay, Jr.] made a speech on Monday [May 12] in disapprobation of the protest [Remark in Senate, April 21, 1834] before a public meeting in which he distinguished himself indeed   I think there is no doubt but that he has extraordinary talents in this way; he seems to be desirous of getting into public life, but of course is too young for the present." ALS. DLC-TJC (DNA, M212, R14). Henry Clay, Jr., and G.R. Tompkins spoke at a "Great Whig Meeting" against "the usurpations of the Executive and the

725

flagrant and repeated violations of the constitution and laws." Lexington *Observer &
Kentucky Reporter*, May 15, 1834.

To John Leeds Kerr, [probably Easton, Md.], May 16, 1834. Comments: "I share
with you fully in the bright prospects which are opening once more on our deluded
Country. I think nothing within the compass of human sagacity can arrest the progress
of the downfall of Jacksonism. It has sufficiently cured us; and the experience which we
have acquired has been most dearly bought. The Senate opened the Campaign in
December and I rejoice that the Country has so patriotically responded. In Virginia
[Clay to Brooke, March 10, 1834]; New York [Berryman to Clay, March 13, 1834];
Ohio; and even in Pennsa. the incubus is thrown off." ALS. ICN. For Kerr, see *BDAC*.
In the 1834 fall elections in Ohio, the Whigs won control of the state legislature, win-
ning a majority of 2 seats in the senate and 16 in the house. *Niles' Register* (November 8,
1834), 47:150. In the Ohio gubernatorial election, the Democratic candidate, Robert
Lucas, defeated the Whig, James Findlay, by a vote of 70,738 to 65,414. *BDGUS*,
3:1199. In the Ohio congressional elections, 10 Whigs and 9 Democrats were chosen.
Guide to U.S. Elections, 563.

Following the Pennsylvania elections of 1834, the Democrats continued to control
the state senate by a margin of 25 seats to 8, just as they had the previous year; however, in the state house of representatives they lost 5 seats, controlling it by a margin of
59 to 41 as opposed to 64 to 36 the previous year. *Niles' Register* (October 26, 1833),
45:131; (November 1, 1834), 47:137. In the Philadelphia ward elections in the spring of
1834, 13 anti-Jackson and 2 Jackson men were elected; whereas, the previous year
there had been 11 Jacksonians and 4 anti-Jacksonians elected. *Ibid.* (March 29, 1834),
46:66. In the Pennsylvania congressional elections 17 Democrats and 11 Whigs were
chosen in 1834. *Guide to U.S. Elections*, 563. Clay may also have felt that the large
number of memorials to Congress from Ohio and Pennsylvania opposing the removal
of deposits was an indication of an anti-Jackson surge. See Clay to Biddle, December
21, 1833; *Niles' Register* (January 25, 1834), 45:372; U.S. Sen., *Journal*, 23 Cong., 1
Sess., 109, 220, 240, 264, 266, 271, 277, 284, 327, 336, 361.

Remark in Senate, May 16, 1834. Brief observations on a claims bill for the relief of
Elizabeth Robinson, only surviving daughter of a deceased veteran of the army during
the American Revolution. *Register of Debates*, 23 Cong., 1 Sess., 1751.

To JOHN SERGEANT   Washington, May 17, 1834
I wish you would ask Mr. [Nicholas] Biddle if he has any objection to furnishing me with a copy of a letter, written by him two or three years ago, to Mr.
[James] Harper, Cashr. of the Lexington office, declining to take any part in
the K. election.[1] I thought it highly judicious and creditable to him. Having
mentioned it to a friend in the H. R. he would like to be at liberty to use it.[2]

Copy, extract. DLC-Nicholas Biddle Papers (DNA, M212, R20). Excerpted from Clay to
Sergeant, May 17, 1834.   1. The Biddle to Harper letter of Jan. 9, 1829, is in Reginald G.
McGrane (ed.), *The Correspondence of Nicholas Biddle Dealing with National Affairs, 1807-1844*
(Boston & N.Y., 1919), 67-68.   2. On May 19, Sergeant forwarded this letter to Biddle,
writing on it: "Can you do what Mr. Clay wishes. I remember the letter very well, and happen to
know it was sincere. Vanderpool [*sic*, Vanderpoel], and the like, I suppose, would say it was a
'humbug.'" For Rep. Aaron Vanderpoel of N.Y., see *BDAC*.

Remark in Senate, May 20, 1834. Speaks to a petition of the principal chiefs of the
Cherokees for relief from the continuing attacks on their nation by President Jackson
and by the state of Georgia, his ally in the matter. Specifically, the chiefs ask for the
resumption of payments of annuities guaranteed them by various treaties with the
United States. Clay dismisses the argument by Sen. John Forsyth of Georgia that the

petition is inadmissable because the Cherokees are a "foreign nation." Remarks that the Supreme Court has defined them as a "domestic nation," and that Congress should see to it that they receive the monies due them—unless it be held that since the president has "taken control of the treasury [Bradley to Clay, October 16, 1832]," Congress no longer has supervision over his spending of the public money. Alludes, in closing, to the treatment of the Cherokees by Jackson and the state of Georgia [Clay to Hammond, October 7, 1829; Johnston to Clay, January 12, 1831; Fendall to Clay, August 27, 1832], calling it a "horrible grievance which had been inflicted upon the Indians, by that arbitrary policy which trampled upon treaties and the faith of the nation." *Register of Debates*, 23 Cong., 1 Sess., 1773; *Cong. Globe*, 23 Cong., 1 Sess., 396.

Speech in Senate, May 21, 1834. Presents memorials and proceedings of various public meetings in Huntingdon County and Bucks County, Pa., and Seneca Falls, N.Y., criticizing President Jackson's fiscal policies [Bradley to Clay, October 16, 1832; Clay to Wilde, April 27, 1833] and praying for relief from the economic distress caused thereby. Examines the facts behind William J. Duane's appointment as secretary of the treasury in May, 1833, his removal in September, 1833, and Roger B. Taney's appointment in his stead. Attacks Jackson for not having yet submitted Taney's nomination to the Senate for its advice and consent, and for similar "high-handed proceedings" with respect to his recess nominations of diplomats. Blames the French rejection of the treaty of indemnity [Brown to Clay, January 24, 1832; Comment in Senate, January 6, 1833] on the politically-motivated turnovers of U.S. diplomats in Paris. Reveals the details of a case of dirty politics on the part of the "Jackson party" in Seneca Falls, N.Y., which so angered some of their followers that "They turned whigs, (a species of conversion which is now proceeding with more activity than any other business in the country)." Charges that Jacksonian legislators in Washington are afraid to go home and face the "frowns" of their "indignant constituents," and that "their party is in a state of rapid and certain dissolution." Asks them "to bear with manly fortitude and Christian resignation the sad reverses which [have] befallen them." *Register of Debates*, 23 Cong., 1 Sess., 1782-87; *Cong. Globe*, 23 Cong., 1 Sess., 397.

Near the end of this day, Clay said he would postpone until another time his further remarks on President Jackson's failure to submit his nominations to the Senate. Meanwhile, he would state that in this connection he "viewed the conduct of the Executive as wholly without precedent." *Register of Debates*, 23 Cong., 1 Sess., 1803.

To Unknown Recipient, May 21, 1834. Notes that P. M. Butler, president of the Bank of South Carolina, is on his way to Kentucky "with a view of endeavoring to effect some arrangement adapted to the existing unfortunate state of derangement of the Currency and of Exchanges, mutually beneficial to the States of Kentucky and South Carolina." LS. NNPM.

Comment in Senate, May 22, 1834. Presents a memorial from Montgomery County, Pa., blaming the severe economic distress in the area on Jackson's removal of the deposits [Bradley to Clay, October 16, 1832]. States that at least 20 percent of the 1,500 to 1,600 memorialists are former Jacksonians. Asserts that the nation can at last see "the beginning of the end" of the "dreadful disease whose alarming symptoms first displayed themselves in 1827, which broke out on the 4th of March, 1829, and ever since has been raging with pestilential violence." *Register of Debates*, 23 Cong., 1 Sess., 1803.

Later on this same day, Clay spoke to a bill to repair the military road at Mars Hill, Maine, and turn it over to the state. Asks whether it was possible that the road would eventually be ceded to Great Britain. Would also "like to know what sort of a road this really was; whether it was a military road, a military-national road, or a military-national State of Maine road?" *Ibid.*, 1804.

To William M. Blackford, Fredericksburg, Va., May 23, 1834. Asks if he might postpone a decision on accepting an invitation to attend a "contemplated Celebration" in Fredericksburg on May 31. ALS. NcD. Letter marked "(Private)."

On May 30, Clay wrote to John S. Wellford *et al.*, regretfully declining the invitation to the "Whig Celebration" in Fredericksburg. Lauds Virginia's recent stands against Jackson's "usurpation" and proposes a toast to be presented to the gathering in his (Clay's) name: "The union of the States, and the union among all Whigs: Both are essential to the preservation of Liberty." ALS. ViU.

Comment in Senate, May 27, 1834. Gives notice that tomorrow he will "introduce a joint resolution, the object of which would be to re-assert what had been already declared by resolutions of the Senate [Bradley to Clay, October 16, 1832; Speech in Senate, March 27-28, 1834], that the reasons assigned by the Secretary of the Treasury to Congress [Speech in Senate, December 26, 1833; Remark in Senate, December 18, 1833], for the removal of the public deposites are insufficient and unsatisfactory; and to provide that, from and after the 1st day of July next, all deposites which may accrue from the public revenue subsequent to that period, shall be placed in the Bank of the United States and its branches, pursuant to the 16th section of the act to incorporate the subscribers to the United States Bank." *Register of Debates*, 23 Cong., 1 Sess., 1813; *Cong. Globe*, 23 Cong., 1 Sess., 404-5. For the outcome of this resolution, see Comment in Senate, May 28, 1834. Section 16 of the 1816 act creating the second B.U.S. states: "That the deposits of the money of the United States, in places in which the said bank and branches thereof may be established, shall be made in said bank or branches thereof, unless the Secretary of the Treasury shall at any time otherwise order and direct; in which case the Secretary of the Treasury shall immediately lay before Congress, if in session, and if not, immediately after the commencement of the next session, the reasons of such order or direction." 3 *U.S. Stat.*, 274.

Comment in Senate, May 28, 1834. Introduces as two separate resolutions, the joint resolution on the deposits issue promised yesterday [Comment in Senate, May 27, 1834]. The first condemns as "insufficient and unsatisfactory" Secretary Roger B. Taney's explanation, dated December 4, 1833, of the removal of deposits [Bradley to Clay, October 16, 1832]; the second demands that beginning on July 1, 1834, all government deposits of its funds be made in the Bank of the United States and its branches. Defends the need, tactical and institutional, for two separate resolutions in this regard. Urges the Senate to proceed with passing them, even in the face of a presidential veto. Demands also of Jackson that Taney's nomination as secretary be submitted to the Senate, as required by the constitution. Successfully blocks an attempt by Sen. Thomas H. Benton (Mo.) to postpone consideration of these resolutions for one week. *Register of Debates*, 23 Cong., 1 Sess., 1817, 1823; *Cong. Globe*, 23 Cong., 1 Sess., 408-10. The first resolution was passed, 29 to 16, on June 3; the second was passed, 28 to 16, on June 4. Both were sent to the House for concurrence. *Register of Debates*, 23 Cong., 1 Sess., 1879, 1895-96. The resolutions were laid on the table in the House on June 13, 1834. U.S. H. of Reps., *Journal*, 23 Cong., 1 Sess., 749-50.

From John McClellan, Fort Monroe, Va., May 28, 1834. Has received Clay's letter and regrets he is disappointed with the jackasses he has purchased from Mr. Taylor's farm in Princess Anne County, Virginia. Explains that the "old Jack I measured myself in December last . . . [and] wishing mainly an approximation to his height, I made a measuring tape, the variations mentioned in your letter of the 24th. from the dimensions I gave you formerly of the Jack, no doubt arises from this circumstance and the bad condition of the animal." States that the jenny is nine years old, and that if she were in good condition, "the impression you now have, that the Jenny is very old, would no longer be sustained." Regrets also that she is not in foal as he had believed. Wants "to do away the impression you *appear* to have, that I had made a misrepresentation," because "I assure you I had no intention to do [so]." Believes that a settlement can be worked out without following Clay's suggestion to refer the matter to friends for arbitration. ALS. DLC-HC (DNA, M212, R5). McClellan graduated sixth in his West Point class of 1826. He was born in Pennsylvania and died in Tennessee on September 1, 1854, at age 49 with the rank of breveted lieutenant colonel. USMA, *Register*, 179.

On June 1, 1834, McClellan wrote Clay that he had learned that "when the asses were delivered to Mr [Henry] Thompson in Baltimore, they were safe." Notes that the colt was very wild and undoubtedly "was choked to death by the halter. . . . Mr Taylor thinks that, as he received Mr Thompson's acknowledgement of the receipt, in safety, of the asses, that the death of the young Jack should not be his loss." However, Taylor is willing "to submit to the decision of two friends mutually chosen" whether "he ought to make a deduction in the price, & if so, what amount." ALS. DLC-HC (DNA, M212, R5).

Clay wrote Henry Thompson on June 13, 1834, stating that Taylor has agreed to take back the two surviving asses Clay had purchased from him and "to submit to arbitration the question whether I shall bear any and what part of the loss" of the young jack which died. Asks Thompson to "engage some trusty man" to take the remaining jacks "to Norfolk and deliver them to Mr. Taylor, at my expense." Also asks that Thompson serve as one of the arbiters in the dispute over the dead jack. ALS. KyU.

Remark in Senate, May 30, 1834. During debate on the U.S. Marine Corps bill, makes it known that he was "opposed to the practice of brevetting for mere length of service." Later, moves that the Senate consider his joint resolutions on the removal and restoration of the deposits [Bradley to Clay, October 16, 1832; Comment in Senate, May 28, 1834]. This motion failing, because of absences of members, announces that he will "press the resolutions to a final passage next Monday [June 2]" regardless of how many members are present or absent. *Register of Debates*, 23 Cong., 1 Sess., 1834; *Cong. Globe*, 23 Cong., 1 Sess., 415.

To FRANCIS T. BROOKE   Washington, June 2, 1834

I regret extremely to learn by your letter of the 31st. Ulto. that you have lost your daughter, the wife of your son, Robert, and I offer you on the occasion my sincere condolence.[1]

I did not go to your festival,[2] and addressed a hasty letter to you by Judge [Samuel L.] Southard, which you had not recd. at the date of yours'. The Judge has returned and was with me last night delighted with his trip. The weather was very unfavorable.

An election for Speaker in the House takes place to day, in consequence of Mr [Andrew] Stevenson's resignation. The issue is uncertain as is that of the decision of the Senate on his nomination.[3]

From some preliminary decisions of the House, on Saturday, [Robert P.] Letcher has a prospect of finally obtaining his seat.[4]

Mrs Clay's health had much improved at the White S. Springs, which she leaves about this time.

I request you to offer my best regards to Mrs. Brooke and assurances of my deep regret for her recent loss with you.

ALS. NcD.   1. Robert's wife was Elizabeth Smith Brooke.   2. Jamestown Celebration of the "Anniversary of the Landing of our Forefathers at Jamestown in May 1607." Richmond *Enquirer*, May 30, 1834.   3. Clay to Brooke, March 11, 1833.   4. Clay to Helm, April 20, 1833; Speech in Senate, March 27-28, 1834.

Remark in Senate, June 2, 1834. Moves to table a New Jersey memorial criticizing President Jackson's removal of government deposits from the Bank of the United States [Bradley to Clay, October 16, 1832], calling attention to the fact that his resolutions pertaining to Secretary Taney's role in the removal policy and the restoration of the deposits in the B.U.S. commencing July 1 [Comment in Senate, May 28, 1834] are pending. Successfully moves that those resolutions now be taken up. Thinks they both can and should be passed today, since the first of them, dealing with Taney, has already been "discussed for several months." *Register of Debates*, 23 Cong., 1 Sess., 1843-44.

Later, moves that Senator Thomas H. Benton's motion to postpone a consideration of the two Clay resolutions be voted upon. They were, and postponement was defeated, 29 to 13. *Ibid.*, 1848.

Later, still, Clay moves a vote on a Benton amendment to Clay's resolution, which asks that the deposits be made in state banks instead of the B.U.S. When that amendment is rejected, 31 to 14, Clay asks for a vote on a similar Benton motion which would permit the continued placing of government deposits in state banks. After that proposal is defeated, 32 to 13, Clay agrees to having separate votes on his two resolutions. On the other hand, he resists a suggestion by Sen. John Forsyth (Ga.) that an investigation of whether the B.U.S. has violated its charter be undertaken in lieu of voting on the resolutions. *Ibid.*, 1858-59; *Cong. Globe*, 23 Cong., 1 Sess., 418, 420.

Comment in Senate, June 3, 1834. Discusses the pros and cons of "an inquiry into the conduct of the bank, by means of a *scire facias*," pointing out the shifting position of Sen. John Forsyth ("a very prompt and ready defender of every Executive measure") on the issue. Warns his listeners to mark well the broadening "state of public feeling" now building against the administration. Defends a memorial from citizens of Harrisburg, Pa., many of them "original Jackson men," who are now critical of Jackson's fiscal policies [Bradley to Clay, October 16, 1832] and his "Executive usurpation." Comments on which Pennsylvanians and how many of them the Harrisburg memorialists really represent. Raises the problem of whether and to what extent committees of citizens waiting upon the president later quote his remarks to them accurately. Cites a recent incident in which Jackson claimed (falsely in Clay's opinion) to have been misquoted by a Baltimore delegation protesting Jackson's fiscal policies. Condemns the president's insistence that in the future such groups must present on paper, and in advance of their interview, the nature of their business with him. This, says Clay, is the "practice" of "monarchs." Launches into a defense of the B.U.S. and an attack on the Jackson administration and all its works. Chides Sen. Forsyth for his predictable support of Jackson on all questions. *Register of Debates*, 23 Cong., 1 Sess., 1871-74, 1879; *Cong. Globe*, 23 Cong., 1 Sess., 423. For the problem with and report of the Baltimore delegation, see *Register of Debates*, 23 Cong., 1 Sess., 3074-75.

Remark in Senate, June 5, 1834. Presents a memorial from citizens of Scott County, Ky., condemning Jackson's "assumptions of unauthorized power" and expressing "sentiments favorable to the Bank of the United States." Remarks in passing that it has now been more than a year since a secretary of the treasury has been "appointed in the constitutional form, by the President, by and with the advice and consent of the Senate." *Register of Debates*, 23 Cong., 1 Sess., 1896; *Cong. Globe*, 23 Cong., 1 Sess., 427.

To CHRISTOPHER HUGHES
Washington, June 6, 1834

I recd. only this morning your note written at Philada. and I commit these lines to the improbable chance of reaching you, prior to your embarkation,[1] merely to assure you of my best wishes, and of my continued esteem.

Your counsel to me to be president, considering the grave and *prudent* source whence it emanates, will be kindly remembered and duly followed.

And I shall not forget to register your application for a certain situation in anticipation.[2]

Mrs. Clay is much better.

I have not yet seen your pompous address in the American.[3]

Did you take me for a penny post when you asked me to deliver your Compliments love &c. to half Congress?

Adieu, my dear Hughes! May you have fair and strong breezes.

ALS. MiU-C.   1. Hughes was on the way back to Sweden where from 1830-42 he was Chargé d' Affaires.   2. Hughes to Clay, August 10, 1834.   3. Hughes's address "To My Fellow Citizens of Baltimore," given on June 1, 1834, was published in the Baltimore *American & Commercial Daily Advertiser* on June 3. In this self-serving address, he discussed the sacrifices he had made to stay in the diplomatic service for twenty years and the problems an American encountered in rearing children in Europe.

To S. DEWITT BLOODGOOD   Washington, June 9, 1834

Mr. Clay's respects to Mr. Bloodgo[o]d, with the enclosed letters. Mr. Dickinson [*sic*, Mahlon Dickerson], our new minister to Russia, is not here.[1] He will probably embark at N. Y. on his mission; and at the time perhaps it will be best to apply to him to take charge of the letters.

Mr. C. must in frankness say that never having had of any Jackson functionary the slightest favor he should feel repugnance in requesting one so inconsiderable as that of even bearing letters; especially when the Minister might apprehend the possibility of some personal inconvenience to himself at the Court of Russia in taking char[g]e of letters from the unfortunate exiles from Poland. He scarcely need say that they have enlisted his warmest sympathies.

AL. CtY. For Bloodgood, see Dorothie Bobbe, *DeWitt Clinton* (New York, 1933), 296.   1. Dickerson declined appointment as minister to Russia. See *BDAC*.

From Thomas Gilmer *et al.*, Charlottesville, Va., June 9, 1834. On behalf of citizens "who are opposed to executive usurpation and misrule," invite Clay to a public dinner in Charlottesville on July 4. They state: "During the series of bold and systematic attempts which have been made and are making, to subvert the well defined, constitutional organization of the several departments of our Federal Government, and to concentrate all power in the executive branch, minor differences of opinion with regard to political measures of principles seem to have subsided throughout the United States, and the American people are, for the first time, divided into two great parties: one of which is determined to sustain, the other to resist these extraordinary executive prerogatives." Copy. Printed in Washington *United States Telegraph*, July 17, 1834.

On June 12, 1834, Clay replied to the committee, declining their invitation and citing his long absence from home and Mrs. Clay's health as reasons for the refusal. Believes, however, that July 4 is an appropriate time for such a dinner and approves its purpose, saying "Our ancestors contended against a foreign monarch: we are combating doctrines which would inevitably lead to the establishment of a domestic monarchy, in its most pernicious form." *Ibid.*

Remark in Senate, June 9, 1834. Successfully moves that Senate records of "the number of the signatures on memorials on the subject of the public distress [Comment in Senate, April 11, 1834]" be brought up to date. *Register of Debates*, 23 Cong., 1 Sess, 1917; *Cong. Globe*, 23 Cong., 1 Sess., 435.

Remark in Senate, June 13, 1834. Supports a bill for the relief of the heirs of Lord Stirling, pointing out that it would make no difference whether the heirs were paid in "land script" or "money," except that if paid in the former, "a strong temptation to speculate in script" might arise. *Register of Debates*, 23 Cong., 1 Sess., 2000; *Cong. Globe*, 23 Cong., 1 Sess., 443-44. For General William Alexander, "Lord Stirling," American Revolutionary War hero, see Alan Valentine, *Lord Stirling*. New York, 1969.

To JAMES BROWN

Washington, June 16, 1834

I am extremely sorry to learn from your letter of the 11h. that you have suffered so much from a renewed attack of Rheumatism. I trust that the more favorable weather which we have had within a few days will re-establish you. I should think that the Hot Springs of Va. if you can comfortably reach them would be serviceable to you.

Mrs. Clay reached home on the 5h. inst. with her strength increased, but her health not entirely restored. She supposed that she derived much benefit from the W. Sulphur Springs. I have proposed to her to return there and meet me early in July, or to come back with me to them in August, and I hope she may embrace one or other of the alternatives.

H[enry]. C. Hart is with me. He has written to you. I am highly gratified with his improvement, altho' I entertain some fears of his being afflicted with the complaint which terminated the life of his mother.[1]

I was greatly surprized and mortified by the misfortunes of Mr. [Martin] Duralde.[2] I am unadvised as to the extent of them, not yet having recd. a letter from him. Judge [Alexander] Porter, [George A.] Waggaman, and Mr. [James] Erwin, all continue to believe that his means are ample, and that he will even be rich, after paying all his debts. I hope such may turn out to be the case. He has applied for a respite, which Judge Porter thinks he will certainly obtain.

Mr Erwin assures me that his own affairs are perfectly snug and safe, and I entertain not the smallest doubt of it. He had re-embursed his advances for real Estate by a sale of about one half of it. As to Mr. Duralde, he had made some advances to him, but he held a mortgage upon property double in value to any amt. which he had advanced or was liable for on his account. I understand from him too that this mortgage provides for a debt due by Duralde to you. I feel perfectly sure that you need entertain no fears on your own account.

We shall adjourn witht. doing any thing corresponding with the just expectations of the public. That is now certain. The Jackson party feels its defeat and is sensible of its overthrow; but the majority in the House cling together with the desperation of drowning men.

[Andrew] Stevenson's nomination is not yet decided. Its confirmation is far from being certain.[3] We rejected [Martin] Gordon the father & [Martin, Jr.] Gordon the son, as Collector of N. O. and finally [James W.] Breedlove was appointed.[4]

I shall leave here probably on the 1st. July via W. Sulphur Springs Va. for Ashland.

ALS. KyLxT.   1. Anna Gist Hart died in Philadelphia on July 10, 1818, after a protracted illness which was probably tuberculosis. Lexington *Kentucky Reporter*, July 29, 1818.   2. Claiborne to Clay, Dec. 4, 1834.   3. Clay to Brooke, June 2, 1834.   4. For Gordon's rejection, see Washington *United States Telegraph*, May 31, 1834. See also *Biennial Register*, 1833, p. 57; 1835, p. 56.

Remark in Senate, June 16, 1834. Moves to refer to the Judiciary Committee a resolution to compensate Elisha R. Potter "for his attendance while claiming a seat in the Senate [Comment in Senate, December 2, 1833]." *Register of Debates*, 23 Cong., 1 Sess.,

2020-21. By a vote of 24-22, with Clay voting in the negative, the Senate approved the resolution to compensate Potter. *Ibid.*, 2037-38.

Remark in Senate, June 17, 1834. Opposes placing a duty of 2 percent on lead ore, but says that the clause in the bill designed "to protect the revenue against frauds ought to pass." *Register of Debates*, 23 Cong., 1 Sess., 2022; *Cong. Globe*, 23 Cong., 1 Sess., 459. The fraud in question concerned the 3 cent per pound duty levied on lead by the Tariff Act of 1833. To avoid this duty, lead was being shipped into the U.S. in busts and other sculptured forms which paid a duty of only 15 percent ad valorem. The bill to prevent this practice passed the Senate on June 18 but was laid on the table in the House on June 28. *Register of Debates*, 23 Cong., 1 Sess., 2024; *Cong. Globe*, 23 Cong., 1 Sess., 462, 478.

Comment in Senate, June 18, 1834. Presents memorials from Huntingdon County and Cannonsburg, Pa., and from Boone County and Bowling Green, Ky., criticizing Jackson's policy toward the B.U.S. Attacks the president for not nominating a secretary of the treasury for the Senate's "consideration and decision" during this session. Explains that the president's shuffling of Louis McLane, William J. Duane, and Roger B. Taney into and out of the Treasury Department is an abuse of executive power and that the removal of Duane violates a constitutional clause requiring the president to "fill up vacancies by commissions which shall expire at the end of the next session." *Register of Debates*, 23 Cong., 1 Sess., 2027-29; *Cong. Globe*, 23 Cong., 1 Sess., 462.

Remark in Senate, June 19, 1834. Speaks to Jackson's message announcing the naval accident in Toulon harbor in which two French seamen were killed and four wounded when the U.S. frigate *United States*, with three of her guns accidentally loaded with shot, fired a salute in honor of the King's birthday. Agrees with the president's recommendation that an indemnity be paid the families of the deceased. Adds that the American gunner responsible should be tried and severely punished. *Register of Debates*, 23 Cong., 1 Sess., 2035, 2039. For legislation authorizing indemnities in the form of pensions to the heirs of the deceased, see *ibid.*, 2041-42, 2075; *Cong. Globe*, 23 Cong., 1 Sess., 464-65.

Later this day, Clay draws attention to the Senate's tally (150,000) of signers of petitions and memorials critical of Jackson's fiscal policies and praying Congress for economic relief [Comment in Senate, April 11, 1834; Remark in Senate, June 9, 1834]. Chides the opposition for not seeing this as "one of the best tests of public opinion, next to the evidences which the ballot-boxes afford." *Register of Debates*, 23 Cong., 1 Sess., 2036-37; *Cong. Globe*, 23 Cong., 1 Sess., 464.

Still later this day, Clay argues that U.S. citizens who had claims against France for property losses prior to 1800 had a "right to indemnity to some extent"; but points out that because of complications inherent in various treaty obligations to France, the claimants' "just right to compensate" should be assumed by the United States. Suggests an appropriation might be made for this purpose, but hopes that the whole subject can be deferred until the next session. *Register of Debates*, 23 Cong., 1 Sess., 2039.

Remark in Senate, June 20, 1834. Asks that documents collected by the Committee on Public Lands having to do with its inquiry into possible fraudulent practices in the buying and selling of such lands be printed. Is convinced that there have been "great and shameful frauds." *Register of Debates*, 23 Cong., 1 Sess., 2044.

Remark in Senate, June 21, 1834. Compares and contrasts the provisions, legality, and long-range costs of two contracts, one let by the administration, the other by Congress, for the publication of the "Diplomatic Correspondence of the United States, from the peace of 1783 to the 4th of March, 1794"; and for the "Documentary History of the American Revolution." Both were multi-volume undertakings. *Register of Debates*,

23 Cong., 1 Sess., 2052; *Cong. Globe*, 23 Cong., 1 Sess., 466. Francis P. Blair published *The Diplomatic Correspondence of the United States of America, From the Signing of the Definitive Treaty of Peace, 10th September, 1783, to the Adoption of the Constitution, March 4, 1789. . . . Published under the Direction of the Secretary of State . . . Conformably to Act of Congress, Approved May 5, 1832. . . .* 7 vols. Washington, 1833-34. With Clay voting in the negative, the Senate voted 23-22 to strike out the appropriation for the proposed "Documentary History of the American Revolution" which was to have been published by Peter Force and Matthew St. Clair Clarke, and to appropriate $15,000 to remunerate the two men for expenses they had already incurred in the project. *Register of Debates*, 23 Cong., 1 Sess., 2044-54.

Remark in Senate, June 24, 1834. Calls Sen. Isaac Hill (N.H.) to order, noting that a motion to take up the resolutions of the New Hampshire legislature was not the proper place for a speech on the reasons why they should be taken up. *Register of Debates*, 23 Cong., 1 Sess., 2066; *Cong. Globe*, 23 Cong., 1 Sess., 469.

Remark in Senate, June 26, 1834. With reference to the date of adjournment, urges the Senate to "economize our time" by ending the talk and beginning action on the reports of committees. *Register of Debates*, 23 Cong., 1 Sess., 2077.

During the evening session this same day, Clay spoke to a bill to pay the city of Washington $70,000 annually for three years, so that it might pay the interest on its canal debt to Dutch bankers [Clay to Watterson, August 8, 1834]. While he was "disposed to give the city something," he felt its "inhabitants had been extremely improvident." Suggests that the subsidy be limited to one year, the form in which the measure was finally passed. *Ibid.*, 2078-79; *Cong. Globe*, 23 Cong, 1 Sess., 473.

Speech in Senate, June 27, 1834. During the evening session on this day, criticizes at length the Post Office Department for the general bribery, corruption, political chicanery, and financial maladministration characterizing all its operations. Points out that the postal system is bankrupt, that Postmaster General William T. Barry of Kentucky ("once, both my personal and political friend") is incompetent, and that the president calmly tolerates the "existing abuses" lying "at the threshold of the Executive mansion." Presents evidence of his charges that the department regularly awards dubious mail contracts to its political friends. Claims that one such award went to the brother of Sen. John M. Robinson (Ill.). Notes that the only senator who has been willing to make "a formal defense of the Post Office Department" has been New Hampshire's Isaac Hill, whose "brother has fifteen [mail distribution] contracts within the limits of that single State!" *Register of Debates*, 23 Cong., 1 Sess., 2113-16.

Earlier this day, Clay presented memorials from York County, Pa., and Bourbon County, Ky., criticizing Jackson's hostility toward the B.U.S. *Ibid.*, 2080-81. He also expressed his intention to vote for an amendment to the harbor bill that would provide a $250,000 subsidy to the Chesapeake and Ohio Canal Company, and he successfully inserted an appropriation into that bill "for the improvement of the Cumberland river." *Ibid.*, 2080-81, 2083.

Remark in Senate, June 28, 1834. Moves repeal of the Senate order establishing a recess from 2:00 to 4:00 p.m. until the session ends; and the order setting apart Fridays and Saturdays each week for the consideration of bills during the remainder of the session. *Register of Debates*, 23 Cong., 1 Sess., 2120-21.

Also moves successfully to reconsider the vote that indefinitely postpones consideration of the appropriation bill for lighthouses and other navigational beacons. *Cong. Globe*, 23 Cong., 1 Sess., 476.

Remark in Senate, June 30, 1834. Since the Senate is "within a few hours of its adjournment," thinks it an "improper time" for Sen. Thomas H. Benton to introduce a resolution to strike "out of the Journals" the Senate resolution of the "20th [*sic*, 28th] of March last" which censured President Jackson [Speech in Senate, December 26, 1833; Remark in Senate, March 28, 1834] for his removal of the deposits [Bradley to Clay, October 16, 1832] from the Bank of the United States. The resolution of censure, according to Benton, was one "imputing impeachable matter to the President, and ought not to be passed except in the regular form of constitutional impeachment." Benton's motion was also opposed by Calhoun and Webster and was defeated 20 to 11. *Register of Debates*, 23 Cong., 1 Sess., 2128; *Cong. Globe*, 23 Cong., 1 Sess., 479. For the long and stormy legislative history of Benton's so-called "expunging resolution" see *Register of Debates*, 23 Cong., 1 Sess., 2128; 23 Cong., 2 Sess., 510, 631, 715, 723, 726-28; 24 Cong., 1 Sess., 722, 877-958, 962, 1593-98; 24 Cong., 2 Sess., 4-5, 128, 380-418, 428-504; also *Cong. Globe*, 23 Cong., 1 Sess., 479; 23 Cong., 2 Sess., 175-77, 189, 259-60, 300, 315, 324-25; 24 Cong., 1 Sess., 159, 162, 226, 259, 266, 271, 275, 280, 299, 308-9, 316, 320, 334-35, 343, 412, 445, 507, 591, Appendix, 188, 230, 406, 534, 679; 24 Cong., 2 Sess., 51, 91, 93, 95, 98-99.

The resolution was finally physically expunged from the U.S. Senate *Journal* of March 28, 1834, by a 24-19 vote on the evening of January 16, 1837. For Benton's own account of the progress of his resolution, see Thomas Hart Benton, *Thirty Years' View*, 2 vols. (New York, 1858), 1:428-32, 524-50, 645-47, 717-31; see also Smith, *Magnificent Missourian*, 150, 152, 163-64; and Chambers, *Old Bullion Benton*, 202, 218-19. For the expunging issue from Clay's perspective see Van Deusen, *The Life of Henry Clay*, 285-86; and Carl Schurz, *Life of Henry Clay*, 2 vols. (Boston, 1887), 2:99-105. A colorful account of the expunging issue is in Bowers, *Party Battles of the Jackson Period*, 325-26, 330-32, 369-71, 465-71.

Later this day, Clay observes that bills for the improvement of the Wabash and Hudson rivers would be dead after adjournment. The Senate adjourned *sine die* at 6:45 p.m. *Register of Debates*, 23 Cong., 1 Sess., 2128.

To FRANCIS LIEBER   Washington, July 1, 1834

I know not how sufficiently to apologize to you for my omission to acknowledge, in due season, your obliging favor of the 29h March, and to express my thanks for the Copy of Mess Beaumont and Toqueville's work on Penitentiaries, with your introduction.[1] I must throw myself on your kindness to excuse me, in consequence of my laborious duties during the Session of Congress, which terminated yesterday. These labors have now ceased, and we have delivered our Country over to Providence and the People. If one or the other do not take care of it, I know not what is to become of it.

I carry with me to Ashland the above work, where I hope to command the leisure to examine it, which I have not found here.

I observe that the Presidency of Transylvania University is still vacant at Lexington. I know not whether its Governors have any one in view to fill it. Desirous myself that the Public should be availed of your services in that situation, I should be glad if you would write me a letter, addressed to me at my residence, communicating your feelings about it. Of course, I should not use it unless circumstances were favorable to the accomplishment of my own wishes.[2]

ALS. CSmH.   1. Alexis de Tocqueville and Gustave Auguste de Beaumont de La Bonniniere, *On the Penitentiary System in the United States and Its Application in France. . . .* Translated from French, with an introduction, notes, and additions, by Francis Lieber. Philadelphia, 1833. 2. After a disagreement with the board of trustees, Benjamin O. Peers had resigned as president on Feb. 1, 1834. John Lutz, a mathematics professor at Transylvania, served as acting president until mid-1835. In the meantime, the post was offered to the Reverend John C. Young, president of Centre College in Danville, but he declined. The Reverend Thomas W. Coit assumed the presidency on July 1, 1835. Peter, *Transylvania University*, 161-62. See also Clay to Lieber, Dec. 3, 1834.

To ALBERT HUMRICKHOUSE[1]

At Mr. John Zombros',[2]
July 6, 1834

I lament extremely to have to communicate to you a most distressing and melancholy accident which has just occurred. In descending a small hill, about one mile from Brucetown,[3] at this house, there being no lock chains, the horses ran away with the Stage, and throwing the wheels on the side of the Bank, overset it on the opposite side. Your son[4] was sitting with the driver, and endeavored to assist him in retaining the command of the horses; but unfortunately got some how entangled fell and received the entire weight of the Stage upon him. The horses pulled off the forewheels, and running away the Driver pursued them There were in the Stage, my servant, a lady[5] and myself. Perceiving that your son was caught under the Stage we got out as soon as we possibly could, raised the Stage, and drew your son out; but alas! it was of no avail. His neck was broke, his entrails seriously injured, he bled profusely at the nose, and never spoke. He breathed, but expired at about 12 O'clock, a few minutes after the accident happened.

I know not how sufficiently to express to you my deep and sincere regret on this sad occasion. I offer you all the condolence which can be possibly felt or tendered under such circumstances. You have lost a fine son. I was much interested by him during our short acquaintance and journey. He manifested a constant desire for my personal comfort, whilst we were together, and I feel grateful for his friendly attentions.

We are now engaged in making the best arrangements we can to have his body taken care of and restored to you and his family.

Except a slight scratch on one of my legs, those of us who were in the Stage, as well as the Driver, escaped without material injury.

Wishing that yourself and your family may bear this heavy affliction with Christian resignation and manly fortitude. . . .

ALS. Courtesy of Edward L. Warner, Charlevoix, Michigan.   1. Humrickhouse (1786-1864) was the proprietor of the stagecoach involved in the accident. He was a resident of Shepherdstown, Va. (W. Va.), where he subsequently held public offices including that of mayor. He later became a merchant and during the Civil War operated a private post office. Millard K. Bushong, *Historic Jefferson County* (Boyce, Va., 1972), 213; Clifford S. Musser, *Two Hundred Years' History of Shepherdstown* (Shepherdstown, 1931), 68, 75-78, 80, 84-85; Martinsburg (W. Va.) *Gazette*, Jan. 23, 1839; Shepherdstown *Register*, Dec. 16, 1854 and Oct. 20, 1860; *Tombstone Inscriptions and Burial Lots Compiled by Bee Line Chapter, National Society Daughters of the American Revolution* (Marceline, Mo., n. d.), 275.   2. Jefferson County, W. Va.   3. Frederick County, Va.; the stage was en route to Charles Town, now W. Va.   4. Albert Humrickhouse, Jr. (March 12, 1811-July 6, 1834). *Tombstone Inscriptions . . .* , 275. For accounts of the accident, see Washington *Daily National Intelligencer*, July 12, 1834; Martinsburg *Gazette*, July 10, 17, 1834.   5. A woman named Coburn. Martinsburg *Gazette*, July 17, 1834.

To Lemuel Bent *et al.*, Winchester, Va., July 7, 1834. Declines an invitation to a public dinner in Winchester, saying: "I am now on my return home, after an absence from it of near ten months, and after a most exhausting session of Congress, and I wish to rejoin my family with as little delay as practicable. I must add, that a sad accident which befel a fellow passenger in the stage on yesterday, and my own narrow escape from danger [Clay to Humrickhouse, July 6, 1834], disqualify me for immediate enjoyment at the festive board." Copy. Printed in Washington *Daily National Intelligencer*, July 12, 1834.

From James Brown, Philadelphia, July 24, 1834. Has heard of Clay's carriage accident [Clay to Humrickhouse, July 6, 1834] and hopes he is well. Discusses his declining health, as evidenced by attacks of vertigo, and concludes: "my life is held by a thread and I am in constant apprehension of a renewed attack, the consequences of which would probably be either fatal or a loss of my remaining intellectual faculties." Complains that "Even interesting conversation on political subjects bewilders me and I am forced to decline the meetings of any of my political friends." Asks Clay's advice on the disposal of his property in Louisiana, saying "You are the Executor of my dear departed wife and her family will own as well by her Will as by my own, the moiety of the half" of the property.

On the subject of politics, states: "The Election here [Clay to Kerr, May 16, 1834] will be warm and Jackson will be in the Minority in the city & northern suburbes. Southerland [*sic*, Joel Barlow Sutherland] may gain his election — He is indefatigable. I must stop here   It is the longest letter I have written since Eleven Months. I cannot see the lines [I a]m writing." ALS. DLC-HC (DNA, M212, R5). Printed in *LHQ*, 24:1170. Sutherland defeated James Gowen for the U.S. House seat from the first (Philadelphia) district by a vote of 3,781 to 2,345. *Niles' Register* (October 18, 1834), 47:104. In the second Pennsylvania congressional district, also in Philadelphia, Whig candidates James Harper and Joseph R. Ingersoll were elected by an average majority of 1,879 over Democrats Henry Horn and Linnard. Also in the second district, Whig candidates were elected to the state senate and assembly and to various city council seats, all by majorities of between 1,700 and 1,800 votes. In the third of Philadelphia's congressional districts, Joseph G. Watmough, a Whig, was defeated by Michael W. Ash, a Democrat, by 5,755 votes. Jacksonian candidates for the state senate and for the state assembly from both Sutherland's and Ash's districts were all elected by large majorities. *Ibid*.

To Benjamin W. Dudley *et al.*, Lexington, July 31, 1834. Thanks them for their invitation to a public dinner in his honor at Brennan & Postlethwait's Hotel, but declines because of "the ill health of a member of my family [Lucretia Hart Clay], the extraordinary heat of the season, and the want of repose, which I feel to be so necessary." Continues: "I am very happy, gentlemen, to learn from you that the course of the senate of the United States at its recent arduous session, commands your approbation. Nothing but an imperative sense of public duty could have induced the senate to assume an attitude of opposition to the executive, and of difference of opinion with the house of representatives, on leading public measures. The people are yet the common umpire in cases of disagreement between their functionaries; and the senate awaits their decision with undoubting confidence. For myself, believing that the measures adopted, and the principles avowed by the executive, involved the safety and existence of free government, I should have regarded myself faithless to the people, and false to the whole tenor of my life, if I had not cheerfully and heartily concurred with the majority of the senate." Copy. Printed in *Niles' Register* (August 16, 1834), 46:417. Among the more important issues on which the Senate had differed from the House and/or from the chief executive during the 23rd Congress, 1st Session, were: its rejections of the nomination of James A. Bayard and others as directors of the B.U.S., of Andrew Stevenson as minister to Great Britain, of Roger B. Taney as secretary of the treasury, of Benjamin Tappan as U.S. district judge in Ohio, and of Martin Gordon as collector of the port of New Orleans; also its passage of a resolution disapproving the removal of deposits from the B.U.S., its related censure of Jackson and Taney, and its attempt to recharter the bank; further, its efforts to distribute to the states income from the sales of public lands; and its attempt to curb the president's power to appoint and remove employees of the executive departments. See Speech in Senate, December 5, 1833; March 7, 1834; Remark in Senate, March 28, 1834; April 21, 1834; Comment in Senate, May 28, 1834; Clay to Wilde, April 27, 1834; Clay to Tazewell, April 5, 1834; Clay to

Southard, May 12, 1834; Clay to Brown, June 16, 1834; U.S. Sen., *Journal*, 23 Cong., 1 Sess., Appendix, 430-32, 442-43, 445-54.

Benjamin W. Dudley *et al.*, had written Clay the day before, July 30, welcoming him home from Washington and inviting him to a public dinner to honor the one who is "foremost in this great struggle" against "Executive usurpation." Copy. Printed in Lexington *Observer & Kentucky Reporter*, August 6, 1834.

To JAMES BROWN   Lexington, August 2, 1834

I duly recd. your favor of the 24h. Ulto. and truly & sincerely regret the continuance of your indisposition. From the description which it contains of your situation, from the experiments in travelling which you have made, and from what I learn from others, I should think it unwise in you to venture far from Philada. There you have medical advice and aid, possessing your confidence, always at hand; and you would not be sure of it any where else.

I returned home a few days ago. The injury I recd. from the Upsetting of the Stage, 'though inconvenient, was slight and is now healed.[1] I found the health of Mrs. Clay a little improved but not re-established. Her case is dyspesia, clearly developed, and it has reduced her to a skeleton. She retains strength remarkably, keeps on her feet, and is even able to take exercise on horseback. It is not a case for medicine, but one which if her health can be restored, it must be effected by diet, exercise and tranquillity of mind. On all these circumstances she bestows all the attention she can. The latter is the most difficult, from her constitution, and the incidents by which she is surrounded. I hope for her recovery, but her condition excites with me great anxiety and solicitude.

[Discusses Brown's request in his July 24 letter for advice concerning the disposal of his property in Louisiana, some of which is owned jointly with his nephew John B. Humphreys. Suggests that Brown "execute a *joint* power of Atto. to your brother[2] and myself authorizing us to sell your interest in the land, slaves, beasts, & implements of husbandry on the Estate, either by private agreement or at public auction." Mentions "several modes by which the Sale might be effected."[3] Continues:]

Mr. [James] Erwin assures me that every one of the notes which he took for you is perfectly secure. He has no apprehension of any difficulty arising out of the rate of 12 per Cent interest. That rate was even less than was frequently taken, but he took it, in consideration of the greater security of the names to the paper.

As to Mr. [Martin] Duralde's debt of $15. 000 he believes it to be secured by a mortgage which he has taken, and a Copy of which I have seen.[4] He thinks it best that you should leave to him, with your approbation, the adoption of such measures as may be necessary to realize that money.

Duraldes case is one in which he exhibits a greater amount of means than of responsibilities; but you know that these estimates are often affected by circumstances, and especially by sacrifices of property.

Whilst his misfortune has grieved me much, I am gratified that the operations of Mr. Erwin, during the period of distress, have been attended with great success. He seems to possess uncommon judgment and discretion.

Lucretia joins me in affectionate remembrance to you.

ALS. KyLxT.   1. Clay to Humrickhouse, July 6, 1834.   2. Apparently a reference to James Brown's brother, John; however, the power of attorney was later given to John Brown's son, Mason Brown. See Clay to Brown, August 7, 1834.   3. *Ibid.*   4. Clay to Brown, June 16, 1834; Claiborne to Clay, Dec. 4, 1834.

To JOHN H. JAMES Lexington, August 6, 1834

I am very thankful for the friendly interest in the health of Mrs. Clay manifested in your letter of the 4th ulto, which I received a few days ago upon my return home. Hers is a case of dyspepsia, clearly developed, in an advanced stage. The best physicians of Philada, Washington and Lexington concur both as to the remedy and the disease. It is not a case for much medicine, but, if cured at all, the cure is to be effected by diet, exercise and tranquillity of mind. This treatment she pursues; but I regret that she continues very low and she is reduced almost to a skeleton. Her condition excites the deepest solicitude. She retains strength, however, most remarkably and keeps on her feet.

I am obliged by your suggestion of the name of Dr. [John] Eberle.[1] I shall propose to her to consult him, if she does not shortly get better, although she has great repugnance to new physicians.

I hope your health continues to improve.

Give my respects to Genl. [Joseph] Vance; tell him that we are in the midst of the election; that [Robert P.] Letcher will be re-elected by several hundred[2] (he had a majority of 280 the first day) and that our elections are all going well. . . .[3]

ALS. Courtesy of Leonard Turley, Louisville, Ky. Addressed to James in Urbana, Ohio. 1. *DAB*. 2. Clay to Helm, April 20, 1833. 3. Speech in Senate, March 27-28, 1834.

To James Brown, Philadelphia, August 7, 1834. Writes that he has talked to John Humphreys about the sale of the Louisiana plantation which Humphreys and Brown own [Clay to Brown, August 2, 1834], and that "He professed a great desire to wind up the concern; thought, for that purpose, the Estate ought to be sold; considered it had depreciated in value; was not very anxious to buy &c." Reports that Robert P. Letcher has been elected [Clay to Helm, April 20, 1833; Speech in Senate, March 27-28, 1834] and that "the Jackson party has sustained a Waterloo defeat in K[entucky]." ALS. KyLxT.

On August 11, 1834, Brown wrote Clay approving "the plan of appointing you *jointly* with my brother [John Brown] to make the necessary disposition to close the concern with my nephew Mr Humphreys." Adds that "John is an honorable man and will deal fairly with you—I would wish him to buy the place if the sacrifice would not be too great." ALS. DLC-HC (DNA, M212, R5). Printed in *LHQ*, 24:1172.

On August 20, 1834, Brown again wrote Clay that Humphreys was visiting him in Philadelphia, but "I have not been able to do any thing to close our affair." Mentions also that the "notes of [Martin] Duralde and Mr [James] Erwin with three years interest . . . are due and in my hands. I hope they may be secured for my heirs and those of my wife. My will is made to divide any thing I may leave equally to both families." Fears he does not have long to live and hopes there will be no difficulties between his "connexions" over the estate. ALS. DLC-HC (DNA, M212, R5). Printed in *LHQ*, 24:1173.

Two days later, August 22, 1834, Brown sent Clay and Mason Brown, John Brown's son, a power of attorney and asked "of you to make the most of my Estate." Adds that "What has been in Mr [James] Erwins hands, with the 15.000 Dollars & interest, four thousand Dollars in Rail road Stock, and the house in N Orleans, part of the joint estate, is all I possess." Continues: "You know all this and will as my oldest and dearest friend not by any use of the power involve me in penury after all the labor and toil which it cost me and the care it occasioned my dear wife [Ann Hart Brown] to obtain what we possessed. I am glad that Mr Erwin thinks he has secured the note of Duralde with his mortgage As Mr Erwin indorsed it I am glad he had tried to secure it. I never looked after it or applied for the interest as I intended it should remain to be divided at my death unless I should be pressed by some engagement." ALS. DLC-HC (DNA, M212, R5). Printed in *LHQ*, 24:1174.

Brown wrote from Philadelphia on October 3, 1834, mentioning that because of frequent "bleeding, cupping and other enfeebling remedies," he has "hardly sufficient strength to write a few lines." Tells Clay, however, "to act as you think you would do were the case your own in conjunction with my dear Nephew in closing as well as you can my affairs." Briefly discusses various business transactions in New Orleans over the last few years, and concludes: "I earnestly entreat all may be adjusted amicably as I love equally all my relatives and connections and wish to die in peace with them and all the world." Recalls that the diamonds among his possessions cost "nine thousand five hundred francs" when purchased. ALS. DLC-HC (DNA, M212, R5). Printed in *LHQ*, 24:1175.

Clay notified Brown on November 9, 1834, that he and Mason Brown had turned over the power of attorney James Brown had given them to James Erwin, because the final stages of the plantation sale must be conducted in Louisiana. Notes that the "family connexions of Mrs. Brown have also given him a similar power; and he will on the 12h. inst proceed to Louisiana cloathed with the authority from all the parties to terminate the concern with Mr. H." Adds that Humphreys "has intimated a willingness to give $45,000 for the moiety held by you," but "This we think too low." Continues: "The time is highly favorable for the sale of the slaves; and if Mr Humphreys will not increase his bid, and Mr. Erwin should be driven to the necessity of dividing the slaves, we believe, unless they are greatly inferior to what he expects to find them, that the slaves alone will realize more than half of Mr. Hs. offer. Whatever may be done, you may be perfectly satisfied that your ease comfort and interest will be consulted." ALS. NcD.

To JAMES CALDWELL
Lexington, August 8, 1834

Mrs. Clay's health continues feeble and precarious. She is averse to leaving home, and, as I cannot separate myself from her, I shall not have the pleasure of seeing you again this Season at the White Sulphur Springs.

Our Elections closed this Week.[1] As far as heard from, the Jackson party is annihilated. In Louisville & Jefferson County,[2] and in the adjacent Counties[3] (which heretofore were Jackson) they are so completely defeated as to almost excite compassion. [Robert P.] Letcher has beaten [Thomas P.] Moore by near 300 votes. His majority last year was less than 50. With fair play, he would have had a majority of upwards of 500.

The little information we have yet recd. from Indiana[4] is good. Louisiana,[5] you know, has done her duty. . . .

ALS. ViHi. Printed in *VMHB* (October, 1947), 55:313.   1. Speech in Senate, March 27-28, 1834.   2. Clay to Gales, August 8, 1834.   3. In Oldham, Shelby, Bullitt, and Spencer counties, all the state representatives elected were Whigs, as was the state senator chosen from this area. Frankfort *Commonwealth*, August 12, 1834.   4. Clay to Mercer, August 13, 1834.   5. Clay to Storer, August 8, 1834.

To JOSEPH GALES
Lexington, August 8, 1834

I thank you for the article from the [Washington *United States*] Telegraph.[1] Its spirit does not surprise me. It is a tirade against parties, in favor of a party; against managers in favor of management; against fallen leaders, in behalf of a prostrate Leader. It in short condemns the very course which it pursues. The Nullifiers as a party are however so weak that I do not think War should be made upon them, at least at the present time. If there is any growling, let their Organs do it.

Our Elections have just terminated in signal success for the Whigs.[2] I doubt whether there will be 30 Jackson out of a 100 members of the H. of R. [Robert P.] Letcher is re-elected by near 300 Votes. If there had been fair play his majority would have been upwards of 500. In Louisville, Jefferson County, and the adjacent Counties (hitherto Jackson) the Jackson party is absolutely annihilated.[3]

Mrs. Clay's health remains precarious. I have recovered from my scratch, occasioned by the Upsetting of the Stage.[4] My respects to Mrs. Gales & Mr. & Mrs. [William] Seaton. P.S. Let me hear from you about the N. Carolina Elections[5]

ALS. NN.   1. The Washington *United States Telegraph* on June 3, 1834, printed a speech of Augustin Smith Clayton of Georgia, given in the House on May 22, 1834.   2. Speech in Senate, March 27-28, 1834.   3. The Whigs were victorious in the city of Louisville and won in Jefferson County by a majority of about 200. Louisville *Public Advertiser*, August 13, 1834. In both Louisville and Jefferson County, Whigs were elected to the state senate and house. Frankfort *Commonwealth*, August 12, 19, 1834; Louisville *Public Advertiser*, August 7, 13, 1834.   4. Clay to Humrickhouse, July 6, 1834.   5. The Whig party controlled the North Carolina legislature by a combined total of 97 seats to 75 for the Democrats, with 12 seats held by members whose party affiliation was unknown. Washington *Daily National Intelligencer*, Sept. 1, 1834.

To BELLAMY STORER   Lexington, August 8, 1834

I am anxious to know what are the prospects of your election, and those of the Whigs in Ohio.[1] Do tell me. I sincerely hope that they are good.

As far as we have heard, the Jackson party has been annihilated in K. at our Elections just closed.   [Robert P.] Letcher is elected over [Thomas] Moore by near 300 Votes.[2]

Judging from the results here, in Louisiana[3] & elsewhere we have much to hope from the Fall elections in Ohio, Pennsa & N. York.[4]

In the Canvass, it seems to me that you should avoid committing yourself against the re-charter of the B. U. S.   The true ground appears to me is to maintain that the institution is necessary; that so far as the public or stockholders are concerned it has been well administered; that its faults are few and venial; that its refusal to submit to the secretary of the Comee. of the H. of R. is to be justified or excused by the party origin and exceptionable constitution of that Comee; that it has since avowed a readiness to submit to an unrestrained investigation of the Senates Comee.;[5] that the H. of R. and the President had each made a previous investigation &c.[6]   I think the only error committed by the Bank, in its recent correspondence with Comee, was that of requiring a specification of breaches of Charter, prior to an exhibition of their Books.

The recharter or not, in my opinion, depends upon the issue of Elections in N. York, Pennsa. Ohio & N. Jersey[7] this fall.

ALS. ViU. Addressed to Storer in Cincinnati, Ohio.   1. Clay to Kerr, May 16, 1834.   2. Speech in Senate, March 27-28, 1834.   3. In the 1834 elections in Louisiana, Edward White, the Whig candidate for governor, defeated John Dawson by 6,018 votes to 4,438. *BDGUS*, 2:561. In races for the U.S. House, two Whigs—Henry Johnson and Rice Garland—were successful, while one Democrat—Eleazer W. Ripley won. *Guide to U.S. Elections*, 562.   4. For Ohio and Pennsylvania, see Clay to Kerr, May 16, 1834. In New York, William L. Marcy, a Democrat, defeated William H. Seward, a Whig, for governor by the margin of 181,905 to 168,800 votes. *BDGUS*, 3:1076-77. In the New York state senate, Jacksonians won 28 seats to 4 for the Whigs, and in the state house of representatives, the Jacksonians won 93 seats to 35 for the Whigs. *Niles' Register* (Nov. 22, 1834), 27:182. In races for the U.S. House, Democrats won 30 seats to 10 for the Whigs. *Guide to U.S. Elections*, 562-63.   5. Biddle had refused to permit the House Ways and Means Committee, chaired by James K. Polk, to examine the books except in the presence of officers of the bank. The committee threatened to cite Biddle and the directors for contempt. Biddle encouraged Sen. Samuel L. Southard to introduce a resolution, which passed on June 30, 1834, calling for an investigation by the Senate Finance Committee. Govan, *Nicholas Biddle*, 268-69.   6. Biddle to Clay, Feb. 8, 1833.   7. In New Jersey, the 1834 elections resulted in the Democrats having a 37-27 seat margin over the Whigs in the total number of seats in both houses of the state legislature. *Niles' Register* (Oct. 25, 1834), 27:118. Peter Vroom was chosen governor in November in a joint meeting of both houses of the Jackson-dominated legislature. *BDGUS*, 3:1014-15. In the U.S. House races, Democrats won all 6 seats. *Guide to U.S. Elections*, 562.

To GEORGE WATTERSON   Lexington, August 8, 1834

I thank you for your Address, transmitted by your letter of the 1st. inst. which I shall seize an early opportunity to peruse.[1]

I am surprized at the ascription to me of unfriendly feelings towards the City [Washington]. My objection to the bill for incorporating the Col[umbian]. H[orticutural]. Society related altogether to time.[2] It came up, I think, the last business day of the Session. We must have either passed it without examination, or it would have taken up some time. I thought it could bear postponement to another Session better than numerous bills pending for individual relief. I had no objection to the principle, certainly none to the object of the bill. The observation about a lurking bank clause in it was playful.[3]

The course I took about the interest on the Dutch loan saved the appropriation for one year. But for the amendment to that effect, I am sure the bill would have miscarried.[4]

The City [Washington] may always expect justice and even liberality at my hands. But I owe some thing to the people of the U. S. generally, and I mean always to perform my duty to them.

I lament the death of Mr– [Thomas] Law, for whom I have always entertained the greatest esteem.

Our Elections have just terminated, and as far as heard from, in a signal triumph to the Whigs. [Robert P.] Letcher is elected by about 300 votes.[5]

ALS. DLC-HC (DNA, M212, R22). Addressed to Watterson in Washington, D.C.   1. Watterson's speech was published under the title *An Address Delivered Before the Columbian Horticultural Society at the First Annual Exhibition*. Washington, 1834. A summary was published by the Washington *Daily National Intelligencer*, June 11, 1834.   2. On the last day of the session, June 30, Clay made a motion that the bill to incorporate the society be tabled. The bill had been introduced in the House on Jan. 29, 1834, and in the Senate on Feb. 5, 1834. U.S. Sen., *Journal*, 23 Cong., 1 Sess., 398; U.S. H. of Reps., *Journal*, 23 Cong., 1 Sess., 258.   3. Reference obscure. 4. In 1829, Dutch bankers had made a $1,500,000 loan to communities in the District of Columbia to finance their puchase of Chesapeake & Ohio Canal stock. When the communities could not meet the payments, their Dutch creditors arrived to collect their money by forcing sales of property in the capital. The bill which was originally introduced in Congress provided for the payment of $70,000 annually for three years to pay the interest on the debt. Clay moved to amend the bill by limiting the subsidy to one year. The bill as amended passed on June 26, 1834. *Register of Debates*, 23 Cong., 1 Sess., 2078-79; Constance McLaughlin Green, *Washington Village and Capital, 1800-1878* (Princeton, 1962), 127, 129.   5. Speech in Senate, March 27-28, 1834.

From Christopher Hughes, London, England, August 10, 1834. Expresses relief on reading of Clay's escape from serious injury in the stagecoach accident of July 6 [Clay to Humrickhouse, July 6, 1834]. Promises to visit Clay in Kentucky, if Congress is not in session, the next time he comes home to the United States. Mentions that his recent passage back to Europe was so "easy & smooth" that "it was like Steam Boat Sailing on one of our *Rivers*."

States that "You may have thought I was joking, when I applied . . . for the Post of private Secretary, when you shall be President [Clay to Hughes, June 6, 1834]. I was in earnest . . . but it is *for you & your* interests; & not for *my own*; I firmly believe and I ardently hope, that you will, one day be President. . . . Strange as it may appear, I dont care one fig about *living, after* I die—id est—in what is called '*History* a pack of balderdash[']; unless with the very most eminent—& gifted (such as you:)   I care for *life* and Comfort: & to aid my friends, in *all* that I *may*; and in my heart, I *believe*, that I could be of *impayable* Service to you, if you were P. & I, *P*-rivate Secy. upon my Soul *I do*. I'd keep you 'all right,' on a 1000 points, that you *think* you understand—& actually *know nothing about*: that's frank! may be blunt! perhaps you'll be offended. No you wont: You know *better*: & you know *me* better, than *ever* to be offended *with me*! I'd be yrs. *fully*, in *Social* concerns, to[o] difficult altogether for a President; as to *Patronage*, I would never meddle with it; no!"

Adds that the only two positions he would prefer over being Clay's private secretary would be as minister to London or Paris. Notes that "I shall never be *either*; as likely to get a Cardinal's Hat, from the Pope, as *either*, from *any President*; even *from you!* I *know*; what publick men *are, when* they get up! No! No! I give in, to *no* such delusion! I should be put off with; 'Why, *Hughes*, the *Nation dont know you!* they dont *think* you *fit: they* would ascribe it, to mere *personal* favors, on *my* part:' To which I answer . . . '*Bah'! There is no man now living in America*, who could render the Country more solid Service, in England France, or *any where* in Europe, than yr. fr[ien]d." ALS. DLC-HC (DNA, M212, R5).

To WILLIAM N. MERCER
Lexington, August 13, 1834

[Thanks Mercer for the "Hogshead of Sherry" which he found in his cellar when he returned home from Washington. Continues:]

Our election has terminated triumphantly.[1] Of the 100 members composing our H. of R. the Whigs will have about 80; and, in the Senate, where we were last year in the minority, we have now a majority of six. Mr. [Robert P.] Letcher was re-elected by more than five times the majority he obtained last year,[2] notwithstanding the introduction into his district of several hundred illegitimate votes against him. As far as we have heard, from Indiana[3] also, the election has gone favorably.

I hope you will return by this way. Besides the pleasure of seeing you, I wish to consult and advise with you in regard to the purchase or establishment of a cotton plantation in Mississippi. My son Henry [Clay, Jr.] wants occupation, and wants to increase his income. The profession of the Law offers but few inducements in K., and indeed he has views not entirely compatible with the pursuit of it. I have a number of surplus slaves here, principally young and well adapted to a Cotton plantation. I have proposed to him to spend three or four months of the ensuing autumn and winter in exploring your State [Mississippi] and Louisiana, and to make a purchase either of new land or an improved plantation, on our joint account. Of course, I could myself do little more than supply some of the Capital. He would have to give it his personal attention for several years, by the end of which one of my two youngest sons [James Brown Clay and John Morrison Clay] might be substituted in interest to me, and assume its management.

If you have leisure, I should be glad to be favored with your opinion, and the benefit of your experience, on the following points:

1. What do you think of the project itself?

2. Will it be best to purchase unimproved land, or an estalished plantation? I have thought that, altho' the latter would possess the advantage of immediate revenue, the former would, in the end, be most profitable, from the augmentation of the value of the Capital. Besides, while our means might be adequate to the purchase of a new place, we could not buy a stocked one in full operation without contracting debt, which I dread.

3. Is Mississippi or the Red River in Louisiana most desirable to make the purchase?

4. What part of the State of Mississippi, as to soil and climate, is the best location?

5. What would be Henry's best route and plan to explore the Country?

I request you to present my best respects to Mr. [James] Caldwell and to Col. Denton, who I presume is yet at the Springs. . . .

Copy. Printed in Pierce Butler, *The Unhurried Years, Memories of the Old Natchez Region* (Baton Rouge, 1948), 38-40. Addressed to Mercer at White Sulphur Springs, Va. (W. Va.).   1. Speech in Senate, March 27-28, 1834.   2. *Ibid.*; and Clay to Helm, April 20, 1833.   3. In the Indiana gubernatorial election Noah Noble, the Whig candidate, defeated the Democratic candidate, Daniel Read, by 36,773 votes to 27,257. *BDGUS*, 1:398-99. The Jacksonians, however, won control of the state legislature. Adam Leonard, "Personal Politics in Indiana, 1816-1840," *IMH* (March, 1923), 19:269.

From Henry Thompson, Baltimore, August 16, 1834. In regard to a cow which Clay has purchased from him, states: "I am sorry that Chloes Calf is paily coloured, but can vouch for its purity of blood, the Gates into my premises are locked every Night & no Bull but Hamlet has ever been with them since Chloe was Calved, a similar occurrence took place with a Calf out of my old Cow two years since & upon showing it to Mr. John Barney of Delaware (one of the best Graziers in this section of our Country) he said it was owing to my having a red & white Cow amongst my Cattle, that he was satisfied of the fact from experience with different animals, but particularly from a Foal out of a Bay Mare by a bay Horse being spotted and having pastured in company with a white Mare—"

Adds that "I sincerely rejoice in your Whig triumph" in Kentucky [Speech in Senate, March 27-28, 1834] and "hope there may be many more." ALS. DLC-TJC (DNA, M212, R14).

To BENJAMIN WATKINS LEIGH   Lexington, August 24, 1834

I wish you would investigate thoroughly at Richmond the subject of Scrip-warrants[1] and come back to the Senate with such information as will enable us, whilst just claimants are provided for, to secure the Government against frauds. Originally I think there was no just foundation for these claims upon the General Government; but the difficulty now is to stop after having undertaken to satisfy some of them.

The result of our recent Elections in K. puts us at east here,[2] on the score of Jacksonism, during the rest of our lives. Seventy six of 100 members of the H. of R. and 10 of the 11 Senators to be elected, were chosen; and Mr. [Robert P.] Letcher was re-elected over Tom Moore by near 300. In Indiana, Illinois and Missouri[3] too the Whigs have done well.

I see that your opponents are making great exertions against you. What will they make of their instructions? On my way home, I saw in the Western part of Va. several members of your Legislature, all of whom assured me that there was no doubt about your election.[4] The member from Greenbriar [*sic*, Greenbrier] may need some looking after.[5]

Can any thing be more stupid than the course of Duff Green?[6] It is suicidal as respects his exclusive object, the election of Mr. Calhoun. Can he suppose that the Whigs are to be driven, nolens volens, into the support of that gentleman? And, then, how he cants about his principles! As, if nobody in the Union had any principles to guide them but himself! And to stir *such* a question at *such* a time! I am almost confirmed in a suspicion which, for some time, I have entertained, that his real purpose is to affect the election of Mr. V. Buren. Such is, at all events, the inevitable tendency of his present course.

I regret to tell you that Mrs. Clays health continues feeble & precarious. Mine remains good, as I hope this will find that to be of Mrs. L. and yourself.

ALS. ViU.   1. This was U.S. Land Office script being issued to Virginia veterans of the Revolution in exchange for warrants in the same amount as the value of the unclaimed or unsatisfied military bounty land to which they were entitled under Virginia law. The problem of possible fraud arose, because under the Script Act of 1830, Virginia veterans not able to produce their original bounty land warrants could assert their ownership of the same by an affidavit merely "stating that such warrant has been lost or mislaid and that the original hath not been sold or transferred." Arrangements to exchange the old warrants for the new script had to be made prior to Jan. 1, 1835. For the Script Act of May 30, 1830, see 4 *U.S. Stat.*, 422-24.   2. Speech in Senate, March 27-28, 1834.   3. For Indiana, see Clay to Mercer, August 13, 1834. Three Democrats were elected to Congress from Illinois, but no Whigs; however, Joseph Duncan, a Democrat-turned-Whig, was elected governor over his Democratic opponent, William Kinney, by a vote of 17,330 to 10,224. *BDGUS*, 1:369; *Guide to U.S. Elections*, 562. Clay's information on Missouri was in error; the only elections there involved members of the state legislature in which the Democrats won by a large majority. Washington *Daily National Intelligencer*, Sept. 11, 1834.   4. Leigh had been elected U.S. senator by the state legislature on Feb. 26, 1834, by a majority of 15 votes over his opponent Philip P. Barbour. Richmond *Enquirer*, Feb. 27, 1834.   5. For William McComas, the Greenbrier member, see *BDAC*.   6. A number of Green's statements at this time suggested that the States' Rights party should not unite with the National Republicans simply for the purpose of defeating Van Buren, but only if the National Republicans would accept states' rights principles. See Washington *United States Telegraph*, July 31; August 4, 7, 11-14, 20, 22, 1834.

To WILLIE P. MANGUM   Lexington, August 26, 1834

You will have heard the result of our K. election.[1] We could not desire that it should have been better — 76 out of the 101 members of the H. of R. Letcher's re-election, and 11 of the 12 Senators to be chosen elected on our side. Indiana has done nearly as well; and Illinois and Missouri are not much behind her.[2] Ohio[3] will bring up the rear gloriously in the West.

How have your fared in N. Carolina?[4] Do tell me. I have seen no satisfactory account; and the [Washington *Daily National*] Intellr. says we shall know nothing until the Legislature assembles; but I presume you are better informed.

Have you not been shocked with the imprudence of D[uff]. Green?[5] To stir *such* a question as that of the Presidency at *such* a time as this! And to stir it as he has done! Poor fellow how much he professes to be devoted to his principles; as if others were less attached to others! Now it is clear that if each element of the Opposition comes to the resolution (and one has just as much right to do it as another) that it will support no Candidate who does not entertain its principles, there can be no union or harmony.

Let me hear from you soon, and say when you go North.

ALS. NcD.   1. Speech in Senate, March 27-28, 1834.   2. Clay to Mercer, August 13, 1834; Clay to Leigh, August 24, 1834.   3. Clay to Kerr, May 16, 1834.   4. Clay to Gales, August 8, 1834.   5. Clay to Leigh, August 24, 1834.

To HAMILTON SMITH   Lexington, September 6, 1834

I recd your letter of the 30h. ulto. regarding my opinion whether the manufacturing business, and especially that of Cotton may be expected to revive.

It would afford me great pleasure to communicate to you any information in my power; but on such a subject, depending upon the combination of so many causes, commercial, competition, and political, one should form and express any opinion with great diffidence. Much depends upon the issue of certain great elections at hand in Pennsa.[1] and elsewhere. If they should be adverse to the Admon, we may look forward with confidence to the restoration of the authority of the Constitution and Laws, and to the settlement of the currency upon some stable footing. If, on the contrary, they should sustain the Admon, we may expect for some time to come a continuance of the derangement of the currency, exchange, &c. with all their train of consequences.[2]

Apart from the acts and measures of the Executive, I see nothing to prevent the success of our manufactures. The Compromise bill[3] assures them, at least until 1843, of a degree of protection, unquestionably adequate. I feared there would be an attempt to get rid of that bill, and further to depress our manufactures, but now I do not think there is any such danger.

If the Fall elections terminate unfavorably to the Admon, you may I think confidently anticipate a revival of prosperity in every branch of business. Otherwise, I cannot answer for any consequences. . . .

ALS. NcU. Smith was a lawyer in Louisville, Ky., by 1840. *NEHGR*, 22:362; Ronald V. Jackson *et al.* (eds.), *Kentucky 1840 Census Index* (Bountiful, Utah, 1978), 204.   1. Clay to Kerr, May 16, 1834.   2. Clay to Robertson, March 28, 1834.   3. Draft Proposal, Mid-Dec., 1832.

To NOAH NOBLE   Lexington, September 8, 1834

I duly recd. your favor of the 2d.   As you do not mention the receipt of a short letter which I addressed to you, of prior date, I presume it had not reached you. I repeat the expression contained in it of my hearty congratulations on your recent election.[1] Considering the opposition you encountered, the result was as gratifying as it is decisive. The course you pursued as to the Presidential election was both judicious & conformable to the general understanding among the Whigs previous to the adjournment of Congress.[2] It was deemed best to designate no Presidential Candidate until after the Fall elections, so as to combine the whole strength of the entire opposition against the Admon and against Mr. V. Buren. In the course of next winter it is to be hoped that there can be an union effected on some Candidate. I think, at last, we have reason to hope that we shall get rid of the miserable concern at the head of public affairs. All my information justifies the belief that the Whigs will succeed in N. York,[3] New Jersey,[4] Pennsa.[5] and Maryland;[6] and there is a strong probability of their success in Maine.[7] Rhode Island[8] has fulfilled our hopes.

I have long wished to visit Indianapolis, and I should be highly gratified to do so; but I regret that it is not in my power to accept your friendly invitation this fall. I have been ten months out of the last twelve from home; and my private affairs require my presence here until the time arrives for me to proceed to Washington. I must therefore postpone the pleasure of seeing your part of Indiana to some more convenient day. I was induced strongly to anticipate the satisfaction of seeing you here this week, at our Cattle shew; and I have not abandoned the expectation. Should it not be in your power to come at that time, I hope you will visit us during the races which take place in the course of the next week. You will see our neighbourhood in a pleasant condition; for after a long and most distressing drought, we have just had fine rains that will restore vegetation, and render our fields once more verdant.

Has [John] Tipton renounced Jacksonism?[9] I fear he is not to be relied on. He affects candor and liberality, but cunning is his predominant quality. What is the political complexion of your Legislature? . . .[10]

ALS. InU.   1. Clay to Mercer, August 13, 1834.   2. Apparently an agreement not to bring the question of an 1836 presidential candidate into the campaign. It was not until late 1835 that William Henry Harrison was brought forward as a candidate in Indiana. Logan Esary, *History of Indiana* (Dayton, Ohio, 1922), 307, 311, 313-14.   3. Clay to Storer, August 8, 1834. 4. *Ibid.*   5. Clay to Kerr, May 16, 1834.   6. In the election for the Maryland state legislature, 37 Whigs won seats in the senate to 11 for the Democrats. In the house 61 Whigs won seats to 16 for the Democrats. Washington *Daily National Intelligencer*, Oct. 9, 10, 1834. The state legislature also reelected James Thomas, an anti-Jackson Democrat, as governor. *BDGUS*, 2:661.   7. In the Maine elections the Democrats won 14 seats in the senate to 11 for the Whigs, while the Whigs won 66 seats in the house to 57 for the Democrats. *Niles' Register* (Sept. 20, 1834), 47:38. The Democrats also won 6 congressional seats to 2 for the Whigs. *Guide to U.S.*

Elections, 562. In the gubernatorial race Robert P. Dunlap, a Democrat, defeated Peleg Sprague, a Whig, by a vote of 38,133 to 33,732. *BDGUS*, 2:600.   8. In the Rhode Island election the Whigs carried the house 41 to 31 and the senate 43 to 38. *Niles' Register* (Nov. 8, 1834), 47:150. 9. For Tipton, see *BDAC*. Tipton, who had been a staunch Democrat, turned against the president when Jackson vetoed a bill to improve the Wabash River after he had signed one to improve the Tennessee River. Nina K. Reid, "Sketches of Early Indiana Senators IV John Tipton," *IMH* (Dec., 1913), 9:259, 268.   10. Clay to Mercer, August 13, 1834.

To FRANCIS LIEBER Lexington, September 15, 1834

I have delayed the acknowledgement of your favor of the 5h. July which reached here before I got home from Congress, under the hope that I could possess myself of the views of the Trustees of Transylvania University, and communicate them to you, in respect to the Presidency of that institution;[1] but they are so dispersed that I have not had an opportunity of conversing with many of them, and I have not felt myself authorized to present your name to the Board formally for the appointment. The office is still vacant, and the Board I believe have designated no one to fill it. Some of the members had turned their attention towards a Clergyman in Pittsburg [*sic*],[2] but there has been no resolution to appoint him. The University at present is not in a very flourishing condition, except in the departments of Medicine and Law. The Salary which the Board can give is $1200 per annum, with apartments in the principal College building for the residence of the President. That sum would probably go as far as $1800 in Philada.   And should the College revive and realize the unquestionable advantages of its location the Salary would no doubt be hereafter augmented.

The City of Lexington, in which the University is situated, contains a population of about 6000. It is distant from the Ohio river 64 miles, and from the Kentucky river 14. It is surrounded on all sides by a rich beautiful Country, unsurpassed in fertility. The City is paved and watched and well built. The population occupies itself with Commerce, Manufactures, the Mechanic arts, the learned professions, and with Seminaries dedicated to the education of the youth of both sexes.[3] It has three Female academies in successful operation. Society is good, hospitable and intelligent. There are seven houses of public worship and four Presses, from three of which News papers are issued.[4]

Mr. [Robert, Jr.] Walsh who has visited Lexington can supply to you any deficiencies in this description of it.

The President presides at meetings of the faculty, has a general superintendance over the University, and lectures in particular departments, usually Moral Philosophy, Belles Lettres &c. to a Class.

Our literary resources and Circles are, of course, not to be compared to those of Philadelphia. Our libraries are very scanty; & the Philosophical Apparatus of the University is inadequate. From this account of Lexington and the University, with such additional information as you can avail yourself of in Philada. you can judge of the advantages which they offer.

Should you determine to apply for the situation, it will afford me pleasure to give any support in my power to your application. In that case however it will be expedient for you to transmit the best testimonials to your qualifications that you can procure, not for me, but for the information of those who possess the appointing power.

I perused, with much sensibility, your description of the 4h. of July festival, and the cordial reception which was given to the annunication of my name. To me, who have been struggling for 16 years, to avert the unhappy state now existing of our public affairs, these manifestations are gratifying. And you, my dear Sir, will share with me the greater pleasure I derive from recent evidences of the returning sobriety of the people generally. A large portion of the West has, in late elections, decisively proclaimed its condemnation of the misrule at Washington;[5] and I think that which is yet to speak (Ohio)[6] will be equally decisive. The favorable changes here bespeak the operation of a general cause, which, it is to be hoped, will shew its influence in the approaching elections of the Eastern States.[7]

I am ashamed to tell you that I have not yet read the Introduction to the Penitentiary &c.[8]   The truth is, that ten months absence from home had prepared me a mass of arrears of business, upon my return, so great that I have had leisure for nothing else; but I hope soon to be able to look into it, and reap from it the instruction which I anticipate.

Mrs. Clay has not regained her health. She continued to decline, after her return, until about a month ago, when she changed the system of her medical treatment. From that period she has improved a little, and we now hope for her recovery.

ALS. CSmH. Addressed to Lieber in Philadelphia.   1. Clay to Lieber, July 1, 1834.
2. Possible a reference to John C. Young, originally of Greencastle, Pa. See *ibid.*   3. Saint
Catherine's Female Seminary; Lexington Female Academy; Mr. & Mrs. Griswald's School for
Young Ladies. Gladys V. Parrish, "The History of Female Education in Lexington and Fayette
County," M.A. thesis, University of Kentucky, 1932, pp. 33, 39, 40.   4. Lexington *Kentucky
Gazette*; Lexington *Observer & Kentucky Reporter*; Lexington *Intelligencer*.   5. For election returns
in Illinois and Missouri, see Clay to Leigh, August 24, 1834; for Indiana, see Clay to Mercer,
August 13, 1834; for Kentucky, see Speech in Senate, March 27-28, 1834.   6. Clay to Kerr,
May 16, 1834.   7. For the key eastern states of New York and Pennsylvania, see respectively
Clay to Storer, August 8, 1834 and Clay to Kerr, May 16, 1834.   8. Clay to Lieber, July 1, 1834.

To JAMES G. BIRNEY   Lexington, September 16, 1834

Mr. Clay presents his respects to Mr. Birney, whose note he has this moment (at six o'clock) rec'd. If Mr. B. will breakfast with Mr. Clay tomorrow morning at 7 o'clock he shall be happy to see him.[1]

Copy. Printed in Dwight L. Dumond (ed.), *Letters of James Gillespie Birney, 1831-1857*, 2 vols.
(N.Y., 1938), 1:135.   1. Endorsed by Birney: "Agreeably to the above invitation, I breakfasted with Mr. C. and had an hour's conversation with him on the subject of emancipation. I
found him, according to my conceptions, altogether wrong—and that he had gone very little
beyond the standard of vulgar reflection on the subject. Altho' we differed radically, yet we parted
on most friendly terms." Birney wrote in his diary after the breakfast with Clay, Sept. 17: "He
said that slavery in Ky. was in so mitigated a form as not to deserve the consideration of a very
great evil—that men's interests in *property* had been found an insurmountable barrier to gradual
emancipation *then*, in '99—that now, they were more formidable—the case was hopeless by any
direct effort, and was to be left to the influence of liberal principles as they should pervade our
land. He spoke of Mr. Robert Breckinridge having put himself down in popular estimation by his
having advocated emancipation,—and that he, and Mr. John Green, two gentlemen of great
worth had disqualified themselves for political usefulness by the part they had taken in reference
to slavery. . . . The impression made upon me, by this interview was that Mr. C. had no *conscience* about the matter, and therefore, that he would swim with the popular current." Note by
Prof. Dumond. For an interpretation of the Clay-Birney breakfast conversation on emancipation
on Sept. 17, see Eaton, *Henry Clay*, 124; also, Comment in Senate, March 28, 1832.

To Noah Noble, September 22, 1834. Thanks Noble for the "very acceptable present of the Tamarack tree" which "came in excellent condition, and I have planted it according to your directions." Invites him to visit. Continues: "There is no doubt that No. Carolina [Clay to Gales, August 8, 1834] has left the administration. In Maine [Clay to Noble, September 8, 1834] our defeat is really a victory, considering the great changes, and the equality of the contest. They have made a nomination of Govr. in N. York on the part of the Whigs which seems to give general satisfaction; and my correspondents speak in a tone of great confidence as to the issue of the struggle in the Empire State upon the whole, I entertain a strong conviction that at last Jacksonism is subdued [Clay to Storer, August 8, 1834]. It will make tremendous efforts this autumn, and will here and there maintain a doubtful ascendancy; but its general march is downward and rapidly." Copy. Printed in *IMH* (March, 1926), 22:211.

From Joseph Ficklin, Lexington, *ca.* October 1, 1834. Submits a bill for postage due on an unidentified pamphlet on gardening, *Drake's Medical Journal, North American Magazine*, and the *Christian Orphan* "to Mrs. Clay." ALS. DLC-TJC (DNA, M212, R17).
    Clay also subscribed to *Western Monthly Magazine* in Cincinnati. Taylor & Tracy to Clay, September 15, 1835. ADS, partially printed. *Ibid.*

To J. S. Evans *et al.*, Louisville, October 3, 1834. Refuses an invitation by "the young whigs of Louisville, to a public dinner," citing the fact that he has "fixed to-morrow for my departure from the city." Mentions that he is "glad . . . to learn that the conduct of the senate of the United States in averting the attacks directed against the constitution and public liberty [Remark in Senate, March 28, 1834], commands the approbation of the young whigs of Louisville," but adds that the "senate . . . can only exert a temperate and negative power, which the people alone can render effectual." Believes that "recent manifestations" of the public will inspire "hopes that the spirit of usurpation will meet with a just rebuke, and the purity of our institutions be successfully vindicated." Copy. Printed in *Niles' Register* (October 25, 1834), 47:121.

To ELIHU CHAUNCEY   Lexington, October 18, 1834

I cannot refrain from the pleasure of communicating the good news which has reached me from the only two points of Ohio from which I have yet heard, Cincinnati, and Zanesville at both of which the Jackson representatives have been turned out of Congress and Whigs elected.[1] At the former place, the prevailing [belief] entertained was that the Whig Candidate for Governor [James Findlay] was elected by not less than 10.000.[2] If, as we have reason to hope and believe, the Whigs have succeeded in Ohio, I think the Republic is safe, whatever may be the result in Pennsa. & New York.[3]
    I have not recd. a definitive answer to the enquiry with which I troubled you as to the practicability of effecting a Loan.[4] At your earliest leisure I should be glad to hear from you, as there is scarcely time remaining, prior to my departure for the City, to receive an answer.
    I am sure you will hear with pleasure that Mrs. Clays health is much improved.

ALS. PHC. For Chauncey, a wealthy Philadelphia landowner and official of the Bank of Pennsylvania, see *PMHB*, 32:420; 66:74.   1. In the Cincinnati district Bellamy Storer, the Whig candidate, defeated Robert Lytle, the Democratic candidate, by a vote of 4,327 to 4,231. In Zanesville, Elias Howell, a Whig, defeated Robert Mitchell, a Democrat, by 4,294 votes to 3,610. *Guide to U.S. Elections*, 563.   2. Clay to Kerr, May 16, 1834; Clay to Leigh, Oct. 22, 1834.   3. Clay to Kerr, May 16, 1834; Clay to Storer, August 8, 1834.   4. Clay may have been attempting to arrange a loan for Henry Clay, Jr. See Henry Clay, Jr., to Clay, June 3, 1833; Clay to Henry Clay, Jr., June 7, 1833; and Feb. 19, 1835.

To Benjamin W. Leigh, Richmond, Va., October 22, 1834. States that "Ohio has acquitted herself nobly. [James] Findlay is supposed to be elected by several thousand, and four or five Jackson members of the H. of R. have been made to yield their places to Whigs." ALS. ViU. Clay's assessment of the Ohio elections was overly optimistic.

Findlay, the Whig candidate, lost the governor's race by more than 5,000 votes. In the 1834 U.S. House elections, the Whigs won 10 seats to 9 for the Democrats; whereas, in 1832 they had won 8 seats to 11 for the Jacksonians — a gain of only 2. See Clay to Kerr, May 16, 1834; *Guide to U.S. Elections*, 558, 563.

To **THOMAS SPEED**   Lexington, November 1, 1834

I am greatly obliged by the information communicated in your favor of the 27h. Ulto. respecting the States of Indiana & Illinois.[1] I scarcely need say that I concur heartily in all you say in regard to Internal improvements and Manufactures. How greatly have the people of the Western & especially N. Western States erred in sustaining the present Admon upon these subjects as well as in relation to the Public lands! We who belong to the minority can only deplore their error or folly. I have been long persuaded that the policy was bad of granting preemptions, but it is so interwoven in our land system, and there is such a wide spread interest in supporting it, in the new States, that it will be found very difficult to eradicate it.

If we have had cause to be gratified with the results of some of the Elections, since the adjournment of Congress, the issue of others (those in Pennsa. and New Jersey in particular)[2] is such as to occasion the deepest regret. Should N. York,[3] as I fear, continue to support this Admon, I see no *present* relief from Jacksonism. In that event, the Bank of the U. S. will be hopelessly gone; and the new Congress will open next year with the parties nearly balanced, perhaps a small majority in both Houses for Jackson.[4] This is not what I hoped & believed would be the condition of the Country. If we add to this that, whilst the Jackson party remains thus powerful, the Whigs are cut up and divided among themselves we shall have a picture of public affairs not a little discouraging.

I shall return this Session to do what I can, but with little anticipation of being able to accomplish any thing for the public good.

ALS. NhD.   1. Letter not found; reference obscure.   2. Clay to Kerr, May 16, 1834; Clay to Storer, August 8, 1834.   3. *Ibid.*   4. See Clay to Robertson, March 28, 1834, for the party strengths in the 24th Congress.

From Francis Lieber, Philadelphia, November 8, 1834. Writes that he has delayed answering Clay's letter of September 15, 1834, because he wanted to be as definite as possible about his interest in the job of president of Transylvania University. Notes that the salary offered "is not large, and I should not be able to incur the expenses of removing thither and furnishing there my house again, if I had not some hope of being able to have some young gentlemen living in my house." Sends a testimonial, as Clay had requested, and suggests that others may be obtained from "any gentleman of note here or in Boston." Continues: "Politics seem, this moment, so sickening that we avoid speaking of them, wherever possible. News, of the very worst kind are here from New York [Clay to Storer, August 8, 1834]. We are already in a revolution, as nations so often are long before they know it. The [Washington] Globe plays very cheering preludes with regard to attacks upon the Supreme Court. My letters from Europe are of the worst kind with reference to the moral influence of our general affairs on those of national freedom and the sway of law in that part of the world." ALS. DLC-HC (DNA, M212, R5). Printed in Colton, *Clay Correspondence*, 4:385-86. In the *United States* v. *Samuel Brewster* (1833), a counterfeiting case, the Court reversed the Circuit Court of the U.S. for the Eastern District of Pennsylvania in holding that the B.U.S. bill of which Brewster's counterfeit bill was a copy, was not a legal bill ("genuine instrument") within the meaning of section 18 of the act of 1816 incorporating the B.U.S. This was because the bill copied was "drawn by the president and cashier of the branch bank of Pittsburgh on the mother bank of Philadelphia," whereas the 1816 act states, in section 18, that a "genuine instrument" must be issued "by order of the president, directors and company" of the B.U.S. in Philadelphia. Hence, no act of counterfeiting had taken place, and the indictment of Brewster was a mistaken one. 7 Peters 164. Francis P. Blair's pro-administration Washington *Globe* revealed in its October 22, 1834, edition that the currency of the hated B.U.S. has thus been brought into question by the Court's decision in that "forgers who thus sell and deliver counterfeit paper of this description, cannot be punished" under section 18.

From John L. Hickman *et al.*, Paris, Ky., November 11, 1834. Invite Clay, on his way back to Washington, "to participate in the joy and hilarity" of a dinner in his honor to be held "at Captain H. Bridges's hotel" in Paris. Say they are "actuated by . . . Whig principles" in their desire to "resist the overbearing spirit of domestic dictation." Add that "For you we feel no personal devotion. We come not to fawn around you as the base parasites of power"; nevertheless, they "feel a just pride and admiration for your transcendant talents." Emphasize that "The principles of Whigism, (in whose support you have spent a long and brilliant life,) we almost adore." They desire to encourage Clay as he contends against "A popular and self-willed military President, a veteran army of 40,000 office-holders, the numerous expectants of office, a pensioned press, and the groundless prejudices of a duped, deceived and injured people" who are conspiring "against the efforts of yourself and your noble compatriots in the American Senate." Copy. Printed in Lexington *Intelligencer*, November 29, 1834.

Clay replied on November 12, 1834, declining the invitation on the ground that his stay in Paris on his return trip to Washington will be short. Continues: "I concur entirely with you, gentlemen, in the justness of the distinction between an attachment to principles, and an attachment to men. And the testimony which you are pleased to render in my behalf is more highly esteemed by me because you place it on the ground of public principles and public services. I believe, with you, that the present contest in the United States is one against power in behalf of the liberties of the country. I will add an expression of my conviction that it involves also the existence both of the constitution and the union of the states." Adds that "history demonstrates that, although . . . military heroes had trampled upon the liberties of the people, and, under the forms of law, they respectively, in the end, received what they merited, the execrations of mankind." Copy. Printed in *Niles' Register* (December 27, 1834), 47:283.

To HENRY CLAY, JR.   Early December, 1834

I was disapp[ointed] [illeg. words] you and my dear Julia [Prather Clay]; but I learn from Anne [Brown Clay Erwin] that you [illeg. words] half an hour of the period of my departure.

I found here, among our political friends, much despondency on account of public affairs; and whilst I have endeavored to rally them, I have not been able to avoid sharing their depression. If among the elements of opposition there could be any union and concert established, all might yet be saved; but I regret to say that no appearance yet exists of accomplishing that desirable object. We shall see if a sense of common dangers will not yet suppress the ambition of individuals and put aside foolish theories and bring us all together.

The most engrossing subject of the Session is likely to be the President's Message relative to our French affairs.[1] His rashness, in advising a warlike measure, without waiting for the decision of the French chambers at their approaching Session, seems to be generally condemned. It is apprehended that, if his message reaches France, as is probable, before any appropriation is made, the Chamber of Deputies will refuse the appropriation, in consequence of the threat which the Message contains. In that event, our difficulties will be greatly encreased. Irritation begets irritation, and I should not be surprized if, in the sequel, two gallant nations, hitherto entertaining for each other the greatest respect, shall be found unexpectedly engaged in War.

The Senate has placed me at the head of the Comee. of F[oreign]. affairs — the most responsible situation of the Session. I shall endeavor to discharge my duty, but I confess I have less heart than ever to exert myself in public business. . . .

ALS. Henry Clay Memorial Foundation, Lexington, Ky. Manuscript is torn.   1. Dated Dec. 1, 1834; see *MPP*, 3:97-123; also, Brown to Clay, Jan. 24, 1832; Remark in Senate, Jan. 6, 1835; Jan. 11, 1836; Speech in Senate, Jan 14, 1835; Undelivered Senate Speech, Late Jan., 1836.

To FRANCIS LIEBER   Washington, December 3, 1834

Your favor of the 8h. Ulto. addressed to me at Ashland, not finding me there, followed me to this place, and in this circuitous way has been received. In the mean time, and prior to the commencement of the Session of Congress, I had gone to Princeton to see my youngest son [John Morrison Clay] at Mr. [Enoch Cobb] Wines's school.[1] This took me through Philada. but my stop there going was only one night, and one day on my return. This short stay prevented me from having the pleasure of seeing you.

The Government of the University of Transylvania is in a Board of 21 Trustees, which appoints the President and members of the Faculties in the institution. I am not now, altho' for a long time I was, a member of that Board. When I recd. your former letter,[2] as it was limited to enquiries, I did not feel myself at liberty to offer, and consequently did not offer, your name to the consideration of the Board, as the President of the Institution. I found, however, on my return home in July, that the office was still vacant, and I had a confidential conversation with one or two persons connected with the institution about you, in which I stated very strongly my views of the advantages of your appointment, if you would accept it. Knowing that the Trustees would probably expect testimonials in your behalf, I wrote you the letter on that subject.[3] Just before I left home, the period approaching of the commencement of the Fall Session of the University, and it being thought absolutely necessary to fill the vacant office of President, the Board appointed a gentleman accordingly.[4] Not knowing that you would accept it, and not hearing from you, I did not feel justified in asking a postponement of the appointment.

Such are the circumstances under which the Revd. Mr. [Thomas W.] Coit of Massachusetts has been appointed President of the University. I have not, since I left home, heard any thing further on the subject. I regret extremely that the opportunity of obtaining your services in that situation is thus, at least for the present, lost. What the Trustees might have done, if your name had been submitted to them, I am not able to say, because it was not submitted, for the reason above stated. What my wishes were I need not repeat.

The testimonial of Judge [Joseph] Story is strong and satisfactory. As the occasion to which it was intended to apply it does not now exist, I return it, thinking that you might possibly have future use for it.

I feel my dear Sir with great sensibility all that you say on our American politics. They are bad enough, and such as to create despair for our Country, if we were not forbidden to entertain that sentiment. . . .

ALS. CSmH.   1. *NCAB*, 1:180.   2. Not found, but see Clay to Lieber, July 1; Sept. 15, 1834; Lieber to Clay, Nov. 8, 1834.   3. Clay to Lieber, Sept. 15, 1834.   4. Clay to Lieber, July 1, 1834.

From William C. C. Claiborne, Jr., New Orleans, December 4, 1834. States that he hopes to save his own "paternal estate from my Uncle's [Martin Duralde] unlucky and extraordinary failure," because the mortgage he holds on Duralde "can only be extinguished by the extinguishment of the debt which occasioned it." Adds that "I consider myself protected by all the spirit and even the letter of our laws, and I shall insist upon my rights." Notes that he, Duralde, and James Erwin are "acting in concert" in the hope of saving "something for Duralde." Attempting to explain Duralde's financial problems, continues: "As to what has brought my poor Uncle to this situation, it is impossible exactly to explain to you, for he does not understand it himself. He has no head at all for business, and is so excessively negligent, that to those who don't know him, it has thrown some shade even upon his integrity. He launched into speculations of all sorts, not upon cash, but upon his credit; and had enormous interests constantly running against him. These speculations were conducted not by himself, but by others for him, and generally failed. His difficulties began with that mill establishment, and brick yard, in which he was probably cheated, and his confidence abused by a rascally partner. . . . In short no one could have more reasons to complain of my poor Uncle than I, but I see he is more to be pitied than blamed, and he may yet get out of the scrape."

On Louisiana politics, mentions that "[George] Eustis is on the ranks for the Senate in opposition to [George A.] Waggaman, but though the former is a connexion, I have lost all confidence in him, and I hope Waggaman will succeed; which will probably be the result [Clay to Storer, August 8, 1834]." ALS. DLC-HC (DNA, M212, R5).

Remark in Senate, December 11, 1834. Gives notice of his intention to introduce a bill on December 15 that would distribute to the several states, for a limited time, the income from the sales of public lands. *Cong. Globe*, 23 Cong., 2 Sess., 29. This bill was introduced by Clay on December 15. *Ibid.*, 36. See Speech in Senate, June 20, 1832; also Remark in Senate, December 16, 1834.

Remark in Senate, December 16, 1834. Informs the Senate that his new land sales distribution bill was "in the same shape exactly" as was the one submitted "last session [Speech in Senate, December 5, 1833; *Register of Debates*, 22 Cong., 1 Sess., Appendix, 117]." Adds that the Committee on Public Lands which had reported it out last session was composed "precisely" of the same members as in this session, and that there is, therefore, no reason "the bill should undergo a second examination by the same committee." *Register of Debates*, 23 Cong., 2 Sess., 15. For the land sales distribution bill introduced by Clay in the 22nd Congress, 2nd Session, see Speech in Senate, January 7, 1833; also Speech in Senate, June 20, 1832.

Remark in Senate, December 22, 1834. Moves that a House joint resolution authorizing the sale of gift horses and a lion presented to the U.S. consul in Tangier by the Emperor of Morocco be referred to the Committee on Agriculture instead of the Committee on Foreign Relations, since the animals were "now in this city and not connected with our foreign affairs." *Register of Debates*, 23 Cong., 2 Sess., 35-36; *Cong. Globe*, 23 Cong., 2 Sess., 54. See Remark in Senate, January 15, 1835.

Remark in Senate, December 23, 1834. Announces the arrangements that have been made for the commemorative oration on the life and character of General Lafayette to be given before the two houses of Congress at 12:30 p.m. on December 31 by John Quincy Adams. *Register of Debates*, 23 Cong., 2 Sess., 44. Lafayette had died May 20, 1834. For Clay's invitation to Secretary of State John Forsyth to attend the Lafayette memorial ceremonies, see Clay and Henry Hubbard to Forsyth *et al.*, December 24, 1834. Copy. DNA, RG59, Misc. Letters (M179, R79).

Later this day, Clay moves that Jackson's instructions to U.S. diplomats in France since July 4, 1831, relating to the Franco-American claims treaty signed on that date, be made available to the Senate; "also all the correspondence" between Paris and Washington "respecting the executor of the said treaty [Brown to Clay, January 24, 1832]." Explains why the Committee on Foreign Relations (of which he was chairman) needs to see this material. *Register of Debates*, 23 Cong., 2 Sess., 45; *Cong. Globe*, 23 Cong., 2 Sess., 61. Resolution was adopted on December 24. *Ibid.*, 70. Correspondence with Secretary John Forsyth carrying out the thrust of this resolution is found in Clay to Forsyth, December 16, 1834. LS. DNA, RG59, Misc. Letters (M179, R79); and in Clay to Forsyth, December 27, 1834. ALS. *Ibid.*

To Ralph R. Gurley, Joseph Gales, & Philip R. Fendall, Washington, December 26, 1834. Regrets that the press of his duties makes it impossible for him to attend the annual meeting of the American Colonization Society on January 19 next. Assures them he entertains "the same sentiments" toward the society he has "always avowed." ALS. KyLxT.

From J. B. Duncan, Lexington, December 27, 1834. Tenders to Clay a receipt for a payment of $45 on three shares of stock in the Winchester and Lexington Turnpike Road Company. ADS, partially printed. DLC-TJC (DNA, M212, R17).

On May 7, 1835, Duncan acknowledged Clay's payment of an additional $30 on the three shares. *Ibid.* The act chartering the company was approved by the general assembly on February 22, 1834. It authorized the construction of "a turnpike road upon the McAdam plan, from Winchester to Lexington," as well as the issuing of capital stock in the amount of $60,000 at $100 per share. The road was completed prior to 1838. Coleman, *The Squire's Sketches of Lexington*, 40; Ky. Gen. Assy., *Acts* . . . 1833-1834, pp. 640-43. See also, Allen, "Turnpike System in Kentucky," *FCHQ*, 28:239-59.

Remark in Senate, January 6, 1835. As chairman of the Committee on Foreign Relations, presents the committee's report [*Register of Debates*, 23 Cong., 2 Sess., Appendix, 208-19] on "that part of the President's message [of December 1, 1834], appertaining to our relations with France [*MPP*, 3:100-108]." The report concludes with a resolution denying to Jackson "authority for making reprisals upon French property" if France fails during the present session of its legislature to make provision to pay the indemnities stipulated by the claims treaty [Brown to Clay, January 24, 1832] signed on July 4, 1831. Defends the committee's resolution, although admitting that neither it nor the report as a whole had been approved unanimously in committee. Notes that he does not know "what France might do when she heard of this threat to make reprisals." But feels that the French response to Jackson's message could range from passionate to prudent. Asks that January 13 be designated as the date on which to commence debate on the resolution. Suggests that 5,000 copies of the committee's report be issued; but supports Sen. George Poindexter's motion that 20,000 copies be printed. *Register of Debates*, 23 Cong., 2 Sess., 104-6; *Cong. Globe*, 23 Cong., 2 Sess., 95-96. For the resolution of the Franco-American claims crisis of 1834-36, see Van Deusen, *The Life of Henry Clay*, 289-94; and McLemore, *Franco-American Diplomatic Relations, 1816-1836*, 132-74. For an opposing interpretation, see William B. Hatcher, *Edward Livingston, Jeffersonian Republican and Jacksonian Democrat* (Baton Rouge, 1940), 423-41. Clay's major speech on the issue was delivered on January 14, 1835. *Register of Debates*, 23 Cong., 2 Sess., 200-205, 213. See also Remark in Senate, January 11, 1836; Undelivered Senate Speech, Late January, 1836; Biddle to Clay, January 4, 1836; and Brown to Clay, January 24, 1832.

Comment in Senate, January 7, 1835. With reference to improvement of navigation on the Wabash River, contradicts President Jackson's contention that the constitution does not authorize "those improvements . . . calculated to advance the interest of our foreign commerce." Will vote for the bill even though the president's construction of the constitution in this regard is wrong. *Register of Debates*, 23 Cong., 2 Sess., 114; *Cong. Globe*, 23 Cong., 2 Sess., 101-2.

Earlier this same day, Clay suggested that since the House had ordered the printing of 50,000 copies of the oration of John Q. Adams on December 31 honoring the memory of Lafayette, the Senate would order but 10,000 more. *Register of Debates*, 23 Cong., 2 Sess., 113-14. Toward the end of the day, he asked that the Senate fill a vacancy on the Committee on Foreign Affairs. *Ibid.*, 117.

To JAMES IREDELL   Washington, January 9, 1835

I have to thank you for the letter which you addressed to me on the 5h. announcing the passage through the H of Com[mons]. of the Land resolutions.[1] It gave me great satisfaction. The proceeds of the sales of the Public lands must be distributed, or the Lands themselves will be soon sacrificed. Of this I entertain not a doubt.

I will take the liberty of sending in a day or two to you a Copy of a Report I recently made on our French Relations.[2]

ALS. NcD.   1. The North Carolina house of commons had voted 82 to 32 in favor of a resolution "instructing her senators and representatives in Congress to vote for . . . 'Mr. Clay's Land Bill.'" The state senate, however, rejected this resolution. *Niles' Register* (Jan. 17, 1835), 47:331. 2. Remark in Senate, Jan. 6, 1835.

From James Kent, New York, January 9, 1835. Asks for "*one* of the 20,000 Copies of your Report [Remark in Senate, January 6, 1835]" when printed. Adds that "I rather guess I shall like it . . . I sympathize with you in all your public feelings & Doings since the beginning of the reign of the present Dynasty." ALS. DLC-HC (DNA, M212, R5). Printed in Colton, *Clay Correspondence*, 4:387.

Remark in Senate, January 12, 1835. Speaks in support of the bill compensating U.S. citizens for French spoliations on their commerce prior to 1800 [Remark in Senate, June 19, 1834]. *Cong. Globe*, 23 Cong., 2 Sess., 118. This bill was introduced by Webster on December 9, 1834, and agreed to in the Senate on February 3, 1835, by a vote of 25-20. It was reported to the House on February 3, where it was tabled on February 21, 1835. U.S. Sen., *Journal*, 23 Cong., 2 Sess., 31, 134; U.S. H. of Reps., *Journal*, 23 Cong., 2 Sess., 318, 426.

Remark in Senate, January 13, 1835. Insists on taking up the question of Franco-American relations [Brown to Clay, January 24, 1832; Remark in Senate, January 6, 1835] on the morrow. *Register of Debates*, 23 Cong., 2 Sess., 199-200.

Speech in Senate, January 14, 1835. Speaks to the resolution concluding the report of the Committee on Foreign Relations [Remark in Senate, January 6, 1835] which reads: "Resolved, that it is inexpedient, at this time, to pass any law vesting in the President authority for making reprisals upon French property, in the contingency of provision not being made for paying to the United States the indemnity stipulated by the treaty of 1831, during the present session of the French Chambers." Believes that the committee and the president are in "entire concurrence" with respect to "the justice of our claim upon France," differing only in approach. Speculates at length on what action the French government might take. Argues that the clause denying to the president the "authority for making reprisals upon French property" unless the claims are promptly paid "could do no mischief" but, instead, was an attempt "to prevent mischief." Considers an amendment to the committee's resolution, presented by Sen. John P. King of Georgia, which reads: "That as the French Chambers have been convened earlier than was expected by the President of the United States at the opening of the present session of Congress, it is inexpedient to pass any law relating to the treaty of 1831 until further information shall be received from France." Suggests to King that his amendment, with which Clay is largely in agreement, is lacking in that it avoids consideration of the substantive reasons listed by the Foreign Relations Committee in support of its decision to limit Jackson's reprisal authority. But agrees with King that nothing further should be done until more information is received from France. If the French legislature flatly refuses to vote the necessary appropriations to pay the claims, he will then consider retaliatory approaches ranging from acts of reprisal against French property to "open and undisguised war." Meanwhile, prefers not to commit the recently elected 24th Congress to specific approaches to resolving the crisis. "The propriety of remaining uncommitted, with our hands untied, must be obvious." Supports a reworded version of King's amendment to the committee resolution which reads: "Resolved, That it is inexpedient, at present, to adopt any legislative measures in regard to the state of affairs between the United States and France." In response to Sen. James Buchanan (Pa.), who interrupts to announce his support of the King resolution, as well as to laud Jackson's handling of the problem ("France, from the tone and language of the President, will have no right to consider this a menace"), Clay remarks that given "the facts and arguments contained in the [committee's] report, he trusted it would not be out of his [Buchanan's] power to defend the reasonings and conclusions of the committee." *Register of Debates*, 23 Cong., 2 Sess., 200-205, 213; *Cong. Globe*, 23 Cong., 2 Sess., 124-26. Printed in Colton, *Clay Correspondence*, 5:632-35. See also, Van Deusen, *The Life of Henry Clay*, 292.

Remark in Senate, January 15, 1835. Suggests that the lion given to the U.S. consul in Tangier [Remark in Senate, December 22, 1834] by the Emperor of Morocco be presented to whatever institution, person, or persons the president may designate. *Register of Debates*, 23 Cong., 2 Sess., 218.

When it was earlier suggested that the surplus lion be presented by Jackson to King Louis Philippe of France, Sen. James Buchanan noted, facetiously, that such a solution "would be a direct declaration of war against France." *Ibid.*; *Cong. Globe*, 23 Cong., 2 Sess., 129.

To FRANCIS T. BROOKE
Washington, January 16, 1835

I recd. your favor of the 13h. I am glad that you approved the French report.[1] You will have seen that the resolution with which it concluded, or rather a broader one, has unanimously passed the Senate,[2] declining to pass at present any Legislative measure whatever. I hope the whole proceeding in the Senate will turn the thoughts of the Nation on peace.

I should rejoice if your Legislature would pass resolutions in favor of the distribution of the proceeds of the Public lands.[3] They would have the best effect. The truth is that they will be wasted, if not distributed, and the whole public domain at no distant day will be thrown away from the old States. It is inconceivable to me (but upon the force of party) that any part of the Union should be adverse to the measure. But most of all am I surprized that the Slave states (which are by my bill to have distributive share regulated by their slaves as well as the number of their whites) should be opposcd to it. Hitherto no objection has been made from the North to that principle.

Here, as with you, so far as I am informed, parties are quiet on the Presidential question. Perhaps, however, as I mean to be perfectly quiet myself, they do not communicate to me what is going on.

I am sorry that I have not one copy of the portrait which you desire. James[4] who promised you one is now at N Orleans. I am not sure that he can perform his promise.

Mrs. Clay's health is restored; and my accounts from home assure me that she is very happy.

Judge [Gabriel] Duval has resigned; and [Roger B.] Taney has been nominated in his place.[5] It is doubtful whether he will be approved. He will not be by my vote.

Genl. [Joseph] Vance this moment tells me that it is apprehended that the Secy of War is dying,[6] and that he has been sent for to see him.

ALS. NcD. 1. Remark in Senate, Jan. 6, 1834. 2. The Committee's French report has initially concluded with a resolution denying the president "authority for making reprisals upon French property [Remark in Senate, Jan. 6, 1835]." It was altered to read "That it is inexpedient, at present, to adopt any legislative measures in regard to the state of affairs between the United States and France." *Register of Debates*, 23 Cong., 2 Sess., 104, 215. 3. The Virginia legislature did pass such a resolution in Dec., 1835. See Clay to Gilmer, Mid-Jan., 1836. 4. Probably James Brown Clay. It is not clear to which portrait Clay refers. One of the most recent was that by James R. Lambdin, which was completed in 1832. "The Portraits of Henry Clay: A Provisional Checklist," by Prof. Clifford Amyx is on file in the office of *The Papers of Henry Clay*. 5. Taney was confirmed by the Senate as chief justice on March 15, 1836, by a vote 29-15. Swisher, *Roger B. Taney*, 321-22. 6. It is unclear to whom Clay was referring; since Lewis Cass, the current Secretary of War, did not die until June 17, 1866. Woodford, *Lewis Cass*, 342.

Remark in Senate, January 19, 1835. Announces his intention tomorrow to move the Senate into consideration of executive business. *Register of Debates*, 23 Cong., 2 Sess., 233.

Remark in Senate, January 21, 1835. Opposes a bill for the relief of Nicholas D. Coleman on the ground that there is "not a particle of evidence" to sustain his claim. *Register of Debates*, 23 Cong., 2 Sess., 236.

Also on this day, agrees to postpone discussion of his distribution bill [Remark in Senate, December 16, 1834] until January 28, and to postpone until tomorrow the bill "graduating the price of the public lands, and providing for the sale of those which have been longest on the market," so that the Senate can proceed to executive business. *Cong. Globe*, 23 Cong., 2 Sess., 145. Says that he will also put off until tomorrow his insistence that the Senate engage in executive business. *Register of Debates*, 23 Cong., 2 Sess., 238. On December 15, 1834, Sen. Thomas Hart Benton had introduced a bill to graduate downward the price of public lands. It was laid on the table in the Senate on February 25, 1835. U.S. Sen., *Journal*, 23 Cong., 2 Sess., 36, 193.

From James Barbour, Barboursville, Va., January 22, 1835. Sends a handbill containing the pedigree of his filly, Allegrante, whose dam "is the mare Phantomia" and whose sire is "My imported horse young Truffle." Asserts that she "has been pronounced wherever she has appeared . . . one of the finest ever seen." Proposes that Clay "should give me $500 and then we would go halves." Adds that if Clay is interested but wants to see the filly before making a commitment, "I will . . . send her to Washington that you may Judge for yourself." ALS. Josephine Simpson Collection, Lexington, Ky.

On February 26, 1835, Barbour wrote Clay that he was sending a servant to Washington with Allegrante, and "I think you can't fail agreeing with me and the public generally that she is the finest filly you have seen." *Ibid*. Phantomia was a bay mare, imported from England by Barbour in 1829. For her decendents through her daughter Allegrante, see M.F. Bayliss, *The Matriarchy of the American Turf 1875-1930* (n.p., 1931), 117, 121.

From **Eleutheros Cooke,** Sandusky City, Ohio, January 22, 1835. Writes to convey "the heartfelt expression of applause with which the report of the Committee on Foreign Relations in reference to our affairs with France, has been received in this quarter [Remark in Senate, January 6, 1835]." Notes that he is not attempting to flatter Clay for having thus again saved the nation, but does so anyway. ALS. DLC-HC (DNA, M212, R5). Printed in Colton, *Clay Correspondence*, 4:387-88. For Cooke, see *BDAC*.

Remark in Senate, January 22, 1835. Opposes bill for the relief of the heirs of Nathaniel Tyler, deceased, Virginia veteran of the American Revolution, and moves that it be tabled. *Register of Debates*, 23 Cong., 2 Sess., 239-40; *Cong. Globe*, 23 Cong., 2 Sess., 151.

Remark in Senate, January 23, 1835. Announces that on Monday next he will move that the Senate "settle at once the executive business before them" whether there are members absent or not. *Register of Debates*, 23 Cong., 2 Sess., 241.

Remark in Senate, January 26, 1835. Moves adjournment at 4:00 p.m., since the reading of the report from the Committee on the Post Office and Post Roads has not been completed, and since a minority report on it is expected. *Register of Debates*, 23 Cong., 2 Sess., 244. The reading of the majority (Whig) report and the minority (Democratic) report on the Post Office bill continued the following day [Remark in Senate, January 27, 1835].

Remark in Senate, January 27, 1835. Urges that the bill to reorganize the Post Office [Remark in Senate, January 26, 1835] be printed at once. Notes that objections to its immediate recommitment to the Post Office Committee for possible amendment, as promised by Sen. Felix Grundy (Tenn.), would not be so strong were members of the Senate at least given an opportunity to examine its provisions in print. *Register of Debates*, 23 Cong., 2 Sess., 245; *Cong. Globe*, 23 Cong., 2 Sess., 169. For the committee's minority report on the Post Office reorganization bill, see *Sen. Docs.*, 23 Cong., 2 Sess., no. 86, pp. 90-119; for the majority report, see *ibid.*, pp. 1-89. The bill passed the Senate on February 10, 1835, and was received by the House the same day. It was tabled in the House on February 13. On February 14, however, the House voted to print copies of the Senate Post Office Committee's majority and minority reports and their accompanying documents. *Register of Debates*, 23 Cong., 2 Sess., 392, 1351, 1391.

Comment in Senate, January 28, 1835. Speaks to resolutions by the Alabama state legislature instructing the state's U.S. senators, William R. King and Gabriel Moore, to employ "their untiring efforts to cause to be expunged [Remark in Senate, June 30, 1834] from the journals on the Senate" the resolution censuring Jackson [Speech in Senate, December 26, 1833; Remark in Senate, March 28, 1834] for his removal of the deposits [Bradley to Clay, October 16, 1832]. Asks King if he plans to submit a formal resolution to the Senate to expunge. If he does, Clay promises to "resist such unconstitutional procedure as the reception of these resolutions, without the expressed wish of the Legislature of Alabama." Hopes King will withdraw Alabama's resolutions "for the present" so that the Senate can continue debate on the important Post Office reorganization bill [Remark in Senate, January 27, 1835]. Following King's refusal to withdraw the Alabama resolutions, because of his certainty that the Alabama state legislature had clearly instructed him to present them, Clay resolves that the Alabama resolutions "not be acted upon by the Senate, nor contain any request that they be laid before the Senate," because to act upon them "cannot be done without violating the constitution of the United States." *Register of Debates*, 23 Cong., 2 Sess., 253, 255-57, 264, 266.

From James Madison, "Montpelier," Va., January 31, 1835. Thanks Clay for the copy "of your Report on our Relations with France [Remark in Senate, January 6, 1835]," and describes the document "as able in its execution, as it is laudable in its object of avoiding war without incurring dishonor." Fears, however, that a danger lurks "under the conflicting grounds taken on the two sides; that taken by the message [Clay to Henry Clay, Jr., Early December, 1834], and by the Report also in a softened tone, that the Treaty is binding on France and is in no event to be touched; and the ground taken or likely to be taken by France, with feelings roused by the peremptory alternative of compliance or self redress, that the Treaty is not binding on her; appealing for the fact, to the structure of her government which all nations treating with her are presumed and bound to understand." Feels, further, that "War is the more to be avoided, if it can be done without inadmissible sacrifices, as a maritime war to which the United States should be a party and Great Britain neutral, has no aspect which is not of an ominous cast. Enforce the belligerent rights of search and seizure against British ships, and it would be a miracle if serious collisions did not ensue. Allow them the rule of 'free ships free goods' and the flag covers the property of France and enables her to employ all her naval resources against us." Adds that France has at present an "advantage over us in the extent of public ships now, or that may immediately be brought into service, whilst the privilege of the neutral flag would deprive us of the cheap and efficient aid of privateers." LS. DLC-HC (DNA, M212, R5). Printed in *James Madison, Letters and Other Writings* . . . , 4:374-75; and Colton, *Clay Correspondence*, 4:388-89.

Remark in Senate, February 2, 1835. Presents a petition from the inhabitants of Louisville asking Congress to purchase stock in the Louisville and Portland Canal [4:33]. *Cong. Globe*, 23 Cong., 2 Sess., 183.

Remark in Senate, February 3, 1835. Says that "until some movement should be made" on the expunging resolutions of the Alabama legislature [Comment in Senate, January 28, 1835], it is not his wish that the Senate act upon them in any way. *Cong. Globe*, 23 Cong., 1 Sess., 189.

To Henry Shaw, February 4, 1835. Expresses confidence in Shaw's "continued friendship." Adds: "I regret extremely to hear of the distractions which you describe as prevailing among the Whigs in Massachusetts & sincerely hope that they may be finally brought to harmonize together." ALS. ViU. Written from Senate Chamber. Whigs in the Massachusetts legislature were in the process of choosing a U.S. senator to replace Nathaniel Silsbee. By mid-January, 1835, Gov. John Davis and Congressman John Q. Adams had become the leading contenders; however, Henry Shaw and Edward Everett, among others, were favored by some. On January 28, 1835, the state house of representatives nominated Davis, but the state senate on February 10 nominated Adams. Davis eventually won the seat. Also causing controversy among Massachusetts Whigs at this time was Daniel Webster's nomination for the presidency by the state legislature on January 21. Some Whigs in that state still supported Clay, while others hoped that some other nationally popular Whig candidate would emerge. Both of these groups had fought Webster's nomination. Wiltse, *Webster Papers*, 4:4-5, 8-9, 11-17, 21, 24, 26-29.

Speech in Senate, February 4, 1835. Presents to the Senate a memorial to Congress from a council of the Cherokees held at Running Waters. Explains that the council represents the wishes of a portion of the Cherokee Nation which is estimated to number in all 15,000 members, some 9,000 of whom still reside in Georgia, the remainder in Alabama, Tennessee, and North Carolina. Points out that "a respectable but also an inconsiderable portion" of them now contemplate voluntary emigration to the West [Fendall to Clay, August 27, 1832] and are asking that the United States assist them in doing so. Traces at considerable length the history of U.S. treaty relations with the Cherokee Nation, pointing out the frequent violations of the treaties by the government. Notes also the scope and operation of the discriminatory legal codes, especially Georgia's, that have systematically stripped the Cherokees of their lands. Compares the present-day social and economic condition of the Cherokee with that of the African slave in the South, to the distinct advantage of the latter. At the behest of the Running Waters council, offers two resolutions: first, to open federal courts to the Cherokees so that they might more effectively protect those of their treaty rights relating to the use and occupancy of their lands; second, to set aside additional land west of the Mississippi to accommodate those Cherokees who seek voluntarily to migrate westward. Asks that the first resolution be submitted to the Judiciary Committee for study and recommendation and the second to the Committee on Indian Affairs. *Register of Debates*, 23 Cong., 2 Sess, 289-300; *Cong. Globe*, 23 Cong., 2 Sess., 195-96, 200. Printed in Colton, *Clay Correspondence*, 5:637-56. The memorial was referred to the Committee on Indian Affairs. On February 5, 1835, Clay's resolutions passed the Senate. They were not taken up by the House; although, the Cherokee memorial had also been presented to the House on January 19 by Edward Everett. *Register of Debates*, 23 Cong., 2 Sess., 1008-10; *Cong. Globe*, 23 Cong., 2 Sess., 138-39, 200. The council at Running Waters had been held for three days, beginning November 27, 1834, and had been attended by only eighty-three Indians who represented the Treaty party, a minority group which viewed removal to the West as inevitable and wished to make a treaty with the United States government on the best terms possible. Elias Boudinot, a Cherokee educated in Connecticut, was chosen as chairman of the council, and a committee was appointed to draft resolutions expressing the views of the group "in regard to the present condition and future prospects of the Cherokee people." John Ridge was largely responsible for drafting both the resolutions and the memorial which was signed by fifty-seven Cherokees. Wilkins, *Cherokee Tragedy*, 255-56. For the split among the Cherokees between those who opposed removal and those who felt it was in their own best interest, see *ibid.*, 207-303.

Comment in Senate, February 5, 1835. Opposes an amendment to the Post Office bill [Remark in Senate, January 27, 1835], offered by Sen. Felix Grundy, that would permit the postmaster general to make "extra allowances" to contractors to "more than double the amoung of postage accruing on the route." Thinks granting this discretionary power to the postmaster general would be productive of monopoly practices and corruption. *Register of Debates*, 23 Cong., 2 Sess., 316-18; *Cong. Globe*, 23 Cong., 2 Sess., 201. William T. Barry (Ky.) was Jackson's postmaster general until May 1, 1835. He was succeeded by Amos Kendall (Ky.).

Remark in Senate, February 6, 1835. Moves that the motion to purchase "certain pictures now in this city, for the President's house," defeated 22 to 20, be reconsidered. Motion tabled. *Cong. Globe*, 23 Cong., 2 Sess., 207. See also *Register of Debates*, 23 Cong., 2 Sess., 312-13.

Speech in Senate, February 11, 1835. Announces he will vote for the $350,000 called for in the Cumberland Road bill [2:188; 4:19-32], because the road needs repairs. Not to do so would cause the road to be abandoned and previous expenditures on it thus wasted. Defends the constitutionality of the bill and of internal improvements in general. Believes also that empowering the federal government to erect tollgates on the road, for the purpose of maintaining the road, is "fitting and suitable" and constitutional. "If the power to make a road were conceded, it followed, as a legitimate consequence from that power, that the general Government had a right to preserve it." Does not, therefore, like the stipulation in this legislation which holds that once the federal government has completely repaired the road it would then be turned over to the states through which it passes for future operation and maintenance. Sees the Cumberland Road as "a great national object" in which all the American people are interested. It should remain under the "guardianship of the general Government." It "ought not to be treacherously parted from it, and put into the hands of the local Governments who felt no interest in the matter." Casts his vote for this bill "very reluctantly." *Register of Debates*, 23 Cong., 2 Sess., 409-12; *Cong. Globe*, 23 Cong., 2 Sess., 228. Printed in Colton, *Clay Correspondence*, 6:7-10.

Comment in Senate, February 14, 1835. Refers to his attempt in the previous session to control, by means of four resolutions [Speech in Senate, March 7, 1834; Clay to Tazewell, April 5, 1834], the president's power to remove public officials from office without senate approval. If the president has such power, then the constitution is "not worth' a sous." Argues that the constitution nowhere confers upon the president the power of removal either expressly or as an inherent power. Offers an amendment to the second section of the bill now under discussion which relates to the president's power of appointment. The amendment proposes that any official appointed by the president with the advice and consent of the Senate may be removed by the president only by the same advice and consent; and that if a removal takes place when the Senate is not in session the president must submit that act of removal to the Senate for its approval or rejection "during the first month of the succeeding session." *Register of Debates*, 23 Cong., 2 Sess., 454-55; *Cong. Globe*, 23 Cong., 2 Sess., 243. Clay's major speech in this session on the removal issue was delivered on February 18. He was speaking here to a bill to repeal the first and second sections of an 1820 "Act to limit the term of office of certain offices therein named [3 *U.S. Stat.*, 582]." Section 1 of this act [Speech in Senate, February 18, 1835] specified the offices to which persons could be appointed for a period of four years, but who "shall be removeable from office at pleasure." Section 2 provided that the commissions for these offices would expire four years from the dates they were granted. This bill to repeal the first two sections of the act of 1820 was suggested in a report of a select committee on executive patronage and brought before the Senate on February 13. It passed the Senate on February 21 by a vote of 31 to 16. When it was brought up in the House, consideration of it was postponed on February 25, and it did not come up again during the session. *Register of Debates*, 23 Cong., 2 Sess., 418-71, 576, Appendix, 219-31; U.S. Sen., *Journal*, 23 Cong., 2 Sess., 178. For Clay's resolutions on the same issue at the previous session, see *Register of Debates*, 23 Cong., 1 Sess., 836.

To ENOCH COBB WINES   Washington, February 16, 1835

Prior to the receipt of your letter dated the 12h. instant, I had received and answered a letter from my son [John Morrison Clay] on the subject of it. But I did not understand his affair had proceeded so far as to occasion his dismission. I requested him to shew you my answer, from which you will perceive that I took nearly the same view of his conduct that you have done.

On one point only I differ with you, that is as to the public apology before the whole school [Edgehill Seminary].[1] I should think, considering the offense and his youth, an apology to Mr. Grundy for the disrespectful contradiction, and an apology to you for violating the rules of order prescribed for the Government of your school ought to be deemed sufficient. Such apologies would soon be known to the whole school; and they would produce all good effect. A public confession of his error, in presence of the whole school, would exhibit him in a mortifying attitude, which would wound intensely the sensibility of any boy and might have a permanent injurious operation upon his future life. Would it not also be a punishment a little disproportionate to the offence?

I know not whether the matter admits now of any accommodation. I should hope it did; but I cannot expect or desire John to remain at Edgehill contrary to your own sense of the interests of the institution.[2]

I shall be glad to hear from him and from you what effect has been produced on his mind by my letter and subsequent reflection.

I take it for granted that John remains in your family under your care until the matter is finally disposed of.

I shall await, with deep anxiety, further information from you and him.

ALS. DLC-HC (DNA, M212, R5).   1. Clay to Lieber, Dec. 3, 1834.   2. He was not expelled. See Clay to Lucretia Hart Clay, March 4, 1835.

Comment in Senate, February 17, 1835. Speaks on the election of a printer for the Senate, and to the growth of the amount of government printing and the expense thereof. States that the reason for the rising cost is "attributal to the abuses of the administration," and that the attempt of the Jacksonians to cover up their abuses in the Post Office and elsewhere "was the cause of the great mass of printing; and the misfortune was that the increased printing could not keep up with the increased abuses." Says, further, that he prefers not to elect a printer for the Senate until the House has chosen its printer. *Register of Debates*, 23 Cong., 2 Sess., 492, 494-95; *Cong. Globe*, 23 Cong., 2 Sess., 255. After seventeen ballots, Gales and Seaton were chosen as the Senate's printer on February 28, 1835, defeating Blair and Rives by 27 to 14. The House voted down a motion on February 25, 1835, to name a printer. They did not choose a printer until the next session when on December 8, 1835, they chose Francis P. Blair and John C. Rives. U.S. Sen., *Journal*, 23 Cong., 2 Sess., 205; *Cong. Globe*, 23 Cong., 2 Sess., 256; *Register of Debates*, 23 Cong., 2 Sess., 1496; U.S. H. of Reps., *Journal*, 24 Cong., 1 Sess., 10.

Speech in Senate, February 18, 1835. Presents an extended and detailed criticism of "the vast expansion of executive power" wrought primarily by President Jackson's patronage policies. Sees the imminent breakdown of checks-and-balances government unless something is done to curb Jackson's power. Claims that the basis of the president's rapidly growing power "is the power of dismission," and argues that such power can best be controlled by requiring that presidential dismissals of civil servants receive the advice and consent of the Senate. Repeats the constitutional arguments outlined in his recent comment in the Senate [Comment in Senate, February 14, 1835], noting that Jackson's dismissals have been based on powers said to be inherent in the Constitution. Asserts that the notion of "inherent power" is merely "a new principle to enlarge the powers of the government," and insists that the "power of removal from office" is not "one of those powers which are expressly granted and enumerated in the constitution." Concludes that since the constitution gives to Congress the power "to make all laws which shall be necessary and proper for carrying into execution the foregoing powers," Congress is therefore the "sole depository of implied power" if such power can be applied to dismission. On the other hand, "if the power of dismission be incident to the legislative authority, Congress has the clear right to regulate it." Either way, the president does not have the absolute power of dismissal. Traces at length the history of the issue and problem of dismissals since 1789, and notes various precedents laid down along the way. Concludes by offering an amendment [Comment in Senate, February 14, 1835] to the second section of the bill to repeal sections one and two of the act of 1820 "commonly called the four years' law." This amendment, which is "substantially the same proposition as one which I submitted to the consideration of the Senate at its last session [Speech in Senate, March 7, 1834]" would require the advice and consent of the Senate in cases of executive dismissal and protect this function while the Senate is recessed. Announces his willingness to vote for the bill with or without the amendment he proposes. *Register of Debates*, 23 Cong., 2 Sess., 513-24; *Cong. Globe*, 23 Cong., 2 Sess., 260-61. Printed in Colton, *Clay Correspondence*, 6:11-26.

To HENRY CLAY, JR.   Washington, February 19, 1835
I recd. a letter from James [Brown Clay], and since one from you informing me of the birth of a daughter [Matilda] from Julia. I congratulate you on the event. It is a great addition to your previous ample means of happiness and I sincerely pray that Julia and you both may justly appreciate it.

I wrote to my friend Mr. [John Jacob] Astor to know if I should want $15 or 20 thousand dollars in the Spring if he could supply me at six per Cent int. upon the most perfect security. He informs me by letter, this day recd,[1] that he can furnish it to me upon 4 or 5 days notice. Should we desire it therefore in the Spring I will obtain it.

I have a strong impression that from the operation of the local banks established and establishing real estate will rise. If Mr. [John W.] Hunt has not sold the [Joseph] Logan farm, and you feel disposed I will unite with you in the purchase of it at the price he proposed last fall.[2]

I am truly sick of Congress.

Give my love to Julia and kiss my dear Grand children.

ALS. Henry Clay Memorial Foundation, Lexington, Ky.   1. Astor to Clay, Feb. 16, 1835. Copy. MH. On April 27, 1835, Henry Clay, Jr., gave bond to his father for $7,500 which he was borrowing from a sum of $20,000 which Clay had in turn borrowed from Astor on March 1, 1835. The Astor loan was for a four-year period at 6 percent interest payable semi-annually. Henry Clay, Jr., promised to pay his father the $7,500 principal on May 1, 1839, and to pay the interest on it regularly in the meantime. DS. DLC-TJC (DNA, M212, R10).   2. On April 30, 1835, Clay entered into an agreement with John W. Hunt and Richard A. Curd, trustees of Joseph Logan, to purchase a tract of land for the sum of $40 per acre. ADS. KyLxT.

Remark in Senate, February 20, 1835. Moves to table a resolution calling for an amendment to the constitution that would permit the overriding of a presidential veto by majority vote. Feels it is too late in the session for such a measure to receive proper consideration. Moves also to table a bill to which he was "disposed to feel favorably," authorizing three branches of the U.S. Mint, now located in Philadelphia, unless it can be taken up right away. Thinks much more information and discussion of the issue is needed. The branches were to be established in New Orleans, La.; Charlotte, N.C.; and Dahlonega, Ga.; and would cost some "half a million annually and in perpetuity" to operate. *Register of Debates*, 23 Cong., 2 Sess., 551-52; *Cong. Globe*, 23 Cong., 2 Sess., 270. The *Cong. Globe's* version of Clay's remarks treats his stance as opposition to the mint-branching bill partly because the measure would add to the "danger and extent of executive patronage." The bill to establish three branches of the U.S. Mint was passed by the Senate on February 24, 1835, by the vote of 24 to 19. Clay voted against it. It was passed by the House on March 3 by the vote of 115 to 60 and was signed by the president the same day. U.S. Sen., *Journal*, 23 Cong., 2 Sess., 188; U.S. H. of Reps., *Journal*, 23 Cong., 2 Sess., 512, 524-26. For the act, see 4 *U.S. Stat.*, 774-75.

Remark in Senate, February 21, 1835. Moves the indefinite postponement of the bill to authorize three branches of the U.S. Mint [Remark in Senate, February 20, 1835]. Says the mint in Philadelphia is fully capable of handling the coinage needs of the nation. Failing in this motion, moves variously and unsuccessfully to postpone consideration of the bill until February 23, to add a branch mint in Louisville to its provisions, to establish one branch only and to amend into its substantial reductions of the projected salaries to be paid employees of the proposed branches. *Register of Debates*, 23 Cong., 2 Sess., 576, 580-81; *Cong. Globe*, 23 Cong., 2 Sess., 276.

Later this day, Clay sharply condemns a rumor linking Sen. George Poindexter (Miss.) to the attempt by one Richard Lawrence on Janaury 30, 1835, to assassinate President Jackson. Calls for a select committee of five to investigate the allegation. *Register of Debates*, 23 Cong., 2 Sess., 582-83; *Cong. Globe*, 23 Cong., 2 Sess., 277. The story of the assassination attempt by the deranged Lawrence, and the alleged Poindexter complicity in it, is in Bowers, *Party Battles of the Jackson Period*, 376-82; see also James, *Andrew Jackson*, 390-91. On March 2 the select committee reported that there was "not a shade of suspicion" that Poindexter "was in any way concerned, directly or indirectly" with Lawrence's assassination attempt. Report adopted by unanimous vote. *Register of Debates*, 23 Cong., 2 Sess., 714.

Speech in Senate, February 23, 1835. Speaks to the bill to consolidate into one circuit the U.S. Circuit Court for New Jersey and Pennsylvania, and that for Delaware and Maryland. Observes that the "new States" are not on the same footing as the original "old States" with regard to the convenience of access to federal district courts. Thinks they should be. Favors this particular bill, however, on grounds of economy. Also, has no objection to increasing the number of U.S. Supreme Court judges, but argues that such judges should be drawn "from all parts of the country, so that they might imbody among them the feelings and sympathies of the people at large." *Register of Debates*, 23 Cong., 2 Sess., 592-93. This bill was amended and recommitted by the Senate on February 23, 1835; in the House it was amended but laid aside on March 3. *Ibid.*, 584-94, 614, 1645-46, 1655.

Comment in Senate, February 24, 1835. Counters the argument that three branch mints [Remark in Senate, February 20, 1835] are needed to reduce the cost of transporting the gold bullion, unloaded at various Atlantic-coast ports, to the mint in Philadelphia. Does not believe that the presumed savings in transportation costs to Philadelphia of gold imported at New Orleans or gold mined in North Carolina will exceed the costs of establishing and staffing the branch mints. Can see no point, save to discomfit the Cherokees, in putting one of the proposed branches in Dahlonega, Ga., "A place which had no existence a few years ago," and one which also legally remains Cherokee under treaty with the United States. Admonishes Calhoun, a Southern proponent of the bill, for introducing sectional arguments into the debate since the issue is basically not sectional. Speaks to the question, raised by Calhoun, of economy in government operations, noting that the costs of fixed coastal fortifications are excessive. Supports "our floating fortifications — the navy — and thought all others ought to be auxiliary to it." Argues that the need for coastal fortifications, as they had existed at the end of the War of 1812, is much reduced. Points out that England, now that Bonaparte's France had been defeated, has "reduced her fortifications and armaments, as unnecessary to be kept up." Hopes "that our own, too, would be unnecessary." Urges that the bill to establish branch mints be returned to committee. *Register of Debates*, 23 Cong., 2 Sess., 603-4, 607-9, 611-13. Motion to recommit failed, 22 to 21; motion to pass carried 24 to 19. *Ibid.*, 613.

Remark in Senate, February 25, 1835. Moves to table an amendment to the bill applying 2 percent of proceeds of sale of public lands in Alabama ("reserved for purpose of making roads to Alabama"), to constructing instead a railroad from the Tennessee River to Mobile Bay. Thinks more information is needed on such a project and that the amendment is therefore "premature." Motion to table adopted. *Register of Debates*, 23 Cong., 2 Sess., 615-16. Section 5, part 3 of the 1819 act authorizing the people of the Alabama Territory to form a constitution and state government and enter the Union, provided that 5 percent of the subsequent proceeds of the sale of public lands in Alabama be applied to the building of public roads and canals, and to the improvement of navigation on the rivers. Of the sum authorized, three-fifths was to be spent in the state, and two-fifths, or 2 percent, on the building of roads leading to the borders of the state. 3 *U.S. Stat.*, 489-92. For the history of this legislation, which was tabled on February 25, 1835, see *Register of Debates*, 23 Cong., 2 Sess., 224-33, 615-16; see also Hibbard, *A History of the Public Land Policies*, 85.

Later this day, Clay declares he will vote for legislation granting funds to Washington, Alexandria, and Georgetown to enable them to make payments on the Dutch loan with which they purchased canal stock [Remark in Senate, June 26, 1834]; hopes, however, that the federal government will eventually buy up the stock and "assume the whole foreign debt." *Register of Debates*, 23 Cong., 2 Sess., 618.

Remark in Senate, February 27, 1835. Opposes bill granting additional public lands in satisfaction of unlocated Virginia military bounty land warrants. Says that the number of acres appropriated is not likely to satisfy all the claims. Explains that the great increase in Revolutionary War claims stems from the fact that since the passage of the act of 1830 [Clay to Leigh, August 24, 1834] "they have found in the attic story of the Capitol a large mass of revolutionary papers, out of which the greater part of these claims have sprung." While there "seems to be no end of these claims," he will nonetheless vote for 550,000 acres, provided it is "to be the last." *Register of Debates*, 23 Cong., 2 Sess., 689. The bill, "granting an additional quantity of land, for the satisfaction of revolutionary bounty land warrants (Virginia)," passed the U.S. Senate on March 2, 1835, as an amendment to the general appropriation bill and was approved by the House on March 3. U.S. Sen., *Journal*, 23 Cong., 2 Sess., 215; *Register of Debates*, 23 Cong., 2 Sess., 1644; 4 *U.S. Stat.*, 760-72.

Remark in Senate, February 28, 1835. Since the House has unexpectedly delayed choosing its printer [Comment in Senate, February 17, 1835], he will no longer oppose Senate election of its own printer. *Register of Debates*, 23 Cong., 2 Sess., 693, 697-98; *Cong. Globe*, 23 Cong., 2 Sess., 308.

From James Brown, Philadelphia, March 2 [1835]. Reports that he has been "so weak that I could not write," and that he "can hardly hope ever to regain, *good health —*" Remarks that from a financial standpoint he has decided "not to leave all my '*eggs* in one *basket*' and that it would be wise to draw to the north, either here or in Kentucky, a portion of them where they could be invested under the guidance of the Counsels of yourself and my good brother [John Brown]." Adds that "Louisiana is filled with bold speculation and it must require great caution to avoid danger of loss — Besides I fear our governments here and at Paris may bring on a war [Brown to Clay, January 24, 1832; Remark in Senate, January 6, 1835; Speech in Senate, January 14, 1835] or some crisis" detrimental to business. Asks Clay to advise him on these financial matters. ALS. DLC-TJC (DNA, M212, R10).

Comment in Senate, March 2, 1835. Supports Webster's amendment to the general appropriation bill striking out the appropriation for any U.S. minister to Great Britain [Clay to Brooke, May 1, 1831] appointed during recess of the Senate. Notes that the president has placed in nomination no name for the post, and warns him not to make a recess appointment. Discusses qualifications which the eventual nominee should have. *Register of Debates*, 23 Cong., 2 Sess., 701-2.

Says, later, he will "not vote an additional cent" for the president's diplomatic contingency fund, for fear that Jackson will misuse it by financing the recess appointment of a minister to England. Continues his criticism of Jackson's failure to nominate a minister to Great Britain while the Senate is in session. *Ibid.*, 705-6.

Adds, still later in this debate, that it is too near the hour of adjournment to expect the president to make a nomination, especially since he surely wants the opportunity to make a recess appointment of a minister to Great Britain as he had in 1831. Only by supporting an amendment denying a salary and outfit to such an appointee can Jackson's instincts in the matter be curbed. Therefore extolls Webster's motion to provide no outfit or salary to any minister not appointed by and with the advice and consent of the Senate. *Ibid.*, 711-13. This amendment became a part of the appropriation act for civil and diplomatic services of government. See 4 *U.S. Stat.*, 768.

Remark in Senate, March 3, 1835. Moves to table the president's veto [*MPP*, 3:146] of a bill which authorizes the secretary of the treasury "to compromise the claims allowed by the commissioners under the treaty [Parry, *Treaty Series*, 83:12-15] with the King of the Two Sicilies [Ferdinand II], concluded October 14, 1832." *Cong. Globe*, 23 Cong., 2 Sess., 326. The legislative history of the vetoed bill can be traced in *ibid.*, 232, 300, 309.

Also submits a report from the Committee on Foreign Relations on the president's message of February 25. In this message [U.S. Sen., *Journal*, 23 Cong., 2 Sess., 194] Jackson transmitted to the Senate copies of all correspondence between the U.S. and French governments since February 6. In this message he noted that he deemed it his duty "to instruct Mr. [Edward] Livingston to quit France with his legation, and return to the United States, if an appropriation for the fulfillment of the convention [Brown to Clay, January 24, 1832; Speech in Senate, January 14, 1835] shall be refused by the Chambers." Report tabled and ordered printed. *Register of Debates*, 23 Cong., 2 Sess., 722.

During the evening session of this date, Clay urges his colleagues to stand by the amendment to the civil and diplomatic appropriation bill [Remark in Senate, March 2, 1835] denying salary and outfit to any minister to Great Britain appointed by Jackson during the coming Senate recess. Argues that such an appointment, made without the advice and consent of the Senate, would be unconstitutional. Urges the Senate's conference committee to stand firm on this amendment when it meets with the House conference committee. Accepts appointment to the former. *Ibid.*, 729-30.

Later in the evening, opposes an amendment to the House version of the Fortifications bill which would provide an additional $3,000,000 for the army and navy to be spent "in whole or in part, under the direction of the President of the United States." Argues that this would place money in Jackson's hands "without any specification whatever of objects." Points out that such an appropriation, "without a specification," had not been made since the "origin of this Government." Opposes placing such undesignated funds in the hands of the president, expecially since there was not "the slightest intimation or prospect of a war." If there is to be a war "it would be a war of our own making — a war to be declared by this country." Specifically, sees no serious threat now of a war with France on the claims issue [Remark in Senate, January 6, 1835; Speech in Senate, January 14, 1835]. Holds, however, that the appearance of preparation for war "might lead to war," because it would "keep up the excitement abroad, and prevent an early settlement of our claims" against France. *Ibid.*, 733-34. The amendment was defeated 29 to 19. *Ibid.*, 738; *Cong. Globe*, 23 Cong., 2 Sess., 326.

To NICHOLAS BIDDLE
Washington, March 4, 1835

I recd. your favor of the 1st. I have understood that the uncommunicated Note of Mr. Serrurier [*sic*, Louis B.C. Serurier], to which you refer,[1] purported to be in conformity with the orders of his Government, but that exception has been taken to some expressions of Mr S not contained in the dispatch of Count de Rigny.[2] I would make a call for it, as suggested, but from an apprehension that it would be refused.

I made yesterday a short report to the Senate on our French affairs, which you will see in the papers.[3] Its tendency is pacific. I think it very fortunate, should the bill be rejected,[4] that Congress has adjourned, without information of that event. There will be time to cool, and for the operation of reason. If there should be a simple rejection of the bill, (which I hope will not be the case) at another Session, the President will find it difficult to goad his party into War.

The closing scenes in the H of R. were very descretable.[5] You will hear of them with mortification, through your members.

My desire to rejoin my family will prevent my returning by Philadelphia.

ALS. DLC-Nicholas Biddle Papers (DNA, M212, R20). Letter marked "(Private)."   1. Biddle wrote Clay on March 1, 1835, saying that Serurier "would be very glad" to have the note published and that he denies there is anything in the note "offensive to Congress or to the nation." Suggests that Clay call for the note from the executive. Adds that Serurier "has looked to you as the statesman best qualified to settle this embarrassing question, as you have settled so many others of vital importance to the country." Copy. DLC-Nicholas Biddle Papers, vol. 5, Supp. Roll 2; AL, draft in Nicholas Biddle Papers (DNA, M212, R20).   2. On Feb. 23, 1835, Serurier wrote Secretary of State Forsyth a note defending the policies of France. It contained a phrase which Forsyth interpreted as an attack upon the integrity of the president, believing it conveyed the "idea that the Chief Magistrate knows or believes that he is in error, and acting upon this known error seeks to impose it upon Congress and the world as truth." McLemore, *Franco-American Diplomatic Relations*, 155-57. The note from Rigny notifying Serurier of his recall was published in the Washington *Daily National Intelligencer* on March 10, 1835.   3. For Clay's report on French affairs, see *Register of Debates*, 23 Cong., 2 Sess., Appendix, 271-72. It was published in the Washington *Daily National Intelligencer* on March 16, 1835.   4. The French Chamber of Deputies began debating the indemnity law on April 9, 1835; and on April 18, by a vote of 289 to 137, they passed the bill with the payment contingent upon an apology or explanation from President Jackson. The news of this action reached the United States on May 26. McLemore, *Franco-American Diplomatic Relations*, 160; Hatcher, *Edward Livingston*, 445-47.   5. The last day of the session was virtually wasted in the House with debates on many topics but little action on any. See *Cong. Globe*, 23 Cong., 2 Sess., 327-32.

To LUCRETIA HART CLAY   Washington, March 4, 1835

Congress adjourned last night, or rather about 3 O Clock this morning, and I am truly rejoiced at it. I feel to day greatly exhausted. Here, we are apparently in the midst of the Winter. The ground is hard frozen covered with snow and it looks more like January than March. On that account, and being also detained by a cause in the Supreme Court,[1] I shall not get off until Saturday. Judge [Alexander] Porter has concluded to go out with me, and we shall try and get along as comfortably as we can. I have got your Moss Rose, and the Public gardener[2] is to put it up with some other plants. Mrs. B. Smith[3] is out of the City and I am afraid I shall not get the roots of which she had the care. Charles[4] will go to Geo. town for the Tea pots.

Poor John [Morrison Clay] had, I am sure, set his heart so much upon returning home that he will feel very sensibly the present moment, when he knows I will be returning without him. I shall write to him to day and comfort him as much as I can. It is I am convinced better that he should remain. He was unwilling that you should know any thing of his affair with Mr. [Enoch C.] Wines,[5] but I wrote him that I had communicated it, at the same time assuring him that I was persuaded you would be highly pleased, as I was, with his manly settlement of it.

I have not heard for some days from Mr. [James] Brown, and I fear greatly that he cannot long survive.[6]

Since writing the above, the Mail has brought me the enclosed letter from him.[7]

My love to all our children.

ALS. Josephine Simpson Collection, Lexington, Ky.   1. Clay, together with Alexander Porter, argued three cases before the 1835 term of the Supreme Court. They were: *The Mayor,*

Aldermen, & Inhabitants of the City of New Orleans, Plantiffs in error v. Christoval G. DeArmas and Manuel Simon Circullu; The Life & Fire Insurance Company of New York v. Christopher Adams; Edward Livingston, Appellant v. Benjamin Story. 34 Peters 224-36, 571-605, 632-61.   2. James Maher. Biennial Register, 1835, p. 162.   3. Possibly Margaret Bayard Smith.   4. His bodyservant.   5. Clay to Wines, Feb. 16, 1835.   6. Brown to Clay, April 7, 1835.   7. Possibly that of March 2, 1835.

To SAMUEL L. SOUTHARD   Baltimore, March 9, 1835

We reached this City [Baltimore, Md.] at 4 O'Clock in about seven hours after we left Washington. The road generally was firm and not broken through, but its condition is such that you had better get over it as soon as you can. The only fear I have about your journey tomorrow is that you may find the stream on the West side of Bladensburg difficult to pass. One abutment of the bridge had given away, & we had to ford it, but without difficulty. It was however rising.

Mr. [David] Barnum[1] had reserved the President's apartments for you, as he says, yesterday and the day before, and had prepared dinners for your family both days. He promises to reserve them for you tomorrow.

I forgot to hand you the Check, as I had intended, for Mr. [Enoch C.] Wines.[2] I shall put it under cover addressed to you at Barnums.

The respects of the Judge [Alexander Porter] and myself for the Ladies.

ALS. NjP. Written from "Barnum's [Hotel]."   1. DAB.   2. On the same date, March 9, 1835, Clay wrote Southard a note saying, "I enclose a check for $150 which I thank you to pay over to Mr. Wines, for the tuition &c of my son [John Morrison Clay]." ALS. NjP.

From Lewis Tappan, New York, March 24, 1835. Sends Clay "a small work on Slavery by Judge [William] Jay," because "Knowing full well the commanding influence you exert in this nation . . . I feel anxious you should be acquainted with the facts contained in this book." Maintains that "As an abolitionist I will do nothing contrary to the constitution & laws of my country, nor the laws of God. . . . I am not more a friend of the poor slave than of the slave holder. The are both men, & are bound to the judgment bar of God."

Admits that while in Washington in 1813, "I conceived a violent prejudice against you & wrote an article for a leading newspaper, libelling your political & personal character." Regrets "that I penned such an article, & deem it my duty to express that regret to you." Adds that "since that period, I have witnessed, with admiration, your eloquent exertions in behalf of the oppressed, and of the rights of man," and if Clay will fight for "the rights of the negro man with equal zeal and ability I should . . . look upon that act as the most glorious of your eventful & brilliant career." ALS. DLC-HC (DNA, M212, R5). Judge William Jay, son of John Jay, wrote An Inquiry Into the Character and Tendency of the American Colonization and American Anti-Slavery Societies. New York and Boston, 1835. For William Jay, see DAB. For Lewis Tappan, noted abolitionist, see Bertram Wyatt-Brown, Lewis Tappan and the Evangelical War Against Slavery. New York, 1971.

From James Brown, Philadelphia, [April] 7, 1835. Writes that his brother, John Brown, "recommends my paying over my dear wifes [Ann Hart Brown] proportion of the sale of the plantation & real estate & Negroes now in the hands of Mr [James] Erwin to her heirs securing to that amount her proportion of the debts should any arise since the marriage and before her death. I mean her share of all they are entitled to under her Will." Adds that "I believe my life will be short. . . . I write with difficulty— but hereby authorize Mr Erwin to make that payment and arrangement as soon as convenient—" ALS. DLC-HC (DNA, M212, R5). Printed in LHQ, 24:1176. The month "April" has been inserted on the letterhead in a different hand; the letter is endorsed by Clay on verso: "7h. Apr. 1835, the day of his death." It may have been the last letter Brown ever wrote.

On April 19, 1835, Charles Ingersoll wrote Clay that the Philosophical Society of Philadelphia has directed Henry D. Gilpin "to prepare a paper to read before them" on the subject of James Brown's life. Asks Clay's help in collecting materials for this project. ALS. DLC-TJC (DNA, M212, R14).

On April 20,1835, James Brown's brother John wrote Clay that "it would be impossible for me to express how deeply how painfull, my feelings have been excited by" news "of the death of my Dear Brother." Feels he should go to Philadelphia "to take charge of my Brothers affects." Adds that "It is certainly important that his papers shall be carefully preserved & that his private correspondence shall not be exposed." States that although he presumes his brother left a will, he does not know "who he has named Executors." Asks Clay's advice on how to proceed. *Ibid.* (R10). Printed in Colton, *Clay Correspondence*, 4:389-90.

An inventory of James Brown's estate, dated June 1, 1835, is in DLC-TJC (DNA, M212, R17).

To Henry Thompson, Baltimore, April 9, 1835. States that he has received Thompson's request "to subscribe in your name for 200 shares in the Northern Bank of K. and to draw upon you for $1000." Promises to do so, but explains that the stock is eagerly sought and that there will be only "one million reserved for subscription in this State," while "three or four times the quantity" will be sought. Warns "that altho' you may subscribe for 200 shares and advance your money upon them, by the process of equalization you may be cut down to ten shares." Notes that "one million of dollars in the Capital of this Bank has been also sent to Philada. & N. York." Asks Thompson in a postscript to check with Erskine Eichelberger & Co. in Baltimore on "a quantity of Brussells Carpeting" he has ordered. ALS. PHC. The Northern Bank of Kentucky was founded in 1835 by John Wesley Hunt and other Lexington financiers who acquired the assets of the Lexington branch of the Bank of the United States. It became the principal depository of federal funds in Kentucky with Madison C. Johnson as president and William Johnson as cashier. Its main office was at the corner of Short and Market Streets in Lexington. Charles Kerr (ed.), *History of Kentucky*, 5 vols. (Chicago, 1922), 2:129; William C. Mallalieu and Sabri M. Akural, "Kentucky Banks in the Crisis Decade," *RKHS* (October, 1967), 65:294-303.

To SAMUEL L. SOUTHARD   Lexington, April 12, 1835

After my departure from Washington, I was taken ill on he road, and detained at Washington (Pennsa) a day; and I have not been well since my return home, but I am gradually recovering and hope soon to find my health re-established.

I was sorry to learn from your letter recd. a few days ago that you too were in ill health. I hope you will take good care of yourself, and that your health will be completely restored.

I have seen that your fine Speech on the Expunging resolution &c. is published, and that the Report of it presents you fairly and advantageously to the public.[1] It is highly spoken of in this quarter.

In this State, and I learn in Ohio also, the course of our political friends is to take no part in the contest between [Hugh L.] White and Van Buren, at present. The Speaker of the last H. of R. of Ohio[2] was with me yesterday, having come here from a great celebration at Cincinnati.[3] He assured me that that was the course of the Whigs in that State; and he added that Judge Burnett [*sic,* Jacob Burnet] (the right hand man of Judge [John] McLean) told him at Cincinnati that Judge McLean would not be a Candidate, his friends having become convinced that he would not be supported. The Speaker also told me that the movement, in the Judge's behalf, during the last Session of the Legislature,[4] was made, in compliance with the earnest entreaties of his friends, and to test the public feeling and sentiment in regard to him. Judge McLean, may I think be looked upon as entirely hors du combat. Genl [William Henry] Harrison does not seem to be making any rapid advance. He is personally very anxious. No movement for Mr. Webster has yet taken place in the West; and I regret to find that the unfavorable opinion of his prospects entertained by my colleagues, in this section, seems to be too well founded.

Judging from all that I see and hear from the South, particularly in Virginia, Judge White seems to be advancing; but the result of this months elections in that State will probably disclose its political condition.[5]

Judge [Alexander] Porter accompanied me home but did not remain long and I suppose is by this time at his own residence.

We look for our daughter [Anne Brown Clay Erwin] next week. Present Mrs. Clay and myself affectionately to Mrs. Southard & Miss Virginia [Southard], and tell Virginia that we should be both highly pleased if she would make us the promised visit this Spring or Summer.

I presume John [Morrison Clay] is now on his Southern excursion,[6] as I have not lately had a letter from him. P. S. Poor contemptible [Richard] Rush has at last sneaked into a pitiful appointment.[7]

ALS. NjP. 1. *Register of Debates*, 23 Cong., 2 Sess., 660-89. Printed under the title *Speech of Mr. Southard, on the Motion to Expunge from the Journal the Resolution of March 28, 1834. . . . Delivered in the Senate of the United States, February 27, 1835.* Washington, 1835; see also Comment in Senate, January 28, 1835. 2. John M. Creed was speaker *pro tempore.* Weisenburger, *The Life of John McLean*, 90. 3. Probably a reference to the balloon ascension of R. Clayton which took place in Cincinnati on April 8, 1835, from the amphitheater on Court Street. Cincinnati *Advertiser & Ohio Phoenix*, April 1, 11, 1835. After completing several segments of his journey successfully, Clayton ascended for the last time in his balloon, "Star of the West," from Lexington in August. As he passed over "Ashland," Clay's home, he dropped a small dog named "Duffy," with a parachute from the balloon. Clayton's trip came to an abrupt halt on the farm of Thomas A. Jones in Clark Co., Ky., when the top portion of his balloon burst. Clayton, however, was not injured. Lexington *Observer & Kentucky Reporter*, August 26, 1835. 4. In Dec., 1834, the "Democratic Republican" members of the Ohio legislature and others in attendance at the circuit court in Columbus had issued an address recommending McLean for president. The address was signed by 57 legislators and 32 other prominent citizens. Weisenburger, *The Life of John McLean*, 89-91. 5. In the election for the Virginia state legislature 68 who favored Van Buren were chosen, 57 who opposed Van Buren, and 9 who favored White; however, Niles stated that "Many *professing* White men . . . are numbered among the Van Burenites." *Niles' Register* (May 16, 1835), 48:186. In the 1835 congressional election in Virginia, 16 Democrats and 5 Whigs were chosen. *Guide to U.S. Elections*, 564-65. 6. Wines to Clay, May 7, 1835. 7. Rush, along with Gen. Benjamin C. Howard, had been commissioned to settle a boundary dispute between Ohio and Michigan. See Rush article in *DAB* and Powell, *Richard Rush*, 236.

From Nimrod L. Finnell, Lexington, Ky., *ca.* May 1, 1835. Bill and receipt on which an entry for June 19 [1834] reads: ". . . inserting an advt for Bristow (Runaway) $1.00." ADS. DLC-TJC (DNA, M212, R17). Finnell was proprietor of the Lexington *Observer & Kentucky Reporter* newspaper. Collins, *History of Kentucky*, 2:437-38.

From Enoch Cobb Wines, Princeton, N.J., May 7, 1835. Sends Clay a bill for $101.83 for John Morrison Clay's tuition at Edgehill Seminary. Reports that John is "in excellent health & spirits" following a three-week trip to Virginia and that "the teacher who accompanied him informed me that his deportment had been uniformly a model of propriety." Inquires also whether John will continue at the school after the next session and "whether you think of sending either or both of your grandsons [Henry Clay Duralde and Martin Duralde III] to Princeton next session." If so, he will save room for them. ALS. DLC-TJC (DNA, M212, R14). Endorsed by Clay on verso: "Sent a check of the Off. B.U.S. at Lexn. on Philada. for the within bal. 24 June 1835 H.C."

An account for John's expenses and tuition from October 30, 1834, to May 6, 1835, is included. D. *Ibid.*

To Washington Irving, Tarrytown, N.Y., May 9, 1835. Announces that his son, Henry Clay, Jr., with his wife and children, is about to depart on a trip to Europe. Asks him to supply letters of introduction. ALS. RPAB.

Sends a similar letter to Nicholas Biddle, May 9, 1835. ALS. DLC-Nicholas Biddle Papers (DNA, M212, R20).

Also sends a similar letter to Aaron Vail, May 10, 1835. ALS. Courtesy of Mme. Jaque de Bon, Geneva, Switzerland.

From William T. Joynes *et al.*, Washington, Pa., May 16, 1835. Inform Clay that they have elected him an honorary member of the "Clay Institute of Washington College." Add that "We offer you this inadequate testimonial of our esteem, not, we hope, from a spirit of man-worship, but from an honest admiration of your virtues as a Statesman, a philanthropist, and a man." LS. DLC-HC (DNA, M212, R5). Printed in Colton, *Clay Correspondence*, 4:390.

To Charles Ingersoll, Philadelphia, June 11, 1835. Has learned that Ingersoll has been named administrator of James Brown's estate [Brown to Clay, April 7, 1835], and expresses "my entire satisfaction with it." States that Martin Duralde's debt "for which Mr. Brown held his note for $15.000 with Mr. [James] Erwin as endorser is secure [Claiborne to Clay, December 4, 1834]." Suggests that Ingersoll have "a suitable monument" erected "over the bodies of our departed friends," and promises "As the Exor of Mrs. [Anne Hart] Brown, I would pay the proportion of the expence with which her estate may be properly chargeable." Adds that "Mr. Erwin will pay over to me the funds in his hands arising from the sale of the part of the Sugar plantation in Louisiana belonging to Mrs. Brown [Clay to Brown, August 7, 1834]." Anticipates no problems in the settlement of the estate if "Mr. [Isaac Trimble] Preston will acquiesce in" Ingersoll's being the administrator. ALS. KyLxT. Charles Ingersoll, son of Charles Jared Ingersoll, was married to Susan Catherine Brown, the daughter of James Brown's brother Samuel. Isaac T. Preston (1793-1852) was the son of Francis Preston, James Brown's first cousin. He was a leading New Orleans attorney who later became a member of the Louisiana house and a judge of the Louisiana supreme court. He renounced the executorship of James Brown's estate in Pennsylvania on June 15, 1835. See John F. Dorman, *The Prestons of Smithfield and Greenfield in Virginia; Descendants of John and Elizabeth (Patton) Preston Through Five Generations* (Louisville, 1982), 11, 56, 149, 169, 218-220. A summary of James Brown's will is in *ibid.*, 11.

On the same day, June 11, Clay wrote John Brown, in care of Charles Ingersoll at Philadelphia, saying that he was satisfied with Ingersoll's being the administrator of James Brown's estate and that "I am persuaded that in this sentiment the whole of Mrs. Browns heirs will coincide." Agrees "without hesitation, to the payment of $100 to each of the two servants who so faithfully attended your brother." Presumes "Mr. Preston will acquiesce in what had been done in Philada. and decline the Executorship" rather than "create some difficulty as to the Louisiana funds in Mr. Erwin's hands." Suggests that it might be more "convenient for Mr. Erwin to pay over" to Mrs. Brown's heirs, all of whom are in the Lexington neighborhood, the funds in his hands "without their passing through the circuit of Philada." Continues: "I shall be happy to concur in any measures for the speedy and friendly settlement of your brohter's Estate. The other heirs of Mrs. Brown will probably be governed by my opinions, as they have been hitherto." ALS. CtY.

Clay wrote Charles Ingersoll on June 19, 1835, explaining that John Hart, who had owed James Brown $3,000, had died in St. Louis and left no estate. Mentions also that James Erwin could probably have secured the small notes Martin Duralde owed Brown, as he had the large note, if he had known about them. ALS. KyLxT.

On June 27, 1835, Clay again wrote Ingersoll that as far as he and Mrs. Clay were concerned the funds belonging to the Brown estate which were now "in the hands of Mess Thomas Biddle & Co. at an interest of 6 per Cent" can remain there "until regularly administered." However, believes it would not be practicable to obtain the consent

771

of the other heirs to absolve Ingersoll of personal liability "in the extremely improbable contingency of their failure." Recommends, if Ingersoll is afraid "to incur any hazard," that he "withdraw the funds and lend them out on good security, or let them sleep in bank." *Ibid.* Clay wrote Ingersoll on July 7, 1835, giving his opinion that it would be better if the administration of Brown's estate "should not be divided, but all be in your hands." Says he has written Col. Preston that since he is a legatee he would have no right to commissions under the laws of Louisiana if he becomes administrator of the estate there. *Ibid.* On July 9, 1835, Clay sent Ingersoll documents dealing with a legal case Brown had been involved in. *Ibid.* Clay wrote Ingersoll on October 1, 1835, discussing various matters concerning the Brown estate and reporting that John Humphreys had died in Lexington "about six weeks ago." *Ibid.* On April 20 of the following year, 1836, Clay wrote Ingersoll discussing lawsuits concerning the Brown estate. Asks "if there exists now any obstacle in the way of distribution of the funds in your hands belonging to the Estate of Mr. Brown." Notes that James Erwin holds the funds from Brown's part of the sugar plantation. Believes "that the *application* of one or the other of the two funds should be made as soon as convenient." *Ibid.*

Clay again wrote Ingersoll on May 3, 1836, suggesting that it would not "be necessary to reserve from distribution the whole funds" until a case pending against the estate is decided. Instead, suggests that Ingersoll retain enough to pay the settlement if the case is decided against the estate and that he distribute the remainder to the heirs. *Ibid.* Clay wrote Ingersoll on October 1, 1835, discussing various matters concerning the Brown estate and reporting that John Humphreys had died in Lexington "about six weeks ago." *Ibid.*

Ingersoll replied on May 28, 1836, enclosing an inventory of the estate, an account, and two memoranda concerning his administration of the estate. Proposes distributing $10,000 to the heirs and reserving the remainding to be used, if necessary, to meet the settlement of the lawsuit. ALS. DLC-TJC (DNA, M212, R14).

Clay endorsed Ingersoll's plans in a letter of May 31, 1836, but suggested that Ingersoll distribute $15,000 rather than $10,000. ALS. KyLxT.

On June 10, 1836, Clay approved the account sent by Ingersoll on May 28 and authorized "any Counsel, in behalf of Mrs. [Lucretia Hart] Clay and the other heirs of Mrs. [Ann Hart] Brown to sign and approve the said account so as to admit it to be officially passed, received and recorded." *Ibid.*

Clay received a letter of August 1, 1836, concerning property James Brown had owned in northern Louisiana near the Boeuf River and Gallion. The writer, who desired to remain anonymous, informs Clay that Brown had owned two tracts of land, comprising about 4,000 acres, and that the Sheriff of the parish, John Williams, had gotten himself appointed curator of the property and had sold it to his brother-in-law Isaiah Garrett for a mere $500 or $600. Recommends immediate action to stop these illegal proceedings. Copy, extract. CtY.

Clay sent an extract of the August 1 letter to Mason Brown on August 27, saying that he is convinced that the communication is true and, in fact, has confirmed it from a second source. Believes the lands are valuable and suggests that Mason Brown or his father [John] look into the matter. Adds that he is writing a similar letter to Isaac T. Preston. ALS. *Ibid.*

Bedford's Administrators v. Clay, June 12, 1835. Sidney Bedford, a minor, had purchased two slaves, paying the vendors for them with a promissory note. Soon after reaching the age of 18, Bedford died, leaving the slaves to his widow. Clay, the surviving vendor and obligee of the note, brought suit against Bedford's estate arguing that the contract of sale was valid even though Bedford was a minor (not yet 18) when he first executed it, and was not yet 21 when he died. The Kentucky Court of Appeals upheld Clay's contention, awarding him "the amount of the note with accruing interest." D. Printed in James G. Dana, *Reports of Select Cases Decided in the Court of Appeals of Kentucky, During the Year 1835* (Cincinnati, 1835), 3:226-28.

To JOHN M. CABANIS[1]   Lexington, June 12, 1835

I duly recd. your favor of the 31st. Ulto. requesting me to inform you if I entertain a preference for Mr. V. Buren as the Presidential Candidate, and for Col. [Richard M.] Johnson as the Candidate for the V. Presidency.

I feel some mortification that any such enquiry should be thought necessary. I have neither felt nor expressed any such preference. Independent of other objections to Mr. V.B. it would be perfectly decisive against him with me, that he is sought to be forced upon the People by Genl. Jackson.

But it is not to be inferred, that I am, therefore, in favor of Mr. [Hugh L.] White. I think the election of either of them would be a great evil. I desire to see a Whig elected; and I think either Mr. [Daniel] Webster or Genl [William Henry] Harrison is greatly to be prefered to either of the others. Whilst there remains any, the smallest, hope of electing a Whig, I will not consider the alternative of choosing between the two Jackson Candidates. Indeed, if the contest be reduced to that alternative, I shall consider it most unfortunate for the Country, and especially the West. We, in the West, will have brought matters to a lamentable pass, if we are compelled to choose between two gentlemen, both of whom are opposed to those measures of policy in which we feel most particularly interested.

In complying with your request, I write for your own satisfaction, with an express injunction that no public use is to be made of my letter. I hope my friends will not disapprove of the resolution which I have formed not to take any active part in the contest for the Presidential office, whatever form that contest may assume.

ALS. NHi.   1. For Cabanis, see Springfield *Illinois Journal*, Jan. 3, 1849. Clay's spelling appears to be "Cabariess."

From Lewis Tappan, New York, June 22, 1835. Replying to a letter from Clay of June 13 and professing to venerate "many parts of your public character . . . and desiring to bring you to a more favorable consideration of the doctrines and measures of emancipationists," submits "some remarks on the great & absorbing topic of slavery." States that "You say Slavery is admitted by all to be 'wrong on principle,'" and asks, "Have you read governor [George] McDuffie's speech in wh[ich] is a defense of slavery as an element of a republican government? Do you know the fact that some leading newspapers at the South are advocating perpetual slavery as authorized by the Divine being, and necessary in the condition in which we are placed by His providence?" Further, "You intimate that the state of things would be infinitely worse than slavery which would follow an immediate emancipation. . . . Does the history of imc. emancipation show this result? Does it not evince the contrary?" To Clay's statement that due to public opinion "the Abolitionists have been compelled to limit their own principles, & to disclaim contending, in behalf of the slaves, for social equality, and intermarriage with the whites," replies that "the abolitionists have ever disclaimed a desire to promote or witness intermarriages between whites & blacks. . . . We contend for the moral equality of the blacks. They are MEN, and we claim for them to be respected and treated as men." As to why colonization and abolition societies cannot exist harmoniously side by side, argues that colonization societies "soak up public sympathy; & they divert attention from the great evil itself" with the ultimate result of tending "to perpetuate slavery." Adds that some have termed colonization "a safety valve, but it is not so. Slavery is rapidly increasing. Colonization has not, nor will it . . . diminish slavery What is to be done? I answer, emancipate."

Complains that "You deprecate the discussion of this question at the north, say it is considered 'a foreign interference,' that, it is considered the non slaveholding states cannot constitutionally interfere with it." Contends that "the question of slavery is not one affecting merely the local policy of a state, its physical condition, its temporal interests . . . but it is a great moral & political question, one in which every citisen of the U.S. has a deep interest, nay one in which every human being cannot but sympathise & act. Do you not then see, dear Sir, that I cannot be a foreigner to a question of this magnitude, affecting so deeply my fellow citisens, my country, & mankind?"

To Clay's remark that "Public opinion in Europe & America, has exerted, is exerting, & will continue to exert, if not checked, a powerful influence on the condition of slavery," replies that "abolitionists are endeavoring here, as they have done in Europe, to correct public opinion, elevate it, improve it . . . to enlighten the public mind; affect the heart & the conscience of this great nation — and thus to bring about a peaceful abolition of slavery." Asks "Is this unconstitutional, is this meddling with what does not belong to us, is this treason?"

Notes also that "I am truly surprised to read the following sentences from yr pen. 'How much, within our recollection, has the condition of slaves been improved for the better! How much has the vigor of the local laws against them been softened! How quietly have they been elevated in the scale of humanity!' Is it indeed so? Is the condition of the slaves, *in the slave states generally*, meliorated? I have thought the reverse. It is unnecessary to refer you to the laws which have been increasing in vigor; to the domestic slave trade which is far greater & more cruel now than ever before." Thinks Clay must have been referring to his own state "which I am happy to know stands first among the slave states in point of humanity."

Appeals to Clay "as a friend of man, a distinguished champion of liberty, a lover of your country" to consider these remarks. "What a close to a brilliant carreer should you assist the cause of human rights in behalf of the oppressed, downtrodden, & dumb in your own land!" ALS. DLC-HC (DNA, M212, R5). McDuffie's inaugural speech in December, 1834, was published in the Richmond *Enquirer*, January 1, 1835, and as a pamphlet under the title *Governor McDuffie's Message on the Slavery Question*. New York, 1835. For Tappan's own publications on slavery, see Wyatt-Brown, *Lewis Tappan*, 350. See also David Donald, "The Pro-Slavery Argument Reconsidered," *JSH* (February, 1971), 37:3-18; William S. Jenkins, *Pro-Slavery Thought in the Old South*. Chapel Hill, 1935; W.H. and J.H. Pease, *The Anti-Slavery Argument*. New York, 1965.

To DAVID F. CALDWELL   Lexington, June 25, 1835

I have to acknowledge the receipt of your obliging letter of the 30h. Ulto. and to thank you for the account which you transmitted of the Celebration of the Mecklenburg declaration of American Independence.[1] I read it with great interest, and with profound admiration of the patriotism and firmness which led to that perilous declaration, so honorable to your State. And I sincerely hope that the recent commemoration of the event may tend to revive and perpetuate the noble spirit of our Ancestors.[2] God knows it is enough wanted in these days of degeneracy.

You justly remark that the moral sense of the Community is constantly shocked by successive acts of the present Administration. One of the most injurious effects is to render the public callous and indifferent to these enormities, by their repeated perpetration, until the people become gradually prepared for any and every change. Another is, that which you notice, that the public becomes disgusted with the Federal Government itself, and in the end may be willing wholly to dispense with this bond of our union. History records long periods, in the progress of Nations, during which depraved & wicked men obtained the sway, and sometimes they have been finally displacd by the revival of public virtue and public spirit. There is a striking resemblance

774

the means which they practised, during the Civil Wars in England, as depicted by Clarendon,[3] and those now at the head of our affairs and their acts. England, after long and great suffering, finally purified herself. This is my only hope now as to our own Country; but I confess I almost despair of living to witness the regeneration.

I feel grateful for your friendly estimate of the value of my public services. Knowing the rectitude of my intentions, I have in my own bosom abundant cause of private satisfaction; but I deeply regret that my efforts, to awaken the people to the danger of entrusting the management of their affairs to such hands as they have confided them to, have not been attended with more success. . . .

ALS. NcD. Caldwell was a lawyer from Salisbury, N.C., a state legislator, and later a judge of the superior court. A Special Staff of Writers, *History of North Carolina*, 6 vols. (Chicago, 1919), 4:222-23.   1. For a discussion of the controversial Mecklenburg Declaration of Independence of May 20, 1775, and an examination of its authenticity, see Hugh T. Lefler, *North Carolina History Told By Contemporaries* (Chapel Hill, 1948), 99; J.H. Moore, *Defense of the Mecklenburg Declaration of Independence*. Raleigh, 1908; W.H. Hoyt, *The Mecklenburg Declaration of Independence*. New York, 1907.   2. For the Mecklenburg celebration in 1835, see Richmond *Enquirer*, June 9, 1835.   3. Edward Hyde, Earl of Clarendon, *The History of the Rebellion and Civil Wars in England Begun in the Year 1641*. Oxford, 1826.

To FRANCIS T. BROOKE   Lexington, June 27, 1835

I duly received your favor of the 27h. Ulto.   My health is now so good, and I feel so quiet and happy at home, and take such an interest in the varied occupations which I find here, that I think I shall not go to the W. Sulphur Springs this summer. Should it be necessary to change the scene, I must visit some of our local watering places.

When I expressed the sentiment that I did not *yet* despair of the Country, I was far from feeling any encouragement with the existing prospect of public affairs. It can hardly be worse. Blackguards, Bankrupts and Scoundrels, Profligacy and Corruption are the order of the day, and no one can see the time when it will be changed. But the history of the Nation from which we sprung records long periods of misrule and abuse, and subsequent regeneration. What a remarkable resemblance between the present times and those of the English Civil Wars![1] Between the men and the means of that period and that through which we are passing! There is nothing wanting, to complete the paralel, but the Religious fanaticism, and that is supplied by the fanaticism towards Genl. Jackson. England emerged, after great suffering, from her troubles. My hope is that we shall, altho' I confess I hardly expect to live to witness it.

In this State, there is great apathy. There is a positive hatred of Mr. V. Buren, and no attachment to Judge [Hugh L.] White. Mr. Webster does not take. The people appear to be disposed to admire but not to vote for him. I am sorry for it; for I should greatly prefer him to either of the other two. I should regard the election of Mr. V.B. as a great calamity; Judge Whites not quite so great. It seems to me that unless a favorable breeze springs up in Pennsa., or unless there be some other Providential interference, V. B. must be elected. Altho' perhaps a majority of the Whigs would prefer White to him, except in the South, it is a cold heartless preference, which will not prompt any vigorous exertion, and vigorous exertion is necessary to defeat V. B. in most of the Western States. You will see that they have gotten my opinions and my preferences in the papers. But I need not say to you that it is impossible for me to support Mr. V.B. and I care little about White. The truth is I take no part, and mean to take no part in the contest. I think I owe this forbearance to my own character, and to my friends.

The time approaches when I must decide whether I return to the Senate. I have a strong disinclination to go back, and am only solicitous to make a decent retreat. Can I not now do it? If indeed our elections should so terminate as to make the election of a Jackson man probable, I should feel bound to hold on; but if they terminate otherwise, as I anticipate, I think no just reproaches can be made against me for retiring.[2]

What will [Benjamin W.] Leigh do? I know he was disinclined to return; but the new and unpleasant condition of your Legislature may possibly induce him to reconsider his determination.[3]

We have been deluged with rain during the last and the present month. Still our half-worked Crops look better than could have been expected. . . .

ALS. NcD.   1. See C.H. Firth, *Oliver Cromwell and the Rule of the Puritans in England.* London, 1901; Clarendon, *The History of the Rebellion and Civil Wars in England.*   2. In the Kentucky state elections in August, 1835, 22 Whigs and 16 Democrats were elected to the state senate while 61 Whigs and 39 Democrats were elected to the house. For the U.S. House of Representatives, 9 Whigs and 4 Democrats were chosen. *Niles' Register* (Sept. 5, 1835), 49:4.   3. Clay to Southard, April 12, 1835; Clay to Gilmer, Mid-Jan., 1836.

To SAMUEL L. SOUTHARD   Lexington, June 27, 1835

I was glad, my dear Sir, to learn by your letter of the 6h. inst. that your health, altho' it had been bad, has improved and that the health of Mrs. S[outhard]. and Miss Virginia [Southard] is good. I sincerely hope that your's may continue to improve, and that no necessity may arise for your retirement from the Senate. I have not positively decided myself upon returning but whether there or not, I should lament exceedingly the public loss of your services.

If I were to write you fully all my sentiments in respect to the Presidential Candidates, I could not do it better than to transcribe yours exactly and return them. A decided repugnance to Mr. V[an]. B[uren]. no attachment to [Hugh L.] White, and a strong preference for Mr. W[ebster]. without any expectations of his success describe, in a few words, the state of my feelings. I believe too such is the general state of feeling among Western Whigs, except that the disinclination to Mr. Webster is even greater than I apprehended last winter; or rather, I should say, the general conviction, among our friends, is stronger than I supposed it would be, that he stands no chance, and that all exertion for him would be fruitless. If there could be a demonstration given, as you say is thought to be possible, that Pennsa may support him, it might alter the aspect of his prospects in the West. [William Henry] Harrison does not appear to take; and [John] McLean is now scarcely spoken of. I have not seen a man in K. since my return who says he thinks the vote of the State can be given to Mr. W. as things now stand. You know I thought last winter that, by great exertion, he might obtain the vote of the State. Most of my friends in Congress thought otherwise, and I regret to find that they thought more correctly. Still, I believe if there could be a belief that the vote of K. would secure his election, he might obtain it.

Our elections come on in August, and notwithstanding the apathy which prevails, I have seen or heard nothing to induce me to believe that we are in any danger of losing the State.[1] There may be, will be, some changes but the relative strength of parties will not I thin[k] be essentially altered.

You may have been right as to a movement in Virginia last winter, seconded by one in Maryland,[2] for me; but that is now past. And as to myself, my views and wishes have undergone no change, since they were fully disclosed to you last winter.

As to the prospects of [George] Poindexter, about which you enquire, I can give no satisfactory information.[3] He is as far from me, you know, as you are. He will be in Lexington, I am told, in a day or two. I understand that [Hugh L.] White is probably in the ascendancy in Mississippi; and that if they can make the elections turn on the Presidential question, he has a good prospect.[4] But I shall learn from himself, I presume, shortly.

Our friend [Alexander] Porter is in Louisiana, where they appear to enjoy great prosperity. Indeed, this appears to be the general condition of the Country. But is not the advance of prices, in a great measure, the effect of the augmentation of the currency? I think it owing to that cause, and the high price of the great Southern staple. Or, to speak more explicitly, it seems to me that the high price of Cotton, preventing the exportation of specie, enables the Banks freely to issue, and that these issues have puffed up every thing. . . .

ALS. NjP.   1. Clay to Brooke, June 27, 1835.   2. Apparently a proposed presidential movement for Clay which was never launched or became visible.   3. Poindexter's term as U.S. senator had expired in March, 1835, and he had declared he would not be a candidate. However, his name was presented to the Mississippi legislature in January, 1836, along with that of Robert J. Walker and Franklin E. Plummer. Walker was chosen on the fifth ballot, with Pointexter running third. Poindexter moved to Kentucky for a time and then moved back to Mississippi, settling in Jackson. See Edwin A. Miles, "Andrew Jackson and Senator George Poindexter," *JSH* (Feb., 1958), 24:51-66; and "Franklin E. Plummer: Piney Woods Spokesman of the Jacksonian Era," *JMH* (Jan., 1952), 14:1-34.   4. Van Buren carried Mississippi over White in the 1836 presidential election by 9,979 votes to 9,688. Arthur M. Schlesinger, Jr. *et al.* (eds.), *History of American Presidential Elections 1789-1968*, 4 vols. (New York, 1971), 1:640.

From HARRIET MARTINEAU

White Sulphur Springs, Va.
(W. Va.), June 30, 1835

Your frank, w[hic]h overtook me at Cincinnati, was highly acceptable on its own account, as well as for the very delightful letters it enclosed from my mother [Elizabeth Rankin Martineau] & the Furnesses.[1] My mother is in excellent health & spirits, & Mr Furness writes me the happy news that his family will be in the neighbourhood of Boston, & that he will preach there during the month of August, at least.

We enjoyed our ten days' visit at Cin[cinnat]i. very much, & found your kind introductions of eminent service.[2] We staid longer there than we had intended, from finding it impossible to travel at all in the interior of the state. A gentleman escaped out of the mud to his home, at last, after travelling at the rate of one mile an hour;–a process w[hic]h does not suit the taste or convenience of Miss [Louisa] Jeffrey[3] or myself. Our voyage & journey were quite prosperous, & the only disappointment we have met with is the non-arrival of Mr & Mrs Smith.[4] As we see & hear nothing of them, & as the Lorings[5] are obliged to go (by Mr L's physician's advice) to the Hot Springs, where we do not want to go, we have accepted the offer of Mr & Mrs [William] Sullivan[6] of Boston to travel together as far as Harper's Ferry. They have engaged an extra, w[hic]h will afford us plenty of room, & have stipulated to be 8 days on the road, seeing the Natural Bridge & Weir's [*sic*, Weyers] Cave[7] by the way. As we are not in need of imbibing Sulphur & this pretty place is soon understood, we have no hesitation in embracing so very advantageous a plan of travelling, though it takes us away tomorrow—The Lorings flew to meet us on our arrival yesterday, & we find quite a throng of friends here from the Atlantic cities, & c[oul]d make ourselves happy for a month, if we c[oul]d stay so long.—We shall leave our Phila address in the Post Office, in case of the arrival of any letters; but we expect no more from you. I almost hope there may be none, we have given you so much trouble already.

Mr [James] Cal[d]well will be most happy to see you; & in the meanwhile, all has been done to fulfill your request about making us comfortable. We shall never forget how much we owe to yourself & very many of your friends to render our stay in this country happy.[8] We shall always love Mr & Mrs [James] Erwin like near & dear connexions of our own. I hope Mrs [Lucretia] Clay & Mrs [Anne Brown Clay] Erwin are both better. Pray present our respects & love to all your circle, & believe me, dear Sir, ever respectfully & gratefully yours   P.S. Mr Prather[9] has been here a few days, improving *hourly* in health. He requests me to mention the safe arrival of the party, & that they are anxiously looking for Mr & Mrs Smith.—I have been introduced to Mr P. since I wrote the first part of this letter.

I have also been weighed; & find my ponderosity to be lb 116;—within two of Mr Erwin's guess; & Louise weighs 110. So now you know another important circumstance about us. Poor Mrs Loring weighs only lb 85. Mr L's eyes are no better. This P.S. is for Mr Erwin, if you will be kind enough to show it him.—

ALS. DLC-HC (DNA, M212, R5). Printed in Colton, *Clay Correspondence*, 4:390-92.   1. Dr. William Henry Furness, a Unitarian minister in Philadelphia. See R.K. Webb, *Harriet Martineau, A Radical Victorian* (London, 1960), 184.   2. On June 12, 1835, Clay wrote a letter of introduction for Miss Martineau and Miss Jeffrey to William Greene of Cincinnati. ALS. NcD.   3. Her companion.   4. Possibly Mr. & Mrs. Samuel Harrison Smith.   5. Ellis Gray Loring, Boston lawyer and abolitionist. See John Spalding Gatton, "'Mr. Clay & I got stung': Harriet Martineau in Lexington," *The Kentucky Review* (Autumn, 1979), 1:55.   6. Mr. & Mrs. William Sullivan of Boston; mentioned in Jeffrey to Clay, July 19, 1835, but omitted by editors.   7. The Natural Bridge, a geological phenomenon, is in Rockbridge County, near Lexington, Va. Weyers Cave is in Augusta County, south of Harrisonburg, Va. William Stevens, *The Shenandoah and its Byways* (New York, 1941), 103.   8. On June 12, 1835, while staying with the Erwins at "Woodlands," Martineau wrote the Rev. Samuel Gilman and his wife Caroline in Charleston, S.C., describing the Clay family's "mournful domestic history." She noted that "his poor son [Theodore W. Clay] is in a lunatic asylum,—driven there, they think, by the violence of his passions. The second son [Thomas Hart Clay] is a sot, the third [Henry Clay, Jr.] so jealous & irritable in his temper that there is no living with him; & the two lads, (fine boys of 17 [James Brown Clay] & 13 [John Morrison Clay]) give no great promise of steadiness. Mrs Erwin is all that they can desire in a daughter; but she is the only survivor of six daughters [Henrietta, Susan Hart Clay Duralde, Lucretia, Eliza, Laura]; Is it not melancholy?" Gatton, "'Mr. Clay & I got stung': Harriet Martineau in Lexington," 52.   9. Probably Julia Prather Clay's brother William Prather.   Kathleen Jennings, *Louisville's First Families, A Series of Genealogical Sketches* (Louisville, 1920), 37.

To WILLIAM B. ROSE   Lexington, July 4, 1835

I recd. your letter of the 29h. Ulto. and tender you my acknowledgements for the favorable and friendly sentiments towards me which it expresses. On the question of your establishment of a News paper, with the view of recommending me as a suitable Candidate for the office of President, respecting which you ask my opinion, I would say that I cannot venture to advise it. I have throughout [words illeg.] had very little to do with the public press, which I have ever thought ought to be left free and unbiased by any person whose elevation it was proposed to espouse. I cannot now depart from that rule.

Upon reflection, too, you will perceive the improp[r]iety of my making any satisfactory response to an individual enquiry whether I would consent to be a Candidate for the office of President. I will however say that, judging from all that I see and hear, the good opinion which you entertain of me is shar[e]d by too few to make it exp[ed]ient to present my name to the public. I have thought it most proper to abstain from all in[ter]ference with the people on a question so delicate, and to [co]ntent myself with whatever decis[i]on they may make. I am fully sensible of the degeneracy and cor[r]uption of which you speak. I have exerted the utmost of my p[o]wers to avert the impending evils; and feel free from all just reproach on account of what ha[s] happened or may happen. Q[u]iet and happy in my own house, whilst I should be as ready now as ever to render any service to my [coun]try, I shall seek no office; and above all, I wish not to appear importunate for any. I could not decline answering your respectful letters; but have to request that you will consider this letter as intended for your own eye only.

ALS, manuscript partially defaced. KyLoF.

To HENRY CLAY, JR.   Lexington, July 7, 1835

Nothing very material has transpired since you left us. Our family and Mr. [James] Erwins enjoy good health, with the exception of your mother who continues pretty much as you left her. James [Brown Clay] has been gone these three weeks past to Missouri and Illinois, and is expected back in 8 or 10 days. Mrs. [Matilda Fontaine] Prather, William [Prather] and Catharine [*sic*, Catherine Prather] are gone to the W. Sulphur Springs, and it is said that Catharine is to marry Mr. Bullitt.[1] At Maple Wood Nollman has not behaved very well. He has cultivated badly, and has had some disputes with Harriet.[2] I threatened to dismiss him, and he will leave the place in September or October. I shall then I think put Beverley[3] there, who appears to be a trusty boy.

Property continues high and is advancing. There is great apparent prosperity, but I fear it is unsolid, and to be attributed largely to the Banks.[4] The Stock of the Northern Bank was sought with the greatest avidity.[5] There were many more names as subscribers than shares. [John] Tilford is appointed President, and the officers of the B[ranch]. Bank of the U.S. officers.   T[homas]. H. Pindell is appointed Teller of the State Bank's Branch at Lexington with a Salary of $1200. Your note was continued, and I do not apprehend any difficulty in its further continuance until your return.

The demand for Cattle and Asses is not abated. I sold Nanette a few days ago with a Calf only a day old to Spencer Cooper for $500; and Nancy's bull calf about nine months old I sold to Genl [William] Thornton for $200. Mr. Erwin sold his Jack for $600, and his Jenny in foal for $600 more; but since she has had a Jack colt by Warrior. I think you would do well to import some first rate Asses and Durham Cattle. If it should not be too late to send two or three heifers in Calf by Genl. [James] Garrard, who would probably select them for you, I would take an interest of half in them. The heifer you designed for Mrs. Prather and another Cow have each very pretty Heifer Calves. We diluted all the milk of the Heifer to be given to her Calf.

I recd. the letters you wrote me just before your departure, with one of the set of Exchange you had procured on England.

Anne [Brown Clay Erwin] has got and is pleased with the woman you dismissed.

I have nothing to communicate on politics. Great apathy prevails in this State; and fears are entertained that we may lose the ascendancy in the Legisature. . . .[6]

779

ALS. Henry Clay Memorial Foundation, Lexington, Ky. Addressed to Henry Clay, Jr., in care of Baring Brothers, London, England.   1. Probably one of the sons of the socially prominent Thomas or Cuthbert Bullitt families of Louisville. However, Catherine did not marry a Bullitt; she married Edward P. Humphrey, a Presbyterian minister. Jennings, *Louisville's First Families*, 27-32, 39.   2. Nollman was evidently an overseer and Harriet a slave.   3. Apparently a slave.   4. Clay to Southard, June 27, 1835.   5. Clay to Thompson, April 9, 1835. 6. Clay to Brooke, June 27, 1835.

From John M. Bailhache, Columbus, Ohio, July 8, 1835. States that he has become "convinced of the absolute necessity of taking some decisive step" for achieving unity "among the different sections of the Whig party" in order to obtain "success in the approaching struggle for the next Presidency." Explains that he opposes John McLean, because he does not have "sufficient positive strength any where to afford a reasonable ground for the hope that he would obtain the electoral vote of a single State"; also, because he fears "that the selection of a gentleman, not known to be a decided Whig, as the candidate of our party, would be productive of more injury than benefit to our cause." Considers other potential candidates, remarking: "Mr Webster, although nominated or recommended by some of the New England States [Clay to Shaw, February 4, 1835], and deservedly popular in that section of the Union, does not, I fear, stand the remotest chance of obtaining even a solitary vote in any of the Southern or Western States. . . . Neither can Judge [Hugh L.] White, who appears to be a favorite with the South. . . . Gen. Harrison, if regularly brought out, with a reasonable prospect of obtaining votes in other States, would doubtless run well in Ohio—far better, I really believe, than either of the gentlemen above named—and I think that, in a contest with the Vice President, the chances would be decidedly in his favor. But although he has zealous friends in Pennsylvania, Kentucky, and Indiana, is he sufficiently popular in those States to beat the Administration candidate in all, or even in any of them?" Considers the possibility that the election might be thrown into the House but thinks Van Buren would likely have the highest number of electoral votes there. Asks: "after what has happened, would it be prudent—would it be safe—to prevent his election, if we had it in our power?" Thinks not, noting that he would be "unwilling, after the experience we have had in this matter, to see anyone but the highest candidate voted for by our friends."

Believes that the present lack of unity could have been avoided if Clay's name, rather than McLean's, had been brought forward at the last session of the Ohio legislature. "All the opponents of the existing Administration," he notes "from Maine to Louisiana, would have rallied for the contest, and stepped forward as one man, to resist the encroachments of arbitrary power. . . . Instead of being divided, we should have presented a bold and solid front, and taken the field with at least a chance of a favorable result. But now, if things remain as they are, we can hardly expect to make even a show of resistance." Feels, however, that the mistake "may perhaps yet be remedied. The great body of the Whigs are still uncommitted. Their attachment to Henry Clay is as warm now as it ever has been; and were he to be announced as a candidate, thousands, who are looking on the approaching contest with absolute indifference, would instantly turn out, and labor zealously and vigorously to insure his success." Emphasizes that "if you cannot succeed, the attempt to elect another must be altogether hopeless."

Asks if it is true "as has been frequently alledged, you have determined in no event to suffer yourself to be taken up as a candidate; and if so, what course, in your opinion, should your old friends pursue in the present emergency?" Continues: "If, as I hope, the allegation is unfounded, will you permit it to be contradicted, should a favorable opportunity present itself for the purpose?" Adds that he does "not mean to ask you to run, unless the chances shall seem to be decidedly favorable. . . . All I wish to know is whether you do not now, as heretofore, consider yourself at the disposal of your friends, and ready to respond to any call which they might be pleased to make on you." ALS. DLC-HC (DNA, M212, R5).

To John S. Snead, July 8, 1835. Mentions that he has looked into the value of the stock of the Lexington and Ohio Rail-Road Company [Clay to Biddle, May 10, 1831]. Reports: "As to the value of the Stock ultimately, one can not speak with positive certainty. I entertain no doubt that it will be good if the Road be extended to Louisville. Limited as it now is to Frankfort, the prospects of the rise of the stock from increased business are encouraging. Sales have been made at 70 per Cent. And it is to be remarked that almost all Rail Road Stock in the U.S. is at or above par." ALS. KyLoF. For Snead, a banker and businessman first in Lexington and then in Louisville, see M. Joblin and Company, *Louisville Past and Present* (Louisville, 1875), 113-14.

To John Jacob Astor, July 9, 1835. Informs Astor that an "act of Incorporation has been obtained from the General Assembly for the erection of a Toll-bridge at Louisville." States that "I do not know what your disposition may be to embark in such enterprises," but recommends it as a sound investment because it is "in the great Western thorough fare." ALS. NN. The Kentucky legislature had passed "An Act to Incorporate a Company to Build a Bridge Across the Ohio River at the Falls," which was approved on December 23, 1831. Ky. Gen. Assy., *Acts . . .* 1831-1832, pp. 216-21. Contracts were let in 1836 to build the bridge, and the cornerstone was laid at the foot of 12th Street, but the work progressed no further at that time. The bridge was not completed until 1870. Ben Casseday, *The History of Louisville From Its Earliest Settlement till the Year 1852* (Louisville, 1852), 194; Johnston, *Memorial History of Louisville,* 1:80.

Speech at Dinner Honoring George Poindexter, Lexington, July 11, 1835. Following Sen. Poindexter's speech of an hour and a half condemning President Jackson and his dictatorial administration, a speech "replete with just sarcasm, severe irony, clear and logical demonstration," Clay spoke, in part, as follows: "I can with truth, as I do with pleasure, bear testimony to the undaunted firmness, ability, and zeal, which he [Poindexter] has displayed in the same cause. In the recent great contest, in which the Senate has been the sole barrier against the daring encroachments of the Executive, he has stood in the front rank, among those who have struggled to preserve the balances of the Constitution, and to maintain unimpaired Public Liberty. I wish that that contest had successfully terminated, but it is still in progress. . . . The late pliant House of Representatives was a mere registry of Executive efforts, totally destitute of all independence, conniving at abuses, and exhibiting spectacles of disorder which would have been disgraceful to any primary assembly of people. The Senate has indeed hitherto stood erect; but it has not escaped the contemptuous treatment of the Executive; and its constitutional share in appointments has been frequently disregarded and trampled upon. The authority of the Supreme Court has been despised and contemned; principles have been avowed by the Executive, which, if practically acted upon, place the execution of all its decisions at his pleasure. . . . The Senate has been the sole, if not the last, refuge of the Constitution and of the Public Liberty. Whether it will be able much longer to impede the march of the Executive to despotic power, remains to be developed. . . . But here, at least, in our own State, its motives and labors have been justly appreciated. And I sincerely hope that, whatever discouragements elsewhere may exist, however gloomy for the moment the prospects of civil liberty may seem to be, Kentucky, whilst a shot remains in the locker, or she has a single gallant son left, will never strike the Whig flag, but, if she stand alone, will faithfully and to the last adhere to her principles. [Great and long continued cheering]. The President is not satisfied with the undisputed and general sway which he has acquired. Like the Monarchs, and Emperors, and Despots, whose story History tells, he is desirous, whilst he is yet in office, in the full possession of all his power and means of influence, to name his successor; and, under forms and veils which the feeblest vision can penetrate, has designated his successor."

Clay concluded with these observations on presidential candidate Martin Van Buren: "With respect to the gentleman who has been thus designated, I feel myself most reluctantly called upon, and this appears to me a fit occasion, to say a few words. The public press, private letters, and other evidences, have reached me, of opinions and preferences being ascribed to me by his friends or partisans, so as to create, I think, a duty on my part, to undeceive the public. My personal relations with the Vice President, before and since he came into office, have been those of civility and courtesy; but they have never for a moment affected my judgment as to the propriety of his election as Chief Magistrate. In no aspect of the contest, in no conceivable contingency, in no imaginable alternative, do I think it would be for the interests or honor of the people of the United States to elevate him to that office. Without stopping to insist upon objections to him, from the exceptionable system of party-tactics which prevails in his own State, and which, in the event of his success, he would endeavor to spread over the whole Union; from the means and the manner by which he has been so far advanced; from my utter inability to comprehend what his principles *now* are, in reference to great measures of National policy; there is one objection to him which, in my mind, is absolutely conclusive. *He is the nominated Candidate of the President and the official corps*, and sought to be forced upon the People by all the weight of the administration. If he were the most pure and perfect of all American Statesmen, this single objection would, in my opinion, be absolutely decisive against him. And I must have been false to every principle which has guided my public life, and faithless in my devotion to civil liberty, if I could have entertained an opinion that, under such circumstances, the vice president should be preferred to any Candidate. [Throughout the delivery of these sentiments Mr. Clay was repeatedly interrupted by animated bursts of applause and cheering.]"

He added: "These expressions have been forced from me. I wished to have enjoyed repose, without taking any part in the Presidential question; but opinions having been often erroneously attributed to me, on that subject, I have not been left at liberty to remain silent. Humble and without influence as my name is, I do not choose to allow it to be applied to unauthorized purposes. I hope this is the last and only occasion in which it may be necessary for me publically to say any thing respecting the contest." Copy. Printed in Washington *Daily National Intelligencer*, July 22, 1835.

To [JOHN M. BAILHACHE]   Lexington, July 14, 1835

I received last night your favor of the 8h. inst.   Having experienced the constancy and fidelity of your friendly attachment to me, and entertaining an high opinion of your discretion and judgment, I shall answer it with all the frankness and freedom with which I would address any friend, on the interesting subject of the next P. election.

After the result of the election of 1832, I have felt no desire to have my name again presented as a Candidate, unless I was satisfied that it was the wish of a probable majority of the people of the U. States. Under the influence of this feeling, far from encouraging any movements in my favor, I have in several instances dissuaded them from being made, when I was consulted. I have indeed some times thought, since that period, that a state of things might arise which would induce a majority of the People to turn their attention towards me; but it has not occurred. It is possible that if the Whigs had manifested no inclination towards other Candidates, and had thought proper to have adhered to me, such a state of things might have arisen. But the solicitude of other Gentlemen, perhaps more entitled than I am to be chosen C. Magistrate, and the discouragement to the use of my name, resulting from the issue of the last contest, have led respectable portions of the Whigs, in different States, to divert their views to other Candidates than myself. The truth is, that I was strongly disinclined to be presented as a Candidate in 1832, forcing the issue which took place, but I was overruled by friends, some of whom have since thought it expedient, in consequence of that very event, that another name should be substituted to mine.

Without meaning to pass any opinion upon the measure adopted by the Whig members of your [Ohio] Legislature, at the last Winter Session, except in regard to its operation upon the prospects of my election, I must say that I think it was highly injurious to those prospects. Ohio had been considered as a State which (Jackson out of the way) would certainly bestow her suffrage on me, if I were a Candidate. It was believed, and probably is yet believed, that no Candidate would unite so much strength in opposition to Mr. V[an]. B[uren]. as I could. When, therefore, it was seen that Ohio instead of manifesting a disposition to support me, was disposed through her Legislature to bring forward another Gentleman [John McLean], it exhibited a division in our party, and a distrust of the extent of my strength which had an unfavorable affect on my pretensions. There were many too who could not see the policy or propriety of selecting, as a Candidate, a gentleman who was an original friend of Jackson, in preference to all who had been uniform in opposition to him. The principle, on which such a selection was founded, looked too much to support expected to be derived from the Jackson ranks, without sufficiently estimating the amount that might be lost in our own, from positive aversion or apathy and indifference.

I have never said that I would not consent, under any circumstances, to be a Candidate. I have said that I did not wish to be a Candidate, except on the condition before mentioned, that is, that I was desired by a probable majority of the Country, or at least that there was strong reason to believe that I should not be again defeated   I could not have declared that my name should not be used, in any contingency, without violating a principle of public duty, which subjects the services of every Citizen of the Country to the call of the majority. But I have reserved to myself the right of controlling and arresting as far as I could any movement which might be attempted in my behalf that was likely to end in defeat.

I must now, in frankness, say that the condition on which I should be willing to be run, has not heretofore existed, and does not seem to me now to exist. I have no reason to believe that I should be elected, if I were brought forward. None to think that I am the wish of the majority of the people. And it is repugnant to my feelings and sense of propriety to be voluntarily placed in an attitude in which I would seem to be importuning the public for an office which it is not willing to confer. It is possible indeed, so many of my friends think, and so I am inclined to believe, from the information I possess, that, if I were the only Whig Candidate, in opposition to Mr. V.B., I would receive a greater support than any other; but I apprehend it would fall short of securing my election.

I have appropriated too much of this letter to myself, the least important part of yours. But I will now give you my candid views as to the state of the Country and the best policy, as it seems to me, for the Whigs to pursue

I will not take up time in dwelling on the calamity of Mr. V.Bs. election. It is enough for me to express my conviction that it would lead to a system of general corruption, and end in a subversion of the Union.

I feel too with you the absolute necessity, to secure his defeat, of union and concert among those who are opposed to him. Can that union and concert be produced on Judge [Hugh L.] White? I think not, for a reason already stated. He has been throughout a supporter of Jackson's administration, and holds no one principle (except in the matter of patronage) as to public measures in common with the Whigs. Altho', for other reasons he is to be preferred to V.B. I apprehend that it would be impossible if we were to take him up as our Candidate, to infuse among our friends the spirit and zeal necessary to ensure success, especially in States where Internal Improvements and the American System have been popular. The Judge, however, seems to be the favorite of the South & S. West; and, from all the lights which we possess, it is probable that he will obtain their undivided support. At least it is so probable as to make it a justifiable basis of future calculation.

Whilst Mr [Daniel] Webster has attainments greatly superior to those of any other nominated Candidate, it is, to be regretted that a general persuasion seems to exist, that he stands no chance. I believe that, if he stood a fair chance else where, by great effort, the vote of this State might be given to him. In this opinion however I differ from many of my friends.

Genl. [William Henry] Harrison could easier obtain the vote of K. than any other Candidate named. Judge [John] McLean has not recently been much spoken of, was never generally popular here, but against V.B. perhaps he might obtain the vote of K.

You will say this is not a very favorable account of the prospects of the several Candidates opposed to Mr. V.B. It is not, and I regret it; but I believe it to be true.

What then is to be done? Nothing towards an union upon either of them, by public assemblies, in my opinion, until after the election in Pennsa. Great confidence exists that the Jackson Candidates for Governor there will be defeated;[1] and as great that, in that event, the States will not support Mr. V.B. Mr. Webster's friends, Genl. Harrison's, and Judge McLeans, each persuade themselves that the vote of the State will be given to their favorite Man, if we can have reasonable assurance that Pennsa. will support either of them, I should think it would be our true policy to rally upon that one, and employ all our energies to give him as great an amount of support as possible.

There would then be three Candidates; Mr V.B. Mr. White, and the Pennsa. favorite And if White gets the S[outh]. & S.W. vote, or nearly all of it, and Pennsa. and the Whig States North of the Potomac and in the West, including Louisiana unite on a Candidate, he would enter the House with the largest vote, and V.B. might have the smallest vote of the three.

I agree with you that whoever is returned to the House will be selected. If his plurality is considerable, after the experience which we have had, and upon general principles, it is desirable that he should be chosen.

On a late occasion of a public dinner given to Govr. [George] Poindexter, I avowed publicly my opinion in opposition to Mr. V.B.[2] This I should not have done, but for the report that I favored his pretensions in a contest with Judge White, which was industriously circulated. You will see what I said, in the public papers. The truth is, that I think the election of either Mr. V.B. or Judge White would be a great misfortune, altho that of the Judge would be the least. I did not express any preference between the other Candidates, which it appeared to me improper to do.[3] But I have no hesitation in saying to you that either Mr. Webster, Genl. Harrison, or Judge. . . .

AL, incomplete. DLC-TJC (DNA, M212, R10). Printed in Colton, *Clay Correspondence*, 4:392-95. From internal evidence, editors have determined that the recipient is John M. Bailhache. Cf. Bailhache to Clay, July 8, 1835. 1. Joseph Ritner, the Whig candidate, won the Pennsylvania governorship over George Wolf and Henry Muhlenberg, both Democrats, by a vote of 94,023 to 65,804 for Wolf and 40,586 for Muhlenberg. *BDGUS*, 3:1302. In the election for the state legislature, 70 Ritner members were chosen, 16 Wolf members, and 13 Muhlenberg members, giving an anti-Van Buren majority of 41. *Niles' Register* (Oct. 31, 1835), 49:141. Van Buren carried Pennsylvania over William Henry Harrison by 91,475 votes to 87,111 and won all 30 of its electoral votes. Schlesinger, *History of American Presidential Elections*, 1:640. 2. The Poindexter dinner was held in Lexington at the Phoenix Hotel on July 11, 1835. Lexington *Observer & Kentucky Reporter*, July 15, 1835. For Clay's speech on this occasion, see above, July 11, 1835. 3. William Henry Harrison was the Whig candidate against Van Buren in the states of Maine, New Hampshire, Vermont, Rhode Island, Connecticut, New York, New Jersey, Pennsylvania, Delaware, Maryland, Ohio, Kentucky, Indiana, Illinois, and Michigan. Of these states, Harrison carried Vermont, New Jersey, Delaware, Maryland, Kentucky, Ohio, and Indiana, winning 73 electoral votes and 548,966 popular votes. Daniel Webster was the Whig candidate in Massachusetts where he won 41,287 popular votes and 14 electoral votes. Hugh L. White was the Whig candidate in the states of Virginia, North Carolina, Georgia, Alabama, Mississippi, Louisiana, Arkansas, Tennessee, and Missouri. He carried Georgia and Tennessee, winning 26 electoral votes and 145,396 popular votes. Willie P. Mangum received the 11 electoral votes of South Carolina. Van Buren carried Maine, New Hampshire, Rhode Island, Connecticut, New York, Pennsylvania, Virginia, North Carolina, Alabama, Mississippi, Louisiana, Arkansas, Missouri, Illinois, and Michigan, winning a total of 762,978 popular votes and 170 electoral votes. In the vice presidential race, Democrat Richard M. Johnson won 147 electoral votes, one less than a majority; Anti-Mason — Whig — Democrat Francis Granger won 77 electoral votes; states' rights Whig John Tyler won 47; and William Smith of Alabama received Virginia's 23 electoral votes. Schlesinger, *History of American Presidential Elections*, 1:640. On Feb. 8, 1837, the U.S. Senate chose Johnson as vice president over Granger by a vote of 33 to 16. For Virginia's dual Whig ticket and an analysis of the election, see Seager, *And Tyler Too*, 120-21.

From Henry W. Drinker, Clifton, Luzerne County, Pa., July 16, 1835. States that "a crisis is now at hand. . . . Shall we be permitted to return to the safe usages & honored days of our former Presidents — Or. shall the present Incumbent [Jackson] appoint His Successor, and the New York Regency Candidate [Martin Van Buren] fasten still further on the Country the Vile System which has already so fearfully taken rout among us and spread Corruption throughout the Land." Asks Clay's opinion "upon this important but most difficult question" of who to support for president in 1836. Continues: "Must we take Judge [Hugh L.] White (who & what is He) — John McClean [*sic*, McLean] — General [William Henry] Harrison — The Talented and patriotic [Daniel] Webster — any of these — or any that have yet been named — Or look we for Another — I fear that not one of these can Succeed — *who* then can —" Mentions that in Pennsylvania the Whigs have "suspended all action" in choosing a presidential candidate until they can elect a Whig governor [Clay to Bailhache, July 14, 1835]. Adds that "I am perfectly clear that we Shall Succeed with our Governor — and that the impulse of Victory and the Vast patronage of the office will decide (General Jackson notwithstanding) the Electoral Contest — one thing alone seems requisite — That we can act understandingly in the selection of a candidate & find out who it is that will with reasonable chance of Success be supported in other parts of the Union —"

Notes that "I was Sir a member Elect — (but did not attend) of the Baltimore Convention [Clay to Brooke, June 23, 1831] which in time, past nominated Mr. [William] Wirt" — and "it is not impossible but that I may be a member of the *next* Convention." Feels that if anyone can advise him who to support, "That man is Henry Clay." ALS. DLC-TJC (DNA, M212, R10). Drinker (1787-1866), sometime resident of Luzerne County, Pa., was involved in the settlement of the townships of Madison, Covington, and Clifton, Pa. He was also the author and forwarder of various public improvements in the state and was a frequent contributor to periodicals. There was no national Whig convention to nominate a presidential candidate for the 1836 election. A group of Harrison supporters in Pennsylvania did hold a convention at Harrisburg in December, 1835, where they nominated Harrison and passed a resolution against holding a national convention. See Henry R. Mueller, *The Whig Party in Pennsylvania* (New York, 1922), 28-31.

To WILLIAM S. WOODS
Lexington, July 16, 1835

I have duly recd. your favor of the 8h. inst. and feel greatly obliged by the friendly sentiments and the constancy with which you have adhered towards me. I regret extremely that I can supply you with no copy of any Speech that I ever made on the Missouri question.[1] The Debate was long, arduous, and, during the late agitation of the question, I spoke almost every day for two or three weeks, on the main or collateral questions. The set or prepared Speech, which I made of three or four hours duration, was never published.[2] Of my share in the debate there is therefore only a meagre amount to be gleaned from the papers of the day.

The question first arose in the Session 1819-20. When the bill for admitting Missouri into the Union[3] was on its passage, Mr [John W.] Taylor of N. York proposed to insert in it a condition on which the State was to become a member of the Confederacy, that it should never tolerate slavery or involuntary servitude.[4] The argument by which that proposition was maintained, by himself and others, was that slavery is contrary to the divine law and to the acknowledged rights of man; that it ought not to exist; that it is an admitted evil; that, if the Genl. Government cannot extirpate it in the old States, it can prevent its extension to the new; that being contracted within a limited sphere it will be less promiscuous and more controllable; that Congress having the power to admit new States may prescrible the conditions of their admission; and that in all preceding instances of the admission of new States some conditions were annexed.

To all this we replied, that the General Government had nothing to do with the subject of slavery, which belonged exclusively to the several States; that they alone were to judge of the evil and the remedy; that every State had such entire control over the matter that those which coluded slavery might abolish it, and those which never had it or had abolished it, might now admit it, without any interference from the General Government; that altho' Congress had the power to admit new States, when admitted, by the express terms of the Constitution, they were on the same footing, in every respect whatever, with the senior States, and consequently had a right to judge for themselves on the question of slavery; that if Congress could exercise the power of annexing a condition respecting Slavery, they might annex any other Condition, and thus it might come to pass that instead of a Confederacy of States with equal power, we should exhibit a mongrel association; that in the case of other new States they were not conditions upon their Sovereignty, but voluntary compacts, relating chiefly to the Public lands, and mutually beneficial; that the extension of slavery was favorable to the comfort of the Slave and to the security of the White race &c.

The proposition by Mr. Taylor (which I think had been made at the previous Session) was defeated by a small majority, and the bill passed, without the obnoxious condition.

Missouri assembled her Convention, formed a Constitution, and transmitted it to Congress. In that Constitution, she unfortunately inserted a clause against free blacks. And, when at the Session 1820-21, it was proposed to admit her into the Union, the same party who had supported the Condition, taking advantage of that exceptionable clause, now opposed her admission.

I did not reach Washington until in January, and when I got there, I found the members from the Slave States, and some from others, in despair.

All efforts had been tried & failed to reconcile the parties. Mr [William] Lowdnes had exhausted all his great resources in vain. Both parties appealed to me; and after surveying their condition I went to work. I saw that each was so committed and so wedded to its opinion that nothing could be effected, without a compromise; and the point with me was to propose some compromise which should involve no sacrifice of principle. I got a Comee of thirteen appointed by the House, and furnished to the Speaker (Mr. Taylor) a list of such members as I wished, embracing enough of the Restrictionists to carry any measure, if they would agree with us. In that Comee, I proposed and, with its Assent, reported to the House a Clause, by way of condition, to be annexed to the act admitting her, substantially like that which was finally adopted. It was defeated in the House by Mr. [John] Randolph, & Mess [Weldon N.] Edwards and [Hutchins] Burton of No. Carolina voting against it.

My next movement was to get a joint Comee of 24 appointed by the two houses. That on the part of the House was chosen by ballot and a list which I made out were appointed with a few exceptions. They reported the resolution, now to be found in the Statute book, which was finally passed 2d. March 1821 and settled the question.

Never did a party put so much at hazard as the Restrictionists did on so small a question, as that was which arose on the second occasion growing out of the Constitution of Missouri. Never have I seen the Union is such danger. Mr. [Rufus] King of N. York was understood to concur in all the measures of the Restrictionists. He was a member of the Senate, spoke largely on the subject, and was most triumphantly refuted, in one of the ablest Speeches of Mr. [William] Pinkney of Maryland that I ever heard.

Besides the topics employed in the first instance, on this second occasion, the main effort of our Opponents was procrastination; they urging that the matter should be put off 'till the new Congress. We believed that their real purpose was to consolidate their party and to influence the Presidential election then appoaching. I never was in better health and spirits; and never worried my opponents more   I coaxed, soothed, scorned, defied them, by turns as I thought the best effect was to be produced. Towards those, of whom there were many from the free States, anxious for the settlement of the controversy, I employed all the persuasion and conciliation in my power.

At the conclusion of the business, I was exhausted; and I am perfectly satisfied that I could not have borne three weeks more of such excitement and exertion.

This account of that memorable question is written for your own satisfaction, and not for publication. It is the first draft, and I retain no copy.[5]

You ask can the Whigs consistently support Judge [Hugh L.] White? Those, in favor of the policy for which I have contended, cannot, except as the last and only alternative. My opinion, is, that the best way to defeat Mr V. Buren is to run two Whig Candidates, one of which shall represent the feelings and interests of each of the two great divisions of the party. Between them there is no common bond, or sufficient force, to call out all their energies zeal and animation in support of any one candidate; or rather the influence of the opinions and principles which are common to them is too much impaired by their differences on certain questions of National policy. The consequence would be that, if Mr. White were run alone agst. Mr. V[an]. Buren, he would be defeated, for the want of Northern or Western support; and if Mr. [Daniel]

Webster, Genl. [William Henry] Harrison or Judge [John] McLean were run, he would be defeated for want of Southern support. Two Candidates therefore are necessary to absorb all the votes of those who are more or less inclined against Mr. V. B.

Your letter has brought on you a great infliction in this long exposition. You must ascribe it to the friendly feelings excited by yours'. I rarely commit this sort of offence. P.S. You will see in the public prints what I have said, on a late occasion, respecting the preference for Mr. V. B. imputed to me.[6]

ALS. MoHi. Addressed to "Major Woods Esqr." For Woods, who had served in the Virginia militia and the state legislature from Albemarle County, Va., see Philip A. Bruce, *History of Virginia*, 6 vols. (Chicago, 1924), 5:251; Gwathmey, *Twelve Virginia Counties*, 314.   1. See 2:669-70, 742-48, 775-77, 778, 785-86, 3:15-16, 18-22, 26-33, 46-47, 49-50.   2. Nor was it printed in the *Annals of Congress*.   3. See Glover Moore, *The Missouri Controversy 1819-1821*. Lexington, Ky., 1953.   4. *Ibid.*, 35, 39-44, 99-103, *passim*.   5. The three lines following have been marked through.   6. Clay to Bailhache, July 14, 1835.

To JAMES HEATON   Lexington, July 18, 1835

My neighbour, our mutual friend, Mr. John Henry has placed in my hands your letter of the 16h. May last, the receipt of which he desires me to acknowledge, and to say to you that his absence from home has delayed his notice of it. He also requested me to say to you a few words on some of the topics of your letter.

The general state of the affairs of our Federal Government is far from being satisfactory to those who have the good of their Country at heart. On the one side, we behold, an active fearless and reckless party composed of official incumbents and others bound by no tye but that of keeping the spoils they have got and acquiring as many more as they can, hurrying our institutions to ruin. On the other, division and distraction unfortunately prevail. If Union and concert could be effected between the members of this latter party; or even if Union could be yet accomplished between those of them who live in the North, the Middle States and the West, I think the attempt of the President to designate his successor would be yet arrested.

Judge [Hugh L.] White, altho' he is to be prefered to Mr. V[an]. B[uren]., is at the same time so utterly opposed to all the measures of the Nat. Republican party, that it will be extremely difficult for them to yield him their support. On the other hand, the South is so averse to any one who heretofore supported the Tariff Internal Improvements and the Bank, that they will probably be not induced to support such a Candidate.

Under these unfortunate circumstances, would it not be best to run two Candidates against Mr V. B., one who would embody the feelings and wishes of the South, and the other those of the N. & West?

Should Pennsa. this fall indicate a disposition not to sustain Mr. V. B.[1] and a proper selection is made of the Whig Candidate of the N[orth]. & W[est]. Mr. V. B. may, in the result, obtain fewer votes than either of them.

As to the person who should be designated for the North and West, I would say that he ought to be that person whom Pennsa. shall clearly manifest a purpose of sustaining, whether it be, [Daniel] Webster, [William Henry] Harrison or [John] McLean.[2]

Since the issue of the election in 1832, I have, in respect to myself, entertained but one feeling, and that is not to desire my name to be used, except in a contingency which has not occurred, and is not likely to arise, that is, that it should be called for by a probable majority of the people of the U. S. If any indication of such a wish by such a majority had been given, I should have regarded it as a duty to obey it. In other words, I am quiet and happy, and shall be content with private life; and I have no desire to engage in a third contest without a prospect of success.

Since the date of your letter, the Legislature of Ohio have adopted measures in respect to your controversy with Michigan which, it is to be hoped, will lead to an amicable settlement of it, without bloodshed.[3]

This letter is written for your own eye only & not for publication. . . .

ALS. DLC-James Heaton Papers (DNA, M212, R21). Addressed to Heaton in Middletown, Ohio.   1. Clay to Bailhache, July 14, 1835.   2. *Ibid.* Harrison and Granger were the Whig candidates for president and vice president in Pennsylvania. Mueller, *The Whig Party in Pennsylvania*, 28-29.   3. For the boundary dispute and its settlement, see Clay to Southard, April 12, 1835; and Weisenburger, *Passing of the Frontier*, 3:297-307.

To WILLIAM HENRY RUSSELL   Lexington, July 18, 1835

[Discusses livestock transactions. Also thanks the Russells for naming their infant after him. Continues:]

You speak of the probability of a convention[1] in which you suppose a leading question that will be agitated is that of emancipation & you ask my opinion of it. As to immediate emancipation, I put it wholly out of the question. It could not be adopted justly without compensation, & it could not be safely, considering the want of qualification in the slaves either to enjoy freedom, or to provide comfortably for themselves.

Gradual emancipation, that is emancipation, at a certain age, of all born after a limited period is a very different question. Thirty seven years ago, this question was made in K. when we were about to reform our Constitution.[2] I was then in favor of it, but we were in the minority and were defeated.

It is a question I think, which depends upon the relative numbers of the white & black races. Where the Black preponderates or is nearly equal, I would not be in favor of it; but where the White greatly preponderates, as in Missouri, it appears to me it may be safely adopted. The proportion of Slaves to the Whites with you [Missouri] is as 22 to 97, or a little more than one fifth. In such a relative condition of the two races there is no danger of the African ever acquiring the ascendancy.

That slavery is unjust & is a great evil are undisputed axioms. The difficulty always has been how to get rid of it. In States where there are comparatively few that difficulty is less. And in Penna.[3] & other Northern States, they have gotten rid of slavery almost without a struggle.

As to compensation, supposing you were to put off the commencement of the period to the year (say) 1850 holding all to be slaves for life born prior to that year, & all subsequent to be free at the age of 28, there would be very little if any diminution in the value of slave property. The measure would operate only on the female, & how much less would a female slave be worth, who, being herself a slave for life, her offspring after 1850 are to be liberated. If there were no prohibition of the removal of slaves prior to 1850, there would be no depreciation in the value. The effect of this measure would be to allow you slave labor, in the infancy of your state, when it is most wanted, & to substitute ultimately free labor for it, when free labor would be abundant. And you would thus gently & gradually free yourself from what has not been inaccurately characterized a great curse.

These are my views, communicated for your own satisfaction, at your request & not for publication.

When Missouri was admitted into the Union, I said to her delegate, Mr [John] Scott, go home, enter the Convention of your State[4] & exert yourself to establish a system of gradual emancipation, similar to that which Dr [Benjamin] Franklin prevailed upon Penna. to adopt in 1779.

I do not conceive that your state would be justly chargeable with violating any pledges to emigrants by adopting the principle of gradual emancipation. The State has never declared that slavery should be perpetual. It tolerates slavery, but retained the power possessed by all slave states to abolish it, when the good of the commonwealth required it. Emigrants went to your state knowing of this power, & knowing that the majority must governs   In making up that majority they have their voices pro or con.

I have now sanguine hopes that Mr V[an]. B[uren]. will be defeated. Judge [Hugh L.] White is likely to obtain the Southern vote; & I think some Whig will get the vote of those states in the North & West, who are in favor of the American system, Internal Improvements & the Bank. If V.B. loses Penna & there are not more than three candidates running, I should not be surprised if he is the lowest of the three. It seems to be generally believed that the Jackson party will be defeated in Penna.[5]

In K. there is not the usual excitement attending the present election.[6] There is perhaps too much apathy prevailing.

Copy. OCIWHi. Endorsed in strange hand: "Copy Henry Clay *to* William Henry Russell—Mr Russel was an ardent friend of Mr Clays   He is now appointed Consul to Cuba, and says he will do what he can to suppress the Slave trade—" Russell was also appointed consul to Trinidad, Cuba, in 1861 by Abraham Lincoln and held the position until after Lincoln's assassination. Anna DesCognats, *William Russell and His Descendents* (Lexington, 1884), 84.   1. In 1835 the general assembly of Missouri submitted to the people the question of calling a convention to revise the state constitution. Some anti-slavery advocates demanded that aboliton be a first order of business, but the vote against calling a convention was almost 2 to 1. William E. Parrish (ed.), *A History of Missouri* (Columbia, Mo., 1972), 2:61.   2. For Clay's role in the Kentucky constitutional convention of 1799, see 1:3-8, 10-14; Bernard Mayo, *Henry Clay, Spokesman of the New West* (Boston, 1937), 64-69, 76-79; Van Deusen, *The Life of Henry Clay*, 20-21.   3. Pennsylvania was the first state to pass a law abolishing slavery. It did so on March 1, 1780. Edward R. Turner, "The Abolition of Slavery in Pennsylvania," *PMHB* (1912), 36:137.   4. For Missouri's constitutional convention of 1820, see Moore, *The Missouri Controversy*, 134-35, 155.   5. Clay to Bailhache, July 14, 1835.   6. Clay to Brooke, June 27, 1835.

From Louisa Caroline Jeffrey, New York, July 19, 1835. Informs Clay that "little insignificant me" is answering his letter to Harriet Martineau [Martineau to Clay, June 30, 1835]. Assures him that the letters and newspapers he has forwarded to them, "including the parcel transmitted through Sir Charles Vaughan" have arrived safely. Details their itinerary to New York and their travel plans in New England. Promises, to write Anne Brown Clay Erwin and tell her "my impressions of Yankee land." Reports that "Miss M——received rather unfavorable accounts of the political state of England from her brother; he appears to think that the Tory influence (used in intimidating & bribing electors) will be too strong for the Whigs." Asks if Clay has seen "that Lord Stanley [Edward George Geoffrey Smith] asserts on the authority of a friend at Washington (of course Mr Murray) that Americans are all conservative, if by conservative he means Tory I think he would find himself mistaken & I cannot think Mr Murray could mean to make such an assertion." Adds that if Clay would "honor me with a few lines," she will "feel more grateful than any lady in whose album you have written in as much, as a few words from Mr Clay's heart, are worth pages of his handwriting." ALS. DLC-TJC (DNA, M212, R14). Printed in Colton, *Clay Correspondence*, 4:395-97. For Lord Stanley, see *DNB*.

On July 4, 1835, Clay wrote Charles Vaughan saying he had transmitted a letter to "Miss Martineau which, as she had left us, I forwarded to the White Sulphur Springs . . . to which she was destined." Comments that "She remained two or three weeks with us and confirmed all the agreeable anticipations which we had formed." Learned from Mr. Murray, who also visited at the same time, "that you had at last obtained your Pension; and consequently had a prospect of that repose the want of which you must feel, after your long and arduous services." ALS. Codrington Library, All Souls College, Oxford Univesity, England. Harriet Martineau had three brothers, James, Henry, and Robert. To which one the reference above is made is not clear. Vaughan left his position in October, 1835, and returned to England, thus ending a ten-year period as British minister to the U.S. *DNB.*

To FRANCIS T. BROOKE   Lexington, July 20, 1835

I hope you will not estimate the constancy of my friendship for you by the carelessness of my correspondence. The truth is that, in this remote quarter, I have but little of interest to write about, and I find myself so much and so agreeably occupied with the avocations of my farm that I dislike writing about nothing. And now my principal object is to say that I can not I believe go to the W. Sulphur Springs this Season; and I presume you are in the same predicament.

I sent you a Newspaper containing some observations I made, on the occasion of a public dinner lately given to Governor [George] Poindexter in Lexington, disavowing any opinion favorable to Mr. V. Buren, in any contingency.[1] I found representations, so extensively and industriously made, of my prefering him eventually, if not to all others, that I could not remain silent; and yet I wished not to have been disturbed.

I begin to think that he can be defeated, if the opposition to him is managed with any discretion and prudence; but I doubt whether his defeat can be effected by an union upon *one* Candidate; or, rather I should say, I believe such a union is impracticable.

In surveying the present condition of the Opposition, it is necessary to go back to pre existing causes. In the South, you have been opposed to the Tariff, to Int. Improvements and the Bank. The first is compromised,[2] the second might be by the Land bill,[3] and the Bank is dead.[4] Still your opposition to those measures influences your judgments and your votes; and altho' many in the South are willing to support Mr. V. B. you will not support any Whig that has espoused those measures. You are unwilling therefore to risk an attempt to sustain any such Whig.

In the Northern, Middle & Western States, where the Whigs predominate, they would support with great reluctance any man who had been opposed to those interests. The intelligent, and perhaps the majority of the party would prefer any Candidate to Mr. V. B; but then, if he had been opposed to their policy and principles, the Canvass would be conducted without animation, and those who might go to the polls would go without spirit. For a similar reason to that which prevents you from sustaining a Northern or Western Whig, they would be unwilling or reluctant to sustain a Southern Whig. The repugnance to a Northern or Western Candidate is probably greater in the South than it is in the N. or West to a Southern Candidate. This is owing to two causes 1st. A difference in character; and 2dly. because you have been in the minority on those questions.

This condition of the two great sections of the opposition to Mr. V. B. indicates what ought to be done in the selection of the Candidates who are opposed to him. There should be one (Judge [Hugh L.] White if you please) to embody Southern interests and feelings; and another on whom the interests and feelings of the Northern, Middle & Western States can rally. Unfortunately the ties between the portions of the Opposition are not sufficiently strong, or rather are improperly disturbed by the collateral cause to which I have adverted. If Judge White were run alone against Mr. V. B. there is no security, from the operation of that cause, that Mr. V. B. might not obtain the votes of the New England Whig States, New Jersey, Delaware, Ohio and even Kentucky. And if Mr. [Daniel] Webster or any other Northern or Western Candidate were run alone there is much reason to apprehend that Mr. V. B. would obtain the votes of all the Southern & South Western States, So. Carolina perhaps excepted.

I have thought therefore from the beginning that the annunciation of Mr. Webster[5] was favorable to Judge White; and that you, in the South, who have called upon him and all others to stand off, and allow the Judge alone to contend with Mr. V. B. have looked too much at home, and too little in other sections of the Union.

Who shall be the Candidate of the Northern Middle & Western States? This is an important question, and I think should be decided early next winter according to the then state of things. Pennsa is undoubtedly much convulsed. The opinion is now confidently entertained that the Jackson party will be prostrated at the approaching election in the autumn,[6] and that [Joseph] Ritner will be elected. Once routed, the opinion is entertained with equal confidence that the party electing Mr. R. will be opposed to Mr. V. B. and will nominate some other Candidate. The friends of Webster, of Genl. [William Henry] Harrison, and of Judge [John] McLean each count upon the vote of that State, in the contingency supposed. Now I would say let the Whig States of the North, West and the Middle unite upon that Candidate whom Pennsa. may thus indicate her intention to support.

Assuming the existence of this triangular contest, and the loss of Pennsa. to Mr. V. B. he would be the lowest of the three Candidates, unless he obtains Southern support.

Upon the supposition of there being three Candidates, it would of course be sound policy to cultivate the best relations of amity between the two sections of the Whig party; since they might find it necessary to co-operate if the election were to devolve on the House   After all, the real differences now existing between them are not of great practical importance. The Tariff being settled, Internal Improvements, always a temporary question, might be easily accommodated; and I take it that there will be no National bank, until that explosion shall take place which I hope will, if ever, be distant but which I believe to be ultimately certain.

You may shew what I have written to [Benjamin W.] Leigh, [Chapman] Johnson, [Robert] Stanard or any other friend confidentially; and I should be glad to be favored with your and their views of it.

ALS. NcD.   1. Clay to Bailhache, July 14, 1835; Speech at Dinner Honoring George Poindexter, July 11, 1835.   2. Draft Proposal, Mid-Dec., 1832.   3. Clay to Wilde, April 27, 1833. 4. *Ibid.*   5. Clay to Shaw, Feb. 5, 1835.   6. Clay to Bailhache, July 14, 27, 1835.

To Joshua Folsom, Bellefontaine, Logan County, Ohio, July 20, 1835. Discusses different varieties of grasses, including orchard grass, timothy, and blue grass. Notes that "blue grass, or more properly speaking the green sward is our most common pasture grass, and it is preferred by Stock to all other grasses." However, recommends sowing timothy or herds grass on wet ground. States that a good Jack can be purchased "for about $1000," and says his "neighbor Genl. [James] Shelby has a good two year old Jack for which he asks that price." ALS. InU.

From Lewis Tappan, New York, July 20, 1835. Writes in response to Clay's letter of July 7, even "Though you decline further correspondence on the subject of slavery." Argues that "your political carreer has placed you in the very front rank of bold defender of equal rights"; therefore, "a man like you has no moral right to stand aloof, on a question of this magnitude." States that "Nearly one half of your letter, Sir, is devoted to an argument that northern interference, on the subject of slavery, is unconstitutional & impertinent. It would be so indeed if northern abolitionists claimed the right of interfering in any way not sanctioned by the constitution. *They do not.* Moral suasion is all they contend for in doctrine or practice." Adds that "On moral subjects, it should be understood, there are no constitutional prohibitions, no geographical lines." Poses the question of how Clay would have responded during the period when he was advocating South American independence [2:492-507, 541-62, 853-60] if a citizen of that region had told him that he had no right to interfere. Asks: "Would you not have repudiated such sentiments? When you knew your fellow-men were suffering under political slavery, and panting for freedom, you generously became their advocate. Is physical servitude, accompanied as it is with the debasement of the mind, and ruin of the soul, of less importance than political thraldom?" Wonders if it is "consistent to give one's self to the advocacy of political equality among foreigners" and also be a defender of slavery.

Argues also against gradual emancipation, saying "As a friend of moral reform I deny the right to pay the debt the nation owes the enslaved by installments. The debt is due. The debtor has the ability to pay at once. And the creditor is wronged by the gradual dispensation of justice. I also deny that there is any obligation to make compensation for the prompt award of justice. Slaveholding is, as we contend, a sin, and men ought not to be paid for ceasing to sin."

Notes that Clay asked "in an urbane manner, if there are no sins at the north to engage the exertions of christian philanthropists," and replies: "I readily answer, yes; and not the least is the sin of upholding slavery in the District of Columbia; the sin of prejudice against our colored fellow-citizens; and the sin of opposing the righteous claims of our enslaved fellow-men." Again wonders how Clay would have responded if a South American had asked him if he should not be tending to problems at home rather than concerning himself with those of a foreign country. ALS. DLC-HC (DNA, M212, R5).

To FRANCIS T. BROOKE
Lexington, July 24, 1835

I recd. your favor of the 16h. inst. and altho' I should have been delighted to have met you at the W. Sulphur Springs, I do not regret, from your account of the Company assembled, my resolution not to visit them this Season.

I wrote a letter — a long letter, for me, a few days ago [July 20] to you addressed at St. Julien, supposing it would find you there, on public affairs. Its principal object was to express the opinion that the defeat of Mr. V[an]. B[uren]. could not be effected by Judge [Hugh L.] White, nor by any other single Candidate alone, but, if accomplished, it must be by two Candidates, one embodying Southern views, interests and feelings, and the other those of the Western States and the Northern; and that the Northern and Western Candidate should be that person (whether [Daniel] Webster, [William Henry] Harrison or [John] McLean) whom Pennsa. shall indicate a disposition to support.[1] I refer you to that letter for an exposition of my views and should be glad to hear from you about it. The times are sufficiently discouraging; but should we not repress any feelings of despair?

You will have heard of the startling occurrences in Mississippi.[2] They have engrossed recently all our thoughts. The lamented death of the C. Justice,[3] having been anticipated, has not diverted attention much from their awful nature. I suppose [Roger B.] Taney or [Edward] Livingston or the presiding Judge of the Virginia Ct. of Appeals [Henry St. George Tucker] will be nominated to the vacancy. . . .[4]

ALS. NcD.   1. Clay to Bailhache, July 14, 1835.   2. Reference to a supposed slave insurrection in Mississippi which was believed to have been scheduled for July 4, 1835. About 10 slaves and 5 or 6 white men were hanged as a result. *Niles' Register* (August 1, 1835), 48:377; Washington *Daily National Intelligencer*, July 27, 29, 31; August 4, 1835; Edwin A. Miles, "The Mississippi Slave Insurrection Scare of 1835," *JNH* (Jan., 1957), 42:48-60.   3. John Marshall died on July 6, 1835.   4. Taney was nominated and ultimately took his place as chief justice on March 16, 1836. Swisher, *Roger B. Taney*, 323.

To SAMUEL L. SOUTHARD   Lexington, July 31, 1835

I regretted very much to learn by your favor of the 18h. inst. that the bad state of your health obliged you to resort to the Virginia Springs, and sincerely hope that their virtues will work an entire cure. I have no sufficient excuse in the state of my health to go so far from home, and I have many occupations to detain me here. When you and Miss Virginia [Southard] have come so near us, will you not come to Ashland? Do; we shall be delighted to see you; and it will afford us an opportunity to thank you in person for your kindness to our John [Morrison Clay], who is himself full of gratitude.[1] Three days and a half will bring you to us, and think what a short time that is.

You appear to think that there is no hope of defeating Mr. V. Buren but by an union upon one Candidate. Undoubtedly if there could be a cordial hearty and spirited union on a single individual it would be the most certain mode of accomplishing that object; but I believe it altogether impracticable and in vain to attempt it. The two sections of the opposition for and against The Tariff, Internal improvements and the Bank will not unite. There is indeed a common bond between them, opposition to Executive power and enmity to V. Buren, but its force is impaired by the difference between them on those subjects. It ought not to be so, but it is so. Go into any of the Whig States, in favor of that policy, and you will be satisfied that Judge [Hugh L.] White cannot unite them. On the contrary, go to the South and you will be convinced that they will not support any Candidate but one who agrees with them on those subjects.

This condition of things suggests, in my opinion, the course of the Campaign—we must run two Candidates, one to unite the Southern votes (let him be White, if they please) and the other to embody the votes of the States in favor of the above policy.

If White can get the South, and the other Candidate can get Pennsa., should there be no popular election, as would be probable, V. Buren would enter the House the lowest Candidate.

I do not know as well as you the prospects in Pennsa.; but at this distance I suppose the divisions of the Jackson party are irreconcilable, and that [Joseph] Ritner will be elected.[2] If that should be the case, it is thought that the state will be adverse to V. B.   Now, whoever it indicates a disposition to support in opposition to him, should be taken up as the Candidate for the Northern and Western States.³ I am told that [William Henry] Harrison is most likely to be the person. He is weak, vain, and far inferior to [Daniel] Webster; but I believe him to be honest and of good intentions. Objectionable as he is, and with me it is not the least that his pretensions are founded altogether on military service, he is preferable to either V. Buren or White. Of all the Candidates, it would require the least exertion for him to secure the votes of Ohio, Kentucky and Indiana.

Should this plan be adopted, it would be requisite to cultivate the best feelings between the two Candidates opposed to V. and their respective friends. In States where one of them is strongest, no ticket ought to be run for the other.

If all the Candidates on our side, that is Harrison, Webster and [John] McLean, would agree to withdraw and unite on me, I do not believe that it is too late, or that any thing will have been lost by the failure to nominate me last winter; but that they will not do, and it is best not to think of me. Indeed if one of them can, and I could not, obtain the vote of Pennsa. that single consideration would be decisive against the presentation to the public of my name.

The horrible events in Mississippi,⁴ and the proceedings of the Northern abolitionists must operate against Mr. V. Buren in the Slave States. Whilst the same proceedings will operate against Mr. White in the free States.

Tell me what you think of these views; and write me if we may expect a visit from you. . . .

ALS. NjP.   1. Clay to Southard, March 9, 1835.   2. Clay to Bailhache, July 14, 1835. 3. Clay to Heaton, July 18, 1835.   4. Clay to Brooke, July 24, 1835.

From JAMES BARBOUR   Barboursville, Va., August 2, 1835
[Briefly discusses personal financial arrangements with Clay. Continues:]

On the subject of politics since our retrograde movement in April in this State¹ I have desponded almost to despair—That our Inglers should should [sic] succeed in Seducing the People into a belief that it was premature to discuss the presidential election and that the issue should be [Benjamin W.] Leigh, The Bank, instructions and all that kind of Stuff² and the moment they had Succeeded turn right round claim a Van Buren victory Send delegates to the Rump Convention³ and immediately demand of their partizans implicit obedience—and all this pigling to be acted in broad day light without producing an immediate and violent reaction seems to me to render our scheme of self Government highly doubtful—Not having left my house scarcely since, personally I know but little—If there have been any changes in The State as yet, I fear, they are few—The Whigs seem generally to have determined to support [Hugh L.] White—A small secession from the Jackson ranks might give us the majority in this State—But the Leaders of the Latter have told those creatures that the Whigs are playing false—they wish to divide the Jacksonians so as to bring the election into the House (of which they express a holy horror—) with a view to elect [Daniel] Webster yourself or some other Whig—It is this which constitutes the the most formidable obstacle to our success in This State—The running of three Candidates they seize upon in conformatism of their charge and it is this that alone gives them hopes of success here—For Van [Buren], apart from this weapon and the endorsement of Jackson, would not obtain 500 votes in The State—But I am quite satisfied that no Candidate can succeed against him here notwithstanding his unpopularity unless it be one maintaining the favorite doctrines of the State—especially one who has been

795

opposed and is now opposed to the Bank—For independently of the long cherished hostility to that institution some Jackson's hostility has been removed—and his party acquiring Success by their incipient clamor or that heard all those in pursuit of office whatever may be their real opinions have Joined in the denunciation—Opposition therefore to this institution is now a fixed maxim in the political creed of this State as much so as the undivided Godhead with a Mahometan—White happens in this respect to Stand well—and therefore I think is the strongest man that can be presented to Virginia—In addition to this the Slave question begins as I learn to incite a Strong Sensation among some of our People—Locality associates Van with the Families of his State and it is not improbable will have a greater influence in the South than any other circumstance in the contest—Webster is out of the question here—[John] McLean is not thought of—[William Henry] Harrison next to White Stands fairest I should conclude—it seems to me however on the whole that we have no prospect of excluding Van but by the plan you suggest of selecting the Two Candidates that will be strongest in three respective Sections—White I apprehend for the South—Webster for the East North and West—or whomso[e]ver Pennsylvania prefers—For in my view She holds the election in her hands—By running two popular men—we have the prospect of retaining or acquiring the ascendancy in the State Governments an object of great importance and almost a compensation for the loss of our Presidential Candidate. For example even here we hope thro' White of regaining our ascendancy whence with an inferior Candidate we should be in a decided minority—Fortunately in Pennsylvania the division in the Jackson ranks promises Success to the Whig Candidate for Governor if he Succeed it will be Sovereign in the contest for President—[4]This election occurring in Octo[b]er will become a beacon to us in the difficulties with which we are Surrounded—with it and the ensuing winter you may decide upon the best course our affairs furnish—Here I threw cold water on [John H.] Pleasants proposed meeting in this State for this month and it has been prudently abandoned—Personally dissatisfied with White—I will support him only because he is a lesser evil than Van—I shall wait patiently the development of events and be prepared to follow any course esteemed best to exclude Van—I read and was much pleased with your remarks touching this Gentleman made at the [George] Poindexters féte—[5]

[Concludes with observations on flower seeds and the failure of one of his trotters to distinguish himself in a recent race.]

ALS. DLC-HC (DNA, M212, R5). Printed in Colton, *Clay Correspondence*, 4:397-99.   1. Clay to Southard, April 12, 1835.   2. Clay to Gilmer, Mid-Jan., 1836.   3. Reference is to the Democratic convention which met in Baltimore on May 20, 1835, and nominated Martin Van Buren for president and Richard M. Johnson for vice president. Since Jackson had already chosen Van Buren as his successor before that convention met, the irrelevancy of its role was not unlike that of the English Rump Parliament dismissed by Oliver Cromwell in 1653. Washington *Daily National Intelligencer*, July 29, 1835; McKee, *The National Convention and Platforms of all Political Parties*, 34-39.   4. Clay to Bailhache, June 27, 1835; Clay to Russell, July 18, 1835. 5. Clay to Bailhache, July 14, 1835.

To FRANCIS T. BROOKE   Lexington, August 19, 1835

I duly recd. your favor of the 7h. inst. and was sorry to hear of Mrs. Brooke'[s] ill-health, which I hope will improve by her excursion to the [White Sulphur] Springs. That of Mrs. Clay and myself remains pretty much as usual.

[William Henry] Harrison is making progress in the West as a Presidential Candidate. Two of the leading papers of K. have declared for him.[1] Our elections have terminated; and notwithstanding the apathy which prevails, decided majorities are elected to both branches of the General Assembly; and nine out of the 13 members of Congress.[2]

There is not one word of truth in Duff Green's statement that Mr. [John C.] Calhoun proposed to me to unite in the support of [Hugh L.] White.[3] Mr. Calhoun never made me any such proposal. On the contrary, in the only conversation I ever had with him respecting the Judge's pretensions, he ridiculed them.

Duff's idea of my having insulted the South is a chimera. I said that I wished to send the Olive branch along with the sword which the Admon was about to send. This was what I meant and substantially what I said.[4] He artfully and perpetually confounds So. Carolina with *the South*. But mark his inconsistency! Whilst he pretends to oppose me upon the sole ground that I would have voted for the Force bill, altho' I did not, he supports Judge White who *did* vote for it and decidedly espouse it.[5]

There is not a more arrant knave and dishonest politician in the Union than this same Duff. Green. His real opposition to me is founded upon his consciousness of injury, which he supposes I never would forgive.

I recd. lately from Ohio a letter signed by several persons stating that popular meetings were about to take place to adopt measures respecting the election of President, and requesting to be informed if I would consent to the annunciation of my name. I answered explicitly declining to yield my consent to the use of my name.[6]

I am more and more convinced that out of the South Judge White can get no popular support; and I adhere to the expediency of the plan of the Campaign suggested in my former letter.[7] The risk in it is, that Whites partizans, perceiving that he will not be supported but in Tennessee and the South, may withdraw him. May he not be appointed C. Justice to get rid of him? Or is Jackson too much enraged against him?

Mr. [Benjamin W.] Leigh may be right about Mr. Calhoun, and *possibly* Mr. Webster.[8] But the latter gentleman several times said to my friends, at the commencement of the last Session, that if it were deemed expedient to announce me as a Candidate he would support me and not allow himself to be brought forward. Policy may have dictated the declaration. . . .

ALS. NcD. 1. Lexington *Observer & Kentucky Reporter*; Frankfort *Commonwealth*. 2. Clay to Brooke, June 27, 1835. 3. Such a statement by Green has not been found either in his Washington *United States Telegraph* or elsewhere. Nor is there evidence that Calhoun ever made such a proposal to Clay. 4. In his speech of Feb. 25, 1833, Clay had said he would have voted, "although with great reluctance," for the Force bill had he been present when it came to a vote. He also stated: "The difference between the friends and the foes of the compromise [tariff], under consideration, is, that they would, in the enforcing act, send forth alone a flaming sword. We would send out that also, but along with it the olive branch, as a messenger of peace." *Register of Debates*, 22 Cong., 2 Sess., 729-42; Colton, *Clay Correspondence*, 5:564, 566. 5. Green had endorsed White in numerous editorials and had called upon Clay to support White. See Washington *United States Telegraph*, March 14; April 9; July 13, 1835. See also Lexington *Intelligencer*, May 30, 1835; Remark in Senate, Jan. 22, 1833. 6. Bailhache to Clay, July 8, 1835; Clay to Bailhache, July 14, 1835. 7. Clay to Brooke, July 20, 1835. 8. Reference obscure.

From Francis T. Brooke, August 21, 1835. Says he recently wrote Sen. Benjamin W. Leigh, enclosing Clay to Brooke of July 20 last. Encloses a return letter to himself from Leigh "with which I think you will be pleased." Reports that in his letter to Leigh he [Brooke] had suggested "that it might so turn out that you would be nominated by your own State, if the elections were favorable, which I see have commenced well, in that event, I think as abolition has ruined V B in Virga [Hugh L.] White and [William

Henry] Harrison would be abandoned, this I [am] sure would be the case in the west I can not See why your friends do not make a move of that Sort, you would get South Carolina I have no doubt, let me hear from you." ALS. DLC-HC (DNA, M212, R5). The Whig convention in Kentucky met on April 19 and 20, 1836, in Lexington, Kentucky, and nominated William Henry Harrison for president and Francis Granger for vice president. They also expressed their regret at Clay's retirement and urged him to continue in the service of his state. Frankfort *Commonwealth*, April 27, 1836.

From Moses M. Henkle, Indianapolis, August 24, 1835. Encloses the first issue of the Indianapolis *Indiana Aurora*, a newspaper "to be devoted to the consideration of subjects of vital importance to our whole country, and to the west specially." Reveals that he is a member of the Indiana Board of Agriculture and asks Clay his opinion of it. Asks also his opinion of what a state board of agriculture should be doing, how it should deal with the state legislature, and how county agricultural societies should be organized. ALS. DLC-HC (DNA, M212, R5). Henkle (1798-1864) was an itinerant minister who vacillated between the Methodist Episcopal church and the Methodist Protestant church. He was also at various times a teacher, reporter, printer, and publisher. He started the *Indiana Aurora* in early September, 1835, but it was soon changed to an agricultural paper. Only one issue of the *Aurora* is extant. See Emily E. F. Skeel, "Not Quite Spurlos Versunkt," in *Bookmen's Holiday* (New York, 1943), 2.

To CHRISTOPHER HUGHES　　　　　　Lexington, August 25, 1835
[Thanks Hughes for ordering the sherry, which has arrived at "Ashland," and apologizes for not having written sooner. Continues:]

I am here surrounded with every comfort, in the possession of great abundance, and enjoying on my delightful grounds as much happiness as falls to the lot of most men. My wife's health is better than when you last saw her, and my own cannot be much complained of. I am becoming more and more attached to the occupations of my grazing farm, and more and more alienated from public life. I think the approaching is the last Session I shall serve in the Senate.

I was not desirous of being presented as a Candidate for the Office of President. The only condition upon which it would have been acceptable to me, that of my being desired by a majority, did not I thought exist; and I felt no inclination to engage in a scramble for it. You know, if not to be declined, neither is it to be sought. And this sentiment I cherished, with unaffected sincerity. Upon a review of my life, altho'. I have been, especially of late years, badly treated, I have much reason to be satisfied with my career, considering the many disadvantages under which I labored at its commencement. I have filled very high offices, and few men have had more success in the measures which they espoused. So much for myself; which I thought it right to say, that you might see there was an end of all your prospects of becoming my private Secretary.[1]

You will feel more interest in knowing what will be the probable issue of the Presidential contest; and I will freely communicate my views of it.

Judge [Hugh L.] White has been taken up by the South; and if he continues to be a Candidate, I think he will obtain its support generally. There will be a great effort there for Mr. V. Buren, but I think it will fail.

Genl. [William Henry] Harrison at present is making far greater progress than any of the Candidates. The belief is gaining ground that he will be sustained by Pennsa. and if he should be he will be formidable, probably the most formidable Candidate. In Ohio, Kentucky and Indiana he is by far the favorite

798

of all the Candidates now before the public. I really shall not be surprized at his election. Should it occur, it will be the consequence of the military spirit excited in the case of Jackson. Nor would it be wonderful, if we had a succession of Military Presidents. In politics as in War a knowledge is acquired of the use of the instruments by which victory is achieved; and the losing party resorts to them.

I do not know whether you are acquainted with Harrison. He is weak, nervous, vain, and excessively susceptible to flattery. But then I believe him to be honest and a gentleman in port and feeling; and, incompetent as he is, deserves to be preferred to V[an]. B[uren].

Webster has not the remotest prospect. I regret it, because, in point of qualification, he stands far ahead of all his Competitors.

Upon the whole, my belief, possibly somewhat controlled by my wishes, is that V. Buren will be defeated. Should you see an account of [Joseph] Ritner's election as Governor of Pennsa. by a considerable majority, you may conclude that V. will certainly fail.[2] In that event, as you are a Courtier, I would advise you to address yourself assiduously to Harrison. He is exactly the man to be reached by flattery, and you are exactly the gentleman to flatter him — that is, unless you will relinquish public life, and come and settle by me at Ashland. I assure you that it is not so difficult as you may imagine to live in retirement, especially if like me, you will cultivate a taste for improved short horn cattle, Saxony Sheep, Maltese Asses and Arabian horses.

You erred in your valedictory published at Balto.[3]   But the regret and surprise which it excited among your friends were momentary, and it is no longer remembered. I shall inflict upon you no criticisms of it.

I have remitted the amt. for the Sherry Wine; and I should receive and take care of it with much more pleasure, if I could persuade myself that the time would ever arrive when you would share it with me, under my own roof. . . .

ALS. MiU-C.   1. Clay to Hughes, June 6, 1834; Hughes to Clay, August 10, 1834.   2. Clay to Bailhache, June 27, 1835.   3. Clay to Hughes, August 10, 1834.

To John Morrison Clay, Princeton, N.J., August 28, 1835. Writes that he expects John home soon from Edgehill School [Clay to Wines, February 16, 1835]. Sends money, telling him to pay his debts in Princeton, but to reserve enough of it to pay his expences on the journey home. Encloses for him a letter of introduction to William D. Lewis of Philadelphia. ALS. Courtesy of M.W. Anderson, Lexington, Ky.

In his letter to William D. Lewis, also dated August 28, Clay asks Lewis to inform young John of anyone with whom he might travel to Kentucky. AL. Josephine Simpson Collection, Lexington, Ky. For Lewis, see *DAB*.

From William F. Dunnica, Chariton County, Mo., September 10, 1835. Discusses taxes on Clay's land in Missouri. Notes that the "nomination for State Officers by the last Jackson legislature will fail I have no doubt—Ashley & Harrison you will see are elected to congress." ALS. DLC-TJC (DNA, M212, R14). The Jackson members of the Missouri general assembly had issued a call for counties to send delegates to a state convention in Jefferson City in January, 1835. The convention adopted a platform and nominated Albert G. Harrison and George Strother as candidates for Congress in the 1835 election. They also nominated candidates for governor and lieutenant governor for 1836 and passed a declaration that no candidates other than those named by the convention should be considered Jackson men—a statement aimed particularly at William Ashley, a congressional candidate who claimed to be a Jacksonian but supported

Clay's American System. James Birch also entered the election for Congress. Since Missouri had no congressional districts, the two at-large candidates receiving the highest number of votes were elected. Ashley handily won with 12,825 votes as did Harrison who received 8,836, the next highest number. *Guide to U.S. Elections*, 564; Leota Newhard, "The Beginning of the Whig Party in Missouri," *MHR* (October, 1930), 25:270-71; Parrish, *History of Missouri*, 2:99.

From James Duplessis, Alexandria, La., September 10, 1835. Thinks that the only *"barely possible"* way to defeat Van Buren is to exploit the "strong probability of a rupture betwixt Van & R. M. Johnson   The suspicions of the latter are awakened; nurse them and you may produce a schism that will destroy the little Dutchman, and without some such plan you are assuredly beaten. It is a fact that [John] Forsyth and others of V.B.'s prominent friends have been so indiscreet as to speak very disparagingly of Dick's qualification's Moral & intellectual, and I know that one of his [Johnson] friends has informed Tecumseh of what is doing. how it will work remains to be seen; but certainly you will not fail to profit by such a contingency: many of the party have gone so far as to say that Dick 'may yet be dropped' and this has also been communicated." ALS. Enclosed in Duplessis to John Tilford (of Lexington), Alexandria, La., September 10, 1835. DLC-HC (DNA, M212, R5). Duplessis was a New Orleans resident who in 1838 resided on "Dauphin st, n Conti." He was a steward of the Louisiana (race) Course and in 1834 had served on a committee to draw up rules and regulations to decrease duelling in New Orleans. Fossier, *New Orleans, the Glamour Period*, 444; John Gibson, *Gibson's Guide and Directory of the State of Louisiana and the Cities of New Orleans and La Fayette . . .* (New Orleans, 1838), 9, 365. Although Richard M. Johnson never married, he had produced two daughters by his mulatto housekeeper, Julia Chinn. This became a campaign issue in 1836, especially in the South. Meyer, *Richard M. Johnson*, 317-23; Robert Bolt, "Vice President Richard M. Johnson of Kentucky: Hero of the Thames—Or Great Amalgamator?" *RKHS* (July, 1977), 75:191-203.

To John M. Bailhache, September 13, 1835. Discusses a mix-up in paying for his subscription to Bailhache's *Ohio State Journal* (Columbus). Continues: "I saw a good deal of General [William Henry] Harrison at Cincinnati. Very little passed between us on the subject of the Presidency. He was very respectful and cordial. . . . I adhere to the opinion expressed in my former letter, that, if Pennsylvania will give satisfactory demonstrations of an intention to support him, it will be expedient, under all circumstances, to run him as the most available candidate against Mr. Van Buren. The issue of the Rhode Island election following that of Connecticut, proves, I fear, that it is in vain to look even to New England for the support of Mr. Webster." Copy. Printed in Colton, *Clay Correspondence*, 4:399-400. In the April, 1835, election in Rhode Island, John Francis Brown, the Democratic candidate, was elected governor over Nehemiah Knight by a vote of 3,888 to 3,774. In the election for the Rhode Island house, the Whigs won 37 seats to 35 for the Democrats. Whigs won 4 seats in the Rhode Island senate, while Democrats won 2, and 4 seats remained vacant because no candidate had a majority. In May the legislature elected Nehemiah Knight to the U.S. Senate over Elisha R. Potter by a vote of 41 to 38. Tristam Burges and Henry Y. Cranston were the Whig nominees for the August congressional election, while Dutee Pearce and William Sprague, Jr., were both nominees for the Democratic and Anti-Masonic parties. The Democratic candidates were elected with the following votes: Sprague—3,924; Pearce—3,901; Burges—3,776; Cranston—3,659. Philip A. Grant, Jr., "Party Chaos Embroils Rhode Island," *RIH* (January, 1968), 27:27-29, 31.

In the spring elections in Connecticut, Henry W. Edwards, a Democrat, was elected governor over Samuel A. Foot, the Whig candidate, by a vote of 22,129 to 19,835. For the state senate 16 Democrats were elected to 5 Whigs, while 126 Democrats and 80 Whigs were chosen for the house. *Niles' Register* (April 25; May 16, 30, 1835),

48:130, 186, 219. The Democrats were also successful in the August congressional election, winning all six Connecticut seats. *Guide to U.S. Elections*, 564.

To Richard Graham, St. Louis, Mo., September 13, 1835. Writes to Graham as his agent informing him that he has agreed to purchase for his son, James Brown Clay, a parcel of land in Missouri. Wants to complete and fill out the parcel, which "wants compactness of form," with an additional nearby piece and asks Graham to assist him in confirming the initial purchase and in effecting the second purchase. Concludes: "My son seems to be very anxious to get to work upon the land. He is rather too young to turn out for himself, and wants experience of course; but he has a remarkable business aptitude, and if he has any vicious habits I do not know them. I hope, my dear Sir, that you will continue your kindness to him, and supply as far as may be convenient, the place of a father, if you find him worthy. He will need advice, and I know no one in whose judgment and friendly dispositions I would more confide than yourself." ALS. MoSHi. Addressed to Graham at "Hazle Patch near St. Louis."

Additional details on this transaction are in Clay to Graham, August 22, 1835. ALS. KyU.

Sometime in 1836, Clay took title to 562 and 91/100 acres he had purchased for James Brown Clay in St. Louis County. D. DLC-TJC (DNA, M212, R15).

The size of the purchase, now said to be 572 and 91/100 acres, and the fact that son James took up residence on the farm and was living in Missouri in mid-1837 is in Clay to Graham, June 1, 1837. ALS. MoSHi.

On October 20, 1835, Clay also wrote John O'Fallon [2:437] asking him to assist in clearing the clouded title of the farm in St. Louis County so that his son could proceed with improving it. *Ibid.*

Clay subsequently paid to have the farm stocked with livestock. John Headley to Clay, October 2, 1836. DS. DLC-TJC (DNA, M212, R18).

From HENRY CLAY, JR.   Bordeaux, France, Sept. 17, 1835
I send today by the ship Tuskina the Spanish ass Don Manuel. Mr. Haggerty [*sic*, James Hagarty][1] in New York will have him put upon grass until he can hear from you. I have written to him to draw upon you for the expenses of transportation. The Capt. carries him for $50 I finding every thing. The Captains bill and the charges in New York and on the way to Ky. will be all that are to be paid. May I beg that you will meet this bill and that you will write to James Haggerty of New York whom you know such directions as will be proper. The ass has been rode and he is as gentle as a dog, so that a small boy, might ride him. He is a very fine ass about 13½ hands and half an inch or one inch high. I am induced to send him because the Tuskina is a large packet and the only fine one in port. I shall go in a few days to the Hautes Pyrennus [*sic*, Pyrénées] department where I hope to procure some good Spanish asses. There is a mistake about them in America. The few I have seen are very handsome.

The expenses of purchasing, putting him on board, food, frame work on the ship &c will amount to about $100. The rest you will know. I wish him sold as soon as possible and the money deposited in the Bank of   so that I may have a fund to draw upon hereafter. If the expenses in New York and on the way out amount to $100 the whole cost will be $200. The Ass is worth in Ky more than Black Hawk, but I desire him to be sold for the highest than can be got. I suppose I can at least double my money. If you find yourself too much engaged to sell him for me I have no doubt that Mr. Smith or James[2] will attend to such directions as you may have the goodness to give.

Your asses have risen in my estimation. Such as Calypso if she be 14 hands and a half as I think you told me are dear in this country. When I speak of this country, I mean not Bordeaux but the high country which lies about 150 miles south. There are found Spanish asses of great beauty and size, but they are dear sometimes selling for 5 or 6 hundred dollars.

I am writing after having sat up several nights with my dear little daughter Matilda who has been ill. She is now much better and I hope will be well soon. Bordeaux though a beautiful town of 100,000 souls, has a wretched humid climate like that of New Orleans. Swamps are behind it, and the rains from the Bay of Biscay are insufferable. This year the vintage will be spoiled by the wet. Tell Anne [Brown Clay Erwin] that the Chasselas de Fontainebleau and the Muscat are considered here the best dessert grapes.

Don Manuel is 5 years old. The little hump upon his back was made by the Spanish saddle.

ALS. Henry Clay Memorial Foundation, Lexington, Ky. First paragraph only printed in Colton, *Clay Correspondence*, 4:400. 1. James Hagarty, a merchant at 26 Broad, resided at 37 Bond in New York City. Thomas Longworth, *Longworth's American Almanac: New-York Register, and City Directory*. New York, 1835. 2. Probably Thomas Smith and James Brown Clay.

From John Jacob Astor, New York, September 21, 1835. Thanks Clay for the $495 interest payment on his loan [Clay to Henry Clay, Jr., February 19, 1835]. Adds: "I note what you say about the Louisville Bridge [Clay to Astor, July 9, 1835]. There is so much demand for money here that it appears doubtful whether I shall have any to invest." LS. DLC-TJC (DNA, M212, R14).

To Maria Cecil Gist Gratz, Lexington, October 3, 1835. Says he has checked the proposed constitution and rules of the Orphan Society, finds them in order, and asserts that the objects of the society "cannot fail to rescue unfortunate Orphans from loss and ruin." Regrets that he cannot attend the initial meeting of the society because of the imminence of his departure "for the Eastward." ALS. Courtesy of Mrs. Lawrence Crump, Lexington, Ky. For M.C.G. (Mrs. Benjamin) Gratz, see 3:11.

To SAMUEL L. SOUTHARD   Lexington, October 12, 1835
My son John [Morrison Clay] returned the day before yesterday, having travelled home by himself. My intention is that he shall return to Edge Hill, with my two grandsons, children of my daughter Duralde.[1]

In a late letter you suggested that your name had been mentioned as a Candidate for V. P. in association with that of Genl. [William Henry] Harrison and asked me if you ought to consent to that use of it. By the time this letter will reach you, the issue of the Pennsa. election will be known,[2] and that will throw light on the future. If Harrison can obtain the vote of that State (and there shall be *soon* a clear indication of it) he will be a formidable Candidate, perhaps the most formidable. If he cannot obtain its vote, I think there will be an end of his pretensions. You cannot desire to run as V. P. without a reasonable prospect of success. There is no one that I would sooner see elected to that office. If therefore you are satisfied that Harrison will receive the vote of Pennsa. I think you might consent to be associated with him; otherwise not.

Can it be possible that Mr. [John Quincy] Adams has written such a letter as is alleged to D. J. Pearce?[3] Unwilling to believe it, I have nevertheless feared it was true. The age of miracles has certainly returned, in these extraordinary times. . . .

ALS. NjP.   1. Martin Duralde III and Henry Clay Duralde, sons of the late Susan Hart Clay Duralde. Wines to Clay, May 7, 1835.   2. Clay to Bailhache, June 27, 1835.   3. Adams had written Dutee J. Pearce, congratulating him and William Sprague, Jr., on their election to Congress from Rhode Island and referring to the Whig party in that state as a combination "of Hartford convention federalism and royal arch masonry" which "is so rotten with the corruption of both its elements, that I hail with joy the victory which you have achieved over it." *Niles' Register* (Oct. 10. 1835), 49:93. See also Clay to Bailhache, Sept. 14, 1835.

To HIRAM KETCHUM   Lexington, October 19, 1835

I duly recd. your favor of the 9h. inst. and feel greatly obliged by the friendly interest you took in the little affair with Col. Wooley [*sic*].[1] It has been much exaggerated, but was nevertheless an unpleasant occurrence. He made every apology and atonement which a gentleman could offer or require, and we were entirely reconciled. However much I regretted the incident, I do not allow myself any longer to dwell on it or any of the circumstances. I sustained no serious injury.

I am not at all surprized at the feelings you express in regard to the Presidential election. The actual state of the contest offers but little gratifying to the hopes of the patriot. It seems to be generally conceded that Mr. [Daniel] Webster, the best qualified of all of the Candidates, stands no chance; and, as to the rest, one can only find among them a choice of evils. Like you, however, I should prefer either to Mr. V. Buren. The issue of the Pennsa. election, yet unknown to us, will probably exercise much influence on the contest. . . .[2]

ALS. MH.   1. Aaron K. Woolley had, for some unreported reason, struck Clay in an incident at the Fayette County Courthouse. Washington *Daily National Intelligencer*, Oct. 23, 1835; Washington *Globe*, Oct. 27, 1835.   2. Clay to Bailhache, June 27, 1835.

To William Garrard *et al.*, Bourbon County, Ky., November 5, 1835. Declines an invitation to celebrate with them the anniversary of the Battle of Tippecanoe on November 7. Thanks them for lauding his public service during the War of 1812, and assures them that those "who gallantly fought our battles" during that conflict deserve the honor the Citizens of Bourbon County have planned to confer upon them. ALS. KyLoF. Some 1,800 people attended the celebration in Paris, Ky. Gen. William Henry Harrison was honored by the group, although he did not attend. Frankfort *Commonwealth*, November 21, 1835.

To LUCRETIA HART CLAY   Maysville, November 19, 1835

I got to Governor [Thomas] Metcalfe's, last night, in good time, and reached here to-day, at two o'clock. The weather has been very fine, and my ride was a very good one. They tell me that a steamboat will be here this evening, in which, when it arrives, I shall embark. I have directed Aaron to go to Governor Metcalfe's to-morrow night, and the next day home.

I feel very uneasy about our dear daughter, Anne [Brown Clay Erwin].[1] I sincerely hope that she may get well, and that all my apprehensions may prove groundless.

I feel too, my dear wife, most sincerely and excessively alive respecting your lonely situation. I regret it extremely, and whatever you may think to the contrary, I should have preferred, greatly, your accompanying me. But I hope and believe that this is the last separation, upon earth, that will take place, for any length of time, between us. And I hope that you will make every effort in your power to be cheerful, contended, and happy.

Copy. Printed in Colton, *Clay Correspondence*, 4:400-401.   1. Anne had given birth to a son—Charles Edward—on Nov. 2, 1835. See also Clay to Lucretia Hart Clay, Dec. 19, 1835.

To John Meany, Philadelphia, December 1, 1835. As a Kentuckian, thinks it inappropriate for him to recommend Meany [5:1034] for the governorship of Pennsylvania, in that "Such a recommendation might be deemed an officious intermeddling on my part." Gives him a letter of introduction instead. ALS. NcU. Written in Philadelphia.

To Lucretia Hart Clay, Lexington, December 3, 1835. Tells his wife that he has visited their son, John Morrison Clay, and their grandsons, Henry Clay Duralde and Martin Duralde III, at Edgehill Seminary in Princeton, N.J. Reports that John has gotten himself straightened out there [Clay to Wines, February 16, 1835] and that all three boys are "now contented with their situations." Visited the Samuel L. Southard family while in Trenton. Assures her he has purchased the oil cloth, stair carpeting, and two dozen each of the dessert forks, knives, and spoons she wants; also "two full blooded Durham Cows (mother and daughter)." Leaves for Washington tomorrow. ALS, part of letter torn off. DLC-TJC (DNA, M212, R11). Written from Philadelphia.

From Rezin D. Shepherd, Boston, December 4, 1835. Asks on what terms or in what manner Clay wants "to receive the Bull Orzimba [*sic*, Orozimbo] and three or four other heifers now at Shepherds Town" in Virginia and get them to Kentucky. ALS. DLC-TJC (DNA, M212, R14). Endorsed by Clay: "About Durham Cattle." Rezin D. Shepherd (spelled Sheppard in the Baltimore City Directory for 1837-38 and in the Baltimore census for 1850) was a merchant and factor in that city who did business in the "Counting House 2nd St. 1 door east of Gay." His ancestors were founders of Shepherdstown, Va. (W. Va.) and he himself later became a benfactor of the town. Samuel Gordon Smyth, *A Genealogy of the Duke-Shepherd-Van Metre Family* (Lancaster, Pa., 1909), 158, 244-45, 408; Millard K. Bushong, *A History of Jefferson County West Virginia* (Charles Town, 1941), 205.

For Orozimbo, a short-horned, red roan, County Durham, English bull out of Rockingham by Thorp, whose grandam was by Wonder and greatgrandam by Wellington, see J.C. Etches to R.D. Shepherd, Liverpool, July 10, 1836.

In addition to the animal's pedigree, Etches also certified that he shipped the three-year-old Orozimbo (born March 20, 1832) from Liverpool to R.D. Shepherd in Baltimore in March, 1835; Shepherd, in an endorsement on the Etches letter, dated April 27, 1836, acknowledged receipt of the pedigree and asserted that the bull was "Now in the possession of Henry Clay Esqr of Kentucky." ADS, by R.D. Shepherd. DLC-TJC (DNA, M212, R18). Endorsed by Clay on verso of Etches letter: "Pedigree of Orozimbo and Five imported Durhams purchased from Mr. Shepherd." For more on Orozimbo [occasionally spelled Orizimbo], see Richard L. Troutman, "Plantation Life in the Ante-Bellum Bluegrass Region of Kentucky," M.A. thesis, University of Kentucky, 1955, pp. 124-25; and Van Deusen, *The Life of Henry Clay*, 272-73.

Clay writes Charles Higbee from Philadelphia December 4, 1835, that his cows and their drover have arrived and will soon proceed on to Shepherdstown via Columbia, Pa., on the Susquehannah River. ALS. NN.

On December 10, John Ridgely, Shepherd's associate in this transaction with Clay, certifies to Clay that the white short-horned bull calf and light roan heifer calf they have sold him are both sired by Orozimbo and are out of thoroughbred County Durham English cows. ADS. DLC-TJC (DNA, M212, R17).

Clay informs Isaac Vanmeter of Winchester, Ky., on December 12 that he is sending out to Kentucky "Two Durham bulls, one imported and the other raised by Col Powell [*sic*, John Hare Powel]." Both are ready to service cows. Copy. Printed in *FCHQ* (January, 1952), 26:42-43.

On December 17, Charles Higbee reports to Clay from Trenton that the drover in charge of Clay's cows has delivered them at Shepherdstown "in good condition." Presumes that Clay has also received "the pedigree I sent you." ALS. DLC-TJC (DNA, M212, R14).

804

R.D. Shepherd informs Clay on December 28 that Hector, the Powel bull he has acquired, was out of Delight by Malcolm. Delight had been imported by Powel from England. *Ibid.* (R17).

Clay writes from Washington to John Hare Powel, then in Baltimore, on December 29, thanking him for the "Very acceptable present of the Durham bull [Hector]," requesting the animal's pedigree when convenient to send it, and reporting that "Owing to his having been conducted injudiciously from Philada. to Shepherdstown his feet had become too tender to proceed immediately to Kentucky." Says Hector will remain in Shepherdstown until March, 1836, "when, by having him carefully shod, I have no doubt that he will safely reach Ashland." ALS. PHi.

On January 6, 1836, Shepherd again writes Clay, stating that "it was not my wish or intention that any alteration should take place in the" contract on the cattle. Promises that if any cattle "Come worthy of being sent to Kentuckey [*sic*], no dispositon shall be made of them until I know your wishes." ALS. Josephine Simpson Collection, Lexington, Ky.

On January 21, 1836, Shepherd writes Clay, quoting from a letter from Capt. Lindsey of his ship *Unicorn* that describes the "three Jacks & their Jennys" Lindsey has purchased for Clay in Malta and has on board the vessel. *Ibid.*

Remark in Senate, December 8, 1835. Presents credentials of John J. Crittenden, Senator-elect from Kentucky, following which Crittenden was sworn in. *Register of Debates*, 24 Cong., 1 Sess., 4.

To LUCRETIA HART CLAY   Washington, December 9, 1835

I arrived here yesterday from Balto. with a bad cold and a good deal fatigued. A few days of rest, if I can get it, will I trust relieve me. Judge [Alexander] Porter and myself have found lodgings in a quiet house, kept by Mr. [M.A.] Clements, on the same street in which we last lived. It cannot accommodate more than another, and we shall therefore not be annoyed with too much company.[1]

Mr. [John J.] Crittenden brings me the latest accounts from Anne [Brown Clay Erwin]. He passed through Lexn. on the 1st. and tells me that he understood she was in better health, and free from danger, altho' not entirely well. My anxiety about her I cannot describe. Our only daughter—and so good a daughter—there is no event that would so entirely overwhelm us as that of her loss.[2] I sincerely hope that we are not destined to experience this sad calamity; and my prayers are daily offered for her preservation. I hope to hear from her by the next mail, and by that Mr. [James] Erwin will continue to keep me informed about her. His letters have relieved me a good deal, but the last was dated the 27h. Ulto.

Henry's [Clay, Jr.] Jack [Don Manuel] will prove, I think, to be a valuable purchase. I sent him from Balto to Shepherdstown yesterday. At that place I am collecting some Eight or ten head of Durham Cattle.[3] Five of them I got from Mr. [Rezin D.] Shepherd on the shares. I shall go with him to Shepherdstown about Xmas, and then send the Stock off to Kentucky, with the Jack.

I have letters from James [Brown Clay] and am happy to find that he continues pleased with his purchase and situation.[4] He bought several articles at the sale of the Roses. He tells me that the negro boys are all contented.

Mr. [John] Bell lost the election as Speaker. It was what was expected. But the majority against him was greater than was anticipated.[5] I met with him and his wife at Philada. She is gone to Boston.

I wrote you after I saw the boys at Princeton.[6] They came down with me to Trenton, and we spent a very quiet and pleasant night at Mr. [Samuel L.] Southards. He and his family are here, and have taken lodgings by themselves at Keyworths, on the [Pennsylvania] Avenue.

I recd. Thomas's [Hart Clay] first letter, and shall write soon to him.

ALS. DLC-TJC (DNA, M212, R10).   1. The Clements house was on C Street. Soon joining Clay and Porter there was Sen. John J. Crittenden of Ky. Goldman & Young, *The United States Congressional Directory*, 291.   2. For Anne's death, see Clay to Lucretia Hart Clay, Dec. 19, 1835.   3. Shepherd to Clay, Dec. 4, 1835.   4. Clay to Graham, Sept. 13, 1835.   5. James K. Polk of Tenn. defeated John Bell of Tenn. for Speaker of the House, 24th Congress. The vote was 132 to 84 with 9 scattered or blank. *Cong. Globe*, 24 Cong., 1 Sess., 2-3.   6. Clay to Lucretia Hart Clay, Dec. 3, 1835.

To JAMES ERWIN   Washington, December 10, 1835

I recd. several letters from you, up to the date of the 26h. of last month. They relieved my anxiety a good deal about my dear Anne [Brown Clay Erwin]; but Thomas [Hart Clay] tells me, in a letter of the 27h. that she was unwell and that his mother [Lucretia Hart Clay] has gone to the Woodlands to see her. On the other hand, Mr. [John J.] Crittenden informs me that he saw you on the first inst. and that she was then better, and in no danger.[1] I sincerely hope his information may prove correct; but I shall not feel easy until I again hear from you.

I bought from the B. of the U.S. a bill on the Mess. Hottinguer & Co. for 5200 franks, the exact amount of $1000 at the existing rate of Exchange, which I have forwarded to Paris, sending one number directly to Henry [Clay, Jr.], and the other to D[aniel] Brent to be delivered to Henry. On reflection, I thought it best to send the memo. of the articles to him, and to say to him that he had better consult with Mad. Serrurier [*sic*, Serurier].

Henrys Jack (Don Manuel) is uncommonly large and fine.[2] I think him superior greatly to Warrior in form, and not much inferior in size.

I have got ten head of Durham Cattle, five my own, and five Mr. [Rezin D.] Shepherd's on the shares. They are, or shortly will be, all at Shepherdstown, to proceed soon to K.[3]

You will have heard of [James K.] Polk's election as Speaker.[4] It is believed that [William Henry] Harrison will be nominated at Harrisburg.[5]

My love to my dear daughter & your children. Tell her that I wish to have from her own hand the assurance that she is well.

ALS. NHi.   1. Clay to Lucretia Hart Clay, Dec. 9, 19, 1835.   2. Clay to Lucretia Hart Clay, Dec. 9, 1835.   3. *Ibid*.   4. *Ibid*.   5. Drinker to Clay, July 16, 1835.

From Thomas Smith, Lexington, December 10, 1835. Discusses legal-financial problems relating to Clay's law practice. Continues: "All are well at Ashland. Mrs. E. [Anne Brown Clay Erwin] is recovering from a relapse. Her physician expects her to be well enough to leave home in a week or two [Clay to Lucretia Hart Clay, December 19, 1835]. — I dread the consequences of a collision between Clarke [*sic*, James Clark] & [James Turner] Morehead for Govr. If it should occur, [James] Guthrie will be elected. Should your friends in Virginia & Maryland second the movement in your behalf in Pa. I cannot see how you will avoid another race — As the question now stands between Van Buren & his competitors [Webster, White, Harrison], the Whigs might as well permit the election to go by default — for he will in all probability get more Electoral votes than all three of them [Clay to Bailhache, July 14, 1835]." ALS. DLC-HC (DNA, M212, R5). James Clark became the Whig nominee for governor of Kentucky in 1836, with Charles A. Wickliffe as the nominee for lieutenant governor. The Democrats nominated Matthew Flournoy for governor and Elijah Hise for lieutenant governor. The vote was: Clark—38,857 and Flournoy—30,491; Wickliffe—35,524 and Hise—32,186. James Guthrie, a Democrat, had been chosen president of the Kentucky senate in 1834. After the local elections of 1835 Whig members of the legislature contended that Guthrie's term was for 1834 only. This became a heated partisan issue. Smith apparently feared that Clark would lose the gubernatorial race if Governor Morehead were the Democratic candidate and that Guthrie would therefore be reelected president of the senate. The Whigs were also victorious in the election for the state legislature, carrying the house 58 to 42 and the senate 24 to 14. Lexington *Observer & Kentucky Reporter*, August 24, 1836; Thomas D. Clark, *A History of Kentucky* (Lexington, 1954), 293-94. The movement for Clay in Pennsylvania which Smith mentions probably refers to the December, 1835, declaration of Clay supporters that they were not bound by the action of the Harrisburg convention's [Drinker to Clay, July 16, 1835] nomination of William Henry Harrison. Mueller, *The Whig Party in Pennsylvania*, 29-32. Although Clay was popular in Maryland, the Whig state convention met in December, 1835, and nominated Harrison. There appears to have been no significant Clay movement in Virginia at this time. Wilbur Wayne Smith, "The Whig Party in Maryland, 1826-1856," Ph.D. dissertation, University of Maryland, 1967, pp. 116-17; Simms, *The Rise of the Whigs in Virginia*, 98-116.

From JAMES ERWIN   Lexington, December 15, 1835
I feel myself scarcely equal to the task which my duty imposes, that of writing you at this time, and speaking of the late dreadful calamity[1] with which it has pleased God to afflict us—by which, at the same fatal blow, has been taken from you a daughter, unequaled in filial devotion and love, and from me a wife, the most devoted, kind, and virtuous, with which man was ever blessed.

Other friends have, I learn, given you the particulars of this sad event, which will spare me the pain of presenting to you the heart-rendering scene which was so unexpectedly produced by the hand of Providence.

My home, lately the happiest, which I have shared for years with a beloved wife, who returned my affection with a devotion almost unknown, who, whether I was worthy or not, honored me with a love and confidence which I would not have exchanged for the whole world beside, that home is now to me insupportable. Every object that presents itself—each tree and flower, once so dear when objects of her care—now serve only to make known to me my loss and my misery. The beloved object who gave life and animation to all, has left me to lament over my wretched fate.

You, my dear sir, I am fully sensible, can and will extend to me more sympathy than any other human being—you who best knew her exalted worth, who have daily witnessed our happiness, not surpassed, I vainly believe, in the annals of wedded life—you who shared our pleasures and our joy, who bestowed upon me the choicest gift of heaven, can feel for me, but who, I fear, will require for yourself all the sympathy of your friends, and all the philosophy with which you are endowed, to support you under this sad bereavement. Mrs. [Lucretia Hart] Clay, although in reality scarcely able to support herself under this severe trial, has suppressed, as far as she was able, her own feelings, intent only in rendering to me and my dear children[2] every kindness which her judgment and affection could suggest. She has abandoned her own home and remained with us, exerting herself to preserve the babe [Charles Edward], which has cost us all so dear.

My children, now ten-fold more dear to me than before, afford me much consolation, yet they are the objects of my greatest solicitude; for me to remain

807

here is impossible, and to part from any of them, at this moment, will be equally trying. Mrs. Clay at once kindly proposed taking charge of all of them, and to have Miss Brulard[3] remove to Ashland, for the present, and teach them as before. Miss B. wishes to return South, and the plan now is, to leave the three youngest at Ashland, the babe, with Lotty[4] and a wet nurse, under Mrs. Clay's care, and for the two boys, Henry and James, to accompany me.

I expect to leave for New Orleans two days hence. My boys will be important to me, and I shall take care not to let any feeling prevent their having the best means for their improvement afforded them.

I shall hope to hear from you very soon after I reach New Orleans.

Copy. Printed in Colton, *Clay Correspondence*, 4:401-2.   1. Clay to Lucretia Hart Clay, Dec. 19, 1835.   2. Henry Clay, James, Jr., Andrew Eugene, Lucretia Hart, and Charles Edward. 3. Apparently the children's governess. See Clay to Southard, Sept. 27, 1836.   4. A slave.

Remark in Senate, December 15, 1835. Declares he will not vote for Sen. Thomas H. Benton's motion to assign seats on the floor to Michigan Senators-elect Lucius Lyon and John Norvell pending Michigan's formal admission into the Union. Wonders what their legal roles and powers would be in the interim. Meanwhile, asserts his readiness to discuss the "principal question . . . the admission of Michigan, as soon as any gentleman might be disposed to move it." *Register of Debates*, 24 Cong., 1 Sess., 8-9. For Lyon and Norvell, see *BDAC*. Michigan was not formally admitted to the Union until January 26, 1837, due to complications resulting from boundary disputes with Ohio and Indiana. For the legislative history of this admissions problem, see *ibid.*, 5-6, 10-11, 36-41, 256-62, 264, 282-90, 1006-22, 1737-39, 1780-81, 1876, 2077-2102, 2145-60, 4206-81; 24 Cong., 2 Sess., 167-172, 204-325, 1312-13, 1414-15, 1434-51, 1479-1500. The final bill passed the Senate on January 5, 1837, the House on January 25, and was approved by the president on January 26. U.S. Sen., *Journal*, 24 Cong., 2 Sess., 93, 163, 165. The act is in 5 *U.S. Stat.*, 144. See also Willis Dunbar, *Michigan Through the Centuries*, 4 vols. (New York, 1955), 1:194-95; and Alec R. Gilpin, *The Territory of Michigan 1805-1837* (East Lansing, Mich., 1970), 193.

To LUCRETIA HART CLAY   Washington, December 19, 1835

Alas! my dear wife, the great Destroyer has come, and taken from us our dear, dear, only daughter![1] My worst forebodings are realized. From the time of her confinement, seeing that she had been nervous and did not sleep well, I have had constant fears, anxieties and forebodings about her. But on the day, when I took leave of her—and she never looked upon me more sweetly or affectionately—she had passed the critical period. Still I left home with strong apprehensions about her. They continued to write me that, altho' occasionally ill, she was getting better. Even yesterday evening, the first letter that I opened from the Western mail assured me that she was much better and would be able in a week or two to accompany Mr. [James] Erwin to New Orleans; but the next, of the same date, from Bishop Smith[2] told me the fatal and melancholy fact. I have prayed for this dear child; night and morning have I fervently prayed for her; but oh! my prayers have not been heard.

If the thunderbolt of H[e]aven had fallen on me—unprepared as I fear I am—I would have submitted, chearfully submitted, to a thousand deaths to have saved this dear child. She was so good, so beloving, and so beloved, so happy, and so deserving to be happy. Then, she was the last of six dear daughters, most of them at periods of the greatest interest and hope, taken from us.[3] Ah! how inscrutable are the ways of providence!

I feel that one of the strongest tyes that bound me to Earth is broken — forever broken. My heart will bleed as long as it palpitates. Never, never, can its wounds be healed.

I know, my dear wife, my duty, but how difficult is it to restrain the sorrows of a broken heart? I know submission to the Will of God is my duty. I have not to sustain me the religious resource which you have, and I regret it; but reason tells me what is my duty. I wish she could enable me to perform it. I know it is my duty not only to submit to Gods will, but to cherish what he has been graciously pleased to leave me. I know I ought to discharge all my duties towards you, my children, and her children who have been left behind by my dear, departed daughter. I shall try to discharge them; but the path may be clear, and yet if we have not feet or legs we cannot move along it.

The particulars of this sad event have not yet reached me. They will come soon enough. All that Mr. Bishop Smith tells me is that it was sudden.

I have not heard from poor Mr. [James] Erwin. The greater magnitude of his sufferings ought to lessen ours. To have lost such a wife as she was! In the midst of youth, with all her plans of happiness and improvements; and her five children!⁴ Poor orphans, what will become of you!

My dear, I ought to endeavor to comfort you, and I am shewing my weakness. I cannot help it. This dear child was so entwined around my heart; I looked forward to so many days of comfort and happiness in her company, during the remnant of my life, that I shall never, never be able to forget her. My tears, and thank God they have flowed almost in a continued stream, have been my only relief. Sleep, food, I have scarcely tasted either.

I have written to Henry and to John.⁵ It is only about ten days ago that I wrote to Henry, and transmitted to him, a list of articles to purchase for his dear sister, to ornament her house and deck her person. Alas! she will never want them more! How little did I then expect that so soon, from such a cause, I should have to countermand the order.

I pray my dear Wife that you may have been able to bear, and may continue to bear, this great affliction better than I have or shall.⁶ I send you the last communication from the school about John [Morrison Clay], which shews how well he is doing, and how worthy he is of our affection.

Give my affectionate regards to Mr. Erwin; tell him that the will of my dear child, written during the period of the Cholera, is at Ashland. And remember me to and kiss my dear grandchildren for your affectionate And afflicted husband

ALS. KyU.   1. Anne Brown Clay Erwin (1807-1835) died on Dec. 10, 1835, from complications following the birth of son Charles Edward on Nov. 2, 1835.   2. Benjamin Bosworth Smith, rector of Christ Church Episcopal in Lexington, later became presiding bishop of the Protestant Episcopal Church in the United States. Ranck, *History of Lexington Kentucky*, 199; *RKHS*, 7:19-22.   3. Henrietta (d. young), Susan Hart Duralde (1805-1825), Lucretia Hart (1809-1823), Eliza (1815-1825), Laura (b. and d. 1816).   4. Julia D. Erwin (1825-1828), Henry Clay Erwin (1827-1859), James Erwin, Jr. (1828-1848), Andrew Eugene Erwin (1829-1863), Lucretia Hart Erwin (1830-1866; m. Frederic Cowles), Mary Erwin (b. May 1832, d. Oct. 1832), unnamed son (stillborn or d. on or soon after Oct. 2, 1833), Charles Edward Erwin (1835-1860).   5. Henry Clay, Jr., was traveling in Europe; John Morrison Clay was in school at Edgehill Seminary in Princeton, N.J.   6. Letters of condolence and Clay's sorrowful responses to them included Clay to Arthur J. Stansbury, Dec. 19, 1835. For Stansbury, see *CAB*. ALS. DLC-HC (DNA, M212, R5).   Margaret Bayard (Mrs. Samuel Harrison) Smith to Clay, Dec. 31, 1835. *Ibid.*   Clay to Margaret Bayard Smith, Dec. 31, 1835. Copy. Printed in Hunt, *First Forty Years of Washington Society*, 375-76.

From Charles W. Morgan, Baltimore, December 19, 1835. Believes that the annual report of Secretary of Treasury Levi Woodbury is so "spun out to the bitter end" and "so gratuitously expressed" as to convey the notion "that it was as much intended to prove the Honble. Secretary's fitness for a future President as Secretary of the Treasury." Announces that he has for sale "a pair of blooded colts—not less than 7/8ths of the Diomede, Archer, Charles, Ratler [*sic*, Rattler] & Star stock—4 and 5, last spring." Will sell them for $1,000. Asks Clay to mention their availability to gentlemen of his acquaintance in Washington, especially Senators Alexander Porter and William C. Preston. ALS, manuscript torn. DLC-James H. Hammond Papers (DNA, M212, R21). The author of this letter was possibly Charles W. Morgan, a U.S. Navy officer from 1809 to 1842, who at this time was in the rank of captain. His Baltimore connection, although he seems never to have lived there, was as brother-in-law to Mrs. John E. Howard, Jr. The Howards, prominent Baltimoreans, looked after his business affairs when he was at sea. Information courtesy of Dr. Frederick Hopkins, University of Baltimore.

From HENRY CLAY, JR.   London, England, December 20, 1835
We arrived in London a few days ago after a somewhat arduous journey. After leaving Bordeaux we directed our course to MontPellier and the South of France. Thence we proceeded up the Rhone to Lyons, and across to Geneva. It had been our intention to penetrate into Italy, but as the cholera still prevailed to an alarming extent we determined to turn our faces northward. Accordingly after having examined some of the curiosities of Switzerland we passed to Basle [*sic*, Basel], and thence along the left bank of the Rhine to Strasbourg Mayence [*sic*, Mainz] and Cologne. At the last place we left this beautiful river and crossed through a part of Western Prussia to Brussels, the Capital of Belgium. Finding ourselves so near the scene of one of the great events of your life we could not resist the temptation of seeing Ghent. Your hotel is at present occupied by the Burgomaster. Quitting Ghent we proceeded to Calais and London. You will perceive from the route I have mentioned that we have made a pretty extensive and very interesting tour. The particulars I must reserve until we meet.

All Europe is awaiting with anxiety the Presidents message.[1] Though I am somewhat inclined to think that the French will at length find it to their interest to give up scruples about honor; still they profess a readiness to engage in war rather than submit upon this point. I feel as much as any one that Genl Jackson's offensive message was uncalled for and only exhibited ignorance of the French Constitution, yet, I hope, as matters stand, that the French may not be allowed to triumph over us.

What prospect is there of opposing Van Buren with success?—Do you not think that the election of another Genl.[2] might have bad consequences? Some of the correspondents of European papers assert that you are again to be a candidate. Much as I should like to see you President, I hope you will not allow yourself to be made a candidate until there be a positive certainty of success.

The agitation of the slave question with the consequences it has had will weaken the credit of America in Europe. Capitalists will not be anxious to invest more money in our country, but as they are not alarmed to such a degree as to make them withdraw what funds they have there, we should perhaps be content.

We would return to America very soon, but we fear the winter storms. I do not know exactly when we can venture. If we wait till next summer, which would certainly be the most agreeable time, Julias [Prather Clay] situation will be such that it will be extremely hazardous. I now think that we shall either sail in February or March or else remain in Europe till next fall. We have good lodgings at present and I think when we are stationary we can live for $500 a month. A serious inroad, I fear, will notwithstanding, be made in our fortune. However I am young and I hope will [ms. torn] able to retrieve it. If you hear of any thing [ms. torn] do in Europe, I should like to have engage [ms. torn] for many vacant hours and would undert [ms. torn] thing which with my limited knowledge of [ms. torn] I should be likely to perform.

When in France I purchased two Jack [ms. torn] Jennies,[3] one of the Jacks I sent in September to [ms. torn] New York, the other three animals were to have [ms. torn] dispatched in Nov. I have not yet heard fr [ms. torn] but I presume they have sailed. I wrote you [ms. torn] about them at the time I purchased them. [ms. torn] Jack and Jennies which went last I do not [ms. torn] have sold, unless $2000 could be got for the Ja [ms. torn] which case, he might be disposed of. I think it will be found on trial that they are perhaps better than other asses for breeding large mules. I repeat to you again after having seen hundreds of mules that the average is as large if not larger than Ky horses. I was prevented by the Cholera and the alarms of cholera from sending any donkeys from the Mediterranean islands. If you think, at the time you receive this letter, that large asses from the Mediterranean or any kind of stock from England could be sent to America with profit, please let me know it

Julia and our little Henry [Clay III], who now talks very prettily are quite well and join me in affectionate regards & love to all the family P.S. No letter nor newspaper — not a word of any kind has reached me from home for months.

ALS, manuscript torn. Henry Clay Memorial Foundation, Lexington, Ky.   1. *MPP*, 3:100-107; Brown to Clay, Jan. 24, 1832; Remark in Senate, Jan. 6, 1835; Speech in Senate, Jan. 14, 1835.   2. Probably a reference to William Henry Harrison.   3. Henry Clay, Jr., to Clay, Sept. 17, 1835.

To JOHN HOWARD PAYNE   Washington, December 23, 1835

I recd. your letter of the 1st inst. with a statement of the outrage recently perpetrated upon you by persons acting under the authority of the State of Georgia,[1] which I have attentively perused. All must unite in opinion as to the enormity of the injury. I wish there could be equal concurrence as to the mode and certainty of Redress. There appears 1st. to have been a violation of the territorial rights of Tennessee. These I suppose she must vindicate. 2dly. Your personal rights. Is there any remedy for you but that which the tribunals of justice can afford? I apprehend not. Thus 3dly. the indian rights, in the person of Mr. [John] Ross. Alas! poor Indians, what rights can they assert against the State of Georgia, backed by the tremendous power of Genl. Jackson?

I wish I could, consistently with truth and my own sense of what becomes our Country and our Age make a reply more satisfactory to you and to myself. I regret that I cannot.

ALS. NNC.   1. Georgia guards had crossed into Tennessee on Nov. 7, 1835, and arrested Payne and Cherokee chief John Ross, accusing them of being abolitionists and charging them with plotting to raise an insurrection among Negro slaves who would then join the Indians in an uprising against the whites. Payne at this time was transcribing Cherokee tribal documents, at the invitation of Ross, preparatory to writing a history of the tribe. Both men were soon released. The incident is mentioned in the *DAB* articles on both men. See also Wilkins, *Cherokee Tragedy*, 273-74; and Moulton, *John Ross*, 69.

To ADAM BEATTY & JAMES BYERS   Washington, *ca.* December 24, 1835

I recd. your favor of the 14h. inst.   At present, I have at home but one Jack, too young for service, and another uncommonly large and fine which has been just imported by my son;[1] but he is for sale, and not for farming. He will be at Maysville in 3 or 4 weeks.

I had expected some Jacks direct from Malta,[2] but they have not yet arrived, and I may be disappointed about them.

Farming Jacks is not very good for the owner, and I do not know, if I receive those I expect, that I can promise you one. It must depend on circumstances.

ALS. Courtesy of Earl M. Ratzer, Highland Park, Ill. Addressed to Beatty and Byers in Washington, Ky. 1. Henry Clay, Jr., to Clay, Dec. 20, 1835. 2. Shepherd to Clay, Dec. 4, 1835.

Speech in Senate, December 29, 1835. Remarks that while he is "borne down by the severest affliction with which Providence has ever been pleased to visit me," he must subordinate his "private griefs [Clay to Lucretia Hart Clay, December 19, 1835]" to the "discharge of my public duties." Introduces a bill to "appropriate, for a limited time, the proceeds of the sales of the public lands of the United States, and for granting land to certain states." Says his bill "conforms substantially" to the one passed by Congress in March, 1833 [Speech in Senate, January 7; December 5, 1833], and pocket vetoed by the president. Explains that in this bill, 10 percent of the proceeds from public lands sold in Ohio, Indiana, Illinois, Alabama, Mississippi, and Louisiana would first be set aside for the use of each of these "new states"; in addition, the seven new states would also receive "the five per cent. reserved by their several compacts with the United States." The remainder of the proceeds would be divided among all of the 24 states "in proportion to their federal population. In this respect the bill conforms" to that which was originated by resolution on March 23, 1832 [Speech in Senate, June 20, 1832], passed by the Senate on June 28, 1832, postponed to December 3, 1832, by the House, and not passed by Congress until March 1, 1833 [Comment in Senate, April 16, 1832; Speech in Senate, June 20, 1832; January 7, 1833]. Says he is willing "to have allowed the new States twelve and a half instead of ten percent.; but, as that was objected to by the President [Jackson] in his veto message [Speech in Senate, January 7, 1833], and has been opposed in other quarters, I thought it best to restrict the allowance to the more moderate sum." Notes that his bill "also contains large and liberal grants of land to several of the new States to place them on an equality with others to which the bounty of Congress has been heretofore extended." Defends at length the contents and purposes of his proposed bill, condemns Jackson's unconstitutional pocket veto of the similar bill passed by Congress on March 1, 1833, and points out that in event of foreign war the distribution of proceeds will cease and those funds will be applied to the prosecution of the war. Laments that had the vetoed bill become law in March, 1833, "about twenty millions of dollars would have been, during the last three years, in the hands of the several States, applicable by them to the beneficent purposes of internal improvement, education, or colonization. What immense benefits might not have been diffused throughout the land by the active employment of that large sum! What new channels of commerce and communication might not have been opened! What industry stimulated, what labor rewarded! How many youthful minds might have received the blessings of education and knowledge, and been rescued from ignorance, vice, and ruin! How many descendants of Africa might have been transported from a country where they never can enjoy political or social equality, to the native land of their fathers, where no impediment exists to their attainment of the highest degree of elevation, intellectual, social, and political! where they might have been successful instruments, in the hands of God, to spread the religion of his Son, and to lay the foundations of civil liberty!"

Concludes with a review of his role in the legislative history of previous public land sales distribution bills ("The affair of the public lands was forced upon me"); remarks that he plans soon to retire from public service; and affirms that in moving into retirement, "I shall carry there no regrets, no complaints, no reproaches, on my own account.

When I look back upon my humble origin, left an orphan too young to have been conscious of a father's smiles and caresses, with a widowed mother, surrounded by a numerous offspring, in the midst of pecuniary embarrassments, without a regular education, without fortune, without friends, without patrons, I have reason to be satisfied with my public career." *Register of Debates*, 24 Cong., 1 Sess., 48-52; *Cong. Globe*, 24 Cong., 1 Sess., 54-55. Printed in Colton, *Clay Correspondence*, 6:27-33, where it is misdated December 20. The *Cong. Globe* prints a copy of the proposed bill and corrects or eliminates several numerical errors in the *Register* version. Colton prints the latter. Jackson's belated (written December 4, 1833) defense of his pocket veto of the distribution bill Congress had passed in early March, 1833, is in *MPP*, 3:56-69. His questioning of the 12½ percent figure is in *ibid.*, 64. For Clay's sponsorship of and activities in behalf of various earlier distribution bills, see his comments, remarks, and speeches in the Senate of April 16; June 20, 1832; January 7; December 11, 1834; also Clay to Wilde, April 27, 1833; Speech in Senate, April 26, 1836. For a brief history of distribution, Clay's and Jackson's attitudes toward it, and the fate of various bills regarding it, see Hibbard, *History of Public Land Policies*, 171-84. For the legislative history of Clay's distribution bill in the 24th Cong., 1 Sess., see *Register of Debates*, 48-52, 810-33, 1172-77, 1299-1313, 1396, 2892-2918, 3201, 3231, 3580-93, 3617-30, 3679-86, 3820-39, 3841-63, 4195-96, 4322-28. The bill passed the Senate on May 4, 1836, by a vote of 25 to 20 but was tabled in the House on June 22. U.S. Sen., *Journal*, 24 Cong., 1 Sess., 330, 1075. Clay introduced it again on December 19, 1836, but moved to table it on February 23, 1837. *Ibid.*, 2 Sess., 46, 276.

Remark in Senate, December 30, 1835. Speaks briefly to Sen. John C. Calhoun's resolution of September 29 to reduce or repeal all duties "consistently with a due regard to the manufacturing interest." This would, Calhoun held, reduce "the immense surplus which was daily accruing in the public treasury." Clay replies that any proposition to lower the duty on wine and silks must carefully be studied. Concurs in Calhoun's statement, however, that there are $21 million of surplus revenue in the U.S. Treasury and that an additional $7 million from the expiring Bank of the United States [Clay to Fendall, August 4, 1832] will soon be added. *Register of Debates*, 24 Cong., 1 Sess., 54-55; *Cong. Globe*, 24 Cong., 1 Sess., 58. Calhoun's double-barrelled bill to regulate the deposits of the public money in private banks, as well as to distribute the surplus in the U.S. Treasury to the states, was introduced on December 29, 1835. It passed the Senate 39 to 6 on June 17, 1836, and the House 155 to 38 on June 21; the president approved it on June 23. *Cong. Globe*, 24 Cong., 1 Sess., 562, 575; U.S. Sen., *Journal*, 24 Cong., 1 Sess., 66, 447, 471, 1071. The act is in 5 *U.S. Stat.*, 52-57. For Calhoun's stance in this matter, see Wiltse, *John C. Calhoun, Nullifier*, 259-60, 265-66. See also Hibbard, *History of the Public Land Policies*, 184; and Comment in Senate, December 21, 1836.

To FRANCIS T. BROOKE Washington, January 1, 1835 [*sic*, 1836]
I recd. your friendly letter of condolence on the occasion of my recent severe affliction,[1] and I thank you for it. The sympathy of no friend that I have could have more soothing effect than the expression of yours; but alas! my dear Sir there are some wounds which nothing can heal, and I feel that such an one has been inflicted on me. My poor daughter [Anne Brown Clay Erwin] was the last of six that God had given us.[2] Never was father blessed with one more filial, more affectionate or who was more beloved by all her connexions. She was my nighest neighbour; all her tastes and pleasures and amusements, especially in improving and beautifying her grounds, were similar to my own. Without an enemy, with a husband [James Erwin] devotedly attached to her, and whom she, in turn, ardently loved; with four sweet children, besides the infant recently born,[3] with a circle of the most warm hearted friends, such is the daughter I

have lost! If I had been asked three weeks ago to point out the happiest female I knew & the happiest family, it would have been my dear daughter, and her husband & children. All my plans of future life; all the prospects before me of passing quietly and agreeably the remnant of my days, comprehended her as a prominent individual. When I left home she was not well but in not the least danger as was supposed. I had nevertheless painful forebodings; and I opened every Western mail with trembling anxiety. The first letter which I opened, in that which brought me the fatal news, assured me that she was well, and had even fixed on the day of her departure for N. Orleans; but the next, of the same date, told the mournful tale. She died suddenly, probably from the rupture of some vital organ.

I feel, my dear friend, as if nothing remained for me in this world but the performance of duties. These I hope, whilst I remain, God will give me strength to fulfill.

ALS. NcD. 1. Clay to Lucretia Hart Clay, Dec. 19, 1835. 2. Henrietta; Susan Hart Clay Duralde; Eliza; Lucretia; and Laura were Clay's other daughters. 3. Henry Clay; James, Jr.; Andrew Eugene; Lucretia; and Charles Edward were the surviving Erwin children. See also Clay to Lucretia Hart Clay, Nov. 19, 1835.

To Thomas Hart Clay, Lexington, January 2, 1836. Reports that he has obtained two Durham bulls, one of which "is an uncommonly fine animal" named Orozimbo [Shepherd to Clay, December 4, 1835]. The other, named Hector, "by Malcolm out of Delight," was raised by Col. Powell [*sic*, John Hare Powell] and presented to me." Discusses selling the jack, Don Manuel, and wonders how Aaron Dupuy is caring for Magnum Bonum. ALS. ICHi. Dupuy was a family slave.

To THOMAS SPEED
Washington, January 2, 1836

I received your favor of the 22d. Ulto. and attentively perused it in the friendly spirit in which it was written.

At the moment when I am considering of an early period of quitting public life altogether, you propose for me a new career upon a new theatre in the Government of Kentucky. The object which you desire to see attained is a great and good one, the gradual emancipation of Slaves *within our State*, and I think of it as I have always thought of it. The principle may be safely applied in our State where the proportion of the African race is too small to create apprehension of their ever becoming, in a state of freedom, the predominant race. In States where, from the number of blacks, that danger might exist, it would not probably be expedient to attempt even gradual emancipation, without the colonization of the blacks.

But I doubt whether the time is auspicious, even in K. to agitate the question of gradual emancipation. I apprehend it is not. The public mind, from the period of the Missouri controversy,[1] has been kept in a state of feverish excitement on the subject of slavery; and recently it has been intensely excited.[2] In such a state of it, any proposition looking even to remote emancipation would be unfavorably received. And we should have most of the Slave states acting on us, if we were to attempt it, as well to prevent the influence of our example, as to guard against the diminution of the weight of the Slave states in the councils of the General Government.

Whether I am right or not in these views, it is not so material in regard to the main object of your letter to me. For there is no conceivable state of things in which I would consent to serve as Governor of Kentucky. I am tired of, not disgusted, with public life. I most unaffectedly desire repose. Measured by my years, I am not very old, and might work some years longer. Measured by the events of my life, I have lived a long time. At any rate, there is no office that possesses any charms for me; and I have regretted that a state of things did not seem to me to exist admitting of my relinquishing before this that which I now hold.

I send you a Copy of a few observations made by me the other day on introducing the Land bill[3] — a measure which I think the most important ever agitated before the National Councils. If the Jackson party oppose it, on party grounds, it cannot pass. My hope is to detach enough of the individual members of it to secure success.

Every thing on the French question[4] awaits the return of Mr. [Thomas P.] Barton; and will probably await until it is ascertained here what effect is produced on the French Government by the Presidents message.[5]

I omitted I believe, before I left home, to thank you for some Grass seeds which you had been good enough to send me. The Wild rye we were familiar with; and we thought we knew the other kind. I directed them to be sowed.

ALS. NhD.   1. Clay to Woods, July 16, 1835.   2. Jackson's Seventh Annual Message [*MPP*, 3:175-76] called on the northern states to suppress the abolitionists and for Congress to pass a law to "prohibit, under severe penalties, the circulation in the Southern States, through the mail, of incendiary publications intended to instigate the slave to insurrection." For the developing slavery/sectional crisis in general, see Freehling, *Prelude to Civil War*; Charles S. Sydnor, *Development of Southern Sectionalism, 1819-1848*. Baton Rouge, 1964; David B. Davis, *The Slave Power Conspiracy and the Paranoid Style*. Baton Rouge, 1969; Louis Filler, *The Crusade against Slavery, 1830-1860*. New York, 1960. For the "gag rule" controversy and Clay's position on the constitutional right of either abolitionists or anti-abolitionists to petition the Senate for their causes, see Remark in Senate, Jan. 11, 1836; Remark in Senate, Feb. 4, 1836; Comment in Senate, March 9, 1836; and Speech in Senate, June 8, 1836.   3. Speech in Senate, Dec. 29, 1835.   4. Brown to Clay, Jan. 24, 1832; Clay to Henry Clay, Jr., Early Dec., 1834; Remark in Senate, Jan. 6, 1835; Clay to Biddle, March 4, 1835; Biddle to Clay, Jan. 4, 1836.   5. For a discussion of Jackson's Seventh Annual Message, see McLemore, *Franco-American Diplomatic Relations*, 185-90.

From Nicholas Biddle, Philadelphia, January 4, 1835 [*sic*, 1836]. Wonders "whether the time has not come when another interposition of yours is not needed to save the country from great trouble." Refers specifically to the negotiations with France over payments they had promised to make under the spoliations claims convention of 1832 [Brown to Clay, January 24, 1832]. Thinks these negotiations have been "mismanaged . . . from the beginning." Finds it "inexplicable" that the "overture of France" has been treated so badly, and observes that the attempt of the Duc de Broglie to defuse the crisis in September, 1835, "ought to have settled the matter in five minutes." ALS. DLC-HC (DNA, M212, R5). Printed in Colton, *Clay Correspondence*, 4:386-87. See Speech in Senate, January 14, 1835; and Undelivered Senate Speech, Late January, 1836.

To JAMES T. AUSTIN   Washington, January 5, 1836
I have received your favor of the 23d. Ulto. and the pamphlet which accompanied it, on the subject of Slavery.[1] I have perused it with great attention and lively interest, and think it distinguished by uncommon ability and eloquence. The Southern public cannot fail to be pleased to recognize in its author one of the ablest defenders of their rights. One of my Mess-mates[2] (the honble Mr. [Alexander] Porter, a Senator from Louisiana) has also read the pamphlet, and coincides with me in the judgment I have formed.

There is one concession common to the pamphlet and to other answers to the Abolitionists, which I am disposed to doubt; and that is their right of free discussion, as it is usually expressed, or, as they really mean, their right at the north, where there is no slavery, freely to discuss the institution of slavery at the South. The right of free discussion of all matters, without reserve, that relate to ourselves, is a very precious and sacred right. But have we a right to discuss that which we have no right to deliberate upon or to decide? Is not the right of discussion limited by the right of action? Is not the *right* to discuss political concerns restrained to those matters on which, in some one of our characters, primary or derivative, we have a right to pass? Throw off all restraint, and what is this right of discussion, exercised beyond the limits of our own State, but the principle of propagandism?

You will readily apply these suggestions.

ALS. MHi.   1. William Ellery Channing had written a book called *Slavery*, which was published in Boston in 1835. Austin wrote *Remarks on Dr. Channing's "Slavery" By a Citizen of Massachusetts.* Charleston, S.C., 1835. This pamphlet was reprinted in 1836, the same year in which Austin wrote *Reply to the Reviewer of the Remarks on Dr. Channing's Slavery.* Boston, 1836.   2. Clay, John J. Crittenden, and Porter occupied rooms at the house of M.A. Clements on C Street during this session.

To NICHOLAS BIDDLE   Washington, January 6, 1836

I recd. your favor of the 4h.   I concur with your entirely in thinking that our Executive has acted with unpardonable impropriety in repelling the French overture to settle amicably the existing difficulty between the two Countries.[1] If Mr. Forsythe [*sic*, John Forsyth] with held the knowledge of that overture from the President, he ought to be dismissed or impeached; and if he communicated it what ought to be the punishment of the President for concealing the fact from the community, in a message which professes to tell the whole truth?[2]

Such an overture ought to have led in ten minutes to an adjustment of the whole difficulty.

I have contemplated calling for a disclosure of the whole state of the case, respecting this affair; but I have thought it best to wait a short time.[3] I believe, through the press and through other channels, that I have learnt all the material circumstances.

There has been a rumor for several days that the President, probably goaded on by the attacks in the [Washington *Daily National*] Intellr., intended to communicate to Congress the whole matter, in the shape of a report to him from the Secy of State.[4] Should he do so, what a triumph will that print have achieved?

Here, among the Admon party, there is a general persuasion that the difficulty will be settled with France, without War, or any restrictive measure. Mr. V[an]. Buren has said to me twice with great apparent confidence, that it would be settled.

The policy of the Opposition, I think, is to wait until the Admon shall prepare some measure, except to make the Call for what passed between Mr. [Alphonse] Pageot and the Secy of State

ALS. DLC-Nicholas Biddle Papers (DNA, M212, R20).   1. Biddle to Clay, Jan. 4, 1836. 2. Undelivered Senate Speech, Late Jan., 1836.   3. *Ibid.*   4. The *Intelligencer* had sharply and frequently attacked the president's French policy. See Washington *Daily National Intelligencer*, Nov. 4, 21, 26; Dec. 3, 8-10, 12, 14-18, 21, 23-25, 29, 31, 1835; Jan. 2, 4, 5, 1836. For Jackson's report to Congress through the secretary of state, see *House Exec. Doc.* 117, 24 Cong., 1 Sess., pp. 1-121.

From John A. Stevens, New York, January 8, 1836. Encloses a letter from a merchant at Havre on the Franco-American crisis. Says he has reason to believe this man "possesses the confidence of the French ministry." Urges Clay to use the letter, subject only to the restriction of withholding the names mentioned in it, "should circumstances render it expedient that it might serve to counteract erroneous impressions from whatever quarter on this side of the affair to which it is related [Brown to Clay, January 24, 1832; Remark in Senate, January 6, 1835]."

Mentions that New Yorkers "are looking with solicitude to Congress for the measures of relief to the City." Believes that "The postponement of the payment of the duty Bonds in Currency here and of all the duties to accrue for a certain period would have extensive and the happiest results." ALS. NHi. See also Clay to Stevens, January 10, 1836; Remark in Senate, January 12, 1836. Stevens was engaged in foreign trade with his father, served as president of the Merchant's Exchange (predecessor to the New York Stock Exchange) for many years, and from 1839 to 1866 was president of the Bank of Commerce in New York City. Bonner, *New York, The World's Metropolis*, 711-12. On December 16-17, 1835, a huge fire destroyed some 674 buildings, including the Merchant's Exchange on Wall Street, and leveled an area of 52 acres, in the heart of the business district of New York City. See Alexander J. Wall, Jr., "The Great Fire of 1835," *NHSQB* (January, 1936), 20:3-22. The U.S. Senate passed "An act for the relief of the sufferers by fire in the city of New York" on January 14, 1836; the House followed suit on March 8, and the president approved it on March 19. See U.S. Sen., *Journal*, 24 Cong., 1 Sess., 97, 239; U.S. H. of Reps., *Journal*, 24 Cong., 1 Sess., 490; *Register of Debates*, 24 Cong., 1 Sess., 104-5; 5 *U.S. Stat.*, 6.

To JOHN A. STEVENS

Washington, January 10, 1836

I recd. your favor of the 8h. inst. with the Copy of the letter endorsed from Havre, for which I am obliged, and of which I will make any good use I can, under the restriction contained in your letter.[1] Our affairs with France seem rapidly leading to a crisis.[2] Never has any thing been worse managed; and as your correspondent justly remarks faults have been committed, on both sides. I hope means may be advised to avert the calamity of War; but the difficulty is daily increased, and sometimes increased too by the indiscretion of both parties, or rather their presses, in this Country. The rashness of the President seems to be contagious.

I know not what may be finally done for the relief of your City.[3] Sympathy with you is strong and general; and if power and policy shall be found commensurate with good dispositions, I presume something will be done for your relief.

ALS. NHi.   1. Stevens to Clay, Jan. 8, 1836.   2. Brown to Clay, Jan. 24, 1832; Remark in Senate, Jan. 6, 1835; Biddle to Clay, Jan. 4, 1836.   3. Stevens to Clay, Jan. 8, 1836; Remark in Senate, Jan. 12, 1836.

Remark in Senate, January 11, 1836. Moves that a petition from Pennsylvania Quakers to abolish slavery and the slave trade in the District of Columbia be tabled. He will "not consent" to having the "time and attention of the Senate" monopolized by "these petitioners." *Register of Debates*, 24 Cong., 1 Sess., 100. The debate over slavery and the right of petition erupted in Congress on December 16, 1835, when John Fairfield of Maine presented in the House a petition from several of his constituents praying for abolition of slavery in the District of Columbia. John Y. Mason of Virginia moved to table the petition without either discussion or referral to committee. The motion carried 180 to 31. For the ensuing debates and controversy which developed following the adoption of the so-called "gag rule" by the House on May 18, 1836, see George C. Rable, "Slavery, Politics, and the South: The Gag Rule as a Case Study," *Capitol Studies* (1975), 3:69-88; James M. McPherson, "The Fight Against the Gag Rule: Joshua Leavitt and the Antislavery Insurgency in the Whig Party, 1839-1842," *JNH* (July, 1963), 48:177; Robert P. Ludlum, "The Antislavery 'Gag Rule': History and Argument," *ibid.* (April, 1941), 26: 203-43; Hecht, *John Quincy Adams*, 545-48, 550-51, 554-58, 562-63, 584-85, 590-91, 597, 614-15.

Later this day, Clay condemned the "nefarious culprits" who had committed land frauds against the Mississippi Indians in violation of the U.S.-Choctaw Treaty of Dancing Rabbit Creek [Parry, *Treaty Series*, 81:122-30]. Demands that the guilty be searched out and punished. *Register of Debates*, 24 Cong., 1 Sess., 101-2. For discussion of the treaty, signed September 27, 1830, and the subsequent land frauds, see Angie Debo, *The Rise and Fall of the Choctaw Republic* (Norman, Okla., 1934), 54-55, 71, 73.

Still later this day, Clay observes that Franco-American relations "are rapidly tending to a crisis" and that war threatens [Brown to Clay, January 24, 1832; Speech in Senate, January 14, 1835]. Insists that under the constitution Congress has a "right to know whatever has passed" between Jackson and the French government, "whether official or not—whether formal or informal [Remark in Senate, January 18, 1836]." Complains that the U.S. press has a document "which this body has not been yet allowed to see." Concludes with a resolution that Jackson turn over to the Senate "any overture" made by France since March 3, 1835, "to accomodate the difficulties between the two Governments" relating to the claims issue, particularly a dispatch from the French minister of foreign affairs, the Duc de Broglie, to Alphonse J. Y. Pageot, French chargé at Washington. Resolves, further, that if such an overture had been made, the president inform the Senate "what answer was given to it." *Register of Debates*, 24 Cong., 1 Sess., 103-4; *Cong. Globe*, 24 Cong., 1 Sess., 84. Published in part in Colton, *Clay Correspondence*, 6:34-35. For Broglie's dispatch to Pageot of June 17, 1835, which Pageot put in the hands of Secretary of State Forsyth on September 11, 1835, see McLemore, *Franco-American Relations*, 152-53, 164-69. The dispatch offered a face-saving formula whereby Jackson is his annual message of December 7, 1835, would appear to apologize to France for the touch language he had used in his annual message of December 1, 1834. In the latter he had threatened U.S. "reprisals upon French property" were the American spoliation claims not promptly paid by the Paris government. For both presidential messages, see *MPP*, 3:100-107, 152-60. The ameliorative language to be put in Jackson's mouth on December 7, 1835, by Secretary of State John Forsyth read: "The conception that it was my intention to menace or insult the Government of France is as unfounded, as the attempt to extort from the fears of that nation what his sense of justice may deny, would be vain and ridiculous." Undelivered Senate Speech, Late January, 1836. Clay's resolutions were amended with an addition suggested by Benjamin W. Leigh and were passed on January 12. *Register of Debates*, 24 Cong., 1 Sess., 106.

Remark in Senate, January 12, 1836. Objects to bill for the relief of the sufferers of loss of property in the New York City fire of December 16, 1835 [Stevens to Clay, January 8, 1836], "in its present shape." Wants to study it further. *Register of Debates*, 24 Cong., 1 Sess., 105. The bill authorized the collector of the Port of New York to lengthen by three to five years the pay-out period of all bonds in amounts exceeding $1,000 that sufferers had put up for payment of duties. But sufferers who had paid off such bonds before the fire were also entitled to the same extension, calculated from the date their bonds had been retired. They would receive an adjusted refund of their payments. *Ibid*. See Comment in Senate, January 13, 1836.

Comment in Senate, January 13, 1836. Objects to the fact that the proposed bill for the relief of New York City fire sufferers [Stevens to Clay, January 8, 1836; Remark in Senate, January 12, 1836] provides relief to those who have incurred no loss. Attempts, unsuccessfully, to amend that discriminatory feature out of the bill. Notes that while there is "an old saying that there [is] no friendship in trade," Sen. Silas Wright and the "mercantile community of New York" have seen to it that "relief was extended to all persons who had imported goods in the port of New York." *Register of Debates*, 24 Cong., 1 Sess., 115; *Cong. Globe*, 24 Cong., 1 Sess., 96.

To THOMAS W. GILMER [Washington, Mid-January, 1836]

I was much gratified to learn from Govr. [James] Barbour, at whose instance I address this letter, that a prospect existed of a favorable vote at Richmond in the Legislature on the project for distributing the proceeds of the public lands.[1] Early next week, the Commee. to which my bill was referred will make a report and bring out some valuable additional information.[2] It turns out, I understand, that the yield of the last quarter of the last year, instead of being only two millions as estimated by the Secy of the Treasury [Levi Woodbury], is five millions!

I am confident that this great National resource will, at no very distant day, be wasted and destroyed if the States do not interpose with a determined spirit to arrest the danger. Such has been long my conviction. Heretofore, I was probably unjustly suspected of motives of a personal nature, in bringing forward this project. Now, I turst, no such imputation can be made.

It is manifest to me that the Admon is aiming to accomplish two purpose 1st to underrate the probable receipts into the Treasury; and 2dly. to squander the surplus. With this view, a War panic is got up, when no one can be foolish enough to believe that France will make War upon us.[3] As a part of the same system, Mr. [Thomas Hart] Benton proposes applying the whole surplus, accrued, and accuring, to the National *defence*.[4] Whilst in the House, they are now discussing a proposition to approporate two millions to the navy, without estimates, and without any report from any head of department.[5] Other schemes will probably be brought forward. The Admon does not feel itself sufficiently strengthened by planning this vast surplus in the possession of favored Banks; it wants the actual employment of it to stimulate and increase partizans.

I will not here discuss the power of distribution, under the deeds of Cession. But I will say that I not only think it exists, but I believe that the very object which Virginia had in view, in her magnanimous grant, can be *only* accomplished by distribution. In no other way can we be sure that each State is benefited in proportion to its contributions and charges resulting from the confederation of the States.

Would it not be most unjust if, after the great sacrifice patriotically made by Virginia, and after the express reservation in her behalf,[6] the Public domain should be now thrown away in visionary graduation projects, or cerded voluntarily to the New States, or used as the means of enticing her sons from her own borders?

I should be highly pleased to see all parties in your Legislature uniting in expressing their approbation of the principle of distribution. And I submit to you whether an effort to produce such an union should not be made. If it fail, and if the Admon party should oppose itself to the scheme, you would then be stronger in your appeal to the people. And I confess it has seemed to me that, if they will draw into the vortex of party, a subject which should be far removed from it; and if the question is properly brought home to the feelings and understandings of the people, your triumph would be certain. No where would it be surer than in Virginia, because no other State made a grant to the General Government so munificent. How much better would it be for you to make such a noble issue as that would be, instead of allowing your opponents to make and compel you to meet them on the miserable issues which they have heretofore tendered?

I have understood that one of your Senators inclines to resign in the event of the passage of a certain resolution before you.[7] Such a course would be against the united judgment of his friends from other States. I know not what effect it would have in Virginia. Every where else it would be bad. And if it should be thought inexpedient at Richmond, would it not be well to address dissuasives to him?

ALS. ViU.   1. On Dec. 31, 1835, the Virginia general assembly passed a resolution instructing its senators and representatives in Congress to vote for the bill to distribute the proceeds from the sale of public lands. This instruction resolution passed the Virginia senate on Feb. 10, 1836. Seager, *And Tyler Too*, 113; Richmond *Enquirer*, Jan. 2, 1836. See also Speech in Senate, Jan. 20, 1832; Dec. 29, 1835.   2. The Land Committee made a report on Clay's bill on Jan. 27, 1836. U.S. Sen., *Journal*, 24 Cong., 1 Sess., 123.   3. Brown to Clay, Jan. 24, 1832; Remark in Senate, Jan. 6, 1835; Biddle to Clay, Jan. 4, 1836.   4. See *Register of Debates*, 24 Cong., 1 Sess., 106.   5. *Ibid.*, 2180-91, 3219. The naval appropriation bill passed the House on April 8, 1836.   6. For the public land controversy at the time of ratification of the Articles of Confederation, see Homer C. Hockett, *The Constitutional History of the United States, 1776-1866* (New York, 1939), 145-46.   7. Benjamin W. Leigh had been reelected to the U.S. Senate in Jan., 1835, by a margin of four votes over Democrat William C. Rives. When it became apparent by mid-1835 that the Democrats would control the Virginia house of delegates at its next session, Leigh made it clear he would neither resign nor obey the legislature if it instructed him to vote for the expunging resolution [Remark in Senate, June 30, 1834]. He maintained this position in February, 1836, when the Virginia legislature formally instructed him to support the expunging resolution, although he resigned later in 1836 for personal reasons. Virginia's other senator, John Tyler, had long supported the concept of state legislative instruction, and therefore felt it necessary to resign his seat since he could not in good conscience vote to expunge the condemnation of Jackson from the Senate *Journal*. He did so on Feb. 29, 1836. William C. Rives was elected to Tyler's seat. Seager, *And Tyler Too*, 112-15; Leigh article in *DAB*.

Remark in Senate, January 18, 1836. Moves that Jackson's special message of January 15 on the status of U.S. relations with France [Brown to Clay, January 24, 1832; Remark in Senate, January 6, 1835; Speech in Senate, January 14, 1835] and accompanying documents, be referred to the Committee on Foreign Relations. Done. *Register of Debates*, 24 Cong., 1 Sess., 168. Jackson's message of January 15, received by Congress on January 18, included copies of pertinent correspondence which had passed between the two governments during the course of negotiations. *MPP*, 3:188-213.

Remark in Senate, January 20, 1836. Requests that the Committee on Foreign Relations be discharged from further consideration of those parts of the president's special message of January 15 on the Franco-American crisis [Remark in Senate, January 18, 1836] dealing with the augmentation of the U.S. Navy and the completion of U.S. coastal defences. Done. *Register of Debates*, 24 Cong., 1 Sess., 211.

To LUCRETIA HART CLAY   Washington, January 23, 1836
I received to day from the good Mrs. [Charlotte] Mentelle, a letter communicating various particulars respecting the death of my dear daughter [Anne Brown Clay Erwin].[1] The perusal of it has occasioned a fresh gust of tears, the only relief which God has yet granted to me in consequence of that sad event. I wish you to thank her for the letter for me. It seems that you only had forebodings of all those about her. I too had them, and they never left me, until they were fatally confirmed.

Poor James [Brown Clay], I infer from a letter which I received from him on the 30h Ulto. had not on that day heard of her death. How much will he be grieved! My information from St. Louis is very favorable about him. He is setting an example of industry that is greatly praised.[2]

I find from a letter received from Majr. [Thomas H.] Pindell that there is a large balance standing to my credit in the Branch of the Northern Bank of K. which I had entirely forgotten. As you may have use for it, I send you a check for the amount, and I request that you will freely use it for any purpose you think proper.

I perceive by a Newspaper at Maysville that my Cattle arrived there on the 14h inst. and of course I presume got to Ashland before this day.[3]

I have argued one of the two Causes in the Supreme Court that made my attendance here this winter necessary.[4] The bill for the relief of Dr. [Benjamin W.] Dudley (in which you know I am concerned) is in progress, and I hope will pass.[5] So that I trust there will never be any occasion of my again returning to this City after this Session. I am truly tired of it

I confine myself almost exclusively to my Room, except when I go to the Capitol. I see no body, except my mess mates [Alexander Porter and John J. Crittenden] and the few who call on me, and I desire to see no one.

Tell Thomas [Hart Clay] to continue to write to me, and I wish also to hear from [John] Headley. Give my love to our dear Grand children, and kiss poor little Charles Edward. . . .[6]

ALS. DLC-TJC (DNA, M212, R10).   1. Clay to Lucretia Hart Clay, Dec. 19, 1835. 2. Clay to Graham, Sept. 13, 1835.   3. Shepherd to Clay, Dec. 4, 1835.   4. Clay argued only one case before this term of the U.S. Supreme Court—*Boone* v. *Chiles* which he had also argued the previous term. 10 Peters 177-255.   5. The bill for the relief of the executors (including Dudley) of Charles Wilkins passed the House on Jan. 29, 1836, and the Senate on Feb. 10. The president signed the bill on Feb. 14. U.S. H. of Reps., *Journal*, 24 Cong., 1 Sess., 78, 252, 326, 366.   6. Clay to Lucretia Hart Clay, Nov. 19, 1835.

To FRANCIS T. BROOKE   Washington, January 25, 1836

I recd. your favor of the 21st. inst. and I should be very glad to be able to communicate to you any satisfactory information on the question of a French War;[1] but I do not know that I can add to what the papers contain. I go out only to the Capitol and mix but little in society. My belief is that the President and his party desire War; and if the Mississipi and Louisiana elections for Senators should be favorable to them,[2] and the two Virginia Senators [Benjamin W. Leigh and John Tyler] or either of them resign,[3] the Jackson party will have a majority in both houses. There is, beyond all doubt, imminent danger of War at no very distant period. It can only, perhaps, be prevented by public opinion, and of that the Administration seems to have the control. Besides all the other elements of War, that party which was opposed to the last War,[4] or, at least, many of its members are supposed to be ready to atone for former errors by supporting a War against France.

You will have seen the dispatch from the Duke de Broglie.[5] It is distinguished by consummate ability; and if it had been recd. with a proper spirit, the whole difficulty might have been accommodated in half an hour. But it was not; and the serious question remains what shall be done? That I am considering; and I have not even yet obtained the documents requisite to the formation of a satisfactory judgment. I think it best to look deliberately on the whole question and to avoid precipitating, or prematurely announcing any opinion. What I now write I wish you to consider confidential.

ALS. NcD. 1. Brown to Clay, Jan. 24, 1832; Remark in Senate, Jan. 6, 1835; Biddle to Clay, Jan. 4, 1836. 2. On Jan. 12, 1835, the Louisiana legislature on the third ballot chose Charles E. A. Gayarre as U.S. senator; however, Gayarre resigned because of ill health and never served in the position. On Jan. 12, 1836, R. C. Nicholas, a Jacksonian, was elected to fill the vacancy caused by Gayarre's resignation. *Niles' Register* (Jan. 31, 1835), 47:370; (Jan. 30, 1836), 49:362; W.H. Adams, *The Whig Party of Louisiana* (Lafayette, La., 1973), 103. 3. Clay to Gilmer, Mid-Jan., 1836. 4. See 1:609-10, 759; 2:6. 5. Biddle to Clay, Jan. 4, 1836; Undelivered Senate Speech, Late Jan., 1836.

To Thomas Hart Clay, Lexington, January 25, 1836. Discusses his stock and other matters related to running Ashland plantation. Instructs Thomas to tell John Headley, his overseer, "to call on Mrs. [Rebecca] Coyle and say to her that I will not consent to her passing through Ashland; that if she will desist and does desist doing so I will not sue her, but that if she perseveres, I wish him to have a suit brought against her for cutting down my bars, and a new suit brought every time she passes through my place." Concludes: "I am in hopes you will do all you can to please your mother, and will not add to her troubles." ALS. DLC-HC (DNA, M212, R5). The property of Rebecca, widow of Cornelius Coyle, formerly a Lexington tailor, adjoined Ashland.

To JOHN FORSYTH   Washington, January 27, 1836
I am directed by the Senate Committee of Foreign Relations to call your attention to a letter from the Duc de Broglie, under date at Paris, the 17h. June, 1835, and published in the [Washington] Globe on the 22d instant, and to enquire whether it be a substantial copy of the letter from that Minister addressed to Mr. [A.J.Y.] Pageot, the late French Charge d'Affaires at Washington which was read to you on the 11th of September last, by Mr. Pageot,[1] and of which he transmitted a copy to you in his note of the first of December, last.—The motive of this request is that the Committee wish, in considering the state of our relations with France, to be assured of the authority of the documents on which they may deliberate.[2]

LS. DNA, RG59, Misc. Letters. 1. Undelivered Senate Speech, Late Jan., 1836; McLemore, *Franco-American Relations*, 152-53, 164-67. 2. The following day, Feb. 28, 1836, Forsyth replied that he had never seen the original letter, because Pageot had read to him a translation; furthermore, the copy he had received was in French, and he had neither read it nor had it translated. States, however, that the "paper in the 'Globe' does not . . . as far as I recollect, differ from the translation read to me." Copy. Printed in Frankfort *Commonwealth*, March 2, 1836.

From GEORGE McDUFFIE   Abbeville, S.C., January 27, 1836
I am from home & you must excuse the foolscap on which I write. Perceiving the message relative to the French indemnity referred to your Committee,[1] & am irresistibly impelled to make a suggestion or two. You again have it in your power for the third or fourth time to save the country from a great calamity. It is perfectly obvious that if the Annual Message of December last[2] had been permitted to reach France before any additional cause of irritation was given by the President, the indemnity would have been promptly paid by the French executive. The King [Louis Philippe] & the Ministry have all along been most anxious to adjust the difficulty & pay the claim. They have had to struggle with a refractory Chamber, who have co-operated with Genl Jackson's rashness & folly, to produce war. Now it seems to me that the course for Congress to pursue, for the interest & true honor of the Country is perfectly plain; and that is to be as courteous & civil as the President has been rude & insulting. State, what is evidently true, a confidence that there is neither a desire on the part of the King & ministry to adjust the matter without

war, & a belief that they will pay the indemnity, when they read the Annual Message and that consequently no preparations for war are necessary. I have not a doubt that such a course would insure a peaceable & prompt adjustment of the existing differences. If war ensues Congress must now be responsible. It will proceed from their acts & not those of the President.[3] Even his last message would be nothing to France if Congress would again adopt the course you recommended last year.[4] If it should fail there will still be time to prepare during the Session for non-intercourse, for I cannot believe a war possible. A non-intercourse act on our part, would not, I am sure, lead to a declaration of war by France. They could not make it a ground of war.

I beg you, my dear Sir, to excuse this liberty. The magnitude of the interests involved must be my apology. A war with France would be utterly ruinous to the Southern States, & God knows what would be its effect upon public liberty. It would be the most signal example of the folly of nations the world ever witnessed. We go to war for five millions, which is sponged out by the declaration, & with a certainty that we shall lose ten times as much, & *never can compel France to pay one cent.*

ALS. DLC-HC (DNA, M212, R5).   1. Remark in Senate, Jan. 18, 1836.   2. Undelivered Senate Speech, Late Jan., 1836.   3. Brown to Clay, Jan. 24, 1832.   4. Remark in Senate, Jan. 6, 1835; Jan. 18, 1836; Clay to Biddle, March 4, 1835; Van Deusen, *The Life of Henry Clay*, 291-92.

Remark in Senate, January 27, 1836. Speaks to a bill from the Committee on Finance appropriating $500,000 "for suppressing hostilities with the Seminole Indians." Notes that Congress has been "altogether uninformed" as to the causes of this war. Wants to know "how this war had burst forth, what were its causes, and to whom the blame of it was to be charged." *Register of Debates*, 24 Cong., 1 Sess., 290. The so-called "Second Seminole War" resulted from removal agreements concluded between the Seminoles and the U.S. government in 1832 and 1833. These agreements, made by a few Indian chiefs, were not accepted by the majority of the Seminoles who opposed removal. Attempts at forced emigration by late 1835 resulted in a guerrilla war that lasted until 1842 and cost the government nearly $40,000,000 as well as countless lives. John K. Mahon, *History of the Second Seminole War, 1835-1842* (Gainesville, Fla., 1967), *passim*; Gary E. Moulton, "Cherokees and the Second Seminole War," *FHQ* (January, 1975), 53:296; Kenneth W. Porter, "Slaves and Free Negroes in the Seminole War," *JNH* (October, 1943), 28:417.

DRAFT OF UNDELIVERED   [*Ca.* Late January, 1836]
SENATE SPEECH

no Foreign power of whose character or conduct it may treat, has any right to complain, to remonstrate, or to ask explanations. If this principle can be established, and we are at liberty to speak without any responsibility in what terms we please of foreign powers, we ought undoubtedly to exercise, with the greatest discretion, such an exclusive privilege. The confidence which Mr. [Edward] Livingston had in this principle does not seem to have prevented him from giving, without the authority of any instruction, an explanation incompatable with it. Whether, it be true or not, to the extent contended for, the [Senate Foreign Relations] Comee. think that no explanation other than those which have been given, under existing circumstances, ought to be given of the message of 1834.[1]

The Comee. cannot but think that it would have been fortunate and proper for the Secy of State [John Forsyth] to have accepted a copy of the despatch of the Duc de Broglie to Mr. [A.J.Y.] Pageot, when it was offered to him on the 11h. of September or on the 1st Decr. last.[2] One obvious use might have been made of it. In the very contingency which has happened, and which must have been forseen on the latter day, that of Congress being advised by the Executive to take the initiative in a system of measures tending directly to War, Congress ought to have been put in possession of the same knowledge of the contents of that despatch as that which the President and Secy of State had acquired. By refusing to receive a Copy, the Executive deprived itself of the means of performing the duty of communicating it to Congress. The omission has been supplied by the publication of that despatch in the American papers,[3] the substantial accuracy of which has been verified by the Secretary. It has been alleged that the publication was made by some person connected with the French Legation; and it is even asserted to have been done in conformity with the orders of the French Government. If so, the publication was most ill-advised, and unnecessary, because by laying it before the Chambers in France it could have readily found its way through the French to the American press.

The despatch displays a spirit, rare in the negotiation which the Committee is considering, of subdued temper, consiliatory spirit, and distinguished ability [word illeg.]. It was communicated in a manner delicate and unobtrusive; and the President justly remarks, in his Special Message, that "no exception was taken to this mode of communication, which is often used to prepare the way for official intercourse". It is certainly not uncommon in diplomacy for the representative of one Government to communicate in extenso his instructions to another. And such a communication, however respectfully made, ought to be deemed, more satisfactory, and to possess more conclusive evidence than any official and formal note embodying the instructions. Yet, whilst the President acknowledges the, conformity to established usage of this mode of inter communication, both he and the Secretary of State are understood to have objected to the reception of it, because it was a deviation from customary form. That deviation, in an affair which partook somewhat of the nature of a personal controversy, was a strong reason for receiving the paper. Why was not the despatch, or the tender of a Copy of it to be regarded as official? It was from the French Minister [Broglie], offered by the French Chargé d' affaires [Pageot], and treating officially a public subject. And so far from considering it a paper, of which the Secretary could have made no use, as stated by the President, besides that which has been already indicated, there were other uses to which it might have been fairly applied.

The Secretary might have prepared a full answer to the despatch, and the Committee [on Foreign Relations] would have been glad to have seen such an answer characterized by the same spirit of consiliation and ability which it displays. This might have been delivered to the Chargé d affaires in the same informal way, or in the ordinary mode, at the option of the Secretary. What was to prevent it? The despatch had been tendered to the Secretary both in a personal interview and in a written official note. Or, receiving the despatch, he might in suitable language have expressed his pleasure in being put in the full possession of the feelings and views[4] of the French Government, and his very great regret that the President cou[l]d not comply with the wishes of the French Government. Or, finally, he might, upon receivng it, have expressed his surprize and regret that the French Government, after Mr. Livingstons official notes of the 29h. day of January and the 25h. April 1835, and the published note of the Secy to Mr. Livingston of the 17 June 1835,[5] should still think explanations were necessary; that the President, anxious to restore the amicable feelings between the two Governments would be most happy to do any thing in his power to effect that desirable object; but that he could not, consistently with his sense of what was due to the people of the U. States and their Constitution, offer to France any other explanations of a message which he had felt himself bound to address to Congress. But he took great pleasure in informing Mr. Pageot[6] that, on the occasion of the Presidents opening message to Congress at the approaching Session[7] it was his intention to lay the present condition of our affairs with France before that body which would afford him a suitable opportunity of declaring that, "the conception that it was my intention to menace or insult the Government of France is as unfounded, as the attempt to extort from the fears of that nation what her sense of justice may deny, would be vain and ridiculous." That the President intended to make such a declaration; and, alluding to what Mr. Livingston had said of the message in his note of the 29h. of January,[8] to add the further declaration that "he had truly declared that it contained, and was intended to contain, no charge of ill faith against the King of the French." These are precisely such declarations as the despatch of the Duc de Broglie had suggested would be satisfactory. This is his language:[9] "We do not care about this or that phrase, this or that allegation, this or that expression; we contend about the intention itself which has dictated that part of the message. If it be true that the President of the U.S., in presenting to Congress a statement of the facts connected with Treaty of the 4h. of July [1831], had no intention to cast any doubt upon the good faith of the French Government; if it be true that the Presdt. of the U.S. in proposing to Congress, to decree the seizure, by force of arms of French property, had not the intention to assume, with regard to France, a menacing attitude, we cannot see how he would find any difficulty in declaring it."

The declarations cited from the message of the 7h. Decr. [1835][10] last are substantially in conformity with those which the French Minister had suggested in his despatch. They were probably intended to be so. And why should not the intention to insert them in the message have been communicated to Mr. Pageot in a friendly interview between him and the Secy of State? Would not such a communication have best corresponded with the President's known character for truth and frankness? And if it had been done can there be a doubt that it would have obviated all difficulty, produced the payment of the debt when it was demanded on the 20h of October, and amicably settled this unfortunate controversy.

Instead of any such communication, the Secy. of State on the 14h. of September,[11] three days after the French Ministers despatch had been read to him, transmits to Mr. [Thomas P.] Barton [U.S. Minister in Paris] his last instructions, preserves in them a studied silence with respect to the friendly overture which he had received, directs a demand to be made for the debt, and if not paid[12] requires him to ask his pass ports and return to the U. States. After the acceptance of a Copy of the despatch had been twice refused at Washington, it was again tendered at Paris by the French Minister [Broglie] to Mr. Barton who replied that, as his instructions had no reference to that question he did not think himself authorized to discuss it.

If it were considered incompatible with the dignity of the U. States to let the French Government know in advance the declarations which the President intended to insert in his message,[13] where was the necessity of closing all diplomatic intercourse by directing the return of Mr. Barton, which would necessarily lead to the withdrawal of the F. representative here before the effect was ascertained of the Message upon the French Government? In the Monarchies of Europe the power of declaring War is vested in their Chiefs and the usual precursor of the declaration is the recall of a Minister. When the monarch has made up his mind for War he recalls his Minister. But in our system the power of declaring is vested not in the Chief Magistrate but. . . .

AD, fragment. DLC-HC (DNA, M212, R6). Dated on basis of the time (end of third week in January, 1836) at which the newspapers published the dispatch mentioned in paragraph 2. See footnote 3, below. Some factual data in this manuscript was apparently used in his Speech in Senate, Feb. 22, 1836. The editors have eliminated insignificant strike-overs and aligned the frequent interlineations found in the original manuscript.   1. Jackson's Sixth Annual Message, Dec. 1, 1834. *MPP*, 3:100-107; Remark in Senate, Jan. 6, 1835.   2. On June 17, 1835, Broglie dispatched a note to Pageot outlining the face-saving conditions under which France would commence payment of the claims and thus defuse the crisis. The solution required an apology of sorts from Jackson (which would be inserted in his annual message on Dec. 7, 1835) for the offensive phrases appearing in his annual message of Dec. 1, 1834 [Remark in Senate, Jan. 11, 1836]. Pageot got the dispatch during the last week of August; but not until Sept. 11, 1835, was he able to communicate it to Secretary of State Forsyth. McLemore, *Franco-American Diplomatic Relations*, 151-53, 164-76; Clay to Forsyth, Jan. 27, 1836.   3. Washington *Globe*, Jan. 22, 1836; Washington *Daily National Intelligencer*, Jan. 22, 1836.   4. Word "wishes" struck over and "views" substituted.   5. McLemore, *Franco-American Diplomatic Relations*, 148, 154, 165.   6. Phrase "the French" struck over and "Mr. Pageot" substituted.   7. Seventh Annual Message, Dec. 7, 1835. *MPP*, 3:152-60.   8. Livingston's note to Rigny of Jan. 29, 1835, attempted to place the president's 1834 annual message [Clay to Henry Clay, Jr., Early-Dec., 1834] in its most favorable light, claiming that it was not intended to increase difficulties or excite irritation with the French. McLemore, *Franco-American Diplomatic Relations*, 148.   9. Broglie to Pageot, June 17, 1835. See footnote 2 above.   10. *MPP*, 3:152-60.   11. McLemore, *Franco-American Diplomatic Relations*, 169-70.   12. Word "by," followed by a space follows "paid."   13. Apparently the Seventh Annual Message. See footnote 7, above.

To NATHANIEL HART   Washington, January 30, 1836

I recd. your favor of the 20h. inst. and thank you for your kind condolence on our late affliction which has plunged me into the deepest distress.[1]

Your check will answer as well as if it had been on an Eastern bank, and I will pay the sum you desire to Mr. [Hezekiah] Niles.

Don Manuel, the Jack to which you allude, I expect is sold or will be before this letter reaches you. If not, I would be willing to selling him to you.

I expect three large and uncommonly fine Jacks from Malta via N. Orleans in the month of March;[2] and I shall be glad to sell one of them to you.

ALS. PPPrHi. Addressed to Hart "near Versailles Kentucky."   1. Clay to Lucretia Hart Clay, Dec. 19, 1835.   2. Shepherd to Clay, Dec. 4, 1835.

Remark in Senate, February 3, 1836. Moves postponement of other business so as to take up his resolution of January 11 calling on the president for certain information on French diplomatic overtures for peace [Remark in Senate, January 11, 1836]. Adds specific documents to those solicited in his earlier resolution. *Register of Debates*, 24 Cong., 1 Sess., 366-67.

Remark in Senate, February 4, 1836. Questions the report of a select committee which explains and evaluates a bill, introduced by John C. Calhoun, that would prohibit any literature "touching the subject of slavery" from being circulated by and in the U.S. mail [Clay to Speed, January 2, 1836]. Argues that such committee reports are "mere argumentative papers" and are "not considered as adopted paragraph by paragraph, by the Senate, in ordering them to be printed." But adds: "If a bill embracing the principles of a report was adopted, the reasoning of the report might . . . be considered as adopted."

Register of Debates, 24 Cong., 1 Sess., 385; *Cong. Globe*, 24 Cong., 1 Sess., 165. See also Comment in Senate, March 9, 1836; and Speech in Senate, June 8, 1836. The Senate rejected Calhoun's bill on June 9, 1836, by a vote of 25 to 19. *Register of Debates*, 24 Cong., 1 Sess., 383, 1737. It was not taken up again during the first or second sessions of the 24th Congress.

Remark in Senate, February 5, 1836. Observes that the bill permitting new states to select a section of land for public school use "instead of being compelled to take every sixteenth section of a township, whether valuable or valueless, would be appreciated by the West." States his belief in the value of education. *Register of Debates*, 24 Cong., 1 Sess., 389-90.

Remark in Senate, February 8, 1836. Moves to refer to the Committee on Foreign Relations the president's message of February 8 [*MPP*, 3:213-24] announcing Britain's offer of mediation in the U.S. dispute with France. *Register of Debates*, 24 Cong., 1 Sess., 390-91. McLemore, *Franco-American Diplomatic Relations*, 182-83. For Britain's role as mediator, see C.K. Webster, "British Mediation Between France and the United States in 1834-6," *EHR* (January, 1927), 42:58-78.

From John Hare Powel, February 10, 1836. Sympathizes with Clay in the loss of his daughter Anne Brown Clay Erwin [Clay to Lucretia Hart Clay, December 19, 1835], saying that he himself has lost two children within the last year to scarlet fever. Reports that he is preparing to leave for Europe, and offers to make any cattle purchases which Clay might desire. Adds the political observation that "I would much more gladly walk up to my knees in C. D . . . g to serve the State under the banner of Clay, than plunge into the little of Pennsylvania politicks, with the same gallant & chivalric leader, in the train of a pompous, weak & vain glorious military coxcomb — But to turn to a more useful, and quite as intelligent an animal, your bull Hector." Notes that Hector "was begotten by my celebrated bull Malcolm on the Cow called Delight" and that "Hector's black nose is his bad point." Mentions that Delight and Malcolm produced Portia that was the dam of Garcia, the dam of Clay's bull Oliver. Contends that the "mellowness of handling among breeders of Short Horns, in Great Britain, is the test of breeding, as the performance upon the turf is the test of pedigree or rather of blood among Race horses — "

Returns to the subject of politics, observing that he has "passed some weeks at Harrisburg — I am convinced that the present administration must sink unless the re-charter of the Bank of U States sustain it — The discontent created among the anti-Jackson men, by the nomination of Mr. [William Henry] Harrison [Drinker to Clay, July 16, 1835] has by I have no doubt operated in favor of the bank by leading Van Buren, to hope that by remaining quiet, & Keeping his friends still, we should be propitiated: — & then some of his adherents worked incessantly — one of them a manly honorable fellow at the head of the Electoral ticket has excited every reserve to promote it — I begin to think, that nothing but your word, can draw off a very large portion of the democrats of the party, who would rather be misled by their Foes than, be humbugged by their friends — I confess that I am one of them — " ALS. DLC-TJC (DNA, M212, R14).

Remark in Senate, February 10, 1836. States that the Committee on Foreign Relations wants to "ascertain the genuineness" of the June 17, 1835, letter of the Duc de Broglie to A.J.Y. Pageot [Speech in Senate, January 14, 1835; Comment in Senate, January 6, 1835; January 11, 1836; Undelivered Senate Speech, Late January, 1836]. Mentions that he had written the Department of State on the subject. *Register of Debates*, 24 Cong., 1 Sess., 464; *Cong., Globe*, 24 Cong., 1 Sess., 175.

From **Rosewell Saltonstall,** New York, February 10, 1836. States that "I Discover with some pain a Man by name of E P Page Esqr with a Petition before Congress to obtain Florida Lands by his Discoveries." Adds that Page "entitles himself the High Priest of Nature & has been months past preach[in]g in Tammany Hall in this City idolized by Regency & Mat V. Buerin [*sic*, Martin Van Buren] administration." Believes "This Man High Priest if in Florida would raise more Rebellion that U S. could stop." Reports that three years ago in New York City, Page "gave me in this City his own Hand writing my Calculations were Right now he comes to supplant I Pray my Discovered Longitude may by Senators yourself &c meet immediate Reward." Continues: "I have wrote the British Minister Mr [Charles] Bankhead on this Subject do see him on this Subject I wish I was near a knowledge of your PeNetrating Eye trys to Console me My Discoveries in London is a Fortune for Three hundred Men   I hold the Magic Square never Discovered in the age of Pythagoras to count either Vertical Horizontal or Diagonal make 7 or 28 & makes 8 x 3   21

8 x 3   24

9 x 3   27"   Concludes: "is there any way for you Senators to have me Nominated Minister to St James Court" ALS. DLC-Willie P. Mangum Papers (DNA, M212, R22). For Saltonstall, who died unmarried in New York City in 1840, see *Ancestry and Descendants of Sir Richard Saltonstall . . .* (New York, 1897), 37, 40. A bill to place Ephraim Page of Vermont on the roll of invalid pensioners passed the Senate on June 27, 1836, and the House on July 1. The president signed it on July 2. U.S. Sen., *Journal*, 24 Cong., 1 Sess., 288, 485, 541; U.S. H. of Reps., *Journal*, 24 Cong., 1 Sess., 1180.

Remark in Senate, February 11, 1836. Argues that the government should assume the mounting interest debt of the cities of Washington, Alexandria, and Georgetown to the Dutch bankers [Clay to Watterson, August 8, 1834] who in 1829 had loaned the three District of Columbia corporations funds with which to purchase Chesapeake & Ohio Canal stock [Remark in Senate, June 26, 1834]. Believes if the government assumes the debt it should also acquire the stock. "We cannot constitutionally subscribe to a work like this, and yet we can assume the debt of others arising out of such subscription. . . . The only proper course [is] to take the stock." *Register of Debates*, 24 Cong., 1 Sess., 467.

To JOHN HARE POWEL   Washington, February 13, 1836

[Thanks Powel for the offer in his February 10 letter to purchase cattle for him in Europe, but declines. Discusses other matters related to livestock. Continues:]

I have never thought that our French controversy would end in War; and now its apsect is decidedly pacific. I should not be surprized if the matter is now in fact settled.[1]

The disgust with which you regard the actual state of the Presidl. contest is very natural. To see such men as Webster put aside, for others who are so greatly inferior to him, is mortifying, and foreboding. Still there may be a choice, first, second and last, among these. And I confess that, looking to the principle on which he is brought out and sustained, Mr. V. B. appears to me to be the last choice.[2] Opposition to that principle perhaps forms the strongest recommendation of either of the two others [William Henry Harrison; Hugh L. White].[3]

You, I presume, will be absent when the question is decided. I sincerely hope, on your return, that you will find a brighter and more cheering prospect of public affairs.

ALS. Phi.   1. Brown to Clay, Jan. 24, 1832; Remark in Senate, Jan. 6, 1835; Biddle to Clay, Jan. 4, 1836.   2. Barbour to Clay, August 2, 1835.   3. Clay to Bailhache, July 14, 1835.

From John Hutchcraft, Paris, Ky., February 18, 1836. States that "You no doubt are regularly advised through the Newspapers of the progress which our legislature with regard to internal improvement in our Country. also the unfortunate political strife that has commenced in the Whig ranks." Believes "It is much to be regretted that Mr. [James T.] Morehead has suffered himself to be drawn before the people as a candidate for next Governor. not but that he is qualified, but Judge [James] Clark had been announced with an understanding by himself and friends. that Mr Morehead would not become a candidate [Smith to Clay, December 10, 1835]." Contends that if they both continue as candidates "Nothing short of a Van Buren Governor will be the result." Continues: "Kentucky is getting wild not only in her politics but in her fiscal affairs. every species of property is at very high rates. Land Negroes and hogs are advancing I may say almost daily. Many tracts have been sold at from $45. to 75 dollars per Acre. One hundred has been offered and refused for particular situations. Can it be possible that this state of affairs can continue long? I think not. The years of 16. 17. 18 are familiar to you alike to the present [1:458, 489; 2:383, 698-701; 3:12, 76, 107, 123, 328, 330, 440, 465, 548-49, 734-35]. A reaction in those years we are familiar with and such in my opinion must be the result of the present unforeseen zeal to acquire property. The products of Kentucky are too high to give to the vendor any thing for his trouble. Without a corresponding rise at the place of consumption the present prices of Kentucky produce can not be sustained." ALS. DLC-HC (DNA, M212, R5). Hutchcraft was born in Culpeper County, Va., in 1791; moved to Bourbon County, Ky., in 1802; and became a noted farmer and horseman. Perrin, *History of Bourbon, Scott, Harrison and Nicholas Counties*, 483. For actions of the Kentucky legislature regarding internal improvements during the period, see Ky. Gen. Assy., *Acts* . . . 1835-1836, pp. 98, 141, 415, 605.

To James Erwin, February 22, 1836. States that "Govr. [Joseph] Kent . . . and two or three other friends of his" have decided to purchase abut 5,000 acres of Erwin's land "at $10 per acre payable, with int. in two three and four years." Remarks that he is "not particularly acquainted with the circumstances of any of them but Govr. Kent," who "is a gentleman of fortune honor & probity." Offers his agency "in completing the business." ALS. NcD.

Speech in Senate, February 22, 1836. Expresses satisfaction over "the amicable termination of our unhappy controversy with France [Brown to Clay, January 24, 1832; Remark in Senate, January 6, 1835; January 11, 1836; Speech in Senate, January 14, 1835]." Attributes the peaceful outcome of the crisis to the patience of the Senate, especially in its unwillingness to support Jackson with legislation "authorizing reprisals upon French property." Blames the origin and deepening of the crisis principally on the president's offensive public remarks about France, and on his unwillingness to accept the peaceful overtures the Duc de Broglie relayed through A.J.Y. Pageot [Undelivered Senate Speech, Late January, 1836] on June 17, 1835. Had war unfortunately broken out it would have been one "highly discreditable to both parties—a war, in which neither civil liberty, nor maritime nor territorial rights, nor national independence, nor true national honor, was involved—a war, of which the immediate cause was an unfortunate message, and the ultimate object an inconsiderable debt, cancelled by the very act declaring it." Comments on "the noble part which Great Britain has acted in this unhappy dispute [Remark in Senate, February 8, 1836]." Concludes: "Our good old President has hardly terminated the French war, before he delcares a new one against the surplus fund [Remark in Senate, December 30, 1835]. I do hope that he will now turn his thoughts on peace; or, if that be impossible, that his friends at least on this floor, cherishing its spirit and its principles, will unite with us in an equitable distribution, upon the principles of the land bill [Speech in Senate, December 29, 1835], of a liberal portion of that fund. I assure them of my thorough conviction that, even for the purposes of defense and war, an investment of a large part of that fund in useful improvements, which will admit of rapid transportation of our means and our strength, will be far better and wiser than profusely to waste it on unnecessary fortifications." *Register of Debates*, 24 Cong., 1 Sess., 588-90; *Cong. Globe*, 24 Cong., 1 Sess., 198-200.

Remark in Senate, February 24, 1836. Speaks to the joint resolution authorizing certain post roads in Florida and Arkansas. Wonders if there is a precedent for establishing post roads by joint resolution and whether such a resolution need not specify what roads should be built but can leave that decision to the discretion of the postmaster general. *Register of Debates*, 24 Cong., 1 Sess., 613.

From Daniel T. Patterson, Norfolk, Va., February 25, 1836. Reports that in response to Clay's request of May 29, 1834, he has "procured at Palma in Majorca a Jack of best Breed three years Old 5 ft. high & will be half a hand higher." Notes that "the Majorca Breed are more esteemed in the Mediterranean than the Malta . . . and are higher priced." States that he could not find "Any Jennets, such as I thought worth bringing." Has housed the jack in a livery stable in Norfolk and asks Clay "what disposition you wish made of him." Adds that he would like "to retain a half interest in the Jack" but has "been Obliged to value upon you, for the Whole Cost and Expenses. One Hundred & ten dollars." ALS. Josephine Simpson Collection, Lexington, Ky.

Clay wrote Henry Thompson at Baltimore on March 2, 1836, asking: "When my Jack arrives at Balto. from Norfolk will you do me the favor to have his height ascertained, and write me what it is, what is his color, what his condition, and what you think of him?" Also requests that the jack be well shod, because "I intend to have him sent to K[entucky]. without unnecessary delay." ALS. Courtesy of J. Winston Coleman, Jr., Lexington, Ky. Printed in *JSH* (February, 1949), 15:96, ed. by James F. Hopkins.

Thompson replied to Clay on March 8, 1836, reporting that "The Jack arrived this morning from Norfolk . . . in better condition than I had expected, he is nearly black, with a good skin, his head & neck are good, with excellent legs & good feet, he is low in the shoulder & you will be disappointed to learn that he only measures 53 Inches." ALS. Courtesy of J. Winston Coleman, Jr., Lexington, Ky.

On March 12, 1836, Thompson wrote again, stating that he had paid Richard Vansant $67 to take the jack to Kentucky. Encloses a receipt for $80 for the total cost of food, care, and transport of the animal. Notes that "The Jack eats uncommonly well, which indicates good health, & I hope he will arrive at Ashland in fine order." ALS. DLC-TJC (DNA, M212, R14).

Patterson, writing from Norfolk on March 16, 1836, informed Clay that on March 7 he had shipped the jack from Norfolk to Thompson in Baltimore. Asserts that the jack is "a very fine One," but "He does not at present appear to his proper advantage. Owing to the Coldness of the weather, his passage &. &." Offers to procure one or two more jacks through "my friend Capt. J. J. Nicholson Com of the Frigate Potomac in the Mediterranean." ALS. Josephine Simpson Collection, Lexington, Ky.

Remark in Senate, February 25, 1836. Suggests postponing discussion of the fortification bill until various printed tables listing the details of the new works being proposed can be provided. *Register of Debates*, 24 Cong., 1 Sess., 614-15.

To FRANCIS T. BROOKE   Washington, February 26, 1836

I recd. your favor of the 23d. inst. and I am glad to see that, after a laborious Session, of the [Virginia Supreme] Court, you are reposing where true repose can only be found, in the bosom of your family.

I had prepared the rough draft of a Report on the French controversy; but as it is happily settled, the Report will now not be made.[1] I had endeavored to throw into it the same calmness which distinguished that of last year,[2] the same American spirit; but censuring, at the same time, both sides where censure seemed to me deserved, and concluding against War or Non-intercourse. I thought it best to invoke the aid of time, at least until all the instalments became due, and to await the expulsion of passion from the councils of both Governments, and the return of Reason.

[John] Tyler, it is understood, certainly resigns and immediately;[3] and [Benjamin W.] Leigh refuses to yield his post,[4] but will intimate his purpose to resign in fulfillment of a previous intention, at the close of this Session. The loss of one vote in Tyler is not at present so great, after the adverse issue of the Elections in Louisiana & Mississippi.[5] On all party nominations, were he to remain, the Admon will probably be able to succeed.

Mrs. Clay's health is better; but her cares, by the late afflicting dispensation of Providence,[6] are greatly increased. . . .

ALS. NcD.   1. Brown to Clay, Jan. 24, 1832; Biddle to Clay, Jan. 4, 1836; Undelivered Senate Speech, Late Jan., 1836.   2. Remark in Senate, Jan. 6, 1835.   3. Clay to Gilmer, Mid-Jan., 1836.   4. *Ibid.*   5. Clay to Brooke, Jan. 25, 1836.   6. Clay to Lucretia Hart Clay, Dec. 19, 1835.

Comment in Senate, February 26, 1836. Objects to appropriating $100,000 for a bridge across the Wabash when bridges across the Ohio or Muskingum would be "far preferable" for improving and continuing the Cumberland Road westward. Complains of Jackson's veto [Johnston to Clay, May 26, 1830] of the extension of the Cumberland Road to Nashville via Maysville and Lexington, Ky., even though Kentucky and Tennessee had received "less benefit from the expenditure of the public moneys than any of the others." Asserts he will continue to support the Cumberland Road project until it reaches the Mississippi, "but not beyond it"; and warns that he will "hesitate" to vote for "enormous appropriations" and for "new bridges." *Register of Debates*, 24 Cong., 1 Sess., 615-16.

Later this day, Clay explains the historical background of the original funding of the Cumberland Road and attacks again the proposed Wabash Bridge. Especially criticizes the suitability of building materials used in grading and preparing various segments of the roadbed and the dollar costs of various construction decisions that are being considered. *Ibid.*, 623-24. Complains particularily that "a Macadamized road is the worst possible road for stock. . . . I had to transport my bull Orizimbo [Shepherd to Clay, December 4, 1835] from Lexington to Maysville. I could not risk the destruction of his feet by putting him on a stone road, and I had to bring him in a wagon." *Ibid.*, 628; *Cong. Globe*, 24 Cong., 1 Sess., Appendix, 159-62. Moves to reduce the Cumberland Road appropriation of $670,000 made last session to $300,000. Motion lost. *Cong. Globe*, 24 Cong., 1 Sess., 208.

Remark in Senate, March 4, 1836. In discussing the Cumberland Road bill [Comment in Senate, February 26, 1836], wants to reduce the $320,000 for building the road in Ohio to $200,000. Claims that the section of road planned from the Wabash to the Mississippi in Illinois, if macadamized with stone materials to be hauled some 13 miles to the construction site, would cost from $10,000 to $15,000 per mile. Asserts that the road from Maysville to Lexington, Ky., had cost only $5,000 per mile. Offers an amendment denying any obligation by Congress to provide funds to macadamize the Illinois segment of the road. "If the object was to make this a Macadamized road, it would be cheaper to make both a railroad and a Macadamized road—a railroad to transport the stone upon for the Macadamized road." Amendment passed. *Register of Debates*, 24 Cong., 1 Sess., 722-24.

From Nicholas Biddle, Harrisburg, Pa., March 7, 1836. Reports that "A resolution passed to-day by more than two thirds of the House of Representatives instructing our Senators to vote against the Expunging resolutions before your House [Remark in Senate, June 30, 1834]. They will pass I believe in the Senate, so that the country will yet be saved from the dishonor of the mutilation of your journals." Adds: "Additional sections were also moved to a bill pending before the House about Banks—declaring that if any State prohibited the circulation of any notes of any Bank chartered by Pennsa. — it should be instantly retaliated upon the Banks of that State and that if any Deposit Bank obeyed any instructions to that effect, its charter should be immediately forfeited." Copy. DLC-Nicholas Biddle Papers (DNA, M212, R20). The Pennsylvania general assembly passed a resolution on March 7, 1836, by a vote of 64 to 25 instructing Senators James Buchanan and Samuel McKean to vote against the expunging resolution. *Niles' Register* (March 12, 1836), 50:17. Although the bank bill passed the state legislature, the "retaliation amendment," which was proposed during the second reading of the bill in the house, was not included in the final enactment. Information supplied by Henry E. Bown, associate archivist of the Commonwealth of Pennsylvania, from *Laws of the General Assembly of the Commonwealth of Pennsylvania, 1836.*

Remark in Senate, March 7, 1836. Moves that the secretary of the treasury report the total amount spent to date on constructing and repairing the Cumberland Road, including bridging costs. Asks that the sums spent on construction east of Wheeling and in the states of Ohio, Indiana, and Illinois be reported separately; also that the sums realized from the sale of public lands in each of those three states be reported separately—especially the monies from such sales that have since been used for the construction of roads or canals leading to those states [Remark in Senate, February 25, 1835; Comment in Senate, February 26, 1836]. *Cong. Globe*, 24 Cong., 1 Sess., 229.

Remark in Senate, March 8, 1836. Presents and supports a petition from Louisville asking for additional federal assistance to the Louisville Marine Hospital [4:779] and similar institutions on the western waters. Points out that the annual federal appropriation of $500 to the hospital has been "quite inadequate." Concludes that the "hardy race of men, who navigate the western rivers, deserved the protection of the Government, on account of their peculiar qualifications for the service of the navy." *Register of Debates*, 24 Cong., 1 Sess., 748-49; *Cong. Globe*, 24 Cong., 1 Sess., 233.

To Leslie Combs, Lexington, March 9, 1836. Reports that James T. Morehead has declined to run for governor of Kentucky, leaving the field to James Clark [Smith to Clay, December 10, 1835]. Mentions that Charles A. Wickliffe will run for lieutenant governor on the Clark ticket. Asserts that "Any arrangement as to individuals ought to be held subordinate to the great object of the prevalence of principles." Expresses "hopes, not unmixed with fears," about the fate of his land bill [Speech in Senate, December 29, 1835; April 26, 1836]. Does not know why Combs's pension bill moves so slowly in the House and states that to speed it up he and John J. Crittenden will introduce a bill in the Senate if need be. Copy. Printed in Colton, *Clay Correspondence*, 4:404. The bill for the relief of Combs was passed by the Senate on May 11, 1836. The

House concurred in it on June 13 and Jackson signed the measure on June 15. U.S. Sen., *Journal*, 24 Cong., 1 Sess., 348, 439; U.S. H. of Reps., *Journal*, 24 Cong., 1 Sess., 992.

Comment in Senate, March 9, 1836. Speaks to a motion not to receive the petition of the Society of Friends in Philadelphia asking for the abolition of slavery and the slave trade in the District of Columbia [Remark in Senate, January 11, 1836]. Expresses his disagreement with Sen. James Buchanan's motion "to receive and immediately reject the petition." Believes, instead, that both the constitutional right of petition and the constitutional provision relating to governance of the District require the Senate to "examine, deliberate, and decide" all petitions. Argues therefore that petitions should be received and fully debated also, that the Senate should state its reasons for whatever decision it makes on a given petition. Feels, however, that there are "certain great subjects that ought to be kept out of the scope of political action: they were the tariff, the great public domain, slavery, and the Union." Also "condemned the movements in a certain quarter on the subject of slavery. . . . [and] expressed the strongest disapprobation of the course of the northern abolitionists, who were intermeddling with a subject that no way concerned them. He expressed himself in favor of a gradual emancipation of the black race, if it could be done without those injurious consequences which would inevitably flow from such a measure. Although he had been taught from his childhood to believe that every man, no matter what was his color or his condition, was entitled to freedom, yet the retaining the black race in slavery was justified by the necessity of the measure. If he were a southern man, he would resist emancipation in every form either gradual or otherwise, because he would go for his own race, which was the superior race of the two; and because emancipation must necessarily give the inferior race, in the course of time, a numerical preponderance." Concludes with an amendment in the form of a resolution, "That the prayer of the petitioners be rejected:

For the Senate, without now affirming or denying the constitutional power of Congress to grant the prayer of the petition, believe, even supposing the power uncontested, which it is not, that the exercise of it would be inexpedient —

1st. Because the people of the District of Columbia have not themselves petitioned for the abolition of slavery within the District.

2d. Because the States of Virginia and Maryland would be injuriously affected by such a measure, whilst the institution of slavery continues to subsist within their respective jurisdictions; and neither of those States would probably have ceded to the United States the territory now forming the District, if it had anticipated the adoption of any such measure, without clearly and expressly guarding against it.

3d. Because the injury which would be inflicted by exciting alarm and apprehension in the States tolerating slavery, and by disturbing the harmony between them and the other members of the confederacy, would far exceed any practical benefit which could possibly flow from the abolition of slavery within the District." *Register of Debates*, 24 Cong., 1 Sess., 778-80; *Cong. Globe*, 24 Cong., 1 Sess., 239. See also Van Deusen, *The Life of Henry Clay*, 310-11, 313-14.

Remark in Senate, March 10, 1836. Speaks to and explains further the three clauses of the amendment he had offered on March 9 [Comment in Senate, March 9, 1836]. Asserts that Congress clearly has the constitutional power to deal with petitions pertaining to the abolition of slavery in the District of Columbia, but reminds the Senate of his view that the particular petition of the Philadelphia Society of Friends is inexpedient. Notes with regret that since his views "had not been received in the spirit in which he expected they would be, he was willing to withdraw" the amendment. Does so. *Register of Debates*, 24 Cong., 1 Sess., 786; *Cong. Globe*, 24 Cong., 1 Sess., 241. On March 11, 1836, the Senate voted 34 to 6 to reject the prayer of the Philadelphia Quakers; Clay voted with the majority. *Register of Debates*, 24 Cong., 1 Sess., 803-4, 810.

Earlier this day, March 10, Clay had requested more time to examine amendments to the bill for the relief of the sufferers of the New York City fire [Remark in Senate, January 12, 1836; Stevens to Clay, January 8, 1836]. *Ibid.*, 783.

Remark in Senate, March 11, 1836. Considers various compromise funding levels for the Cumberland Road segments in Indiana and Illinois; also estimates the appropriations that have been voted for the road in the past few years, and explains that the "two per cent. fund [Remark in Senate, February 25, 1835]" is exhausted. *Register of Debates,* 24 Cong., 1 Sess., 801, 803; *Cong. Globe,* 24 Cong., 1 Sess., 246.

To Samuel L. Southard, Washington, March 11, 1836. Writes: "I am pretty confident that [Albert G.] Harrison is for the Land bill [Speech in Senate, December 29, 1835], and think he told me so last fall; but I cannot be positive." ALS. NjP. Harrison was a member of the Committee on Public Lands.

To THOMAS HART CLAY   Washington, March 13, 1836

I received today your letter of the 4h.   I am perfectly satisfied with the Sale of our Hemp made by you and Mr. [John] Headley, and I think it better be delivered as fast as gotten out.

I sent yesterday the imported Jack "Delaware" to Kentucky where he ought to arrive about the 25h. inst.   If Don Manuel is sold Majr. Smith[1] is to keep Delaware, who I understand is in fine condition. I have written to him; and if the Don is not sold, Majr. Smith is to take him and keep him; and Delaware will in that case remain at Ashland; but if you can get $1500 for him he may be sold.

About the time this letter reaches you, I expect six Maltese Asses (three Jacks and three Jennettes) will arrive at Ashland. from N. Orleans, the property of R. D. Shepherd Esq., consigned to me; and I now give directions about them.

One of the three Jacks is four years old this Spring, and I am informed, he is 4 feet 11 inches high. Another is three years old, four feet nine inches high, and the youngest is two years old four feet eight inches high. I fear there is some inaccuracy in the measurement. And immediately on their arrival I wish you, Majr. Smith and Mr. Headley accurately to measure them, and also the Jennetts, and send me their heights and your opinion of them.

I wish the best of the three Jacks reserved for me, and the other two sold, provided you can get $2000 a piece for them, or as much more as you can. The three Jennetts I wish put to the best of the Jacks as they come in Season. They may run and be fed with my Jennetts, and as they have been so long at Sea it will be desirable for them to run on a Rye pasture, as soon as it is in a condition to be grazed.

As to the Jacks, I think it would be best to keep them at Ashland, if it can be done with convenience, until they are otherwise disposed of. And if Abraham[2] can be trusted for faithful attention to them, they might be put under his care. They ought to be daily groomed, well fed, bedded &c.   If you and Mr. Headley conceive that they can not be well taken care of at Ashland, and would be better provided for in town at a Livery Stable, they may be put there. I wish you would think of and give some suitable names to the Jacks.

I do not know whether Genl. [James] Shelby has returned; but if he has, I should like his opinion of the Jacks obtained; and if he wishes to take charge of the one reserved for me, he may do so, and we will hereafter arrange the division of the profits of the Season.

834

I have heard nothing as to the Sale of Don Manuel; but I suppose he has been taken by Mr. Swanson of Tennessee[3] or Dr. White of Madison.[4]

I will attend to the request of your Mama respecting the roots of the Moss Rose. P.S. The business of this letter is very important, and it ought to have and I hope will your best attention. If the Jacks are of the description given to me they will sell readily and at high prices. Perhaps it might be well to advertise them. Mr. Tho. Smith will assist you.

ALS. Henry Clay Memorial Foundation, Lexington, Ky.   1. Probably Thomas Smith. 2. A slave.   3. Possibly Edward Swanson, founder of Nashville, or a member of his family. William McRaven, *Life and Times of Edward Swanson* (Nashville, 1937), *passim.*   4. Probably Dr. Jacob White, a large landowner in northern Madison County and son of Capt. James White. In the 1820s he was a guardian of the Madison County orphanage and in 1821 a justice of the peace. Information courtesy of Prof. Henry Everman, Eastern Kentucky University, Richmond, Ky.

From Rezin D. Shepherd, Baltimore, March 13, 1836. Writes of his pleasure in hearing "that Orozimbo is admired in Kentucky." Believes the cows Clay has purchased will also be admired when they have had time to become acclimated. States that he will not sell the Broken Horn Cow for less than $300. Reports that the jacks Clay has purchased [Shepherd to Clay, December 4, 1835] have made "quite a sensation in New Orleans," and sends a paragraph about them which he wants delivered to the office of the Washington *Daily National Intelligencer.* ALS. DLC-TJC (DNA, M212, R10). For notice of the arrival of the jacks and jennies, see *Niles' Register* (March 26, 1836), 50:53.

On March 15, 1836, Shepherd wrote Clay informing him that "you will do as you please regarding the Broken Horn Cow, or if it would suit you better she may go into the agreement with those you now have to Breede on shares." Presumes she is now in calf to Orozimbo. Notes that Clay has decided "to take half Interest in the Six Asses imported in the [vessel] Unicorn at the rate of 3000$ for the whole or 1500$ for the half." ALS. Josephine Simpson Collection, Lexington, Ky.

Shepherd wrote again on March 17, 1836, reporting that he has "debited your account with 1.500$ for your half Interest in the Six Asses Imported in the Unicorn." As he has "no Use whatever for the money and it Can lay as long as you please," promises to keep a running account "so that there will be no necesity of your remitting only when it is perfectly Convenient to do so." Urges Clay to accept any good offers for the jacks, because several ships have gone out from New Orleans to Malta to bring back jackasses, so "Another year you will no doubt be inundated with them." ALS. Courtesy of M.W. Anderson, Lexington, Ky.

On March 24, 1836, Shepherd notified Clay that "your account has Credit for Four hundred & ten Dollars for Brick in Philadelphia." Also says he has made arrangements to deliver the Broken Horn Cow "and you must decide whether she goes into the Partnership or to take her on your own account." Promises to send the pedigrees on the animals sold to Clay as soon as his agent returns form the north of England. ALS. DLC-TJC (DNA, M212, R14).

James Shelby wrote Clay on April 2, 1836, that the shipment of six Maltese jacks and jennies have arrived at Ashland and have been measured. Discusses their conformation, comparing them to jacks already at Ashland such as Ulysses, Magnum Bonum, and Achilles. ALS, manuscript torn. Courtesy of M.W. Anderson, Lexington, Ky.

On April 27, 1836, R.D. Shepherd wrote from Baltimore that he has received "the Pedigrees of my Importation of 13 Heifers and two Bulls." Sends those he thinks correspond to the ones Clay has purchased, and says if the descriptions are "not exact, send me one that is so and I shall no doubt be able to trace out from the various Certificates in my possession every Heifer you have." ALS. DLC-TJC (DNA, M212, R14).

Shepherd wrote on May 5, 1836, offering Clay possession of "two Thorough bred mares" immediately and of the stallion named Derby in a month's time. ALS. Josephine Simpson Collection, Lexington, Ky.

Two days later, May 7, Shepherd wrote Clay describing the mares and the stallion Derby. Notes that Derby still shows the effect of a bad injury to his left hind leg received on board ship. Concludes, therefore, that the animals "may not appear as Valuable as you thought them, should they not prove equal to your expectations after you get them home, put them all under the Hammer & sell them for whatever they will bring." ALS. DLC-TJC (DNA, M212, R10).

On May 9, 1836, Shepherd acknowledged receipt of $5,500 of Clay's money to be invested at 6 percent interest. Discusses sending the horses to Kentucky in the care of Richard W. Vansant. *Ibid.* (R14).

Shepherd wrote on May 12 giving the pedigree of Derby which "you will find . . . in Skinner's edition of the English Stud Book Page 843, dam Urganda foaled in 1831 by Peter Lely & bred by Lord Derby, his memoir will be found in the 10 Vol of the Sporting Magazine April No 1835, — The English Mare you will also find in the English Stud Book page 874 — dam Dodo, foaled in 1828 by Ardrossan, bred by Mr Read of Denham [*sic*, Mr. Read Denham]." Promises to have the pedigree of the Virginia mare in a few days. Notes he is closing his business at Shepherdstown, Va. (W. Va.), and invites Clay to visit him in Baltimore and stay at "My Very humble abode" on "No. 28 Second Street Corner of Gay." ALS. Josephine Simpson Collection, Lexington, Ky. See *The [Skinner] General Stud Book, Containing Pedigrees of English Race Horses, &c. &c. . . . Three Volumes In Two* (Baltimore, 1834), 1:843, 873-74.

Shepherd, in a letter of July 26, 1836, authorized Clay to sell any of the stock he had received from Shepherd. Suggests sending the stallion Derby along with other "Stock in the neighborhood of Shepherds Town that . . . will be removing to Kentuckey [*sic*] in the Fall." ALS. Josephine Simpson Collection, Lexington, Ky.

On October 24, 1836, Shepherd wrote acknowledging that he had received from Clay "502 ½ $ . . . for my half of the Jack sold — @ 1000$," and noting that "I observe you have also sold another of them for 1500$ which I think a good price." Reports that Derby is now in good condition, but states that if he does not do well "put him up under the hammer & sell him for whatever he will bring." ALS. Courtesy of M.W. Anderson, Lexington, Ky.

On December 15, 1836, Shepherd wrote Clay, enclosing the pedigree of the two calves and two brood mares Clay had purchased. Says that Derby's season "will not be out before the 1st July," and "he Cannot possibly be deliver[e]d before that time." *Ibid.*

From Nimrod L. Lindsay, North Middletown, Ky., March 15, 1836. Accepts Clay's offer to sell one-half interest in the bull, Hector, for the sum of $250, "provided I will engage a suitable hand and be at half the expense of bringing him Out" from Shepherdstown, Va. (W. Va.). States that he will send a young man to Shepherdstown "a few days hence" on the mission. Also wants to purchase through Clay "a full blooded imported Cow" for "John Hutchcraft my neighbor." ALS. DLC-TJC (DNA, M212, R14). Lindsay had served in the legislature from Bourbon County in 1827-28 and was a Mason. Collins, *History of Kentucky*, 2:772; Perrin, *History of Bourbon, Scott, Harrison and Nicholas Counties*, 136.

Comment in Senate, March 17, 1836. Questions the security of $30,000,000 of public funds "reported to be in the deposite banks." Points out that "the aggregate amount of all the capitals of those institutions was only forty-two millions of dollars, whilst the public had, or ought to have, in their vaults thirty millions. In various instances the amount of the public deposite far exceeded the capital of the banks. . . . Now, the security of this vast sum of public money is an object of great importance. Let us see what it is. Those deposite banks are under total liabilities to the enormous amount of nearly seventy-eight millions of dollars, for payment of which they may be called on any one of the 365 days of the year. And what amount have they to meet these liabilities, in the event of any such immediate call? Only about ten millions of specie! Only one dollar in about eight! The principal part of their other means consists of notes discounted and bills of exchange negotiated. But if there come any sudden pressure, if that convulsion in the paper system of which every considerate man feels a consciousness shall take place, there means will be found altogether unavailable to enable the deposite banks to fulfil their engagements." Harks back to the more secure days "when the Bank of the United States was the financial agent of the Government." *Register of Debates*, 24 Cong., 1 Sess., 840-42; *Cong. Globe*, 24 Cong., 1 Sess., 262.

Remark in Senate, March 23, 1836. Does not believe that referral to the Committee on Foreign Affairs of the resolutions of the Massachusetts legislature relating to the boundary between Maine and New Brunswick can "lead to any useful or practical result." Moves that the resolutions be tabled. They were. *Register of Debates*, 24 Cong., 1 Sess., 962.

Remark in Senate, March 24, 1836. Hopes for an early adjournment of the session, perhaps as early as May 30. Indeed, "So anxious" is he "individually on this subject" that if Congress does not "adjourn before that time," he will be "obliged to adjourn himself." Thinks, however, that since the single issue of Sen. Thomas Hart Benton's expunging resolution [Comment in Senate, January 28, 1835] will occupy five or six weeks of the Senate's time, May 30 is probably an unrealistic adjournment date. *Register of Debates*, 24 Cong., 1 Sess., 962-63. The 24th Congress, 1st Session adjourned on July 4, 1836.

Later this day, Clay asks for enough additional information on a bill confirming claims to lands in Missouri "to satisfy Congress" that it is "not giving away these lands in the dark." *Register of Debates*, 24 Cong., 1 Sess., 965-66.

To DANIEL WEBSTER   Washington, March 24, 1836

Nothing very material has occurred in the Senate since you left us. But a bill has been introduced for the admission of Michigan forthwith, has been made the order of the day for tuesday next, and will probably be pressed by the Administration party.[1] I understand that there is a probability we shall have the votes of the Indiana Senators [William Hendricks; John Tipton], [Samuel] McKean and [Hugh L.] White against the immediate admission, and in favor of the passage of a prior law, according to regular usage. It will occasion no doubt debate, both on the principle, and the proposed boundary of the new State. How long the debate will be protracted is uncertain; but your presence by wednesday or thursday at farthest is very important.

ALS. NcD.   1. Comment in Senate, Dec. 15, 1835.

Remark in Senate, March 25, 1836. With reference to a bill extending the time for issuing script certificates on U.S. military land warrants, moves that the land granted by this legislation be limited to 20,000 acres. *Register of Debates*, 24 Cong., 1 Sess., 978.

Remark in Senate, March 28, 1836. Moves to fix May 23 as the date of adjournment. Adopted. *Register of Debates*, 24 Cong., 1 Sess., 981.

To Thomas Hart Clay, Lexington, Ky., March 29, 1836. Is disappointed that he has not heard from Henry Clay, Jr., "for so long a time." Believes "he will arrive soon." Would "be glad if you could make some arrangement for sowing down in Oats and clover & timothy all his ground next to [Richard H.] Chinn, except that which was in hemp last year, and which I wish again put in hemp." Concludes: "I have not heard of

837

the arrival at Ashland of my N. Orleans Asses [Shepherd to Clay, December 4, 1835; March 13, 1836]. Delaware [Clay to Thomas H. Clay, March 13, 1836] will get there by the time this letter does." ALS. Mary Clay Kenner Collection, Rogersville, Tenn.

To LEWIS TAPPAN
Washington, March 29, 1836

I recd. your letter stating that there are defects in the laws which were intended to suppress the African Slave trade; and that some further legislation is necessary to secure their object. I feel quite sure that Congress would readily correct any such defects, on being informed of them; and you do me no more than justice in supposing that I would cordially co-operate in that endeavor.[1]

But your letter does not state what the defects are, and I have no knowledge of them. Perhaps it would be best for the District Attorney[2] to communicate them either to the Atto. General [Benjamin F. Butler] or to some member of Congress.

The effectual suppression of that trade is an object on which we can all unite, without the danger, as in the case of slavery within the States, of any imputation of improper interference.

ALS. ICN.   1. Congress did not take up this subject during the 1st or 2nd sessions of the 24th Congress.   2. William M. Price was district attorney for the Southern District of New York. *Biennial Register*, 1835, p. 156.

From David G. Burnet, Harrisburg, Texas, March 30, 1836. Announces that "Texas has pronounced a final Separation from the miserable and always revolutionary government of Mexico." Notes that "The causes which have led to this momentous act are too numerous to be detailed in a Single letter—but one general fact may account for all—the utter dissimilarity of character between the two people, the Texians and Mexicans—The first are principally anglo-americans—the others a mongrel race of degenerate Spaniards, and Indians more degenerate than they." Predicts that "We may be driven to the bank of the Sabine. yea—beyond it—and Still we will be independent of the unprincipled, priest-ridden, faithless Mexicans—Our rights in the Soil of Texas, are founded in the holiest guarantees of national faith, and we will not relinquish them, except with our lives—Such is the predominant feeling in Texas, and it is backed by many Strong arms and Stout hearts, who Know how to poise a rifle or wield a Sabre—" Admits, however, that "we are few in comparison with our enemies—and we need all the external aid, that can be had." States: "To You Sir whose voice is always eloquent and never more powerful, than in Swaying the Sympathies of men and of governments, we look with confidence, for an advocate and a friend—To You, who took the feeble, distracted and vascillating governments of the South by the hand [2:541-62, 853-60], and introduced them to the great audience of nations—to You, the government of Texas appeals and asks a Similar favor."

Argues that "An early recognition of the independence of Texas, by the government of the United States, would redoud greatly to our advantage—Save the Shedding of much genuine *American* blood—and, if not add a new and brilliant Star to the constellation that illuminates the northern Republic, it would at least give confidence and energy to a gallant people who will be always found in harmony, as in juxtaposition to that Republic—The voice of Henry Clay has never been raised in a more righteous cause than this, and none, in which humanity has been more outraged—The merciless massacres that have Succeeded every little advantage of our enemies, would afford a Sufficient answer to all the objective Suggestions of Mexico, and put her diplomatic minions to Silence." ALS. DLC-HC (DNA, M212, R5). Endorsed by Clay on verso "David S. Burnet [*sic*, David G. Burnet]   Presidt of Texas." For the Texas Revolution, see William C. Binkley, *The Texas Revolution*. Baton Rouge, 1952; John Holmes Jenkins (comp.), *The Papers of the Texas Revolution, 1835-36*. Austin, 1973. See also

Austin to Clay, April 13, 1836; Comment in Senate, May 4, 1836; Van Deusen, *The Life of Henry Clay*, 294-96.

From James Erwin, New Orleans, March 30, 1836. Writes that he did not get to measure "the height of the Asses," because "they were Crowded up in the ship, so that it was impossible for me to do so [Shepherd to Clay, December 4, 1835; March 13, 1836]." Believes, however, that "they are of good size" and estimates a good purchase price as $300 for the "Jennets . . . & the best Jack will be worth $1000—the others 700 each."

Reports that [Isaac T.] Preston did not qualify as James Brown's executor "until yesterday," but there "has been no loss by delay, property has advanced, I can now obtain $10.000, for the house for which we supposed 8000 a fair price [Ingersoll to Clay, June 11, 1835]. Discusses other financial transactions, adding that he has been delayed in returning to Kentucky by his attempt to get "my childrens rights established as separate from mine in such manner as to enable me to sell off such of my property as I may wish to get clear of." Adds: "The passion in the money market is very great almost equal to that which followed the removal of the deposits [Bradley to Clay, October 16, 1832]—yet property is increasing daily in Value—I have purchased Cautiously, almost too much so." ALS. DLC-HC (DNA, M212, R5).

Remark in Senate, March 31, 1836. With reference to Mississippi Sen. Robert J. Walker's bill "to reduce and graduate the price of the public lands to actual settlers alone, &c.," argues that it is "in fact a bill to give every thing to the new States, and leave nothing for distribution among the older States of the confederacy. That, with its graduation clause and donation clause and pre-emption clauses, it might as well be called by its true name—a bill to give the whole of the public lands to the new States, or to the settlers that would roam over them." *Register of Debates*, 24 Cong., 1 Sess., 1028. This observation elicited a "burst of eloquence" from Walker, in which he objected to having "actual settlers" called squatters and claimed that had 1,000 of these "much-abused squatters, these western riflemen" been at Bladensburg in 1814 under Jackson's command, "never would a British army have polluted the soil where stands the Capitol. . . . [Here Mr. W. was interrupted by warm applause from the crowded galleries.]" When quiet was established, Clay "disclaimed any intentional disrespect to squatters, but hardly thought they would have saved the Capitol unless they had given up their habits of squatting." *Ibid.*, 1029-30; *Cong. Globe*, 24 Cong., 1 Sess., Appendix, 217. For the provisions of Walker's graduation and preemption bill, see *Cong. Globe*, 24 Cong., 1 Sess., 309. The bill was referred to a select committee which reported it favorably, although the Senate did not act on it. *Ibid.*, 310; *Register of Debates*, 24 Cong., 1 Sess., 1031-32; U.S. Sen., *Journal*, 24 Cong., 1 Sess., 254, 350.

Remark in Senate, April 1, 1836. Suggests changes in wording in the bill establishing the northern boundary of Ohio and admitting Michigan Territory into the Union [Comment in Senate, December 15, 1835]. *Register of Debates*, 24 Cong., 1 Sess., 1046-48; *Cong. Globe*, 24 Cong., 1 Sess., 311.

Remark in Senate, April 2, 1836. Supports motion of Sen. Alexander Porter to recommit the bill to establish the northern boundary of Ohio and admit Michigan into the Union [Comment in Senate, December 15, 1835]. Porter sought to amend the section on suffrage in Michigan and better secure the rights of the United States to public lands in the new state. *Cong. Globe*, 24 Cong., 1 Sess., 313.

To Luke Tiernan, Baltimore, April 5, 1836. Assures Tiernan that "I feel very much as you do in respect to public affairs. They present very little gratifying to patriotism, and

I regret to say that the prospect before us is not very encouraging. Sometimes, however, in the dispensations of Providence, when all seems to be lost, in His mercy he sends us unexpectedly relief. This is now my hope." ALS. NcD.

Remark in Senate, April 6, 1836. On the question of paying Revolutionary War pensions, thinks it is better not to tamper with the law requiring the creditors of the government to take nothing but gold and silver in payment rather than "bank notes of every description." Reminds his colleagues in this regard that the notes of the Bank of the United States "were never legal tender; the laws only authorized them to be received in payment of debts due the Government." Points out, however, that if any senator wants to get rid of his B.U.S. notes, he will be glad to exchange "the notes of any of these small banks, or even specie, for them." *Register of Debates*, 24 Cong., 1 Sess., 1095-96; *Cong. Globe*, 24 Cong., 1 Sess., 325-26.

To JOHN PATTON *et al.*   Washington, April 7, 1836
I have duly received your favor[1] transmitting the proceedings of a public meeting of the citizens of Bolivar, in which they do me the honor to express a wish that I would reconsider the resolution which I had formed to retire from the public councils to private life. They are pleased to believe that my public services cannot be dispensed with at the present time. And you, gentlemen, are good enough to add many kind and friendly expressions, for all of which, I am very thankful.

This is the thirtieth year since I first entered the service of the Federal Government.[2] My labors for the public have been various and often arduous. I think they give me some title to repose, which I feel to be necessary on many accounts. I believe with you that the present period in the affairs of our country is imminently critical. It requires all the wisdom, the virtue and the energy among us to avert impending danger. — If I were persuaded that, by remaining longer in the public service, I could materially aid in arresting our downward progress, and in communicating additional security to civil liberty and our free institutions, I should feel it a duty not to quit it. But I am not sure that my warning voice has not been already too often raised. Perhaps that of my successors may be listened to with more effect. I sincerely hope it may be.

These, Gentlemen, are briefly my motives for retirement. It is my purpose, if my health will allow me, to remain in Congress during the present session. I reserve for future consideration whether I shall serve out the term for which the Legislature of my State did me the honor last to elect me;[3] and your wishes will have due weight in any decision I may form. Beyond that term, I can conceive of no probable contingency which would reconcile me to a farther continuance in the Senate. . . .

Copy. Printed in Columbus *Ohio State Journal*, May 21, 1836.   1. On March 16, 1836, Patton *et al.* wrote Clay on behalf of the citizens of Bolivar, Ohio, urging him not to retire from public life. If he retires, "to whom shall the friends of the Constitution appeal for a correction of those abuses and usurpations, which have characterized the most prominent acts of the present Chief Magistrate?" Assert that the people of the country are becoming more convinced each day "that the President has been induced, by the intriguing influence of the *man* who now claims to be his *legitimate* successor [Van Buren], and who officially declared that the present Administration was the friend of the *British Government*, to abandon those republican principles, by which he declared, anterior to his election, this nation should be governed." Urge Clay to remain in the Senate "until, at least, the expiration of the term for which you were last elected." *Ibid.*   2. See 1:254-55. 3. Clay to Beatty, June 8, 1830.

Remark in Senate, April 8, 1836. Since a bill granting public land to Missouri for internal improvements has no chance of passage, moves that it be indefinitely postponed. *Register of Debates*, 24 Cong., 1 Sess., 1121.

To HENRY CLAY, JR. Washington, April 11, 1836

I wrote you a few days ago, and, altho' I am not sure of this letter reaching you, I now write principally to inform you that two of the Poitou Asses[1] (the Jack and one of the Jennettes) have unfortunately died at Sea, and the third is in such condition as to make her recovery uncertain. I get this information from Mr. [James] Hagarty. They were shipt on board the Geo. Turner on the 22d. Feb. and their loss is attributed to a long rough and inclement voyage. I fear there has been neglect; as the six Asses shipt by Mr. [Rezin D.] Shepherd[2] in Novr. did not arrive at N. Orleans until March (being four months at sea) and were in better order, all agree, than any animals had been ever known to have been brought over in before. It is true they had the advantage of the Trade winds. I do not know whether your insurance will cover the loss. I fear it will not; but I have requested Mr. Hagarty to have due proof of it, in proper form, made. As I know not where the insurance was effected, I have not directed where the proof is to be sent. If he does not know he will await your orders on that point. Should the loss fall on you, I hope the $1500 which I am to receive from Dr. [Jacob] White for Don Manuel will, with the surviving Jennett, indemnify you. If you are not deceived as to the superiority of the Poitou Asses, it would be very desirable to get two or three of the Jacks of a large size of that race; but they ought to be shipt at a good season and in careful hands. Can you make any arrangement to get them?

I have late letters from home, and all were well at Ashland. Your woman Harriet[3] had lost her child.

Hemp continues high. It was selling for ten dollars. I have not been informed Whether they have been able to have your ground again put in Hemp, but I hope and suppose it will be done. Thomas [Hart Clay] was busily at work on the Logan farm, and I trust is doing better.

The vacation at Mr. [Enoch C.] Wines's school [Edgehill Seminary] continuing, the boys[4] will remain with me until its termination. . . . P.S. It will be probably at least the first of June before Congress adjourns. Nothing very important has yet been done. The Virginia elections[5] are in progress and their issue is doubtful; or, I should rather say, I am afraid it will be against us.

ALS. Henry Clay Memorial Foundation, Lexington, Ky. 1. Henry Clay, Jr., to Clay, Dec. 20, 1835. 2. Shepherd to Clay, Dec. 4, 1835; March 13, 1836. 3. A slave. 4. Martin Duralde III; Henry Clay Duralde. 5. The Democrats carried the Virginia house of delegates by 77 seats to 56 for Whigs and the senate by a margin of 20 seats to 12. Richmond *Enquirer*, May 17, 1836.

Comment in Senate, April 12, 1836. Speaks to the fact that Arkansas, seeking admission into the Union, has in its proposed state constitution a clause prohibiting any future legislation that would abolish slavery in the state. Points out that the Missouri Compromise gave any state or territory "south of 40 degrees" north latitude the "entire right . . . to frame its constitution, in reference to slavery, as it might think proper." Presents petitions from Philadelphia that dispute his personal view of the matter. Does this because of his belief that he has a duty to present petitions, a duty of "a constitutional, almost a sacred character," even if the only action on them by the Senate be "the mere laying of them on the table." Asserts that the adoption of the U.S. Constitution, the settlement of the Missouri question [Clay to Woods, July 16, 1835], and the adjustment of the tariff [Draft Proposal, Mid-December, 1832; Comment in Senate, February 12, 1833; Speech in Senate, February 25, 1833] all illustrate a "principle of compromise" that was "highly desirable" to continue. *Register of Debates*, 24 Cong., 1 Sess., 1134-35; *Cong. Globe*, 24 Cong., 1 Sess., 346-47. The *Congressional Globe* version varies somewhat in language. It does not employ the reference to "south of 40 degrees"; instead, it refers to the Missouri Compromise "line." The *Register of Debates* version is printed in Colton, *Clay Correspondence*, 6:36-37 where it is misdated as April 11. Arkansas was admitted to the Union on June 15, 1836. The controversial part of the Arkansas constitution was article 7, section 1 which provided that the "General Assembly shall have no power to pass laws for the emancipation of slaves, without the consent of the owners"; nor could it "prevent emigrants to this State from bringing with them such persons as are deemed slaves by the laws of any one of the United States." Orville W. Taylor, *Negro Slavery in Arkansas* (Durham, N.C., 1958), 42-46.

From Henry Austin, New Orleans, April 13, 1836. Writes to enlist Clay's support on behalf of Texas independence [Burnet to Clay, March 30, 1836]. Reports that "rumors which have been circulated, that the despot of Mexico [Santa Anna], could have uttered, much less have seriously intended to carry into effect threats to exterminate the people of Texas" are "lamentably true." States: "Texas, from the River Nueces, to the Brazos, presents nothing to the view, but a desolated wilderness, polluted by the colored Savages of Mexico and Smoking with the blood of their victims; Who are now marching forward, under the blood red flag of the Tyrant, destroying and to destroy, without regard to age, or sex, or condition, without even Mercy for the innocent, helpless, unoffending children[.]" Argues that the natural instinct of United States citizens, who are "the friends of human rights and human liberty," is to aid "the people of Texas, before all are slaughtered." They cannot do so, however, without committing a crime under "the 6 section of the act of congress, passed 20 April 1818 [2:492-507]," which "constitutes it a crime against the US, 'to set on foot, or provide, or prepare, the means, for any Military expedition, or enterprise, to be carried on from thence against the territorys, or dominions of any foreign Prince or state.[']" Since "This law renders the disposition, of the benevolent, and the brave, to extend aid to suffering humanity, and to the support and extention of civil liberty almost nugatory," suggests that it be repealed. Asks Clay to consider "that our dwellings are in flames, our properties laid waste, our women and children flying, destitute to the Sabine for safety, the mass of our citizens concentrated upon the east bank of the Brazos, about to hazard all in a decisive battle with the whole force of the tawny-butcher of Mexico, and unless all obstacles to the obtaining [of] aid from the people of this republic be removed, in case of defeat the torch of liberty in Texas, will soon be extinguished in the blood of its inhabitants." ALS. DLC-HC (DNA, M212, R5). See also Comment in Senate, May 4, 1836. Henry Austin was the brother of Mrs. Horace Holley, wife of the former president of Transylvania University in Lexington, and a cousin of Stephen F. Austin of Texas fame. Eugene Barker, *The Austin Papers* (Austin, 1926), 371, 377. A bill to alter or amend the act of April 20, 1818, did not come before the Senate during the 24th Congress.

Comment in Senate, April 14, 1836. Defends the provisions of his land bill [Speech in Senate, December 29, 1835] dealing with the size of land grants to Louisiana, Missouri, and all the new states except Ohio. Argues that these grants are governed by "the principles of equalisation and compromise." Is willing, however, to vote "to expunge from the bill the grant to any new State, whose two Senators concurred in desiring it to be so expunged." Notes that Jackson has taken divergent stances in the past on the distribution of public land sales proceeds to the states and that his action on this bill cannot be predicted. It should be debated and decided on its merits. Announces that when the question of land grants to new and old states alike comes up he will "Vote for them as part of a great compromise." But if they come up as separate bills for each state, he will "vote against them, as being without precedent or principle." Makes it clear that he opposes the bills before Congress "making large grants to the new States, and not one acre to the old ones." *Register of Debates*, 24 Cong., 1 Sess., 1172-76; *Cong. Globe*, 24 Cong., 1 Sess., 357-58. Clay's main speech on land sales distribution in the 24th

Congress, 1st Session was delivered on April 26, 1836; see also Speech in Senate, June 30, 1832.

Remark in Senate, April 15, 1836. Speaks to petition of David Melville protesting his removal as a customs officer in Newport, R.I. Says that if Melville's facts are true, they reveal "an instance of flagrant injustice and abuse of power." Would like to know if Jackson or Secretary of the Treasury Levi Woodbury had authorized the removal. Since Melville's petition levels "some charges" against "those high functionaries," wonders wryly whether "those Senators who adopted the expunging principle [Remark in Senate, June 30, 1834]" were really interested in this particular petition. *Register of Debates*, 24 Cong., 1 Sess., 1178; *Cong. Globe*, 24 Cong., 1 Sess., 361.

Comment in Senate, April 18, 1836. On the question of the bill to authorize contracts for the movement of the U.S. mail on railroads, reminds his colleagues of his long-standing support of the "power of the Government to construct roads." Believes that this particular legislation will "end in a complete revival of the system of internal improvements." Warns, however, of the dangers of the "spirit of speculation, both in England and in this country, in regard to railroads." Feels that U.S. mail contracts will stimulate "this system of fancy speculation" in railroad stocks, contribute to inflation, and injure further a national currency already becoming a "paper system." Agrees that "the Government must avail itself of the use of these roads in some way," but thinks that the whole question of such mail contracts with the railroad companies needs careful study. *Register of Debates*, 24 Cong., 1 Sess., 1206. In moving and opening debate on this bill, Sen. Felix Grundy argued that it was well above party concerns, quoting in support of his opinion a "patriotic sentiment expressed some days since by the Senator from Kentucky, [Mr. CLAY] 'that, whatever political or party differences might be, still there were some subjects paramount to all party considerations, and upon them, at least, we should act without reference to party.'" *Ibid.*, 1199.

To THOMAS H. CLAY   Washington, April 20, 1836

I recd. the enclosed letter from Mr [Benjamin] Gratz and shall send him today $150 to pay Heiskills [*sic*, Hieskell's] debt.[1]

I enclosed to Thomas Smith yesterday a proxy for you to represent me at the meeting of the Stockholders of the Rail Road Co.[2]

My brother P[orter]. Clay is now here. He tells me that he did not think the portion of my Stock of Cattle which he saw looked in very good order. How do they generally appear?

I think all my heifers, and the English Cows had better be put in the lower pasture at Mansfield.[3] If any of the English Cows want the bull, care should be taken that he serves them. Lafayette may be used, altho' I should prefer Orozimbo, if he were not too far off.

ALS. Mary Clay Kenner Collection, Rogersville, Tenn. Endorsed on side sheet: "I ought to have enclosed this letter in mine of today. H.C. 19h. Apl."   1. Clay wrote Benjamin Gratz on April 20, 1836, that Hieskell "has consented to receive $150 in discharge of Thomas's [H. Clay] debt." Thanks him "for the trouble you have taken in that affair, and I will as soon as I can get a check today for the amt. transmit it to you." ALS. PHi. See Wharton to Clay, March 6, 1829.   2. Lexington & Ohio Railroad Co. See Clay to Biddle, May 10, 1831.   3. The farm, one mile east of Lexington on Richmond Road, on which Clay built Thomas a house, "Mansfield," in 1846. James B. Kittrell, Jr., *Thumbnail Sketches of Old Lexington (Ky.) Today* (Lexington, 1959), 13. At his death Clay left the farm and house to Thomas "In trust however that it shall be retained free from all debts or incumbrances, as a home for the residence of himself his wife, and the Children that he has or may have. . . . And upon the death of my said son Thomas, I give and devise Mansfield to such of his children or their descendants as he may by his last Will and Testament direct and appoint." Clay's Last Will & Testament dated July 10, 1851; Codicil dated Nov. 14, 1851. DS. Fayette County Will Book T.

Speech in Senate, April 21, 1836. Continues the discussion and defense of his land bill [Comment in Senate, April 14, 1836]. Attacks an amendment by Sen. Robert J. Walker that would insure the graduation of the price of public land downward over a period of years. Says he would rather see the bill fail than see the principle of graduation amended into it. "It would be much better to increase than diminish the price of public lands," he argues. Presents statistical evidence to sustain this contention. Discusses also the failure of preemption in Kentucky and Tennessee "at an early day" to attract and hold permanent settlers in those states. Notes the fraudulent devices by which speculators come to acquire public lands through manipulated pre-emption techniques. Asserts that graduation can only reduce the value of marginal land and, eventually, the value of the better land as well. *Register of Debates*, 24 Cong., 1 Sess., 1248-49; *Cong. Globe*, 24 Cong., 1 Sess., 381.

Remark in Senate, April 22, 1836. In response to Sen. Isaac Hill's assertion that he has discovered a corrupt government clerk who promotes dubious Revolutionary War claims, Clay asks if it is possible that in the five years Hill has been in Washington "one little clerk was the only corrupt officer he had found in the Government?" Suggests that if Hill "would look into the Post Office and other Departments, he would find many more instances of corruption." Further, on the issue of distributing the Treasury surplus, he informs and assures Hill that there is $27,000,000 to distribute and no constitutional difficulties impeding distribution. *Register of Debates*, 24 Cong., 1 Sess., 1252-53; *Cong. Globe*, 24 Cong., 1 Sess., 384.

To CHARLES JOHN HUGHES   Washington, April 24, 1836

I received a letter from your father [Christopher Hughes] dated at Stockholm in February last; and supposing it might be later than any intelligence received by you from him, I have thought it would be agreeable to you to have this information. He was then slightly indisposed with a bad cold contracted in a Royal Elk Hunt, but appeared nevertheless to be in good spirits, and speaks of you with the greatest affection.

I hope you are pleased with your situation in the Academy,[1] and that you are embracing with assiduity the fine opportunities for improvement which it affords. These are very great and unsurpassed. I have remarked, however, one disadvantage attending a West point education, that the Cadet goes forth into the world with too much contempt for mankind, and that he consequently marks his aversion from its follies and indiscretions with too strong an *expression* of his disapprobation. Too much he *cannot feel* for actual vice; but it is not always prudent or proper to give utterance to all one's feelings. . . .

ALS. MiU.   1. Hughes entered West Point in 1834 and graduated in 1838. He died in Florida on August 22, 1839. USMA, *Register*, 189-90.

Remark in Senate, April 25, 1836. Citing the wording of Virginia's deed of cession of her public lands to all the "States then in the Union" [i.e. the states adhering to the Articles of Confederation], opposes as unconstitutional an amendment by Sen. Robert J. Walker to the land bill [Speech in Senate, December 29, 1835; Remark in Senate, March 31, 1836]. The amendment would shift the mathematical basis of the distribution of public land revenues to the states from the census figures of 1830 to the total number of house and senate members each state has in Congress. Notes that while Walker's formula "nearly tripled" the amount "little Delaware" would receive, he could only compliment Delaware Sen. John M. Clayton's "sense of justice" in resisting such crude inducements. Asserts that "distribution according to the basis of federal population was the only just one." *Register of*

Debates, 24 Cong., 1 Sess., 1282-83, 1285-86; *Cong. Globe*, 24 Cong., 1 Sess., 397-98. The Walker amendment failed by a vote of 37 to 6.

To ROBERT WALSH, JR. Washington, April 25, 1836

I duly received your favor of the 18h. inst. You do me the favor to desire an adequate notion of my services and views whilst I was in the Department of State. I regret that the bad state of my health, and my various public duties here oblige me to be very brief.

Besides the discharge of the current duties of the office, I negotiated various treaties. Several of these (those for example with Austria[1] and Mexico[2]) were agreed upon, but not actually signed, and were subsequently concluded in the name of the succeeding Administration.

In the treaty with Central America[3] was first introduced the great principle that the national and foreign vessel should be equally allowed to introduce into their respective Countries merchandize without regard to the place of its *origin*. The principle had been adopted in the Convention with England of 1815,[4] negotiated by Mess. [John Q.] Adams, [Albert] Gallatin and me, of permitting the vessels of the two Countries to import the productions of the *two Countries*, on terms of entire equality; but it was restricted to the productions of G. B. & the U. S. It did not admit of an English vessel importing into the U. S. the produce of any Country other than G. B. nor vice versa. By the treaty with Central America, which I negotiated, on the contrary, an American vessel may carry into its ports the produce of any Country of the four quarters of the world on the same terms as it can be imported by a National vessel, and vice versa. This has been a model treaty, which has been followed in several treaties afterwards negotiated.

My instructions to Mr. [James] Brown, on our claims against France,[5] cost me much labor, and were favorably thought of by others.

But my great work was the preparation of the instructions intended for our Commissioners who were to meet first at Panama,[6] and afterwards at Tacubaya. If you could take the trouble to read them, you would obtain a better conception of my views than any I can now give you, as to the liberal basis on which the Commerce of the world should be placed. I there argue and endeavor to have established the principle that *private* property on the Ocean shall enjoy the same safety and protection to which it is entitled on land. And all the maritime principles in favor of free trade, against spurious blockades &c. for which we have so long and so earnestly contended, are sought to be established at the proposed Congress.

These instructions are almost exclusively my sole work. Without consulting any body particularly, I engaged in their preparation, and afterwards submitted the draft of them to the President [John Q. Adams] and his Cabinet. They run into about eighty pages of manuscript, and I do not think that the alterations which, on the scrutiny of those Gentlemen, they underwent amounted altogether to one page; and those related chiefly to the projected connection between the Atlantic and Pacific Oceans. I was disposed to go a little farther than my colleagues.

The relations in which I stood to the Diplomatic Corps, during the whole of Mr. Adams' Admon, and to every member of it, were of the most cordial and friendly character. It was impossible, I think, that business could have been transacted more satisfactorily to all parties. I have reason to believe that, up to this moment, the members of that Corps who were associated with me retain lively recollections of our amicable feelings and intercourse.

I will not dwell on this subject, but must refer you, for any deficiencies, to my public acts and the transactions of the day.

I will add that I introduced into the Department, as vacancies from time to time occurred, (I created none) some most accomplished assistants, several of whom were found to be so necessary that they escaped the general proscription.[7]

I think it very probable that your feelings towards me have been sometimes misunderstood and misrepresented. Certainly in our personal intercourse, I never discerned any evidence of hostility or prejudice. Candor oblige[s] me to say that I have sometimes seen in your paper [Philadelphia *National Gazette & Literary Register*] what I thought bore testimony of an inimical spirit; but your frank assurances now convince me that I was mistaken. We have been in the midst, during these late years, of the most exciting scenes in our public affairs. I did not much underrate the power which I was opposing — certainly not its disastrous tendency. I felt that I was struggling for the Country, for its civil liberty, its institutions, its property, its virtue. I felt that I had a good title to the support of all honorable & intelligent men. Perhaps I have been sometimes too sensitive, when I thought that support was not yielded, and have censured too hastily when I supposed a measure of zeal in the public cause was not displayed by others equal to my own. . . .

ALS. DLC-HC (DNA, M212, R5).   1. See 7:453.   2. See 7:21-22, 114-15; Parry, *Treaty Series*, 81:381-416.   3. See 7:200-203.   4. See 2:30-37, 57-59.   5. See 6:596-603, 611-13.   6. See 5:314-44; 6:127.   7. For a comparison of the clerks in the State Department in 1827, 1829, and 1833, see *Biennial Register*, 1827, p. 9; 1829, p. 9; 1833, pp. 1-2.

Speech in Senate, April 26, 1836. Gives a detailed and extensive explanation and defense of his land bill [Speech in Senate, December 29, 1835]. Assures his colleagues that the $40,000,000 surplus in the Treasury, now deposited in 34 state banks of dubious stability, makes necessary the distribution of the proceeds of public land sales to the states, old and new, before the existing paper currency system collapses. Recounts the history of the panic and depression of 1819 and the rapid growth of the number of unregulated state banks from about 300 to about 800 since 1830. Observes: "No man of ordinary prudence and forecast could contemplate the existing state of things without the most serious alarm. It was impossible that they should continue; that eight hundred banks should go on, from day to day, to issue so much paper, and that the twenty-four sovereignties [states] should submit to it. It was utterly impossible but that an explosion must come; though when it would come, he could not pretend to say. They might differ there about the cause of it, but come it certainly would." Develops this theme with specific illustrations. Adds the thought that not even substantially increased expenditures on national defense can absorb the surplus. Presents arguments, historical and constitutional, for including all the states in the distribution process. Outlines the many expected social, economic, and educational advantages the distribution of public lands and the proceeds from the sales of public lands will bring to each and every state, and defends his proposed ten percentage formula [Speech in Senate, June 20, 1832] for determining the level of distribution to the new and old states. Says that while it is certainly desirable to reduce the surplus, he cannot support any downward changes in the existing protective tariff structure other than those provided in the Compromise Tariff Act of 1833 [Draft Proposal, Mid-December, 1832], legislation which he was "delighted at having borne an important part" in formulating. Presents a summary of arguments for the expediency of distribution and against the principle of graduation and the practice of preemption [Speech in Senate, April 21, 1836]. Notes that there are still 700,000,000 acres of public land "lying outside of the States, unappropriated," some of it encumbered "by the unextinguished title of the natives." States, however, that "from the moment the white man put his foot on the rock at Plymouth, or on the shores of Jamestown, commenced the entire extinction of that unfortunate race of people; and the Indian lands might all be counted on as a source of distribution." Concludes: "By passing this bill, that greatest of all interests, the interest in preserving the Union, would be greatly advanced . . . and could they conceive a tie more strong to bind the Union together than the fact that every year each State would share [land sales receipts] with its co-States?" *Register of Debates*, 24 Cong., 1 Sess., 1288-98; *Cong. Globe*, 24 Cong., 1 Sess., Appendix, 305-7.

Remark in Senate, April 27, 1836. Says he has not yet read the "voluminous papers" related to the House bill to raise additional troops for the Seminole War [Remark in Senate, January 27, 1836] in Florida. *Register of Debates*, 24 Cong., 1 Sess., 1299; *Cong. Globe*, 24 Cong., 1 Sess., 403.

Later this day, Clay continues his defense of his land bill [Speech in Senate, December 29, 1835; April 26, 1836]. Opposes a graduation amendment that would reduce to fifty cents per acre all land that had been in the market for twenty years, this reduction to be made at the rate of ten percent a year for a period of five years. Argues that the anticipation of such reductions would quickly render them political issues in the new states and would also "tend to increase speculation" in public lands. Later this day, Clay opines that "the minds of the Senators were all made up" on the land bill and that "no changes would probably be made." *Register of Debates*, 24 Cong., 1 Sess., 1303,1310; *Cong. Globe*, 24 Cong., 1 Sess., Appendix, 318.

Remark in Senate, April 28, 1836. Thinks the debate on James Buchanan's resolution "to inquire into the expediency of contracting with Luigi Persico for two groups of statues to complete the ornaments of the east front of the Capitol" is really much ado about very little. Proclaims Persico to be "well known as a superior artist." *Register of Debates*, 24 Cong., 1 Sess., 1317-18; *Cong. Globe*, 24 Cong., 1 Sess., 407. Persico (1791-1860) had been engaged in 1825 to execute several pieces of sculpture for the U.S. Capitol, particularly the classical "War" and "Peace" figures for the east portico. These were completed and delivered in 1834. There is no evidence that he was commissioned to do any additonal pieces for the government. George C. Groce & David H. Wallace, *The New York Historical Society's Dictionary of Artists in America, 1564-1860* (New Haven, 1957), 501.

From Enoch Cobb Wines, Princeton, N.J., April 30, 1836. States that Clay's grandsons, Martin Duralde III and Henry Clay Duralde, arrived at Edgehill Seminary "in safety about nine o'clock last eveng, a good deal fatigued by their journey." Notes that they "seem a little sad at the prospect of being deprived of the society and counsel of their uncle [John Morrison Clay], to whom they are passionately attached," but thinks "that their spirits will soon regain their wonted elasticity." Suggests that John visit "them at Edgehill instead of their going to the college to see him," because "they are too young to be allowed to go by themselves to a place where they can hardly fail to see & hear much that they ought not to witness." Continues: "We part with regret from your son [John Morrison Clay], towards whom we feel a strong attachment. Without meaning to flatter either yourself or him, I cannot permit him to leave the institution without expressing to you the very high regard & respect with which his talents & conduct have inspired me. I consider him decidedly one of the most promising young men I have ever had under my care. He posseses fine capacities, excellent principles, great independence & strength of character, a nice sense of honor, & is, so far as I know, very correct in his habits. He only lacks *religion,* to make him almost every thing that you could desire. If any thing could console you under the loss of a daughter, in whom your affections were bound up, it would be the possession of such a son."

Expresses his concern about "intimations in the public prints of your intention to retire from public life." Believes "Your loss from the public councils at this particular time could not but be severely, perhaps disastrously, felt by the whole Country." Contends "that there is no man living to whom the nation is so deeply indebted as to you," and predicts that "history will do you ample justice." ALS. DLC-HC (DNA, M212, R5). Following an illness of typhoid fever during the summer of 1836, John Morrison Clay failed to return to New Jersey to go to college there as was apparently planned. Instead, he attended Transylvania University in 1836-37.

Wines also included with the letter two receipts, both dated April 30, 1836, one for $329.26 and one for $172.06. These were for payments Clay had made to Wines for the schooling of Martin and Henry Duralde. ADS. *Ibid.*

Comment in Senate, May 4, 1836. Argues that the defense appropriation bill passed this morning by the House, authorizing an increase in the size of the regular army and the calling out of 10,000 volunteers, must be viewed by the Senate in the light of actual events in Mexico [Burnet to Clay, March 30, 1836; Austin to Clay, April 13, 1836; Lindsey to Clay, May 22, 1836]. Points out that as yet we have received nothing but "rumors of the inhuman scenes" said to have occurred there, so there is "no ground for engaging in hostilities with any foreign power." Opposes increases in army strength until more is known. Says he had hoped that a final vote on the land bill [Speech in Senate, December 29, 1835] might be held today but is willing to postpone it for more pressing business. Notes that "He had been told that we had lately at Tampa Bay seven thousand men engaged in a contest with six or seven hundred miserable Indians [Remark in Senate, January 27, 1836]: these we had neither conquered nor found; and unless we could show a somewhat better capacity for war, we had better refrain from engaging in one. If Santa Anna should commence hostilities with us, if he should invade our frontier—and he had, as yet, shown no such intention—what was to prevent our transporting this force from Tampa Bay to the Sabine, to prevent any violation of neutrality and of existing treaties in that quarter? But, unless there was an actual or threatened invasion, we were not called upon for any active measures." At any rate, the Senate needs more information. That information lacking, suggests proceeding to consideration of the land bill. *Register of Debates,* 24 Cong., 1 Sess., 1387-88; *Cong. Globe,* 24 Cong., 1 Sess., Appendix, 404. The *Cong. Globe* of this date reported the fact (unreported in the *Register*) of Clay's resolution to amend the tariff law in order to bring the duty on all hemp imported into the country to the level of that levied on Russian hemp. *Cong. Globe,* 24 Cong., 1 Sess., 416. The "inhuman scenes" involved the massacres of revolutionary Texas forces at The Alamo (March 6) and at Goliad (March 27) by Mexican General Antonio Lopez de Santa Anna.

Remark in Senate, May 5, 1836. With reference to the passage of the land bill [Speech in Senate, December 29, 1835] at the end of yesterday's session by a vote of 25 to 20, doubts that the yeas and nays had actually been called for, but rather had been taken "under an impression that they had been ordered." *Register of Debates,* 24 Cong., 1 Sess., 1396; *Cong. Globe,* 24 Cong., 1 Sess., 418.

Later this same day, Clay defends his resolution of May 4 to bring the duty on all imported hemp to the level of that on Russian hemp. Cites the manner in which "Bengal hemp" currently evades the tariff on hemp. Denies his resolution is a measure to increase hemp duties. Charges that those who wish to avoid increases in the tariff had best stop making "extravagant appropriations" such as "Ten millions for the Navy, and fifteen millions for the War Department!" Urges reductions in military spending so that surplus public funds being held in the state deposit banks to pay for an elaborate and entirely unnecessary coastal defense improvement program can be released for distribution to the states. *Register of Debates*, 24 Cong., 1 Sess., 1397-99; *Cong. Globe*, 24 Cong., 1 Sess., 419.

To JULIA PRATHER CLAY   Washington, May 9, 1836

We (John [Morrison Clay] and myself) attended the Rail Road depot on several successive arrivals of the Cars, and at length was gratified the evening of friday to find Henry [Clay, Jr.] in them; and I was rejoiced to find him in good health and spirits; but we were greatly disappointed in not meeting you also. I have been much grieved to learn from Henry that you met with a misfortune at Sea;[1] but I sincerely hope that his assurances of your entire recovery from it are well founded. I am most anxious to see you, my dear daughter, and your little Son [Henry Clay III]. Henry tells me that you remained in N. York only to recover from the fatigue of the Voyage, and he talks of leaving here tomorrow to bring you and my little name sake to us. I had promised John to let him accompany his brother, and gratify his fervent desire to see you; but, poor fellow, he is taken ill, altho' not in any apparent danger, and I fear will be unable to leave me. We are both most eager to see you, and hope you will come to us as fast as you can consistently with your health and comfort.

I will thank you to make my respects to Mr. [James] Hagarty, and say to him that I am greatly obliged by his kind invitation to visit N. York, which I should be happy to do, but my public duties will not allow me to leave the Senate. . . .

ALS. Henry Clay Memorial Foundation, Lexington, Ky. Addressed to Julia in New York City in care of James Hagarty.   1. Henry Clay, Jr., to Clay, Dec. 20, 1835.

To Alfred Beckley, "Allegheny Arsenal near Pittsburgh Pennsylvania," May 10, 1836. States that he will "be happy to furnish you with any Durham Cattle, or other stock . . . whch you may want." Suggests that Beckley visit Ashland and select them himself. Adds that "I have been a long time in public life, and think I may shortly retire without being liable to any reproach for leaving it." ALS. Courtesy of Turner McDowell, Glenn Falls, N.Y.; also ViU. Written from the Senate Chamber. For Gen. Beckley, son of John James Beckley, of Beckley, Va. (W. Va.), attached to the 4th Regiment of Artillery, see *Biennial Register*, 1835, p. 104; *PMHB*, 72:55; *WVH*, 9:128, 133, 205-6, 215; 10:241-42, 249-50.

Remark in Senate, May 10, 1836. Moves adoption of the House bill, as amended by the Committee on Foreign Relations, to carry into effect the convention between the United States and Spain. *Register of Debates*, 24 Cong., 1 Sess., 1427. The Senate amendment provided that the attorney general would divide and distribute the money obtained under the treaty. The House version called for a board of three commissioners to perform this function. See Remark in Senate, May 31, 1836. The "Claims Convention between Spain and the United States" had been signed at Madrid on February 17, 1834. The bill in question was to implement the first article of the convention which provided that "the proceeds thereof, shall be distributed by the Government of the United States among the claimants entitled thereto, in such manner as it may deem just and equitable." Parry, *Treaty Series*, 84:144-48 (espec. 144).

Remark in Senate, May 11, 1836. As chairman of the committee on Foreign Relations, speaks to the thrust of Jackson's brief message of May 6 which observes that the act of July 12, 1832, does not enable the president to carry into effect the "recently negotiated additional article to the treaty of limits with Mexico" and requests the necessary legislative corrective. Reports that the committee wants a corrective bill that will revive the boundary survey commission, authorization for which had expired on April 3, 1836, when the April 3, 1835, convention had expired. Observes: "A survey was to be made; and we were endeavoring to ascertain, as precisely as possible, the true [Sabine] boundary line between that country and our own. In the mean time, the General [Edmund P. Gaines] commanding our forces in that quarter had taken up a position in or near this disputed territory. Existing circumstances were such as to make it absolutely necessary that proper officers should be authorized to carry out the provisions of the treaty; thereby evincing the sincerity of our intentions, and the fidelity with which we adhered to our engagements." *Register of Debates*, 24 Cong., 1 Sess., 1409, 1427. Maj. Gen. Edmund P. Gaines commanded American forces on the Sabine. See Francis Paul Prucha, *The Sword of the Republic: The United States Army on the Frontier, 1783-1846* (New York, 1969), 307. The continuing problem with Article II of the U.S.-Mexican boundary treaty of January 12, 1828 [2:678, 816; 4:171-73, 666-67; 7:21-22] can be traced in Parry, *Treaty Series*, 78:35-42; 85:101-5; 86:103-6.

To HENRY CLAY, JR. Washington, May 12, 1836

John [Morrison Clay] continues very ill — high fever, head ache &c. Yesterday he was cupped, bled, blistered and took calomel. This morning I think he is a little better. He is free from head ache, but his fever (9 OClock) is rising, and he has a constant drowsiness. I do not perceive any immediate danger, but I am nevertheless quite uneasy about him. This situation will prevent me from meeting you and Julia [Prather Clay] at Baltimore; I hope you will come to us as soon as you can. My love to Julia and Henry [Clay III]

ALS. Henry Clay Memorial Foundation, Lexington, Ky. Addressed to Henry in New York City in care of James Hagarty.

To MARGARET BAYARD SMITH Washington, *ca.* May 14, 1836

Dr. [Henry] Huntt thinks John [Morrison Clay] better this morning; but his fever continues, without any alarming symptoms. We hope to break it to day, and for the purpose of watching him and seeing that his medicine is properly administered, I shall remain with him and not attend the Senate.

Many thanks for the Jelly &c and especially for your friendly offer of service. He rests well at night, and Charles [Dupuy][1] and I sleep in the same room with him, without much disturbance to any party. In the day, he is attended by a good female nurse. I look moreover to day or tomorrow for his brother [Henry Clay, Jr.] and his wife [Julia Prather Clay], who will be with me a week or ten days. So that, whilst I am exceedingly grateful for your obliging tender of your personal attention, it will be unnecessary at present to tax your kindness. Should a different and unfortunate state of things arise, I will avail myself of your goodness.

ALS. DLC-J. Henley Smith Papers (DNA, M212, R22). Printed in Hunt, *First Forty Years of Washington Society*, 157-58. 1. Clay's bodyservant.

To THOMAS HART CLAY Washington, May 19, 1836

John [Morrison Clay] is still confined by his fever, which is very stubborn. He has not at present any dangerous sympton, but of course my solicitude about him is extreme. The fever was bilious, without intermission, but it has become typhoid. Dr. [Henry] Huntt is his attending physician, and Drs. Linn and Causin[1] his consulting physicians. They agree perfectly in the course of treatment and assure me that they think he will recover. I wish his mother was present with us to assist in nursing him, but he does not suffer for nurses; and many offer to set up with him at night on whom I have not called. Henry [Clay, Jr.] prefers setting up half of the night, which he has done for the last three.

I recd. your letter of the 9h. You mention that you have not Stock for your grass. It is much better to have too much grass than too little. When I go out, we will make some arrangement for supplying you. In the mean time if you could get 15 or 20 four or five year old Steers to fatten on grass and sell this fall, perhaps it would be well. Perhaps Majr. [Thomas] Smith could assist you in procuring them. If you cannot get any, and you find that I am over-stocked, I would be glad that you would take some of mine, for which I would pay you

I have sent two blooded mares to K[entucky]. and they are now on the way. They are both supposed to be in foal by Derby the imported horse that I am to get after the present Season.[2] On their arrival, I will thank you to ascertain from [Richard W.] Vansant[3] whether either of them was horseing on the journey. If either of them was, or should shew a want of the Horse after their arrival, I wish the imported mare sent to Bertrand,[4] and the other to Stamboul. They are both Browns, but the imported mare has a lump or swelling on one of her forelegs about the knee from an injury which happened to her at Sea. If both of them should prove to want the horse (and I wish Mr. [John] Headley to have them frequently tried) and Bertrand cannot serve the imported mare, let them both go to Stamboul. They ought not to run where there is much clover. I am afraid in the new pasture at Mansfield[5] there is too much clover for breeding mares or Jennies, but of that Mr. Headley and you must judge.

Along with the mares, there will be Eight or ten Asses of Mr. White's[6] which, if the man, in charge of them, desires it, may be allowed to remain at Ashland some days to rest.

Is Nancy (the Quaker Cow) in calf? Are all my other English Cows that I sent out last winter also in Calf?

I do not wish any Heifers that have never had Calves put to the Bull until my return. . . .

ALS. Henry Clay Memorial Foundation, Lexington, Ky. 1. For Dr. Lewis F. Linn, a physician and senator from Missouri, see *BDAC*. Dr. Nathaniel P. Causin was a Washington physician who in 1827 was located on the "north side Pen, av near 14w." *The Washington Directory* . . . (Washington, 1827), 19. 2. Shepherd to Clay, March 13, 1836. 3. *Ibid*. 4. John Hutchcraft advertised the services of his stallion, Bertrand, at stud in the Lexington *Observer & Kentucky Reporter* of Feb. 24, 1836. 5. Clay to Thomas H. Clay, April 20, 1836. 6. Probably Dr. Jacob White of Madison County. See Clay to Thomas H. Clay, March 13, 1836.

From Thomas N. Lindsey, Frankfort, May 22, 1836. Discusses matters relative to the James Morrison estate. Continues: "The only excitement we now have in Ky and it is not much, is in relation to Texas [Burnet to Clay, March 30, 1836] Some few Companies of volunteers will leave in the Course of a month Less stir in politics than I have known at this season of the year for many years [Smith to Clay, December 10, 1835]. Produce is rather declining in price, & labor advancing. I know not how Ky is to progress with her system of internal improvements [Hutchcraft to Clay, February 18, 1836] unless some means can be decided, to induce a heavy emigration. The progress of the land bill [Speech in Senate, December 29, 1835] excites a good deal of interest here." ALS. DLC-TJC (DNA, M212, R14). For Kentucky's reaction to the Texas war for independence against Mexico, see James E. Winston, "Kentucky and the Independence of Texas," *SHQ* (July, 1912), 16:27-62. Lindsey was a Frankfort lawyer and sometime member of the Kentucky legislature. He also served as a delegate to the 1849 state constitutional convention. Kerr, *History of Kentucky*, 4:315.

To SAMUEL L. SOUTHARD   Washington, May 23, 1836
There has been a slight improvement with John [Morrison Clay] yesterday morning and this, but no decisive change. The physicians think the chances of recovery are on his side.

The news of the overthrow of St. Anna and his army and his capture are confirmed and I think may be credited.[1]

ALS. NjP.   1. The defeat of Santa Anna at San Jacinto on April 21, 1836. See Burnet to Clay, March 30, 1836.

To LEWIS TAPPAN   Washington, May 23, 1836
I have recd. your favor of the 20h. inst. and I submit it to you whether the enquiry you make of me[1] does not imply a little want of charity on your part, towards the N. Y. Colonization Society.

The truth is that I was earnestly requested to attend and address the Society, at its annual meeting; and, retaining all my convictions in favor of the object of the Society, I should have been glad to have done so, but was obliged to decline the invitation. After my letter was recd. at N Y. I recd. another acknowledging it but at the same time renewing the invitation and pressing my attendance, with great earnestness. To this second application I made no reply; and my *silence* no doubt lead to the expectation of my attendance.

ALS. DLC-Lewis Tappan Papers (DNA, M212, R22).   1. Reference obscure; letter not found.

Remark in Senate, May 31, 1836. Notes that the House has disagreed with the Senate's amendment to the bill to carry into effect article I of the Claims Convention of February 17, 1834, with Spain [Remark in Senate, May 10, 1836]. Urges his colleagues to insist on the Senate amendment when the issue is discussed in the Senate-House joint conference committee. *Register of Debates*, 24 Cong., 1 Sess., 1647. The compromise eventually reached in conference was to appoint a single commissioner, rather than three commissioners or the attorney general, to distribute the funds received under the convention. *Ibid.*, 1694 (June 4, 1836). See also Remark in Senate, June 4, 1836.

Remark in Senate, June 2, 1836. With reference to a bill authorizing the purchase of the private stock in the Louisville and Portland Canal, urges a "high, just, and generous policy on the part of the United States." *Register of Debates*, 24 Cong., 1 Sess., 1674.

Remark in Senate, June 4, 1836. Supports resolution, which fails, to puchase the library of the late Count Bourtoulin of Florence, Italy. *Register of Debates*, 24 Cong., 1 Sess., 1694. For Count Dmitrii Petrovich Buturlin (or Boutourlin), a native of St. Petersburg, Russia, and a military historian and rare book collector, see *Great Soviet Encyclopedia*; and *Catalogue de la biblioteque de Son Exc. M. le Comte D. Boutourlin*. Florence, 1831.

Later this day, Clay, in his capacity as a Senate member on the joint Senate-House conference committee on the convention with Spain [Remark in Senate, May 10, 31, 1836], reports on the compromise reached and recommends its acceptance. The compromise was "to appoint one commissioner instead of three commissioners, to execute the duties, and to reduce the time allowed for the performance of the duties from eighteen months to one year." *Register of Debates*, 24 Cong., 1 Sess., 1694.

Speech in Senate, June 8, 1836. Opposes the bill [Remark in Senate, February 4, 1836] to prohibit deputy postmasters from receiving and transmitting any printed or pictorial material "touching the subject of slavery" in any state, territory or district where, by law, such circulation is prohibited." Argues that this bill [Clay to Speed, January 2, 1836] is "totally unnecessary and uncalled-for by public sentiment," and is also "unconstitutional." Charges that Jackson's message on the subject [*MPP*, 3:175-76] has "met with general disapprobation," and that if not unconstitutional, contains "a principle of a most dangerous and alarming character." Notes that the principle involved applies not only to the slaveholding states; indeed, it can "be applied to all the States, and to any publication touching the subject of slavery whatever, whether for or against it, if such publication was only prohibited by the laws of such State." Wants to know, too, "whence Congress derived the power to pass this law." Claims that if the doctrine in this bill prevails, "the Government might designate the persons, or parties, or classes, who should have the benefit of the mails, excluding all others." Challenges Sen. James Buchanan's argument that the post office power in the Constitution gives Congress the "right to regulate what should be carried in the mails." Agrees that "dangerous consequences" might flow from transmitting "incendiary publications" in the slave states that are "calculated to promote civil war and bloodshed." Concludes, however, that "Congress had no power to pass beyond the constitution for the purpose of correcting it. The States alone had the power, and their power was ample for the purpose. . . . the bill was calculated to destroy all the landmarks of the constitution, establish a precedent for dangerous legislation, and to lead to incalculable mischief. There was no necessity for so dangerous an assumption of authority, the State laws being perfectly competent to correct the evil complained of. He must say that, from the first to the last, he was opposed to the measure." *Register of Debates*, 24 Cong., 1 Sess., 1721, 1728-31; *Cong. Globe*, 24 Cong., 1 Sess., Appendix, 455-56. The bill was rejected by a vote of 25 to 19. *Register of Debates*, 24 Cong., 1 Sess., 1737. For the constitutional dimensions and political implications of Clay's attitudes toward the "gag rule" and "incendiary publications," see Remark in Senate, January 11, 1836; Comment in Senate, March 9, 1836; Van Deusen, *The Life of Henry Clay*, 309-11, 314-19; and Eaton, *Henry Clay*, 115-36, espec. 127.

Comment in Senate, June 9, 1836. Opposes a "peculiar feature" in the supplementary bill to the act to admit Michigan to the Union [Comment in Senate, December 15, 1835] which was designed to curb speculative land purchases. This feature was its failure to include the "usual exemption from taxation for five years of lands purchased by individuals from the United States." Moves an amendment to insert this exemption which, he says, is "a powerful motive to purchasers" who would be "actual settlers" rather than speculators. Amendment defeated. *Register of Debates*, 24 Cong., 1 Sess., 1737-39; *Cong. Globe*, 24 Cong., 1 Sess., 540.
    Later this day, Clay attacks the "nefarious system of pre-emptions" with all of its "glaring abuses." Opposes a bill to extend the time for receiving proof of certain pre-emption claims under the act of June 19, 1834. *Register of Debates*, 24 Cong., 1 Sess., 1741. The June 19, 1834, act is in 4 *U.S. Stat.*, 678.

Remark in Senate, June 10, 1836. Sees no need to increase the army and smiles at the picture drawn of dangers to the nation when actually the only threat on our frontiers was that from "a few miserable Indians." *Register of Debates*, 24 Cong., 1 Sess., 1756.

Remark in Senate, June 11, 1836. Supports a bill to authorize a "liberal appropriation" for marine hospitals to serve sick and disabled seamen on the western waters. *Register of Debates*, 24 Cong., 1 Sess., 1759. See Remark in Senate, March 8, 1836.

Remark in Senate, June 13, 1836. Presents a memorial from Shelby County, Ky., signed by many "respectable" citizens, some known personally to him, asking for recognition of the independence of Texas [Burnet to Clay, March 30, 1836]. Takes no personal stand [Comment in Senate, May 4, 1836] on this issue since the Committee on Foreign Relations, which he chairs, is presently considering it. *Register of Debates*, 24 Cong., 1 Sess., 1759; *Cong. Globe*, 24 Cong., 1 Sess., 546.

Remark in Senate, June 15, 1836. States he has not yet had time to read the diplomatic correspondence on the Northeastern Boundary dispute with Britain [1:1006; 4:181-82; 6:1100-1101] submitted by President Jackson. Believes that this correspondence should not be printed until the senators from Maine and Massachusetts are consulted about it. Moves to refer Jackson's message and the enclosed documents to the Committee on Foreign Relations. *Register of Debates*, 24 Cong., 1 Sess., 1779; *Cong. Globe*, 24 Cong., 1 Sess., 556.

Remark in Senate, June 16, 1836. Opposes the report of the Committee on Pensions adverse to the Revolutionary War claim of Humphrey Marshall [1:397-402]. *Register of Debates*, 24 Cong., 1 Sess., 1780-81. Marshall had presented a petition "praying that certain parts of his pension, improperly withheld, may be paid." The Committee on Pensions recommended that it not be paid; this was amended to read "That the petitioner is not entitled to pensions or allowances under both the acts of Congress of the 7th of June and 5th of July, 1832," but that the Treasury had no power to "detain the sums becoming due on pensions accruing to reimburse sums erroneously paid on the other." The memorial itself was neither passed nor rejected. Finally on January 18, 1838, the committee was discharged from further consideration of the memorial. U.S. Sen., *Journal*, 23 Cong., 2 Sess., 289, 440, 459-60; 24 Cong., 2 Sess., 151. See also *Register of Debates*, 24 Cong., 1 Sess., 1854. For the pension acts of June 7 and July 5, 1832, see 4 *U.S. Stat.*, 529-30, 563-64.

Later this day, with reference to the bill to regulate the deposits of public monies and distribute the Treasury surplus to the states [Remark in Senate, December 30, 1835] Clay moves an amendment to require the banks to pay 4 percent interest on the government deposits instead of 2 percent. Withdraws motion. *Register of Debates*, 24 Cong., 1 Sess., 1784.

Also on this day, the Senate, by votes of 39 to 4 and 39 to 7, defeated amendments by Senators Silas Wright, John Black, and John Tipton that would have served to weaken the political appeal of the public deposits segment of the bill by requiring the government to pay interest on public funds deposited, and by separating it from that section of the bill that would reduce the Treasury surplus. *Ibid.*, 1784-87.

Speech in Senate, June 17, 1836. Congratulates the Senate for defeating amendments yesterday to separate the regulation of the public deposits question from the reduction of the treasury surplus issue [Remark in Senate, December 30, 1835]. Thinks this will increase the appeal of the public deposits proposal. Holds that "the Republic is safe, the Constitution is safe, the Country is safe from the corrupting influences of a vast Surplus" of $46,400,000 which should now be cautiously and safely transferred to the states. Points to the surplus as a product of "the flourishing state of our manufactures," and claims that "our present e[n]viable condition is the triumph of the American System," particularly its protective tariff feature. Argues, nonetheless, that if "the bill, which three years ago passed Congress for distributing the proceeds of the Sales of the public lands, had not been unfortunately defeated [Speech in Senate, June 20, 1832; January 7, 1833; December 5, 1833; Clay to Wilde, April 27, 1833], we should not now be troubled with questions about the disposition of Surpluses." Affirms that to pass the pending land bill [Speech in Senate, December 29, 1835] would "distribute the whole or greater part" of the surplus, but notes that the bill "languishes in the other House." Argues, on the other hand, that the "present bill proposes to take it [surplus], at reasonable periods, out of the deposite banks, and to deposite it with the States, without interest, to be returned to the General Government when its wants require it." Sees no incompatibility between the two measures were the pending land bill to pass, since the latter would "exhaust the surplus" and leave "nothing for the other measure to operate upon." Examines and dismisses various "schemes" to spend away the surplus — on fortifications, the army, the navy, "Splendid edifices," and even on "Steam Engines on Rail Roads!" AD, by Clay. DLC-HC (DNA, M212, R6). Manuscript is apparently an incomplete rough draft. The *Register of Debates* for this date mentions only that Clay spoke "at length" in favor of the bill to regulate the public deposits and reduce the treasury surplus. The *Cong. Globe* of June 17 does no more than list Clay as a speaker on the issue. At the end of this day the bill went to its final vote and was passed 39 to 6. *Register of Debates*, 24 Cong., 1 Sess., 1845-46; *Cong. Globe*, 24 Cong., 1 Sess., 562.

Speech in Senate, June 18, 1836. Presents the report of the Committee on Foreign Relations on the recognition of the independence of Texas [Burnet to Clay, March 30, 1836; Comment in Senate, May 4, 1836] and the related recommendation and resolution of the committee. Gives a brief history of the practice of recognition, noting that "Its exercise gives no just ground of umbrage or cause of war." The United States has in the past extended recognition to new governments "in practical operation"; it has not inquired "whether the new Government has been rightfully adopted or not." Asserts that the U.S. government "has taken no part" in the war between Mexico and Texas. Indeed, "It has avowed its intention, and taken measures to maintain a strict neutrality towards the belligerents." Points out, too, that the government has not authorized the activities of any of the U.S. citizens who have fought in the war "impelled by sympathy for those who were believed to be struggling for liberty and independence against oppression and tyranny." Calls attention to popular sentiment in the U.S. favoring recognition of the independence of Texas, declaring that "The committee shares fully in all these sentiments; but a wise and prudent Government should not act solely on the impulse of feeling, however natural and laudable it may be. It ought to avoid all precipitation, and not adopt so grave a measure as that of recognising the independence of a new Power, until it has satisfactory information, and has fully deliberated. The committee has no information respecting the recent movements in Texas, except such as derived from the public prints." Agrees that the brilliant victory of the Texans at the Battle of San Jacinto and the capture of Santa Anna there must be considered as "decisive of the independence of Texas." Explains the various ways the U.S. might go about effecting its recognition of Texas independence. Does not believe that President Jackson has been tardy in taking the initiative in this matter, since the Texas government has been in existence only three months and "it is not unreasonable to wait a short time to see what its operation will be." The committee thus unanimously recommends: "*Resolved,* That the independence of Texas ought to be acknowledged by the United States whenever satisfactory information shall be received that it has in successful operation a civil Government, capable of performing the duties and fulfilling the obligations of an independent Power." *Register of Debates*, 24 Cong., 1 Sess., 1846-48; *Cong. Globe*, 24 Cong., 1 Sess., 564-65. Serving on the Committee on Foreign Relations with Clay, its chairman, were John P. King (Ga.), Willie P. Mangum (N.C.), Nathaniel P. Tallmadge (N.Y.), and Alexander Porter (La.).

Remark in Senate, June 20, 1836. Speaking to an amendment to the bill to fund and reorganize the Post Office, states that the whole "matter of perquisites" for postmasters, such as income from box rentals, is "inconsistent with the genius of our government." Urges his colleagues not to view the income of postmasters in such light that it will serve to authorize their "exactions" as a legitimate part of their salaries. *Register of Debates*, 24 Cong., 1 Sess., 1851; *Cong. Globe*, 24 Cong., 1 Sess., 567. The Post Office reorganization bill passed the House on June 2, 1836, and the Senate on July 2. *Register of Debates*, 23 Cong., 2 Sess., 244-53, 309-12, 392, 1351, 1364-92; 24 Cong., 1 Sess., 1769-75, 3779-88, 4106-35; U.S. Sen., *Journal*, 24 Cong., 1 Sess., 553.

Later this day, Clay opposes augmentation of the army by an additional regiment of dragoons, because the present Indian wars [Remark in Senate, January 27, 1836] would be over before the increase could take effect and because the militia is the "proper constitutional force for repelling all insurrections and invasions." *Register of Debates*, 24 Cong., 1 Sess., 1851; *Cong. Globe*, 24 Cong., 1 Sess., 567-68.

To JAMES WOLCOTT Washington, June 21, 1836

I have received your favor communicating the wish of the Managers of the American Institute[1] that I would deliver an Address at the Annual fair in the City of New York. Feeling a deep interest in the success of the Institute, and an anxious desire for the promotion and prosperity of our domestic manufactures; I would take great pleasure in contributing to these ends any exertion in my power which I could make without too great personal sacrifices. But I have now been absent from my family and home seven months, Congress has fixed the 4h. of July for its adjournment, and I hope to reach my residence by the middle of that month. Should I return at the next Session of that body (which is a question that I have not decided)[2] the short vacation will hardly, be sufficient for necessary attention to my private affairs. If I do not return, I know not when I shall again pass the mountains. Under these circumstances, I regret that it is not in my power to contract the engagement proposed by the Managers of the Institute. I beg that you will make this communication to them. . . .

ALS. NcD.   1. The purpose of the American Institute which originated in 1828 in New York City, was to encourage and promote industry throughout the Union by bestowing rewards and other benefits on persons excelling in agriculture, commerce, manufactures, and the arts. The first annual fair was held in 1829. Lamb, *History of the City of New York*, 2:717.   2. Clay was reelected on Dec. 15, 1836, and continued in the Senate until 1842. The vote in the Kentucky legislature was 76 for Clay and 54 for James Guthrie. *Niles' Register* (Dec. 31, 1836), 51:273.

Remark in Senate, June 22, 1836. Asserts that the House amendment to section 13 of the bill to regulate the deposits and reduce the treasury surplus [Remark in Senate, December 30, 1835] has actually strengthened the bill, because it now contains "a restriction on the Treasury in calling in the money, so that it would not be in the power of the Treasury to distress the [deposit] banks." *Register of Debates*, 24 Cong., 1 Sess., 1859.

Later this day, Clay joins in criticism of Jackson's veto on June 9 of the bill to fix by law the date of future meetings and adjournments of Congress [Remark in Senate, March 24, 1836]. *Ibid*. For Jackson's veto message, see *MPP*, 3:231-32.

Comment in Senate, June 23, 1836. Reports that the Committee on Foreign Relations has examined the correspondence with Great Britain on the Northeastern Boundary controversy [Remark in Senate, June 15, 1836] and that the senators from Maine and Massachusetts have also read it. All agree it can "be safely published." Regrets that the negotiation, while not entirely ended, "does not promise to result in any satisfactory adjustment of the boundary question." Three thousand copies ordered printed. *Register of Debates*, 24 Cong., 1 Sess., 1864.

Later this day, Clay opposes an appropriation for a Patent Office building. Says the proposed plan calls for 4,000,000 bricks and that the total cost would be $400,000 to $500,000. Suggests buying an existing building instead. *Ibid.*, 1866. For the Senate bill to authorize a Patent Office building to cost no more than $108,000, see *ibid.*, 1853, 1898. A bill authorizing the purchase of the "old brick capitol [Remark in Senate, June 28, 1836]" for housing the Patent Office was incorporated into an appropriations bill which passed both houses of Congress and was signed by the president on July 4, 1836. U.S. Sen., *Journal*, 24 Cong., 1 Sess., 494-95, 1193, 1225. See also Green, *Washington: Village and Capital*, 137.

Still later this day, Clay supports the bill to change the mode of conducting public lands sales so as to eliminate "fraud and violence" from the present procedure. Bill postponed indefinitely. *Register of Debates*, 24 Cong., 1 Sess., 1869.

To Noah Webster, New Haven, Conn., June 23, 1836. Thanks Webster "for the little book which you have done me the favor to present me." Adds: "My speech on the Land bill has not been published; and I regret therefore that I cannot comply with your request for a Copy of it." ALS. NN. Reference is either to Clay's speech of December 29, 1835, or that of April 26, 1836, neither of which was published. During 1836, Webster published *History of the United States*. . . . (324 pp.); *An Improved Grammar of the English Language* (192 pp.); three spelling books; and a genealogy of the family of John Webster (8pp.). Which one, if any of these, he had sent Clay is not known.

Remark in Senate, June 24, 1836. Defines as "gratifying" and a cause for "great rejoicing" Jackson's message of this date announcing his approval of the bill to regulate the public deposits and reduce the Treasury surplus [Remark in Senate, December 30, 1835]. But deplores the fact that the president's act was also "announced this morning in the [Washington] Globe, in an editorial article which bore an authorized character." Characterizes the leak as "not according to established usage, nor respectful towards Congress." *Register of Debates*, 24 Cong., 1 Sess., 1870; *Cong. Globe*, 24 Cong., 1 Sess., 583.

Later this day, Clay points out that on June 23, in response to the Senate resolution of June 18 [Speech in Senate, June 18, 1836], Jackson had "signified a desire to wait for further information before he acts" on recognition of the independence of Texas [Comment in Senate, May 4, 1836]. For this reason there is no need now to refer to the Committee on Foreign Relations a related State Department report to the president on the issue. Informs Sen. William C. Preston (S.C.) that he does not agree with him that the "sole fact" governing recognition is the "termination of the war" in Texas. Another consideration is whether there is a Texan "Government existing in full and successful operation." *Register of Debates*, 24 Cong., 1 Sess., 1870-71; *Cong. Globe*, 24 Cong., 1 Sess., 583.

Remark in Senate, June 25, 1836. Opposes Sen. Thomas H. Benton's bill, first brought up on April 8, as amended by Sen. Robert J. Walker, on that same day, to grant 500,000 acres of land to Indiana, Alabama, Mississippi, and Missouri for internal improvement purposes. Bill tabled. *Register of Debates*, 24 Cong., 1 Sess., 1120-21, 1876.

Following his continued opposition, not recorded, to Benton's bill, Clay moves his bill to settle the claim of Richard W. Meade. Passed. *Ibid.*, 1876. For a discussion of Meade's claim and its outcome, see the Meade article in *DAB*.

Remark in Senate, June 27, 1836. Supports an annual salary of $1,800 for the proposed federal district judge in the state of Michigan [Comment in Senate, December 15, 1835]. *Cong. Globe*, 24 Cong., 1 Sess., 585. Later, moves to proceed to the consideration of executive business. *Register of Debates*, 24 Cong., 1 Sess., 1884.

Remark in Senate, June 28, 1836. Votes against Sen. Hugh Lawson White's resolution to rescind the Senate's censure of President Jackson dated March 28, 1834 [Speech in Senate, December 26, 1833; Remark in Senate, March 28, 1834], and suggests that "it would be proper to take up the other [Benton's expunging] resolution on the same subject [Remark in Senate, June 30, 1834] and dispose of it also." *Register of Debates*, 24 Cong., 1 Sess., 1897. For White's resoultion to rescind Jackson's censure, see *ibid.*, 1897-98.

Later this day, Clay participates in a discussion of the renewal of Joseph Grant's patent on a machine to make hat bodies and to exempt from prosecution those who have used the machine since the patent expired in 1834. *Cong. Globe*, 24 Cong., 1 Sess., 591; *Register of Debates*, 24 Cong., 1 Sess., 1897-98.

Still later this day, Clay calls for the reading of a communication offering to sell the "old brick capitol" to the government for the use of the Patent Office [Comment in Senate, June 23, 1836]. Votes to reject for this purpose the purchase of the "building formerly used for the temporary accommodation of Congress." *Register of Debates*, 24 Cong., 1 Sess., 1898. The "Brick Capitol" was a building erected as a temporary meeting place for Congress after the Capitol was burned by the British in 1814. The 14th Congress convened there in December, 1815, and it continued to be used for that purpose until the new Capitol was ready for occupancy in 1819. Green, *Washington: Village and Capital*, 67.

Remark in Senate, June 29, 1836. Presents a petition from Kentucky members of the American Colonization Society asking Congress for aid to the Society. While the petition comes too late for action at this session, Clay trusts "that the society would hereafter receive a larger portion of the public favor" that it has formerly enjoyed. Tabled. *Register of Debates*, 24 Cong., 1 Sess., 1901.

Later this day, Clay delivers extended comments on the Fortification bill. Supports efforts to reduce military expenditures and calls attention to "the enormous and alarming amount of appropriations . . . during the session." Calculates these at "about twenty-five millions" as of May 27 and "up to forty millions" to date. "Forty millions of dollars in one year, when we have no debt, and no foreign war!" Claims this is larger than the annual British military appropriation "for similar objects." Asks the "friends of the administration" to "stay these extravagant appropriations," as promised, as an act of "devotion to party." Says he has heard that it is "intended to withdraw the appropriations from the public Treasury, place them to the credit of disbursing officers, in the custody of local banks, and thus elude the operation of the deposite bill which has recently passed [Remark in Senate, December 30, 1835]." Notes that annual average appropriation for fortifications has been about $750,000 to $800,000, but that this year "we shall have appropriated" $4,500,000. Demands a reduction of this sum by half. Following further debate, moves to recommit the bill "with instructions to reduce the appropriations one third." *Ibid.*, 1903-4, 1906. The bill was recommitted without instructions, 24 to 18. Printed in Colton, *Clay Correspondence*, 6:38-40.

Comment in Senate, June 30, 1836. Reports that "after the fullest reflection," his initial judgment on the March 28, 1834, resolution to censure Jackson [Speech in Senate, December 26, 1833; Remark in Senate, March 28, 1834] "remained unchanged," because Jackson's behavior was "an exercise of illegal and unconstitutional power, and dangerous to the liberties of the people of this country." Thinks it is too late in the session to "protract the discussion" of Sen. Thomas H. Benton's resolution to expunge the resolution of censure from the journal of the Senate [Remark in Senate, June 30, 1834]. Also alludes to a precedent in the Pennsylvania house of representatives, dated February 10, 1816, which, he holds, sustains the unconstitutionality of "mutilating and expunging the journals of the Senate." *Register of Debates*, 24 Cong., 1 Sess., 1907-8.

Later this day, moves to consider the resolution reported by the Committee on Foreign Relations on the independence of Texas [Burnet to Clay, March 30, 1836; Comment in Senate, May 4, 1836]. Postponed until tomorrow. *Ibid.*, 1908.

Still later this day, Clay questions the inordinate size of the Fortification bill, calling attention to one item for $200,000 that could be procured for $25,000. *Ibid.*, 1910.

From George Tucker, Charlottesville, Va., June 30, 1836. Notes that by now Clay "will have learnt the death of our venerated friend, James Madison." Writes to give "you a further proof of the high place you held in his estimation." Continues: "When I was last with him — a few days after the short interview I had with you in Washington — we were conversing on the affairs of the nation — and especially on the then agitating question of the efforts of the abolitionists — when, with that absence of his habitual reserve on political topics, of which he had of late afforded me many flattering proofs, he said 'Clay has been so successful in compromising other disputes, I wish he could fall upon some plan of compromising this — and then all parties (or enough of all parties I forget which,) might unite & make him President' — Knowing his desire to be at peace with all, and to escape the coarse & reckless vituperation of the newspapers, I never ventured to mention this except to one or two discreet friends — nor would I now do it to any one who would make it public, as in the virulence of party feeling it would operate with many prejudiced minds to abate the respect that the nation will be disposed to shew to his memory, and by thus detracting some what from the weight & influence of his good opinion, deprive you of your just rights — I never however intended that such a remark such [*sic*, should] be buried, as that would have been a still greater injustice to you, and meant & still mean in good time to make it known."

Asks if it would be practicable, safe, and prudent to extend the franking privilege to Mrs. Dolley Madison. Adds: "You must have a mix[e]d feeling of triumph, contempt & amusement that the majority have been obliged virtually, to pass your land bill [Speech in Senate, December 29, 1835] under another form [Remark in Senate, December 30, 1835] — " ALS. DLC-TJC (DNA, M212, R10). Printed in Colton, *Clay Correspondence*, 4:405-6. James Madison died on June 28, 1836. Congress soon passed a bill to give Dolley Madison franking privileges, and it was approved by the president on July 2, 1836. U.S. Sen., *Journal*, 24 Cong., 1 Sess., 519, 534, 541.

Speech in Senate, July 1, 1836. Favors Sen. William C. Preston's amendment to the resolution that the United States should recognize Texas when it is known that the Texans have "in successful operation a civil government, capable of performing the duties and fulfilling the obligations of an independent power [Burnet to Clay, March 30, 1836; Comment in Senate, May 4, 1836]." The Preston amendment expressed gratification with President Jackson's efforts to obtain information on the actual political and military situation in Texas. States that he, like Preston, favors a resolution supporting immediate independence; but says he is reluctant to go that far until it is clear that a competent civil government is in operation there. Suggests that it would be appropriate, too, were Mexico to be forced by the military valor of the Texans to recognize their independence prior to U.S. recognition. Further, U.S. recognition must also take into account the problem of future good relations with Mexico and give evidence of the nation's ability to distinguish between Mexico's 8,000,000 "unoffending" citizens and "Santa Anna — the blood-thirsty, vain, boasting, military tyrant" who has been "exercising military sway" over them. Points out that many U.S. citizens, "impelled by a noble devotion to the cause of liberty," have assisted Texas in achieving her independence and that this fact may strengthen the hostile attitudes of those European powers inclined to "attribute to our Union unbounded ambition, and a desire of aggrandizing ourselves at the expense of our neighbors." Asks, therefore, "Is it not better for all parties that we should wait a little while longer?" Concludes that "we should stop with the resolution and proposed amendment" and wait until the president has further information. Printed in Colton, *Clay Correspondence*, 6:41-44. A summarized version of this speech, substantially shorter than that printed by Colton, is found in *Register of Debates*, 24 Cong., 1 Sess., 1915. The *Cong. Globe* of this day did not carry Clay's remarks. No manuscript version of the speech has been found.

Comment in Senate, July 2, 1836. Recommends on behalf of the Committee on Foreign Relations that a long-standing claim stemming from a military attack on two U.S. citizen traders by New Mexican authorites in 1817 be revived and pressed, and that the Mexican government now be held legally responsible for the outrage. The incident, which occurred on U.S. soil, had resulted in the arrest and imprisonment of the American traders and the confiscation of their merchandise in the value of over $30,000. *Sen. Docs.*, 24 Cong., 1 Sess., no. 284, p. 424. See *MPP*, 3:229.

During this day's session, Clay also participated in a brief discussion of the Harbor bill. *Register of Debates*, 24 Cong., 1 Sess., 1935.

From P. & C.L.L. Leary, Louisville, July 15, 1836. Send "a drab Beaver Hat of our own manufacture . . . as a testimonial of our gratitude to one, whose aim . . . has been solely directed to the advancement of his country's prosperity." Laud Clay's efforts on behalf of "the manufacturers of the United States." Copy. Printed in Louisville *Daily Journal*, July 21, 1836. The Learys were merchants in hats, furs & materials, located at the second door west of 6th Street on Main in Louisville. *Ibid.*, June 4, 1836.

On July 19, 1836, Clay wrote, thanking the Learys for the sentiments expressed in their letter and for the beaver hat. Notes that in "my past public career, no part of it affords me more satisfaction than my humble endeavors to place the manufacturers of our country upon a Sol[i]d foundation." Adds that this policy "has laid the real Independence of our country upon broad and deep foundations." *Ibid.*, July 21, 1836; *Niles' Register* (August 13, 1836), 50:395.

To RICHARD BARTLETT
Lexington, July 25, 1836

I have received you letter requesting information in respect to the public archives of Kentucky, and take pleasure in answering it.

The capital of this state has been twiced destroyed by fire.[1] The public records not having been kept in it, except within a limited extent, were fortunately preserved. They are kept in distinct buildings, not, I believe, fireproof, which remain unconsumed.[2]

The original statutes of the General Assembly (the denomination given to our state legislature) are engrossed on parchment, and carefully filed away and preserved in the office of the secretary of state. Both those of a private and public nature, as annually passed, are annually published.

Deeds, mortgages, and other conveyances of land, ordinarily, are recorded in the clerks' offices of the several counties within which the land conveyed is situated. There are about one hundred. Several of them have been occasionally destroyed by fire. That of the county of Fayette, (including the city of Lexington) was burnt thirty-two years ago,[3] and its destruction produced much inconvenience. The extent of such a calamity is not always at first known, but is develped in the process of time.

Copy. Printed in Richard Bartlett, *Remarks and Documents Relating to the Preservation and Keeping of the Public Archives* (Concord, N.H., 1837), 51. 1. On Nov. 25, 1813, and again on Nov. 4, 1824. Willard R. Jillson, *Early Frankfort and Franklin County, Kentucky* (Louisville, 1936), 80. 2. A great many state documents were, nevertheless, destroyed. See Kerr, *History of Kentucky*, 1:310; 4:59; *Niles' Register* (Nov. 27, 1824), 27:198; also 3:878-81. 3. The Fayette County Courthouse, along with most of the county's records, burned on the night of Jan. 31, 1803. Ranck, *History of Lexington Kentucky*, 52.

Speech at the Woodford Festival, Versailles, Ky., July 26, 1836. Speaks for about two house at a public dinner "in his accustomed manner, fervent, solemn, sometimes pathetic, sometimes playful, convulsing his audience with laughter." Discusses the treasury surplus, produced principally by the tariff, and his efforts to provide for its "just disposition" in the form of his land bill [Speech in Senate, June 20, 1832; December 5, 1833; Clay to Wilde, April 27, 1833]. Criticizes Jackson's veto of that bill.

Explains the details of the bill jointly to regulate the deposits and distribute the treasury surplus [Remark in Senate, December 30, 1835] which in principle was similar to the land bill in that "Both bills were in fact bills for the distribution of the Surplus." Criticizes the Jacksonians for their "constant tampering with the currency." Indeed, "One rash, lawless and crude experiment succeeds another"; specifically, the recent "Treasury order by which all payments for public lands were to be made in specie." Considers this a "most ill-advised, illegal and pernicious measure. In principle it [is] wrong, in practice it will favor the very speculation which it professes to endeavor to suppress." Believes that the new policy will require "specie, at great hazard and expense, to be transported from the Atlantic cities across the mountains, that the pleasure may be enjoyed of transporting it back again . . . at similar expense and hazard. Or, what will be still more injurious to the Western States, it subjects their banks to perpetual drafts of specie to meet the wants of purchasers of the public domain." As for Jackson's role in this unfortunate decision, "HIS WILL . . . becomes the law, and the law has lost its equal, general, and impartial operation." Predicts a happy time for land speculators and "abuses of all kinds." Castigates Jackson's policy toward the Indians, a policy "productive of fraud, violence and injustice" and the trampling upon treaties made with them. "By our ill-treatment to them, they are goaded into acts of desperation; and then the sympathies of the white people are appealed to on account of Indian depredations." Calls particular attention to outrages against the Cherokees [Fendall to Clay, August 27, 1832]. Points out that he had "again and again warned his countrymen of the danger, illustrated by all history, of elevating to the Chief Magistracy, a man possessing no other than mere military qualification." He has certainly been incompetent in handling the civil government of the nation; but also in directing the military affairs of the country. "We had a right to expect that the military affairs of the Union would be administered with skill and ability." However, the "miserable Black Hawk war [Henry Clay, Jr., to Clay, April 22, 1832]" and the "more disgraceful Seminole war [Remark in Senate, January 27, 1836]" point to a pattern of military inefficiency, high cost, and tactical failure. Announces that he intends to retire from the U.S. Senate at the end of his present term. Feels that "perhaps his voice had been too often raised, was too familiar to the public ear; perhaps one less known of more buoyancy and elasticity may be heard with more salutary effect." Is convinced that "foul corruption had penetrated almost every branch of adminstration and was gradually poisoning the whole government." For this reason he feels that the "public good" he might accomplish in the future in public life would not be "at all proportionate to the private sacrifices" he would have to make. Copy. Printed in Louisville *Daily Journal*, August 23, 1836.

For the invitation to speak at a public dinner to be held near Versailles, Ky., on July 26, see Samuel M. Wallace *et al.* to Clay, July 13, 1836, in Lexington *Observer & Kentucky Reporter*, July 20, 1836. Clay's acceptance, dated July 15, is in *ibid*. For the so-called Specie Circular, drafted by Sen. Thomas H. Benton, which Jackson ordered Secretary of the Treasury Levi Woodbury to issue on July 11, 1836, one week after Congress had adjourned, see Benton's resolution of April 22-23, 1836, requiring specie payments for public land, in *Register of Debates*, 24 Cong., 1 Sess., 1254-59, 1267. See also Van Deusen, *The Life of Henry Clay*, 288, 305; James, *Andrew Jackson*, 414, 426, 439-41; Govan, *Nicholas Biddle*, 298-316, 327, 333-34; and Arthur M. Schlesinger, Jr., *The Age of Jackson* (Boston, 1953), 130-31, 218, 222-24, 262.

From Charles J. Cabell, Harrodsburg, Ky., July 31, 1836. States that "My father [Edward B. Cabell] has requested me to enquire of you whether you would sell him" a tract of land "lying in the military bounty lands in the state of Missouri —" Adds that his father has authorized him "to offer you one hundred & sixty dollars for the tract," and "Should you be willing to make a sale upon these terms, I shall visit Fayette next summer for the purpose." ALS. DLC-TJC (DNA, M212, R14). Charles Joseph Cabell

(1813-1882) became a lawyer and a surveyor of public lands in the new states, expecially in Louisiana. In 1837 he married Susan B. Allin, daughter of Mercer County (Ky.) Court Clerk Thomas Allin. See Alexander Brown, *The Cabells and Their Kin* (Boston, 1895), 462-63, 465.

To PHILIP R. FENDALL
Lexington, August 8, 1836

I recd. your favor of the 19h Ulto but did not get the two numbers of the [Washington *United States*] Telegraph which you forwarded until last night. Prior to the receipt of your favor I had perused Vindex,[1] and rightly conjectured its friendly author.

[Duff] Green's malevolence towards me is now so notorious, and he has become so contemptible, that I do not know that it is worth while seriously to notice any thing he says of me.[2] He pays no regard to truth. His persevering attempt to attribute to me the expression that I wished to send the sword along with the olive branch is a proof at once of his malignity and his falsehood[3] My real expression was that I wished to send the olive branch along with the sword, which *others* were sending. That such must have been my idea is manifest from my whole course, during the passage of the Force bill.[4] It was no measure of mine. I took no lead in it. I took no part in the debate. I endeavored once or twice to soften its severity by an amendment. How then could I have said that *I* wished to send the sword &c. Still I would have voted, reluctantly, for the measure — reluctantly, not on account of any doubt I had or now have about the propriety of suppressing resistance by force to any law of the U.S. whether that resistance proceed from a State, or part of a State, but in consequence of my want of confidence in the Admon which was to execute the force bill. My sentiments in this respect were well known to the Senate, and expressed by me in that body[5]

I left the Senate the night the force bill passed about Eight OClock, whilst Mr. [Daniel] Webster was speaking, after the Chamber was lighted up. I left it, because I cannot endure the atmosphere of the room when lighted. I did not expect moreover that the vote would be taken that night. On the next day, without any sort of allusion from Mr Webster or any body else to the fact of my absence the previous night, I took an early occasion to say that if I had been present I would have voted for the bill.[6] This was not necessary for the Senate, as my opinion was well known to that body, but was said for the public. The allegation of Green therefore that Mr Webster intimated that I had dodged the bill is a fabrication, without any foundation. When did I ever dodge any measure?

His story about Mr. Webster having taken up his hat and walked off, when I consulted him about the Compromise bill is also a fabrication. Mr Webster was not, as is well known, in favor of that measure; but in all our private intercourse nothing passed between us which was not perfectly and mutually respectful.[7]

He asks why was the compromise, as he calls it, of Genl [Robert Y.] Hayne declined in 1832,[8] and that in 1833 proposed.[9] In 1832, I did not believe that the Protecting policy was in such danger as it appeared to be in by the result of the Presidential election, and other elections in the fall of that year. I did not moreover think that So. Carolina would proceed to the extravagant length which she did, after the long Session terminating in 1832.[10]

I proposed the compromise of 1833 therefore 1st to save the Tariff and 2dly. to save the Country from Civil War. Both objects were accomplished. It is not true that I ever abandoned the American System. It is not true that it is abandoned by the Compromise of 1833. It was, on the contrary, preserved by that compromise. The Manufacturers so understood it and yet understand it. They are flourishing beyond all example, under this alleged abandonment of it. They are flourishing in peace & security, without being annually threatened & harrassed. It is modified but not abandoned after the year 1843. My views on all these matters are to be collected from the brief notices of the debates in Feby and March 1833.

Green says that he is not now to learn that I am personally vindicitive. On what does he found his assertion? My relations to him? He has been abusing me all his life, certainly from 1825, and I suppose I am vindictive because I did not prefer him, a political enemy, as public printer, to Gales & Seaton political and personal friends.[11]

Should you think proper, my dear Sir, further to notice in the public prints, this matter, I wish no doubt to be excited about my firm convictions being utterly opposed to nullification; nor any that I should have voted for the Force bill, as I have repeatedly declared. I do not wish any appeal to the Nullifiers to be made which shall throw doubts, in that respect, on my opinions.

Then, I wish it distinctly understood that *I* have never abandoned the American System. I proposed, by the compromise, to modify, not to destroy it. I believe in its wisdom now as much as I ever did. It is the real source of the Surplus. It paid the N[ational]. debt. All this it did, against the predictions of its opponents, who maintained that we should be obliged to resort to direct taxes to supply the ordinary wants of the Government.

Can any thing demonstrate more strongly Green's malignity towards me than the fact of his assailing me, who took no part in supporting the Force bill, for that measure, and his supporting Judge [Hugh L.] White, who took a leading part in supporting the bill? Or has he the covert object of attacking Judge White through me, and prejudicing the Nullifers against him? If they ought to be dissatisfied with me for what *I* did, what ought to be their feelings towards him, for what he did?[12] There are not wanting persons who believe that Mr Calhoun, Green &c. really desire Whites defeat, and V[an]. Burens' election, looking to future results. Green's movement now is analogous to his movement about the same time in 1832.[13] He can endure the election of no Presidential Candidate of similar politics other than Mr Calhoun, and his feeling has lost no force by the marriage which has taken place between members of their respective families[14]

I will not pursue this subject. . . .

ALS. MiDW. 1. An article by "Vindex" appeared in the Richmond *Enquirer* on June 21, 1836; however, it is uncertain that this is the article to which Clay refers. 2. On July 20, 1836, Green wrote in the Washington *United States Telegraph* that Daniel Webster had been the first to charge that Clay had dodged a vote on the Force bill. He added that at this charge "Mr. Clay lost his self command, and, with more of passion than we have ever witnessed in him, said that if he had been present, he would have voted for the bill, because he would *have sent the sword along with the olive branch.*" 3. Clay to Brooke, August 19, 1835. 4. Remark in Senate, Jan. 22, 1833. 5. *Ibid.*; Clay to Brooke, August 19, 1835. 6. Clay to Brooke, August 19, 1835; Van Deusen, *The Life of Henry Clay*, 269. 7. For Webster's position on the Compromise Tariff of 1833, see Fuess, *Daniel Webster*, 1:392-96. 8. Hayne had proposed on Jan. 16, 1832, a modification of Clay's proposed tariff bill which would "be so reduced that the amount of the public revenue shall be sufficient to defray the expenses of Government according to their present scale, after the payment of the public debt; and that, allowing for the gradual reduction of present high duties on articles coming into competition with similar articles made or produced within the United States, the duties be ultimately equalized, so that the duty on no article shall, as compared with the value of that article, vary materially from the general average." Hayne's amendment was referred to the Committee on Manufactures, along with a number of other proposed amendments. Clay's bill, along with the amendments, was tabled on March 30. In July the Senate took up, and ultimately passed with some modification, the House tariff bill. *Register of Debates*, 22 Cong., 1 Sess., 77, 678, 1154; Van Deusen, *The Life of Henry Clay*, 249-52; Webster to Clay, Jan. 8, 1832.   9. Draft Proposal, Mid-Dec., 1832.   10. Stoddard to Clay, Nov. 12, 1832. 11. Comment in Senate, Feb. 17, 1835.   12. White voted for the Force bill. *Register of Debates*, 22 Cong., 2 Sess., 688.   13. Fendall to Clay, Oct. 9, 1832.   14. Calhoun's son, Andrew, had married Duff Green's daughter, Margaret.

To Nicholas Biddle, Philadelphia, August 13, 1836. On behalf of his son, Henry Clay, Jr., sends a check for $6,000 "which he wishes remitted to Messrs Baring Brothers & Co of London by the purchase of a bill at the market price, or in such other mode as may be convenient or customary." ALS. DLC-Nicholas Biddle Papers (DNA, M212, R20).

Biddle replied on August 24, 1836, assuring Clay that he had carried out the request. Copy. *Ibid.*

From Benjamin B. Smith, Lexington, August 16, 1836. Reports that Clay's "pithy remark" of the previous evening "that the duty of the Clergy is to lash the vice and spare the man" has given him the hope "that you may be employed, in the Good Providence of God, as a peace maker amongst us." States that Clay's comment to him "has presented the affair of Charlton Hunt Esqr and the Stage Coach conversation to my mind in a new point of view." Adds that "I now see that I was wrong," and "although as a citizen I have an undoubted right to repeat strictures upon character circulated in a political canvass," it would have been "more delicate and christian" to have foregone exercising that right. Mentions that he wants "to convey to that whole family the assurance . . . that I have never in thought, record, or deed gone back from the reconciliation which, sometime since, were exchanged between us." ALS. Archives of the Episcopal Church, Austin, Texas.

Clay replied on August 17, 1836, promising that when Hunt returns to town, "I will endeavor to effect a pacific object with it." Believes that "the views contained in it are just, and ought to be satisfactory, at least on the matters of which it treats." *Ibid*. At this time Bishop Smith was embroiled in a controversy within the Episcopal Diocese of Kentucky which resulted in 1837 in his being tried on a variety of charges centering on alleged maladministration. He was acquitted by the diocesan convention. His primary counsel at the diocesan trial was Charles Morehead, assisted by Robert Wickliffe, but he also occasionally consulted Clay during the course of the dispute. Charlton Hunt was a leading member of Christ Church Episcopal in Lexington. The exact nature of the conflict between Bishop Smith and Hunt is not known; however, Hunt had refused the Whig party's nomination for a seat in the state legislature due to "circumstances beyond my [Hunt's] control." Lexington *Observer & Kentucky Reporter*, April 27, 1836. For a complete account of the dissension within the diocese, see Frances K. Swinford and Rebecca S. Lee, *The Great Elm Tree, Heritage of the Episcopal Diocese of Lexington* (Lexington, 1969), 108-45; W. Robert Insko, "The Trial of a Kentucky Bishop," *FCHQ* (April, 1961), 35:141-58.

To JAMES ROBERTSON[1] *et al.*   Lexington, September 3, 1836
I have the honor to acknowledge the receipt of your letter of the 24th [*sic*, 22d.] ulto[2] stating that in consequence of the languishing condition of the cause of Colonization at Louisville, the Auxiliary Society formed in that City, had by a resolution adopted on the 16 ulto. determined to apply to me to aid in its revival; that you are appointed a Committee to make the application to me; and you accordingly request me to address the Citizens generally & publicly [illeg. words] at such time as may be most convenient to me.

I am extremely sorry to learn that the Colonization Cause should be in a languishing condition in your intelligent & enterprizing City. In my opinion the project of Colonizing the free blacks on the Coast of Africa is entirely practicable; and only requires the necessary pecuniary aid to ensure it complete success. That aid the Governments of the Union and of the States are fully competent to render. Indeed, I think that the measures & success of the Colonization Society have demonstrated that whenever the several states or any of them shall be disposed to find a foreign Asylum for any portion of the African race, bound or free, residing within their respective limits, the coasts of Africa offer a certain one within their reach & within their means . . . gradually & judiciously applied. It is greatly to be regretted that our Governments have not taken more efficient hold of the scheme; & given it their countenance, sanction, & patronage. I think they will sooner or later, ultimately do it. In the mean time the cause of Colonization addresses the most powerful motives of humanity religion & patriotism to our Country men. And I sincerely hope that the spontaneous contributions by benevolent individuals will be continued until the General or local Governments shall come forward to its support. With this view, as well as for the purpose of enlightening the public mind as to the objects & progress of the Colonization Society, I think the formation of Auxiliary Societies is deserving of all encouragement. The advantages of Louisville are very great for such a Society; and I would gladly render it any aid in my power; but I regret Gentlemen that consistently with other engagements and avocations, I cannot assume the task of delivering the public address which [illeg. words] me to make. Appreciating highly the honor done me in naming me for that [illeg. words] should hesitate in declining your request, as I am obliged to do, if I were not persuaded that amidst the genius, talents, ability, and piety with which Louisville abounds, some one could be selected who would confer as much eclat, & render as essential services to the cause, as I could possibly do. . . .

Copy, manuscript torn. DLC-Records of the American Colonization Society (DNA, M212, R20). 1. Probably James Robertson, a Louisville attorney. For his obituary, see Louisville *Daily Journal*, May 30, 1840. 2. Robertson *et al.* of Louisville, Ky., had written Clay on August 22, 1836, presenting a resolution of the local branch of the American Colonization Society which asked Clay to "visit our City, & endeavor to awaken by a public address, the Citizens around us, from that lethargy, into which, they seem unfortunately to have fallen upon the great subject of Colonization." They add: "We think that the present time is peculiarly favorable to a regeneration of the Society, & that the public mind is in a fit condition to receive proper impression, to be made by the just & comprehensive which it is in your power, so eloquently, to present." Copy. DLC-Records of the American Colonization Society (DNA, M212, R20).

To JOHN M. CLAYTON
Lexington, September 9, 1836

Prior to the receipt of your favor of the 29h. Ulto. a letter had reached me from [Walter] Lowrie announcing his purpose to resign his office of Secy of the Senate. I am not in the habit of committing myself prior to an appointment of this kind, but, on this occasion, I will say that, if I am in the Senate, I will vote with great pleasure for Dr. [Arnold] Naudain,[1] and you may tell him so. I will thank you also to tell him that I received his letter. Judge [Alexander] Porter is now here, and I communicated to him the Dr's wishes, and he concurs heartily with me; but he has some fears that he may not be able to reach the Senate in time. I will see [John J.] Crittenden on the same subject. Should the Dr. be successful, it will be the first time that the Senate had a Secy. that can *read* and *write*.[2]

I rejoice in the assurances you have given me as to the certainty of the course of Delaware.[3] I really think that there is a fair prospect, with due exertions, of defeating Mr. V[an]. B[uren].[4]

ALS. DLC-John M. Clayton Papers (DNA, M212, R20).   1. For Naudain, see *BDAC*. 2. Asbury Dickins became secretary of the Senate. U.S. Sen., *Journal*, 24 Cong., 2 Sess., 32. 3. Clay to Bailhache, July 14, 1835.   4. *Ibid.*

To MARTIN DURALDE III &   Lexington, September 16, 1836
HENRY CLAY DURALDE

I have written to your uncle [James] Erwin requesting him to bring you out with him to Ashland; and if you cannot come when he does, I have written to Mr. [Enoch C.] Wines to let one of the tutors accompany you to Philadelphia and look out for some person returning to Kentucky for you to travel with. As it is my intention that you should go back to Edgehill, it will not be necessary for you to bring your books nor more clothes than may be requisite during the month that you will be absent. Mr Erwin will supply money for the expences of your journey, if you come with him; and if you do not, Mr Wines will supply you.

Your uncle James [Brown Clay], who has been with us upwards of two months, will leave here in a few days for Missouri. Your uncle John [Morrison Clay] has apparently good health, altho' he occasionally complains   The family are generally well.

ALS. DLC-HC (DNA, M212, R5).

To SAMUEL L. SOUTHARD   Lexington, September 27, 1836

I was very glad to learn by your favor of the 10h instant that your sons had graduated with so much credit.[1] I sincerely hope that in their future life they may realize your fondest expectations. I was happy also to hear of your own health and that of Mrs. Southard and Miss Virginia [Southard]. Ours is reasonably good. John [Morrison Clay] has entirely recovered, and is occupied with studies at home, under the direction of the tutor of Mr. [James] Erwins children, a very competent person.[2] Should my grandsons [Martin Duralde and Henry Clay Duralde] not return to Ashland, as I expect, with Mr. Erwin, I shall be very happy to hear of their being under the protection of your family during the vacation.

I think the political signs are highly auspicious. I have now very great confidence in the defeat of Mr. V[an]. Buren.[3] I should not be surprized if he should be beaten as far as Angoura was in her late race with Rodolph, that is doubly distanced.[4] Under these encouraging circumstances, I should regret extremely to find New Jersey in the minority.[5]

Not being able to find any sufficient reason for remaining at home, I think it probable I shall attend the next Session of the Senate. And if I do I shall, with great pleasure, vote for Dr. [Arnold] Naudain. . . .[6]

ALS. NjP.   1. Samuel Lewis Southard and Henry Lewis Southard both graduated from Princeton in 1836.   2. Probably a reference to "Miss Brulard." See Erwin to Clay, Dec. 15, 1835.   3. Clay to Bailhache, July 14, 1835.   4. In a race in Louisville called Kentucky vs. Tennessee, Rodolph had easily beaten Angoura to win a $5,000 purse. Rodolph was then barred from tracks at Lexington because he was too fast. John Hervey, *Racing in America* (New York, 1944), 134.   5. Clay to Bailhache, July 14, 1835.   6. Clay to Clayton, Sept. 9, 1836.

To BENJAMIN W. DUDLEY *et al.*   Lexington, October 13, 1836

I have received your note of yesterday,[1] stating that the honorable R[ichard]. M. Johnson asserts, as of his own knowledge, that his competitor for the vice presidency, Francis Granger, esq. is an abolitionist, that he was the organ of that party, and that he maintained abolition principles and opinions on the floor of congress last winter; and you requested me to communicate his opinions on that subject, under the supposition that I had every opportunity of becoming possessed of them.

I regret that the short interval between the present time and the period of the election does not admit of your obtaining from Mr. Granger himself a statement, under his own signature, of his real sentiments, and laying them before the people. — This consideration reconciles me in giving an answer, in compliance with your request.

I cannot but persuade myself that you must have been misinformed as to the assertions attributed to col. Johnson. I think he could hardly have made such a great mistake in imputing opinions to a distant and absent competitor, who had no opportunity of answering him.

Abolition was an engrossing topic of private conversation and public debate during the last session of congress. I had frequent opportunities in social intercourse with Mr. Granger, and in his public discussions, of learning his opinions. I understood him clearly and distinctly to disapprove of all interference with slavery, as it exists in the states tolerating that institution, either on the part of congress or the northern states. And I am perfectly sure that it is altogether inaccurate to say that he is either an abolitionist or the organ of the abolitionists.

Numerous petitions were presented to both houses of congress, praying for the abolition of slavery within the District of Columbia, over which congress has a right, by the constitution, to legislate in all cases whatever. Mr. Granger and many other members were charged with presenting some of these petitions. Some of them were sent to me, and I felt it a duty, as probably others did, to present them, when couched in respectful language. It was the subsequent duty of congress to dispose of them as might seem to it to be right. A question having been made as to the reception of these petitions, it was decided by a very large majority in the senate that the petitioners had a constitutional right to offer them. The same opinion prevailed in the house.[2]

I was well acquainted with Mr. Gideon Granger, the late postmaster general, appointed by Mr. [Thomas] Jefferson. He was the father of Mr. Francis Granger. During part of the years 1813 and 1814 my family and that of Mr. Gideon Granger resided in Washington near to each other. We were very intimate, and I then became acquainted with Mr. Francis Granger, whom I have known ever since. And I should not do justice in concluding this note, without bearing testimony to his high character, his great abilities, his manly and uniform correct deportment. I have found him, whether in the senate of New York or the house of representatives, with unflinching firmness, supporting those great measures of national policy which appeared to me best adapted to strengthen the union and advance the common prosperity. . . . .

Copy. Printed in *Niles' Register* (Nov. 5, 1836), 51:151.   1. On Oct. 12, 1836, B.W. Dudley, James E. Davis, Charlton Hunt, George C. Thompson, George W. Anderson, Leslie Combs, Robert Wickliffe, Jr., and Aaron K. Woolley, all of Lexington, wrote Clay to ascertain the truthfulness of Richard M. Johnson's campaign charge that the Whig vice presidential candidate, Francis Granger, "is an *abolitionist*," and "one of the organs of that party." *Ibid.*   2. Remark in Senate, Jan. 11, 1836; Comment in Senate, March 9, 1836.

From Nimrod L. Lindsay, North Middletown, Ky., October 14, 1836. States that "As the efforts of Hector continue to be ineffectual," he proposes "that you pay me $25 and I will relinquish any further claim to Hector." Believes "this proposition" is "liberal on my part," because the "actual expences in bringing, Hector and your cow from Shepperdstown [*sic*, Shepherdstown, Va. (W. Va.)] to my house" totaled $127.50. Makes it, however, "to insure a rescinding of the contract [Lindsay to Clay, March 15, 1836], being satisfied that if he possesses the power of propagating his species at all, that it is but very seldom." ALS. DLC-TJC (DNA, M212, R14).

To Adam Beatty, Washington, Ky., November 5, 1836. States: "The fact in regard to the P. Election will now so soon supersede all speculations upon the event that I will trouble you with none [Clay to Bailhache, July 14, 1835]. I have strong hopes, but not unmixed with fears." ALS. Courtesy of Earl M. Ratzer, Highland Park, Ill.

To Philip R. Fendall, Washington, D.C., November 5, 1836. States: "Not being able to find any satisfactory reason for not serving this the last Session of my term in the Senate, I intend going to Washington." Asks Fendall, if possible, to find rooms for him at Mr. [Robert] Keyworth's on Pennsylvania Avenue. ALS. NcD. Clay boarded instead with M.A. Clements on Pennsylvania Ave. Living in the same house during this session were John J. Crittenden, Samuel L. Southard, and John Calhoon (Ky.). Goldman and Young, *The United States Congressional Directories*, 303.

From DOLLEY PAYNE TODD MADISON

"Montpelier," November 8, 1836

The continued and very severe affection of my eyes[1] not permitting but with much difficulty even the signature of my name, has deferred, dear friend, the acknowledgments due for your very kind and acceptable letter of August 18th. I should sooner have resorted for this purpose to the pen of an amanuensis but that the failure of my general health combining equal, and sometimes greater suffering, rendered dictation very painful, and hope still flattered me that I might yet use my own. So much time however having elapsed with but little improvement in my situation, I can submit to no longer delay in offering this explanation of my silence, nor omit the expression of my deep sensibility to that pure and true sympathy which I am conscious I receive from such highly valued friends as Mrs. [Lucretia Hart] Clay and yourself.

The sources of consolation in my bereavement[2] which you suggest, are those which my heart can most truly appreciate. The reflected rays of his virtues still linger around me, and my mind now dwells with calmer feelings on their mellowed tints. He left me too a charge, dear and sacred; and deeply impressed with its value to his fame, and its usefulness to his country, the important trust [has] sustained me under the heavy pressure of recent loss, and formed an oasis to the desert it created in my feelings.

In fulfilment of his wishes I have therefore devoted myself to the object of having prepared for the press the productions of his own pen — it will form the surest evidence of his claim to the gratitude of his country and the world.

With the aid of my brother [John Cole Payne] who had prepared copies of the Debates in the Revolutionary Congress and in the Convention under Mr Madison's eye, triplicates have been completed for publication here and abroad.[3] My Son [John Payne Todd] went in July as far as New-York and remained there for the purpose of negotiating with the most eminent publishers, and I have had communication with those in other Cities; but no offer has been made by any entitled to confidence, which would free me from heavy and inconvenient pecuniary advances and the risk of impositions and eventual loss. Under these circumstances I have been advised by a friend to offer the work to the patronage of Congress asking their aid so far as to relieve the work from the charges upon it, principally for literary and other benevolent purposes, and, after their use by Congress, to give me the stereotype plates. This would at once allow me to throw them into general circulation on a scale that would remunerate me more in accordance with the expectations entertained by their author, and would also allow the price to be so graduated as to ensure their general diffusion.

As this plan was suggested by one favorable to the administration[4] he advised also that the channel of his friends, as the majority of those who were to decide on the proposition, should be employed in making it, and pledged their support. This work being a record only of what passed preceding the existence of present parties, cannot associate the name of Mr Madison with either, and therefore its introduction and advocacy by the one can be no bar to the favor of the other. On your part, I am sure that, in my yielding to it this direction, you will perceive no deviation from the high respect and friendly regard I entertain towards yourself; but approving an adoption of this course, as most conducive to success, you will, with your friends, ensure it on the merits of the work alone, uninfluenced by adversary feelings towards the source from whence the measure originated.

It was my intention to have gone to Washington principally with a view to obtain in personal conference the advice of my best friends, but my protracted ill health and the approach of an inclement season I fear may prevent the journey.

In addition to the three volumes of Debates (near 600 pages each), now ready for the press, matter enough for another volume is expected, and nearly 400 pages copied, of writings and letters on Constitutional subjects — considerable selections have also been made from his early correspondence which may form a volume on the legislative proceedings of Virginia and historical letters of the period from 1780 up to the commencement of the new Government. His Congressional and Executive career may furnish two more.[5] His writings already in print as "Political observations" a pamphlet in 1795, "Examination of the British doctrine" &c. it is thought should be embodied with his other works for more permanent preservation.[6]

It is important that these manuscripts should be prepared and committed to the press as early as they can follow the Debates, and the success of the latter will much facilitate the publication of the former, even if Congress should decline a like patronage to them, a mode which would be much preferred.

The near approach of the time which will call you to your senatorial duties rendering it uncertain whether this would reach you ere your departure from home, I deem it safest to address it to Washington, whence I hope, on your safe arrival, you will favor me with an acknowledgment of its receipt and any suggestions your friendship may offer. . . .

LS. InU. Printed in Colton, *Clay Correspondence*, 4:406-8.   1. Dolley Madison long suffered from inflamed eyes which gave her violent headaches. Virginia Moore, *The Madisons* (New York, 1979), 443.   2. Tucker to Clay, June 30, 1836.   3. A bill "to authorize the purchase of certain manuscripts of the late James Madison" passed the Senate on Feb. 20, 1837, by a vote of 32 to 14. In the House it came "to no resolution" before the end of the session. U.S. Sen., *Journal*, 24 Cong., 2 Sess., 28-29, 36, 128, 265, 268; U.S. H. of Reps., *Journal*, 24 Cong., 2 Sess., 34, 280, 606; *Sen. Docs.*, 24 Cong., 2 Sess., no. 9. Nevertheless, the transfer of documents took place, and Mrs. Madison received payment of $30,000. In 1840 *The Papers of James Madison*, 3 vols., were published in Washington by order of Congress. They included debates of the confederation congress, and debates in the constitutional convention of 1787. Many subsequent editions were published in later years. See Wilson, *Calhoun Papers*, 8:445-50; Irving Brant, *James Madison*, 6 vols. (Indianapolis, 1940-1961), 6:523; William T. Hutchinson *et al.*, *The Papers of James Madison*, 14 vols. to date (Chicago, 1962-), 1:xvii.   4. Sen. William C. Rives. See Brant, *James Madison*, 6:523.   5. In addition to the three volumes of debates (see footnote 3), various editions of *Selections from the Private Correspondence of James Madison, from 1813 to 1836* were published in Washington from 1853-59; and under the sanction of Congress Jonathan Elliot edited in Washington from 1836-59, *The Debates in the Several State Conventions on the Adoption of the Federal Constitution . . . the Journal of the Federal Convention . . . and other illustrations of the Constitution.*   6. James Madison, *Political Observations*. Philadelphia, 1795; and *An Examination of the British Doctrine Which Subjects to Capture a Neutral Trade Not Open in Time of Peace*. London, 1806. Numerous other items had been published before Madison's death.

To HENRY CLAY, JR.   Washington, December 10, 1836

I received your letter of the 3d. inst. with the note and check enclosed, which are now returned executed as you desire.

I am sorry to learn that Blossom was not in Calf as I supposed she was, and still hope that notwithstanding she has taken your bull, she may be yet in Calf; but if not, I shall be glad to get a Calf from her by Lord Althorp. Whenever my Cows are done with him (which will be ascertained by Xmas) I wish you to relieve yourself from their care by sending them to Ashland.

I wrote you a few days ago and refer to that letter. It is as warm here to day as a September day. . . .

ALS. Henry Clay Memorial Foundation, Lexington, Ky.

To DOLLEY PAYNE   Washington, December 13, 1836
TODD MADISON

Your letter of the 8h. Ulto. was handed to me the day before yesterday by Mr. [Richard] Cutts to whom you had confided it; and I was extremely sorry to find in it a confirmation of the account which I had previously received of your indisposition. I trust that this letter will reach you, in better health & with prospects of its speedy re-establishment.

You were perfectly right in selecting the channel which you did for submitting to Congress the subject of the Debates in the Convention, prepared by Mr. Madison.[1] I am persuaded that no person of any party will feel his disposition to afford needful aid, in the publication of that valuable work, at all diminished by that selection.

On reflecting upon the best and most practicable mode of rendering you assistance, in the publication of the Debates, it appears to me that the simplest will be for Congress to purchase at once, at a liberal price, the Manuscript report of Mr. Madison.[2] No greater objection, on principle, can apply to such a purchase than to any other form of assistance that might be proposed. Nor would there, I think, be greater difficulty in carrying through Congress a measure of purchase than any other.

I do not comprehend in the idea of such a purchase any other of his works but the Debates, and, perhaps, what he may have written or reported respecting the Articles of Confederation.

In suggesting this plan, I have been influenced by considerations of what is due to the character of Mr. Madison, the great interest and value of the Debates, as connected with the Constitution, and what I think would most redound to your own benefit.

Highly as I am prepared to appreciate the value of the work, I am apprehensive that you might be disappointed in the profits of the sale of Copies of it. The purchase and perusal of it would be principally confined to the politicians of the Country; and the demand from that source, I fear, would not be sufficiently great to make it very profitable, at least in any short time. I ventured to express this impression to several friends, in my mess, before Mr. [William C.] Rives shewed me, as he did yesterday, the letter of Mr. [Jared] Sparks, the facts communica[ted] in which tend sharply to confirm it.

I have mentioned to my Colleague Mr. [John J.] Crittenden, and to Mr. [Samuel L.] Southard (who both lodge with me) the idea of a purchase as being in my opinion the preferable mode of aiding the publication, and they entirely coincide with me. There is an example for it, in the purchase two Sessions ago of the papers, or rather some of the papers of Genl. [George] Washington.[3]

I have also conferred with Mr. Rives, and I understood him to agree with me in thinking that it would be best to purchase the work, for a gross sum to be paid to you.

But, my dear Madam, whilst I have thought it right, from the terms of your letter, and our friendly relations, thus frankly to express my own views, I beg you to count upon my humble support of any mode of assistance which you may finally decide to apply for.[4]

Mrs. Clay is not with me. Melancholy events in my family hav[e] devolved upon her the care of seven grand children;[5] and altho' the task is great, I am happy to tell you that I hope her improved health will enable her to go through it.[6]

ALS. Courtesy of Maurice R. Large, Farmville, Va.   1. Madison to Clay, Nov. 8, 1836. 2. *Ibid.*   3. A "bill making provision for the purchase of the fac simile of General Washington's accounts" was passed by the House on Feb. 9, 1835, and read for the first time in the Senate the following day. It was referred to the Committee on the Library of Congress which reported it without amendment. The Senate, acting as Committee of the Whole, tabled it on Feb. 28, 1835. U.S. H. of Reps., *Journal*, 23 Cong., 2 Sess., 330, 351; U.S. Sen., *Journal*, 23 Cong., 2 Sess., 151, 153, 162, 209.   4. Madison to Clay, Nov. 8, 1836.   5. See 4:658-60; Clay to Lucretia Hart Clay, Dec. 19, 1835.   6. On Dec. 16, 1836, Dolley Madison wrote Clay that she felt "much gratified by your approbation of the course I have pursued" and by "the favorable dispositions entertained by yourself and our friends . . . towards the plan I so much preferred, of the complete purchase by Congress of the manuscript debates." Encloses an "abstract" of "a hypothetical estimate of the sum to be allowed me." ALI, draft. DLC-James Madison Papers (DNA, M212, R22). Mrs. Madison's brother, John Cole Payne, wrote Clay on the same day, estimating that probable sales of "the Debates in Convention" would number 50,000 and "their product would be $150,000 — deducting one third for prompt instead of continuous payments & for the payment of the legacies charged in the Debates in Convention, this calculation would eventually net $100,000." Notes that "I cannot refrain [from] the remark that the Debates in Convention derive an enhanced value over other works from the circumstance of their being unique. They are not only the solitary complete record of the formation of our Confederacy, but they were at the time of their completion the only full account existing of the formation of any confederacy ancient or modern." Copy. *Ibid.* Madison had provided in his will that proceeds from his *Notes on the Debates in the Federal Convention* would be divided into five legacies: $2,000 to the American Colonization Society; $6,000 to three great-nephews; $1,000 to Princeton; $1,000 to Madison College in Uniontown, Pa.; and $1,500 to the University of Virginia. Moore, *The Madisons*, 470.

From James Clark, Frankfort, Ky., December 15, 1836. Certifies that "The Legislature of this Commonwealth, on the fifteenth day of December, one thousand eight hundred and thirty-six, having in pursuance of the Constitution of the United States of America, chosen Henry Clay Esquire, a Senator." DS. DNA, RG46, 11B-B2. This was read in the Senate, March 4, 1837. See Clay to Wolcott, June 21, 1836.

Remark in Senate, December 15, 1836. Suggests that the Committee on the Post Office and Post Roads be invested with the power "to send for persons and papers" during its investigaton of the fire [Clay to Henry Clay, Jr., December 16, 1836] that destroyed the building that housed the General Post Office, the city post office, and the Patent Office. *Register of Debates*, 24 Cong., 2 Sess., 19.

Also gives notice that he intends tomorrow to introduce a bill "to appropriate for a limited time, the proceeds of the sales of the public lands, and to grant lands to certain States, and for other purposes [Comment in Senate, December 19, 1836]." *Cong. Globe*, 24 Cong., 2 Sess., 26.

To HENRY CLAY, JR.   Washington, December 16, 1836

I received today your favor of the 7h. inst. and now return enclosed the note you transmitted with my signature. You are right in not placing yourself under obligations to others by getting them to endorse for you. I shall always perform that office for you, with pleasure, whilst I live. And I think you would be wise to decline endorsing for others generally. The refusal of the first favor of that kind will do you less prejudice than to have to stop, after you once begin.

I have recd. no letter from Ashland, since I left home; and therefore had not heard of the Shepherd Cow[1] dropping a dead Calf. I regret it, but hope it has not proceeded from any neglect. You do not tell me whether the Hector calf has recovered from its lameness altho' you speak of its improvement.

Yesterday the Genl. P[ost]. Office House was burnt. Suspicions are afloat as to the cause of it, but it is not ascertained whether they rest on any solid foundation.[2]

I feel less interest than ever in public affairs. Indeed I should be very happy if I were not restrained by a sense of duty from returning home. There alone, if any where, I must look for repose and tranquillity, during the residue of my life. . . . P. S. I sent in a former letter the other note you forwarded.

ALS. Henry Clay Memorial Foundation, Lexington, Ky.   1. Probably the Broken Horn Cow. See Shepherd to Clay, March 13, 1836.   2. The House Committee on the Post Office and Post Roads reported that the fire started in the cellar and might have been caused by the custom of depositing ashes in the cellar. The floors of the building were all of wood, and fuel, consisting of both coal and wood, was stored in the vaults underneath the first floor. This undoubtedly added to the combustibility of the building. *Niles' Register* (Dec. 17, 1836), 51:242; (Jan. 28, 1837), 51:344.

To FRANCIS T. BROOKE   Washington, December 19, 1836

I was glad to learn by your favor of the 15h. inst. that Mrs [Mary Champe Carter] Brooke's health is improving, and sincerely hope that it may be soon entirely re-established.

Your objection to the immediate organization of an Opposition, upon the principles stated by me, applies rather to the time of its commencement than the principles themselves. Undoubtedly such an Opposton should avail itself of the errors of the new Admon; but it seems to me that it would acquire greater force by availing itself also of that fatal error in its origin, which resulted from the President elect [Martin Van Buren] being the designated successor of the present Encumbent [Jackson]. If a president may name his successor, and bring the whole machinery of the Government, including its 100.000 dependents, into the canvass; and if by such means he achieves a victory, such a fatal *precedent* as this must be rebuked and reversed, or there is an end of the freedom of election. No one doubts that this has been done. And no reflecting man can doubt that having been once done, it will be again attempted, and unless corrected by the people, it will become, in time, the established practice of the Country. Now I think that no wisdom or benefit in the measures of the new adminstration can compensate or atone for this vice in its origin. Still, this point may be pressed or not, according to circumstances, in different States. As for Virginia, I am afraid another Generation must arise before she regains her former high rank. Henceforward, at least during our lives, I apprehend she will be only a satellite of N. York.

I am obliged greatly to Mr. Pleasants[1] for cherishing his friendly sentiments towards me, and request you to assure him that they are cordially reciprocated.

Nothing of interest has occurred here since the burning of the G. P. Office.[2] I understand that the opinion is general among the inhabitants of the City that it was accidental.

ALS. KyU. Printed in Colton, *Clay Correspondence*, 4:409 with minor variations.   1. Probably John H. Pleasants.   2. Clay to Henry Clay, Jr., Dec. 16, 1836.

Comment in Senate, December 19, 1836. Reintroduces his bill to distribute the proceeds of the sales of public lands to the states which has "heretofore several times passed the Senate, and once the House." Announces a major change in this bill based on the fact that the Deposit Act of the previous session [Speech in Senate, December 29, 1835] "had disposed of so large a part of the divisible fund under the land bill." For this reason, it would be unwise to base the distribution formula on the net proceeds from public land sales during the period December 31, 1832 to December 31, 1837, as had his previous distribution bills. His new bill eliminates "that retrospective character." However, the period of its duration, as in former land bills, would be for five years — from December 31, 1836 to December 31, 1841. The 1841 date of termination is demanded by the fact that the Tariff Act of March 2, 1833 [Draft Proposal, Mid-December, 1832], "commonly called the compromise act," provides at that time the "reduction of one half of the excess beyond twenty per cent. of any duty then remaining." Also, "By that time, a fair experiment of the land bill will have been made," and Congress can decide whether to continue distribution or apply the public land sales proceeds to the current expenses of government. Notes finally that the provision requiring the states to spend the income from public lands granted and transferred to them by the federal government solely on "the great Objects of education, internal improvement, and colonization," a requirement contained in his original plan for distribution [Speech in Senate, June 20, 1832; December 29, 1835] has been "restored in this draught." Otherwise, "the bill is exactly as it passed this body in the last session [Speech in Senate, December 29, 1835]." *Register of Debates*, 24 Cong., 2 Sess., 20-21; *Cong. Globe*, 24 Cong., 2 Sess., 30. On February 23, 1837, Clay moved to table this bill. Motion approved. U.S. Sen., *Journal*, 24 Cong., 2 Sess., 276. On Clay's other land (distribution) bills, see Speech in Senate, June 20, 1832, note.

Earlier this day, Clay presented the petition of a number of Revolutionary War pensioners asking that their pensions be increased. *Cong. Globe*, 24 Cong., 2 Sess., 29.

Comment in Senate, December 21, 1836. Listens to Calhoun's suggestion that in addition to depositing Treasury surpluses with the states, beginning on January 1, 1838, as provided by the Act to Regulate the Deposit of Public Money of June 23, 1836 [Remark in Senate, December 30, 1835], the reductions called for in the compromise tariff legislation of 1833 might also be accelerated in order to help solve the surplus problem. Such reductions, he argues, would "avoid the great and rapid descent" of tariff levels in the years 1841 and 1842 that were written into the 1833 act [Draft Proposal, Mid-December, 1832; Speech in Senate, February 12, 25, 1833]. Indeed, Calhoun concludes, it would now be "wise to distribute the remaining reduction equally on the six remaining years of the act."

To this suggestion, Clay responds that Calhoun's proposal would "disturb" the compromise tariff act of 1833. "In faith of adherence to the provisions of that act, large investments have been made, and under its beneficent operation every interest has prospered, the manufacturing not less than other great interests." Explains that at the time he drew up the compromise he had seen the "probability of a large surplus" and had "endeavored, simultaneously with the passage of the act, to provide for it by the introduction of the land bill [Speech in Senate, January 7, 1833]." That bill "unfortunately had encountered the veto of the President." Argues vigorously against adjusting the schedules of the compromise tariff to handle the treasury surplus. "Any essential alteration in the measure of protection secured by that act" could only lead to a "reopening of the wounds which had been so happily healed." Announces he will "cooperate in no such object" and will "steadily oppose any material change in the provisions of the act." Reiterates that the "complete remedy for a surplus . . . is to be found in the land bill [Comment in Senate, December 19, 1836]." *Register of Debates*, 24 Cong., 2 Sess., 79-84.

To **RALPH RANDOLPH GURLEY**   Washington, December 22, 1836

I have the honor to acknowledge the receipt of your note of the 19h. inst. informing me that, at the last annual meeting of the American Colonization society, in this City, I was unanimously elected its President.[1] I receive, with very great sensibility, this distinguished proof of the confidence of the Society, and request you to communicate my acceptance of the Office, and my respectful acknowledgements to those who have bestowed it.

Regarding the American Colonization Society as the only practical scheme ever presented to public consideration for separating, advantageously to all parties, the European descendants upon this Continent from the free people of Color, the descendants of Africans, with their own consent; and of ultimately effecting a more extensive separation of the two races, with the consent of the States and individuals interested, I shall continue to cherish the highest interest in the success of the Society, and will contribute whatever is in my power to promote its prosperity.[2]

ALS. NHi.   1. The American Colonization Society had met in Washington on Dec. 15-17, 1836. Clay remained its president until 1849. *Niles' Register* (Dec. 24, 1836), 51:259; Staudenraus, *The African Colonization Movement*, 187.   2. This letter is the subject of James M. Gifford, "Some New Light on Henry Clay and the American Colonization Society," *FCHQ* (Oct., 1976), 50:372-74.

From O. T. Reeves *et al.*, Chillicothe, Ohio, December 24, 1834 [*sic*, 1836]. Express gratification at Clay's recent election [December 15, 1836] to the U.S. Senate [Clark to Clay, December 15, 1836] by the Kentucky legislature. Urge him to remain in the Senate despite the personal sacrifice it entails, adding that "you must not leave us, near as the country may be to the dreadful vortex of corruption which has hitherto swallowed up republics, and threatens the existence of this." Believe that although "party animosity and political envy" have "warped or defeated" most of Clay's projects, "we are no less of the opinion that the influence of your eloquence may still have its weight in the assembled senate of this great union." Copy. Printed in *Niles' Register* (April 22, 1837), 52:119. This letter is misdated in *Niles' Register* as December 24, 1834. Clay replied to it on March 6, 1837.

To Jacob Snider, Jr., Philadelphia, December 27, 1836. States that he has become very interested in the manufacture of sugar from beets due to "the patriotic endeavors of yourself and others in Philada to introduce it in the U. States." Reports that he himself distributed "some of the Siberian beet seed brought from France last spring . . . and I

874

caused some of them to be sowed at Ashland, my residence." Notes that "they grew very large, and were more productive than any other beets which I have ever tried." Believes they are well adapted to the climate of the United States, and "What is now wanted is a knowledge of and experience in conducting the processes by which Sugar is extracted from the Root." Thinks also that "In my opinion, the establishment of the Manufacture of Beet Sugar in the U.S. eminently deserves the liberal patronage of Government," but "Owing to the diversity of opinions which exist as to the powers and duties of the Genl. Government, which otherwise would be the most fitting to bestow the proper patronage, perhaps an appeal had better be made to the liberality of one of the State Governments; and I know of none to which it can be addressed with more propriety than that of Pennsa." Adds that "with or without the aid of Government. . . . I believe that at no distant day a great part of this necessary of human life will be derived from this new source." ALS. PPAmP. Snider resided at 32 Walnut Street, Philadelphia, and was president and secretary of the Beet Sugar Society. Lexington *Kentucky Gazette*, June 27, 1836. The Beet Sugar Society had been organized in Philadelphia in 1830, and although there is no evidence it received aid from the Pennsylvania legislature, it sent James Pedder to Europe in 1836 to make a thorough study of the industry. United States Beet Sugar Association, *The Beet Sugar Story* (Philadelphia, 1959), 14-15.

CALENDAR OF UNPUBLISHED
LETTERS AND OTHER DOCUMENTS

Letters deemed to have slight historical importance to an understanding of Henry Clay and his career are listed below. Copies of them are on file in the offices of *The Papers of Henry Clay* at the University of Kentucky, Lexington, and may be consulted by interested persons. The locus of the original manuscript of each letter has been included below, as has an indication of the general subject matter of each. Subject classification code numbers have been employed as follows:

1　Requests for general assistance and government assistance, information, documents, reports, correspondence, books and other printed materials.

2　Transmission of routine information, and documents, including that between the Executive and Legislative branches.

3　Applications, recommendations, appointments, and resignations pertaining to government employment and political office.

4　Correspondence and transmission of information relating to the claims of private citizens against the U.S. and foreign governments:
　a.　United States
　b.　Great Britain
　c.　France
　d.　Spain
　e.　Holland
　f.　Other European nations
　g.　Latin American nations.

5　Correspondence and transmission of information relating to land grants, pensions, and related legal actions.

6　Routine correspondence relating to:
　a.　Forwarding of mail
　b.　Interviews and audiences
　c.　Introductions & character references
　d.　Invitations, acceptances, regrets, condolences
　e.　Appreciation, gratitude, social pleasantries
　f.　Subject matter not clear
　g.　Application, recommendations pertaining to private employment.

7　Routine legal correspondence and documents relating to:
　a.　Clay's law practice as counsel or executor
　b.　Cases in which Clay was plaintiff, defendant, witness, or deponent
　c.　James Morrison Estate management
　d.　Eliza Jane Weir guardianship
　e.　James and/or Ann Hart Brown Estate management.

8   Routine correspondence and documents (including deeds, agreements, leases) relating to Clay's land purchases and sales, livestock transactions and breeding, and investments.

9   Routine bills, receipts, checks, bank drafts, promissory notes, loans, payments, rents, mortgages, tax documents.

10   Correspondence relating to routine political and professional services rendered constituents, colleagues, friends, other politicians.

11   Miscellaneous.

1829
ca. From J.M. McCalla, DLC-TJC, 7a, 9. From S.S. Nicholas, KyLxT, 7c. To Robert Scott, DLC-TJC, 8.

MARCH 1829
 9 To BUS-Wash. branch, DLC-TJC, 9.
12 From Gales & Seaton, DLC-TJC, 9.
23 From F.M.L. Phelps, DLC-TJC, 7a.
31 From Edmund P. Banks, DLC-HC, 11.

APRIL 1829
 8 From H.I. Bodley, DLC-TJC, 7d, 9.
 9 From George W. Dawson, DLC-TJC, 7b, 9.
14 From Forsyth & Co., DLC-TJC, 9.
15 To BUS-Lex. branch, DLC-TJC, 9.
22 To BUS-Lex. branch, DLC-TJC, 9.
23 To Lafayette, NNPM, 6c.
24 From Bryant & Sturgis, DNA, 6a, 9. To George Rapp, PPiU, 6c. To Estate of H. Seeley, DLC-TJC, 9.
25 To Peter B. Porter, NBuHi, 9.
26 From P. Dudley & Co., DLC-TJC, 9.
30 From T.K. Layton & Co., DLC-TJC, 9.

MAY 1829
 1 From J.H. Holeman, DLC-TJC, 9. From Charles A. Potter, DLC-TJC, 9.
11 From William George, DLC-TJC, 8, 9. From Macy Thwaits, DLC-TJC, 9.
15 To BUS-Lex. branch, DLC-TJC, 9. From William Shackleford, DLC-TJC, 9.
16 To BUS-Lex. branch, DLC-TJC, 9.
18 From Lewis Webster, DLC-TJC, 8, 9.
19 From John Tilford, DLC-TJC, 9.
21 To BUS-Lex. branch, DLC-TJC, 9.
26 From William Gibson, DLC-TJC, 8, 9. From John R. Price, DLC-TJC, 9. From S. Wymore, DLC-TJC, 8, 9.
27 To BUS-Lex. branch, DLC-TJC, 9. From S.S. Nicholas, KyLxT, 7c.
30 To BUS-Lex. branch, DLC-TJC, 9. From John Oliver, DLC-TJC, 8, 9. From Samuel Pilkington, DLC-TJC, 9.
Late May To Episcopal Church, DLC-TJC, 9.

JUNE 1829
n.d. To Edward Everett, MHi, 6d.
 1 From Ozborne Henley, DLC-TJC, 9. To S.S. Nicholas, KyLxT, 7c.
 6 From Logan & Hord, DLC-TJC, 9.
 8 To BUS-Lex. branch, DLC-TJC, 9. From William Bell, DLC-TJC, 9. To Edward Everett, MHi, 6d.
 9 From William Challen, DLC-TJC, 9. From B.R. McIlvaine & Co., DLC-TJC, 9.
10 From D. Warner, DLC-TJC, 9.
11 From John H. Kerr, DLC-TJC, 9.

12   To Leslie Combs, KyU, 6d. From John Puthuff, DLC-TJC, 9.
13   From John H. Kerr, DLC-TJC, 9.
16   From Lewis Bryan, DLC-TJC, 9.
17   To Bruce & Gratz, KyLxT, 7a. From William R. Morton, DLC-TJC, 8, 9.
18   From William C. Dunn, DLC-TJC, 9.
29   From J. Edrington, DLC-TJC, 9.

JULY 1829
 3   From William Shackleford, DLC-TJC, 8, 9.
 4   To Lafayette, NNPM, 6c.
 6   From J. Bruen, DLC-TJC, 9.
 9   From Joseph Ficklin, DLC-TJC, 9.
10   From Alexander Hodge, DLC-TJC, 9.
13   From S.S. Nicholas, KyLxT, 7c.
16   To Thomas Law, KyU, 7a. From Robert Scott, KyLxT, 9.
18   From Samuel L. Richardson, DLC-TJC, 7c. From Robert Scott, KyLxT, 7c. From Robert
     Scott, KyLxT, 7c.
19   From S.S. Nicholas, KyLxT, 7c.
20   With Daniel Bradford, DLC-TJC, 8. With James A. Brooks, DLC-TJC, 8. From Joseph &
     George Boswell, DLC-TJC, 9.

AUGUST 1829
n.d. From James Erwin, DLC-TJC, 8, 9.
 3   From James Castleman, DLC-TJC, 8.
 4   From Francis T. Brooke, DLC-HC, 7a.
 7   From Gideon Wood, DLC-TJC, 8, 9.
10   To BUS-Lex. branch, DLC-TJC, 9. From William S. Dallam, DLC-TJC, 10.
12   From Robert Scott, DLC-TJC, 8.
17   With George Lansdowne, DLC-TJC, 7a, 8.
28   From Robert Wilson, DLC-TJC, 9.

SEPTEMBER 1829
 1   From R. Smith, DLC-TJC, 9.
 8   To George M. Bibb, KyLxT, 7a. To Committee of Warren Co., Louisville *Public Advertiser*,
     Sept. 19, 1829, 6d.
10   From William C. Dunn, DLC-TJC, 9. From John H. Kerr, DLC-TJC, 9.
14   From Richard A. Buckner, DLC-HC, 6d.
15   From S.S. Nicholas, KyLxT, 7c.
24   From Daniel Webster, NhD, 6c.
26   From Samuel Hanson, DLC-TJC, 7b.
28   From P.B. Atwood *et al.*, Lex. *Ky. Reporter*, Oct. 7, 1829, 6d. To P.B. Atwood *et al.*, Lex. *Ky.
     Reporter*, Oct. 7, 1829, 6d.

OCTOBER 1829
n.d. From John Clark, DLC-TJC, 9.
 5   From H.I. Bodley, DLC-TJC, 7c, 9. From S.S. Nicholas, DLC-TJC, 7c.
 9   From Ahmed Rucker, DLC-TJC, 7a. From Jonathan Taylor, DLC-TJC, 7a.
12   From Gabril Hume, DLC-TJC, 8, 9.
14   From Philosophical and Literary Society of Centre College, DLC-TJC, 6d. To Richard
     Smith, PHi, 9.
20   From Daniel Bryan & William Rowan, DLC-TJC, 7a.
26   From John S. Hart, DLC-TJC, 9.

NOVEMBER 1829
 1   With John C. Sullivan, DLC-TJC, 9.
22   From S.S. Nicholas, KyLxT, 7c.
23   From Hart & Curd, DLC-TJC, 9.
25   From John Kirkpatrick, DLC-TJC, 9.
28   From S.S. Nicholas, DLC-TJC, 7c. From Robert Scott, DLC-TJC, 7c. To James Strong,
     NcD, 4a, 7c. To Daniel Webster, NhHi, 4a, 7c. From John Wirt, DLC-TJC, 9.

29　From John H. Kerr, DLC-TJC, 9.
30　To E.C. Berry, ViU, 9.

DECEMBER 1829
2　From E. Carey & A. Hart, DLC-TJC, 9.
7　From January & Huston, DLC-TJC, 8, 9.
8　With Ozborne Henley, KyLxT, 8.
9　From James A. Brooks, DLC-TJC, 8, 9. From Ozborne Henley, KyLxT, 8.
11　To E. Cary & A. Hart, KyU, 9.
12　From A. Gibney, DLC-TJC, 9. From William North, DLC-TJC, 9.
13　From Theodore Wythe Clay, DLC-TJC, 7b. To Hezekiah Shields, Fleming Co. Deed Book, p. 482, 7a.
14　From Macy Thwaits, DLC-TJC, 9.
17　From Amos Kendall, DNA, 7c.
19　From Samuel Weisinger, Ky. Court of Appeals, Book Z, pp. 7-8, 7c.
25　To Elisha Whittlesey, OClWHi, 4a, 6c, 7c. To Alva Woods, KyLoF, 6b.
29　To BUS-Lex. branch, DLC-TJC, 9. From T.K. Layton & Co., DLC-TJC, 9.
31　From Joseph Ficklin, DLC-TJC, 9. From Estate of H. Seeley, DLC-TJC, 9.

JANUARY 1830
1　From Macy Thwaits, DLC-TJC, 8, 9.
4　From John W. Hunt, DLC-TJC, 9. To U.S. House of Representatives, DNA, 4a, 7c.
5　To Bryan & Roman, DLC-TJC, 7b., From John C. Sullivan, DLC-TJC, 9.
7　From Ozborne Henley, KyLxT, 9.
8　*Clay* v. *Owings*, DLC-TJC, 7b. From Andrew F. Price, DLC-TJC, 8, 9. From Robert Scott, KyLxT, 9.
9　From Samuel Pilkington, DLC-TJC, 9. From Drs. Richard Pindell & Thomas P. Satterwhite, DLC-TJC, 9. From Edmond H. Taylor, DLC-TJC, 7c.
11　To BUS-Lex. branch, DLC-TJC, 9. From H.I. Bodley, DLC-TJC, 9. From John H. Kerr, DLC-TJC, 9. From T.K. Layton & Co., DLC-TJC, 9, From Drs. Richard Pindell, & Thomas P. Satterwhite, DLC-TJC, 9. From Robert Scott, DLC-TJC, 9.
12　To BUS-Lex. branch, KyLxT, 9.
20　From Logan & Hord, DLC-TJC, 9.
25　From Nathaniel Dick, DLC-HC, 6d.

FEBRUARY 1830
5　*Clay* v. *Lytle*, Ky, 7b. From John H. Savage *et al.*, Washington *Daily National Journal,* April 12, 1830, 6d.
8　From Levi Pierce *et al.*, Lynchburg *Virginian,* March 8, 1830, 6d.
9　To BUS-Lex. branch, KyLxT, 9. To Levi Pierce *et al.*, Lynchburg *Virginian,* March 8, 1830, 6d.
13　From Daniel Vertner *et al.,* Washington *Daily National Journal,* April 5, 1830, 6d.
18　*Wickliffe* v. *Clay*, Ky, 7b.
20　To Daniel Vertner *et al., Washington Daily National Journal,* April 5, 1830, 6d.
22　To Elisha Whittlesey, OClW, 4a.

MARCH 1830
1　Answer to Interrogatories, KyLxT, 7c.
7　From James Allen, DLC-TJC, 9.
8　From Forstall & Co., DLC-TJC, 9.
12　To John H. Savage *et al.*, Washington *Daily National Journal,* April 12, 1830, 6d.
13　From William Martin, DLC-TJC, 9.
20　From Thomas B. Megowan, DLC-TJC, 9.

APRIL 1830
n.d.　From Ozborne Henley, KyLxT, 9.
1　From H.I. Bodley, DLC-TJC, 7c, 9. From Joseph Ficklin, DLC-TJC, 9.
2　To James Sudduth, Sue Bascom Steele Collection, Lexington, Ky., 8.
3　From H.I. Bodley, DLC-TJC, 9.
6　From Joseph Ficklin, DLC-TJC, 9.
14　From Caldwell & Ernest, KyLxT, 9. With Ozborne Henley, KyLxT, 9.

15 From S.S. Nicholas, KyLxT, 7b, 7c.
24 From Lucy Weisinger & son, DLC-TJC, 9.
28 From Henry Chiles, KyLxT, 7b, 7c. *Clay* v. *Nicholas's heirs,* DLC-TJC, 7b, 7c. To Richard Hawes, Jr., KyLxT, 7b, 7c.
29 From Martin Van Buren, DNA, 2.

MAY 1830
 1 To BUS-Lex. branch, Mary Clay Kenner Collection, Rogersville, Tenn., 9.
 3 From William S. Dallam, DLC-TJC, 8.
 5 *Wickliffe* v. *Clay,* Ky, 7b.
 6 From Henry Chiles, KyLxT, 7b, 7c. From George Graham, DNA, 7c.
 7 From William C. Dunn, DLC-TJC, 9.
12 With Mrs. M.J. Ratel, DLC-TJC, 8.
14 From Porter Clay, DLC-HC, 8, 9.
15 With Edward Bateman, DLC-TJC, 8. From P. Delahoussaye *et al.,* DLC-TJC,1.
17 From William Master, DLC-TJC, 9.
18 With Francis Walker, DLC-TJC, 8.
24 From Thomas Gray, DLC-TJC, 9.
25 To Martin Van Buren, DNA, 2.
26 From William C. Dunn, DLC-TJC, 9.
29 From Robert P. Letcher, NN, 9.
31 To BUS-Lex. branch, Henry Clay Memorial Foundation, Lexington, Ky., 9. From Robert Scott, DLC-TJC, 9.

JUNE 1830
 1 From John Porter, DLC-TJC, 9. From Jordan Sisk, DLC-TJC, 9.
 3 To James Madison, Maurice R. Large Collection, Farmville, Va., 6c.
 4 From William Alexander, DLC-TJC, 9.
 5 From Logan & Hord, DLC-TJC, 9.
18 From Logan & Hord, DLC-TJC, 9.
20 From Logan & Hord, DLC-TJC, 9.
23 From Joseph Anderson, DLC-TJC, 2, 7c. From William Henry Harrison, DLC-TJC, 6c.
24 From John Postlethwaite, DLC-TJC, 9.
26 From William S. Dallam, DLC-TJC, 8. From John Kirkpatrick, DLC-TJC, 9.
30 From Unknown Sender, DLC-TJC, 9.

JULY 1830
 1 From H.I. Bodley, DLC-TJC, 9.
 5 To Joseph Anderson, DNA, 7c. From William C. Dunn, DLC-TJC, 9.
12 From S. Mason *et al.,* Washington *Daily National Journal,* August 7, 1830, 6d.
15 To S. Mason *et al.,* Washington *Daily National Journal,* August 7, 1830, 6d.
20 From Crutchfield & Tilford, DLC-TJC, 9.
26 To Peter B. Porter, NBuHi, 6c.

AUGUST 1830
 9 To Whom It May Concern, MHi, 6c.
10 To James Lloyd, PPL-Ridgeway Branch, 6c.
14 To Joseph Anderson, DNA, 7c. From Abner Spears, DLC-TJC, 9.
16 From William C. Dunn, DLC-TJC, 9.
18 From Norman Porter, DLC-TJC, 9.
23 From John Q. Adams, MHi-Adams Papers, 6c.
25 From J.M. Moore, DNA, 2.
27 From George Lansdowne, DLC-TJC, 9.

SEPTEMBER, 1830
n.d. Account, KyLxT, 7c. From Logan & Hord, DLC-TJC, 9. From Hezekiah Niles, DLC-TJC, 9. From John Wirt, DLC-TJC, 9.
 4 From William Martin, DLC-TJC, 9.
10 From Logan & Hord, DLC-TJC, 9.
13 From Robert Scott, DLC-TJC, 7c. To Robert Scott, MoHi, 7c.
17 From Joseph Anderson, DNA, 7c. With William C. Dunn, DLC-TJC, 8, 9. From James S. Rollins *et al.,* Lexington *Ky. Reporter,* Dec. 1, 1830, 6d. From Archer Smith, DLC-TJC, 8, 9.

21 To BUS-Phila., Henry Clay Memorial Foundation, Lexington, Ky., 9.
22 From Robert Scott, DLC-TJC, 9. From Robert Scott, KyLxT, 9.
25 To James S. Rollins *et al.*, Lexington *Ky. Reporter*, Dec. 1, 1830, 6d.
27 From R.S. Todd, KyLxT, 9.

OCTOBER 1830
 1 From H.I. Bodley, DLC-TJC, 7c, 9.
 5 From George L. Gregg, DLC-TJC, 9.
15 To Nicholas Biddle, MB, 6g.
16 With Daniel Bradford, DLC-TJC, 8.
20 From J.W. Houston, KyLxT, 7c.
25 From Conover & Thomas, DLC-TJC, 9. From Daniel Drake, DLC-TJC, 9.
27 To Richard B. Jones, DNA, 6c.
29 To ? Crawford, DLC-TJC, 6f.

NOVEMBER 1830
 2 To BUS-Lex. branch, DLC-TJC, 9.
 4 From Joseph Anderson, KyLxT, 7c.
 6 From G.W. Allen, DLC-TJC, 9. From James Erwin, DLC-TJC, 9. From Robert Ramsey, DLC-TJC, 9.
 8 From Robert Scott, DLC-TJC, 9
 9 From Logan & Hord, DLC-TJC, 9.
11 To Elisha Whittlesey, OClWHi, 10.
13 From William Frazer, DLC-TJC, 9. To Thomas M. Hickey, KyLxT, 7c.
19 From William Martin, DLC-TJC, 9.
20 To BUS-Lex. branch, DLC-TJC, 9. From James A. Brooks, DLC-TJC, 9. From Logan & Hord, DLC-TJC, 9. From Robert Wilson, DLC-TJC, 9.
23 From Joseph Robb, DLC-TJC, 7a.
25 From William Martin, DLC-TJC, 9.
29 From William North, DLC-TJC, 9. From Tilford & Anderson, DLC-TJC, 9.
30 From Logan & Hord, DLC-TJC, 9.

DECEMBER 1830
 7 From Robert Scott, KyLxT, 7c.
10 From George W. Morton, DLC-TJC, 8, 9.
11 From Logan & Hord, DLC-TJC, 9.
14 From E.W. Craig, DLC-TJC, 9. From John R. Shaw, DLC-TJC, 9.
15 To William C. Rives, DLC-Rives Papers, 6c.
16 To BUS-Lex. branch, DLC-TJC, 9. From William S. Dallam, KyU, 9. From William Martin, DLC-TJC, 9.
17 From Logan & Hord, DLC-TJC, 9.
18 From A.S. Elliott, DLC-TJC, 9. From S.S. Nicholas, DLC-TJC, 7c. From Samuel Pilkington, DLC-TJC, 9. From H.M. Seeley, DLC-TJC, 9.
20 From John Anderson, DLC-TJC, 9. From John Kirkpatrick, DLC-TJC, 9. From Thomas McCracken & Samuel Long, DLC-TJC, 9. From George W. Morton, DLC-TJC, 9. From Robert Scott, KyLxT, 7c.
21 From Robert Scott, KyLxT, 7c.
24 From T.K. Layton & Co., DLC-TJC, 9.

JANUARY 1831
n.d. To BUS-Lex. branch, DLC-TJC, 8. *Clay* v. *Pike*, Ky, 7b. *Clay & Craig* v. *Hart*, Ky, 7b. To Thomas Ewing, DLC-Ewing Papers, 2. From Thomas Smith, DLC-TJC, 8, 9. *Wickliffe* v. *Clay*, 7b. *Wickliffe* v. *Clay*, Ky, 7b.
 1 From Thomas P. Hart, DLC-TJC, 9. From Ozborne Henley, KyLxT, 9.
ca. 2 From Macy Thwaits, DLC-TJC, 9.
25 With Alfred G. Boyer, DLC-TJC, 8.

FEBRUARY 1831
13 From Judge Pitus, DLC-TJC, 7e.
21 *Wickliffe* v. *Clay*, Ky, 7b.
29 From Hezekiah Niles, DLC-TJC, 9.

MARCH 1831
4 From William Prentiss, DLC-TJC, 9.
10 From Robert Crittenden, DLC-TJC, 9.
12 From Gales & Seaton, DLC-TJC, 9.
15 From ? Wallenstein, DLC-HC, 6e.
18 To John W. Hunt, KyU, 6g.
23 From Robert Wickliffe, Ky, 7b.
29 From Joseph Ficklin, DLC-TJC, 9.
31 From Timothy C. Twitchell, DLC-HC, 9.

APRIL 1831
1 From H.I. Bodley, DLC-TJC, 7c, 9. From H.I. Bodley, DLC-TJC, 7c, 9. From G.R. Tompkins, DLC-TJC, 9.
2 From Ward & Stokes, DLC-TJC, 9.
4 From Jacob Rynear, DLC-TJC, 9.
8 To BUS-Lex. branch, Henry Clay Memorial Foundation, Lexington, Ky., 9. From Susan Price, ViU, 9.
11 From J. Hamilton, DLC-TJC, 9. From William North, DLC-TJC, 8.
12 From William North, DLC-TJC, 8, 9. From Robert Scott, KyLxT, 9.
15 From William Henry Russell, DLC-HC, 6c.
20 To BUS-Lex. branch, Mary Clay Kenner Collection, Rogersville, Tenn., 9.
21 Clay v. Marshall et al., Ky, 7b.
25 From Daniel Bradford, DLC-TJC, 9.
26 From Thomas Grant, DLC-TJC, 8. With Thomas Grant, DLC-TJC, 8.

MAY 1831
5 With Richard Hawes, Jr., DLC-TJC, 7c. Nicholas's heirs v. Clay, DLC-TJC, 7c.
8 From Henry Chiles, KyU, 7a.
11 To BUS-Lex. branch, DLC-TJC, 9. To BUS-Lex. branch, DLC-TJC, 9.
16 From Peter Dudley & Co., DLC-TJC, 9.
18 Nicholas's heirs v. Clay, DLC-TJC, 7c.
20 To BUS-Lex. branch, DLC-TJC, 9. From Robert Scott, DLC-TJC, 8.
22 From Robert Scott, KyLxT, 7c.
25 From Pleasants & Abbott, DLC-TJC, 9. From Robert Scott, KyLxT, 9.
26 From BUS-Lex. branch, DLC-TJC, 9.
31 To BUS-Lex. branch, Mary Clay Kenner Collection, Rogersville, Tenn., 7c. 9. To BUS-Lex. branch, DLC-TJC, 9.

JUNE 1831
n.d. From E. Denning, DLC-TJC, 9.
1 From M. Fishel, DLC-TJC, 9.
3 To Illeg. Name, DLC-TJC, 9.
11 To BUS-Lex. branch, Mary Clay Kenner Collection, Rogersville, Tenn., 9.
20 From Thomas M. Ewing, DLC-HC, 3.
22 To BUS-Lex. branch, DLC-TJC, 9. To Richard Hawes, Jr., DLC-TJC, 9.
24 To Nicholas Biddle, DLC-Nicholas Biddle Papers, 6g. To Edward Everett, MHi, 6g.
27 Nicholas's heirs v. Clay, DLC-TJC, 7c.
30 To BUS-Lex. branch, Henry Clay Memorial Foundation, Lexington, Ky., 7c, 9.

JULY 1831
2 Wickliffe v. Clay, KyLoF, 7b.
4 To Esther Morrison, Henry Clay Memorial Foundation, Lexington, Ky., 7c, 9.
7 To BUS-Lex. branch, DLC-TJC, 9. To BUS-Lex. branch, Mary Clay Kenner Collection, Rogersville, Tenn., 7c, 9.
8 Wickliffe v. Clay, Ky, 7b.
18 To BUS-Lex. branch, DLC-TJC, 9. To BUS-Lex. branch, DLC-TJC, 9. From T.K. Layton & Co., DLC-TJC, 9.
19 From Simon Bernard, DLC-HC, 6e. To BUS-Lex. branch, DLC-TJC, 9.
20 To BUS-Lex. branch, DLC-TJC, 9.
21 To BUS-Lex. branch, DLC-TJC, 9. From Drs. Richard Pindell & Thomas P. Satterwhite, DLC-TJC, 9. From Drs. Richard Pindell & Thomas P. Satterwhite, DLC-TJC, 9.

ca. 22 Acct. for Hart Estate, DLC-TJC, 7a, 9.
26 From Benjamin Parsons, DLC-TJC, 6c.
29 To BUS-Lex. branch, DLC-TJC, 9. From Thomas Sacrey, DLC-TJC, 9.

AUGUST 1831
1 To BUS-Lex. branch, Mary Clay Kenner Collection, Rogersville, Tenn., 7c, 9.
2 From John Wirt, DLC-TJC, 9.
9 From January & Huston, DLC-TJC, 9.
ca. 12 From T.K. Layton & Co., DLC-TJC, 9.
12 From John Rohrer, DLC-TJC, 9.
13 From Henry Chiles, DLC-TJC, 7a, 9.
ca. 17 Acct. for Hart Estate, DLC-TJC, 7a.
17 From George Lansdowne, DLC-TJC, 9.
22 To Peter B. Porter, NBuHi, 6d.
27 From Thomas Secrel, DLC-TJC, 9.
28 To Thomas Metcalfe, W. Richard Metcalfe Collection, Ga. Institute of Technology, 6c.
30 To BUS-Lex. branch, DLC-TJC, 9.

SEPTEMBER 1831
2 To William S. Dallam, NcD, 8, 9. From Thomas McCracken & Samuel Long, DLC-TJC, 9.
10 From Thomas McCracken, DLC-TJC, 9. From Susan Price, DLC-TJC, 7a.
14 From Thomas P. Hart, DLC-TJC, 8. With Lexington & Ohio Railroad Co., KyLxT, 8.
16 From G. Christy, DLC-TJC, 9.
17 To Bruce & Gratz, Fayette Co. Court, Deed Book 7, p. 186,7c. To Bruce & Gratz, Fayette Co. Court, Deed Book 7, p. 186, 7c.
ca. 22 From William W. Worsley, DLC-TJC, 9.
ca. 26 From John Anderson & John Kirkpatrick, DLC-TJC, 9.
26 To Andrew Stainton, KyLxT, 7c.
27 From Thomas McCracken & Samuel Long, DLC-TJC, 9.
30 *Clay* v. *Lytle*, Ky, 7b.

OCTOBER 1831
1 To BUS-Lex. branch, Mary Clay Kenner Collection, Rogersville, Tenn., 7c, 9.
3 From Madison C. Johnson, DLC-TJC, 7c, 9. *Wickliffe* v. *Clay*, Ky, 7b.
ca. 4 From Joseph Ficklin, DLC-TJC, 9.
4 To Lafayette, NIC, 6c. To Whom It May Concern, Mrs. Henry Jackson, Sr., Collection, Danville, Ky., 7c.
8 To BUS-Lex. branch, Henry Clay Memorial Foundation, Lexington, Ky., 9.
10 To BUS-Lex. branch, Mary Clay Kenner Collection, Rogersville, Tenn., 7c, 9.
12 From W.S. Archer, DLC-TJC, 11.
21 From P. Seeley, DLC-TJC, 9.
27 From P. Seeley, DLC-TJC, 9.

NOVEMBER 1831
7 From Samuel Long & son, DLC-TJC, 9.
11 From Lucy Weisinger & son, DLC-TJC, 9.
14 To BUS-Lex. branch, Mary Clay Kenner Collection, Rogersville, Tenn., 7c, 9. From William Dunlap, KyLxT, 9.
16 To BUS-Lex. branch, DLC-TJC, 9. To BUS-Lex. branch, DLC-TJC, 9.
17 To BUS-Lex. branch, DLC-TJC, 9. To BUS-Lex. branch, Mary Clay Kenner Collection, Rogersville, Tenn., 9. To BUS-Lex. branch, DLC-TJC, 9. From William S. Dallam, KyU, 8, 9. From Thomas McCracken, DLC-TJC, 9. From Thomas McCracken & Samuel Long, DLC-TJC, 9.
18 From Thomas M. Hickey, DLC-TJC, 7c, 8. From A. Logan, DLC-TJC, 9. From Andrew Stainton, KyLxT, 7c. To Trustees of Transylvania University, DLC-TJC, 7c, 8.
19 From William Martin, DLC-TJC, 9. From Samuel Redd, DLC-TJC, 9.
21 From John R. Shaw, DLC-TJC, 9.
22 To Joseph T. Farrow, Fleming Co. Deed Book R, pp. 153-54, 7a. To David Likes, Fleming Co. Deed Book R, pp. 98-99, 7a. To James McGregor, Fleming Co. Deed Book R, p. 32, 7a. To William Proctor, Jr., Fleming Co. Deed Book R, p. 111-12, 7a. To William Proctor, Sr., Fleming Co. Deed Book R, pp. 37-38, 7a. To Ferdinand Vannatten, Fleming Co. Deed

Book R, pp. 216-17, 7a.
29 To BUS-Lex. branch, DLC-TJC, 9.

DECEMBER 1831
n.d. To Henry A.S. Dearborn, Justin G. Turner Collection, Hollywood, Ca., 6f.
 3 From F.H. Gallandet, DLC-TJC, 10.
 5 From William L. Miller *et al.*, DLC-HC, 6d.
12 From Peter H. Leuba, DLC-TJC, 6g. To Levi Woodbury, DNA, 6a.
13 From Levi Woodbury, DNA, 6a.
16 To Peter B. Porter, NBuHi, 6d.
17 From William Nourse, DLC-HC, 10.
18 To Thomas Cope, OCHP, 7b.
22 From Elijah Hayward, DNA, 2.
23 From John Marshall, Jr., DLC-HC, 3.
25 To George C. Washington, NN, 6d.
26 To Henry A.S. Dearborn, Justin G. Turner Collection, Hollywood, Ca., 2. From J.C. Wright, DLC-TJC, 7c.
27 From Lewis Cass, DNA, 2. To Henry A.S. Dearborn, *MVHR*, 2:424, 2.
29 From P.N. Nicholas, DLC-TJC, 8.

JANUARY 1832
ca. 1832 To Coster & Berryman, Josephine Simpson Collection, Lexington, Ky., 8. From J. Edrington, DLC-TJC, 9. From Samuel Long, Jr., DLC-TJC, 9.
 1 From James Dill, DLC-HC, 4a, 5.
 6 From S. Deardorff, DLC-TJC, 7c. From Elijah Hayward, DNA, 4a, 5.
 7 To William Greene, OCHP, 6c.
13 To Elisha Whittlesey, OClWHi, 7a.
16 To Elisha Whittlesey, OClWHi, 7a.
19 From Lewis Cass, DNA, 2, 4a, 5.
24 From Nathan Smith, DLC-TJC, 9.
30 From Lewis Cass, DNA, 2, 5.

FEBRUARY 1832
 1 From Willilam Potter, DLC-TJC, 4a.
 4 From Richard Rush, DLC-HC, 6e.
 6 From T. Cleaveland *et al.*, DLC-HC, 6d.
 7 From Andrew Marschalk, DLC-HC, 1.
10 From Thomas Norvell, DLC-HC, 11.
14 From Loubry Pellerin, DLC-HC, 4c.
18 From James T. Morehead, DLC-TJC, 10.
23 From Francis Taylor, DLC-HC, 2, 4a, 5.
29 From George W. Morton, DLC-TJC, 10.

MARCH 1832
 2 From Joseph Meades, DLC-HC, 4c.
 3 To D.S. Dickinson, ICN, 6e. To Workingmen of Annapolis, Lexington *Observer & Ky. Reporter,* March 23, 1832, 6d.
 5 To Peter Hagner, DNA, 5.
 7 From George W. Spotswood, DLC-TJC, 2.
10 From Edward Dyer & Co., DLC-TJC, 9. From Byrd Monroe, DLC-TJC, 1, 5.
11 From Robert Walsh, DLC-HC, 6e.
12 From William H. Underwood, DLC-HC, 1, 10.
13 From James L. Edwards, DNA, 5.
14 To John Q. Adams, MHi-Adams Papers, 6d.
16 From David W. Nowlin, DLC-HC, 1, 10.
17 To Elijah Hayward, DNA, 2, 10.
19 From Elijah Hayward, DNA, 2, 10.
20 To Mrs. John Barney, NjP, 3, 6d.
22 From BUS-St. Louis branch, MoSHi, 9.
26 From Thomas Hart, DLC-TJC, 9.
31 From William North, DLC-TJC, 9.

APRIL 1832
10   From Thomas Hart Clay, DLC-TJC, 8, 9.
11   From Thomas P. Hart, DLC-TJC, 9. From R.B. Maury, DLC-HC, 1, 10.
16   From W.F. Dunnica, DLC-TJC, 7c, 9.
18   To Levi Woodbury, DNA, 1,2.
19   From Levi Woodbury, DNA, 2.

MAY 1832
 4   From John Sergeant, InU, 6c.
 6   From Charles McDougal, DLC-HC, 3.
10   From Elisha Meredith, DLC-HC, 1.
15   To John I. DeGraff, NcU, 2.
17   From Charles F. Mayer, DLC-HC, 2. From Francisco de Paula Santander, DLC-HC, 6f.
18   From James L. Edwards, DNA, 5. From George McCormick, DLC-HC, 6c, 6g.
22   From Harriet Barney, DNA, 4c. From Nathan Smith, DLC-TJC, 9.
27   From Thompson P. Ware, DLC-HC, 1, 3.
28   From J. Elliot, DLC-TJC, 9.

JUNE 1832
 2   From E.G. Emack, DLC-TJC, 9.
 5   From Willis Morgan, DLC-TJC, 5.
12   From Robert Mickle, DLC-HC, 4c, 7a.
20   From R.J. Curtis, DLC-HC, 5. From Hiram Ketchum, DLC-HC, 6c.

JULY 1832
14   From Nicholas Biddle, DLC-HC, 6f.
16   From David Barnum, DLC-TJC, 9. From Peter R. Stith, DLC-TJC, 9.
17   From Elijah Hayward, DNA, 2.

AUGUST 1832
 4   From Estate of F. Walker, DLC-TJC, 9.
11   To Charles R. Baldwin *et al.*, Wv-Ar, 6d.
14   From W.H. Plumb, DLC-TJC, 9.
22   From Porter, Biddle & Co., DLC-TJC, 9.
24   From T.W. Ducondray Holstein, DLC-HC, 6f.

SEPTEMBER 1832
 4   To James Erwin, Mary Clay Kenner Collection, Rogersville, Tenn., 9.
 7   To BUS-Lex. branch, Mary Clay Kenner Collection, Rogersville, Tenn., 7c, 9.
 8   From Susan Price, DLC-TJC, 7a, 9.
 9   Executor's Bond, Fayette Co. Executor's Bonds, No. 3 (1827-38), p. 85, 7a.
13   To BUS-Lex. branch, DLC-TJC, 9.
14   From Harrison Blanton, DLC-TJC, 7c.
17   To Fielding Bonham, Fleming Co. Deed Book R, pp. 222-23, 7a. To Francis R. Davis, Fleming Co. Deed Book R, p. 226, 7a. To William Estill, Fleming Co. Deed Book R, pp. 312-13, 7a. To George Latham, Fleming Co. Deed Book R, pp. 221-22, 7a. To Nat. Randall, Fleming Co. Deed Book R, p. 227, 7a.
18   To BUS-Lex. branch, DLC-TJC, 9.
20   From Benjamin & Ann M. Cassell, DLC-TJC, 8.
21   To BUS-Lex. branch, DLC-TJC, 9.
22   To Fielding L. Turner, Fayette Co. Deed Book 8, pp. 263-64, 7a.
27   To BUS-Lex. branch, Mary Clay Kenner Collection, Rogersville, Tenn., 9.

OCTOBER 1832
 6   To BUS-Lex. branch, Mary Clay Kenner Collection, Rogersville, Tenn., 7c, 9.
15   From J.R. Jackson, DLC-HC, 6c.
18   From W.P. Roper, DLC-TJC, 7a.
20   To BUS-Lex. branch, Mary Clay Kenner Collection, Rogersville, Tenn., 9. To BUS-Lex. branch, Mary Clay Kenner Collection, Rogersville, Tenn., 9.
21   To Andre B. Roman, KyU, 6c.
24   To David Daggett, CtY, 6c. From John W. Hunt, DLC-TJC, 9.

26 To BUS-Lex. branch, Mary Clay Kenner Collection, Rogersville, Tenn., 9.
30 From Dewees & Grant, DLC-TJC, 9. From W.J. Minor, DLC-TJC, 7a.
31 From John R. Shaw, DLC-TJC, 9.

NOVEMBER 1832
2 From Samuel Hanson, Josephine Simpson Collection, Lexington, Ky., 6g.
3 To John Q. Adams, MHi-Adams Papers, 2. From James Clark, Josephine Simpson Collection, Lexington, Ky., 6c, 6g. From N.F. Clarke, DLC-TJC, 11. From Isaac Cunningham, Josephine Simpson Collection, Lexington, Ky., 6c, 6g.
8 From Samuel Smith, DLC-TJC, 8.
12 To BUS-Lex. branch, Burton Milward Collection, Lexington, Ky., 9.
13 To George W. Morton, Mary Clay Kenner Collection, Rogersville, Tenn., 9. From Benjamin O. Peers, DLC-TJC, 9.
14 To BUS-Lex. branch, DLC-TJC, 9.
19 From Thomas P. Hart, DLC-TJC, 9. From William North, DLC-TJC, 9. From Smith & Hart, DLC-TJC, 9.
24 To Esther Morrison, DLC-TJC, 7c, 9. With Trustees of Transylvania University, KyLxT, 7c, 8.
25 From Richard Graham, MoSHi, 7c.
26 To BUS-Wash. branch, DLC-TJC, 9. With Thomas B. Megowan, DLC-James O. Harrison Papers, 8. From John Wirt, DLC-TJC, 9.
27 From Sarah Hall, DLC-TJC, 9.
28 To BUS-Lex. branch, Henry Clay Memorial Foundation, Lexington, Ky., 9.

DECEMBER 1832
1 From Benjamin O. Peers, DLC-TJC, 9.
17 From J. Andrews, NN, 9. To Samuel L. Southard, NjP, 11.
20 To Lynde Catlin, Lexington *Observer & Ky. Reporter*, Jan. 10, 1833, 6d.
22 From Samuel Franklin, DLC-TJC, 9.

JANUARY 1833
ca. 1833 From John Clark, DLC-TJC, 9. *Clay* v. *Bedford*, Ky, 7b. From Philip B. Hockaday, M.W. Anderson Collection, Lexington, Ky., 8. To Joseph S. Jenckes, InHi, 6d. Toast to Van Buren, DLC-HC, 11.
1 From George W. Anderson, DLC-TJC, 9.
4 To BUS, KyLoF, 8.
5 From Nathan Smith, DLC-TJC, 9.
12 To Tristam Burges, NBuHi, 6c.
22 From Pishey Thompson, DLC-TJC, 9.

FEBRUARY 1833
2 From Nathan Smith, DLC-TJC, 9.
4 From William Wirt, DLC-William Wirt Papers, 6c.
6 To John Y. Mason, ViHi, 6c.
9 From William B.L. Hopkins, DLC-TJC, 9.

MARCH 1833
2 From Nathan Smith, DLC-TJC, 9.
3 From Willie P. Mangum, DLC-HC, 11.
7 To BUS-Wash. branch, Mary Clay Kenner Collection, Rogersville, Tenn., 9.
11 From Duff Green, DLC-TJC, 9.
13 From Gales & Seaton, M.W. Anderson Collection, Lexington, Ky., 9. From Charles Polkinhorn, DLC-TJC, 9.
15 From BUS-Wash. branch, DLC-TJC, 9.
18 From Nathan Smith, DLC-TJC, 9.
29 From John Ruth, DLC-TJC, 9.

APRIL 1833
1 To BUS-Lex. branch, Henry Clay Memorial Foundation, Lexington, Ky., 9. From Joseph Ficklin, DLC-TJC, 9. From H.A. Griswold, DLC-TJC, 9. From George T. Morton, DLC-TJC, 9. From Transylvania University, DLC-TJC, 7c, 9.

4 From William A. Leavy, DLC-TJC, 9.
8 From William Martin, DLC-TJC, 9.
12 To Edmund H. Taylor, KyHi, 9.
15 To Levi Woodbury, DNA, 6a.
20 To William Pickerell, Fleming Co. Deed Book R, pp. 435-36, 8.
24 From John Boyle, DNA, 6a.
26 From Craig & Cochran, DLC-TJC, 9.

MAY 1833
1 To James Erwin, DLC-TJC, 9. From Thomas McCracken, DLC-TJC, 9.
6 From Peter Hagner, DNA, 7a.
11 From Thomas H. Pindell, DLC-TJC, 9.
13 Executor's Bond, Fayette Co. Executor's Bonds, No. 3 (1827-38), p. 100, 7a.
16 From Enoch Clark, DLC-TJC, 9. From James Garrard, DLC-TJC, 8.
20 To Edmund H. Taylor, KyHi, 9.
22 To Edmund H. Taylor, KyHi, 9.
24 To John J. Crittenden, KyLoF, 6c, 10.

JUNE 1833
1 From John Jones, DLC-TJC, 9. From Stephen Swift, DLC-TJC, 9.
3 To Edmund H. Taylor, KyHi, 7a.
7 From Porter Clay, M.W. Anderson Collection, Lexington, Ky., 8.
28 From Frederick Montmollin, DLC-TJC, 9.
29 From Frederick Montmollin, DLC-TJC, 9. From H. Shurlds, DLC-TJC, 9.

JULY 1833
9 To Frederick Montmollin, DLC-TJC, 9.
12 From James Shelby, DLC-TJC, 7a.
14 From Joseph Boswell, DLC-TJC, 9.
15 To BUS-Lex. branch, DLC-TJC, 9. To BUS-Lex. branch, DLC-TJC, 9. To Nicholas Biddle, DLC-TJC, 6g. From Richard Pindell, DLC-TJC, 7a, 9. From Susan Price, DLC-TJC, 7a, 9.
17 From January & Huston, DLC-TJC, 9.
18 From Eliza Ross, DLC-TJC, 7a, 9.
23 From J. Edrington, DLC-TJC, 9. From John Myers, DLC-TJC, 9.
26 From William Martin, DLC-TJC, 9.
31 From Benjamin Gratz, DLC-TJC, 9. From Phineas L. Tracy, DLC-TJC, 9.

AUGUST 1833
16 To William Dunlap, KyLxT, 8.
20 From J. Clarke & Co., DLC-TJC, 9.
29 From Augustus Hall, DLC-TJC, 9.

SEPTEMBER 1833
n.d. Endorsement, DLC-TJC, 7c.
6 From Thomas Rankin, DLC-TJC, 9.
9 From Thomas McCracken, DLC-TJC, 9.
11 From S. Swift & Co., DLC-TJC, 9.
12 From William Hawkins, DLC-TJC, 9.
13 From Abraham K. Smedes, DLC-TJC, 9.
14 From Smith & Hart, DLC-TJC, 9.
19 From John R. Shaw, DLC-TJC, 9.
23 From John Tilford, DLC-TJC, 9. From John Wirt, DLC-TJC, 9.
25 To BUS-Lex. branch, DLC-TJC, 9. From Thomas H. Pindell, DLC-TJC, 9.
26 From Thomas Bradley, DLC-TJC, 9.

OCTOBER 1833
ca. 1 From G.W. Pinnell, DLC-TJC, 9.
22 To General & Mrs. Lyman, MH, 6d. From Harrison Gray Otis, DLC-HC, 6e.
26 From Kitham, Mears & Co., DLC-TJC, 9.
28 To Samuel Elliott, MH, 6d.

NOVEMBER 1833

7　To ? Oakes, CtY, 6e.
12　*Wickliffe* v. *Clay* & *Clay* v. *Wickliffe*, *Reports of Select Cases Decided in the Court of Appeals of Ky.
　　. . . 1833*, p. 585-94, 7b.
14　To John M. Griffith *et al.*, Lexington *Observer & Ky. Reporter*, Dec. 5, 1833, 6e.
15　From Elijah Boardman, DLC-TJC, 9.
16　To ? Milford, NIC, 11.
23　From John Kirkpatrick, DLC-TJC, 9.
24　From Elisha Lee, DLC-TJC, 9.
29　To John Tuttle *et al.*, Richard Maass Collection, White Plains, N.Y., 6d.
30　From Samuel C. Owings, DLC-TJC, 9.

DECEMBER 1833

6　From Jesse Brown, DLC-TJC, 9.
12　From Nicholas Biddle, DLC-Nicholas Biddle Papers, 2.
14　From John Sergeant, DLC-TJC, 9. From C.H. & J.F. White, DLC-TJC, 9.
19　From Charles Polkinhorn, DLC-TJC, 9.
21　To C.C. Clay, Sr., NcD, 6a.

JANUARY 1834

ca.　1834To H.I. Bodley, DLC-TJC, 7a. *Burton* v. *Executor of John Gilmore*, KyLoF, 7a. From
　　heirs of Thomas Hart, DLC-TJC, 7a. To Henry Clay Walker, Kansas City *Kansan*, June ?,
　　1954, 11.
4　From January & Huston, DLC-TJC, 9.
7　To Levi Woodbury, DNA, 6a.
17　To Nicholas Biddle, DLC-Nicholas Biddle Papers, 9.
18　To BUS-Wash. branch, DLC-TJC, 9.
27　From Robert Keyworth, DLC-TJC, 9. From Thomas McCracken, DLC-TJC, 9.
30　From James K. Polk, DLC-James K. Polk Papers, 6a.

FEBRUARY 1834

3　To James Brown, KyLxT, 7a.
6　To ? Coke, Joseph V. Vanmeter Collection, Chillicothe, Ohio, 6c.
12　From King Holbrook & Co., DLC-TJC, 9. To George W. Lay, DLC-George W. Lay
　　Papers, 2.
18　From John Clements, DLC-TJC, 9. To John Floyd, Vi, 6c.

MARCH 1834

4　From Whitney & Co., DLC-TJC, 9.
14　From John Hutchcraft, DLC-TJC, 9.
15　To BUS-Wash. branch, DLC-TJC, 9.
17　To BUS-Wash. branch, DLC-TJC, 9.
20　To BUS-New York branch, NN, 9. To BUS-Wash. branch, DLC-TJC, 9.
21　To Robert J. Breckinridge, DLC-Breckinridge Family Papers, 6c.
22　From King Holbrook & Co., DLC-TJC, 9.
24　To BUS-Wash. branch, DLC-TJC, 9.
25　*Wickliffe* v. *Clay*, Ky, 7a.
26　To BUS-Wash. branch, DLC-TJC, 9.
29　To BUS-Wash. branch, DLC-TJC, 9.
31　*Wickliffe* v. *Clay*, Ky, 7a.

APRIL 1834

1　To BUS-Lex. branch, DLC-TJC, 9. To Lewis Cass, NN, 5. From Madison C. Johnson,
　　DLC-TJC, 7c, 9.
2　From Isaac Bartlett, DLC-TJC, 9.
4　From King Holbrook & Co., DLC-TJC, 9.
11　To BUS-Wash. branch, DLC-TJC, 9.
16　From Uriah F. Hyde, DLC-TJC, 9.
17　From Isaac Bartlett, DLC-TJC, 9.
19　From John E. Foulke, DLC-TJC, 9.
28　To BUS-Wash. branch, DLC-TJC, 9. From Lewis Hardon, DLC-TJC, 8, 9.
29　To BUS-Wash. branch, DLC-TJC, 9.

MAY 1834
12 From Gales & Seaton, DLC-TJC, 9.
13 From Levi Pumphrey, DLC-TJC, 9.
14 To H.V.R. Schemmerhorn, NHi, 10. From Nathan Smith, DLC-TJC, 9.
15 From Tucker & Thompson, DLC-TJC, 9.
16 From Pishey Thompson, DLC-TJC, 9.
18 To Elijah Hayward, DNA, 5, 6a.
22 From Tucker & Thompson, DLC-TJC, 9.
26 *Clay* v. *Marshall et al.*, Ky, 7b. To Esther Morrison, DLC-TJC, 7c, 9.
29 To Jacob Burnet, Dr. Holman Hamilton Collection, Lexington, Ky., 6c. From Patrick
    Byrne, DLC-TJC, 9. To Levi Woodbury, DNA, 6a.
30 From Levi Woodbury, DNA, 6a.

JUNE 1834
 1 To Hugh Mercer, J. Winston Coleman, Jr., Collection, Lexington, Ky., 6d.
 3 To Nicholas Biddle, DLC-Nicholas Biddle Papers, 6c.
 6 From Duff Green, DLC-TJC, 9.
16 To Unknown Recipient, MB, 9.
21 To Maria Ewing, DLC-Thomas Ewing Papers, 6e.
27 To James Caldwell, ViHi, 6c.
28 To Thomas Biddle, NN, 6c. From Thomas H. Jacobs, DLC-TJC, 9. From Derrick Warner,
    DLC-TJC, 9.
29 To January & Huston, KyU, 10.
30 From Levi Pumphrey, DLC-TJC, 9.

JULY 1834
n.d. To Mr. & Mrs. Samuel L. Southard & Virginia Southard, NjP, 6c.
 1 From Nathan Smith, DLC-TJC, 9.
 5 From John Nitchie, Colton, *Clay Correspondence*, 4:384, 11. From John Cotton Smith, DLC-
    HC, 11.
11 From Thomas Huggins, DLC-TJC, 9. From Levi Woodbury, DNA, 7c.

AUGUST 1834
n.d. From John Anderson, DLC-TJC, 9. From William North, DLC-TJC, 9. *Wickliffe* v. *Clay*,
KyLoF, 7b.
 7 From William Martin, DLC-TJC, 9.
 9 From J. Norse, DLC-TJC, 9.
11 From Benjamin Chapeze, DLC-TJC, 7a. From Thomas McCracken, DLC-TJC, 9.
22 From Abraham K. Smedes, DLC-TJC, 9.
24 To January & Huston, Maysville (Ky.) Public Library, 7a.
25 From Levi Woodbury, DNA, 7c.
26 From Richard H. Chinn, DLC-TJC, 9. From Thomas McCracken, DLC-TJC, 9. Thomas
    McCracken, DLC-TJC, 9.
29 From Coster & Berryman, Josephine Simpson Collection, Lexington, Ky., 8, 9.

SEPTEMBER 1834
 3 From Henry Clay Hart, DLC-TJC, 9.
 4 From Richard Pindell, DLC-TJC, 7a, 9. From Eliza Rosse, DLC-TJC, 7a, 9.
10 From January & Huston, DLC-TJC, 9.
12 From Levi Woodbury, DNA, 7c.
ca. 14 From January & Huston, DLC-TJC, 9.
15 From James Shelby, DLC-TJC, 7a, 9.
16 *Clay* v. *Morris*, Ky, 7b.
18 From Micajah Harrison, DLC-TJC, 7a.
20 From William Rockhill, DLC-TJC, 9. To Charles R. Vaughan, Codrington Library, All
    Souls College, Oxford, England, 6c. From Levi Woodbury, DNA, 7c.
23 From James Erwin, DLC-TJC, 9.
27 *Wickliffe* v. *Clay*, Ky, 7b.
28 From Buckner H. Payne, M.W. Anderson Collection, Lexington, Ky., 8.
30 From Buckner H. Payne, Josephine Simpson Collection, Lexington, Ky., 8.

OCTOBER 1834

n.d. To Fayette Co. Court Clerk, DLC-TJC, 8. To Fayette Co. Sheriff, DLC-TJC, 7a.

20 *Wickliffe* v. *Clay*, Ky, 7b. From Elijah Hayward, DNA, 2. From Levi Woodbury, DLC-TJC, 7c.

21 *Wickliffe* v. *Clay*, Ky, 7b.

22 To BUS-Lex. branch, DLC-TJC, 9.

23 *Wickliffe* v. *Clay*, Ky, 7b.

24 *Wickliffe* v. *Clay*, Ky, 7b.

27 To BUS-Lex. branch, Mary Clay Kenner Collection, Rogersville, Tenn., 7c, 9.

28 From G.W. Laudeman, DLC-TJC, 9. To John Milton, DLC-TJC, 7c.

29 To William S. Dallam, DLC-TJC, 9.

30 To Robert Wickliffe, Ky, 7b.

NOVEMBER 1834

6 To BUS-Lex. branch, Mary Clay Kenner Collection, Rogersville, Tenn., 9.

7 From Robert Wickliffe, DLC-HC, 7c.

8 From Susan Price, DLC-TJC, 7a, 9.

10 To BUS-Lex. branch, Mary Clay Kenner Collection, Rogersville, Tenn., 7c, 9, To BUS-Lex. branch, Henry Clay Memorial Foundation, Lexington, Ky., 9. To Sidney Edmiston, DLC-TJC, 9. From Joseph Ficklin, KyLxT, 7d, 9.

11 From H.I. Bodley, DLC-TJC, 7b. From John Headley, DLC-TJC, 9. From Madison C. Johnson, DLC-TJC, 7b. From Matthew T. Scott, DLC-TJC, 9.

12 From Thomas McCracken, DLC-TJC, 9. From Thomas H. Pindell, DLC-TJC, 19. From Samuel Redd, DLC-TJC, 9.

13 From Gales & Seaton, DLC-TJC, 9.

ca. 15 From Richard Cole, DLC-TJC, 8.

18 To Gideon Shryock, DLC-TJC, 7c.

24 From Sanford Vanpelt, DLC-TJC, 9.

26 To Gideon Shryock, DLC-TJC, 7c.

DECEMBER 1834

10 From S.L. Fairfield, DLC-TJC, 9. From W.R. Senter, DLC-TJC, 9.

12 From Ambrose Young, DLC-TJC, 9.

16 From Erskine Eichelberger & Co., DLC-TJC, 9. From Elijah Hayward, DNA, 2, 5.

20 To John Forsyth, DNA, 1.

22 To James L. Edwards, NN, 1. From Erskine Eichelberger & Co., DLC-TJC, 9. From A.J.W. Jackson *et al.*, DLC-TJC, 6d.

23 To John Forsyth, DNA, 1, 2.

24 To John Q. Adams, MHi-Adams Papers, 6d.

25 From James Hamilton, DLC-TJC, 9.

26 From Baltimore & Washington Stage Co., DLC-TJC, 9.

27 From O. Farra, DLC-TJC, 9.

30 From ? Dowden, DLC-TJC, 9. From Mrs. ? Pilkington, DLC-TJC, 9.

31 From J. Durham, DLC-TJC, 9. From Joseph Ficklin, DLC-TJC, 9.

JANUARY 1835

1 From William Martin, DLC-TJC, 9.

5 To John Q. Adams, MHi-Adams Papers, 2, 6e. From John S. Mitchell, DLC-TJC, 7a, 9.

8 To January & Huston, MHi, 8.

15 From Sidney Smith, DLC-TJC, 11.

18 From Sidney Smith, DLC-TJC, 9.

20 From Craig & Warner, DLC-TJC, 9.

30 From John Scott, Nj P, 6c.

FEBRUARY 1835

n.d. To Nicholas Biddle, DLC-Nicholas Biddle Papers, 6c.

11 From Thomas P. Hart, DLC-TJC, 7e.

13 From Elijah Hayward, DNA, 5.

20 To Francis T. Brooke, NcD, 2, 6c.

22 From BUS-Phila. branch, DLC-TJC, 9.

MARCH 1835

n.d. From John Bailhache, DLC-TJC, 9. To Fayette Co. Circuit Court Clerk, KyLxT, 7d. From Todd & Co., DLC-TJC, 9.
 4 From T.K. Layton & Co., DLC-TJC, 9.
 5 From Robert Fleming, DLC-TJC, 9. From Norman Porter, DLC-TJC, 9. From Enoch Tucker, DLC-TJC, 9.
 8 From Nathan Smith, DLC-TJC, 9.
10 From William & James Crook, DLC-TJC, 9.
18 From Stephen Simpson, DLC-TJC, 9.
20 From Samuel Smith, DLC-TJC, 8, 9.
23 From J.B. Hockaday, DLC-TJC, 8, 9. From H. Maguire, DLC-TJC, 9.
25 To Henry Clay Hart, Benjamin H. Branch, Jr., Collection, Arlington, Va., 9.
27 From Esther Morrison, DLC-TJC, 7c.
30 From John Headley, DLC-TJC, 9.

APRIL 1835

 1 From Madison C. Johnson, DLC-TJC, 7c, 9.
 2 From John W. Hunt & son, DLC-TJC, 9.
 3 From Lemuel Franklin, DLC-TJC, 9. From Gideon Shryock, DLC-TJC, 8.
 6 From Gales & Seaton, DLC-TJC, 9. From ? Milton, DLC-TJC, 8, 9. From Gideon Shryock, DLC-TJC, 8, 9.
11 From Thomas Bradley, DLC-TJC, 9.
12 From Finnell & Zimmerman, DLC-TJC, 8, 9.
13 To David Daggett, CtY, 6c. From John W. Hunt & son, DLC-TJC, 9.
18 To Nicholas Biddle, DLC-Nicholas Biddle Papers, 6c.
20 From Walter Smith, DLC-TJC, 9.
21 To Thomas H. Genin, KyU, 6e.
23 To BUS-Lex. branch, DLC-TJC, 9.
25 To Robert J. Breckinridge, DLC-Breckinridge Family Papers, 6c. To Aaron Vail, Jaques de Bon Collection, Geneva, Switzerland, 6c. To Whom It May Concern, DLC-Breckinridge Family Papers, 6c.
27 From George & Robert Blackburn & Co., DLC-TJC, 9. From George & Robert Blackburn & Co., DLC-TJC, 9. From Daniel Webster, MH, 6c.
29 To BUS-Lex. branch, DLC-TJC, 9.
30 From J.B. Boswell, DLC-TJC, 9.

MAY 1835

 6 From Walter Smith, DLC-TJC, 9.
 9 From L.H. Van Doren, DLC-TJC, 9.
11 To BUS-Lex. branch, Mary Clay Kenner Collection, Rogersville, Tenn., 9.
12 From Gideon Shryock, DLC-TJC, 8.
13 From Samuel Peel, DLC-TJC, 8, 9.
16 To Gideon Shryock, KyHi, 8.
18 To BUS-Lex. branch, DLC-TJC, 9.
28 From Thomas Huggins, DLC-TJC, 9.

JUNE 1835

 2 From Alexander Gibney, DLC-TJC, 9. From T.K. Layton & Co., DLC-TJC, 9. From T.K. Layton & Co., DLC-TJC, 9.
 5 From Thomas Smith, DLC-TJC, 8, 9.
 9 To BUS-Lex. branch, DLC-TJC, 9.
10 From William Boner, DLC-TJC, 9. From January & Huston, DLC-TJC, 9.
16 From George Ballard, DLC-TJC, 8, 9.
26 To Daniel Webster, John Mason Brown Collection, New York, N.Y., 6c.
29 From John Anderson, DLC-TJC, 9. From Thomas McCracken, DLC-TJC, 9. From Elijah Noble, DLC-TJC, 9.
30 From J. Durham, DLC-TJC, 9. From H. Maguire, DLC-TJC, 9. From Stephens, Winslow & Stephens, DLC-TJC, 9.

JULY 1835
 6 From James H. Lewis, DLC-TJC, 9.
 8 From Thomas Huggins, DLC-TJC, 9. From Thomas Huggins, DLC-TJC, 9.
13 To BUS-Lex. branch, DLC-TJC, 9.
18 To BUS-Lex. branch, DLC-TJC, 9. From William Buford, DLC-TJC, 8.
22 From Patrick Doyle, DLC-TJC, 9.
23 From J. Edrington, DLC-TJC, 9.
24 To BUS-Lex. branch, DLC-TJC, 9. From Thomas Theobald, DLC-TJC, 9.
28 From P. Dudley & Co., DLC-TJC, 9.
29 From Prime, Ward, King & Co., DLC-TJC, 9.

AUGUST 1835
 1 From A. Fisk, Watt & Co., DLC-TJC, 9.
 3 To Bus-Lex. branch, DLC-TJC, 9.
 4 To Ariss Throckmorton *et al.*, Frankfort *Commonwealth*, August 15, 1835, 6d.
12 From Walter Smith, DLC-TJC, 9.
20 From D.K. Minor, DLC-TJC, 9.
23 From J.T. Frazer & Co., DLC-TJC, 9.
24 From John S. Hart, DLC-TJC, 7e.
28 To BUS-Phila. branch, KyU, 9. From William North, DLC-TJC, 9.
29 To BUS-Lex. branch, DLC-TJC, 9.
31 From Prime, Ward, King & Co., DLC-HC, 9.

SEPTEMBER 1835
n.d. To H.I. Bodley, KyLxT, 7d. Endorsement, DLC-TJC, 7e. From J.C. Rodes, KyLxT,
      7d. From J.C. Rodes, KyLxT, 7d.
 1 From James B. Duncan, DLC-TJC, 8, 9.
 4 From Willcox & Feam, DLC-TJC, 9.
21 From Alexander R. Atchison, DLC-TJC, 8, 9. From Henry Daniel, KyLxT, 7d.
26 From John Love, KyLxT, 9.

OCTOBER 1835
n.d. From J.C. Rodes, KyLxT, 7d.
 1 From Madison C. Johnson, DLC-TJC, 7c.
 3 From John McCauley, DLC-TJC, 9.
 5 To Benjamin Kellogg, Jr., DLC-Benjamin Kellogg Papers, 7a.
 6 From T.K. Layton & Co., DLC-TJC, 9.
 7 From Joseph Goss, DLC-TJC, 9. From Thomas McCracken, DLC-TJC, 9. From Thomas
      McCracken, DLC-TJC, 9.
12 To John Forsyth, DNA, 1, 2.
20 To Norborne B. Beall, KyLoF, 7a.
21 From Benjamin Warfield & Thomas Smith, DLC-TJC, 8.
24 From John Hutchcraft, DLC-HC, 6a, 10.
27 From Richard H. Chinn, KyLxT, 7d. To Unknown Recipient, Bibliotheque de L'Arsenal,
      Paris, France, 10.
28 From John Jacob Astor, DLC-TJC, 9. To William Grundy, Union Co. Circuit Court,
      Morganfield, Ky., 7c.

NOVEMBER 1835
n.d. From Jacob Swigert, KyLxT, 7d.
 4 From Thomas P. Satterwhite, DLC-TJC, 9.
 7 From John W. Hunt & son, DLC-TJC, 9.
11 From Joseph George, DLC-TJC, 9.
12 To Robert Fisk, DLC-TJC, 9. To Northern Bank of Ky., Mary Clay Kenner Collection,
      Rogersville, Tenn., 9.
13 To Trustees of Transylvania University, KyLxT, 11.
14 To Northern Bank of Ky., DLC-TJC, 9. To Northern Bank of Ky., DLC-TJC, 9. To
      George S. Still *et al.*, NjR, 6d. From Robert Wickliffe, DLC-TJC, 7a.
16 From John Atkinson, DLC-TJC, 9. From T.K. Layton & Co., DLC-TJC, 9. From John
      McCracken, DLC-TJC, 9. From William North, DLC-TJC, 9. From William Rockhill

DLC-TJC, 9. To Trustees of Transylvania University, DLC-TJC, 7c, 9.
17 To George W. Anderson, DLC-TJC, 9. To Thomas N. Lindsey, KyLoF, 7c.
18 From Gales & Seaton, DLC-TJC, 9.
20 To Asbury Dickins, DLC-Asbury Dickins Papers, 2.
26 To James E. Davis, DLC-TJC, 7a, 9. From Henry Clay Hart, DLC-TJC, 7a. From Susan
    Price, DLC-TJC, 7a.

DECEMBER 1835
 1 From Levi Pumphrey, DLC-TJC, 8, 9.
 8 From J.H. Page, DLC-TJC, 9.
 9 To Thomas N. Lindsey, KyLoF, 8.
14 From S.L. Fairfield, DLC-TJC, 9.
18 To Margaret C. Meade, ViU, 6a, 10.
21 From James Stuart, KyLxT, 7d.
23 To S. Jaudon, Robert H. Goldman Collection, Springfield, Ill., 9.
29 To James Taylor, OCHP, 7a.
30 From Ethan A. Brown, DNA, 2, 5, 7a. To Ethan A. Brown, DNA, 1, 5, 7a. Notice, NcD, 6d.
31 To Ethan A. Brown, DNA, 5, 7a. To James Ronaldson, KyU, 6f.

JANUARY 1836
ca. 1836 *Clay* v. *Commonwealth of Ky.*, Ky, 7b.
 2 To John Ridgely, DLC-TJC, 7c, 9.
 6 From James Ackland, DLC-TJC, 9. From Daniel F. Patterson, Josephine Simpson Collec-
    tion, Lexington, Ky., 9.
23 To Littleton W. Tazewell, KyU, 6c.
30 To Northern Bank of Ky., OC, 9.

FEBRUARY 1836
 3 To John Forsyth, DNA, 1, 6a.
 4 From John Forsyth, DNA, 2.
 8 From Richard Higgins, DLC-TJC, 9.
 9 From John Forsyth, DNA, 10. To John Forsyth, DNA, 1, 2.
11 To John Harvie, ViU, 6c.
16 To Logan, Frazer & Co., DLC-TJC, 8.
17 To Whom It May Concern, DLC-HC, 9.
20 From Levi Woodbury, DNA, 2, 5.
24 To John Forsyth, DNA, 1.
25 From John Forsyth, DNA, 11. From Levi Woodbury, DNA, 7a.

MARCH 1836
 2 From Mahlon Dickerson, DNA, 2.
 9 From A. Favier, DLC-TJC, 9.
10 From Louisa Caroline Jeffrey, Colton, *Clay Correspondence*, 4:404-5, 6e.
11 To James L. Edwards, NN, 1.

APRIL 1836
n.d. From E.E.J. Swigert, KyLxT, 7d.
 6 To John Headley, Josephine Simpson Collection, Lexington, Ky., 8.
16 From Rezin D. Shepherd, DLC-TJC, 9.
21 From Duff Green, DLC-TJC, 9.
22 To Nicholas Biddle, DLC-Nicholas Biddle Papers, 6c. To Edward Everett, MHi, 6c.
25 From Charles Ingersoll, KyLxT, 7e.
28 From John Jacob Astor, MH, 9. From Madison C. Johnson, DLC-HC, 7c, 9.
29 From Richard W. Vansant, DLC-TJC, 8, 9.

MAY 1836
 2 From Duff Green, DLC-TJC, 9. From Enoch C. Wines, DLC-TJC, 9.
 4 From John M. Clay, DLC-TJC, 9. From M.A. Clements, DLC-TJC, 9.
 7 From James B. Clay, DLC-TJC, 9.
14 To James Caldwell, ViHi, 6c.
20 To Siler, Price & Co., Robert H. Ferrell Collection, Bloomington, Ind., 9.

21 To Joseph Lancaster, ICHi, 2.
26 To Virgil David, ICU, 6e.
31 From Richard W. Vansant, DLC-TJC, 9.

JUNE 1836
 6 From Charles Ingersoll, DLC-TJC, 7e.
 7 To John Fane, 11th Earl of Westmoreland, DLC-James H. Hammond Papers, 6c. From John & Anne Marie Farrell, DLC-TJC, 8.
 9 To Thomas Biddle, DLC-Nicholas Biddle Papers, 6c.
20 To Nicholas Biddle, DLC-Nicholas Biddle Papers, 6c. To Lawrence Lewis, J. Winston Coleman, Jr., Collection, Lexington, Ky., 6c.
21 From Nathaniel P. Causin, DLC-TJC, 9.
23 From Nathaniel P. Causin, DLC-TJC, 9.
25 To J.W. Ware, OFH, 6d.
27 *Wickliffe* v. *Clay*, DLC-TJC, 7b.
28 To Edward Everett, MHi, 6c.
29 From Desangue & Huber, DLC-TJC, 9.

JULY 1836
n.d. From H.I. Bodley, KyLxT, 7d.
 2 To Grant & Stone, DLC-TJC, 9. From Enoch Tucker, DLC-TJC, 9.
10 From January & Huston, DLC-TJC, 9.
16 From January & Huston, DLC-TJC, 9. To Northern Bank of Ky., DLC-TJC, 9. To Levi Woodbury, DLC-Levi Woodbury Papers, 6c.
18 From James Crawford, DLC-TJC, 7a.
21 To Northern Bank of Ky., DLC-TJC, 9.
26 From Harriet Martineau, DLC-HC, 6e.
28 From Thomas L. Winthrop, DLC-HC, 6e.

AUGUST 1836
 1 To Robert Wickliffe, DLC-TJC, 7b.
 6 To Matthew L. Bevan, DLC-Nicholas Biddle Papers, 6c. To Conway D. Whittle, ViU, 10.
11 From Charles Higbee, DLC-TJC, 8.
15 From Bell & Hale, DLC-TJC, 9.
24 From John Dement, DLC-TJC, 9.
30 From John Headley, DLC-TJC, 9.

SEPTEMBER 1836
14 To Northern Bank of Ky., DLC-TJC, 9.
15 From Ethan A. Brown, DNA, 7c.
16 To Northern Bank of Ky., DLC-TJC, 9. To Northern Bank of Ky., DLC-TJC, 9.

OCTOBER 1836
n.d. From James Erwin, DLC-TJC, 9.
 1 From John W. Hunt, KyLxT, 9. To John Raush, DLC-TJC, 9.
 7 From John Jacob Astor, DLC-HC, 9. From Moore, Morton & Co., DLC-TJC, 9.
 8 To Samuel C. Reid, KyU, 6c. To Henry Thompson, Edgar E. Hume, Jr., Collection, n.p., 6c.
19 From John Wirt, DLC-TJC, 9.
22 To Northern Bank of Ky., Mary Clay Kenner Collection, Rogersville, Tenn., 9.

NOVEMBER 1836
 8 From Morehead & Brown, KyLxT, 7d.
12 From Edmund Grayson, DLC-TJC, 9.
14 From Thomas Smith, DLC-TJC, 9.
19 To Northern Bank of Ky., Mary Clay Kenner Collection, Rogersville, Tenn., 9.
21 From Moore, Morton & Co., DLC-TJC, 9.
22 From Thomas Broadus, DLC-TJC, 9. To Northern Bank of Ky., Mary Clay Kenner Collection, Rogersville, Tenn., 9.
23 From William R. Morton, DLC-TJC, 9.
30 From William Botts, DLC-HC, 7a.

DECEMBER 1836
 7 From Allen & Grant, DLC-TJC, 9.

7 From James Whitcomb, DNA, 5.
15 To Nicholas Biddle, DLC-Nicholas Biddle Papers, 6c. To James Kent, DLC-James Kent Papers, 6c.
27 To James Whitcomb, DNA, 5.
28 To Edward A. Lesley, PCarlD, 6e.

NAME & SUBJECT INDEX: VOLUME 8

The editors present here a combined name and subject index similar to that found in Volume 7, pages 651-90, and do so with the reminder that the Subject Index for Volumes 1-6 is to be found in Volume 7, pages 691-777. Primary responsibility for the subject entries rests with the senior editor. The name entries are the work of Margaret Spratt-Wyatt, assisted by Caroline Parrish Seager.

The editors also present, for the historical record, Henry Clay's views on the general subject of indexes. Asked on April 11, 1832 to support an amendment to the general appropriation bill that would provide $2500 each to the secretaries of state, treasury, war, and navy "to have the papers in their departments arranged and indexed," Senator Clay characterized the idea as "a most extraordinary and useless appropriation of money," since "it had never, within his knowledge, taken five minutes to find any document, unless it was, perhaps, an old revolutionary [war] paper."

Allen (Michael) & Grant (George) Commission Merchants: from, 89; mentioned, 31
Allin, Susan B., 862
Allin, Thomas, 862
American Annual Register, 231
American Civil War, 736
American Colonization Society: of Ky., 127, 157-58, 161-62, 167, 169, 625, 858; of N.Y., 852; mentioned, 7, 34, 132, 138, 147-48, 151-52, 155, 234, 258, 313, 390, 471, 483, 537, 653, 754, 865, 874
American Farmer & Turf Register, 232
American Hotel (New York City), 663
American Hotel (Washington), 667
American Institute, 856
American Revolution, 141-42, 148, 430, 509, 576, 679, 690, 695, 726, 732-34, 744, 758, 765, 840, 844, 854, 873
American System
—general: newspaper support for, 82; Ky. support for, 109, 113, 238; lower classes relationship to, 120, 243; Jefferson said to be father of, 258, 271; early C. support for, 258; C. lauded as father of, 307; C. first employs term, 252 (*see also* 3:701); South's opposition to, 105; New England support for, 307; coastal defense needs related to, 458; support for among Anti-Masons (*see* Anti-Masonic party)
—domestic manufactures: C. support of, 11-13, 280, 345-46, 375; slump in level of, 108; decrease in price of, 544; growth of New England textiles industry, 352; U.S. competition with British cotton textiles, 352; growth of in West, 352; attitudes in South toward, 69; in R.I., 105; in Pittsburgh, 345-46; in Louisville, 860; manufacturers laud C., 254, 280; American Institute promotes, 856. *See also* Congress of the United States: 22, 23, 24 Cong.–various entries on tariff issue
—internal improvements: C. support of roads, 2, 20, 375; C. on Maysville Road, 70, 122-23; Maysville-Lexington Turnpike, 347-48; macadam process, 123; Delaware & Chesapeake Canal, 239; Louisville Canal, 238, 759, 852; Ohio Canal, 452-53;

hold nation together, 249, 422, 635; national security dimensions of, 105, 239, 244, 829-30; permanency of system of, 59; tariff surplus investment in, 377; Adams administration support of, 57-58, 69; attitudes of South toward, 69; interest of West in, 20, 238; relationship of national railroad development to, 843; railroad development in Ky. (*see* Kentucky)
—protective tariff: C. support of & arguments for, 1-2, 14-15, 58, 81, 101, 105, 124-25, 243, 280, 324-25, 345-46, 374-75 (*see also* Congress of the United States); produces economic prosperity, 11, 12-13, 108-9; on sugar, 324-26; demands for on woolens, 356, 403; farmers' stake in on woolens, 550-51; produces treasury surplus problem, 813, 854; relationship of to public debt, 403; support for in Ky., 113; support for in New England, 70-71, 307; attitudes toward in South, 57-58 (*see also* Congress of the United States; Tariff); Anti-Masonic attitudes toward, 248; mentioned, 10, 19, 21, 52, 77, 83, 94-95, 106, 121, 137, 173, 177, 180, 200-201, 240-41, 260, 267, 269-70, 278, 282, 286, 294, 303, 310, 314, 350-51, 366, 381, 405-6, 419, 430, 445, 455, 475, 477, 487, 492, 505, 507, 515, 549, 606, 618, 624, 626, 666, 720, 784, 790, 800, 863. *See* Congress of the United States: 22, 23, 24 Cong.
American Whig and Knoxville Enquirer, 94
Anderson, George W. & Co., 86, 867
Anderson, Joseph, 262, 688, 690
Anderson, Richard C., Jr., 2
Angoura (horse), 866
Annals of Congress, 788
Annapolis, Md., 223
Anne Arundel Co., Md., 104, 237
Anthony (slave), 85
Anti-Masonic Party
—general: Lockport trials, 353, 354, 362; principles of, 195, 267-68, 290-92, 300-302, 303-4, 388, 390, 393-95, 398, 414-15, 436; aggressiveness of, 254; party organization, 300-302; political tactics of, 290-92,

300-302, 303-4, 409-10, 411-12, 413-14, 414-15, 416; growth of in U.S., 127, 195, 361, 406; opposition to Jackson in, 254, 256, 260, 270, 492; opposition to Van Buren & Regency in, 393; splits within, 301; alliances with Jacksonians, 301, 303; political components of, 500-501; character of, 411; support for American System within, 248, 303, 414; possible choices for nomination of a presidential candidate for 1832, 361, 364-65, 367, 374, 383, 384, 392-93, 393-95, 398, 404, 404-5; nominates Wirt for president (*see* Election (presidential) of 1832: William Wirt role in); John McLean relations with and as possible candidate of (*see* McLean, John); support for Calhoun within, 291 (*see also* Calhoun, John C.). *See also* Election (presidential) of 1832: Anti-Masonic role in
—campaign activity, prognoses, influence & political problems of in various states & sections: Kentucky, 506; Maryland, 362; Massachusetts, 586; New England, 353, 385, 394; New Jersey, 318, 404, 573, 575, 595, 601-2; New York, 107-8, 195, 204-5, 240-41, 246-48, 254, 260, 267, 270, 278, 283-84, 290-92, 293, 294-95, 296, 297, 300-302, 302, 303-4, 305, 306, 308, 311, 317, 331, 340, 353-54, 361, 362, 364-65, 381, 383, 393-94, 401, 404, 422-23, 443, 492-93, 512, 519-20, 573; Ohio, 303, 361, 577-78 (*see also* Ohio); Pennsylvania, 78, 127, 164, 195, 256, 260, 270, 293, 303-4, 305, 306, 346, 356, 362, 364, 365-66, 367-68, 381, 383, 399, 469-70, 513, 514, 519, 519-20, 522-23, 568, 569, 573-74, 588-89, 593; Vermont, 353, 423; mentioned, 118, 172, 286-87, 299, 310, 343, 387, 425, 430, 432, 462, 505, 517, 526, 528, 532, 534, 541, 562, 564-67, 575, 582, 592, 597, 612, 618, 648, 683, 725, 785, 800
—Clay relations with and attitudes toward: sounds out C. on his views, 197; C. on Masons & Masonry (*see* Masonic Order); C. on constitutional rights of, 381, 384,

Baltimore, Md., (continued)
447, 500, 458-59, 462, 483,
494, 507, 513, 516, 523, 527,
533-34, 542, 584-85, 606-7,
631, 663-66, 668, 715, 719,
729-31, 796, 799, 804-5, 810,
830, 835-36, 850
Baltimore *Chronicle & Daily
Marylander*, 183-84
Baltimore Co., Md., 669
Baltimore & Ohio Railroad,
209, 670
Baltimore & Wheeling Transportation Line Co., 606
Bancroft, George, 282, 285
Bankhead, Charles, 828
Bank of the United States
(BUS): C. opinion of,
129-30, 552-53; C. shift
(1816) of opinion on (*see
espec.* 2:200-205), 342-44,
413-14, 552-53, 697-98, 723;
C. work for & connection
with, 129-30, 680, 721; C.
denies later connection with,
721; proposed charter
change, 426; C. on early
renewal of charter of (see
Election (presidential) of
1832: issues, charges & counter-charges in campaign–
BUS charter renewal);
Jackson attacks on (*see* Congress of the United States: 21
Cong., 2 Sess., 22 Cong., 1
Sess., 23 Cong., 1 Sess., Election (presidential) of 1832;
Jackson administration); C.
loans from, 556-57; reaction
to cholera epidemic, 685; C.
solicits turnpike road financial
aid from, 129-30, 160,
165-66, 347-48, 351, 490 (*see
also* Lexington, Ky.); C.
solicits financial aid for Transylvania University from,
129-30; branch in Lexington,
265; power in Ky., 129-30;
constitutionality of, 365-66;
unpopularity in Pa., 595-96;
Exchange Committee of,
680-81; Nashville branch of,
628; Washington branch of,
581; status of notes issued by,
840; Senate investigation of,
619, 623-24; C. pronounces
"dead," 791-92; bill to sell
govt.-owned stock of, 623-24;
U.S. v. *Brewster* on currency
of, 750-51; brokerage fees in
Ky., 452; problem with
govt.-appointed directors of,
680-81, 682; issue in 1834
mid-term elections, 742;
begins winding up business
after U.S. deposit with-
drawals, 696, 724; men-
tioned, 17, 103, 138, 195-96,
205, 210, 217-18, 223-24,

233, 242-43, 263-64, 282,
287-88, 320, 343, 356, 363,
366, 375, 415, 420, 423, 432,
434-35, 437-39, 443-46, 450,
453, 455, 458, 468, 470,
473-74, 477, 480, 483, 493,
495, 498-500, 504, 506-8,
513, 515, 521-24, 526-29,
532, 546-47, 549, 551, 558,
562-64, 566, 574, 577, 583,
588, 592, 613, 627, 630,
640-41, 655, 668, 672-75,
678-79, 683-84, 686-89,
691-93, 695, 700, 702, 705,
708, 712, 714, 717, 720, 722,
725, 728, 730, 733-35, 737,
741, 750-51, 769-70, 779,
794-96, 806, 813, 827, 837.
See also Biddle, Nicholas;
Jackson administration
Banks, Linn, 397
Banta, Henry (not identified),
613
Baptist Church, 582
Barbara (slave), 87
Barbour, James: returns home
from Europe, 127; testimonial
dinner for, 131; on Jackson
administration, 158; on C.
presidential candidacy in
1832, 158; president of National Republican nominating
convention (1831), 431; C.
visits, 558; offers slaves for
sale, 681; offers thoroughbred
horse for sale to C., 757; analysis of Va. presidential politics
(1836) for C., 795-96; from,
158, 470, 757, 795; to, 127,
430, 472, 629; mentioned, 61,
86, 100, 131, 410-11, 418,
434, 463, 474, 486, 526, 531,
543, 574, 683, 819
Barbour, Philip P.: appointed
to U.S. Supreme Court,
406-7; as possible vice presidential candidate on Jackson
ticket (1832), 557-58; mentioned, 745
Bardstown, Ky., 39, 81, 113,
200, 216, 479, 592, 625, 653
Barger, John L.: from, 6
Baring Brothers & Co., 864
Baring, Me., 562
Barnard, Isaac D., 286
Barnes, Lewis L.: to, 280
Barnes, Samuel: to, 183;
mentioned, 13
Barnett Shorb & Co.: from,
346; to, 345
Barney, John: to, 357; men-
tioned, 24-25, 744
Barnum, David, 768
Barnum, H. L., 277-78, 352
Barnum's Hotel (Baltimore),
664
Barren Co., Ky., 470
Barry, Catherine Mason (Mrs.
William T.), 135

Barry, William T.: role in
Peggy Eaton affair, 126-27,
135-36; work as postmaster
general, 137-38; accused of
corruption as postmaster
general, 288-89, 734; men-
tioned, 29, 68, 159, 172,
176, 181, 360, 631, 680,
760
Bartlett, Ichabod, 332
Bartlett, Richard: to, 860
Barton, David, 253, 257, 287,
293, 308, 312, 388
Barton, Thomas P., 815,
825-26
Bascom, Henry B.: from,
132; mentioned, 234
Basel, Switzerland, 810
Bassett, Burwell, 411
Bates, Edward: from, 105
Bath Co., Ky., 592, 650
Baton Rouge, La., 178, 181
Batture controversy, 344
Bayard, James A., 681, 737
Baylies, William, 282
Baylor, Robert E. Bledsoe, 177
Bay of Biscay, 802
Bayonne, France, 178
Beach, Samuel: from, 232
Beal, William, 457
Beall, Norborne B.: to, 450;
mentioned, 35, 451
Beall, Samuel T.: to, 655
Beardsley, Samuel, 292
Beasley, Frederick, 319, 324
Beatty, Adam: C. supports un-
successfully for U.S. House
(1829), 63-64, 66, 75, 89-90;
to, 11, 37, 63, 66, 75, 201,
220, 236, 357, 366, 373, 569,
589, 811, 868; mentioned,
74, 78
Beatty, Martin, 68
Beaumont de La Bonniniere,
Gustave Auguste de, 735
Beauvais, Armand, 178,
190, 214
Beckley, Alfred: to, 849
Beckley, John James, 849
Beckley, Va. (W. Va.), 849
Bedford, Sidney, 772
Bedinger, George M., 64, 90
Beet Sugar Society, 875
Belfast, Ireland, 719-20
Belgium: independence of,
288-89, 338-39, 552; C. op-
poses recognition of, 491;
mentioned, 249, 605
Belize, British Honduras, 374
Bell, John, 805-6
Bell, Samuel: to, 696; men-
tioned, 93, 697
Bell, William: to, 168
Benjamin Franklin (ship), 37
Benning, Thomas R., 9-10, 115
Bent, Lemuel: to, 736
Benton, Thomas Hart:
snubbed socially in New
Orleans, 40; presidential

ambitions of, 171-73; fist fight with Jackson, 553, 563; rumored duel with C., 554; trades insults with C., 553; public land distribution proposal, 531; at Jefferson Day Dinner, 195; alliance with Calhoun, 195, 203; spokesman for West claim challenged, 484; plan to separate West and Northeast politically, 171-73, 178, 196, 204-5, 206; reelection (Nov. 1832) to U.S. Senate, 570, 576; sees public land debate as West-South political alliance, 172-73; in campaign of 1832, 172-73, 181-82, 195; on public land sale graduation, 757; sponsors expunging resolution, 735, 749; mentioned, 190, 193, 198, 312, 448, 493, 540, 562, 566, 615, 672, 680, 685, 728, 730, 808, 819, 837, 857-58, 861

Berks Co., Pa., 701

Berlin, Germany, 313

Berrien, John M., 99, 159, 172, 176, 181, 187, 234, 288, 360, 368, 370, 380, 386, 388

Berry, Joseph: to, 649; mentioned, 650

Berryman, Edwin Upshur: from, 415, 560, 593, 704; mentioned, 401-2, 607

Berthoud, Nicholas, 165

Bertrand (horse), 851

Betsey (slave), 86

Beverly (slave), 779

Bibb, George M.: on Maysville Road veto, 220-21, 230, 261; on tariff, 230; on Indian removals to West, 230, 261; does not contest U.S. Senate seat (1835), 221; supposed reconciliation with C., 467; mentioned, 60, 110, 171, 527

Biddle, James, 456

Biddle, Nicholas: C. advises on BUS recharter, 165-66, 263-64, 432-33, 694; on congressional reports on BUS, 218; on early BUS recharter, 287-88, 435, 444; on Jackson's veto of BUS recharter bill, 556, 562; on removal & restoration of BUS deposits, 673, 675, 681, 691; quality of govt.-appointed BUS directors, 680-81, 682; solicits aid & advises C. on BUS-related political issues, 627-28, 694, 694-95; salutes C. for 1833 compromise tariff, 627-28; assists Lexington, Ky. turnpike road projects, 160, 351; on Maysville Road bill, 218, 351; opinion of C., 435;

abstinence from politics, 348, 726; C. asks financial favor of for important Whig, 694; C. defends in Senate speech, 697-98; from, 160, 218, 287, 351, 363, 435, 556, 557, 619, 627, 634, 682, 691, 693, 694, 815, 832; to, 129, 130, 165, 223, 263, 265, 347, 432, 490, 562, 623, 630, 636, 680, 694, 766, 771, 816, 864; mentioned, 130, 366, 443, 490, 563, 581, 588, 648, 658, 672, 683. *See also* Bank of the United States; Congress of the United States: 23 Cong., 1 Sess.

Biddle, Thomas, 366, 388, 772

Big Sandy River, 53

Billy (slave), 649, 657, 659

Binney, Horace, 633, 680-81

Binns, John: from, 399; mentioned, 25

Birch, James, 800

Birney, James G.: to, 748

Black Hawk (jackass), 801

Black Hawk War, 497, 531, 861

Black, John, 854

Black Rock, N.Y., 202, 247, 473

Black Sea, 127

Blackburn, Patsy Watkins (Mrs. William B.), 131-32

Blackburn, William B., 132

Blackford, William M.: to, 728

Blair, Francis P.: role in "corrupt bargain" charge against C., 219, 225; starts Washington *Globe* to support Jackson, 297, 305-6, 313; attacks C.'s character, 448-49; conflicts with Gales & Seaton publications, 670; mentioned, 205, 324, 380, 450-51, 624, 734, 751, 762

Blaize (cow), 668

Blake, George, 423

Blake, Thomas H.: from, 22, 100; mentioned, 23

Bland, John B., 386

Blanton, Harrison: from, 40; mentioned, 608

Bledsoe, Jesse, 177

Bledsoe, Simeon & Co., 507

Blodget, Rebecca Smith (Mrs. Samuel), 525

Bloodgood, S. DeWitt: to, 731

Blossom (cow), 870

Blunt, Joseph: to, 231; mentioned, 302, 306

Bodley, Breckenridge, 650, 654

Bodley, Thomas: to, 462; mentioned, 442, 650, 652, 654

Boeuf River, 772

Boggs, Lilburn W., 570

Bogota, Colombia, 50, 191, 211

Bolivia, 4-5

Bolivar, Ohio, 840

Bolivar, Simon: C. writes critical letter to, 185, 191; mentioned, 5, 169, 211, 840

"Bolling Hall," 555

Bolling, William, 554-55

Booker, William O., 77

Boon, Ratliff, 199, 389, 538

Boone Co., Ky., 733

Boone, Daniel, 538

Bonaparte, Napoleon (France), 1, 45, 137, 425, 717, 764

Bordeaux, France, 802, 810

Boston, Mass.: depression in, 110, 692; Jackson patronage policy in, 82-83; Anti-Masonry in, 385; C. son gets job in (*see* Clay, James Brown); morals of young men in, 579; campaign (1832) support for C. in, 592; mentioned, 87, 95, 98, 117, 228, 288-89, 354, 374, 394, 417, 476, 516, 602, 606, 633, 638, 644, 651, 663-66, 668, 676, 694, 705, 777, 805

Boston *Atlas*, 570

Boston *Bulletin*, 99

Boston *Courier*, 83, 354-55, 478

Boston *Daily Advocate*, 476, 593

Boston *Federalist*, 116

Boston *Sentinel*, 94

Boston *Statesman*, 99

Boswell, George, 648

Boswell, Joseph, 650, 652, 654

Boswell, Thomas Edward, 321

Boudinot, Elias, 760

Bouldin, J. W., 707

Bouldin, Thomas T., 697, 706-7

Bouligny, Dominique, 359

Bourbon Co., Ky., 64, 66, 74-75, 272, 734, 803, 829, 836

Bourtoulin, Dmitrii Petrovich (Count de), 852

Bowling Green, Ky., 21, 39 53, 733

Boyd, John P. (not identified), 98

Boyle, John, 21

Bracken Co., Ky., 64, 201

Bradford, Daniel, 439, 538

Bradford, John: to, 168; mentioned, 538

Bradish, Luther, 291-92

Bradley, Phineas, 121

Bradley, William A.: from, 583

Branch, John, 99, 126, 137, 159, 167, 171-73, 176, 181, 187, 198, 234, 342, 351-52, 359-60, 368, 370

Brand, Eliza, 228-29

Brand, John, 229, 443, 520

Brand, William Moses, 228-29, 443

Brandywine (ship), 502

Brazil, 146

Brazos River, 842

Breathitt, John T., 453, 470, 506, 520, 565, 568-69, 596

Breckinridge, John, 116, 134

Clay, Henry (continued):
nature of despotism, 81; on
his thorny public life, 393;
satisfied with his political
career, 798, 812-13; future of
free government in U.S.,
212; on various reform movements in U.S., 379, 381;
heavy workloads of U.S.
presidents, 531; tailoring
speeches for later publication,
251; anonymous newspaper
articles by, 197, 199; compares Jacksonism with
cholera, 725; accepts collective rather than single-state
nullification, 243; on nullification (see South Carolina);
as saviour of his country,
724-25; no interest in being
governor of Ky., 814; will
not meddle in politics of
other states, 804; issues that
should be kept out of
American politics, 833; God
assists U.S., 839-40; criticized for publishing speeches,
245; criticized for making too
many speeches, 89; criticized
for mentioning personal
problems in his speeches,
242; criticized for writing too
many revealing letters to
strangers, 367; faith in virtues & intelligence of the
people, 59; triumphant political journey home (March
1829), 2, 3, 4-6, 8, 8-9, 9,
10-11, 18, 19, 20, 23, 25, 31,
33, 35, 36, 55; brilliant
political career of, 244-45; on
nationalism & patriotism,
483; political plans & prospects & possible return to
Congress, 3, 8-9, 11, 21, 26,
26-27, 27, 28-29, 32, 33,
34-35, 36, 38, 39, 52-53, 56,
59, 62, 72, 167; ponders retiring from political life, 88,
776, 798, 812-13, 814-15,
821, 840, 848, 849, 856, 861,
866, 868, 872
—slaves & slavery: transactions in slaves (1829-1836),
85-87, 663-64; has surplus
slaves at Ashland, 743; in-
herits slaves from his father,
207; slavery in Ky. constitution, 85, 789; mildness of
slavery in Ky., 482, 650,
748, 774; believes U.S.
government has no power to
deal with slavery, 482-83 (see
also Constitution of the
United States); on slave
traders, 85, 774; on slave
insurrections, 397, 794; on
emancipation in South, 641,
643, 656; on emancipation &

civil war, 641, 653; mixed
views of emancipation—immediate, gradual, & compensatory, 85, 258, 390, 478, 482-83,
641, 648, 650, 789-90, 814,
833; slave "Lotty" (see also
7:622-24, 631-33), 72, 198,
253, 261, 309, 441; helps
recover runaways, 271, 350;
advertizes for runaway, 770;
overseer-slave relationships at
"Ashland," 319; attitudes
toward slaves at "Ashland,"
497; on racial inferiority of
slaves, 833; fears numerical
preponderance of, 833; improvement in treatment of
slaves, 774; Christianity &
slavery, 773; would use
treasury surplus to finance
emancipation, 478, 535-37;
on dangers of abolitionism,
815-16, 833; on restrictions
of abolitionists' free speech,
815-16; on right of petition
for abolitionists, 817-18, 833,
853; on abolition of slavery
in D.C., 7, 817-18, 833, 867;
exchange with Lewis Tappan
on emancipation, colonization, abolition, slave trade,
773-74, 793, 838, 852; on
progress toward abolition,
650; on slavery in Ark. &
Mo., 789-90, 841-42; com-
pares conditions of slaves &
Cherokees, 760; compares
conditions of slaves & European serfs, 167; European
opinion of slavery, 774; on
U.S. slavery & Latin
American independence, 793;
on emancipation of slaves in
British West Indies (see espec.
641), 390, 641, 643, 650,
653, 656; decline of economic
relevance of in South, 641;
on economics of sectionalism,
643; sentiment for in North,
656; suppression of African
slave trade, 838; support of
colonization concepts and the
American & Ky. Coloniza-
tion Societies, 127, 128-58,
161, 162, 165, 169, 234, 258,
390, 471, 477-78, 482-83,
535-36, 625, 650, 653, 754,
773-74, 812, 852, 858,
864-65, 874; colonization
paid for with land sales
receipts, 812; on production
of cotton per slave, 466;
slave beaten to death, 429,
438; figures slave population
into public land (distribution)
bill formula, 756. See also
Slavery.
Clay, Henry, Jr. (son): future
plans of, 18, 55, 118, 216,

228, 229, 231, 232, 256-57,
265, 298-99, 315, 330, 336,
346-47, 428; C. career advice
to, 30, 91, 118, 132, 231,
256-57, 265, 285, 329, 435,
600; C. advice to on life,
256-57, 600; character &
personality of, 40, 437, 778;
on his own character,
427-28, 456-57, 509; as example to brothers, 228, 266;
C. hope for & confidence in,
185, 213, 231; academic performance at West Point,
66-67, 91, 103, 226, 256-57,
265, 336; honors received at
West Point, 184, 216, 228,
230, 232, 256, 265, 285;
cadet officer at West Point,
91, 228, 232, 235; persecution at West Point, 235,
256-57; Uncle James Brown
advises to stay at West Point,
234, 257; graduates second
in class from West Point,
363; criticism of Superintendent Thayer, 234-35, 256;
resigns from U.S. Army,
298-99, 346, 410; gets M.A.
degree from Transylvania
University, 18; gift to Transylvania University, 91; on
father's forensic skills, 298;
submissiveness to C., 103,
346-47, 363; C. recommends
reading to, 265-66; on marriage, 231; on nature of
genius, 347; on Jackson, 18,
725; oratorical skills, 298; on
wealth v. poverty, 457; on
his brother Theodore (see
Clay, Theodore Wythe); proposes establishment of
"American Institute," 163;
quotes C. on slavery, 85; job
on Maysville Road, 118;
visits New Orleans, 401, 431;
on New Orleans, 427, 428;
studies law in New Orleans,
401, 411, 427, 438, 441, 446,
451, 457, 465, 469, 480, 488,
518; passes New Orleans bar
exam, 632; urges C. to speculate in New Orleans property, 457; practice of law, 509,
519, 604, 743; little aptitude
for law, 743; considers practice of law in New Orleans,
604, 607, 632, 638; courtship
& marriage to Julia Prather
(see espec. 529, 560, 587), 555,
588, 595, 600-601; takes over
wife's estate, 607, 648; on
presidential election of 1832,
518; on presidential election
of 1836, 810; public political
discourses & orations, 667,
725; delegate to state Whig
convention, 724; European

906

trips, 451, 457, 465, 480, 771, 801-2, 810-11, 849; buys Spanish jackasses in France, 801-2, 811, 811-12; love of "Ashland," 315, 498; thinks "Ashland" needs lake, 298; manages "Ashland" in C. absence, 481, 489, 490, 493-94, 495, 496-97, 498, 501, 504, 508-9, 518, 529-30, 560; buys & works farm ("Maplewood") in Lexington, 638, 657, 659, 676, 704, 714, 718, 841, 870; C. advises on buying, selling & raising livestock, 669, 779; C. advises to buy slaves, 657; as slave owner, 841; personal financial situation, 648, 743, 872; C. largely supports, 509; C. financial assistance to, 714, 763, 864, 872; C. helps stock farm of, 698, 805; C. offers to help buy more land for, 743, 763; informs C. of conditions at "Ashland," 675, 690; from, 17, 55, 91, 103, 117, 216, 227, 231, 234, 265, 298, 315, 330, 346, 363, 426, 433, 456, 468, 480, 489, 493, 496, 498, 504, 508, 517, 521, 529, 555, 595, 600, 632, 648, 675, 724, 801, 810; to, 29, 91, 131, 160, 162, 184, 213, 229, 231, 256, 284, 309, 329, 336, 435, 437, 446, 465, 468, 488, 495, 501, 508, 560, 600, 606, 607, 648, 657, 659, 667, 669, 670, 690, 692, 697, 698, 699, 704, 705, 714, 718, 751, 763, 779, 841, 850, 870, 872; mentioned, 100, 214, 226, 270, 429, 482, 486, 567, 608, 644, 649, 654, 656, 681-82, 749, 806, 809, 837, 850-51
Clay, Henry III (grandson): birth, 659; mentioned, 669-71, 676, 692, 697, 704, 706, 811, 849-50
Clay, James Brown (son): enters Transylvania University prep department, 30; enters Transylvania University, 285, 329; C. high hopes for, 213; prospects of, 777-78; education, 30, 285, 319-20, 425, 452, 491; literary skills, 441; plays flute, 319; early interest in politics, 469; C. considers financial career for, 391, 410-11, 579, 602, 603, 606; joins commercial house in Boston, 579, 602, 606, 660; quits Boston job, 704, 705, 705-6; C. considers a Philadelphia job for, 705, 710; C. buys Mo. farm for him to work (*see espec.* 801),

801, 805-6, 820-21, 866; C. provides slaves for Mo. farm of, 805-6; from, 319, 425, 469; mentioned, 231, 256, 266, 321-22, 441, 480, 486, 490, 509, 567, 604, 644, 656, 664, 718, 724, 743, 757, 763, 779, 802
Clay, John (brother): death, 130, 161, 162; leaves slave to brothers, 207
Clay, John (father), 207
Clay, John Morrison (son): C. high hopes for, 213; prospects, 778; character, 847-48; education of, 215, 285, 319-20, 321, 454, 491, 752, 761-62, 866; sent away to Edgehill Seminary (N.J.), 752, 761-62, 768, 770, 799, 802, 804, 809, 841, 847-48; gets into trouble at Edgehill, 761-62, 767; attends Transylvania University, 847-48; suffers typhoid fever, 847-48, 849, 850, 851, 852, 866; from, 321; to, 799; mentioned, 30, 231, 256, 266, 308-9, 329-30, 425, 438, 452, 469, 480, 486, 490, 509, 567, 664, 667, 682, 743, 794, 803
Clay, Julia Prather (daughter-in-law): marriage to Henry Clay, Jr. (*see* Clay, Henry, Jr.); estate rights after marriage, 607; pregnant with Henry Clay III, 638, 644, 656; birth of Henry Clay III, 659; birth of daughter Matilda, 763; health of daughter Matilda, 801-2; sister Catherine, 779-80; to, 638, 649, 654, 704, 849; mentioned, 529, 555, 587-88, 595, 600-601, 603, 608, 658, 669-71, 676, 692, 697, 706, 714, 718, 751, 778, 810-11, 850
Clay, Julie Duralde (Mrs. John), 428, 436, 441, 451, 466
Clay, Laura (daughter), 778, 809, 814
Clay, Lucretia (daughter), 778, 809, 814
Clay, Lucretia Hart (wife): born in Md., 209; dislike of farm life, 391; homesick for "Ashland," 491; mother (Susannah Gray Hart) dies (*see espec.* 566-67), 563, 566-67, 568, 569, 570, 571, 577, 584; receives bequest, 633; buys china for use in D.C., 680; serious stomach disorder, 698, 704, 705, 705-6, 710, 714, 715-16, 718, 723, 724, 729, 732, 738, 740, 741, 744, 748; does not accompany C. to D.C., 803-4;

raises grandchildren, 871; to, 767, 803, 804, 805, 808, 820; mentioned, 7, 17, 23, 32, 100, 195, 169, 182, 184, 203, 207-8, 227, 256, 269, 285, 303, 308, 321-22, 330, 351, 401, 410, 425, 428-29, 431, 441-42, 446, 452, 454, 458, 466, 469, 481-82, 486-87, 494-96, 498, 502, 505, 518, 556, 600, 602-4, 608, 636, 638, 643-44, 657, 659-60, 664, 668, 673, 676, 678, 682, 731, 739, 749, 757, 770-72, 779, 796, 798, 806-8, 822, 831, 868
Clay, Matilda (granddaughter), 763, 802
Clay, Porter (brother): conveys slave to C., 207; marriage, 208; slaves owned by, 658; advises C. on land purchase, 658; from, 207, 658; to, 608; mentioned, 117, 660, 843
Clay, Sophia Grosch (wife of brother Porter), 117
Clay, Susan Hart (daughter). *See* Duralde, Susan Hart Clay (Mrs. Martin)
Clay, Theodore Wythe (son): bored at "Ashland," 30; looks for something to do, 231; personality & bad habits, 215, 298; causes C. pain, 231; mental problems, 284; committed to Lunatic Asylum of Ky. (*see espec.* 442-43), 442-43, 453-54, 462, 489-90, 530-31, 675-76, 718, 777-78; on his own illness, 454, 489-90, 495, 496, 509, 520, 530-31; C. attitude toward insanity of, 462, 489, 498, 502, 530-31, 671; family attitudes toward insanity of, 603, 675-76; medical treatment of, 530-31; attempts to leave asylum, 520; allowed visits home from asylum, 603; sent back to asylum, 675-76, 725; from, 442, 453, 520; mentioned, 18, 120, 185, 213, 319, 329, 480, 668
Clay, Thomas Hart (son): imprisoned in Philadelphia, 3, 843; returns home from prison, 3, 30, 36; bored at "Ashland," 30; C. thinks unstable, 131; H. Clay, Jr. opinion of, 676; causes C. pain, 231; C. admonishes, 822; bad habits (liquor) of (*see espec.* 671), 2-3, 30, 213, 298, 450, 671, 676, 681-82, 777-78; corn speculation deal, 329; has responsibility for "Ashland" in C. absence, 668, 822, 834-35, 837-38, 843, 850-51; runs C.-owned

Northeast boundary dispute, 477, 552 (*see also* Great Britain); military appropriations, 444; State Department appropriations, 487, 491, 495; outfit of U.S. minister to France, 491, 495; railroad construction subsidy, 472; Columbian College subsidy, 521; Revolutionary War claims & pensions, 509; private relief bills, 479, 481; unclaimed dividends on public stocks, 455, 481; centennial birthday of and proposed reburial of George Washington, 462, 464, 465, 466; Calhoun faction opposition in, 465; C. on compensated emancipation of slaves, 478, 483; colonization of free Negroes, 478, 482-83, 535-36; disbursement of public lands & internal improvements relationship, 538-39; sectional vote trade-off on tariff & public lands issues, 481, 496; Van Buren nomination and rejection as U.S. minister to Britain (*see espec.* 342, 344, 450), 342, 344, 365, 369-71, 440, 443, 445, 446, 448, 450, 455, 458-59, 460, 463, 466, 468, 473, 475, 488, 597, 598; debate on public lands (distribution) bill (*see espec.* 494, 539-41), 429, 445, 482, 494, 495, 496, 500, 506, 507, 508, 513, 521, 522, 527, 531, 535, 539-41, 544, 546, 547, 548, 549, 551; content and circulation of Committee on Manufacturers land bill report (*see espec.* 494), 482, 494, 507, 535, 539, 546, 547, 552, 576; C. prayer & fasting resolution about cholera, 545, 546, 548, 549, 554; C. on successes during session, 551. *See also* Jackson administration; Van Buren, Martin —22 Cong., 2 Sess., (12/3/32–3/2/33): bitterness in, 602; C. considers resigning seat in next Congress (*see*, below, 23 Cong., 1 Sess.); secret of eternal life discovery, 613; C. on recess hours of Senate, 625; debate on public lands (distribution) bill (*see espec.* 494, 539-41, 609-10), 602, 603, 609-10, 612, 613, 614, 615, 615-16, 617, 621, 629, 629-30, 630, 632, 639, 640, 644, 646, 652, 854; Jackson pocket veto of land (distribution) bill (*see espec.* 610), 629-30, 630, 632, 642, 643,

646, 652, 677 (*see also* Jackson administration); Benton's public land bill, 615; congressional investigation of BUS, 619, 623-24; removal & manipulation of government deposits in BUS, 583-84, 623 (*see* below, 23 Cong., 1 Sess.); French spoliations issue, 613 (*see also* France); debate on Force— "Collection of Revenue"—bill (*see espec.* 615), 609, 616, 623, 624, 625, 626, 628, 629, 675, 686, 688, 862; S.C. nullification and Jackson handling of, 597-98, 602, 609, 611, 622, 624; C. opinions of nullification (*see* South Carolina); rumored C.-Calhoun alliance to oppose Jackson attack on nullification, 605-6, 612; Calhoun attempt to repeal Force bill, 686-87, 689, 713, 715; criticism of C. failure to vote on Force bill, 688; C. explains failure to vote on Force bill, 625, 686, 797, 862; Webster-Poindexter confrontation on Force bill, 629; debate in H. of R. on Verplanck tariff bill (*see espec.* 608), 609, 610-11, 614, 615, 616, 616-17, 624; Clay's Compromise Tariff Bill/Act of 1833, 604, 619-21, 621-22, 626-27; C. urged to fashion a compromise tariff bill, 610, 611; C. willingness to effect a compromise, 609, 610, 613-14, 615, 617, 624, 626; sectional politics in tariff schedules of, 640, 653; Senate debate on compromise tariff, 604, 608, 621-22, 624-25, 625, 626-27, 627, 628; Senate switch to identical H. of R. bill, 608, 627; C. authorship, introduction, explanation, & defense of his compromise tariff, 604, 613, 613-14, 617, 619-21, 621-22, 622, 623, 624, 625, 626, 626-27, 627, 628, 629, 631, 633, 636-37, 639, 653, 862-63; C. willing to renounce public service if bill is passed, 624-25; publication & circulation of C. compromise tariff speeches, 633, 635, 636, 639; opinions on & reactions to C. compromise tariff proposal, 622, 623, 624-25, 626, 628, 631, 633-34, 635, 636, 636-37, 640, 641-42, 646, 647; New England attitudes toward C. compromise tariff, 623, 633-34, 635, 647, 653; C.

evaluation of his tariff compromise handiwork, 628, 629, 631, 632, 633, 636-37, 639, 640, 643, 653, 862-63; election of public printer, 623-24. *See also* Jackson administration —23 Cong., 1 Sess. (12/2/33–6/30/34): party strengths & lineups in (*see espec.* 577-78), 578, 617, 670-71, 672-73, 673, 674, 678, 681, 691, 696, 697, 699, 706, 711-12, 712; C. considers resigning seat in, 607, 639, 642, 643, 644, 647, 652; C. committee service in, 674, 679, 680, 681-82; debate on adjournment date, 734; removal & replacement of H. of R. clerk, 670-71, 672; *Register* v. *Globe* issue in, 670; disputed R.I. Senate seat election (*see espec.* 670), 670, 702, 710, 732; investigation of post office, 680, 734; internal improvements, 674-75, 734, 735; military roads, 727; subsidy to city of Washington, 734; public land sales by Jackson administration, 702, 721, 733; private claims bills, 726; Indian affairs issues, 702, 726-27 (*see also* Indians); maritime navigational aids, 734; historical publications, 733-34; Senate v. House disagreements during, 737; debate on Senate appointment of its own committees, 670, 672, 673, 674, 675, 678, 679; attempt to repeal Force Act (*see espec.* 686, 713), 675, 686, 688, 689, 713, 715; C. demand that Jackson submit executive document dealing with Taney removal of U.S. deposits from BUS (*see espec.* 583-84), 673, 673-74, 674, 680; constitutional question of executive power & privilege, 673, 673-74, 674, 682, 693, 699-700, 701, 703, 710-11; Jackson-Taney removal of deposits from BUS & debate on resulting C. resolution to censure both (*see espec.* 583-84, 684-85, 687, 708, 728), 673, 673-74, 679, 680, 680-81, 682, 684-85, 685, 685-86, 687, 688, 690, 690-91, 692, 692-93, 694, 694-95, 695, 696, 697, 697-98, 698-99, 701, 702, 703, 705, 706, 707, 708, 709, 710, 713, 714-15, 721, 723, 725, 727, 728, 730; Senate & H. of R. votes to censure Jackson & Taney, 708, 710, 711-12, 749; Taney role in removal of deposits

Congress of the US (continued): issue (*see* Taney, Roger B.); publication & circulation of C. speech of 12/26/33 opposing Jackson's removal of deposits, 690-91, 692, 694; attempt to restore U.S. deposits in BUS & sentiment therefore (*see espec.* 583-84, 684-85, 728), 681, 686, 688, 694, 695, 696, 697, 698, 701, 703, 704, 705, 714, 720, 728; restoration of deposits effort by joint resolution (*see espec.* 728), 728, 729, 730; reactions to Senate censure of Jackson, 735, 749; Jackson's protest of his Senate censure (*see espec.* 716-17, 722, 724), 716-17, 717, 717-18, 718, 721, 722, 724; circulation of Jackson's protest statement, 725; C. speech attacking Jackson's protest, 722; vote against receiving Jackson's protest of his censure, 724; Benton crusade to expunge Jackson's censure from Senate *Journal*, 735, 749; C. on doctrine of instructions, 717; Jackson's appointment of incompetent government directors of BUS, 681, 682, 723; BUS & pension agency fund issue (*see espec.* 695), 691, 695, 698-99; limit on denominations of BUS notes, 700; distribution of revenue from public land sales (*see espec.* 539-41, 609-10, 671), 640, 671, 673, 677, 721, 723; continuing debate on compromise tariff, 653, 655, 700; adjustments of existing tariff schedules, 733; mixed interpretations of 1833 tariff schedules & port of entry valuations (*see espec.* 688-89), 688, 688-89, 690, 700; Jackson's recess appointments policy, 727, 730, 733; efforts to curb executive's power of appointment to & removal from office (*see espec.* 710-11), 693, 699-700, 708, 710-11, 712, 722; problem & extent of national depression & currency derangement, 683, 685-86, 689-90, 691, 692, 696, 697, 697-98, 700, 701, 703, 706, 707-8, 725, 727, 733; attempts to alleviate impact of depression by stretching out revenue bonds payments (*see espec.* 689-90), 689, 689-90, 696, 699; statistical analysis of relief petitions linking national depression

to Jackson's removal of deposits (*see espec.* 713), 721-22, 731, 733; obligation to indemnify U.S. citizens for French spoliations prior to 1800, 733, 755; election of new Speaker (John Bell, Tenn.) of H. of R., 729, 732; defeat of Jackson party in, 732. *See also* Jackson administration
— 23 Cong., 2 Sess. (12/1/34–3/3/35): possible Whig divisions in, 750; C. pessimism about, 750; mood of Whigs, 751; C. committee appointments, 752; presidential politics during, 757; public land (distribution) bill (*see espec.* 539-41, 609-10, 671, 753), 753, 755, 756, 757; Benton's bill to graduate public land prices, 757; disposal of horse & lion gifts to U.S., 753, 756; military bounty land warrants, 765; commemoration of life of Lafayette, 753, 755; obligation to indemnify U.S. citizens for French spoliations prior to 1800, 755; internal improvements, 755; Cumberland Road bill, 760-61; Alabama roads bill (2% fund), 764-65; Fortification bill, 764, 766; consolidation of federal courts, 764; investigation of attempt to assassinate Jackson, 764; recess appointment of U.S. minister to Britain, 765, 766; Cherokee removal issue, 759-60; expunging resolution (*see espec.* 735), 758, 759, 769; C. on status & reorganization of post office, 758, 760; personal claims bills, 757, 758; curbing executive power of appointment & removal of public officials, 703, 761, 762; subsidy (for Dutch loan) payment to D.C., 742, 765; election of Senate & H. of R. printers, 762, 765; constitutional amendment to limit veto power of executive, 763; bill to establish branches of the U.S. Mint, 763, 764; diplomatic crisis with France over spoliation claims, 754, 755-56 (*see also* France: U.S. relations with). *See also* Jackson administration
— 24 Cong., 1 Sess. (12/7/35–7/4/36): party strengths in (*see espec.* 709), 750, 821, 831; C. ponders retirement from, 776, 814, 849, 856; post

office reorganization bill, 855-56; post roads legislation, 830; movement of U.S. mail by railroad, 843; C. on specie payment (Specie Circular) for public land, 860-61; procedures used in selling public lands, 857; Walker's public land graduation & preemption bill, 839, 844, 853; public lands for public-school use, 827; public land (distribution) bill (*see espec.* 539-41, 609-10, 671, 753, 812-13, 846-47), 812-13, 815, 819, 832, 834, 842, 844, 846-47, 847, 848, 859; land claims in Mo., 837; public land grant to Mo., 840; military land warrants, 837; public land grants to states for internal improvements, 840, 857; bill jointly to regulate the deposits and reduce (distribute) the treasury surplus — Deposit & Treasury Surplus Act of 1836 (*see espec.* 813), 813, 829-30, 836-37, 844, 854, 854-55, 856, 857, 858; admission of Mich. to Union (*see espec.* 808), 808, 837, 839, 853; admission of Ark., 841-42; duty on hemp, 848; debate on abolition of slavery/slave trade in D.C., 817, 833, 867; C. on right of petition as applied to ("gag rule") abolition of slavery and/or slave trade in D.C., 817, 833; debate on excluding slavery materials from U.S. mails, 815, 826-27, 853; congressional aid to American Colonization Society, 858; war with Seminole Indians, 823, 847, 848; violations of U.S.-Choctaw treaty (1830), 818; expunging resolution (*see espec.* 735), 820, 832, 837, 843, 857-58, 858; relief for New York City fire sufferers (*see espec.* 817, 818), 817, 818, 818-19, 834; defense (fortifications) appropriation bill, 819, 830, 848, 848-49, 853, 856, 858; harbor bill, 860; Cumberland Road, 831, 831-32, 832, 834; D.C. canal debt to Dutch bankers, 742, 828; need for marine hospital at Louisville, 832, 853; request to purchase stock in Louisville & Portland Canal, 852; U.S. recognition of Texas independence (*see espec.* 838-39, 855), 842, 848, 853-54, 855, 857, 858, 859 (*see also* Texas); insecurity of

Election of 1832 (continued): 401, 404, 485, 501, 573, 577, 590-91, 592, 593; vice presidential nominees considered, 56, 80, 85, 92-93, 187, 230, 271, 289, 306, 321, 341, 353, 401, 404, 409-10, 428, 437, 458, 465, 506, 513, 527, 543, 555, 558, 579; post-election analysis of results, 595-96, 597-98, 599, 599-600, 601-2, 610, 613, 618

—Anti-Masonic role in: 195; C. on third party candidates, 324; possible Anti-Masonic withdrawal from, 365, 590; possible alliance or cooperation with National Republicans, 492-93, 495, 505, 522, 542-43, 588 (*see also* Anti-Masonic party: National Republican alliance or cooperation with; and, below, campaign activity in specific states–New York, Pennsylvania); McLean declines Anti-Masonic nomination, 367, 405-6. *See*, below, nominating conventions: Anti-Masonic party; also, below, William Wirt role in: Anti-Masonic party

—issues, charges & countercharges in campaign: Jackson incompetence, corruption, misrule, tyranny, radicalism, etc., 104, 197, 200, 242, 312, 328, 342, 350, 369, 377, 378, 380, 382, 383-84, 411, 419, 447, 450, 500, 501, 509-10, 512, 516, 521, 539, 548, 562, 582, 585, 586, 589, 595, 599, 602; Jackson cabinet turmoil & resignations, 159-60, 171-72, 176, 187, 189, 305-6, 341, 342, 347, 348, 349, 351-52, 353, 359, 365, 368, 369, 370 (*see also* Eaton, John; Eaton, Margaret (Peggy) O'neal; Jackson administration); tariff issue (*see espec.* 455-56), 77, 79-80, 96, 108-9, 112, 114, 124, 125, 136, 177, 193, 198, 200, 202, 202-3, 204, 208, 216, 220, 227, 228-29, 230, 239, 243, 248, 260, 270, 283, 307, 322, 323, 324-25, 337, 348, 356, 369, 375, 377, 405, 411, 412-13, 417, 419, 422, 423, 436-37, 440, 443, 444, 445, 446, 448, 452, 453, 455-56, 456, 459, 460, 465, 466, 466-67, 468, 469, 470, 471, 472, 474, 475, 477, 481, 482, 483, 487, 492, 499, 501, 502-3, 503-4, 505, 515, 526, 527, 529, 539, 543-44, 546, 547, 549, 551; internal

improvements, 93, 112, 128, 193, 200, 202, 209, 216, 220, 224, 225, 227, 230, 237-40, 241, 242, 244, 307, 404, 413, 419, 422; American System (general), 105, 237-40, 241, 243, 248, 258, 260, 278, 282-83, 303, 310, 350, 381, 422, 430, 455-56, 458, 475, 477, 487, 492, 505; Maysville Road bill veto, 204, 209, 214, 215, 219, 220, 221, 223, 224, 225, 227, 230, 237-40, 243-44, 261, 271, 282, 350, 351, 381, 549; Jackson single-term pledge & the single-term issue, 62, 95, 102, 123-24, 136, 158, 159-60, 167, 169, 170, 172, 174, 182, 189, 193, 195, 196, 197, 200, 210, 259, 320, 321-22, 365, 582; public land (distribution) policy (*see espec.* 539-41), 112, 171, 195, 197, 413, 415, 419-20, 429-30, 481-82, 491, 492, 494, 500, 506, 527, 539-41, 551, 544; tariff level & public land sales (distribution) relationship, 413, 419-20, 481-82, 492, 494, 539-40; how to spend expected surplus revenue, 320, 337, 375, 377, 405, 412-13, 415, 419-20, 422, 535-37; Jackson's Indian removal policy (*see espec.* 112), 112, 202, 208, 219, 222, 224, 225-26, 226, 227, 230, 231, 241, 250, 255, 261, 282, 320, 323, 358-59, 460, 466, 563; Jackson's & Georgia's defiance of Supreme Court Cherokee decision, 320, 323, 472, 473, 473-74, 475, 475-76, 477, 483 (*see also* Georgia; Jackson administration); Jackson's proscription & patronage policy, 112, 128, 133, 167, 187, 196, 197, 198, 242, 411, 450, 458 (*see also* Jackson administration); Jackson's appointment of printers & editors to government offices, 125-26, 128, 171, 172, 196, 198, 211 (*see ibid.*); BUS charter renewal (*see espec.* 263, 434, 443, 552, 640-41), 166, 205, 208, 210, 218, 223-24, 242, 242-43, 263-64, 265, 283, 287-88, 375, 413, 418, 423, 431-32, 432-33, 434, 437, 443, 444, 446, 452, 453, 455, 458, 468, 473-74, 477, 483, 498, 499, 503, 504, 506, 515, 523, 527, 546, 547; Jackson's veto of BUS recharter bill (*see espec.* 434, 443, 552, 640-41), 263, 287, 434, 455, 468, 527, 546,

547, 549, 551, 552, 552-53, 553, 556-57, 557, 561, 562, 563, 564, 566, 574, 577, 579, 583, 596; U.S. exclusion from British West Indies trade, 81, 219, 270, 282, 380, 435, 440, 450, 520 (*see also* 4:179-81; 5:630-32); Jackson's trade treaties, 520; Van Buren nomination & rejection as minister to Britain (*see espec.* 342, 344), 349, 388, 440, 446, 448, 450, 455, 458-59, 459, 460, 460-61, 465, 466, 466-67, 468, 472, 474-75, 475, 562 (*see* Van Buren, Martin); constitutional issues, 320, 332-33, 335, 344 (*see*, below, S.C. nullification threat); proposed constitutional amendment to limit presidential veto power, 220, 220-21, 221-22, 223, 224, 225, 230; S.C. nullification threat, 195-96, 196, 197, 208, 227, 238, 241, 243-44, 245, 271, 282, 307, 320-21, 344, 349, 351, 388, 404, 405, 406, 417, 419, 434, 473, 506, 527, 596, 602, 603 (*see also* South Carolina); C.'s connection with Masons (*see espec.* 381-82, 383), 335, 348, 353-55, 356, 367, 376, 381-82, 383, 384, 388, 390, 393-94, 403, 409, 420, 436, 476, 500-501, 512-13 (*see also* Masonic Order); Jackson's age & health, 100; purchase of Texas, 132; Eaton-Berrien correspondence, 380, 382; French spoliation claims & treaty, 448 (*see also* France: U.S. relations with); C. personal character, 244-45; C. connection with Aaron Burr, 258; C. earlier connection with J.Q. Adams, 62, 186; C. "corrupt bargain" with J.Q. Adams (*see espec.* 4:143-66), 105, 173, 205, 219, 225, 239, 327, 340, 348, 372, 420, 484, 484-85, 548, 591; C. as duelist, 448-49, 450-51, 456; slavery & colonization, 471, 478, 535-37 (*see also* Slavery; Henry Clay: slaves & slavery). *See also* Jackson administration; Congress of the United States: 22 Cong., 1 Sess., 22 Cong., 2 Sess.

—newspapers, journals, printed speeches & pamphlets: political use & influence in campaign, 102, 104, 106, 128, 128-29, 133, 164, 170, 171, 172, 175, 183-84, 197, 199-200, 204, 205-6, 207, 208, 222, 241, 242, 244-45,

914

Royal Navy, 458; Municiple Reform bill, 720; Court of St. James's, 370, 371, 828
—U.S. relations with: status of U.S. relations with in March 1829, 11-12; fears of war with, 15-16; would drag U.S. into her wars, 338; Indian rights in Ghent treaty, 358-59; Convention of 1815, 845-46; impressment issue with, 453; Northeast boundary dispute (*see also* 1:1006; 4:181-82; 6:1100-1101), 9, 447, 543, 552, 837, 854, 856; West Indies trade controversy with U.S. (*see also* 2:839; 3:729; 4:179-81, 417, 941-42; 5:630-32, 831-35; 6:316), 105, 219, 247-48, 342, 344, 380, 389, 440, 450, 475, 520-21; offers mediation in Franco-American claims dispute, 827, 829-30; cotton textile production competition between, 352; trade treaty with, 81; mentioned, 1, 7, 61, 67, 92, 116, 122, 139, 141, 146, 162, 180, 200, 207, 230, 270, 330, 335, 368, 390, 402, 445-46, 449, 459, 466, 476-77, 480, 545, 547, 630-32, 643, 650, 656, 700, 727, 737, 743, 757, 759, 764-66, 775, 779, 791, 796, 811, 835-36, 839-40, 858, 869
Great Lakes, 683
Greece, 7, 127, 165
Green, Charles F. (not identified), 323
Green, Duff: proscribes Adams appointees, 17; criticizes C.'s Panama Instructions (*see also* 5:313-44), 16; role in Jackson administration, 74, 96, 98-99; tension with Jackson administration, 369, 581; C. opinions of, 56, 79, 862-63; Webster attacks, 178; proposed removal from office, 288, 297, 313; role in 1832 election, 862-63; supports Wirt's candidacy (1832), 581; on C. withdrawal from 1832 presidential race, 579, 581; hypocrisy of, 581; works to organize workingmen for McLean's presidential bid, 666-67; works for States' Rights party & Calhoun presidential nomination, 744-45, 745; supports Force bill, 862-63; charges C.-Calhoun alliance to support White (1836), 797; C. hatred of, 797, 862-63; supports White in 1836 election, 797; alliance with Calhoun,

862-63; mentioned, 32, 89, 380, 383, 412, 485, 864
Green, John, 748
Greenbrier, Va. (W. Va.), 744
Greencastle, Pa., 748
Green Co., Ky., 470
Green River, 110, 113, 580
Greene, William: from, 253; to, 201, 251, 283, 295, 424, 438, 513; mentioned, 251, 778
Greenfield, Mass., 440
Greenleaf, _____, 647
Greenville, S.C., 434
Gregory, _____, 389
Grey, Earl, 249
Griffin, Samuel Stuart: to, 63
Griffith, John T., 369, 371
Griffith, William, 371
Griswold, George, 461
Griswold's School for Young Ladies (Lexington, Ky.), 748
Grove, _____, 663
Grundy, _____, 761
Grundy, Felix: C. opinion of, 188; elected to U.S. Senate, 407; defends Jackson's protest of censure, 722; supports national bank (1814), 723; mentioned, 182, 623, 674, 758, 760
Grymes, John Randolph, 400-401
Guatemala. See Centre of America, Federation of
Guerrero, Vincente, 5
Guiramand, Jean Marie Morel, 281, 310
Gulf of Mexico, 20, 143, 157, 204, 696
Gunter, John: to, 358; mentioned, 359
Gunter's Landing, Ga., 359
Gurley, Ralph R: to, 313, 625, 754, 874
Guthrie, James, 386, 439, 600, 806-7, 856
Guyandotte River, 91, 560
Gwathmey, John, 449-50
Gwin, Samuel, 560

Hagarty, James, 801-2, 841, 849-50
Hagerstown, Md., 9-10, 13, 16-17, 25, 68, 94, 104, 120, 362, 618
Haiti, 152-53
Haley, Elizabeth (not identified), 86
Hall, _____, 481
Hall, Joseph, 648
Hall, Nathan H., 29
Hall, Sarah, 321, 491
Hallett, Benjamin Franklin, 476, 593
Halsey, Abraham, 242
Hamilton County (Ohio) Agricultural Society, 272, 721
Hamilton Co., Ohio, 721
Hamilton *Intelligencer*, 94

Hamilton, James A., 279, 288, 340-41, 417
Hamilton, William S., 178, 214
Hamlet (bull), 744
Hammond, Charles: on outcome of 1828 presidential election, 59; comments on possible nominations for president in 1832, 88-89, 97-98, 100-101, 104, 111-112, 114, 170, 404-5, 533-35; aid to C. in 1832 campaign, 253; C. criticizes Hammond article on C. nomination, 296, 533-34; on Ky. state elections of August 1831, 542-43; on National Republican nominating convention in Baltimore, 542-43; on 1832 Ky. gubernatorial election, 563-65; C. begins to doubt loyalty of, 384, 533-34; criticized for erratic political course, 404-5, 515; break with C., 533-34, 542-43; calls for C.-Calhoun-Anti-Masonic coalition for 1832 presidential election, 506-7; endorses Wirt & Anti-Masons in 1832, 542-43; from, 533, 561; to, 59, 87, 96, 111, 541, 563, 599; mentioned, 120, 128, 177, 222, 390, 418, 514
Hammond, Jabez D.: to, 333
Hampton Roads, Va., 28, 458
Hancock, Md., 9
Hannah (slave), 87
Hanover, Ind., 396
Hanover, Pa., 722-23
Hanover Co., Va., 539, 548, 555, 720
Hardin, Benjamin: elected to U.S. House (1831), 345; mentioned as C. opponent for U.S. Senate seat (1831), 395; mentioned, 439, 652-53, 655
Hardin, John J.: to, 658
Hardin, Mark: advice to C. on political plans, 28-29, 34-35; on healing Old Court v. New Court schism, 29, 35; as possible candidate for U.S. Senate, 395; from, 28, 34; mentioned, 208
Hardin, Martin Davis, 658
Harding, Chester, 676
Hardy, Nathaniel: to, 69
Harlan, James, 649
Harold, William, 216
Harper, James, 130, 160, 165, 220, 263, 726, 737
Harper's Ferry, Va., 242, 777
Harriet (ship), 28, 34
Harriett (slave), 779-80, 841
Harrisburg, Pa., 192, 196-99, 201, 234, 236, 260, 270, 356, 470, 472-74, 513-14, 519, 524-26, 561, 730, 785, 806-7, 827

Harrison, Albert G., 799-800, 834
Harrison, Burr, 652-53
Harrison Co., Ky., 463
Harrison, James O., 231, 604
Harrison, Jesse Burton: writes anti-slavery pamphlet, 576; from, 11, 116; to, 64, 166, 313, 377, 399, 401, 575; mentioned, 30, 65, 166, 428
Harrison, John H., 434
Harrison, Margaretta Ross (Mrs. James O.), 604
Harrison, William Henry: criticism of Bolivar, 191; C. declines attending dinner for, 201, 314; U.S. Senate ambitions, 313-14; Ohio gubernatorial ambitions, 313-14; C. low opinion of, 795, 799; C. sees as militarist in Jackson mold, 795, 798-99; honored in Ky., 803; C. on as 1836 presidential candidate, 773, 776, 784, 788, 795 (see also Election (presidential) of 1836: William Henry Harrison candidacy); from, 191; mentioned, 9, 14, 16-17, 61, 185, 746, 770, 780, 785, 789, 792-93, 796, 800, 802, 806-7, 811, 827-28
Harrisonburg, Va., 778
Harrodsburg, Ky., 77, 94-95, 112, 137
Hart, Anna Gist, 732
Hart, Henry Clay (nephew of wife): borrows money from C. sans permission, 594; service in U.S. Navy, 594; health, 732; from, 594; mentioned, 185, 289, 305, 330
Hart, John, 771
Hart, Nathaniel (first cousin of wife): to, 826
Hart, Susannah Gray (mother-in-law), 281, 309, 319, 321-22, 482, 486, 489-90, 497, 563, 566, 568-71, 577, 584
Hart, Thomas, 86, 321, 496, 520
Hart, Thomas Pindell, 454
Hartford (Conn.) American Mercury, 94
Hartford, Conn., 666
Hartford Convention, 803
Harvard University, 95, 257, 265
Harvey, Matthew, 170, 189
Hassler, Ferdinand R.: from, 9
Hatter, James (not identified), 86
Havana, Cuba, 351
Hawes, Albert G., 358
Hawkins, James L.: from, 2
Hawley, William (not identified): from, 169
Hayne, Robert Y.: speech (1832) against tariff, 446,

448, 453, 459, 487; on 1832 tariff bill, 862-63; from, 459; mentioned, 193, 196, 204, 238, 279, 455-56, 464, 466, 468-69, 544, 548, 553
Haynes, Charles, 325
Haywood, Elijah, 121, 583
Headley, John: employed as overseer at "Ashland," 676; mentioned, 821-22, 834, 851
Heady, Stillwell, 345
Heard, Morgan A., 513
Heaton, James: to, 642, 788
Hector (bull), 805, 814, 827, 836, 867-68, 872
Helena, Arkansas, 130
Helm, _____, 86
Helm, Thomas: to, 609, 638
Hemphill, Joseph, 362, 411
Hendershott, Isaac (not identified): from, 68
Henderson, Stephen, 428
Hendricks, William: vote in U.S. Senate on confirming Jackson's appointment of printers & editors, 191-92, 198, 206; mentioned, 199, 287, 323, 837
Henkle, Moses M.: from, 798
Henley, Osborne, 86, 127
Henry (slave), 86
Henry (ship), 311
Henry, Gustavus A., 21, 28
Henry, John F.: from, 20; to, 27; mentioned, 21, 788
Henshaw, John P.H., 549
Herkimer, N.Y., 246, 248, 278, 524-25
"Hermitage," 32, 226
Herring, James; to, 454; mentioned, 455
Hertell, Thomas, 248
Hickman, John L.: from, 751; to, 751
Hieskell's City Hotel (Philadelphia), 3
Hieskell, Thomas, 3, 843
Higbee, Charles (not identified): from, 804; to, 804
Higgins, Richard, 520
Hill, Isaac: Jackson appoints second comptroller, 16-17; U.S. Senate votes down appointment of, 170-71, 187-88, 191-92, 193, 196; slanders Adams & wife, 16-17; power of in N.H., 312; elected U.S. Senator by N.H. legislature (1830), 193, 227; attacks on, 182, 187, 191-92, 196; mentioned, 20, 22, 198, 702, 734, 844
Hill, Leroy L. (not identified), 85-86
Hiriat, Sebastian: from, 178
Hise, Elijah, 807
Hith, _____, 526
Hitchcock, Ethan Allen, 235, 310

Hitchcock, Peter, 577
Hobbie, Selah R., 121
Hockaday, Edmund W.: from, 607; mentioned, 705
Hockaday, Philip B.: from, 607; mentioned, 697, 705
Hogan, William, 292
Holley, Mary Austin (Mrs. Horace), 40, 228, 842
Holman, Jesse L., 567
Holmes, John, 190, 204-5, 217, 520-21, 539, 566, 647
Hopkinsville, Ky., 27, 39, 101, 110, 112-13, 576
Horn, Henry, 737
Horn, John, 461
Hornblower, Joseph C., 573
Hottinguer & Co., 1, 806
Hot Springs, Va., 732, 777
Houston, George Smith: from, 121
Houston, Sam, 463, 493, 500, 513
Howard, Benjamin C., 25, 770
Howard, George: from, 55; mentioned, 585
Howard, Horton: from, 434
Howard, Mrs. John E., Jr., 810
Howard, Joseph: from, 452
Howell, Benjamin B.: from, 458
Howell, Elias, 749
Hoxie, Joseph, 323, 461-62
Hubard, William James, 479
Hudson River, 735
Hughes, Charles John: to, 844; mentioned, 207, 249
Hughes, Christopher: replaced as chargé in Holland, 71, 193; blames removal on Gallatin, 106, 161; C. supports as minister to Mexico, 161-62, 168; considers running for Congress, 162; on meager salary as U.S. diplomat in Sweden, 436; son Charles as artist, 207, 251; son Charles as West Point cadet, 844; on 1830 revolution in France, 251; on reform movement in England, 251; predicts C. defeat in 1832 election, 436; wants to be private secretary to President Clay, 731, 742-43, 798-99; urges C. to run for president, 730; ego of, 742-43; philosophy of life, death & history, 742-43; as sycophant to C., 742-43, 798-99; from, 105, 106, 193, 249, 436, 742; to, 161, 664, 730, 798
Humphrey, Edward P., 780
Humphreys, John, 739-40
Humrickhouse, Albert, Jr., 736
Hunt, Charles, 469, 495
Hunt, Charlton, 439, 442, 656-57, 864, 867

922

Hunt, John Wesley: to, 462; mentioned, 520, 763, 769
Hunt, Jonathan, 513
Hunter, Andrew (not identified): from, 242
Hunter, Charles G., 198
Huntingdon Co., Pa., 721, 727, 733
Hunton, Jonathan G., 170
Huntress (ship), 124
Huntt, Henry: from, 561; mentioned, 691, 715-16, 850
Huston, Felix: from, 501
Huston, William, Jr.: to, 122
Hutchcraft, John: from, 829; mentioned, 836, 851
Huygens, Mme. C.D.E.J. Bangeman, 135
Hyde, Edward (Earl of Clarendon), 775

Iberville Parish, La., 178
Illinois: Jacksonian patronage power in, 130-31; hemp raising potential, 271-78; general assembly elections (1830) in, 250-51, 251, 252, 254, 268-69; U.S. Senate election (1830) in, 259, 281-82, 286-87, 292-93, 307-8; U.S. House elections (1831) in, 365-66, 387-89, 401; public land distribution in, 481-82; C. land purchases in, 658; Indian incursions (Black Hawk War) into, 496-97, 529-31; elections (August 1834) for governor, general assembly, U.S. House in, 744-45, 745, 747-48; C. sets up son Thomas on farm in (*see* Clay, Thomas Hart); mentioned, 81, 132, 185, 213, 231, 253, 368, 391, 394, 409, 424, 429, 450, 454, 539-40, 575, 579-80, 586, 588, 590-91, 734, 750, 785, 812, 832, 834
Imlay, Gilbert, 538
Independence (ship), 718
India, 662
Indiana: general assembly elections (August 1829) in, 100-101, 125-30; C. on campaigning in, 420, 422; C. as landowner in, 131-32, 161; hemp raising potential of, 278; National Road reaches, 422; railroad charters authorized in, 458; state legislature nominates C. for president, 100-101; seeks BUS branches, 458; general assembly elections (August 1830) in, 250-51, 251, 252, 254, 268-69; U.S. Senate election (1830) in, 259, 287, 307-8; general assembly elections (August 1831) in,

389-90, 403-4, 455; U.S. Senate election (1832) in, 567; general assembly elections (August 1832) in, 567; C. popularity & presidential political support in, 100-101, 579-80, 589-91 (*see also* Election (presidential) of 1832: campaign & related political activity in specific states & sections–Indiana); National Republicans in choose C. electoral slate, 458; presidential campaign organization in, 458; elections for governor & general assembly (August 1834) in, 740, 743-44, 744-45, 745, 746-47, 748; anti-Jacksonism in, 746-47; legislature of, 388, 568, 798; mentioned, 192, 197-98, 206, 215, 231, 253, 368, 388, 394, 401, 409, 436, 500, 512, 538-40, 568, 570-72, 575, 586, 588, 592, 597, 750, 780, 785, 795, 798, 812, 832, 834, 857
Indianapolis, Ind., 422, 458, 746
Indianapolis *Indiana Aurora*, 798
Indians
—general: removals to West (*see espec.* 112, 563), 112, 136, 320, 563, 726-27, 759-60 (*see also* Congress of the United States: 21, 22, 23 Cong.; Election (presidential) of 1832: issues, charges & counter-charges in campaign–Jackson's Indian removal policy; Jackson administration: Indian policy & attitudes; U.S. Supreme Court); C. support of, 255, 726-27 (*see,* above, removals to West); *Worcester* v. *Georgia*, 318-19, 320 (*see also* U.S. Supreme Court); Indian rights in Treaty of Ghent, 358-59; Treaty of Greenville, 140; U.S. violations of treaties with, 221-22, 726-27; C. on dim future for all Indian lands, 846-47; Running Waters, Council of, 759-60; Indian Territory, 548
—Black Hawk: war of (*see espec.* 496-97), 496-97, 529-31, 531, 640-41, 860-61
—Cherokees: C. attempts to assist Cherokees, 759-60; C. on history of Cherokees, 811; Ga. attack on Cherokee Chief Ross, 811; mentioned, 112, 266, 358, 368, 460, 466, 473, 677, 726-27, 764, 861
—Chickasaw: treaty, 31-32; mentioned, 17
—Choctaw: C. condemns land

frauds against, 817; land sales to U.S., 701-2; treaty of Dancing Rabbit Creek, 818; mentioned, 702
—Creek: land sales to U.S., 701-2; mentioned, 112
—Fox, Sac, & Shawnee: 497, 679
—Seminoles: war with U.S. (*see espec.* 823), 104, 219, 318, 341, 823, 847, 860-61
Ingalls, William, 99
Ingersoll, Charles: from, 769; to, 771; mentioned, 425, 664, 772,
Ingersoll, Charles Jared, 771
Ingersoll, Edward, 380, 737
Ingham, Samuel D., 22, 99, 102, 136-37, 159, 167, 171-72, 174, 176, 181, 187, 234, 305, 320, 324, 326, 342, 351-52, 359, 365-66, 368, 370, 372-73, 425, 581
Inman, Henry, 702
Institut de France, 163, 184
Ipswich, Mass., 169
Iredell, James: to, 755
Ireland, 719-20
Ireland, William H. (not identified), 323
Irish, 15, 25, 69, 558-59
Irving, David, 286
Irving, George Washington: to, 771; mentioned, 333
Irwin, David, 447
Italy, 7, 249, 451, 810

Jackson administration (person, party, & problems): social & class composition of, 25, 79-80, 92, 120, 133, 169, 233, 313, 355, 501, 513, 548, 556, 581, 695; analysis of election of, 11; C. doubts intentions of, 11-12, 14, 55-56, 59-60, 61-62, 64-65, 79-80, 82-83, 108-10, 252-53; C. counsels acceptance of election victory of, 4, 13, 14-15; Jacksonism as revolution, 232, 236, 242, 245, 320, 342; compared to French revolutions, 22, 312, 411, 750; compared with English Civil War, 774-75, 775; charged with seeking civil war, 582, 609; European opinion of, 750; popularity of, 230, 661, 750; Jacksonian tyranny, militarism, dictatorship, 4-5, 14, 37, 61, 65, 67, 678, 684-84, 686, 717, 751 (*see also* Election (presidential) of 1832: issues, charges & counter-charges in campaign); Jackson's handling of personal interviews, 730; Houston's attack on Stanbery, 500; unpopularity

923

924

McLean, John (continued):
on C. prospects in 1832 elections, 421; relations with, attitudes toward & nomination by Anti-Masons (1831), 195, 268, 293-94, 305, 306, 345, 365, 366, 384, 392-93, 393-95, 398-99, 404, 404-5, 408-10, 412-15, 582; declines Anti-Masonic nomination, 405-6; betrays National Republican cause, 582; as presidential candidate in 1836, 666-67, 677-78 (see also Election (presidential) of 1836); C. on presidential candidacy of, 776-77, 783-85; Ohio legislature nominates for president in 1836, 783-85; mentioned, 29, 92-93, 97, 100-102, 106, 111, 114, 133, 165, 170, 174, 182, 187, 189, 227, 230, 282-83, 287, 318, 343, 349, 353, 355, 367, 371, 373, 375, 383, 390, 396, 401, 418, 572, 690, 769-70, 780, 788, 792-93, 795-96
McMahon, John Van Laer, 24-25, 68
McNair, John, 309
McNairy, Boyd: from, 206, 407; mentioned, 661
Macy, John B., 683
Madison, Dolley Payne (Mrs. James): from, 868; to, 870; mentioned, 269, 636, 643, 859, 868-71
Madison, James: defense of Va. Resolves (1798), 279, 282; C. on Va. Resolves of, 343; role in Va. constitutional convention, 116; supports American Colonization Society, 870-71; on increase in slave labor, 636; on problems of economic sectionalism, 635-36, 646-47; congratulates C. on Cincinnati speech (8/3/30), 279; on C. tariff speech (2/2/32), 475; on the South & the tariff, 479, 646-47; on need for sectional compromise on tariff, 479; on C. compromise tariff of 1833 (see espec. 621-22, 626-27), 635-36, 643, 646-47; on S.C. nullification, 279-80, 636; on disunion, 646-47; on U.S. Constitution & pocket veto, 646; on U.S. population growth, 646; tobacco culture in Va., 647; recommends candidate for Transylvania University presidency, 328; on claims crisis with France, 759; on maritime law & neutral rights, 759; C. visits at "Montpelier" home, 558, 574;

declining health, 574; hopes C. can compromise abolition issue & gain presidency, 859; death, 859, 868; legacies provided by will of, 871; wife Dolley as literary executor of, 868-70, 870-71; franking privileges for Dolley, 859; Congress acquires & publishes papers of, 868-70, 870-71; from, 279, 328, 479, 635, 646, 759; to, 269, 643, 662; mentioned, 65, 190, 298, 344, 595
Madison, Pa., 785
Madison College (Pa.), 871
Madison Co., Ky., 66, 272, 835, 851
Madison Co., Va., 397
Madisonville, Ky., 76, 93
Madrid, Spain, 849
Magazine of Useful and Entertaining Knowledge, 242
Magill, Alfred T., 662
Magnum Bonum (jackass), 835
Mahmud II (Turkey), 456
Maine: doubtful support for C. (1832), 164-65; C. popularity & support in, 562; confusion of Jacksonians in, 169-70; gubernatorial election (1830) in, 170; legislative elections (1830) in, 267, 282, 297, 314; state elections (1832) in, 562, 577; state elections (1833) in, 647-48; gubernatorial & legislative elections (1834) in, 746-47, 749; Anti-Masons in, 385; Jackson visits, 647-48; strength & discipline of Jackson party in, 647-48; removal of deposits from BUS issue in, 691, 717-18; military road at Mars Hill, 727; mentioned, 43, 73, 96, 161, 254, 259, 320, 368, 385, 394, 423, 481, 543, 552, 570, 572, 586, 668, 780, 785, 817, 837, 854, 856
Major (slave), 87
Majorca, 830
Malcolm (bull), 805
Malker & Co., 8
Mallary, Rollin C., 355
Mallory, Daniel: from, 122, 386, 456; mentioned, 241, 252
Malta, 805, 812, 826, 835
Mangum, Willie P.: to, 745; mentioned, 682, 697-98, 785, 855
"Mansfield," 843, 851
Mansion Hotel (Washington, D.C.), 3, 6
"Maplewood," 704, 779
Marblehead, Mass., 665
Marcandier, _____, 167-68
Marcy, William L.: on patronage politics (victors & spoils),

450; nomination for governor of N.Y., 500, 524-25; mentioned, 248, 304, 487, 626, 694, 709, 741
Marigny, Bernard de, 441
Marks, William, 287
Marriner, Maj. _____, 687
Marshall, Eliza Price (Mrs. Thomas A.), 321, 704
Marshall, Humphrey, 448, 538, 854
Marshall, James K., 201
Marshall, John: mentioned as presidential candidate in 1832, 392; disinterest in presidential nomination, 406; on C.'s report on distribution of public land sales revenue, 506; asks personal favor of C. for nephew, 632; health, 406, 417; death, 406, 794; from, 632; mentioned, 65, 190, 298
Marshall, Thomas A., 66, 74-75, 78, 388-89, 437, 458, 563, 568, 667
Marshall, William, 632
Mars Hill, Me., 727
Marston, Stephen W. (not identified): from, 83
Martin, John G. (not identified), 75
Martin, Samuel: from, 470
Martin, William (overseer): conveys cattle to & from "Ashland," 585, 597, 602, 609; instructions to on management of farm, 663-64, 668; C. displeased with work of, 676, 681-82, 692, 714; to, 663; mentioned, 86, 184, 192, 319, 321, 469, 488-89, 495, 497, 502, 504, 508, 529, 602, 671, 675, 704
Martineau, Elizabeth Raykin, 777
Martineau, Harriet: C. courtesy to, 777-78; family of, 790-91; travels in Va., 777-78, 791; visits C. in Lexington, Ky., 777-78, 791; weight of, 778; opinions of C.'s children, 778
Martinsburg, Va. (W. Va.), 94
Martinsburg (Va.) Gazette, 94
Mary (two slaves by same name), 85, 86
Maryland: Lucretia Clay born in, 209; poor roads, 2; C. praises politics of, 13, 209; Bank of, 707, 709-10; Historical Society of, 447; University of, 662; C. popularity & political support in, 24, 237, 368, 447, 483, 549; C. political tactics in, 293; Jackson political tactics in, 266; doubtful C. political

932

Natural Bridge, Va., 777
Naudain, Arnold, 865-66
Navy. *See* U.S. Navy
Nelson Co., Ky., 386, 391
Nelson Co., Va., 544
Netherlands: Belgian civil war against, 605; King William and Northeast boundary arbitration, 552; mentioned, 161-62, 164, 193, 734
Newark, N.J., 666
New Brunswick, Canada, 837
New Court party (Ky.), 35
New England: early support for C. presidential candidacy in, 67, 76-77, 95-96, 107-8, 118-20, 122, 164-65 (*see also* Election (presidential) of 1832: campaign & related political activity in specific states & sections); decline of Jacksonism in, 95-96; support for Maysville Road bill in, 204-5, 206; tariff issue in, 70-71, 95-96; depression in, 108-10, 110; Southern dislike of, 108-10; C. likes people of, 108-10; Anti-Masonry in, 353-54, 385, 394; mentioned, 16, 33, 55-56, 84, 88, 93, 101, 117, 139, 159, 169-70, 186, 199, 202, 210, 249, 257, 299, 307, 313, 333, 337, 374, 393, 447, 603, 623, 626, 628, 635, 647-48, 655, 665, 673, 696, 780
New Granada, South America, 490
New Hampshire: doubtful C. support in for 1832, 164-65; Jacksonism in, 188-89, 312, 384-85; Anti-Masonry in, 384-85; gubernatorial & legislative elections (1830) in, 169-70, 189; state legislative elections (1831) in, 332; power of Isaac Hill in, 312; removal of deposits from BUS issue in, 691; legislature of, mentioned, 17, 84, 93, 172, 193, 227, 320, 368, 374, 394, 423, 586, 697, 702, 785
New Hampshire Sentinel, 94
New Haven, Conn., 516, 665-66
New Jersey: C. support in, 1-2, 99-100, 164-65, 219, 368; Jacksonism in, 120, 318-19; support for American System in, 1-2; nomination of C. for president, 404; legal conflict with N.Y., 474; cholera epidemic in, 561; removal of deposits from BUS issue in, 583, 684-85, 691, 692, 706-7; Anti-Masonic sentiment in, 318,

404, 573, 575, 595, 601-2; state elections (1829) in, 99-100, 120, 132-34; state elections (1830) in, 245, 256, 260, 267, 297-98, 308, 309, 318, 321-22, 323-24; U.S. House elections (1830) in, 297; state elections (1831) in, 444; state elections (1832) in, 573, 584-85, 587-88, 595, 601-2; U.S. House elections (1832) in, 601-2; U.S. Senate election (1833) in, 601-2; state elections (1834) in, 741, 746-47, 750; legislature of, 246, 691, 692, 717; mentioned, 24, 26, 31-34, 36, 72, 80, 93, 132, 147, 159, 210, 227, 257, 311, 371, 410, 423, 430, 456, 474, 503, 512, 528, 539, 562, 592, 628, 679, 688, 704, 730, 785, 792, 848, 866. *See also* Southard, Samuel L.
New Market, Va., 645-46
New Orleans: C. business affairs in, 23; Battle of, 179; C. opinion of, 399-400; C. visits to, 66, 289; C. on law practice in, 399-400; H. Clay, Jr., studies law in & considers law practice in, 603-4 (*see also* Clay, Henry, Jr.); cosmopolitanism of, 400; speculative opportunities in, 457-58; C. interest in real estate in, 629, 642; property values in, 839; C. popularity in, 178, 179, 427-28 (*see also* Louisiana); yellow fever in, 587; cholera in, 587, 602, 649, 650, 651; character of population, 575-76; Creole hostility to Jackson in, 66; military depot at, 444; mentioned, 18, 30, 40, 65, 113, 130, 134, 136, 161-63, 165-69, 172-73, 177, 181, 184-85, 189-92, 209, 211, 214, 257, 261, 281, 285, 298-99, 303, 309, 311-16, 319, 322, 325, 329-30, 332-33, 336-37, 344, 350, 357, 369, 401, 410, 425, 429, 431, 433-35, 437-38, 448, 451-52, 468-69, 480-82, 487, 490, 495, 499, 502, 509, 518, 579, 600, 607, 632, 638, 640, 652, 665, 681, 732, 737, 739-40, 757, 763-64, 771, 800, 802, 808, 814, 826, 834-35, 837, 841. *See also* Louisiana
New Orleans *Courier*, 401
Newport, Ky., 571
Newport, R.I., 843
Newspapers: attempts to save pro-C. Washington *Daily National Journal*, 104, 128-29,

130, 185, 197-98, 203-4, 326-27, 350-51, 369-71; C. on *Niles' Register*, 355-56; Redwood Fisher launches N.Y. *American Advocate and Journal*, 386-87; Louisville *Focus* supports C. for U.S. Senate, 421; collapse of Albany *Daily Morning Chronicle*, 440; Washington *National Union* launched, 520-21; Jackson's appointment of editors & printers to public office, 20, 47-48, 61, 121, 124-25, 188, 751. *See also* Election (presidential) of 1832: newspapers, journals, printed speeches & pamphlets
New York *American Advocate*, 387
New York City: opposition to Van Buren banking plan in, 90; opposition to Albany Regency in, 240-41; Van Buren rejection by, 458-59, 459-60, 461-62; opposition to Jackson in, 240, 578, 715, 726; political factionalism in, 240-41; size & character of electorate, 283, 290; pro-C. sentiment in, 122, 128, 283, 362; organization of C. party in (*see espec.* 306-7), 306, 306-7, 308, 312, 323, 327, 348-49; newspaper support for C., 241; state elections (November 1830) in (*see espec.* 248), 240-41, 242, 248, 283-84, 289; C. defeat in fall 1830 elections in, 289-92; Workingmen's party in (*see* Workingmen's party); Anti-Masonic movement in, 240-41; city-wide elections (April 1831) in (*see espec.* 289-92), 289-92, 331-32, 348-49, 353-55; 1832 presidential campaign in, 455, 578; Masonic Hall in, 460, 578, 594; C. for president rallies in (1832), 594; city-wide charter elections (April 1834) in (*see espec.* 704-5), 704-5, 705, 709, 710, 712-13, 714, 714-15, 715, 726; economic distress in, 704-5; great fire (December 1835) in & aid to sufferers of, 817, 818, 818-19; C. criticism of merchants of, 818-19; American Institute organized in, 856; mentioned, 87, 177, 212, 247, 334, 344, 356, 364, 369, 374, 401, 422-23, 443-44, 483, 490, 511, 532, 544-45, 632, 635, 664, 666-67, 683, 696, 706, 711, 802, 828, 834, 849-50. *See also* New York State

933

935

Paris, France, 1, 116, 122, 166, 193, 216, 230, 249, 265, 270, 289, 295, 401, 452, 495, 605, 727, 743, 754, 765, 818, 825
Paris, Ill., 132, 658
Paris, Ky., 319, 321, 333, 402, 458, 654, 751, 803
Park, Roswell, 226
Parker, Daniel, 434, 607-8
Parks, Gorham, 648
Parks, James, 92, 201
Patrick, Thomas C. (not identified): to, 655
Patterson, Daniel T.: from, 830
Patterson, Joseph W., 357
Patterson, Robert M., 280
Patterson, Thomas: from, 67, 120, 137, 362, 372; mentioned, 68, 138
Patton, John M.: to, 840; mentioned, 410
Paulding, James Kirke: from, 632; to, 632
Pawling, William: from, 395
Payne, Buckner H.: from, 464, 574, 582, 658, 663; mentioned, 402
Payne, John, 286
Payne, John Cole, 868, 871
Payne, John Howard: Ga. outrage against, 811; to, 665, 811
Payne, John R.D.: to, 692; mentioned, 693
Payne, Susan Bryce (Mrs. John R.D.), 693
Pearce, Dutee J., 96, 802-3
Pearce, Isaac, 248
Peck, James H., 317, 321
Peck, John (not identified): from, 350
Pedder, James, 875
Pedraza, Manual Gomez, 5
Peel, Robert, 37
Peers, Benjamin O.: C. sons attend school of, 285, 319, 321, 425, 452, 491; president of Transylvania University, 753; resigns as Transylvania University president, 735
Peggy (slave), 86
Pendleton, Edmund H.: to, 659, 663
Penn, Shadrach, 23
Pennsylvania: Jackson support in, 64-65, 281-82, 315, 522; decline of Jacksonism in, 79-80, 233-34, 279, 335, 347, 365-66, 367-68, 439-40, 527, 569, 726; Jackson party in splits, 365-66, 367-68, 516-17, 522-23, 532, 557-58; breakdown of parties in, 25, 78; C. support in, 80, 107-8, 120-21, 132, 258, 260, 351-52, 355, 362, 522-23, 558; nomination of Jackson

in, 191-92, 197-98, 199-200, 347; nomination of C. in, 259-60; C. party overoptimism in, 260; key to halting Jacksonism, 320; gubernatorial election (1829) in, 78, 126-27; tariff issue in, 131, 196, 198, 315, 321-22, 502-3, 505, 525-26, 527; state elections (1830) in, 259-60, 267, 286, 306; U.S. Senate election (1830) in, 286-87, 315; internal improvements issue in, 315; BUS issue in, 527, 827; Bank of, 439, 749; Van Buren support in, 159-60, 525-26; Calhoun faction in, 365-66; state elections (1831) in, 378-79, 424-25; Anti-Masonic party in, 78 (see also Anti-Masonic party); Anti-Masonic alliance with National Republican party in (see espec. 514-15), 303-4, 514-15, 522-23, 524, 558-59, 561, 562, 568, 589-92; gubernatorial election (1832) in (see espec. 514-15), 514-15, 516-17, 522-23, 524, 525, 527, 557-58, 569, 575, 580-81, 584, 586, 587-88, 588-89, 589; state & U.S. House elections (1832) in, 580; local inspector elections (1832) in, 579-80, 580-81, 581, 585-86, 586, 589; Anti-Masonic nominating convention (1831) in (see espec. 513-14), 356-57, 469-70, 514-15; National Republican nominating convention (1832) in (see espec. 514-15), 444-45, 469-70, 513-15, 516-17, 519, 519-20, 522-23, 525, 525-26, 526-27, 557-58, 561; Democratic Jackson nominating convention in, 472-73, 473-74; nomination of Van Buren in, 515; National Republican presidential campaign (1832) in, 549; C. party cannot carry (1832), 279; C. party holds (1832) balance of power in, 505; Irish role in politics of, 557-58, 559; cholera epidemic in, 558-59, 561; Governor Wolf on BUS issue, 720-21, 721-22, 723; removal of deposits from BUS issue in, 701, 705, 720-21, 721-22, 723, 727, 730, 734; state elections (1834) in, 726, 737, 740-41, 745-46, 747-48, 749, 750; gubernatorial election (1835) in, 775-76, 785, 792, 796,

798-99, 802-3, 803; key to Harrison 1836 presidential hopes, 800; Harrison nominating convention (1835) in, 785, 806, 806-7, 827; presidential movement for C. (1835) in, 806-7; presidential election (1836) in, 788-89; emancipation of slaves in, 789-90; U.S. senators of instructed on expunging resolution, 832; Academy of Fine Arts of, 479; general assembly of, 832; hospital of, 618; house of representatives in, 858; Society for Promoting the Abolition of the Death Penalty in, 667; state legislature of, 80, 192, 315, 347, 425, 440, 502, 503, 527, 593, 722, 723, 785, 875; university of, 319; mentioned, 20, 81, 91-92, 101-2, 106, 137, 139, 142, 144, 155, 164-65, 170-72, 176, 186, 195, 205, 215, 219, 221, 256, 262, 270, 293, 305, 324-25, 331, 339, 343, 346, 353, 355, 361, 364, 371-72, 375-76, 381, 383-84, 394, 399, 408, 410, 417, 422-23, 430, 448, 460-61, 498, 500, 506, 510, 512, 528, 543, 546-47, 553, 555, 560, 564, 572-74, 576-77, 582, 585, 594-95, 597, 599, 628, 687, 696-97, 729, 756, 771, 780, 784, 793-95, 804. See also Election (presidential) of 1832: campaign & related political activity in specific states & sections-Pennsylvania; Election (presidential) of 1836: campaign & related political activity in specific states & sections-Pennsylvania
Pensacola, Fla., 34
Perkins, T.H. (not identified): to, 665
Perrault & Allain, 337
Perrow, Charles: to, 543; mentioned, 544
Perisco, Luigi, 847
Peru, 5-6
Peter Lely (horse), 836
Peterson, William F. (not identified): from, 364, 374, 384
Petit, Nathaniel, 497
Pettis, F.H.: from, 313
Pettis, Spencer C., 313, 366, 388
Pettit, William N. (not identified): from, 361
Phantomia (horse), 757
Philadelphia, Pa.: class background & activities of Jackson party in, 695; Anti-

936

Schenectady, N.Y., 680, 714
Scholefield, John: from, 666; mentioned, 667
Science: meteor shower (11/13/33), 696-97; C. on phrenology, 722; medicine (see Lexington, Ky.: cholera epidemic in)
Scioto River, 204, 399
Scotland, 449
Scott, Charles, 649, 652
Scott, Gustavus H.: from, 3
Scott, Henley & Co., 127
Scott, John, 790
Scott, Judith Cary Bell Gist (Mrs. Charles), 649, 652
Scott, Lucius H. & J.: from, 492
Scott, Robert: alleged business scandal involving R.W. Wickliffe, 329, 334-35, 341-42; mentioned, 122, 127, 329, 454
Scott, Winfield: interest in H. Clay, Jr., 363; mentioned, 298, 411
Scott Co., Ky., 730
Seaton, William W.: from, 2, 582; to, 2, 448, 449, 453; mentioned, 104, 172-73, 313, 382, 395, 450-51, 458, 477, 623, 633, 635, 670, 741, 863
Seaton, Mrs. William W., 741
Selden, Dudley, 292, 687
Selden, Joseph Dudley, 687
Semmes, Benedict J., 104
Seneca Co., Ohio, 452
Seneca Falls, N.Y., 727
Seneca River, 600
Sergeant, John: on C.'s political future, 78, 229-30; on Jackson administration, 78, 229-30, 232-34, 367-68; informs & advises C. on Pa. politics, 78, 232-34, 367-68, 444, 516-17, 522-23, 524, 525, 525-26, 569; on C. prospects in 1832 election, 229-30, 232-34, 431; declines to run for U.S. Congress, 229-30; advises C. on campaign style, 229-30, 367-68; says C. writes too many letters, 367; campaigns for C., 362; pre-election analysis & predictions, 367-68, 411-12, 431, 516-17; on Jackson's cabinet officers, 368; on early recharter of BUS, 444; on National Republican convention (1831) events, 431; nomination for vice president on National Republican ticket (1832), 431, 433, 434, 458, 516-17, 522-23; prospects for election as vice president (1832), 516-17, 524; opposes C.'s compromise

tariff bill (1833), 630, 633; from, 78, 229, 232, 260, 264, 367, 411, 431, 444, 516, 522, 524, 525, 527, 557, 561, 569, 680, 682; to, 726; mentioned, 2, 97, 365-66, 372, 406, 418, 439, 474, 532, 543, 553, 557, 562, 575, 681
Serurier, Louis B. C.: from, 549; mentioned, 766-67, 806
Seward, William H., 568
Seymour, Horatio, 539
Shackelford (Shackleford), William, 504, 508, 518
Shadrack (slave), 86
Shakespeare (horse), 475, 495
Shaler, Charles: from, 618
Shannon, James, 228, 382, 462
Sharpsburg, Ky., 650
Shaw, Henry: from, 407; to, 666, 759
Shelby, Alfred, 604
Shelby, Isaac, 31-32, 596
Shelby, James, 31-32, 352, 657, 834-35
Shelby, Richard, 117, 185
Shelby, Thomas H., 31-32
Shelby Co., Ky., 124, 272, 596, 853
Shelbyville, Ky., 53, 124-25
Shelbyville, Tenn., 207, 213
Shelton, Edwin: from, 633
Shelton, John, 633
Shelton, Susan E. Oliver (Mrs. Edwin), 633
Shepherd, Rezin D.: from, 804; mentioned, 805-6, 834, 836, 841
Shepherdstown, Va. (W. Va.), 736, 804-6, 836, 868
Shepley, Ether, 647
Shinn, William N., 602
Shippen, Edwin, 557
Short, Charles, 319
Shulze, John A., 78
Sibby (slave), 86
Sibley, John: from, 642
Sierra Leone, Africa, 34
Silsbee, Nathaniel, 337, 443, 759
Simpson, Eveline (not identified): to, 203
Simpson, John G.: from, 85; mentioned, 86
Simpson, Stephen, 383, 385, 524
Singleton, Richard, 464
Sir Lovel (horse), 415
Skidmore, Thomas, 248
Skinner, Frederick, 232
Skinner, John S., 68
Slade, William, 355
Slavery: Nat Turner rebellion, 397; British responsibility for in U.S., 7-8; total value of U.S. slaves, 535-37; freeing Abduhl Rahaman, 28, 34; compensatory emancipation,

535-37; financing colonization with public land sales revenues, 535-37; William Jay on, 768; and purchase of Texas, 132; role in Mo. Compromise issue, 786-88; American slaves & Russian serfs, 167; brutality toward, 428-29; supported by God, 773-74; solving national problem that is, 471. See also Clay, Henry: slaves & slavery
Sloane, John: from, 404, 419; to, 61, 235, 340, 414, 424, 585, 586; mentioned, 420, 564, 583
Smiley, _____, 389
Smilie, John, 472
Smith, _____, 700
Smith (William S.) & Mason (Daniel M.) Commission Merchants, 277-78
Smith, Benjamin B.: from, 864; mentioned, 808-9
Smith, Daniel, 343
Smith, Francis O. J., 647
Smith, Hamilton: to, 745
Smith, John (not identified): from, 436
Smith, Margaret Bayard (Mrs. Samuel Harrison): to, 850; mentioned, 768, 777-78, 809
Smith, Maslin, 86
Smith, Nannette Price (Mrs. Thomas), 487, 655-57
Smith, Nathan, 515
Smith, Oliver H., 389
Smith, Richard, 253
Smith, Samuel, 106, 161, 196, 198, 218, 443, 498, 551
Smith, Samuel Emerson, 170, 577, 647
Smith, Samuel G., 464
Smith, Samuel Harrison, 777-78
Smith, T. R., 248
Smith, Thomas: from, 439, 806; mentioned, 161, 206, 226, 319, 443, 518, 560, 649, 656-57, 801-2, 834-35, 843, 851
Smith, William, 171-72, 785
Smyth, Alexander, 48-49
Snead, John S.: to, 781
Snider, Jacob, Jr.: to, 874
Snowden, Edgar: to, 405
Somerset Co., Md., 104
South: dislike of New England, 108-10; disappointment with Jackson administration, 119-20; need for industry, 501; attacks on tariff in, 57-58, 131 (see also Congress of the United States: 22 Cong., 2 Sess.; Election (presidential) of 1832: issues, charges & counter-charges in campaign); opposition to Maysville Road bill in, 204-5;

943

U.S. Congress. *See* Congress of the United States

U.S. diplomacy: C. performance as secretary of state, 244-45, 845-46; C. lauded for support of Latin American independence, 490; C.'s Panama Congress Instructions, 16, 19; C. sees U.S. under Jackson as aggressive, 766. *See also* individual nations

U.S. District Court: for the District of Columbia, 278; for Kentucky, 713; for Louisiana, 630; for Missouri, 317; for New Jersey, 764; for Ohio, 599; for Pennsylvania, 750, 764

U.S. General Land Office: impact of 1830 Script Act upon, 744-45; mentioned, 89, 545, 583

U.S. House of Representatives committees: Judiciary, 333; Post Office & Post Roads, 872; Ways & Means, 196, 325-26, 608, 619, 624, 687, 699

U.S. Marine Corps, 729

U.S. Military Academy: pressure on H. Clay, Jr., 234-35, 256-57 (*see also* Clay, Henry, Jr.); opposition to within board of visitors, 228; C. on Sylvanus Thayer, 256; C. opinion of graduates, 844. *See also* West Point, N.Y.

U.S. Mint, 761

U.S. Navy: status at end of Adams administration, 12; Jackson dismisses dueling officers, 194, 197-98, 199-200; sectional interests in, 238; security against British impressment, 453; loyalty to civilian rule & civil liberties, 717; proposed increase during French crisis, 820; western river seamen join in time of crisis, 832; C. sees as floating fortification system, 764; mentioned, 17, 105, 155, 169, 277, 280, 289, 413, 491, 583, 631, 766, 848

U.S. Patent Office: C. opposes new building to house, 856-57, 858; mentioned, 89, 872

U.S. Post Office: C. distrust of, 220, 585-86; suppression of mail for political purposes, 585-86; C. attacks corruption & politics in, 734; bill to reorganize, 758 (*see also* Congress of the United States: 23 Cong., 2 Sess., 24 Cong., 1 Sess.); contracts to move mail by railroad, 843; building

of in Washington burns, 872, 873; attempt to exclude slavery materials from mail, 814-15, 826-27, 853; mentioned, 137, 175, 187, 525, 583, 629, 680, 760, 844, 855

U.S. Senate, Journal of the, 717-18, 735

U.S. Senate committees: Agriculture, 753; Bank, 495, 499, 619, 623; Claims, 550; Commerce, 521; Finance, 196, 435, 443, 498, 689-90, 694, 741, 823; Foreign Relations, 448, 753, 754, 755, 756-57, 759, 766, 820-24, 827, 837 849, 854-59; Indian Affairs, 760; Judiciary, 687, 713, 725, 732, 760; Library of Congress, 871; Manufactures, 477, 481-82, 484, 494, 499, 502, 504, 507, 535, 539-40, 546-47, 549, 552, 679, 689, 864; Pensions, 854; Post Office & Post Roads, 758, 872; Public Lands, 112, 494, 502, 507, 521, 535-36, 539, 540-41, 546, 610, 679, 702, 723, 733, 753, 820, 834; Roads & Canals, 472, 521; Select, 623

U.S. State, Department of, 9, 34, 51, 61, 105, 173, 370, 491, 555, 562, 583, 827, 845-46, 857

U.S. Supreme Court: cases argued by C. before, 767-68, 821; number & geographical distribution of justices, 764; C. on *Worcester* v. *Georgia*, 320, 323-24, 678 (*see also* Indians; Jackson administration); C. against Webster in *Minor* v. *Tillottson* (1833), 629-30, 631-32, 633; *Cohens* v. *Virginia* (1821), 623; *BUS* v. *Osborne* (1824), 623; *U.S.* v. *Brewster* (1833), 750-51; *Boone* v. *Chiles* (1835), 821; attacks on, 750; mentioned, 17, 22, 89, 92, 190, 278, 333, 406, 472, 474-77, 482, 587, 614, 678, 727, 781. *See also* Constitution of the United States

Ustick, T.W., 79

U.S. Treasury, Department of, 9, 17, 22-23, 137, 169, 174, 193, 278, 370-71, 381, 474, 487, 491, 551, 608, 619, 621, 630-31, 684, 688, 690, 699, 707-8, 711, 717, 721, 727, 733, 813, 846, 854-57

U.S. War, Department of, 134, 229, 242, 329, 336, 491, 589, 691, 848

Utica, N.Y., 311, 504, 510, 524-25, 532, 556, 558, 568, 586

Vail, Aaron, 771

Valparaiso, Mexico, 594

Van Buren, Martin: ambition to be U..S minister to Britain, 92; role in Jackson administration, 73-74, 119, 159-60, 164-65, 176, 195; motive for supporting Jackson, 92, 131, 205; opinion of Jackson, 174-75; political liabilities, 202; weak political support in South, 529; political prospects in Ga., 136-37, 158; political prospects in N.C., 137, 158; political prospects in N.J., 80; political prospects in N.Y., 158, 202, 466, 474-75, 475; political prospects in Pa., 525-26; political prospects in Va., 100, 137, 158, 205, 209, 210, 218, 316, 327, 529; political prospects in West, 158; presidential ambitions & prospects, 104, 136, 137, 158, 159, 164, 164-65, 167, 170-71, 187-88, 189, 191-92, 194, 197-99, 199-200, 202, 205, 210; conflict with Calhoun within Jackson administration, 80, 104, 119, 120, 126, 138, 164, 167, 170, 187, 189, 191-92, 194, 195, 196, 198, 201, 218-19, 230, 288-89, 318, 322, 349; hostility toward McLean, 322; early support of BUS, 366; opposition to BUS, 263; politics of BUS issue, 672, 683, 686-87; on tariff issue, 465; role in Peggy Eaton crisis, 126, 136, 138, 159, 164, 171-72; role in cabinet resignation crisis (1831), 370-71; resigns as secretary of state, 338, 342, 349, 359; reputation as secretary of state, 368; performance as secretary of state, 368, 562; instructions to McLane (*see* McLane, Louis); as vice presidential nominee in 1832 (*see* Election (presidential) of 1832: Martin Van Buren role in); nomination of & Senate rejection as U.S. minister to Britain, 342-44, 365, 370-71, 443-44, 445-46, 448, 450, 455, 458-59, 460-62, 463-64, 465, 466, 466-67, 468, 475, 488, 547-48, 597-98; performance as minister to Britain, 453; designated successor to Jackson in 1836, 547-48, 661-62; C. criticizes as designated successor to Jackson, 706, 782, 782-83; reaction to

The Virginia Advocate, (Charlottesville), 76
Vroom, Peter D., 245, 741

Wabash Canal, 458
Wabash River, 132, 161, 450, 735, 747, 755, 831
Wager, Peter, 681
Waggaman, George A., 86, 189, 359, 365, 369, 419, 434, 482, 681-82, 732, 753
Walker, Robert J.: elected to U.S. Senate, 777; graduation and preemption land bill, 839; mentioned, 844, 857
Wallace, D. C. (not identified): to, 721
Wallace, David, 389
Walsh, Robert, Jr.: criticizes C. acceptance of Senate seat, 425; misunderstands C. stance on S.C. nullification, 616, 630, 633; C. extends olive branch to, 846; solicits C.'s evaluation of his career as secretary of state, 845; to, 845; mentioned, 627, 747
War: C. on principles of, 87; C. on threat of general war in Europe, 338; C. thinks preparation for threatens, 766
Ward, Henry Dana, 290-91, 301-2, 304
Ward, Richard R., 284, 290
Warden, David B., 116
Warfield, Elisha, 576
Warfield, George F.: from, 23
Warfield, Margaret Wilson (Mrs. Walter), 271
Warfield, Walter, 271
Warm Springs, Va., 556
War of the American Revolution: C. involvement in pension claims of veterans & heirs, 509, 730-31, 757, 758, 840, 844, 873; claims issuing from, 690, 726; mentioned, 141-42, 148, 430, 509, 576, 679, 690, 695, 726, 732-34, 744, 758, 765, 840, 844, 854, 873
War of 1812: Wellington asked to command British armies, 1; C.'s 1830 view of, 179; C. on Treaty of Ghent, 179; impact of on BUS recharter (*see espec.* 2:200-201), 723; disastrous nature of, 552; massacre at River Raisin, 679; C. public service during, 803; C. on burning of U.S. Capitol, 839; mentioned, 20, 190, 458, 764
Warren Co., Ky., 217, 564
Warrenton, Va., 716, 718, 724
Warrior (jackass), 665, 670-71, 697, 704, 779, 806
Washington (slave), 87

Washington, George: proposal to remove remains of to Washington City, 462, 463, 464, 465, 545; centennial birthday dinner honoring, 466; statue of, 545; disposition of personal papers of, 871; mentioned, 8
Washington, George Corbin: to, 208, 377
Washington, John A., 464
Washington, D.C.: social life in under Jackson, 78, 80-81, 96, 98, 135, 317, 368, 691; C. withdraws (1836) from social life of, 821; depression in, 81, 317; cholera in, 581; furnishing & furbishing of White House, 135, 760; paintings & statues for Capitol, 702, 847; C.'s farewell (1829) speech in, 4-6, 252; C. lodging & housekeeping arrangements in, 437-38, 667, 672-73, 680, 682, 868; congressional support of Columbian College in, 521; acoustical problems in U.S. House chamber, 385; "Temple of Liberty" proposed for, 385; repayment of Dutch loan used to buy canal stock (*see espec.* 742), 734, 742, 765, 828; free bridge across Potomac at, 531, 532-33; National Republican young men's nominating convention in, 507-8, 547-48, 572, 581; C. takes plants home from, 767; issue of slave trade & slavery in, 793 (*see also* Congress of the United States: 24 Cong., 1 Sess.–abolition of slavery/slave trade in D.C.); post office fire in, 872, 873; C. on corrupt atmosphere of, 638; mentioned, 2-3, 7-8, 10, 16, 18, 20, 22-23, 25, 32-35, 37, 50-51, 59-62, 65, 67, 69, 71, 74, 76, 79, 82, 84, 86, 89-90, 95, 100, 104, 106, 110-11, 114, 120, 123, 126, 130-32, 136-37, 147-48, 158, 162, 164, 168-69, 174-76, 186, 188-89, 191-94, 197, 199-202, 204-5, 208-10, 212-14, 218, 220-21, 229-30, 234, 237, 244, 261-62, 267, 295, 301, 306, 310-13, 321, 323, 327, 331-32, 341-43, 349, 351, 362, 365, 371-72, 374, 376, 378-79, 383, 390, 396, 402, 404, 407, 410, 416, 422, 425-27, 429, 433-34, 440-41, 444, 448, 451, 455, 460-67, 473, 476, 479, 481, 490, 494, 516-18, 520, 522,

525, 529, 537, 545, 550, 557, 559-60, 563-64, 567, 580-85, 588, 595, 597, 599-601, 603, 606, 617, 622, 626, 630-32, 634, 636, 642, 644, 648, 655, 662, 666, 668, 670, 676, 695-96, 705, 710, 713-15, 738-39, 743, 746, 748, 751-54, 757, 768-69, 786, 804-5, 810, 818, 822, 833, 844, 851, 859, 867, 869-70, 874
Washington, Pa., 9, 38, 371, 618, 769
Washington (bull), 668
Washington Bridge Co., 533
Washington *Chronicle*, 79
Washington *City Gazette*, 90
Washington College (Md.), 771
Washington Co., Ky., 653
Washington Co., Md., 104
Washington Co., N.Y., 118, 387
Washington Co., Pa., 63, 471, 492
Washington *Daily National Intelligencer*, 2, 16, 55, 94, 154, 189, 271, 296, 394-95, 448, 450-51, 456, 458, 464, 569, 582, 609, 670, 685, 745, 816, 835
Washington *Daily National Journal*, 2, 6, 16-17, 19, 79, 82, 94, 104, 106, 128-30, 171-72, 185, 197, 203, 252, 262, 295, 326-27, 350-51, 369, 534-35
Washington *Globe*, 297, 313, 322, 324, 327, 380, 449-51, 453, 558, 582, 670, 678, 750-51, 857
Washington *National Union*, 520, 563
Washington-Rockville Turnpike, 549
Washington *United States Telegraph*, 32, 90, 98-99, 201, 260, 288, 327, 380, 581, 643, 740-41, 797, 862-63
Watkins, Caroline Milton, 438, 487
Watkins, Elizabeth Clay (mother): death, 131-32, 161, 162
Watkins, Henry (stepfather): death, 131-32, 160, 162
Watkins, Tobias, 16-17, 19-20, 60, 72-73, 76, 80-81, 84, 89, 120, 174
Watmough, Joseph G., 737
Watson, James A. (not identified): from, 396; to, 396
Watson, Lyman (not identified): from, 244
Watterson, George: replaces Fendall as editor of Washington *National Journal*, 171, 172-73, 197-98, 203-4; to, 79, 203, 268, 742; mentioned, 129

946

947

Wickliffe, Robert, Sr.
(continued):
duel, 115; linked to alleged
business failure involving
Robert Scott, 329, 334-35,
342; on tariffs & internal improvements, 475;
horsebreeder, 475; slaves of,
475; acquires wife's estate,
607-8; from, 9, 57, 342, 475,
521; mentioned, 205, 219,
344, 395, 443, 530, 607, 864
"Wickliffe Mare" (horse), 489,
495, 502, 504, 509
Wilde, Richard Henry: to,
639; mentiond, 712
Wilkins, James C., 257
Wilkins, William: mentioned
as vice presidential candidate
on the Jackson ticket (1832),
555, 558; mentioned, 287,
315, 368, 423, 448, 474, 500,
502, 506, 525, 553, 631, 687,
696-97
Wilkinson, Celestine Laveau
Trudeau (Mrs. James):
from, 271
Wilkinson, James, 271, 550
William I (Netherlands),
161, 552
William IV (England), 352
Williams, _____, 355
'Williams, Abraham J. (not
identified), 570
Williams, Benjamin, 16
Williams, John, 176, 257, 772
Williams, John S.: to, 200;
mentioned, 123
Williams, Lewis: to, 352
Williams, Micajah T., 286
Williams, Nathaniel F.: to,
416, 636
Williamsburg, Va., 63
Willis, Nathan, 332
Wilmington, Delaware,
554, 668
Wilson, Alexander: to, 9
Wilson, Ephraim K., 104
Wilson, George, 233-34
Winchester, Ky., 177, 697,
754, 804
Winchester, Va., 176, 736
Winchester & Lexington Turn-
pike Road Co., 754
Winchester (Va.) *Republican*, 251
Wines, Enoch Cobb: from,
847; mentioned, 752, 767-68,
770, 841, 848, 866
Winston (slave), 86
Winter, Elisha I., 401
Winthrop, Robert Charles:
to, 694
Winthrop, Thomas L., 332
Wirt, William: character,
411-12; friendship for C.,
421; role in 1832 election (*see*
Election (presidential) of
1832: William Wirt role in);

mentioned, 266, 304, 365,
368, 407-10, 417-20, 422-25,
430-31, 440, 446, 448, 450
455, 468, 475-76, 497, 501,
506-7, 510, 512, 515-16, 542,
547, 572-73, 577, 581, 584,
587-88, 590-93, 785
Wisconsin, 683
Wissett, Robert, 167
Wolcott, James: to, 495, 856
Wolf, George, 78, 102, 315,
470, 515, 517, 522-26, 532,
543, 557-58, 569, 581,
587-88, 720, 722-23, 785
Woodbridge, William: from,
679
Woodbury, Levi: annual report
as secretary of treasury
(1835), 809-10; mentioned,
159, 359-60, 631-32, 819,
843, 861
Woodford Co., Ky., 124-25,
131, 221
Woodford Festival, Clay
speech at, 860-61
"Woodlands," 357, 401, 486,
494, 496, 498, 502, 638,
648-49, 654, 657-58, 662,
778, 806
Woods, Alva: from, 363;
mentioned, 319
Woods, William, 512, 786, 788
Woodward, George: from, 642
Wool: Ky. prices (1831), 352;
problems of U.S. manufac-
turers of cloth of, 117, 356.
See also Tariff: Act of 1828,
Act of 1832
Woolley, Aaron K., 803, 867
Worcester, Mass. 598, 666
Worcester Co., Md., 104
Worsley, William W.: from,
421
Worthington, Madison G. (not
identified), 217-18
Wright, Francis (Fanny),
248, 290
Wright, John C.: to, 216;
mentioned, 217
Wright, Silas, Jr., 474, 702,
818, 854
Wyer, Ned, 632
Wyk, Olof (not identified):
from, 221

Yale College, 440
Yancey, Joel, 21-22, 62, 388-89
Yellow Springs, Ohio, 236
York, Pa., 355, 494
Young, John C., 735, 748
Young, Samuel, 307-8
York Co., Pa., 705, 707,
720, 734
Young, Aquilla, 582

Zanesville, Ohio, 371, 463, 749